V!

TRAVEL GUIDES

Ecuador
&
the Galápagos Islands

7th Edition
January 2014

VIVA Travel Guides' Guarantee:
We guarantee our guidebook to be the most up-to-date printed guidebook available. Visit www.vivatravelguides.com/guarantee to learn more.

VIVA Travel Guides Ecuador.

ISBN-13: 978-1-937157-22-7

Copyright © 2014, Viva Publishing Network.
Website: www.vivatravelguides.com
Information: info@vivatravelguides.com

Travel is inherently dangerous. While we use a superior process for updating guidebooks and have made every effort to ensure accuracy of facts in this book, Viva Publishing Network, its owners, members, employees, contributors and the authors cannot be held liable for events outside their control and we make no guarantee as to the accuracy of published information. VIVA encourages travelers to keep abreast of the news in order to know the safety situation of the country. Please travel safely, be alert and let us know how your vacation went!

◊ Cover Design: by Jason Halberstadt

◊ Cover Photo: by Robert Gibson Z.

Photographs: All photographs in this book were taken by the author unless otherwise indicated. Exceptions are licensed under the Creative Commons license (see http://creativecommons.org/licenses/by/2.0/ and http://creativecommons.org/licenses/by/3.0/ for details) and contain authroship labels.

"Centro histórico de Quito, Ecuador" (La Ronda) by Carlos Adampol Galindo ©, http://www.flickr.com/photos/cadampol; "Pululahua" (Volcanic Crater) by Rinaldo Wurglitsch ©, http://www.flickr.com/photos/wurglitsch; "Cayambe" by Marcio Ramalho ©, http://www.flickr.com/people/caneladeurubu; "Otavalo-3" (Market) by funkz ©, http://www.flickr.com/people/funkz; "Mujeres de Cotacachi" (Women on street corner) by alele ©, http://www.flickr.com/photos/alele; "Huacos, La Mama Negra - Latacunga" by Jose Pereira ©, http://www.flickr.com/people/jpereira_net; "El Nariz del Diablo" (Devil's Nose) by Dan Nevill ©, http://www.flickr.com/people/dnevill; "Quilotoa" by Marcio Ramalho ©, http://www.flickr.com/people/caneladeurubu; "Quilotoa to Chugchilán" by Casey ©, http://www.flickr.com/people/ramblurr; "Catedral de la Inmaculada Concepcion" by Alex Proimos ©, http://www.flickr.com/photos/proimos/3964966114; "Casablanca - Same" by Ximena ©, http://www.flickr.com/people/ximenacab; "Canoa Beach" by Athena Lao ©, http://www.flickr.com/people/inmyflippiefloppies; "Ayangue" by wogo24220 ©, http://www.flickr.com/people/wogo24220; "Galapagos Islands" by Michael R Perry ©, http://www.flickr.com/people/michaelrperry.

CONTENTS

6

Ecuador

About this Book

At V!VA, we believe that you shouldn't have to settle for an outdated guidebook. You can rest assured that in your hands is the most up-to-date guidebook available on Ecuador & the Galapagos Islands because:

--The final research for this book was completed on September 1, 2013.
--Each entry is "time stamped" with the date it was last published.
--V!VA's hyper-efficient web-to-book publishing process brings books to press in days or weeks, not months or years like our competitors.
--V!VA's country guides are updated at least once per year.

When you buy a V!VA Guide, here's what you're getting:

--The expertise of professional travel writers, local experts and real travelers in-country bringing you first-hand, unbiased recommendations to make the most out of your trip.
--The wisdom of editors who actually live in Latin America, not New York, Melbourne, or London like other guidebook companies.
--Advice on how to escape the overly-trodden "gringo" trail, meet locals and understand the culture.
--The knowledge you'll need to travel responsibly while getting more for your money.

Contribute to V!VA

V!VA is an online community of travelers, and we rely on the advice and opinions of vagabonders like yourself to continuously keep the books accurate and useful.

Take part in this ongoing effort by reviewing the places you have been to on the website, www.vivatravelguides.com.

Other travelers want to know about that rarely visited town you stumbled upon, about that bus company you will never take again, about that meal you just can't stop thinking about.

Together, we can help enhance each other's travel experiences and share in our love and passion for exploring Latin America.

Go ahead! Log on and create a free user account to help make the best guidebook series to Latin America even better.

! = Recommended by Viva!

About VIVA Travel Guides

We began VIVA Travel Guides back in 2007 because we simply wanted a better travel guide to our home country of Ecuador. All the guidebooks at the time were years out of date and weren't nearly as helpful as they should have been to real travelers. We knew we could do better.

We asked the question: "What would the travel guidebook look like if it was invented today from the ground up in the era of Google, Facebook, Wikipedia and nearly ubiquitous Internet connectivity?"

We concluded that the key to creating a superior guide is a knowledgeable community of travelers, on-the-ground professional travel writers, local experts and street-smart editors, all collaborating together on the web and working toward the goal of creating the most helpful, up-to-date guide available anywhere.

Continuously Updated
Traveler reports come in daily via the web and we take advantage of highly efficient 'web to book' technology and modern digital printing to speed the latest travel intelligence to the printed page in record time. We update our books at least once per year—more often than any other major publisher. We even print the date that each piece of information in the book was last updated so that you can make informed decisions about every detail of your trip.

A Better Way to Build a Guidebook
We're convinced we make a better guidebook. It's a more costly, painstaking way to make a guidebook, but we think it's worth it, because you're be able to get more out of your trip to Peru. There are many ways that you can get involved in making VIVA Travel Guides even better.

Help other travelers by writing a review
Did you love a place? Will you never return? Every destination in this guidebook is listed on our website with space for user ratings and reviews. Share your experiences, help out other travelers and let the world know what you think.

Make corrections and suggestions
Prices rise, good places go bad, and bad places go out of business. If you find something that needs to be updated or improved in this book, please let us know. Report any inaccuracies at www.vivatravelguides.com/corrections and we'll incorporate them into our information within a few days. As a small token of our thanks for correcting an error or submitting a suggestion we'll send you a coupon for 50 percent off any of our E-books or 20 percent off any of our printed books.

Make your reservations at www.vivatravelguides.com/hotels
You can support VIVA's mission by reserving your hotels at www.vivatravelguides.com/hotels. When you buy from our website, we get a commission, which we reinvest in making our guides a better resource for travelers.

We sincerely hope you enjoy this book, and your trip to Peru even more.

Happy Trails,

Jason Halberstadt
Founder, VIVA Travel Guides

Join VIVA on Facebook! Hit the Like button at www.facebook.com/VTGEcuador

ABOUT THE AUTHORS & EDITORS

Christopher Klassen is the Managing Editor at VIVA Travel Guides and oversaw all of the work done for this edition of VIVA Ecuador & the Galapagos. With parents that worked for the U.S. Foreign Service up until he graduated from high-school, Chris was raised to have the heart of a nomad throughout his life. He has lived in Honduras, Guatemala, Colombia, Panama and Ecuador throughout his years, and just recently spent the past four up in Canada finishing his Bachelor's Degree in Philosophy at the University of British Columbia.

Jason Halberstadt is the founder of VIVA Travel Guides and VIVA's parent company MetaMorf. He has lived in Ecuador since the mid 1990's and has traveled extensively in the Galapagos, and throughout Ecuador. He has trained writers and editors in VIVA's Travel Writing Boot Camps throughout Latin America and currently runs Metamorf's Silicon Valley office.

Jorge Alberto G. Fernández was born in Havana, Cuba. He collaborated with this edition of Viva's Ecuador book by updating a plethora of entries and contact information for many of the places listed throughout the country. He is a playwright currently based in Quito, as well as a Spanish editor and translator. Presently, he continues to work for MetaMorf S.A, the mother company of Viva Travel Guides, as a translator and online-marketing consultant.

At age 29, **Lorraine Caputo** packed her trusty knapsack, Rocinante, and began traipsing throughout the Americas, from Alaska to Tierra del Fuego, and widely in Peru. Her work appears in a variety of publications in the US, Canada and Latin America. Her Andina Aquarelles (Snark, 2002) includes poetry about Peru, and her artwork is in the founding collection of Chachapoyas' Museo de Arte Contemporáneo. In addition to writing the Northern Andes chapter, for this edition Lorraine traveled extensively from the North Coast to Lake Titicaca.

Dr. Christopher Minster, PhD, is a graduate of Penn State University, The University of Montana and Ohio State. He is the resident VIVA Travel Guides expert on ruins, history and culture, as well as spooky things like haunted museums. He worked for the U.S. Peace Corps in Guatemala as a volunteer from 1991 to 1994 and has traveled extensively in Latin America. He currently resides in Quito.

Jena Davison was a former staff writer and editor at V!VA. Shortly after graduating from University of Wisconsin-Madison with a BA in Journalism and Mass Communication, Jena packed her backpack and headed across the equator to travel solo through South America. Born and raised in New Jersey, Jena's itch for travel has previously brought her to 20 countries, mostly in Europe and Latin America. She currently lives in Florida.

Martha Crowley is one of the Editors for this edition of VIVA Peru. After graduating with a BA in Language and Communication, Martha has spent much of the past five years working and traveling in Latin America, including teaching English in the Galapagos Islands, managing non-profits in Bolivia and Ecuador, and writing travel guides to Peru and Bolivia. She is now based in Quito, Ecuador.

10

MANY THANKS TO:

Jesua Silva, VIVA's staff cartographer; **Pedro Vasconez**, our talented in-house graphic designer; and **Daniela Viteri**, who was a valuable asset during the updating process. Also, thanks to the Techie Team, the programming masterminds who keep our parent website www.vivatravelguides.com running smoothly and always lend a hand to the not-always-computer-savvy staff. A big thank you to the whole Metamorf team for their support.

Thanks also to all the former editors and writers who helped build the foundation of this book over the years, including: Paula Newton, Ricardo Segreda, Margaret Rode, Karen Nagy, Michelle Lillie, Laura Granfortuna, Alison Isaac, Tom Ravenscroft, Andrea Davoust, Rachael Hanley, Chris Hughes, John Howison, Erin Helland, Caroline Bennett, Katie Tibbetts, Kristi Mohrbacher, Amanda Massello, Katie Hale, Jordan Barnes and Blessing Waung.

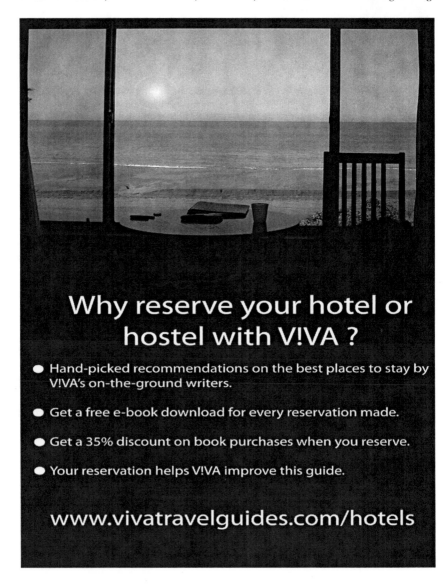

Why reserve your hotel or hostel with V!VA ?

● Hand-picked recommendations on the best places to stay by V!VA's on-the-ground writers.

● Get a free e-book download for every reservation made.

● Get a 35% discount on book purchases when you reserve.

● Your reservation helps V!VA improve this guide.

www.vivatravelguides.com/hotels

Join VIVA on Facebook! Hit the Like button at www.facebook.com/VTGEcuador

Regions of Ecuador
Quito (p. 86)
Quito, the bustling capital of Ecuador, is more than just a place to pass through en-route to other spectacular sites, such as the Galápagos, Otavalo or the Amazon Basin. Most visitors to Quito are struck by how the modern and the traditional exist side by side: The city has everything from Baroque cathedrals to TGI Friday's. The colonial city center, named by UNESCO as the first World Heritage site because of its well-preserved, beautiful architecture, is a great place to take a stroll or even spend the night if you don't mind a little more noise. A downtown highlight is La Compañia church: the interior is one of the most striking in the world, as there is a vast amount of gold leaf covering all of the intricate woodwork on the walls and ceiling. You'll want to visit El Panecillo, a small hill n ear colonial Quito where an impressive statue of an angel overlooks the city. The view is fantastic.

The Mariscal district, beloved by international visitors, is where you'll find all of the chévere (cool) places: nightclubs, bars, internet cafes, bookstores and hip restaurants. Shoppers won't want to miss out on the indigenous artisan markets in and around El Ejido park: they're the best place to find a bargain south of Otavalo. Visitors of all ages will want to visit Quito's highest attraction, the Telefériqo, a gondola-style cable car that whisks visitors from downtown Quito to the top of Pichincha volcano, climbing several hundred meters in the process—the complex also features an amusement park, restaurants and shops.

Quito is the cultural and artistic heart of Ecuador—here is where you'll find all of the best museums, restaurants and upscale shops and malls. If you're interested in culture, Quito has it in abundance. Visitors can see shows and concerts at the elegant and newly restored Teatro Sucre or catch the world-famous Jacchigua national folkloric ballet. No visit to Quito is complete without a stop at Mitad del Mundo, a small "village" for tourists about twenty minutes north of the city where the equatorial line is marked by an impressive monument. Take your photo with one foot in each hemisphere, then enjoy local cuisine at the restaurants in the complex as you listen to impromptu concerts by Andean bands.

The Andes (p. 159)
The majestic Andes Mountains bisect Ecuador along a north-south line, effectively dividing mainland Ecuador into three zones: the rainforest, the highlands, and the coast. The Andes region is home to several of the most interesting places to visit in Ecuador, including the country's most charming cities, one of the best markets in the Americas, several volcanoes and many opportunities for adventure travel, such as rafting and hiking.

No visit to Ecuador is complete without a trip to the famous indigenous crafts market at Otavalo, located just north of Quito. South of Quito, the mellow tourist town of Baños attracts visitors from around the world who want to test the thermal baths, which supposedly have divine healing powers. Most travelers try to find time to fit in at least a day trip to Cotopaxi, one of the highest active volcanoes on earth. On a clear day, it can be seen towering over Quito. If remote is your thing, head to the Quilotoa Loop where you will find a spectacular crater lake and opportunities to observe rural life. Cuenca should not be missed with its well-preserved colonial center and opportunities for hiking and shopping in the surrounding area. If you have the time, head down south to Vilcabamba where you will quickly see why its inhabitants claim to live long lives and the pace of life is sublimely relaxed.

The Amazon Basin (p. 303)
Much of the water that flows eastward through South America along the Amazon river and its tributaries originates in the mountains of Ecuador. The Ecuadorian Amazon Basin is a fantastic place to visit—you can expect to see monkeys, birds, caimans, butterflies and more on a trip to the jungle. Most visitors to the Amazon take advantage of the services offered by the various jungle lodges, who arrange everything from transportation to guides and food throughout the day. Other travelers go to the city of Tena, a ramshackle jungle city not too far from Quito, where it is possible to set out to visit the rainforest nearby. Puyo is up-and-coming as an alternative jungle entry point. If you want to see lots of wildlife, head deep into the primary rainforests (Cuyabeno or Yasuni) to spend time at any one of the numerous outlying, isolated lodges.

The Coast (p. 337)

Ecuador's Pacific coast is long, largely undeveloped (apart from major ports at Esmeraldas, Manta and Guayaquil), and dotted with many excellent beaches.

One of the routes to the beach passes through the small town of Mindo, located in the tropical cloud forest. Mindo is a prime destination for birdwatchers, who can expect to see hundreds of species in a very small area. Mindo is also known for rafting and adventure travel. Ecuador's biggest city, Guayaquil, is located in the coastal region as well. While the northern coastline is lined with greenery, the southern coast is typified by countless shrimp farms and drier scrubland. Banana plantations and swampy mangroves are found along pretty much the entire length of the coast.

Coastal highlights include the beach towns of Esmeraldas province, such as Atacames, which have good nightlife but can get overrun on weekends and public holidays with quiteños escaping the city. The laid-back surfing town of Montañita, and the stretch of beach in between known as La Ruta Del Sol—the route of the sun is a journey worth embarking on if you're a fan of the beach.

The portion of coast around the Machalilla National Park is particularly stunning with many a pretty white-sand beach to laze on. Canoa is a town in the province of Manabi that's been getting increasingly popular recently and it's not hard to see why with its divine beach and very laid-back atmosphere. If you're ready for some fun in the sun after shopping in the highlands or hiking through the jungle, then it's time to hit the beach. Don't forget the sunscreen!

The Galápagos (p. 451)

If you've ever switched on the Discovery Channel, chances are you've heard of the Galápagos Islands—the archipelago is certainly Ecuador's most hyped-up and famous tourist destination, attracting thousands of visitors annually from around the world. Visitors are never disappointed; if anything, they find that the islands are even more special and unique than they had initially anticipated.

Santa Cruz, the main port of entry for most Galápagos visitors, is home to the largest city in the islands: Puerto Ayora. It is also where you'll find the world-renowned Charles Darwin Research Station, where scientists continue Darwin's work on evolution and natural selection and protect imperiled Galápagos species. Remote Genovesa, known by its nickname as the "bird island," is home to large colonies of frigate birds, boobys, swallow-tailed gulls and more. San Cristobal is where you'll find Puerto Baquerizo Moreno, the capital of Galápagos Province, as well as several good beaches and Isla Lobos - one of the best places in the islands to snorkel or dive with sea lions. Española is the only nesting place in the world of the waved albatross, the largest bird found on the islands. Floreana is a good place to see flamingos and where you'll find The Devil's Crown, considered by many to be the best snorkeling site around the islands. Isabela, the largest island, boasts no less than five volcanoes, each of which is home to a different species of giant tortoise. Fernandina, the youngest island, is where you'll find the flightless cormorant, a remarkable bird endemic to Galápagos. Whether you've come for history, science, the wildlife or just to relax, Galápagos will not disappoint.

Introduction

Ecuador might be the smallest of the Andean countries, but size is a hardly a factor in light of what it contains. The entire country covers the Coast, Andean Highlands and the Amazon Basin - all packed into its small surface area. Not to mention, there's the Galapagos Islands sitting right off the coast. As a result of this, Ecuador - in many ways - boasts a little bit of everything that South America has to offer, and its relatively small size and wide diversity ultimately become its most enticing qualities.

Get stoked, and plunge right into the sparkling blue waters of the Galapagos Islands where playful sea lions swim through your legs and hammerhead sharks slither by without even a glance in your direction.

Relax, and sip a cappuccino in the capital's historic colonial center while taking in the beauty of Spanish cathedrals built over the ruins of the Inca Empire - all of which is set against the majestic backdrop of the Andes.

Finally, awe yourself, and pull up to a remote jungle lodge in a dugout canoe - carved out using the same techniques that Amazon tribes have used for thousands of years - and allow yourself to be lulled to sleep by the sounds of toucans, parrots and howler monkeys that inhabit the dense forest surrounding you.

Hard to believe, but it's all possible here in Ecuador.

It's so enticing that , in recent years, Ecuador has become a hotspot for expats and retirees from all over the world to come and establish new roots in. The country itself is still incredibly cheap to reside in, and you'll find that an abundance of affordable travel services - along with luxury travel options - are readily available.

However, the country still remains largely undiscovered even by the seasoned traveller and there are still plenty of opportunities for remote adventure travel. Some of the most popular activities in Ecuador include birdwatching, mountain biking, kayaking and hiking.

Other travelers come to volunteer, often as language teachers; either to help with reforestation (the rainforest is being stripped at an alarming rate) or to work with one of

Ecuador Quick Facts

Population: 15 million (2011)

Capital: Quito

Religion: Roman Catholic (80.4%)

People: mestizo 72%, montubio 7.4%, African descent 7.2%, indigenous 7%, white 6.1%, other 0.3%

Language: Spanish, Kichwa, Shuar

Government: Republic; executive branch dominates government structure. President Rafael Correa Delgado (since January 15, 2007); Vice President Lenín Moreno Garcés (since January 15, 2007). (The president is both the chief of state and head of government).

Literacy Rate: 93.2%

Economic Facts: As of 2012, unemployment is 4.1%,and underemployment 46.7%. Public debt is 22.1% of GDP. In 2011, 28.6% of the population lived below the poverty line.

Agriculture: flowers, bananas, coffee, cocoa, rice, potatoes, manioc (yucca / cassava and tapioca), plantains, sugarcane; cattle, sheep, pigs, beef, pork, dairy products; balsa wood; fish, shrimp.

Main exports: petroleum, bananas, cut flowers, shrimp.

Main industries: petroleum, food processing, textiles, wood products, chemicals.

Provinces (24 in total): Azuay, Bolívar, Cañar, Carchi, Chimborazo, Cotopaxi, El Oro, Esmeraldas, Galápagos, Guayas, Ibabura, Loja, Los Ríos, Manabí, Morona-Santiago, Napo, Orellana, Pastaza, Pichincha, Santa Elena, Santo Domingo de los Tsáchilas, Sucumbíos, Tungurahua, Zamora-Chinchipe

Time: Mainland = GMT minus 5; Galapagos = GMT minus 6

Lowest point: Pacific Coast (0 m / 0 ft)

Highest point: Volcán Chimborazo (6,310 m / 20,697 ft)

Electricity: 110/120 Volts AC, US 2 pin plugs are used.

Enter V!VA Photo Contests: vivatravelguides.com/photography-contests/

Photo by: Chris Klassen

Cotopaxi

also choose to spend a few weeks studying Spanish in Quito - currently the biggest language-learning center in South America.

But whatever it is you're in search of throughout Latin America, this might very well be the place to find it.

Geography of Ecuador

At 283,560 square kilometers (176,196 sq mi), Ecuador is about the size of the US state of Nebraska and slightly larger than the United Kingdom. Bordered by Peru to the south and Colombia to the north, the nation forms a small bulge off the Pacific northwestern coast of South America, with the equator cutting across the northern part of the country.

Ecuador is divided into four distinctive regions, making it one of the most varied countries in the world for its small size. Pacific coastal lowlands lie to the west, the extremely bio-diverse jungles of the Amazon basin form the east, and the arresting peaks of the Andes cut down through the center of the country and constitute the central highland region. The country also holds the unique archipelago of the Galápagos Islands some 1,000 kilometers (621 mi) off-shore to the west, accesible only by air and giant sea tortoise

Almost all rivers eat of the Andes in Ecuador drain to the Amazon. The major waterways are: the Napo, Pastaza and Putumayo, which all drain to the east; and Daule-Guayas and Guayllabamba-Esmeraldas, which flow into the Pacific Ocean.
Updated: Sep 03, 2012.

Weather and Climate

Ecuador has two seasons, wet and dry, which have much to do with the part of the country you are in. Generally speaking, the temperature is dictated by altitude. **Quito** and the Andes enjoy spring-like weather year-round, with highs of around 20-25° C (68-77°F) and lows of about 8-10°C (45-50°F). Weather in the **Galápagos** varies between misty and cool, and steamy and sunny. The Amazon region is generally either hot and humid, or hot and rainy.

The wet season or *invierno* (winter) in the highlands is from October until April (with a short dry period from mid-November to the end of December), and the dry season, *verano* (summer), lasts from June until September. However, no matter what season it is said to be, the weather is ultimately unpredictable. Warm sunny mornings can often lead to bone-chilling, rainy afternoons, hence the *sierra*'s adage "four seasons in one day."

The Pacific Coast is at its coolest from June to November, when it is often cloaked in *garúa*, a thick, foggy mist. Generally, the region is warm and humid year round, with temperatures averaging 25-31°C (77-90°F). The rainy season—from December to May—is warm and muggy. The dry season is less humid, but by no means dry. It tends to be wettest in the north (Esmeraldas) and driest in the South near the Peruvian border.

Temperatures in the Amanzon (*Oriente*) hover around the high 20s to low 30°sC (high 80s to low 90s°F). It rains most days in this area, but the wettest months are April to September. Some secondary roads may be closed due to flooding at this time, which can put off a trip if it involves road travel off the main roads. Many of the lodges in the Oriente are reached by canoe. During the dry months, especially December to February, many of the subsidiary rivers completely dry up and lodges are reached by foot instead of canoe. This provides a completely different experience and you may want to check with your tour operator before lugging your bags along the dried-up river bottom.

In the Galápagos there is a rainy season, a dry season and a transition season. The months of June to December tend to be characterized by cool garúa (mist) and temperatures averaging 22°C (72°F). From January to May, the climate is more typically tropical: hot air temperatures, wide stretches of blue sky, and occasional brief downpours. Because many of the islands are covered in black (bare) lava rock, you may feel yourself baking (and burning) in the heat. Updated: Aug 06, 2012.

Flora and Fauna in Ecuador

Nature lovers from around the world are drawn to the rainforests, jungles, cloud forests, deserts, islands, volcanoes and snow-capped peaks of Ecuador, one of the world's most bio-diverse nations. This tiny country holds 46 different ecosystems. Many private and public organizations work to protect Ecuador's biodiversity, which includes 44 national parks and reserves, and several UNESCO Natural Heritage sites. The most notable of these regions are Ecuador's portion of the Amazon Rainforest and the enchanted Galápagos Islands.

Whether you are interested in seeing some of the 2,725 orchid species growing in the wild in the Andes, or the 25,000 different species of trees in the northeastern Amazon Rainforest, Ecuador has what you're looking for. The Amazon is particularly rich in flora, partially because of its geographical advantage; the Andes sharply drop off into the Amazon River basin, feeding rich nutrients right into the rainforest basin.

The Andes feature cloud forests rich in orchids, *bromeliads* and tropical plants and trees. In total, the Andes have an estimated 8,200 plant and vegetable species. Although the Galápagos Islands were volcanically formed and are largely barren, they are home to over 600 native plant species, and many more have been introduced.

The small country is also home to more bird species than exist in North America and Europe combined: a total of 18 percent of the world's birds and 15 percent of its endemic bird species can be found in Ecuador. A million species of insects, 4,500 species of butterflies, 350 reptiles, 375 amphibians, 800 fresh water fish, 450 salt water fish species, and 1,550 mammal species crawl, climb, fly and swim throughout this incredibly biodiverse wonderland. Updated: Sep 03, 2012.

National Parks And Reserves

Ecuador is one of the most beautiful, biologically diverse countries in the world, and fortunately its countless natural wonders are protected in 44 national parks and reserves, as well as a number of private reserves.

In total, about 20 percent of the country is protected (which is one of the highest rates in all of Latin America).

Within these areas you can and will certainly experience unmatched scenery along with an incredible array of flora and fauna. Whether you find yourself in a misty grasp of a cloud forest reserve, paddling through countless mangroves on the coast, or breathing thin air on the summit of the world's highest active volcano, you will soon discover why Ecuador is one of South America's most popular outdoor adventure destinations.

The nation has a total of eleven national parks (Parque Nacional), as well as a wide variety of wildlife, ecological, biological and marine reserves (Reserva). Another series of preserves consists of the Áreas de Recreación Nacional, or national recreation areas. They are, by region:

ANDES

Parque Nacional Cajas

About 48 kilometers (30 mi) west of Cuenca, the park is a páramo high up in the mountains. While trekking you'll wade through cloud patches, smell the tiny-yet beautiful-flowers, watch birds fly overhead. Bring a jacket!

Reserva de Producción Faunística Chimborazo

Home to the tallest volcano in all of Ecuador, standing at 6,310 meters (20,702 ft). The reserve lies between the areas surrounding Riobamba and Ambato.

Reserva Ecológica Cotacachi-Cayapas

In the Esmeraldas region, this part Andean, part rainforest reserve is home to many condors.

Parque Nacional Cotopaxi

Less than two hours south of Quito, this park is home to an active volcano.

Reserva Ecológica El Ángel

This high altitude grassland reserve in Carchi is the birth of many rivers.

Reserva Ecológica Los Illinizas

In the northwest Andes, this largely unexplored area of deep craters and tall peaks has beautiful scenery and is rich in natural resources.

Reserva Geobotánica Pululahua

Lying on the "Middle of the World," this caldera (crater) is known for its diverse flora and fauna.

Parque Nacional Podocarpus

Located in Southeast Ecuador, the park is a complex natural system of over 100 lagoons.

Reserva Ecológica Antisana

The reserve got its name from its volcano, Antisana. In the Napo Province, this protected area has numerous wildlife species on the verge of extinction.

Parque Nacional Llanganates

Fragmented into four provinces south of Quito, and separated into two ecological zones: páramo and the slopes of the Andes with abundant flora and fauna.

Other federal nature preserves in the highlands are Refugio de Vida Silvestre Pasochoa and Área Recreacional El Boliche.

AMAZON

Reserva de Producción de Fauna Cuyabeno

Split between the Sucumbios and Orellana Provinces, this reserve is recognized for its impressive biodiversity.

Reserva Ecológica Cayambe-Coca

Situated about 97 kilometers (60 mi) from Quito, great for fishing and birdwatching; especially spotting the Andean Condor. The Papallacta hot springs are here.

Reserva Biológica Limoncocha

Birdwatching is a popular attraction in this reserve that has a lagoon-style landscape, located in Sucumbios Provice.

Parque Nacional Yasuní

This is Ecuador's largest national park, in the easternmost region of rainforest. You will spot very rare wildlife here.

Parque Nacional Sangay

This park has been listed as a UNESCO World Heritage Site, and has also been threatened due to over-poaching, grazing and a proposed highway. After years of protection, the park is again thriving.

Parque Nacional Sumaco Napo-Galeras

A largely unexplored national park, there are very unique biological conditions to be found here.

Other protected areas in the Amazonía are the reserves El Zarza, RE Cofan-Bermejo and El Quimi, and the national parks El Cóndor and Yacuri.

COAST

Parque Nacional Machalilla National Park

This coastal park has been largely threatened by deforestation, commercial fishing and poaching and the tourist industry. This is the only habitat outside of the Galápagos where you can see waved albatross.

Reserva Ecológica Cayapas Mataje

A mangrove forest near Esmeraldas, the reserve holds a series of formations of aquatic communities, the cluster of which helps in protecting the area from experiencing sea-erosion. The mangroves are home to many natural resources as well, used in large part by the locals to make a living.

Did a unique trek? Tell other travelers at vivatravelguides.com

Reserva Ecológica Mangalares-Churute

Located in Guayas province, about 40 kilometers (24 mi) from Guayaquil. There's an abundance of exotic aquatic creatures here. Other wildlife refuges along the coast are La Chiquita, Isla de Santa Clara, Estuario del Río Muisne, El Morro, Manglares Estuario del Río Esmeraldas River, Isla Corazón y Fragatas, Pambilar, Manglares El Salado and Puntilla de Santa Elena. Also in the region are two Reserva Ecológica, Arenillas and Mache-Chindul; marine wildlife refuge, Refugio Silvestre Marino Costero Pacoche; marine reserve Galera-San Francisco and recreational areas Parque Lago, Isla Santay, Isla Del Gallo and Los Samanes.

GALÁPAGOS
Parque Nacional Galápagos

Comprising 97 percent of the Galápagos archipelago, this UNESCO Heritage of Humanity site protects dozens of species found nowhere else on the planet.

Reserva Marina de Galápagos

Created in 1996 and also included in the UNESCO designation, Ecuador's first marine reserve protects 13,300,000 hectares (32,865,015 ac) of sea around the Galápagos Islands.

The Galapagos Islands were designated as Ecuador's first national park in 1959; the first mainland park, Cotopaxi, was established in 1975. Ecuador also has numerous private nature reserves, like Bosque Protector Cerro Blanco, located about 15 kilometers (19 mi) out of Guayaquil, aimed at preserving tropical dry forest and some 200 species of birds.

It should be noted that while Ecuador has been vigilant about creating parks, it has not always proved serious in maintaining its protected areas. The country's wonders, even within national parks and reserves,

are not safe from development and environmental degradation. Due to this, visitors are encouraged to travel responsibly and be mindful of the different customs, ecosystems and environmental regulations of Ecuador during their journey.

As of January 2012, entry into all national parks—with the exception of Galápagos—is free. The use of cabañas, camp sites and naturalist guides will still be charged a fee.To learn more about Ecuador's national parks and reserves, visit the Ministerio de Medio Ambiente's website (URL:www.ambiente.gob.ec).
Updated: Oct 03, 2012.

Social and Environmental Issues in Ecuador

In the 21st century, Ecuador has experienced a change of consciousness in regards to environmental and social issues, which often go hand-in-hand. The new Constitution of 2008 expands the guaranteed rights of both humans and the environment. Articles 56-60 address the rights of indigenous, *montubio*, Afro-Ecuadorian and other ethnic communities have guaranteed rights to maintain their language, customs and identity. Articles 71-74 provides rights to Mother Earth (*Pacha Mama*), including protection from environmental damage and of native species, be restored to its original state if damage has occurred and the restriction of introduced species.

Nonetheless, Ecuador still faces a number of social and environmental challenges as the nation tries to balance conflicting obligations of repaying international debt, developing industry and keeping the poorest sectors of society alive. Below are the most pressing issues.

OIL EXPLOITATION

Oil was discovered in Ecuador in the 1960s, followed by large-scale production began in the 1970s. Oil has been a huge boost to the nation's economy. However, development has not been sustainable. Ecuadorian Amazon is one of the most bio-diverse regions on the planet and oil companies are a serious threat to the rainforest. Petroleum exploitation has been particularly detrimental on the region's fragile ecosystems, vulnerable indigenous populations and public health. Even at lodges deep in the jungle, plumes of smoke emanating from oil refineries smudge the otherwise untouched horizon.

Bartolomé Island

The hardest-hit area is the Lago Agrio and Yasuni rainforest in Sucumbíos Province, where Texaco (now Chevron) operated from 1964 to 1994. Here, year after year, Chevron dumped 16 billion gallons of toxic waste and crude oil spilled into the waterways of the Amazon. Furthermore, it abandoned over 900 unlined waste pits that stored carcinogenic "produced water," thus contaminating the soil. Local residents began exhibiting miscarriages, birth defects, and leukemia and other cancers, as well as cultural upheaval. The jungle was also deforested. The extent of the damage is estimated to be far greater than that caused by the Exxon Valdez disaster in Alaska in 1989. Communities near Lago Agrio filed suit against Chevron in 1993. In February 2011, Ecuadorian courts ruled Chevron must pat $18.2 billion in damages.

Additionally, there have been instances of drilling on ancestral land. The Ecuadorian government sold exploration rights in two areas of the jungle without consulting the indigenous communities to whom those areas were considered ancestral: in 1989, Block 23, a 200,000-hectare (494,211-ac) field in the homeland of the Kichwa ancestral lands of Sarayaku, in Pastaza Province; and in 1998, the 200,000-hectare Block 24 in the Shuar and Achuar peoples' Transkutuku region in Morona Santiago Province.

Community groups demonstrated and local workers held strikes with some limited success. Protests in Sucumbíos and Orellana provinces in 2005 caused the state-owned oil company Petroecuador to halt production for several days. While consequences were dire on the economy, the local people gained some concessions in terms of health and infrastructure investment in these areas. In addition to guarantees in the 2008 Constitution, President Correa's administration has implemented a cap-and-trade policy. In this scheme, billions of barrels of oil are kept underground, in exchange for monetary benefits collected from developed countries These funds, in turn, will be used for renewable energy sources research and installation.

SUSTAINABLE TOURISM

Ecuador suffered a severe economic crisis in the late 1990s, which plunged over half of the population into poverty, which has led to high levels of migration to cities and foreign countries. The economy has since rebounded (in 2011, the poverty figure had dropped to 28.6 percent), due in part to tourism. This important source of income brings in over $1.2 billion of annual revenue to the country, contributing 1.8 percent to the GDP (World Tourism and Travel Council, 2011). The tourism and travel industry provided an estimated 273,700 jobs in 2011, representing 4.5 percent of total employment. Thus, tourism has the ability to decrease poverty in Ecuador in a manner that is potentially less damaging to the environment and more sustainable than other revenue generating enterprises such as export agriculture and petroleum extraction.

Many of the tourist operations in the Andean region of Ecuador promote the beauty and indigenous culture of the area, yet only a handful classify themselves as ecological and try to meaningfully engage in conservation and community awareness. Key factors determining the success of pioneering eco-lodges are conservation and community development. Most tourist operations recognize the importance of sustainable practices but do not have sufficient technological or financial resources to engage in them.

One model for encouraging sustainability is through outreach by non-governmental organizations (NGOs). The Ecuadorian NGO Conservación y Desarrollo (C&D; URL: www.ccd.ec) has a program called Smart Voyager which is aimed at training and certifying operations in sustainable tourism. The Smart Voyager program increases the efficiency and profitability of tourism operations, which provides an economic incentive for the operations to become certified. Certification helps to ensure that growth in tourism has a positive impact on the environment, workers, communities and the fight against poverty. It also provides consumers with independent information on the environmental and social standards of an operation. Moreover, through workshops and training sessions run in collaboration with C&D's partner Rainforest Alliance, tourism operators are able to share ideas and learn new methods of conserving the environment, promoting social programs and reducing poverty in their own areas.

There are severak ways you can leave a positive mark on the places you visit: practicing responsible tourism and using companies that have received ecotourism certification are two of the most important measures to ensure the country and its people benefit from your travels as much as you do.

THE INDIGENOUS MOVEMENT IN ECUADOR

For over three decades, a strong and largely united indigenous movement has been developing in Ecuador and it is considered to be among the strongest in Latin America. Indigenous political groups wield significant power in Ecuador, including nation-wide strikes and the tumbling of elected officials.

In the 1980s, the Amazonian and highland federation CONAIE (Confederation of Indigenous Nationalities of Ecuador) was formed, bringing together 11 Ecuadorian ethnic groups (approximately 3.5 million people) with a united purpose. The group focuses on high-level key aims for all of its member groups such as human rights, consolidation of territory and education. In 1990, thousands of indigenous people held a three-week strike, the first major indigenous uprising against the government. This was the first time that such power had been wielded by these groups and came as a shock to the establishment. Roadblocks were placed in the Andes and a march took place in Quito to demand land rights and bilingual education. In the aftermath of the 1990 uprising, CONAIE began to gain real political influence as the indigenous people saw that it was possible to have a say and gain rights, if they united in their goals. This led to a number of massive protests and finally in 1995, Pachakutik, the indigenous political party, was formed, to drive the rights of the people forward in the political arena. It played a role in the ousting of Abdalá Bucaram from the presidency in 1997.

A decade of unrest, lack of social reform and government corruption in the 1990s came to head in early 2000 as the indigenous people had been left in poverty. When demonstrating again in Quito, troops were called in to break up the demonstrations. Lucio Gutiérrez (at the time an army colonel) did not follow orders and instead, provided mobile army kitchens to support the indigenous protesters and let them overtake the congress building, declaring a "Parliament of the People." Gutiérrez worked with the indigenous to unsuccessfully try to form a new government to replace ousted president Jamil Mahuad. Gutiérrez then was arrested and imprisoned for six months and deputy Gustavo Noboa was installed as president. Despite the failure of the indigenous movement to form a new government, this was landmark news. Failure of the Noboa government to take notice led to further uprisings in January and February 2001. These united not only the indigenous groups but also the urban and rural poor, who had many of the same problems. Many marches were held in Quito. After stating he would not negotiate, Noboa was eventually forced to concede to end ten days of protests. This significantly weakened his political position, strengthening that of the indigenous movement and setting the scene for the election of Gutiérrez in 2002.

Gutiérrez' power-base was built on siding with indigenous Ecuadorians, unhappy with a government that appeared to be out of touch with the poor. When he turned his back on this base his power began to disintegrate. Due to disagreements regarding IMF recommendations and his apparent out-of-touch with the poor, he lost his indigenous allies' support. In April 2005, popular uprisings would topple him from power.

The provisional government, led by Alfredo Palacio also faced opposition in March 2006, in response to free trade negotiations with the United States. Indigenous groups feared such an agreement would cripple small-scale farmers in rural communities, especially those who produce rice, potatoes, beans, meat, cheese and maize. During the March protests, indigenous groups blocked the Pan-American Highway north and south of Quito. A state of emergency was declared in five central sierra provinces. These protests set the pace for political movements in the October 2006 presidential elections.

Running as a candidate of Alianza País, a coalition of over 30 parties and organizations, including Pachakutik, Rafael Correa won the 2006 elections. A major component of his platform was to call an Asamblea Constituyente, to write a new constitution which was voter-approved in 2009. In the country's new Magna Carta, indigenous and other ethnic groups have the right to practice their traditions, language and identity. In 2010, however, the indigenous political party Pachakutik broke with Alianza País over issues of water rights, teacher certification and other issues. Pachukutik has joined the MUPP (Movimiento de Unidad PluriNacional) in the 2013 presidential elections.

THE GALÁPAGOS FISHING WAR

There is constant tension in Galápagos between the two main industries in the islands: fishing and tourism. Those in the fishing industry are always pushing for ecologically questionable concessions from the government such as long-line fishing, long seasons for valuable species such as lobsters and sea cucumbers, and removal of protections on marine reserves.

Long-line fishing is particularly destructive—it involves baiting several hundred hooks on the same heavy line. Used to catch swordfish and tuna, it also results in a lot of "by-catch," or unintended catch, including sea turtles, sharks, rays, sea lions and even marine birds such as the albatross, all of which are protected in Galápagos. Ecologists are aghast that this fishing method is even being considered in such a fragile ecosystem.

Catch levels are way down in recent years, yet short-sighted fishermen continue to push for longer seasons and larger catch limits. What is worse, there is a lot of illegal fishing being done in Galápagos, both by foreign vessels fishing in Ecuadorian waters near the islands as well as local boats engaged in poaching out of season or of illegal species. In particular, sharks in Galápagos are being hunted to near extinction: they are caught for their fins, which bring a lucrative price in Asia. Sharks are caught by unscrupulous fishermen (sometimes using chopped-up sea lions as bait), their fins are cut off, and they are dumped back into the water. There is a ban on shark fishing, but Ecuador does not have the resources (or desire, apparently) to enforce it.

The tourism operators in the islands favor stringent restrictions, as unchecked fishing is severely detrimental to the ecosystem. For example, the sea cucumber, one of the most highly sought-after species in Galápagos, is a key link in the marine food chain. Most Galápagos life ultimately depends on the sea: many birds feed on fish, and if the marine ecosystem collapses, there will be no more boobies, frigates or albatrosses for tourists to come and see. Therefore, tour operators are constantly pressuring the Ecuadorian government to enact and enforce strict rules for those who want to fish in Galápagos.

Most of the residents of the islands are either fishermen themselves or have family members who fish. This is true of many of the park rangers, who are charged with enforcing the rules: they often look the other way if they catch family or friends doing something illegal. The fishermen are very powerful in the islands: on more than one occasion, they have blockaded whole islands from tour vessels to protest a new ban or law, and once they even took over the Charles Darwin Research Station, held the scientists hostage, and threatened to kill Lonesome George.

Although the two sides seem beyond any sort of agreement, there are those who are working on compromises and new solutions; large tour operators Metropolitan Touring and Lindblad Expeditions support projects such as the "Teachers on Board" plan, in which schoolteachers from Galápagos spend time on cruise ships, learning about the islands from a tourism perspective. Metropolitan also has a project in which fishermen are paid to pick up trash off the islands. Perhaps in the future, fishing, wildlife and tourism will be able to coexist in these fragile islands. Updated: Sep 07, 2012.

Ecuadorian History
PRE-INCA TIMES
Although the earliest evidence of man in Ecuador can be traced back to 10,000 BC, there are few concrete facts about the country's history before the invasion of the Inca in the mid-15th century. Research is ongoing, and the **Museo Nacional** in Quito has some fascinating artifacts that are laid out to chart the probable development of the country before the Inca, from the age of hunter-gatherers to the dawn of pottery and ceramics, agriculture and fixed settlements. By 1480, dominant indigenous groups included Imbayas, Shyris, Quitus, Puruhaes and Cañaris in the highlands; and the Caras, Manteños and Huancavilcas along the coast.

THE INCA INVASION
The Inca began dominating present-day Peru in the early 13th century, but it was not until the mid-15th-century that they began to expand into what is now Ecuador. Pachacútec led the invasion with his son Túpac Yupanqui. Native resistance was fierce, particularly in the north, but they eventually arranged peace terms with one dominant group in the south, the Cañari.

Túpac Yupanqui extended the empire further after the death of his father, establishing himself at Ingapirca before conquering the Quitu-Caras nation at present-day Quito. He then built an impressive network of roads stretching the length of his empire from Cusco in southern Peru all the way up north to Quito. Some of these roads survive today and are popular with hikers, with some taking a number of days to traverse.

Túmac Yupanqui was succeeded by his son, Huayna Cápac, who had been born at Tomebamba (also called Tumipampa; modern-day Cuenca), who established another administrative seat at Quito, where his son Atahualpa was born. Problems arose when Huayna Cápac died, setting off a war of succession between two of his sons, Huáscar and Atahualpa. Huáscar, Huayna Cápac's eldest son, was based at Cusco, while Atahualpa, Huáscar's younger brother, governed his half of the empire from Quito. Both brothers were power hungry, and soon after their father's death civil war broke out. In 1532, Atahualpa secured victory over his brother.

THE SPANISH INVASION AND CONQUEST

The Inca ruler Atahualpa governed for less than a year before the Spanish arrived, led by Francisco Pizarro. Atahualpa—foolishly as it turns out—thought of Pizarro and his band as an innocent bunch of foreigners. He welcomed them into his empire and befriended them, only to be captured and held hostage by them. Fearing for his life, Atahualpa offered a huge ransom of gold and silver in return for his release. Pizarro accepted, then beheaded the leader anyway. Knowing that the Spanish had assassinated Atahualpa, the Inca, led by General Rumiñahui, chose to destroy Quito rather than leave it in the hands of the Conquistadores. Within one bloody year, hundreds of thousands of Incas had been slaughtered and the whole empire had fallen to the Spanish.

Pizarro founded his capital at Lima, Peru, while his lieutenants Sebastián de Benalcázar and Diego de Almagro founded **San Francisco de Quito** in 1534, on the charred remains of the Inca city. Following a local legend of great riches in the lands to the east, Pizarro sent an expedition down into the Amazon Basin in 1540. Pizarro placed his brother, Gonzalo, in charge of the expedition, which departed from Quito. Having found nothing after several months, and running out of food, Gonzalo Pizarro sent Francisco de Orellana ahead to see what might be found. Orellana never returned. Instead he had floated down the entire Amazon River, through Brazil, out to the Atlantic Ocean. This marked the first crossing of the continent by a white man in a canoe, and the event is still celebrated in Ecuador today.

Meanwhile, the Spanish had been busy dividing up Ecuador's land among themselves. The encomienda system was established by the Spanish crown to reward conquistadores by granting them huge estates upon which they could force the indigenous people who happened to occupy the land into slavery. In exchange for their back-breaking labor, the slaves were given room, board and religious instruction. The food was so meager and the work so hard that many starved to death or died from diseases. As a result, the indigenous population decreased dramatically. About half of Ecuador's Indian population was forced to live in this manner for a number of centuries.

Although the encomienda system was theoretically outlawed in the 17th century, in practice, the oppression of the indigenous population continued under various guises until 1964 when the Agrarian Reform Law was passed. Two sectors of the indigenous population escaped the encomienda system. Some were rounded up to live in specially constructed indigenous towns and forced to work in textiles or agriculture (it is for this reason that **Otavalo** became so famous for its weaving), or lived so deep in the Amazonian lowlands that they completely escaped all the implications of Spanish rule, both good and bad. One positive legacy of this troubled time is Ecuador's beautiful haciendas, elaborate country mansions built by the wealthy Spaniards. Today, many of these haciendas have been converted into some of Ecuador's most memorable and unique hotels.

INDEPENDENCE FROM SPAIN

Spanish rule continued with relative peace until the late 18th century, when creole (Spanish born in the New World) leaders started to resent Spain for its constant interference and its demand of high taxes. The creoles began working toward independence. When Napoleon placed his brother Joseph on the throne of Spain in 1807, many creoles saw it as the opportunity for independence they had been waiting for. After a couple of failed attempts to defeat the Spanish armies, the first real victory was won at Guayaquil, which gained independence in October 1820. At this point an urgent request for backup was sent to the South American liberator, Simón Bolívar.

To help prevent the Spanish from regaining power, Bolívar swept into action by sending his best general, Antonio José de Sucre, to take command of the rebel army based in Quito. Sucre and his forces won the pivotal battle of Pichincha on May 24, 1822, ending Spanish rule in Ecuador. Bolívar declared Quito the southern capital of a huge new

MANUELA SAENZ

Born in Quito in 1795 (some sources say 1797) as the illegitimate daughter of a married Spanish nobleman, Manuela Sáenz led one of the most fascinating lives in the history of Latin America. After her mother's death, she entered a convent for schooling and left at the age of 17 when it was discovered that she was carrying on an affair with a Spanish military officer.

Her father arranged for her to marry James Thorne, a wealthy Englishman who was much older than she. They moved to Peru, where Manuela lived as an aristocrat and became involved in the planning of the independence movement. She was a member of the revolutionary army, and fought alongside Mariscal Antonio José de Sucre at the battles of Pichincha (1822) and Ayacucho, Peru (1824), thus earning the rank of colonel.

In 1822, she left her husband and moved back to Quito and worked in the independence movement. There she met Simón Bolívar, the hero of South American independence, and they began a torrid affair. Although she lived with Bolívar for a short while, they spent most of their time apart as he traveled a great deal in pursuit of independence. On September 25, 1828, she saved his life by helping him escape an assassination attempt.

Bolívar died two years later of tuberculosis. After his death, anti-Bolívar factions in Colombia and Ecuador conspired to exclude her from any position of influence. She was exiled, first to Jamaica, then to the small port town of Paita in northern Peru, where she lived by selling tobacco and translating letters that North American whalers wrote to their lovers in various ports of Latin America. She died penniless in 1856 during a diphtheria epidemic.

Today, Ecuadorians (and Quiteños in particular) have embraced Manuela Sáenz as one of their own. She is considered a national heroine and is the subject of the first ever Ecuadorian opera, which opened in 2006. You can visit the Museo de Manuela Sáenz in Quito.

INTRO & INFO

nation, Gran Colombia, which included present-day Ecuador, Colombia, Panama and Venezuela. His dream was to make the whole continent into a single, independent nation. However, his idea went down badly with the residents and in 1830 the Quito representatives won independence for their own republic, calling it Ecuador because of its location on the equator.

CIVIL WAR AND COAST-SIERRA RIVALRY

Fresh disputes emerged between the conservative residents of the highlands, who were content with Spanish rule, and the liberal costeños, who wanted complete independence. To some extent this rivalry still continues, albeit in the form of lighthearted teasing: The coastal residents call the highlanders boring and backward, and the highlanders call their coastal counterparts *monos* (monkeys) and tease them for being loud and obnoxious. In the mid-1800s, different cities and areas attempted to declare their own set of rules. Guayaquil gave itself over to Peruvian rule, and much of Ecuador was close to being taken over by Colombia. However, in 1861, Gabriel García Moreno, a fearless leader and devout Catholic, became president. The most significant legacy of his rule was to turn Ecuador into a Catholic republic and force his beliefs on all of its residents by denying official citizenship to those who rejected Catholicism.

Moreno was assassinated in the streets of Quito by political rivals in 1875. After Moreno's death, the equally fearsome but liberal president, Eloy Alfaro, took over and immediately started undoing Moreno's work by secularizing the state and education. His decades-long reign came to a bitter end in 1911, when he was overthrown by the military. The following year, while leading a revolt, he was captured and found guilty of treason. His body was dragged through the streets of Quito and publicly burned around the square. This event marked the beginning of a 50-year battle for power between the liberals and conservatives, which cost the country thousands of lives and numerous presidents (some of whom lasted only days). Taking advantage of Ecuador's weakened state, Peru challenged Ecuador in a border dispute from 1941 to 1942, which resulted in Ecuador losing almost half of its land to Peru in a 1948 treaty.

BANANAS AND OIL

Ecuador went through a relatively peaceful period in the 1950s and 60s, helped by both the popular president, Galo Plaza Lasso, and the beginning of the banana boom, which created thousands of jobs and had a positive impact on the economy. It was during this period that the Agrarian Reform Law put a halt on the virtual slavery that the indigenous people had been subjected to since the 16th century. Unfortunately, in the 1960s, banana exportation was abruptly nullified by a fungal disease that affected the country's entire crop, evoking a short period of economic decline in Ecuador.

This decline ended when large oil reserves were found in the Oriente in 1967 by Texaco, an U.S. oil company. The Ecuadorian military, led by General Guillermo Rodríguez Lara, managed to block the swarms of money-hungry oil companies waiting to pounce on the land and negotiated fair contracts for oil extraction. Though at the cost of ghastly damage committed on the environment, the economy began to prosper and new wealth was being pumped into education, health care, urbanization and transport. Even with the new oil money, Ecuador was unable to pay off its enormous debts, and foolish decisions by Lara to overcome this problem (such as raising taxes to absurd levels) resulted in his overthrow in 1976. A stable democracy was reinstated soon after.

ECUADORIAN-PERUVIAN BORDER DISPUTE

The border dispute between Ecuador and Peru lasted over 160 years and was the longest armed conflict in the Western Hemisphere. Amazonian land was the source of the conflict.

After Simón Bolívar liberated Gran Colombia (present-day Colombia, Venezuela, Panama and Ecuador) in 1819, he had the bold ambition to unite all of South America into the republic. However, Peruvian president José de la Mar wanted to be the sole ruler of Peru. De la Mar incited anti-Colombian sentiment within Peru and Bolivia and the Colombian army was expelled in 1828. De la Mar went even further after all this by invading southern Ecuador.

This caused the Gran Colombian-Peruvian War. Peru officially lost Guayaquil to Gran Colombia. The two countries agreed to recognize the viceroyalty-era boundaries between them, delineated by the Marañón and Amazon rivers.

In 1830, Ecuador succeeded from Gran Colombia. In 1857, Ecuador planned to repay its debt with British creditors, which it had accumulated from the war for independence, by giving Britain land in the Amazon. Peru claimed this land as its own and this set off the Ecuadorian-Peruvian War of 1859. The Peruvian navy blockaded Guayaquil until Ecuador signed a treaty to agree not to sell the Amazonian land to Britain. Still, it was debatable what country owned the land.

From 1860 to 1941, a number of treaties were signed to settle the territorial dispute, but the two countries took up arms again in 1941. Peru claims Ecuador invaded its Zarumilla Province, while Ecuador claims Peru launched attacks on Ecuadorian troops around the border. The war lasted less than a month until Ecuador requested a cease fire and Peruvian forces withdrew from Ecuador's El Oro Province. The Protocol of Rio de Janeiro of 1942 ended the war, and Ecuador lost nearly half of its Amazonian holdings, an area rich petroleum, gold, uranium and other minerals.

In 1960, Ecuador's President José María Velasco Ibarra stated that the 1942 protocol was null, as Ecuador had been forced to sign under duress. Tensions flared again in the Cordillera del Cóndor region, briefly in 1981 and again in 1994-1995. This later conflict also involved the headwaters of the Río Cenepa. The conflict came to an end February 28, 1992, with the signing of the Montevideo Declaration and the later Itamaraty Peace Declaration, which reaffirmed the Rio Protocol.

Finally, on October 26, 1998, the two nations signed a comprehensive border agreement, which was ratified by both nations' congress. Ecuador and Peru established Parque Binacional El Cóndor in the Cordillera del Cóndor. Today the borders are clearly defined, but there is still a residual bitterness between the two countries.
Updated: Sep 11, 2012.

DOLLARIZATION AND BEYOND

From 1979 until 1996 a string of governments attempted (and failed) to stabilize the delicate economy—which swung dramatically back-and-forth due to fluctuating oil prices and severe debt. The perilous state of the economy provoked the indigenous people to rise up against the government through their new organization, Confederación de Nacionalidades Indígenas del Ecuador (CONAIE), and make their voice heard.

In 1998, the situation worsened. Ecuador suffered its most severe economic crisis; the GDP shrank dramatically, inflation rose and banks collapsed. The citizens of Ecuador were furious with their leaders, whose corruption and ineptitude had contributed to the crisis. Roads were blockaded and virtually the entire country went on strike.

In 1999, then-President Jamil Mahuad decided nothing could be done to protect the national currency, the sucre, from failing completely, and he concluded that the only answer was to transfer to the U.S. dollar. Although this move had the immediate desired effect of stabilizing the economy, it brought numerous other problems for the Ecuadorian people. The cost of living skyrocketed and poverty worsened. The indigenous population suffered greatly, and in 2000, thousands of protesters stormed Congress, backed by the military, and ousted Mahuad from office in just three hours.

He was replaced immediately by his vice-president, Gustavo Noboa, under whom the economy slowly started to recover. On April 20, 2005, President, Lucio Gutiérrez, elected in 2002, was overthrown by popular protest and a vote in Congress, and was replaced by his vice-president, Dr. Alfredo Palacio. Updated: Apr 23, 2013.

Politics

Ecuador has been a constitutional republic with a democratic government since 1976. The government consists of three main branches: executive, headed by the president, currently Rafael Correa Delgado (since January 2007); legislative, the National Assembly, with representatives from dozens of political parties that are constantly interchanging; and judicial.

Between 1996 and 2007, political instability plagued Ecuador once again. The country witnessed a procession of incompetent and/or corrupt leaders. Eight different presidents rose to and fell from power in that decade, three of them elected and subsequently overthrown.

Ecuadorians were generally frustrated with their politicians, as is often demonstrated in street protests these days. In April 2005, popular protest against unconstitutional actions by former President Lucio Gutiérrez brought an early and abrupt end to his term as president.

Then Vice President Dr. Alfredo Palacio took over shortly after congress voted to remove Gutiérrez from office. U.S.-trained economist Rafael Correa was elected president in November 2006 and sworn-in to replace Palacio as president in January of 2007. Later that year, several elected members of Congress were charged with violating campaign laws and were subsequently thrown out.

In September 2007, a constitutional assembly was voted into power and drafted a new constitution—Ecuador's 20th since gaining independence—which was then approved by voters in September 2008. The new constitution grants the executive branch more control, and allows two consecutive four-year terms for the president, vice president and National Assembly members. While supporters welcome the idea of a more stable government with longer elected terms, opponents fear the president's increase in power could lead to autocracy.

The new constitution also includes a world first: a bill of rights extending unalienable rights to nature using a cap-and-trade strategy. Although this could certainly benefit this biologically diverse and dense country, some skeptics wonder how successful the government will be in terms of implementing this unprecedented concept.

Correa led congress to rewrite the constitution to reflect the progress of Ecuador in 2009, which includes free education through university and provides social security to stay-at-home mothers, as well as extends the rights of the president. It also pioneered an "eco-constitution," extending inalienable rights to nature.

As a result, the Ecuadorian government has been working toward an initiative to keep underground billions of barrels of oil in order to collect monetary benefits from developed countries using a cap-and-trade policy, of which is intended for innovation in renewable energy sources. It is questionable whether or not this initiative holds enough strength to be sustained however, and only time will be the test of such a system.

Political disputes over oil exploration in the Amazon continue to persist, honing in on the Yasuni rainforest in recent years and continuing to seek payment of $18.2 billion courts have ruled Chevron owes for environmental damages incurred. Updated: Aug 22, 2012.

Ecuador's Economy

Ecuador's economy is based on exports from the agricultural industries, such as bananas and shrimp; money transfers from native employed abroad; and petroleum production, which accounts for 40 percent of export earnings and one-third of the central government budget revenues.

The economy delved into a frightening free-fall in the late 1990s when the nation suffered the natural disasters of El Niño and the eruption of Pichincha volcano, in addition to a sharp decline in world petroleum prices. Poverty worsened (over half the population lived below the poverty level) and the banking system collapsed. Bankers fled the country in 1999 without honoring their clients' accounts.

When the sucre—the nation's currency—depreciated by about 70 percent in the same decade, then-President Jamil Mahuad made the wildly unpopular announcement that he would adopt the U.S. dollar as the national currency. A military coup in January 2000 ousted Mahuad. With few alternatives to save the struggling economy, Congress went on to approve the adoption of the U.S. dollar in March of that year.

Since then the nation's economy has been relatively solid. Economic growth reached 7.2 percent in 2008, but dropped to 0.4 percent in 2009 due to the global financial crisis. Soon it rebounded, achieving 6.5 percent growth in 2011. An estimated 28.6 percent of the population still lives below the poverty line (2011).

At the start of Correa's term the President was outspoken about his reluctance to Free Trade Agreement talks with the U.S., and stated that Ecuador will acknowledge its external debt—and only what it deemed to be "legitimate debt"—only after successfully funding domestic social programs. The government implemented income transfers to the poor and announced plans to increase spending on health and education.

Talks have resumed between Correa and the European Union over fair trade development, which Correa has publicly stated does not have anything to do with the Free Trade Agreement, and still opposes arriving at any agreement over the official act.

In 2009, Ecuador joined the Alianza Bolivariana para las Américas (ALBA), an alliance of the leftist South American countries that promotes fairer trading and other relationships between nations.

- **Unemployment**: 4.1 percent (as of 2012)

- **Underemployment**: 44.8 percent (as of 2013)

- **GDP Per Capita**: $8,800 (as of 2012)

- **Public debt**: 23.3 percent of GDP (as of 2012)

- **Chief agricultural exports**: flowers, bananas, coffee, cocoa, rice, potatoes, manioc (yucca / cassava and tapioca), plantains, sugarcane; cattle, sheep, pigs, beef, pork, dairy products; balsa wood; fish, shrimp.

- **Export commodities**: petroleum, bananas, cut flowers, shrimp.

- **Main industries**: petroleum, food processing, textiles, wood products, chemicals.

Updated: Aug 22, 2012.

Population of Ecuador

The estimated population of Ecuador is 15 million (2011). Annual population growth is currently two percent (2012). Half of Ecuador's population is under 25 years and over 30 percent under 14 years.

Because many Ecuadorians do not know their precise ethnic heritage, the 2010 national census asked Ecuadorians with which culture or customs they related. Almost 72 percent stated mestizo (European-indigenous mix), and 6.1 percent as white. Afro-Ecuadorians, who reside mostly in Esmeraldas Province, but also in the Valle del Chota in the northern Andes, constituted 7.2 percent of the respondents.

For the first time ever, Ecuadorians could choose to identify themselves as *montubio* - a mestizo ethnic-cultural group of the coastal mountains of Manabí, Los Ríos and Loja provinces; 7.4 percent of chose this classification. Approximately seven percent of the population is indigenous, almost two-thirds of whom live in Chimborazo and Imbabura provinces.

Morona Santiago, Pastaza and Napo provinces also have large indigenous populations. Other ethnicities constitute less than half-percent of the population.
Updated: Sep 03, 2012.

Ecuador's Languages

The 2008 Constitution establishes Spanish (*castellano*) as the official language of Ecuador, with Kichwa and Shuar as additional official languages for intercultural relations. Other ancestral, indigenous languages may be used as the official and legal language in areas where they are spoken.

Almost all Ecuadorians speak Spanish as either a first or second language. Ecuadorian Spanish varies according to each region. On the coast, the Spanish is slurred and final consonants are dropped. In the Andes, the Spanish is slower and clearer-making it one of the easiest places to learn the language.

See our Spanish Schools section for more information.

Quichua (*kich-wa*) is the most common indigenous language, with almost 600,000 speakers; most live in the sierra, and about one percent in the jungle.

The most common Amazonian languages are Shuar, with over 79,000 native speakers, and Achuar, with over 7,000. Of the 15 languages spoken in modern-day Ecuador, three have fewer than 700 speakers.

English is taught from an early age in schools, but is not taught well. Most Ecuadorians understand much more English than one would imagine, but relatively few are fluent.
Updated: Sep 03, 2012.

Religion in Ecuador

Indigenous groups once practiced different religions across Ecuador, but the arrival of the Spanish wiped out much of this diversity. Using fear, intimidation and bribery, the country was almost completely converted to Catholicism. Today, even those Amazon villages that have never seen a car have Catholic churches. Many rural villages that once practiced other religions still blend old traditions with the practice of Catholicism. Native

religious celebrations are still occasionally held at Ingapirca, the most important Inca site in Ecuador.

Other Christian denominations with temples in Ecuador are Eastern Orthodox, Anglican, Episcopalian, Methodist, Lutheran, Presbyterian, Mennonite, Baptist and Mormon, as well as a number of evangelical and Pentecostal churches. Other faiths represented in Ecuador are Judaism, Islam, Buddhist, Hinduism and Spiritualism.

In 2012, the Instituto Ecuatoriano de Estadística y Censos (INEC) conducted a study that revealed that 80.4 percent of Ecuadorians are Catholic, and 19.6 percent of the population belong to another religion, or is atheist or agnostic.
Updated: Sep 03, 2012.

Culture in Ecuador

Elements of *cultura* (culture) are everywhere you go in Ecuador. From the gilded, glittering 19th-century theaters of Quito to the raucous parades and dancing in the streets of tiny Andean towns, Ecuadorians across the nation love to celebrate their heritage and traditions.

Ecuador brandishes a rainbow of cultures: the native inhabitants had a well-developed sense of cultural identity before the arrival of the Spanish, who added their own traditions to the mix. Later, Africans came to the region—primarily the coast—and brought with them their own unique culture. Today, Ecuador has even embraced international traditions, such as Halloween.

Ecuador's culture ranges from upscale (opera at Teatro Sucre in Quito) to low-key (cockfights in rural towns), and from very old (religious processions for Holy Week) to new (*chivas*—party buses with a loud band on top—driving through the streets of Quito). No matter what aspects of Ecuadorian culture you choose to explore, you can be sure that it will be colorful, boisterous and lots of fun. Ecuador takes its art and music very seriously.

The nation—and Quito in particular—was a thriving artistic center during the colonial period, and the people of Ecuador developed a love for art that continues to this day. Quito's museums and galleries should not be missed if you are an art aficionado. Music is also important to Ecuadorians: you won't go anywhere in Ecuador without seeing a small Andean band playing traditional tunes, hoping to sell a CD to tourists.

Ecuador has the wonderful Casa de la Cultura Ecuatoriana (URL:www.cce.org.ec) that promotes the visual and performance artists of the country. The main complex is in Quito; but every provincial capital has a *nucleo*, or a branch, where regional artists are highlighted. The casas host literary readings, concerts, art exhibits, films and other cultural events—many of them free. Many also have shops where books and recordings may be purchased.

Keep your eyes and mind open: there are opportunities everywhere in Ecuador to sample local culture. The people of Ecuador are excited when a foreigner wants to participate in a town festival or other local celebrations: let the locals be your guides and enjoy! Updated: Sep 13, 2012.

ECUADORIAN LITERATURE

Before the Spanish conquest, literature was an oral affair in Ecuador. During the colonial period, the written tradition began. One notable work of that era is *Elegía a la muerte de Atahualpa*, written in Quichua and attributed to *cacique* Jacinto Collahuazo (18th century).

In the years leading up to Independence, several important writers emerged on the scene: **Eugenio Espejo** (1747-1795), the country's first journalist, and poet **José Joaquín de Olmedo** (1780-1847), who wrote *Canto a Bolívar* and *Canción del 9 de octubre*, which would become Guayaquil's anthem.

In the mid-19th century emerged two of Ecuador's most important writers: **Juan Montalvo** (1832-89) and **Juan León Mera** (1832-94). Montalvo was principally an essayist who wrote about social, political, historical and cultural issues. His works include *Cosmopolita, Geometría moral, Las Catilinarias* and his masterpiece, *Siete Tratados*. A collection of his oeuvre, published by Arizona State University, is available in English. Mera is credited with writing the first Ecuadorian novel, *Cumandá* (1879), a Romantic genre story set in Ecuador's jungle. This writer was also a musician, and composed the lyrics for Ecuador's national anthem.

The next important Ecuadorian novel was written by **Luis A. Martínez** (1869-1909). His work, *A la costa*, launched the Realism movement in the Andean country. This novel vividly displays the social changes Ecuador experienced at the end of the 19th century. Of the same genre is *Plata y bronce* (1927) by **Fernando Chávez**, which examines race and social class relations between the Indigenous and whites.

Chavez' work ushered in Ecuador's next literary movement, Social Realism. Its most famous representative is **Jorge Icaza** (1906-79), who penned *Huasipungo (in English,The Villagers*, 1934). This controversial Indigenismo novel portrays the Indigenous struggle against exploitation. It is widely acclaimed as one of the most significant works in contemporary Latin American literature.

Another noteworthy work of this period is *Los que se van* (1930) by **Joaquin Gallegos Lara** (1911-1947), **Demetrio Aguilera Malta** (1909-1981) and **Enrique Gil Gilbert** (1912-1973). This collection of stories focuses on the social reality of Ecuador's Indigenous and Montubio peoples. These three writers, along with **José de la Cuadra** (1903-1941) and **Alfredo Pareja Diezcanseco** (1908-1993), formed the Guayaquil Group. All became famous in their right.

Contemporary Ecuadorian writers continue to focus on social and political issues. **Jorge Carrera Andrade** (1903-1978) is considered to be one of Latin America's most important 20th-century poets; most of his works have been published in English. **Jorge Enrique Adoum** (1926-2009) wrote *Entre Marx y una Mujer Desnuda* (1976), which is not yet available in English; it was turned into a movie by Camilo Luzuriaga in 1995. An English collection of Adoum's poetry, *Disinterred Love*, was released in 2012 by Salt Publishing. **Demetrio Aguilera Malta** is widely translated into English. His magisurrealist novels include: *Don Goyo* (1980), *Seven Serpents and Seven Moons* (1981) and *Babelandia* (1985).

Influential Afro-Ecuadorian writers are Nelson Estupiñán Bass, (1912-2002), Antonio Preciado (1944-) and Adalberto Ortiz (1914-2003), who wrote *Juyungo* (1942) which appears in English.

Other 20th and 21st century wordsmiths from this Andean nation to check out are: Abdón Ubidia, Alicia Yánez Cossío, Eliécer Cárdenas, Enrique Gil Gilber, Mariana Falconí, Nuria Rengifo and Raúl Pérez Torres.

The books of these and many others may be purchased at the bookstores of the Casa de la Cultura Ecuatoriana, which has branches throughout the country.
Updated: Oct 03, 2012.

Art and Painting in Ecuador

Ecuador has always been a nation of painters and artists. During the colonial era, Quito built a solid reputation as a center for religious art in the New World, and has never looked back. Today, Ecuador is still one of the best places in the world to appreciate and purchase beautiful works of art.

THE QUITO SCHOOL OF ART

Within a few years of arrival in Quito, the Catholic Church began constructing houses of worship—from small chapels to huge cathedrals. These churches, emulating their European counterparts, featured elaborate, impressive interiors with hand-carved decorations and pillars, paintings and arches. Rather than import artistic works such as crucifixes, paintings and statues of saints from Europe, the priests began training local artists to produce them.

For the first hundred years or so, the copies of European art made by Ecuadorians were skilled and workman-like, if uninspiring in nature. But then, something happened that the priests did not foresee: The local artists began to develop their own techniques and styles. Their art became more visceral and detailed than that of the original European works they had now copied.

The crucifixes, which had previously portrayed a stoic Christ on the cross with a single wound over his heart, now were of a Christ in agony; his flesh shredded, his ribs showing, his skin flayed and blood running down his sides. Few who view crucifixes from this period can resist an involuntary shudder as they see Christ's pain and torment—the pain and torment of the conquered, enslaved native people who produced the crucifix.

The Quito (Quiteño) school is also known for highly detailed statues. The saints and other religious figures that were depicted were made from finely carved local wood, painstakingly whittled into shape before being painted with incredible attention to detail. The cheeks of the saints were given a rosy glow, and fake glass eyes were included to improve the sense of realism. Some even had real hair, and many had robes of fine local cloth.

The Quito style of art became well-known in the region and in the world, and by the middle of the 18th century, there were more than 30 art guilds operating in Quito, producing art full-time. With the advent of independence and the resulting loosening of the Catholic Church's stranglehold on art and culture, the Quito school of art began exploring their roots, blending what they knew with their own culture. From this period come paintings of Christ wearing Andean clothes and even eating *cuy* (guinea pig) at the last supper.

INDIGENOUS MOVEMENT

In the early twentieth century, a new artistic movement swept the country: the indigenous movement. Inspired by the Quito School of Art as well as by the suffering of native peoples in the Americas, artists from Ecuador began producing works which reflected the sorry state of native populations in South America. Artists such as Oswaldo Guayasamín, Eduardo Kingman and Camilo Egas gained world-wide fame with their portrayals of the trials and tribulations of native life, contact between natives and Spaniards and pressures of modern life. Their works can be seen in Quito at the Casa de la Cultura and the museums dedicated to Guayasamín, Egas and Kingman. See the museums section for locations and hours.

TODAY'S ART SCENE IN ECUADOR

Today, Ecuador—and Quito in particular—is home to a vibrant art scene. Several impressive art galleries in Quito feature work by local artists. The capital's Centro Cultural Metropolitano and Centro de Arte Contemporáneo hold special exhibits. The annual salon, Mariano Aguilera, is the national art competition. A neat place to see local artists showcasing their work is El Ejido Park (across from the Hilton Colón) on Sunday morning, when dozens of local artists unpack their canvases for everyone to see and (hopefully) purchase.

If you're interested in other forms of art, such as tapestries, check out the fancy boutiques on Amazonas and Juan León Mera. The few art galleries in Mitad del Mundo offer touristy paintings. There are several galleries (the term is used loosely: some are converted family living rooms) in Otavalo. On that town's market day (Saturday), you can choose from a wide array of local art, mostly watercolors. Prices are reasonable, but be persistent in your bargaining. Art sellers in Otavalo tend to jack up their initial prices relatively

JULIO JARAMILLO

Born in Guayaquil in 1935, Julio Jaramillo would become the most famous Ecuadorian singer and a major cultural icon—sort of like an Ecuadorian Elvis Presley. Like Elvis, he became famous at a young age, and died young at the age of 42 in 1978. Because Ecuador was considered something of a musical backwater, he spent much of his career elsewhere, mainly in Venezuela, Columbia, Mexico and Uruguay. Jaramillo recorded songs in several different genres, including boleros, pasillos, waltzes, tangos and rancheras. He is most famous for the boleros, which are commonly referred to as *corta-venas*, or "vein-cutters," in Ecuador because they are remarkably depressing.

At the height of his career he sold records from Mexico to Argentina and was greeted by huge crowds wherever he went. His most famous song was "Nuestro Juramento" ("Our Oath"). It became so famous that he was known as "Mr. Juramento" for most of his career. He returned to Ecuador in 1976.

By then, he was very popular in his native land, and was treated like royalty. When he died two years later, thousands of sorrowful fans filled the streets near his home. Today, he is still widely popular, particularly in his native Guayaquil: Whenever someone plays a Jaramillo song on the jukebox in a bar—and every jukebox has at least one of his songs—the crowd will stop whatever they're doing and sing along. Updated: Sep 03, 2012.

more than other merchants. You may find yourself paying less than half the original price for a piece of art if you bargain well.

One local form of art that is popular with visitors is the Tigua painting. Tigua is a tiny town high in the Andes known for small, colorful paintings made on stretched sheepskin. The paintings usually feature tiny figures of Andeans about their daily life herding llamas, attending local fairs and the like. Some feature mythological elements, such as condors, faces in the mountains, and volcanoes. Be sure to ask the vendor (who is often also the artist) about any element in the painting that you don't understand: often, the artist offers and interesting explanation. Tigua paintings are available almost everywhere: you'll see them in any market you visit.

OSWALDO GUAYASAMÍN

Born in 1919 to humble, indigenous parents, Oswaldo Guayasamín would later mature into Ecuador's most famous artist. His striking art portrays the humanity and suffering of the repressed classes and people of the Americas. Considered an expressionist, Guayasamín used bright colors, symbolism and images of pain and torment to create truly unique and memorable works.

By the time he was middle aged, Guayasamín was awarded numerous artist and humanitarian honors and his art had been exhibited in the U.S., Italy, Spain, France, Brazil, the Soviet Union, Cuba, China, and other countries. Some of these exhibits were in prestigious locations, such as the Palais de Luxembourg (Paris, 1992) and the L'Hermitage Museum (Saint Petersburg, 1982). In 1978 he was named to the Royal Academy of Fine Arts of Spain and in 1979, to the Academy of Italian Arts. The United Nations Educational, Scientific and Cultural Organization (UNESCO) gave him a prize for "an entire life of work for peace."

In spite of these lofty awards, Guayasamín never lost his connection with the common people of Ecuador, who adored him. Toward the end of his life he began work on La **Capilla del Hombre** (The Chapel of Man), which he dedicated to the races of Latin America, although he never lived to see it finished. He passed away in 1999. Artists from around the world continued to complete the master's plans. Nor did Guayasamín never lose his artistic edge. Commissioned to do a series of murals for the Ecuadorian Congress in 1988, he painted 23 panels depicting his nation's history. One of the panels features a black-and-white painting of a horrid, skeletal face wearing a Nazi-style helmet with the letters CIA on it. The painting caused an international incident between Ecuador and the U.S. The artist held firm and the painting remains.

Today, Guayasamín is still very popular. His works are on display in his **museum** and at the Capilla del Hombre. If you go shopping in the Mariscal area, you're likely to see many knockoffs of his works for sale in a variety of mediums. His works are easy to spot: They are colorful and feature people with distinctive twisted hands and faces.

Music in Ecuador

Ecuadorians love music. On the streets, in homes, at parties, and on buses—if you're traveling in Ecuador, you're going to hear plenty of sound.

In tourist areas such as Otavalo or Baños, you're bound to encounter a native band (called a *grupo* or *conjunto*) composed of anywhere from four to 10 Ecuadorians, often dressed in native clothing, playing folkloric songs on traditional instruments. The group is bound to have at least one guitarist, a drummer and at least one musician producing a haunting melody on a panflute, a traditional Andean instrument composed of varying lengths of bamboo lashed together.

In towns like Baños, the groups make the rounds of the more expensive tourist restaurants, stopping by and playing three or four songs, then passing the hat for tips and selling CDs of their music. Some fancier places, such as haciendas that have been converted into hotels, have their own native bands that play for guests in the evening and during dinner (they'll probably have CDs, too).

If you're lucky enough to get invited to a private party or make it to a local festival, you may see a *banda del pueblo*. These bands are composed of locals who get together on special occasions to play mostly traditional music. The instruments are often old and fairly beat up, and occasionally the musical talent is questionable, but whatever they may lack in skill or instruments they more than make up for in exuberance and volume.

Ecuadorians also perform modern genres, like *cumbia, reggaetón* and *salsa* as well as *electronic* and *metal*. Paulina Aguirre and her producer-husband Pablo Aguirre were the first musicians of this Andean nation to win a Latin Grammy, in 2009, for Best Christian Album.

Ecuadorians have diverse musical tastes in regards to international music. If you spin the dial on a radio in Quito, you'll find different stations playing salsa, rap, Spanish oldies, elevator music, pop, rock, reggaetón and everything in between.

Some stations consider "music in English" to be its own genre, which means that the same station plays music that would never be played together in the U.S., such bizarre blending involves the likes of Britney Spears, Eminem, Korn and the Bee Gees.

International Spanish-language music is widely popular in Ecuador. Salsa, merengue and cumbia—all different forms of dance music from Latin America—can be heard around the nation. Each is a different genre of music that requires different dance moves, but to the untrained ear they can be difficult to tell apart. If you plan on visiting a *salsateca* (salsa dance club) while in Ecuador (and you should, they're a lot of fun) you may want to take a dance class or two first. The Mariscal area in Quito (see Quito section) is full of dance schools. Alternatively, check out a dance show if you can. They're hyped up by the tour companies for a reason. You should also see what is happening at major cultural centers such as the Casa de la Cultura and Teatro Sucre, as they often have special events and shows.

Dance, Theater and Comedy

Ecuador's deeply rooted history, variety of cultures and geography has treated its artistic expressions no differently: The evolution of dance, theater and comedy has taken many forms. All these can easily be combined, because dance often takes the form of theater and vice-versa, and comedy is a great artistic expression.

DANCE

Marimba, the official dance of Ecuador, was created and popularized by the Afro-Ecuadorian population. The *currulao* portion of the dance performance corresponds with the rhythm of the marimba instrument, which resembles a xylophone, and has strong roots in West African Bantu and Mande heritage. The dance signifies freedom from colonizers.

Afro-Ecuadorians were able to fend off the Spaniards in the coastal city of Esmeraldas until the mestizo encroached on their land in search of mineral resources. The mestizos regulated the Afro-Ecuadorians' use of the *currulao* dance, prohibiting them from performing unless they possessed a specific license. But in the 1970s the Afro-Ecuadorians reclaimed their power and formed dance troupes, in order to spread and preserve the knowledge and technique of their music and dance to new generations. Often this music and dance is combined with theater to tell the rich history of the Afro-Ecuadorian culture.

Ballet has swept into Ecuador in colossal form, especially in the capital city of Quito. One of Ecuador's ballet companies, Ballet Folklórico Ecuatoriano de Virginia Rosero

Did a unique trek? Tell other travelers at vivatravelguides.com

has, in recent years, traveled around the world representing the indigenous culture of Ecuador. Ballet companies usually encompass folkloric dances portraying all traditions, including Inti Raymi, Amazonian dance, mestizo dance, and bombas from Chota. In larger towns and cities salsa has become the modern dance of choice. Salsa is usually performed by partners, moving to a brisk beat.

THEATER

Ecuador's history of theater and modern productions offers insight into its true culture. During the pre-Columbian period, plays were once pure creations of improvisation. Theater was banned by the Spanish colonists because the leaders deemed the artistic expression to pose too much a threat to their succinct society. But through it all, theater has helped preserve the perils and hardships the country has had to face, and expresses it in all its beauty.

In the past couple of decades, theaters have experienced cutbacks in funding, hindering their ability to function at a high level. This could be due to the rising trend in film production or a simple lack of interest, but there is an esoteric triumph of individuals working to keep the tradition very alive.

An example of this is "Malayerba," a politically and economically independent theater group. For more than 30 years, it has traveled, addressing relationships between men and women and domestic violence.

A lot of great theater houses and productions can be found in cities, especially in Cuenca, the cultural capital of Ecuador.

COMEDY

Comedy in the form of theater, stand-up and performances have not made too large of a break in Ecuador. In terms of international influence, Comedy Central is now an Ecuadorian channel, however.
Updated: Sep 03, 2012.

History of Ecuadorian Cinema

The history of Ecuador's film industry can be divided into two periods: pre-1999 and post-1999. With regards to pre-1999, Ecuador's sporadic attempts at movie making were, to paraphrase Samuel Johnson, like a dog walking on his hind legs. Indeed, it was not done all that well, but one was surprised to find it done at all.

With the exception of Mexico, Brazil and Argentina, no Latin American country was ever capable of establishing a substantial, independent and durable film industry. This was partly due to the hegemonic dominance of Hollywood and Europe in movie theaters, and partly due to the three aforementioned countries, whose industries were subsidized by their governments, going after what was left of the remaining market share.

While there was little in the way of actual Ecuadorian filmmaking in the 20th century, there was no shortage of popular enthusiasm for the new medium from its beginnings. In fact, the visible presence in foreign films of Victrolas, gas stoves, cosmetics and modern sanitation prompted a new market for such items among Ecuador's emerging middle-class, thus helping Ecuador move more quickly out of its feudal origins.

The Golden Age of Ecuadorian cinema is generally considered the 1920s, with one notable entrepreneur-auteur, Augusto San Miguel. He not only made two feature films, "El Tesoro de Atahulpa" (Atahualpa's Treasure) and "Un abismo y dos almas" (An Abyss and Two Souls),but who was politically progressive as well. The latter film decried the exploitation and abuse of the country's impoverished indigenous majority at the hands of its greedy, land-owning aristocracy.

Almost all Latin American countries had their own, similar pioneers in this period, yet the arrival of the talkie, with its attendant high production costs, crushed what nascent potential these countries had for their own film industries, especially with Spanish-dubbed Hollywood fare flooding local theaters.

Thus, for the next fifty years, what scant filmmaking occurred in Ecuador was mostly in the realm of the documentary, a genre whose budget and, unfortunately, whose audience, were both modest. Between 1947 and 1959, four feature films were made with local actors and sought to reach a popular audience. Their value today, however, is sociological-historical rather than aesthetic or even pleasurable.

The seeds of Ecuador's modern film movement were planted in the 1970s, when universities began to offer film study curricula and local television stations sponsored short-film contests. Even before then, the government-sponsored Casa de la Cultura, under the direction of Ulises Estrella, presented showings of non-commercial films for a club of art-of-film enthusiasts. In 1977, Ecuador saw the formation of its first representative body of filmmakers, an organization known as Asocine.

A new generation of ambitious and passionate writer-directors was able to find the funding for their dream projects, most notably Camillo Luzuriaga, whose film, "La Tigre" (The Tigress), based on a fictional allegory by Ecuadorian author, José de la Cuadra, won the Best First Film award at the Cartagena International Film Festival in 1989. On television, American-trained, Yugoslav director Carl West adapted a series of historical Ecuadorian novels into skillfully-made television films.

However, in 1999 it was a young man from Cuenca, Sebastian Cordero—fresh out of the UCLA film program—who gave birth to Ecuador's modern film movement when his tough, gritty crime thriller, "Ratas, Ratones, Rateros" (Rats, Mice, Thieves), was honored with awards and nominations across the world, including a nomination for the Spanish Goya for Best Spanish Language Foreign Film. Cordero's next Ecuadorian film, "Crónicas," was co-produced by the Mexican-Hollywood directorial superstars Alfonso Cuarón and Guillermo del Toro, and starred John Leguizamo.

In 2006, Ecuador's congress established the National Film Council to subsidize and encourage local filmmakers. In 2007 another Cuenca director, Tania Hermida, scored a major critical and commercial success, both locally and internationally, with "¿Que tan lejos?" (How much further?), which starred Ecuadorian singer Fausto Miño.

The last few years have validated the aspirations of Ecuador's filmmakers with the creation of original and deeply felt works, both in the realm of fiction and documentary.

Of the latter, "Con mi corazón en Yambo" (With My Heart in Yambo), a passionate, angry investigation by María Fernanda Restrepo of the disappearance and probable torture and murder of her two adolescent, Colombian-immigrant brothers who were mistakenly identified as "terrorists" under the scorched-earth "anti-terrorist" policies of former Ecuadorian president, León Febres-Cordero.
Updated: August 1, 2013.

Holidays and Fiestas
CARNAVAL
Carnaval, which is celebrated each year in February or March the week before Lent, is Latin America's version of Mardi Gras. The celebrations that take place in Ecuador the four days preceding Ash Wednesday may not be as crazy as some countries, but if you happen to be in the area during this holiday it is worth checking out.

During the four days before Ash Wednesday, Quito is almost a ghost town. Many of its residents head to the coast to soak up the sun. Atacames is particularly busy. Children run around at all hours of the night, spraying the random passerby with foam in a can while their parents are busy dancing in one of the many bars along the beach.

The main component of any carnaval celebration in Ecuador is abundant water, used for soaking people. Beware, foreigner, as you are a very attractive target. Without a doubt you will be drenched with water and silly string by hoards of children. Quito is no exception. It can be vexing, but try to accept that it is simply their way of celebrating this holiday.

If you prefer a bit dryer holiday weekend, head to Ambato, where water throwing is prohibited. Here, the huge festival is called Fiesta de la Fruta y de las Flores. This event is filled with colorful parades, bullfights and handicraft exhibits.

Another town that has an impressive carnaval celebration is the town of Guaranda, located in the central Andes. Usually this is your average sleepy Ecuadorian town, nothing remarkable for a tourist. However, carnaval transforms it into a four day non-stop party, filled with parades, music and fun. Also the locals tend to be very hospitable, many prepare large feasts and invite anyone on the street into their homes to celebrate with them.
Updated: Sep 03, 2012.

SEMANA SANTA (EASTER AND HOLY WEEK)
February sees religious processions and an endless supply of *fanesca* (a typical stew made of different grains and seafood eaten throughout the week) mark Palm Sunday, Holy Thursday, Good Friday, Holy Saturday and Easter Sunday. While Holy Saturday is technically the only official holiday during which stores ought to be closed, many businesses are closed the whole week. Be advised

that pretty much all of Ecuador goes to the beach during Holy Week, consequently prices go up and rooms are scarce. The Ceremonia de Reseña or Vísperas is celebrated in only three cities around the world, and Quito is one of them. If you are in Quito on Miércoles Santo be sure to check it out. Updated: Aug 23, 2012.

GOOD FRIDAY

One of the most grandiose events for Quito's religious community, the great procession of Santo Viernes (Good Friday) follows the morning *Via Crucis* prayer on the final Friday of Holy Week, observing the crucifixion of Jesus Christ. Tens of thousands—many donning purple robes and coned hoods reminiscent of the Ku Klux Klan—flock to the city's historic center and wind through the streets in a solemn procession. It's a colorful scene definitely not to be missed. Watch it from a balcony or join the masses walking through the streets.

The procession begins at midday at Iglesia San Francisco, making its way through the Centro Histórico to the Basílica and back to San Francisco. Traditional purple-hooded *cucuruchos* (penitents, many donning thorny headpieces, massive crosses and chains around their feet demonstrating their will to change) and robed *Verónicas* (also wearing purple dresses and black shrouds as they pay tribute to the woman who wiped the sweat and blood from Jesus' face as he was carried on the cross) encircle a figure of Jesus and the Virgen Dolorosa (Our Lady of Sorrows), further surrounded by the solemn masses.

The procession ends at 3 p.m.—the hour of Jesus' death—and is followed by a ceremony reenacting the Descent from the Cross at six in the evening. Some Quito churches make quite an ordeal of this, with the priest recounting the story of the apostles performing the sepulcher of Christ from his pulpit. Finally, designated men remove the nails from the crucified Christ, passing the body along to a group of women who lay him to rest in a white tunic and flowers.

In addition to watching the procession, Quiteños typically go to church on the morning of Good Friday and spend the rest of the day at home, perhaps watching religious movies about Jesus. In the evening, the extended family gets together for dinner, where *fanesca*, a traditional Easter-time soup made with twelve grains and fish, is usually served.

Many families also go to the coast for Good Friday and Semana Santa because children have off school and adults have time off work. Updated: Aug 23, 2012.

CEREMONIA DE RESEÑA O VÍSPERAS

The Ceremonia de Reseña o Vísperas in Quito's Catedral is one of the oldest and rarest ceremonies in the Catholic Church. The centuries-old procession happens the Wednesday before Easter, *Miércoles Santo*, in only three churches in the world: in Sevilla, Spain; Lima, Peru; and Quito, Ecuador.

The procession, consisting of six priests and the Archbishop, represents the life, death and subsequent resurrection of Jesus Christ.

Way back in the days of colonization, Lima's Catedral operated beneath Sevilla. Quito, in turn, operated under Lima. Given the hierarchy of the Catholic Church, the Ceremonia de Reseña o Vísperas is only allowed to be practiced in churches given permission from Sevilla. Witnessing the Quito ceremony is a chance to see this rare religious service driven by centuries of history.

The procession begins with the six priests filing into the front of the Catedral. Their elaborate black robes represent the collective darkening of humanity due to sinning. They are followed by the Archbishop, who wears a purple robe. Initially, the six priests, flanked by two altar boys bearing lit candles, walk a loop around the outside edge of the Sanctuary. The Archbishop follows last, surrounded by altar boys. The altar boys carry a small, square tent which represents protection of the church from evil. The Archbishop carries a small cross, said to be a relic from the original cross on which Jesus died.

After completing a full lap around the perimeter of the sanctuary, the six priests arrive at the front of the church and kneel with their faces to the floor. This represents the death of Christ. Thus begins the second part of the ceremony. It is thought that the inspiration for this part of the ceremony was derived from the funeral traditions of the Roman Army.

A major feature of the ceremony's second half is the solid black flag with a red cross on it, which symbolizes the powers and wisdom of Jesus. The congregation sings a hymn as the Archbishop waves the flag over the altar. The altar represents the body of Christ and the waving of the flag is intended to pick up the merits of Christ. The Archbishop then

Important Dates in Ecuador

January 1—New Year's Day

January 6—Three Kings Day (a.k.a. Feast of the Epiphany)

February 12—Anniversary of the Discovery of the Amazon River; Province Day (Galápagos)

February 27—National Community Spirit Day

May 1—Labor Day. Processions fill the streets and plazas to honor workers nationwide.

May 24—Battle of Pichincha. Military and civilian parades show the nation's pride of the day in 1822 when the country's most important battle in the war for independence from Spain was fought.

June—Corpus Cristi. Usually celebrated on the ninth Thursday after Easter, this religious holiday / traditional harvest celebration of the highlands includes ceremonies and dancing.

June 24—Saint John the Baptist. Celebrations in Otavalo and the surrounding highland communities.

June 29—Saints Peter and Paul. Celebrations in Otavalo and the surrounding highland communities. Communities in Manabí Province and elsewhere on the coast fête these patron saints of fishermen with boat processions.

July 24—Simón Bolívar's Birthday. A nationwide celebration of the birthday of South America's great liberator.

July 25—Founder's Day. Guayaquil's biggest party - the city shuts down for two days to celebrate Simón Bolívar's birthday and the foundation of Ecuador's most populous city.

August 10—Quito Independence Day: Quito celebrates with outdoor concerts, plays and special events the whole month of August. September - Various harvest festivals throughout the country

September 1-15—Fiesta del Yamor: An annual festival in the highland town of Otavalo.

September 23-24—Festival of the Virgin of Mercy

October 9—Guayaquil Independence Day: Once again, Guayaquil combines holidays (Independence Day and Columbus Day) to ensure a multi-day festival.

October 12—Columbus Day: Also known as Día de la Raza (Day of the Race), Columbus Day celebrates the day in 1492 on which Christopher Columbus (Cristóbal Colón) first set foot on American soil in what is now known as the Dominican Republic. In the last decade, with more and more people recognizing the negative effect of the conquistadores that followed Columbus, the celebration is a time to focus on the indigenous groups and their significant contributions.

November 1—All Saints' Day

November 2—All Souls' Day (a.k.a. Day of the Dead): All Souls' Day is a day during which families visit cemeteries to dance, drink, eat and leave flowers and other offerings for deceased friends and relatives in a convivial ceremony designed to celebrate the lives of those who have passed on.

November 3—Cuenca Independence Day: The culmination of three days of festivities, this is the final day of Cuenca's biggest annual celebration.

November 11—Latacunga Independence Day andFestival of the Mama Negra: Parades and parties precede a Catholic-Pagan religious procession.

December 6—Founder's Day (Quito). The air in the capital takes on a more festive spirit throughout the first week of December as Quiteños watch parades, attend street dances, and ride around Quito atop *chivas* (open-air party buses complete with live music and drinks). Also known as Fiestas de Quito, this week, in reality, is just the opening act to a month-long gala for many.

December 24—Christmas Eve

December 25—Christmas Day

December 28-31—Year End Celebrations. Starting with the Day of the Innocents, the entire nation symbolically prepares to enter a new year by burning human effigies in the streets as Quiteños end a nearly month-long party. In some parts, men dress up as *viudas* alegres (happy widows).

Did a unique trek? Tell other travelers at vivatravelguides.com

INTRO & INFO

turns around to face the kneeling priests (and the congregation) and waves the flag over the priests.

The kneeling six priests, covered by their black robes, resemble a large black space. This blackness is meant to symbolize mankind's sins. At the end, while singing the final verse of the hymn, the Archbishop hits the flag three times on the floor and the six priests rise to their feet, symbolizing the resurrection of Christ. Updated: Sep 03, 2012.

FIESTA DE LA MAMA NEGRA

The *Fiesta of the Mama Negra* (the Black Mother), which takes place biannually in the city of Latacunga, is one of the most fascinating cultural events in Ecuador.

This public celebration of civic pride rivals Brazil's festivals as an emblematic "melting pot" of wildly divergent cultural traditions: Spanish, Inca, Aymara, Mayan, African and, most recently, homosexuality.

The fiesta originated with the colonization of Latacunga by the Spanish for its rich mineral resources. The native inhabitants were forced to convert to Catholicism, but the conversion was not entirely pure, with the result that indigenous elements, such as a polytheistic belief in "spirits," became part of the new religion.

The Spanish conquerors brought in additional populations from Bolivia, Guatemala and ultimately Africa as slaves, and they too, brought their own beliefs and traditions to Latacunga. What set the holiday in motion was the eruption of the Cotopaxi volcano in 1742. The citizens of the region petitioned the Virgen de la Merced (Virgin of Mercy), who had been designated the patron of the volcano. When Latacunga was spared, an annual celebration was set in place to honor her.

The festival was traditionally held during the last weekend in September. It was on the verge of dying out in the early 1960s, until Cotopaxi Governor Virgilio Guerrero proposed preserving it by hosting a dual celebration of the festival with Latacunga's official celebration of the city's independence on November 11.

The now-official holiday had the ironic effect of reviving interest in the traditional religious celebration of the Virgen de la Merced on September 23-24, which is when the first annual Mama Negra festival takes place. However, the larger and more colorful celebrations are in November. Dates vary from year to year—sometimes coinciding with Latacunga's independence day and sometimes with the days surrounding Day of the Dead—so be sure to ask around.

The event constitutes a parade of characters, such as the Angel of the Stars, the Moorish King and Los Huacos, who represent Latacunga's pre-Columbian heritage, and the Camisonas (colorful transvestites), in a parade that attracts many, including dancers, musicians and marching bands, all leading up to the arrival of the Mama Negra, who is a combination of the Virgin with African deities. The Mama Negra, bearing dolls representing her "children," is elaborately costumed, and performs by spraying milk and water on parade goers.

Candy and wine containers are also tossed to the crowds, and restaurateurs feature Latacunga's most famous contribution to Ecuadorian cuisine, *chugchucaras*: deep fried pork, pork rinds, popcorn potatoes, maize and plantain. Updated: Sep 17, 2012.

THE DAY OF THE DEAD IN ECUADOR

Celebrated throughout Latin America as a result of the combination between indigenous beliefs and Catholic religion, the Day of the Dead (Día de los Muertos) takes place on November 2 around the continent. In Ecuador the holiday is interpreted as a day to "catch up" with the ones who are no longer with us but have a life in a different world. People pack lunches of traditional food, flowers and offerings and head for the cemeteries where they spend the day as a family talking, eating and performing routine maintenance on the grave site.

The staple food of the season is the famous *colada morada*, a thick purple drink, and *guaguas de pan*, sweet bread in the shape of dolls. Weeks before the holiday, supermarkets and bakeries begin selling the ingredients and store-made versions these items.

Colada morada is made out of black corn flour, blackberries, cinnamon, and pineapple, among other ingredients that are cooked together and served hot or cold with the sweet bread. To some people, the reddish-purple drink symbolizes blood, which in turn symbolizes life of the ones who have moved on from this existence.

There are as many versions of colada morada and guaguas de pan recipes as there are households, because whether a family visits their long-time gone relatives at cemeteries or not, the great majority of Ecuadorians will taste their version of the traditional food. The tradition of spending the day at cemeteries has declined in urban areas of Ecuador. However, once you leave the city behind it is easy to find entire communities mingling at the local cemetery for the occasion.

It is probably best to catch this holiday in the southern provinces of the Sierra, since November 3 marks the Independence of Cuenca and colorful festivities of the two consecutive holidays can be enjoyed in the area.
Updated: Sep 10, 2012.

FIESTAS DE QUITO

If you are in Quito during the last days of November and during the run-up to December 6, you cannot fail to notice a distinctly fiesta-ish atmosphere in the city. During these days, Quiteños let their hair down to commemorate the Spanish founding of the city on the same date in 1534.

Fiestas de Quito celebrate Ecuador's Spanish roots, so traditional Spanish culture is appreciated and enjoyed during these days. Traditional food like *fritadas* (fried, chopped pork) and *llapingachos* (potato pancakes with cheese), as well as copious amounts of wine, are commonly consumed. *Pasillos*, or traditional Spanish music, is widespread and games like *trompos* (spinning of tops) and *carros de madera* (wooden car racing) are played. Joke-telling in theaters and *cuarenta* card game competitions are two other traditions during the festivities.

For the ten days running up to and including December 6, there are also bull fights at the Plaza de Toros, the only time during the year when the bull ring is actually used for bull fighting. The fights are considered by most to be a high-class social event, and Quito's elite flock to the fights, dressed in their finest smart-casual wear, donning cowboy or panama hats to keep the sun off. Many also have *botas* (wineskins). Those who can't afford to go inside linger outside and in the surrounding streets in groups drinking beer and whiskey and dancing in makeshift discos.

In late November, the festivities start with the election of the Queen of Quito. From this point onwards, in the streets you can see *chivas*, or colorful open-topped buses driving through the streets, carrying as many as 50 people who may be dancing to the *banda del pueblo* (town band) which play on the top, or drinking *canelazo*, a potent alcoholic drink with a sugar cane alcohol and cinnamon base. This happens night and day, and chivas are reserved well ahead of time for the early days of December.

On the night of December 5, the partying reaches a climax and there are street parties all over Quito. The Mariscal district is more alive and crowded than usual as bars and clubs overflow with revelers. Large parties in haciendas in the surrounding valleys are also common occurrences. A good place to head is Carolina Park, where there will often be open-air concerts and fireworks.

In some of Quito's traditional neighborhoods, like the Centro Histórico, roads are closed for dancing and candelazo drinking as *vacas locas* (crazy cows), or cows made out of fireworks, spark in the streets. If street parties are your thing, head to Vancouver and Polonia streets (located behind the Petrocomerical gas station on Amazonas), where there is usually a DJ, decent music and plenty of dancing to be enjoyed.

Those with leftover stamina will continue to party throughout the day and night of December 6 into the morning of December 7. Street parties persist throughout the city and in the valleys as more dancing and drinking takes place. Some places serve breakfast on the morning of December 7 for a small cover, so those who stay up all night can enjoy some food with friends as a farewell to the year's festivities. However, for many, December 6 itself can end up being a fairly quiet day, as many Quiteños and foreigners sleep off their hangovers.

NEW YEAR'S EVE

A New Year's Eve, or *Año Viejo*, spent in Ecuador provides a fascinating insight into local culture and folklore. During the week or so preceding the day itself, you will see effigies for sale in the streets, made from wood, paper, cloth and firecrackers. These effigies will usually represent international political figures that are hated, locally despised politicians, or icons from popular music or culture, from the old year. These figures are dressed up in the family's clothing and with masks of the personalities they seek to depict. They are then burned on New Year's Eve to banish the bad and welcome in the new - a flaming catharsis, so to speak.

In Quito, Avenida Amazonas is the place to head early in the evening to check out the stalls and the open-air entertainment. Themed effigy displays line the road along with live music and street food. You may see effigies being burned here and you will certainly see fireworks. Outside of Quito, the coastal town of Salinas is a popular Ecuadorian New Year's Eve haunt. In the countryside, many people light fires in the street, upon which they burn the effigies. This happens in Quito too, but more frequently in the suburbs.

Similar to Halloween in the States, New Year's Eve is a day when children and adults alike dress up in costumes, wigs and masks. Throughout the country, a popular pursuit is for men to dress up as women—the *viudas alegres*, or merry widows —and beg for money. Also, outside of the main cities, especially on roads to the smaller countryside towns, you may come across children holding string across the roads. They are trying to stop the traffic with the aim of relieving you of your small change.

Midnight tends to be a family affair, indulging in a meal served at home with relatives. A local tradition is to eat twelve grapes (*uvas*) at the stroke of midnight, which is supposed to bring luck throughout the year. The streets become ablaze with little fires as each family burns its own effigy. After dinner, younger people head off to clubs or parties to see in the New Year with style.

Ecuador Visa Information

NOTE: The following information should be confirmed with the Ecuadorian Embassy or Consulate in your own country, or the Ministerio de Relaciones Exteriores (Ministry of Foreign Affairs) website (www.mmrree. gob.ec/eng/services/visas.asp). Visa policies and regulations change frequently, and can vary from one office to another. Sometimes the best sources are other travelers who have gone through the process themselves. The Ministry of Foreign Affairs is located in Quito, at Carrión E1-76 y Av. 10 de Agosto (Tel: 593-2-299-3200).

U.S. citizens need to have passports that are valid for at least six months prior to departing Ecuador as well. This only applies if you have an international stopover, though. If your flight is direct to the United States, departure will not be denied in the instance of less than six months validity.

TOURIST VISAS

Most travelers to Ecuador will not need to obtain a visa before departure. Citizens of Afghanistan, Bangladesh, Eritrea, Ethiopia, Kenya, Nepal, Nigeria, Pakistan, the People's Republic of China and Somalia require a visa to enter Ecuador.

As of August 2011, visitors need to have at least six months valid on their passport prior to travel in order to enter the country. When you arrive, the migration officials will stamp a tourist visa valid up to 90 days. If you plan to stay the entire 90 days, be sure to request the full visa limit as migration officials will sometimes give a visa for less time. They will also give you give you an embarkation card. Save this. You will need to present it when you leave the country.

If you come from a country that requires a tourist visa, you will need to apply for a 12-X visa. The fee for this visa is $30, plus a processing charge of $30 which you have to present at the Ministerio de Relaciones Exteriores, along with: two copies of the completed *formulario de solicitud de visa de no inmigrante* (non-immigrant visa application form; print off from the Ministry's website), two passport photos (in color, with white background), an economic guarantee (print-out of your bank account), your original passport with at least six months validity, a photocopy of your passport, a photocopy of your round-trip plane ticket and a *solicitud de visa* (an explanation of why you want to extend your stay, in Spanish).

Extending Your Tourist Visa

Your 90 day visa can be extended for a further 90 days by applying for a 12-IX visa, the Commercial Activities Visa. It is valid for up to six months and allows you to change your visa status. It allows the foreigner to engage in tourism, sports, health, education, science, art or commercial transactions. The fee for this visa is $200, plus $30 processing charge.

The paperwork entails: two copies of the completed *formulario de solicitud de visa de no inmigrante* (non-immigrant visa application form; print off from the Ministry's website), two passport photos (in color, with white background), an economic guarantee (print-out of your bank account), your original passport with at least six months validity, a photocopy of your passport, a photocopy of your plane ticket and a *solicitud de visa* (an explanation of why you want to extend your stay, in Spanish).

Embassies and Consulates in Ecuador

Here is a list of foreign embassies in Ecuador. Because information for embassies in Ecuador may change at any point, please let us know of any updates by e-mailing us at: books@vivatravelguides.com

---

Argentina
Av. Amazonas 21-147 and Roca, Building Río Amazonas, 8th Floor, Quito. Tel: 256-2292 / 252-7624, E-mail: embarge2@uiosadnet.net / feecua@mrecic.gov.ar.

Bolivia
Av. Eloy Alfaro 2432 and Fernando Ayarza, Zona El Batán, Quito. Tel: 458-863 / 458-868, E-mail: emboliviaquito@andinanet.net.

Brazil
Av. Amazonas 1429 and Colón, Edificio España, 10th Floor, Quito. Tel: 256-3086, E-mail bec-ecu@trans-telco.net.

Canada
Av. Amazonas 4153 and Unión Nacional de Periodistas, Eurocenter Building, 3rd floor, Quito. Tel: 245-5499, E-mail: quito@dfait-maeci.gc.ca.

Chile
Juan Pablo Sanz 3617 and Amazonas, Edificio Xerox, 4th Floor, Quito. Tel: 246-6780, E-mail: embachileecu@uio.satnet.net.

China
Atahualpa 349 and Amazonas, Quito. Tel: 244-4362, URL: ec.chineseembassy.org/esp.

Colombia
Colón 1133 and Amazonas, Edificio Artistas, 7th Floor, Quito. Tel: 222-2486, E-mail: equito@minrelext.gov.co.

Costa Rica
Isla San Cristóbal N44-385 and Guepi, Quito. Tel: 225-2330, E-mail: embajcr@uio.satnet.net.

Cuba
Mercurio 365, between La Razón and El Vengador, Quito. Tel: 245-6936, E-mail: embajada@embacuba.ec, URL: www.cubadiplomatica.cu/ecuador.

Dominican Republic
Av. de los Shyris 1240 and Portugal, Edificio Albatros, 5th Floor, Quito. Tel: 243-4275, E-mail: emrepdom@interactive.net.ec.

Finland
Flores Jijón E 17-87 (280) and Hernan Sotomayor, Quito. Tel: 244-6052, E-mail: renecruz@hotmail.com.

France
Leonidas Plaza 107 and Patria, Quito. Tel: 294-3800, E-mail: francie@uio.satnet.net, URL: www.ambafrance-ec.org.

Germany
Av. Naciones Unidas, Edificio Citiplaza 14th Floor, Quito. Tel: 297-2820, E-mail: info@quito.diplo.de, URL: www.quito.diplo.de.

Guatemala
República del Salvador 733 and Portugal, Edificio Gabriela III, 3rd Floor, Quito. Tel: 245-9700, E-mail: mbecuador@minex.gob.gt, URL: www.guatemala-ecuador.org.

Honduras
Av. 12 de Octubre 1942 and Cordero, World Trade Center, Building Torre A, 5th Floor, Quito. Tel: 222-0441, E-mail: embhquito@yahoo.com.

Israel
Av. 12 de Octubre 1059 and Francisco Salazar, Plaza 2000 Building, 9th Floor, Quito. Tel: 397-1500, E-mail: info@quito.mfa.gov.il, URL:quito.mfa.gov.il.

Italy
La Isla 111 and Humberto Albornoz, Quito. Tel: 256-1077, E-mail: archivio.quito@esteri.it, URL:www.ambquito.esteri.it.

Japan
Juan León Mera 130 and Av. Patria, Corporación Financiera Nacional building, 7th Floor, Quito. Tel: 256-1899, E-mail: japembec@uio.satnet.net.

Korea
Av. Naciones Unidas and República del Salvador, Citiplaza Building, 8th Floor, Quito. Tel: 297-0625, E-mail: ecuador@mofat.go.kr.

INTRO & INFO

Lithuania
Pasaje Frederico Paredes 555 and 10 de Agosto, Quito. Tel: 243-9450, E-mail: blasonlit@andinanet.net.

Mexico
Av. 6 de Diciembre N36-165 and Naciones Unidas, Quito. Tel: 292-3770, E-mail: embajadamexico@embamex.org.ec, URL: www.sre.gob.mx/ecuador.

Netherlands
Av. 12 de Octubre 1942 and Cordero, World Trade Center Building, Torre A, 1st Floor, Quito. Tel: 222-9229, E-mail: nlgovqui@ebajadadeholanda.com, URL: www.embajadadeholanda.com.

Panama
Alpallana 505 and Whimper, Edificio ESPRO, 6th Floor, Quito. Tel: 224-5871, E-mail: pmaemecua@interactive.net.ec, URL: www.embajadadepanamaecuador.com.

Peru
Av. Republica del Salvador 495 and Irlanda, Irlanda Building, Quito. Tel: 246-8410, E-mail: cperuloj_s@easynet.net.ec, URL: www.embajadadelperu.org.ec.

Russia
Reina Victoria 462 and Roca, Quito. Tel: 252-6361, E-mail: Embrusia@accessinter.net, URL: www.ecuador.mid.ru.

Sweden
Juan Severino E8-38 y Diego de Almagro, Edificio Argentina Plaza, piso 2, oficina 201, Quito. Tel: 380-0630, E-mail:vconsuec@uio.satnet.net.

Switzerland
Juan Pablo Sanz 120 and Av. Amazonas 3617, Xerox Building, 2nd Floor, Quito. Tel: 243-4948 / 243-4949, E-mail: vergregungatqui.ret.admin.churl_desk, URL: www.eda.edmin.ch/quito.

Spain
La Pinta 455 and Amazonas, Quito. Tel: 256-4373 / 256-4390 / 256-4377, E-mail :embespec@correo.mae.es.

Uruguay
Av. 6 de Diciembre 2816 and Paul Rivet, Josueth González Building, 9th Floor, Quito. Tel: 254-4228, E-mail: emburug1@emburuguay.int.ec.

United Kingdom
Av. Naciones Unidas and República del Salvador, Citiplaza Building, 12 and 14th Floor, Quito. Tel: 297-0800 / 297-0801, E-mail: consuio@satnet.net, URL: www.fco.gov.uk.

United States of America
Av. Avigiras E12-170 and Ave. Eloy Alfaro (next to SOLCA) Quito. Tel: 256-2890, E-mail: contacto.usembuio@state.gov, URL:ecuador.usembassy.gov.

Venezuela
Av. Amazonas N30-240 y Eloy Alfaro, Edificio Comonsa, 8th floor, Quito. Tel: 255-7209, E-mail: embve.ecqto@mppre.gob.ve, URL: www.ecuador.embajada.gob.ve.

WORK, STUDY AND OTHER NON-RESIDENT VISAS

If you want to work, study (long-term) or just travel for more than 180 days, you will need to look into a different visa. There are two main types of visas: resident and non-resident (referred to as immigrant and non-immigrant on the Ecuadorian government website).

Student visas, work visas, volunteer and religious work visas, cultural exchanges and tourist visas all fall under the category of non-resident and will set you back between $50 and $200, plus $30 processing fee. All of these visas have to be applied for before you arrive in Ecuador at the consulates in you native country.

Work visas are extremely hard to obtain and are much more complicated than tourist visas and are best arranged with your employer. Student visas are less complicated but are also best obtained with the help of your school or study program, which will undoubtedly have experience in jumping through the necessary bureaucratic hoops.

NOTE: All non-resident visas, except for the 12-X Tourist, that were applied for overseas must be registered at the Dirección de la Extranjería (Av 6 de Diciembre, between Colón and La Niña) within the first 30 days of arrival. Failure to do so will result in a hefty $200-2,000 fine. If you applied for it in Ecuador, you do not need to register it.

Censos are no longer issued to foreigners. Instead you are supposed to carry your passport at all times. A photocopy of the photo, visa page and visa registration pages may suffice in most circumstances.

OVERSTAYING YOUR NON-IMMIGRANT VISA

As of April 20, 2010, foreigners are no longer fined for overstaying their non-immigrant visas; nonetheless, some travelers reports being charged upon leaving the country. Re-entry into the country will be banned for nine months; your name will appear on a list.

If you are caught overstaying you can be deported.

IMMIGRANT (RESIDENT) VISAS

If you are planning to stay for more than a year, and want to be able to work and have unlimited exit and entry status, you may want to look into a resident visa. Any non-Ecuadorian over the age of 18 who applies for an immigrant visa (type 9) in either Ecuador or abroad, must obtain a criminal record for the past five years, before applying for the visa. The record must be translated into Spanish. Depending on the country of residence, the record may need to be legalized as well. More details on these visas and the processing fees (in Spanish only) can be found at the Ministerio de Relaciones Exteriores' website (www.mmrree.gob.ec/servicios/req_visas_inm.asp).
Updated: Oct 02, 2012.

REGISTERING WITH YOUR EMBASSY

When traveling or living in Ecuador, it's a good idea to register with your embassy so that you can be contacted and assisted in the event of an emergency in Ecuador, such as civil unrest, terrorism or a natural disaster, or informed of a family emergency in your home country.

Registering with your embassy is free and can be done online before you arrive in Quito or at your embassy once you arrive. All you need to do is provide certain travel information and personal details, including your passport number, and address and contact info in Quito, as well as emergency contact details in your home country. If you choose not to register with your embassy, it is recommended that you leave a detailed travel itinerary and contact details with family or friends at home, and provide them with the Quito-based embassy's contact information.
Updated: Sep 11, 2012.

Travel Insurance in Ecuador

Travelers to Ecuador would be well advised to take out a travel insurance policy. There is a wide range of policies that cover a variety of potential problems, including transportation delays, cancelation, loss of luggage, theft, hijacking and legal expenses.

A lot of different insurers are out there and they offer a variety of products, so it is best to research each policy to decide which one fits your trip. Before you start, check to see if you already have coverage through your bank or credit card company. These companies sometimes provide basic travel insurance. If you already have renter's or homeowner's insurance, your policy most likely covers travel. This is also true for health insurance or life insurance policies.
Updated: Oct 02, 2012.

MEDICAL INSURANCE IN ECUADOR

Medical coverage is the most important part of any travel insurance policy. Medical treatment costs for serious injuries can pile up fast. Find out how much your insurance will pay for emergency expenses and what treatments or procedures are included (e.g., helicopter rescue and emergency evacuation). If you need to return home for medical attention you'll want to know if that is covered. Most hospitals in Ecuador require that you pay for medical treatment upon entrance.

Ecuadorian hospitals often only accept cash. If you pay cash at a hospital, be sure to ask for receipts for any medical care you receive, this way you can provide copies when you make your insurance claim. Before you travel, make sure your travel insurance policy covers all the things you are interested in doing. Some activities may be considered "adventurous activities" and therefore are not covered under a basic travel policy (e.g., mountain biking, climbing and zip-lining).

LOST OR STOLEN ITEMS IN ECUADOR

Most of the insurance claims made by travelers relate to stolen or lost items. If you plan on taking valuable belongings such as laptops, cameras or mp3 players to Ecuador, there is a possibility that these items will be stolen or damaged.

When buying a travel insurance policy, make sure that it offers a level of protection that will cover the combined value of all the items you intend to bring to Ecuador. If this is not possible, consider leaving any extremely valuable items at home.

INTRO & INFO

Did a unique trek? Tell other travelers at vivatravelguides.com

If you are robbed while traveling through Ecuador, make a police report within 24 hours. Make sure to obtain a copy of the report, as your insurance company may require this type of documentation (they may also need a receipt for the stolen item) in order to process your claim.

The general rule is that the more money you spend on travel insurance, the more protection you will have. Basic travel insurance policies often don't cover lost or stolen valuables so you'll need to do your homework and you may have to be willing to spend a decent amount of money. If you buy a comprehensive policy, as opposed to a basic policy, your deductible will be lower, limits on single items will be higher, and you may even receive coverage for cash and passports fees. Look over the details of your policy very closely to make sure the level of coverage works for you.

STUDENT TRAVEL INSURANCE IN ECUADOR

If you are studying in Ecuador, it is important to be covered by the appropriate travel insurance policy. Several study abroad programs require their students to have medical insurance or special policies before departure. If you need to buy insurance coverage yourself, look around for the policy that fits your needs.

Students living abroad may be able to collect additional benefits that are not included in normal travel insurance policies. These may include benefits that go towards refunds for tuition in the event that you need cancel your courses for medical reasons.

It can be easier to insure valuables under study abroad insurance policies, and you may also be able to get coverage for jobs, sports or other activities while you are in Ecuador.

ECUADOR TRAVEL TIPS ON INSURANCE

Make sure you have your insurer's 24-hour emergency contact number on hand along with a copy of your policy number. If you keep your insurance details in an email account, you can access the information easily from anyplace you happen to be, even if someone steals your belongings.

Insurance companies recommend having written records of medical conditions and the names of any medications you take, plus copies of prescriptions, just in case.
Updated: Sep 11, 2012.

Getting To and Away from Ecuador
BY AIR

Two international airports are in Ecuador. The majority of international flights touch down at the new **Mariscal Sucre International Airport (UIO)**, located about 19 km (12 mi) east of Quito. It takes approximately one hour to get to the city of Quito from the airport.

Some airlines offer service to the southern coastal city of **Guayaquil.** Flights to Guayaquil touch down at the **Aeropuerto Internacional José Joaquín de Olmedo (GYE)**. Formerly known as Simón Bolívar International Airport, it was renamed in 2006 to honor the former Ecuadorian president, poet and first mayor of Guayaquil.

If you want to book a flight, go to www.vivatravelguides.com/flights/ecuador.

International flights to Quito and/or Guayaquil:

- Aerogal
- Copa Airlines
- American Airlines
- Avianca
- Continental
- Delta Airlines
- Iberia
- KLM
- LAN
- Lacsa
- TACA
- Tame
- United Airlines

Flights to Ecuador from the United States

Continental Airlines and **United Airlines** offer flights to Quito from Houston, while **American Airlines** flies out of Miami and offers direct service to both Quito and Guayaquil. **Delta Airlines** flies out of Atlanta with year-round service to Quito and seasonal service to Guayaquil.

Flights to Ecuador from Europe

Iberia offers international flights to Ecuador with a stopover in Madrid. **KLM** also offers flights from Europe to Ecuador with a stopover in the Netherlands. Europeans can also fly **American Airlines** or **Continental**; however, KLM and Iberia are much better for finding cheap flights to Ecuador from Europe.

Flights to Ecuador from Canada

Avianca Airlines offers service to both Quito and Guayaquil with a stopover in Bogotá, Colombia, and operating through codeshares with Air Canada. **Delta Airlines**

operates out of Montreal and Toronto and offers service to Quito and Guayaquil, with at least one stopover in the United States (Atlanta and/or Detroit). A final option for Canadians is **Continental Airlines**, which offers service to Quito from both Toronto and Montreal, with a stopover in Houston (and sometimes multiple stops in various other U.S. cities).

Flights to Ecuador from Latin America

From Quito, various regional carriers provide service to Latin American Countries. **Lan** offers flights to Lima, Peru; Medellín and Cali, Colombia; Buenos Aires, Argentina; and Santiago, Chile. **AeroGal** also flies to Lima and Bogotá. **Tame** services Bogotá, as well as La Habana, Cuba and Panama City, Panamá. **AeroRepública** is another airline that goes to Bogotá. **Copa** flies to Panama City, Panamá. **Taca** has flights to Medellín, Colombia, and San Salvador, El Salvador. **Lacsa** flies to San José, Costa Rica.

Many of these airlines fly from Guayaquil to various Latin American cities.

Cheap Flights to Ecuador

If you're looking for cheap flights to Ecuador, **visit during the low (wet) season** (October-November and February-June); ticket prices are much more reasonable during these times. If you purchase your return ticket in Ecuador, call the airline or travel agency where you purchased your ticket 72 hours before your flight to confirm, or you may be bumped from the flight. If you are traveling to Ecuador during the high seasons, from the beginning of July to the beginning of September and December to mid-January, you will find that airfare to Ecuador is much more expensive; expect a bump in ticket price and limited availability. When planning a trip during the high season, be sure to reserve your ticket well in advance.

Ecuador Airport Departure Tax

The airport departure tax (*Tasa Aeroportuaria or Impuesto de Salida Internacional*) for flights out of Quito and Guayaquil are now included in your airline ticket.

BY LAND

Ecuador may be reached by land from Colombia and Peru. For specifics on border crossing, see the respective cities. Taking a reputable international bus company is ideal because it eliminates the potential

complications that can occur at border crossings. Some of these companies also have service to other Latin American capitals. The borders are also open to private vehicles for those who are crossing the border by bicycle, motorcycle or car.

Getting to Ecuador from Colombia

At present, only two border crossings are open to international travelers. The most commonly used one is Rumichaca, on the Pan-American Highway, connecting **Tulcán**, Ecuador, and Ipiales, Colombia. The second option is through the jungle, at San Miguel. This journey begins in **Lago Agrio**, Ecuador, and ends at Mocoa, Colombia.

Getting to Ecuador from Peru

Three major border crossings exist between Ecuador and its southern neighbor, Peru. The fastest option is **Huaquillas, Ecuador**, a coastal city south of Machala by the Río Zarumilla to Aguas Verdes, Peru. Another popular route—and the safest—is at **La Tina**, south of Macará, Ecuador.

Both borders are open 24 hours and have international bus service. The third choice is a beautiful, several-day journey through jungle mountains from **Vilcabamba** to the La Balsa border south of Zumba. This is worth it if time is not of the essence.

International Buses

Taking a reputable international bus company to and away from Ecuador is ideal because it eliminates potential complications, like excess fees and rip-off money changers that tend to occur at border crossings. Buses will stop at the border and wait for passengers to complete immigration procedures before heading onwards.

Rutas de America (URL:www.rutas-america.com) offers direct service between Quito or Guayaquil and Lima, Peru (24 hr, $50-60). It also has direct trips to: Colombia (Bogotá, $60; Cali, $30) and Venezuela (Caracas, $90), and indirect trips to: Bolivia (La Paz, $145), Chile (Santiago, $160), Argentina (Buenos Aires, $200), Brazil (Río de Janeiro, $300).

The company has two Quito offices in Quito (Selva Alegre OE1-72 and Av. 10 de Agosto. Tel: 593-2-254-8142, E-mail:quito@rutas-america.com). In Guayaquil, the office is at La Garzota 3, Manzana 84, Villa 1 (Tel: 593-4-223-8673, E-mail:guayaquil@rutas-america.com).

Panamericana Internacional also provides direct service between Ecuador and Caracas, Venezuela, and indirect services to Colombia (Bogotá, Cali), Peru (Lima), Chile (Santiago) and Argentina (Buenos Aires). The company's Quito office is in the La Mariscal neighborhood (Av. Colón 852 and Reina Victoria. Tel: 593-2-255-7133).

Expresso Internacional Ormeño (URL:www.grupo-ormeno.com.pe) operates buses to Colombia (Cali, Bogotá, Cúcuta) and Venezuela (Caracas). Southern destinations are Peru (Lima, Cusco, Puerto Maldonado), Brazil (Rio Branco, São Paulo), Bolivia (La Paz), Chile (Santiago), Argentina (Mendoza, Buenos Aires). Its Quito office is near Parque Carolina (Av. Los Shyris 34432 and Portugal, Centro Comercial La Carolina. Tel.: 593-4-213-0847, E-mail:adm.quito@grupo-ormeno.com.pe). In Guayaquil, Ormeño's offices are near the Terminal Terrestre (Av. de Las Américas, C.C. El Terminal, Bloque C, Oficina C-34. Tel.: 59 3-4-214-0487, E-mail: adm.guayaquil@grupo-ormeno.com.pe).

Loja Internacional (cooperativaloja. com, Quitumbe Tel: 023824872, Colón 022224306, located at Orellana between Juan de Velazco and 9 de Octubre has several buses per day from **Loja** to Piura, Peru.

Other companies that offer service from Guayaquil and Machala to Tumbes, Máncora and other destinations on Peru's northern coast, via the Huaquillas / Aguas Verdes border crossing are: **CIFA Internacional** (URL:www.cifainternacional.com), **Civa** (URL:www.civa.com.pe) and **Cruz del Sur** (URL:www.cruzdelsur.com.pe).

BY BOAT

Traveling to and away from Ecuador by boat can be both expensive and inconvenient, but is inarguably the most adventurous method of transportation.

To Peru

The river crossing from Ecuador to Peru on the Río Napo is becoming popular once more. The trip goes from **Coca** (Francisco de Orellana) to Nuevo Rocafuerte and then to Pantoja and Iquitos, Peru.

To Colombia

Presently, the river journey up the Rio Putumayo into Colombia is not recommended, as it passes through the red zone of Colombia's civil war area. Filled with guerrillas and many of anti-government factions, it's quite dangerous. By sea, a cargo-passenger service ploughs the waters between **Esmeraldas** and Tumaco, Colombia.
Updated: Aug 31, 2012.

Border Crossings in Ecuador

The three border crossings from Ecuador to Peru are at three seperate towns along the frontier: **Macará**, **Huaquillas**, and **Balsas**.

For Colombia, the border at **Tulcán/Ipiales** is the best place to cross into or out of Ecuador. **Tulcán** is the border town in Ecuador six kilometers away from the border and Ipiales in Colombia. Change money in a large Colombian or Ecuadorian city before crossing any border. The money -changers at the border often pass false bills and will rip you off on the exchange rate.

At each border post you will need to show your passport in order to be given an entry stamp, which will state the number of days you are allowed to stay in Ecuador. Most foreigners receive 90 days free of charge, whereas citizens of the Andino Pact countries receive up to six months. See Ecuador Visa Information for more information on entry requirements (p. 38).

Border crossings are generally only open 6 a.m.-8 p.m., so plan accordingly if traveling with local transportation. The major border crossings—at **Huaquillas / Aguas Verde** and **La Tina**—are open 24 hours for international buses only. Upon arriving at the border, locals may offer to assist you with forms, taxes and other border paperwork. They will charge a fee for their services. It is best to avoid these unnecessary costs, and deal only with verifiable immigration and border officials. Change money only at banks or legitimate *casas de cambios* (exchange houses). Updated: Apr 22, 2013.

ECUADOR-PERU BORDER CROSSINGS
Macará, Ecuador / La Tina, Peru
This is the safest of the border crossings between Ecuador and Peru. La Tina is directly south of Macará, Ecuador. It has historically been a laid-back border, where the officials often have lunch on the other side and (as legend says) played chess together during their nations' war in the mid-1990s. Border posts are only about 200 meters from each other. The border is open 24 hours; during business hours banks operate on either side of the border. Money changers also operate near the market in Macará.

The road from **Macará** heads south to **La Tina** and then **Sullana** beyond to the border crossing. Scenery passes from mountain forests to oasis and bare desert. From Macara you can take a pick-up truck ($0.50) to the border or cab it there ($1). From the border you can take a mototaxi to La Tina ($1). Bus from La Tina to Sullana (1.5-2 hours, $4), and then to Piura (40 minutes, $1). Be careful in Sullana, as it's a rather unattractive and dangerous city.

Huaquillas, Ecuador / Tumbes, Peru

The faster border crossing is along the coast. It's the road that goes along the coastal plains from Huaquillas, Ecuador to Tumbes, Peru and beyond.

Your best bet is to depart from **Machala,** Ecuador so you can get to **Tumbes,** Peru via bus (the bus will even wait for you as you do immigration). From here you can get to other such places like **Máncora** via bus or taxi. Just know that this is a border crossing with some lurking issues. Besides the to-be-expected contraband running, certain dangers await the unsuspecting. For many decades, travelers of all nationalities have reported that they were given counterfeit notes by border money changers, robbed on the route between border posts, charged extra fees by corrupt border officials (all official transactions are supposed to be free) and taxi drivers (who may demand a $20 "road tax" spontaneously) and unfortunately even assault and rape. Many international travelers are beginning to go the other route, through La Tina. However, for those whose next destination is on Ecuador's coast, this is the most logical one.

Balsas, Ecuador / San Ignacio, Peru

Due south of **Vilcabamba** is a crossing into Peru, convenient for getting to Cachapoyas, Peru. This journey has been described as adventuresome and beautiful, through a landscape of cloud-bathed jungle mountains strewn with orchids. Expect delays due to landslides (especially December-April) and roadwork. You will need two days; hotels exist in every transfer point, though Jaén is best.

From Vilcabamba, starting at 6-6:30 a.m. there are several buses called Cooperativa "Sur Oriente" that pass in front of Hosteria Izhcayluma and head to Zumba (5-6 hrs, $6.50). From Zumba to La Balsa there are several open-air buses called "rancheras" or "chivas" that will take you there (1.5 hrs, $1-2). Once in La Balsa, either catch a bus

to the border or take a taxi there for $20. The border is open on both sides from 6:00 a.m. to 6 p.m., and there are money changers available as well.

From the border Peruvian border you can get to **San Ignacio** via a colectivo taxi (2 hrs, 15 soles/$5.50). Then from San Ignacio take a *combi* (microbus) to **Jaén** (3 hrs, 12 soles/$4.50). From Jaén head to a **Bagua Grande** in a one hour-hour taxi colectivo ride (8 soles, $3). From Bagua Grande you can get to **Chachapoyas** via colectivo taxi (3 hrs, 25 soles/$9); or alternatively, catch a*combi* to **Pedro Ruiz** (1 hr, 22 soles/$8) and then ride another *combi* to Cachapoyas (2 hrs, 8 soles/$3).

ECUADOR-COLOMBIA BORDER CROSSINGS
Tulcán/Ipiales

The principle border crossing between Ecuador and Colombia is at the Rumichaca bridge, just seven kilometres (4.4 miles) north of Tulcán and three kilometres (1.8 miles) south of Ipiales, Colombia.

Immigration for both countries is open 6 a.m.-10 p.m. but it is recommended to cross during the day for security reasons. Most travelers (from Europe and North America) do not need a visa in advance. Simply make sure the Ecuadorian authorities give you an exit stamp and then you can get a 90-day tourist visa on the Colombian side. Minibuses ($0.75) and taxis (colectivos or shared taxis, $0.85; private $4) may be caught at Tulcan's bus terminal or from Parque Ayora. The taxi or van will drop you off in the parking lot across from Ecuador immigration.

If you are entering Ecuador, a maximum of 90 days (within a 365-day period) is given. After going through Ecuador immigration, cross the river to Colombia migración. Usually only 60 days are given upon entering, but go ahead and ask for 90. There is one line for entry stamps, and another for exit stamps. The immigration building also has the offices for travellers crossing in private vehicles, bathrooms and an exchange house. Combis (mini-vans, $0.80) to Ipiales' bus terminal or a taxi to Parque La Pola downtown ($3) leave from the parking lot in front of the steps to immigration. Freelance money changers work on both sides of the border. Be sure to check all calculations for accuracy and bills for authenticity, and count your money well. Transportation fares on either side can be paid in dollars or Colombian pesos.

Getting Around Ecuador

Viajero Contento (URL: www.ecuador-schedules.com) lists all the Ecuador bus, train and flight schedules. It covers more than 2,600 routes and 25,000 departures all over the country. For a small yearly fee, you receive phone numbers and other contact information for over 300 bus companies, airlines and the national railroad. It's a convinient little site packed with schedule info.

BY PLANE

Four carriers provide domestic air service in Ecuador.

Tame (URL:www.tame.com.ec) has the most extensive schedule. From Quito, it flies to Baltra (Galápagos), Coca, Cuenca, Cumbaratza, Esmeraldas, Guayaquil, Lago Agrio, Macas, Manta, San Cristóbal (Galápagos), Santa Rosa, Tena and Tulcán. From Guayaquil, Tame has flights to Cuenca, Esmeraldas, Loja, Latacunga and Quito.

Aerogal (URL:www.aerogal.com.ec), flies from Quito to Baltra (Galápagos), Coca, Cuenca, Guayaquil, Manta and San Cristóbal (Galápagos); and from Guayaquil, to Quito and the two Galápagos airports.

Lan Ecuador (URL: www.lan.com) offers services from Quito to Baltra (Galápagos), Cuenca, Guayaquil and San Cristóbal (Galápagos). From Guayaquil, it flies to Quito and the Galápagos.

Saereo (URL:www.saereo.com) has flights from Quito to Lago Agrio and Macas, and offers inter-island flights in the Galápagos Islands (Isabela, Baltra, San Cristóbal).

Flying within Ecuador is not always cheap considering the short distance from point-to-point, but it can save you hours of travel time. For example, a flight from Quito to Guayaquil takes about 50 minutes and costs $110-200 round trip, while the bus takes over 10 hours (each way) and costs about $24 round trip. Student and senior discounts may apply for both land and air travel, so be sure to ask. It is easiest to stop at a travel agency to book your flight, but be sure to call the airline to confirm a couple of days before you travel.

BY BUS

Traveling by bus is the most common method of transportation for Ecuadorians as well as the cheapest and often the most convenient. Long-distance buses charge $1 per hour on average, slightly more for the Ejecutivo or First-Class buses. Bus drivers, especially in the sierra, are fearless. If you have a queasy stomach, sit near the front, but you may not want to sit at the very front where you can see exactly what the driver is doing. Sometimes it is better not to know! Most long-distance buses are equipped with DVD players and TVs so you can enjoy Jean Claude Van Damme, Arnold Schwarzenegger and many more action stars dubbed in Spanish as you speed around curvaceous two-lane mountain roads. Ecuadorian bus drivers tend to like action flicks, so don't get your hopes up for anything in the line of sappy dramas or romantic comedies.

The major cities have extensive public bus service available. Buses in Quito cost $0.25 and fall under two categories: the regular buses and the trolleys or trams that are more of an express service. The Ecovía, the Trole and the Metro Bus System run north and south and then have extension routes that stretch out farther into the valleys and neighborhoods to the north and south. Other buses weave throughout the city and can be confusing for travelers, especially those not fluent in Spanish. The best way to orient yourself on these buses is by reading the major destinations on the placards on the front window of the bus, and asking the driver and/or driver's assistant if they will be passing by your destination. The buses are numbered, but in no apparent order: it is best to ignore the numbers and focus on the placards.

BY TRAIN

The construction of a railway from the sierra to the coast in 1873 was initiated by President Gabriel García Moreno. The 461-kilometer (288-mi) line from Durán on the coast to Quito, which took 35 years to complete, was essential for commerce and trade within the country. The El Niño phenomenon of 1993 destroyed the Riobamba-Durán line at Río Chanchán, near Aluasí. In 2008, the federal government initiated an intense program to bring the Quito-Durán and Otavalo-San Lorenzo trains back on line.

At present, 10 tourist routes operate, some using steam locomotives and other *ferrobuses*. The most popular thrill ride is the El Nariz del Diablo (the Devil's Nose), a 12-kilometer (7-mi) series of switch back rails between Alausi and Sibambe. Ferrocarriles del Ecuador lists the timetables and prices for these trips on its website (Tel: 1-800-873-637, URL:www.ferrocarrilesdelecuador.gob.ec).

BY TAXI

In Quito and Guayaquil, taxis will be an important way for you to get around. They are quite cheap, reliable and safe. There are a few rules and tips you need to familiarize yourself with first, however. Before you get in the cab, you should agree on the price for your destination. Never simply get in and ask how much the ride costs once you get to your destination. The rate will go up if you're sitting in the back seat when you begin to negotiate, it seems drivers are fond of having company. City buses stop running about 8 p.m. or so, and after that it is safest to travel in taxis, even for very short distances.

In Quito (but not in Guayaquil), taxis are required to have a *taximetro* (taxi meter), which measures how much the passenger must pay. Generally, the drivers keep it in the center of the dashboard, below the radio. During the daytime, the taxis must use the meter if the passenger asks. Especially in the Mariscal or when dealing with foreigners, some less scrupulous taxis will hide it or claim that it doesn't work. Rule of thumb: once you flag down a cab, ask to see the taximetro before you get in. If the driver starts mumbling something about it being broken, wave him on and get the next cab.

There are some exceptions: Taxis at the airport are not required to use the taximeter and negotiate directly with passengers. They'll charge as much as they can, so if you don't have much baggage, cross the street and catch a cab there. After 9 p.m., Quito cabs are allowed to disconnect their taximetros and wheel and deal with passengers. Expect to pay about a dollar more than you would for the same trip in the daytime.

BY CAR AND MOTORCYCLE

The general philosophy of drivers in Ecuador is, "I have the right of way." In practice, whoever is bigger goes first. As a result, you will hear lots of horns blaring, brakes screeching, insults flying and pedestrians running for their lives. That said, renting a car while you are traveling in Ecuador has its advantages. There are many spots where buses dare not venture and can only be reached by four-wheel drive, on bicycle or by foot. In order to legally drive in Ecuador, you need an international driver's license used in conjunction with a driver's license from your home country. It's a good idea to also have good insurance coverage when booking your car. There are four car rental companies operate in Ecuador, these are:

Avis: www.avis.com.ec
Budget: www.budget-ec.com
Hertz: www.hertz.com
Localiza: www.localiza.com

You'll need to rent a car in one of the larger cities in Ecuador: Cuenca, Guayaquil or Quito.

HITCHHIKING

In a country full of pickup trucks, hitchhiking is a fairly common way to get around, especially in small towns and the jungle where there is no established bus system. Some drivers, especially in the larger pickup trucks with seats and wooden walls to block the wind, will charge a small fee. You should always ask about price before hopping in. While hitchhiking is more common in Ecuador than in many other countries, it is still not guaranteed to be safe. Use common sense, especially if you are a woman or traveling alone.

BY BIKE

A lot of enthusiasts choose to travel the Ecuadorian landscape on a mountain bike, just make sure when you travel you have a bike-repair kit, because there will be obstacles along the way. It's best to buy your kit at home, for the only place in Ecuador with bike parts is Quito, and even those stores have a limited supply. Quito is also the only place to buy bikes, and they're usually pretty expensive. It would seem that Ecuador is not the most biker-friendly nation. However, on Sundays in Quito the busy streets are shut down so peddler enthusiasts can cruise through the city at ease.

BY BOAT

Boats will navigate through the far-reaching areas of the jungle not accessible by any other mode of transportation. For this reason, traveling by boat may be inescapable if you're visiting the Amazon. Canoes are usually dugouts, following the techniques of ancient Amazonian traditions, and can transport up to a couple dozen travelers. Be sure to bring something to sit on and some sunscreen, as six hours in a canoe can leave you with burns and a sore bottom. Because of the variety of tour companies in the Amazon, you may choose to go by canoe, or for more comfort, by yacht. Yachts also frequent the Galapagos. If you choose to bring your own yacht, you'll most likely have to dock in for the remainder of your stay on the islands, as there are strict limitations on boater licenses. Tour companies operate boats that range from simple sailboats to yachts with private bathrooms and air-conditioning.

Did a unique trek? Tell other travelers at vivatravelguides.com

INTRO & INFO

Responsible Tourism

Tourism is a vital source of income to Ecuador and one that will long outlast the petroleum industry. Support this struggling nation by encouraging local industries. Eat at local restaurants and stay at locally-owned hotels as opposed to foreign-owned businesses or international chains.

There is a wide selection of comfortable, clean and reasonably priced hotels all over the country owned and operated by Ecuadorians. V!VA Travel Guides usually mentions if the owners are foreign, so choose wisely.

Use water and electricity carefully. When city officials cut down on the community's supply, travelers are usually given preference, so don't abuse the privilege.

BEGGARS
Don't give money or candy to children begging. You are just encouraging this destructive cycle by financing parents willing to send their little ones out onto the streets to work. Many disabled adults and senior citizens also beg; you can decide if you want to help them out or not. Most Ecuadorians do.

PHOTOGRAPHY
ALWAYS ask before taking photographs or videos of people. Just because people look and dress differently doesn't mean you're in a zoo. Show your respect by talking to people before making them a souvenir of your vacation. For more information, see p. 77).

ENVIRONMENTAL AWARENESS
An eco-tourism movement is slowly but surely making its way through Ecuador. The habits of throwing trash out bus windows and littering in general are deeply ingrained in Ecuadorian collective consciousness. Be responsible by not participating in these bad habits and make a point of leaving camping sites, nature walks and picnic areas cleaner than you left them.

Ecuadorian cities have started putting up "Do Not Litter" signs, but there is still a long way to go. Use recycle bins where available, or participate in "garbage bags for cocktails" at certain hostals on the beach even.

Consider staying at an eco-lodge or volunteering for an organization working to educate the community and preserve the environment. See our eco-tourism page box for more information.
Updated: Sep 05, 2012.

THE SOUTH AMERICAN EXPLORERS' CLUB
The Quito branch of the South American Explorers' Club is a lively hub. It has a lot to offer to both travelers and ex-pats, and is a great place to meet people. For travelers, the club is an excellent source for maps, guidebooks and general up-to-date safety and travel information. Regular weeknight events include pub quizzes, Spanish and cooking classes. The club also regularly organizes good-value beach or hiking excursions. Club members get discounts on all of this, plus cheaper deals in many bars, restaurants and tour agencies in Ecuador. Jorge Washington E8-64 y Leonidas Plaza, Tel: 02-222-5228, URL: www.saexplorers.org, E-mail: quitoclub@saexplorers.org.

Adventure Travel in Ecuador
Ecuador is a great destination for adventurous visitors itching to get off the tourist track. This country features a fairly well developed infrastructure for activities like climbing, hiking, mountain biking, rafting, horseback riding, surfing, scuba diving and birdwatching. Whether you decide to ramble out on your own or hook up with a local guide service, the logistics of planning excursions in Ecuador are simpler and the planning time shorter than in other, more remote areas of the world. Updated: Sep 04, 2012.

HIKING IN ECUADOR
There are a number of excellent trips through the Andean páramo (grassland) which features spectacular views of Ecuador's volcanic peaks.

The most popular, longer treks are the Trek de Condor, which passes the often cloud-shrouded Antisana and ends at the Cotopaxi Volcano; and the Ingapirca Trek which takes you along an old Incan trail to Ecuador's most important Inca site. There are some great hikes from lodges along the Napo River in the Amazon.

For the intrepid trekker there are several multi-day Andes-to-Amazon hikes that take you from the grassy plains of the high altitude páramo, through cloud forest, and finally to lowland rainforest. During your descent, as you pass through one ecosystem to another, you'll see dramatic changes in the flora and fauna while you are peeling off layer after layer of clothing. Scents change, as does the culture. Rainforest hikes are also possible, but it's a good idea to hire a local guide to ensure you don't become lost.

Enter V!VA Photo Contests: vivatravelguides.com/photography-contests/

Ecotourism in Ecuador

Ecotourism has risen to become the new, more socially and environmentally conscious method of travel, and Ecuador has a unique geographical advantage.

In this small country with four strikingly diverse ecosystems, responsible tourism is omnipresent. But because this stamp increases the credibility of a company, there are façades galore.

The Asociación Ecuatoriana de Ecoturismo (Ecuadorian Ecotourism Association, URL:www.ecoturismo.org.ec) decided to define the branding, grounded in the belief that many companies tend to market any type of tourism that involves nature as "ecotourism"-and, being Ecuador, there needed to be more strict regulation. Ecotourism is now defined as tourism that benefits the community, the wildlife, the ecosystem and the traveler. In the ideal situation, a majority of the profits collected by an ecotourism company is funneled back into environmental conservation and restoration projects. The easiest way to know if a venue is actually eco-friendly is if it's owned by the local community.

The Galápagos, being the most highly chosen destination in Ecuador, has specialized in ecotourism and set a benchmark for others to meet. But there are façades there, too.

The idea of ecotourism has become more deeply ingrained in the Amazon. Indigenous cultures are using ecotourism as a way to spread awareness about their culture in an attempt to preserve their land and way of life. The Achuar people, for instance, are running an eco-lodge in order to fend off oil exploration and exploitation in their region, using the income from the lodge to fund their political struggle.

So while you're planning your trip, if your goal is to remain as eco-friendly as possible, do your research. "Eco" in a company's doesn't necessarily mean the company uses just practices. Check the company's philosophy, research their eco-practices, read reviews and act accordingly.

You can also download the Ecuadorian government's Ecotourism Standards (in Spanish) or visit the National Ecotourism Portal of Ecuador (URL:www.amigosdelasaps.org) for more information.
Updated: Sep 12, 2012.

RAFTING AND KAYAKING IN ECUADOR

Ecuador is considered one of the best destinations in the world for whitewater sports due to the steep drop-offs from snow-capped peaks to rich lowland areas connected by one of the highest concentrations of rushing rivers per square kilometer.

In addition, its tropical location provides for year-round water sports. Whether you are interested in whitewater rafting or kayaking, Ecuador has the tours, isolated destinations and heart-racing rapids.

Where to Go

Tena is the biggest kayak and rafting destination in Ecuador; some say it offers the best kayaking rapids in all of Latin America. Many travelers choose to start in Quito and shop around the dozens of tour operators that base their operations in the capital before heading out. Santo Domingo also has a developed whitewater community, and offers warmer water than mountain rivers at higher altitudes. For something a bit more low-key, head down to Baños and give rafting a go on the Río Pastaza.

Packing List

Swimsuit, tennis shoes or Teva-like sandals with secure ankle straps, T-shirt (quick-drying material is best), easy-dry shorts or running tights, safety strap if wearing glasses, and waterproof cameras are all suggested.

Don't forget a waterproof bag for anything you want to keep dry during your trip, not to mention - a dry change of clothes for the trip back to Quito.
Updated: Sep 10, 2012.

Did a unique trek? Tell other travelers at vivatravelguides.com

MOUNTAIN CLIMBING IN ECUADOR

Ecuador offers an incredible diversity of mountains to explore. Within a day's drive from Quito are glaciated peaks which rise over 5,000 meters (16,400 ft) and one over 6,000 meters (19,680 feet), all of which are volcanoes. The highest Andean summits in Ecuador are located primarily along the Avenida de los Volcanes (Avenue of the Volcanoes), a fertile central valley just south of Quito, which is buttressed by two mountain ranges, the Eastern and the Western Cordilleras.

Some of the summits are young, cone-shaped volcanoes like Cotopaxi (5,897 m / 19,342 ft) with technically straight-forward climbs offering the novice a chance to get near to or above high altitudes. Others are deeply eroded, older volcanoes with challenging rock and ice routes that ought to be summited by the more experienced, such as the glorious ring of peaks on El Altar (5,319 m / 17,446 ft).

For your first few days in Ecuador, you should acclimate by ascending some of the smaller mountains, such as Illiniza Norte (5,126 m / 16,813 ft), Imbabura (4,610 m / 15,121 ft) or Pichincha (4,794 m / 15,724 ft) to avoid developing AMS (Acute Mountain Sickness) or the more severe Pulmonary Adenoma or Cerebral Adenoma. (See Health for more information.) These lower peaks are non-glaciated, easily accessible within a day's travel from Quito, and offer either hut facilities or nearby hostels that can be used as a climbing base.

Once your body has adjusted to the altitude, you are ready to try one of Ecuador's four classic glaciated peaks: Chimborazo (6,310 m / 20,697 ft), Cotopaxi, Cayambe (5,790 m / 18,991 ft) or Tungurahua (5,023 m / 16,475 ft). Although the standard routes are technically straightforward, people do die every year-primarily from avoidable mistakes. Novices should hire a guide.

Experienced mountaineers can attempt the more remote and / or more difficult peaks of El Altar, Antisana (5,705 m / 18,712 ft) and Illiniza Sur (5,248 m / 17,213 ft), or choose more challenging routes on other mountains.

As a relatively recent playground for climbers, Ecuador still provides many opportunities for ascents on new routes. There are three anomalous volcanoes (Reventador, Sumaco and Sangay) that do not belong to either of the Cordillera mountain ranges, but rather thrust up from dense jungle east of the Andes. These climbs have the added attraction of giving you a chance to test out your machete skills, as you must blaze trails through dense cloud forest or rainforest just to get to the base of these giants. Sangay (5,230 m / 17,154 ft) is also noteworthy for its healthy population of woolly mountain tapirs.

V!VA Update: As of this writing, Tungurahua, Sangay and Reventador (3,485 m / 11,431 ft) are highly active. We do not recommend that you try to climb them at this time. Check with your climbing outfitter and guides for up-to-the-minute information, especially before going out for a climb. Updated: July 5, 2013

Entrance Fees
Mainland park entrance fees generally run from $5-20, but Cotopaxi National Park is the only one that strictly enforces its entrance fee; all others are hit or miss.

Climbing Huts (Refugios)
There are huts at Cotopaxi, Chimborazo, Cayambe, the Ilinizas and Tungurahua. Almost all huts have bunks, stoves, pots / pans and toilets. Some even have electricity. The cost per night is around $10. The hut at Cotopaxi has a cellular number for weather information and emergencies: 09-963-8344. Plans to install cellular phones at the other refuges have also been discussed as part of future improvements.

Guide Services
Guide services in Ecuador are a classic example of "you get what you pay for," so we recommend avoiding the cheapest ones. There are many agencies and individuals who will take you up to Cotopaxi at the expense of a few nickels, but they don't know the first thing about mountaineering, and they could embed you in a dangerous situation.

Cotopaxi

Photo by: Jason Halberstadt

Equipment and Packing

Climbing and hiking gear can easily be purchased or rented at reasonable prices in Quito, and with a bit more difficulty in Baños, Riobamba and Ambato. Helmets are the general exception to this rule; if you have your own helmet, bring it.

Packing List

Below are supplies you will need on a two day non-technical climb up mountains such as Cotopaxi and Chimborazo. The more technical climbs will require more specialized equipment. For nearly all tours, the items listed under Equipment (below) are provided by the tour company. All equipment may be rented in Quito as well. Helmets are the exception to both of these statements, they are rarely provided and are also very difficult to rent.

Equipment: Mountaineering boots, crampons, ice axe, carabineers, climbing ropes, harness and gaiters. Recommended personal gear: Water, headlamp, 3 sets of batteries, glacier glasses, lip balm, sunscreen, knife, two water bottles, two insulating layer tops: one thin, one thick, insulating layer bottoms, Gore-Tex type hooded coat, Gore-Tex type bottom, glove liners, Gore-Tex gloves, two pairs of socks, warm hat, camera (keep it in your inside pocket or it will freeze) extra change of clothes, shoes for around camp. Updated: Sep 05, 2012.

MOUNTAIN BIKING IN ECUADOR

Ecuador offers the cyclist seemingly endless back roads and trails to explore.

The Incas, who were legendary road builders, and their living descendants have been carving scenic paths for centuries. Today, mountain bikes are used by rural communities as a major form of transportation in many areas.

The Andes create a playground of huge vertical descents and lung-bursting climbs where the snow line and the equator meet. For most people, the extreme cycling environment of the Andes is best enjoyed going downhill. Descents of 3,000 meters (10,000 ft) in a single day can be done in several areas of the country.

The world-class descent directly down the slopes of Cotopaxi Volcano, the technical descent down Pichincha Volcano and trips that take riders from the heights of the Andes to the Amazon Basin are all highly recommended.

Biker-friendly buses and pickup truck taxis, plus readily available lodging and food in most rural areas make cross-country independent bicycle travel in Ecuador extremely appealing, but careful planning is essential. The lesser-traveled back roads make the best routes.

Avoid the Pan-American Highway, and most other paved roads in Ecuador, as you will encounter reckless bus and truck drivers who are not used to seeing bicycles on the road. Most parts of Quito are extremely biker-unfriendly, and should be avoided. The city is often packed with bumper-to-bumper traffic. Cars will rarely give bikers the right-of-way. The city does have some bicycle trails, however, and hosts the 27-kilometer (16.2-mile) Ciclopaseo bicycling circuit on Sunday mornings, which runs from Parque de los Recuerdos in the North, down Avenida Amazonas, into the Centro Histórico and South as far as Quitumbe.

Bike rental is available in Quito and Baños, but quality varies widely. Check your bike carefully before heading out. Shocks and strong aluminum rims are essential as the high-speed descents on potted terrain will otherwise lead to unwanted bent wheels.

Packing your bike up at home and bringing it with you on the plane is one alternative to rental. Be sure to bring a strong lock and always leave your bike locked in a secure location. Pack wisely and bring plenty of spare parts, including extra tubes and tires, and a tool kit, as well as a first-aid kit if you'll be pedaling in remote areas. Updated: Sep 05, 2012.

HORSEBACK RIDING IN ECUADOR

Ecuador provides riding enthusiasts with a surprising range of excellent opportunities. You can jaunt high in the Andes through the *páramo* (grasslands) and plains with snow-capped volcanoes as a backdrop; through lowland tropical rain forest; or even through the many unique ecosystems of the Galápagos Islands. Ecuador's extensive hacienda system makes it possible to ride through quilted pasture land from one hacienda to another, many of which now operate as country inns and send riders out with scrumptious picnics.

Ecuador has a number of stables that rent good horses, and if you know where to look you can find pure Peruvian Pasos, Andalusians and Arabs. Beginning riders

Did a unique trek? Tell other travelers at vivatravelguides.com

INTRO & INFO

are advised to hire the tough, mixed-blood Criollo horses. Be forewarned: even healthy horses will generally look thin in the Sierra. At these altitudes, the horses cannot afford to carry extra weight-so you will rarely find well-padded mounts.

Rules of Riding

Stable standards, ethics and horse-care policies vary tremendously in Ecuador. Horse owners and trainers change regularly, which means that training and care also changes. It's rare that you'll find a passionate owner. Common sense is therefore essential. When considering a horse for hire, follow these basic rules:

1. If a horse appears ill, lame or abused, REFUSE to ride it. Change horses or leave. Please let Viva Travel Guides know if you find inhumane conditions at any stables.

2. If you cannot control the horse or do not feel safe, it's best to change horses or to not ride. If you are on a trail when a problem arises, do not hesitate to dismount.

3. If the tack (saddle & bridle) looks ill-fitted, old, cracked or damaged, ask to have it changed, or a fall could ruin your entire trip.

4. Check the tack adjustments before getting on the horse. Is the girth band tight? Are the reins and stirrup leathers in good condition? Most importantly, take the time to set your stirrups for the right length. Stirrups that are too short will hurt your knees and can be dangerous, as can stirrups that are too long. Western tack is typically used in Ecuador, although some stables offer English saddles.

Western saddles are recommended as they are safer going up and down steep terrain and are generally more comfortable for long rides. Few stables offer riding helmets, so if you are planning on doing any serious riding, bring your own.

Where to Ride

There are many places in Ecuador that offer horseback riding. The central highlands have the best scenery, including snowy volcanoes, wide valleys and stark high-altitude grasslands known as páramos. It is also in the highlands where you'll find most of the best haciendas, which generally offer horses. Baños has a number of good riding trails nearby, although shop for horses carefully as there are many disreputable stables in the area.

When to Ride

In Ecuador you can ride year-round, although some months are better than others for certain areas. The coastal areas and semi-tropical Baños have a tendency to be muggy. In the Sierra north of Quito, the month of May can be rather wet. During the rest of the year it typically rains only in the late afternoons and by this time the horses are back in the stables and you are fireside enjoying a pre-dinner cocktail.
Updated: Sep 04, 2012.

BIRDWATCHING IN ECUADOR

Ecuador is a popular destination for bird watching. With upward of 1,500 species, it has as many species as in Europe and North America combined. Ecuador's top birding spots are in the Oriente region, with over 600 species, and the Galápagos with its abundant endemic species. However, other regions birders may wish to explore include the bird-rich cloud forest area surrounding Mindo. Many unusual species can also be found in the páramo region. Because Ecuador is small and has a decent infrastructure, it is possible to access many of these areas fairly easily. It is recommended to hire the services of local guides for the best birding experiences, as they have good local knowledge and know exactly where to look in the undergrowth to locate that rare bird. Don't forget your binoculars!

Birdwatching in the Amazon

To spot the widest variety of species of birds in the Amazon, it is worth heading there during the transitions between the dry and wet months. The worst time is during the dry months (December, January and August).

Species to be spotted in the Amazon include the Rufous-headed Woodpecker, Fiery Topaz, Harpy Eagle and Zigzag Heron, as well as various species of tanagers, toucans and parrots and antbirds, to mention just a few. The best birdwatching opportunities in the Amazon region are found by staying at one of the many jungle lodges. Be sure to select one with an observation tower: these are built around the tall kapok trees and allow climbing above the forest canopy to spot a great variety of species.

Sacha Lodge is unique for its 40-meter (131-ft) tower, from which it is possible to spot many species. From the tower, a wild cacophony greets you as you spot a wide variety of colorful birds, including parrots and macaws. Sacha boasts that it is possible for a guide to spot as many as 80 species in a single morning from this tower. With 500 recorded species in the area, this could be true. For an alternative birding experience, take a motorized canoe for one and a half hours to the Yasuni Parrot Lick. Here, in a colorful spectacle, several species of parrots gather in the early morning to eat the exposed salty clay, which is vital for their digestion. Hope for a dry, sunny day; because that's when you'll see more parrots.

Kapawi Lodge is another alternative for great birding. In a stay of ten days, it is possible for a keen and dedicated spotter to see up to an astounding 400 species. The building of the lodge was one of the biggest community-based projects in Ecuador and there is a wish to provide genuine ecotourism. River islands close to Kapawi are home to Horned Screamers, Orinoco Geese and Muscovy Ducks. Other birds in the locality include Brown Jacamars, Plumbeous Antbird, Buckley's Forest Falcon and the Blue-winged Parrotlet, to name just a few. It is possible to observe species here that cannot be found at other lodges.

At **La Selva**, native birding experts are hired to assist those interested in birdwatching. While their English is not great, their birding skills more than make up for this. Close to the lodge it is possible to see many varieties of birds just by walking around.

However, for a great view, La Selva offers an observation tree tower. La Selva is also close to parrot salt licks, and it is a great place for spotting the Cocha Antshrike and Zigzag Heron.

Birdwatching in the Galápagos

Where else could birdwatching be easier? Even for an amateur, it is possible to spot most of the species with little effort or patience. The coastline, where most visits take place, is quite biologically diverse, allowing visitors to view a large cross-section of Galápagos bird life. A typical shoreline might contain sandy and rocky beach, mangroves, and brackish tidal pools. There are countless opportunities for observing the life rituals of these birds, including courtship and nurturing of the young.

The most famous of the Galápagos Islands for bird-watching is probably Tower (Genovesa). This remote northern island was never colonized by many land animals, which left it almost completely open to birds. If you visit Tower, you can expect to

see a wide variety of birds including boobies, frigates, gulls and the Short-eared Owl. Red-footed Boobies and frigates nest at one of the visitor sites, so you may get the opportunity to view chicks.

You will doubtless not leave the Galápagos without observing all three types of booby – Blue-footed, Red footed and Masked (also referred to as Nazca). Blue-footed Boobies are famous for their intriguing courtship dance which you may be lucky enough to see. Frigate birds are common as well. They spend a lot of time offshore, and often there will be two or three in flight, curiously accompanying your boat.

If you are keen to see the Waved Albatross, visit the islands between April and December; during the other months you may be disappointed. An unforgettable sight is watching the albatross make its way to the cliffs at the southern end of the island in order to launch their large, heavy body into the air. The Waved Albatross can only be seen on Española Island, so plan your trip accordingly.

Photo by: Jason Halberstadt

The Galápagos Penguin is one of the smallest species of penguin and is unusual in that it lives north of the equator, unique in the penguin family. If you are lucky you may spot penguins fishing underwater, while you are snorkeling–don't forget your underwater camera! Flightless Cormorants are found on some islands. It is interesting to observe them stretching out on the rocks to dry after swimming.

Greater Flamingos are a bright pink, stark contrast to the volcanic backdrop of the islands and can be found inhabiting the lagoons that are found slightly inland in some locations. The mockingbirds on the islands are arguably the tamest creatures of all. They will land on you and clamor to get into your water bottle. Don't let them! Last but not least, and famed for inspiring Darwin's theory of evolution, the thirteen varieties of Darwin Finches can be spotted on the islands.

Did a unique trek? Tell other travelers at vivatravelguides.com

Birdwatching in the Cloud Forest and surrounding areas

In the subtropical cloud forest regions, the humid conditions and high biodiversity create a birdwatcher's paradise. Of particular note, the town of **Mindo** has been designated an Important Bird Area since 1997, the first area in South America to be attributed this honor. **Bosque Protector Mindo-Nambillo** supports over 350 species of birds, over 50 of which are endemic to the area. The Mindo area is home to more than 500 species of birds. Some of the more spectacular ones include the Golden-headed Quetzal, Yellow-collared Chlorophonia, Choco Toucan, Club-winged Manakin and Cock-of-the-rock.

Mindo is a two-hour drive from Quito and the best months for birdwatching are early September until the very end of January. There are many lodges to choose from in the Mindo area. It is worth heading a bit further out, 29 kilometers (18 mi) from Mindo, to the **Bellavista Cloud Forest Reserve**, for a stay at the Bellavista Lodge, where 263 species have reportedly been observed. Unusually, the Tanager Finch has been spotted here—Bellavista is the only known place in Ecuador where this species resides.

Alternatively, if interested in observing the birds of the lowland forests, head west of Mindo to Santa Domingo, which is a two to three-hour drive from Quito. Note: This is for keen birdwatchers only, as there is not a lot else to see or do in Santa Domingo. However, it is worth a stay in **Tinalandia** close by, as more than 270 species of birds have been spotted, including the Long-wattled Umbrella Bird, Golden-winged Manakin and Glistening-green Tanager.

The area surrounding Tinalandia is considered by ornithologists and botanists to be one of the most biodiverse areas in the world. There are opportunities to birdwatch just walking around the grounds, and those staying for a while can take trips to see birds such as Torrent Duck and Black Phoebe.

Another option, 50 kilometers (30 mi) from Santa Domingo, is the **Río Palenque Science Center**, located on the Palenque River. This reserve has 360 species of bird to see, including the Yellow-tailed Oriole, Ecuadorian Trogon, Northern Barred Woodcreeper, Orange-billed Sparrow and varieties of hawks and kites. The center has a capacity for 26 guests.

Birdwatching in the Páramo

Above the cloud forest region sits the páramo, the barren zone above the tree line, (3,100-4,700 meters / 10,170-15,419 ft a.s.l.). Birds here are easy to spot due to the lack of vegetation.

Ecuador's national symbol, the Andean Condor, can be found here, along with the Tawny Antpitta and the Andean Snipe. Condors can also be spotted on the road to Papallacta from Quito. Areas of the páramo worth visiting include the national parks of El Ángel,Cajas and the highland areas of Cotacatchi-Cayapas and Cayambe-Coca.

Parque Nacional Cajas is home to 125 species, including the condor and Violet-tailed Metaltail, an endemic hummingbird.

Parque Nacional Cotapaxi is also a good place for páramo birding, with 90 species to spot, including the Black-chested Hawk-eagle, Andean Coot, Andean Lapwing and Páramo Pipit. Other birds that make their home in the páramo include the Rufous-bellied Seed Snipe and Stout-billed Cinclodes.

Shopping in Ecuador

Shopping is a varied experience in Ecuador. From dusty, noisy animal markets to craft markets to sterile, glossy malls, there is something for everyone here. Ecuador produces an interesting array of products that can be purchased as souvenirs.

Arts and crafts (in Spanish, *artesanía*) such as weavings, wood carvings, rugs, toys and clothes can be picked up all over Ecuador. Prices are reasonable and bargaining is highly encouraged.

WHAT TO BUY

Special to Ecuador and of note is the so-called "Panama" hats. Despite their name, their origin is Montecristi, Ecuador. Good quality hats can be rolled up and will spring back into shape. Beware of the hats available in Otavalo market, cheap does not equate to a bargain.

Vegetable ivory (*tagua*) items are a nice buy and can be both cheap and small—helpful for getting them home. An unusual and colorful purchase is a bread dough ornament. It is possible to buy bread dough fridge magnets, nativity and Christmas decorations (available year-round) and other figures such as llamas for a cheap price in Calderón, just north of Quito.

Enter V!VA Photo Contests: vivatravelguides.com/photography-contests/

The Otavalo region is known for its excellent quality textiles which are sold daily in its famous market. Good quality, cheap leather goods are also a good bet in Ecuador.

If you plan on picking up some souvenirs in the Enchanted Islands, it's a good idea to choose carefully: avoid purchasing items that appear to have been made from endangered plant or animal species.

WHAT NOT TO BUY

It is not possible to export animal products out of Ecuador, and in fact it is not usually permissible to import them to most countries, either. Thus avoid products manufactured from animals, endangered or otherwise. This includes insects and feathers. Take care with antiques; it is difficult to export these too. The export of archaeological artifacts is also prohibited.

WHERE TO BUY

For artesanía, Otavalo is the most famous and possibly the best place to bargain for some high quality products, such as weavings, woodwork and jewelry. And while it is possible to pick up Panama hats all over Ecuador, Montecristi and Cuenca arguably hold the best stock. For bread dough ornaments, head to the small town of Calderón, located just to the north of Quito.

HOW TO BUY

Bargaining is the name of the game in Ecuadorian markets and often in the craft shops too. Indeed, in the markets no prices are displayed. You will need to bargain prices with the stall holder. Wait until the seller suggests a price, and then offer to pay half to two-thirds of that price and take it from there.

To find out the lowest price that a vendor will accept, ask "el último?" It is worth checking out prices on a few different stalls with similar products before entering into bargaining, to get a good idea of value. Also recommended for some super discounts is to buy a lot of things at the same stall.

Sellers will often discount prices for those buying in bulk. Stalls away from the main arteries of markets will often have better bargains than those near strategic corners. Most importantly, don't pass up that unique sweater for the sake of a dollar. In the end, understand that that dollar will mean more to the stall holder than to you, and you will surely regret it when you get home. Updated: Sep 04, 2012.

Markets in Ecuador
OTAVALO MARKET

Colorful and buzzing, Otavalo market is the biggest indigenous market in South America. It is held daily, but the most important day is Saturday. The market is based in Plaza de los Ponchos and extends far into the local streets on a Saturday. During the rest of the week, the market is pretty much confined to the Plaza, but you'll still find a variety of fine products, fewer stalls and foreigners to contend with, and a more relaxed atmosphere. It is often possible to barter for better prices on days other than Saturday due to the smaller number of buyers.

For a unique cultural experience visit the animal market held in a field on the outskirts of Otavalo. It starts in the wee hours on Saturday mornings. This is not for late-risers—if you get there after 9:30 a.m. there will be little left to see. For a few hours the field is a throng of pigs, sheep, goats, cows, chicken and bartering, along with a rather unsavory-looking selection of food stalls. It you want to visit the animal market it is probably best to stay overnight in one of the many Otavalo hotels.

COTACACHI LEATHER TOWN

The leather-making town of Cotacachi, about 11 (6 mi) km from Otavalo, is worth a stop. Market day is Sunday, but if you can't get there on a Sunday it's not a big deal because on Calle 10 de Agosto, which is at the center of the Sunday market, it is possible to pick up all variety of good quality leather items all week long. Products available include jackets, shoes and boots, bags, wallets and belts.

SAN ANTONIO DE IBARRA

Also near Otavalo is the small town of San Antonio de Ibarra. This village, located about mid-way between Otavalo and Ibarra, is known for woodcarvings. There is no market per se, but several shops sell a variety of intricately carved wooden items, such as

INTRO & INFO

bowls, religious figures, boxes, chess sets and flowers. The gallery of Luís Potosí is located on the main square and in general probably has the best items, although there are little treasures to be found in each of the shops. As usual, bargaining is the norm: Never pay the first price offered, even in the fancier galleries. Check out hotels in Otavalo or Ibarra as an overnight stay is recommended.

SAQUISILÍ MARKET

At Saquisilí, about 2.5 hours from Quito the market kicks off at 7 a.m. on Thursday mornings and is pretty much over by 2 p.m. This is one of the largest markets in the Ecuadorian highlands and vendors travel from miles around to display their wares. It is possible to get a bus from Quito, or there are tours available. Alternatively, stay nearby overnight in one of the hotels in Latacunga. As well as food, there are a wide variety of arts and crafts on sale. There is also an animal market a short walk from the main market, best visited before 10 a.m.

MERCADO ARTESANAL LA MARISCAL

In Quito, visit the Mercado Artesanal at Reina Victoria and Jorge Washington to pick up arts and crafts. Panama hats can be purchased here, along with woodwork, weaving, jewelry and *tagua* items. The Market is open between 10 a.m. and 6 p.m. daily.

PARQUE EL EJIDO MARKET

In Quito's Parque El Ejido, opposite the Hotel Hilton Colón, a small market is held on Saturday and Sunday mornings. Paintings are the main focus here, and if this is your interest, it is worth a visit. A number of stalls also sell sweaters and other crafts. Other hotels in Quito are nearby if the Hilton is out of budget.

MERCADO SANTA CLARA

For a taste of the real Ecuador in Quito, stop at Mercado Santa Clara at Versalles and Ramírez Dávalos. This is just hopping distance from the conveniently-named "Santa Clara" *trole* stop on 10 de Agosto. On the ground floor, sellers vie for your attention to sell you a mysterious-looking selection of fruits and vegetables, many of which don't have English translations.

If your stomach can handle it, upstairs is the meat and fish market. It is better to visit before 2 p.m. as the market starts to wind down after that. You can also find some basic *artesanía* here, such as fine hand-made baskets. Updated: Sep 04, 2012.

Studying Spanish in Ecuador

Ecuador's excellent selection of Spanish schools is unmatched in South America. Prices are low, averaging $4-10 per hour for individual classes. Most schools also arrange home-stays with a local family, and some offer excursions, salsa dancing or cooking classes as part of the package. Either way, they are a great way to learn spanish.

Although Quito has the biggest choice of Spanish schools, you can also sign up for classes in numerous other towns and cities in Ecuador. Baños, Otavalo, and Cuenca are all popular places to take classes. If you'd rather be at the beach, then check out the schools in Puerto López and Montañita. Updated: Sep 04, 2012.

Living in Ecuador

Many travelers passing through Ecuador fall in love with the country and decide to stay for an extended period of time. According to the U.S. Embassy, about 30,000 Americans live and work in Ecuador. Undoubtedly, even more Europeans make this beautiful country their home. The most popular cities for resident foreigners are Quito, Cuenca and Vilcabamba.

Quito has a large expatriate community and lots of options for furnished apartments, jobs for English speakers and volunteer projects. Expect to pay upward of $250 a month for a one-bedroom apartment and $500 per month for a luxury one-bedroom apartment in the north of Quito or in one of the valleys like Cumbayá with beautiful furnishings and often a common pool, hot tub and terrace with mountain views.

Outside of Quito, the prices drop almost half for apartments, but it will be harder to find a furnished place. For apartment listings, local newspapers, such as El Comercio, are

an excellent source, though you will have to be able to read Spanish, or know someone who does. Another great option for travelers looking to stay a bit longer is living with a family. Many families in Quito (and around Ecuador) offer rooms in their homes as an alternative source of income, or for inter-cultural exchange. Prices for homestays vary drastically, ranging from $200-450 per month, and usually include two or three meals per day.

If you plan to stay in Ecuador longer than three months, you will need to look into getting a non-resident or resident visa. See our visa section for more information. Many people enjoy the options for work in Ecua-dor. Salaries are somewhat low for the cost of living, and some might find it a struggle to keep up with the costs of living while work-ing in the city. Expect to earn between $400-1,000 in Quito, and much less outside of the city. For more information on the topic, see our work and volunteering section (p. 60).

For retirees interested in stretching their re-tirement savings the extra inch, Ecuador is an excellent place to live. Property is fairly easy to purchase and makes for a relatively safe investment. Be sure to get a good lawyer and / or real estate agent, though. The climate of this tropical country is ideal with spring-like weather year-round in the Andes and steamy hot weather year-round on the coast. It is not possible to buy land in the Galápagos Islands due to strict restrictions in place to protect the flora and fauna in the national park. Updated: Sep 05, 2012.

IMPORTING GOODS INTO ECUADOR

Importing goods into Ecuador from the United States or Europe can be a time-consuming, costly and frustrating process. However, with the guidance of good lawyers and reputable companies, many—but cer-tainly not all—of these annoyances can be alleviated.

Start the process way ahead of time and don't count on goods arriving according to a strict schedule. Many things can go wrong along the way. Guidelines are constantly changing and a lot depends on which par-ticular customs officials you are dealing with at any given time.

The first real step entails figuring out what type of visa entitles importation of goods. This is very important, as getting the wrong type of visa will cost you extra money, time

and overall hassle. Keep in mind that you cannot import goods into Ecuador with a student visa. Then there are other visas like the investment visa—which requires a $25,000 minimum in the bank to keep it valid—that do allow importation, but are not recommended for doing so.

Once you get have secured a visa at your local Ecuador consulate, the next big—and very important—step is finding a reputable importer. Take the time to do thorough re-search and make sure the company is aware of the specific provisions for importing into Ecuador before you get started. Many claim they know them, yet few have any real expe-rience with Ecuador importation, and the requirements for Ecuador are very different than they are for other countries.

The extra splurge on a reliable importer may be worth it, simply because it is usu-ally bound to save you money as well as cut down on inconvenience down the road. The importer will usually handle export docu-ments, but at an extra cost.

You will also need to set up an agent in ad-vance to supervise customs at the port in Guayaquil, and to transport your items to Quito. It is also possible to pick the stuff up yourself in Guayaquil instead. INSA (URL: www.insa.com.ec) is a reputable company with English-speaking employees.

One of the most important measures you will need to take is creating your *Menaje de Casa*, or an official, extremely detailed list of each item you are importing. The list must be translated into Spanish, and you need to include descriptions of, serial and model numbers of, and the values of each thing in your shipping container.

After this has been completed, you will need to get a Certificado de Menaje de Casa de Extanjeros at your nearest Ecuadorian con-sulate. You will have to get the signature on your Menaje de Casa notarized and then will need to get a letter written at the consulate that says you haven't left the country in the last 30 days and that you will live in Ecuador for more than a year, which will then have to be notarized by someone in the consulate building.

Once notarized, the letter will have to have an apostille afixed at the state or provincial capital building and then will need to be taken back to the consulate another time.

Approval of the Menaje de Casa costs about $100. Make sure to make lots of copies of all these documents (and that goes for all documents throughout the entire process). Also, take your passport with you everywhere because you will most likely be asked for it each step of the way.

Costs are highly dependent on the importer you use, but keep in mind that you are charged per shipping container, not per pound, so empty space is wasted space. However, make sure that all items in the container, which will then be reflected on your Mensaje de Casa, total less than $4,000 or else you will be subject to much higher taxes. On a value of slightly under $4,000, you can expect to pay about $700 in taxes, or about a fifth of the total value. Importing one shipping container from New York City to Guayaquil will cost around $3,000, and then an additional $1,300 or so for customs clearance and transport from Guayaquil to Quito.

The entire process from start to finish can take close to a year, or even longer. Sometimes you will need to wait a few months for a boat to even come in the direction of Guayaquil before you will be able to send your belongings.

Other times, your shipping container may sit inexplicably in customs for weeks or months. Therefore, don't plan for anything to arrive on time. Also, don't be surprised if items are missing, as there have been many reports of stolen goods.

This is where hiring a reputable agent should payoff, as it should oversee the wellbeing of your goods and reduce the chances of this happening. Finally, importing, like many other things in Ecuador is all about who you know. Therefore, if you can hook up with someone who imports regularly through business or otherwise, putting your stuff with theirs is a significantly better and cheaper option. Updated: Sep 11, 2012.

MOVING PETS
Bringing pets into Ecuador from the United States or another country is often a complicated affair, but it is not impossible by any means.

In fact, if you do comprehensive pre-research and have all the documents in order, the process should go pretty smoothly. Make sure to contact the Ecuadorian consulate for the most up-to-date information, because requirements are always changing.

Ten days prior to coming to Ecuador, you will need to take your pet for a travel health check-up in your native country. It will need to be treated for parasites at least 21 days before departure, and have a certificate of this. Don't forget to keep all vaccine documentation, both the copies and the originals. At the veterinarian, you should be able to get a pet travel certificate as well; just inquire about this during the check-up.

After the check-up, you must go one step further and receive a certification from the state veterinarian's office to confirm that your veterinarian is registered in your state. This documentation must then be notarized before it will be considered valid. All documents must be in English and in Spanish. make copies if possible.

Once you have completed these steps, you will have to go to the Ecuadorian consulate nearest to you and register your pet for travel purposes. Check ahead with the consulate and come prepared, as there are instances when the pet owner must be there in person when photos of the pet will suffice. Also, keep in mind that there will likely be a fee of $30 or more, typically paid in cash.

At least 72 hours before arriving in Quito, you should contact the Ecuadorian Agency of Quality Assurance in Agriculture (AGROCALIDAD) with flight arrival and carrier information (Tel: 5939-565-0556). A representative from this office will supposedly meet you once you arrive in Quito. Updated: Sep 04, 2012.

Setting Up A Business in Ecuador
It is not too difficult to start a business in Ecuador. Many expatriates decide to create a small business in order to both earn an income and sometimes to stay longer in Ecuador if it's too difficult to meet the requirements for an investor or retirement visa.

However, it is necessary to talk to a competent lawyer who has experience working with foreigners setting up a business in the particular city where the business will be located.

A competent lawyer should explain all the steps involved in advance and should not (by any means) require the lump fee paid in full before any action is taken, although it's customary to pay a partial advance to get the paperwork started.

A large incentive to creating a business in Ecuador is that foreigners are permitted to own 100% of an Ecuadorian business in most sectors. Luckily, you don't need a huge amount of money to start a small business, but you do need some, and a lot of creativity and patience. Expect in many cases to have to be in daily contact with your lawyer and to have small delays with all the municipalities.

This is somewhat customary in Ecuador, but make sure your lawyer has a good reputation with expatriates and is managing everything properly.

What kinds of businesses can you start?

Many expatriates choose to start an export company and ship either natural resources like roses, or crafts made by artisans, to their country of origin. Regarding exports, those foreign companies that solely export Ecuadorian goods and do not own and operate a local facility, do not necessarily need to establish a business in Ecuador. However, if a foreigner does own a local facility, is involved with an Ecuadorian company in a joint venture, or ships goods to an Ecuadorian company that does not take ownership of the goods, the foreigner must establish a business legally.

Either way, before embarking on an export business, consult a lawyer to make sure you are acting in accordance with the laws. Keep in mind as well that with certain types of visas it is illegal to earn money while in Ecuador.

Another popular company model is investing in real estate. In general, the most lucrative option in the real estate game is to buy a house on the coast near Salinas or Montañita, or other places popular with expats, remodel the homes, and then sell them for profit. Ecuador is already a very attractive destination for retirees and designing properties with this in mind can be financially rewarding. Many other expatriates choose to open restaurants, hotels, bed and breakfasts or small shops. Whichever business model you choose, the first step of course is to create a business legally.

How to start a business

In order to start a company there must be either an Ecuadorian partner involved, or a foreign partner with a current visa. The process for a small business takes about two months and costs $1,500- 2,000 and requires clarity about what operations the company will perform. Starting a larger company, or establishing a branch in Ecuador of a pre-existing foreign company, is a bit more complicated and costs more money.

Most types of companies need to be registered with, and are regulated by, the Superintendence of Companies which is governed by the Companies Law. Typically a deed of incorporation, company by-laws, and proof of tax payment, along with various other forms depending on the type of business, must be submitted to the Superintendence of Companies.

Once a company is officially incorporated, it must file a return with the Superintendence of Companies annually which includes financial statements and reports by the external auditors, the legal representative, and the corporate controller. In addition, public companies must also publish their financial statements in a local newspaper twice per year.

Steps for starting a business

In general, the process of beginning a business looks a little like this:

One should hire a lawyer to prepare the minutes of incorporation which should only take one day and cost $500-900. These minutes should include the constituting contract, articles of incorporation and the bylaws of the company and the formation of capital. These documents must be signed by the lawyer and notarized by a third party.

The next step is to reserve the company name at the Superintendent of Companies (Superintendencia de Compañías, URL: www.supercias.gob.ec). This is free of charge, but have a couple of different names in mind for your company as Ecuadorian law requires that a business' name not be similar to that of an existing company. The foreigner should then deposit 50 percent of paid-in capital into a bank account set up under the name of the company.

After the notary has notarized the bylaws of the company and charter of incorporation the lawyer needs to present these documents to the Superintendent of Companies for approval. This step can take up to a week or two and the notary normally charges about 0.2 percent of the capital and around $300 for the stamp duty. The company must then publish an abstract of the charter in a local daily newspaper so as to make the deal public and then inscribe the charter and resolutions, along with all the names of the legal representatives that make-up the Mercantile Registry.

Once those steps are finished, the company must apply for the Registro Único de Contribuyentes, print invoices and VAT forms at an authorized printing shop, and sign up at the Instituto Ecuatoriano de Seguridad Social (IESS) to obtain approval of payroll forms at IESS and get issued an employer's identification number. Employees must all sign contracts with the company and the contracts must be registered with the Ministry of Labor to prevent exploitation or misuse of employees.

The municipality will then inspect everything and make sure everything is in order which can take up to a month. Once the municipality has finished with their inspection, the foreigner must obtain a commercial patent for the company and after all that can finally begin working.
Updated: Sep 11, 2012.

ECUADORIAN TAXES

Visitors to Ecuador should expect to pay 12 percent value added tax (IVA) to most goods and services. Usually the tax is included in the price quoted, although in some restaurants and hotels it may not be. Drugs, food products in their natural state and veterinary products are tax-exempt.

Property tax is significantly cheaper in Ecuador than in many other countries and is usually only 1 percent of the assessed value of the property, though rates vary from city to city. To pay these taxes, the owners or someone acting on their behalf, must go and pay at the Distrito Metropolitano of the city where the property is owned. Obviously, you must bring the Número de Predio, or official house registration number, with you. The process normally takes an hour including waiting time.

The Ecuadorian government taxes individuals and businesses only on money earned in Ecuador. The scale ranges from 0 percent to a maximum of 35 percent, depending on your income. The standard corporate income tax is 23 percent. Like Ecuadorians, foreigners living in Ecuador must file through SRI (URL: www.sri.gov.ec), the Ecuadorian Internal Revenue Service. Although it's possible to file on one's own, if you do not speak Spanish fluently and own your own business, or have a complicated filing, it's best to get

help from an accountant. Refunds can be directly deposited into bank accounts if the person meets certain requirements.

On sums of money over $1,000 leaving the country for a foreign bank account, a five percent expropriation tax is levied. This is to prevent capital flight.
Updated: Sep 26, 2012.

Volunteering and Working in Ecuador

Ecuador has seen an explosion in voluntourism recently. There is a huge choice of organizations, both in and out of Ecuador, which can set you up with voluntary work. Popular options are working with children (generally teaching English at a school or helping out at an orphanage) or ecology-based projects such as reforestation, research or conservation projects.

Some organizations offer free accommodation and food in return for your labor, while others charge a small fee. If you're planning to stay for a while (generally a month or longer) the price goes down. If you are in Quito, check with the South American Explorers Club, which can give you up-to-date information on organizations that offer volunteer work.

There are also numerous possibilities for working in Ecuador, although this is more difficult to arrange from home. Your best bet is to turn up and see what you can find.

There are vacancies year-round for English teachers in Quito and Guayaquil (less so in other cities) and most of the teachers we spoke to had no problems finding a job. The best way to find work is to print off a few copies of your résumé / CV and visit a few language schools in person.

Pay ranges from $3-8 per hour. Schools that teach business English pay the best, but tend to require certification such as CELTA or International TESOL. Some bilingual high schools require native English speakers (with the relevant experience and qualifications) to teach English as well as other subjects. Private schools generally hire in September and their pay is probably the best you will find as a foreign teacher in Ecuador.

Your second best bet is to get a job in the tourism industry, such as at a travel agency or hotel work. Pay is not as good as the top-end English schools but pay often includes accommodation and food so you can live rather cheaply. For these jobs you need a good level of Spanish.

If you want to work in business, it may be worth checking out the notice boards in the Mariscal as there are often vacancies for jobs in the flower and oil industries. Again, your chances will be far better if you have a good level of Spanish and English. Updated: Sep 04, 2012.

ECO-FRIENDLY FARMSTAY TOURS

Stay with a local family on a homestay tour in this rural area of Ecuador and experience life on the farm for yourself. Guided farm tours available, and you're encouraged to get involved and help pick coffee, chocolate, bananas, oranges, etc. You can also visit sugarcane farmers to see them produce alcohol from sugarcane and get a taste of the results.

For the more adventurous, ask for a local guide in Salinas de Guaranda and take the 2-day downhill hike to San Luis de Pambil, the hometown of Eco-Friendly Farmstays and Tours.

The cost per night is $15 per person in double/twin accommodation, $18 in single accommodation. It includes breakfast and the planting of one tree. 4-day all-inclusive trips: $135-178 include accommodation, all meals, excursions, guide, transport and tree-planting.

This eco-tourism project is run by a reforestation charity (www.progresoverde.org), so you're invited to plant a tree for each night that you stay there. It's a fun, friendly way to get a tour off the beaten track. San Luis de Pambil, Tel: 03-265-6216, URL: www.farmstaysecuador.org.
Updated: Mar 19, 2013.

Casa Mojanda

Lodging in Ecuador

Visitors to Ecuador will find plenty of options when it comes to accommodation. There are enough hotels, hostels, haciendas, eco-lodges and campgrounds to cater to everyone from penny-pinching backpackers to those with money to burn. Most towns have hostels and/or hotels, which tend to cost anywhere from $5 to the low $100s. Generally speaking, you get what you pay for.

ECUADOR BUDGET LODGING

All across Ecuador, in rural areas, small towns and cities, you will find hostels (*hostales* in Spanish) that are geared toward budget travelers. Some have dormitories, which cost as little as $5 per night per person (up to $10 per night for a Quito hostel). Many hostels have private rooms as well, with shared or private baths. Hostels in Quito will run you a little more than hostels in Otavalo or Baños or more rural areas.

ECUADOR LUXURY HOTELS

International four- and five-star hotel chains exist mostly in the major cities of Quito and Guayaquil. A stay in Quito offers plenty of options for luxury with prices that are lower than most international cities.

HACIENDAS

Historical Haciendas are a unique experience which let you step back in time – including back to colonial time – hundreds of years ago. Haciendas are generally pricey, but provide an authentic Ecuadorian experience.

In colonial times, the mountainous countryside was divided up among rich landowners, who ruled Indian villages like medieval dukes. The landowners usually built an hacienda, a sort of rural mansion, as a place to live and oversee the work done on their lands. The system was in place for centuries, and the Ecuadorian countryside is dotted with old haciendas in varying states of upkeep. In the past decade, many of the most picturesque ones have been converted into hotels and guest homes. The area to the north of Quito, near Otavalo, is particularly known for excellent converted haciendas.

The spacious rooms, beautiful gardens and centuries of history have proved irresistible to thousands of visitors every year. The best of them have not lost their rural charm: they still feel like a home. While the area north of Quito near Otavalo is known for its haciendas, the scene to the south, towards

Did a unique trek? Tell other travelers at vivatravelguides.com

Tunguragua and Chimborazo, is equally as beautiful. From volcano vistas to first-class facilities the haciendas stretching across the central Andes are certainly worth the trip.

Haciendas are not meant for the backpacker crowd, as it is hard to reach many of the best ones without private transportation and the prices are significantly higher than the hostels and smaller hotels common in tourist areas. Travelers with a higher budget, however, should make a point of visiting at least one hacienda while in Ecuador, as each is unique and memorable, and the value for the money is usually quite good. Most Ecuadorian haciendas offer horseback riding, mountain biking, and gardens where their guests can wander and relax. Most also have an on-site restaurant. Many of them plan and host special events such as conferences and weddings. The least expensive haciendas run about $30-40 per room per night, whereas the more expensive ones can cost over $200 per person per night. Most of them fall into the mid-range of about $70-90 per night. Guests can often negotiate discounts for large groups or extended stays.

RAINFOREST LODGES & ECO-LODGES

Spending time in a lodge in the Amazon or cloud forests of Ecuador is an experience that really shouldn't be missed. The quality and price vary widely, so choose your lodging with care.

In recent years, eco-lodges have proliferated across Ecuador. Basically, these are environmentally-friendly hotels often set in large, protected areas of forest. In theory, the lodges use the profits they receive from tourism to help conserve their particular area of forest, and many also work with local communities to improve schools, build paths and improve the quality of life for the locals. However, while there are many bona fide eco-lodges around, there are also plenty of fakes that think they can boost their popularity simply by tacking "eco" onto their name. (One place we visited claimed to be an eco-lodge because it had a papaya tree!) Have a look at our page on ecotourism to find out some of the basic principles that lodges should abide by in order to use this title.

The Amazon rainforest basin, or El Oriente, is a popular tourist destination, and a number of jungle lodges are located here. Most of them are centered around Tena, Puerto Francisco de Orellana (Coca), or Nueva Loja (Lago Agrio), which are transportation hubs in Ecuador's eastern lowlands. Although each is quite unique, activities and basic features don't vary too much, unless you splurge on a high-end option.
Updated: Aug 13, 2012.

Food in Ecuador

While Ecuador isn't very internationally known for its cuisine, the small country does have a few delectable dishes you must try during your stay.

TYPICAL ECUADORIAN CUISINE

Usually each lunch and dinner will begin with a traditional Ecuadorian **soup**, all of which are highly nutritious. The main course will consist of a meat dish, with rice and raw vegetables. Corn is also a main crop in Ecuador, and comes to your plate in many different forms. *Choclo* is the most well-known variety of cultivated corn. You'll undoubtedly top your meal with ají, the Ecuadorian hot sauce, at some point during your trip, if not during every meal.

Restaurants and cafeterias offer *desayunos* (breakfasts), *almuerzos* (lunches) and *meriendas* (dinners) which tend to come with soup, a main course, juice and dessert at an economical price. Food sold on the street is quite cheap and smells appetizing, but hygiene is often questionable. When assessing a street vendor or small local restaurant, a good rule to follow is that if the place is frequented by many locals, the food probably merits joining the crowd.

Ají (chili) is a hot sauce made from a spicy red pepper. Although food in Ecuador isn't as spicy as in other Latin American countries, this hot sauce is extremely popular in Ecuadorian food recipes and complements the traditional diet of rice, potatoes and meat. Most Ecuadorian restaurants and homes have their own version of ají. Some types are mild, while others are incredibly spicy, so be sure to sample a bit before smothering it all over your food. If you don't see a little bowl of ají on your table, just ask—they're sure to have it.

In addition to ají, *platos fuertes* (main dishes) are often accompanied by a mountain of rice, a small salad, and potatoes or *patacones* (squashed, fried green plantains). On the coast and in the Amazon however, potatoes are often supplemented or replaced by *menestra* (beans or lentils) and/or steamed *yuca* (manioc).

Other traditional Ecuadorian dishes include *seco de pollo*, a stewed chicken accompanied by rice and avocado slices; *lomo salteado*, a thin beef steak covered with onions and tomatoes; and *seco de chivo*, a goat (though most often made with lamb or mutton) stew served with a mound of rice.

Brave travelers in Ecuador can try native foods like *cuy* (guinea pig), a traditional Andean dish that dates back to before the days of the Inca. It is generally fried or cooked over an open fire. There is not a lot of meat on a cuy, which tastes like a cross between chicken and pork.
Updated: Aug 13, 2012.

ECUADORIAN SOUP

Soup *(sopa)* is by and large the most common and diverse type of food from Ecuador. The first course of most lunches and dinners is a savory soup, rich with grains, vegetables and chicken or beef. Locro, made with cheese, avocado and potato, sounds a bit odd, but is surprisingly tasty. *Chupe de pescado*, a fish and vegetable soup with coastal origins, is becoming popular throughout the country. Bolder diners can try *yaguar locro*, a special potato soup made with sprinklings of cow blood.

And bizarre food in Ecuador includes one final soup: Those ready to throw their inhibitions completely to the wind should dip their spoon into *caldo de pata*, a broth containing chunks of boiled cow hooves, considered a delicacy by locals and believed by some hopeful men to increase virility.
Updated: Aug 13, 2012.

Fanesca

Fanesca is a traditional soup served almost everywhere in Ecuador during Easter week. A large bowl of the rich, milk-based broth is a pretty much a full meal as it is very heavy. Fanesca is made from 12 different beans and grains, including green beans, fava beans, kidney beans, *chocho* beans and corn *(choclo)*. The soup can be served with or without salt cod, which is used instead of meat because it is believed that meat should not be eaten during this time. Fanesca also contains chunks of ripe plantain *(plátano)*, boiled egg, fried bread, cheese and peanuts. It is thought that the 12 grains in the soup symbolize the 12 disciples and the 12 tribes of Israel, while the fish symbolizes Christ. Countrywide, but especially in the Andes, you will see signs outside restaurants advertising that fanesca is on the menu. A bowl of

the soup such as this kind will set you back anywhere between \$5 and \$10, depending on the restaurant and the region.
Updated: Aug 07, 2012.

FOOD IN THE ANDES

The main staples in the Andes are rice, potatoes, corn and meat (chicken, beef and pork). Your dish will most likely include a simple salad or lentils. Locals in the Andes also prepare *quinua*, a native, high-protein grain. Also, the famous *cuy* (guinea pig) is roasted in the Sierra, as Ecuadorians think of the furry companion as a prime delicacy. In some cases you might even have the awkward opportunity to pick your guinea pig. *Llapingachos* are one of Ecuador's most popular food recipes. The hearty dish centers around a generous mound of cheesy mashed potatoes and is often accompanied by sliced avocado, fried egg, plantains and some form of meat. You can find this highland specialty at local markets, as well as in restaurants in the popular tourist towns of **Quito**, **Otavalo**, and **Ambato** (where it's most famous).

Llapingachos

FOOD IN THE AMAZON

In remote areas of the Amazon you'll find hunter-gatherer type methods of collecting and eating food, so you'll be sampling exotic endemic fruits, fish and meats eaten only in the jungle.

FOOD ON THE COAST

Seafood is a popular and plentiful food choice in Ecuador, not only along the coast but also in the highlands. Lobster *(langosta)* dinners can be enjoyed in major coastal cities, at low prices. Plate varieties of *camarones* (shrimp) are also widely popular. The coast has tons of fish *(pescado)* to feast on, including *corvina* (white sea bass) and *trucha* (trout). Crab and some other seafood have *vedas* (bans), seasons when fishing is prohibited. Much shrimp is farmed, which is damaging to mangroves; consider ecological implications of that before ordering.

In **Esmeraldas**, on the northern coast, try the signature seafood specialty *encocados,* an elegant mix of seafood prepared in coconut milk. In Manabí province, seafood is presented with a spicy peanut sauce. *Encebollado* is a cooked, spicy soup made with tuna, tomatoes, onion and yucca.

Another popular seafood choice in Ecuador is *ceviche*, a cold soup of raw seafood marinated in a broth of lime juice, onions and tomatoes. Ceviche is often accompanied with popcorn or *chifles*, thin slices of fried plantains. Ceviche can be made with fish, shrimp, *concha* (shellfish), *calamar* (squid) or all of the above. Exercise caution, however, as improperly prepared ceviche has become one of the primary culprits of cholera and other nasty bacteria. Most restaurants are aware of this and act accordingly, but choose your dining establishment wisely.

To to top it all off, the coast offers cocada which comes across as more of a macaroon, except it's made of coconut shards and melted brown sugar.

FOOD IN GALÁPAGOS

Because migrants to the Galápagos come from all three regions of the mainland, the islands' culinary fare is a blend of those cuisines, using whatever ingredients that is available. Only certain foods are grown on the islands, and much needs to be imported to fill tourist demand. Fish, of course, is a staple. Galápagos beef is succulent and flavorful.

INTERNATIONAL FOOD

If after your share of guinea pig you find yourself hankering for a familiar burger, burrito or pizza, don't panic. Major cities feature (for better or worse) U.S. fast food chains such as Pizza Hut, Taco Bell, McDonalds and KFC as well as some higher-quality chains like TGI Fridays, Applebee's and Tony Roma's. As an up-and-coming cosmopolitan city, **Quito** also offers a good selection of international cuisine.

If you fancy Argentine steak, Italian pasta, Japanese sushi or French fondue, you won't be disappointed. Expect prices lower than those in the United States or Europe but higher than local cuisine. Chinese, Mexican, Cuban, Arabic, Indian and vegetarian meals are available in Quito at reasonable prices. However, if you're looking for Thai cuisine, you'll be hard pressed to find any decent options around.

VEGETARIAN AND VEGAN FOOD

Vegetarians traveling in Ecuador will be pleasantly surprised by the wide selection of vegetarian and vegan food options in popular tourist destinations like **Quito** and **Baños**. In smaller towns, however, you will often be stuck eating some combination of rice, oily salads and eggs. Strict vegans will have a tough time finding acceptable food in Ecuador and should plan on doing a lot of grocery shopping, as restaurants in Ecuador don't really understand the concept of a meal without some sort of animal product. Most vegetarian options include milk, eggs or cheese. Packets of locally produced, pure peanut butter (*pasta de maní*) are available at most grocery stores.

Drinks in Ecuador

FRUIT DRINKS

With the mouth watering selection of exotic fruits, Ecuador has many delicious (and cheap) fruit juices, or *jugos*. Popular fruits native to Ecuador include *naranjilla*, a tangy, orange-colored fruit; *tomate de árbol*, a fruity tree-grown tomato with a kick; *mora* (blackberry); *guanabana* (soursop), an almost milky, sweet, white fruit; and tangy *maracuya* (passion fruit). If you're staying in a home with an Ecuadorian family, chances are good you'll be treated to a fresh *jugo* with breakfast every day. Most restaurants offer a variety of juices as well; be sure to ask for what's fresh. *Jugo naturales* are straight-up fruit juice, while *batidos* are fruit smoothies mixed with yogurt and / or milk.

COFFEE, TEA AND SODA

Bottled and canned fizzy drinks (including Coca Cola, Sprite and Fanta) are widely available throughout the country. The Peruvian sodas Kola Real (KR) and Big Cola are also bottled in Ecuador.

Ecuador produces good coffee, but surprisingly, most Ecuadorians seem to prefer instant over brewed coffee. *Café pasado* is a super-concentrated coffee brew served in a small cruet; add this to the cup of hot water or milk you are served. If you are willing to pay slightly more, you can usually find a well-brewed cappuccino in the bigger cities and most popular tourist haunts. Tea and herbal tea are also popular and widely available; most restaurants serve tea of some sort.

It's five o'clock.... Nowhere

Most people would agree that democracy is a nice thing, but what if it gets in the way of a good party? That is exactly what happens with Ecuador's Ley Seca or "Dry Law." Designed to prevent drunk voting and people sleeping through election day, the Ley Seca in Ecuador bans the sale and consumption of alcohol during a period stretching from 36 hours before voting starts to 12 hours after it ends. Since voting almost always occurs on a Sunday, this covers pretty much a whole weekend.

The Ley Seca also applies on *any* Sunday of the year. Stores may not sell liquor on that day. Restaurants may serve it with food only until 4 p.m. If you want a bottle of wine or beer to accompany your Sunday meal at home, be advised to buy it the day before.

Businesses that sell alcohol face harsh penalties, and most bars and clubs (and even some restaurants) are shuttered for the weekend during elections and on Sundays year-round. If you scratch the surface a bit you will find bars and liquor stores that are still open, but the punishment for purchasing or consuming alcohol is a stay in the drunk tank and a fine, so you are wise to lay off the booze during Ley Seca.
Updated: Sep 12, 2012.

ANDEAN SPECIALTY DRINKS

Chicha is a traditional concoction found throughout the Andes, made from fermented corn, rice or yucca. In some rural parts of Ecuador the fermentation process is augmented by human saliva. Chicha-makers (traditionally women) chew the ingredients before putting them back in the pot to brew!

Not to be missed is the Andean specialty drink *canelazo* (or *canelito*), a popular fiesta drink similar to a hot toddy made of boiled water, sugar cane alcohol, lemon or orange, sugar and cinnamon.

ALCOHOLIC BEVERAGES

Most Ecuadorian wine is sweet and made from grape, apple, peach or other fruit. Some good, dry wines are now being locally produced. Wine from Chile and Argentina is widely available. The cheapest way to enjoy it is from a *cartón* (yes, a box) from the local supermarket. Clos is a good brand.

If your palate is a bit more finicky, fine wines from Chile, France, Spain and Italy are also available. Most bars in Ecuador serve local beers of average quality and very good value. The most popular brand is **Pilsener**, which generally comes in a large bottle. Local rum is quite cheap and good. Imbibing too much of this liquor, though, might leave you with a mighty case of *chuchaqui* (hangover) the next morning.

Note: Remember that tap water is frequently used in ice, so request that your beverages be served *sin hielo* (without ice) in restaurants. Güitig is a trustworthy national brand of bottled water.

Media in Ecuador
NEWSPAPERS:
El Comercio
www.elcomercio.com.ec.
One of the largest print daily news publications in Ecuador, based out of Quito. Covers national and international news.

El Financiero
www.elfinanciero.com.
Another national paper, with a focus on the economy.

El Universo
www.eluniverso.com.
Competes with El Comercio in daily publications. Based out of Guayaquil.

Diario Extra
www.diario-extra.com.
Self publishing newspaper from Quayaquil, specializing in feature-driven news.

Hoy
www.hoy.com.ec.
A morning-edition daily newspaper characterized by its openness to different schools of thought and its free print version.

La Hora
www.lahora.com.ec.
An umbrella news company that prints in 12 regions throughout Ecuador, publishing regional news in the area.

MAGAZINES:
Analisis Semanal
www.ecuadoranalysis.com.
Offers in-depth analysis of economics in Ecuador.

Did a unique trek? Tell other travelers at vivatravelguides.com

Cosas Ecuador
www.cosas.com.ec.
A sophisticated celebrity gossip newspaper with in-depth feature articles on politics and culture.

Generacion XXI
www.generacion21.com.
A very popular celebrity magazine for Ecuador's teenager market.

La Cometa
www.cometa.com.ec.
A magazine about children, for children.

Vistazo
www.vistazo.com.ec.
Feature-length local and national news stories.

TV:
Considered the most important source of the country's mass media. *Telenovelas*, which can be compared to American soap operas, take up most of the air-time in Ecuador.

There are 10 private channels and three operated by the state, as well as regional stations. Cable is becoming increasingly popular. Among the private networks are:

Ecuavisa: www.ecuavisa.com.
Teleamazonas: www.teleamazonas.com.
Telerama: www.telerama.ec.

The national public (state-run) television stations are:

Ecuador TV: www.ecuadortv.ec.
Gama TV: www.gamatv.com.ec.
TC Televisión: www.tctelevision.com.

RADIO STATIONS:
Listening to the radio is a very popular passtime in Ecuador, and each town has at least one of their own, local radio stations broadcasting nearby. Most stations produce a mix of music and conversation. While most are in Spanish, it's possible to find a few in English stations as well.

For top hits in Quito, listen to **Los 40s Principales** (97.7 FM), or **Alfa Radio** (98.5 FM); and for local music and adult contemporary themes, listen to Ecuador **Inmediato Radio,** which is best online. **Radio Sucre** (www.radiosucre.com.ec) is a national network.
Updated: Sep 12, 2012.

Money
While Ecuador is not as cheap as it was before converting to the U.S. dollar in 2000, it is still quite affordable for most travelers.

CASH
Travelers in Ecuador should have no problem withdrawing money from local banks using a debit or credit card with **VISA, MasterCard, Cirrus** or **Maestro** representation. **Travelers checks** can be difficult to exchange, even in major cities, so it's a good idea to always have an emergency stash of cash.

Most travelers find it best to bring a combination of cash, credit or debit cards and travelers checks. Several banks in Ecuador can help with international transfers, wiring money and taking money from an **ATM** (*cajero*).

ATM WARNINGS AND ADVICE
Your home country bank will likely **charge a hefty amount** for each time you use an ATM in Ecuador, even if you are just looking at your balance. Also, at times Ecuadorian bank will not acquire a good connection to your home bank and will tell you that you have insufficient funds.

Sometimes this is true, but often it is not, so before making an expensive and frustrating international call to your home bank, try another ATM or wait a day. In general, however, **using ATMs are the easiest way to stay supplied with cash in Ecuador**. If your country does not use the U.S. dollar, an exchange rate fee will also be charged to your account, as the ATMs in Ecuador only deal in dollars.

NOTE: Criminals sometimes target foreigners at ATMs. Be careful after dark or in very busy or deserted areas. Always use ATMs located inside banks or malls with a guard nearby. Some ATMs in tourist areas, such as Quito's Mariscal, are staffed by security guards. If someone is standing too close to you, he or she may be trying to look over your shoulder at your PIN code. When in doubt, walk away and use another machine later.

TRAVELERS' CHECKS
It is a good idea to come with **an emergency stash of travelers' checks**. Many hotels accept travelers' checks (American Express is best; VISA is not always accepted) even in remote areas where you have to travel for hours to reach a bank. While hotels may accept them, you are likely to have a difficult time cashing travelers checks for

dollars at a bank. **Always bring your actual passport. Banco de Guayaquil,** which is American Express' representative in Ecuador, is your best bet for cashing such checks, but be prepared to pay an exchange fee.

WIRE TRANSFERS
MoneyGram (URL:www.moneygram. com) and **Western Union** (URL:www. westernunion.com) agents are common in Ecuador, as they form alliances with local banks around the country. Check the websites for the nearest office. Fees vary and tend to be high, so this option is best for emergencies.

CREDIT CARDS
All international hotels and most higher-priced hotels and restaurants accept **Visa** and **MasterCard**. Many also accept **Diners Club** and **American Express** cards. Beware: an extra 10 percent is often added to your total bill if you pay with a credit card.

Depending on the price, you may be better served withdrawing the cash from an ATM and stashing the credit cards. In general, most Ecuadorian shops do not accept credit cards. Some exceptions are mall stores, and high-end gift and *artesanía* stores.

If your card is lost or stolen, be sure to report it: **American Express** (Tel: Ecuador, 02-256-0488; U.S. collect, 905-474-0870), **Diners Club** (Tel: Ecuador, 02-298-1300; U.S. collect, 303-799-1504), **MasterCard** (Tel: U.S. collect, 636-722-7111), **Visa** (Tel: U.S. collect, 410-581-9994).'

CHANGING MONEY
If you come with **Euros, British pounds, Colombian pesos** or other such foreign currencies, you will be able to change them — but only in very few places. Most Quito banks only have one single branch which will do currency transactions, usually the branch in the more touristy part of town.

A *casa de cambio* (exchange house) usually do not give good exchange rates and are few and far between. Remember to bring ID (or a photocopy) if you do find yourself needing to go to one. In Quito, a couple of *casas de cambio* can be found in Mariscal along Av. Amazonas, like **MegaCambios** on Amazonas N24-01 and Wilson. There's also a place that does change in the Centro Histórico, on the corner of Venezuela and Plaza de la Independencia.

Costs
BUDGET TRAVELERS
Budget travelers easily can survive in Ecuador on about $25-30 per day, staying in hostel dorm rooms, eating at *almuerzo*-style restaurants and traveling on buses. If you are traveling in a group or watch your spending, you can cut daily costs down to $12-15 per person.

Hostels usually range from $8-15 per night, depending if you are in a city or a rural area. Budget $5 per day for food, granted you can cook a meal at the hostel and you eat an almuerzo lunch for $1.50-$4. Pack some oatmeal and fruit for snacks. You'll have to board economy-priced buses, which can be rather unsafe but may also unravel a great travel story.

MID-RANGE TRAVELERS
This class of travelers will get the most value for their dollar. For $35-75 per day, you'll have the luxury of staying at modest, yet comfortable low-end hotels or hostels, which usually have complementary WiFi and may even include a breakfast in the packet.

You'll be able to eat out, and won't have to scour the entire town or city to find the cheapest option; budget $5-10 per meal. At the end of the day, you'll also get to have a little money left over to enjoy the nightlife or embark on weekend day trips that involve rafting, hiking or horseback riding.
Updated: Sep 07, 2012.

LUXURY TRAVELERS
On the other hand, if money is no object you can travel very comfortably using private transportation and have a lot of fun eating out. Quito offers some world-class restaurants throughout its city, many of which are located in stunning colonial buildings. Nice dinners in Ecuador range from $15-30 per person. If you add drinks the price may amount to a bit more.

You can tour the Galápagos and Oriente in style with a highly reputable company and include an itinerary of shopping to your heart's content at Ecuador's many craft markets. Luxury hotels start at about $75 per night International hotels like the Marriott and Hilton cost $160-300 per night.
Updated: Sep 07, 2012.

See our Travel Tips for Ecuador section for more detailed guidelines pertaining to budget, mid-range and luxury travelers (p. 74).

Did a unique trek? Tell other travelers at vivatravelguides.com

INTRO & INFO

Mail, Shipping and Customs in Ecuador

SENDING AND RECEIVING MAIL IN ECUADOR

In general, mailing out packages and letters from Ecuador is easy to do, but receiving mail is more complicated. You can find post offices and couriers in major cities like **Quito**, **Guayaquil** and **Cuenca**.

Ecuador's national postal service, **Correos del Ecuador** (Tel, toll-free: 1-700-CORREO / 267736, URL.www.correosdelecuador. com.ec), has a variety of mailing options: EMS (express,priority), certified and regular.

Locales are typically open Monday-Friday 8 a.m.-6 p.m. and Saturday 8 a.m.-noon. Mail usually takes the following amount of time to reach its destination:

United States: 8–10 business days.

Europe: 10–15 business days.

Asia and Middle East: 18–22 business days.

Latin America and Caribbean: 5–6 business days.

To receive a letter at the *poste restante* (general delivery) - where the post office holds mail until the recipient calls for it - have the sender address the letter to you like this:

LAST NAME, First Name
Lista de Correos
Correo Central
City, ECUADOR

Your name should appear as it is in your passport, which you will need to retrieve the letter or parcel. The city is where you will pick the mail up.

In the major cities, the main post office branches are:

Quito: Japón N36-153 y Av. Naciones Unidas. Also, in the Central Histórico: Venezuela y Chile, Local 25, Centro Comercial Palacio Arzobispal

Guayaquil: Aguirre 301, entre Chile y Pedro Carbo

Cuenca: Borrero y Gran Colombia esq.Additionally, Correos del Ecuador rents post office boxes.

If you are a member of the **South American Explorers Club** (p. 48), you may also receive mail at its Quito clubhouse.

If you are mailing something urgent or important, then it's best to stick with a reputable courier. Most of the time, Ecuador's national postal service does the trick, but you can expect greater delays in sending packages overseas.

The international couriers that have offices in Ecuador's large cities are the following:

Fedex (URL:www.fedex.com/ec)
Tomas Berlanga E-1080, between Avenida Los Shyris and 6 de Diciembre (Tel: 593-2-601-7818). The office is open Monday-Friday 9 a.m.-7 p.m. Fedex also has branches in Cuenca, Guayaquil and Manta.

DHL (URL:www.dhl.com.ec)
La Mariscal: Av. Colon 1333 y Foch (Tel: 593-2-250-8088)

New Town: República 433 y Diego de Almagro (Tel: 593-2-226-5077)

Mariscal Sucre Airport
(Tel. 593-2-292-2687)
All Quito offices are open Monday-Friday 8:30 a.m.-6:30 p.m.; the first two are open Saturday 9 a.m.-5 p.m. DHL also has offices in Cuenca, Guayaquil and Manta.

UPS/LAAR Courier Express S.A. (URL:www.laarcourier.com)

Calle de los Cipreses, Lote 26 y de las Avellanas (Tel: 593-2-396-0000)

Major hotel chains in Quito, like the Hilton, also offer express mail service, so be sure to check with them if you plan on staying at one.

CUSTOMS AND SHIPPING COSTS IN ECUADOR

Correos del Ecuador offers the least expensive service in the whole country.

To mail a postcard or letter (0-20 gr) to Canada, the US or any other place in North, Central or South America costs $2 ($4.00 certified); a letter weighing 21-100 grams costs $4.75 ($7.75 certified). If your correspondence is destined for Europe, the costs are $2.25 ($4 certified) and $5.50 ($8.25 certified), respectively. Note that for a little extra you can also track your parcel too.

Packages should be sent directly from post offices in Ecuador, and it's safest to send them via the **main post office in Quito** (Japón N36-153 y Av. Naciones Unidas). Don't close your packages before you get to the post office: the staff is required to check the contents before the envelope or box is mailed.

It is technically prohibited to mail jewelry, cash or other valuables, so use some discretion when choosing to mail something. Reseal the package yourself before leaving it to be sent.

If you receive a package from overseas, and it weighs over two kilograms, you will have to pick it up at *aduanas* (customs). *Flete* (transportation) fees and other import taxes are calculated according to the declared value of the package; these fees can be quite high. Some ex-pats recommend having the sender declare a $0 value.

The international couriers—DHL, FedEx and UPS—charge are at least triple what the national postal service does. Check the companies' websites for shipping cost calculations. With these services, stamps aren't necessary. The companies can also help with customs paperwork.

Ecuador Phones
ECUADOR COUNTRY CODE:
+593

EMERGENCY NUMBERS:
Emergency: 911
Fire Department: 102
Police: 101

It is easy to keep in touch by phone in Ecuador, thanks to the spread of cellular phone and internet technology. Visitors have a number of options for calling Ecuador, calling home from Ecuador and placing calls within the country. If you do not have your own fixed (land) line or cellular phone, then drop by a *locutorio* or *centro de llamadas* (call center) and use a booth there.

ECUADOR CELL PHONES
It seems wherever you go in Ecuador, mobile phone use is rampant, and those travelers who will be in the country for more than a few days may want to join in. Three companies provide service in Ecuador: Claro, Alegro and Movistar. All three offer monthly plans as well as pre-paid services.

For most travelers in Ecuador, pre-paid plans make the most sense; phones can be purchased at retailers throughout the country, and phone shops will also sell SIM cards that will give you a local phone number and allow you to place and receive calls. After that, all you have to do is buy phone credits to load onto your phone (*recargar*); this usually comes in the form of scratch cards which contain a secret code you enter into your phone. The cards are sold in convenience stores and shops throughout the country. Alternatively, they ask for your cellphone number so that they can add credit to it electronically.

Movistar credit is usually the easiest to find in Quito, while Claro is typically the easiest to find in the provinces and Alegro, the most difficult. Also note that in Ecuador, phone calls that are made within cell networks (for example, Claro to Claro) are considerably cheaper than calls between different networks (as in, Movistar to Claro).

It may be possible to use your cell phone from home while traveling. Ecuador's cell carriers operate on GSM networks; Claro and Movistar use the 850 MHz band and Alegro uses the 1900 band. That means that dual-band phones from Europe, Africa, Asia and Oceania will not work, but GSM-enabled phones from the North or South America likely will. All quad-band, and most tri-band, phones will work in the country.

Remember that phones from outside the western hemisphere will need a plug adapter and 120-volt converter in order to charge safely. Some foreign phone carriers will allow you to use your existing phone plan while in Ecuador, while incurring hefty foreign roaming charges. Others may allow you to unlock your phone and use a local SIM card (from Claro, Movistar or Alegro) while you are in the country. You should contact your phone carrier to check.

Cell coverage in Ecuador is relatively good. The main cities, like Quito and Guayaquil, have blanket coverage. In the Andes, valleys often have very spotty coverage, while a signal can usually be found on top of hills and ridges.

The main coastal resort areas are well-served, while smaller communities may have weak or no coverage. Remote parts of the Amazon basin do not, generally, have coverage. As companies build more cell towers, expect coverage across the country to improve.

INTRO & INFO

Did a unique trek? Tell other travelers at vivatravelguides.com

INTRO & INFO

Ecuador Provincial Phone Codes

Pichincha (including Quito) and Santo Domingo de los Tsáchilas – **2**

Bolívar, Chimborazo, Cotopaxi, Pastaza and Tungurahua – **3**

Guayas (including Guayaquil) and Santa Elena – **4**

Galápagos, Los Ríos and Manabí – **5**

Carchi, Esmeraldas, Imbabura, Napo, Orellana and Sucumbíos – **6**

Azuay, Cañar, El Oro, Loja, Morona Santiago and Zamora – **7**

Note: On September 30, 2012, all cellular phone numbers are 10 digits. Existing numbers add a "9" after the initial "0." For example: if calling from within Ecuador, the number 0-8-9272-700 would be 0-98-9272-700; or if calling to Ecuador from overseas: 593-8-9272-700 would be 593-98-9272-700

This change affects not only cellular phones, but also mobile devices (like smart phones and tablets) that use an internet connection via cellular number.

CALLING ECUADOR

The country code for Ecuador is 593. To call Ecuador from overseas, follow these directions:

Calling Ecuador from the USA and Canada:

Dial 011 + 593 + The One-Digit Province Code (see below) + The Seven-Digit Phone Number

Calling Ecuador from the UK, Western Europe, New Zealand, Peru, Bolivia and most of Latin America:

Dial 00 + 593 + The One-Digit Province Code + The Seven-Digit Phone Number

Calling Ecuador from Australia:

Dial 0011 + 593 + The One-Digit Province Code + The Seven-Digit Phone Number

Calling Ecuador from Colombia:

Dial 009 + 593 + The One-Digit Province Code + The Seven-Digit Phone Number

To make cheap calls to Ecuador, you can either use a voice-over-internet system like Skype, or buy a phone card. In North America, phone cards with cheap rates to Ecuador are widely available in Hispanic grocery stores; otherwise, they can be found online.

CALLING WITHIN ECUADOR

The procedure for making domestic calls in Ecuador depends on the location of you and the person you are calling, as well as whether the phones are on fixed (land) lines or cellular lines. For calls from one land line to another within a single province, all you have to do is dial the seven-digit phone number.

Calling to or from a cellular number, or across provinces, requires the phone number to be preceded by the number 0 and the provincial code. For example: To call the Guayaquil number 232-7100 from Quito, you would dial 04-232-7100. When calling another mobile number, it must always be dialed with 098 or 099 followed by the seven-digit phone number.

Calling Home from Ecuador

To make an international call from Ecuador, you must dial 00, then the country code for the nation you are calling, then area code for the city, and finally the phone number.

To Call the US or Canada from Ecuador:

Dial 00 + 1 + Area Code + Phone Number

To Call the UK from Ecuador:

Dial 00 + 44 + Area Code + Phone Number

To Call Australia from Ecuador:

Dial 00 + 61 + Area Code + Phone Number

To Call Peru from Ecuador:

Dial 00 + 51 + Area Code + Phone Number

To Call Colombia from Ecuador:

Dial 00 + 57 + Area Code + Phone Number

The telephone directory (*guía telefónica*) lists the codes for most countries and their major cities.

Enter V!VA Photo Contests: vivatravelguides.com/photography-contests/

International rates on landlines and cell phones in Ecuador tend to be quite high. One cheaper option is to call over the internet, either by using a service like Skype or by making a call from a *cabina* (phone center) Expect to pay $0.10-0.25 per minute to the US or UK; rates are higher to other parts of the world. Porta, Movistar and Andinatel also have phone booths from which you can make calls using a pre-paid phone card, but the rates tend to be significantly higher than on internet calls.
Updated: Apr 16, 2013.

Internet Access, WiFi and Internet Cafes in Ecuador
ECUADOR INTERNET ACCESS
Internet accessibility in Ecuador is improving, but still has a long way to go. If you are bringing a laptop to Ecuador, you can find WiFi hotspots in major cities like **Quito** and **Guayaquil**. However, once you venture outside the larger cities, you will find internet sporadic and pricey.

WIFI IN ECUADOR
WiFi is becoming more common in Ecuador; however, signal strength widely varies. Not only do many mid- to high-end hotels in have WiFi on-site, but also foreign-targeted hostels; simply ask for the password to gain access. Several nicer cafes and restaurants in **Quito**, **Cuenca** and **Guayaquil** also offer free WiFi access. If having WiFi is important for your trip, be sure to research and plan your accommodation in advance, as it's not as widely available here as in other European or North American countries. Also, **check with VIVA Travel Guides**: we normally state whether a lodging or restaurant has WiFi on-site. **Quito** has installed free WiFi zones at several of the city's plazas and parks; see: www.quito-wifi.com for a listing of access points.

ECUADOR INTERNET CAFES
Internet cafes are cheap and ubiquitous in major cities like Quito and Guayaquil. Internet costs $0.50-1.50 per hour, though cafes in smaller towns tend to be a bit pricier than that. The quality of Ecuador internet cafés widely varies: some offer broadband connection and flat-screen monitors, while others are painfully slow and have keypads loosely dangling off the keyboard. Many Ecuador internet cafes come equipped with headsets, web cams and Skype, and some come with international keyboards. It pays to shop around and find a good café that suits your needs and budget. Additionally, in many areas, connection gets slow 3-10 p.m., when kids get out of school and hop on the Internet. To access the @ sign, type Alt Gr + 2 or Alt Gr + q.
Updated: Sep 25, 2012.

Health in Ecuador
While traveling in Ecuador, it is important to feel safe and at ease. Do not focus on all the potential diseases you could contract. Follow our preparation guidelines and you should be fine. However, should you have a medical emergency, remember that after Cuba, Ecuador has the best private health care system in Latin America. So even if it might cut into your budget, you will receive the best of care. Pharmacies in Ecuador are conveniently located and common. As with most Latin American countries, if you tell the pharmacist your symptoms, then he / she will often be able to recommend what you need, helping to avoid a costly visit to the doctor. Reliable national chains are Fybeca and Pharmacys.

Minor Health Problems
Altitude Sickness
When traveling in the Ecuadorian Andes it is important to rest the first few days and drink lots of bottled water, limit fatty foods and avoid alcohol. Take things slowly; don't immediate go running around sightseeing. Should you feel a severe headache, drowsiness, confusion, dry cough, and / or breathlessness, rest. If the symptoms continue, you may want to move to a lower altitude. Anyone planning to hike at high altitudes is advised to relax in a high altitude city such as Quito for a few days before any physical exertion.

Note that altitude sickness, locally called *soroche*, can come on suddenly if you experience a sudden change of altitude. You may get it if you ride the Teleférigo to the top of the mountain or take a bus to the refuge at Cotopaxi, even if you've been in Quito or another highland city for a while. Even native Quiteños have been known to occasionally pass out at the top of the Teleférigo, so take care!

Sunburn / Heat Exhaustion
Ecuador straddles the equator; therefore, even at high altitudes where cool breezes constantly blow and snow can accumulate, the sun is incredibly strong. Apply sunscreen with at least an SPF of 30 every few hours

INTRO & INFO

you are outside. The sun in Galápagos and on the coast is particularly strong and unprepared visitors get badly burned all the time. If you get severe sunburn, treat it with a cream and stay out of the sun for a while.

To avoid overheating, wear a hat and sunglasses and drink lots of liquids. Overweight people are more susceptible to sun stroke. The symptoms of heat exhaustion are profuse sweating, weakness, exhaustion, muscle cramps, rapid pulse and vomiting. If you experience heat stroke, go to a cool, shaded or air conditioned area until your body temperature normalizes and drink a lot of liquids. If the symptoms continue, consult a doctor.

Note: Drinking only water is not enough, as your body loses salts when you sweat. Drink sports beverages like Gatorade or coconut milk; in a pinch, mix six teaspoons of sugar and a half-teaspoon of salt in a liter of purified water.

Motion Sickness

Even the hardiest of travelers can be hit by motion sickness on the buses in the Andes and boats in the Galápagos. Sit near the front of the bus or stay above deck on the boat and focus on the horizon. If you are prone to motion sickness, eat light, non-greasy food before traveling and avoid drinking too much, particularly alcohol.

Over-the-counter medications such as Dramamine can prevent it: in Ecuador, go to a pharmacy and ask for Mareol, a liquid medicine similar to Dramamine. Some travelers also say that ginger candies or tea is helpful. If you suffer from severe motion sickness, you may want to get a prescription for something stronger, like the patch.

Traveler's Diarrhea

This is probably the most common disease for travelers. There is no vaccine to protect you from traveler's diarrhea; it is avoided by eating sensibly. Contrary to popular belief, it is usually transmitted by food, not contaminated water. Eat only steaming hot food that has been cooked all the way through in clean establishments.

Avoid raw lettuce and fruit that cannot be peeled, like strawberries. Vegetables are usually safer than meat. An inexpensive vegetable wash (known as *vitalín*) may be purchased at any supermarket and is a good way to ensure clean fruit and vegetables if you are cooking your own meals.

Make sure any milk you drink has been boiled. Avoid ice cream that could have melted and been refrozen, such as anything for sale in the street. *Helado de paila* does not contain milk and is safer. If you do get diarrhea, the best way is to let it run its course while staying hydrated with clear soups, lemon tea, Gatorade and soda that has gone flat. Bananas are also a good source of potassium and help stop diarrhea. If you need to travel and can't afford to let the illness run its course, any pharmacy will give you something that will make you comfortable enough for a bus trip. If the diarrhea persists for more than five days, see a doctor.

More Serious Health Problems
Hepatitis

If you are planning to live in Ecuador for more than six months or work in a hospital or with children, it may be a good idea to get a vaccination against Hepatitis A and B. The vaccine is not considered necessary for short-term travelers. Avoid situations where you could be subject to being punctured by a dirty needle.

One of our writers was on a local bus on the coast where a nurse was giving out free measles shots while the bus was in motion. Needless to say, it is a good idea to stay away from any sort of questionable injection. It is also not a good idea to get a piercing while traveling, especially at the popular outdoor markets.

Malaria

Most doctors around the world will tell you that if you travel anywhere in Ecuador, you must take pills to prevent malaria. This is not true. Malaria is only found on the Pacific Coast (but not in the Galápagos Islands) and in the Amazon Rainforest. If you are only traveling in the Andes and to the Galápagos, you run no risk of contracting malaria.

However, if you plan to spend a lot of time along the Pacific Coast or in the Amazon Rainforest, it is a good idea to take the proper measure to prevent the disease. Mosquitoes carrying malaria are evening and nighttime biters.

If you are planning to go to the Amazon rainforest for a couple of days, you might want to ask the staff of the lodge for recommendations. Many areas of the Amazon are relatively mosquito-free because black-water rivers are inhospitable breeding grounds to mosquitoes.

Thoroughly apply insect repellent with at least 30 percent DEET. Applying it to your hair is good way to make the scent stay on your body longer. Sleep under a mosquito net. Wear light colored clothes and avoid shiny jewelry. Avoid using scented deodorants, soaps or perfumes.

Rabies
There are stray dogs throughout Ecuador that are usually harmless. However, many home-owners train guard dogs to attack trespassers. On long hikes in rural areas, always carry a walking stick to defend yourself if a dog starts to attack. In case you are bitten by a dog, rabies vaccinations are readily available in Quito and other major cities.

Typhoid
An oral capsule or injection should be taken before travel if you are planning to travel in Ecuador or South America for an extended period of time (six months or more). The oral vaccine needs boosting every five years, and the injection every three years.

Yellow Fever
This mosquito-borne disease is endemic to Ecuador and many other parts of South America. Talk to your doctor before taking the vaccine, as it is not recommended for people with certain allergies, pregnant women and other special cases. The vaccine is effective for up to ten years.

Safety in Ecuador
As is true in most Latin American countries, travelers tend to stand out in Ecuador. There is a good chance you will stand a head taller than the crowds on rural buses throughout the country, and people will notice that you're foreign. As a result, travelers are easy targets for petty crime. Although crime in Ecuador is rarely violent and many travelers have escaped sketchy situations by yelling and running away, good street sense and awareness must be exercised. In crowds, always hold your bag close to your body and in front of you where you can see it. Most thieves work in teams; one will distract you while the other slashes your bag or picks your pocket. If you are approached by a suspicious person asking for money or the time, just walk away quickly. Don't let yourself get cornered.

Distribute important documents into at least two stashes. Keep your passport, at least one credit card and most of your cash well protected under your clothes and against your skin –either in a money belt, in-sewn pocket or other contraption. Keep a wallet or coin purse within easy reach (but NOT in a hip pocket) with a small amount of money and perhaps a second credit card for daily food and shopping, so that you don't have to reach into your main reserve when you aren't in a comfortable space.

In most cities in Ecuador the dodgy neighborhoods are easy to identify: They are around bus stations and major outdoor markets. Lodging is usually slightly cheaper in these areas, but for a dollar or two more a night, you can get a substantial upgrade worth the peace of mind. Researching the perfect spot beforehand is the best way to avoid being stuck in a neighborhood that makes you uncomfortable.

Earthquakes are common in Ecuador and three volcanoes are presently active (Tungurahua, Sangay and Reventador). To keep informed on these situations, visit the Instituto Geofísico's website (URL:www.igepn.edu.ec). Tsunamis can occur along the coast. In the case of any of these disasters, be sure to follow local authorities' instructions.
Updated: Sep 10, 2012.

Etiquette & Dress in Ecuador
Ecuadorians are polite: When entering a store, or a restaurant or even browsing goods at an outdoor market, it is expected to greet the staff with a *buenos días, buenas tardes* or *buenas noches,* depending on the time of day, and to say *gracias* or *hasta luego* when you leave. Greetings involving women are a kiss on the right cheek and a handshake between two men. In a business meeting and when meeting an indigenous person, a handshake is sufficient for women.

How to Dress
Ecuadorians tend to be better dressed than most North Americans and Europeans. So if you are wearing old, tattered travel clothes and flip flops, you will invariably get some stares. That said, Ecuadorians are infinitely patient with the ways of the foreign traveler and will treat you respectfully regardless of how raggedy your outfit—as long as you aren't trying to get into a nice restaurant, bar or club dressed like a bum.

In the Andes, people tend to cover up a lot more than on the coast, partially because it is much colder and partially because the culture tends to be a bit more conservative. You will rarely see an *serrano* (person from the sierra, or mountains) wearing shorts off the *fútbol* field, and flip flops are an oddity. Men should never plan to travel bare-chested in the Andes. Likewise, women should never wear just a sports bra or swimsuit around town.

If blending in is important to you, then wear pants more often than shorts, don't wear flip flops; and when going out at night, men should wear collared shirts (no hats!) and women should wear clean, stylish clothes—pants are fine.

Dress outside of cities and at the beach is much more casual, but the same basic principles apply.

FOOD MANNERS
Like all countries, there is a certain way to eat all typical meals. In Ecuador, for example, people toss popcorn and fried banana chips into ceviche. Table manners are more relaxed, though, so don't worry too much about them. Tables at casual, crowded restaurants are often shared. When you get up to leave or join someone's table, it is appropriate to say *buen provecho* (bon appétit).

ETIQUETTE WHEN VISITING SOMEONE'S HOME
If visiting someone's home for a party or meal, it is polite to bring a small gift like a cake for dessert or a bottle of wine. Bigger gifts can be overwhelming and the host may feel like he or she needs to give you something in return, so stick with something small. Ecuadorians are incredibly generous by nature and will want to feel one ahead in gift exchanges, so try not to overwhelm your host with expensive presents.

If you are staying with your host for an extended period of time, offer to help out with groceries and bring fresh flowers. A memento from your hometown like a photo, post card or small book will be appreciated. Also remember that, unless you are staying with a rich family, your visit will probably be something of a financial strain. You can make it less so by taking short showers—hot water is expensive—and minimizing electricity use—also extremely expensive. Phone calls to cell phones should never be made from land lines; they cost up to $1 per minute. Phone and internet service in general tends to be very pricey, so be conscious of its use.

Business Hours
Banks vary their hours but are generally open from Monday-Friday 9 a.m.-4:30 p.m. around the country. Hours for money and travelers check exchange are often different. See our Banks and ATM and Money and Costs sections for more information.

Restaurants often shut down between meals. Breakfast is generally served 8-10 a.m.; lunch, noon-3 p.m. and dinner, 6-10 p.m. In smaller towns, dinner will end earlier. In Quito, Guayaquil and cities with high tourist traffic, it is not uncommon to eat at 10 p.m. Restaurants, especially in small towns, are often closed on Sundays and public holidays. In Quito and Guayaquil, the international chains always stay open on these days. Hotels are a good option when restaurants are closed; they are almost always prepared to serve food.
Updated: Aug 22, 2012.

Travel Tips for Ecuador
Travel has different meanings for different people. Why are you traveling? Some travel for business, some for pleasure. Some are backpackers with limited budgets, some have money to burn. Some travelers have special needs, such as handicap access or child-friendly facilities. In order to provide you with the best service possible, our writers here at V!VA Travel Guides have included this section on Ecuador Travel Tips. In it, you'll find all the travel tips, advice and suggestions that you'll need to custom-fit your trip to best suit your needs.

Are you a woman traveling alone? If so, you'll want to check out our page on tips for women travelers. Traveling with kids? You'll want to see our section on Ecuador travel for families. Gay / lesbian? Don't go without first looking at out Gay/Lesbian travel tips page. Senior citizens will also find useful advice, as will handicapped travelers. Planning on taking some photos while in Ecuador? Photographers will want to take a look at our Photography in Ecuador page. All of this information is available starting on page 77.

So, how much is this trip going to cost you? Depending on how much you'd like to pay, we have tips for travelers in every price range in the following couple of pages. You can also check out our Money and Costs page for more further information regarding financing (located on pages 66 and 67).

Tips for Budget Travelers

Traveling in Ecuador is ideal for the budget traveler, and essentials such as food, lodging and transportation are reasonably priced wherever you go.

Lodging

Every major or minor tourist destination in Ecuador has at least one or two hostels that cater to the budget traveler set. In some, you can find decent, dorm-style lodging for as little as $5 per night, though in some areas you'll have to budget $8-15. Ten or fifteen years ago, finding a good place was a crap shoot. You showed up in a town and started looking, guidebook in hand. Maybe you would get lucky and find a nice, clean place with a vacancy, maybe you wouldn't. Word of mouth among travelers was the best way to find a good recommendation. Today, many of the better hostels accept reservations via the internet or by phone: V!VA's website is a good place to begin your search.

In many hostels, the most inexpensive lodging option is a bunk room. Bring a padlock to secure your belongings while you explore. Most of the better hostel dorm rooms have small lockers for guests to keep their things. Above all, don't settle for just a clean bed and place to lock your things. Ecuadorian budget hostels often have game rooms, TVs with DVD libraries, friendly cafés and more. Often, doing a little homework beforehand can make a big difference when you finally find a place to stay.

Transportation

Buses in Ecuador are what trains are in Europe: The cheapest way to get around. You may feel some nausea while traveling throughout the country on buses, so bring some medication. We also recommend you become familiar with the inner-city bus routes.

Quito has a great transportation system, with the Trole, Ecovia and Metrobus running parallel north-and-south.

Food

A true budget traveler can get by on as little as $5 a day. If you don't need a sit-down meal, try bargaining with the little old ladies selling produce at fruit and vegetable stands. Sometimes you can cut deals coming away with five avocados for a dollar. You can always stop at a food cart, but you are taking a gamble with your health. Often times the risk is very worth it, though. Ecuador is also home to the *almuerzo ejecutivo*, where you'll receive a predetermined three-course meal for $1.50-$4.

Another hint is to familiarize yourself with local foods, like the *empanada*. In Ecuador, empanadas are pastries, folded-over with chicken, beef or cheese inside, then baked or deep-fried. Yummy and cheap, you can find them in most bakeries for under a dollar each, and there are bakeries everywhere. One is a snack, two are a meal.

Tours

If you're on a super-tight budget, chances are you won't be able to afford a long, extended tour. However, there may be some exceptions. If you want to take a big-ticket tour, like a visit to a jungle lodge or even Galápagos, you can consider going last-minute.

Travel agencies in Quito often have last-minute deals. If the tour hasn't filled up two or three days before departure, they'll often dramatically cut their prices, sometimes by as much as half. Obviously, this option is more likely in low tourist seasons. You can also try a web search to find last-minute deals, too.

In addition to last-minute deals, you may want to look into day trips suck as horseback riding, whitewater rafting or mountain biking. These day trips can cost anywhere from $35-$80 or so, and if you go with a reputable company you're sure to have a good time.

Tips for Mid-Range Travelers

Good news! Ecuador is a fabulous place for mid-range ($30-$75 daily budget) travelers. Of all of our three categories, you'll be the ones who get the most bang for your buck.

Lodging

Mid-range travelers get to enjoy the best lodging options available in Ecuador, which consist of everything from converted colonial homes and haciendas to bed and breakfasts and adventurous eco-lodges. Most of these carry the two-to-three star perks: free breakfast, travel info desk, adventures such as mountain biking or horseback riding, cable TV, private bathrooms, 24-hour hot water and more. Some even have spas, swimming pools, free internet and free airport pickups. One huge bonus is internet presence of hotels: most of the best mid-range hotels have a website or at least an e-mail address so that you can make reservations. Some of the sites are better than others, but most offer at least basic contact information, rates and location.

If you're e-mailing back and forth to a hotel before your trip, you can even negotiate the price a little, especially if you're coming in low tourism season (September-May) or if you're going to stay more than one night. For those who are interested, the best eco-lodges in Ecuador, such as the Black Sheep Inn and Al-Andaluz Hotel, are mid-range hotels: you may want to consider spending the night at a place that makes a difference!

Transportation

Buses are still probably your best option for traveling throughout Ecuador. Even if you can afford a rental car, it's a bad idea. Quito and Guayaquil are terrible cities to drive in, as there are no street signs and one-way streets are not always labeled. Guayaquil is worse than Quito. After a few minutes in Guayaquil, you will wonder who left the asylum door open and let all the lunatics out. When you're not in the city, there are no road signs, so you may come upon an intersection in a remote location with no indication of which way you need to go. Roads are bad, and breakdowns, flat tires and other automotive problems are very common.

As an option, buses are pretty easy and comfortable and allow you to rest between adventures. An even more comfortable option is to book a tour, which is pretty affordable in Ecuador. In cities, take taxis because they're safe and cheap. See our taxis in Ecuador section for tips on dealing with cabbies (p. 47).

Food

The restaurants in Ecuador are excellent, safe and reasonably priced. Almost all of them should be within your price range, especially if you save a little money here and there, on breakfast and lunch, in order to splurge on dinner. In Quito, which is considered expensive by the rest of Ecuador, dinner at a very nice restaurant, such as a steakhouse, will cost you $15-$20 per person, all inclusive. Be sure to check out fancy restaurants offering Ecuadorian cuisine, and avoid street food.

Tours

The best part about booking a trip through a tour agency is not having to deal with pesky matters like airport transfers, worrying about the security of your luggage and not

having an emergency number to call when you need it. Many mid-range travelers arrive to Ecuador with a tour already booked, which is definitely preferable. Reputable agencies such as Metropolitan or Lindblad are more expensive, but your satisfaction is almost assured. If you want to save a little money, you may want to look for a newer, up-and-coming agency looking to win a good reputation.

Some mid-range travelers like to leave a few days at the end of their stay to hang out in Quito or add on optional shorter tours such as shopping or adventure trips. This is a great option for those who have a little extra time and money. Travel desks at hotels can be quite helpful for making your plans.

Tips for Luxury Travelers

Great news! Hotels, restaurants, visitor sites and travel agencies in Ecuador have the professionalism, attention to detail and elegance that the first-class traveler has come to expect.

In the major cities, internationally renowned hotels such as the Hilton and the Marriott have modern, attractive branches. In Galápagos, some of the finest cruise ships in the world, luxuriously outfitted and staffed with the best guides Galápagos has to offer, await you. Even some of the remote jungle lodges, often uncomfortable and rustic, now have fine dining, air conditioning, and other amenities which allow you to visit the Amazon without having to sacrifice any comfort. Updated: February 12, 2013

Lodging

First-class travelers will find a wide array of lodging options in Ecuador. There are super-deluxe hotels in every major Ecuadorian city: Quito, Cuenca and Guayaquil. These are modern, five-star hotels that have every imaginable luxury: room service, in-room internet, mints on the pillows, you name it.

If you have some flexibility with your luxury travel, you may want to consider some options. Many of the upper mid-range hotels are cheaper and more charming than the large luxury chains.

If you can choose, say, between a large international chain and an elegant converted seventeenth century hacienda, you may want to choose the latter if you're interested in history and want a more memorable experience, as well as a romantic atmosphere.

Speaking of haciendas, you'll definitely want to check out one of the converted haciendas to the north of Quito: they're truly unique and memorable and offer first-class service. For more information, visit our Haciendas In Ecuador page (p. 61).

Transportation

No buses or cars for you, luxury travelers! If money is no object, you'll definitely want to arrange a very complete tour that includes all transfers and trips. Buses in Ecuador are convenient, comfortable and cheap, but they can be somewhat limiting and dealing with them will take up valuable time: if you can afford it, going with a tour is definitely the way to go.

Also, if you're traveling to the Oriente – the eastern jungle – you may have the option of overland or air travel to Coca or Lago Agrio. The overland trip is interesting but long and somewhat grueling, as the roads are terrible. Flying will also change a ten-hour trip to 45 minutes: quite a difference.

Food

You will greatly enjoy the quality of food in Ecuador's finest restaurants. In the larger cities, such as Quito, Cuenca and Guayaquil, there are world-class restaurants that boast fine cuisine and excellent service. Some of the cruise ships in Galápagos offer fine dining as well: Metropolitan's M/N Santa Cruz offers lobster thermidor and filet mignon. The best news is the price: even in the finest restaurants, it is uncommon to pay more than $60 or so for a dinner for two (not counting alcohol). Remember, when calculating price for a meal in Ecuador, add 22 percent: 10 percent for service (offering a tip is optional) and 12 percent for taxes. Outside of the cities and cruise ships, fine international cuisine is difficult to find, but that's not all bad: it gives you an excuse to sample Ecuador's delicious traditional plates. Nearly everywhere you go, there will be a local restaurant or two that is a cut above the rest: your guide or tour agency will see to it that you find your way into them for a good meal.

Tours

If you can afford them, there are a variety of tour options available to Ecuador. The most famous part of Ecuador, is, of course, the Galápagos, and there are numerous tour operators who specialize in nothing but the islands. When booking a Galápagos tour, one thing to bear in mind is the luxury / comfort level of the vessel: there are many ships working the islands, and some of them are much more luxurious than others. Another thing to consider is the quality of your guide: an exceptional guide can make all the difference in the world on a Galápagos trip: the more expensive ships generally pay their guides better, which in turn attracts the best guides.

Don't simply spend a couple of days in Quito, fly to Galápagos and assume you've seen all there is of the country. There are many other tours and trips available in Ecuador to the country's fascinating places and sites. Do some research and figure out which ones are the best for you to see. Tour agencies commonly offer trips to favorite places like Baños, Otavalo, Cuenca and the jungle. Their prices are a little bit higher than they would be if you did them by yourself, but you pay for convenience. Having the travel agency van pick you up and drop you off at your hotel is probably worth it. Tourism services in Ecuador, at least the ones at the top of the travel food chain, are excellent, and the value for the money is usually very good. Updated: Sep 07, 2012.

Photography in Ecuador

Anyone with even a passing interest in photography will love Ecuador. It is one of the most scenic countries in the world, with several places—Galápagos, the Otavalo market, the waterfalls near Baños, to name a few—being truly exceptional and unique places to take photos. Take care with your cameras: They are one of the items most stolen from visitors.

For any camera, make sure you have extra batteries. They can be difficult to find in Ecuador unless they're a common type like AA. If you use rechargeable ones, be sure to bring your battery recharger. Bring filters if you use them, as lighting and weather conditions in Ecuador can often be extreme. Talk to an expert at the local photo shop about filters if you don't know much about them. Tell him or her that you'll be going to a place with very strong sunlight. A waterproof camera bag is a must, as is camera cleaning equipment.

If you use print film, it is possible to purchase it fairly easily in Ecuador. Common 35mm film is easy to find. The best prices are usually at the little photo developing shops that you'll find almost everywhere. Prices for decent 100, 200, and 400 speed film are a little bit higher than in the States, but the quality

INTRO & INFO

is the same and the convenience factor probably makes it worth it to purchase film in Ecuador, especially when you consider that you won't have to pass your film through several x-ray machines as you go through airport security. Specialized film, such as 160 speed film for portraits, black-and-white film or any film that is not 35mm, may be difficult to find. If you run out and you're at a tourist destination like Mitad del Mundo, film will be easy to find but more expensive.

It is possible to develop your print film in Ecuador, but many visitors complain about quality. Stories of lost photos, botched developing and scratched negatives are common enough for concern. Black-and-white processing is nearly impossible.

Of the various developing chains in Ecuador, Ecuacolor (URL: www.ecuacolor.com) seems to have the most satisfied customers. There are several Ecuacolor branches in Quito, and they are easily identified by their bright yellow color scheme. Ask about special deals. Most photo places offer daily specials such as two rolls for the price of one, a free new roll of film with developing, etc.

If you use a digital camera, be sure to have more than one memory chip. You'll take a lot of photos, and downloading them to a disc or computer may be difficult. If your chip is full, internet cafés may be able to put all of your photos on a disc for you for a minimal price. Many of the high-end tourist places, such as the nicer hotels and Galápagos cruise ships, also offer this service. Before you go, be absolutely sure to bring all appropriate cables, chargers and other accessories. Do not expect any computer places to have them. Spare batteries is also a good idea, as you may be away from a wall socket for a while.

If you're planning on downloading your photos somehow before returning home, be aware that the CDs themselves can be sometimes difficult to find. You may want to pack one or two just in case. Photo shops in Quito and Guayaquil will be able to make prints for you if you can't wait to get home.

If you use a video camcorder, bring as many tapes or mini DVDs as you think you're going to need, as it may be hard to find them in Ecuador. Assume that you will not be able to download the tapes onto any disc or DVD until you get home, although some of the better internet cafés might be able to do it. Best to take a hard drive with you if you can.

UNDERWATER PHOTOGRAPHY

Galápagos is a fantastic place to take underwater photos, as the water is often clear, there are many opportunities to dive and snorkel, and there are species of marine life found nowhere else in the world. Plan on bringing all of your own equipment, though. Dive shops in the Galápagos tend to be very basic and probably won't be able to lend you any gear.

It is a good idea to bring along one or two disposable cameras. If you're going out with friends to dance and drink, they're perfect: small, handy and replaceable if stolen. Disposable cameras are available in the larger cities and in photo shops, but they're more expensive than they are in the States: a decent one with flash will cost you around $15-20 in Ecuador. Semi-waterproof cameras are also a good idea: they're fun to bring on rafting trips and while snorkeling in Galápagos (tip: get close or the picture won't work). Disposable water cameras are available in Quito, but a little bit expensive.
Updated: Sep 07, 2012.

Travel Tips for Specific Groups
WOMEN TRAVELERS

Machismo is alive and well in Ecuador. Ecuadorian men endlessly call out to women in public. Ignore the comments and they won't go any further.

Ecuadorian women usually travel with family or friends. A lone female traveler is an odd sight. Use the time-honored ploys, if you don't want to attract advances: Wear a wedding ring, and a cross or Star of David necklace. Carry a picture of your "husband" and if asked, say he is nearby. Dress conservatively.

Women travelers interested in meeting men will run into more complications, however. *Gringueros*, or Ecuadorian men who habitually prowl the tourist scene, have quite a reputation throughout the country. Be careful and don't expect to be friends with an Ecuadorian man. There will almost always be ulterior motives.

In general, women should have no problems with safety, even if traveling alone throughout the country. Be smart, though: take cabs after dark and don't go to a club or bar alone, watch your drink at all times and never accept a drink offer from someone else. See our section on safety in Ecuador for more information (p. 73).

GAY AND LESBIAN TRAVELERS

Ecuador, like most Latin American countries, has well-defined, stereotypical roles for men and women: Men like to be seen as strong, macho figures and the women as dependent homemakers. That is not always practiced, and the younger generation is rapidly changing that image. However, the image does not lend to open acceptance of homosexuality.

Politically, Ecuador is fairly accepting of homosexual citizens. Before the 1998 constitutional reforms, which protected citizens from discrimination against sexual orientation, citizens could be arrested for any action which offended "public morality," for example, patronizing a gay bar. The new Constitution of 2008 went one step further, by legalizing same-gender civil unions.

In practice, Ecuador has a long way to go on the road to acceptance. The coast tends to be more liberal. Guayaquil has a fairly active gay scene. Quito and Cuenca also host growing gay scenes, but is still fighting the very conservative Catholic culture of the sierra. There is widespread bias against homosexuality. *Maricón*—a negative term for gay man—is a common insult for a man acting at all effeminate.

Gay and lesbian travelers will be surprised on New Year's and other holidays like Latacunga's Mama Negra festival in September, when men cross-dress as women to ask for money, join in parades and act generally goofy. Unfortunately, this is seen more as a joke than a widespread acceptance of sexual alternatives.

See quito.queercity.info and http://paiscanelaguia.blogspot.com for guides to the gay scene and general information about gay and lesbian travel in Ecuador.

DISABLED TRAVELERS

Unfortunately, Ecuador has extremely undeveloped infrastructure for disabled travelers, especially those on a tight budget. The internationally-owned hotels in Quito and Guayaquil are recommended for disabled travelers, but still not perfect. Sidewalks are often cobblestone with a generous helping of potholes and cracks. Much of the activity for travelers in Ecuador is active-- hiking, biking and the like—and is not open to wheelchairs. Even the Galápagos, which is the most developed tourist destination in Ecuador, requires a certain level of agility to get on and off the boat and to explore each different island. Disabled persons qualify for discounts on transportation and entry fees to museums, parks and other attractions.

SENIOR TRAVELERS

Active, adventurous senior travelers will be pleasantly surprised with the level of respect and consideration they will be greeted with. Older citizens are greatly respected in Ecuador. Most live with their children. Nursing homes and care facilities are all but nonexistent and considered a shameful and embarrassing "gringo" practice.

Many travelers wait a lifetime to visit the world's most diverse cageless zoo: the Galápagos Islands. As a result, many of the travelers to the Galápagos Islands are active senior citizens. The activities in the Galapagos do require someone with a certain level

A Cultural Note on Photography in Ecuador

Some Ecuadorians are uncomfortable having their photo taken, particularly the indigenous people from the highlands and rain forests. It is always polite to ask before you take someone's photo. In common tourist places like Otavalo and Baños, locals (particularly children) sometimes dress up for the express purpose of letting visitors take their picture: in this case, they'll expect to be paid. Again, the best way is to ask first. If the photo is worth fifty cents or a dollar to you and you don't mind encouraging the money-for-photo attitude, go ahead. One good way to get photos in Otavalo is to make a purchase first at a particular stall. The local's attitude toward a photo may change very quickly if you're a paying customer! Powerful zoom lenses can also let you take some excellent photos of people without making them uncomfortable. If you're taking a general photo, such as a market street, it is not necessary to ask anyone first.

Also, it may be illegal to take photos in certain areas. Be careful when taking photos near any sort of official or military installation. If there is a soldier or policeman nearby, it is best to ask first if photography is permitted.

of stamina and agility—many of the hikes require wet landings where you wade onto the beach and climb around rocks on your walks. However, a number of tour operators and cruise boats cater their itinerary to your specific needs, so be sure to ask before booking your cruise.

Travelers over 65 are eligible to discounts throughout the country on buses, planes and tourist attractions like museums and national parks, so be sure to ask.

TRAVELERS WITH CHILDREN

Children under 12 will often get discounts on buses, planes and hotels when traveling throughout Ecuador, so do ask before paying full price. On Quito city buses and trolleys, children up to age 16 pay only $0.12. Ecuadorian children are generally treated with extra special attention, and travelers with children will be greeted with friendly care and interest.
Updated: Sep 05, 2012.

ECUADOR PACKING LIST

The difficult thing about packing for Ecuador is that you have to be prepared for every type of climate if you are going to travel extensively throughout the country. The easy part is that everything you need can easily be purchased in Quito, Guayaquil and other tourist cities.

Climbing and camping gear is a little more expensive, but sunglasses, hats, hand-knit items like hats, gloves, sweaters and other basic supplies are plentiful and cheap. We have divided the packing list into regional lists and included extra sections for backpackers and adventure travel.

Some basic things to consider: the voltage in Ecuador is the same as in the United States, 110 volts 60 cycles. However, many older buildings require a converter for plugs with three prongs. A small medical kit and extra personal supplies, like tampons are a good idea, since they can be hard to find outside of Quito and Guayaquil.

The seasons on the coast and in the Amazon Basin are divided between wet and dry. December to July is sunny and dry on the coast, while the rest of the year is foggy and cooler. November to March in the Amazon is the driest part of the year and some lodges are unreachable by boat during this time. The

weather in the Andes is unpredictable, so be prepared for hot, cool, wet and dry on any given day.

Sunglasses and sunscreen are a must throughout the country, as is bug repellent. Malaria is only found on the coast (but not in Galápagos) and in the Amazon Rainforest Basin.

Take extra safety precautions. Petty theft is commonplace, especially in Quito and Guayaquil, but it can be easily avoided. Leave copies of important documents like your passport, credit cards and the numbers from your travelers checks, if you are using them, in a separate part of your luggage.

It's also a good idea to store important information, including the international phone number for your credit cards online somewhere easy to access, like in an e-mail account.

Traveler's insurance is an excellent idea, especially if you are bringing expensive camera equipment or electronics that you want to

Photo by: Chris Klassen

Guápulo & Cumbayá

feel comfortable using frequently. Keep all important documents, credit cards and most of your cash inside your clothing and a separate wallet or coin purse within easy reach for small purchases and meals. Updated: Jun 27, 2012.

Adventure Sports Packing List

RIVER RAFTING

Swimsuit; tennis shoes or Teva-like sandals with secure ankle straps; t-shirt (quick drying material is best); easy-dry shorts or running tights; safety strap if wearing glasses; waterproof camera; plastic bags for anything you want to stay dry; dry clothes for after the trip; and lots of adrenaline.

MOUNTAIN CLIMBING

Below are supplies you will need on a two day non-technical climb up mountains such as Cotopaxi and Chimborazo. For the more technical climbs, more specialized equipment is needed. For nearly all tours, the items listed under "Equipment" are provided by the tour company. All equipment may be rented in Quito as well. Helmets are the exception to both of these statements, they are rarely provided and are also very difficult to rent.

Equipment

Mountaineering boots; crampons; ice axe; carabineers; climbing ropes; harness; and gaiters.

Personal

Food; water; headlamp; three sets of batteries; Glacier Glasses; lip balm; sunscreen; knife; two water bottles; two thick insulating layer tops; one thin, one thick; insulating layer bottoms; Gore-Tex type hooded coat; Gore-Tex type bottom; glove liners; Gore-Tex Gloves; two pairs of socks; warm hat; camera-keep it in your inside pocket, it'll freeze; extra change of clothes; and shoes for around camp. Updated: Jun 27, 2012.

ANDES PACKING LIST

Because of the rapid change in seasons, bring lots of layers of fast-drying clothes. Fleece and other synthetic fabrics are perfect. Water proof shoe are also a good choice.

Hiking boots and comfortable sandals are also essential. Hiking in the páramo, or high grassland, requires rubber boots, which cost only around $5 in any part of Ecuador.

GALAPAGOS PACKING LIST

Clothes

There is no dress code on most boats or in island towns, so pack **casual, yet comfortable clothing**. Bring **lightweight, breathable** items for day hikes and a **sweater** or **jacket** for cool evenings on the boat. Terrain on some islands is rough and rocky, so bring **comfortable sneakers** or **hiking boots** with good traction. **Tevas, Chacos** or any other types of sandal with a security strap are great for beach sites and less rugged trails. On the boat, you will keep your shoes in a communal bin and either walk barefoot or in **flip-flops**.

Luggage

If you are on a cruise tour, it is a good idea to **pack as lightly and compactly as possible**, since there is only a finite amount of space in your cabin and on board. **Backpacks** are the most portable through all of the required land-water transfers, but **suitcases** and **duffel bags** are fine. Your boat will send representatives from the crew to meet you at the airport, collect your bags, deliver them to the boat, and ultimately place them in your cabin. So if you have bulky or awkward pieces of luggage, the burden of transporting them will fall upon the helpful and gracious members of the crew. Because you will have day excursions on the islands, it is essential that you bring a **day pack** or **fanny pack** so that you can have **water, sun protection, photographic equipment, rain gear** and any other items you may need with you at all times.

Swimming/Snorkeling Gear

If you like the water, you will have a number of opportunities to swim, snorkel, or scuba dive in the Galápagos, oftentimes more than once a day. As such, you should bring **more than one swimsuit**, a **towel** (some boats may provide beach towels but others will not), and **beach attire** (a sarong or beach wrap is perfect for women). Because you can get cold and sunburned very easily in Galapagos waters, it is also a good idea to bring a lightweight neoprene **wetsuit** or **dive skin**, if you have one, or some other quick-dry outfit (that you don't mind wearing in the ocean), like long underwear or **sport clothes. You** can rent wetsuits in Quito, Guayaquil, Puerto Ayora or sometimes directly on your boat for a reasonable daily price. Many boats have their own snorkeling equipment, which is complementary or available for rent, but the quality and maintenance may be sub-par

INTRO & INFO

Galapagos 'Essentials' Packing List

- **sunhat**
- **sunglasses**
- **sandals** (for the boat)
- **sneakers** (for dry landings and rocky shores)
- **teva-style sandals** (for wet landings)
- **swimsuit**
- **umbrella** (for sun protection during island hikes or the occasional downpour)
- high factor, waterproof **sunscreen**
- **flashlight** or **head lamp**
- **water bottle**
- **plastic Ziploc bags** to keep things from getting wet
- **snorkel and mask** if you aren't renting
- **beach towel** and **bath towel**
- **wind resistant jacket**
- **light sweater** or **sweatshirt** (nights can get rather cool and you don't want to miss stargazing on deck)
- twice as much **film** or **memory cards** as you think you will need;
- **extra batteries**
- **underwater camera**
- **motion sickness pills**
- Water can be very cold so you may want to bring a **dive skin** or **wetsuit**

and the sizes available may be limited. If you are on a boat with scuba diving capability, you will probably have more luck, but you should still bring your own if you have it.

Scuba Diving Equipment

If you plan on scuba-diving and have your own **equipment**, bring it. You will need at least a **6mm wetsuit**, **boots**, **gloves** and possibly a **hood**, in addition to a **regulator**, **BCD**, **computer**, **weight belt**, **fins** and **mask**. All of the dive shops will include equipment in the price of their packages, but the quality and size availability varies from place to place. Some dive shops replace their equipment every year, keep a variety of sizes and styles and maintain their gear in stellar condition. Others have older, worn-out equipment-a sticky regulator, a leaky BCD, ill-fitting apparel, etc.-that is still usable but less desirable for many recreational divers, so don't come in expecting lavish equipment.

The conditions in the Galápagos can be challenging for many divers, so if you are at all nervous about your abilities, ease some of your worries by bringing your own gear.

Photography

The Galápagos are an excellent place—even for novices—to take magazine-quality photographs and to make exciting home-videos. Because much of the wildlife in the Galápagos is stationary and close to the trails, you can get very good results with **digital**, **manual** and even **point-and-shoot** cameras. Although you probably don't need

anything larger than a hand-held lens, you can get some very good close-up results if you bring a zoom lens. You should also bring an **underwater casing** for your camera (if you have one) or an **underwater camera**. Although capturing the underwater landscape and bigger creatures is best with a **video-camera** or a camera with a strobe, the smaller **digital cameras** with flash are great for macro shots of fish, eels, or coral.

Extras

Keep in mind that facilities for recharging batteries on boats are limited (some have 110-V outlets), so it is a good idea to invest in some **long-life batteries** or bring along a lot of spares. It is also a good rule to bring twice as much **film** or **memory** than you think you will need.

If you know you will be making a stop in Puerto Ayora during your cruise, you can plan to download photos from your memory card onto a CD at any of the internet cafes in town.

Updated: Jun 27, 2012.

AMAZON RAINFOREST PACKING LIST

Rubber boots are a must and are almost always provided at the lodge or through your tour company, up to size 10 (US), or can be purchased in advance.

Also bring: insect repellent (with DEET); malaria pills; antihistamine tablets and an epi-pen for people with serious allergies to stings; binoculars (invaluable in the rainforest - it's worth spending a bit of extra money to get a good pair -8 x 40 are excellent for poor light conditions under the forest canopy); plastic bags for keeping your clothes dry; swimming suit; lightweight, quick-drying clothes; at least one long-sleeved shirt; one pair of loose-fitting pants (no jeans); a light sweater (it gets surprisingly chilly in the rainforest, especially on boat trips); poncho that fits over you and your pack (the cheap plastic knee-length type coats are better than Gore-tex, which will soak right through in a real rainforest deluge); bandanna; at least one pair of socks per day - or more; Teva-like sandals or sneakers for around camp; and Ziploc bags for food, books, maps and anything else you hope to keep dry.

All clothes (undergarments included) should be loose fitting to help keep you cool and to reduce your chances of being bitten by chiggers. Updated: Mar 24, 2013.

BACKPACKERS' PACKING LIST

While this is not to be considered an authoritative packing list, here are a few items that we have found handy when backpacking around Ecuador:

Flashlight; clothesline; mosquito net; Swiss Army Knife or Leatherman (but don't forget to put it in your checked luggage!); watch with alarm clock; toilet paper; plastic bags for separating dirty and clean clothes and shoes; needle and thread; biodegradable soap; notebooks and pens/pencils; hat; and poncho. Antibacterial hand gel is less wasteful than wet wipes. Tents and sleeping bags can be easily rented and you will find that camping is often the same price as a budget hostel.

Information Resources

Here are a few websites to check out before your trip to Ecuador:

GOVERNMENT PAGES
Ecuadorian Presidency:
www.presidencia.gob.ec

Ministry for External Relations:
www.mmrree.gob.ec

National Assembly of Ecuador:
www.asambleanacional.gob.ec

US Embassy in Ecuador:
www.ecuador.usembassy.gov

TOURISM PAGES
Official Ecuador and Galapagos Travel Guide:
www.ecuador.travel.com

South American Explorers Club:
www.saexplorers.org

GENERAL
Couchsurfing:
www.couchsurfing.com.
Homestays and free accomodation.
Expatriate Information Ecuador:
www.internations.org.
A worldwide expatriate community.

Information on Living in Ecuador:
www.livinginecuador.com
By a host family offering a glimpse into life in Ecuador.

The Latin American Network Information Center:
www.lanic.utexas.edu/la/ecuador .
The website provides links to all things Ecuador, including to organizations, practical information and cultural studies.

NGO PAGES
Alternet:
www.alternet.org.
World-wide humanitarian news.

Amnesty International:
www.amnesty.org/es/region/ecuador.

Ecopapel:
www.ecopapel.org.
Makes stationery out of recycled paper as a community development project.

Fundación Jatun Sacha (Jatun Sasha Foundation):
www.jatunsacha.org.
An NGO running 10 sustainable conservation projects around the country, with about 800 volunteers.

Human Rights Watch:
www.hrw.org.
Human rights work throughout the world)

Ecuador Bibliography

If you cannot find these works at your local vendor or for purchase on-line, ask your public library if you can obtain them through interlibrary loan (there may be a small fee for this service). Libri Mundi bookstores in Quito also carry many of these titles.

This is just a sample of works about Ecuador. Please write us with more of your suggestions.

Guides and Travelogues

Crowder, Nicholas. *Cultureshock Ecuador: A Survival Guide to Customs & Etiquette.* Tarrytown, NY : Marshall Cavendish Editions, 2009. – A crash course in how to behave in Ecuadorian society.

Nelson,Tyrel. *Stories from Ecuador.* [Minnesota?] : T. Nelson, 2009. – Nelson came to Ecuador to teach English and ended up traveling off the beaten track.

Pombo, Connie. *Living and Retiring in Cuenca: 101 Questions Answered.* Amazon Digital Services, 2011. – A how-to guide about setting down roots in Cuenca.

Rachowiecki, Rob and Mark Thurber. *Ecuador: Climbing and Hiking Guide.* Quito: VIVA Travel Guides, 2009. -- The updated classic guide for mountain climbers and hikers.

Thomsen, Moritz. *Living Poor: A Peace Corps Chronicle.* Seattle: University of Washington Press, 1990. – A Peace Corp volunteer's experiences in one of the poorest parts of Ecuador. Later, Thomsen settled in Esmeraldas and wrote *The Farm on the River of Emeralds* (Boston : Houghton Mifflin, 1978).

Literature

Benner, Susan E., Kathy S. Leonard and Marjorie Agosín, ed. *Fire from the Andes: Short Fiction by Women from Bolivia, Ecuador and Peru.* Albuquerque: University of New Mexico Press, 1998.

Carrera Andrade, Jorge. Century of the Death of the Rose: Selected Poems. Montgomery, Ala. : NewSouth Books, 2002.

Icaza, Jorge, and Bernard M. Dulsey. *The Villagers.* Carbondale: South Illinois University, 1964.

Levitin, Alexis and Fernando Iturburu, ed. and trans. *Tapestry of the Sun: an Anthology of Ecuadorian Poetry.* San Francisco, Ca.: Coimbra, 2009.

Mera, Juan León. *Cumanda: The Novel of the Ecuadorian Jungle.* Bloomington, Ind. : AuthorHouse, 2007.

Wishnia, K.J.A. *Twentieth-century Ecuadorian narrative : new readings in the context of the Americas.* Lewisburg, Pa. : Bucknell University Press, 1999.

Nature Guides

Herrmann, Steven. *Birding Northwest Ecuador (Birding Areas of Ecuador).* Amazon Digital Services, 2012.

Jiggins, Chris, Pablo Andrade and Eduardo Cueva. *Equador Nature Guide: Southwest Forests.* Canada: Lone Pine Publishing, 2001.

Quintana, Catalina Medina., and Adela Tobar. *Wild Plants in the Dry Valleys around Quito, Ecuador: An Illustrated Guide.* Quito: Herbario QCA, PUCE, 2010.

Pearson, David, Les Beletsky, and Priscilla Barrett. *Travellers' Wildlife Guides Ecuador and the Galapagos Islands.* Northampton, MA: Interlink, 2010.

Policha, Tobías. *Plantas de Mindo: Una Guía de Bosque Nublado del Chocó Andino / Plants of Mindo: A Guide to the Cloud Forest of the Andean Choco.* Eugene, Or.: American Herbal Dispensary Press, 2012.

Ridgely, Robert S., Paul J. Greenfield and Frank Gill. *The Birds of Ecuador: Field Guide.* Ithaca: Cornell University Press, 2001.

Non-fiction

Becker, Marc. *Pachakutik: Indigenous Movements and Electoral Politics in Ecuador.* Lanham, Md. : Rowman & Littlefield, 2011. – The modern history of Ecuador's indigenous movements and politics.

Cruz Cevallos, Ivan. *The World of Spirits in Precolumbian Ecuador.* Milan: 5 Continents Editions, 2013. – An examination of spiritual beliefs in pre-conquest Ecuador.

Hemming, John. *The Conquest of the Incas.* London: Macmillan, 1971. – An historical explanation of the 16th century Spanish conquest led by Francisco Pizarro.

Hurtado, Osvaldo, and Barbara Sipe. *Portrait of a Nation: Culture and Progress in Ecuador.* Lanham: Madison, 2010. – A nonfiction tale about the nature of development in Ecuador.

Kane, Joe. *Savages.* New York: Knopf, 1995. – A critically-acclaimed "must read" for anyone interested in visiting the Amazon. An anthropological field-guide into the conflicts between isolated Amazonian tribes and the Oil Industry.

Klein, Daniel and Ivan Cruz Cevallos, ed. *Ecuador: The Secret Art of Precolumbian Ecuador.* Milan: 5 Continents, 2007. – A beautifully illustrated guide on Ecuador's pre-Columbian art.

Lourie, Peter. *Sweat of the Sun, Tears of the Moon: A Chronicle of an Incan Treasure.* New York: Atheneum, 1991. – Lourie travels into the Andes in search of a long-lost Inca treasure.

Robarchek, Clayton Allen, and Carole Robarchek. *Waorani: The Contexts of Violence and War.* Fort Worth: Harcourt Brace College, 1998. – A study of human violence, relating case studies of villages across the globe; one based in Ecuador. The Waorani tribe is again explored.

Striffler, Steve. *In the Shadows of State and Capital: The United Fruit Company, Popular Struggle, and Agrarian Restructuring in Ecuador, 1900-1995.* Durham: Duke University Press Book, 2001. – Ecuador's saga as a banana republic.

Tidwell, Mike. *Amazon Stranger.* New York: Lyons & Burford, 1996. – A natural history about the Cofan people and oil exploration.

Torre, Carlos De La, and Steve Striffler. *The Ecuador Reader: History, Culture, Politics.* Durham: Duke UP, 2009. – An anthology of writings by and interviews with Ecuadorians.

Did a unique trek? Tell other travelers at vivatravelguides.com

Quito

 2,850 m  2,239,191 02

Travelers worldwide are drawn to Quito for its spectacular mountain setting, its colonial historical center, near-by adventure travel opportunities, international cuisine, and the gentle, generous quiteño culture. The city is known for being home to some of the best Spanish schools in South America; there is a great backpacker community; and, the area offers plenty of activities to help you escape the typical tourist crowds. Don't miss out on or be shy about socializing with the locals either, quiteños tend to be relaxed, friendly and eager to make friends.

This rapidly growing capital city has a past that stretches back to before the Incas made Quito the second capital of their empire. It appears that only the mountains that cradle the city remain unchanged. The historic Old Town features colonial architecture which the Spanish constructed over the charred remains of the Inca city. Just north of Old Town, towering concrete and glass structures show off the modern structures of the business and tourist center of the city.

Planning a trip from Quito to other parts of Ecuador, or to neighboring South American countries, is also fairly easy. Most Quito hotels, travel agencies and tour operators can be found in the neighborhood of La Mariscal and are within a five block radius of each other. Transportation by land and air is also plentiful and generally inexpensive, depending on the time of year.

History of Quito
PRE-INCA CIVILIZATION

Despite its high altitude and scarcity of easily cultivable land, the area around Quito has been the scene of human settlement for nearly 10,000 years, dating back to the Quitu (who gave the city its name), Cara, Shyri and Puruhá indigenous groups. With it's central location, Quito flourished as a permanent commercial trading center for the people residing in the Amazon basin, the sierra and on the coast. The merchants traded products like salt, cotton and shells from the coast for cinnamon, medicinal herbs and precious metals from the Amazon region. Traders from the sierra sold potatoes, corn and other agricultural products native to the area.

INCA RULE

Those early inhabitants of Quito fiercely resisted the Inca invasion of the late 15th century; however, after more than a decade of fighting, Quito fell to Inca rule under Túpac Yupanqui and became an important part of his empire. Túpac Yupanqui's son, Huayna Capac, was born near Quito, making him the first Inca ruler to be born outside the confines of Cusco. A generation later, Atahualpa, one of Huayna Capac's sons, used Quito as his capital during his war against his brother. No architectural evidence of the pre-Columbian city remains, however, because it was destroyed by the Inca general Rumiñahui to keep it out of the hands of the Spanish conquistadors.

SPANISH RULE

Colonial officials rebuilt Quito in the style of a Spanish city, featuring a grid of narrow streets dotted with public squares, still largely intact today as the city's Centro Histórico. While it remained a compact city, colonial Quito was the capital of an administrative district larger than present-day Ecuador. The city also made an enormous contribution to the arts of the Spanish empire. Originally used as a means of inculcating the indigenous inhabitants of the region into Christianity, religious painting and sculpture flourished in the city. The so-called "Quito School" of the 17th and 18th centuries was marked by the use of dramatic, often quite gruesome, images to depict Biblical stories. Many of these works can still be viewed in Quito's art museums and colonial churches. Over time, Quito's native-born population chafed under the rule of the Spanish crown. This frustration resulted in the quiteños' declaration for independence in 1809. Quito's - and Ecuador's - independence from Spain was sealed on the slopes of Volcán Pichincha, high above the city, when José Antonio de Sucre's army defeated the Spanish garrison on May 24, 1822. Today, the site of the battle is commemorated by the military museum La Cima de la Libertad.

1869 - PRESENT

In 1869, President Gabriel García Moreno altered the constitution to make Catholicism the official state religion of Ecuador and required all voters and political candidates to be Catholic. The liberal opposition despised him for this, especially the self-exiled writer Juan Montalvo. Shortly after he began his third term, Moreno was attacked on the steps

Quito Highlights

Centro Histórico's Churches (*p. 43-45*): Visit Quito's colonial past in the Old Town, home to several stunning, well-preserved churches, including the dazzling, over-the-top golden interior of La Compañía. Not merely for the faithful, these timeless churches are a constant reminder of the cruel splendor of the height of the Spanish Empire.

Museo Guayasamín and the Capilla del Hombre (*p. 74*): Now combined into one complex, modern artist Oswaldo Guayasamín's personal art collection can be seen alongside his own impressive masterpieces. The highlight is the Capilla del Hombre, or "Chapel of Man," a powerful statement against human violence, which houses Guayasamín's most provocative works.

Guápulo (*p. 70-71*) : Come wander along Guápulo's charming cobblestone streets lined with swaying palm trees for a taste of what old Spain must have been like. Afterward, rest your aching feet and brush elbows with local artists and expats sipping espresso in the bohemian cafés.

TeleferiQo (*p. 72*): One of Quito's newest attractions, the gondola-like TelefériQo takes you up the side of Volcán Pichincha to a panoramic view of Quito and its surroundings. Go early in the morning, before the clouds roll in. From the lookout, you can hike to the summit of Rucu Pichincha.

Mitad del Mundo (*p. 82-83*): The 30-meter-tall (98 ft) Mitad del Mundo monument was actually erected 240 meters (787 ft) north of the real equatorial line, yet tourists come by the busloads to visit it. After taking photos straddling the fake equatorial line, visit the interesting Museo del Sitio Intiñan, located on the actual line of the equator, where you can see shrunken heads, balance an egg on a nail, and see the Coriolis effect on both sides of the equator.

Updated: Feb 15, 2013.

of the Palacio de Gobierno and hacked to death by a machete-wielding assassin in 1875. When Montalvo heard of Moreno's death, he proclaimed, "My pen has killed him!"

The conservatives continued their reign in the country, especially under the dictator General Ignacio de Veintimilla. Conservative rule ended in 1897 with the election of Eloy Alfaro. He was a revolutionary and fought against García Moreno's government during his youth. During his two terms as president, from 1897 to 1901 and 1906 to 1911, Alfaro separated church and state, severed ties with the Vatican, instituted divorce, and kicked out foreign clergy. He also helped complete the Quito-Guayaquil railway. In between terms, Alfaro's adversary General Leónidas Plaza became president. Plaza caused civil unrest amongst conservative Catholics and liberals and Alfaro's second term saw nearly half of the budget go towards the military for security reasons along with the overwhelming fear of an uprising.

Civil war broke out when Alfaro's successor, Emilio Estrada, died shortly after his inauguration in 1911. Plaza's forces proceeded to defeat and kill Alfaro and his supporters, dragging them through the streets of Quito and finally burning their corpses at the Parque El Ejido.

Loved it? Loathed it? Write a review and help other travelers

QUITO

Leonidas Plaza's son, Galo Plaza Lasso, became president in 1948. He had strong ties to both Liberal and Conservative parties, and strongly advocated democracy and freedom of speech, which caused him to become the first Ecuadorian president to serve a full term since 1924. The banana boom in the 1940s helped fund Quito's undertaking of new schools, an airport, hospitals and universities. It was also during this time, following the Second World War, that Quito expanded dramatically. The wealthy abandoned the Centro Histórico for new neighborhoods farther north. Meanwhile, the difficulty of earning a living through agriculture and the availability of jobs in the city lured many people from the countryside to settle in the Quito's poorer neighborhoods, a migration which continues to this day. It was later, in the 1970s, that saw the oil boom transform Quito into the second most important financial center in the country.

By 1991, the population of the city hit one million; and as the population began approaching two million in the new millennium, Quito implemented the Metrobus (Ecovia) which currently facilitates the commute across the city from north to south. In 2005 the renovation of La Mariscal - which was formerly considered a zona roja (red-light district) - saw the creation of new bars, cafes, hostels and restaurants.

2013 welcomed the new, larger airport for the city located on its outskirts to the east – an idea which took nearly 50 years to come to fruition.

Famous People From Quito
EUGENIO ESPEJO

Eugenio Espejo is considered one of the most influential figures in colonial Ecuador. Born to a Quechua father in 1747, Espejo became both a lawyer and a doctor. In 1785, the town council asked Espejo to write a medical report on small pox. In his greatest work, Espejo denounced the way the colonial government handled sanitation. His work was sent back to Madrid and published in a medical journal, which made him many enemies because of his criticism of the physicians in the colonial government. This forced Espejo to flee Quito until 1790. He returned to serve as both the director of Quito's first public library and as the director of the Patriotic Society. The society was set up by the church for influential thinkers to discuss the social, economic, political and educational problems in Quito. The society also published Quito's first newspaper with Espejo serving as the editor. King Charles IV of Spain dissolved the society in 1793 and the newspaper quickly folded forcing Espejo to take a job as a librarian. His liberal views landed him jail and he died of dysentery in 1795. Today he is considered Ecuador's first journalist and a medical pioneer.

JUAN JOSÉ FLORES

Juan José Flores became the Supreme Chief of Ecuador in 1830 after its separation from Gran Colombia. Born in Puerto Cabello, Venezuela in 1800, Flores became a renowned military leader before becoming the first president of Ecuador. He first ruled from 1830 to 1834 and served two more terms from 1839 to 1845. Flores' popularity declined after intervening in the politics of Nueva Granada. While his popularity steadily declined with his increased use of military, Flores replaced the 1835 constitution with a new one that Ecuadorians nicknamed the "letter of slavery." He was finally overthrown by future president Vicente Ramón Roca in 1845 and died in 1864 while under house arrest of President Gabriel García Moreno. He is still referred to as "the founder of the Republic."

GABRIEL GARCÍA MORENO

Gabriel García Moreno served three terms as the president of Ecuador from 1861 to 1875 and is known for strengthening the power of the Catholic Church in the country. Moreno was born in 1821 in Guayaquil. He studied theology and law at the University of Quito and seriously considered becoming a priest. He became a lawyer and a journalist, and opposed the liberal government of the 1840s.He entered the political realm as a senator in 1856 and then ruled as president for four years starting in 1861. He returned to office in 1869. He changed the constitution and made Catholicism the official state religion and required all voters and candidates for office to be Catholic. This caused hatred amongst his liberal critics. Shortly after re-election in 1875, Moreno was attacked on the steps of the Palacio de Gobierno. He was hacked to death by a machete and his final words were, "God does not die!" He is still highly regarded in Ecuador for stabilizing the country and uniting the country through religion.

MARIA AUGUSTA URRUTIA

Maria Augusta Urrutia is considered one of Ecuador's most influential humanitarians. Born into an aristocratic family from Quito in 1901, Urrutia spent much of her youth in Europe. After her husband's death in 1931, Urrutia dedicated her life to charitable activities. She was known for helping the street kids of Quito and her influence is still felt today through volunteer programs throughout Quito. Because of her work with the poor of Quito, President Osvaldo Hurtado recognized Urrutia as one of the top 100 Ecuadorians in 1982. She died in 1987.
Updated: Apr 29, 2013.

When To Go to Quito

Quito has two seasons: spring with rain (September–April), and spring with sun (May–August). The city's location, about 40 kilometers (about 25 mi) south of the equator and at an altitude of 2,800 meters (9,180 ft) above sea level, makes for some startling temperature changes in a 24-hour period.

The city gets downright cool when the sun is down (from 6:30 p.m.- 6 a.m. every day of the year) and when it rains. When the sun is out, however, you will find yourself in need of shorts and shade. Consequently, wearing layers is fundamental to being comfortable in Quito. Pants, a light T-shirt or tank top layered with a long-sleeve shirt and jacket or sweater should be fine throughout most of the year.

Travelers coming from colder climates will be amused at the winter garb of most quiteños from September-April, which often includes jackets, scarves, gloves and hats. Winter is a strong word, but during these months, afternoon storms are common and tend to drop the temperature to around 10°C (50°F). During sunny days, the temperatures can rise up to 30°C (85 °F).

In addition to climate, things in Quito tend to heat up socially and culturally during *fiestas* (festivals) and cool down during *feriados* (holidays). The latter is ideal for visitors who wish to see Quito in a softer, quieter light - for it's during this time that the capital empties out as quiteños head to the coast to either party or rest. Carnaval (second week of February) and Semana Santa (Holy Week, end of March) specifically provide said windows of time.

Fiestas on the other hand are much more abundant and have the city bustling with parties, concerts and fireworks. Fiestas de Quito is perhaps the most iconic time of the year as quiteños celebrate - from the end of November to the 6th of December - the foundation of their capital. From bullfights to opera and theater shows commemorating Quito's history and culture, quiteños party hard during this time, riding Chiva's (open party buses) or attending block parties and concerts hosted by the city.

Christmas and New Years might pale in comparison to the above, but these days still hold their own energy as the city goes into a shopping tizzy right before Christmas day, calming down for a week right after, and then jumping into the New Year with copious amounts of food, liquor, fireworks, and the traditional burning of the Año Viejo (a human mannequin with your choice of a politician or celebrity's mask, done to symbolize the letting go of the previous year).
Updated: Feb 28, 2013.

Getting To and Away from Quito

Quito is one of two main transportation hubs within the country, the other being Guayaquil. From the capital, you can pretty much get to anywhere inside of Ecuador, either by bus or plane.

In addition to being the center of the domestic transport network, Quito is also well connected to international locations by both air and long-distance buses.

BY AIR

All international and domestic flights arrive and depart from Quito's Mariscal Sucre International Airport (Code: UIO) which is 18 kilometers (11 mi.) east of the city, near the small town of Tababela.

TRANSPORTATION BETWEEN THE AIRPORT AND QUITO:

The company Aeroservicios S.A. (www.aeroservicios.com.ec) runs WiFi equipped buses 24/7, leaving every 15 minutes at rush hour (7-10a.m., 4-7p.m.), or every 30 minutes during normal hours. Buses depart from the old airport to the new one at a rate of $8 per passenger, taking about one hour to an hour-and-a-half in getting there. Tickets can be bought online or before boarding.

Loved it? Loathed it? Write a review and help other travelers

QUITO

QUITO

Alternatively, public transit will provide buses departing from the Rio Coca terminal to the new airport every 15 minutes for $2. The catch is that you'll have to patiently wait through 5 brief stops before finally getting there. Estimated transport time between the two points will be at least an hour-and-a-half to two-hours until traffic conditions improve - specifically once the bypasses are constructed (the main Collas-Tababela highway that is being built from the city to the airport is not expected to be completed until April of 2014).

The third option is to take a Taxi, which will cost an estimated $25 to get to the airport from most places in Quito (and vice-versa).

From Quito it is possible to fly directly (non-stop) to the following destinations:

INTERNATIONAL FLIGHTS
In Latin America:
- Bogota or Medellín (Colombia)
- Caracas (Venezuela)
- Lima (Peru)
- Santiago (Chile)
- Saõ Paulo or Manaus (Brazil)
- San Jose (Costa Rica)
- Panama City (Panama)

In the United States:
- Miami
- Houston
- Atlanta

In Europe:
- Madrid (Spain)
- Amsterdam (Holland)

DOMESTIC FLIGHTS
Served by three airlines: TAME (www.tame.com.ec), LAN (www.lan.com), and Aerogal (www.aerogal.com.ec). AeroGal and LAN are somewhat more expensive than their competitors, but generally receive high marks from travelers. The following are popular cities that have direct flights to and from Quito:

- Bahía
- Coca
- Cuenca
- Esmeraldas
- Guayaquil
- Galapagos
- Lago Agrio
- Loja
- Macas
- Machala
- Manta
- Portoviejo
- Tulcán

These national flights cost about $60-100 each way, except to the Galapagos where a round trip ticket will cost around $400. There are no departure taxes for flights within Ecuador except for trips into and out of the Galapagos.

BY BUS
Instead of one, centrally-located bus station, Quito has two terminals located at the north and south ends of Quito. These newer stations are intended to make travel more efficient and cost-effective, as well as reduce the number of long-distance buses passing through the city.

In the far north is Carcelén (Av. Eloy Alfaro and Av. Galo Plaza Lasso), with buses that go typically go north from Quito. At the southern tip is the brand new Quitumbe station (Av. Cóndor Ñan and Av. Mariscal Sucre), this terminal is most useful for buses heading south from Quito.

Some bus companies have locations in the Mariscal part of town, making the purchase of tickets in advance significantly easier thanks to its proximity. In many instances it is possible to simply turn up at the appropriate bus terminal and buy a ticket to your chosen destination.

However, those wanting to travel over public holidays are best advised to book tickets in advance (up to several days in advance to secure a seat).

Buses From The Quitumbe Terminal
This modern, new bus terminal is located at the Southern end of Quito. From here you can get to the Amazon, coast or any of the surrounding Mountain regions such as Baños and Cuenca. You can get to this station via the Trolebus or Ecovia ($0.25, 1 hour) or taxi from La Mariscal ($10-15, 30 minutes), for more info see Getting Around Quito (p. 96). Av. Cóndor Ñan and Av. Mariscal Sucre.

Photo by: Pepe Valdez

Quitumbe Departures

Transportes Patria leaves from booths 1 and 2 to **Riobamba, Cuenca** and **Guayaquil** every hour until 7:30 p.m.

Ecuador Ejecutivo leaves to **Riobamba** from booths 3 and 4 every 30 minutes until 8:30 p.m.

Transportes Ecuador leaves to **Guayaquil** from booths 43 and 44 every hour from 7:30 a.m. to 1:00 a.m.

Cooperativa Chimborazo leaves to **Riobamba** from booth 5 every hour until 7 p.m.

Transvencedores leaves to **Tulcán** and **Riobamba** from booth 7; and to **Santo Domingo, Pedernales,** and **Jama** from booth 57 every 1 to 2 hours.

Cooperativa Alausí leaves for **Alausí** from booth 9, at 7:25 a.m., 9:25 a.m., 12:10 p.m and 5:25 p.m.

Transportes Andina leaves to **Otavalo** and **Ibarra** from booth 11, every 40 minutes from 4:20 a.m. to 7:50 p.m.

Transportes 20 de Diciembre leaves to **Riobamba** from booth 8 at 2:30 a.m., 2:30 p.m. And 8:45 p.m.

Union Provincial de Carchi leaves to **Otavalo, Ibarra, San Gabriel,** and **Tulcán,** from booth 12, every 30 minutes a day.

Transportes Latinoamerica Express leaves to **Puyo** at 5:45 p.m. and **Macas** at 12:30 p.m. and 8:45 p.m. from booth 15

Macas Limitada leaves to **Baños, Puyo** and **Macas** from booth 17 at 9 p.m.

Transportes Putumayo leaves to **Lago Agrio, Sacha,** and **Coca** from booth 18 and 19 on 8 buses (6 a.m., 8:30 a.m., 11 a.m., 12:40 a.m., 4 p.m., 5:45 p.m., 8 p.m., 8:45 p.m. and 9 p.m.)

Tranportes Putumayo leaves to **Shushufindi** from booth 18 and 19 at 7:15 a.m., 9:30 a.m., 8:30 p.m. and 10:30 p.m.

Transportes Putumayo leaves to Puerto **El Carmen, Dureno, Pacayacu, Tarapoa, Tipishca, San Sahuari** and **Cuyabeno** at 8:30 a.m., 7:00 p.m., and 9:30 p.m.

Transportes Putumayo leaves to **Coca** and Tigüino at 8 p.m. daily.

Transportes Asotrial leaves to **Latacunga** from booth 20 and 21 every 10 minutes between 5 a.m. to 9 p.m.

Transpores Unidos San Miguel, Primavera and Salcedo leaves to **Santo Domingo, Quevedo, Moraspungo,** and **El Corazón** from booth 22 every 20 minutes starting at 5:30 a.m.

Tranportes Illinizas/Reina de Sigchos leaves to **Toacaso** and **Sigchos** from booth 23 as follows: Mon. 8 a.m. and 2 p.m. / Tue., Wed. and Thu. 2 p. m. / Fri. 2 p.m., 5 p.m. and 5:45 p.m. / Sat. 8 a.m., 9 a.m. and 2 p.m / Sun. 4:30 p.m and 6:30 p.m.

Transportes Ambateños leaves to **Parque Nacional Cotopaxi, Latacunga, Salcedo,** and **Ambato** from booths 24 to 26 every 5 minutes starting at 5:30 a.m. until 10:30 p.m.

QUITO

QUITO

Unión de Cooperativas de Tungurahua leaves to **Lasso, Salcedo, Latacunga, Ambato, Tena, Baños,** and **Puyo** from booths 27 and 28 every 5 to 10 minutes daily.

Cooperativa Amazonas leaves to **Ambato, Baños, Tena, Puyo** and other destinations from booth 29 almost all day and night long very frequently.

Flota Pelileo leaves to **Tena** through **Baeza** from booth 30 at 3:00 a.m., 6:00 a.m.; 8:00 a.m., 11:00 a.m., 1:00 p.m., 10:00 p.m., and 12:00 a.m.

Flota Pelileo leaves to **Baños** and **Puyo** from booth 30 at 9:00 a.m., and 7:25 p.m.

Expreso Baños leaves to **Baños** from booth 31 once per hour from 6:00 a.m. to 5:00 p.m.

Expreso Baños leaves to **Papallacta, Baeza** and **Tena** from booth 31 at 7:00 a.m., 9:00 a.m., 9:30 a.m., 2:30 p.m., and 4:00 p.m.

Expreso Baños leaves to **Puyo** through **Baños** from booth 31 at 6:30 a.m., 7:30 a.m., 8:30 a.m., 1:30 p.m., 2:30 p.m. and 8:30 p.m.

San Francisco leaves to **Ambato, Baños** and **Puyo** from booth 32 once per hour from 4:00 a.m. to 10:30 p.m.

San Francisco leaves to **Sucúa** from booth 32 at 4:05 p.m. and 10 p.m.

San Francisco leaves to **Macas** from booth 32 at 6:45 a.m., 10:00 a.m., 2:15 p.m., 4:05 p.m., 6:15 p.m. and 10:00 p.m.

Tranportes Bañós leaves to **Lago Agrio, Coca, Loreto, Shushufindi, Sacha, Tarapoa, Tipishca, Puerto El Carmen, Tiguino, Limoncocha, Puyo, Macas, Tena, Baños** and **Ambato** from booths 33, 34, 13 and 14 every 30 to 60 minutes, from 4 a.m. to 11:30 p.m.

Pillaro leaves to **Latacunga, Salcedo,** and **Pillaro** from booth 35 at 10:00 a.m., 12:00 p.m., 2:00 p.m., and 4:00 p.m.

Flota Bolívar leaves to **Guaranda, San Miguel,** and **Chillanes** every hour from 5:30 a.m. to 4:30 p.m. from booth 36.

Flota Bolivar leaves to **Babahoyo** and **San Luis** from booth 36 at 11:30 a.m. and to **San Luis** at 6 a.m.

Express Atenas leaves to **Guaranda, Chillanes, San Juan, Tambo, San Pablo** and **Guayaquil** from booth 37 at various times.

San Pedrito leaves from booth 38 to **Latacunga, Salcedo, Ambato, Guaranda, Chimbo,** and **San Miguel**, but also to **San Pablo, Montalvo, Babhoyo, Guayaquil, Santo Domingo, Quevedo, Ventanas** and **Echeandía**, between 7:00 a.m. to 6 p.m. every half hour.

Transportes San Pedrito leaves to **San Pedrito** from booth 38 once a morning.

TransEsmeraldas leaves to **Esmeraldas, Atacames** and **Muisne** from booths 39 and 40 every 1.5 hours between 7:30 a.m. to 11:40 p.m.

Buses leave to **Machala** and **Huaquillas** from booths 39 and 40 at 9:15 p.m.

Buses leave to **Portoviejo** and **Manta** at 9:30 p.m.

Buses leave to **Lago Agrio** at 11 p.m.

Buses leave to **El Coca** at 9:30 p.m.

Buses leave to **Borbón** and **San Lorenzo** at 5:30 a.m. and 10:20 p.m.

Transportes Occidentales leaves to **Esmeraldas** from booths 41 and 42 every hour from 7 a.m. to 10:30 p.m.

Transportes Occidentales leaves to **Atacames** and **Muisne** at 11:45 a.m.

Buses leave to **Huaquillas** through **Guayaquil, Salinas** and **Machala** at 8:45 a.m., 1:15 p.m., 4 p.m., 6 p.m., 7:30 p.m., 9:30 p.m. and 10:15 p.m.

Panamerica Internacional leaves to **Guayaquil, Manta, Huaquillas, Tulcán, Machala, Cuenca, Loja, Milagro, Santa Rosa, Atacames, Esmeraldas** and **Ambato** from booths 45 and 46 at various times.

Flota Imbabura leaves to **Cuenca** from booths 47 and 48 at 6:30 a.m. and there are 7 buses that leave from 5:00 p.m. To 11:00 p.m.

There are 17 buses that leave between 7:00 a.m. to 12:30 a.m. to **Guayaquil** from Flota Imbabura.

Flota Imbabura leaves to **Manta** at noon, 9:00 p.m., 10:00 p.m., 10:30 p.m. and 11:30 p.m.

Transportes Zaracay leaves to **Esmeraldas** at 11:00 a.m.

AeroTaxi leaves to **Santo Domingo, Esmeraldas, Atacames, Quevedo, Babahoyo**, and **Guayaquil** every 3 hours between 3:30 a.m. to 11:00 p.m. from booth 49.

Transportes Zaracay leaves to **Guayaquil** from booth 50 and 51 at 3:35 a.m. and 4:25 a.m.

Transportes Zaracay leaves to **Santo Domingo** every 20 minutes until 9 p.m.

San Cristobal leaves to **Santo Domingo, Quevedo, Babahoyo** and **Guayaquil** every two hours between 10:30 a.m. to 12:15 a.m. from booth 53.

Macuchi leaves to **Santo Domingo, Quevedo, La Maná, El Corazón. El Empalme, Ventanas, Balzar, Echeandía, San Luis**, and **Chaso Juan** every 5 minutes between 6:00 a.m. to 9:00 p.m. from booth 54.

Cooperativa de Transportes Salcedo leaves to **Santo Domingo, Quevedo, Quinsaloma, Moraspungo, El Corazón** at 6:20 a.m., 7:45 a.m., and 12 p.m. 11:15 a.m. and 6:15 p.m. from booth 56.

Viajeros leaves to **Cuenca, Oña, Saraguro** and **Loja** at 3:30 p.m., 4:30 p.m., and 6:30 p.m. from booth 58.

Cooperativa de Transporte Loja leaves to **Loja** from booths 59 and 60 at 12:50 p.m., 3 p.m., 5 p.m., 6:15 p.m., 7 p.m., 7:15 p.m., 8 p.m., and 8:40 p.m., 8:55 p.m., 9:15 p.m. and 9:30 p.m. / The bus leaving at 3 p.m. goes through the Coast.

QUITO

Sucre Express leaves to **Ambato, Riobamba, Alausí, Chunchi, Cañar, Azogues**, and **Cuenca** every hours between 7:30 a.m. to 10:45 p.m. from booths 61 and 62.

Turismo Oriental leaves to **Alausí, Chunchi, Cañár**, and **Azogues** from booth 63 at 6:00 a.m., 8:10 a.m., 11:30 a.m., 8:00 p.m., 8:45 p.m., and 11:45 p.m.

Super Taxis Cuenca leaves to **Ambato, Riobamba, Alausí, Chunchi, Tambo, Cañar, Azagues** and **Cuenca** from booth 64 at 7:00 a.m., 2:00 p.m., and 8:15 p.m.

Jahuay leaves to **Cuenca** at 7:15 p.m. and 10:15 p.m. from booth 65.

Santa leaves to **Machala** and **Huaquillas** from booths 66 and 67 at 5:10 p.m. and 9:00 p.m.

Santa leaves to **Guayaquil** through **Bucay** and **El Triunfo** from booths 66 and 67 at 10:00 a.m. and 9:00 p.m.

Santa leaves to **Cuenca** at 10:45 a.m., 2:45 p.m., 6:15 p.m., 9:30 p.m. and 11:00 p.m.

Santa leaves to **Cariamanga** at 3:45 p.m. (through the Coast) and 5:30 p.m. (Through the Highlands).

Santa leaves to **Loja** at 1:40 p.m., 4:00 p.m., 6:00 p.m., 7:10 p.m. (through the Coast), 7:45 p.m. and 8:40 p.m.

Ciudad de Piñas leaves to **Machala, Santa Rosa, Balsas, Marcabeli, Zaracay, Piñas, Portovelo, Zaruma** and **Paccha** from booth 68 at 6:15 p.m. and 11:30 (through the Coast) and at 5: p.m. and 8:00 p.m. (through the Highlands).

TAC leaves to **Machala, Santa Rosa, Piñás, Portovelo, Zaruma, Arenillas**, and **Huaqilllas** from booth 69 at 7:00 a.m., 5:00 p.m., 7:30 p.m., and 8:45 p.m.

Reina del Camino leaves to **Junín, Manta, Tosagua, San Vicente, Chone, Puerto Lopez, Bahía de Caraquez**, and **Portoviejo** at various times from booths 70 to 72.

Carlos Aray leaves to **Jipijapa** and **Puerto Lopez** at 10:10 a.m., and 7:00 p.m. from booth 73.

Carlos Aray leaves to **El Carmen, Flavio Alfaro, Chone, Tosagua, Rocafuerte, Portoviejo**, and **Manta** at 9:00 a.m., 1 p.m., 3 p.m., 5:20 p.m. and 11:30 p.m. from booth 73.

Reales Tamarindo leaves to **El Empalme, Represa, San Sebastian, Buena Fé, San Placido, Manta, Santo Domingo, Quevedo** and **Portoviejo** from booth 75 at 5:00 a.m. and 11:00 p.m.

Coactur leaves to **Portoviejo** from booth 76 at 10:30 a.m. and 1:30 p.m.

Coactur leaves to **Manta** from booth 76 at 9:15 p.m. and 10:40 p.m.

Buses leave to **Guayaquil** and **Salinas** from booths 39 and 40 at 8:50 p.m. and 10:10 p.m.

Buses From The Carcelén Terminal

The northern bus terminal in Carcelén is smaller and more grimy than the southern terminal. Buses here head north from Quito, the main reason to come here is to get to Otavalo or Mitad del Mundo. To get to this bus terminal via public transit you'll need to take the Metrobus and transfer at Estación Ofelia, which will take approximately one hour. From here you will have to take the "feeder buses" to get there. To get to the terminal via taxi will cost approximately $8 from La Mariscal, more during busier periods. The journey will take just 20 minutes or so with no traffic, longer during rush hour periods.

At this bus terminal you will find baggage storage, food stalls and telephone and Internet. There are 16 booths from which to buy a ticket. All have their destinations listed on the wall above each individual booth. Sometimes you can pick up a bus outside the terminal that is already leaving and just get on there, paying the driver instead of the company representative at the booth. Av. Eloy Alfaro and Av. Galo Plaza Lasso.

Bus companies and destinations from Carcelén:

Unión de Nor-Occidente
Leaves to **Los Bancos, Puerto Quito, Santo Domingo, Mindo, Perovicente** from booth 3 every 30 minutes from 5:00 a.m. to 10:00 p.m.

San Cristobal
Leaves to **Tulcán** from booth 6 every hour from 2:00 a.m. to 12:00 a.m.

Expreso Tulcán
Leaves to **Tulcán** from booth 7 every hour from 1:00 a.m. to 12:00 a.m.

San Gabriel
Leaves to **San Gabriel** from booth 10 every 30 minutes from 5:30 a.m. to 8:00 p.m.

Espejo
Leaves to **Masquerida, Mira, San Isidro, El Angél, Otavalo, Ibarra and Tabacundo** from booth 11 every hour from 4:30 a.m. to 7 p.m.

Flota Imbabura
Leaves to **Atuntaqui, Otavalo, Ibarra,** and **Tulcán** frequently from booth 12.

Taca Andina
Leaves to **Ibarra** and **Santo Domingo** every 20 minutes from 5 a.m. to 10 p.m. from booth 13.

Buses From The Mariscal

Buses that leave from the Mariscal are usually the most convenient for travelers or expats who want to get out of Quito for a while. This part of town is fairly central and easy to access, unlike the major bus terminals.

There are eight bus providers in the Mariscal, and they capitalize on their good location by charging a little more for their tickets than if you'd travelled from Quitumbe or one of the northern bus terminals. In a lot of cases, it is possible to get air conditioned buses that are non-stop from the Mariscal to your chosen destination.

The following is a list of long-distance bus companies, their destinations and contact information. The price for these companies varies between $8-15, one-way.

Transportes Occidentales
Buses from this company go from Quito to: **Santo Domingo, Quininde, Esmeraldas, Tonsupa, Atacames, Sua, Muisne, San Lorenzo, Guayaquil, Salinas, Machala, Pasaje, Santa Rosa, Huaquillas, Lago Agrio, Riobamba.** 18 de Septiembre and Versalles. Tel: 02-250-2735

Reina del Camino
This company's buses go from Quito to: **Canoa, Junín, Manta, Tosagua, Pedernales, San Vicente, Chone, Puerto Lopez, Bahía de Caraquez**, Portoviejo. 18 de Septiembre and Manuel Larrea. Tel: 02-321-6633

Flota Imbabura
Flota Imbabura's buses head from Quito to **Guayaquil, Cuenca, Manta, Ibarra and Tulcán.** Portoviejo and Manuel Larrea. Tel: 02-256-5620

Transportes Aray
Transportes Aray has buses that head from Quito to: **Manta, Santo Domingo, Chone, Ambato, Pedernales, San Vicente, Portoviejo, Bahía de Caraquez, Manta, Esmeraldas, Lago Agrio, Quevedo, Jipijapa, Jama, Rocafuerte, Tosagua, Puerto Lopez.** Portoviejo and Manuel Larrea, Tel: 02-275-0424.

Panamericana International
Buses from Quito to **Guayaquil, Manta, Huaquillas, Tulcán, Machala, Cuenca, Loja, Milagro, Santa Rosa, Atacames, Esmeraldas.** This company also has buses that go to Colombia and Peru.

La Mariscal Station: Av Colón, E7-31, between Reina Victoria and Diego de Almagro. Tel: 02-255-7133/7134. Tickets: ext.131, Secretary: ext.132. Fax: 02-251-5414. Quitumbe Terminal: Av. Condor Ñan and Av. Guayanay. No. 45 Y 46. Tel: 02-382-4751.

TransEsmeraldas
Buses head from Quito to: **Muisne, Atacames, El Coca, Machala, Esmeraldas, Lago Agrio, Huaquillas, Santo Domingo, Guayaquil, Portoviejo, Salinas.**

La Mariscal Station: Santa María y 9 de octubre. Tel: 02-250-5099

Quitumbe Terminal: Av. Condor Ñan and Av. Guayanay. Tel: 02-382-4791

BY TRAIN
Resurrected in late 2008, Ecuador's railroad system is back in full force and – starting June 2013 – provides affluent travelers with trips from Quito all the way to Guayaquil over the course of four to five days. Since 1975, the railroad system in Ecuador gradually decreased in popularity due to the growth of highway transportation and dwindling interest and investment on behalf of the government, inevitably leading to its demise and neglect. Back in April of 2008 however, attention to the old railroad system grew within government as it came to be regarded as a cultural and historical hallmark of the country, and as a result, they saw it fit to rehabilitate its lanes and trains.

From Quito, it's possible to take day trips to **Machachi, Boliche** & **Latacunga** for about $10-30, round-trip. Estación de Trenes Chimbacalle, Sincholagua and Maldonado. Tel: 1-800-873637. www.trenecuador.com Updated: Apr 12, 2013.

Getting Around Quito
GETTING AROUND QUITO BY BUS
The blue buses of Quito crisscross the city in every imaginable direction and, like other forms of public transportation, cost $0.25 cents (non-transferable).

Easiest to navigate are the **Trolebus, Ecovia** and **Metrobus,** each of which run from north to south (and vice versa) across Quito on a dedicated pair of lanes that are sandwiched between the major avenues: 10 de Agosto, 6 de Diciembre, and La Prensa. Each trip costs $0.25 like the blue buses, regardless of the length of the journey. These three tend to be much more crowded than the blue buses due to their popularity. Updated: Apr 12, 2013.

Blue Bus
To figure out where a particular blue bus is headed, you'll have to quickly read the long, multi-colored destination list that's posted on the front window (as the bus is barreling toward you). If the bus is the one you want, simply wave it down and jump aboard. If you're not able to read the sign in time, or don't manage to catch the tout's (the driver's partner who shouts out destinations and collects money) attention, don't worry - another bus will come along shortly.

Some buses have cashiers (behind a wooden desk to the left of the door) or touts who will take your 25 cents as you get on. Should you need a little more time to gather your payment, all operators will accept the fare as you leave or come to collect them during the trip. Make sure you have small change when you take the bus. Most operators are unable or unwilling to give change for currency larger than $5.

To get off the bus, stand up, walk to the front and indicate to the tout that you want to disembark. The bus should pause long enough for you to step off quickly to the curb, mind you the bus may still be slowly moving.

Bus routes are so numerous and so varied that not all of them can be detailed here. but it's safe to say: if there's a part of the city you'd like to get to, then there's probably a bus that will take you there. Ask a local (most quiteños are very helpful) what bus you need to take to get to where you want to go. Intercity buses typically stop operating shortly after 8 at night.

Trolebus

The Trole system runs down **6 de Agosto** from the southern **Terminal Quitumbe** station to the northern **Estación La "Y"** (Tel: 593-2-243-4975). Along its trajectory, and worth noting, are three stops: Colón (outskirts of La Mariscal neighborhood), Plaza del Teatro and Plaza Santo Domingo (in the Old Town).

Troles have dedicated lanes and green, glass booths as their stops. Like the Metrobus and Ecovia, the ride to any point along the Trole route costs $0.25 cents in exact change. If need be, you can get change for small bills or coins at the attendant's kiosk at any stop. Troles are handicap accessible, but the doors usually open and close quickly, so be prepared. Also, watch your valuables carefully, particularly if the popular Trole buses are jammed with people. If any one Trole seems too full, just wait for the next one.

Serving the city everyday is the Trole that runs from the northern terminal La "Y" to the southern station El Recreo. The schedule for getting from these two places, and vice-versa is:

Monday-Friday:
5 a.m.-Midnight (every 8-15 minutes)

Weekends & Holidays:
6 a.m -10 p.m. (every 10-15 minutes)

Note: After midnight on any day of week, all the buses still continue to run once every thirty minutes; however, they do so with limited service, stopping only at every other (second or third) stop along the line. Starting at 2a.m., they run once every hour. On weekends the same applies after 10 p.m, but only running once every hour.

At three of the following main stations, the Trole splits off into a number of supplemental bus routes.

- At **Marán Valverde** you can continue on along Camal Metropolitano, Cdla. Ejército, Guamaní and San Martin de Porras.

- **El Recreo** serves Solanda, Chillogallo, Lucha de los Pobres, Oriente Quiteño (ending at Vilcabamba) and Ferroviaria.

- **La "Y"** connects to Cotocollao, Rumiñahui, Carapungo, Kennedy, Comité del Publo (ending in Jiménez) and Los Laureles (to Rio Coca and Eloy Alfaro).

If need be, many Trole stations have route maps posted to help you find your destination. If you're still unsure, ask at one of the main stations for directions and a "*mapa de rutas y paradas del Trole*" (map of Trole routes and stops).

Ecovia

The Ecovía consists of a series of very popular, articulated buses that operate along **Av. 6 de Diciembre**. The Ecovía is one part of Quito's North-South public transportation triumvirate, and runs between **Rio Coca** to the north, and **La Marin** to the south. Like the Trolebús and Metrobus, the Ecovías have dedicated lanes, covered stops and always cost 25 cents (no matter your destination). Conductors usually call out the next point along the line, but each Ecovía *parada* (or stop) is also indicated by a large, brown marker and pictographic signs. To use the Ecovía, walk into any of the stops along 6 de Deciembre. Each stop is a glass, rectangular booth. You will need to insert correct change into a machine to pass through the turnstile. If you don't have 25 cents, the booth attendants can convert coins and small bills for you. (Just don't ask them to change anything larger than $5).

Be sure to get on quickly, as the doors don't stay open for long. If you are confronted with an Ecovía that appears extremely full (which happens often), wait for the next one. Once you're on, make sure you grab one or two of the many handholds, since Ecovías stop abruptly. Food and uncovered drinks are not allowed on the Ecovias. Keep an eye and hand on your valuables at all times; if you're using a backpack or large bag, shift it to your front when you get on. Pickpockets have been known to target Ecovía passengers, particularly on crowded buses.

Ecovias pass by very regularly during their operating hours of 5 a.m. to 11 p.m., Monday through Friday, and 6 a.m. to 9:30 p.m. weekends and holidays. Outside of those hours (midnight-dawn), the Ecovía runs hourly Monday-Friday, and half-hourly Friday-Saturday.

QUITO

QUITO

Metrobus

Of all three lines, Quito's Metrobus line is the one that reaches farthest north. Barreling down **America** & **La Prensa**, the metrobus makes several stops within walking distance of several areas such as: Mañosca St., La Gasca, Iñaquito Alto, Urb. Granda Centeno, Quito Tennis, El Bosque, Pinar Bajo, Pinar Alto, and La Concepción. Terminus station to the south is **Estacion Varela**, and to the north is **Estacion La Ofelia**. The cost is $0.25.

In addition to taking you farther north, the Metrobus is actually your first step in getting from Quito all the way to Mitad del Mundo via public transit. Transfer at the final stop up north in Estación La Ofelia, making sure to check (by asking) which buses are leaving to Mitad del Mundo from there.

The Trole, Ecovia and Metrobus offices are located at Av. Vicente Maldonado y Miguel Carrión sector El Recreo in Quito. To reach the main line, call: 593-2-266-5023; fax: 593-2 266-5019; email:info@trolebus.gov.ec; or visit www.trolebus.gov.ec.

GETTING AROUND QUITO BY TAXI

If you are looking for a relatively inexpensive, safe and convenient way to travel, tapping into Quito's extensive taxi network is a good way to get around the city.

During the day, taxi drivers are required to use a taximetro (or meter) when they drive you around. When you climb in, the initial rate should be 35 cents. Always ask for the taximetro, which is typically located just in front of the emergency brake, between the driver and front passenger seats. You should always be able to easily see the meter and should check the amount as you arrive at your destination (before the taxista turns it off).

Some drivers have been known to tell passengers that their meter is broken or that they don't have one, particularly around large hubs such as Terminal Terrestre. Taxis are plentiful enough that, if your driver won't use his meter (or has a meter that seems to be going extraordinarily fast), tell him to stop, get out and hail a more honest cabbie. Most daytime trips around the city cost between $1.50 and $3. Given the distance, trips to the airport cost a lot more. The price of taxis to the airport are calculated by a fixed price chart (not a taximetro) which is based

on the neighborhood you are departing to/from. For the most part, a trip to the airport will cost around $25-30 from most places in Quito (and vice versa).

At night, within the city itself, rates increase by $1 (since few other public transportation services are available) and taxi drivers do not use their meters. Make sure to negotiate a price before you get into a cab. If the price is too steep, ask for a more reasonable rate or hail a different taxi. Drivers charge per ride, not per person. Make sure when you're taking a taxi that you have roughly the correct fare in small change. Most cab drivers won't have much money on hand and will not be able to handle large bills. Tips are also accepted but usually not expected

GETTING AROUND QUITO BY CAR

Renting a car can be a good way to get out of Quito and explore the surrounding, spectacular countryside. Whether it be for a short trip or a longer vacation, car rental is a good option for those who are prepared to brave the interesting traffic "rules" that Ecuador has. When renting a car, be sure to consider that in some cases, roads may not be in top condition, and a vehicle with 4-wheel drive might be the best option.

In order to rent a car, you must be at least 25 years of age. Drivers must hold a valid driver's license and own an international credit card. As a general rule, those renting cars can expect to pay anything from $50 to $120 per day.

Avis (tel. 02/2440-270; www.avis.com.ec), Budget (tel. 02/3300-979; www.budget-ec. com), Hertz (tel. 1800/227-767 toll-free within Ecuador, or 02/2254-257; www. hertz.com.ec) are the main car rental agencies, with offices at both Quito and Guayaquil airports.

GETTING AROUND QUITO BY BICYCLE

BiciQ is Quito's new public bicycle system, which aims to promote everyday cycling for both Quito residents and visitors to the city. Twenty five bicycle stations are located around the city, with a total of 425 bikes for use, allowing for easy mobility throughout Quito. In order to have access to the public bikes, you need to subscribe to the service, which costs $25 for the year; visitors can arrange monthly payments instead. Once registered—either online, at one of the BiciQ stations, or at the BiciQ administrative office—you will receive a BiciQ card that you will need to present at each station in order to borrow a bike.

BiciQ users have 45 minutes of free use between stations to return their bike, at which point they can trade it for another. Other rules do apply, including the city confines in which the bike can be used. You must be at least 18 years old to sign up; those who are 17 or 16 years old can register if a parent signs for them. BiciQ operates daily between 7 a.m. and 7 p.m. The main administrative office is located on Calle Venezuela, between Chile and Espejo streets in the Centro Histórico (Tel: 02-395-2300, E-mail: biciq@quito.gob.ec, URL: www.biciq.gob.ec). Updated: Jan 4, 2013.

Safety

As in an any major city, it is important to be aware of your belongings and to be attentive, but not overly paranoid, about your surroundings. Avoid walking alone at night or in remote areas, and always take taxis after dark (after 7 p.m.), even for only a distance of two blocks. Especially on crowded city buses, pickpocketing and bag snatching or slashing are fairly common. In general, don't bring out anything you cannot afford to lose. On inter-city and international buses, sometimes other people pose as conductors and tell you to put your bag somewhere just out of sight, while items from your bag are stolen. Always keep your belongings close to you and within reasonable vision (never put them under a seat or in the overhead racks).

COMMON SCAMS

Thieves tend to work in small groups and often use distractive ploys to rip off their victims. One popular method involves spilling mustard or another substance on a victim and then offering to help, while another robber steals the victim's bag. Unfortunately, children are also involved in these schemes and may pose a fight, try to sell candy or beg for money as a way to distract, while another child takes some belongings.

Drugging has also been used to subdue victims and steal their items. Thieves have put the date rape drug, which is colorless and odorless, in food, drink and on fliers, and have even laced perfumes and flowers with it, making the victim succumb to their every command and wish.

Be especially cautious when using ATMs. If you are in an enclosed ATM and a few local men or woman surround you and insist that you swipe your card once more in order to unlock the door, then a popular scam is probably at work. Numerous travelers have run into this same problem, particularly in the Mariscal, and subsequently have had their card information and money stolen.

Try to use ATMs in daylight and be aware of who is watching you while withdrawing money. There have been reports of some ATMs not dispersing money and spitting out receipts claiming that no money has been withdrawn, while the entered amount has actually been taken out of the person's account. If this happens, keep the receipt from the transaction and contact your bank immediately.

Pico & Placa

Quito's *Pico y Placa* (literally: peak and plate) system was created in order to reduce traffic during peak travel hours, but also to generally encourage public transport over use of private vehicles within the city. It works according to the last number of the vehicle's license plate and only applies during the week in the mornings from 8-9:30 a.m. and in the evenings from 4-7:30 p.m. On Mondays, plates ending in 1 and 2 cannot be on the road; on Tuesdays, those ending in 3 and 4; on Wednesdays, those ending in 5 and 6; on Thursdays, those ending in 7 and 8; and on Fridays, those ending in 9 and 0. The government claims that there has been a 3.5% reduction in total cars on the road in Quito during peak hours since the application of Pico y Placa.

Vehicles who do not follow the Pico y Placa rules are subject to fines that increase after each offense. First-time offenders pay $97.33 and have their vehicle detained for one day; second-time offenders pay $146 and have their vehicle detained for two days; third-time offenders pay $292 and have their vehicle detained for three days. For more information on Pico y Placa, call 1-800-EMMOPQ or visit http://www.epmmop.gob.ec/epmmop/index.php?option=com_content&view=article&id=91

Loved it? Loathed it? Write a review and help other travelers

QUITO

More recently, express kidnappings—when taxi drivers drive a passenger to one or more ATMs and force the person to withdraw money—have become more common in Quito, so be sure to take only yellow, registered cabs with orange license plates and 4-digit numbers plastered on their windshields and car door. Another, safer option is to call a radio taxi, which will meet you at your location. Even though these taxis are often not yellow, either the driver will know your name from the call or the cab company will relay the number of the taxi due to show, which will confirm that it is yours. Keep in mind that taxis are supposed to use meters before dark, but many will claim that they don't have one or that theirs is broken, in which case, you should always negotiate the price before getting in. Even those with meters may pull some tricks on passengers by unplugging the meter right before arriving at the destination and charging a bit more.

It is wise to avoid using or buying illegal drugs in general. Often times, those who you are buying drugs from or who you are using drugs with have connections with the cops and are looking for bribes. Bribes or not, these types of activities may land you in some serious legal trouble.

Also, some local men and women seek relations with foreigners for the sole purpose of having access to their money, citizenship or both. Foreigners are stereotypically pegged as wealthy, and thus are seen as an impetus to a better life. Therefore, be careful who you become romantically involved with while in Ecuador, and know you can be a target of one of these phony relationship scams.

Finally, know that fake tour operators do exist and that you run the risk of being scammed if you are not careful about checking the reputation and credentials of certain companies.

UV RADIATION

At an elevation of 2,850 meters (9,350 ft) and a location just 25 kilometers (15 mi) from the equator, it is no surprise that Quito gets blasted by the sun's rays. The Ecuadorian Civil Space Agency (EXA), however, has discovered that these problems have been exacerbated by a thinning of the Ozone layer over Ecuador, Colombia and Peru. Quito is subjected to UV radiation measured at 24 UVI; anything over 11 UVI is considered

unsafe. Extended exposure to such high levels of UV radiation can lead to skin cancer, vision problems and cell mutation. The wisest preventative measures are to wear long sleeves and pants, wear a hat that covers your face and neck, and bring along a pair of good UV-resistant sunglasses. Covering any exposed flesh with sunblock is also a great idea. EXA's website has a real-time UV radiation meter, which can give you the current reading in Quito and a handful of other cities. Updated: Feb 08, 2013.

Quito Lodging

Quito has accommodation options for travelers of any economic stature and for travelers with specific interests, whether it's history, art, trekking or partying. Quito hostels are abundant and range in price, depending on whether you want a dorm bed or a spacious room with a private bathroom. Hostels are the best places to meet fellow travelers, so stay in one if you're looking for a traveling companion or a social atmosphere.

Keep an eye out for some basic amenities when looking for accommodations, especially when deciding on cheaper places to stay. Evenings are cool throughout the year and heat in hotels is pretty rare, so hot water and thick blankets are a necessity. Many hotels have rooms with beautiful views of the Pichincha volcanoes or city skylines at no extra charge, so it never hurts to ask.

There are also large, more luxurious hotels with solid reputations, great restaurants and safe locations, many of which are located outside the Mariscal neighborhood. If you want to avoid the impersonality of large hotels, another luxury option is the bed and breakfast. Quito boasts some very nice B&Bs, many of which are housed in renovated colonial buildings in or near the Old Town.

Anyone who wants to be in a central location, with easy access to the restaurants and bars of the New Town as well as the sights and charm of the Old Town, the Mariscal is a good place to stay. However, since this is where much of the city action is, you may find many places to be a bit noisy.

Those who want to be in the heart of cultural Quito, surrounded by museums, cobblestoned streets, and expansive plazas with impressive colonial buildings will want to stay in the Old Town. Business travelers often prefer to stay in the northern sector of the city, which is more modern and well-connected by transport, or in La Floresta.

Quito is a large city with much to see and do. Don't be surprised if you find yourself staying longer than anticipated. If you stay for more than a couple of days, ask for a discount on your room. Bargaining is always appropriate. Updated: Jan 18, 2013.

Quito Restaurants

It'll take more than just a quick glance at this guide book to really figure out what Quito's culinary scene looks like from the inside, but in a nutshell: it's extraordinarily varied. Ranging anywhere from traditional mote or *chocho* (Andean beans and corn) being served on the curbside for just a few quarters, all the way to Lebanese delights being catered to your table for a much higher (but well spent) price at Balbeek. There is no need to feel overwhelmed however.

For the most part, La Mariscal offers visitors a place to travel across the gamut of the culinary world that Quito has to offer. Given that the neighborhood itself has a reputation for offering affordable lodging to tourists from all over the world, it's here that you'll find the greatest variety in prices and dining from place to place, and just over the expanse of a couple of blocks too.

La Ronda on the other hand will veer you away from the rest of the world (in a gastronomic sense) as it funnels you down its cobblestone streets past a number of cafés and restaurants all set on serving you the hallmarks of Ecuadorian cuisine. Prices here vary as well, but that usually depends on how hungry and restless you are. Grab an empanada or *canelazo* (a warm, cinnamon-infused alcoholic beverage that is guaranteed to raise your spirits on cold nights) for a dollar or so on the street if you feel like eating on the go; or settle down inside any one of the numerous restaurants to be treated with an array of choices on the menu, along with live music - albeit for a substantially higher price.

While wandering throughout the sites of Old Town, be sure to go to the Palacio Arzobispal courtyards. Once the former residence of Quito's Archbishop, it's now two conjoined courtyards that host multilevel restaurants.

Hasta la Vuelta Señor is one that has exquisite local dishes and a charming legend that elaborates on its name.

Dinner with a view? Absolutely. Quito has a couple of restaurants definitely worth going to that are perched on the slopes that cradle the city. Worth noting are Café Mosaico and El Ventanal, both of which have a wonderful vantage point of the city (from the east and west, respectively). It's here that you'll be able to peruse Quito's intricate design of streets and buildings against a mountainous backdrop, all with a drink in hand and food in front. Mind you that at these pricey places it's the view that you're paying for rather than quality of the food (which is still filling!).

Venture down the hills that uphold the bohemian neighborhood of Guápalo to dine at a cute café or a yummy pizzeria, like Ananké, for great views of the valley and the church at the bottom of the hill. Or stroll back up to the top and devour one of Quito's drunkenly sought hot-dogs at Los Hot Dogs de la Gonzales Suarez.

Lastly, if Ecuadorian or Western fast food is what you crave, then rest assured that any one of the shopping malls around Quito will provide you with your fix at any one of their food courts. Updated: Mar 08, 2013.

Things To See and Do in Quito

If you have a limited period of time in Quito, don't miss a tour of the Centro Histórico at night or the weekend market at Parque el Ejido (especially if you can't make it to the market in Otavalo). If you have more time, be sure to take a trip to El Panecillo, which offers excellent views of the narrow Andean city.

Take a trip to Parque La Carolina, where you will get a true taste of the relaxed, life-loving Ecuadorian culture as families putt around the boat pond, send their little ones biking or skateboarding over concrete peaks in the skate park and dirt bike track, play sports or just lounge and enjoy the day. Alternatively, the parque Metropolitano is one of the biggest Metropolitan parks in all Latin America.

Some museums not to miss while in Quito are Guayasamin's Capilla del Hombre and the Museo Nacional del Banco Central.

Loved it? Loathed it? Write a review and help other travelers

QUITO

Nightlife Schedule

Almost every night of the week there is something fun going on in Quito, but it is all a matter of knowing where to go and when. Of course, some places are better than others on certain nights and in general, drink specials tend to be reveler magnets. Many drink specials run throughout the week, but it will be difficult to find much happening on Sunday and Monday nights, because most places are closed. As far as weekends go, no particular places stand above the rest on most nights so grab your friends and head to your favorite establishment.

On Tuesday nights, No Bar is the hotspot and is by far the best place to go if looking for a rowdy time. The crowd is a mix of both Ecuadorians and gringos, and most fall between the ages of 18-25. Admission costs $4, which includes one free drink. If you are more up for singing than dancing, head to Aguijón, because Tuesday night is karaoke night! Or, if mingling with expats and testing your knowledge is more your thing, check out the pub quiz at Finn McCools every Tuesday at 8 p.m. Participation costs $2, and all proceeds go the Bruce Ecuador charity.

Wednesday night is a surprisingly popular night to go out, providing some mid-week relief. Bungalow 6 is especially a crowd magnet, mostly due to the fact that it is Ladies' Night, meaning females drink whatever they want for free for two hours, from 8-10 p.m. Males are not even allowed in until after 10 p.m., but often start lining up at the door beforehand, scoping out the general attractiveness and level of drunkenness of the women inside.

Wednesday is also Salsa Night at Aguijón, where hordes of salsa dancers and those looking to learn some salsa moves go. It is usually packed and sweaty and salsa beats stay pumping until well into the middle of the night. Entrance is free before 10 p.m., but jumps to $6 thereafter.

Mulligan's also has its Wings Night on Wednesday nights, where its buffalo wings drop to the extremely affordable price of $0.15 per wing. Finally, the South American Explorer's Club hosts a pub quiz at Turtle's Head Pub every other Wednesday evening at 8 p.m. The cost is $2 for members and $3 for non-members, and the top three placing teams win a free pitcher of beer, while the first-place team receives beer and free meal

vouchers. Questions range in topic and issue, but are all recited in English.

Thursday night is *the* night to go to Seseribo, one of Quito's best and well-known salsa clubs. Admission costs $8. Rockers will also be pleased to know that Thursday night is Rock night at Blues, where the club's usual techno, house and electronic beats make way for rock music. Ladies get in for free before midnight and drink for free until 1 a.m. On Thursday night, Mulligan's also has a pub quiz of its own. The cost is $1 and the questions are read in both English in Spanish. Updated: Apr 19, 2012.

Gay Quito

Politically, Ecuador is relatively progressive. With the creation of a new constitution in 1998, Ecuador banned any type of discrimination based on sexual orientation, becoming the first country in the Americas - and the third country worldwide - to do so.

This was a huge step in the right direction for acceptance and tolerance of sexuality across the nation. In 2008, Ecuador officially recognized same-sex civil unions, although same-sex marriage is constitutionally banned. Unfortunately, despite the political progression, it is still best to downplay any public displays of affection while out with your partner in Ecuador - even in the gay friendly areas.

Travelers may be surprised to see men dressing as women and asking for money during the Mama Negra festival and New Years Eve, but far from showing an acceptance of fluidity in gender, this is seen as more of a joke. Like many other South American countries, Ecuador has defined stereotypical gender roles assigned to both men and women. Men are expected to be macho, while women are expected to take care of the home, the children, and be somewhat dependent on men. A negative term for a gay man is a "maricón" and it is often used as an insult for any man acting effeminate.

Of course, this is slowly changing with the younger population and the larger cities like Quito and Guayaquil are more accepting in general. Quito's ever-expanding gay pride parade takes place at the end of June (or early July) in the Mariscal, and goes down Avenida Amazonas to Plaza Foch.

A wonderful resource for gay/lesbian day trips and tours is Zenith Travel. The owners are full of information about gay-friendly places in Ecuador and are overall nice people. Each year they offer 3 lesbian-only and 3 gay-only 11 day tours around Quito and the Galapagos. The lesbian tours correspond with Valentines Day, Halloween, and Independence Day and the gay tours correspond with Mardis Gras, Ecuadorian Independence Day, and Thanksgiving. The tours are very popular and they do fill up quickly, so reserve well in advance. Ask for Marcos. Juan León Mera N24-264 Y Cordero 02-252-9993 / 290-5595 www.zenithecuador.com. Updated: Mar 13, 2013.

Gay Quito Nightlife & Dining

BARS:

Suzette (no cover)
A picturesque terrace, lounge and bar in the very heart of Plaza Foch, right behind the fountain. You'll identify it by the colorful walls, lamps and tables. Owners Juan Manuel and Edison will be sure to host and serve you. Suzette, as they describe it, is a "hetero-friendly" place where (gay or straight) one can eat and drink in a relaxed and integrated atmosphere. Should you have a desire to purchase one, the paintings on the walls are for sale too.

Dionisios (Cover: $4-6)
Surrounding the bar and dance floor are walls covered with photograph's of men. They frequently host drag shows, cabaret, and comedy nights. The cover includes a drink. Tue. - Sat., 9 p.m.-2 a.m., Manuel Larrea 550 and Riofrio, América. Tel: 02-255-7759, E-mail: dionisioskfe@latinmail.com

CLUBS :

Tercer Milenio, a.k.a "El Hueco" (Cover: $7)
Mixed gay and lesbian club, very welcoming, and easy to meet people. Baquedano 188 and Reina Victoria.

Living (Cover: $6)
Located inside the Zodiacal Club, this is a popular place for people in their teens to thirties and hosts strippers and go-go dancers on certain nights. Plays Electronic music and some Reggaeton. Wilson E4-229 y Amazonas. Opens Friday and Saturday from 10 p.m - 3 a.m.

Magenta (Cover: $8)
A dance club. Open Monday through Saturday. Reina Victoria N26-32 and Santa Maria

Buddah (Cover: $1 after 10 p.m.)
Frequented by young gays and lesbians interested in dancing to electronic music (this is not to say that they play it all the time!). Foch between Amazonas and Juan Leon Mera.

Six (Cover $10 2 drinks)
Very nice environment and decoration. Only Electronic music. Opens at 10 p.m. Corner of 6 de diciembre and Orellana, next to Subway.

RESTAURANTS:
The places listed below are not gay places per se, just gay-friendly.

La Mariscal
El Cafecito
A simple café popular at night with good vegetarian food. Cordero 1124 and Reina Victoria, Tel: 593-2-223-4862

La Boca del Lobo
A very popular restaurant in the heart of the Mariscal with kitchy décor. Mon-Sat 5 p.m.-midnight. Calama 284 and Reina Victoria, Tel: 593-223-4083, E-mail: labocadellobo@hotmail.com

Centro Histórico
La Ronda street has a nice selection of art galleries and hosts live music in the evening, along with vats of hot wine and canelazo. A great option for low-key evenings.

Loved it? Loathed it? Write a review and help other travelers

QUITO

Studying Spanish in Quito

Quito is a major hub for travelers who want to study Spanish. Most Spanish schools offer homestays, excursions and even other types of classes like cooking classes and salsa lessons. You will usually have a choice between group or private instruction, and many schools recommend or require a minimum hours per week. Rates range from around $5-10 per hour, but rates often reflect quality. If even the lower end of the scale is out of your budget, many schools will hire you as an English teacher and either give you a discount on your Spanish lessons or let you take classes for free. Classes are rarely less than one week and run as long as several months in length. Updated: Jan 22, 2013.

Yanapuma Spanish School

Yanapuma Spanish school is a unique, nonprofit school whose proceeds benefit Yanapuma Foundation and its sustainable development projects in Ecuadorian communities. It combines in-class learning with a wide variety of optional activities, including culturally and socially oriented weekday and weekend excursions, community-based Spanish study, and volunteering in poor neighborhoods of Quito. The school is located at the edge of the Mariscal (New Town), with many restaurants, bars, and other tourist amenities a short walk away. It offers free WiFi or limited use of its computers, a language lab, and a TV and DVD player for watching Spanish movies and videos. All materials are included in the class price. Veintimilla E8-125 and 6 de Diciembre, Tel: 02-254-6709, E-mail: spanish@yanapuma. org, URL: www.yanapumaspanish.org

Academia de Español Guayasamín

(Weekly Cost: $150, four hours for one week to seven hours in eight weeks) Academia de Español Guayasamín offers affordable hourly group classes. Teachers are native Spanish speakers and all have at least seven years of experience. All materials are included in the price, along with salsa classes, city excursions, volunteer opportunities, and assistance with securing accommodation in a hotel or homestay. Class schedules are flexible. Programs are also offered on the coast and in the Amazon Jungle. Calama E8-54 and 6 de Diciembre, Tel: 02-254-4210, E-mail: info@guayasaminschool.com, URL: www.guayasaminschool.com. Updated: Feb 21, 2013.

Academia Latinoamericana de Español !

($165-290 per week, includes host family) At Academia Latinoamericana de Español, you will find yourself quickly learning Spanish amid friendly Ecuadorians and the mix of Spanish and indigenous history that defines Quito. Regardless of your proficiency level, you will find a program that suits your needs, goals and learning style here. The maximum number of students per class is four, and you will learn using the four language skills: listening, grammar, oral and written comprehension. The school arranges homestays with native, middle-class families within a 10-minute bus ride of school, providing a cultural complement to your language learning. Additionally, you can combine your Spanish study with volunteer programs and excursions in and around Quito. Noruega N10-31 and 6 de Diciembre, Tel: 02-225-0946/226-7904/7905, Fax: 02-226-7906, E-mail: info@latinoschools.com, URL: www.latinoschools.com. Updated: Jan 08, 2013.

Amazonas Language School

(Weekly Cost: $450-630, Hours per Week: 20-35) Amazonas Language School features private or group Spanish classes for 20 to 35 hours per week. Since the school is paired up with a travel agency, students have the advantage of learning about the country and language as they travel. Founded in 1989, the school is well-established and all teachers have degrees in language and literature, along with a minimum of six years of teaching experience. There are various options for study around Ecuador, including classes in Quito, the Galápagos Islands and the Amazon jungle. English, French and German language classes are also offered.

Prices include homestay in a private bedroom with three meals a day and laundry service, airport transfer upon arrival, cultural activities once a week, study materials, salsa classes once a week, luggage storage and more. Those who commit to at least 100 hours of study also get access to the Hilton Health Club for two weeks, which has a pool, sauna, gym and Jacuzzi. Jorge Washington E4-59 and Av. Amazonas., Edificio Rocafuerte, Washington Tower, 3rd. floor, Tel: 02-254-8223/250-4654, Cel: 09-8328-0302/8321-1923, E-mail: info@eduamazonas.com / Messenger: languages.travel@hotmail.com, URL: www.

eduamazonas.com/www.ecuadorandgalapagosislands.com/Facebook:www.facebook.com/amazonaseducation.
Updated: Feb 21, 2013.

Andean Global Studies

(Weekly cost: $200) Andean Global Studies is a Spanish school based in Quito and offers foreign students a wide variety of programs, such as: spanish immersion, medical Spanish, and volunteering. The school facilities are deigned with comfort in mind, providing Wi-Fi and computer access for their students. The school has multiple classrooms, cafeteria and a recreational room with audiovisual material. It's also conveniently located in the heart of the city, surrounded by banks, parks, shopping malls and restaurants. If you would like to travel and study throughout Ecuador, AGS is a pretty good option given they have programs in Manta, Cuenca, and Montañita. El Mercurio 346 y La Razón, Tel: (593 2) 225 4928, E-mail: info@andeanglobalstudies.org, URL: www.andeanglobalstudies.org.
Updated: May 18, 2012.

Cristóbal Colón Spanish Language School

Private classes at Cristóbal Colón are reasonably priced and no registration fee is necessary, just pay as you go. Its library offers a selection of materials for your classes and you have the option of changing teachers each week to practice a variety of accents and teaching styles. There are several ways you can get discounts at this language school, including working in the office, staying at the hostel next door, or printing out a brochure from their website. Extra services offered include excursions, English teacher placements around Quito, host family accommodation and more. Salsa classes, cooking classes, Internet facilities, and city excursions with your teachers are all included in the price. Av. Colón 2-56 and Versalles, Tel: 02-250-6508/222-2964, E-mail: info@colonspanishschool.com, URL: www.colonspanishschool.com.
Updated: Jan 08, 2013.

Simón Bolivar Spanish School 』

Located just three blocks from the center of the Mariscal area, Simón Bolívar Spanish School offers a wide range of extra services such as free Internet, airport pick-up, city tours, two salsa classes per week, cooking classes, and classes on culture, economy and other Ecuadorian subjects. Its flexible class schedules are also a plus. Simón Bolívar also has branches in Cuenca, just south of Puerto López on the coast, and in the Amazon rainforest. Homestays can be also be arranged on a weekly basis, with all meals included. Mariscal Foch E9-20 and 6 de Diciembre, Tel: 02-254-4558/223-4708, Fax: 02-254-4558, E-mail: info@simon-bolivar.com, URL: www.simon-bolivar.com.
Updated: Jan 08, 2013.

Volunteering in Quito

On point with the growing trend toward "voluntourism"—or supplementing travel experiences with volunteer work—thousands of people come to Ecuador each year looking to volunteer. Lots of programs exist in and around Quito, but these opportunities vary greatly in type of work involved, cost, and minimum length of commitment. Most volunteer opportunities are in the health care, education and conservation fields, though you are likely to find some program in line with your particular interests and backgrounds. Schools, orphanages, hospitals, childcare centers, organic gardens and farms, and indigenous communities are all popular placements.

Many programs offer homestays, low-cost or free accommodation options, and some will even provide food, transportation and Spanish language classes. Depending on the volunteer work, required commitments can span from one day to one year. Some programs and organizations charge little to nothing, while others have high registration, weekly or monthly fees. Keep in mind that the reputations of some organizations are questionable, so it's best to check out credentials and personal testimonies before deciding on a volunteer opportunity.
Updated: Jan 18, 2013.

Center for the Working Girl (CENIT) Volunteer

The Center for the Working Girl (an acronym in Spanish known as CENIT) is a nonprofit association that uses educational and job training to overcome poverty and improve the lives of young girls and their families. Participants are asked to work three to eight hours a day and there is no cost to the volunteer, however donations are greatly appreciated. Huacho 150 and Jose Peralta, Tel: 02-265-4260, URL: www.cenitecuador.org.

Loved it? Loathed it? Write a review and help other travelers

QUITO

Yanapuma Foundation

Yanapuma Foundation is a cooperative non-profit organization driven by the enthusiasm of its national and international staff and volunteers working toward the realization of its vision: marginalized communities achieving equity and well-being; ecological, social and economic sustainability; and developing a sense of the uniqueness of their culture in a global context. The foundation has a great volunteer program called Volunteer Ecuador. It pairs interested volunteers with worthwhile projects from the coast to the Amazon, as well as in and around Quito. It also provides orientation information, on-site support and after-care. Yanapuma Foundation does have a one-time volunteer set-up fee, which ranges from $85-185, depending on the location of the project. Veintimilla E8-125 and Av. 6 de Diciembre, Tel: 02-290-7643, E-mail: volunteer@yanapuma.org, URL: www.yanapuma.org. Updated: Jan 22, 2013.

South American Explorers' Club

The South American Explorers (SAE) club-house offers several unpaid internships every year. Internships last at least 12 weeks and candidates who can stay longer are given preference. Interns usually participate in all aspects of SAE, such as assisting members, performing general office tasks, planning events, maintaining the library and performing other tasks that come up. Special internships for development, web marketing, etc. can also be arranged. SAE prefers volunteers who have some experience in Latin America and who speak some Spanish. Although the internships are unpaid, the clubhouse provide tons of fringe benefits. Jorge Washington 311 and Leonidas Plaza, Tel: 02-222-5228, E-mail: quitoclub@saexplorers.org, URL: www.saexplorers.org/volunteer. Updated: Jan 22, 2013.

Quito Tours

Quito is where almost all tours are organized throughout Ecuador, and the streets of the-Mariscal Sucre neighborhood are lined with every type of tour operator imaginable.

Some of the most popular tours booked in Quito are: Galapagos last minute tours, trips to lodges in the Amazon region or cloud forests of Mindo, day trips to the Otavalo market, Papallacta hot springs, and Cotopaxi National Park.

Adventure activities like mountain biking, white water rafting, mountain climbing, trekking and birdwatching are also popular and best booked in Quito.

It's recommended to reserve Galapagos tours well in advance before you arrive, especially in the high season of summer and around Christmas and New Years when boats book up months or even years in advance. Last minute bargains do exist, but are rare. Quito city tours are offered by a handful of travel agencies and tend to focus on Quito's Historical City Center. The history of Quito is fascinating, so contracting a city tour guide who knows the history instead of just wandering around the Old Town is highly recommendable.

There's a new red double decker tour bus that passes by the most interesting tourist attractions that goes from Parque Carolina, through the Mariscal and to the Historical City Center. Updated: Jan 16, 2013.

Quito Tour Bus

(TICKETS: $12 adults, $6 children, seniors and disabled people) The Quito Tour Bus is a convenient and comfortable way to see all of the city's main attractions. Each day, the modern two-story tour buses leave from Avenida Naciones Unida (diagonal to the Quicentro Shopping mall, in front of the park by the pedestrian bridge) at 9 a.m., 10 a.m., 1 p.m., 2 p.m., 3 p.m. and 4 p.m. The bus makes a thorough three-hour journey through the city with stops at 12 different sights, including the Botanical Garden, Plaza Foch, La Basílica, El Panecillo, Centro Histórico's Plaza Grande, and the TeleferiQo cable car.

Passengers can hop on and off at any of the stops within 24 hours of their ticket purchase. On the way, you will also learn important historical and cultural information about the various places through a pre-recorded audio commentary in english.

There is also an evening ride that leaves at 7:30 p.m. if you would like to see the city lit up at night. You can pay for the bus as you board or buy tickets in advance. El Quinde Tour office located on Ca. Japón and Naciones Unidas, Tel: 02-243-5458/245-8010, URL: www.quindetour.com. Updated: Mar 12, 2013.

Columbus Travel ✏

Norwegian owned and based in Quito, Columbus Travel has access to a wide range of boats and cruises, providing an excellent booking service for Galapagos tours. As a result of selling more Galapagos cruises than any other company, they're able to negotiate some excellent discounts and prices which they make widely available to all travelers. They also know a lot about dive tours, hotels, island-hopping and can set up a wide variety of itineraries catered to their clients' tastes. The service they provide is honest and reliable, and they're a good place to start if you find yourself having trouble on deciding what to do and where to go.

In addition to offering tours of the Galapagos, Columbus also provides tours of Quito, Guayaquil, Otavalo, Papallacta, Mindo, Baños and Cuenca. There are also longer tours offered through the different regions of mainland Ecuador (across the Andean sierra and its Colonial Towns or the Pacific Coast, to name a few). Mariscal Foch 265 and 6 de Diciembre Avenue, Sonelsa Building 2nd and 3rd floors, Quito, Ecuador, Tel: 02-602-0851, URL: www.columbusecuador.com. Updated: Mar 12, 2013.

Ecuador Adventure

Ecuador Adventure provides what some might say is a more adrenaline-centered tour of the country, offering a range of places to go see and activities to do en route. They arrange trips that typically end up being a healthy mix of exposure to indigenous communities, ancestral traditions and outdoor adventuring over a period of days and nights. The accommodations they pick for their adventurers tend to be on the more eccentric side, but nevertheless well selected and quite comfortable. In addition to this, they provide leaders and guides that are sure to keep you venturing forth. Their tours span Cotopaxi, the Amazon, the Andes and the Galapagos. Tel: 1-800-217-944 / 02-2604-6800, URL: http://www.ecuadoradventure.ec/. Updated: Mar 12, 2013.

Quito City Tour and Travel

A local and savvy tour operator that provides thorough guides of the Old Town as well as tours of landmarks on the outskirts of the city, such as the Teleferiqo or Mitad del Mundo. But if you're bent on venturing even further out: Cotopaxi, Otavalo, Mindo or Papallacta are among the more distant tours that they provide. With all this in mind, you can contact them to have them arrange a custom itinerary based on the sights and places you'd like to see in and around Quito. Orellana y 12 de Octubre, Lincoln Building, First Floor, Office: 102., Tel: 09-9882-9941, Fax: 02-604-2429, E-mail: info@quitocitytour.travel, URL: http://www.quitocitytour.travel. Updated: Mar 12, 2013.

TribuTrek

TribuTrek is a Dutch/Ecuadorian tour operator located in Quito specializing in tours and trekking around the Quilotoa Loop, Cotopaxi and Chimborazo, as well as general tours in Ecuador. Gregorio Munga and Portete (two blocks west of 6 de Diciembre), Tel: 085-737-829, E-mail: info@tributrek.com, URL: www.tributrek.com. Updated: Sep 06, 2012.

Tour Operators in La Mariscal

If you're looking to take a tour from Quito, whether it is a week in the Galapagos or a day in Old Town, La Mariscal is the place to book. Travel and tourism agencies have popped up around La Mariscal (specifically near Plaza Foch, the area's central meeting point) making it easy to book once you arrive and have figured out exactly what you would like to do while in and around Ecuador's capital. While it can't hurt to book ahead, as tours are popular from Quito and often fill up, there are definitely risky but rewarding benefits in trying to catch last minute deals, specifically filling spots on Galapagos cruises. Many tour agencies offer a range of options, from half-day trips to week-long excursions; be sure to shop around as something will surely meet your needs.

Ec Travel Tours

Ec Travel, based in Quito, features friendly staff and great prices. The company offers tours to all around the country and to the Galápagos Islands. The establishment is owned by young Ecuadorians that personally attend every tour. From time to time, they can be overbooked, but it is a safe bet that if they are; they will find a way to accommodate you. Scuba diving, whale watching, community tourism and other tours are available. 6 de Diciembre 2130 and Av. Colón, Building Antares, 12th floor, office 1201, Tel: 02-252-3945, Fax: 02-252-3945, E-mail: 02-252-3945, URL: www.ectravel.com.ec. Updated: Jan 08, 2013.

QUITO

Galapagos Travel Center

The Galapagos Travel Center is perhaps one of the best places to reserve your Galápagos cruise due to having one of the widest selection of boats and highly-competitive prices available on the GalapagosIslands.com website. Its website is highly informative and useful for trip planning, and its British-lead staff have an excellent reputation. The GTC office is at a new location right off of Plaza Foch in the Mariscal. Mariscal Foch E-612 and Reina Victoria, Tel: 02-602-0851, URL: www.galapagosislands.com.
Updated: Jan 16, 2013.

Gulliver Expeditions

Gulliver Traveloffers a wide range of options for exploring this beautiful country, from guided vehicle tours to extreme outdoor pursuits such as mountain biking, horseback riding, hiking and climbing in the Avenue of the Volcanoes. Ecuador has much to offer its visitors: very diverse climatic zones spread over a relatively small area easily accessible from Quito, diverse indigenous populations, impressive historic city centers and excellent safety conditions. Every Gulliver tour offers high-quality, personalized service, competitive prices, high standards in safety procedures, and professional, qualified guides. Juan León Mera N24-156 and Calama, Tel: 02-252-9297, URL: www.gulliver.com.ec.
Updated: Jan 08, 2013.

Biking Dutchman Cycling Trips

Since 1991, Biking Dutchman has been offering great cycling trips all throughout Ecuador, helping travelers enjoy the beautiful surrounding landscape. Whether you're a beginner or expert, Biking Dutchman has a variety of cycling adventures to suit your level of experience, comfort and interests. Trip lengths range from convenient and fun day trips to exciting week-long expeditions across the Andes and the Amazon. Foch 714 and Juan Leon Mera, Tel: 593-2-256-8323 / 593-2-254-2806, Fax: 593-2-256-7008, E-mail: biking.dutchman@gmail.com, URL: www.bikingdutchman.com
Updated: Dec 04, 2012.

Yacu Amu Rafting

If you've never tried whitewater rafting before, or even if you have had the pleasure, Yacu Amu Rafting will provide an adventure that you'll never forget. Yacu Amu trips run the gamut, from week-long stays with prearranged activities to simple day trips.

Professional tour guides will instruct you in the proper etiquette, safety rules, etc. After a thorough tutorial, you're on your way! Whether you're bumping down the Blanco River or being tossed around on the Toachi, you are bound to have a good time. The company also provides fresh meals during the day to refuel adventurers. End the long day by scribbling in the tour guide's "blah blah book," where weary adventurers recap their day along the river. Check out the company's website to choose exactly which excursion is perfect for you. Shyris N34-40 and Republica de El Salvador, Tapia Building, Office 104, Tel: 02-246-1511, URL: www.yacuamu.com.
Updated: Jan 08, 2013.

Opuntia Eco Journeys

Contrary to all the hype and fuss over cruises, Opuntia aims to organize a well-rounded experience that's based around taking in the wildlife, nature and adventure that's to be found in land-based tours of the islands. The moments you do spend in the water will only involve either going from island to island quickly or checking out the wildlife below with snorkeling, rather than spending it on a cruise. As added karma, Opuntia is also recognized by the Rainforest Alliance as a sustainable tour operator. Their guides are top-notch and the tours are meant to give you a thorough experience of the Galapagos islands and its highlights, rather than just a passing visit which cruise-based tours are prone to giving. Manuel Sotomayor E17-105 and Flores Jijón Tel: 1-800-217-9414, URL: www.opuntiagalapagostours.com.
Updated: Jan 08, 2013.

Andean Discovery

Experts in putting together your Andean "dream trip," Andean Discovery sets out to take care of all the logistics involved in arranging an itinerary for you and filling your time in Ecuador (or even Peru). Their interest and devotion in taking you off the beaten path is what makes them quite exceptional, showing you places many others rarely get to see. Their itineraries can also convert just about any set of variables (budget, interests, schedule, group size, etc.) into an unforgettable and solid experience. The guides are well-trained English speakers and will be there to offer you a safe and memorable experience as well. Tel: 1-800-893-0916, E-mail: info@andeandiscovery.com, URL: www.andeandiscovery.com.
Updated: Jan 08, 2013.

Centro Histórico

The Centro Histórico (also known as the Old Town) is Quito's extensive colonial center that was built over the ashes of what was once a major part of the Inca empire. One of the first areas to be named a World Heritage Site by the United Nations in 1978, Old Town will send you across centuries of history as you stroll down its cobblestone streets and alleyways, filled by local residents and *vendedores ambulantes* (street vendors).

At the beginning of the 20th century, Quito fit within the boundaries of this entire neighborhood. Today however - following decades of expansion - it's only a small piece of the entire city, but still undoubtedly the most iconic one. Filled with a rich past, it's here that some of Ecuador's most famous battles and executions took place in the plazas, only to be replaced now by the much more peaceful but lively bustle of residents, tourists, businessmen, street vendors, and protesters; not to mention - all the noisy cars and buses that wind through its single-lane streets.

Once considered dangerous, Old Town has drastically changed over the past few years. Beggars and pushy merchants have dwindled in numbers, the façades of old buildings have been repainted, streets and the plazas are better illuminated at night now, and the Trole and Ecovia have managed to cut down on bus traffic and fumes. Most significant is the fact that the police force is a much stronger presence now, notably helping deter pickpockets and other criminals. It's still advised to be cautious and discreet though, as the streets tend to fill up quickly with locals during lunch-time and at the end of the day, and tourists are still a bit of an oddity in this area of Quito.

For some extra fun, veer off from the guided tour and spend some quality time in the plazas or side streets that feature exquisite colonial architecture and winding pathways that open up into lovely courtyards.
Updated: Feb 28, 2013.

Centro Histórico Services
TOURISM
Quito Turismo
A friendly and helpful spot for information about Quito and Ecuador in general. You'll find information pamphlets and maps. On the corner of Venezuela and Espejo, Tel: 02-257 0786, E-mail: info@quito-turismo.com.

MONEY
Banco de Pichincha
Guayaquil, between Olmedo and Manabi. Tel: 02-295-5700, Open Hours From: 08:30 a.m. to 5:00 p.m., Monday-Friday, Days Closed: Sundays but open Saturdays from 9:00 a.m. to 1:00 p.m..

MEDICAL
Farmacias SanaSana (Pharmacy)
Venezuela N1-84 and Bolivar, Tel: 02-396-8500, Open Hours From: 9:00a.m., Open Hours To: 5:00p.m..

SHOPPING
Tianguez Gift Shop
The Tianguez Gift Shop supports the entrepreneurial spirit of Ecuador. There are handmade crafts from around 350 groups and individuals in the country; from Panama Hats to blow guns, precolombian ceramics, tapestries and Tigua paintings. Aspiring to pay fair prices to the original artists, you will find the prices here higher than most outdoor markets, however the variety and quality is exceptional. Plaza de San Francisco cuenca y sucre under the church's atrium, Tel: 593-2-257-0233 / 593-2-954-326, E-mail: administracion@sinchisacha.org, URL: www.tienguez.org /www.sinchisacha.org/ www.mindalae.com.
Updated: Jan 08, 2013.

Things To See and Do in the Old Town
You will need more than one afternoon to see and do all that Quito's Centro Histórico has to offer. The hilly cobblestone streets take you back to the era of the Spanish Empire, with large central plazas, sprawling green parks, beautiful colonial buildings and elaborate Catholic churches. With so much to gaze at, you just might find yourself wandering in awe throughout the pleasant neighborhood.

When you do, however, you will be instantly amazed. Check out the gold ornamented Iglesia de La Compañia, or wander through the President's Palace in Plaza Grande. Pay a visit to one of Centro Histórico's many interesting museums, with exhibits on colonial and indigenous art, military memorabilia, and relics that chart the country's checkered history from pre-Inca times to the present. When in Quito, it is definitely worth your while to spend time embracing one of Ecuador's most historic areas.

QUITO

Loved it? Loathed it? Write a review and help other travelers

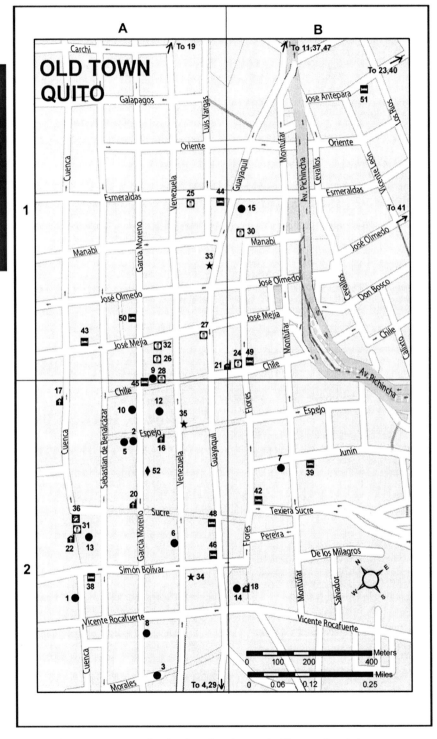

Activities ●

1 Casa del Abalado A2
2 Centro Cultural Metropolitano A2
3 La Ronda A2
4 Mirador El Panecillo A2
5 Museo Alberto Mena Caamaño A2
6 Museo Casa de Sucre A2
7 Museo Casa Manuela Sáenz B2
8 Museo de la Ciudad A2
9 Palacio Arzobispal A1
10 Palacio de Gobierno A2
11 Parque La Alameda B1
12 Plaza de La Independencia A2
13 Plaza de San Francisco A2
14 Plaza de Santo Domingo B2
15 Plaza del Teatro Sucre B1

Churches and Cathedrals ♙

16 Iglesia de La Catedral
   (The Cathedral) A2
17 Iglesia de La Merced A2
18 Iglesia y Museo de Santo
   Domingo B2
19 La Basilica del Voto Nacional A1
20 La Compania A2
21 Monasterio de San Agustín B1
22 Monasterio de San Francisco B1

Eating 🍴

23 Café Mosaico B1
24 El Cafeto B1
25 Govindas A1
26 Hasta la Vuelta Señor A1
27 Heladería San Agustin A1
28 Mea Culpa A2
29 Pim's A2
30 Theatrum Restaurant B1
31 Tianguez Café A2
32 Vista Hermosa A1

Services ★

33 Banco de Pichincha A1
34 Farmacias SanaSana
   (Pharmacy) A2
35 Quito Turismo A2

Shopping 🛍

36 Tianguez Gift Shop A2

Sleeping 🛌

37 Casa Bambu B1
38 Casa Gangotena A2
39 Casa San Marcos B2
40 Chicago Hostel B1
41 Colonial House Quito B1
42 Hotel Boutique Plaza Sucre B2
43 Hotel Catedral Internacional A1
44 Hotel Internacional Plaza
   del Teatro A1
45 Hotel Plaza Grande A2
46 Hotel Real Audiencia A2
47 Hotel Revolution Quito B1
48 Hotel San Francisco de Quito A2
49 Hotel Viena Internacional B1
50 Patio Andaluz A1
51 The Secret Garden B1

Tours ♦

52 Los Coches de La Colonia:
   Horse-Drawn Carriage Tours A2

QUITO

Loved it? Loathed it? Write a review and help other travelers

Quito's historic center takes you back to the era of the Spanish Empire, with its beautiful colonial buildings and elaborate churches such as the Monasterio de San Francisco and the Compañia de Jesus. There are also several interesting museums in this area that house colonial and indigenous art, military memorabilia and relics that chart the country's checkered history from pre-Inca times to the present.

Los Coches de La Colonia: Horse-Drawn Carriage Tours

What better way to enjoy the colonial center of Quito than in the preferred method of transportation of a century ago, a horse and buggy! Quito's colonial founders would be surprised to hop into one of these carriages as soon as the MP3 player starts bumping, the headlights flick on and the high-tech brakes kick in. The tour is about 15 minutes long and runs from near the Plaza de la Independencia (Plaza Grande) to the Plaza de San Francisco and back. Go after dark when the cathedrals are lit up, traffic is less horrendous, and the cool breeze will require snuggling to stay warm! Ca. García Moreno, between Ca. Espejo and Sucre, Tel: 099-030 3216, Open Hours From: Monday-Wednesday 4 p.m.-10:30 p.m. Updated: Jan 24, 2013.

CITY PLAZAS, STREETS AND PARKS
Plaza Santo Domingo

Toward the south of the Centro Histórico, the wide open Plaza de Santo Domingo is dominated by the Iglesia de Santo Domingo on the southeastern edge. There is a statue of marshal Mariscal Sucre in the center, his arm outstretched to Volcán Pichincha where he led the winning battle for Ecuador's independence in 1822.

Being slightly out of the way of the main attractions in the neighborhood, many tourists miss the plaza altogether. This is a shame, as it's certainly worth at least a quick detour, especially on weekends when hundreds of quiteños congregate here to be entertained by storytellers, jugglers, acrobats and magicians (all of which are of dubious skill but unquestionable enthusiasm). They're free, but appreciate a donation.. Unfortunately this area is a prime target for muggers in the evenings. If you want to see the domes of the church lit up, it's advisable to go with a group of people or get a taxi to take you there and wait for you.

Plaza de la Independencia

As you wonder around the Centro Histórico, you'll probably find yourself walking into the majestic Plaza de la Independencia (Plaza Grande), at some point, even if you haven't been looking for it. The plaza is as much a local hangout as a tourist hot spot, and is always buzzing with life, regardless of the time or the weather. You could comfortably spend half a day here, exploring the attractions around the edges of the plaza. Take your time; there's a lot to see.

Among the plaza's attractions is the 19th century Iglesia de la Cathedral on the southwestern side; opposite the cathedral is the *Palacio Arzobispal* (Archbishop's Palace). The building on the northwestern side of the plaza, above the row of arched, hole-in-the-wall shops, is the *Palacio de Gobierno* (Presidential Palace). On the corner between the presidential palace and the cathedral is the Centro Cultural Metropolitano, and inside the cultural center is the Museo Alberto Meno Caamaño.

The changing of the guard happens twice daily at the palace: If you are in town on a Monday make sure to get to the plaza at 11 a.m. to see the impressive weekly military ceremony. On García Moreno, between Ca. Chile and Espejo. Updated: Jan 18, 2013.

Plaza San Francisco ♪

The cobbled Plaza de San Francisco is one of Quito's oldest and most impressive sights, including, as it does, views of the magnificently white Monastery of San Francisco and, in the distance, the towering peak of Volcán Pichincha.

The plaza is located on the site where the palace of the Inca ruler Atahualpa's son, Auqui Francisco Tupatauchi, once existed and was used for centuries by indigenous groups as a trading center, or tianguez. The current plaza and church, both of which you can visit, were constructed between 1536 and 1580. Built on a slight incline, the plaza also affords fine views over the rooftops of southern Quito, and you might find yourself passing an hour or two taking in the view and watching the ever present throng of strolling quiteño families, wide-eyed tourists, shoe-cleaning kids and thousands of pigeons. The Café Tianguez, in the northern corner of the square, is a good place to park yourself for people-watching, offering a comfortable seat and a good coffee. The café is expensive by Quito standards, but what you're really paying for is the location. Cuenca and Bolivar. Updated: Jan 18, 2013.

Plaza del Teatro Sucre

The Plaza del Teatro is a pleasant, low-key alternative to the bustling Plaza Grande, and serves as a hub for a wide array of theatrical and musical activities. On the south side stands Teatro Sucre, which was built between 1879 and 1887 and serves as Ecuador's national theater. It is the premiere performance center for acclaimed plays and operas. In the northeast corner is the more local and experimental Teatro de Variedades Ernesto Albán. Additionally, the comfortable and modern Café del Teatro hosts frequent musical performances, most notably jazz, and the coffee there is better than in most of Quito. Finally, culture lovers can enjoy the plaza's free outdoor concerts, including week-long jazz fests in April and September as well as religious music during holy weeks. A bronze statue of the deceased theatrical comic Ernesto Albán watches the action from his perch on one of the benches. Corner of Ca. Manabí and Guayaquil. Updated: Jan 18, 2013.

Parque La Alameda

Between Old Town and New Town, the small triangular Parque Alameda is the closest open space to the Centro Histórico, and therefore one of the busiest in the city. The grassy banks of the boating lake are particularly popular with picnicking families during the weekends, while other areas are taken up with various ball games and smooching teenage couples escaping their parents for the day. Scores of food vendors make their way around the park with carts of ice cream, hot dogs, candy floss and the likes, ensuring you don't go hungry.

In the middle of the park is the Quito Observatory, which is open to the public on weekdays and still houses a German telescope, reputedly once among the most advanced in the world. Although the park is fine during the day, it's unwise to hang around after dusk, when muggings are common. Ave. Gran Colombia and Luis Sordiro. Updated: Jan 18, 2013.

Calle La Ronda !

Parting from Calle Benalcázar, the downhill walk along Calle La Ronda is a short journey through a very significant representation of colonial life in Quito. The term ronda refers

QUITO

A Walking Tour of the Centro Histórico

The Centro Histórico is Quito's best neighborhood for exploration, but its collection of hilly little streets can be confusing to a first-time visitor. Here, however, is a simple walking tour of Quito's Centro Histórico that takes in most of the neighborhood's leading attractions. It begins at the Plaza del Teatro, easily accessibly by Trole, and ends at the Basilica del Voto Nacional.

Start at the Teatro Sucre and the lively Plaza del Teatro. Continue southwest along Calle Flores. At the intersection with Chile, theSan Agustín monastery will be to your right. Continue straight on Flores for five blocks until you reach the little-visited Plaza Santo Domingo and the Iglesia de Santo Domingo.

Continue up hill and west (your right, as you entered the plaza) on Simón Bolívar for three blocks, passing the Casa Museo María Augusta Urrutia, until you reach the Plaza San Francisco, with its impressive views and imposing Monasterio de San Francisco. From the eastern corner of the plaza, walk one block down Calle Sucre, then turn left on Calle García Moreno. On your left, you will find the breathtaking old Jesuit church- La Compañía.

Continue down Moreno and you reach the Plaza de la Independencia, Quito's main square. The Palacio del Gobierno is on your left, the city's cathedral is on your right, and the Archbishop's palace is across the plaza from you.

Cut diagonally across the plaza to Calle Venezuela, and keep walking north along Venezuela. After seven blocks, you will arrive at the Basilica del Voto Nacional, a massive neo-Gothic cathedral. After you've climbed to the top of the church, you can cross the park and walk down Calle Caldas to reach the Trole. Updated: Jan 18, 2013.

Loved it? Loathed it? Write a review and help other travelers

QUITO

to a small alleyway within the walls of a city, and although Quito was never walled, the street once marked the southern boundary of the city. In the 20th century, the neighborhood took on a bohemian flair as the street was the home and hang-out of artisans, painters, musicians and poets.

In recent years, La Ronda was infamous for its trash, crime and prostitution. In 2006, thanks to the help of the local government, represented by FONSAL (Fondo de Salvamiento del Patrimonio Cultural), and families in the area, the street was finally cleaned up and its colonial atmosphere restored. The original cobblestones are still intact, and the white-walled buildings feature wooden doors, balconies and hanging flower baskets. The narrow pedestrian-only lane is now home to small art galleries, candy and souvenir shops, and cafés and restaurants serving traditional food. There is often live music and street theater, particularly during citywide festivals. The best time to visit La Ronda is around sunset and in the evening, when the streetlights come on.

MUSEUMS AND MONUMENTS
Centro Cultural Metropolitano
(ADMISSION: FREE) The Centro Cultural Metropolitano is a great place to see colonial art and temporary modern art exhibitions on display throughout the building, which is a renovated colonial complex. The building also has a huge Spanish library comprised of literature, sciences and economics. One of the most appealing attractions of the building are the third-floor patios, which are perfect areas to people-watch in the Centro Histórico and to admire the architecture of the churches that surround the building. There is also a café on the first floor; and once a month, the Centro Cultural hosts an evening "inauguración" (art opening), which is free and open to the public (often with free drinks and hors d'ouvres). Ca. García Moreno and Espejo, Tel: 02-395-2300 ext 15502, URL: www.centrocultural-quito.com. Updated: Jan 22, 2013.

Museo Alberto Mena Caamaño
(ADMISSION: $1.50) Hidden up some stairs at the back of the Centro Cultural Metropolitano with no signs in sight, this museum can be tricky to find. Formerly known as the Antiguo Cuartel de la Real Audencia, thanks to its former function as a cuartel

(army barracks), the museum underwent a large-scale expansion and refurbishment in 2002 and was subsequently renamed after its biggest donor, Alberto Mena Caamaño. He bequeathed his impressive collection of painting and sculptures to the museum in the 1950s, most of which is colonial art from the 16th and 17th centuries, attributed to well-known artists from the Quito School, including Miguel de Santiago and Joaquín Pinto. However, there are several more modern works as well. Espejo Oe5-43 and García Moreno, Tel: 02-395-2300 ext 15535, URL: www.centrocultural-quito.com. Updated: Jan 22, 2013.

El Palacio Arzobispal (The Archbishop's Palace)
Opposite the cathedral in the Plaza Grande, the former Palacio Arzobispal (Archbishop's Palace) now houses a row of shops, ranging from delicatessens to clothing stores. During the last few years, the central courtyard of the palace—with its whitewashed walls and wooden balconies—has been converted into a food court offering everything from a quick burger to first class dining. One of Quito's most famous restaurants, Mea Culpa, overlooks the plaza from its first floor location, and is a great place for a splurge. On Friday evenings, locals pour into the courtyard to watch the free performances of dancing and singing. Ca. Chile and García Moreno. Updated: Jan 18, 2013.

Palacio del Gobierno
(ADMISSION: FREE) The building on the northwestern side of the plaza above the row of arched, hole-in-the-wall shops, is the Palacio del Gobierno (Presidential Palace), also called Carondelet. The palace is open to the public. The half-hour to 40 minutes tours take visitors into several lavishly decorated salons. Tours are given every 15 minutes. Queue up on Calle Espejo, across from the Centro Cultural Metropolitano. The mural by one of Ecuador's most famous artists, Guayasamin, in the stairwell illustrates Francisco de Orellana's celebrated descent of the Amazon. A placard on the García Moreno side marks the spot where President García Moreno was assassinated. It's also possible to see the presents that were given to President Rafael Correa in several cities and locations. Espejo and García Moreno, Plaza de Independencia (Plaza Grande), URL: www.presidencia.gob.ec. Updated: Jan 18, 2013.

Museo Casa de Sucre

(ADMISSION: $1) The Casa de Sucre, or Sucre residence, is a museum located in the old home of Mariscal José Antonio de Sucre, one of the greatest heroes of Ecuadorian independence. The ground floor houses an impressive array of weapons and military relics, some of which belonged to Sucre himself. The second floor has been restored to what it might have looked like in Sucre's time. Corner of Venezuela and Sucre, Tel: 02-295-2860.
Updated: Jan 08, 2013.

Museo Casa Manuela Sáenz

(ADMISSION: $4) Without a doubt, the most important woman in South America's Independence Wars was Manuela Sáenz. She is known by most as Libertador Simón Bolívar's confidant, but she was a military commander in her own right. The museum's 11 rooms recount the life of this Quiteña, from birth until her death in Paita, Perú. On exhibit are not only her items, but also those of Antonio Sucre and Bolívar. Museo Manuela Sáenz also displays a series of paintings by Adriana Méndez, dipicting the lives of Sáenz, Bolívar and Sucre. Junín Oe113 and Montúfar, Barrio San Marcos, Tel: 02-228-3908, Cel: 09-9873-7387.
Updated: Jan 08, 2013.

Casa del Abalado

(ADMISSION: $4) Casa del Abalado welcomes you to the worlds of the ancient peoples of Ecuador. On the first floor, explore the Underworld, that of the ancestors and death. The next floor takes you through the Middle World, where we mere mortals reside, and then into the Supramundo, learning about the shamans' spiritual life and the way of the elites. This private collection has excellently preserved pieces that rival those in the Museo Nacional. Touch-screen computers give detailed explanations on techniques and another room has videos on the major pre-Columbian cultures of the region. Casa del Alabado is in a restored 16th-century house. Cuenca 335 and Bolívar, Tel: 02-228-0940, URL: www.alabado.org.
Updated: Jan 08, 2013.

Mirador El Panecillo

El Panecillo—or to use the Inca name, Yavira—is a lush green hill visible from many different points in Quito. La Virgen del Panecillo, the winged virgin sitting atop the hill, is essentially the main religious symbol of Quito. As a result, when visiting the monument, guides tend to quote scriptures as opposed to emphasizing historical or structural facts. The view is incredible, especially on a clear day, so even if aren't interested in listening to a recital of Revelations 12, you will enjoy the trip. The best way to get there is by cab. From the Centro Histórico, you shouldn't pay much more than $5. Alternatively, you can arrange a tour that includes a trip to the Panecillo at any travel agency. The bus that goes up to the Panecillo is the same green bus you can take to Mitad del Mundo (but on the southern end of the loop, obviously). Be careful at the bottom of the hill and on the roads leading up the Panecillo as there have been many reports of muggings.
Updated: Jan 18, 2013.

Museo de la Ciudad

(ADMISSION: $3) Housed in a spacious and attractively restored old hospital building just east of Plaza de Santo Domingo, the Museo de la Ciudad is certainly worth a visit, and is a good starting point if you are new to Quito and unfamiliar with its history. Two floors of models, interactive displays and memorabilia—from horse-drawn carriages to 17th-century pots and pans—map out Quito's chequered past century by century in clear, unfussy displays. Beside each one is a written explanation in Spanish; if you don't read Spanish, a guided tour is recommended, and these are available in English, French, German, Italian and Spanish for an extra cost.

Another draw of the museum is the peaceful leafy courtyard around which it is built, offering a welcome respite from the bustle of Quito's city center, and fantastic views over southern Quito and of the Panecillo. The reasonably priced café looks onto the courtyard, and is open to the general public as well as to museum visitors. García Moreno S1-47 and Rocafuerte, Tel: 02-295-3643, ext.108, URL: www.museociudadquito.gob.ec.
Updated: Jan 08, 2013.

CHURCHES AND CATHEDRALS
Monasterio de San Francisco

(ADMISSION: $2) The bored-looking stone chap in the northern corner of the Plaza de San Francisco is Franciscan missionary Joedco Ricke, who set to work in the Monasterio de San Francisco soon after the foundation of Quito in 1534. It took him and his

QUITO

team 70 years to complete, but it remains Quito's largest colonial structure, though much of it has been destroyed and rebuilt over the years. However, its gold interior retains its grand and imposing feel and it's certainly worth a visit.

Some of the monastery's most precious and delicate relics have been re-housed in the Museo Franciscano. Much of the artwork on display dates back to the early 1600s, and the museum also houses one of the best collections of indigenous art in the city. The furniture, with its intricate detail and encrusted with pearls, is another highlight. The building is interesting too, with its long, sweeping corridors and hidden internal courtyards. The entrance to the museum is just to the right of the main monastery door. Ca. Cuenca 477 and Sucre, Plaza de San Francisco, Tel: 02-295-2911.
Updated: Jan 24, 2013.

Monasterio de San Agustín
(ADMISSION: $1) Constructed by Spanish architect Francisco Becerra in 1573 and then rebuilt after the earthquake in 1868, this beautifully designed church and monastery holds political and artistic significance to Ecuador. The nation's Declaration of Independence was signed here in on August 10, 1809, and the interior contains gigantic, gorgeous depictions of St. Augustine's life by painter Miguel de Santiago, famous in the Quitan school of art. Ornately designed altars and cloisters fill the multi-level building, including the main altar brought in from Rome. Of powerful significance is a golden crucifix by Olmos, an 18th-century Quiteno artist. Chile 924 and Guayaquil, Tel: 02-295-5525, URL: www.migueldesantiago.com/contacto.html.
Updated: Jan 08, 2013.

La Basílica del Voto Nacional !
(ADMISSION: $2) A relatively new addition to the Quito skyline, and now one of its most striking landmarks, is the del Voto Nacional, or simply "the Basilica." Consecrated in 1988 (though still technically unfinished), the church stands on a steep hill to the northeast of the Centro Histórico and can be seen from almost everywhere in the city, particularly at night when it is illuminated, beacon-like, in bright green and blue.

The highlight of a visit here is undoubtedly the climb up the tower, which offers several vantage points along the way. The first flight of stone stairs leads to a balcony where you can look down on the nave, its stone arches mottled in the bright colors of the stained glass windows. The second flight leads up to a southern viewpoint with a telescope, offering a close-up inspection of some of the old town's other landmarks, including the Virgin perched on the Panecillo opposite. From here you have to head down a tenuous-looking (though perfectly safe) causeway and exposed iron ladder to get to the top. If you can manage it, you will be rewarded with excellent views that, on a clear day, stretch for miles over both the new and old parts of the city—something even the Panecillo can't claim. Ca. Carchi 122 and Venezuela, Tel: 02-228-9428
Updated: Jan 24, 2013.

Iglesia y Museo de Santo Domingo
(ADMISSION: $2) The Iglesia de Santo Domingo may at first seem like one of those churches that is far more impressive from the outside. However, step into its dimly lit, moody interior and you'll find some surprising treasures; numerous paintings from the Quito School of Art hang in its side chapels, one of which also houses the church's showpiece: a statue of the Virgin de Rosario, a gift from King Charles V of Spain.

Unfortunately, the tower, which gives great views over Quito, is now unsafe to climb and will be closed for the foreseeable future until enough funds are raised to carry out the restoration work. Its museum is also worth a visit, housing an interesting collection of 16th and 17th century religious art around an intimate courtyard. The entrance is about 15 meters (49 ft) to the left of the main church door. Ca. Flores 150 and Bolívar, Plaza de Santo Domingo, Tel: 02-228-0518.
Updated: Jan 24, 2013.

La Compañía !
(ADMISSION: $3) Carved entirely out of volcanic stone, the ornate Baroque façade of this Jesuit church is probably the most exquisitely executed in Quito. From the arresting outside, walk inside and you'll be awed by the sculptured interior, shimmering beneath 120 pounds of fine gold leaf.

A stunning display of art and architecture, appointed with a community of cherubs, angels and saints, keeps the eyes busy as the feet shuffle between the skyward stretching Corinthian pillars, soaring arches and

QUITO

carefully decorated cornices. Jesuits began work on the church in 1605, but it wasn't complete until 1765 (a lucky coincidence considering the Spanish expelled the order just two years later). Today, some of the most important, and impressive artifacts to grace the interior are housed in the vaults of the Banco Central; one such piece is the stunning emerald-framed painting of the Virgin Dolorosa. García Moreno and Sucre, one block south of Plaza de la Independencía, Tel: 02-258-1895/4175, URL: www.fundacioniglesiadelacompania.org.ec. Updated: Jan 08, 2013.

Iglesia de La Merced

(ADMISSION: FREE) With its plain white exterior, handsome bell tower (the highest in colonial Quito) and tiled domes, the church of La Merced is a good example of the Moorish influences in Spanish architecture in the late 18th century, and is a pleasure to stumble upon while exploring the backstreets of the Centro Histórico.

The rather conservative-looking exterior, however, does little to prepare you for what is inside; a sea of pink and white plasterwork covering every surface provides the backdrop for surely some of the most imaginative and dramatic paintings in Quito, while bleeding, neon-lit Jesus statues occupy shiny gold-sided chapels around the edge. Not to everyone's taste, but certainly worth a look if you're passing by. Ca. Chile and Cuenca. Updated: Jan 24, 2013.

Iglesia de la Catedral
(The Cathedral)

(ADMISSION: $1.50) On the southwestern side of the Plaza de la Independencia (Plaza Grande) is the Iglesia de la Cathedral. It is unusual in Ecuador, in that it's refreshingly free of the top-to-toe decoration that adorns most churches, though it does feature several interesting paintings by artists of the Quito School.

Although it is considered relatively austere by Ecuadorian standards, the 16th-century cathedral is probably the most important church in Ecuador, and is the location for state funerals of the country's political and cultural heroes. It is here that Quito's liberator, Mariscal Sucre, is buried. Ca. Venezuela N3-117 and Espejo, Plaza de la Independencia, Tel: 02-257-0371. Updated: Jan 24, 2013.

Centro Histórico Lodging

Centro Histórico is what most people think of when they envision Quito. Every year, the neighborhood attracts thousands of tourists and locals to its narrow streets and lovely plazas. Centro Histórico hotels are rapidly being renovated and becoming more popular as Quito tries to re-establish the historical center as the main tourist hub but there is still work to be done. For now, most hotels are based in the newer parts of Quito. However, there are still options for travelers who want to stay in this neighborhood.

Since Centro Histórico is an older part of town, the hotels are often in colonial buildings, which are much more charming—but sometimes more rundown and weathered— than hotels and hostels in the newer parts of time. Several hotels are kept up very well though, so it's a good idea to ask to see the rooms before you decide. In fact, a few of the city's most luxurious accommodation options can be found here. The neighborhood is centrally located and there are plenty of buses and taxis, so getting around Quito from Centro Historico is fairly easy. Updated: Jan 22, 2013.

BUDGET
Casa Bambu !

(DORMS: $7, ROOMS: $25) Casa Bambu is one of Quito's best values with clean dorm rooms and shared rooms. This small hotel is full of character and homey touches. The lounges are spacious and have comfy couches, flowering plants, and a collection of books, games and DVDs for guests to use. Its several outdoor patios provide excellent views of Quito. We recommend you take a cab when you first arrive, as the hotel is located up a steep hill not conducive to luggage. It's just a block from several main bus lines, so transportation isn't a problem once you stash the heavy stuff. Casa Bambu also locations in Mindo and Canoa. Solano E527 and Av. Colombia (up a steep hill from the southernmost corner of Parque el Ejido), Tel: 02-222-6738, E-mail: hotelbambuecuador@hotmail.com, URL: www.hotelbambuecuador.com/pages/casaquito.html. Updated: Jan 08, 2013.

Hostel Revolution Quito

($8.50-25 per person) Hostel Revolution Quito is a cool backpacker hostel in the Old Town created by and for backpackers who want to socialize, take in the historical sights and culture, exchange info, and go out and have a great time. The hostel is located in a renovated colonial-type house with wooden floors and decorative plaster ceilings, and has a bar, lounge, shared kitchen and rooftop terrace with great views. It is within walking distance of most of the city's historical sites: colonial houses, plazas, museums, churches and monuments. Hostel Revolution can also help with arranging volunteering, Spanish lessons or work teaching English. Los Rios N13-11 and Julio Castro, Tel: 02-254-6458, E-mail: stay@hostelrevolutionquito.com, URL: www.hostelrevolutionquito.com. Updated: Jan 09, 2013.

Colonial House Quito

(ROOMS: $10-25) With a great location and affordable rooms, Colonial House Quito provides a comfortable base camp (that's over 200 years old) for getting around the city. If you're planning on exploring the country, it's also conveniently located between both major bus terminals to the North and South, costing about $10 to get to either one via taxi. Owners and volunteers that run place are friendly and helpful too, helping you with any questions you might have. Rooms are well maintained, and the courtyard provides a nice little common area for travelers to swap stories. Mind you, it's not located in the cleanest or most appealing of neighborhoods, and you shouldn't come expecting Western lodging given it'll only disappoint you with what it has to offer in comparison. Nevertheless, it's a great place for backpackers. Free Wi-Fi and computers are available, as well as tea and filtered water. You can also order a pretty good breakfast and drinks for an affordable price too, or simply make your own in their communal kitchen space. Olmedo 432 and Los Rios, Tel: 02-316-3350 / 09-951-6687, URL: http://www.colonialhousequito.com. Updated: Mar 11, 2013.

Chicago Hostel

($10-22 per person) Chicago Hostel is conveniently located in a traditional neighborhood called San Blas, on the border between the Old Town and La Mariscal. It is also well-connected by public transportation, so you can either walk or easily take a city bus to most of the major city sights. The hostel has a communal kitchen on a covered rooftop terrace, 24-hour hot water, lockers where you can stash your important stuff, and a friendly, bilingual staff. Private rooms also come with TVs with either local channels or DirecTV cable, depending on the type. There is also an on-site tour operator, laundry service and WiFi. Breakfast is included in the price and is served each morning on the rooftop terrace, which has a pretty view of Quito. Los Rios N11-142 and Briceño, San Blas, Tel: 02-228-1695, E-mail: chicagohostel_customerservice@live.com, URL: www.chicagohostalecuador.com. Updated: Jan 18, 2013.

Hotel Internacional Plaza del Teatro

($13-16 per person) This is a perfect serviceable hotel, ideally located for visiting Centro Histórico. The rooms, which all have private bathrooms and TVs, are clean and modern. Some have views over Plaza del Teatro. However, these tend to be quite noisy, so if you want quiet, ask for one in the back. The restaurant is open for breakfast and lunch. It has a very popular fixed lunch and is therefore packed between about noon and 2 p.m. Ca. Guayaquil 8-75 and Esmeraldas (corner), Tel: 02-295-9462, URL: www.hotelplazadelteatro.com/index.html. Updated: Jan 08, 2013.

The Secret Garden ♪

($11.75-40 per person) Set in a converted colonial building in Quito's Centro Historico district, the Secret Garden is a favorite among backpackers. It's main selling points are the stunning view over the colonial district from the roof terrace restaurant/bar, and the friendly, laid-back atmosphere. Dinner is a particularly sociable occasion; there is a set-menu option (always with a vegetarian alternative) and everyone eats together at a long table. The rooms are more expensive than other hostels in the area, but it's worth it for the incredibly comfortable mattresses and real duvets. Breakfast is served every morning on the terrace for an extra cost. There are also regular day trips to Cotopaxi from the hostel. Antepara E4-60 and Los Ríos, San Blas, Tel: 02-295-6704, Cel: 09-8149-1849, E-mail: hola@secretgardenquito.com, URL: www.secretgardenquito.com. Updated: Jan 08, 2013.

MID-RANGE
Hotel Viena Internacional

($24-76 per person) This hotel is popular with Ecuadorian and foreign visitors alike. Although it is set in an old, colonial building, the interior is modern and clean. Rooms are fairly standard and look out onto the central patio. Some, however, are quite dark. All have private bathrooms with new, fully functioning fittings. The hotel is centrally located and provides a good launching point for seeing the major sights of Quito's historic center. The staff is friendly and willing to answer any queries. Ca. Flores 600 and Chile (corner), Tel: 02-295-4860, Fax: 02-295-4633, E-mail: reservas@hotelvienaint.com, URL: www.hotelvienaint.com. Updated: Jan 09, 2013.

Hotel San Francisco de Quito

(ROOMS: $27-58) San Francisco de Quito offers simple, clean rooms in a very central part of the Old Town. Many sights are within easy walking distance. The hotel is located on the second and third floors of a pleasant inner courtyard. All rooms are equipped with private bathrooms, a telephone and television. Decorations are sparse, although the dark wood furniture is aesthetically pleasing. Rooms on the third floor are very quiet, with high ceilings, although you might consider bringing a sleeping mask given the skylights. Note also that hot water and water pressure can take a while to pass through the pipes on the upper level.

The price includes free internet and breakfast at the restaurant downstairs, including bread, tea or coffee, and eggs (fruit salad costs 1 dollar extra). The hotel has taken serious safety precautions; a guard monitors the entrance, and you must be buzzed in through a wrought-iron gate. However, since Quito can be dangerous, if arriving late, take a taxi and make sure the driver stops right outside the entrance and have him stay until someone lets you in. Sucre 217 y Guayaquil, Tel: 02228-7758, URL: www.sanfranciscodequito.com.ec. Updated: May 18, 2013.

The Secret Garden

Hotel Catedral Internacional

(ROOMS: $60-90) Apparently named due to its proximity to the cathedral, this hotel is on a busy street right in the center of the Centro Histórico. Its approximately 20 rooms are set around a leafy courtyard and all have private bathrooms and a TV. There is a good restaurant downstairs, which is open from 8 a.m. to 9:30 p.m. Breakfast is not included in the price. The hotel was refurbished a few years ago. Mejia OE6-36, between Cuenca and Benalcázar, Tel: 02-295-5438, E-mail: info@hotelcatedral.ec, URL: www.hotelcatedral.ec. Updated: Jan 8, 2013

Hotel Real Audiencia

(ROOMS: $45-118) Set just off the Plaza Santo Domingo, the Real Audiencia Hotel is filled with dusty but decent rooms. The highlight is the top-floor restaurant and bar with large windows looking out onto the Plaza. The hotel makes an effort to work with the city to protect the historic buildings, like itself, in the area. Discounts for Ecuadorians are available. Transportation can be arranged from the airport, just be sure to make arrangements with the hotel in advance. Bolívar Oe3-18 and Guayaquil, Tel: 02-295-2711/0590, Fax: 02-258-0213, E-mail: hotel@realaudiencia.com, URL: www.realaudiencia.com. Updated: Jan 23, 2013.

Hotel Boutique Plaza Sucre

(ROOMS: $50-150) The hotel is stylishly embedded in an 18th century building within walking distance of all the major hot spots (La Ronda, Plaza de la Independencia, El Panecillo) in Old Town. Safe and well kept, the hotel also hosts a number of eccentric yet charismatic Ecuadorian artwork throughout its halls. There is no café or restaurant in the hotel itself, but breakfast is still provided in the morning. The hotel also offers free wifi, computers as well as tea & coffee for their guests. The staff are very friendly and will be more than pleased to store your baggage before your check-in time; or, after your checkout time. Rooms come equipped with a safe, hairdryer, shampoo, conditioner, body lotion, soap and bottled water. Bathrooms had a shower, but no bath. Sucre Oe2-42, between Guayaquil and Flores, Tel: 02-295-4926/228-6633, E-mail: reservaciones@hotelplazasucre.com, URL: http://www.hotelplazasucre.com. Updated: Mar 05, 2013.

Loved it? Loathed it? Write a review and help other travelers

QUITO

QUITO

HIGH-END
Patio Andaluz ⚑

(ROOMS: $200-250) Patio Andaluz is located in the heart of the Centro Histórico in an over 400-year-old-house that was once owned by the first president of Ecuador, Juan José Flores. The hotel was renovated almost a decade ago but retains its classic colonial style. The rooms are beautiful, with hardwood floors and views onto the courtyard. You can play chess on handcrafted tables overlooking the courtyard, relax in the hammocks, read magazines and books in English and Spanish in the peaceful Guayasamin Lounge, or spend your free time in the sauna and fitness room in the back. Some guests have complained about the lack of ventilation, as the only windows in rooms look out onto the indoor courtyard. There is also an on-site restaurant and gift shop with local artisan crafts. Ask about package deals, which include all meals and tours around the Centro and to featured museums. Av. García Moreno N6-52, between Olmedo and Mejia, Tel: 02-228-0830, Fax: 02-228-8690, E-mail: info@hotelpatioandaluz.com, URL: www.hotelpatioandaluz.com.
Updated: Jan 09, 2013

Hotel Plaza Grande

(ROOMS: $500-2,000) Located in the heart of Quito's Old Town, Hotel Plaza Grande is surrounded by fascinating historical sights, including the Presidential Palace. This luxury hotel offers 15 suites including Royal, Plaza View and Presidential options. All rooms have air conditioning, VIP treatment and many additional premium amenities. Other services include 24-hour room service, spa and fitness facilities, and meeting facilities.

Fine dining is available at three restaurants as well as a variety of entertainment. If your budget can't accommodate these extravagances, show up with a smart appearance and a polite demeanor and the staff will be happy to invite you on a free tour of the elegant facilities. The fourth floor balcony offers an unbeatable view of the Plaza Grande below. Take a moment to absorb the hustle and bustle of the square, while a rose-filled fountain trickles gently beside you. To your right, you'll get a great view of the Presidential Palace. Ca. García Moreno N5-16 and Chile, Tel: 02-2-251-0777, Fax: 02-251-0800, E-mail: recepcion@plazagrandequito.com, URL: www.plazagrandequito.com.
Updated: Jan 09, 2013

Casa San Marcos

(ROOMS: $100-200) Casa San Marcos is an ornately decorated museum, gourmet restaurant, and botique hotel all rolled into one. Offering a quiet place to stay near the heart of the historical center (as well as a great view of El Panecillo), San Marcos will provide you with a warm welcome and rooms that follow suit. The owner too, is a delight to have around, treating travelers as if they were guests in her own home. Food is prepared exquisitely by the in-house chef Cathy, and served in the dining room with a wonderful view of the city. Junín E1-36 and Montúfar, Tel: 02-228-1811/02-257-2297, E-mail: casasanmarcosecuador@hotmail.com, URL: www.casasanmarcosquito.com. Updated: Mar 05, 2013.

Casa Gangotena

(ROOMS: $375-750) One of the highest ranked hotels in all of Quito, and undoubtedly so. This three-story mansion is a gem for the eye to behold, and a place where the rest of your senses will be pleased as well. Starting from the top-notch service that the hotel offers all the way to the exquisite meals they serve at their restaurant, you'll find that in many cases it's the attention to detail and the small things that make this place what it is. Incredibly comfortable atmosphere, amenities and beds as well as a delightful courtyard, library and incredible view of the Centro Historico from the rooftop terrace. This place will not disappoint, especially given the price! Bolivar Oe6-41 and Cuenca, Tel: 098-800-0100, E-mail: info@casagangotena.com, URL: www.casagangotena.com. Updated: Mar 05, 2013.

Centro Historico Restaurants

The Centro Histórico offers everything from elegant restaurants with traditional live music, dress codes and waiters in tuxedos, to small locally owned places that sell cheap fixed-price lunches for under $2. In the last few years, several international restaurants have opened, especially in the area around Plaza de la Independencia (Plaza Grande).

There are also quite a few fast food joints. La Ronda is lined with cafés and restaurants that sell canelazo (warm drink made with sugar cane alcohol, fruits and cinnamon), empanadas and other local specialties like *seco de chivo* and *guatita*.
Updated: Jan 18, 2013.

Theatrum Restaurant

(ENTREES: $14-20) Located on the second floor of the historic Teatro Nacional Sucre, the Theatrum Restaurant is a must-see while in the Centro Histórico. With its soaring ceilings and muted décor, it is a fancy atmosphere befitting an equally posh menu. With offerings such as baby Ecuadorian banana with warm chocolate soup and rabbit risotto, travelers are infused with a feeling of international cuisine made with Ecudorian ingredients.

Don't be afraid to splurge when it comes to Theatrum. The restaurant even offers free transportation when you make a lunch or dinner reservation online, so be sure to take advantage of this offer. Ca. Manabí, between Guayaquil and Flores, 2nd floor of Teatro Nacional Sucre, Tel: 02-257-1011/228-9669, E-mail: reservas@theatrum.com.ec, URL: www.theatrum.com.ec.
Updated: Jan 09, 2013.

Café Mosaico ¶

(ENTREES: $7-20) Ecuador goes international at this lively restaurant and café, perched high above the city, having one of the best restaurant views in Quito! Originally from New York, the owners clearly packed their stylish city instincts and gastronomical intuition. Café Mosaico offers an extensive menu, including sandwiches, salads, burgers, Ecuadorian specialties and Greek dishes.

The food is wide-ranged but overpriced and nothing to write home about. However, the amazing view is really the selling point here (and what you truly pay for), so it is still worthwhile to come for a meal, dessert, coffee or glass of wine. Manuel Samaniego N8-95 and Anteparra, Itchimbia, Tel: 02-254-2871, Fax: 593-2-254-2871, E-mail: cafe@cafemosaico.com.ec / julia_charpentier@hotmail.com, URL: www.cafemosaico.com.ec.
Updated: Jan 09, 2013.

Vista Hermosa

(ENTREES: $11-30) As its name suggests, Vista Hermosa's (Gorgeous View) biggest selling point is its spectacular 360-degree view of Quito from its romantic roof terrace. Located on the sixth floor of a colonial building, Vista Hermosa has a simple but slightly pricey menu featuring Ecuadorian plates, pizzas, and meat and seafood mains, in addition to a full bar list. Come and enjoy a bowl of locro de papas (traditional potato

soup topped with cheese and avocado), seco de chivo (goat stew), or corvina en salsa de mariscos (sea bass in seafood sauce) while gazing out over Centro Histórico's colonial building tops. Ca. Mejía 453 and García Moreno, Tel: 02-295-1401, E-mail: info@vistahermosa.com.ec, URL: http://vistahermosa.com.ec.
Updated: Jan 18, 2013.

Hasta la Vuelta Señor

(ENTREES: $8-15) Set in the Mediterranean courtyard of Edificio Arzobispal facing the cathedral in the Plaza de la Independencia. The location is ideal and the atmosphere is warm and inviting. Hasta la Vuelta feaures traditional Quiteño dishes.

You can definitely find a slightly less sanitary version of the same fare for a much cheaper price in dozens of cafes in this same area. The atmosphere is what makes this restaurant special. Calle Chile OE-422 and Venezuela, Palacio Arzobispal, third floor, Tel: 02-258-0887/5812, E-mail: reservas@hastalavuelta.com, URL: http://www.hastalavuelta.com.
Updated: Jun 07, 2013.

Mea Culpa

(ENTREES: $15-23) This lovely and spacious restaurant on the second floor of the Edificio Arzobispal on the northern side of the Plaza de la Independencia (Plaza Grande) has a wide selection of Mediterranean food, featuring seafood and an extensive tapas menu. Chile and Venezuela, Palacio Arzobispal, Plaza de Independencia, Tel: 02-295-1190, E-mail: reservaciones@meaculpa.com.ec, URL: www.meaculpa.com.ec.
Updated: Jan 09, 2013.

El Cafeto

(DRINKS: $2-6) This small and open-air café serves deliciously rich coffee, made from 100 percent organic Ecuadorian beans. In addition to buying coffee, take-home bags of coffee beans can be bought for a reasonable $8. Food is rather basic, with a small selection of breakfast, sandwiches and cake. Still, you're here for the genuinely delicious coffee, which is hard to come by in Quito. For a quiet escape, head up to the second-floor balcony, which offers people-watching views of the streets down below. Open Daily 8 a.m.-7:15 p.m. Located on Ca. Chile 930 and Flores, Tel: 02-257-2921, URL: www.elcafeto.com.
Updated: Jan 24, 2013.

QUITO

Loved it? Loathed it? Write a review and help other travelers

QUITO

Tianguez Café

(ENTREES: $8 and up) Set right in the Plaza de San Francisco, this is the perfect spot to try out some traditional Ecuadorian dishes in one of the most traditional colonial plazas in the Old Town. Its also a great place to relax, sip a cappuccino and people-watch. Try the *plato típico*, with *mote* (Andean white corn), *maduro frito* (fried plantain), *llapingacho* (a type of cheesy potato pancake), fresh avocado, lettuce and tomato, and your choice of chicken or *fritada* (fried pork bits). The restaurant—which is also connected to a small gift shop/museum in a cave-like structure underneath the church—is named after the Nahuatl word for market. Before the Spanish arrived, the plaza was used as a market for tribes from all over Ecuador. When the Spanish constructed the church between 1536 and 1580 over the ruins of an Inca palace, the market continued for centuries more. Today, besides the items for sale at the Tianguez Café and gift shop, pretty much only wares for purchase are shoe shines and newspapers. Plaza de San Francisco, under the San Francisco Monastery, Tel: 02-257-0233, E-mail: tianguez_reservas@hotmail.com / administracion@sinchisacha.org, URL: www.tianguez.org.
Updated: Jan 09, 2013.

Govindas

(Set Lunch: $2.50) Vegetarians can get inexpensive meals at Govindas, located within the Hare Krishna's Academia Vaisnava in Quito's colonial center. At this restaurant, meals are presented cafeteria-style, with a choice of the day's well-seasoned offerings, including brown rice. The three-course meal includes soup, main dish, with plenty of sides and dessert, as well as tea or a fresh juice. Dining is in the main front room, or the small courtyard in back. Academia Vaisnava also has evening classes in vegetarian cooking, yoga and other topics, and a bakery-shop. Esmeraldas Oe3-119 and Venezuela, Tel: 02-295-7849.
Updated: Jan 09, 2013.

Heladería San Agustin

Featuring the delicious helados de paila, ceviche, traditional food and pastries, the Heladería San Agustín has been making the same excellent dishes for an unbelievable 140 plus years and has never used preservatives or artificial coloring! You can't leave without trying the helado de paila (ice cream that tastes more like sorbet). The owner is almost always on-site and will happily recommend her favorite dishes, or tell you some of Quito's history, as seen from the doorway of this classic café. Ca. Guayaquil N5-59 and Mejía, Tel: 02-228-5082, Cel: 09-8351-4580, E-mail: heladeriasanagustin@yahoo.com.

Pim's

(ENTREES: $17-25) Pim's provides an elegant view of the city from the inside and out. Despite its spacious two-level dining area inside and plenty of outdoor seating with space heaters, reservations are highly recommended, especially for weekends. With an extensive menu that starts with a page of Quichua vocab translated into Spanish and English, you may be surprised that the most recommended dish is the hamburger! There are five different steak preparations, seafood, pork, salads and a few traditional dishes. On Sundays there is only an all-day buffet for a set price. Gral. Aymerich, Top of El Panecillo *or* Parque Itchimbía Palacio de Cristal, Calle Iquique, Tel: 02-317-0878, E-mail: reservacionespanecillo@grupopims.com, URL: www.grupopims.com.
Updated: Jan 09, 2013.

Centro Historico Nightlife

La Ronda ⚡

As nightfall creeps over the city, La Ronda lights up its cobblestone alleyway with live music, bubbling vats of canelazo, freshly-made empanadas, and crowds of people. Along it's narrow, white-walled path are a number of bars and restaurants that open their doors to tourists and quiteño's alike. With a wide variety of cuisine offerings, ambiance and invigorating spirits, La Ronda serves up an overwhelming palette of choices. Ultimately, it is up to the traveler that wanders down its alleyway to discover where to go and what to choose from; and trust us, there's plenty to pick from. Starting on Benalcázar and Calle Morales, La Ronda crosses Venezuela and Guayaquil and ends at Maldonado.

Photo by: Carlos A. Galindo

La Mariscal

The Mariscal neighborhood of Quito, or "Gringolandia" as it has come to be known, is the main tourist hub of Quito. It runs from Parque El Ejido in the south up to Avenida Orellana in the north, and is centered around the roads Juan Leon Mera and Reina Victoria. Most of Quito's budget hostels are located here; as well as every tourist service you could possibly want and a wide array of international and local cuisine to savor.

For the tech-savvy travelers, Mariscal has many Internet cafés offering speedy connections and Skype. The neighborhood also offers other basic services like banks, laundromats and mini-marts. Most<bold>Quito travel agencies also have their offices in Mariscal, so it's a good place to find a tour, whether you're looking for an international or domestic flight from Quito, a Galápagos cruise, an Amazon lodge stay or an Andean hiking adventure. Quality and prices vary a lot, so be sure to shop around before making any final decision.

In La Mariscal, you will also find the city's best selection of international restaurants and nightlife, all concentrated within a few blocks. It is a good place to meet up with friends and hop around from place to place. The Mariscal is also home to some of the best artisan markets in Quito: one that is near Parque El Ejido, one that is on Jorge Washington between Juan León Mera and Reina Victora, and one that takes place in Plaza Foch on Saturdays.
Updated: Mar 13, 2013

La Mariscal Services

While other areas of Quito, such as Centro Histórico and the New Town, offer many services -- supermarkets, laundry, internet and banking -- La Mariscal has the most concentrated and easiest to access number of resources.

While these services may cost a bit more (they're used to foreigners arriving with a different concept of what qualifies as 'expensive'), the convenience is tough to beat. There are laundry and wireless internet services in many hostels (ask when you book a room), though it's also easy to find cafes or laundry services on various Mariscal streets (look anywhere around the plaza at Reina Victoria and Foch).

As far as supermarkets go, La Mariscal has an abundance of small corner stores (tiendas), usually found near/along Juan Leon Mera and José Calama. If you're in need of a fully stocked supermarket, just walk several blocks up Lizardo Garcia (east of 6 de Diciembre) to 12 de Octubre and you can't miss the large red and white sign indicating Supermaxi, which is Quito's main and biggest grocery chain.
Updated: Mar 11, 2013.

MONEY
Banks open from 9a.m. to 5pm. and remain closed on weekends.

ATM
On Reina Victoria (between Calama and Foch)

Banco de Guayaquil
Av. Amazonas N22-147 and Veintimlla

Banco del Pacifico
Av. Amazonas, between Carrion and Veintimilla

Producambios
Ave. Amazonas 350 and Vicente Ramon Roca

Western Union
Mariscal Foch and Colon (with DHL)

Casas de cambio specifically deal with international money, so if you didn't manage to change what you needed to at the airport (or gotten enough cash via machine) you can find a couple around the neighborhood (search down Amazonas).

KEEPING IN TOUCH
Internet Cafes are ubiquitous in the Mariscal, and you can find a couple on every other block; specifically along Amazonas Ave. Although they all charge under $2 an hour, the quality of the hardware and connection speed vary from place to place. If you find one cafe that doesn't offer satisfactory service, there is probably an alternative right down the street.

DHL Express
Colon 1333, between Amazonas and Foch, Tel: 1-800-345-345, URL: http://www.dhl.com.ec/en.html, Open Hours From: 8:30a.m., Open Hours To: 7:00p.m, Day Closed: Sundays.

Loved it? Loathed it? Write a review and help other travelers

QUITO

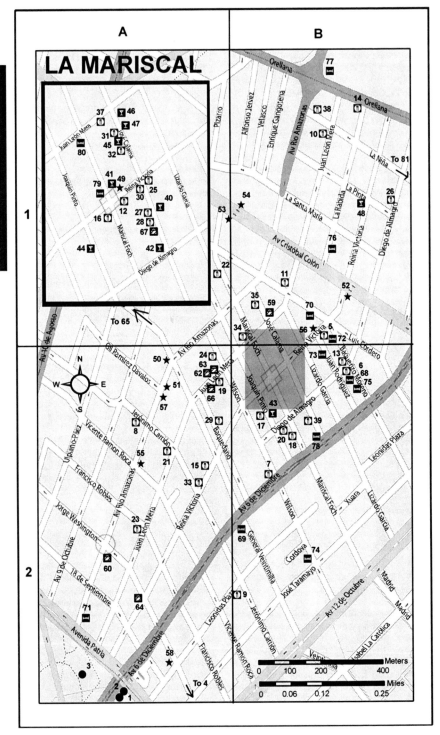

Activities ●

1 Casa De La Cultura A2
2 Museo Nacional A2
3 Parque El Ejido A2
4 Rocódromo A2

Eating 🍴

5 Achiote B1
6 Aladdin (See Insetmap)
7 Balbeek B2
8 C.A.C.T.U.S. A2
9 Café Libro B2
10 Cevichería Marisquería
   Los Siete Mares B1
11 Chandani Tandoori B1
12 Coffee Tam Plaza
   Foch (See Insetmap)
13 Cosa Nostra B2
14 Crepes and Waffles B1
15 El Arabe A2
16 El Español (See Insetmap)
17 El Maple B2
18 El Rincón del Gaucho B2
19 Este Café A2
20 Finn McCool's B2
21 Formosa A1
22 Fried Bananas A1
23 Fuji Sushi A2
24 Kallari A2
25 La Boca del Lobo (See Insetmap)
26 La Bodeguita de Cuba B1
27 La Canoa Manabita (See Insetmap)
28 La Creperie (See Insetmap)
29 Le Arcate A2
30 Mama Clorinda (See Insetmap)
31 Mongo (See Insetmap)
32 Mulligan's B1 (See Insetmap)
33 Punto Cubano A2
34 Red Hot Chili Peppers B1
35 The Great India Restaurant B1
36 The Magic Bean (See 80)
37 Tomato Pizza Bar Restaurante B1
38 Turtle's Head B1
39 Uncle Ho's B2

Nightlife 🍸

40 Aguijón (See Insetmap)
41 Azuca (See Insetmap)
42 Bungalow 6 (See Insetmap)
43 Cherusker B2
44 Dirty Sanchez B2
45 Fragola Fusion
   Hookah Lounge
   (See Insetmap)
46 No Bar (See Insetmap)

Services ★

49 ATM (See Insetmap)
50 Banco de Guayaquil A2
51 Banco del Pacifico A2
52 Correos Del Ecuador B1
53 DHL Express &
   Western Union A1
54 Pharmacy's B1
55 Producambios A2
56 Quito Turismo B1
57 Sana Sana (Farmacy) A2
58 South American
   Explorers Club A2

Shopping 🛍

59 Confederate Bookstore B1
60 Espiral Shopping A2
61 Galería Ecuador Gourmet (See 56)
62 Galería Latina A2
63 Libri Mundi A2
64 Mercado Artesanal
   de La Mariscal A2
65 Santa Clara Market A1
66 Tatoo Adventure Gear A2
67 The English
   Bookshop (See Insetmap)

Sleeping 🛏

68 Antinea Apart-Hotel B2
69 Casa Helbling B2
70 El Cafecito B1
71 Hilton Colón Ecuador A2
72 Hostal Arco del Sol B1
73 Hostal Backpackers' Inn B2
74 Hostal Fuente de Piedra I B2
75 Hostal Posada Del Maple B2
76 Hotel La Rábida B1
77 JW Marriott Hotel Quito B1
78 La Casa Sol B2
79 Nü House B2
80 The Magic Bean
   Hotel (See Insetmap)
81 Vieja Cuba B1

QUITO

Loved it? Loathed it? Write a review and help other travelers

Correos Del Ecuador

Ecuador's Official Postal Service that's actually quite reliable in sending mail and/or packages in and around the country, as well as internationally (United States, Canada, Australia, Brazil). Colon and Reina Victoria, Torres almagro, Tel: 02-250-8980, URL: www.correosdelecuador.com.ec/index.htm, Open Hours From: 8:00 a.m. to 6:00 p.m. Updated: Mar 11, 2013.

MEDICAL

Pharmacy's

Av Colon 1310 y Foch, Tel: 02-222-2278, URL: http://www.pharmacys.com.ec, Open Hours From: 8:00a.m. to 9:00p.m. Updated: Mar 11, 2013.

TOURISM

The South American Explorers Club

The Quito branch of the South American Explorers' Club is a lively hub. It has a lot to offer to both travelers and ex-pats, and is a great place to meet people. For travelers, the club is an excellent source for maps, guidebooks and general up-to-date safety and travel information.

Regular weeknight events include pub quizzes, Spanish and cooking classes. The club also regularly organizes good-value beach or hiking excursions. Club members get discounts on all of this, plus cheaper deals in many bars, restaurants and tour agencies in Ecuador. Jorge Washington E8-64 and Leonidas Plaza, Tel: 02-222-5228, E-mail: quitoclub@saexplorers.org, URL: www.saexplorers.org. Updated: Mar 08, 2013.

Quito Turismo

For information about Quito and Ecuador in general, the knowledgeable and friendly staff here at Galeria Ecuador Gourmet will be sure to help you out. They offer anything from tour bus tickets to maps of the city. Reina Victoria and Cordero, Tel: 02-255-1566. Mar 08, 2013.

Shopping in La Mariscal

Shopping-wise, La Mariscal has a number of arts and craft stores scattered throughout its streets that are worth dropping into, if only to see what sort of nifty things are on sale. Otherwise, the spiraled shopping mall down Amazonas Ave. will provide you with an array of stores inside.

The English Bookshop

The English Bookstore has been in Quito since 2005. It's collection is only second to Confederate Books, and its prices are much more reasonable. It is easy to find a book for $5.50 here. The bookstore also has a four-shelf selection of what the owner considers the best books in the store. These books can be rented for $5 for two weeks, which is a great bargain, considering that many of these books cost upwards of $15. The bookstore also has some great non-fiction books on South America that are available. José Calama, close to Diego de Almagro.

Galería Ecuador Gourmet

A mix of modern and quaint, the two-story Galería Ecuador offers travelers a ritzy store and cafe to come peruse its goods and aromas. Ranging from clothing to arts and crafts, the gallery here pridefully displays it's country's fruits of labor and imagination. From sampling spirits and coffee to perusing an entire room filled with photography books about Ecuador, the store has a draw that most tourists won't be able to resist.

Prices for clothes and items here are a lot steeper than the ones at the Mercado Artesanal, but for a special reason - nearly all of the items here are brand-name and of a higher quality. Reina Victoria N24-263 and Lizardo García, Tel: 02-223-9469, URL: http://www.galeriaecuador.com. Updated: Apr 04, 2013.

Galería Latina ⟨

Sporting what is probably the finest collection of arts and hand-made crafts throughout Quito, it is here that you'll find a beautiful array of high quality pieces from across Latin America. Most of it comes at a hefty price however, so do bring a large wallet if you're interested in acquiring the wonderful items that it has to offer. Juan León Mera N23-69 (833) and Veintimilla, Tel: 02-254-0380, URL: www.galerialatina-quito.com. Updated: Mar 11, 2013.

Libri Mundi

Established in 1971, Libri Mundi is a popular bookstore chain with a number of stores in and around Quito, and also in Cuenca and Guayaquil. They stock a wide variety of books but for the traveler, the most important thing is that they sell English-language books, including novels. Libri Mundi stocks some of the best quality reads, from art history to mystery and biographies to Ecuadorian literature. Not least, they sell guidebooks, and V!VA is proud to partner, so you can buy your V!VA guide here! Juan León Mera N23-83 y Wilson, Tel: (593-2) 252-1606, 223-4791, 252-9587. Updated: Mar 08, 2013.

Mercado Artesanal de La Mariscal

Mercado Artesanal is a small and bustling market full of artisan handiwork, which is located on Calle Reina Victoria (on the edge of La Mariscal) and close to Parque El Ejido. The market is home to permanent stalls that sell Ecuadorian hand-knit goods, wood carvings, silver, jewelry and native musical instruments, among other items.

The Mercado Artesanal de La Mariscal is a significantly smaller version of the famed indigenous market in Otavalo, but you can find most everything here that you would there, without having to make the 3.5-hour journey. All things can, and should, be bartered for, whether you're looking for souvenirs or an addition to your alpaca sweater collection. Jorge Washington, between Juan León Mera and Reina Victoria. Updated: Jan 21, 2013.

Confederate Bookstore

An American second-hand bookstore that has been in Quito for over 18 years. It has a great selection to choose from, especially in classics, mystery and science fiction. Used books usually cost anywhere from $7-15. It probably has the best English selection in Quito, but don't browse too long, or the owner may kick you out for not buying anything. Corner of Juan Léon Mera and Calama, Tel: 02-252-7890. Updated: Jan 18, 2013.

Tatoo Adventure Gear

Tatoo Adventure Gear is a top source for brand-name sportswear, trekking and camping equipment, biking accessories and lots more. The Tatoo Mariscal outlet stocks guidebooks and maps, and the knowledgeable staff provides information on mountaineering courses and seminars, and offers tips on everything from the best routes to climb to buying the perfect hiking boot. Be sure to ask about second-hand gear if you'd like something on the cheap. Juan León Mera N23-54 and Wilson, Tel: 02-290-4533/3983, URL: www.tatoo.ws. Updated: Jan 09, 2013.

Andes 6000

This store is conveniently located for travelers in the Mariscal part of Quito. The store is fairly small, but reasonably well stocked with outdoorsy products, such as clothing, knives, cooking equipment, head lamps and more. Good quality rain gear can also be bought here. Since the store is a bit small, the range of sizes available may also not be that large at times. The staff is generally friendly and knowledgeable, able to give decent advice on the purchase that you should make. Ventimilla and Juan Leon Mera, Tel: 02-254-0861, URL: http://www.andes6000.com. Updated: Mar 08, 2013.

Santa Clara Market

A few blocks east of the bustling center of La Mariscal, Santa Clara market is just as much a cultural experience as a place to pick up cheap groceries. Here locals sell mounds of fresh fruits and veggies, herbs, flowers, meats, cheeses and seafood, making it a great place to buy ingredients for the week. On the bottom floor there are also a bunch of small fresh fruit stands and restaurants selling local specialties like *hornado* (roasted pork), *fritada* (fried pork), *llapingachos* (potato pancakes topped with a fried egg), fish soups and *seco de chivo* (goat stew); don't be alarmed if you see full roasted pigs staring back at you.

As with other Ecuadorian markets, all the products are local so don't expect to see imported items here; you can head diagonally across the street to Santa María grocery store for those. It is best to buy as much as you can at one stall instead of buying one or two things at each so that you can barter a better price. Ca. Versalles, between Ramírez Dávalos and Marchena. Updated: Jan 22, 2013.

Espiral Shopping

Spiraling upwards inside this large structure are a number of stores and services (163 in total) that offer a variety of goods - some even pirated! - for a relatively cheap price. It's also an interesting relic to behold, given that it was one of Quito's first ever shopping centers to be built in 1980. As always is the case with crowded and commercial places such as this - be sure to keep an eye on your belongings at all times. Amazonas and Jorge Washington, Tel: 02-256-6221, URL: http://elespiral.net/home.html. Updated: Mar 11, 2012.

Loved it? Loathed it? Write a review and help other travelers

QUITO

Things To See and Do in La Mariscal

Parque El Ejido

On the southern edge of the Mariscal, the big, grassy Parque El Ejido is fairly empty on weekdays, but fills up at weekends with whole extended families and their lunches—though with the scores of footballing youths that also frequent the park, it can't make for very relaxing picnicking. Most tourists come for the Saturday and Sunday handicrafts market, which stretches around the semicircular path at the northern end of the park. It has a good selection of stuff, with vendors from all over the country coming to sell their wares. Prices are slightly higher here than in the larger markets such as Otavalo, but lower than in the shops and other markets in Quito during the week. Make sure to check out the local art that lines the park on Sundays. 6 de Diciembre. Bounded by Avenida Patria, Avenida 6 de Diciembre, Avenida 10 de Agosto and Avenida Tarqui.

Casa De La Cultura

Other than the impressive museum it holds, the Casa de la Cultura has a cinema, various theaters, the Eugenio Espejo national library, a few auditoriums, and a grassy field that usually is a popular spot for schoolchildren to play soccer. The building is dated and is not in the best condition, but the field is a good place to relax on a sunny day. The original Casa de la Cultura, built in 1946, is worth visiting for the murals on its walls by Oswaldo Guayasamín. Av. 6 de Diciembre N16-224 and Av. Patria, Tel: 02-290-2272/252-5679/222-3392, E-mail: info@cce.org.ec, URL: http://cce.org.ec. Updated: Jan 09, 2013.

Museo Nacional

(ADMISSION: Free) If you only visit one museum in Ecuador, make it this one. Even if you're not an avid museum visitor, it's easy to spend an hour or two getting lost in the maze of exhibits, from ancient artifacts to contemporary paintings. There are five main sections in the museum: Perhaps the best known is the Sala Arqueología, which features artifacts from all over the country stretching back to pre-Columbian times. Some of the home exhibits taken from ancient tribes—tools, decorated plates and furniture, etc.—are particularly interesting if you have visited or plan to visit any of Ecuador's indigenous communities, where they still use similar objects and imagery today.

Other areas are the Sala de Oro, which has a good collection of gold objects from before colonization, The Sala de Arte Colonial, the Sala de Arte Republicano and the Sala de Arte Contemporáneo, each with a good cross-section of work from it's respective period. All five areas are very well laid out, with explanations in English and Spanish alongside each display. Av. Patria, between Av. 6 de Diciembre and Av. 12 de Octubre., Tel: 02-222-3258, URL: www.museos-ecuador.gob.ec. Updated: Jan 09, 2013

Rocódromo

(ADMISSION: $5) The impressive Rocódromo climbing complex (Complejo de Escalada Ciudad de Quito) is near the southeast edge of the Mariscal, across from Coliseo Rumiñahui. The main 25-meter-high (82-ft) brown climbing structure has climbing routes on three faces; two of the faces feature overhangs and have very challenging routes (lead routes are class 5.7-5.11).

In addition, there's a fortress-like natural rock wall, topped with metal poles for anchoring, as well as an indoor climbing gym and bouldering area. You can rent harnesses, carabiners, ropes, shoes and chalk, just be sure to bring someone to belay! Calle Queseras del Medio, near La Catolica University, Tel: 02-250-8463. Updated: Jan 22, 2013.

La Mariscal Lodging

Backpacker's take note: La Mariscal is the place to stay. The so-called Gringolandia of Quito is loud and energized, chock-full of bars and clubs, international restaurants and cafés, Internet hot spots, and plenty of laundry service options. This is undoubtedly the hub for most gringos, as anything you may need can be found within a few-block radius.

Mariscal hostels are some of the cheapest in the city, but the area is worth checking out for its mid-range hotels and upscale spots as well. One of the setbacks of staying in this neighborhood is its questionable safety, but if you are smart and aware of your surroundings and belongings, especially at night, you should be fine.

La Mariscal has a lot to offer in many ways, but the benefits come with some shady characters every once in a while. Updated: Jan 12, 2013

BUDGET
El Cafecito ♪

(ROOMS: $7-22) With two popular locations (Cuenca being the other) Hostal Cafecito is a good place to crash in Quito. The hostel is Canadian-owned with rooms upstairs and a candlelit café and restaurant downstairs, making it a great spot to meet other travelers and locals.

El Cafecito offers a 24-hour reception, luggage storage and an international book exchange. Definitely a trendy choice, it's not known to disappoint.Luis Cordero E6-43 and Reina Victoria, Tel: 02-223-4862, E-mail: quito@cafecito.net, URL: www.cafecito.net. Updated: Feb 28, 2013.

Hostal Backpackers' Inn

(ROOMS: $7-24) This charming little hostel is located right in the heart of the bustling Mariscal, still manages to be quiet. It is clean and has comfortable beds. The well-equipped kitchen is for communal use and is one of the better ones you will find among hostels in Quito. Juan Rodriguez 748 and Diego de Almagro, La Mariscal, Tel: 02-250-9669, E-mail: info@backpackersinn.net, URL: www.backpackersinn.net. Updated: Jan 09, 2013.

Hostal Posada Del Maple

(ROOMS: $20-36) Located alongside busy streets, this hostel is a dream for every tired traveler: clean, nicely decorated rooms, hot water, helpful staff, and a cozy/inviting atmosphere. It has a common room with cable TV, a mini-library to exchange books, a garden to chill-out, a well-equipped kitchen, and a living room with a fireplace. Additionally it provides Internet access, telephone boxes, a safety box and free luggage storage for those heading out for a couple of days. For security, the front door is always locked.

The staff is extremely friendly and will help you out whenever it can. Because the hostel is quite popular among travelers, it's best to try to arrange a room in advance. The hostel regularly offers discounts during the off season (March, April and May) and for students, SAE members and longer stays; be sure to ask when making a reservation. The hostal is located on Juan Rodriguez E8 - 49 and 6 de Diciembre, Tel: 02-290-7367, Fax: 02-290-6367, E-mail: admin@posadadelmaple.com, URL: www.posadadelmaple.com. Updated: Jan 09, 2013.

The Magic Bean Hotel

(ROOMS: $14.50-30) This hostel is not the best value in town, but dorm rooms (which sleep three or four people) are clean, the beds are comfortable, and there are big lockers in each room for you to store your stuff. There's also a great American-style restaurant/café below, which sometimes hosts live music. The central location is convenient for the Mariscal's best bars, clubs and restaurants—though it can get a bit noisy at night when music from numerous locations filters through the windows until well into the early hours. Mariscal Foch E5-08 and Juan Leon Mera, Tel: 02-256-6181/290-6105, E-mail: info@magicbeanquito.com, URL: www.magicbeanquito.com.

Casa Helbling

(ROOMS: $9-30) Popular with German and Swiss guests but warmly welcoming all worldly travelers, La Casa Helbling is a spacious home offering a variety of bright rooms, each with its own name, color and character. Single, double and triple rooms come with either private or shared bathrooms. The shared bath is a bit out of the way, so it may be worth your while to pay the extra few dollars for your own. Additionally, the inn will store your luggage and keep your valuables safe in a deposit box. All guests have access to cooking facilities, the internet and book exchanges. This is an affordable and comfortable bed and breakfast just steps from the Ecovia and the heart of La Mariscal. General Veintimilla E8-152 and 6 de Diciembre, Tel: 02-256-5740 / 222-6013, E-mail: reservierung@casahelbling.de, URL: www.casahelbling.de. Updated: Mar 07, 2013.

MID-RANGE
La Casa Sol ♪

(ROOMS: $39-99) A quaint, homey hostel on a side street away from most of the noise of the Mariscal, La Casa Sol has comfortable rooms, a couple of cozy sitting areas, a book exchange, a fireplace and a peaceful central courtyard. With a strong emphasis on native culture, decorations create a uniquely Ecuadorian atmosphere. Cultural events the last Friday of every month add to this. The 24-hour café boasts that it has some of the best coffee in Ecuador. Calama 127 and Av. 6 de Diciembre, Tel: 02-223-0798, Fax: 02-222-3383, E-mail: info@lacasasol.com, URL: www.lacasasol.com. Updated: April 06, 2013.

QUITO

Loved it? Loathed it? Write a review and help other travelers

QUITO

Antinea Apart-Hotel ♪

(ROOMS: $42-134) Declared a cultural heritage site, this charming and unique French hotel is located in the very heart of Quito. Antinea offers spacious rooms, suites and furnished apartments, all decorated with good taste and class, making it a popular home away from home for leisure and business travelers alike. Antinea is located close to the city's best restaurants, bars, and shops, and is situated only 15 minutes from both Quito's historic center and the airport. All rooms have WiFi access. Ask about their extended stay and/or corporate discounts. Juan Rodríguez E8-20 and Diego de Almagro, Tel: 02-250-6838, Fax: 02-250-4404, E-mail: info@hotelantinea.com, URL: www.hotelantinea.com.
Updated: Jan 09, 2013.

Antinea Hotel

Hostal Arco del Sol

(ROOMS: $18-40) Cozy and comfortable, Hostal Arco del Sol is an ideal place for weary travelers to rest their tired heads. Rooms are tidy and pleasant and—except for the dorm—come with a private bathroom and cable TV. Breakfast is included in the price, and visitors are welcome to use the hostel's well-equipped kitchen. Hostal Arco del Sol also offers a variety of helpful services, including daily bilingual tours to local points of interest, transfer to the airport, laundry service, and free Internet. Group student discounts are available. Juan Rodríguez 7-36 and Reina Victoria, Tel: 02-223-7755, E-mail: info@hostalarcodelsol.com, URL: www.hostalarcodelsol.com.
Updated: Jan 09, 2013.

HIGH-END

Hostal Fuente de Piedra I

(ROOMS: $57-81) Hostal Fuente de Piedra looks more like a luxury hotel than a hostel, with its efficient 24-hour reception and cozy but comfortable rooms for two. The en-suite bathrooms are sparkling clean, while the restaurant welcomes guests for traditional Ecuadorian fare served at polished wooden tables. Although a bit pricey, the cost includes breakfast, and trips can be arranged to a jungle lodge along the Napo River and to Otavalo's El Hotel Coraza, both also owned by Ecuahotel. Hot water is available all day, every day, and visitors can take advantage of the laundry service, a multilingual book exchange and a free Internet facility. A mostly European and North American clientele has left favorable comments in the guestbook. Wilson E9-80 and Tamayo, Tel: 02-252-5314, Fax: 02-255-9775, E-mail: fuente1@ ecuahotel.com / ecuahotel@ecuahotel.com, URL: www.ecuahotel.com.
Updated: Jan 09, 2013.

Nü House

(ROOMS: $95-189) The swankiest of newcomers in the area, walking into this boutique hotel makes you feel like you could be in a trendy high-class hotel anywhere in the world. Shiny elevators take you to rooms and suites with modern red and white décor, flat-screen TVs and mini-bars. This place screams posh down to the fancy shampoos and loofahs in marble-tiled bathrooms. If this is your style, you might also check out its sister restaurant and club, Q Café to the right toward Foch Plaza, and The Loft to the left. All three are owned by the same, and guests of the hotel receive a 10 percent discount at the others. Mariscal Foch E6-12 and Reina Victoria, Tel: 02-255-7845, E-mail: reservas@nuhousehotels.com, URL: www.nuhousehotels.com.
Updated: Jan 09, 2013.

Vieja Cuba

(ROOMS: $55-107) Vieja Cuba is full of character and class, and its rooms are spotless and sunny. Conveniently located in a corner house in La Mariscal, each room is slightly different, with personality oozing from every corner. The owners are an Ecuadorian/ Cuban couple who also own the Cuban restaurant downstairs. La Niña N26-202 and Diego de Almagro, Tel: 02-290-6729, Fax: 02-252-0738, E-mail: info@hotelviejacuba. com / viejacuba@hotmail.com, URL: www. hotelviejacuba.com.
Updated: Jan 09, 2013.

Hotel La Rábida

(ROOMS: $61-93) This small, Anglo/Italian-owned boutique hotel has a clean, colonial feel with friendly service, great food and lots of personal touches that make it unique. It is one of only a few hotels in Quito awarded with the *Distintivo Q*, a certificate of quality and sustainable tourism. Hostal de La Rábida is an old traditional house recently restored into a first-class South American boutique hotel. It offers guests the gracious atmosphere and style of a beautiful home located in the heart of Quito, near most places of historical and tourist interest as well as restaurants, banks, travel agencies and shops. With only 11 charming and tastefully decorated rooms, Hostal de la Rábida is a very special hotel in which to enjoy your stay in Quito. La Rábida 227 and Santa Maria, Tel: 02-222-1720/2169, E-mail: info@hostalrabida.com, URL: www.hostalrabida.com. Updated: Jan 09, 2013.

JW Marriott Hotel Quito

(ROOMS: $189-1,500) The newest of Quito's luxury international hotels, the JW Marriott Quito is a gigantic, modern pyramid in the northern end of La Mariscal. With spacious, sunny and elegantly decorated rooms with excellent city and mountain views, two excellent restaurants, a tropical pool area that will make you forget you are in the middle of a polluted city, and relaxing common areas including an indoor waterfall, the Marriott is well-worth the price for travelers desiring a luxurious stay. Each of the over 250 rooms has safes, cable TV, data ports and minibars, and some also have in-room hot tubs. Av. Orellana 1172 and Av. Amazonas, Tel: 02-297-2000, Fax: 02-297-2050, E-mail: businesscenter.quito@marriothotels.com, URL:www.marriott.com/hotels/travel/uiodt-jw-marriott-quito. Updated: Jan 09, 2013.

Hilton Colón Ecuador

(ROOMS: $179-329) The Hilton Colón is one of Quito's older international luxury chains and it is beginning to show its age. Nonetheless, it is a beautiful hotel with extensive amenities and great city views. Located in the southern end of La Mariscal, right in front of Parque el Ejido (home to a weekend outdoor market with crafts from all over Ecuador) the Hilton Colón is a blockish concrete structure. Services include a small but modern gym and heated outdoor pool. Two restaurants downstairs offer ample buffets and spacious seating areas. Av. Amazonas N19-14 and Av. Patria, Tel: 02-256-1333, E-mail: reservations.quito@hiltoncolon.com /frontdesk.quito@hiltoncolon.com, URL: www.hiltoncolon.com. Updated: Jan 09, 2013.

La Mariscal Restaurants

Finding a place to eat is no problem in La Mariscal—it's deciding where to go that can be a challenge. Whether you're in the mood for a hearty steak, spicy Mexican food, sushi or traditional Ecuadorian fare, this area is prepared to appease your gastronomical cravings. Entrée prices range across the board, as you can just as easily get a cheap almuerzo or burger and fries combo somewhere as you can enjoy a fancy sit-down meal. Either way, La Mariscal's offerings are accessible and abundant; plan to grab a bite here while you're in Quito. Updated: January 18, 2013

ECUADORIAN
Achiote]

(ENTREES: $15-25) Specializes in preparing exquisite Ecuadorian plates that you simply cannot miss out on if you're staying in Quito. Located on the fringe of the Mariscal's bustling nightlife (but still within it's borders) the restaurant presents a haven of sorts for those interested enjoying a night out, minus the rowdiness that's typical of the neighborhood at night. Serving a range of typical dishes all the way from seafood to delicacies of the highlands (including guinea pig!) Achiote provides your palette with an abundance of choices. The appetizers come in small or large portions so you can easily sample a number of items on the menu. The services on top of it all is delightful, with waiters holding a near perfect command of English and an extensive knowledge regarding everything that's on the menu. Juan Rodriguez 282 and Reina Victoria, Tel: 02-250-1743, E-mail: lcastro@achiote.com.ec, URL: http://achiote.com.ec. Updated: Mar 11, 2013.

Mama Clorinda

(ENTREES: $8-23) A decent restaurant with standard Ecuadorian food. The large restaurant has two levels, and is a good place for large groups to gather. Mama Clorinda is also a safe place to try out some typical dishes you may hesitate to taste in other places such as *cuy* (roasted guinea pig). Vegetarians have two options: the *llapingacho* (cheesy potato pancakes) platter, salad and veggies or *locro de queso* (a delicious and creamy cheesy potato soup). Reina Victoria 1144 and Calama, Tel: 02-254-2523, E-mail: info@mamaclorinda.com, URL: www.mamaclorinda.com. Updated: Jan 16, 2013.

Loved it? Loathed it? Write a review and help other travelers

QUITO

C.A.C.T.U.S.

(ENTREES: $5-20) In a neighborhood filled with pizzerias, Chinese restaurants and shawarma joints, C.A.C.T.U.S. serves authentic, honest-to-goodness Ecuadorian food. Specializing in the traditional cuisine of the Sierra's indigenous population, the restaurant cooks up delicious *llapingachos*, tasty trout, and a number of bean, corn, *cuy* and vegetable salads.

The restaurant is tiny and the atmosphere is intimate, with groups of friends crowded around the small tables drinking beer and cocktails. On especially festive nights, the patrons have been known to engage in some traditional Otavalo-style dancing. Carrión, between Av. Amazonas and 9 de Octubre, Tel: 02-254-9591.
Updated: Jan 16, 2013.

Fried Bananas

(ENTREES: $5-15) Fried Bananas Restaurant & Cafe is small, off the beaten track, and what some might call "cute" thanks to its ambiance. What really steals the show however, is the combination of simplicity and imagination in their plates as they serve up some incredibly delightful Ecuadorian cuisine. From avocado cream to shrimp bathed in wonderful sauces, spaghetti with saffron or some incredibly tender beef, Fried Bananas does its name justice by getting you to its glorious desert via some wonderful entrees along the way.

Cozy and with prices much lower than one would expect given the elegant atmosphere, you can't pass up coming here at least once. Open Monday to Saturday, 12 p.m. to 9 p.m. Mariscal Foch E4-150 and Amazonas, Tel: 02-223-5208 / 09-970-7695, E-mail: info@newfriedbananas.com.
Updated: Mar 13, 2013.

ARGENTINIAN
El Rincón del Gaucho

(ENTREES: $20-25) This Argentinean steakhouse has huge portions of excellent steak cooked on a charcoal grill on the premises. Try the *parrillada* (BBQ platter) to share in a group; it's served on a mini grill that keeps your meat warm. The service is great. A good wine selection is another plus. Diego de Almagro 422, between Lizardo García and Calama, Tel: 02-254-7846/222-3782, E-mail: info@rincondelgaucho.net, URL: www.rincondelgaucho.net.

ASIAN
Uncle Ho's

(ENTREES: $7-10) Uncle Ho's brings Vietnamese food to Quito in a fun, casual atmosphere. The owner is part-Vietnamese and unlike most of the Asian food in Quito, the food is very authentic. The restaurant combines delicately flavored, mouth-watering food with friendly, though slow, service. For a real taste of Vietnam, slurp on the *pho*, which is a Hanoi-style beef noodle soup. Other options include summer rolls, coconut curry chicken, lemongrass beef kebabs over a rice or noodle plate, and sea bass in lime and chili sauce. Finish up with a round of stuffed fried bananas, flambéed at your table. *Que rico!* José Calama E8-40 and Diego de Almagro, Tel: 02-511-4030, E-mail: kevinheehee@gmail.com, URL: http://unclehos.com.
Updated: Jan 16, 2013

Mongos

(ENTREES: $10-15) Right in the heart of the Mariscal, Mongos Mongolian BBQ has quickly become a firm favorite with travelers and Ecuadorians alike. Go for the all-you-can-eat option, where you can choose any combination of meats, veggies, sauces and other add-ins. For this price, you also get a soup or salad starter thrown in. For those not feeling creative, there are also plenty of meals on the menu. One of the best features here is the excellent drink specials. It is worth being patient with the somewhat sullen staff for the excellent value food. Also, check out the set lunch menu, with choice of soup or salad, full-sized entree, and dessert and beverage. Mongos can get busy but usually clears out quickly, so hang around. José Calama and Juan León Mera, opposite No Bar, Tel: 02-255-6159, E-mail: mongosgrill@gmail.com.
Updated: Jan 16, 2013

Chifa Chang Man Lou Sushi

(ENTREES: $3-10) Chifa Chang Man Lou Sushi's underwhelming location, on the ground floor of a worn Mariscal apartment building, makes it easy to dismiss the restaurant as just another of Quito's poor Asian joints. Step inside, however, ignore the bland interior, and you'll find that it serves generous portions of excellent Japanese and Chinese food. Take your time and explore Chifa Chang Man Lou Sushi's multiple menus, which feature sashimi and rolls, grilled and teriyaki entrées, and Chinese rice

and noodle dishes. They also have bottles of Sapporo. Robles 609 and Juan León Mera, Tel: 02-254-0330.
Updated: Jan 16, 2013.

CAFES

Kallari ❗

($3-6) Kallari is a community-owned coffee shop and crafts shop owned by an association of Quechua communities in the Napo province, mostly from the Amazon Rainforest. Organic coffee and organic chocolate in brownies and hot chocolate accompany tasty snacks. Wilson E4-266 and Juan Leon Mera, Tel: 02-223-6009, URL: www.kallari.com.
Updated: Jan 18, 2013.

Café Libro ❗

($5.50-13.50) Founded in 1992, this bohemian hotspot is one of the few remaining hip coffee shops in the Mariscal area that has yet to be discovered by the gringo masses. There are regular live music performances, rotating art exhibits and a book exchange. The menu is mostly drinks (coffee and a number of cocktails); however, hungry visitors can munch on appetizers or sandwiches. Leonidas Plaza N23-56, between Wilson and Veintimilla, Tel: 02-250-3214/252-6754, Fax: 593-2-223-4265, E-mail: cafelibro@cafelibro.com, URL: www.cafelibro.com.
Updated: Jan 09, 2013.

El Español

($4-7) A sandwich shop with several locations around Quito, El Español has excellent imported cheeses, olives and meats (available on sandwiches and separately). Order your cold cuts on a baguette or soft roll. Some locations have rotating lunch specials that feature a sandwich of the day, which comes with a small salad or potato chips, and fresh-squeezed orange juice or a frozen coffee drink. There is not usually much seating at El Español; food is generally meant to go. Juan León Mera and Wilson, Tel: 02-255-3995, URL: www.elespaniol.com.
Updated: Jan 09, 2013.

Este Café

($4-8) Lovers of coffee shouldn't pass up a quick glimpse at the gourmet drinks on offer at Este Café. Whether you settle into one of the colorful couches with a frozen Oreo cappuccino, soak up some funky break beats over a steaming cup of chai, or peruse the book exchange with a Baileys iced latte, it's easy to chill at this artsy coffee spot.

The drinks selection is varied and impressive, ranging from wholesome natural juices to wicked hot chocolates with marshmallows or cheese, to a variety of caipiriñhas with a twist. The mix of traditional Ecuadorian and international food choices also makes Café Este a popular haunt for students, travelers and businessmen with eccentric ties. Be sure to catch one of Café Este's monthly exhibitions featuring the works of Ecuadorian artists or one of its regular live music and theater performances. Flyers and information about what else is on in Quito are also available. Juan León Mera n23-94 and Wilson, Tel: 02-254-2488, E-mail: eventos@estecafe.com, URL: www.estecafe.com.
Updated: Jan 16, 2013

Coffee Tam Plaza Foch

($10-15) With four branches in the Mariscal, Coffee Tam has become a neighborhood institution. Coffee Tam Plaza Foch is THE spot for people-watching and pre-game drinks, or catching a fútbol match or late-night bite on the always-hopping plaza. A slew of outdoor tables are always full of a mixed gringo/Ecuadorian crowd clamoring to be heard over the pulsing pop and electronic music. Drinks are reasonably priced (there's a different 2-for-1 cocktail every day); its overpriced food is pretty varied and comes in big portions. Mariscal Foch and Reina Victoria, Plaza Foch, Tel: 02-252-6957.
Updated: Jan 09, 2013

CUBAN

La Bodeguita de Cuba

(ENTREES: $10-15) A classy restaurant-come-bar, this place serves excellent food, accompanied by live Cuban music most nights. On Thursday to Saturday nights, it stays open until 2 a.m., when different live bands play to a packed room. Drinks are fairly expensive, but you pay for the atmosphere. Varadero, which is next door, is run by the same owners and also has live music on Friday and Saturday nights, and appeals to a more mature clientele. Reina Victoria N26-105 and La Pinta (next to Varadero), Tel: 02-254-2476, E-mail: evarcuba@yahoo.com.
Updated: Jan 09, 2013

Punto Cubano

(ENREES: $4-12) This is a great little place to drop in and have some lovely cuban cuisine, with various dishes consisting of beef, chicken or even seafood. Their Cuban specialty *ropa vieja* (pulled beef) is quite

QUITO

QUITO

delicious, and is definitely worth ordering. Come here early to get good seats at lunch. Reina Victoria and Jerónimo Carrion, Tel: 02-378-345.
Updated: Mar 12, 2013

FRENCH
Crêpes de París
(ENTREES: $3-5) This cozy restaurant in the Mariscal specializes in French food, especially, as its name hints, in crepes. It is a bit pricey for Quito, but in reality a value compared to French restaurants in other countries. The food is very good but the service is not always great. If you are craving French food, this is an excellent option in Quito. José Calama 362.
Updated: Jan 18, 2013

INDIAN
The Great India Restaurant ♪
(ENTREES: $3.50-8) Situated in the buzzing café thoroughfare of Calle Calama, The Great India Restaurant holds its own in the Mariscal restaurant scene as a longtime favorite haunt whose cheap and authentic Indian food lure a stream of budget diners, both local and foreign. Simple and low-key in its setting, the restaurant is brightened up by bustling student crowds and the occasional woman adorning colorful saris.

For vegetarians, The Great India Restaurant is heavenly, with the menu arranged by the separation of meat and veggie dishes. There is a wide range of curry dishes, with meat options of beef, chicken and goat. All meals are accompanied by rice or naan bread. Smaller appetites can order pakoda, shwarma or falafel. It is also popular for its bargain beer combo specials. It is also one of the only restaurants in town reliably open on Sundays. Calama E4-54, between Juan Leon Mera and Amazonas, Tel: 02-223-8269, Cel: 09-9418-0183.
Updated: Jan 09, 2013

Chandani Tandoori
(ENTREES: $4-7) Could this be the best Indian/ Hindu restaurant in the Mariscal? In Quito? In Ecuador? Very likely! The Chandani Tandoori serves a menu of extremely cheap mouth-watering curries—sauces range from mild to so spicy it will make your nose run. The large variety of curries are served either as a vegetarian option, with chicken, or, for an extra few dollars, with beef. The curries come with either rice or naan and go

perfectly with cold Brahma beer. The restaurant's lunch menu is an extremely good value and includes a curry, rice or naan, pakora or bhaji and a fruit juice. Juan León Mera 1312 and Luis Cordero, Tel: 02-222-1053.
Updated: Jan 09, 2013

ITALIAN
Le Arcate
(PIZZAS: $8-10) Le Arcate is an authentic Italian restaurant with great service, a nice interior and amazing prices for the food it serves. There are over 60 types of pizzas here, with options ranging from simple four cheese pizzas to pizzas topped with mixed seafood. All of the pizzas are made in an actual stone oven, and all of the pasta at the restaurant is homemade and can also be bought for home use. If the restaurant was in the United States or Europe, it would be one of the more expensive places to eat, but it is possible to get a great meal here for less than $10. Delivery is also available. Andrea Bocelli plays throughout the restaurant at no extra cost. Baquedano 358 and Juan Leon Mera, Tel: 02-223-7659/252-9211, E-mail: info@le-arcate.com, URL: www.le-arcate.com.
Updated: Jan 16, 2013

Tomato Pizza Bar Restaurante
(PIZZAS: 4-8) Conveniently located at a busy intersection of Mariscal, this place is the spot for a cheap grab-and-go slice of yummy pizza. Slices are only $1 each from the takeaway window. However, with airy windows, Latin fusion music and a laid-back atmosphere, the place is great for eating in, too. While pizza is undoubtedly the house specialty, Tomato also serves a variety of Italian cuisine, including calzones, lasagna and spaghetti. It has a fixed price lunch on weekdays that includes a soup/salad, entree, dessert and drink. On Tuesdays, pizzas are 2x1. There are sometimes 2x1 beer and drink specials as well. Juan León Mera N24-148 and Calama, Tel: 02-290-6201.
Updated: Jan 09, 2013.

Cosa Nostra ♪
(PIZZAS: $10-14) What some proclaim to be one the best italian pizzerias in all of Quito, Cosa Nostra is a restuarant that accurately hits the the bullseye when it comes to delicious and authentic Italian cuisine. Attracting foreigners and locals alike, this pizzeria offers dozens of thin-crust, brick-oven pizzas with lots of typical and gourmet toppings to choose from. Cosa Nostra also offers a

variety of homemade pastas such as ravioli, gnocchi and lasagna. The place has an near perfect balance across price, quality, charisma and service - including a "buongiorno!" from the owner when you walk in through the door (sometimes, not always!).

The restaurant only uses high-quality ingredients and also incorporates local products, including organic tomatoes and cheese from Cayambe. With an ambiance that's incredibly relaxed and classy, Cosa Nostra is a gem lying right near the heart of La Mariscal that you shouldn't pass up on. Baquerizo Moreno E7-86 and Diego de Almagro, Tel: 02-252-7145, E-mail: pizzeria.cosanostra@yahoo.com. Updated: Mar 13, 2013

INTERNATIONAL
Crepes and Waffles
(ENTREES: $8-12) This Colombian chain is found in several locations around Quito and has reliably tasty food that comes in good-sized portions. The waffles are not meant to be breakfast, but rather dessert; they are piled high with ice cream, whipped cream, nutella, fruit and more. Crepes are served with sweet or salty fillings and are full of flavor. The salads are gigantic and delicious, while the pita sandwiches are stuffed with a number of combinations of veggie and meat options.

The atmosphere is casual, almost diner-style, but attracts a gringo and classy Ecuadorian crowd. If for nothing else, stop by for a scoop or two of Crepe and Waffles' delicious ice cream, which is served in either a cup or homemade waffle cone! This is the main restaurant in La Mariscal, but there are also locations in the Quicentro and El Jardin malls. Rábida N26-249 and Francisco de Orellana, Tel: 02-250-0658, E-mail: servicioalcliente@crepesywaffles-ec.com / smosquera@crepesywaffles-ec.com, URL: www.crepesywaffles.com.ec.
Updated: Jan 09, 2013

La Boca del Lobo 🍴
(ENTREES: $12-25) Featuring a brightly lit, colorfully painted glass-encased patio with funky chandeliers, hanging bird cages, and faux renaissance portraits, La Boca del Lobo sticks out as the most flamboyant joint in the Mariscal's somewhat low-key gringo scene. It's no surprise, then, that La Boca del Lobo is also gay-friendly, and you'll find Quito's "beautiful people" here mixed in with upper-scale gringo tourists. With a huge menu of Mediterranean-fusion appetizers and entrées and a long list of fruity cocktails all made with Absolut Vodka, La Boca del Lobo is the kind of place you can lounge in for hours. Calama 284 and Reina Victoria, Tel: 02-223-8123/254-5500, E-mail: eventos@labocadellobo.com.ec, URL: www.labocadellobo.com.ec.

The Magic Bean
(ENTREES: $5-14) From the "Have a nice day" sign by the bar to the huge pancakes served for breakfast, there's nothing Ecuadorian about this place. Unless you're seeking an authentic dining experience, you're unlikely to be disappointed. The cozy patio café is always packed with travelers so it's a great place to meet people. All the dishes on the huge menu are delicious; the smoothies are a must! Some menu options include omelettes, French toast and huevos rancheros for breakfast, and salads, sandwiches, burgers and chicken kebabs for lunch or dinner. Mariscal Foch E5-08 and Juan León Mera; also Portugal E9-106 and República del Salvador, Tel: 02-256-6181, Fax: 593-2-290-6105, E-mail: info@magicbeanquito.com.
Updated: Jan 09, 2013.

MEXICAN
Red Hot Chili Peppers
(ENTREES: $7.50-11) Red Hot Chili Peppers is a great Tex-Mex restaurant with the best fajitas in Quito and possibly the best margaritas in Ecuador. Right in the heart of the Mariscal, this place's flavors and portions are American style: full of taste and huge portions for reasonable prices. All dishes can also be served vegetarian. Mariscal Foch E4-314 and Juan Leon Mera, Tel: 02-255-7575, Cel: 09-8552-3548, E-mail: fierro.fabian@gmail.com. Updated: Jan 17, 2013.

MIDDLE EASTERN
Aladdin
(ENTREES: $3-5) Aladdin is popular for its spacious outdoor seating, cozy indoor couches, late hours, tasty hookahs, and of course, its cheap and delicious Middle Eastern food. The Iranian owner has lived in Ecuador for over 20 years and has established this Mariscal institution well. Try the falafel or shawarma sandwiches or platters. Diego de Amagro and Baquerizo Moreno, Tel: 02-222-9435.
Updated: Jan 17, 2013.

Balbeek

(ENTREES: $12-25) For a taste of authentic Lebanese cuisine, Balbeek is where it's at. If you're not familiar with Lebanese food, rest assured that the delightful owner will take care of any questions you have, as he himself takes your order. Beware however, for he might take over ordering for you if you allow him to! This can (and will) rack up the bill considerably.

Portions are on the smaller side for appetizers specifically, given that the idea is to order a variety of things to taste and sample. There are main courses however, for those desiring larger portions of food, but these are considerably more expensive. Arabic dancing is featured on Thursday nights as well, so come early! 6 de Diciembre N23-103 and Wilson. Quito, Ecuador, Tel: 02-255-2766, E-mail: info@restaurantbaalbek.com, URL: www.restaurantbaalbek.com. Updated: Mar 07, 2013.

El Arabe

(ENTREES: $5-8) Despite a newly remodeled interior that gives it a more middle-eastern ambiance, El Arabe has always been on track with the authenticity of its warm and filling meals. In addition to offering exotic cuisine, El Arabe is actually a restaurant that caters to the vegetarian-scene quite well; all in all, it offers a nice change of pace beginning with its wonderful hummus all the way to the filling shawarma's they serve up. Reina Victoria 627 and Carrion, Tel: 02-549-414.
Updated: Mar 12, 2013

PUBS

Finn McCool's

(ENTREES: $7-10) Finn McCool's is one of the the few places in Quito where many travelers are likely to feel at home. European and North American sporting events are regularly shown, and there's a free pool table, great drinks (especially beer), and excellent pub food, including Irish stew, bangers and mash, and fish and chips. Finn McCool's is a great place to meet fellow travelers, expats and Ecuadorians, and this Irish pub often has DJs on weekends (turning it into a quasi-night club) and hosts the city's best St. Patty's Day party every year. Diego de Almagro N24-64 and Joaquin Pinto, Tel: 02-252-1780, E-mail: info@irishpubquito.com, URL: www.irishpubquito.com.
Updated: Jan 09, 2013

Turtle's Head

(ENTREES: $5-10) An excellent Scottish-owned pub in Quito's Mariscal district and one of the only spots in Quito to get home-brewed beer. Three varieties of micro-brewed beers are for sale from the on-site brewery, which provide a nice break from the national beers. The Turtle's Head also has great hamburgers and snacks, along with pool, darts and foosball. The pub is very British in look and feel, enhanced by cartoon strips from the adult comic Viz, that are displayed on the walls and in the toilets. There is also a new Turtle's Head in Cumbaya near Quito. La Niña 626 and Juan León Mera, Tel: 02-256-5544, E-mail: tthquito@hotmail.com.

Mulligan's

(ENTREES: $8-19) Mulligan's, despite its Irish name, is an American-style sports bar. It has several TVs— usually tuned into soccer or basketball—spread out throughout the place and sports memorabilia up on the walls. The relatively pricey food is normal American bar fare, with burgers, mozzarella sticks and jalapeño poppers all making an appearance on the menu.

The chicken crunchers are a crowd favorite, and the buffalo wings cost $0.19 each on Wednesday from 6-9 p.m. The beer menu is fairly long for Quito, but you might find the imports prohibitively expensive. José Calama E5-44 and Juan Leon Mera (next to the Calama parking lot), Tel: 02-254-0876, E-mail: mulligansinfo@gmail.com, URL: www.mulligans.com.ec. Updated: Jan 17, 2013

SEAFOOD

Cevichería Marisquería Los Siete Mares

(ENTREES: $5-7) Cevichería Marisquería Los Siete Mares has excellent *ceviche*, other seafood soups, and lunch platters in a variety of combinations. Don't forget to fill up a basket with popcorn and *chifles* (fried plantain chips) to dunk in your soup of choice. Corner of Juan León Mera and La Niña.
Updated: Jan 18, 2013

La Canoa Manabita

(ENTREES: $4-6) By far one of the most overlooked holes in wall in the Mariscal area, La Canoa Manabita is easy to miss, but unjustifiably so. Offering incredibly delicious plates from the coast, ranging anywhere from fried and breaded fish to yummy ceviches, La Canoa Manabita is an oasis for seafood lovers in the city that want an authentic taste of the delicious plates that the coast of Ecuador has to offer, all for a cheap price too. Updated: Mar 12, 2013.

VEGETARIAN

El Maple

(ENTREES: $3-7) El Maple serves up a variety of vegetarian and even entirely vegan dishes. It's a simple and convinient little place located in la Mariscal that serves up their meals rather quickly too, specifically their executive lunch specials (appetizer, soup, entree, dessert and juice) which cost a mere $3-5. With food that's always fresh and flavorful, it's hard to go wrong here, especially if your a vegan or vegetarian. Joaquin Pinto E7-68 and Diego de Almagro, Tel: 02-229-0000, URL: http://www.elmaple.com. Updated: Mar 13, 2013.

Formosa

(ENTREES: $3-6) Offering a tasty vegetarian meal of the day for an incredibly cheap price, this Taiwanese restaurant is a smash hit at lunch-time. Serving a delicious selection of tofu and beans along with flavorful corn and noodles or rice. The door is on Carrion and the restaurant is up a flight of stairs on the 1st floor. Mind you, it gets busy during the lunch hours! There's also one located in La Floresta as well. Juan Leon Mera and Carrion, Tel: 02-234-828. Updated: Mar 12, 2013.

La Mariscal Nightlife

The Mariscal is undoubtedly Quito's nightlife hot spot. With an overwhelming number of bars and clubs on every street, this is definitely the best place to head to on Friday and Saturday nights (sometimes Tuesdays, Wednesdays, and Thursdays as well). Despite its name, Gringolandia is the place to go out for quiteños just as much, if not more, than backpackers.

Technically all bars in the Mariscal area must close by 2 a.m., in accordance with a law passed a few years ago. However, many stay open until three, or later if they think no one's looking. There are also a number of "clubs", which open later, often until 6 or 7am. Note: If you're planning on pre-drinking, liquor stores "legally" close at 10 p.m. Updated: Mar 07, 2013.

Bungalow 6

(COVER: $5-10 for men, FREE for women on most nights) Bungalow 6 is the most famous club in Quito among expats and visitors, and odds are that at some point you will find yourself on its crowded dance floors, in its lounge or leaning over its pool tables. Bungalow's playlist is dominated by last year's Top 40 hits and reggaeton, while the clientele is dominated by gringos and the Ecuadorians who would like to pick them up. The meat market atmosphere is amplified on Wednesdays, Ladies' Night, when the place is opened only to women from 8-10 p.m. After plying the girls with free drinks for two hours, the staff opens up the doors to men, who charge in like bulls stampeding through the streets of Pamplona. Wednesday-Saturday 8 p.m.-3 a.m. Corner of José Calama and Diego de Almagro, E-mail: bungalow-6disco@gmail.com. Updated: Jan 17, 2013

Strawberry Fields Forever

(Drinks: $4-10) If you love the Beatles and Classic Rock, you'll love Strawberry Fields. If you're not looking carefully, you might miss it. Strawberry Fields is tucked away next to the popular No Bar. Take a seat in the cozy alcove in the back, and rock out to the amazing playlist, which includes songs by the fab four and their peers. Drinks are named after the best of the Beatles, from their signature Strawberry Fields margarita to the eclectic Octupus's Garden. Be sure to check out the Yellow Submarine-themed restroom, and chat up the friendly, young owners, who are usually sitting by the bar. Strawberry Fields Forever also has another location in La Floresta (Gonzalez Suárez 171 and 12 de Octubre). Calama E5-27 and Juan Leon Mera, Tel: 09-9903-1592. Updated: Jan 18, 2013.

Aguijón

(COVER: $6-8) A local favorite among hipsters and trendsetters, Aguijón also manages to maintain a down-to-earth, chilled out vibe, unlike some of its dressier neighbors. A wide variety of music keeps an eclectic crowd dancing to ever-changing beats of salsa, hip-hop, jazz, alternative rock and top 20. The place is bit tricky to find, look for the white and red entrance and sign with a scorpion emblem. Aguijón is also well-known for its salsa night every Wednesday night, when the place fills up with locals and tourists looking to learn or practice salsa dancing. Admission

QUITO

Loved it? Loathed it? Write a review and help other travelers

QUITO

for salsa night is free before 10 p.m. and $6-8 after 10 p.m. Bring an ID if you want to get in. Calama E735 and Reina Victoria, Tel: 02-256-9014, Updated: Jan 09, 2013.

Cherusker

(DRINKS: $4-10) Cherusker is the first German brew pub in Ecuador, and it offers a variety of German craft beer at reasonable prices. Beer options range from wheat beer (Hafeweizen) to dark stout beer and can be sampled in a few different sizes. You can accompany your pint with typical German food, including bratwurst and currywurst. Cherusker's ambiance is friendly and comfortable, with lounge-type seating indoors as well as tables outdoors for a beer garden atmosphere. Monday-Thursday 3 p.m.-midnight, Friday-Saturday 3 p.m.-2 a.m. Closed Sundays. Joaquin Pinto E7-85 and Diego de Almagro, Tel: 02-601-2144, URL: www.facebook.com/CheruskerCerveceriaAlemana. Updated: Jan 17, 2013

Dirty Sanchez !

(DRINKS: $2-8) Run by a couple of friendly foreigners, Dirty Sanchez is an excellent addition to Quito's café and scene. Just one block from Plaza Foch, this café/bar/gallery serves good coffee (a rarity in the city), wine, beer and cocktails, including the "Dirty Sanchez," a mix of tequila, Baileys and Kahlúa, served in a towering shot glass; roll a die to determine how much you'll pay ($1-6). Dirty Sanchez is decorated with comfy furniture and quirky artwork—be sure to check out the washrooms. This small space hosts Poker Nights on Mondays and often has live electronic DJs on weekends, disco ball and all. Sometimes there is cover when there are events. Joaquín Pinto, between Reina Victoria and Diego de Almagro. Updated: Jan 18, 2013.

No Bar

(COVEr: $5) Hot, sweaty and crowded, this place appeals almost exclusively to the very young and the very drunk. The Ecuadorian to foreigner ratio is about 50-50, mainly aged between 16 and 25, who come for the cheap drinks and the school disco/meat market atmosphere. The music is a mix of Latin and western chart cheese. It could be anywhere in the world, but if you want to dance the night away and forget that you're in Ecuador, it might be the place for you. Calama y Juan León Mera, Tel: 02-254-5145.

Varadero

(COVER: $5-6) This small Cuban bar/club is very similar to its neighbor, La Bodeguita de Cuba. The long, skinny bar stretches the length of the room, giving the impression that the bar is always packed full. The tiny dance floor is almost always at least half-occupied by a live band playing Cuban dance tunes. There is usually a cover of $5-6, which includes a free drink, usually a Cuba Libre or Mojito. Reina Victoria N26-105 and La Pinta (next to La Bodeguita), Tel: 02-254-2575, E-mail: bodevarcuba@yahoo.comhotmail.com. Updated: Jan 09, 2013

Azuca

Azuca, located right on Plaza Foch, is blatantly noticeable from the second you walk down Calle Mariscal Foch. Decked out in a neon color scheme, the self-dubbed Latin Bistro serves up an eclectic mix of seafood and meat dishes. The "aphrodisiac rice" is something you should definitely give a try, seeing as it could be the best seafood rice dish to be had so far from the coast. Although the restaurant may not be as crowded as Coffee Tam, the privacy of the booths in the back is a welcome hiding spot from the masses, and not to mention - an entire deck filled with sand. It also has frequent drink specials, though the drinks are pricey to begin with. Mariscal Foch E6-11 and Reina Victoria, Plaza Foch, Tel: 02-290-7164. Updated: Jan 09, 2013.

Fragola Fusion Hookah Lounge

(DRINKS: $4-6) Definitely not providing the fastest service in the world, what La Fragola lacks in speed it makes up for in atmosphere. The hip red and yellow décor is certainly a draw for this sweet little night spot on always-happening Calama Street in the heart of La Mariscal. This is a prime spot for people-watching, as this bar and restaurant is perched on the second floor, with a great view of the night's (drunken) activities below. The all-you-can-drink deal for $10.99 for three hours of mojitos, caipirinhas, vodka tonics, and Cuba libres is another draw for those looking to get drunk, as are the hookahs - the billowing and growing white-smoke of which adds to the dazed decor and colorful ambiance of the place. Calama E5-10, between Reina Victoria and Juan León Mera, Tel: 02-255-6159, E-mail: mongosgrill@gmail.com. Updated: Jan 17, 2013.

La Floresta

Located east of La Mariscal, La Floresta is a more residential and less touristy district. Nonetheless, it's a neighborhood that still offers a wide variety of mid-range to luxury hotels as well as many of the city's trendiest restaurants, cafés and bars; and not to mention - Quito's only independent movie theater 'Ocho y Medio'. It's core is on 12 de Octubre and Coruña (Plaza Artigas roundabout) near the Swissotel and "The Strip" of apartments-with-wonderful-views that is Gonzales Suarez.
Updated: Mar 13, 2013.

Things To See and Do in La Floresta

Cine Ocho y Medio (Indie Movie Theater) ♪

(TICKETS: $4.80) Ocho y Medio is Quito's only independent movie theater and is a great spot to catch a flick. Located east of the Swisshotel in the La Floresta neighborhood, the artsy film spot has two comfy rooms (one with throw pillows in front of the screen) to view movies and is teamed up with the trendy and delicious La Cafetina Galería Restorán out front, where you can grab a bite to eat or a drink before or after the showing. Ocho y Medio screens indie and second-run films and documentaries from around the globe in a variety of languages (with Spanish or English subtitles), and hosts film festivals and the occasional live theater, music or dance show. Valladolid N24-353 and Vizcaya, URL: www.ochoymedio.net.
Updated: Jan 22, 2013.

El Mercado De La Floresta

Just down and around the block from the Swissotel, you'll find some incredibly cheap groceries for sale at the outdoor and indoor market of La Floresta. Search amidst foods, flowers, vegetables, or meats to find what you need and barter for how much you believe its worth! Arriving earlier gets your fresher goods, and cheaper prices as well. Open everyday except Sundays, 7 a.m. to 1 p.m. Galavis Street, between Isabel La Catolica and Andalucia.
Updated: Mar 13, 2013.

La Floresta Lodging

Accommodations run the gamut in La Floresta, with budget hostels existing side-by-side fancy hotels practically. Hostels here are typically cozy bunkhouses that start at $10/person. In La Floresta you'll also find the Swissotel (Quito's most expensive hotel) with room prices starting at well over $200. It's just a short walk from La Mariscal, but the two neighborhoods are worlds apart given that you're less likely to be running into tourists, and you'll be avoiding the nightly noise and chaos as well.
Updated: Mar 13, 2013.

BUDGET

Hotel Folklore ♪

(ROOMS: $29-49) Hotel Folklore is a colorfully decorated, intimate hotel. The rooms include a private bath and a home-cooked breakfast served every morning in its pleasant dining room. You're even welcome to use the kitchen to whip up a specialty from your home country! It is located close enough to the Mariscal area to be close to the action but far enough to be quiet. Madrid E13-93 and Pontevedra, Tel: 02-255-4621, Cel: 09-8927-2700, Fax: 02-255-4621, E-mail: reservaciones@folklorehotel.com.
Updated: Jan 09, 2013.

Casona de Mario

($12-14 per person) Hostal La Casona de Mario is a quaint home with a spacious garden, two community kitchens and two comfortable lounges. All bathrooms are shared, and rooms are spacious and clean with lots of natural light; most have private balconies. The Internet cafe a few doors down gives guests a 10 percent discount on Internet and international phone calls. Andalucía 213 and Galicia, two blocks east of 12 de Octubre, Tel: 02-254-4036, Fax: 02-223-0129, E-mail: lacasona@casonademario.com.
Updated: Jan 09, 2013.

MID-RANGE

Hostal Sur

(ROOMS: $25-64) A larger house in a quiet neighborhood in La Floresta, Hostal Sur has comfortable, if slightly overpriced, rooms. The rooms are basic, with no frills, but all have private bathrooms and cable TV. Its good service is one of the major perks of this family-run hotel; the staff is friendly and helpful, and has a working relationship with travel agencies nearby if you want to plan day trips near Quito or overnight adventures in other parts of Ecuador. There is a computer in the common area with Internet for hostel guests to use, but it has an hourly cost. Francisco Salazar 134-E10 and Tamayo (corner), Tel: 02-255-8086, E-mail: jparedesguz@gmail.com.

QUITO

QUITO

Aleida's Hostal
($12-25 per person) Aleida's Hostal has recently opened in the laid-back neighborhood of La Floresta. It is a restored private residence with great views of Quito and a pretty garden where you can drink complimentary coffee. The staff speaks English and can help arrange trips and/or tours to several locations in Quito and the surrounding areas. Rooms come with either private or shared bathrooms. Discounts of 10 percent are given for groups of over 10 people staying longer than a week. Andalucia 559 and Francisco Salazar, Tel: 02-223-4570, E-mail: info@aleidashostal.com.ec, URL: www.aleidashostal.com.ec.
Updated: Jan 09, 2013.

HIGH-END
Hotel Quito
(ROOMS: $57-80) Hotel Quito is a large luxury hotel in La Floresta with some of the best views over the city and the valleys to the east. The hotel offers all of the services one would expect of an international chain, but charges a much lower price. The exterior is somewhat obtrusive and outdated, but inside, the hotel feels spacious, comfortable and clean. The outdoor pool is a highlight; like the rooms and rooftop restaurant, the pool offers excellent views. If you feel like exercising, there also tennis courts, playing fields and walking trails, among other options. Most rooms feature a balcony with a view, and all of them have WiFi, cable TV and room service. The rooftop restaurant (El Techo del Mundo) is a big plus and is worth a visit even if you aren't staying at the hotel. Gonzales Suarez N27-142, Tel: 02-254-4600, Fax: 02-3964911, E-mail: reservaciones@hotelquito.com, URL: www.hotelquito.com.
Updated: Jan 09, 2013.

Swissotel
(ROOMS: $230-500) Undoubtedly one of Quito's most elegant hotels, the Swissotel has full facilities, including a lovely outdoor pool and spa area with beautiful views of the city and nearby Pichincha and Cotopaxi volcanoes. Most of the rooms are spacious, over-sized suites catering to upper-class business customers and travelers willing (and able) to spend almost double that of other high-end hotels in Quito. The hotel has six exquisite restaurants that can cater to any palate. Av. 12 de Octubre 1820 and Cordero, Tel: 02-256-7600/7128, URL: www.swissotel.com/hotels/quito.

Casa Aliso
(ROOMS: $110-135) Casa Aliso is a beautifully preserved private residence, with plenty of furnishings and colors to keep the senses pleased. The hotel is actually a renovated and heartily decorated home, with 10 rooms to spare and garden out back, offering travelers the luxury of spending their time in an ambiance that feels more like a friend's home than it does a mere place to rest, really. With tonnes of character, decor and excellent service here to keep your spirits lifted, the hotel goes the extra mile by providing its guests with its scrumptious meals over at its restaurant. Given all this, it's hard to go wrong with Casa Aliso. Francisco Salazar E 12-137 y Toledo, Tel: 02-252-8062, info@casaaliso.com, URL: www.casaaliso.com.
Updated: Aug 1, 2012

La Floresta Restaurants
Some of Quito's finest restaurants can be found in the La Floresta neighborhood, most of which are concentrated on Avenida Isabel La Católica, Avenida Coruña, Avenida Whymper and Avenida 12 de Octubre. Restaurants in La Floresta tend to be high-end and cater to a clientele to match, so you will find sleek atmospheres, elegant food and elevated prices here. Excellent French, Chinese, Japanese, Peruvian, Italian and Ecuadorian cuisine can all be enjoyed here.

ECUADORIAN AND LATIN AMERICAN
El Pobre Diablo   ❢
(ENTREES: $7.50-15) El Pobre Diablo is a well-decorated jazz bar, popular with artsy intellectuals and local bohemian types. Live music lights the place up most Wednesday, Thursday and Saturday nights, with jazz and soft Cuban beats on other nights. Its food is pricier than local norms, but dishes are decent and the atmosphere more than makes up for the extra cents. You can order a portion of fried yucca, empanadas, or a meat-and-cheese plate to pick at as you drink and enjoy the music, or a full-on main course. It also has a set lunch menu on weekdays for $7, which includes a soup, entree with a side, dessert and juice. When there is a live show, there is usually a cover of $6.50-8. Drinks are also very expensive here, especially compared to other Quito bars. Av. Isabel La Católica N24-274 and Francisco Galavis (corner), one block south of Swissotel on Isabel La Católica, Tel: 02-223-5194/222-5397, E-mail: eventos@elpobrediablo.com, URL: www.elpobrediablo.com.

Barlovento

(ENTREES: $10-15) Barlovento is an elegant place to try Ecuadorian cuisine. Guests can lounge on the outdoor terrace or, for a more upscale feel, sit on the upper floor, which has live music on select days. The menu includes empanadas and soup for lighter appetites, as well as hearty entrees. Main dishes include local favorites such as *fritada* (fried pork), *seco de chivo* (goat stew with rice), and a variety of *ceviches* (cold seafood broth marinated with lime, onion and tomato). 12 de Octubre N27-09 and Orellana, Tel: 02-222-4683, URL: www.grupobarlovento.com. Updated: Jan 09, 2013.

Restaurante La Choza

(ENTREES: $10-12) La Choza has all the classic Ecuadorian and Quiteño dishes. It is easy to construct a vegetarian dish with *llapingachos* (cheesy potato pancakes), *mote tostado* (different preparations of Andean corn), cheese-filled empanadas and more. There are also several meat and fish dishes which are excellent. 12 de Octubre N24-551 y Cordero, Tel: 593-2-250-7901 / 2230839, E-mail: info@lachozaec.com, URL: www.lachozaec.com. Updated: Jan 3, 2013.

ASIAN
Formosa ♩

(ENTREES: $3-6.50) Sitting quietly two blocks off the main avenue of 12 de Octubre, and just behind the Swiss Hotel, is this quaint little hole in the wall which at midday is bustling inside. Serving meals consisting solely of vegetarian food, Formosa boasts a daily buffet fit for the ravenous, and serves you a selection of 3-4 items of your choice from a variety of options - all for an incredibly cheap price ($3-4, including juice and soup). There are à la carte plates and entrees that you can order for a bit of a higher price as well, but whatever you do, don't miss out on their tasty tofu! Andalucia and Luis Cordero. Updated: Mar 13, 2013.

Noe Sushi

(ENTREES: $6-34) Sushi lovers rejoice when they discover Noe Sushi Bar, which serves a mix of high-quality traditional and special rolls (many of which can also be ordered as half rolls), sashimi, and combination plates. Even if you don't like sushi, there are some satisfying Asian mains on the menu, such as grilled beef in ginger sauce, udon noodles with prawns and tempura veggies, and chicken teriyaki. Top it all off with a dessert like guanábana meringue or Toblerone cheesecake. Noe Sushi has several locations in Quito: in the shopping centers Quicentro, El Jardin and Plaza Las Américas, and in La Floresta; it also has a restaurant in Cumbayá in Plaza Cumbayá. In Quito, the La Floresta location has the nicest ambiance. Isabel La Católica 24 and Coruña, Tel: 02-395-5400, URL: www.noesushibar.com. Updated: Jan 18, 2013.

FRENCH
Chez Jerome Restaurant

(ENTREES: $15-30) This French cuisine in town combines a bit of Ecuadorian culture with the most classic French cuisine. The restaurant is in a remarkable and magical location with a very comfortable ambience, as well as decent prices. Whymper N30-96 y Coruña, Sector La Paz, Tel: 02-223-4067, E-mail: secretaria@chezjeromerestaurante.com / chezjero@uio.satnet.net, URL: www.chezjeromerestaurante.com. Updated: Jan 09, 2013.

ITALIAN
La Briciola

(ENTREES: $4-8) This Italian-owned restaurant located in a quiet neighborhood in La Floresta is a perennial favorite and great value for your money. Service is friendly, the food is delicious and the prices are very reasonable. There aren't many choices for vegetarians though; non-meat eaters will be limited to salads and plain pasta dishes. Toledo 1255 and Luis Cordero, Tel: 02-254-7138, E-mail: labriciolaquito@hotmail.com, URL: www.labriciolaquito.com. Updated: Jan 09, 2013.

SEAFOOD
Segundo Muelle ♩

(ENTREES: $11.50-20) Excellent Peruvian food comes in tiny portions at the sleek Segundo Muelle, one of Quito's finest restaurants. Although your pocketbook may not thank you when the check arrives, your palate certainly will. Prepare your taste buds with a fruit-infused *pisco* sour followed by the *ceviche mixto en salsa de tres ajís* (mixed ceviche made with three different chilis), a *tacu tacu*, or tortellini filled with crab and ricotta. Although heavy in seafood, the menu has a few different beef and pasta options as well. Segundo Muelle has restaurants in Peru, Panama and Spain, with two locations in Quito: one in La Floresta and the other in Quicentro

QUITO

shopping. Av. Isabel La Católica N24-883 and Gangotena, Tel: 02-222-6548, Cel: 09-9846-9287, E-mail: quito@segundomuelle.com, URL: www.segundomuelle.com. Updated: Jan 09, 2013.

La Jaiba

(ENTREES: $8-18) A restaurant with over 37 years of tradition in Quito, La Jaiba's menu contains a fantastic selection of seafood—all served by an attentive staff. Staying true to the claim that their ingredients "slept in the sea yesterday," the food is extremely fresh and tasty, making it worth the price. Av. Coruña and San Ignacio, Tel: 02-254-3887, E-mail: xponcem42@andinanet.net, URL: www.restaurantelajaiba.com. Updated: Jan 09, 2013.

Guápulo

Located behind Hotel Quito, the neighborhood of Guápulo runs down the winding cobblestone Camino de Orellana, from Gonzalez Suárez to Calle de los Conquistadores, the main road out of Quito, and to the neighboring suburbs of the Tumbaco Valley. Guápulo is nestled more or less on the side of a large hill, between Bellavista, an affluent residential area to the north, and the affordable yet trendy, La Floresta to the south.

Often considered Quito's artsy, bohemian neighborhood, Guápulo is home to many local artists, hip expats and a couple of hipster cafés/bars. These cafés lie in the middle of the neighborhood, halfway up the road from the famed Iglesia de Guápulo. This 15th-century church, built in honor of the Virgin of Guadalupe, is undoubtedly the focal point of this enchanting area, and combined with the stucco mountainside homes, towering palm trees, and cobblestone streets, it creates a picturesque remembrance of old Spain.

Aside from the local community, Guápulo is also inhabited by a couple of embassies and their elite. Right on Camino de Orellana is the Spanish Embassy, and in the northern valley, you will find the British Embassy, both easily marked by high-flying flags. It is this juxtaposition of high and not-so-high society, as well as a layout that breaks free from the grid and a gorgeous geographical position that makes Guápulo so special. It's no wonder that fireworks fly from the church most weekends and every year on September

7th, when *guapaleños* honor their neighborhood with the Fiestas de Guápulo, a fantastic celebration complete with costumes, parade, food, drink, song, dance, and even early morning orange throwing. Updated: Jan 18, 2013.

Things To See and Do in Guápulo

While Guápulo is small and somewhat hidden beneath the posh Avenida de Gónzalez Suárez, the bohemian neighborhood is worth the trip. You can begin walking from the Mirador de Guápulo - a restaurant and lookout point - which by day offers local *artesanías* to tour buses that stop to see the sprawling green valley below and by night pumps out live music and a full menu of Ecuadorian fare. Views of the valley from here are quite remarkable at night (with Cumbaya's sparkling lights off in the distance).

Take the stairs (as long as there's still daylight), as the view is unbeatable. At the bottom of the stairs, you'll hit a small *tienda* (shop), which is a perfect place to grab water or a snack for the rest of your walk.

As you head down the winding Camino de Orellana, you'll pass five or so small cafés, most open for dinner. There are a couple more *tiendas* along the way; one has Internet and a phone booth for national or international calls.

At the bottom of the great hill is the Iglesia de Guápulo, a gorgeous sanctuary with a museum and monastery inside. There are also park benches for relaxing in this church square below, which you will want to take advantage of before making the long hike back up. Updated: Jan 18, 2013.

Museo "Fray Antonio Rodríguez" de Guápulo

(ADMISSION: $1.50) Museo "Fray Antonio Rodríguez" de Guápulo is housed inside the Iglesia de Guápulo. A history lesson along with a tour of the sanctuary can be arranged. Small religious momentos can also be purchased in the museum shop, ranging from posters of the Last Supper to silver rosaries; compared to other religious paraphernalia in town, the prices are cheap and the variety is plenty. The Iglesia is located at the very bottom of the Guapulo hillside. Tel: 02-256-5652/254-1858. Updated: Jan 09, 2013.

Guápulo Restaurants

Guápulo is home to a number of independently-run family restaurants and cafes. You'll often step into one and instantly begin recognizing the features and layout of what was once a house. Note however, that such a business model has its perks. In many cases, these places provide a number of scrumptious entrees and drinks that all come with that (often neglected) home-made-taste and authenticity.

Cafe Arte Guápulo

(ENTREES: $6-7) With hot chocolate, hot wine, hot canelazo, and giant drip candles on the tables, Cafe Arte Guápulo is a good place to warm up on chilly Quito nights. This funky spot is home to a friendly kitty, and the red walls are covered in old music posters and sketches as well as drawings by local artists and café patrons.Come on the weekend, when the usually laid-back café and outdoor patio fill up with a crowd of hipsters and hippies. Café Guápulo sometimes has live music and other events, and has hosted events by big-name bands like Manu Chao in the past. Monday-Thursday 6 p.m.-midnight, Friday-Saturday 6 p.m.- 2 a.m. Closed Sundays. Camino de Orellana N27-492, Tel: 02-513-2424, URL: www.facebook.com/cafe-arteguapulo.

Café ChiQuito ♪

($3-5) Although its menu is small, this artsy café has big personality. With paintings depicting quiteño life, a wide variety of board games and cards, and a few cozy tables, Café ChiQuito is the perfect place to spend a rainy afternoon with friends, sipping chai and eating slices of walnut caramel pie while playing an old German version of Chutes and Ladders or Scrabble.

ChiQuito also serves a few tasty sandwiches on focaccia bread: try the roast beef, arugula, and cream cheese, or the toasty mozzarella with pesto and tomato. ChiQuito opens in the afternoon around 2 p.m. and stays open until the crowd leaves, around 10 or 11 p.m. This is the only Guápulo café open on Sundays. Updated: Jan 09, 2013.

Pizzeria Ananké ♪

(PIZZAS: $5-10) A small converted bungalow that feels more like a hipster's home than a restaurant, Ananké has a stunning view of Guápulo from its upstairs outdoor patio. This artsy dive specializes in inexpensive, delicious homemade wood-oven pizzas and calzones.

The menu also includes an array of appetizers and mixed drinks, including a fresh watermelon vodka cocktail. If you're lucky to drop in at the right time, they have live music playing every so often. Camino de Orellana 781, Tel: 02-255-1421, Cel: 09-9561-3074, E-mail: anankepizzeria@hotmail.com. Updated: Jan 09, 2013.

Los Hot Dogs De La Gonzalez Suarez

(HOT DOGS: $1-4) Quito is a city that takes its hotdogs seriously, and many quiteños swear by the offerings at Los Hot Dogs de la Gonzalez Suarez. You won't find anything here that you wouldn't at another hotdog stand around town, but "Los Hot Dogs" has consistently good dogs and toppings, including pineapple marmalade and crushed potato chips.

The atmosphere at all of the restaurants is pretty informal, and there really isn't any seating; after the bars and clubs shut down, you will see people outside Los Hot Dogs, leaning against cars and buildings, trying not to spill the sauce off of their cherished hotdogs. Located on Gonzalez Suarez and San Ignacio, at the very top of Guapulo where the street bends downwards. Updated: May 31, 2013.

QUITO

Loved it? Loathed it? Write a review and help other travelers

QUITO

Northern Quito

The area north of La Mariscal and before the drop-off into the valleys is generally referred to as "el Norte de Quito." Here you will find two of Quito's most beautiful parks, Parque Carolina and Parque Metropolitano, as well as some of the city's nicest restaurants, hotels, malls, office buildings and neighborhoods. In contrast with the Centro Histórico, the northern sector is very modern and developed, with a strong North American influence.

Things To See and Do in Northern Quito

The Northern part of the city provides the grounds for some posh, Western-priced shopping as well as a number of more extravagant touristy sites. With 3 major shopping malls, Northern Quito delivers a wide array of designer brands and commercial goods to the public:

-**Quicentro:** Av. Naciones Unidas entre 6 de Diciembre and Shyris.

-**El Jardín:** Av. Amazonas N36-152 and Naciones Unidas.

-**C.C.I Shopping Center:** Avenida República No. 6-114 and Amazonas.

In addition to this, there's still a lot to explore in terms of scenery, culture and history in the Northern area despite it's modernity. So don't think that Northern Quito is completely dominated by consumer culture! It isn't! And you'll find beautiful parks and sites to visit here as well.
Updated: Mar 13, 2013.

TelefériQo !

(ENTRANCE: $8.50) Quito's best-known tourist attraction offers some of the most spectacular and most easily accessible views of the city. There are 18 gondolas that soar up the side of Quito's western mountain range along the Pichincha Volcanoes. The ride lasts only 10 minutes but takes you to an altitude of 4,050 m (13,300 ft). At the top, there is a lookout platform complete with coffee, snacks, horse rental and oxygen for the faint of breath. Walk up the hill from the platform and you'll find some excellent hiking trails that lead to more views of Quito and the Pichincha Volcanoes, which are visibly snow-capped from time to time throughout the year.

In spite of the thin air, the hike up toward Rucu Pichincha is not technically challenging, and you can reach the Cava del Oso ("bear cave"...but no bears in sight!) in about an hour and a half. There have been reports of assaults on the path, though, so it is best to hike in a group. Because the mountain tends to cloud over very quickly, try to go as early as possible for clear views.

At the base of the TeleferiQo, there is popular Vulcano Park, an amusement park, and a slew of restaurants, cafés and gift shops, though some of them are closed now that the initial excitement over the TeleferiQo opening has died down.

The easiest way to get to the ride entrance on Avenida Occidental is by taxi; the cab ride costs about $4-6 from anywhere in Quito. Tel: 02-222-2996.
Updated: Jan 24, 2013.

Parque La Carolina

Almost two kilometers (1.2 miles) in length, Parque Carolina is situated between residential and commercial districts in the northern part of Quito. It is the number one choice for sports enthusiasts, housing several athletic facilities, including a football field, basketball and tennis courts, volleyball nets, a skating area, and some of the only bicycle lanes in the city. A boating lake and children's playground make this park popular with families, too. Unsurprisingly, it's busiest during weekends, but despite its weekend popularity, Carolina is still probably your best bet for finding your own private patch of grass amid the city. Something that you shouldn't pass up on if you plan on visiting the park is the Jardin Botanico (Botanical Garden) that's filled with all kinds of orchids and flowers, located on the Southeastern end of the park itself. Parque Carolina is great during the day, but after dark it's best to not pass through. The park can be reached by any of its four bordering streets: Avenida Shyris, Avenida Eloy Alfaro, Avenida Amazonas or Avenida Naciones Unidas.
Updated: Jan 22, 2013.

Parque Metropolitano !

This is Quito's biggest park and one of the largest city parks in Latin America. Set up on a hill overlooking Quito on one side and the valleys outside of Quito on the other, Parque Metropolitano is a maze of forest paths, roads, sports fields and picnic areas.

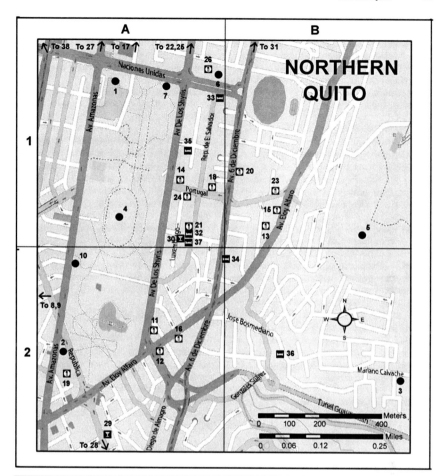

Activities ●

1 C.C.I. Shopping Mall A1
2 El Jardín Shopping Mall A2
3 Museo Guayasamín and
  La Capilla del Hombre B2
4 Parque La Carolina A1
5 Parque Metropolitano B1
6 Quicentro Shopping Mall A1
7 Quito Tour Bus A1
8 Rumipamba Archeological
  Park A2
9 TeleferiQo A2
10 Vivarium A2

Eating 🍽

11 Al Forno Pizzeria A2
12 Capuleto Deli Café A2
13 Carmine B1
14 Cyrano's Bakery A1
15 Il Risotto B1
16 La Maison Du Fromage A2
17 Las Conchitas Asadas A1
18 Mister Bagel A1
19 Raclette A2
20 Restaurante Mi Cocina B1
21 Romolo E Remo A1

22 Rusty's Hamburgers A1
23 San Telmo B1
24 Sushi-In A1
25 Swiss Corner A1
26 T.G.I. Friday's A1
27 Taqueria La Michoacana A1
28 Zazú A2

Nightlife 🍸

29 BLUES A2
30 Pideme La Luna A1

Sleeping 🛏

31 Casa Vida Verde B1
32 Dann Carlton A1
33 Four Points Sheraton Quito A1
34 Hotel Akros B2
35 Hotel Finlandia A1
36 Hotel Mirador De Bellavista B2
37 Le Parc Hotel A1
38 Lupe Coronel A1

Loved it? Loathed it? Write a review and help other travelers

QUITO

Most of the trees are eucalyptus, which produce a heavenly scent year round. There are a couple of access roads to the park; the main one is Diego Noboa just up the hill from the Olympic soccer stadium. URL: www.parque-metropolitano.ec.
Updated: Jan 22, 2013.

Museo Guayasamín &La Capilla del Hombre !

(ADMISSION: $4) As of November 29, 2012, marking the 10-year anniversary of the opening of the Capilla del Hombre, the Museo Guayasamín has been moved and integrated into the Capilla del Hombre complex.

Museo Guayasamín houses an extensive collection of the artist's own work, from the beginning of his "career" at the age of 7, right up until his death in 1999. He is famous for his abstract humanist works, that both reflect and denounce the violence of the 20th century with its world wars, civil wars, genocide, concentration camps, dictatorships and tortures. The museum is also home to some of the artist's extensive collection of archaeological, colonial and contemporary art, which he bequeathed to the city of Quito shortly before he died.

Guayasamín's most ambitions work, however, is the Capilla del Hombre, or "Man's Chapel," located in the same complex as the museum. Unfortunately it is still unfinished (the artist was still working on it when he died), but it still contains some powerful imagery that reflects his own grim view of Latin American history since the arrival of the Spanish. He wanted to dedicate it to the pre-Columbian man and his 500 years of quiet resistance and struggles against the conquerers. The chapel's altar holds an eternal flame in defense of peace and human rights. Lorenzo Chávez EA18-143 and Mariano Calvache (corner), Bellavista, Tel: 02-246-5265/244-8492, Fax: 02-333-0723, E-mail: 02-333-0723, URL: www.capilladelhombre.com.

Quito Tour Bus

(TICKETS: $12) The Quito Tour Bus is a convenient and comfortable way to see all of the city's main attractions. Each day, the modern two-story tour buses leave from Avenida Naciones Unida (diagonal to the Quicentro Shopping mall, in front of the park by the pedestrian bridge) at 9 a.m., 10 a.m., 1 p.m., 2 p.m., 3 p.m. and 4 p.m. The bus makes a thorough three-hour journey through the city with stops at 12 different sights, including the Botanical Garden, Plaza Foch, La Basílica, El Panecillo, Centro Histórico's Plaza Grande, and the TeleferiQo cable car.

Passengers can hop on and off at any of the stops within 24 hours of their ticket purchase.

On the way, you will also learn important historical and cultural information about the various places through a pre-recorded audio commentary in english. There is also an evening ride that leaves at 7:30 p.m. if you would like to see the city lit up at night.

You can pay for the bus as you board or buy tickets in advance. Buses leave from Avenida Naciones Unidas, diagonal to the Quicentro Shopping mall, in front of the park by the pedestrian bridge. Bring a hat and sunscreen. Tel: 02-243-5458/245-8010, URL: www.quindetour.com.
Updated: May 08, 2013.

Rumipamba Archeological Park

An archeological site that holds artifacts and ancient shelters dating from 1500 B.C. all the way to 1500 A.D. You'll find some incredible evidence regarding the lives and societies of the indegenous people that once governed this land, long before Quito was even its official name.

Walk beside the remains of Inca walls and houses, and travel down the incredible trenches that the Inca's made to access the coast from the Andes. There's a lot to soak in as you walk across the expanse of this archeological park. Mariana de Jesús Ave. and Occidental.
Updated: Mar 13, 2013.

Vivarium

(ADMISSION: $3) The Vivarium, which opened in 1989, is considered one of the premiere reptile houses in Latin America. There are 87 reptiles and amphibians, but it primarily houses snakes of all kinds. Other than the king cobra, every animal in the Vivarium is native to Ecuador. It houses boas, iguanas, tortoises and even the fear Equis, which is one of the deadliest snakes in Ecuador. Tuesday-Sunday 9:30 a.m.-5:30 p.m. Av. Amazonas 3008 and Rumipamba (Parque Carolina), Tel: 02-227-1799, URL: www.vivarium.org.ec.
Updated: Jan 22, 2013.

Northern Quito Lodging

"New Town" Quito tends to cater to business travelers more than the backpacker community. Hotels here have spacious, luxurious rooms and international chains are the majority, so don't expect to find an abundance of budget-priced hotels or hostels. like La Mariscal. If you're looking to stay a bit longer in the city, the north is also a good place to find shared housing, home-stays and private apartments. Prices vary, so be sure to scout out a few options before settling down. Updated: Mar 06, 2013.

BUDGET
Casa Vida Verde

(ROOMS: $20-25) Casa Vida Verde is a fully furnished residential hostel, created to provide a safe and comfortable residence for foreign students, workers and tourists who would like both independence and the opportunity to socialize with others. The Casa Vide Verde means "The House of Green Living," which unfortunately sometimes means no hot water or heating, and can make for some chilly nights.

Both English and Spanish are spoken, and nightly or long-term stays can be arranged. The hostel has a great view of Quito and the mountains from the roof-top terrace and a kitchen complete with all basics items. All bills are included in the cost of a room, and all cleaning costs are included with the exception of your dish washing, which you are expected to do yourself. In addition, Spanish lessons can be arranged through the Vida Verde Spanish School. Those with experience in teaching English can inquire about possible paid teaching opportunities. Vida Verde has contacts with several local schools and can help set up interviews. Gonzalo Noriega N39-221 y Gaspar de Villaroel, Tel: 02-226-0471, URL: http://www.vidaverde.com/casavidaverde.html.
Updated: Mar 07, 2013.

Lupe Coronel

(ROOMS: $18-25) If you're looking for a homestay with a recommended family, stay with Lupe. The family is friendly, will assist you with your Spanish, and always makes an effort to include you. They are a warm family of four (mother, father, daughter and son), offering two private rooms at $18 a day each. This price includes breakfast, as well as access to a washing machine, Internet and a park nearby, which is great for evening jogs. Located in the neighborhood San Pedro Claver, near the old airport. Machala 5676 and Carlos V, Tel: 02-229-7431 / 098-400-8158.
Updated: Mar 07, 2013.

MID-RANGE
Hotel Mirador De Bellavista

(ROOMS: $30-72) Situated beside the steep, cobblestone slopes of the road that leads up to it, Mirador de Bellavista is a quiet little hotel that's perched on the western slopes overlooking the city. What's really convenient about this place is that it's located within walking distance of the Museo de Guayasamin and Parque Metropolitano, and is surrounded by a neighborhood that has it's charm as well. Rooms are tidy and some even have a decent view of Quito but they're nothing to boast about, although they do offer hot water 24/7, private bathrooms and a restaurant downstairs as well. The reception also functions as an impromptu tour desk, so don't be afraid to ask questions if you have any! Bosmediano E14-194,(between Gonzáles Suárez y Pasaje Lafayet), Tel: 02-245-4741 / 09-202-7627, E-mail: info@hotelmiradorbellavista.com, URL: www.hotelmiradorbellavista.com.
Updated: Mar 13, 2013.

Hotel Finlandia

(ROOMS: $60-83) Located close to the city's financial district and popular tourist destinations, Hotel Finlandia is a friendly, modern hotel with 25 smartly styled and comfortable rooms with amenities like mini-fridges and cable TV. The cozy atmosphere, surrounding gardens and welcoming staff are a pleasant complement to any international trip, whether you're just passing through on business or about to embark on an adventure in Ecuador. The hotel also has a restaurant, La Tuka, and offers 24-hour reception, city tours and WiFi. It is only a block away from one of city's main parks, Parque Carolina, a good place to unwind on weekends. Finlandia 227 and Suecia (corner), Tel: 02-224-4287/8/9, E-mail: info@hotelfinlandia.com.ec, URL: www.hotelfinlandia.com.
Updated: Jan 09, 2013.

HIGH-END
Four Points Sheraton Quito

(ROOMS: $90-110) The Four Points Sheraton Quito is a beautiful multi-story luxury hotel in the northern part of the city, right across from the popular mall, Quicentro.

Prices are reasonable for the services offered and plenty of extras are included. There's a spa and gym but no pool. Av. Naciones Unidas and República de El Salvador, Tel: 02-297-0002, Fax: 02-243-3906.
Updated: Jan 09, 2013.

Dann Carlton

(ROOMS: $130 and up) Hotel Dann Carlton is a Colombian chain offering luxury standards and catering to business travelers. Prices tend to be a bit lower than other international chains, and special rates are given to businesses. It is located in a quiet neighborhood, just a block from the Parque Carolina and closer to the airport than Mariscal hotels. Av. República de El Salvador N34-377 and Irlanda, Tel: 02-224-9008, Fax: 02-244-8808, E-mail: reservas@danncarltonquito.com, URL: www.danncarltonquito.com.
Updated: Jan 09, 2013.

Hotel Akros

(ROOMS: $92.50-160) Hotel Akros is an aging luxury hotel in the north of Quito that offers 128 rooms and suites. Rooms are well-appointed and include all of the amenities one would expect from a luxury class hotel. The staff is warm, welcoming and always prepared to lend a hand with bags or to answer questions about the city. The on-site restaurant, The Promenade, is open for lunch and dinner, and serves a variety of Ecuadorian and international cuisine. Breakfast is served at the indoor café, and guests can enjoy live music at La Boheme, the hotel's piano bar. Av. 6 de Diciembre N34-120, Tel: 02-243-0600, Fax: 02-243-1727, E-mail: akros@hotelakros.com, URL: www.hotelakros.com.
Updated: Jan 09, 2013.

Le Parc Hotel ♩

(ROOMS: $160-280) Located in the financial disrict of Quito, Le Parc Hotel offers its guests spacious rooms (each is a suite, 4 rooms per floor) with modern decor, incredibly comfy beds and a large bath. Locationwise, it's actually pretty close to all the major places in the city, with taxi's costing no more than $2-3 to get to where you need to go.

The hotel also houses a bar and restaurant which are on the pricier side of what's available in other parts, but they do serve some delicious food. Also, within walking distance is the Quicentro shopping mall. República de El Salvador N34-349 and Irlanda, Tel:

02-227-6800 / 1-888-790-5264, Fax: 02-227-7870, E-mail: reservas@leparc.com.ec.
Updated: Mar 07, 2013.

Northern Quito Restaurants

The restaurants to the north of Quito tend toward international cuisine and fast food. With three of Quito's larger malls, El Jardin (at Amazonas and República), CCI (Amazonas and Naciones Unidas) and Quicentro (6 de Diciembre and Naciones Unidas), food courts are wildly popular; you will be hard-pressed to find a seat on weekends.

There are also several nicer restaurants along Portugal from Eloy Alfaro down to Shyris. The crowds are less touristy at these spots, but that doesn't mean the prices are any less than at restaurants in Mariscal.
Updated: Jan 18, 2013.

ARGENTINIAN
San Telmo

(ENTREES: $16-39) San Telmo is expensive by Ecuadorian standards, but it is worth every cent. The atmosphere is elegant and peaceful, the service is excellent, and the steaks are thick, juicy and delicious. There are no vegetarian dishes, but there is a good selection of steaks, seafood and chicken. Both indoor and outdoor seating is available, and there is a cozy fireplace inside. Portugal 440 and Francisco Casanova, Tel: 02-333-1944, Fax: 593-2-246-5434, E-mail: santelmo@santelmorestaurante.com, URL: www.santelmorestaurant.com.
Updated: Jan 09, 2013.

ASIAN
Sushi-In

(SUSHI: $4.25-12.55) Sushi-In offers up decent sushi at a reasonable price. Located in Quito's northern district, the ambiance of the place can best be described as what you'd expect from a fast-food sushi place—clean, efficient and with no frills. In addition to the relatively cheap sushi, a few other limited menu options are available.

There are vegetarian rolls available for those who do not eat fish. You can also order anything off the menu for delivery or take-out. Half rolls can also be prepared if you want to try a few or several different ones at once. Portugal N34-340, between Shyris and República de El Salvador, Tel: 02-333-0929, URL: www.sushi-in.com.ec.
Updated: Jan 18, 2013.

ECUADORIAN
Restaurante Mi Cocina
(ENTREES: $15-20) A semi-elegant restaurant in the north of Quito a couple of blocks from the Parque Carolina, Restaurante Mi Cocina offers typical Ecuadorian cuisine like *empanadas* and *fritada* (fired pork). There is outdoor seating and plenty of indoor seating for big groups. Try the *chocolate caliente* (hot chocolate); its made from real chocolate and served with the traditional slice of *queso fresco* (fresh farmer's cheese). Monday-Saturday 9 a.m.-9 p.m., Sunday 9 a.m.-8 p.m. Av. 6 de Diciembre and Alemán (Megamaxi), Tel: 02-224-1210, E-mail: micocinamegamaxi@hotmail.com. Updated: Jan 09, 2013.

ITALIAN
Il Risotto
(ENTREES: $8-16) For an authentic Italian banquet and elegant atmosphere with stunning city views, Il Risotto is your spot. The friendly, Italian owners create a pleasant service atmosphere and the buffet ($12-18) will make anyone start to drool. There is outdoor seating on a small balcony in the back. It has a second location on República del Salvador, near Portugal. Eloy Alfaro N34-447 and Portugal, Tel: 02-224-6850, E-mail: ilrisotto1@puntonet.ec. Updated: Jan 09, 2013.

Romolo E Remo
(PIZZA: $2.50-8) If it's high quality Italian-cuisine that you're in search of, then be sure to get your fix at this joint. From salads to pizzas, Romulo e Remo excels in providing its hungry clientele with exquisite Italian dishes for a price that falls in line with quality. Sink into your chair and revel in the coziness of the place as you wait for your order. Just know that you can't add ingredients to any pizza you choose from the menu, which makes for a fixed and rather unmalleable list. But that's not to say its not extensive or delicious! Republica del Salvador N34-399, Tel: 02-600-0683. Updated: Mar 13, 2013.

Al Forno Pizzeria
(PIZZA: $4-9) With a warm and inviting atmosphere along with staff to add to it all, Al Forno serves up a wholesome selection of Italian cuisine and artisan pizza. Don't worry about having a lack of choices to satisfy your hunger either, as this joint has an array of different pizzas to satisfy just about

anybody's watering palette. Prices are quite reasonable as well. Belgica E9-35 and Shyris Ave., Tel: 02-333-0681, E-mail: info@alfornopizzeriaitaliana.com, URL: http://alfornopizzeriaitaliana.com/index.php. Updated: Mar 12, 2013.

Carmine
(ENTREES: $17-32) Head to Carmine in the northern sector of the city for a unique take on Italian cuisine. Hip and modern, dishes here include a variety of tasty pastas, seafood and meat mains cooked in a Mediterranean style. Owner and chef, Bill Carmine, translates the menu board and describes dishes in English for those with only a smattering of Spanish. Although the plates are pretty pricey, especially compared to many of the restaurants in Quito, it is well worth the splurge. Servings are generous and of high quality, with options like pappardelle in pesto sauce, gnocchi in rabbit sauce, veal ravioli, and salmon in a balsamic sauce. The restaurant's interior is classy and features modern artwork on its walls. Monday-Saturday noon-11 p.m., Sunday 12:30-5 p.m. Catalina Aldaz N34-208 and Portugal, Tel: 02-333-2829/2896, Cel: 09-9796-4646, E-mail: reservquito@carmineristorante.com / carmine@carmineristorante.com, URL: www.carmineristorante.com. Updated: Jan 17, 2013.

Capuleto Deli Cafe
Capuleto is a lovely Italian restaurant and deli with a large garden patio that has ample seating and a strange family of parrakeets. Prices are on the expensive side, but the food is full of flavor and portions are generous. Av. Eloy Alfaro N32-544 and Bélgica, Tel: 02-255-0611, E-mail: ristorante@capuleto.com.ec, URL: www.capuleto.com.ec. Updated: Jan 09, 2013.

SEAFOOD
Zazú
(ENTREES: $15-39) Offering a modern interpretation of Peruvian cuisine, this stylish restaurant is filled nightly with diplomats, oil expats and Quiteño high society. Stand out appetizers include thinly sliced octopus served with a creamy olive dip, and crispy mushroom and artichoke "empanadas" encased in wonton-style wrappers. There are plenty of main dishes to choose from for meat eaters, including tender New Zealand lamb chops, but the house specialty is seafood. The unusual combination of tuna in a

QUITO

spicy pineapple sauce is spectacular. Accompany your meal with a perfectly made pisco sour or a bottle of wine ($16-400). Service is attentive and you may even be lucky to get a visit from the chef himself. Call ahead to reserve if you want to be sure to find a seat at one of the 10 or so tables. Mariano Aguilera 331 and Martin Carrion, La Pradera, Tel: 02-254-3559, E-mail: info@zazuquito.com, URL: www.zazuquito.com. Updated: Jan 09, 2013.

Las Conchitas Asadas

(ENTREES: $3.50-5) Las Conchitas Asadas is an inexpensive seafood restaurant with a casual atmosphere and big portions in the north of Quito. Isla Floreana 510 and Fernandina, Tel: 02-246-5444. Updated: Jan 09, 2013.

SWISS

Swiss Corner

($10 and up) Craving a delicious and filling home-cooked meal? Then check out this eatery, which serves up some of the tastiest and heartiest meals in Quito. This Swiss restaurant specializes in delectable breakfast bites such as pastries, omelets and french toast. However, dinner guests will not be disappointed, either: The evening menu includes heavy comfort foods like stroganoff and tortellini. Ask for the *platos típicos* (typical plates) menu to browse the evening's entree specials.

The restaurant has two locations in Quito, both in the northern part of town. The original, on the corner of Avenida de los Shyris and El Telegrafo, includes both a deli and restaurant. A second deli can be found further north on the corner of Avenida Eloy Alfaro and Avenida de los Helechos. Av. de los Shyris N38-41 and El Telégrafo (corner); Av. Eloy Alfaro (lot 10A) and De los Helechos (corner), Tel: 02-246-8007/280-5360 ext. 102, E-mail: ventas@swisscorner.com.ec, URL: www.swisscorner.com.ec. Updated: Jan 09, 2013.

Raclette

(ENTREES: $15-20) Both tasteful and tasty, Raclette is an elegant restaurant located in the food court of El Jardin mall near Parque La Carolina. The house specialty, of course, is raclettes, served with cheese, chicken and fine beef; a vegetable alternative is also available. The restaurant also serves up an assortment of delicious fondues. Other popular dishes include savory steak favorites like filet mignon and Chateaubriand. If possible, save room for the extensively rich dessert menu. Mall El Jardín, Patio de Comidas, Tel: 02-298-0266, URL: www.raclette.com.ec. Updated: Jan 09, 2013.

INTERNATIONAL

Mister Bagel

(BREAKFAST: $3-5) Mister Bagel is a great breakfast and lunch spot not only because it has the best bagels in Quito, but also one of the biggest book exchanges. With any purchase, you can exchange an unlimited number of books, contingent on the approval of one of the employees. Try the *aji* bagel with the famous Ecuadorian hot pepper or the quinoa bagel, in addition to classics like cinnamon raisin, everything, sesame and whole wheat. The lunch specials are a pretty good deal: soup of the day with bagel chips, a bagel sandwich (pizza bagel, chicken salad or tuna salad) and a fresh fruit juice. There are also a few different breakfast options, some of which include eggs and bacon. Av. Portugal E10-95 and Av. 6 de Diciembre, Building Oporto, Tel: 02-224-0978, E-mail: hughgillis@yahoo.com. Updated: Jan 09, 2013.

Taquería La Michoacana

(ENTREES: $10-15) Tiny and unappealing from the outside, La Michoacana is a little hole in the wall that serves up some big and exquisite Mexican cuisine on the inside. Starting anywhere from their delicious taco combos to an assortment of Mexican entrees, you'll find it hard to find a place in Quito that nails it as well (and as cheaply) as La Michoacana does with Mexican food. Elialiut and Brasil Ave., Tel: 02-246-5199. Updated: Mar 13, 2013.

T.G.I. Friday's

(ENTREES: $8-20) Friday's is wildly popular among Quiteños and has a slightly more formal reputation than it does in the United States, partially because the people in Quito that can afford it have more money than the average citizen. Offering a wide selection of grilled meats, chicken, salads, fried food, huge scrumptious desserts and a gigantic drink menu, Friday's offers all-American food. Happy hour is from 4-9 p.m. on weekdays, when drinks and appetizers go two for the price of one. Quicentro Shopping Mall, Naciones Unidas, Tel: 02-226-4638. Updated: Jan 09, 2013.

Rusty's Hamburgers !

(COMBO: $5-6) As far as hamburger joints in Quito, this is probably the best around. Owned by a Californian transplant, Rusty, it has been a fixture in Quito since the 1970s. It serves up all the fare you would expect for a diner: hamburgers, French fries, onion rings, milk shakes, even root beer! Sometimes you will find Rusty at the till taking orders, he is hard to miss with his handlebar mustache. It is a bit on the pricey side for Quito; a simple meal costs around $5, but if you really need your greasy food fix it is a great place to go. Av. De Los Shyris, N43-157 and Río Coca, Tel: 02-245-1098/244-0080.
Updated: Jan 09, 2013.

CAFE'S
Cyrano Bakery

While there are hundreds of *panaderías* and *pastelerías* in Quito, one of the best fresh-baked bread shops in town is Cyrano Bakery. Cyrano offers up more of a gourmet selection than other shops, with whole grain, yucca and quinoa breads in loaf and roll varieties, as well as garlic and herb focaccia. Cyrano also sells traditional cinnamon rolls, sweet orange rolls and chocolate croissants. A selection of scrumptious party-pleasing sized cakes and pies are also on hand, as are the small individual pieces of cake and delicious fruit turnovers. There are also Cyrano branches in some of the city's upscale malls, including Quicentro Shopping (Av. de Los Shyris and Naciones Unidas. Tel: 02-225-9314). Portugal E9-59 and Av. de Los Shyris, Tel: 02-289-2143/02-224-3507.
Updated: Jan 10, 2013.

FRENCH
La Maison Du Fromage

(SET LUNCH: $6.50) After spending the morning at Carolina Park or the Alliance Française, have lunch at La Maison du Fromage (Casa de Quesos). This bistro lives up to its name, offering a variety of dishes highlighting cheeses. Try one of the pasta dishes, or opt for a chicken or beef *milanesa* (breaded cutlets) with mashed potatoes. Grilled chicken in honey sauce or grilled beef in cheese sauce are also on the menu. All is served with a delightful salad and your choice of fresh fruit juice or wine.

La Maison du Frommage uses only Ecuadorian ingredients. It also sells artisanal cheeses, wines and other products. In the evening, you can also bring some friends along and order cheese fondu. Rusia N3-21 and Eloy Alfaro, Tel: 02-227-5938, Cel: 09-9502-5681/9549-0660.
Updated: Jan 28, 2013.

Northern Quito Nightlife

Less tourist-oriented is the nightlife scene in Northern Quito, bringing in all the cool cats from the ritzier parts of town to bars and clubs that are, to say the least, more 'extravagantly' priced. Clubs in this area will charge upwards of $20 just as a cover charge, whereupon drinks inside the clubs can skyrocket to $10 for a cocktail, to $4 for just a bottle of water.

BLUES (a.k.a Siete) !

(COVER: $12-25) A home away from home for privileged Ecuadorians, Blues is one of the few clubs in Quito that is of international caliber and can stay open late—usually until 6 a.m. The club, open Thursday-Saturday, has resident DJ nights and weekly special events, such as classic and alternative rock tributes, featuring live music, and various themed parties. The music is an eclectic mix of Euro- and '80s-pop, punctuated with popular Latin-Caribbean tunes, though Blues is best known for its electronic music, from downbeat to house. Weekend sets by international DJs are the highlight, when the hipsters and well-heeled clientele sip expensive imported spirits in dimly lit corners and mingle on the dance floor. Women get in free before midnight on most nights, men have to pay up regardless. Open Thursday, Friday and Saturday. República Ave. 476 and Pradera. URL: www.clubblues.com.
Updated: Mar 15, 2013

Pideme La Luna

(DRINKS: $8-15) With an incredibly dazzling display of ambiance and character, this bar and restaurant is located just around the block from Quito's main business district. Pideme La Luna offers a variety of fancy drinks made with high quality liquor, and will surround you with decorations and a mood that'll be sure to keep your senses tingling with wonder and excitement. Prices (given the area its located in) are rather high though, but every now and then there's some good drink promotions in effect that one should definitely take advantage of - their cocktails are quite good. Luxemburgo N34-166 and Holanda. Tel: 02-603-6273. URL: www.pidemelaluna.com.
Updated: Mar 15, 2013.

QUITO

Loved it? Loathed it? Write a review and help other travelers

QUITO

Around Quito

Those looking to escape the capital city do not have to venture far: Enveloped by a stunning landscapes of golden grasslands, volcanic peaks and plunging valleys, Quito makes journeys from its bustling borders both convenient and plentiful. On weekends quiteños flee the city to soak in Papallacta's thermal springs or take a family trip to the pretty *pueblos* dotted along the quietly quaint Valle de los Chillos.

Many travelers optimize their stay in Quito by taking day trips to Quito's surrounding region. In less than two hours, travelers can transport themselves to the tranquility of the pretty *páramo*. Adrenaline-seekers can take their pick of a variety of volcanoes, including the ultimate rush of conquering the perfectly conical Cotopaxi.

Many trips can be organized through tour operators in town or in all-inclusive packages offered by the highlands' numerous haciendas. However, independent spirits can simply arm themselves with a map and an open mind. A variety of buses from the city's northern bus stations (Ophelia and Carcelén) head out into Quito's surrounding area. Updated: Jan 21, 2013.

Things To See and Do Around Quito
HIKING AROUND QUITO

Few large cities can top Quito when it comes to nearby hiking and climbing opportunities. Just 65 kilometers (40 mi) from the capital, dozens of volcanoes and mountains jut forth from the rich tapestry of cultivated fields and high-altitude grasslands that extend north and south across the 400-kilometer (249 mi) long "Avenue of the Volcanoes."

Some favorite day hikes among Quito's outdoors community include Fuya Fuya, Pasachoa, Papallacta and Rucu Pichincha. None of these require any technical skills and since they are day hikes, you won't need much more than a good pair of boots. Hikes and non-technical climbs that can be done in a long day (mostly because of the drive) include Iliniza Norte, Imbabura, Rumiñahui and Sincholagua. If you are out to tackle snow-capped volcanoes, Cayambe and Cotopaxi await, just 60 kilometers (37 mi) north and south of Quito respectively. Summiting

either of these two glaciated beauties requires an overnight stay and, unless you are an expert, the help of one of Quito's numerous guiding companies.

Two volcanoes are located about 10 kilometers (6 mi) west of Quito — Guagua and Rucu Pichincha, 4,776 meters (15,670 ft) and 4,627 meters (15,180 ft), respectively. Guagua, which means "baby" in the Quichua language, is higher than its neighbor and currently active: it covered the Ecuadorian capital with ash in 1999. Inactive Rucu, meaning "old," is slightly lower and closer to Quito. Updated: Mar 15, 2013.

Hiking Pasochoa Volcano

At 4,199 m (13,766 ft), Pasochoa's lushly vegetated crater and slopes make for an unforgettable day hike. In recent years, due to its beautiful setting and convenient location just 30 kilometers (18.6 miles) south of Quito, Pasachoa has become one of the most popular hiking excursions just outside the capital.

The mountain can be climbed from every side but the west face, which is steep and composed of unstable rock. The two most easily accessible routes are via the Refugio de Vida Silvestre (Pasochoa Forest Reserve) or the Central Hidroeléctrica, which provides easier access to the peak but a much less picturesque ascent.

Getting To and Away from Pasachoa Volcano
Regardless of the route you ultimately choose, you need to travel south out of Quito on the Pan American Highway to Amaguaña. Public buses leave frequently from the Plaza La Marín station, which you can get to by Ecovia. In bus or car, the trip takes about one and a half hours.

Hiking the Refugio de Vida Silvestre Route
The get to the Reserve, travel to Amaguaña and then take a left on to a cobblestone road just across the main entrance to the town. Drive about 100 meters up to a church with a double bell tower (which is visible from the highway) and make a right. Follow the road for approximately six kilometers (3.7 miles) up to the Reserve's main entrance. There is a fee of $2 for Ecuadorians and residents and $7 for foreigners. This fee gets you in

and buys you a good map of the Reserve's trail system. It's also possible to camp for $2 per person. About 100 meters up the hill from the caretaker's house and parking lot, there is an environmental education center. A number of trails that range in difficulty and duration begin here. Sometimes there are also naturalist guides available to accompany you on the shorter walks.

To reach the summit, or most often just the cliff that's an hour short of the summit, you should follow the relatively well marked "green" trail for about two hours through a bamboo forest, a splendid stretch of cloud forest, and a pine grove until you reach the *páramo*. From here, follow the footpaths to the left of the crater for about an hour to an hour and a half until you come to a steep rock cliff. At this point you are at approximately 3,950 meters (12,959 feet). It's possible but not recommended to continue up the cliff and onto the peak, mainly because it's steep and the rock is unstable.

Hiking Rucu Pichincha

Climbing Rucu Pichincha used to require hiring a truck or making a long, and sometimes dangerous, three-hour slog through eucalyptus forest and sponge grass up to Cruz Loma. Fortunately, Quito's Teleférico makes these less appealing options unnecessary. The gondola ride departs from a station on Avenida Occidental and Avenida La Gasca and costs $8 for foreigners and $4.50 for Ecuadorians. See Quito's Teleférico for more information (p. 144).

The hike from Cruz Loma to Rucu's peak consists of a one and a half hour walk along a grassy ridge that steadily rises toward a rocky base beneath the summit. Once you reach the rock, you can either go right and traverse the cliff until you reach a sandy slope that leads to the summit or go straight up the rock. Both of these routes require an additional one and a half hours. The second option should not be attempted by inexperienced climbers unless they are accompanied by a guide equipped with ropes and harnesses.

Hiking Guagua Pichincha

Guagua Pichincha is best accessed from Lloa, a village located south of the two volcanoes. Take a bus or cab south on Avenida Mariscal Jose Antonio de Sucre to Calle Angamarca, where you will find transportation to Lloa. You can also hire a cab to take you all the way to Lloa and even to the refuge, which is just an hour walk from the crater. If you decide to hike all the way from the village to the crater, head west out of town and follow a meandering road up to the refuge. It takes between five and six hours of steady walking. From the refuge, there is a clear trail to the crater. It was once possible to walk down into the crater; however since the eruption of Guagua Pichincha in 1999 and the possibility of renewed emissions of noxious volcanic gases, this is not recommended.

HORSEBACK RIDING AROUND QUITO

If your legs just aren't up for a massive hike or trek, another great way to enjoy the stunning scenery just outside of Quito is from the back of a horse. A number of larger tour agencies and smaller private companies offer horseback riding trips for all ages and skill levels. Single and multi-day trips are available, depending on how long you (and your bum) want to spend in the saddle. Popular places for horseback riding include Cotopaxi National Park, in Pululahua Crater, in Antisana Ecological Reserve and near Quilotoa. Updated: Jan 21, 2013.

Green Horse Ranch ♪

(PRICE: $85-1,550) Green Horse Ranch is located at the bottom of a volcanic crater just outside of Quito. The ranch specializes in trail rides throughout the Western Andes, and offers one- to 12-day trips venturing into the heart of the Ecuadorian Andes. All trips are tailor-made, based on your experience and interest. Astrid Müller, the German owner, has been running the ranch since 1995. Working with horses was her childhood dream, and her knowledgeable international and local staff has lifelong riding experience.

The horses are well-treated and healthy. With luscious green fields to run around and with constant access to fresh streams, this place is not only a paradise for the horses but also for any animal-lover. Astrid takes time to explain each horse's personality and past, so that you'll be sure to feel relaxed and comfortable with your companion. You'll also get a choice between European and Western saddle.

The scenery reveals the outstanding landscape that has made Ecuador famous: cloud forests, desert-like landscapes, deep river canyons and steep mountain slopes. The

QUITO

QUITO

tracks are no problem for beginners and no bore for experts. Due to the remoteness of the area, overnight stops are mainly basic, though always carefully chosen. The price includes pick-up and return to Quito, and involves an optional photo stop by the famous Mitad del Mundo monument. Each way takes about 1.5 hours, depending on the traffic. Day trips or weeklong trips can be arranged. Pululahua Crater, Tel: 02-380-6338, Cel: 09-8612-5433, E-mail: ranch@gmx.net, URL: www.horseranch.de.
Updated: Jan 10, 2013.

Lodging Around Quito

While further from the action and sufficiently more expensive, accommodations outside of Quito are definitely worth checking out if your schedule and budget allow. For the most part, these hotels aren't your usual South American hard mattress, breakfast-not-included types of places. Rather, you are more likely to find authentic haciendas, luxurious spa accommodations, ecological reserves and lodges that are at your service to relax and soothe you.

These locales are not just for sleeping, but for full relaxation, for day-trip exploration, and for a taste of Ecuador outside, but still within reach, of the hustle and bustle of the capital city.
Updated: Jan 9, 2013.

La Carriona

(ROOMS: $109-195) Located a mere half hour south of Quito, La Carriona is a viable option for the traveler who needs to stay within close reach of the capital but who still wants to have the hacienda experience (at a reasonable rate). A traditional hacienda—over 200 years old—the 25 rooms and eight junior suites are elegant and ample, with large windows for guests to enjoy nice views of the gardens.

Facilities at the hacienda include a conference area, sauna, steam room, Jacuzzi, pool, tennis court and soccer field. There is even a small bullring, and bullfights in the local tradition can be arranged with advance notice. Breakfast is included in room prices as well. Km 2 1/2 via Sangolquí - Amaguaña, Sangolquí, Tel: 02-233-1974/233-2004, Fax: 02-233-2005, E-mail: info@haciendalacarriona.com, URL: www.lacarriona.com.
Updated: Jan 21, 2013.

Hacienda La Alegría

(ROOMS: $65-180) Situated an hour south of Quito, on the slopes of the Corazón Volcano, Hacienda La Alegría is in the heart of the "Avenue of the Volcanoes." On a clear day, you can see not only Corazón but also four other volcanoes from the courtyard. Still a working organic farm (guests can participate in farm-related activities such as cow milking, etc. if they wish), La Alegría specializes in horses. It offers a variety of tours, ranging from one-day trips without lodging to multiday trips that include overnight accommodations and meals.

Although La Alegría's horseback excursions are more expensive ($75-320) than those you can find in a town like **Baños**, you can rest assured that the hacienda takes excellent care of its horses. La Alegría also offers hiking, mountain biking and excursions to the nearby cloud forest, and hosts an annual summer camp for Ecuadorian children. La Alegría only has space for 18 guests, so if you wish to visit, you may want to make reservations ahead of time. Tel: 02-223-3213, Cel: 09-9980-2526, E-mail: info@alegriafarm.com, URL: www.haciendalaalegria.com.
Updated: Jan 10, 2013.

DAY TRIPS AROUND QUITO

MITAD DEL MUNDO

Just half an hour north of Quito, you'll find the Mitad del Mundo (the middle of the world), a monument marking the location of the equator. In actuality, the monument called Mitad del Mundo was inaccurately reported as the equator line by a group of international explorers in the 19th century. The original monument is worth a visit for its three-story museum (entrance $3) which goes into great detail on all of Ecuador's indigenous tribes' typical dress, food and customs. Ask for a guide, they almost always have someone that speaks at least passable English, and its difficult to understand the exhibits otherwise. The area around the monument has become something of a downtown Disney with touristy shops, a main plaza with occasional performances and lots of cafes and restaurants. Access to the area costs $2.

Today anyone with access to a GPS can tell the line is about 100 meters off. There is a small sign at the actual equator now in an outdoor museum called Museo del Sitio Inti-ñan, or Intiñan Museum, which is dedicated to experiments and a 45-minute tour for $2.

To get there, take the Metrobus ($0.25) to Ofelia station, where you board a blue Mitad del Mundo bus ($0.40). Alternatively, take a $10 cab ride from Quito. For more information see Getting Around Quito (p. 96).
Updated: Jan 24, 2013.

Things To See and Do In Mitad del Mundo
Museo de Sitio Intiñan

(ADMISSION: $4) Just 200 meters (656 ft) north of theMitad del Mundo monument you will find Ecuador's actual "middle of the world," marked by the Museo de Sitio Intiñan, or Intiñan Musuem. The museum showcases what modern-day GPS has proven to be the true site of the equator line, for it's here that your device will actually read zero degrees latitude and zero degrees longitude. Unlike the monument at Mitad del Mundo (a complex that features a multi-story museum, food court and small shopping center), the museum at Intiñan is rather quaint and set in a scenic cactus garden.

Information is presented through a guided tour—which is included in the entrance fee and conducted in English or Spanish. The tour takes visitors through the museums highlights: small artifacts (a real shrunken head!), local history, and best of all, scientific experiments. Although these experiments are reportedly fake, you can still have fun trying to balance an egg on a nail (a feat for which you will receive a certificate), seeing water spin both clockwise and counterclockwise (depending on which side of the line it's on), and trying to walk in a straight line on the equatorial line.

Intiñan also offers information about some of Ecuador's indigenous tribes, and houses a replica burial chamber (bones and all). In addition to all this, they'll stamp your passport with an authentic equator stamp (Note: like anywhere else, traveling with your passport on public transport to and from the museum can be dangerous). The entrance for the museum is off the main highway, less than a block north of the entrance to Mitad del Mundo, on Autopista Manuel Córdova Galarza., Tel: 02-239-5122, Cel: 09-9730-9508, URL: www.museointinan.com.ec.
Updated: Mar 13, 2013.

PAPALLACTA
Papallacta is dusty little town known for its relaxing hot springs and deliciously fresh trout. It's located about three kilometers (1.9 mi) off the main road an hour and a half east of Quito on the road to Tena. Just before the main entrance to the pools, there is a luxury hotel and spa with private hot springs. Otherwise, you can pay less than half the cost of the private hot springs to use the public ones, which are also very nice and well-kept, though more crowded. Within walking distance there is a handful of restaurants serving cheap plates of fish or meat and some cheap hostels.
Updated: Feb 18, 2013.

Getting To and Away from Papallacta
To get there, catch a bus from Río Coca, the northernmost Ecovia stop, to Cumbaya (30 minutes, $0.25). You'll be dropped off at a gas station near Supermaxi. From the supermarket, catch a bus bound for Tena (1.5 hours, $2) and ask to be let off at Papallacta. You'll be dropped off on the roadside. Continue along on foot until you see a large sign for the hot springs off the highway and a road leading up the hill. Follow the road for about 3 kilometers to the spa entrance. Getting there on foot can be a bit confusing, but it is possible to take a camioneta, or covered pick-up truck, if you can flag one down. You can also take a bus from the Quitumbe terminal. Bus companies with service to Tena and Lago Agrio (Transportes Baños, Occidental, Ecuador and Putumayo) will also drop you off at Papallacta at the end of a road. From there, take a camioneta up to the hot springs. If you're heading back by bus, try to find a ride all the way back to the main highway. Stand on the left (there is a triangle of grass in the road). Buses to Quito go by roughly every 30 to 45 minutes and you can flag them down.
Updated: May 31, 2012.

Things To See and Do In Papallacta
Thermal Hot Springs !

The hot springs are the main attraction at Papallacta. Just behind the Termas de Papallacta hotel and spa (which has its own, private hot springs), these pools are heated by the Antisana Volcano, and are known for their relaxing, medicinal qualities. For just $7.50 a day (or $3.50 for children and senior citizens), you can soak in these clean

and well-maintained public baths. Take your pick from 8 different pools that range from icy-cold to scalding-hot, or make that 9 if you're daring enough to jump into the rolling river that pummels beside the facilities. Termas de Papallacta, 5-10 minutes uphill from town in car.
Updated: Mar 15, 2013.

Hiking in Papallacta !

Papallacta, located approximately 60 kilometers east of Quito, is best known for its magnificent volcanic hot springs. Nevertheless, there is a rewarding three-hour hike through páramo and patches of cloud forest just behind the Termas de Papallacta Resort.

On the hill just to the right of the entrance to the hot springs is a visitor information and environmental education center where you will have to pay a small entrance fee to access the trail. From the education center, follow the marked trail for about 10 minutes until you reach a wooden bridge that takes you onto a small island amidst the mountains. Continue up the trail for a few minutes to a fork. Go right for about 15 minutes until the two paths merge again at another bridge. Walk another 100 meters up to a dirt road and concrete bridge. Here you will see another gate. Go in and follow the trail until you reach a patch of cloud forest.

About 20 minutes from the gate, you will come to an intersection of trails. Take the trail that goes east and then north into the cloud forest. Continue north for about half an hour until you reach yet another intersection. Here you can either go left on the main trail or continue north on a secondary trail for about 40 minutes until you reach a waterfall tumbling down the east slope of the valley. If you choose to go north in search of the waterfall, you will have to feel out the route as you go, which can be difficult because it's not well trodden. The round-trip takes about three hours.

Papallacta Lodging
Termas de Papallacta

(ROOMS: $144-650) The Termas de Papallacta Spa, Resort and Convention Center is quite literally a world unto its own. For a city escape, make the trip to this inviting retreat perched high in the Andean valley. Stay at the hotel or in one of the cabins and enjoy the mountain-view private thermal pools day and night.

When you've had enough poolside relaxation, dry off and head to one of the resort's other pamper-yourself facilities. You can choose to revitalize your body with a variety of therapies, massages, and tailor-made treatments—its exclusive "Thermal Club" is a great opportunity to really relax and revamp.

The area is also home to an abundance of flora and fauna, which can be explored via a number of walking trails. Guided ecological tours are also available. As if the pools themselves were not enough of a draw, the resort also has an on-site restaurant, where you can soak your senses in both local and international fare.

Thanks to its beauty and promise of a relaxing getaway, this place is packed on weekends and during holidays, so be sure to reserve in advance. The most economical way to stay at the Termas de Papallacta is to share one of the six or eight-person cabins. It's best to come as a group, as the place offers no dormitory-style lodging for solo travelers. Quito office: Foch E7-38 and Reina Victoria, Tel: 02-256-8989/250-4787/223-0156, E-mail: termasuio@termaspapallacta.com, URL: www.termaspapallacta.com.

Papallacta Restaurants

After a long day of either lounging in the baths or exploring the great outdoors that Papallacta has to offer, there's no doubt you'll be hungry. You'll find that many of the local restaurants around the town specialize in steamed trout more than anything, but if you're not a seafood fan they have other options too. Just know that prices within the Termas de Papallacta hotel and spa will be considerably more expensive than what you'll be able to get just outside its walls or in town - where prices can drop to just $4-5 for a bountiful meal.

PULULAHUA VOLCANIC CRATER !

Pululahua is a volcanic crater just north of the equator. Set at an elevation of 3,356 m (11,010 ft) it offers spectacular views of a patchwork golden and green farms and forests cradled inside the miniature valley. Hikes, horseback riding and relaxing are the main activities at this now dormant 3 km-wide crater. The last eruption was about 2,400 years ago.

You need a private vehicle to reach the crater, which is about 15 minutes up from the main highway just north of Mitad del Mundo and about 25 km (15 miles) north of Quito. The road is mostly unpaved, so a 4-wheel drive is recommended. The weather is sunny and warm most of the year, but clouds can move in quickly, so come with layers.

Photo by: Rinaldo Wurglitsch

There are very few places offering food and lodging in Pululahua, but many tour operators based out of Quito offer daytrips and activities in the area. Entrance to Pululahua Botanical Reserve costs $1 for Ecuadorians and foreign residents, $3 for non-resident Latin Americans, $5 for other non-resident foreigners, $0.50 for children under 12 and seniors above 60.

Things To See and Do at Pululahua Volcanic Crater

The Pululahua reserve is a very tranquil place, inhabited only by a handful of corn farmers and a few hacienda owners. The main thing to do here is to relax while soaking in the silence and scenery, and then hike along the paths that lead up the crater. You can also bring a mountain bike and follow the dirt roads, which are pretty safe, considering how few cars come out here. There's also the option of simply asking the hotel and restaurant about bike-rentals or even horseback riding (for more information on horseback riding in the area see Green Ranch, p. 153) .

Pululahua Lodging
Pululahua Hostal
(ROOMS: $12-60) Hostel Pululahua is a small resort surrounded by nature and set inside a Geobotanical Reserve. It is a quiet and mystic place near Quito, only 10 minutes away from La Mitad del Mundo. Guests can relax or explore the area doing hiking, horseback riding or mountain biking. There private and shared rooms. Outside there is a beautiful jacuzzi. The meals are very healthy, since most of the ingredients are produced in the organic farm. Tomatoes, lettuce, carrots, alfalfa, beets, cabbage, corn, beans and potatoes are only some of the vegetables produced in the garden. Chickens, pigs, guinea-pigs and rabbits are also raised on the farm. Vegetarian meals are available. Pululahua Geobotanical Reserve, Tel: 0999-466-636, E-mail: info@pululahuahostal. com, URL: www.pululahuahostal.com.

El Crater Hotel
(ROOMS: $95) A small all-suites hotel with space for just 24 people—two per suite—has the feel of a modern luxury spa more than a hotel. The open, fresh rooms are decorated with minimalist décor, using over-sized picture windows as the main attraction and soft tones with wood balancing out the natural feel. The views are the main attraction: each suite has two spectacular views, the edge of the Pululahua Volcano Crater and the mountains on the other side of the volcano. The suites are all one room with a divider between the sitting area and the bed. Beds are outfitted with plush down-mattress and pillows, and thick feather blankets facing the picture window overlooking the crater. Large tubs are in each bathroom. The hotel is designed for complete relaxation. You can even request aromatherapy treatments and personal massages in the comfort of your own suite. El Crater can arrange for personal guides to take you around the many hikes in the area. There is also an on-site restaurant. Mirador de Pululahua, 25 km/15 mi north of Quito, Tel: 02-243-9254, E-mail: mbaca52@ hotmail.com / info@elcrater.com, URL: www.elcrater.com.
Updated: Jan 10, 2013.

Pululahua Restaurants
El Crater Restaurant
(ENTREES: ~$25) A visit to this restaurant can easily be a vacation highlight. It offers one of the most spectacular views of any restaurant in Ecuador. Perched literally on the edge of a spectacular Pululahua crater, the view will blow you away. The food comes in a very close second. The theme is contemporary Ecuadorian cuisine with excellent steaks, trout and other traditional dishes. Be sure to walk around the crater after filling up on tasty Ecuadorian food. There are some excellent nature paths to explore. Mirador del Pululahua, about a 15-minute drive from Mitad del Mundo., Tel: 02-243-9254, E-mail: mbaca52@elcrater.com, URL: www. elcrater.com.
Updated: Jan 10, 2013.

Valleys Around Quito
CUMBAYÁ

Little more than a decade ago, Cumbayá consisted mostly of open pastures and country cottages where Quito's elite escaped the hustle of the capital. Though the farms and rolling fields have been largely displaced by upscale suburbs and open-air shopping malls, the city has maintained some of its rustic charm and a decidedly slower pace than Quito.

Cumbayá sits at the edge of the Valley of Tumbaco, some 20 kilometers east and several hundred meters below the capital. Its location in an inter-Andean valley provides for a climate that is both warmer and considerably drier than Quito's. Like Quito, Cumbayá has two centers, a new one and an old one, located just a few kilometers apart.

The new city center consists of two strips of chain stores, including a Supermaxi and Fybeca, that parallel the Via Interoceanica underpass. At the end of these outdoor malls is the even newer and bigger Paseo San Francisco shopping mall, which is right at the crux of the Interoceanica mini-tunnel and Diego de Robles bypass. Right beside it is the University of San Francisco de Quito (USFQ), a private and well respected liberal arts college that caters to Quito's upper class, the old town, and the City of Tumbaco.

If you continue down through the Interoceanica mini-tunnel you'll eventually end up in Tumbaco. If you take the bypass however (the lane to the right of the tunnel) you'll end up in the Old Town of Cumbayá. To get to the town plaza, just go down the bypass and turn left at the corner of Paseo San Francisco, go past USFQ and turn right on Pampite Ave., follow this street down to the reservoir and turn right on Chimborazo, and then left on Orellana. The plaza has been recently renovated and boasts a wide assortment of good restaurants and high-end shops.
Updated: Mar 13, 2013.

Getting To and Away from Cumbayá

Taxis to Cumbaya can cost anywhere from $8-12 depending on the time of day, with the trip typically lasting around 30 minutes. Green buses for Cumbayá frequently depart from a bus station just next to the Ecovia terminal at Río Coca. Follow signs at Río Coca to lead you there. These same buses pick up passengers at the southeast corner of Avenida Eloy Alfaro and Via Interoceánica (frequently referred to as Avenida Los Granados) before heading to the valley. The ride costs $0.25 and takes about 30 minutes. Otherwise, you can take a taxi between Quito and Cumbayá, which costs about $8-10 each way.

If you have your own vehicle, you can also drive to Cumbayá on an adventurously winding road that begins just north of Hotel Quito and follows Avenida de Los Conquistadores through Guápalo and over a narrow bridge spanning the Machángara River Canyon. Alternatively, you can take the two-kilometer (1.2-mi) tunnel that connects Quito with Cumbayá. The tunnel enters Quito at La Plaza de Argentina on Avenida 6 de Diciembre and Diego del Almagro.
Updated: Feb 18, 2013.

VALLE DE LOS CHILLOS

Sitting in a lush, sunbathed valley just a quick bus ride southeast of Quito is Valle de los Chillos, a popular weekend retreat for quiteños. Significantly warmer and more laid-back than the city, this area is perfect for anyone looking to relax and unwind without having to venture far from Quito.Sangolquí, the largest town in the valley, has a few accommodation options, as well as a Spanish school. The town's lively Sunday market is a good place to pick up fresh fruits and vegetables without bumping elbows with other tourists.

Northeast of Sangolquí, but still in the valley, are El Tingo and La Merced's thermal pools - if you're up for a steamy soak. Llaló, located just 4 kilometers past La Merced, offers privately owned pools, which are cleaner and less packed. To reach the pools catch one of the La Merced buses from La Marin. For a tropical escape, head to Rincón Amazónico, a gorgeous gem of a restaurant near the thermal baths of El Tingo. Anyone hoping to get out and about in the hills outside Quito should make their way toward Alangasi and Pintag. The privately owned Reserva Ecológica Antisana, which includes the magnificent Volcán Antisana (5758m), is a prime spot for hiking, trekking, horseback riding and condor-watching.

!!!!!

Northern Andes

The Northern Andes region in Ecuador begins at the edges of Quito and continues all the way up to the jagged line defining the Colombian border. This mountainous and hilly region features a wide range of ecosystems that run the gamut from dry to wet, playing host to a land filled with some unbeatable Andean fauna, culture and landscapes.

It's here that you'll be able to withdraw from the tourist mainstream, humbling yourself with the magnificent scope of *Volcán Cayambe* (the country's third-highest volcano) while drawing nearer to witnessing the heart and source of all kinds of artisan goods in towns like Otavalo. And to the west, birdwatchers from around the world and weekenders alike heed the call of Mindo, as they flock to indulge in its abundance of bird species as well as experience its incredibly relaxing rainforest ambiance.

Whether it's ice-climbing, trekking through unspoiled *páramo* (grasslands), exploring rural villages (where the pace of life remains the same after centuries), getting the best deals and widest selection of artisan goods or simply soaking in the *Arco Iris* hot springs, the Northern Andes is a region you won't want to miss.

NORTHERN ANDES

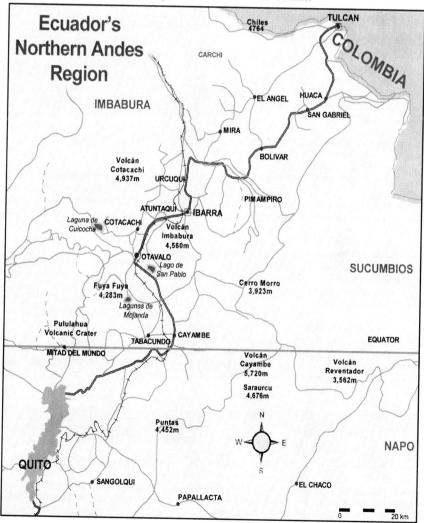

Ecuador's Northern Andes Region

Chiles 4764
TULCAN
CARCHI
COLOMBIA
IMBABURA
EL ANGEL   HUACA
SAN GABRIEL
MIRA
Volcán Cotacachi 4,937m   URCUQUÍ
BOLIVAR
ATUNTAQUI   IBARRA
PIMAMPIRO
Laguna de Cuicocha   COTACACHI
Volcán Imbabura 4,560m
OTAVALO
Lago de San Pablo
SUCUMBIOS
Fuya Fuya 4,283m
Cerro Morro 3,923m
Lagunas de Mojanda
Pululahua Volcanic Crater
TABACUNDO   CAYAMBE
EQUATOR
MITAD DEL MUNDO
Volcán Cayambe 5,720m
Volcán Reventador 3,562m
Saraurcu 4,676m
Puntas 4,452m
N
W E
S
NAPO
QUITO
SANGOLQUI
EL CHACO
PAPALLACTA
0   20 km

Did a unique trek? Got way off the beaten path? Tell other travelers at vivatrav-

CAYAMBE

Cayambe is a medium-sized Andean town, located at the foot of the volcano of the same name. Most visitors to Ecuador will get to see the town, at least in passing, as Cayambe is squarely on the route between Quito and Otavalo. There are a couple of good restaurants in town, and most Ecuadorians will not drive through Cayambe without picking up a bag of freshly made bizcochos, the specialty of Cayambe.

Bizcochos are long, thin, yellowish-orange biscuits, made by hand and baked in ovens similar to pizza ovens. They are not sweet but salty, and many Ecuadorians like to eat their bizcochos dipped in *manjar de leche*, a milk product similar to caramel.

Things To See and Do in Cayambe

Hiking Cayambe

Cayambe, a massive glaciated volcano is the third highest peak in both Ecuador and the Americas north of the equator. It also enjoys the distinction of being the highest point on the earth's surface through which the equator directly passes. Although technically not very difficult, it is dangerous due to crevasses and avalanches. A refuge is located on the southwest flanks of the mountain at 4,600 meters (15,090 ft) and is named after the three French climbers who died in an avalanche on Cayambe. Getting to the refuge will require a car with 4-wheel drive. Once there, you'll find it has a permanent guardian, running water, gas stove, cooking facilities and toilets. It is now under the administration of the San Gabriel Climbing Club and the overnight charge is $20.
Updated: Mar 15, 2013.

Cayambe Lodging

When looking into Cayambe hotels, you may be surprised that most accommodations are akin to B&B's and cabañas. Cayambe is also sprinkled with backpacker hostels, all of which tend to be moderately priced. If you're searching for Cayambe hotels with a little something extra, seek out an eco-reserve.
Updated: Mar 15, 2013.

Hacienda Guachalá

(ROOMS: $44-88) Hacienda Guachalá dates back to 1700 and has a chapel that was originally built in 1580. In its heyday, Guachalá was the administrative center for about 22,000 hectares (54,360 ac) of land and employed 500 workers, who created textiles to be shipped to Spain. It was converted to a hotel in 1993, and offers one of the more affordable options for those who wish to have a true hacienda experience. The complex has attractive gardens, ample rooms (all with private bath and fireplace), a swimming pool, chapel and restaurant. There are a number of activities available as well including, but not limited to, horseback riding and fishing. Panamericana Highway Km 70 (Quito - Cayambe), Tel: 236-3042, Fax: 236-2426, E-mail: info@guachala.com, URL: www.guachala.com.
Updated: Oct 31, 2012.

OYACACHI

Located two hours east of the town of Cayambe, Oyacachi is hidden just below the paramo in a lush cloud forested valley that serves as the cusp of the upper rim of the Amazon basin. Nearly everyone that visits Oyacachi goes to the Termas de Oyacachi. They are excellent, uncrowded hot springs where, with a little luck, on weekdays you might even end up having the place all to yourself.

There are no hotels in the area, but a few families in town have begun to take in travellers as homestays (inquire at the hot spring ticket booth). There is excellent camping at the hot springs (running water and bathrooms are adjacent) for a few dollars per tent. A few basic restaurants are in town but they rarely seem to open. There are usually a couple of stands that sell trout outside the hot springs, but otherwise, the food selection at small *tiendas* (food stores) is very limited, so bring your own supplies (especially alcohol, it's a dry town!).

Oyacachi is one of the best places in Ecuador to find the Andean Deer and Spectacled bears, but observe them at a distance, as there have been reports of bear attacks on locals. There is excellent hiking around Oyacachi and the roads are great for mountain biking.
Updated: Mar 15, 2013.

Getting To and Away from Oyacachi

Driving from the town of Cayambe head south on the main highway to Quito (or if coming from Quito to Cayambe go just north

Northern Andes Highlights

Otavalo Market (*p. 164-165*): This market is famous for a reason. If you're looking for souvenirs and gifts, you will find an incredible variety of options, including rainbow-colored textiles, hand-woven tapestries, alpaca wool sweaters, and tagua seed jewelry. Even seasoned hagglers may find themselves a bit tongue-tied at the end of a day spent wandering from stall to stall bargaining with the local vendors.

Lagunas de Mojanda (*p. 171-172*): Just 17 kilometers (10.5 mi) from Otavalo, Lagunas de Mojanda are a group of calm, beautiful lagoons set high in the páramo grassland. The area is one of the best spots for hiking in the region, with the ability to climb up several peaks (like Fuya Fuya) for impressive overhead views or to complete a three- to four-hour circuit around part of Laguna Grande, Laguna Negra and Laguna Chiquita.

Cotocachi (*p. 179-183*): Resting at the foot of the towering Cotocachi Volcano, the charming town of Cotocachi is best-known for producing cheap but high-quality handmade leather goods. You can spend hours perusing the variety of leather belts, boots, jackets and more sold in the dozens of shops lining its main streets. Cotocachi is also a base for exploring the nearby Cotocachi-Cayapas Ecological Reserve.

El Ángel Ecological Reserve (*p. 191-193*): One of Ecuador's most interesting natural reserves, El Ángel consists of 15,700 hectares (38,795 ac) of wild páramo in the northern part of Carchi province. The reserve is best known for its iconic *frailejón* plants, which freckle the landscapes, and for its forests of polylepis trees, also known as paper trees for their thin, paper-like bark. Animals like condors, foxes, deer and rabbits call the reserve home, and activities like hiking and camping can be enjoyed by visitors.

Cayambe (*p. 160*): Both the small town and the volcano itself are worth checking out; the former for its charm and biscuits, the other for the awesome scenery it provides should you choose to ascend its slopes.

Lago San Pablo (*p. 174-175*): With the Imbabura Mountain rising up from behind it, Lago San Pablo offers some great scenic hiking along its frigid waters, which actually do nothing to stop people from going water-skiing in them. Take a paddle boat or walk along its circumference to soak in the scenery and rural towns that surround it.

NORTHERN ANDES

of the new Mitad del Mundo) until you see the signs for Hacienda Guachala. Go past the hacienda and the town of Cangahua and follow the signs to Oyacachi.

Buses from **Quito** to **Cayambe** leave every thirty minutes from the bus station called La Ofelia. There are buses that leave daily but early in the mornings from the Cayambe Plaza to Oyacachi.
Updated: Mar 15, 2013.

Things To See and Do in Oyacachi
Oyachachi Hot Springs

(ADMISSION: $2) Be prepared to be as relaxed and *tranquilo* as the easygoing locals when come here and immerse yourself into the baths it has to offer. The steaming ferrous-sulphur are said to cure muscle pains, and if that doesn't sedate you enough, the panoramic views and sound of the river below are guaranteed to lull you into a near co-

Did a unique trek? Got way off the beaten path? Tell other travelers at vivatrav-

NORTHERN ANDES

matose state. Oyacachi is an excellent, more remote alternative to the Termas de Papallacta hot springs East of Quito.
Updated: Mar 15, 2013.

Hiking around Oyacachi

There are several walking trails accessible from the town, including a pre-Columbian stone path that will take you a few kilometers down the valley from the town all the way to the town of Chaco in the Oriente, a 3-day hike. Two kilometres (1.2 miles) out of town on this road is a collection of ruins consisting of several stone houses and a cemetery that were abandoned around a hundred years ago probably because of high landslide risks. An hour or so down the trail, there are some land forms that look suspiciously like Caranqui pyramids (but locals cannot confirm this), and a few hours more on the trail will take you to El Pueblo Viejo, the "old town", which is now nothing more than a few flat clearings that make for an excellent camping spot on the trek to the Oriente.
Updated: Mar 15, 2013.

OTAVALO

2,530m   43,000   06

Set in a valley a couple of hours north of Quito, Otavalo is at the top of any traveler's must-see list. It is famous for its weekly market, reportedly the largest of its kind in Latin America, where one can find an overwhelming variety of Andean crafts. Every Saturday from about 7 a.m., the local craftsmen pour into the town and unfold their wares along Plaza de Ponchos and in the surrounding streets. The whole area explodes into a hodgepodge of colorful rugs, clothes, paintings and other crafts. There is also a chaotic early Saturday morning animal market which is well worth a visit.

Photo by: funkz

During the week Otavalo is a sleepy little town, which can be hard to believe if you've seen it during Saturday's mid-market frenzy. But rest assured you'll find something regardless, for there's always a number of market stalls in the Plaza de Ponchos.

Architecturally speaking, Otavalo is relatively modern (if you count 1960's and 70's vintage cinder block as modern), although there are a few colonial buildings left, mainly at the southern end of town around the Plaza Bolívar. There are also a couple of museums that are worth a peek.

Nightlife is virtually nonexistent during the week, but come the weekend a healthy number of venues open up, particularly traditional *Peñas* that play live Andean music.

Despite its quietness - or perhaps because of it - many travelers opt for an extended stay here, often to study spanish, volunteer for a few weeks, or explore the surrounding area with its lakes, waterfalls and ancient Inca trails that weave in and out of the mountains.

Getting To and Away from Otavalo

Otavalo's bus terminal, on Calle Atahualpa and Calle Ordoñes (an easy 10-minute walk from the Plaza de Ponchos), is basically a giant and very chaotic parking lot.

There are no actual bus company offices: to locate the right bus, simply wander around and listen out for the name of your destination. On Saturdays, get to the bus terminal early, as buses fill quickly.

Note that on all days, buses generally run between 6 a.m.-6 p.m.

To Cayambe (40 min, $0.50): Buses leave every 20 to 30 minutes. Alternatively, take a Quito-bound bus which will drop you off at the turnoff to Cayambe, a 15 minute walk away from the town center.

To Ibarra (40 min, $0.45): Buses leave every 10 to 15 minutes.

To Lago Cuicocha: Take a bus to Quiroga (see below). From there, hire a taxi or truck to the lake for $6.

To Lago San Pablo (20 min, $0.25): Buses leave every 10 to 15 minutes.

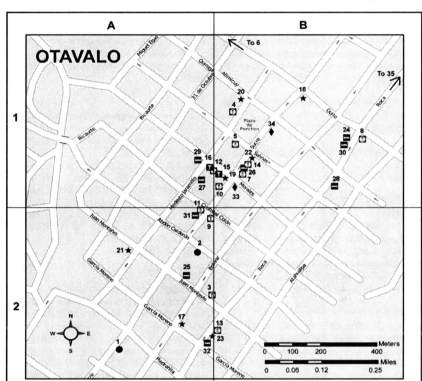

Activities ●

1 El Obraje Museo A2
2 SISA A2

Eating 🍴

3 Árbol de Montalvo A2
4 Balcon de Imbabura B1
5 Buena Vista B1
6 Café Pachamama B1
7 Green Coffee Shop B1
8 Juanita Marquez B1
9 La Casa del Intag A2
10 Mi Otavalito B1
11 Oraibi A2
12 Pizza Siciliana A1
13 Quino B2
14 Tabasco's B1

Nightlife 🍸

15 La Taberna B1
16 The Red Pub A1

Services ★

17 Banco del Pacífico A2
18 Banco del Pichincha B1

19 Lavandería B1
20 La Mia Supermercado B1
21 Mercado 24 de Mayo A2
22 Post Office B1
23 The Book Market A2

Sleeping 🛏

24 El Rincón del Viajero B1
25 Hostal Doña Esther A2
26 Hostal El Indio B1
27 Hostal María A1
28 Hostal Runa Pacha B1
29 Hostal Tama Tiaki A1
30 Hostel Valle del Amancer B1
31 Hotel Flores A2
32 Hotel Riviera – Sucre A2

Tours ◆

33 Ecomentes Tour B1
34 Runa Tupari Nature Travel B1

Transportation 🚌

35 Bus Terminal B1

NORTHERN ANDES

To Peguche (10 min, $0.15): Buses leave every 20 minutes or so. Note that rather than leaving from inside the terminal itself, buses to Peguche pass by the terminal on Ca. Atahualpa.

To Quiroga/Cotacachi (15/20 min, $0.20/$0.25): Buses leave every 10 minutes, stopping at Quiroga first.

To Quito (2 hr, $2): Buses leave every 10 to 15 minutes.
Updated: Oct 24, 2012.

Otavalo Services
TOURISM
The tourism office, **iTur** (Monday to Friday 8 a.m.-12.30 p.m. and 2.30-6 p.m., Saturday 8 a.m.-4 p.m.), is located on Calle Quiroga and Jaramillo, on the corner of the Plaza de Ponchos. Staff can provide information on the surrounding area, and have free maps.

MONEY
Just off the Plaza de Ponchos is a branch of **Banco Pichincha** (Ca. Sucre 1413, near the corner of Quiroga. Monday to Friday 8.30 a.m.-4 p.m., Saturday 9 a.m.-12 p.m.) which has an ATM that accepts international cards; the ATM is only accessible during banking hours however. 24-hour ATMs that accept VISA and Mastercard can be found at the **Banco de Guayaquil** on Calle Calderon between Roca and Bolívar, and at the **Banco del Pacifico** on the Parque Central(corner of Garcia Moreno and Bolivar).

KEEPING IN TOUCH
There are an abundance of Internet cafés in Otavalo, almost all of which also have phone cabins. Internet rates run at around $0.70 per hour. Calles Roca, Bolivar and Sucre in particular have several Internet cafés. The **post office** (Ca. Sucre 12-18, corner of Salinas. Go through the corridor and up the stairs) is open Monday to Friday 8 a.m.-6 p.m. and Saturday 8 a.m.-12 p.m. (there is no outward mail service on a Saturday however).

MEDICAL
You'll have no problem finding a pharmacy in Otavalo. Conveniently located on the Plaza de Ponchos is the **Farmacia Santa** (daily 8 a.m.-9 p.m.). The public hospital, **Hospital San Luis**, is located on Sucre and Estados Unidos, a 10-minute walk from the Plaza de Ponchos.

LAUNDRY
There is a coin laundromat on the corner of Morales and Sucre, next to La Taberna bar. Rates are $0.50 per pound, for both washing and drying.

SHOPPING
Otavalo's best shopping opportunities can be found-of course-in its markets (see Things To See and Do In Otavalo). For day-to-day items though, there is a supermarket, **La Mia**, on the corner of the Plaza de Ponchos (on Jaramillo and Quiroga), and a **Supermercado Tia** on Calle Sucre between Calderon and Montalvo. For fresh fruit, dried goods and cheap *almuerzos*, head to **Mercado 24 de Mayo** on the corner of Montalvo and Jaramillo.
Updated: Oct 17, 2012.

The Book Market
The Book Market is squeezed into a tiny store next to the Hotel Riviera Sucre. It's the place to come to buy new books (guide books, non-fiction and literature) and to exchange any books you've finished with (the exchange works on a bring two, get one basis). Books are available in English, Spanish and German. Also sells maps and stamps. Monday to Saturday 9 a.m.-1 p.m., 2.30-7 p.m. Ca. Roca, corner of Garcia Morena., Tel: 292-8535/0991-754-656.
Updated: Oct 17, 2012.

Things To See and Do in Otavalo
Otavalo Markets ♩
The Otavaleños have been long renowned for their weaving skills, and over the last few decades have become the most successful indigenous group on the continent, thanks to the popularity of their weekly craft market. Although most still live in the hills around the town and wear traditional clothing, this doesn't mean they are poor–it is not unusual to see families of six or seven loading rugs into their brand new Toyota Land Cruisers at the end of the day, or women carrying baskets of grain up the hill while talking on their cell phones.

The market itself offers a fantastic wealth of crafts, especially alpaca goods (sweaters, hats, scarves, gloves, etc.), weavings, jewelry, hammocks, rugs and more. The main market takes place on Saturday, when stalls appear in the Plaza de Ponchos and on the surrounding streets. Although you can visit the market in a day from Quito (the trip is approximately two hours by bus), many tourists also choose to arrive on Friday night. Getting to town early will not only give you a chance to enjoy an almost empty craft market before the day trippers arrive (and prices rise), but will also give you a chance to visit the weekly animal market (see below).

When you go to the market, remember to try to bargain for what you're buying. **Haggling** may feel uncomfortable at first, especially if you're not used to debating prices, but remember that negotiating for sales is commonplace here, and locals do it all the time. Knowing what an item should cost is difficult, but you can generally expect to pay half to two-thirds of the original asking price. Offer half of the original price that the vendors quote and settle at just above.

Saturday is the main market day, but the craft market on the Plaza de Ponchos does continue throughout the week (albeit in a much smaller and less frenzied fashion). If you do come during the week, you'll benefit from lower prices and lack of crowds, but the range of products won't be quite as varied as on Saturday.

The **animal market** also takes place on Saturday on the outskirts of town, west of the Panamericana (just follow the stream of locals, squealing piglets and braying donkeys up Calle Colón and over the river). It's a fascinating and noisy spectacle, starting at 5 a.m. and finishing around midday.
Updated: Oct 29, 2012.

Parque Cóndor Otavalo

(ADMISSION: $3.75) Parque Cóndor is a non-profit wildlife refuge for owls and raptors, including the endangered Andean Condor. It seeks to rescue, protect and rehabilitate these birds and, if possible, release them back into the wild. Those that cannot be released become the stars of an educational bird show held twice a day (at 11:30 a.m. and 4:30 p.m., though times may change depending on the weather). The show gives visitors the opportunity to observe these beautiful creatures in flight, and allows the park to inform visitors about the importance of environmental conservation.

From Parque Cóndor you get stunning views of the Imbabura and Cotacachi volcanoes, San Pablo Lake and the towns of Otavalo and Cotacachi. The park also has a small restaurant and a playground. You can get there by taxi (about $3-4 from Otavalo) or take the exit to San Pablo Lake off the Panamericana Highway.

If you're up for a little physical exertion, you can hike from Otavalo up to the park (around an hour); just ask the locals for the best way to head toward its entrance. It can get cold in the park even at noon, so dress appropriately. Sunscreen and bug spray are also a good idea. Comunidad de Pucará Alto, Parroquia Eugenio Espejo, Tel: 0984-311-769, URL: www.parquecondor.org.
Updated: Oct 30, 2012.

Museo De Tejidos El Obraje

(ADMISSION: $2) The small but delightful Museo de Tejidos El Obraje is the place to come to if you wish to learn about traditional weaving methods used in and around Otavalo. Proprietor Luis Maldonaldo talks visitors through the weaving process and the techniques used. It can be easy to miss the museum; it's at the back of a small courtyard. You may also need to ring the bell a few times to get somebody's attention. Monday to Saturday 9 a.m.-12 p.m. and 2-5 p.m. Ca. Sucre between Colón and Calderon
Updated: Oct 16, 2012.

S.I.S.A

(ADMISSION: $3) S.I.S.A (Sala de Imagenes, Sonido and Arte, which translates as Room of Images, Sound and Art) is an indigenous-owned complex featuring a small movie theater, shops, and a couple of cafés (the top floor café is particularly popular due to its excellent coffees and desserts). The movie theater shows both Ecuadorian and international movies, with showings thrice-daily on Fridays, Saturdays and Sundays. Fridays are two-for-one. Check the facebook page for up-to-date listings. Ca. Calderon 4-09, Tel: 292-5624, URL: https://www.facebook.com/pages/CINE-SISA-OTAVALO/261924650499597.
Updated: Oct 16, 2012.

Cotacachi-Cayapas Ecological Reserve

The Ecological Cotocachi-Cayapas Reserve, in the Western Andes, encompasses 204,420 hectares (505,133 ac) that widely ranges in elevation from the summit of Cotacachi (4,939 m/16,200 ft) to coastal rainforest (300 m/980 ft).

Access to the reserve is difficult since most of the area is covered by thick vegetation, with the exception of the eastern edge, which is páramo. Most people choose to access the reserve from Otavalo or Ibarra, but it is also possible to gain entry by traveling up the Cayapas River from the coastal Afro-ecuadorian community of Borbon.

The Piñan area, a section of high, unspoilt páramo, is located at the eastern end of the Cotacachi-Cayapas reserve. For incredible views, which many consider to be the best in Ecuador, try summiting the Yanaurco in the Piñan. The trek takes between three and four days and begins at the small village of Iruguincho, northwest of Ibarra. A stop in the village will give you an insight into the traditional farming practice in the area, which has remained largely unchanged for centuries.

As you climb high into the páramo, you may notice herds of wild horses, an abundance of small lakes and spectacular local vegetation that includes a variety of wild flowers. Due to the isolation and unspoiled nature of the area, the Piñan is one of the best places in Ecuador to see condors and white-tailed deer. For those interested in birds, there are also caracaras, finches, flycatchers and a large number of hummingbird species that live around the area. From the Yanaurco summit, the views are breathtaking. On a clear day you can see the whole of the Ibarra/San Pablo valley and a scattering of more than 40 lakes.

To get to the reserve head to Otavalo's bus terminal, take a green-colored bus heading to Quiroga/Cotacachi and get off in Quiroga ($0.20, 15 min). From Quiroga, you can hire a taxi or truck to the reserve (and the lake) for $6. If you are heading to the reserve or lake from Cotacachi, you can also hire a taxi for around $6. Campus Trekking Agency, which is based just outside of Quito, is one of the Ecuadorian operators that offers guides and services for the Piñan trek. Contact: Campus Trekking Tel: 234-0601, URL: www.campus-trekking.com.
Updated: Oct 24, 2012.

Otavalo Tours

For a town that draws such large numbers of tourists, Otavalo is surprisingly short on local tour operators. This can largely be attributed to the fact that most people arrange a tour of Otavalo and the surrounding area from Quito. There are a couple of excellent and helpful tour operators here, however; both offer a wide range of activities, from Otavalo city and market tours to adventure sports trips and overnight stays in indigenous communities.
Updated: Oct 29, 2012.

Ecomontes Tour

The friendly Ecomontes tour operator offers trips all over Ecuador, with a specialty in ecotourism. This family-run agency is the operator of the Cuyabeno River Lodge and offer various multi-day trips to the Amazon. Around Otavalo, options include trips to Laguna Cuicocha, the Pecughe waterfall, trekking or cycling to the Lagunas Mojanda, and hiking or horseback riding up the Fuya Fuya mountain. It also has an office in Quito. Corner of Sucre and Morale, Otavalo, Tel: 06-292-6244/6235, Cel: 09-9547-7918, URL: www.otavaloguide.com / www.ecomontestour.com.
Updated: Jan 08, 2013.

Runa Tupari Nature Travel

Runa Tupari works with indigenous communities around Otavalo, offering tourists the opportunity to stay with local families and experience day to day life. They also arrange volunteer programs, at a cost of $15 a day (including room and board). Other excursions include visits to the Laguna Cuicocha, hiking the Imbabura volcano, horseback riding, downhill biking, and hikes in Intag's cloud forest. Monday-Saturday 9 a.m.-6 p.m. Ca. Sucre, 3rd floor, Plaza de Ponchos, Tel: 2922-320/097-286-756, URL: www.runatupari.com.
Updated: Oct 08, 2012.

Otavalo Lodging

As you might expect from such a tourist hot spot,Otavalo hotels and hostels come in all shapes, sizes and price ranges, and, in particular, there are several budget and midrange accommodations. If you're heading to the Saturday market the day before, don't be tempted to stay in one of the basic hostels on the Plaza de Ponchos; it may seem convenient, but it's noisy and prices aren't any lower.

Most of the nicest hostels and hotels are located a couple of blocks or a quick, five-minute walk from the plaza. Some of the nicest hotels in Otavalo are a few miles outside of town (see Lodging Around Otavalo). These relatively luxurious hotels, spas and haciendas tend to be a bit more expensive but there are a couple of options to suit backpackers, too. Haciendas are a particularly unique experience, with several exceptional options in the Lago San Pablo, Cotocachi and Laguna Mojanda areas.

BUDGET

Hostal María

($8-15 per person) The Hostal María is a unremarkable but friendly place, conveniently close to the Plaza de Ponchos. The medium-sized rooms lack character, but they're clean and all have private bathrooms and cable TV. The price is fixed per person, whether you want a single, double or triple, which makes the hostel a good deal for single travelers. There's no common area or café, so when you're in the hotel you're pretty much restricted to your room, and breakfast isn't included. Ca. Modesto Jaramillo between Morales and Colon, Tel: 06-292-0672.
Updated: Apr 24, 2013.

Hostal Valle del Amanecer

($12-15 per person) A gem of a hostel, this is a chilled out little place with lots of perks: friendly owners, a helpful travel desk, a café/restaurant that is open all day and a central patio with a huge avocado tree, lots of plants and hammocks. Rooms have WiFi but are small and basic, and it can get quite noisy if there are a lot of people staying, which there invariably are on weekends. A few of the rooms have private bathrooms but most are shared. The hostal also rents mountain bikes. Corner of Ca. Roca and Quiroga, Tel: 292-0990, Fax: 292-1159, E-mail: www.valledelamanecer.com, URL: valledelamanecer@hotmail.com.
Updated: Jan 9, 2013.

Hostal Tamia Taki

($6-10 per person) Hostal Tamia Taki is about as basic and dingy as they come, but if you're on a serious budget, you're not going to get much cheaper than this in Otavalo. Rooms are dark-they have no outside windows-and come with either shared bath (a tiny room with shower and toilet) or, for a dollar more, private bath. Spend a few more dollars however, and you can find a far more pleasant hostel altogether. Ca. Jaramillo, between Morales and Colón, Tel: 06-920-684.
Updated: Apr 24, 2013.

Hotel Flores

(ROOMS: $15) For the price, Hotel Flores is a respectable option-rooms are comfortable and each has a private bathroom, cable TV and WiFi, and some have balconies. The hotel itself is simple but pleasant, with colorfully-painted walls and an airy indoor courtyard. It's located on a busy road though, so it does get noisy, and breakfast, though offered, isn't included in the room rate. Ca. Sucre between Colón and Calderón, Tel: 06-292-6827.
Updated: Apr 24, 2013.

Hostal Runa Pacha

($7-9 per person) The stuffed calf in the lobby might put you off, and the staff could be friendlier, but with bright, spacious rooms and some of the cheapest rates around, this is a good choice for those on a budget. Some rooms have small balconies overlooking the street and all have cable TV and WiFi. Single rooms are on the small side though, and the cheaper rooms-those with shared bath-are a little neglected. There's no breakfast. Ca. Roca 10-02, corner of Quiroga, Tel: 06-292-5566/099-237-8202.
Updated: Apr 24, 2013.

Hotel El Indio

(ROOMS: $15) The Hotel El Indio's concrete and glass façade and tired neon signs do little to tempt tourists. But those who do make it through the front door will be rewarded with a warm welcome from the Otavaleño owners and with spotlessly clean rooms, all with private bathrooms and cable TV. The decoration is a curious mix of 70s kitsch–think black leather armchairs and bright strip lighting–and Otavaleño, with large, brightly colored murals and wall-hangings. Breakfast isn't included, but the hotel's restaurant next door offers it for an extra $3. Don't confuse this place with the more expensive Hotel El Indio Inn, which is located a couple of blocks away. Ca. Sucre between Salinas and Morales., Tel: 292-0060/0993-199-408/0992-526-263.
Updated: Oct 08, 2012.

Rincon del Viajero

($11.50-15 per person) El Rincon is one of the best backpacker options in Otavalo, with friendly staff and an equally friendly clientele. There are a number of attractive facilities: a rooftop terrace with hammocks, pool table, restaurant, communal living room, and a cozy cabin that, by night, is heated by a log-fire. A hearty breakfast is included in the

Did a unique trek? Got way off the beaten path? Tell other travelers at vivatrav-

NORTHERN ANDES

room rate. Simple rooms have either shared or private bath, and-very importantly-the water in the showers is lovely and hot. Roca N11-07 between Quito and Quiroga, Tel: 292-1741, URL: www.hostalrincondelviajero.com. Updated: Oct 29, 2012.

MID-RANGE
Riviera Sucre

(ROOMS: $10-52) Otavalo's oldest hotel, Hotel Riviera Sucre, located in a beautiful, 150 year old colonial house, is hands-down the loveliest hotel for this price range. It's deceptively spacious, with a courtyard filled with greenery and hammocks, gardens, an area for washing and drying clothes, a communal kitchen with oven, and a living room with a fireplace and book exchange. Rooms are substantial, with high ceilings and large bathrooms, and some have balconies. All have cable TV. WiFi is available in the courtyard and communal areas only.

Note that the one room with shared bath is a little dark and poky, and also set outside in the garden. Breakfast isn't included, but is offered for an extra $3. All in all, Riviera Sucre is a wonderful and reasonably-priced hideaway. Garcia Moreno 380 and Roca, Tel: 2920-241/2925-682, E-mail: rivierasucre@hotmail.com, URL: www.rivierasucre.com. Updated: Oct 10, 2012.

Hotel Doña Esther ▮

(ROOMS: $28-55) Set back from the street, this lovely hotel has a friendly, homey feel, and is blissfully quiet. Three floors of moderately-sized en-suite rooms are arranged around a leafy courtyard. If you can stretch to it, the top-floor suite is a gem, with gorgeous views from the kitchenette, sitting area and double bedroom. Rooms have WiFi, but no television: if you do feel the urge to watch TV, you can do so by heading over and settling down in the comfort of the snug communal living room.

While you're here, take advantage of the hotel's restaurant, which is justly famous for its delicious, thin crust pizzas among the other tempting entreees they offer. Breakfast is available for guests, but costs extra. Juan Montalvo 4-44 y Bolivar, Tel: 2920-739/2925-381, E-mail: hostalesther@yahoo.com, URL: www.otavalohotel.com. Updated: Oct 09, 2012.

HIGH-END
La Posada del Quinde

(ROOMS: $48-200) La Posada del Quinde (previously the Hotel Ali Shungu), though located just a few blocks from the Plaza de Ponchos, has the feel of a country inn, due to its gorgeous gardens and sunny patio. Rooms, though simply furnished, are spotlessly clean and decorated with local weavings.

American owner Maggie provides friendly and excellent service. A scrumptious breakfast is included in the price, and the hotel's restaurant, Café Pachamama, is one of the best in town. By night, cozy up to the inviting open fire in the dining room. The one drawback is its location near to the highway: ask for a room furthest away from the road. Ca. Quito and Ca. Miguel Egas, Tel: 06-292-0750, E-mail: maggie@posadaquinde.com, URL: www.posadaquinde.com. Updated: Apr 24, 2013.

Otavalo Restaurants

Otavalo has an array of international eateries, fitting for the huge numbers of international tourists it receives. These restaurants offer everything from pizza and Mexican food to seafood and vegetarian dishes; prices also tend to reflect the tourist influx however, and can be a little high. For more budget-priced meals, head to any of the rice-with-everything joints or fast-food restaurants that can be found on every other corner. At night, cheap food stalls light up the Calle Jaramillo side of the Plaza de Ponchos.

Buena Vista ▮

(ENTREES: $6-8.50) Buena Vista certainly lives up to its name (Good View), with its prime spot (and balcony) overlooking the Plaza de Ponchos. It has a homey feel, with paintings and hammocks decorating the walls, and candles add to the atmosphere at night.

Buena Visa also has a small book exchange (take one, leave two), and the restaurant plays daily movies in Spanish and English. The menu features pasta, meat dishes, nachos, burgers, and seafood, and there's nightly cocktail specials. Note that Buena Vista is closed all day Tuesday. 2nd Floor, Ca. Salinas, Plaza de Ponchos, Tel: 2925-166, URL: www.buenavistaotavalo.com. Updated: Oct 10, 2012.

Pizza Siciliana

(ENTREES: $4-15) Pizza Siciliana's warm ambiance, boosted by its wood-burning stove and open fireplace, has been enticing both foreigners and locals for years. Pizzas are decent, if rather heavy on the crust, and though pizza prices are high, other options such as salads, hamburgers and sandwiches are more reasonable. Pasta dishes are also available. Service is on the slow side, but friendly. Come here on a Friday or Saturday night, and you'll have live Andean music to entertain you while you eat. Morales 5-10 y Sucre, Tel: 593-6-2925999 / 2920431.
Updated: Oct 10, 2012.

Tabasco's

(ENTREES: $6-9) Tabasco's location, three floors up, is superb, as it provides the opportunity to have your lunch on the rooftop terrace overlooking the plaza. The friendliness of the owner and his wife add to the restaurant's charm. The food is the usual Mexican fare, and though it's decent, it can be a little hit and miss. Prices are a little higher than average: you pay for the smiley service and the superb people-watching. Monday to Saturday 8 a.m.-9 p.m., Sunday 11 a.m.-9 p.m. Salinas 617 and Sucre, Plaza de Ponchos, Tel: 0999-314-615/292-8027, E-mail: tabascosmexicanfood_777@hotmail.com.
Updated: Oct 09, 2012.

Café Pachamama

(ENTREES: $8.50-10) Café Pachamama, located within the hotel La Posada del Quinde, serves healthy and excellent fare, which can be enjoyed by the open fire in the attractive, art-filled dining room, or, on a sunny day, outside on the beautiful garden patio. Dishes make use of local ingredients-try the delicious quiona-encrusted shrimp. The stuffed peppers are also a hit. Pizzas, steaks, seafood, pasta and sandwiches are also on the menu, as are a refreshingly wide variety of vegetarian dishes. American owner Maggie is friendly and always happy to chat. Come on a weekend and you may encounter live local music. Daily 7 a.m.-8 p.m. Ca. Quito and Miguel Egas, Tel: 292-0750, E-mail: maggie@posadaquinde.com, URL: www.posadaquinde.com.

Árbol de Montalvo

(ENTREES: $6.80-9.60) Árbol de Montalvo is located in the Hotel Doña Esther and has a cozy bistro-like atmosphere, which is at least partly due to the big wood-burning oven in the middle of the restaurant. Árbol de Montalvo serves Mediterranean food, specializing in delicious wood-fired pizzas (which some claim are the best pizzas in town). Typical Ecuadorian dishes are also on the menu. Note that the restaurant is open for dinner only. Tuesday to Sunday 5.30-9.30 p.m. Juan Montalvo 444, Tel: 2920-739, Fax: 06-2920739, E-mail: info@otavalohotel.com, URL: www.otavalohotel.com.
Updated: Oct 10, 2012.

Shanandoa Pie Shop

(PIES AND SANDWICHES: $2-5) Owner Aide Garzon started making pies over 25 years ago, after purchasing a book on pie recipes and experimenting until she found the perfect one. And perfect they are: team a slice of apple pie (or blackberry, or strawberry, or one of the many other flavors) with a couple of scoops of ice-cream, and you're in heaven. Aide also makes wonderfully huge, over-stuffed sandwiches and salads, along with milkshakes, fresh fruit juices and breakfasts. Ca. Salinas, Plaza de Ponchos.
Updated: Oct 09, 2012.

Mi Otavalito

(ENTREES: $6.50-8) An old favorite, Mi Otavalito has an extensive and consistently good menu of steak, chicken, fish, and vegetarian dishes, as well as a children's menu. The spacious, attractive dining room and traditionally dressed and smiley staff add to the appeal, and there's live Andean music Friday and Saturday nights. Daily 8 a.m.-9 p.m. Ca. Sucre between Colón and Morales, Tel: 2920-176.

Juanita Marquez

(ENTREES: $ 3-6) The Colombian-owned Juanita Marquez, which opened in March 2012, is a quiet retreat from busy Otavalo, with tables set around a peaceful outdoor courtyard. It's a good option for a decent *almuerzo*; also on the menu are typical Colombian plates (including the *bandeja paisa*, a generously-sized dish made up of pork, sausage, ground meat, rice, red beans, avocado, eggs and plantains), as well as hamburgers, sandwiches and a children's menu. Daily 12-7 p.m. Ca. Roca and Quito, Tel: 0991-645-020.

Balcon De Imbabura

(ENTREES: $3-6.50) For a convenient spot to rest feet weary from hours of shopping, you can't beat Balcon de Imbabura: it's right

NORTHERN ANDES

on the square, overlooking the market. Run by a friendly family, Balcon de Imbabura offers a menu of (so it claims) entirely organic food, with pasta, sandwiches, Mexican dishes, baked potatoes and steaks on offer. The breakfasts (pancakes, French toast, granola with fruit and yogurt) make a nice change from the usual bread roll with eggs, but, as the restaurant doesn't open until 10 a.m., it'll be more like brunch. Daily 10 a.m.-10 p.m. Ca. Jaramillio 7-29, Plaza de Ponchos., Tel: 0984-864-825. Updated: Oct 08, 2012.

Green Coffee Shop and Diner

(ENTREES: $5-7) The tiny Green Coffee Shop & Diner features a scattering of tables in a rustic but sunny courtyard, the walls of which are brightened by colorful murals. Aimed firmly at tourists, the organic menu features breakfasts, sandwiches, salads, pasta and nachos. The fresh juices are particularly good. Ca. Sucre 12-10, Tel: 0992-508-537, E-mail: vguzman87@yahoo.com. Updated: Oct 09, 2012.

La Casa De Intag

(ENTREES: $2.75-4) Fair-trade coffee shop La Casa de Intag sells real coffee (both whole bean and ground varieties) from the beautiful Intag region, an area of cloud forest a few hours north-west of Otavalo. Sit down and sip on a steaming hot cup of coffee, or buy some to take home; in addition, you can purchase artisan crafts, handmade soap, and natural shampoos and creams. Breakfasts, pancakes and sandwiches are also on the menu at this cute little café. The owners also give some of their profits to benefit the communities in the Intag region. Open Monday to Saturday 8 a.m.-6.30 p.m. (may sometimes close for half an hour or so). Ca. Colón 465, on the corner with Ca. Sucre., Tel: 2920-608/0981-949-893/0994-929-861. Updated: Oct 10, 2012.

Peña Amauta

Peñas-bars that play live Andean music while you sip on a drink or two-are popular in Otavalo, and Peña Amauta is an old favorite. Weekend nights see excellent folkloric groups playing, kicking off at around 10 p.m. There's a small cover charge, which generally includes the price of your first drink. Friday and Saturday 8 p.m.-4 a.m. Ca. Morales 511, between Jaramillo and Sucre, Tel: 292-2435, E-mail: amauta64@hotmail.com. Updated: Oct 10, 2012.

Quino

(ENTREES: $4-8.50) Run by an Afro-Ecuadorian family, the unpretentious Quino is known for its excellent seafood, particularly its ceviches, grilled trout and seafood goulash. Each dish is freshly made, so don't expect quick service-but it's worth the wait. Ca. Roca 740, between Garcia Moreno and Montalvo. Updated: Oct 16, 2012.

Oraibi

(ENTREES: $3-10) The adorable Oraibi has a decent and completely vegetarian menu, with good breakfasts, pizzas, pasta, sandwiches and salads on offer. Enjoy your meal in either the cozy indoor dining room or the delightful courtyard garden. Note that though the restaurant claims to be open all day, it has a tendency to shut at random hours. Wednesday to Friday 8 a.m.-10 p.m., Saturday 7.30 a.m.-9 p.m. Ca. Sucre 10-11, corner of Ca. Colón, Tel: 292-1221, E-mail: eplattner@hotmail.com. Updated: Oct 17, 2012.

Otavalo Nightlife

La Taberna

La Taberna does serve food but, with loud music blaring as early as midday, it's more suited to an evening drink or two. It's a small and cozy bar; thick red walls and muted lighting. If you do get hungry though, you can nibble on some nachos, a steak or a burger. The service is remarkably good given how much the place fills up on weekends especially. If downstairs is full, head upstairs where there's another seating area-but even this can get full as well. Monday to Thursday noon to midnight, Friday and Saturday noon to 2 a.m. Ca. Morales 5-01 and Sucre, Tel: 2928-236. Updated: Oct 09, 2012.

The Red Pub

The Red Pub is a popular watering-hole, frequented by the younger demographic of the Otavalo crowd. Needless to say, it's still cheerful, perhaps a little bit rowdier that other bars in the area, but the wooden bar and wooden stools really do help to give it the pub-like feel it deserves. Food is also served: choose from sandwiches, snacks, steak or pasta. In addition to this, hookah pipes are also available and seem to be quite popular drinking companions. Located on Morales 5-07, Tel: 2927-871. Updated: Oct 10, 2012.

AROUND OTAVALO

Although many travelers come to Otavalo just for the market, there's plenty more to do outside of town. Otavalo is surrounded by extinct volcanoes, rugged Andean peaks and fertile highlands, as well as an abundance of lakes and waterfalls. Getting around is fairly easy; the combination of ancient Inca trails, cobbled roads and tracks make the possibilities for walking and cycling almost unlimited.

There are a couple of tour agencies in the town that can arrange trips from Otavalo; the most popular tours are visits to local villages where you can visit indigenous residents in their homes, watch carpets being woven the traditional way, and learn about the weaving process. Hiking, cycling and horse-riding trips are also available.

If you're going hiking, the area around **Lagunas de Mojanda** is an excellent spot–beautiful, yet not at all crowded. The high páramo land, just 17 kilometers (10.56 mi) south of Otavalo, has numerous trails, lasting from just a few hours to a whole day. There are a few hotels along the road that provide easy access to this area and both can recommend good routes (see Lodging Around Otavalo on the next page for more information).

Laguna San Pablo (p. 174), southeast of Otavalo, is another good choice, with several places to eat fresh fish, get involved in water sports, or stay the night. There's a paved road encircling the lake, and you can walk around it in a day; the views are beautiful.

Another good excursion is to the gorgeous **Laguna de Cuicocha** (p. 178), a volcanic crater lake which is a haven for wildlife. There's a trail around the lake, but the path very eroded in places and can be difficult to follow. On a clear day the views are stunning. You can also take a boat trip around the lake.

A popular walking or cycling trip from Otavalo is to the waterfall at **Cascada de Peguche** (p. 178). Follow the railway tracks north to the town of Peguche (about 3 km/1.86 mi), where you may be lucky enough to see weavers at work. Keep going another 2 kilometers (1.24 mi) along a trail southwest to reach the waterfall. The area can be fairly busy with locals during the weekend, but quieter during the week.

Things To See and Do Around Otavalo
FUYA FUYA

Fuya Fuya is located 20 kilometers (12.4 mi) south of Otavalo. Trails on the mountain offer straightforward climbs with spectacular views of the Lagunas de Mojanda, three pristine lakes located at the base of the mountain, and wide expanses of páramo grasslands.

Getting To and Away from Fuya Fuya

From Quito, take the Pan-American Highway north toward Otavalo. From Otavalo, take any bus heading to Quito or Lago San Pablo (see Getting To and Away from Otavalo for more information, p. 172). After you reach Lago San Pablo, you will pass a Repsol gas station on the right. Just beyond the gas station, you should see a sign for Mojanda where you turn left and follow the cobblestone road for about 15 minutes until you come to the lakes. Fuya Fuya is easily visible from here. Or, simply hire a taxi to the Lagunas from Otavalo (approximately $15 one-way; you can pay more to have the taxi wait).

Hiking Fuya Fuya

You can follow any of the various footpaths up to the pass or to the peak at 4,263 meters (13,986 ft). The hikes take two to three hours to summit from the lakes, and the total elevation gain is approximately 550 meters (1,804 ft), making Fuya Fuya a good, quick mountain for climbers hoping to acclimatize for some of Ecuador's higher peaks.

Plan to take a topographic map of the region if you decide to hike in the areas beyond the lakes, as trails in the more remote regions are not always well marked.

LAGUNAS DE MOJANDA

The area around Lagunas de Mojanda is one of the most popular spots for hiking in the Northern Andes.

Getting To and Away From Lagunas de Mojanda

The lakes are located 17 kilometers (10.5 mi) from Otavalo and are set in high páramo grassland at an altitude of about 3,500 meters (11,482 ft). A taxi up to the lake from Otavalo costs about $15. Expect to pay another $7-10 per hour if you want the taxi to wait. If you come hiking up here, make sure you take some warm clothes and a wind-proof jacket–the altitude and the exposure make it a lot colder than the sheltered town of Otavalo a ways below.

Hiking Lagunas de Mojanda

The cobbled road between the lake and the town is itself a pleasant walk–it has great views of the valley and passes through several little villages. There's no transportation up there, so if you walk, you should order a taxi to pick you up at the top (the walk takes five to seven hours with breaks), or be prepared to walk back as well. Alternatively, take a taxi to the top and walk back down. It's best to go in a group; some parts are isolated and there have been reports of robberies on the route.

There are two main places to stay along this road. On the right hand side, 3 kilometers (1.86 mi) from Otavalo, is the top-end hotel Casa Mojanda. About 1 kilometer (0.6 mi) further on, on the left, is La Luna, which is more geared to backpackers. Both hotels have great views into the valley. See Lodging Around Otavalo for more information.

Once you reach the lake, there are numerous possibilities for hiking. A good hike (well, half hike, half scramble) is from the lakeside (close to where the road stops) up to the top of Fuya Fuya, an extinct volcano–at 4260 meters (13,976 ft), it's the highest point around the lake, and, on a clear day, the views from the top are stunning.

A shorter walk is to the top of the first hill on the left, as you face the lake from the parking area. You'll see the trail leading upwards from the lakeside. The climb is rather steep and takes between 20 to 30 minutes to get to the highest point. From the top, you can make your way along the ridge. Take one of the paths down the hill to the lakeside, from where you can walk back to the parking area.

Although there is a trail around the lake, hiking it in a single day is almost impossible–unless you run. Most people simply walk along the trail for a couple of hours then backtrack. There are also several circular routes that start off on the lakeside trail then bend into the mountains–these can take anywhere from a couple of hours to a full day. Both of the hotels mentioned above can suggest good walking routes and arrange tours, or just enquire at one of the tour agencies in Otavalo. Updated: Oct 30, 2012.

Lodging Around Otavalo

The area around Otavalo is home to some of the country's most beautiful converted haciendas and hotels. Rates for these often luxurious mountain accommodations vary widely, but tend towards mid-range and high-end prices. Haciendas, as a general rule, offer beautiful views, direct access to walking routes, excellent restaurants, and can be wonderful places in which to escape the bustle of town. Updated: Oct 31, 2012.

La Luna ⚑

(ROOMS: $12-26) Perched up in the quiet hills a few miles south of Otavalo, La Luna feels like a home away from home and is an excellent choice for backpackers who want to chill out for a few days. Depending on your budget, choose between a camping, a bed in a dorm, a room with shared bath or a room with private bath and warming fireplace. The charming lodge-style hostel offers beautiful views of the valley–particularly from the hammocks on the terrace. The cozy restaurant serves basic but wholesome food, and there's a wood-burning stove for colder evenings. The lounge has plenty of games and DVDs to keep you occupied. There are several good walks in the area, and the helpful English/Ecuadorian owners can provide you with a map and suggest some good routes. They can also arrange transport to the Lagunas de Mojanda, as well as organize horseback riding and mountain-biking trips. Kilometer 4 1/2 via route to Mojanda (from Otavalo), Tel: 0993-156-082/0998-294-913/0999-737-415, E-mail: lalunaecuador@yahoo.co.uk, URL: www.lalunaecuador.com. Updated: Oct 31, 2012.

Cabañas Rose Cottage

(ROOMS: $12-100) Set up in the hills three kilometers (2 mi) outside Otavalo, Rose Cottage offers guests a beautiful base from which to explore the surrounding area. It offers a range of clean and cozy options in its seven distinct cabins, and those on a tighter budget can stay in dorms or camp. You can also rent an entire cabin or house. Located around the grounds are table tennis, TV, DVD selections, a book exchange, safe storage and a large library. Active travelers can take advantage of the on-site tennis court (free) or enjoy pleasant walks, including one to the beautiful Taxopamba waterfall, just 40 minutes away on foot. Horse riding excursions can also be arranged, and the staff organizes free transport to the Saturday

morning markets. Breakfast is included. From Otavalo, a taxi to Rose Cottage costs around $3-4. 3.5 kilometers south of Otavalo, Tel: 0997-728-115, E-mail: info@rosecottageecuador.com / rosecottageecuador@btinternet.com, URL: www.rosecottageecuador.com.
Updated: Oct 31, 2012.

Santa Agua de Chachimbiro

($50 per person) Previously known as Hostería Termas de Chachimbiro, Santa Agua de Chachimbiro (Holly Water of Chachimbiro) used to be a community-based ecotourism spa and resort run by the Cordillera Foundation (a local NGO), but is now run by the Provincial Government of Imbabura. The *hosteria* has thermal water pools and offers massage services that include hydromassage. At the resort, you also have access to numerous activities such as horse riding, canopy tours, a zip-line and a cable car. The hosteria is a good starting point for the Piñan trek, which can also be arranged with a tour operator who works with the them. Hosteria Termas Chachimbiro is located in the Urcuqui county Imbabura province, 50 Km north west of both Otavalo and Ibarra. Ibarra office: Pedro Moncayo, between Rocafuerte and Maldonado (World Computers Building), Tel: 06-264-8063/8308/8435, Ibarra office: 06-261-0250, E-mail: santaaguareservaciones@hotmail.com, URL: www.imbabura.gob.ec/chachimbiro.
Updated: Feb 15, 2013.

Hacienda San Francisco

(ROOMS: $57-140) Located in the Imbabura province in the Salinas Valley, just 40 minutes from Ibarra, Hacienda San Francisco has been in the same family since 1640. The establishment is close to a variety of places of interest; nearby is the Chachimboro thermal springs and the hacienda also has its own, natural hot spring and thermal bath. San Francisco has cobblestone patios surrounded by spacious, well-kept gardens, and beautiful, sunny rooms. Activities include swimming, tennis, and horseback riding. The horseback riding tours visit the scenic Cotacachi-Cayapas reserve and the 'paramo of Piñar,' a highland plain. Meals are not included, but the traditional, full service restaurant offers breakfast, lunch and dinner. Tel: 2648-442/0994-783-964, E-mail: info@hosteriasanfrancisco.com, URL: www.hosteriasanfrancisco.com.
Updated: Oct 31, 2012.

Casa Mojanda

(ROOMS: $122-292) Casa Mojanda, located in the hills on the road to Lagunas de Mojanda (just over 3 km/1.86 mi from Otavalo), is a delightful mix of hacienda experience and modern responsible tourism. Casa Mojanda is not a historical hacienda; rather, the accommodations are relatively modern. It prides itself on making the experience as genuine as possible: the home-cooked meals are excellent, using local recipes made from traditional ingredients, and a band is often around to play Andean music.

Otavalo is only a ten-minute drive away, or an hour if you'd rather hike. The staff can also arrange for horseback riding, hiking tours in the Mojanda Lakes, artisan villages tours and bird watching, as well as visits to local places of interest. Rates include breakfast and dinner. Mojanda Lakes Road Km 3.8, Tel: 098-033-5108, E-mail: casamojandainn@gmail.com, URL: www.casamojanda.com.
Updated: Feb 19, 2013.

Hacienda Pinsaqui

(ROOMS: $112-175) Located between the market towns of Otavalo, Cotacachi and San Antonio de Ibarra, Pinsaqui is the perfect place to come to to visit the markets while enjoying the comfort of one of the most beautiful haciendas in the north of Ecuador. Pinsaqui has a long history of famous visits: Simón Bolívar used to stop at Pinsaqui when he would travel between Ecuador and Colombia (the 'Simón Bolívar Room' is the most elegant suite in the hotel).

It feels more like a home than a hotel; the staff is friendly, helpful and courteous. The hacienda is a maze of well-kept, beautiful gardens, patios, airy hallways, unique guest rooms (all of which have private bath and either a wood stove or a fireplace), fountains and a charming, cozy bar. Pinsaqui also owns a small number of horses and can arrange for rides along trails in the hacienda's grounds. Breakfast is included, and lunch and dinner are also offered in the hotel's restaurant. Panamericana Norte KM 5, Tel: 06-294-6116/6117, E-mail: info@haciendapinsaqui.com, URL: www.haciendapinsaqui.com.

Hacienda Primavera

(ROOMS: $83) Raved about by travelers, Hacienda Primavera is a gorgeous eco-lodge tucked in the El Choclo rainforest reserve.

The hotel, which has been owned by the same family for over 90 years, is located an hour and a half from Otavalo. The hacienda is a working ranch with several animals, and is surrounded by a lush forest with prolific bird life. There are eight suites with exquisite views of the rainforest, all with private bathrooms and balconies.the proprietors make every effort to keep their lodge eco-friendly through organic recycling and other earth-conscious efforts. The restaurant serves gourmet meals, using organic crops from the hacienda and local farms. The lodge organizes activities such as horseback riding, hiking and Ecuadorian cookery classes, and there are also opportunities to participate in the day-to-day running of the hacienda. Rates are all-inclusive and include lodging, three meals, all activities and use of the swimming pool. Caserio La Primavera, Carchi, Tel: 301-1719/0993-708-571, URL: www.haciendaprimavera.com.
Updated: Oct 31, 2012.

The Ali Shungu Mountaintop Lodge

(ROOMS: $87.50-95) The Ali Shungu Mountain Top Lodge has an idyllic setting on a hilltop with gorgeous views of Otavalo and the surrounding countryside. The staff is extremely friendly and do their best to ensure their guests feel at home. Visitors stay in private (and very spacious) guesthouses, which can accommodate up to four people. Each of the cozy guesthouses has a living area with sofas, board games and books, kitchenette, private bath, and patio. Room prices include breakfast, dinner, and two hours' horseback riding with a guide around the lands surrounding the hacienda. Meals are served in the gourmet restaurant, and there are several organic and vegetarian options, with many of the ingredients coming from the hotel's garden. If you need to stay connected, there is free WiFi in the main lodge. Note that there is a minimum two night stay at the hacienda. You can have a taxi can take you to the lodge from Otavalo for $5, or staff may be able to pick you up with prior arrangement. Casilla 34, Otavalo, Ecuador, Tel: 0989-509-945, E-mail: mountainlodge@alishungu.com, URL: www.alishungumountaintoplodge.com.
Updated: Oct 31, 2012.

Las Palmeras Inn

(ROOMS: $60-120) Las Palmeras is a 150-year old hacienda just a few minutes outside of Otavalo. The establishment, set in gorgeously landscaped gardens, has spectacular views of Imbabura and Cotocachi Volcanoes. Most of the inn's rooms are located in cozy cabins, set apart from the main house. There are larger, more luxuriously appointed rooms available too however, as well as an entire private house which can be rented by the week or month. Rooms have log-fires and hot water is available for tea and cocoa if nights get really chilly. Rates include breakfast as well. 3 km west of Otavalo, from the Interamerican Highway in front of the Animal Market, follow the signs to Las Palmeras. Tel: 292-2607, E-mail: palmeras@cusin.com.ec, URL: www.laspalmerasinn.com.
Updated: Oct 31, 2012.

LAGO SAN PABLO

Lago San Pablo, located a few miles southeast of Otavalo, is another good hiking destination in the Northern Andes. One of the most visited lakes in Ecuador, you'll find that there are several places to stay on the edge of the large lake offering a number of activities anywhere from sailing to waterskiing.

You can also take a day hike around the circumference and take in the beautiful view of the Imbabura volcano.

Getting To and Away from Lago San Pablo

To get to Lago San Pablo you'll have to take any one of the buses from Otavalo ($0.25) that depart in that direction every 15-20 minutes. The journey there shouldn't take more than 20 minutes.
Updated: Mar 15, 2013.

Lago San Pablo Lodging
Hacienda Cusin

(ROOMS: $90-180) Hacienda Cusin, one of the most elegant and prestigious haciendas in the northern highlands, is a complex of beautiful buildings, gardens and patios. Some of the buildings date back to the colonial era, when the owners of Cusin oversaw more than 40,470 hectares (100,000 ac) in the nearby valleys.

Hacienda Cusin is now a luxurious favorite and also hosts numerous weddings and special events. Cusin is only about a half hour from Otavalo, and the hacienda tends to fill up on weekends with tourists headed to the market. The establishment offers horseback

riding and mountain biking trips, as well as a game room and sports courts. There are a variety of room types, for one to four people, and breakfast is included; there is also the option to pay a special "umbrella" rate which includes all meals and activities. Lago San Pablo, Tel: 291-8013/8136/8317, Fax: 291-8003, E-mail: hacienda@cusin.com.ec, URL: www.haciendacusin.com.
Updated: Oct 31, 2012.

Cabañas del Lago

(ROOMS: $122-205) Located on the east side of the San Pablo lake, only 15 minutes from Otavalo, Cabañas del Lago is an oasis of luxury tucked between the small lake towns. The resort-style hotel offers a variety of lodging options including: single rooms, cabins, suites and family cottages. Each room is equipped with a working fireplace, which is lit for you in the evenings, completing the rustic look of this well-built establishment.
The hotel also includes a mini golf course, boat rides, volleyball courts, a gift shop, water sports and a full-service restaurant on the shore of the lake.

Even if you are not planning to stay for the night, this place is a perfect stop for lunch, coffee or an early dinner before heading back to Quito. The entrees range from $8 to $13, and, in case you already spent all of your cash in the Otavalo market, you can charge the meal to your Mastercard or Visa. Make sure to finish the experience with a glass of chocolate liquor –a specialty of the region– in front of the fireplace. Lago San Pablo, Tel: 06-291-8108 / 06-291-8001, E-mail: info@cabanasdellago.com.ec, URL: www.cabanasdellago.com.ec.
Updated: Feb 14, 2013.

Hostería Puerto Lago

(ROOMS: $60-95) On the shore of San Pablo Lake, about fifteen minutes south of **Otavalo**, sits Puerto Lago hotel and restaurant. The establishment is an attractive complex of well-manicured lawns, spacious rooms, and also features one of the most elegant restaurants in the area. There are 27 rooms in the complex, the best of which have a magnificent view of the lake and Volcan Imbabura.

The rooms are cozy, neat, and comfortable, with fireplaces and cable TV. Puerto Lago owns a motorboat and can offer tours of the lake, as well as fishing and water skiing trips.

There are llamas on the grounds for photos, and a gift shop. On weekends, women from Otavalo set up small stands in the gadens of the parking lot to sell their wares to tourists who pass through to eat at the restaurant. Lago San Pablo y Panamericana Norte, P.O. Box 10 02 100, Tel: 593-6-292-0920, E-mail: puertolago@andinanet.net, URL: www.puertolago.com.
Updated: Apr 15, 2013.

Lago San Pablo Restaurants

Puerto Lago

The restaurant is probably the best part of Puerto Lago. Since the dining room was constructed right along the shore, if you're seated at the window, you have excellent views over the water. The food is outstanding, and many of the tour buses going to and from Otavalo regularly stop for lunch.

Puerto Lago specializes in traditional food, but has a wide array of menu options. There are also conference facilities, and Puerto Lago can host special events. Lago San Pablo and Panamericana Norte, Tel: 06-263-5400, URL: http://www.puertolago.com/eng.
Updated: Apr 15, 2013.

PEGUCHE

Within hiking distance from Otavalo, Peguche makes a welcome break for those looking for some peace and quiet after a hard day's bargaining Otavalo Market. The town is sleepier than it once was, as the train tracks have been abandoned ever since the late 1980s, but Peguche is still very friendly and welcoming despite its rather unkempt appearance.

The town is home to a nearby and sacred waterfall, along with a number of artisan stalls that line the path to the entrance. Here, vendors will try to persuade you to part with your cash before you head to Otavalo. A number of musicians also live in town whom you may see out in the open playing their pan pipes, accompanied by local dancers and artists.

The facilities in Peguche are limited to just a couple of hotels with adjacent restaurants and just one or two grocery stores in the center, so its advised that you stock up on anything important that you might need while in Otavalo before head out here.
Updated: Mar 18, 2013.

NORTHERN ANDES

Getting To and Away from Peguche

Peguche is just a few kilometers from Otavalo and it's possible to walk between the two. Just head north along the Pan-American Highway, in the direction of Ibarra. You will come across signs for Peguche, which is a right turn off the highway. The walk takes about 40 minutes. Alternatively, you can take a bus there from Otavalo: either hop on one of the Peguche-bound buses that run past the bus terminal on Calle Atahualpa (10 min, $0.15) or take a north-bound bus along the Pan-American Highway in the direction of Ibarra, and get off at the turn for Peguche (where the traffic lights are). Taxis will take you from Otavalo for around $4.
Updated: Mar 18, 2013.

Things To See and Do in Peguche

Peguche Waterfall

If you're staying the night in Peguche, it's worth it to take the 20 minute walk to the town's sacred waterfall. About 2 kilometers (1 mi) long, the trail has an array of sellers, hoping that you will buy their jewelry and dream-catchers. Along the way, you'll also pass through a eucalyptus-forested area where you can camp. The waterfall is not spectacular, but it is serene - particularly if few other travelers are around; during the June festival of Inti Raymi however, this site becomes the place for ritualistic baths conducted by the locals, whom come and bathe under its freezing waters. Just on the outskirts of Peguche.
Updated: Mar 18, 2013.

Peguche Lodging

La Casa Sol !

(ROOMS: $49-139) La Casa Sol is more than a hotel, it is a home integrated into the daily life of the indigenous communities of the sector. La Casa Sol is located inside the "Cascada de Peguche" (Waterfall of Peguche) Protected Forest. The Kichwa de Peguche community is a privileged and energetic place where guests will be able to enjoy evenings and sceneries that will leave them breathless.

Brightly colored walls and artwork adorn the entire property. Most rooms have expansive views of Cotocachi Volcano and the valley below. Traditional local food served in the cozy dining room rounds off the full sensory Andean experience.

Casa Sol coordinates a community tourism project which provides tours of workshops and cooperatives in and around Peguche. Local artisans show you how their traditional handicrafts are made and offer a behind-the-scenes look into the making of the Otavalo market. The hotel is owned by Marcos Lema, an Otavaleño musician and entrepreneur who also started the original Casa Sol Bed and Breakfast in Quito. Both are highly recommended. Cascada de Peguche 3 Km north of Otavalo, Tel: 06-269-0500, Fax: 06-269-0448, E-mail: info@lacasasol.com, URL: http://www.lacasasol.com/casaotavalo.
Updated: Feb 14, 2013.

Aya Huma

(ROOMS: $20-56) The hostel Aya Huma is a decent and economical option for those who would prefer to stay outside of Otavalo after a long day at the market. Rooms are basic, but clean, and the ones with bathrooms have very hot showers. Rooms along the edge of the road can be a little noisy at night, so try to get one that is located down below, away from the traffic. Aya Huma has a book exchange, lots of information for travelers, and a pleasant gift shop with good quality, locally-made products for sale. The hotel also has an adjoining restaurant. Hostal Aya Huma is a traditional indigenous house, located along the train tracks in Peguche, a 1 km (.62 mi) distance of the Waterfalls and 2.5 km (1.6 mi) outside of the town center of Otavalo. Peguche-Otavalo 110 km. north of Quito, Tel: 06-269-0333, Fax: 06-269-0164, E-mail: ayahuma@ayahuma.com, URL: www.ayahuma.com.
Updated: Feb 14, 2013.

Peguche Restaurants

Aya Huma Restaurant

(ENTREES: $.350-7) In Peguche there aren't a whole lot of options for food, but the adjoining restaurant to the Aya Huma hostel is decent. The menu is a respectable size, with lots of the typical Ecuadorian fare (including *cuy*, or guinea pig), as well as some international and vegetarian alternatives. Portions are hearty and served with organic vegetables. Service is leisurely, so while you wait for your food, sit back and listen to the pan pipe band that regularly plays, or watch local kids putting on a traditional dance show. Outskirts of Otavalo. Tel: 06-269-0333, E-mail: ayahuma@ayahuma.com, URL: www.ayahuma.com.
Updated: Feb 14, 2013.

ILUMAN

In the shadow of Volcán Imbabura, at an altitude of about 2,600 meters (8,500 feet), is the village of Iluman, home to artisans and healers. If you've noticed felt hats at the markets in Otavalo and want to see how they are produced, Iluman is the place to go. It's located between Otavalo and Ibarra, and you can get there simply by taking a 20-minute bus ride from Otavalo.

In local workshops, wool is transformed into the coveted headgear using a series of irons, presses and molds. The hats are finished with distinctive braided headbands before being shipped off to stores and markets around the country.

The village is also known for the number of spiritual healers residing there (some estimates put the number at more than 200). The healers are often referred to by the Quichua term *yachac taitas*, or wise fathers.

Visitors who want to undergo healing rituals at the hands of the yachac taitas can do so, but should be prepared to be doused in a spray of alcohol, tobacco smoke and herbs. The rituals are meant to cleanse the recipient spiritually and remove curses - such as the 'evil eye' - more than being used to cure physical diseases (although they're reported to be able to do that too).
Updated: Mar 15, 2013.

IRUGUINCHO

Iruguincho is a small, poor, rural village close to the Cotocachi-Cayapas Reserve where people rely on subsistence agriculture. The community has become involved in eco-tourism around their area, and can provide visitors with local guides and horses. You can get to Iruguincho by catching a bus from Ibarra.

In the village you can arrange a day hike to *Churo* (Quechua meaning snail, or sea shell), one of the best preserved pre-columbian temples in the area (the trip takes three hours). Historians and locals believe that the form of the temple, which corresponds to the shape of a shell, suggests that the temple was used to worship the volcano, Cayambe. The community also offers shorter walks to the nearby cloud forest and a beautiful local waterfall. You can even enjoy a dip in the Timbuyacu hot springs (a very basic

facility that's owned by the community). Ask for Galo Vargas in the village. He can arrange horses for longer trips and can act as a guide for the Cotocachi-Cayapas Reserve (in Spanish only).

There are currently no accommodation option available in Iruguincho, but the community is planning to open their homes to visitors in the near future. In the meantime, you can camp near the village or stay in Tumbabiro.
Updated: Mar 18, 2013.

TUMBABIRO

Tumbabiro is a small, rural village located approximately 40 minutes northwest of Ibarra. Most of the people who live in this area still cultivate crops using largely traditional methods. Many of the buildings in and around the main square are very old and were originally constructed using adobe mud bricks and local timbers. There are also a number of very old adobe walls that surround the nearby fields.

The area around Tumbabiro has numerous paths and roads, many of which are free from traffic and good for walking. On the weekends, you can watch local men playing a traditional ball game, Pelota en Mano, at the village's main square. From Tumbabiro, you can also catch buses to Urcuqui, Cahuasqui and Ibarra.

About 4 km north of Tumbabiro, close to Ajumbuela village, there is a complete, double-ramped Caranqui pyramid. Although the edifice is covered with vegetation, the pyramid is in excellent condition; many pottery fragments dating from 500-1500 BC have been found in the area. More information -- in English, German and Spanish -- is available at Hostería Pantaví. The hotel can also arrange for guide to take you on a tour.
Updated: Oct 30, 2012.

Tumbabiro Lodging
Hostería Pantaví

(ROOMS: $46-1310) Hostería Pantaví has 12 lovely rooms in a beautiful, peaceful setting. There is a variety of ethnic art on the walls of the main house, painted by the owner, Camilo Andrade. Many of these pieces have been inspired by his interest in the local archeology and Ecuadorian mythology. Pantaví is located near a variety of interesting places to

NORTHERN ANDES

NORTHERN ANDES

visit: the Cotacachi-Cayapas Reserve, Arco Iris and Chachimbiro hot springs, El Ángel Ecological Reserve and a number of Caranqui archeological sites. The hacienda isn't far from Chota, where the Afro-Ecuadorian inhabitants produce interesting masks.

The hostería has a swimming pool and conference facilities, as well as areas for tennis and volleyball. The dozen rooms vary in capacity and bed size, so make sure to ask to see your room when you arrive or check ahead of time when you make reservation. Km. 7 on the road to Salinas, Tel: 2347-476/2934-185, E-mail: info@hosteriapantavi.ec, URL: www.hosteriapantavi.com.
Updated: Oct 30, 2012.

CAHUASQUI

Cahuasqui is a beautiful, but remote village where the residents depend largely on subsistence agriculture. Their farming techniques employ methods which have remained unchanged over the course of centuries. The area's main draw is the Cahuasqui plateau, which has about 20 burial and ceremonial mounds scattered around. The plateau was a strategic stronghold of the Caranqui culture between 500 and 1,500 BC; ancient agricultural terraces can still be identified where they cut into the land.

In times past, cotton and maize were grown on the terraces. Nowadays, the land continues to be used by the local people for the cultivation of maize and other vegetable food crops.

Cahuasqui also has a huge ceremonial pyramid, which was partially destroyed by bulldozers in order the use the ground for agriculture, but is nevertheless worth a visit if you are in the area. In the smaller Cahuasqui park, there is evidence of the last Caranqui calendar that exists in Ecuador. The calendar was carved on a huge stone and, in order to protect the archaeological piece, the local people mounted the stone in cement. Now, all you can see is half of the main façade.

There is also a small, private, archaeological museum in the main plaza close to the church. Ask for Pablo Montalvo, a young enthusiast (collector of archaeological pieces) who will be happy to show you his museum for free—but might expect a small tip. He only speaks Spanish, but can also act as a guide for *tolas* (mounds) and pyramids in the areas. The town is located about 45 kilometers (28 mi) from Ibarra, and takes about two hours to get there via public bus.

CUICOCHA LAKE

Cuicocha, which means "guinea pig lake" in Qechua, is a crater lake situated at the foot of Cotocachi Volcano, at an altitude of 3200 m. Emerging from the dark waters of the 3 kilometer wide lake are four spectacularly perfect vegetation-covered domes which were formed by the last eruption over 3,000 years ago. Boats, which depart every half hour or so, will take you around the islands, near which you can observe bubbles of sulfur gas escaping to the surface and turning the water lukewarm. The ride costs about $2 and includes a voucher for a free canelazo at the cafeteria. If you are up for a three-to-four hour hike, you can also follow the path along the rim of the crater, which offers spectacular views of the surrounding volcanoes and of Otavalo valley.

Getting To and Away from Cuicocha

By car or taxi, Cuicocha is about 20 minutes from Cotacachi, which in turn is about 20 minutes from Otavalo.

Things To See and Do at Cuicocha Lake
Boating Around Cuicocha Lake

If you're not up for the hike, you can take a scenic tour of the lake by boat. Boats, which depart every half hour or so, will take you around the islands, near which you can observe bubbles of sulfur gas escaping to the surface and turning the water lukewarm. The ride costs about $2 and includes a voucher for a free canelazo at the cafeteria.
Updated: May 07, 2013.

Hiking around Cuicocha Lake   !

The hike around Cuicocha Lake can be completed anywhere between 3.5 and 5 hours, depending on your general level of fitness. Most people walk around the lake anticlockwise from the restaurant. Be aware that the hike has steep sections, especially at the beginning if you take the anti-clockwise route. The walk is probably best done in groups, as in the past there have been reports of robberies. The hike's highlights include countless species of pretty orchids and flowers and great views of the lake and its islands.

COTACACHI

 2,377m   10,000 📞 06

This pleasant pastoral town rests at the foot of the dormant Cotacachi volcano. It is best known for producing cheap but high-quality handmade leather goods, and attracts a good number of tourists for this reason. The area is also rich in biodiversity, making Cotacachi an attractive place to go for outdoor activities and adventures, both around the volcano and in the nearby Cotacachi-Cayapas Ecological Reserve.

The diverse cultural and ethnic makeup of the Cotacachi population has become a central focus for the town, as well as a great source of pride. Great effort has been put into creating tolerance and solidarity among the indigenous, black, and mestizo residents. In 1996, Cotacachi became the first town in Ecuador to elect an indigenous mayor.

The town has even received awards from UNESCO (United National Educational, Scientific and Cultural Organization) and other international organizations for its focus on integration, education, and urban development. Walk into town though, and you'll first find a dusty, potholed road. Keep going and you'll see what all the praise has been about. Cotacachi is clean and well-maintained. Charming plazas are surrounded by huge buildings painted pink, yellow and green. Not all buildings have been refurbished-some are still dirty, crumbling and supported by decaying infrastructure-but Cotacachi has been taking steps in the right direction.

On the weekends travelers flock to the town to browse its famous "Leather Street" (10 de Agosto), where leather craftsmen (and women) sell their quality leather goods that include wallets, purses and jackets.
Updated: Oct 24, 2012.

Getting To and Away from Cotacachi

Cotacachi is served by frequent buses to and from Otavalo and Ibarra. The town's bus station is located on 10 de Agosto and Salinas; if you're closer to the main plaza, Parque La Matriz, you can also catch the bus to Otavalo or Ibarra from here (buses stop on Calle Modesto Peñaherrera-look out for the green bus stop).

To Ibarra ($0.30, 25 min): buses leave every 10 to 15 minutes between 6 a.m.-6 p.m.

To Otavalo ($0.25, 20 min): buses leave every 10 to 15 minutes between 6 a.m.-6 p.m. If you're planning on heading to Laguna Cuicocha from Cotacachi, note that there is no public transport. Instead, you can hire a taxi or truck to take you there for around $6 per car (taxis line up around Plaza la Matriz and also on the corner of 10 de Agosto and Bolivar).
Updated: Oct 24, 2012.

Things To See and Do in Cotacachi

Leather Shopping

Shopping for Cotacahi's famed leather goods is the reason most people come to this little *pueblo,* and to do so, simply walk up and down Calle 10 de Agosto, which runs all the way through town (starting at the bus station).

Here you will find shop after shop jam-packed with leather: jackets, shoes, belts, purses, wallets and vests and more. This is the best spot in Ecuador for buying genuine, handmade leather. Though the shops are almost identical in the type of goods they have to offer, quality does vary from store to store, so shop around before making any purchases.

Most stores are open daily from 9 a.m.-7 p.m., though several shut for a *siesta* between 12-3 p.m. Major credit cards are accepted in the majority of the shops, but note that you'll generally receive a discount if you pay in cash.

Photo by: Ale

If you end up sticking around town for a few days (and this pleasant town has that sort of effect on travelers), you can ask the leather-workers to tailor or customize your purchases.
Updated: Oct 24, 2012.

NORTHERN ANDES

Did a unique trek? Got way off the beaten path? Tell other travelers at vivatrav-

Parque la Matriz

Parque la Matriz can be found beneath the gaze of a towering sculpture of Jesus. La Matriz is Cotacachi's main plaza and is ringed by the flags of a dozen diverse nations. A large glass plaque marks Cotacachi's status as a UNESCO world heritage sight, and another nearby monument honors the city's "democratization of municipal management."

One of the more notable features of the park is a statue of Santa Ana de Cotacachi wearing strings of local beads. Walk towards Iglesia Matriz (the church) and you'll see several more statues of local religious figures. The church is beautiful, but you may have to be content with admiring the exterior, as Iglesia Matriz not always open to tourists. The sights of Parque la Matriz can be enjoyed in the course of a brief stroll around the square. But one of the most rewarding things to do is just sit on a shady park bench to people-watch and enjoy the refreshing afternoon breeze. Parque La Matriz, just follow the towering statue of Jesus that stands on top of the cathedral. The figure is visible from anywhere in the city.
Updated: Oct 24, 2012.

Casa De Las Culturas

Cotacachi's Casa de las Culturas (House of Culture) is set in a beautifully restored building where (in some places) the ceilings are impressively high and the walls are 1.3 meters (4.5 ft) wide. The Casa has many facets: it's an educational center (with classrooms and a library), has an arts area (there are frequent art exhibitions, as well as an original painting by Guayasamin, Ecuador's most famous contemporary artist), and the town's radio station is also located here, which features talkshows and daily music. There is also a lovely café, Cafeteria Toisan, and a very helpful tourist information center, where staff can give free tourist information and maps of Cotacachi. You can rent bikes here to go to Laguna Cuicocha ($8 a day gets you the bike, helmet, and a welcome drink on your return. Staff recommends renting a van to take you to the lake, then cycling the 1.5 hour journey back). Corner of Bolivar and 9 de Octubre, Tel: 255-4122/0999-316-887, Updated: Oct 24, 2012.

Verde Milenio

The Verde Milenio Foundation is a non-profit organization dedicated to protecting the environment and preserving the cultural heritage of native communities where the traditional ways of life are in danger of dying out. Verde Milenio operation is currently based in El Chocó, in the Cotocachi-Cayapas Ecological Reserve. The non-profit works in collaboration with the local Chachi and Afro-Ecuadorian communities to support the development of eco-tourism projects. The projects provide the communities with sustainable development alternatives that are ecologically and culturally sound.

In addition to eco-tourism, Verde Milenio also manages education, health, conservation, small business development and volunteering projects. Obs. Miguel y Solier # 122 & Selva Alegre, Tel: 02-290-6192 / 099-984-2256, E-mail: info@verdemilenio.org, URL: www.verdemilenio.org.
Updated: Feb 14, 2013.

Cotacachi Services

MONEY

You'll find a few branches of national banks in Cotacachi, including **Banco de Guayaquil** (Ca. 10 de Agosto and Rocafuerte, on the corner of Parque San Francisco) and **Banco Pichincha** (Ca. Imbabura, on Parque San Francisco).

Both banks have ATMs which accept international cards such as VISA, Mastercard, Diners Club and Cirrus.

MEDICAL

Small pharmacies are dotted around town. **Farmacia Vitalpharma** is conveniently located on Calle 10 de Agosto, directly opposite La Marqueza restaurant 7 a.m.-10 p.m.).

KEEPING IN TOUCH

There are several Internet cafés around the main plaza, Parque la Matriz, as well as along Calle Bolivar. Most also have cabins for making phone calls.

TOURISM

The city's tourism office is now located in the building of the Gobierno Municipal on the Plaza la Matriz (Monday to Friday 8 a.m.-5 p.m.). Go inside the building's main entrance, and the tourism desk is to your right. It's not always manned, however, and though the staff is friendly, they don't have a lot of resources or much to offer the curious tourist. The tourism desk in the Casa de las Culturas (See Things to See and Do in Cotacachi) tends to be more useful, frankly.

SHOPPING

Shopping for leather, of course, is the reason most people visit Cotacachi (see Things to See and Do in Cotacachi for information), but there are other types of shopping here too. For groceries, head to either the **Tia** supermarket on Calle 10 de Agosto, between Bolivar and Sucre, or the **Mercado de los Andes** (Ca. 10 de Agosto and Salinas, by the bus station). For traditional artisan goods, you'll find a small artisan market on Parque San Francisco (walk all the way down 10 de Agosto until you reach Rocafuerte); there are stalls here every day, but numbers increase on the weekends.
Updated: Oct 24, 2012.

Cotacachi Lodging

Cotacachi hostels and hotels offer accommodation to suit any budget. For those watching their money, there are a couple of comfortable hostels which offer the basics; if you have a bit more to spend, there are several up-market options, including a couple of luxury (and expensive) haciendas outside of town.
Updated: Oct 24, 2012.

BUDGET
Hostal-Posada Munaylla
(ROOMS: $15) Munaylla is a quiet hostel close to the center of town. The hostel itself has a dark, slightly depressing feel, but the rooms are bright and pleasant and have cable TV and WiFi. The rooms that don't have outside-facing windows should be avoided however. Since Munaylla is the tallest building for some distance, there are great views from the rooftop. The hostel is popular with Ecuadorian families, but there aren't any real common areas, so don't expect to meet many fellow travelers. Corner of 10 de Agosto and Sucre, Tel: 291-6615/291-6169, E-mail: munaylla@imbanet.net.
Updated: Oct 18, 2012.

La Cuadra
(ROOMS: $15-30) La Cuadra has everything going for it: a central location (half a block from the main plaza), large and spotlessly clean rooms, friendly service from owner Jairo (who also speaks English), gorgeous views from the rooftop terrace, and low prices. The well-equipped and spacious communal kitchen and the living area with sofas, large-screen TV and DVD player are a real plus too. Rooms all have private bath and cable TV. WiFi is available in some of the rooms, as well as the communal areas. The only downside is the lack of breakfast. Modesto Peñaherrera 11-46 (half a block from the Plaza Principal), Tel: 291-6015/0991-969-936, E-mail: jairo@lacuadra-hostal.com, URL: www.lacuadra-hostal.com.
Updated: Oct 23, 2012.

MID-RANGE
Hostal El Arbolito
(ROOMS: $30-50) Hostal El Arbolito blends elegant charm and modern comfort with old-fashioned friendliness. Each room is decorated with finely handcrafted wood and comes equipped with private bath, cable TV and WiFi. Staff is extremely friendly and can help arrange tours. El Arbolito's central location (just off Parque San Francisco, where the artisan market is) is convenient for strolling around town. Unfortunately there's no breakfast, but you can pop next door to the adjoining restaurant Colors & Flavors. Ca. Imbabura 911, just off Parque San Francisco, Tel: 291-6892/291-4388/0986-059-420, E-mail: hostalarbolito@hotmail.com, URL: www.hostalelarbolito.com.
Updated: Oct 23, 2012.

Hostería Oro Azul
(ROOMS: $60-90) Hosteria Oro Azul is a really nice place, in the middle of the nature, localized in the beautiful city of Cotacachi between the 2 volcanos Cotacachi and Imbabura. It's an old centenary "Hacienda" transformed. There are nice rooms with private bathrooms and one bathroom with Jacuzzi. The environment of the hotel is relaxing, with nature all around, possibilities of trekkings and horses renting. The breakfast is included in the price, and those responsible are working directely with local "organic" producers from the communities around the place. It's a recommended place for nature lovers and people who need to get fresh ideas and relax. El Rosario Campo Andino, Tel: 06-291-6020, E-mail: hosteriaoroazul@gmail.com, URL: www.hosteriaoroazul.com.
Updated: Feb 03, 2013.

Hotel Tierra Del Sol
(ROOMS: $59-99) Half a block from the main plaza is the lovely Hotel Tierra del Sol (previously Hotel El Meson de las Flores). It is set in an elegant 180-year old colonial building, with spacious rooms dotted around an indoor courtyard. Rooms are pleasant, and have private bath, WiFi, and heaters for

Did a unique trek? Got way off the beaten path? Tell other travelers at vivatrav-

the chilly nights. Climb up to the top of the building, and you'll be rewarded with beautiful views. There's a small sauna and massages are available at $30 an hour. If you can, splash out on the top suite, which is huge and includes a four-poster bed and massive bathroom with tub (no kitchen though). Rates include breakfast and use of the sauna. Be warned that creaky wooden floorboards and nearby church bells generate some unwelcome noise. Ca. Garcia Moreno 13-67, Tel: 291-6009, Fax: 291-5828, E-mail: hotel.landofsun@gmail.com, URL: www.hoteltierradelsollandofsun.amawebs.com. Updated: Oct 23, 2012.

HIGH-END
La Mirage

(ROOMS: $355-732) One of Ecuador's most elegant and upscale resorts is located at the end of a nondescript dirt road just outside-Cotacachi. La Mirage was once an elegant colonial hacienda, but since the establishment was purchased and renovated by the prestigious French hotel chain Relais & Chateaux, Mirage has become an exclusive spa and retreat. There are 23 suites, each of which features a fireplace, original paintings on the walls, elegant four-poster bed, TV, and tasteful decorations.

The Mirage spa is one of the main attractions. The treatments are expertly done: options range from a simple massage to a "purification treatment," in which a massage is combined with a real fire-breathing local shaman who conducts a traditional spiritual cleansing. Remote, yes. Expensive, yes. But life is short and if you're the sort of person who can afford the best–the very best–it is hard to find a hotel in Ecuador that outdoes the Mirage. Rates include breakfast and sumptuous three-course dinner. Ca. 10 de Agosto, Tel: 291-5237/in the U.S.:1-800-327-3573, Fax: 593-291-5065, E-mail: mirage1@mirage.com.ec, URL: www.mirage.com.ec. Updated: Oct 31, 2012.

Cotacachi Restaurants

Due to it's popularity with both expats and tourists, there's a number of unpretentious but pleasant cafés and restaurants here, serving a mix of local and international dishes. For those on a budget, head down to the area around the bus station where you'll find cheap market-stall meals. While you're in Cotacachi, be sure to try *carne colorada*, the town's typical plate, which consists of beef cooked with *achiote*, a natural red seasoning (hence the name, "colored meat"), accompanied by plantains, potatoes, rice and avocado.

El Leñador

(ENTREES: $6.70-16) Spanish for "The Woodcutter", El Leñador is a mecca for meat lovers, serving a juicy array of steak, seafood and chicken (vegetarians will have to settle for an appetizer or soup). Hearty carnivores are challenged to try one of the giant grilled platters, which offer salad, four to seven different cuts of meat, potatoes, mote (dried corn), and, if you still have room, ice cream. While a bit pricey by local standards, the delicious food, speedy service and elegant atmosphere make it one of the best restaurants in town. Daily 8 a.m.-9 p.m. Ca. Sucre 10-12, between 10 de Agosto and Juan Montalvo, Tel: 291-5083/291-5122/0986-731-781, E-mail: info@restaurantellenador.com. Updated: Oct 23, 2012.

Colors and Flavors

(ENTREES: $3.50-9.50) It's small and a little dark, and the rather eccentric decor may not be to everyone's taste (the ceiling seems to covered in flowing curtains, though the artwork on the walls-designed by the owner's son, Jiovanni-is beautiful), but the food is delicious and the owner, Susannah, is lively and friendly. Travelers rave about the personal pizzas and sinfully rich chocolate mousse, and the hamburgers are enormous. They also do an excellent three-course *almuerzo*. Colors and Flavors is squeezed next to the Hostal El Arbolito, just off Parque San Francisco. Daily 7.30-10 a.m., 12-3.30 p.m., 5-10.30 p.m. Ca. Imbabura 911 (next to Hotel El Arbolito), Tel: 291-4066.

El Jardín de los Andes

(ENTREES: $1-4) Looking for a quick and budget-priced meal? Then go where the locals go. Located next to the bus station, El Jardín de los Andes serves traditional Ecuadorian fare in an outdoor food court-like setting. "The Garden" is not a single restaurant, but rather a line of a dozen or so individual food stands. Come here to fill up on local favorites like grilled chicken, fried fish, *ceviche*, or *carne colorada* (steak cooked in a natural red seasoning), a regional specialty. Note that most stands start to shut down around 3 to 4 p.m. Ca.10 de Agosto (next to the bus station).

La Marqueza

(ENTREES: $7-9.50) La Marqueza offers traditional Ecuadorian dishes (including *cuy*!) as well as more international fare (steaks, chicken and seafood). Though the large dining room, with its worn furniture, fake flowers and out of place cabana-style bar is a bit shabby, the quick and cheery service more than makes up for the décor. La Marquez is very much tourist-orientated however (you'll often see large tour groups), and the prices, which are high for Cotacachi, reflect this. A four-man Andean band occasionally stops by to serenade you while you dine. Ca. 10 de Agosto 12-65, between Ca. González Suarez and Ca. Bolívar, Tel: 291-5488/0994-948-712, E-mail: lamarqueza_rest@yahoo.com.
Updated: Oct 23, 2012.

Café Rio Intag

(SNACKS: $1-3) A recent addition to Cotacachi, Café Rio Intag is a delightful respite for weary shoppers. Located on Parque San Francisco (where the artisan market is), it's light, airy and charming, and an excellent place to satisfy your sweet tooth (with a cake, muffin and brownie) or get a caffeine hit from a cup of fresh coffee. Choose between a comfortable sofa or sit outside and people-watch.There's also a one-for-one book exchange, and cocktails and wine if you´re looking for something a little stronger. Monday to Friday 8 a.m.-8 p.m., Saturday 10 a.m.-10 p.m. and Sunday 10 a.m-6 p.m. Ca. Imbabura (on Parque San Francisco), Tel: 264-8489/0990-958-242, E-mail: aacri@andinanet.net, URL: www.aacri.com.
Updated: Oct 23, 2012.

Trebol Cotacachi

(ENTREES: $3.25-4.50) Since it opened in April 2012, the American-run Trebol has quickly become popular, and for good reason. Owners David and Wendy have made this unpretentious café into a local meeting spot for expats, drawn in by the excellent food and friendly service. The hamburgers are said to be the best in town, and, as well as the menu's offerings of sandwiches, stir-fries, chicken wings and *fajitas*, there's daily specials such as lasagna, home-made soup and *tacos*. Sports games and occasional movies are shown on the café's TV. Note that Trebol is closed on weekends. Ca. Gonzalez Suarez, near the corner of Ca. 10 de Agosto, Tel: 0988-179-179.
Updated: Oct 23, 2012.

Mercado De Los Andes

(ENTREES: $1-4) Mercado de los Andes is the city's main food market and includes a large produce section, with every type of fruit you've heard of and likely a few that you haven't. The market itself is nothing special, and would really only be of interest to those planning on cooking (or a few hat-aficionados). But the market's food court has some surprisingly tasty dishes, with variety to suit most palates, and prices are kind on the wallet. Ca. 10 de Agosto and Ca. Salinas.
Updated: Oct 24, 2012.

IBARRA

 2,225m   109,000   06

Ibarra - Imbabura's provincial capital and the most populated highland city north of Quito - is also known as the "White City," due to its colonial whitewashed buildings (though some visitors find it a bit more lackluster than it sounds).

Cobblestone streets and red-tiled roofs add to the historic ambiance. In the past, busloads of travelers came to Ibarra to hop aboard the train which rolled its way down to the coastal town of San Lorenzo; unfortunately, this route is currently under construction (and has been for some time).

There is an alternative however, and visitors can now opt to take the train on the beautiful, 30-kilometer (18.6 mi) route to the Afro-Ecuadorian town of Salinas. It's slower, but well worth the trip if you're in no hurry.

Ibarra is a peaceful, pleasant place to spend a day or two, with its pretty plazas, sunny climate, relaxed café culture and excellent sweets treats (such as the famous *helado de paila*, a sorbet-like dessert, which is sold everywhere). It also serves as a good jumping off point from which to explore the surrounding countryside, including nearby Laguna Yahuarcocha and the highland hamlet of La Esperanza, which sits at the foot of Volcan Imbabura.

Getting To and Away from Ibarra

Ibarra's **Terminal Terrestre** is located on Avenida Espejo and Avenida Teodoro Goméz de la Torre (a $1 taxi ride or 20 minute walk from the center of town). Inside,

Did a unique trek? Got way off the beaten path? Tell other travelers at vivatrav-

you'll find the usual *tiendas* selling snacks and drinks, as well as a food court. There is a $0.05 tax for using the terminal. Unless specified, buses generally run between 6 a.m. to 6/7 p.m. For shorter bus rides (e.g. to Quito, Otavalo, Cotacahi, etc.), you don't need to buy your ticket inside the terminal; instead you can simply pay on the bus.

To Cotacachi (20 min, $0.30): leave every 15 minutes.

To El Angel (1.5 hr, $1.50): leave every two hours between 6 a.m.-5.30 p.m.

To Guayaquil (11 hr, $13): leave every hour.

To Otavalo (40 min, $0.45): leave every 15 minutes.

To Quito (2.5 hr, $2.50, 2.5 hr): leave every 15 minutes.

To San Lorenzo (4 hr, $4): leave every two hours between 4 a.m. and 6 p.m.

To Tulcan (2.5 hr, $2.50): leave every hour If you're planning on going to **La Esperanza** (the village at the base of the Imbabura volcano), note that buses don't leave from the terminal. Instead, head to Parque Germán Grijalva, on Calle Sánchez Cifuentes (from Oviedo, walk directly down Sánchez for eight blocks). Buses leave every 20 to 30 minutes (25 min, $0.25).
Updated: Oct 30, 2012.

Ibarra Services
MONEY
There are several branches of national banks in Ibarra, including **Banco del Pacifico** (corner of Olmedo and Moncayo) and **Produbanco** (Parque Pedro Moncayo, on the corner of Flores and Sucre). Both have 24-hour ATMs that accept international bank cards.

KEEPING IN TOUCH
The **post office** is located on Calle Juan de Salinas, between Pedro Moncayo and Oviedo (Monday to Friday 8 a.m.-6 p.m., Saturday 8 a.m.-12 p.m.). For Internet or phone calls, there are plenty of Internet cafés scattered around, particularly around the main plaza and on Calles Oviedo, Olmedo and Bolivar. Most also have phone booths.

MEDICAL
You'll have no trouble finding pharmacies in the center of Ibarra; try **Farmacias Cruz Azul** on Olmedo, between Oviedo and Flores (daily 8 a.m.-9 p.m.). In case of a medical emergency, head to **Clinica Imba Medical** on Calle Oviedo (between Olmedo and Sanchez); there's a 24-hour emergency ward.

TOURISM
The helpful tourism office, **iTUR**, is located on the Plazoleta del Coco, next to La Hacienda restaurant (corner of Sucre and Oviedo). Spanish and English-speaking staff can provide maps and have all sorts of information on activities in and around Ibarra (Monday to Friday 8 a.m.-5.30 p.m. Tel: 260-8489).

SHOPPING
For groceries, go either to **Super Tia**, a large supermarket on Avenida Alfredo Perez Guerrero, or the **Mercado Amazonas**, a typically chaotic market that sells, well pretty much everything. It's also located on Avenida Alfredo Peresz Guerrero, on the corner of Cifuentes. For artisan goods, there's a small artisan market on the Plazoleta Francisco Calderón (on Sucre and Pedro Moncayo).
Updated: Oct 26, 2012.

Things To See and Do in Ibarra
Much of what there is to do in Ibarra involves wandering around its plazas, churches and museums, while snacking on *nogadas* and *helado de paila,* some of Ibarra's sweeter specialties. To start, take a stroll to the tree-filled Parque Merced on Calle Flores, and visit the *Basílica de La Merced* (open at mass times only: daily at 6.30 p.m. as well as 7 a.m.-12 p.m. on Sundays), with its lofty red-and-gold altarpiece. After, wander to the beautiful Parque Pedro Moncayo where you'll find the cathedral (open during mass and confession times only), where portraits of the 12 disciples, painted by Rafael Troya (one of Ecuador's most celebrated artists) are displayed. From the plaza, walk a few blocks north to the Iglesia Santo Domingo (open all day) which has a small collection of religious paintings.

Ibarra's main museum, Museo Banco Central, is well worth a visit, as is the suburb of Caranqui, two kilometers (1.24 mi) south of the center, rumored to be the birthplace of the Inca King Atahualpa; here you can visit the engaging Iglesia Señor del Amor (which is said to be built on the top of an Inca temple) as well as the Museo de Atahualpa. For day tripping outside the city, head to the peaceful shores of Laguna Yahuarcocha, or the woodcarving capital of San Antonio de Ibarra. Ibarra is also en route to Esmeraldas, if you want a quick dip in the ocean.

Laguna Yaguarcocha

If you're looking to escape the city, Laguna Yaguarcocha is a pleasant side-trip on the outskirts of Ibarra. What is now a peaceful lake set among rolling green hills, was once the site of a bloody massacre of the indigenous Cara people by Huayna Capac and his Inca army. The 1495 slaughter marked the climax of Capac's 17-year military campaign. Up to 50,000 people were killed during the event. As a result, the lake's name was changed to a Quichua word meaning "lake of blood." Visitors are now greeted by crystal-clear water, shores filled with totora reeds and the occasional call of a herons. You'll find a number of places to eat around the lake (tilapia is a favorite) and places to fish, rent bicycles, or take a boat ride around the lake. The setting is only slightly marred by a massive race track that has been constructed around the lake; competitions are now held in September during the Ibarra fiestas. To get to Laguna Yaguarcocha, head to Oviedo at the corner of Sánchez y Cifuentes and hop on a bus (every 15 min, $0.25), or walk, following the path that heads east from Oviedo, over the bridge and along the Panamericana.

Volcán Imbabura

This long-extinct volcano is located just south-west of Ibarra. The 4,630-meter (15,190-ft) high summit can be climbed in one long day (around 10 to 12 hours round trip) and, although not technically difficult, the loose rock at the top can make the traverse somewhat treacherous. It's a tiring but rewarding climb, with gorgeous views. You can choose to do the climb with a tour operator (agencies in Otavalo offer it), or go independently. For the latter, head to the tiny village of La Esperanza (just outside of Ibarra) which sits at the foot of the volcano. Here you can either climb solo or hire a guide from one of two hotels. To shorten the climb, you can take a hired camioneta (truck) for $5 from La Esperanza to the water tank, at which point it is around a three hours' climb to the top of the volcano.
Updated: Oct 30, 2012.

Museo Central Cultural

The excellent Museo Central Cultural consists of a number of rooms containing over 350 Ecuadorian archaeological finds, including prehistoric ceramics, gold artifacts, and masks. There are also two rooms of colonial art, and temporary art exhibitions. Displays are labelled in both Spanish and English, and guides are available at no charge (some guides speak English). There is also a library and bookshop. Monday to Friday 8.30 a.m.-5.30 p.m. and Saturday 10 a.m.-4 p.m. Ca. Sucre 7-21 between Pedro Moncayo and Oviedo.
Updated: Oct 30, 2012.

Tren De La Libertad

(PRICE: $10-15) It may no longer be possible to go to San Lorenzo by train from Ibarra, but, since 2011, there has been an alternative: the scenic tourist train to Salinas, an Afro-Ecuadorian community some 30 kilometers (18.6 mi) north. This gorgeous ride goes through sweeping valleys as it makes its way down to Salinas, passing through a series of tunnels and over bridges, one of which is 80 meters (262 ft) wide and sits at a staggering 100 meters (328 ft) high over the river Ambi.

The train ride itself is about two hours long, which leaves tourists with a couple of hours to get to know Salinas; a tour of the town and a visit to Salinas' Museo Comunitario are included in the price of the ticket. The train leaves at 10.30 a.m. Wednesdays to Sundays (and holidays), arriving back in Ibarra at 5 p.m. (it is also possible to travel one-way only and stay in Salinas). You can buy tickets over the phone or in person at the station; the beautiful new Estacion de Ferrocariles is open daily from 8 a.m.-4.30 p.m.

As the trains tend to fill quickly, it is advisable to reserve your ticket at least a week in advance; there are also ticket offices in Quito (Venezuela and Espejo, in front of the Plaza Grande) and Guayaquil (Malecón and Calle Aguirre). Estacion de Ferrocariles, Av. Eugenio Espejo and Cristóbal Colón, Tel: 1800-873637/228-8696, URL: www.trenecuador.com.

Guayabillas Animal Rescue Center

(ADMISSION: $1.25) Set in a park of 4.6 hectares (11.36 ac) overlooking Ibarra, the Guayabillas Animal Rescue Center is a wonderful place to visit. Founded in 2005, the

Did a unique trek? Got way off the beaten path? Tell other travelers at vivatrav-

NORTHERN ANDES

center houses dozens of animals, most of whom were rescued from being traded illegally. Over 900 animals have been brought to the center since it began, with the majority being successfully released back into the wild. Species include monkeys, lions, Galapagos tortoises, sloths, parrots and more. If you'd like to stay longer than a day, the center also has a volunteer program; volunteers help to feed and care for the animals while staying with a local host family or at the center itself (minimum stay one week; contact the center for prices and more information). To get to Guayabillas, ask a taxi to take you to Loma de Guayabillas (no more than $2), from where you can walk to the center. Parque Guayabillas, E-mail: rescate_guayabillas@hotmail.com / ecostur_adin037@hotmail.com, URL: www.guayabillas.com. Updated: Oct 30, 2012.

Ibarra Lodging

Ibarra doesn't generally receive large numbers of tourists, and as a result hotels here cater mainly to local visitors. Though there are a few budget options (and more midrange ones), there's no real backpacker hostels. For those with more money to spare, there are several charming haciendas outside of town that are mostly located along the Panamericana. Updated: Oct 26, 2012.

Imbabura

($8-12 per person) Travelers on a budget, or those interested in spending the night in a charming but run-down colonial house, should make their way to Imbabura. The hotel has an interior courtyard, soaring ceilings and a distinct monastery-like feel. Rooms are simple, and all have shared bath (the bathrooms could definitely do with a good clean), and some boast excellent views of the stunning Ibarra scenery. Imbabura attracts a largely backpacker crowd, but anyone who values character will fall in love with Imbabura's charisma and its friendly owner, who will happily show you his collection of historic Ibarra photos and miniature bottles of spirits. There's no breakfast. Ca. Oviedo 9-33 and Av. Chica Narváez, Tel: 295-1155/295-8522. Updated: Oct 25, 2012.

Hostal El Ejecutivo

(ROOMS: $8-21) Hostal El Ejectivo has been owned and operated by the Chacon family of Ibarra for over 30 years, and is a clean, comfortable establishment with hospitable staff. There are 16 rooms in total, all with private bath and cable TV (there's no WiFi though). Some rooms have a balcony overlooking the city. The combination of amenities, low rates and friendliness all make this one of the best places to lay your sleepy head in Ibarra (meaning you may want to make a reservation in advance, as it can fill up). There's no breakfast though. Bolivar 9-69 (between Velasco and Colón)., Tel: 295-6575, E-mail: mchaconf@yahoo.com. Updated: Oct 24, 2012.

Hotel Montecarlo

(ROOMS: $27-80) Centrally located, Hotel Montecarlo is a spacious establishment with 33 rooms and two suites, all of which have private bathrooms, cable TV and WiFi. While not a luxury retreat, the establishment is a solid option in the mid-range category, and the facilities (jacuzzi, Turkish Spa, sauna and swimming pool) are a bonus. The on-site restaurant serves up a decent mix of national and international cuisine, and breakfast is included in the room rate. The hotel is located on a busy road, so it may be wise to ask for a room at the back if you're a light sleeper. Av. Jaime Rivadeneira 5-55 and Oviedo., Tel: 295-8182/8266, E-mail: montecarlohotel@gmail.com, URL: www.hotelmontecarloibarra.ec. Updated: Oct 26, 2012.

Hotel Ajavi

(ROOMS: 64-98) Hotel Ajavi is one of Ibarra's nicest hotels, with rates that are lower than would be expected from a hotel of this quality. It has many luxury features, including a huge outdoor pool, gym and spa facilities, playing fields and games rooms. Rooms are spacious and light, and come with private bath, cable TV, WiFi, desk and ironing facilities. Though located a little out of the town center, it is only a quick taxi ride or 20-minute walk away from the action. Ca. Mariano Acosta 1635, Zip: , Tel: 295-5555/5221, E-mail: hotelajavi@andinanet.net / h-ajavi@andinanet.net, URL: www.hotelajavi.com. Updated: Oct 30, 2012.

Hotel Nueva Estancia

(ROOMS: $20-45) Hotel Nueva Estancia is a deceptively spacious hotel overlooking the pleasant Parque La Merced. Unfortunately, its location is probably its best asset however, as inside it feels a little run down; rooms are gloomy, and most only have internal windows. But staff is cheerful and, for the price (especially if you're a couple or in a group) the facilities-rooms with private bath, cable TV and WiFi-aren't to be sniffed at. Breakfast is included, and there's also a garage. Garcia Moreno 7-58 (on the Parque La Merced), Tel: 295-1444/260-5556. Updated: Oct 24, 2012.

Hotel Lago Azul

(ROOMS: $17-30) If El Ejecutivo is full, head up the road to Hotel Lago Azul. The rates are more than double but, considering breakfast is included and are all rooms have private bath, cable TV and WiFi, are still reasonable. The location is convenient too. Rooms err on the basic side though and are somewhat garishly decorated, but comfortable enough. Ca. Pedro Moncayo between Bolivar and Sucre, Tel: 264-1851, E-mail: info@hotellagoazul.com, URL: www.hotellagoazul.com. Updated: Oct 25, 2012.

Hotel Ajavi

Ibarra Restaurants

Ibarra has a decent number of restaurants, with a variety of cuisines: seafood, Chinese, Italian and international (steaks and hamburgers especially) all feature heavily. If you want *almuerzos* or fast food, you won't have to go far; a good spot is on the Calle Olmedo side of Parque Merced, where (by night) there is stall after stall of *comedores* cooking up $1 plates of soup, rice and meat (a couple are also open during the day). For seafood, head to Calle Oviedo between Calle Chica Narvaez (on the roundabout) and Rivadeneira, where you'll find a row of *cevicherias* selling cheap bowls of *ceviche* and plates piled high with fried fish and shrimp.

For dessert, try Ibarra's specialty, *nogadas* (traditional sweets made from sugar, milk and walnuts), which are also sold at a number of stands on the Olmedo side of Parque Merced, just down from the food stalls. And no trip to Ibarra would be complete without sampling its most famous specialty: *helados de paila*. This sweet, fluffy sorbet-like treat is whipped up in oversized copper pans, known as pailas, and sold at a number of *heladerias* in town. Updated: Oct 26, 2012.

Donde El Argentino

(ENTREES: $7.50-19.50) Donde El Argentino is a outstanding restaurant tucked away in the corner of the pleasant Plazoleta Francisco Calderón. It serves up heavenly Argentinean-style dishes literally dripping with flavor. Beef (grilled and served with heaps of spicy sauces and mouth-watering sides) is the specialty here, and you're guaranteed to leave with a full belly. This place is an absolute find, and a well-kept Ibarra secret; it's generally not frequented by tourists, so shhh...don't tell anyone! The inside of the restaurant is tiny, with only a few tables squeezed in, but there is more seating tucked away upstairs as well as a spacious, covered (and heated if necessary) seating area outside on the plaza. Plazoleta Francisco Calderón Local 4, Sucre and Pedro Moncayo, Tel: 0999-459-004, E-mail: dondeelargentino@hotmail.com.

Café Pushkin

(SNACKS: $1.50-$3) A great place to enjoy an early breakfast or mid-afternoon snack. In the mornings, Ibarran locals filter in to grab a bite to eat before starting the day, and the small café quickly comes to life with conversation. Although there is no official menu, set dishes include traditional fare, such as sandwiches, *quimbolitos* and *café con humitas*. Breakfasts are served with a heaped basket of bread still hot from the oven. A variety of fresh juices are also available, and the fruit salads are enormous. Daily 6.30 a.m.-10 p.m. Olmedo 7-75, Tel: 295-0205/0991-176-436. Updated: Oct 24, 2012.

La Esquina

(SNACKS: $1.60-3) The clean and colorful La Esquina is one of the more modern cafés in Ibarra that, in addition to traditional Ibarra ice cream (fluffy ice cream with a consistency similar to sherbet), has a short menu of Ecuadorian specialties, such as *humitas*, *quimbolitos* and *empanadas*, as well as sandwiches, desserts, and breakfasts. The café has been decorated with a bright orange and green décor and Ikea-like furnishings, and there's a plastic play gym for toddlers on the second floor. There's a second, smaller La Esquina across the road serving up sandwiches, fruit salads, cakes, juices and coffee- but no ice-cream. Corner of Olmedo and Flores, Tel: 295-1874, E-mail: laesquinaibarra@hotmail.com. Updated: Oct 24, 2012.

Heladería Rosalía Suárez

(ICE-CREAM: $0.80 and up) This is the oldest and most famous of Ibarra's *heladerías de paila*, dating back to 1896, when 16 year-old Rosalía Suárez began creating her now legendary *helados*. There's a full range of delicious flavors, and you can even watch them being made. Note that though there are two shops directly across the road that are also named *Heladería de Rosalía Suárez*, this is the original. Corner of Oviedo and Olmedo, Tel: 295-0107. Updated: Oct 24, 2012.

San Café

(ENTREES: $3-8) San Café is a cozy pub-like hangout that is equally suitable for a spot of comfort food or a cold beer. The atmosphere is friendly, and owner Andrea ensures you feel at home as soon as you walk in the door. There's board games to play, and the walls are covered in caricatures. Sweet and savory crepes are popular, and there's also pizzas, sandwiches, salads and deserts. Monday-Thursday 7.30 a.m.-11 p.m., Friday and Saturday 7.30 a.m.-1 a.m., Sunday 5-8 p.m. Ca. Oviedo, between Olmedo and Bolivar, Tel: 0987-939-952, E-mail: andreacuevasuárez@hotmail.com. Updated: Oct 24, 2012.

La Hacienda

(ENTREES: $3.80-18) Ask an local to recommend a place to dine in Ibarra, and La Hacienda will very likely receive a mention. This hugely popular restaurant is decorated to resemble a barn, with benches stuffed full of hay and booths that are built like horse-stables (if you prefer cozier seating, head upstairs). The menu offers enormous baguette sandwiches, *tablitas* (cheeses, meats, olives, etc.), tapas and vino combos, pizzetas (mini pizzas which are basically posh and very yummy cheese on toast), and

salads. The coffee is said to be the best in town, and the desserts (especially the blackberry cheesecake) are delicious. Plazoleta del Coco, corner of Sucre and Oviedo, Tel: 260-5881/0995-028-439, E-mail: cafela.hacienda@ymail.com. Updated: Oct 25, 2012.

Aromas Café

(ENTREES: $7-14) The location of Aromas Café (at the back of a courtyard, on a side street) makes it an ideal courtyard, which is often home to temporary art exhibitions (there's also more seating here). Yes, Olor de Café is undoubtedly a little on the expensive side, but it's worth coming here even for a relaxing cup of tea or an Irish coffee. If you do want to splash out, sandwiches, steak, pasta, ribs and hamburgers are available, as well as a variety of substantial breakfasts. Service can be slow, but comes with a smile. Monday to Saturday 8 a.m.-9 p.m., closed Sundays. Corner of Bolivar and Flores, Parque Pedro Moncayo, Tel: 295-4505. Updated: Oct 25, 2012.

El Horno Pizza

(ENTREES: $7.40-14.80) Superb food and a warm, easygoing atmosphere make this Ibarra's best Italian restaurant, though, ironically, it's run by an Ecuadorian who learnt the ropes of Italian cooking during his 12 years in France. The wood-fired pizza is the specialty, though the lasagna and steaks are excellent too, as are the deserts (try the banana *flambée*). There's often live music on Saturday nights, or you may even catch the owner rehearsing with his own band. Note that it's open for dinner only. Tuesday to Sunday 6-11 p.m. Ca. Rocafuerte 6-38, between Flores and Oviedo, Tel: 295-9019. Updated: Oct 25, 2012.

Ibarra Nightlife

Café Arte

(ENTREES: $6-7) Local hotspot Café Arté lives up to its name with good food, great art and eclectic music. A variety of rotating artwork-from modern paintings to photo exhibits-cover the walls. The funky decor includes mosaic floor tiles, candles and rustic wooden tables. On Friday and Saturday nights the place transforms into a live music mecca, with excellent local, national, and even international musicians. There's also a free movie night every Tuesday at 7 p.m. The menu includes a range of options, from lavish salads and sandwiches to Mexican dishes and steaks, and there's also a reasonably-priced *almuerzo*. Monday to Thursday 12.30-3 p.m. and 5 p.m.-12 a.m., Friday and Saturday 12.30-3 p.m. and 5 p.m.-2 a.m. Ca. Salinas 5-43, Tel: 295-0806/0997-250-589. Updated: Oct 25, 2012.

Santo Pretexto

Rock bar Santo Pretexto is one of the most favored night-time spots in town. The pub-like bar has plenty of seating, happy hours, a big-screen TV for sports games, and occasional karaoke nights. Pub food (nachos, burgers, steaks, etc.) is available too. There's frequent live rock music, usually on Fridays. Generally there's no cover, except after 10 p.m. when there's a band playing. Tuesday to Thursday 5 p.m.-12 a.m., Saturday and Sunday 5 p.m.-2 a.m. Ca. Oviedo 7-52, Tel: 295-8747, E-mail: santopretexto@hotmail. com, URL: facebook.com/santopretexto. Updated: Oct 25, 2012.

AROUND IBARRA

Outside of Ibarra you'll find an eclectic mix of towns and haciendas with a number of distinguishing features that either run the gamut of art and crafts and/or time and tradition. These are towns that are off the beaten path and the locals are sometimes (benignly) struck by the presence of outsiders, and are places that definitely deserve a venture into if you have the time and curiosity.

The haciendas are all about welcoming people from all over the world into the time capsules they represent, or simply the scenery and tranquility that they provide a vantage point for.

Lodging Around Ibarra

Hacienda Piman ♪

(ROOMS: $90) Located a half an hour outside of Ibarra, Hacienda Piman is an excellent example of an historical Ecuadorian hacienda, founded in the 1620's and remaining in the same family from the 1680's until today. Recently renovated and opened in 2013 as a luxurious inn and all-inclusive hacienda, Piman successfully mixes the old and the new.

You can choose to stay in the historical house's guest rooms or the new tastefully designed super-sized rooms. Historical features include a church, arches and gateways. The new parts feature an all-glass restaurant that serves exceptional international and traditional cuisine, much of which comes out of the haciendas organic gardens. The wait service is excellent. The hacienda is nestled in an oasis like valley and the mountainous area surrounding the hacienda is perfect for scenic hikes and mountain bike rides. Its isolation makes it an exceptionally quiet, peaceful escape from the modern world. Calle Piman, old highway Ibarra - Chota, Tel: US Toll Free: 1-800-706-2215 Rest of the World: 00.593.2.256.6090, Fax: 00.593.2.223.6521, E-mail: info@haciendapiman.com, URL: www.haciendapiman.com. Updated: Apr 25, 2013.

Rancho de Carolina

($25-30 per person) The peaceful Rancho de Carolina is set back on a small dirt road, away from nearby Pan-American Highway. The ranch, located among the green mountains of the Imbarabura province, offers a place to retreat from the hustle of Ibarra and Quito.

The hotel has a pool, hydro massage, tennis court and pool tables with horseback riding trails in the surrounding hills. The hotel has 18 rooms, all with private baths, TV, telephones and hot water. Panamericana Sur Km 4., Tel: 06-293-3113, E-mail: info@ranchodecarolina.com, URL: www.ranchodecarolina.com. Updated: Feb 15, 2013.

Hacienda Lulunqui

($85 per person) Nestled in the rugged Andes Mountains of northern Ecuador, Hacienda Lulunqui is a working dairy farm and hacienda offering spectacular accommodation, coupled with scenic views and the option of touring nearby sites like Otavalo, Cuicocha and Cotacachi. Surrounded by stunning scenery, the Hacienda also plays host to resident birds and butterflies, and herds of llama, horses and dairy cows. The grounds feature extensive gardens, boasting a variety of fruits and vegetables, which guests are certain to enjoy at mealtimes. Rooms are cozy and comfortable and the friendly staff will cater to your every need. Whether you come to relax or to adventure into the surroundings, Hacienda Lulunqui is a good place to spend some time and rest your head. Price includes transport, tours, room, and meals. Tel: 06-261-1059, E-mail: tgturner3@hotmail.com.

NORTHERN ANDES

Hacienda Zuleta

(ROOMS: $204-345) Located about an hour from Otavalo, Zuleta is a good option for travelers who are looking for an authentic hacienda experience. Like the haciendas of old, Zuleta is a working, 1620-hectare (4,000-ac) farm with a stable of over 90 horses. There is an embroidery workshop and a working dairy farm on the premises.

Unlike most of the other converted haciendas in the region, Zuleta considers tourism and guests as a secondary source of income; the establishment is still primarily a large farm, though you will find spacious guest rooms, fine dining (using food mainly produced at the farm), and beautiful gardens. Rates are all inclusive and include three meals, snacks and non-alcoholic drinks.

Several activities are offered, and the owners pride themselves on their horses, offering classes and week-long riding programs. Hacienda Zuleta, Angochagua, Tel: 2662-182, E-mail: info@haciendazuleta.com, URL: www.zuleta.com.
Updated: Oct 31, 2012.

Bosque De Paz

(ROOMS: $13-18) This eco-conscious bed and breakfast located in the village of El Limonal, 43 kilometers (27 mi) northwest of Ibarra, is committed to sustainability, education, and the comfort of their guests. Not only do they offer freshly made meals, a swimming pool and spacious rooms, they also work hard to teach their guests about ecological restoration, permaculture, and agro-forestry—principles that guide their business practices. Guests have a choice of private or shared rooms.

Each room has a porch and hammock for relaxing. Breakfast is included in the price of the room but lunch and dinner are available for an added fee. In addition to lodging, Bosque de Paz offers horse rental and guide services. There are also volunteering opportunities for a monthly fee of $235, which includes room and board. El Limonal, Km 42 from Ibarra to San Lorenzo, Tel: 301-6606, URL: www.bospas.org.

Hacienda Chorlavi

(ROOMS: $70-103) If you interested in rustic accommodation that's still comfortable and charming, then Hacienda Chorlavi is the place to come to. The hotel consists of a converted colonial hacienda, complete with whitewashed buildings and a monastery-converted cocktail bar, and is bursting with character.

Set among manicured gardens and palm-fringed grounds, the buildings evoke another era. Rooms are appointed with period furnishing, big beds and private bathrooms, as well as flat-screen TVs and WiFi. There's a spa, with pool, sauna, jacuzzi, as well as sports fields and a movie room.

Even if you don't plan on spending the night, stop by and dine in the locally famous restaurant, a popular spot for Ecuadorian families. On weekends you can indulge in local fare while enjoying live music, though, be warned, this place fills to the brim on Saturdays and Sundays so make a reservation. Panamericana Sur Km 4.5, Tel: 293-2222/2223, Fax: 293-2224, E-mail: reservaciones@hacienda-chorlavi.com / sugerencias@haciendachorlavi.com, URL: www.haciendachorlavi.com.
Updated: Oct 30, 2012.

SAN ANTONIO DE IBARRA

San Antonio de Ibarra, located on the southern outskirts of Ibarra, is a village where roughly 25 percent of the 15,000 residents are involved in some form of sculpting or wood carving.

Carpentry shops are located throughout the town -- along the main plaza, in homes and in small artisan workshops. Due to the number of people devoted to the industry, the village has come to be known primarily as a place where tourists can go to buy carved furniture, religious statuary or souvenirs.

San Antonio was founded in March 1693 and became an center for art following the creation of the Liceo Artístico school in 1880. Besides carpentry, the Liceo Artístico taught painting, sculpture and other forms of artistic expression. Although San Antonio de Ibarra is now primarily known for its wood products, residents also use cement and metal in their sculpture, which can be ornately painted.

The town has several small churches (such as Santo Domingo or San Vincente) and places to walk, such as near El Dique (the Dam), but the main draw is definitely the woodwork.

SALINAS VALLEY

Salinas, located just 30 kilometers from Ibarra, gets its name from the high concentration of mineral salts in the area soils. Up until fairly recently, people were still extracting mineral salt by traditional methods. You can visit one of the salt mines and see for yourself how this was done. Ask in the village for more information.

Although the valley is now mostly dedicated to the cultivation of sugar cane, Salinas was once a meeting point and market for indigenous groups from all different directions. The valley has been a location of strategic importance throughout history as it provides one of the easiest passages from the coast to the Amazon (by way of two Andes ranges). Updated: Oct 30, 2012.

CHOTA VALLEY

The Chota Valley, located 34 kilometers to the north of the Imbabura Province, is arguably best known for being home to a large Afro-Ecuadorian community. Many of the current Chota residents are descendants of slaves that were brought to Ecuador by Spanish land owners. Agricultural work, such as sugarcane production, still figures prominently in the area, and the locals have also maintained a unique Chota identity, mainly through music and dance.

Bomba, one of the regional dances, includes a mixture of African and highland Indian components (as an indigenous-hispanic-African hybrid). Women wear wide colourful skirts and men dress all in white. The music is rhythmic and based around the "bomba," a drum played with both hands.

The community also welcomes tourists, and it's not uncommon to see groups of photography students visiting the area. The community provides basic, clean accommodation for $8 per night, including breakfast.

The locals also sell various craft products, including wonderful clay masks, candelabras and other objects. The community also has a volunteer program, and can arrange for either dance classes or a variety of other activities. For more information contact: Mirium Ghysselinckx, Tel: 09-449-4029, E-mail: miri2002es@hotmail.com. Updated: Oct 30, 2012.

EL ÁNGEL

 3,000m   5,000   06

The sleepy little village of El Ángel, nestled high amid the pretty rolling green pastures of the Carchi province, is the starting-off point for visiting the ecological reserve of El Ángel 17 km away.

The most basic services like telephone, tourist information and pharmacies are available in the streets around the main square. Beyond that, and apart from strolling up and down the Monday food and clothing market, you will not find much to do in the village. If you have your own wheels, you can drive to the waterfalls and pools in the surrounding area. But the major attraction nearby, the Reserva Ecológica, can only be reached by 4x4 or by hiring a pick-up from the town center.

There are a couple of cheap accommodation options in town, plus the well-kept El Ángel Hostería, then a luxury lodge, the Polylepis, much further out, and a few simple eateries scattered around.

El Ángel was named after the Indian chief Blas Angel, whose statue you can see on the Botijuela monument located in the middle of the roundabout at the entrance of town. The 1926 church and the main park with clipped cypress trees are about the only other noteworthy landmarks that distinguish this otherwise simple little village.

Getting To and Away from El Angel

The white and orange buses of the Cooperativa Espejo (tel. 06-297-7216) leave from the main square to :

Quito (5 hours, $3.70) every hour from 3 a.m. to 6 p.m.

Ibarra (2 hours, $1.25) at 7.30 a.m., 11.30 a.m., 12.30 p.m., 1.30 p.m., 7 p.m.

Tulcán (1.5 hours, $1.50) at 5.30 a.m., 7 a.m., 8.30 a.m. and 1 p.m.

The white and green buses of TransMira also stop in El Ángel on their hourly services to Tulcán and Mira (30 minutes away). Updated: Mar 18, 2013.

NORTHERN ANDES

Did a unique trek? Got way off the beaten path? Tell other travelers at vivatrav-

El Ángel Services
TOURISM
The InfoTur tourist information center on the main square (on the Esmeraldas side) is open Monday – Friday, 8 a.m. – 12 p.m. and 2 p.m. – 6 p.m., and can deluge you with brochures about the area. Tel: 06-2977-147.

The office of the Reserva Ecológica just a few meters away on Salinas and Esmeraldas is much more knowledgeable and helpful when it comes to organizing a tour of the reserve and can give you maps of the park. Open Monday – Friday, 8 a.m. – 1 p.m. and 2 p.m. – 5 p.m. Tel. 06-2977-597.

KEEPING IN TOUCH
Andinatel is on the corner of Espejo and José B. Crijalva and there are cabinas Porta on the same street one block before the main park.

MEDICAL & SAFETY
Hospital
Tel. 06-2977-166

Police
Tel. 06-2977-101
Updated: Apr 15, 2013.

Things To See and Do in El Ángel
El Ángel Ecological Reserve
(ADMISSION: $10) The 15,700 hectare reserve of El Ángel is a wild area of golden páramo (spongy grasslands) which lies in the northern region of the Carchi province, at an altitude ranging from 3,700 to 4,800m. The reserve is best known for the curious *frailejón* flowers that dot the landscape. The frailejón, which resembles a pineapple with oversized furry leaves growing on the end of a meter-high stick, is only found in this region of Ecuador. Another curious plant is the polylepis, also known as the "árbol de papel" because it sheds papery bark. Some visitors to the park have also been lucky enough to spot condors, foxes, deer and rabbits.

There are two main circuits in the park. The one going through the Bosque de Polylepis starts on the small private property of the Polylepis lodge, which is in fact operating without a license in the reserve, and charges visitors for access. The other circuit (about one hour long) takes you past the El Voladero lakes and on clear days offers views of the Chiles volcano on one side, of the valleys towards San Gabriel on the other. The

park ranger office at the entrance of the El Voladero area gives out maps and information. There also are two rooms with bunk beds (one of two, one of four) where you can stay overnight. Camping (for free) is also permitted on the grounds of the reserve.

To get there, the road to the reserve is an unpaved one, full of potholes, accessible only in a 4x4, and the ride takes just under an hour. You can hire a camioneta (pick-up truck) from El Ángel for about $15-20 (return trip + two-hour wait). There is no other form of public transport.

El Ángel Lodging
You won't exactly be spoiled with choices when looking for a hotel in El Angel. Ecuador has plenty of picturesque towns to visit and this one is no exception, it's just that accommodations are rather limited here. There are a couple of budget options and one luxury lodge (illegally) located within the reserve - that's about it. Most offer guided tours, hikes and other activities including horseback riding and mountain-biking. If you decide to stay in El Angel itself, no matter which place you pick, you won't be more than a ten-minute walk from the main square and its eateries.

Residencial Las Chimeneas
($5-8 per person) This quiet little hole-in-the-wall place offers just four rooms for rent on the first floor of the owner's house. The

wooden rooms are pretty basic, with sagging beds and thin walls, and the cement-floor shower in the shared bathroom spits out coldish water, but what the residencial lacks in comfort it amply makes up for in warmth and friendliness. The cheerful owner, señora Oliva, will happily make you herb tea at night in the carpeted bar downstairs and will whip up breakfast. Segunda transversal and Av. Espejo, Tel: 098-513-9934.

Hostal San Blas

($6-8 per person) Right on the roundabout at the entrance of the village, Hostal San Blas offers very basic and somewhat dark rooms with tiled floors. Some have a private bathroom. While distinctly lacking in charm, this place may be convenient for people just passing through and who don't want to bother going into town. There is a very large parking area. La Botijuela roundabout, Av. Espejo and Panamericana, Tel: 06-297-7346.

Polylepis Lodge

(ROOMS: $45-75) Polylepis is a unique eco-lodge tucked inside El Ángel Ecological Reserve. The reserve protects 30 acres of rare polylepis forest that dates back to about 2 million years. The lodge has a mix of 14 huts and cottages with private bathrooms, fireplaces and, for some - private jacuzzis. Each of the locations can accommodate between two and 12 guests. The lodge also has a restaurant, bar and game room, which makes Polylepis a perfect places to unwind at the end of a long day of hiking and climbing. Located in the buffer zone of the Ecological Reserve El Angel (Carchi province) to 170 km., Tel: 06-263-1819 / 099-522-7472, E-mail: info@polylepislodgeec.com, URL: www.polylepislodgeec.com Updated: Feb 14, 2013.

El Ángel Restaurants

You will find a few cheap eateries on the main streets, like Asadero Rico Pollo on Espejo and Segunda Transversal, or Doña Mary which serves $1.50 set lunches, on the corner of Crijalva and the main square.

The only place that deserves to be called a restaurant is La Pozada Café-Deli, on Río Frio and Segunda Transversal (Tel. 06-2977-371, E-mail: cibel890@yahoo.com) which offers burritos and enchiladas from $1.60 as well as sandwiches and salads ($1.30-1.80) and breakfasts ($1.50-2.50). Updated: Feb 14, 2013.

TULCÁN

 2,980m 86,498 06

The city of San Sebastian de Tulcán is a drab border city, which you are most likely to use only as a crossing point into Colombia. Because natural disasters destroyed most colonial architecture, it is composed mainly of featureless modern buildings, and the sole interesting attraction of the city is its topiary garden. A regional culture museum is due to open in the former customs building on the Rumichaca bridge in the summer of 2009.

The border into Colombia is best crossed during daytime, so if you need to stay overnight in Tulcán, there are plenty of hotels to choose from. The very cheap options tend to be a bit dreary, but if you can't afford the better places like Sara Espindola or Machado, the Unicornio and the España are clean and reasonably-priced alternatives. Eating options are limited to chifas and cheap chicken places, but a few Colombian restaurants offer variety, unless you prefer to sit down at a market stall.

Nonetheless, the rolling pasture land around the city is pretty and worth taking a small detour through if you have the time, for example to visit the Aguas Hediondas hot springs. Updated: Apr 15, 2013.

When To Go

Because of its altitude, Tulcán tends to be a chilly city all year-round, regularly doused in drizzle. Daytime temperatures reach only to16-17°C (61-63°F) and at night it gets to a chilly 4-5°C (39-41°F). June-September are the dryer months; more rain falls March-April and October-December. In the course of a year, Tulcán receives 956 millimetres (38 in) of rain.

The fiesta de Tulcán is on April 11th and the Carchi provincial holiday on November 19th. If you happen to go through town on a Tuesday or a Sunday, you will see the markets on Sucre and Tarqui liven things up a little. Updated: Oct 08, 2012.

Safety in Tulcán

Like any border city in the world, Tulcán has its share of smuggling – in this case, drug trafficking - and is not the safest place in the country. Always keep an eye on your

Did a unique trek? Got way off the beaten path? Tell other travelers at vivatrav-

NORTHERN ANDES

belongings, take taxis after nightfall and you should be fine. Also, while the Colombian guerilla is not present in the immediate surroundings, it is not advised to hike in the more remote border areas beyond the Volcán Chiles, near Maldonado and Chical.

Getting To and Away from Tulcán

BY ROAD

El Tulcán is about 120km from Ibarra and 260km from Quito on the Panamericana.

BY AIR

The airport is a few kilometers outside the city. TAME offers services from Quito for approximately $100 return. Seewww.tame.com.ec for more information.
Updated: Oct 09, 2012.

BY BUS

The Terminal terrestre is inconveniently located on the far end of Bolívar, 1.5km from the town center. A taxi ride should not set you back more than $1. Plenty of cooperatives run regular services to Quito (5 hours), Ibarra (2.5 hours), Mira (2 hours) and a few even go to Cuenca (14 hours) or Guayaquil.

San Cristobal (tel. 2980-273) goes to Quito every hour for $4.80.

Expreso Tulcán has 20 buses **to Quito** from 1.30 a.m. until 10.15 p.m.

Velotax has 25 buses **to Quito** from 2.25 a.m. until 10.35 p.m., trip costs $4.80.

Expreso Turismo (tel. 2980-831) goes **to Ibarra** ($2.50) and **Quito** ($4.50) every hour from 6 a.m. until 5.30 p.m.

Flota Imbabura (2986-831) goes **to Guayaquil** ($13) at 11 a.m. and 7 p.m., **to Cuenca** at 4.30 p.m.

Panamericana (2980-339) goes **to Guayaquil** ($13) at 4 p.m., to Manchala ($13) and Milagro ($12).

Transmira has 9 buses **to Mira** (2 hours) via El Angel (1.5 hours, $1.50) from 6 a.m. to 6 p.m.

Crossing Into Colombia

The Rumichaca Border Crossing

The principle border crossing between Ecuador and Colombia is at the Rumichaca bridge, just seven kilometres (4.4 miles) north of Tulcán and three kilometres (1.8 miles) south of Ipiales, Colombia. Immigration for both countries is open 6 a.m.-10 p.m. but it is recommended to cross during the day for security reasons. Most travelers (from Europe and North America) do not need a visa in advance. Simply make sure the Ecuadorian authorities give you an exit stamp and then you can get a 90-day tourist visa on the Colombian side.

Mini-buses ($0.75) and taxis (colectivos or shared taxis, $0.85; private $4) may be caught at Tulcán's bus terminal or from Parque Ayora. The taxi or van will drop you off in the parking lot across from Ecuador immigration. If you are entering Ecuador, a maximum of 90 days (within a 365-day period) is given.

After going through Ecuador immigration, cross the river to Colombia migración. Usually only 60 days are given upon entering, but go ahead and ask for 90. There is one line for entry stamps, and another for exit stamps. The immigration building also has the offices for travellers crossing in private vehicles, bathrooms and an exchange house.

Combis (mini-vans, $0.80) to Ipiales' bus terminal or a taxi to Parque La Pola downtown ($3) leave from the parking lot in front of the steps to immigration.

Freelance money changers work on both sides of the border. Be sure to check all calculations for accuracy and bills for authenticity, and count your money well. And know that Transportation fares on either side can be paid in dollars or Colombian pesos.
Updated: Oct 09, 2012.

Getting Around Tulcán

Tulcán is organized lengthwise, along the parallel streets Sucre and Bolívar. The city is compact enough that you can run most errands on foot, otherwise, taxis are plentiful, mostly congregating on the two main squares, Parque de la Independencia and Parque Isidro Ayora. City buses ($0.10) run up Bolívar to the bus terminal and the Obelisk, and down Sucre towards the airport. If you need to call a taxi, try Cooperativa Rápido Nacional 06-298-0444.

Tulcán Services

Most services are concentrated around the main square (Parque de la Independencia) and on Sucre and Bolívar, the two main arteries of the city. Be aware that many shops and services in Tulcán tend to close for a lengthy lunch break.

MONEY

There are several banks, all located on or around the Parque de la Independencia, which all have ATMs. None change money or travelers' checks.

ATM

outside Cooperativa financiera CoopCCQ (corner of Olmedo and 10 de Agosto, open 8.30 a.m. – 5.30 p.m.) accepts Visa, Cirrus and Mastercard.

Banco del Pichincha

Cannot be missed with its giant yellow sign in the middle of 10 de Agosto on the southern side of the main square, has two ATMs which accept BanRed, Diners Club International, MasterCard, Visa and Plus. Open 8.30 a.m. – 5 p.m.

Banco del Austro

On Ayacucho, has an ATM which takes Visa, Plus, Cirrus and BanRed. To change money, you have to go through money-changers (*cambiastas*). You should have no trouble spotting them: they are all the men hanging around the Parque Isidro Ayora and Parque de la Independencia, casually flipping bank notes and hissing "cambio! Dolares, pesos!" Just make sure you check their "carnet de identificación" which provides legal proof that they belong to the official Asociación de cambistas.

KEEPING IN TOUCH
Post Office
On Bolívar 53-027 and Junin.

Phone

There is a plethora of shops offering "cabinas", among which Andinatel on Bolívar and Atahualpa, and Porta and Movistar cabinas just up the street.

Internet

Cybercafés can be found in abundance on the main streets of Tulcán. The one on Rocafuerte and Sucre, open 9 a.m. – noon and 3 p.m. – 9 p.m., has headphones if you need to make a Skype call.

MEDICAL

The Clinica del Volante, on Bolívar 48-056 and Rocafuerte, offers 24-hour attention. A basic visit costs $10 and there is an English-speaking doctor, usually on duty in the afternoon. Tel: 06-298-1889. There are pharmacies just about on every street corner.

POLICE

The general emergency number is 101, the phone number for the most central unit of policía comunitaria, on Parque Ayora, is 06-298-2022.

TOURIST INFORMATION

The tourist information center is located in the building at the entrance to the cemetery. The staff will helpfully hand out brochures and give you information about Tulcán itself, but is a little clueless regarding attractions any further than Tufiño. If they happen to run out of city maps, you can check out the giant mural on the outside wall facing the topiary. Open daily 8 a.m. – 1 p.m. and 3 p.m. – 6 p.m. Tel: 06-298-5760

Colombian Consulate

You should be able to cross the border into Colombia without having to resort to the Colombian consulate, but in case you do need to, it is located on Rafael Arellano and Roberto Sierra and open 8 a.m. – 2 p.m. Tel: 06-2980-559

Things To See and Do in Tulcán

Tulcán is a mere stopover on the way to Colombia; the only sight worth seeing in town is the topiary garden at the cemetery. The blue and white colonial cathedral and the market are both worth a brief visit, should you come upon them on your way through town. If you have a little more time, the ride to the Aguas Hediondas hot springs beyond Tufiño (40 minutes away) is a nice one.

Did a unique trek? Got way off the beaten path? Tell other travelers at vivatrav-

Topiary Garden

(ADMISSION: Free) Tulcán's sole worthwhile attraction is the lovely topiary garden in the cemetery at the far end of town. The cypress hedges which line its paths have been clipped into hundreds of carved arches, rotund birds, chubby monkeys and squat pre-Columbian figures. With any luck, while taking a stroll around the quiet garden, you will come across the head gardener shearing away, and he will happily point out the most recent creations. The first bushes were made into *esculturas en verde* (green sculptures) in 1936 by Don José María Franco Guerrero, who based his creations on ceramics involving pre-Columbian and Egyptian motifs. His son keeps the legacy alive, which has inspired some neighboring villages - like El Angel - to clip the trees of their squares as well. Av. del Cementerio.

Aguas Hediondas

(ADMISSION: $2) If you have a few hours to kill or happen to be suffering from a rheumatism or poor circulation, you might want to pay a quick visit to Aguas Hediondas. This small hot springs complex of "smelly waters" (so called because of the strong rotten-egg smell given off by the sulfur-rich waters) is located outside the village of Tufiño - a scenic, thiry-minute drive from Tulcán. The locale is made up of three milky-white pools which supposedly cure the above ailments, and while the facilities are a little rundown (broken tiles and grim changing rooms), wallowing outside in 35-degree water while looking up at the surrounding mountains is not an unpleasant experience altogether. There also is a 45-minute path ("sendero frailejón") which takes you through the páramo vegetation, including the peculiar frailejón tree, which resembles a leafy pineapple on a stick. 6km past Tufiño. Take a Co-operativa TransNorte bus from the corner of Roberto Sierra and Rafael Arellano ($0.40, 35 minutes, every hour) to the village of Tufiño. There, unless you have your own 4x4 or want to hike 6km along the dirt road, hire a camioneta for $6-10.

Updated: March 13, 2013

Archaeological Museum

(ADMISSION: $1) This mural-covered edifice is home to several pre-Colombian artifacts and Ecuadorian artistry, ranging anywhere from ceramics all the way to modern art that encompasses the nation. One block south of the topiary garden.

Tulcán Lodging

Tulcán Hotels may be cheap and plentiful but you tend to get what you pay for. The standard is generally average with a select few offering good value for money. While hotels near the bus station may seem convenient, the area isn't the safest in Tulcán. It's usually just worth it to pay the extra few dollars and stay in the center of town.

Hotel Machado

($25 per person) One block from the main square and all the money changers, on one of the main arteries of Tulcán, Hotel Machado is one of the decent, if pricy, options in town. The 12 rooms, some doubles and some singles, are cozy, with comfortable beds and small but clean tiled bathrooms. There is a dark lounge with couches for watching TV. Ayaucho 403 and Bolívar, Tel: 06-298-4221.

Hotel San Francisco

($6-8 per person) If you are looking for the cheapest place possible, the Hotel San Francisco is your last half-decent option before you fall into the category of downright dingy places. The 11 simple, double and five-bed rooms are equipped with beds ranging from firm to squishy, and some have private bathrooms – more spacious and a little cleaner than the shared bathrooms. Try to get a room on the last floor, which is brighter and quieter than the lower floors. Bolívar and Roberto Sierra, across the street from the San Francisco church, Tel: 06-298-0760.

Hotel Sara Espindola

(ROOMS: $22.50-37.50) Climb the tiled staircase into the reception area, and you'll find nice carpeted hallways leading to bright and cheerful double and triple rooms, each one with a spotless private bathroom, TV and wireless internet. There is a bar, karaoke and dance floor downstairs, plus a sauna and Turkish bath, which are free for guests and $3 for visitors. Also, Sara Espindola is conveniently located right on the corner of the main square. Sucre y Ayacucho, corner of Plaza de la Independencia, Tel: 06-296-0071.

))))

NORTHERN ANDES

Central Andes

To the south of Quito, the Central Highlands area is reached by the Avenue of the Volcanoes, characterized by striking volcanic peaks and rugged Andean scenery. Some of Ecuador's most visited sites lie in this area, including the Cotapaxi National Park, the lively little holiday town of Baños, the hot springs at Papallacta, the Laguna de Quilotoa, the huge crater lake on the route of the popular 'Quilotoa Loop' and, of course, Ecuador's highest peak, Chimborazo.

LATACUNGA

 2,800m 63,842 03

A medium-sized city about an hour south of Quito, and the capital of the Cotopaxi province, Latacunga appeals to the traveler interested in visiting an authentic Ecuadorian city, where tourism isn't the be-all and end-all. It's also a good base for visiting Cotopaxi, the Quilotoa Loop, and the nearby Saquisilí market. Many people, however, bypass the

Ecuador's Central Andes Region

PICHINCHA

Volcán Atacazo 4463

QUITO

Volcán Pasochoa 4200

Parque Nacional Sumaco-Galeras

Volcán Antisana 5758

Volcán Corazón 4788

MACHACHI

Volcán Sincholahua 4893

Volcán Rumiñahui 4712

NAPO

Volcán Iliniza Norte 5263

SIGCHOS

Volcán Cotopaxi 5897

Volcán Quilindaña 4878

CHUGCHILÁN

THE QUILOTOA LOOP

SAQUISILÍ

Parque Nacional Cotopaxi

QUILOTOA   QUILOTOA CRATER

LATACUNGA

PUJILÍ

SAN MIGUEL

COTOPAXI

EL CORAZON

PILLARO

Parque Nacional Llanganates

AMBATO

PATATE

TISALEO

PELILEO

CEVALLOS QUERO

BAÑOS

Carihuairazo 5020

MOCHA

Volcán Chimborazo 6310

Volcán Tungurahua 5016

MER

BOLIVAR

CALUMA   GUARANDA

GUANO   PENIPE

TUNGURAHUA

S. J. DE CHIMBO

SAN MIGUEL

RIOBAMBA

VILLA LA UNION (CAJABAMBA) CHAMBO

Altar 5319

2 0   20 km

N
W   E
S

Central Andes Highlights

Baños (*p. 233-245*): This adventure-sports haven is the perfect place to unleash your inner risk-taking tendencies, with opportunities to go canyoning, white-water rafting and puenting (swing jumping). Rent a mountain bike or 4x4 for the day and explore the many waterfalls surrounding town. Then, soothe your sore muscles in the town's hot springs or treat yourself to a massage at one of the many spas.

Cotopaxi National Park (*p. 221-228*): Dominated by the perfectly coned and snow-capped Cotopaxi Volcano, this national park should be on the top of any visitor's list while in the Central Andes. Whether you want to merely awe at the view of Cotopaxi from afar, or challenge yourself to climb to its peak (or to the refuge), it is bound to be breath-taking.

Quilotoa Loop (*p. 203-206*): This rewarding, off-the-beaten-path circuit starting near Latacunga passes through several small indigenous artisan towns, where local markets can be visited. The biggest attraction, though, is the magnificent Quilotoa crater, with jagged rock walls encircling a beautiful turquoise lagoon. Descend to the crater's bottom or spend several hours walking around the crater's edges for an unforgettable experience.

Nariz del Diablo (*p. 257-258*): The Devil's Nose's is a picturesque 2.5-hour train ride from Alausí to Sibambe that passes through part of the country's impressive "Avenue of Volcanoes." The highlight of the ride is a series of switchbacks that climb from 1,800-2,600 meters (5,905-8,530 ft) by going forward and backward up the tracks. Sit on the right side of the train for the best views.

Carnaval in Guaranda (*p. 255*): Ecuador's biggest Carnaval celebration takes place in Guaranda, mixing Catholic religion with Inca rituals. Starting the week before Ash Wednesday, this otherwise sleepy town comes alive with droves of tourists, traditional dances, parades and water-throwing. Typical food, drink and music is enjoyed in excess for a rather rowdy time.

city on the dusty Panamericana highway on the edge of town, thereby missing out on the other side of Latacunga: a surprisingly charming historic center, with cobbled streets, tranquil plazas and a sprinkling of intimate cafés. Despite its low numbers of visitors, Latacunga still has a decent tourism infrastructure.

Latacunga was destroyed by earthquakes and eruptions of Cotopaxi on three occasions: in 1742, 1768 and 1877. In spite of the repeated destruction, it has a well-preserved colonial downtown. Once a somewhat grungy city, Latacunga municipality has done a great deal in recent years to beautify itself, improving gardens in the town squares and

adding ornate metalwork to the bridges that connect the city to the highway.

Latacunga's biggest claim to fame is its bi-annual festival, La Fiesta de la Mama Negra, held in both September and October, attracting huge crowds and featuring parades, fireworks, and dancing.

Photo by: Jose Pereira

Getting To and Away from Latacunga

BY BUS

It's easy to get to Latacunga from **Quito**; it's a quick 1.5 hour journey. Latacunga is also a convenient place to travel from if you're heading to Cotopaxi or the **Quilotoa Loop**, including the popular market town of Saquisilí.

Latacunga's bus terminal is located on the Panamericana Highway, about a 15 to 20-minute walk to the town center. Yellow, registered taxis buzz around the bus terminal, and charge $1 for the short ride into the city. Note that several buses also go to and from Quito and Ambato via Latacunga and, instead of dropping Latacunga-bound passengers off at the bus terminal, stop on Avenida 5 de Junio and Cotopaxi. If you get dropped off here, don't panic: the bus terminal is a quick five-minute walk east on Avenida de Junio; from here you can either move on to your next destination or carry on into the city center. If you have a lot of luggage, you can generally flag down a passing yellow taxi.

Buses run to the following destinations:

To **Ambato** (45 min, $1): depart every 10 to 15 minutes until 6 p.m. It is also possible to hop on the Ambato-bound bus from Quito on Avenida 5 de Junio (see above for more information). These buses run later in the evening, but be sure to take care.

To **Quito** (1.5 hr, $1.50): depart every 10 to 15 minutes until 6 p.m. It is also possible to hop on the Quito-bound bus from Ambato on Avenida 5 de Junio (see above for more information). These buses run later in the evening.

To **Saquisilí** (25 min, $0.30): depart frequently (every 10 to 15 minutes). For transport to and around the Quilotoa Loop, see Getting To and Away from the Quilotoa Loop (p.203).

BY TRAIN

If you prefer a more serene way of getting to Latacunga, then take one of the scenic tourist trains run by Ferrocarriles del Ecuador, which go between **Quito** and Latacunga every Thursday, Friday, Saturday and Sunday. Latacunga's train station is on Avenida Marco Aurelio Subia (a few blocks west of the bus terminal). Seewww.ecuadorbytrain.com for more information.

Getting Around Latacunga

Latacunga is a small city, and it's fairly quick and easy to find your way around. In fact, it's really small enough to walk anywhere if you're in the mood; even the bus terminal is only a 15-minute walk from the city center.

Registered yellow taxis buzz around the city, charging around $1 for a short ride (at night, ask your hotel to call you one, to be on the safe side).

Another transportation option is bicycle: Bike Life rent out bicycles by the day; $8 a day will get you a bike, protection, helmet, and local map routes (Sánchez de Orellana 16-85 and Guayaquil. Tel: 224-5245/097-700-999, E-mail:joaquin-echeverria@hotmail.com. Monday to Saturday 9 a.m-7.30 p.m.).
Updated: Sep 06, 2012.

Latacunga Services

TOURISM

The town's tourism office (Monday to Friday 8 a.m.-1 p.m. and 2-5 p.m. Tel: 280-8494) is on Sánchez de Orellana, in the same building as Casa de los Marqueses (upon entering the courtyard, the office is the first door on your left). The Spanish-speaking staff can provide you with free maps of the city.

MONEY

A number of banks have branches on Parque Vicente León. Banco Pichincha (Monday to Friday 9 a.m.-5 p.m., Saturday 9 a.m.-1 p.m.) has two; the branch on Calle Quito has 24-hour ATMs. There are also two 24-hour NEXO ATMs next to Banco Pichinca, which accept VISA and Mastercard.

KEEPING IN TOUCH

Internet cafés, many with phone cabins, are everywhere, particularly on Calle Quito-you will find a good two or three on Quito between Guayaquil and the Plaza. The post office (Ca. Belisario Quevado, near the corner of Maldonado) is open Monday to Friday 8 a.m.-6 p.m. and Saturday 8 a.m.-12 p.m.

MEDICAL

If you need a pharmacy, go to Farmacias Cruz Azul (Monday to Saturday 7.30 a.m.-9 p.m. Ca. Quito 16-49, next to Hotel Rosim) or Farmacias Económicas (Monday to Saturday 8 a.m.-8 p.m. Corner of Belisario Querado and Maldonado, one block west of the main plaza). The Hospital Provincial General de Latacunga is on Calle Hermanas Páez and 2 de Mayo.

CENTRAL ANDES

SHOPPING

For artisan goods, head to Calle Guayaquil between Quito and Sanchez de Orellana, where there is a row of stores selling crafts and souvenirs. The town's main market takes place on Tuesdays, Fridays and Saturdays (Saturday's market is the most impressive) around the streets of Avenida Amazonas and Echeverría.
Updated: Sep 05, 2012.

Things To See and Do in Latacunga

Aside from strolling around with an ice-cream, there is not a whole lot to do within Latacunga, and most of the tourists that come here use the city as a base for visits to Cotopaxi and the Quilotoa Loop. There are a couple of museums, however, and also a lively market, which takes place on Tuesday, Friday and Saturday (Saturday's market is the most impressive). You'll find the market stalls spread around the streets of Avenida Amazonas and Echeverría. The main plaza, Parque Vicente León, provides a pleasant spot to sit and people-watch in front of the white-washed cathedral (which is disappointingly plain both inside and out, and often shut). For good views of the city, head up to the Mirador El Calvario on Avenida Oriente and Isla Fernandina (from the main plaza, walk up Maldonado for about 10 minutes, then turn left onto Avenida Oriente).

Casa De Los Marqueses

The Casa de Los Marqueses is a restored colonial mansion (one of the few that has survived the earthquakes and eruptions of the nearby Cotopaxi volcano) that was built over 250 years ago, and which now accommodates traditional furniture and colonial art. It houses three small museums, the Museo de Numismática y Filatelia, the Museo de Arte Religioso y Arqueología, and the Biblioteca Municipal. You'll also find the town's tourism office here. Sánchez de Orellana, between Juan Abel Echeverria and Guayaquil. Tel: 280-8494.
Updated: Sep 17, 2012.

Casa De La Cultura

(ADMISSION: $1) Latacunga's Casa de la Cultura is housed on the site of a former Jesuit watermill that was constructed in 1676; much of the original buildings have been lost to natural disasters and flooding, but some parts still remain. Nowadays, there is an interesting collection of pre-conquest artifacts as well as an art gallery with rotating exhibits. Ca. Antonia Vela and Padre Salcedo.

Latacunga Tours

Tour agencies mainly focus on trips to the surrounding volcanoes, with day trips and two-day trips (which include the summit) of Cotopaxi being the most popular, as well as visits to the Thursday morning Saquisilí market (this is usually included on the one-day Cotopaxi tour, though can be done separately).

Tours to the Quilotoa Lagoon and Quilotoa Loop are also favorites. There are a number of agencies along Calle Guayaquil which all offer fairly similar programs (in terms of both destinations and rates).
Updated: Sep 06, 2012.

Neiges Travel Agency

The friendly Neiges Travel Agency offers one-day and multiple-day tours to Quilotoa, Illinizas, Chimborazo and more, as well as one day tours to either the north or south side of Cotopaxi and two-day summits of Cotopaxi.

The one-day Cotopaxi tour costs $50 per person, with a minimum of two people. Daily 8 a.m.-6 p.m. Guayaquil 6-25 and Quito (next to Santo Domingo church), Tel: 281-1199/098-376-220/0988-960-315, URL: www.ecuadorneigestours.com.ec.
Updated: Oct 31, 2012.

Greivag Turismo

The helpful Greivag Turismo run a myriad of tours, with day trips (or longer) to Quilotoa, Cotopaxi, Illinizas and Chimborazo, as well as tours to the market town of Saquisilí. A one day tour to Cotopaxi, including Saquisilí, costs $40 per person (minimum two people). Guides speak Spanish, English and German. Monday to Saturday (and holidays) 9 a.m.-7 p.m., also open some Sundays. Ca. Guayaquil (corner of Sánchez de Orellana), Tel: 281-0510/0998-647-308.
Updated: Oct 31, 2012.

High Andes

High Andes specializes in adventure travel, with climbing and hiking tours to the many surrounding volcanoes. They offer several one-day tours as well as six and seven-day Cotopaxi acclimatization programs. Guides speak Spanish and English. Don't miss the office-it's up a winding staircase, and located in the same space as the High Andes coffee shop. Guayaquil 6-72 (2nd floor), E-mail: highandescoffeeshop@gmail.com, URL: www.high-andes.com.
Updated: Sep 06, 2012.

Latacunga Lodging

Latacunga hotels and hostels tend to hover around budget to mid-range prices; for those seeking more luxurious accommodation, head outside of town to one of several converted haciendas. Most hotels in the city are scattered around the central plaza, Parque Vicente León. Note that accommodations are often fuller (or full) on Wednesday nights, as people arrive in Latacunga in time for the Thursday morning market in nearby Saquisilí. Prices tend to double during the local Fiesta de La Mamá Negra, which takes place every year on the 23rd and 24th of September and again around November 8th; be sure to reserve a room in advance.
Updated: Sep 05, 2012.

Hostal Tiana

($10-15.50 per person) Hostal Tiana is a pleasant surprise in Latacunga. It's aimed at backpackers, and does its job well. Set in a large colonial house, there's dorms as well as private rooms, a rooftop terrace, and a spacious outdoor courtyard that is perfect for socializing, with a lounge and dining area, TV, open kitchen, and computers with free Internet access (it's a shame this area is uncovered though, as it's the only communal space and nights get chilly in Latacunga). The free breakfast (bread, jam, tea and juice-eggs cost extra) is also served in the courtyard. There's also free WiFi, a book exchange, free hot drinks, and lots of activities going on: the hostal runs tours to Quilotoa and Cotopaxi. Staff are friendly enough but don't exactly go out of their way to make you feel and home, and rates are overly expensive for Latacunga, but it's a great place to meet other travelers. Luis Vivero 1-31 and Sánchez de Orellana, Tel: 03-281-0147, E-mail: info@hostaltiana.com, URL: www.hostaltiana.com.
Updated: Feb 06, 2013.

Villa De Tacvnga

(ROOMS: $45-100) Villa de Tacvnga is one of the nicer places to stay in Latacunga. It's not a luxurious hotel, but rooms, which are set around a small, sunny courtyard, are agreeably decorated, airy, and comfortable, with WiFi and cable TV. The hotel itself is set in a lovely colonial house that dates back more than 200 years. Staff are friendly and laid-back. Breakfast is included and served in the hotel's charming restaurant. Corner of Sánchez de Orellana and Guayaquil, Tel: 281-2352/0987-987-391., E-mail: gerencia@villadetacvnga.com, URL: www.villade-tacvnga.com.

Hotel Rosim

($12 per person) Centrally located just off the main square, Hotel Rosim is cool and quiet, with simple but well-maintained rooms. The prices are reasonable for what you get: rooms with private bath, WiFi, and cable TV, though there's no breakfast. Quito 16-49 and Padre Salcedo., Tel: 280-0853/280-2172/281-3200/280-1517, E-mail: hotelrosim@hotmail.com, URL: www.hotelrosim.com.
Updated: Sep 04, 2012.

Hotel Rodelu

(ROOMS: $29-70) The rooms are comfortable, with private bathrooms, cable TV and WiFi, and there's free use of communal computers if you don't have your own, but considering the lack of both breakfast and light (several rooms have internal windows only), Rodelu seems a little overpriced. The place is clean and modern however, and there's a good international restaurant and cafeteria downstairs. Quito 1631 and Padre Salcedo, Tel: 280-0956/281-1264, Fax: 281-2341, E-mail: rodelu@andinanet.net, URL: www.rodelu.com.ec.
Updated: Sep 04, 2012.

Hotel Central

($7-10 per person) On the corner of the main square, the Hotel Central has been around for 30 years, run by cheerful owner Viola. It has built up a healthy reputation in that time, particularly with tour groups. It's not hard to see why: even though the hotel and its furnishings are simple, rooms are large and light, and all have private bath, cable TV and Wifi. Some rooms sleep up to eight people. The rates are some of the lowest around, though don't include breakfast, which is an extra $2.50. Rooms at the front overlook the plaza, while rooms at the back are more peaceful. Sánchez de Orellana and Padre Salcedo (on Parque Vicente León), Tel: 280-2912, E-mail: hotelcentralatacunga@hotmail.com.
Updated: Sep 05, 2012.

Latacunga Restaurants

Latacunga is known for chugchucara, a heavy dish of fritada (fried pork), chicharrón (fried pork skin), maduras (fried plantains), cheese empanadas, and potatoes. If you're up for the challenge (portions tend to be huge), head downtown to Calle Quijano & Ordoñez between Calle Tarqui and Avenida Ruminahui, where there are a number of traditional chugchucara restaurants. Ice-cream parlours are also wildly popular; indulge your sweet tooth in one of the several heladerias around Calles Guayaquil and Quito. Besides fried pork and ice-cream, there's numerous eateries with cheap set-lunches, as well as fast-food joints and restaurants offering international cuisine; pizza seems to be a particular favorite.

La Fornace

(ENTREES: $4) La Fornace is a warm and inviting pizzeria that unfortunately belies its popularity by churning out rather disappointing thin-crust pizza: bases taste a little of cardboard, and toppings are hardly generous. Service is quick and efficient though, and, if you really must satisfy that pizza craving, it'll do. For dessert, choose from the wide selection of ice-cream. Ca. Quito 1749. Updated: Sep 05, 2012.

Guadalajara Grill

(ENTREES: $3.50-6) By day, this clean, unpretentious and budget-friendly restaurant prepares filling almuerzos (set-lunches) with huge bowls of scorching hot soup. By evening, Guadalajara Grill lives up to its namesake by turning into a Mexican joint and serving up tacos, burritos and other Mexcian dishes. Sánchez de Orellana, corner of Guayaquil., Tel: 280-6100/0987-889-568. Updated: Oct 31, 2012.

El Copihue Rojo

(ENTREES: $7-24) Ask a Latacunga local to recommend a place to eat, and many will point you in the direction of El Copihue Rojo (the Copihue is Chile's national flower). It's a little struggle to find the place, but worth the search: walk down Calle Quito from the Cathedral, and, half-way down the block on your left, you'll find a red sign adorning a narrow passageway: El Copihue is at the back of the courtyard. Don't expect a fancy restaurant though; it's straightforward and traditionally furnished, but it's the food that keeps people coming back (you'll find steak, chicken, fish, and pasta on the menu). The set-lunches are popular too. Monday to Saturday 10 a.m.-9 p.m. Quito 14-38 and Tarqui, Tel: 280-1725. Updated: Sep 05, 2012.

Brocolini

(ENTREES: $2.50-19) Brocolini is Latacunga's only vegetarian restaurant. It's a small and friendly café that aims to provide healthy, fresh food for those who, for whatever reason, want to steer clear of anything meat-related. There's pastas, pizzas and sandwiches, as well as soya burgers,

vitamin-packed fresh juices and a daily setlunch. It has limited opening hours though: come after 7 p.m. on a weekday or any time on the weekend, and you'll find it closed. Ca. Quito (corner General Maldonado), Tel: 0987-613-169. Updated: Oct 31, 2012.

El Sol De Manta

(ENTREES: $3-7.50) By and large, if a restaurant is consistently brimming with locals, then it's a sign of first-rate food. El Sol de Manta is no exception. Several tables are crammed into a basic room, where popular Ecuadorian seafood dishes such as ceviche, encebollado (fish stew) and fried fish are dispensed with speed. Daily 8.30 a.m.-3.30 p.m. Juan Abel Echeverria (between Ca. Quito and Ca. Belisario Quevedo), Tel: 0988-663-159. Updated: Oct 31, 2012.

El Templario

Hidden away on a pedestrian thoroughfare, El Templario is a delightful discovery for those who chance upon it. The friendly Spanish owner, who opened the place in June 2012, has made this small bar/café into a relaxing refuge, with live acoustic music (particularly jazz) on the weekends, and an inviting room full of sofas. Uniquely in Latacunga, there's stout and ale on tap. Hot drinks, snacks and sandwiches are on offer. Luis F Vivero 1-02 and Sánchez de Orellana, Tel: 0998-504-456, URL: www.cafebareltemplario.com. Updated: Oct 31, 2012.

Neiges Café

If you're looking for somewhere relaxed to have a drink (alcoholic or otherwise) on a chilly Latacunga night, head to Café Neiges by the church. Run by the nearby Neiges Travel Agency, this cozy joint has beer, cocktails and good coffee, and an informal atmosphere. There's not much in the way of food if you're hungry, though you can always fill up on a sandwich or slice of chocolate cake. Guayaquil 6-07 and Quito, next to the Santo Domingo church., Tel: 281-1199/098-376-220/0988-960-315, E-mail: neigestours@hotmail.com. Updated: Oct 31, 2012.

La Casa De Juan

(ENTREES: $5-19) Just off the main square, the Hotel Rodelu's charming, cozy restaurant is open to the public for breakfast, lunch and dinner. It serves up a mix of wood-fired pizza, steak, chicken, pasta, and salads. There is also a small cafeteria that, as well as pizza, offers sandwiches, hamburgers, snacks and ice-cream. Hotel Rodelu, Ca. Quito 1631 and Padre Salcedo, Zip: 281-2341, Tel: 280-0956/281-1264, E-mail: rodelu@andinanet. net, URL: www.rodelu.com.ec. Updated: Sep 06, 2012.

Villa De Tacvgna

(ENTREES: $6-12) Fancy injecting a bit of class into your afternoon? If so, head to the Villa de Tacvgna, where you can dine in the hotel's delightful courtyard restaurant set in the middle of a restored 200 year-old building. Set-menu almuerzos (lunches) are surprisingly reasonably-priced (from the outside, the restaurant looks like it might be alarmingly expensive), and by night you can choose from a menu of international cuisine (steak, fish and pasta). Daily 7.30 a.m.-8.30 p.m. Hotel Villa de Tacvgna, corner Sánchez de Orellana and Guayaquil., Tel: 281-2352/0987-987-391, E-mail: genercia@villadetacvnga.com, URL: www.villadetacvnga.com. Updated: Oct 31, 2012.

QUILOTOA LOOP

The region that has come to be known as the Quilotoa Loop boasts some of the most breathtaking scenery in Ecuador, and is perfect for travelers seeking a taste of indigenous farm life and spectacular mountain landscapes that are a bit off the usual path.

Starting in Latacunga, the Quilotoa Loop winds for 200 kilometers (124 mi) of mostly unpaved road through patchwork hills and along riverbeds, connecting tiny mountain villages, before circling back to Latacunga. Though riding the entire loop in one fell swoop would take about eight hours by bus, the real thrill of the expedition is in hiking

and bumping along the dusty road from village to village, staying the night and hanging out with both the locals and fellow travelers.

Many choose to travel the loop in a circle, walking, busing or riding horses from village to village in either direction, staying in a different place each night. Another option is to base yourself in either Chugchilán,Isinliví or Tigua, which all have delightful accommodation options.
Updated: Sep 13, 2012.

Getting To and Away from The Quilotoa Loop

Public transport to the Quilotoa Loop originates in Latacunga. You can choose to either travel around the loop clockwise (covering first Zumbahua, then Quilotoa, Chugchilán, Sigchos and Saquisilí), or counter-clockwise, covering the towns in the reverse order.

Note that for many destinations, there is only one bus a day, often leaving at an alarmingly early hour (in order to allow local people to get to the morning markets). If you can't drag yourself out of bed at 3 a.m., you can always hire a private car or, in some cases, hop on the daily milk truck. See each separate town in the Quilotoa Loop for more detailed transport information (e.g. place of departure, private car hire).

Several of the Quilotoa Loop buses, including those going to Chucghilán, are operated by **Transporte Illiniza**, who have a stand in the Latacunga bus terminal.

Depending on road and weather conditions, journey time can be significantly extended, and bus times may change frequently.

Transport from Latacunga to the various towns in the Quilotoa Loop is as follows:

Latacunga to **Chugchilán** via **Sigchos** (3.5 hr, $2.50): Buses depart Monday to Friday at 11.30 a.m., stopping in **Saquisilí** at around 12 p.m. and Sigchos around 2 p.m. Buses also run Saturday at 3 p.m. and Sunday at 11.30 a.m. and 12 p.m.

Latacunga to **Chugchilán** via **Quilotoa** (3.5 hr, $2.50). Buses depart Monday to Saturday at 12 p.m., stopping in **Zumbahua** at 2 p.m. and in Quilotoa at 2.30 p.m. On Sunday, buses run at 7 a.m., 9 a.m. and 2 p.m.

Latacunga to **Isinliví** (3 hr, $3): Daily departues at 12.15 p.m. and 1 p.m. (on Satur-

Quilotoa

day, buses leave at 11.15 a.m. instead of 12.15 p.m.). On Thursdays, there are no buses from Latacunga; instead, they leave from the market town of Saquisilí at 11 a.m. and 12 p.m. (buses to **Saquisilí** leave Latacunga every 15 minutes).

Latacunga to **Saquisilí** (25 min, $0.30): depart frequently (every 10 to 15 minutes).

Latacunga to **Sigchos** (2.5 hr): Buses depart Monday-Friday at 9.30 a.m., 10.30 a.m., 11.30 a.m., 12 p.m. and 1 p.m. (on Tuesday, Thursday and Friday there is an additional service at 3 p.m.). Saturday and Sunday buses leave at 9.30 a.m. and 5 p.m.

Latacunga to **Zumbahua** (2 hr, $2): Depart hourly. Note that buses go via Zumbahua on their way to Quevedo, stopping on the hill above Zumbahua.

Latacunga to **Pujili** and **Tigua**: Depart hourly (take the Quevedo-bound bus that goes to Zumbahua, stopping in Pujili and **Tigua** on the way).

Transport from within the Quilotoa Loop to Latacunga and other towns is as follows:

Chugchilán to Latacunga via **Sigchos** (3.5 hr, $2.50): Buses leave Chugchilán daily at 3 a.m. (note that buses sometimes leave as late as 4 a.m., but be there at 3 a.m. just in case), stopping in Sigchos around 4 a.m. and arriving in Latacunga at 6.30 a.m. You can also hop on the 9 a.m daily milk truck for $1, which goes to Sigchos only; from there, you can take a bus onto Latacunga (see Sigchos to Latacunga for more information).

Chugchilán to Latacunga via **Quilotoa** (3.5 hr, $2.50): Buses leave Chugchilán daily at 4 a.m. (note that buses sometimes leave as late as 5 a.m., but try and be there at 4 a.m. just in case), stopping in Quilotoa at 5 a.m., Zumbahua at 5.30 a.m. and arriving in Latacunga at 7.30 a.m. On Wednesdays and Fridays, buses also leave Chugchilán at 6 a.m., stopping in Quilotoa at 7 a.m., **Zumbahua** at 7.30 a.m. and arriving in Latacunga at 9.30 a.m.

Looping the Loop

Gettting around the Quilotoa Loop via public transport is doable with a little patience, planning, and some very early morning rises. The destinations more than make up for the arduous journeys, and the scenery is stunning by golden dawn light. Below are some must see places along the way.

• The magnificent **Quilotoa Volcanic Crater Lake** is one of the most striking sites in Ecuador and one of the most beautiful craters in Latin America, with lustrous emerald waters and excellent hiking paths.

• The indigenous market at **Sasquisilí** is considered by many to be the best market in Ecuador. You won't find many souvenirs, but it's certainly one of the most authentic. Filled with locals bartering for everything from pigs' ears to fresh produce, Thursdays in Saquisilí transform into a colorful spectacle for the senses.

• The tiny, charmingtown of **Chugchilán** offers a few fantastic hostels, and its popularity as a base for exploring the area continues to rise. With some of the region's most incredible vistas, an array of hiking and horseback riding trails into canyons and cloud forests, and exceptionally warm and hospitable people, it's no wonder that business in this tiny mountain town has flourished.

• The artisan village of **Tigua** is probably best known for the unique style of colorful paintings made locally and sold all over the country. In addition to visits to local art galleries and workshops, there are many hikes in the area and an excellent working-farm that you can visit.

Pujili and **Tigua** to Latacunga: Buses from **Quevedo** stop in Pujili and Tigua hourly on their way to Latacunga.

Saquisilí to Latacunga (25 min, $0.30): depart frequently (every 10 to 15 minutes).

Sigchos to Latacunga (2 hr): Daily buses run to Latacunga at 2.30 p.m. and 4 p.m.; on Sundays they run every hour from 9 a.m.

Quilotoa to **Zumbahua** (20 min, $0.50): Buses leave daily at 1 p.m. and 4 p.m.

Zumbahua to **Quilotoa** (20 min, $0.50): The Quilotoa-bound bus from Latacunga stops in the center of Zumbahua daily at 2 p.m.

Zumbahua to Latacunga (2 hr,m $2). Latacunga-bound buses from Quevedo stop on the hill above Zumbahua every hour. The daily bus from Quilotoa also stops in the center of Zumbahua on its way to Latacunga at around 1.15/1.30 p.m.
Updated: Sep 13, 2012.

Things To See and Do in the Quilotoa Loop
Hiking in the Quilotoa Region

The Quilotoa region presents some of the best hiking in Ecuador, from traversing deep rugged canyons, volcanic crater lakes and cloud forests, to gentle walks through rolling patchwork hills and on to high-mountain cheese factories. If you have a few days, walk the whole loop from village to village, hopping on the bus or a local milk truck when you've had enough. Alternatively, base yourself in Chugchilán, Tigua, or Quilotoa and indulge in several fantastic day hikes.

The walk from the Quilotoa crater to Chugchilán is undoubtedly one of the best short hikes in Ecuador. The trek takes four to five hours depending on how long you stop to let your jaw drop at the alternating views between glistening green volcanic crater lake and endless green pastures backed by distant jagged mountains. Another good five-hour hike is from Isinliví to Chugchilán, which passes through the small village of Guantualo, and offers plenty of opportuni-

CENTRAL ANDES

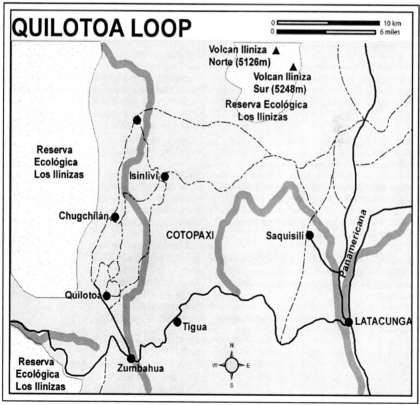

CENTRAL ANDES

ties to stop and admire the landscape. Hit the Monday market in Guantualo if you can. The hike from Tigua to Quilotoa is four to five hours of breathtaking views and gentle trekking, rewarded with the glimmering waters of the Quilotoa Crater Lake at the end. Look up specific towns to find out more about hikes there, and ask around to determine which trails are currently best while you're in the region. Any of these trips can be made in reverse. Always pay attention to the notoriously rapidly-changing weather, and be sure to leave ample time to complete hikes well ahead of afternoon rains and before dark falls.
Updated: Sep 13, 2012.

Photo by: Casey

Biking in the Quilotoa Region

The Quilotoa Loop presents some awesome trips for cyclists, with gentle inclines and awe-inspiring views around nearly every corner. Most people begin the journey in Latacunga, though you can also enter the region from Lasso or Zumbahua. Biking any good part of the loop takes a comfortable three-five days, depending on your speed. While the route is easy going in most places, watch out for cobbled stones and steeper hills around the Sigchos area.

A few popular routes that diverge from the typical towns on the loop are:

In the North: Latacunga-Guingopana-Guangaje-Guantualo-Isinliví-Sigchos. From Sigchos you can take a bus back to Latacunga.

To the South: Zumbahua-Angamarca-Shuyo-Moraspungo-Quevado or Salinas.

Renting bikes on the loop itself is difficult; instead, you will need to enquire with tour agencies or bike rental shops in either Quito or Latacunga.
Updated: Sep 13, 2012.

SAQUISILÍ !

The small town of Saquisilí is gaining fame for its bustling local Thursday market. Only two hours south of Quito by bus and less than half-an-hour from Latacunga, the market's accessibility and authenticity are making it an increasingly popular stop with tourists.

Each Thursday, the town is transformed by a lively sprawling display of goods brought in by locals from surrounding villages in all directions. Unlike the Otavalo market that is primarily a show for tourists, the Saquisilí market is truly a local event which has existed since pre-Columbian times. Men and women from surrounding villages swarm in at the crack of dawn, toting every item imaginable, from household necessities to baskets full of squawking chicks.

The market takes up eight main plazas and offers everything from reed mats and herbal remedies to the squealing livestock itself. To explore the latter, walk for about 10 minutes past the market's main plaza along the dirt road that leads out of town. Come early, as the animal market excitement begins to subside by about 9 a.m. As well as the main squares, every adjoining street see vendors selling more random items, from painted key rings to cell phones and electronics.

Like many local highland markets, the market at Saquisilí is not only for commerce; it is also a very important social and cultural affair. Indigenous men and women can be seen donning traditional dress and felt fedora hats, bartering with their neighbors and mingling over lunch.

For the traveler, much of the market is of little interest (though there is a growing artisan section of colorful local crafts, with prices that are cheaper than in Quito and Otavalo); instead, the essence of the market is in its authenticity, as well as its food, animal market, and general lively atmosphere. Though you're not likely to be in the market searching for a dish rack or a new alpaca, Saquisilí provides a genuine look at native life and culture, and photographic opportunities abound.
Updated: Sep 13, 2012.

Saquisilí Services
MONEY
Banco Pichincha (Monday-Friday 9 a.m.-5 p.m., Saturday 9 a.m.-1 p.m. Mariscal Sucre, corner of 9 de Octubre) has a 24-hour ATM that takes VISA and Mastercard.

KEEPING IN TOUCH

If you need to send a quick email while in Saquisilí, head to one of the many Internet cafés around Parque Central. Cyber and Cabinas Gabycita (corner of Mariscal Sucre and 24 de Mayo) is open daily 8.30 a.m.-8.30 p.m. and charges $0.60 an hour for Internet; it also has several phone cabins.

TOURISM

There is no tourist office in Saquisilí. For information on tours of the market and the surrounding area, visit a travel agency in Latacunga (see Latacunga Tours).

MEDICAL

You'll find a pharmacy on the Calle 24 de Mayo side of Parque Central (daily 8 a.m.-10 p.m.). There's also a medical clinic on Mercado 18 de Octubre on Calle Bolivar (walk one block up Bolivar from Parque Central).

SHOPPING

Aside from the more obvious shopping locations-the market-you can pick up snacks and groceries at the Micro Mercado Saquisilí on Ca. Barreno and 25 de Mayo (on the corner of Parque Central).
Updated: Sep 07, 2012.

Getting To and Away from Saquisilí

Because the Thursday morning market starts bright and early (and it's best to get there before 8 a.m.), many people stay in **Latacunga** the night before and hop on the bus to Saquisilí the next morning.

It's also possible to take a bus directly from **Quito**'s Quitumbe bus terminal, but the two-hour ride means you'll need a seriously early start to make it in time for the market.

To **Chugchilán** (3 hr, $2.50): The daily Chugchilán bus from **Latacunga** passes through Saquisilí at 12 p.m. Monday to Friday, 3.30 p.m. Saturday and 12 p.m. and 12.30 p.m. Sunday.

Latacunga to Saquisilí (25 min, $0.30): Buses leave frequently (every 15 minutes or so) from the Latacunga bus terminal, beginning at dawn. In Saquisilí, buses drop you off on Calle Barranco: from here, walk down to the Parque Central, from where you can access many of the markets.

To **Latacunga** (25 min, $0.30): Buses to Latacunga leave regularly from the corner of Bolivar and Imbabura (two blocks down from the clothing market).

To **Quito** (2 hr, $2): Buses leave when full from Plaza Gran Colombia (the food market). The last bus to Quito leaves around 4 p.m. Alternatively, you can take a Latacunga-bound bus and asked to be dropped off at the highway, then flag down a bus heading to Quito.

To **Sigchos** (2 hr, $2): Buses from Latacunga stop in Saquisilí on their way to Sigchos in Plaza Kennedy (walk one block up Calle Bolivar from Parque Central) at 10 a.m., 11 a.m., 12 p.m., 12.30 p.m. and 1.30 p.m. (on Tuesday, Thursday and Friday there is an additional service at 3.30 p.m.). On Saturday and Sunday, Sigchos-bound buses leave Saquisilí at 10 a.m. and 5.30 p.m.

Several tour agencies in both Latacunga and Quito also offer trips to Saquisilí, including private transport to the market. Agencies in Latacunga generally include the market in their one-day Cotopaxi tour. See Latacunga Tours for more information. If you make your way to Saquisilí in your own vehicle, you can park it at the parking lot on Plaza Gran Colombia (where the food market is), on Calle Abdon Calderon.
Updated: Sep 07, 2012.

Saquisili Lodging

Though many travelers prefer to stay in nearby Latacunga and take a crack-of-dawn bus to the Thursday market, there are some accommodation options in Saquisilí, though most are basic. Places fill up on Wednesday nights, so reserve in advance if you can.

Hostería Ecologica Gilocarmelo

(ROOMS: $17.50-20.80) With 14 rooms set around a pretty garden and large grounds with 70 tree species, Hostería Ecologica Gilocarmelo is a tranquil and naturally beautiful retreat, complete with a covered swimming pool and sauna. Staff aim to make their guests feel at home. Packages with meals are offered, and activities such as horse-riding and fishing can be arranged. The hotel is located just outside Saquisilí, a 10-minute walk from the Plaza Gran Colombia. Ca. Chimborazo y Bartolomé de las Casas, Saquisilí, Tel: 272-1634/340-0924/0999-669-734/0992-517-327, E-mail: gilocarmelo@hotmail.ec, URL: www.hosteriagilocarmelo.com.
Updated: Oct 31, 2012.

Salon Pichincha

($5 per person) Salon Pichincha is a quiet and very simple option, which is reflected in the low rates. Bathrooms are shared, and

CENTRAL ANDES

there is no breakfast. There's no phone, so you can't reserve a room in advance; instead, if you're in town for the market, arrive early as rooms tend to fill up fast on Wednesday nights. The restaurant's hotel is a favorite with locals for almuerzos. Ca. Boliviar, corner of Pichincha (1 block from the clothing market).
Updated: Sep 07, 2012.

San Carlos

($10 per person) If you can handle the cheesy décor and a little Jesus paraphernalia, you'll find that this is one of Saquisilí's nicer hostels. Rooms are simple and dark but will do the trick for a night, and all have private bath and cable TV. Even if you're not staying at San Carlos, for $1 you can save your weary shoulders and store you r backpack here for the day. Bolivar and Sucre (Parque Central), Tel: 272-1981.
Updated: Sep 07, 2012.

Saquisili Restaurants

The most popular place to eat in Saquisilí is, of course, in one of the many food markets, and there's no shortage of traditional food to sample; some options are quite tasty, while others can be a bit nauseating to the unaccustomed stomach. Locals will tell you that you haven't experienced the real Saquisilí if you don't try tortillas de maiz-a sizzling hot corn pancake oozing with cheese and smothered in sauce. If you haven't yet tried cuy (guinea pig), Saquisilí is a well-known place to do so. If you can't stomach the market cuisine, you will find a handful of simple but adequate restaurants around the main square that offer fried chicken and almuerzos. There are also a number of bakeries selling fresh bread on the corner of Parque Central (24 de Mayo and Mariscal Sucre).

Cevicheria Paty

(ENTREES: $1.50-2) A popular spot next to the San Carlos hotel on the plaza, this modest seafood joint offers ceviches, encebollados and almuerzos at low prices (though sometimes the seafood options are non-existent). Daily 7 a.m.-5 p.m. Corner of Simon Bolivar and Barranco, Parque Central.
Updated: Sep 10, 2012.

Coffee Bambu's

(ENTREES: $1.50-12) Coffee Bambu's is Saquisilí's only tourist-orientated eatery. It's an amiable little café that serves up coffees and hot drinks, desserts, and pizzas in a variety of sizes. Ca. Barranco (Parque Central), Tel: 272-1355/0984-456-615.

Asados Isaac

(ENTREES: $2.50-3) If you don't have the stomach for what's on offer in the market itself, try Asados Isaac for generous portions of fried chicken and french fries, as well as almuerzos. Daily 7 a.m.-8 p.m. Ca. Bolivar (corner of Barreno).
Updated: Sep 07, 2012.

PUJILI

 2,800m n/a 03

A small market town located only a few miles away from Latacunga and the Quito-Ambato highway, Pujili has a rich culture and history. Most of the inhabitants of Pujili are indigenous, and the best time to see native customs and clothing are the market days: Wednesdays and Sundays. Unlike Otavalo, which is aimed mainly at tourists, the market in Pujili is still a local affair.

Men and women from surrounding villages will pack up their llamas and burros early in the morning and head to the market to sell their extra produce for whatever money they can make. Professional vendors also bring their wares, which are generally basic essentials such as rope, knives, dishes, batteries, clocks, and so on.

Like the market in Saquisili, this is more than simply a place to shop: going to the market is an important social activity, and locals will dress up and take time to mingle. Tourists are discovering Pujili, meaning more stalls dedicated to Otavalo-style weavings and other popular crafts are popping up. The town itself is known for clay pottery and ceramics, which are also sold at the market.

Of particular interest in Pujili is the Corpus Christi festival in June, which features the El Danzante parades. This fiesta is a fascinating mix of Catholic and ancient native religious practices. Pujili's location makes it an ideal place to combine with other day trips to the Cotopaxi area, and is easily reached from Latacunga or Quito.

For a small town, this place has an interesting history: the citizens of Pujili fought bravely in the war of independence. One of Ecuador's presidents, General Guillermo Rodríguez Lara, was a native of Pujili. The town was devastated by an earthquake in 1996, but has since been reconstructed.

CENTRAL ANDES

Pujili is undeveloped in terms of tourism, but there are a few very simple hospedajes and restaurants dotted around town. The market is also a great option for sampling local dishes.
Updated: Sep 13, 2012.

Getting To and Away from Pujili

Pujili is easily reached from Latacunga; it's around a 15-20 minute ride, and buses run frequently (every 15 minutes or so) between the two city's respective bus terminals. You can also hop on a Quevedo-bound bus in Latacunga, which will drop you off in Pujili on the way; these buses leave hourly (buses returning from Quevedo on their way to Latacunga also stop hourly in Pujili).
Updated: Sep 13, 2012.

QUILOTOA

 3,914m n/a 03

Just off the Quilotoa loop road about 14 kilometers (8.7 mi) north of Zumbahua lies the tiny, windswept village of Quilotoa, and the mysterious emerald waters of its illustrious volcanic crater lake. Steep cliffs of the caldera's walls drop 400 meters (1312 ft) down from a fully encircling rim to meet the massive reflective pool below. The opaque-green of the lake paired with the distant snow capped peaks of Iliniza Sur and Cotopaxi create a truly awe-inspiring scene.

A single stretch of dirt road and the scattering of houses and tiny businesses that line it make up the small village of Quilotoa, which lies just before the crater lake and seems to only exist in response to tourism. There are several basic hostels that also serve as restaurants, and a few stores, but not much else. Quilotoa is a good place to find local indig-

Photo by: Marcio Ramalho

enous art, especially paintings in the famous Tigua style. There are a few shops where artists sell their work. If the doors are locked, ask around and someone will likely come let you in. You'll also find traditional woven goods and crafts sold in a small row of artisan stalls, by the top of the steps that lead down to the lake.

Be aware that Quilotoa is cold (and feels even colder due to the strong wind). Nights can be very cold at 3850 meters (12600 ft) high, and some simple accommodations may not be sufficiently equipped to keep you warm; bring adequate clothing.

Note that are no services to speak of in Quilotoa, including no Internet or phone cabins. Be sure to bring a sufficient amount of cash with you.

Getting To and Away from Quilotoa

Buses to Quilotoa originate from **Latacunga**, leaving Latacunga's bus terminal once a day (note that this bus stops in Quilotoa on its way to **Chugchilán**. NOTE: There is also a daily bus from Latacunga to Chugchilán via Sigchos - *do not* get this bus, as it won't take you anywhere near Quilotoa!. The buses that run between Latacunga and Quilotoa are operated by **Transporte Illiniza**, who have a stand in the bus terminal.

There are also buses between Quilotoa and the nearby town of **Zumbahua**.

In Quilotoa, all buses leave from or close to the checkpoint at the entrance to the village. **Latacunga** to Quilotoa (2.5 hr, $2.50): The **Chugchilán**-bound bus leaves Latacunga's bus terminal Monday to Saturday at 12 p.m., stopping in Quilotoa at 2.30 p.m. On Sunday, buses leave Latacunga at 7 a.m., 9 a.m. and 2 p.m., stopping in Quilotoa at 9.30 a.m., 11.30 a.m., and 4.30 p.m.

Quilotoa to **Latacunga** (2.5 hr, $2.50): The bus from **Chugchilán** stops in Quilotoa at 5 a.m. daily. On Wednesdays and Fridays, there is an additional bus that stops in Quilotoa on the way to Latacunga at 7 a.m. Note that buses are often delayed in Chugchilán, leaving up to an hour late; they also sometimes leave on time however, so it is best to assume that they will leave on time rather than miss the bus!

Quilotoa to **Zumbahua** (20 min, $0.50): Buses leave daily at 1 p.m. and 4 p.m.

CENTRAL ANDES

Zumbahua to Quilotoa (20 min, $0.50): If you're in Zambahua, hop on the Quilotoa-bound bus from Latacunga which stops in the center of Zumbahua daily at 2 p.m. Otherwise, you can hire a camioneta (truck) for around $5.

If you need to get from Quilotoa to **Latacunga** but can't face the 5 a.m. start, take the bus to **Zumbahua** in the afternoon (or catch a ride in a camioneta from Quilotoa to Zumbahua for between $2-5), then from the center of Zambahua walk 10 minutes uphill to the highway, where you can hop on the Latacunga-bound bus that passes by every hour (2 hr, $2).

Alternatively, hiring a truck/taxi to take you between Quilotoa and Zumbahua costs between $10-15 one-way and to Chugchilán $25 one-way (with up to five passengers; each additional passenger incurs an extra $5). A private truck/taxi between Quilotoa and Latacunga will set you back around $40-50.
Updated: Sep 11, 2012.

Things To See and Do in Quilotoa

Quilotoa activities center-of course-around its dazzling crater lake. The first thing many people do is to head straight down to it: from the village, walk up the hill and to the row of artisan stalls, from where the steps down to the lake begin.

In 30 minutes, you can climb down to the shore; the steep, literally breathtaking return trip takes at least two or three times as long, or for a few bucks you can hop on a donkey and save weary legs (be sure to contract the donkey above in the town before you leave). Take plenty of water with you. This is an extremely environmentally sensitive location: take great care to not contaminate the lake in any way.

Kayaks are available for rent at the end of the trail, though the lake has no outlet and you shouldn't swim or drink from the stagnant alkaline waters. Paddling five minutes to the east (towards the right from the shore) reveals hot springs and fumaroles bubbling up from the lake bottom.

Hiking inside the crater is somewhat limited due to the steep terrain, but up at the top of the rim, relatively fit hikers can make the four to five-hour trek around the entire circumference of the crater.

Another popular activity available in Quilotoa is to hike or go horseback riding a third of the way around the lake and then carry on to Chugchilán.
Updated: Sep 12, 2012.

Hiking From Quilotoa To Chugchilán

This 12 kilometer (7.5 mi) mile trek is one of the most astonishingly beautiful day hikes in Ecuador. Depending on fitness levels, the hike takes between four to five hours, passing by Quilotoa's volcanic crater lake, down into the valley through the town of Guayama, and finally up the canyon into Chugchilán. While the hike is not extremely challenging, pay close attention to the route and, as always, the weather. Note that, doing this hike in reverse (Chugchilán to Quilotoa) is far more challenging, as much more of it is uphill, and it takes at least a couple of hours longer.

The route begins in the tiny town of Quilotoa. Signs used to mark the hike, but they have since been removed or blown over. From El Mirador-the lookout over the crater-look left across the lake to where three sandy patches will be visible along the ridge. Your aim in this first section is to make it to the third sandy spot (the lowest along the ridge-line) where you will descend from the ridge into the valley. From El Mirador, walk to your left along the ridge on the well-defined path. At the beginning of the path, a sign with helpful hints also has a map painted on the back of it.

The path will wind along the top of the ridgeline, giving the hiker breathtaking views of the emerald lake and patchwork valley. Be sure to have reached the lowest sandy spot before turning down into the valley. This third sandy patch has a rock cairn in the middle of it, with an empty signpost sticking out.

From the sandy spot you will be able to see your next objective, the small town of Guayama. Take the path that descends straight down the hill, past a small house. Once you reach the bottom of the hill, a road will take you through the middle of the town. The wee village here has few amenities, though there is a basic shop with drinks and a small hostel (Hostal El Chucurito) by the cemetery. At the far end of town, the road will curve left past the cemetery. You will find the continuation of the path to Chugchilán at the third right.

In the final section of the hike, the path will wind through beautiful pastures and then steeply down into the river basin, before climbing up into the town of Chugchilán. The path is obscured a bit in one spot, where three options present themselves in a small grassy clearing. Take the middle route that looks like a tunnel, which leads down into the canyon on a narrow path with tall steep rock walls. Once at the bottom, just keep following the well-trodden trail past local dwellings and up and into Chugchilán.

This hike is mostly downhill, however the final section is steep and challenging. It also can be difficult to find your way, especially if the weather is cloudy. Only undertake this adventure if you are confident in your sense of direction.

Make sure that you have enough time to complete the hike before the afternoon weather moves in; never leave from Quilotoa after 1:30 p.m. If you have any doubts, hire a local guide for $15-20.

It is also possible to do this route on horseback, for around $20 (including the guide). Ask at your hostel.
Updated: Sep 12, 2012.

Quilotoa Lodging

Quilotoa hotels are generally humble ramshackle shelters that offer small rooms (some with fireplaces to help ward away the very cold nights) and not much else. There are a couple of more comfortable options if you don't mind forking out a few more dollars, though neither are by any means luxurious.

If you have your own tent, camping is also possible at the Princesa Toa hostel by the lakeside, but be aware that it will be freezing. Note that all places include breakfast and dinner in the room price, which, considering Quilotoa's almost complete lack of restaurants, is highly necessary.
Updated: Sep 10, 2012.

Hostal Conejito

($10 per person) Staying at the Hostal Conejito (literally, the Little Rabbit hostel) is more like staying in somebody's tiny home; in fact, spend the night here and you are staying in somebody's home. Up a steep, precarious wooden staircase, there's three very small rooms (each with a double bed that pretty much takes up all the floor space) that share a shower room and toilet with both fellow guests and the owners. Downstairs is a sparse dining/living room where breakfast and dinner are served (both meals are included in the price), as well as a store selling snacks and cervezas. It's very compact and basic, but the owners are friendly and charge less than any other place in town. It's the last house at the end of the village, by the crater. Tel: 0982-604-720.
Updated: Oct 31, 2012.

Hosteria Alpaca

($25 per person) One of the newer accommodation options in the village, the Hosteria Alpaca has some of the most pleasant rooms of any of the Quilotoa hotels, with comfy beds, wood-burning stoves and beautiful views (for the latter, ask for an upstairs room). There's a large communal living area where breakfast and dinner (included in the price) are served, and you can hang out on the sofas and watch TV. However, the place is a little gloomy, the staff isn't very forthcoming and, with the highest rates in town, it's overpriced. Opposite the checkpoint at the village's entrance. Tel: 0992-125-962, URL: www.alpacaquilotoa.com.
Updated: Oct 31, 2012.

Hostal Chosita

($12 per person) Hostal Chosita is a pink two-storey building halfway up the hill to the crater. Rooms have private bath and rates include breakfast and dinner, but the place is bleak and lacks the rustic charm of other similarly-priced hotels. Halfway up the hill on your right as you walk towards the crater. Tel: 0988-520-156.
Updated: Oct 31, 2012.

Pacha Mama

($12 per person) A basic but decent option run by an amicable local family, Pacha Mama is the second to last stop on the left as you approach the crater. Four upstairs rooms are surprisingly warm for the area as heat is carried up and radiated through a large metal pipe. That said, it's still downright chilly at night, so be sure to bring plenty of warm clothes. The rooms come with hot water, but they often keep water shut off until a guest requests it be turned on (so check before undressing for the shower!). Rates include breakfast and dinner as well, which are served on the first floor next to a warm furnace. Non-guests can also come and eat here for $3 a meal. At the top of the hill toward the rim of the crater. Tel: 0980-410-675/0992-125-962.
Updated: Oct 31, 2012.

Princesa Toa

($15 per person) The only hostel located down on the actual lakeside, Princesa Toa is organized by the Fundacion Ecuatoriana del Habitat. It is run by local community members and all profits are invested back into the community. Though accommodations are rustic (bathrooms are outdoors), the indigenous locals who work there are friendly and proud. Prices include breakfast and dinner as well.

If you have your own tent, you can camp for free, though be sure to bring plenty of warm clothes and a well-insulated sleeping bag, as temperatures are extremely cold (even during the day). However there have also been multiple reports of campers' items being stolen, so don't leave your things unaccompanied. Down by the lakeside (next to the row of artisan stalls is a flight of steps leading down to the lake).
Updated: Sep 11, 2012.

Quilotoa Crater Lake Lodge

($20 per person) A diamond in the rough of the concrete village that is Quilotoa, the Crater Lake Lodge is undoubtedly the nicest place to spend a cold, windy Quilotoa night. The hacienda-style lodge was built with respect for the environment and lush surrounding area in mind, and offers clean and comfortable double and triple rooms. The highlight is the large but cozy restaurant that is somewhat reminiscent of a ski-chalet lodge, with its panoramic views and a massive stone fireplace. Rates include breakfast and dinner. Up on the hill, before the entrance to the village., Tel: 0985-023-559/305-5816, URL: www.quilotoalodge.com.ec.
Updated: Oct 31, 2012.

Quilotoa Restaurants

Restaurants are very scarce in Quilotoa; in fact, there's only one restaurant that is actually a restaurant in its own right, rather than the dining room of a hotel. Travelers therefore eat in their respective accommodations, as all hotels offer packages that include breakfast and dinner; many also offer lunch as an extra or can make up a packed-lunch for hikers.

From midday onward, you'll find a few food carts at the top of the hill, on the other side of the row of artisan stalls. To stock up on snacks and drinks for a long trek, head to one of the handful of tiendas on the main road.

Kirutwa Mushak Wasi

(ENTREES: $5) The community-run Kirutwa Mushuk Wasi is the only actual restaurant in town. Perched on the rim of the crater, the restaurant is set inside a sparkling wooden building that was opened in 2009. It is operated in the same way as the lakeside hostel Princesa Toa, with profits invested back into the Quilotoa community. The restaurant itself is a welcome refuge from the harsh wind: there's an open fire, and, if you head up to the second-floor dining area, gorgeous views of the lake. Snacks, sandwiches, hot drinks and main meals (a typical plate of meat, rice, french fries and salad) are available. Portions are generous and the food itself is decent enough, though overcooked sometimes. Daily 8.30 a.m.-5.30 p.m. Located by the rim of the crater, at the top of the hill, Tel: 0981-179-321.
Updated: Oct 31, 2012.

TIGUA

 3,396m n/a 03

Climbing up from Pujilí, the rolling hillsides ascend towards the jagged peaks of Cotopaxi and the Ilinizas. Here lies the tiny village of Tigua, which has become world famous for a special style of painting of the same name. Colorful pieces depicting Andean life can be bought directly from the artists at the Galería de los Pinturas de Tigua, run by the association of indigenous painters of Tigua. Be on the lookout for paintings by the Toaquiza family, who originally conceptualized the Tigua style.

There's not much of a town center, more a scattering of several clusters of houses and the occasional shop, but Tigua is close to the larger town of Zumbahua. There are pretty walks in the area, and two excellent lodging options make Tigua an appealing place to base yourself in while exploring the region. Both of these accommodations provide meals, as there are no restaurants to speak of in Tigua.

Mount Amina hovers over the eastern side of the village, which, according to local Quichua legend, is a giant who came from the coast to rest in Tigua and has been sleeping there ever since. Every summer locals tradionally gather on the mountainside for a ceremony in reverence of the sleeping giant.
Updated: Sep 13, 2012.

Getting To and Away from Tigua

To get there, take a Quevedo-bound bus from **Latacunga**, and asked to be dropped off in Tigua (1.5 hr, $1). Buses leave Latacunga's terminal every hour.

From Tigua, you can hop back on this bus and carry on to **Zumbahua** (30 min). To get back to Latacunga, wait on the main road for the return bus from **Quevedo**, which passes through hourly.
Updated: Sep 13, 2012.

Things To See and Do In Tigua

Most of the activities in Tigua are outdoors, and local guides can take you on breathtaking hikes with views of the mountains. But there's also the option to visit a local home, or to see a workshop of one of Tigua's painters. Good day trips from here include a visit to the volcanic crater at Quilotoa, and the traditional Saturday market in the town of Zumbahua.
Updated: Sep 13, 2012.

Galería De Los Pinturas De Tigua

This gallery is home to an impressive collection of art by local indigenous painters, run by the friendly artist Alfredo, who is president of the Association of Indigenous Painters of Tigua. Located on the main highway just outside of the village, this is arguably the best place to purchase authentic Tigua art. If the door's locked, ask around, and somebody will come open it up for you. Kilometer 53, Tigua.
Updated: Sep 13, 2012.

Tigua Lodging

There are very few accommodations in Tigua; in fact there, are just two: one is a working farm and the other a community-run hosteria. Although in no way luxurious, both places are perfect if you are looking to experience real Ecuadorian culture.
Updated: Oct 31, 2012.

La Posada de Tigua

($25-35 per person) An old sprawling hacienda, La Posada de Tigua is a working farm-turned-guesthouse with an authentic feel and a warm host. While this place may sound a bit pricey for the region, it's worth it, and rates include a delicious breakfast and dinner. Cozy rooms of varying décor and layout make up the first floor of a large farmhouse, convening in a snug living room with a woodstove and old west feel.

The farm works to fuel the posada, providing fresh veggies, milk, yogurt and meats that the family transform into some tasty meals that would give your grandma a run for her money. Be sure to try the yogurt made on-site mixed with manjar de leche-an incredible caramel treat! Hosts are more than happy to show you the farm, send you off on horses, or even have a go at milking the cows or riding a llama. 15 minutes walk down from the highway, Tel: 281-4870/0991-612-391, E-mail: laposadadetigua@latinmail.com
Updated: Oct 31, 2012.

ZUMBAHUA

Located along the loop, about halfway between tiny Tigua and the Quilotoa crater, lies the sleepy town of Zumbahua. Sitting low and surrounded by mountain peaks and quilted hills, the town seems as if it has sprung up out of nowhere. Though you may be the only tourist around on any given weekday, the area is pleasant, with great hiking and stunning views, though the town itself offers very little to do.

On Saturdays Zumbahua springs to life, as locals from surrounding villages stream in with goods and livestock to sell at one of the most colorful and authentic markets in the area. The real highlight is watching the town transform early in the morning, as traditionally dressed families come parading by with llamas or goats. Though you probably won't find too much interesting stuff to buy while you're there, it's a lively scene and a photographer's delight.
Updated: Sep 11, 2012.

Getting To and Away from Zumbahua

There's frequent bus service between Zumbahua and **Latacunga**, and less frequent service from Zumbahua to **Quilotoa** and **Chugchilán**.

Note that most of the buses between Latacunga and Zumbahua are actually on their way to and from **Quevedo**, meaning that rather than stopping in the center of Zumbahua itself, they pass by on the highway just above the town. If you're heading to Zumbahua and get off the bus on the highway, look for the gas station and walk down the hill beside it, following the road downhill for about five minutes; when it forks, turn left, and you will reach the town center. To go from Zumbahua's plaza to the highway, walk up Calle Zumbahua Quilotoa, passing Hotel Oro and the tiny police station. Follow the road around to your right and all the way up the hill, until you're on the highway. Wait for the passing bus outside the little row of shops, opposite the public bathrooms.

Latacunga to Zumbahua (2 hr, $2): Depart hourly from Latacunga's bus terminal. Note that buses go via Zumbahua on their way to **Quevedo**, stopping on the hill above Zumbahua.

Zumbahua to **Latacunga** (2 hr, $2). Latacunga-bound buses from Quevedo stop on the hill above Zumbahua every hour. Additionally, the early-morning bus from **Chugchilán** to Latacunga stops in the center of Zumbahua at around 5.30 a.m., and the twice-daily bus from **Quilotoa** also stops in the center on its way to Latacunga at around 1.15/1.30 p.m. and 4.15/4.30 p.m.

Quilotoa to Zumbahua (20 min, $0.50): Buses leave daily at 1 p.m. and 4 p.m., or you can catch a ride in a passing truck for around $2-5.

Zumbahua to **Quilotoa/Chugchilán** (20 min/1 hr, 20 min): The Chugchilán-bound bus leaves Latacunga's bus terminal Monday to Saturday at 12 p.m., stopping in the center of Zumbahua at around 2 p.m., before heading to Quilotoa (arriving at 2.30 p.m.) and **Chucghilán** (arriving 3.30 p.m.). On Sunday, buses leave Latacunga at 7 a.m., 9 a.m. and 2 p.m., stopping in Zambahua at 9 a.m., 11 a.m. and 4 p.m. before heading on to Quilotoa and Chugchilán.

Alternatively, you can hire a private taxi from Zumbahua to **Quilotoa** for between $10-15, and to **Chugchilán** for around $30-35. Updated: Sep 11, 2012.

Zumbahua Services

There's no tourism office in Zumbahua (which, considering the town's lack of activities, isn't surprising) and no bank facilities, but there is an Internet café on the main square opposite the church that charges $0.80 an hour for internet; it also has several phone cabins (daily 9 a.m.-6/7 p.m. Ca. Zumbahua Quilotoa). If you need to stock up on medicines, visit the tiny pharmacy two doors down from the Hostal Condor Matzi (Monday to Saturday 8 a.m.-6 p.m., Sunday

8 a.m.-12 p.m. Ca. Angel Maria Umajinga, on the main plaza). For more serious health issues, there's also a medical clinic, Hospital Claudio Beneti(walk down Calle Zumbahua Quilotoa from the main plaza, and turn right; the hospital is 300 m/985 ft along the street). Updated: Sep 11, 2012.

Zumbahua Lodging

There are a handful of hostels around the central plaza. The standard is pretty basic but most offer a warm bed and hot water. As market day is Saturday, accommodation options tend to fill up fast at the weekend, especially on Friday evenings, so try and book ahead or turn up early. Beware that nights can be chilly-be sure there are plenty of blankets available when choosing a room. Updated: Sep 11, 2012.

Hostal Richard

($6 per person) Hostal Richard is a small but friendly family-run place on the corner of the square opposite the church. Two large dorm rooms, a double, and a triple share bathrooms and a kitchen. Ca. Zumbahua Quilotoa (on the main plaza opposite the church), Tel: 0987-949-364. Updated: Oct 31, 2012.

Hostal Condor Matzi

($8 per person) Though this hostel seems a little worn and tired, the top balcony offers great views for people-watching during the weekend market, and a generous supply of blankets is provided to ward off the chilly nights. Ask around at the corner store if you arrive and no one is there to let you in. Even if you aren't staying at Condor Matzi, for a dollar the hostel staff will let you store your backpack there while you wander around the market. Ca. Angel Maria Umajinga (on the right-hand side of the plaza, if facing towards the church). Updated: Sep 11, 2012.

Hotel Oro Verde

($7-10 per person) Above one of the village's most popular lunch spots is one of the larger hostels in Zambuhua, the Oro Verde. Staff are a little brusque and despite the attached restaurant breakfast isn't included in the price, but the rooms have a private bath and are pretty fair for a night or two. Ca. Zumbahua (just off the plaza, on the opposite side to the church), Tel: 280.2548/267-2095/0095-980-047, E-mail: hotelz_oroverde@hotmail.com. Updated: Oct 31, 2012.

Zumbahua Restaurants

You'll find a few very simple restaurants in Zumbahua, mostly around the main plaza. They serve typical meals (soup followed by rice, meat and potatoes) at very low prices. If you want super-fast (but perhaps a little questionable) food, there are a row of food stands on the plaza opposite the Hotel Condor Matzi.

Restaurante Oro Verde

(ENTREES: $2) The bottom floor of the Hotel Oro Verde is taken up by a spacious dining area that, come lunchtime, is buzzing with locals filling up on typical dishes and cheap almuerzos. It also offers breakfast. Daily 7 a.m.-8.30 p.m. Ca. Zumbahua Quiloatoa (just off the main plaza, opposite the church), Tel: 280-2548/267-2095/0995-980-047.

Restaurante Zumbahua

(ENTREES: $2) The petite Restaurante Zumbahua has friendly owners and opens early, convenient if you want a desayuno americano (eggs, bread, coffee and juice) before setting off on a morning hike. Lunch and merienda (supper) are also available. Daily 6 a.m.-6 p.m. Ca. Zumbahua Quiloatoa (next to the Hotel Oro Verde).

CHUGCHILÁN

 3,200m   n/a   03

Sitting high to the west between Sigchos and Quilotoa, tiny Chugchilán is a real Andean gem with friendly locals, stunning scenery, hikes into plummeting canyons, primary cloud forests, cheese factories and some of the homiest accommodations in Ecuador. Chugchilán should not be missed. Chugchilán landed on the map because of a few fantastic hostels, and its popularity as a base for exploring the area continues to rise.

Built into the mountainsides and overlooking the impressive Río Toachi canyon, the village is one of those places where people pass through and end up staying for days. There are excellent lodges in and around the town, each with its own warm touches and all offering hearty home-cooked meals, horseback riding trips, and hiking information. The town itself consists of a small square in front of a church, surrounded by a few simple houses, and little else. Hotel accommodation can be found by heading down the hill from the main square.

Getting To and Away from Chugchilán

Daily buses go around the Quilotoa Loop in both directions, beginning at **Latacunga** and ending in Chugchilán. These buses are operated by **Transporte Illiniza**, who have a stand in the Latacunga bus terminal. In Chugchilán, buses depart from the teeny-tiny bus station opposite the hotel Posada Blanquita.

Latacunga to Chugchilán via **Sigchos** (3.5 hr, $2.50): Buses depart Monday to Friday at 11.30 a.m., stopping in Saquisilí at around 12 p.m. and Sigchos around 2 p.m. Buses also run Saturday at 3 p.m. and Sunday at 11.30 a.m. and 12 p.m.

Latacunga to Chugchilán via **Quilotoa** (3.5 hr, $2.50). Buses depart Monday to Saturday at 12 p.m., stopping in Zumbahua at 2 p.m. and in Quilotoa at 2.30 p.m. On Sunday, buses run at 7 a.m., 9 a.m. and 2 p.m.

Chugchilán to **Latacunga** via **Sigchos** (3.5 hr, $2.50): Buses leave Chugchilán daily at 3 a.m. (note that buses sometimes leave as late as 4 a.m., but be there at 3 a.m. just in case), stopping in Sigchos around 4 a.m. and arriving in Latacunga at 6.30 a.m. You can also hop on the 9 a.m daily milk truck for $1 (ask at your hotel for information), which goes to Sigchos only; from there, you can take a bus onwards to Latacunga (see Sigchos to Latacunga for more information).

Chugchilán to **Latacunga** via **Quilotoa** (3.5 hr, $2.50): Buses leave Chugchilán daily at 4 a.m. (note that buses sometimes leave as late as 5 a.m., but be there at 4 a.m. just in case), stopping in Quilotoa at 5 a.m., **Zumbahua** at 5.30 a.m. and arriving in Latacunga at 7.30 a.m. On Wednesdays and Fridays, buses also leave **Chugchilán** at 6 a.m., stopping in Quilotoa at 7 a.m., Zumbahua at 7.30 a.m. and finally arriving in Latacunga at 9.30 a.m.

If you get stuck or aren't eager to brave the early mornings, you can hire a private pickup: ask at your hostel, or try Transportes de Caminetas (Tel: 091-037-363) by the bus station in Chugchilán.

A pickup to Quilotoa costs $25; to Sigchos $20; and to Latacunga $60 (prices are per-truck and are based on a maximum of five people; for each extra person, there is a $5 additional charge).
Updated: Sep 12, 2012.

CENTRAL ANDES

Chugchilán Services

Services are sparse in Chugchilán; there's no tourism office, bank or medical facilities.

KEEPING IN TOUCH

Surprisingly though, for such a tiny town, there are two Internet cafés: one is on the main road opposite the bus station, in the same building as the hotel Posada Blanquita; it also has phone booths and charges $1.50 an hour for Internet (daily 7.30 a.m.-6.30 p.m.). The other is the Info Centros (which, at first glance, seems like it may be a tourism office, but really isn't) where Internet is completely free. To find it, walk up the hill and past the plaza; it's located on the 2nd floor of the first building to your right (Monday to Friday 10 a.m.-1 p.m. and 1.30-6.30 p.m.). Updated: Sep 12, 2012.

SHOPPING

Artesanias Grupo de Mujeres Chugchilán

The organization runs a small shop filled with lovely hand-knit goods made by local women. The proceeds of sales benefit the community. To find it, face the church from the road, and you'll spy it on the right side of the church. The store is very often shut, so ask around and someone will come open it up for you.
Updated: Sep 13, 2012.

Things To See and Do in Chugchilán

Aside from relaxing in a hammock while admiring the mountain views, hiking is the number one thing to do here, and there are a variety of fantastic hikes. The walk from the Quilotoa crater to Chugchilán is undoubtedly one of the best short hikes in Ecuador (see Quilotoa Activities for more information).

Even if you're based in Chugchilán, you can take the bus or hire transport to Quilotoa in the morning, and hike back (it is possible to hike from Chugchilán to Quilotoa, but, as it's mostly uphill, it's longer, more challenging, and not as much fun). Another good hike is from Chugchilán to Isinliví, which passes through the small village of Guantualo and offers plenty of opportunities to admire the landscape.

Other hikes include a four-hour trip to the nearby Bosque Nublado (cloud forest) where you can visit a rural fabrica de quesos (cheese factory) and sample some local cheeses (also try the ice-cream!). A shorter, two to three-hour hike is to the Cañon del Toachi, a ca-

yon that was created some 1,800 years ago from the flow of heated gas and rock from the nearby Quilotoa volcanic crater lake.

Most hikes can be attempted solo, with some good instructions and ideally a map, but don't expect the route to be crystal clear. If you're worried about getting lost, or just prefer somebody else to take the lead, you can hire a local guide-ask at your hotel.

Alternatively, you can hire horses to take you on any of the above hikes. Whether hiking or horse-back riding, always pay attention to the notoriously quickly changing weather, and be sure to leave ample time to complete hikes well before afternoon rains and darkness falls.
Updated: Sep 12, 2012.

Horseback Riding

The landscape around Chugchilán is fascinatingly diverse, and great for exploring by horse. The relatively small region is home to the Paramo highlands, vast expanses of Andean farmland, the lowland riverbed of the Río Toachi, and both primary and secondary cloud forests. Within just a few hours, you can experience several dramatically different terrains and climate zones, visit a highland cheese factory and stick your toes into one of several nearby waterfalls. Rides costs between $15-25, including the guide. Either ask at your hostel, or, if you prefer to spread your money around the community a little more, find the tiny sign advertising horse-riding (on your left as you walk down the hill from the square, before you get to Mama Hilda), and follow the small path up to a one-storey house where horse-back riding guide Humberto Ortega lives. Humberto (Tel: 081-881-820/270-8078) runs a number of horse-riding tours, including down into the Quilotoa crater lake. He can accommodate from 1-20 people.
Updated: Sep 12, 2012.

Chugchilán Lodging

Chugchilán is tiny, so its excellent lodging options-easily the best in the whole Quilotoa Loop-come as a pleasant surprise. All offer home-cooked meals (generally included in the price), and can arrange horseback-riding tours, guides, and private transportation.
Updated: Sep 12, 2012.

The Black Sheep Inn Ecolodge !

(ROOMS: $35-80) This gorgeous mountain lodge, though only a brisk 15-minute walk from the village of Chugchilán, has rambling

CENTRAL ANDES

grounds, a remote feel and dazzling views. The lodge makes a strong effort to promote environmental awareness in the local community and with guests. Vegetarian meals, permaculture practices, compost bathrooms and more all work toward that goal.

The lodge doesn't skimp on comfort however, and rooms (which have private or shared bath) are cozy and warmed by wood-stoves, and facilities include a sauna and hot tub, yoga studio, decks with hammocks, a tree house, and even WiFi. For those on a lower budget, there's a bunkhouse-style dormitory which sleeps 10. The lodge staff are helpful and can happily help you plan your day's activities, and arrange for transportation, guides and horseback rides. Rates include breakfast, lunch, dinner and hot drinks. Note that the Black Sheep Inn requires a minimum two-night stay.

Chugchilán-Sigchos Road: If you're coming on the Latacunga-Chugchilán bus via Sigchos, tell the driver you want to be dropped off at the entrance to the Black Sheep Inn (La Oveja Negra). If you're coming from Chugchilán, walk down the hill for 10 minutes and you will see the sign for the hostel on your left.At the entrance, its a steep 5-minute walk up to the lodge. Tel: 281-4587/270-8077, E-mail: info@blacksheepinn.com, URL: www.blacksheepinn.com. Updated: Sep 12, 2012.

Hostal Cloud Forest !

($12-15 per person) The cheapest of Chugchilán's hotel options, but comparable in quality, the Hostal Cloud Forest is well-run and great value. Its cozy and inviting atmosphere is comforting amid the freezing and unforgiving Andean air. The owners and staff are extremely friendly and attentive; they definitely like to keep their guests happy and warm! Rooms (some are a bit small-you can pay a few dollars more for a bigger room) have private baths and thick blankets, and open on to spacious balconies with hammocks.

There is a communal area with ample seating, a fireplace, pool table, ping-pong table, and two computer terminals with Internet ($1 a go). Excellent meals are served in a blessedly-warm communal dining area (vegetarians are very well-catered for). If you fancy spending a little longer in Chugchilán, the Hostal Cloud Forest will give you free room and board in return for teaching English or computer skills at the local school

(minimum three month stay). Just down the hill, on the left, past Mama Hilda's as you head out of town., Tel: 270-8181/270-8016/0989-545-634, E-mail: josecloudoforest@gmail.com. Updated: Oct 31, 2012.

Hostal Mama Hilda

($16-36 per person) A lovely complex of clean and cozy rooms with spectacular views and the warmest of hosts, you're sure to be taken care of and then some at Mama Hilda's. Running the place is a full-out family affair with hearty group meals in a homey dining room, and Mama herself seemingly everywhere at once, ensuring that everything is up to par. Vegetarians are well-catered for. Comfy brick-walled rooms, some with wood-stoves and private bath, all share decks with colorful hammocks that look out over Mama's flower garden and sunny terraces, as well as the green patchwork hills beyond. The owners will happily arrange horseback tours, hikes and private transport. The hostal is located on the left as you start walking down the hill from the center of town. Tel: 270-8005, E-mail: reservations@mamahilda.com, URL: www.mamahilda.com. Updated: Sep 12, 2012.

Posada Blanquita

($12-15 per person) Posada Blanquita is a relatively new addition to Chugchilán's smattering of hotel options. You'll find it in a pleasant, airy building opposite the bus terminal. The hotel's restaurant takes up the first floor; head upstairs (don't be put off by the scruffy back courtyard) and you'll find spacious and sparkling clean quarters which comprise a communal living room with TV and a handful of dorm and private rooms, all with balconies overlooking the street below as well. Dinner is included in the rate, but breakfast is extra. While Posada Blanquita is a perfectly decent option, it doesn't have the extra facilities, space and charm of the other Chugchilán hotels, and rooms aren't any more competitively priced. A good choice if the other hostels are full. Opposite the bus terminal, Tel: 270-8006/0987-721-656/0997-272-358, E-mail: gblanquita@gmail.com / lourdesguamangate@yahoo.ec, URL: www.posadablanquita.com. Updated: Oct 31, 2012.

Chugchilán Restaurants
There are no restaurants in Chugchilán. Instead, travelers eat at their respective hotels, which offer meal plans that include dinner and breakfast. For lunch, or if you're

CENTRAL ANDES

just passing through, head to either Posada Blanquita (opposite the bus station) or the Hostal Cloud Forest; both can provide lunch for non-guests.

If you need something to keep you going until dinner-time, there are a couple of dusty tiendas on the main road that sell water, snacks and drinks. At night, a couple of street stalls by the main square dish out simple plates of rice and meat.
Updated: Sep 12, 2012.

ISINLIVÍ

 2,900m n/a 03

This tiny village is just off the Quilotoa Loop southeast of Sigchos. The town is only really on the map due to the fantastic Hostal Llullu Llama. There's not much else here-a small woodshop and a handicraft store are worth a quick visit-but the area is stunning and makes for a good hiking destination or base despite its barren nature. Hikes to or from Isinliví from Sigchos or Chugchilán are particularly popular among visitors.
Updated: Sep 13, 2012.

Getting To and Away from Isinliví

Daily buses run between **Latacunga** and Isinliví:

Latacunga to Isinliví: (2.5-3 hr, $3). From Latacunga's bus terminal, buses depart at 12.15 p.m. and 1 p.m. (on Saturday, buses leave at 11.15 a.m. instead of 12.15 p.m.). On Thursdays, there are no buses from Latacunga; instead, they leave from the market town of **Saquisilí** at 11 a.m. and 12 p.m. (buses to Saquisilí leave Latacunga every 15 minutes).

From Isinliví to **Latacunga** (2.5-3 hr, $3): Buses make the return journey to Latacunga bright and early at 3 a.m. on Tuesdays, Thursdays, Fridays and Saturdays. On Wednesdays the bus leaves at 7 a.m., on Sundays at 12.45 p.m. and Mondays at 3 p.m.

There are also daily buses between **Sigchos** and Isinliví (45 min, $0.75) but times vary; ask around for exact departure times. You can hire a pick-up truck to take you from **Sigchos** to Isinliví for $10. A private pick-up truck between Latacunga and Isinliví costs $60.
Updated: Sep 13, 2012.

Isinliví Lodging

Apart from the famed Hostal Llullu Lama, there are few lodging choices in Isinliví, and, as options are limited, rates tend to be fairly high. You may be able to find a local family offering you a room in their home; be sure to negotiate the price in advance.
Updated: Sep 13, 2012.

Hostal Llullu Llama   ❗

($18-25 per person) Once a traditional farmhouse, Hostel Llullu Lama is now a beautiful mountain lodge. Due to its location, the hostel is a prime spot to start hikes and treks. Pick up free hiking maps or organize a multiday tour. Head out to nearby indigenous markets and communities, check out hidden valley trails or just enjoy the local flora and fauna, including orchids and hummingbirds. The hostel is known for its scrumptious food, and prepares hearty three-course meals, including a substantial breakfast to start the day (both breakfast and dinner are included in room rates), and There are dorm rooms and more expensive private rooms. The hot showers and wood stove are the perfect way to warm up and get rid of that Andean chill. Isinliví, Cotopaxi Province, Tel: 281-4790/0985-737-829, E-mail: info@llullullama.com, URL: www.llullullama.com.
Updated: Oct 31, 2012.

SIGCHOS

 2,800m n/a 03

Aside from catching an onward bus or visiting the small Sunday market, there's really not much to see or do in the dusty town of Sigchos. People are friendly and there is very basic accommodation if you need somewhere to stay the night, but, with Isinliví and Chugchilán's fantastic lodging options both less than 25 kilometers (15.5 mi) away, it's hard not to simply pass through Sigchos en route.
Updated: Sep 06, 2012.

Getting To and Away from Sigchos

In comparison with some of the other towns around the Quilotoa Loop, Sigchos has fairly frequent bus transport:

Latacunga to Sigchos (2.5 hr): Buses depart from Latacunga's main bus terminal Monday-Friday at 9.30 a.m., 10.30 a.m., 11.30 a.m., 12 p.m. and 1 p.m. (on Tuesday,

Thursday and Friday there is an additional service at 3 p.m.). Saturday and Sunday, buses leave at 9.30 a.m. and 5 p.m.

Sigchos to **Latacunga** (2.5 hr): Daily buses leave Sigchos' plaza at 4 a.m., 7 a.m., 2.30 p.m. and 4 p.m.; on Sundays they run every hour from 9 a.m. Note that the 4 a.m. bus is the bus from **Chugchilán**, so it may reach Sigchos later (sometimes even as late as 5 a.m.) than planned.

Sigchos to **Chugchilán** (1 hr): Monday to Friday, the bus from **Latacunga** passes through Sigchos on its way to Chugchilán around 2 p.m. On Saturdays, it stops in Sigchos at around 5.30 p.m. and Sundays at 2 p.m. and 2.30 p.m.

Chugchilán to Sigchos (1 hr): Buses leave Chugchilán daily at 3 a.m. (this can sometimes be as late as 4 a.m., but be there at 3 a.m. just in case), stopping in Sigchos at 4 a.m. If you want a little extra sleep, you can hop on the daily milk truck ($1 per person) which leaves Chugchilán around 9 a.m. daily. There are daily buses to and from **Isinliví**, but times change so ask around for exact departure times. If you're in a hurry, you can hire a private pick-up truck to take you to Isiniliví for $10.
Updated: Sep 13, 2012.

Sigchos Services

There are very limited services in Sigchos. There's a bank on Calle Guayaquil (one block up the hill from the plaza), but it has no ATM, so be sure to bring sufficient cash with you. Internet café Cybernet has computers and phone cabins (corner of the plaza, Ca. Carlos H Paeza and Guayaquil).
Updated: Sep 13, 2012.

Sigchos Lodging

As in much of the Quilotoa Loop, Sigchos hostels are simple and threadbare. They are cheap, though, and provide all the basic necessities.

Hostal Jardín de los Andes

($7 per person) A large colorful sign hanging above the corner store near the center of town marks Hostal Jardín de los Andes (formerly called Residencial Tourismo). This is about the only shop in town and probably your best bet for sleeping and eating if you decide to stay overnight in Sigchos. The large building caters to groups passing through and can house 30-40 guests in simple but clean rooms, some with a private bath.

Meals are also available and the owner and shop runner Yolanda will take care of you with a smile. Corner of Ca. Tungurahua and Ca. Ilinizas, Tel: 03-271-4114, Cel: 09-9287-7968, E-mail: rapaugoee@hotmail.com.
Updated: Feb 06, 2013.

Hostal Tungurahua

($5 per person) This three-story house offers very basic rooms for $5 a night. Let them know in advance if you'd like meals during your stay, and they'll make arrangements. Calle Tungurahua.
Updated: July 7, 2013.

SINCHOLAGUA VOLCANO

Sincholagua is an inactive volcano located 45 km (28 miles) southeast of Quito and about 15 km (9 miles) northeast of Cotopaxi Volcano. The mountain is less frequently climbed than any of others listed here, for the simple reason that it's difficult to access. Nevertheless, those who make the effort to get to Sincholagua will be well rewarded with a beautiful hike and spectacular views of Cotopaxi, Rumiñahui, and Pasochoa.

Getting To and Away from Sincholagua

Drive one hour south on the Pan American Highway to the town of Machachi. Go to the main plaza in Machachi and then turn right just after you pass the plaza's northeast corner. This road will take you through town to a cobblestone road that continues on into the countryside. About five minutes outside of town, the road dips down into a river valley and then winds up for approximately one hour through a number of small villages and past the Guitig factory on the left. Stay on the main road; there a number of secondary roads that can be hard to distinguish from the principal one. You will eventually come to a "T". Go right for about another 10 minutes until you reach the north entrance to Cotopaxi National Park.

Even though Sincholagua resides outside of the National Park's boundaries, rangers will likely charge you a fee of either $2 or $10 (depending on whether you are a resident or foreign visitor) per person to drive through the Park.

Immediately after the ranger station, take a left on the dirt road and follow it east and south for 10 to 15 minutes. When you start driving downhill, to your right you will see a collection of small white buildings at the bottom of a gulley. Take the switchback left and then right to get down to these buildings. There is a gate but it is generally not locked. Continue on about 500 meters past the building to a well constructed concrete bridge spanning the Río Pita. If the gate is open, drive across the bridge and park along side the dirt road. If it's closed, park in the grassy area adjacent to the bridge and continue on foot.

Things To See and Do at Sincholagua
Hiking Sincholagua

Once you have crossed the bridge, follow the vehicle tracks northeast up the ridge through a series of pine groves and meadows. After about one and a half hours of steady walking, you will find a concrete survey marker from where you should be able to see a clear approach along a rocky ridge to the mountain. Make your way across this ridge and then traverse the right side until you reach the barren base of the mountain. From here, traverse left and up the northwest face. You will drop down into a basin and then climb up to a saddle below the summit. The final ascent and the summit itself are exposed and require good scrambling skills.

For rock enthusiasts, a great nearby climb is Pico Hoeneisen, which is the prominent peak below Sincholagua. Hoeneisen should only be done by experienced climbers with technical gear. Updated: Apr 12, 2013.

ilinizas

ILINIZA VOLCANOES

The twin peaks of Iliniza Norte (elevation: 5,126 m, 16,817 ft) and Sur (elevation: 5,248 m, 17,220 ft) are in sharp contrast to the Páramo 55 km (34 miles) south of Quito. Today the two mountains are connected by a one-kilometer long saddle, but in prehistoric times, they were one solid volcano.

Though similar in height they vary greatly in technical difficulty. Norte requires no technical skills or equipment (unless there has been considerable snowfall, in which case you may want rope and even crampons). On the other hand, Iliniza Sur is one of Ecuador's more technical climbs and should only be attempted by experienced climbers.

Getting To and Away from the Ilinizas

To reach the Ilinizas, drive south on the Pan American Highway and turn right (west) eight kilometers after Machachi onto a cobblestone and dirt road that leads to the community of El Chaupi. Go seven kilometers on this road until you reach El Chaupi's main plaza. Go right out of the plaza on a road to the right of the church. Travel three kilometers up this road and make a left turn. Continue on until you reach a series of switchbacks that take you up a hill to a parking area marked by a shrine to the Virgin Mary.

From the parking area, follow a dirt road that leads to a well trodden trail. Follow the trail as it winds upwards to a steep ridge, and then climb the ridge until you reach a simple refuge made of cement blocks. On a clear day, you will see Iliniza Norte to the northwest and Iliniza Sur to the southwest. Updated: Apr 12, 2013.

Things To See and Do at the Ilinizas
Hiking Iliniza Norte

To climb Norte, walk approximately 45 minutes up the left side of the southeast ridge. You will be on a slope of sandy scree and loose rock until you reach a ridge of solid rock. Follow this ridge of solid rock to a false summit at 5,060 meters, and then traverse right across a number of sandy ledges, including one called the Paso de Muerte, or "death pass." These can be intimidating to inexperienced climbers, especially when they are covered with snow. Continue on until you reach a gully. Ten minutes more of scrambling up loose rock will lead you to the true summit marked by an iron cross.

The danger of falling rock during the last part of the climb should not be understated; wearing a helmet is always a good idea. It takes between two and three hours to reach the summit from the refuge, and the total climbing time to the summit and back to the shrine is approximately eight hours. Updated: Apr 12, 2013.

Climbing Iliniza Sur

This relatively steep and crevassed mountain is one of the more difficult climbs in the country and is not for beginners. The Normal Route is currently the most frequently climbed route to the summit. The Direct or Ramp Route is no longer climbed due to disappearance of the glacial ice and increased danger from rockfall. Front pointing may be necessary on the Normal Route. This is a tiring technique, particularly at over 5,000 meters (16,400 ft), and should be learned and practiced at lower elevations if possible (in the Alps or the Rockies for example).

It is best to bring an assortment of ice screws, flukes and snow stakes. Rockfall can be hazardous and a helmet is recommended. Avalanches occur often enough to pose a danger and a detailed route description is difficult due to de-glaciation from global climate change.

It is possible in the next decade that this peak may lose most of its glaciers. For more information on this route, consult Ecuador: Climbing and Hiking Guide. Updated: Apr 12, 2013.

EL CORAZÓN

El Corazón is yet another eroded and extinct volcano located about 40 kilometers (25 mi) southwest of Quito. The route is straightforward and requires no rock climbing equipment or experience. The first recorded ascent was in 1738 by La Condamine and Bouguer, and this easy peak has been climbed many times since. Pre-conquest ruins have been reported on the northeast slopes, but they are very overgrown and have yet to be investigated.

The name El Corazón means "heart" in Spanish and is said to refer to two gullies on the northwest slopes which, when seen from a distance, appear to join together in the shape of a heart. For more information on this route, consult Ecuador: Climbing and Hiking Guide.

COTOPAXI NATIONAL PARK

An hour and a half south of Quito, along the Avenue of the Volcanoes, is the dominant image on the Ecuadorian national psyche: the perfectly conical Cotopaxi volcano (altitude 5,897 m / 19,350 ft), one of the world's highest active volcanoes and a mecca for mountain climbers. The volcano lies within Parque Nacional Cotopaxi, a 33,393-hectare (82,515-ac) national park created in 1975 to protect the fragile wet forest and páramo habitat of the endangered Andean condor and spectacled bear. It is the most popular of Ecuador's reserves.

The national park has two types of mountain ecosystems: cloud forest, or montane forest, up to the timberline (3,600-3,000 m / 11,808-12,464 ft) and páramo (4,000-4,500 m / 13,120-14,760 ft). Andean blueberries, lupine, bromeliads, mountain roses and other flora cover the landscape. Fauna species entail 17 mammals, including puma, white-tailed deer, weasel, an endemic marsupial mouse and wild horses; and almost 100 species of birds, including Andean gull, shrike-tyrants, brush finches and snipes.

Cotopaxi last erupted in 1942. The volcano is monitored by Ecuador's Instituto Geofísico (URL:www.igepn.edu.ec). Besides Cotopaxi, the park is also home to other mountains and volcanoes: Rumiñahui (with three peaks: 4,722 m / 15,488 ft, 4,631 m / 15,190 ft and 4,696 m / 15,403 ft), Morurco (4,849 / 15,905 ft) and Chiguilasin Chico (4,876 m / 15,993 ft). Just northeast of the park boundary is Sincholagua (4,873 m / 15,983 ft), which also can be summited. Volcán Cotopaxi's glaciers feed the Guayllabamba, Cutuchi and Daule rivers, which flow to the Pacific Ocean, and the Río Napo, which flows towards the Amazon.

Parque Nacional Cotopaxi may beaccessed at three entrances: the northern (called Pedregal), near Machachi; El Boliche, where the train arrives; and the main entrance (Caspi), six kilometers (3.6 mi) north of Lasso. The roads from the latter two meet and head to the southern ranger station. About five to six kilometers (3-3.6 mi) beyond the main station is Estación Mariscal Sucre, a complex that has a restaurant, lodging, a small museum displaying the park's flora and fauna, and a self-guided hiking trail. The climber's refuge is another 15 kilometers (9 mi) uphill.

The national park offers a wide variety of outdoor activities, including climbing Cotopaxi and other mountains, hiking, horseback riding and mountain biking. Laguna Limpiopungo, which lays midways between the two ranger stations, just west of the turn-off for Volcán Cotopaxi, provides excellent birdwatching and vistas of the various volcanoes. Several pre-Columbian ruins scatter the park, the most impressive of which is the Inca fortress, El Salitre (Entry: $5).

If spending the night under Cotopaxi's starry skies, you have a choice of lodging options: camping, refuges and a variety of inns, from hostels to haciendas.

The national park service of the Ministerio del Ambiente publishes a downloadable interpretive guide (in Spanish) about Parque Nacional Cotopaxi (URL:www.ambiente.gob.ec/wp-content/uploads/downloads/2012/07/Parque-Nacional-Cotopaxi.pdf). For more details about hiking and climbing in Parque Nacional Cotopaxi, check out Ecuador Climbing and Hiking Guide (in English).

No entry fee into the park is now charged, although one must still pay for camping, refuges and other services. You may entire the park 365 days of the year, between 8 a.m. and 3 p.m. Cell phone reception is difficult to nonexistent in this area.
Updated: Oct 26, 2012.

When To Go to Cotopaxi National Park

The park has a damp climate with warm days and cold nights. Daytime temperatures reach 18-20°C (64-68°F), and at night can drop to freezing. Temperatures are colder at higher altitude. Rain, sleet and hail, accompanied by strong winds, are also likely. The drier months are June-July (but winds can be strong, especially on the volcanoes) and December-February (when winds are calmer). The park receives 500-1500 millimeters (20-60 in) of precipitation per year.

As this is Ecuador's most popular park, it receives thousands of visitors at holiday times and on weekends. To lessen your impact on the reserve's environment, go at the low times.
Updated: Oct 25, 2012.

Safety

Campers, hikers and other visitors should be prepared: warm clothing that is wind and rain resistant; and water and high energy snacks.

Hypothermia and altitude sickness are serious concerns. Be sure to acclimatize properly before attempting any physically demanding sport. For further information, see Health in Ecuador. Avalanches and falling into a crevasse are additional safety hazards in the park.

Potable water is available at only a few of the campsites and refuges. Any other water should be treated by filter or boiling. Purification drops are less effective when water is cold.
Updated: Oct 25, 2012.

Getting To and Away from Cotopaxi National Park

Parque Nacional Cotopaxi has three access points: Lasso, El Boliche and Machachi. The roads between the entry stations are being paved. Many lodges have and offer private transport service.

Lasso Entrance

The main entrance to Cotopaxi National Park, Caspi, is just a few kilometers before the town of Lasso. From Quito, drive south on the Pan-American Highway for approximately two hours, until you see a large sign: Parque Nacional Cotopaxi. Turn left (east) at the sign, immediately cross a set of railroad tracks, and follow a dirt road east for 15 kilometers (9 mi) until you get to the park's main entrance. The route is well-marked.

If you don't have your own car, buses run regularly along the Pan-American Highway from Quito. Ask to be let off at the entrance and walk or hitchhike (easier on weekends) to the entrance. Often times there are taxis waiting at the park entrance turn-off. It costs about $10 to hire a taxi to take you to the museum, but many hikers opt to hire a ride to the Laguna Limpiopungo. This is about a 15-kilometer (9-mi) trip from the Pan-American Highway.
Updated: Oct 25, 2012.

El Boliche Entrance

El Boliche is about 1.5 hours south of Quito and is also the turn-off to the Clirsen NASA minitrak station. The road, which may be closed to vehicles but accessible to hikers and mountain bikers, is marked with a huge sign and the tracking equipment is plainly visible from below. Take a bus as far as the turn-off from the Pan-American Highway.

The road is asphalted for the first two kilometers (1.2 mi); after the old tracking station, it is gravel. There are signs most of the way, but stay right following the railroad tracks for 0.5 kilometer (0.3 mi). You pass the railway station, cross the tracks and continue to the Río Daule campsite, which is about seven kilometers (4.2 mi) beyond the tracking station.

Alternately, take the train, the Ruta Páramo Infinito, which arrives at Área Nacional de Recreación el Boliche, near Parque Nacional Cotapaxi. (See the site of the national railways for more information:www.ferrocarrilesdelecuador.gob.ec.) Ecuadorians have the curious habit of riding on the roof of trains and a small rail is set up around the edge of the bus-looking train to keep passengers from flying off.

From the train depot, the dirt road continues climbing gradually. One to two kilometers (about 1 mi) beyond Río Daule, it passes a hairpin bend with a stable and a thatched hut. After a further one to two kilometers, take an unmarked left-hand turn (look for herds of llamas; the animals are being studied in the area) down the main road to the park entrance station. Just before the station, you'll meet up with the road from the Lasso entrance.

Machachi Entrance

The third entry point into the park is south of Machachi. This is the closest turn-off from Quito, favored by those with private vehicles and better for bicyclists, but involves a rougher road to the less-used North Entrance Station, Pedregal. You can take a bus to Machachi and hire a camioneta (pick-up truck) to the refuge for about $35.

The route follows a cobble road to the left out of the main plaza in Machachi and climbs around the north side of Rumiñahui. The road first drops down to a river valley 3 kilometers (1.8 mi) from the plaza, then follow signs another 12 kilometers (7.2 mi) to Hacienda El Porvenir (Volcano Land).

Continue another four kilometers (2.4 mi) to the North Entrance Station. From here head south first passing by Tambopaxi, and eventually arrive at the turn-off to the climber's refuge.

Things To See and Do at Cotopaxi National Park

Cotopaxi is Ecuador's most popular national park for a reason: It offers a bit of something for everyone, whether they are looking to take a vacation or just escape from the city for the weekend. Adventure enthusiasts can summit Cotopaxi, Rumiñahui and other volcanoes, do multi-day hikes, mountain bike through the area or take it easy and horseback ride. If you are not one to undertake rigorous outdoor activities, you can check out the museum and stroll the nearby interpretive trail, visit the archaeological ruins and birdwatch at Laguna Limpiopungo. Updated: Oct 25, 2012.

Summiting Cotopaxi

Even novice climbers can summit the glacier-topped peak with the help of a good guide, glacier climbing equipment and a hardy jacket. The views from the top on a clear day are incredible, providing dreamy views of the mountainous Andean landscape for hundreds of kilometers in every direction.

Even so, it's a physically demanding climb (if not technically demanding), depending on snowfall and current glacier conditions. Proper acclimatization, good fitness and training are essential. A week in Quito or any other Andean town with ample walking and summiting of a lesser peak or two should be sufficient.

Though the route has changed over the years due to recession and shifting of the glacier brought about by global climate change, you generally head up the right (east) side of the volcano's north face to the huge rock wall called Yanasacha, and then the route cuts back left (west), traversing a steep slope to the summit.

The ascent along this route, which is usually well-marked by footprints and wands, takes between five and seven hours, and the descent approximately half that time. If there is any doubt about your pace and climbing time, start earlier rather than later, as the snow becomes sticky and difficult to traverse soon after sunrise. Climbers usually stay at the José Ribas refuge and depart from there 11 p.m.-midnight.

CENTRAL ANDES

CENTRAL ANDES

Another, less frequent route is on Cotopaxi's southern slope. It's lower popularity comes from the fact that this route is usually tougher to navigate.

Cotopaxi may be climbed any time of the year, though June-July tends to be windy and December-February has calmer winds. Though not very technical by mountaineering standards, Cotopaxi is not without its dangers. Along the lower section of the mountain you will encounter a number of large crevasses spanned by ice bridges and, just after Yanasacha, you must climb a short but steep, nearly vertical, wall of ice and snow in order to access the final stretch of glacier leading up to the crater. This last part is quite possibly the hairiest moment of all.

Climbing tours of Volcán Cotopaxi can be booked with a number of agencies in Quito. Additionally, several of the hotels and haciendas in the national park also offer these expeditions.

Note that, in certain scenarios, it may not be possible to make it all the way to the top, typically due to weather but also sometimes because of a weak member of the group. Updated: Oct 25, 2012.

Hiking To Cotopaxi's Refuge

Cotopaxi's main refuge, Refugio José Ribas, is popular destination not only for those willing to take on the challenge of reaching the top of the volcano, but also for day trippers who want to get closer to the mountain and touch the snowline. Guided hiking tours to the refuge can be booked through the park's hotels.

From the main park entrance, follow the road for about 20 kilometers (12 mi) to a parking area below the refuge. The Park Service has placed signs at most of the key intersections and, unless it's foggy, you will see Cotopaxi and the road leading up to it on your right.

From the parking area, situated at 4,500 meters (14,760 ft), it is a steep, one-hour climb to the refuge (4,800 m / 15,648 ft). If you intend to climb to the peak, it's wise to settle into the refuge by mid-afternoon as you will have to leave the comfort of your sleeping bag between 11 p.m. and 2 a.m.

Guided tours (when booked through a park hotel) can cost anywhere from $30-80. Updated: Oct 25, 2012.

Other Hikes Around Cotopaxi

Besides the hiking up to and around Refugio José Ribas, visitors to Parque Nacional Cotopaxi have several other treks they may undertake to discover the natural beauty, fauna and fauna of this landscape.

Volcán Rumiñahui – From the campground between Estación Mariscal Sucre and Laguna Limpiopungo, you can access a trail that goes to Volcán Rumiñahui. This spectacular walk takes 6-8 hours round trip.

In reality, walking most any path through the páramo from either the campgrounds or Lago Limpiopungo, towards the ridge to the right of the southernmost peak of Rumiñahui, will lead you to the peak.

Vuelta al Cotopaxi – This is a moderate, six to seven-day trek around the base of Volcán Cotopaxi. The 75-kilometer (46-mi) circuit, which begins at the Lasso entrance and ends at Mulaló, is best done June-January.

Trek of the Cóndor – Considered one of the best treks in Ecuador, this challenging, 60-kilometer (36-mi) hike begins at El Tambo, near Papallacta, and ends at Laguna Limpiopungo in Parque Nacional Cotopaxi. The three- to five-day expedition goes past Antisana and Sincholagua volcanoes, through cloud forest and across páramo.

For complete details on these and other treks, see Ecuador Climbing and Hiking Guide. Updated: Oct 25, 2012.

Mountain Biking

Mountain biking in Cotopaxi is a spectacular once-in-a-lifetime experience. The biking routes begin at the parking lot near Refugio José Ribas, at 4,600 meters (15,088 ft) altitude, and head along the main roads northward and westward, towards the park entrances. You descend, cutting through the thin air at bone-chilling speed. Most of the park is, ironically, very flat due to historical eruptions that caused the glacier to melt and form lake beds around the volcano. This is all good news, since riding uphill at this altitude, you could bust a lung – or two.

All of the tourist routes are day rides. Some of the park's hotels loan bicycles to their guests for free or a charge; a guided tour costs extra. In November is the 140-kilometer (86-mi) Vuelta al Cotopaxi (www.cotopaxi.cikla. net), an internationally renowned mountain,

two-day bike race around the base of Volcán Cotopaxi. Stay on the approved routes; do not cut cross country, as this can damage the delicate environment. Because you will be sharing the roads with vehicular traffic, keep an eye out for cars and buses..
Updated: Oct 25, 2012.

Horseback Riding

Another great way to see the park is on horseback. Many of the routes, which for the most part are the same as those for trekking, present opportunities to spot domesticated llamas, wild horses, raptors, Andean gulls, deer and other wildlife, as well as to see the geologic and archaeological riches of the park. The tours are offered by the park's hotels. Lodges outside the reserve have excursions lasting eight to 10 hours. Some also allow tourists to learn about the chagra – or Ecuadorian cowboy – way of life.

Contact the park hotels for details and to arrange excursions (which usually must be done with at least 24-hour notice), they charge about $10 per hour, or $30-160 for a guided excursion. Because of the terrain, it is recommended that riders have an intermediate skill level. Daytrippers may arrange excursions ahead of time, if they will not be overnighting in the park.
Updated: Oct 25, 2012.

Cotopaxi National Park Tours

Tour operators in Quito and other cities offer packages to Parque Nacional Cotopaxi. Most climbing expeditions are also arranged through these agencies. Lodges within and outside the park also offer a variety of tours, including climbing, hiking, mountain biking and horseback riding. These are not only for their guests, but also for people only spending the day in the reserve (reservations must be made in advance). All guides must be licensed, follow the environmental protection norms of the park and be in good physical condition (including not drunk or hung over).
Updated: Oct 25, 2012.

Cotopaxi National Park Lodging

Cotopaxi National Park hostels and hotels are generally good value for money with many offering combined accommodation, meal and excursion packages. For those with a bit more money to spend, staying at a hacienda is definitely the way to go. The atmosphere at these is generally homely, authentic and in many, luxurious. Another option for visitors to Parque Nacional Cotopaxi is camping. Budget travelers, groups and families may choose from official campsites with the accompanying facilities and spectacular views of the park. Several of the park's lodges also offer camping. Those summiting Cotopaxi may stay at one of the refuges. The albergues are open to all visitors.
Updated: Oct 25, 2012.

Camping In Parque Nacional Cotopaxi

Travelers on a budget or those wanting a more intimate relationship with nature have several choices of camping at Parque Nacional Cotopaxi. Be sure to have a wind and rain-resistant tent, good sleeping bag and thermal sleeping mat, as well as a cook stove that is fitted for high altitude. Within the park, campfires are ONLY allowed in campsites and picnic areas.

Near the El Boliche train depot, on the other side of the railroad tracks, is the Río Daule campsite (free). It has plenty of flat tent spaces, two small picnic shelters (unsuitable for sleeping in) and fireplaces. Drinking water is available from the river about 0.5 kilometers (0.3 mi) past the campground, beyond a bend in the road. This is a good place to spend your first night. The dirt road continues climbing gradually and one to two kilometers beyond Río Daule, it passes a hairpin bend with a camp by it; there is a stable and a thatched hut, but no water.

The national park service provides several designated campgrounds inside the park. One zone is past the Estación Mariscal Sucre, about 0.5 kilometers (0.3 mi) before the Plains of Limpiopungo, on the left side. The site has two latrines. A second campground is at the crossroads to Laguna Limpiopungo. A third camping area is at Laguna de Santo Domingo, northeast of Cotopaxi volcano. All three of these campgrounds cost $3 for Ecuadorians and $5 for foreigners. No camping is allowed around Laguna Limpiopungo.

Trekkers doing the Vuelta al Cotopaxi, Trek of the Cóndor or other hikes may wild camp. Be sure to take precautions to not damage the fragile páramo environment.

Several of the lodges in Parque Nacional Cotopaxi have campgrounds available for a relatively cheap price, such as: Tambopaxi, Hacienda El Porvenir, Hacienda Santa Rita and Cuello de Luna.
Updated: Oct 25, 2012.

Cotopaxi Refuges

Within Parque Nacional Cotopaxi are three refuges that offer dorm-style lodging for $20-25 a night. The two on the flanks of Volcán Cotopaxi are limited only to those who will be climbing the volcano. You should bring your own sleeping bag.

Albergue Paja Blanca – Located that the Estación Mariscal Sucre complex (3,600 m / 11,808 ft), this refuge has two cabins, with capacity for 20 persons total. It has a common bath with one hot-water shower.

Refugio José Ribas – This mountain refuge on the northern slope (4,850 m / 15,912 ft) of Volcán Cotopaxi is the most-used facility in the park. Restricted to those who will summit the volcano, the Alpes-styled hut has room for 60 people. The first floor has two dining halls and equipped kitchens. On the second story are the dorm-style accommodations and bathrooms. The hut has electricity only for two hours at night. Do not expect to have a quality sleep due to noise from other climbers and the high elevation. Most alpinists wake at 11 p.m. to start their trek up the mountain. Refugio Ribas is also exceptionally damp and cold, so a good sleeping bag is necessary. Lockers provide reasonable security for your gear, but be sure to bring your own padlock. The refuge is a 30 minute high elevation walk from the top parking lot.

Refugio Cara Sur – This refuge, perched on the south face of Volcán Cotopaxi, has two parts, depending on the type of activity the tourist will do. At 4,000 meters (13,120 ft) is Albergue Cotopaxi Cara Sur: two cabins with rooms for two, three and five persons (total capacity: 10), that have bathrooms, common room with fireplace and restaurant. Cara Sur's second refuge, Campamento Alto (4,780 m / 15,679 ft) is a three-hour climb above the albergue. This refuge provides large tents for climbers attempting the mountain from this side. To reach this refuge, enter the park at the Lasso entrance off the Pan-American Highway, and travel to the community of Ticatilín; from there it is a three-hour walk to the albergue.
Updated: Oct 25, 2012.

Hacienda El Porvenir (Volcano Land)

(CAMPING: $5, ROOMS: $35-139 per person) Hacienda El Porvenir (a.k.a. Volcano Land), an old hacienda set on a 1,000 hectare (2,471-ac) spread in the foothills of Volcán Rumiñahui, offers lodging for all bud-

gets. Suites have magnificent views, sitting room, fireplace and private bath. Traditional hacienda rooms have heating and private bath. Machai rooms, set up in typical Quichua fashion, have thatched roofs and woven-reed walls, and share four bathrooms. The campground has bathhouses and hut.

The hacienda also presents a dining hall and five living rooms, all with fireplaces, restaurant, bar and shop. El Porvenir is still a working farm, and guests can roll up their sleeves with the chores when not taking one of the lodge's many tour offerings. The hacienda supports local projects and takes volunteers. 21 kilometers (13 mi) south of Machachi and four kilometres (2.5 mi) from the north entrance of Parque Nacional Cotopaxi: From Quito, take a bus to Machachi (1 hr), buses for El Pedregal depart from the main square four times per day; ask to be dropped off at Hacienda El Porvenir. A private pick-up from Machachi to the hacienda costs approximately $12 one way. Quito office: Vía Láctea 350 y Chimborazo, Cumbayá, Tel: 593-2-204-1520 / 600-9533, Cel: 0994-980-121, E-mail: info@volcanoland.com, URL: http://english.tierradelvolcan.com.

Hacienda Hato Verde

(ROOMS: $134-244) The Mora-Bowen family opens the doors of their 150-year-old country home, Hacienda Hato Verde, to discerning travelers. In keeping with the original style of the old house, there are 10 luxurious rooms, each one with beds dressed in goose-feather pillows and comforters, private bathroom and fireplace. Built of impeccable masonry evoking the region's colonial-cum-rustic style, the farm lies just on the western edge of Parque Nacional Cotopaxi, thus giving guests easy access to exploring the reserve on horseback. The inn also offers hiking, biking and vehicle tours of the park, as well as excursions to market towns. Panamericana Sur Km 55, turn off for Mulalo, Tel: 593-3-271-9348, Cel: 0995-978-016. Quito office: 593-2-254-4719, Fax: 593-3- 271-9902, E-mail: info@hacienda-hatoverde.com, URL: www.haciendahatoverde.com.
Updated: Oct 26, 2012.

Hostería La Ciénega

(ROOMS: $63-190) Over its almost 500-year history, this old hacienda played host to many famous people, including many Independence heroes and Alexander von Humboldt. The walls, made of volcanic rock, have withstood countless tremors from its active volcanic neighbor. The spacious house offers 34 luxurious rooms and suites for the discerning international traveler. All accommodations have private bathrooms, hot water, telephones and heaters. The hacienda's restaurant serves international cuisine. Other facilities include a chapel – mainly used for weddings, two seminar rooms, a bar, sports facilities and gardens. Among the activities available at La Ciénaga are sport fishing, hikes, horseback riding, as well as a variety of tours. 74 km (45 miles) south of Quito, past Lasso, on road to Cuicuno, Quito office: Cordero 1442 and Av. Amazonas, Edif. Fuente Azul, Tel: Hacienda: 593-3-271-9052 / 271-9093, Quito: 593-2-254-9126 / 254-1337, Fax: Hacienda: 593 3-271-9182, Quito: 593-2-222-8820, E-mail: info@hosteria-lacienega.com / reservaciones@hosteriala-cienega.com, URL: www.hosterialacienega.com, Getting there: Updated: Oct 25, 2012.

Hostería Papagayo !

($15-110 per person) Papagayo is a beautiful hostería that presents a variety of rooms with superb views of the volcanoes, as well as a cabin. Its relaxing atmosphere makes it the perfect place to acclimatize before or after summiting the mountains. Amenities include Jacuzzi, BBQs, WiFi and an excellent restaurant. In addition to climbing, mountain biking and horseback riding excursions, the lodge also offers tours to Laguna Quilatoa, the indigenous markets at Saquisilí and Machachi, Volcán Illinizas hot springs, Santa Martha Animal Rescue Center and Ecoroses rose plantation. Papagayo sometimes accepts volunteers to work at the hostel in exchange for free room and board.Hacienda La Bolivia, Panamericana Sur Km 26: You can take a bus from the Quitumbe bus terminal to Machachi. From Machachi take a bus to El Chaupi and get off it when it arrives to Agriconsultores. , Tel: 593-2-231-0002 / 2-367-0042, Cel: 0939-014-711 / 0980-448-812, Fax: 593-2-231-0002, E-mail: Info@hosteria-papagayo.com, URL: www.hosteria-papagayo.com. Updated: Oct 25, 2012.

Hotel Cuello de Luna

($18-95 per person) Cuello de Luna, four kilometers (2.4 mi) west of the main entrance to Parque Nacional Cotopaxi, is a convenient base for exploring the national park, climbing Cotopaxi, visiting the indigenous markets of Saquisili and Zumbahua, hiking around the Quilotoa crater, as well as leisurely day hikes and acclimatization. The lodge offers these tours, as well as mountain biking and horseback riding. The beautiful mountain landscape is the backdrop for Cuello de Luna's 25 rooms all with private bath and fireplace. Budget backpackers can stay in the seven-bed hostel dorm or use the hotel's campgrounds. From Quito, take the Panamerican Highway South on the way to Latacunga. When you reach the blue and white sign for the Cotopaxi National Park Entrance "El Chasqui" at Km 44, turn right and follow the small road for 1.5 km (1 mi) to Hotel Cuello de Luna. Tel: 593-3-271-8068 / 593-2-290-6039 (Quito office), Cel: 0999-700-330 / 0999-727-535, E-mail: www.cuellodeluna.com. Updated: Oct 25, 2012.

San Agustín de Callo

(ROOMS: $228-398) San Agustín de Callo is one of the most intriguing haciendas in Ecuador. Originally the site of a 15th-century, the Spanish conquerors built on the site, which was given to the Augustinian religious order in 1590 before becoming private property. It has been in the Plaza family (which boasts two Ecuadorian presidents) since 1921. The University of Texas has an ongoing archaeological project at the hacienda. The most impressive sights in the area are the perfectly carved volcanic stone walls of two of the Inca rooms that now serve as the chapel and dining rooms. San Agustín de Callo has spacious, elegant rooms, beautiful gardens, full dining and good service. It offers horseback riding, trekking, biking, fishing and organized trips to the traditional indigenous markets in Pujilí and Saquisilí. Panamericana Sur highway, 77 kilometers (47 mi) south of Quito and near the Park's main entrance; the hacienda is about 5 kilometers (3 mi) east of the highway, Tel: 593-3-271-9160; Quito office: 593-2-290-6157, E-mail: info@incahacienda.com, URL: www.incahacienda.com. Updated: Oct 26, 2012.

Secret Garden Cotopaxi

(ROOMS: $32.50-79.50) Tranquil Secret Garden Cotopaxi is located in a breath-taking, mountainous setting on the northern boundary of Parque Nacional Cotopaxi. This hostel offers several types of lodging, including dormitories, tent cabins and honeymoon suites. The all-inclusive package includes three delicious meals per day, prepared with ingredients from the Secret Garden's farm. In addition to paid hiking, horseback riding and climbing tours, the hostel offers several free ones to its guests, as well as free use of

bicycles and maps. Secret Garden Cotopaxi's international and Ecuadorian staff is exceptionally friendly and hospitable, and ready to ensure you spend a few memorable days here. Approximately 20 kilometers (12 mi) south of Machachi and 4 kilometers (2.5 mi) from the north entrance of Parque Nacional Cotopaxi; The Secret Garden organizes regular shuttles departing from its Quito hostel ($5-20 per person, depending on number of persons, minimum 2 persons. If you are traveling alone, you can share a van with others). Tel: Cel: 0993-572-714; in Quito: 02-295-6704, Cel: 0991-980-027, E-mail: hola@secretgardenquito.com, URL: www.secretgardencotopaxi.com.
Updated: Oct 26, 2012.

Tambopaxi

(CAMPING: $6, ROOMS: $19-150 per person) Set just inside Parque Nacional Cotopaxi, Tambopaxi is an acclimatization center that advertises itself as "the best place to stay and climb Cotopaxi." At 3,720 meters (12,202 ft) altitude, Tambopaxi offers two huts hosting private rooms with private baths, and dormitories, as well as campsites. Whilst the buildings are the only ones visible for miles, the careful use of construction materials and close attention to aesthetic detail mean they blend into the natural environment. Day trippers may enjoy Tambopaxi's restaurant which offers delicious, hearty set meals with a stunning view of Cotopaxi on clear days. Parque Nacional Cotopaxi: from the Panamericana Sur highway, take the turn-off to the town of Machachi, and then south to the North Entrance of the national park. Tambopaxi is just a few kilometers further on.. Quito office: Diego de Almagro N26-105 and La Pinta, office 9, Tel: 02-222-0241, Cel: 0999-448-223, E-mail: reservas@tambopaxi.com, URL: www.tambopaxi.com.
Updated: Oct 25, 2012.

Cotopaxi National Park Restaurants

The only independent restaurant in Parque Nacional Cotopaxi is at Estación Mariscal Sucre, where the museum is. The great majority of thelodges in and near the national park have their own restaurants, and offer all-inclusive packages to their guests. Some of the hacienda and hotel restaurants accept non-guests, with prior arrangements. Campers and trekkers should plan to be self-sufficient and pack all food in. Only some of the refuges and albergues have equipped kitchens. Bring a camp stove that works at high altitudes.

AMBATO

 2,500m 329,856 03

The Central Andes' biggest city, located a couple of hours south of Quito, tends to be more of a bus stopover than a tourist destination, and most travelers choose to continue on to the livelier and more appealing town of Baños, a mere hour away. This is partly due to the destruction of the 1949 earthquake, which killed 6,000 people and destroyed the city's colonial center.

Much of Ambato is modern and rather plain as a result. But Ambato isn't without attractions though, and there a couple of decent museums and appealing parks. In addition, nobody can argue that Ambato doesn't present visitors with an authentic Ecuadorian experience, particularly when it comes to its busy markets.

When To Go to Ambato

Carnival, held annually in February or March, is when Ambato really comes alive. The city's festival, Fiesta de las Flores y las Frutas (festival of flowers and fruits), has grown tremendously in reputation, if not in reality. The festival is advertised as a two-week-long celebration with colorful parades, festivities and bullfights. If there was ever such a huge festival in Ambato, though, there isn't now. What you get, instead, is four nights of dancing and drinking (and afternoon bullfights) in the build up to Ash Wednesday, a Roman Catholic observance that kicks off Lent. Plan to book early if you want to spend the weekend in Ambato, as accommodations fill up quickly.
Updated: Sep 18, 2012.

Getting To and Away from Ambato

Ambato is one of the country's major transport hubs, with daily buses to and from **Quito, Guayaquil, Baños, Cuenca, Latacunga, Riobamba, Guaranda**, and other cities. The Terminal de Buses is located two kilometers (1.24 mi) north of the center of city on Avenida de las Americas. There is a tax to use the terminal ($0.20 for adults, $0.10 for children) which you must pay before entering the boarding area outside of the terminal.

For buses to a number of destinations, including Quito, Latacunga, Riobamba and Guaranda, there is no need to buy your ticket at one of the many ticket booths; instead, you can simply pay on the bus itself. The easiest way to get between the bus terminal and the town's center is to hop in a yellow, registered taxi (taxis wait outside the terminal), which should cost no more than $1.50.

Buses run to the following destinations:

To **Cuenca** (7 hr, $8): leave at 9.45 a.m., 1.15 p.m., 5.15 p.m., 10.15 p.m. and midnight.

To **Guaranda** (2 hr, $2): leave every hour.

To **Guayaquil** (6 hr, $7): leave every hour.

To **Latacunga** (45 min, $1): leave every 15 minutes. Note that some buses go directly to the Latacunga terminal, while others drop you off on the highway before continuing on to **Quito** (when the bus stops at a road filled with buses and people, get off!). If you do get dropped off on the highway, walk down Avenida 5 de Junio for five minutes until you see the terminal.

To **Quito** (2 1/2 hr, $2.50): leave every 15 minutes.

To **Riobamba** (1 1/2 hr, $1.25): leave every 15 minutes.
Updated: Aug 30, 2012.

Ambato Services
MONEY
There are several branches of national banks (many with 24-hour ATMs that accept international cards) throughout the city, particularly around Parque Cevallos.

Banco de Guayaquil: The bank's ATMs, which accept Mastercard and Visa, can be found outside on Calle Sucre. Corner of Sucre y Juan Leon Mera.

Banco Pacifico: ATM takes Visa. Monday to Friday 8.30 a.m.-4 p.m., Saturday 9 a.m.-2 p.m. Bolívar 17-58 and Montalvo (ATM on Montalvo).

Banco Pichincha: Note that the ATMs are inside the bank, so are only accesible during business hours. Monday to Friday 9 a.m.-5 p.m. Lalama, between Sucre and Av. Cevallos.

KEEPING IN TOUCH
You'll have no problem finding an Internet café in Ambato, and there are several around Parque Cevallos and Avenida Cevallos. Ca-

binas Internet (Daily 7 a.m.-9 p.m. Lalama, next to Banco Pichincha) has several computer terminals, Skype facilties, and phone cabins. The post office (Parque Montalvo, opposite the Cathedral on the corner of Mariano Castillo and Bolívar) is open Monday to Friday 8 a.m.-6 p.m. and Saturday 9 a.m.-1 p.m.

MEDICAL
You will find numerous pharamacies along Avenida Cevallos. Farmacia Metropolitana (Cevallos between Juan Leon Mera and Matinez) is open Monday to Friday 8 a.m.-9.30 p.m., Saturday and Sunday 8.15 a.m.-9.30 p.m.

Farmacias Comunitarias (Cevallos and Montalvo) is open daily 8 a.m.-9 p.m. The public hospital, Hospital del IESS, is located on Calle Himno Nacional, north-east of the center and one block from the highway that circles Ambato. There is also a medical clinic, Clinica del Salud 1, two and a half blocks north of Parque Cevallos (Lalama 429, between Calles Rocafuerte and Cuenca. Tel: 242-3504).

TOURISM
The tourism office, Dirección Provincial de Turismo de Tungurahua (Monday to Friday 8.30 a.m.-5.30 p.m. Guayaquil 01-08 and Rocafuerte, by the entrance to Hotel Ambato. Tel: 282-1800) has maps and Spanish-language brochures for the city and surrounding areas.

SHOPPING
Ambato is known for its many markets. The biggest market day is Monday, when vendors line the main streets around Calles Benigno Vela and 12 de Noviembre, Avenida Cevallos, and Parque Cevallos. You will find just about everything on sale here, though there are less artisan goods and more groceries, clothing and, of course, the fruits and flowers that Ambato is famous for. Daily markets include the large Mercado Modelo (Av. Cevallos between Espejo and Mariano Eguez), which sells meat, fruit, vegetables and dry goods on the first floor, and clothing, artisan goods, and food stalls (with filling $1-2 almuerzos) on the second floor. Another market is the Mercado Central on Marieta de Veintimilla and 12 de Noviembre, which has a similar, but smaller, collection of goods. A more modern market is the Supermercado Tia, just across the road from the Mercado Modelo on Espejo and Benigo Vela.
Updated: Aug 30, 2012.

Things To See and Do in Ambato

Ambato is known as the "city of the three Juans", due to it being the birthplace of three notable figures: Juan León Mera, a prolific author (and the writer of Ecuador's national anthem); Juan Montalvo, a writer and essayist; and Juan Beningo Vela, a journalist. The legacy of the three Juans can be seen around Ambato, in its plazas and street names, and also in Mera's and Montalvo's former homes, which have been turned into museums.

The main Plaza, Parque Montalvo, is Ambato's prettiest, and, with its many trees and fountains, it's a nice spot to perch on a bench and people-watch. From here you can also wander around the Catedral, a modern, white construction that sits on the site of the original cathedral, which was first built in 1698 and subsequently destroyed by the 1947 earthquake. Ambato is also the most convenient point from which to head to Quisapincha, a tiny town famous for its leather goods.
Updated: Sep 18, 2012.

Casa De Montalvo

(ADMISSION: $1) The birthplace of one of Ambato's most distinguished authors, Juan Montalvo, a controversial novelist and essayist who was born in 1832, is also his resting place; his coffin is displayed to the public on a tiered platform. The museum aims to promote Montalvo through a display of personal effects, photos and manuscripts. Montalvo 03-50 and Bolívar (on the corner of Parque Montalvo), Tel: 282-4248/4987.
Updated: Sep 18, 2012.

Museo De Ciencias Naturales

(ADMISSION: $2) One side of Parque Cevallos is taken up by the imposing Instituto Tecnológico Superior Bolívar, which houses the city's rambling Science museum.

This engrossing museum, which was inaugurated in 1920, has a diverse assortment of displays, including coins and medals (including macuquinas, hammered coins from the 16th century), 20th century photographs of Ecuadorian landscapes, indigenous musical instruments, a ceramic collection dating back to 700 A.C., human fetuses and skeletons, and a large collection of stuffed animals, with species from Ecuador's four ecosystems: Galapagos, coast, Andes, and Amazon. Ca. Sucre (right next to Plaza Cevallos), Tel: 282-7395 Ext. 197.
Updated: Sep 18, 2012.

Museo de la Provincia de Tungurahua

(ADMISSION: Free) The Museo de la Provincia de Tungurahua is housed in the airy Casa de Portal, neighboring the cathedral on Parque Montalvo. The Casa de Portal, built in 1900, is a beautiful example of republican architecture, and was mostly recently-and lovingly-restored in 2011. The museum is dedicated to the art and culture of the Tungurahua province, and consists of paintings, photographs and archaeological finds from the region. Ca. Sucre (on Parque Montalvo).
Updated: Sep 18, 2012.

Parque Provincial De La Familia

The 57-hectare (140-ac) Parque Provincial de la Familia, located on the outskirts of the city, is a welcome break from dusty Ambato. The park has great views, and consists of several wide green spaces, gardens, basketball, volleyball and football courts, children's play areas, a lake, picnic areas, and a small farm with a number of animals including llamas, guinea pigs, and donkeys. Note that pets and bicycles are not allowed in the park, and it is open Thursday to Sunday only, and national holidays. Via a Quisapincha, Tel: 277-2604/282-0244.
Updated: Sep 18, 2012.

Quinta De Juan León Mera

(ADMISSION: Free) A couple of kilometers (1.2 mi) north of the city center is the former residence of a prominent Ecuadorian novelist and intellectual, Juan León Mera, who was born in Ambato in 1832. This riverside villa was built in 1874, and is home to a small museum that houses modern and historic art, as well as some of Mera's manuscripts and photographs. The gorgeous and extensive gardens are the main attraction though, and it's easy to while away a relaxing hour or two wandering around them. There's a botanical garden with over 250 flower species (including seven that are endemic to Ambato). To get there, either hop in a taxi ($2) or take a bus from Parque Cevallos. Av. Pachano Lalama.
Updated: Sep 18, 2012.

Quisapincha

10 kilometers (6 mi) west of Ambato is the tiny, windswept village of Quisapincha, which may as well be called Leatherville: its main street is devoted to store after store bursting with genuine cuero (leather) goods. You'll find jackets, shoes, wallets, bags and more, in every style and color imaginable. Prices are much lower than in the cities, and even lower than in the more

well-known leather-crazy town of Cotacachi, in the Northern Andes. From Ambato, it's a 20 minute bus ride from the plaza Primero de Mayo (from Parque Montalvo, walk seven blocks east on Bolivar, then four blocks north on Tomas Sevilla) to Quisapincha. In Quisapincha, buses head back to Ambato from the main road.

If shopping makes you hungry, be warned that Quisapincha isn't overflowing with restaurants; instead, you'll a few street food stalls and a bakery. 10 kilometers (6 mi) west of Ambato.
Updated: Sep 18, 2012.

Ambato Lodging

Although there are plenty of accommodation options in Ambato, hotels for the most part are overpriced and many seem to have been decorated at the height of the 70's. However, if you can look past the décor, they are fairly comfortable for a night or two, and there are some nicer, higher-priced places if you can afford it. Budget hotels, however, are scarce, and there are certainly no backpacker-style hostels. There are a number of hotels around Parque 12 de Noviembre that, though grotty, are cheap, and are bearable for a night or two. Most of the hotels are located in the center of the city, so if you get to town without a reservation, cruise around and find a place. They are rarely booked out, with the exception of during Carnival, when a reservation is necessary for any hotel in Ambato.

Quinta Loren

(ROOMS: $47-108) This small but pleasant hostería is surrounded by beautiful gardens and fruit orchards—a nod to Ambato, the town in which it is located, home of the nationally famous Festival of Fruits and Flowers during Carnival week. Elegant and clean, the colonial architecture and decorations give the place an upscale yet intimate atmosphere.

Its nine rooms are clean, cozy and equipped with WiFi. Guests can take a stroll along the beautiful grounds, taking in scenic views of the snow-capped mountains and volcanoes of Tungurahua, Altar and Chimborazo. In the evening, guests can dine at the restaurant then unleash their inner rock star at the on-site karaoke bar. Av. Guaytambos and Taxos, Loren neighborhood, Tel: 03-246-1275/0699, Cel: 09-9543-9723, E-mail: ventas@quintalorenhosteria.com, URL: www.quintalorenambato.com.
Updated: Feb 06, 2013.

Gran Hotel

(ROOMS: $16-39) The Gran Hotel is better than it looks from the outside: it's housed in a shabby, nondescript building, so it's a relief to step into the shiny, modern lobby. The foyer is rather deceptive however, as rooms are disappointingly simple. But still, it's one of the cheaper places in town, and extras (rooms have cable TV and WiFi, and breakfast is included) help make up for it. Rocafuerte 10-45 and Lalama., Tel: 282-4235/0987-400-350, E-mail: granhotelambatoecu@hotmail.es.
Updated: Oct 31, 2012.

Hotel Señorial

(ROOMS: $22-34) Look past the odd decor that's reminiscent of a bad 80´s film, and you will see that this is actually a perfectly agreeable and well-kept hotel. The rooms have big beds, cable TV and WiFi, and large windows that provide a good amount of light. The top floor houses four suites, complete with bath tubs with hydro massage; the layout of the suites' bathrooms however doesn't exactly allow for much privacy, as you can't completely shut the bathroom (and, more importantly, the toilet) off from the room.

Staff are courteous, but could be friendlier, and the hotel's location on Avenida Cevallos, though convenient, is noisy-ask for a room away from the street. Breakfast is included. Av. Cevallos and Ca.Quito, Tel: 282-5124/282-6249, E-mail: reservas@hoteleniorial.com, URL: www.hoteseniorial.com.
Updated: Aug 31, 2012.

Hotel Ambato

(ROOMS: $56.80-81.20) Hotel Ambato is the easily the cushiest place in town (with prices to match). If your budget allows it, you'll be rewarded with a glossy, modern hotel that offers spacious rooms and suites, a quiet location that's pleasantly peaceful but still only a few blocks from the main plaza, and sleek communal areas, including an ample outside terrace with lovely views of the hills.

Other facilities in the hotel include a café, restaurant belwo, parking spaces if you have a car and 200-person conference room. Rooms have cable TV, WiFi, room service, and the rates include breakfast as well. Guayaquil 01-08 y Rocafuerte, Tel: 242-1791/1792/1793/0992-557-459, E-mail: info@hotelambato.com / ventas@hotelambato.com, URL: www.hotelambato.com.
Updated: Oct 31, 2012.

Hotel Roka Plaza

(ROOMS: $49-120) Hotel Roka Plaza provides the nearby Hotel Ambato with some healthy competition when it comes to the nicest place to stay in the city. It doesn't have the facilities or space that Hotel Ambato possess, but what it lacks in amplitude, it makes up for in charm and character. This small hotel is housed in a renovated 150 year-old colonial building that has been lovingly and thoughtfully decorated. The room finishings are excellent. Opt for a suite if you can-they're they same price as a double, but twice the size. The only downside is that rooms-apart from the suites-are small, and lack light: the windows look out onto an indoor courtyard. There's a gourmet restaurant in the courtyard serving up lunch and dinner, and breakfast is included. Bolivar (between Quito and Guayaquil), Tel: 242-3845/2360, E-mail: ventas@hotelrokaplaza.com / recepcion@hotelrokaplaza.com. Updated: Aug 31, 2012.

Hotel Del Sol

($9 per person) Travelers in need of a cheap place to crash for the night head to Parque 12 de Noviembre, where a handful of shabby hotels line the plaza. Hotel del Sol is one of the slightly more desirable ones. It's a little dingy, with simple rooms set around dimly-lit and deserted communal areas. But if you just want a place to lay your head for the night, it's fine, and you'll at least have a private bath with warmish water and cable TV. There's no breakfast. Ask for a room at the back to avoid the noise of the overpass that flows past the front of the building. Ca. Luis A Martinez and Av. 12 de Noviembre, Tel: 282-5258, E-mail: hoteldelsol77@hotmail.com. Updated: Aug 31, 2012.

Hotel Cevallos

(ROOMS: $21-57) It's conveniently located right in the middle of the city center (ask for a back room if you're worried about noise), and rooms are spacious, clean and comfortable, and the staff is amiable. All rooms have private bath, cable TV and WiFi, and breakfast is included. Groups of eight people or more receive a 10% discount. Av. Cevallos 05-76, corner of Montalvo (entrance is on Montalvo)., Tel: 242-2009/282-4877. Updated: Aug 31, 2012.

Hotel Piramide

(ROOMS: $16-26) Just one block away from Parque Cevallos, Hotel Piramide is one of the city's better budget-priced options. Rooms are snug and have cable TV and WiFi, and breakfast is included. Rooms away from the street are quieter, though they have no external windows. A simple but agreeable option. Mariano Eguez and Av. Cevallos, Tel: 242-1920/0991-495-889. Updated: Oct 31, 2012.

Ambato Restaurants

Ambato's center, El Centro, has the greatest concentration of restaurants: as well as typical Ecuadorian food, you'll find a number of places offering international cuisine-think pizza, pasta, steak, fried chicken and even shawarma. Make sure you wander downtown for a helado (ice cream). There are several places that sell this frozen treat, and their offerings are all delicious and cheap.

One dish not to miss is Ambato's most famous, llapingachos: potato pancakes stuffed with cheese, and typically accompanied by sausage, a fried egg, avocado and salad. Now enjoyed by people across the county,this plate originated in Ambato, and you will find it everywhere in the city. If you want a quick snack, street stalls serve up freshly-cooked llapingachos for a dollar or two. Updated: Sep 03, 2012.

El Gaucho

(ENTREES: $3.50-22) El Gaucho has been an Ambato staple for years, serving sizzling and tender Argentine-style steaks at affordable prices. Although the decor is sparse (the experience is more like eating in a cafeteria than a restaurant), it's a great place to relax and enjoy a quality steak without having to dress up. Demanding appetites can try the generous combo plates. Monday to Saturday 12-10 p.m. Bolivar, between Ca. Quito and Ca. Mariano Castillo, Tel: 282-8969/284-1070/0998-307-631. Updated: Oct 31, 2012.

Oasis Café

(ENTREES: $2.65-6.50) This lovely café specializes in helado (ice cream), which comes in a variety of yummy flavors. If you're looking for a place to spend a few hours relaxing with dessert and a coffee you've found the spot. The café also has a food menu, with hearty breakfasts, sandwiches, burgers and plato fuertes (main dishes) such as filet mignon and camarones a la plancha (grilled shrimp).

However, make sure to save room for the ice cream, as it's hands-down the tastiest in all of Ambato. Service is refreshingly speedy.

Monday to Friday 8 a.m.-10 p.m., Saturday and Sunday 9 a.m.-9 p.m. Sucre 04-10 and Mariano Eguez, Tel: 282-5535, E-mail: heloasis@interactive.net.ec, URL: www.heladeriaoasis.com.
Updated: Aug 31, 2012.

La Fornace

(ENTREES: $4-15) This highly popular joint serves delicious wood-fired pizza, made from scratch and cooked in a massive antique brick oven. The thin crust and fresh ingredients easily make it a town favorite, and there's pasta, meat and fish dishes if you don't have a pizza craving. The atmosphere is cozy and, at night, the restaurant is lit by candles and warmed by an open fire. Service is attentive. Delivery is available if you're not in the mood to venture out into the chilly Ambato night. Daily 11 a.m.-11 p.m. Av. Cevallos 17-28, between Montalvo and Mariano Castillo., Tel: 282-3244, E-mail: info@lafornace.com.ec, URL: www.lafornace.com.ec.
Updated: Aug 31, 2012.

El Álamo Chalet Restaurante

(ENTREES: $5.80-9) As you're wandering down Av. Cevallos, El Álamo Chalet will likely catch your eye, simply because it really does look like a mountain chalet-albeit on a busy Ambato street. While El Álamo aspires to be affordably posh (and the restaurant's interior is just as aesthetically appealing as its exterior), the food, though decent, tends to fall a little short of expectations. The menu is varied, ranging from breakfast options and lunch specials to steak, fish, chicken, pasta and typical Ecuadorian dishes. In terms of service, you might find that your order arrives quickly, but flagging down a server for the bill is nearly impossible. Avenida Cevallos 17-19 y Montalvo, Tel: 282-4704.
Updated: Aug 31, 2012.

Ambato Nightlife
El Portal Cafetería

(SNACKS: $1.50 and up) El Portal Cafeteria is a sweet little café/bar located on the pretty Parque Montalvo, which by day offers a cozy environment in which to enjoy a coffee while using the free WiFi, and by night the chance to sip on a cocktail while listening to live music. There's also snacks, sandwiches and hamburgers if you get peckish. You'll find live music being played daily (except on Sundays) between 6-9 p.m., as well as from 9 p.m. on Wednesday to Saturday. Sucre and Mariano Castillo (on Parque Montalvo), Tel: 242-4507.
Updated: Aug 31, 2012.

BAÑOS

 1,815m   18,000   03

Baños is one of the most popular tourist destinations in the Ecuadorian Sierra. The town's full name, Baños de Agua Santa (literally, "baths of the holy waters"), comes from the natural hot springs that run off of neighboring Volcán Tungurahua (5,023 m, 16,480 ft). The town is surrounded by a curtain of bright green mountains, and is an area rich in waterfalls, flora and fauna.There are natural hot springs under the waterfall splashing into town which are a chocolate brown color and are almost always packed to capacity. Baños is full of hotels, hostels,restaurants and cafes.

With myriad hiking, bike trails, spas and tours, there are plenty of activities to keep you entertained around Baños.

Safety

Baños is a small and safe tourist town. The biggest threat to safety here is the activities themselves, as Baños is known for its adventure sports. Tons of tour operators offer these activities but it is always important to check the company's safety reputation and see the equipment before committing to jumping head first off of a bridge. Tungurahua Volcano, which sits just outside of town, could pose another safety concern in Baños, since the volcano is very active and is often erupting. Check with the U.S. embassy before traveling to confirm that you will not be in danger. Otherwise, you will find that Baños is a very hospitable place and if you exercise common sense, you will leave here without any issues.
Updated: Feb 08, 2013.

Getting To and Away from Baños

Baños is a popular weekend trip from Quito, so there are many options and frequent departures from **Quito** to get here. The bus ride from Quito takes approximately 3.5 to 4 hours, and costs abour $3.50-4. Almost all buses leave from the Quitumbe bus station in the south of Quito. Some of the companies that make the trip are **Transportes Baños**, **Transportes Amazonas** and **Transportes Alausí**. Transportes Baños also has two buses per night (8:30 p.m. and 9:30 p.m.) that leave from its office in the **Mariscal**, making it a convenient alternative than going all the way to Quitumbe.

CENTRAL ANDES

CENTRAL ANDES

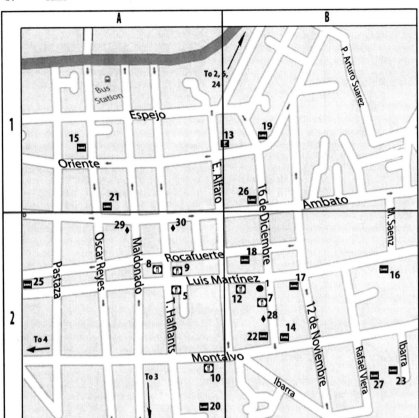

Activities ●

1. Chiva Night Tour (B2)
2. El Refugio Spa (A1)
3. Hiking to Bellavista (A2)
4. Virgen del Agua Santa (A2)

Eating 🍴

5. Blah Blah Cafe (A2)
6. Café del Cielo (See 24)
7. Cafe Hood (B2)
8. Casa Hood (A2)
9. Jota & Jota (A2)
10. Mariane (A2)
11. Pancho Villa (See 14)
12. Swiss Bistro (B2)

Nightlife ⅄

13. Leprechaun Bar (B1)

Sleeping 🛏

14. Gala Hotel (B2)
15. Hostal Alcazar (A1)
16. Hostal Chimenea (B2)
17. Hostal Plantas y Blanco (B2)
18. Hostal Residencial 'Lucy' (B2)
19. Hostel Transilvania (B1)
20. Hotel Monte Selva (A2)
21. Hotel El Belen (A1)
22. La Petite Auburge (B2)
23. La Posada del Arte (B3)

Tours ◆

28. Imagine Ecuador (B2)
29. Rainforestur (A2)
30. Geoturs (A2)

From Baños, buses frequently go to **Quito** (3.5 hr, $3.50-4), **Riobamba** (2 hr, $2), Tena (3 hr, $4) and **Puyo** (1 hr, 15 min; $2), and less frequently to **Cuenca** (6 hr, $6-10), **Guayaquil** (6-7 hr, $8), **Ibarra** (6 hr, $6), **Coca** (8 hr, $10) and **Macas** (5 hr, $7). All buses that go to **Tena** pass Puyo on the way and can drop you off on the highway outside of town. The buses to Cuenca all switch buses in Riobamba. Transportes Baños has one bus per day, at 2 p.m., that goes to the Mariscal, instead of Quitumbe.

The following is the updated bus schedule from the bus station in Baños:

Cooperativa de Transportes y Turismo Sangay

To **Riobamba**: 19 per day, every 20-35 minutes 6:25 a.m.-9 p.m.; To **Tena**: 8:15 a.m., 12:15 p.m., 3:15 p.m.; To **Puyo**: 10 per day, every 30 minutes 7:45 a.m.-7 pm., last bus at 9 p.m.; To **Cuenca**: 6 per day, 6:45 a.m., 8:45 a.m. 9:45 a.m., 1:50 p.m., 3:45 p.m., 6:40 p.m. Tel: 03-274-1037, URL: www. transangay.com.ec

Flota Pelileo:

To **Puyo**: 11:10 a.m., 1 p.m., 2:10 p.m., 11 p.m.; To **Tena**, passing through **Puyo**: 4:45 a.m., 9:40 a.m., 12:40 p.m., 10 p.m.; To Coca: 4 a.m., 7:30 p.m.; To **Guayaquil**: 9 a.m., 11:30 a.m., 2 p.m., 4 p.m., 7 p.m., 10:30 p.m.; To **Macas**: 10:30 a.m., 9:30 p.m.

Cooperativa de Transportes y Turismo Riobamba:

To **Riobamba**: 14 per day 6 a.m.-9 p.m.; To **Guayaquil**: 6 a.m., 1:10 p.m.; To **Cuenca**: 7:15 a.m., 11 a.m., 5 p.m.; To **Tena**, passing through **Puyo**: 5:30 a.m., 6:40 a.m., 9:30 a.m., 10 a.m., 11:30 a.m., 1:40 p.m., 4:30 p.m. Tel: 03-274-0133

Cooperativa Expreso Baños:

To **Quito**: 6:40 a.m., 9:45 a.m., 10:20 a.m., 11:15 a.m., 4:10 p.m., 4:30 p.m., 7:50 p.m.; To **Ibarra**: 4 a.m., 2:40 p.m.; To **Tena**, passing through **Puyo**: 3:30 a.m., 5:30 a.m., 7:40 a.m., 10:40 a.m., 4:30 p.m., 6:40 p.m., 7:30 p.m.; To **Puyo**: 8:10 a.m., 10 a.m., 6:10 p.m.; To **Riobamba**: 8:05 a.m., 10:10 a.m., 12:40 p.m., 4:25 p.m.

Cooperativa de Transportes Amazonas:

To **Quito**: 20 buses depart per day, from 1:30 a.m.-6:20 p.m.; To **Puyo**: 9 a.m., 3:30 p.m., 4 p.m., 7 p.m., 8:20 p.m.; To **Tena**: 1:30 p.m., 8:30 p.m.

Transportes Baños:

To **Quito**: 20 per day, 4 a.m.-6:40 p.m. The 2 p.m. bus goes to the **Mariscal**. To **Tena**: 6:30 a.m., 8:30 a.m., 11:30 a.m., 2:30 p.m.; To **Coca**: 5:30 p.m., 9:30 p.m., 10:40 p.m.; To **Macas**: 1 p.m.; To **Guayaquil**: 1:15 a.m., 5:30 p.m., 7:15 p.m., 11 p.m.; To **Riobamba**: 2:20 p.m.
Updated: Dec 03, 2012.

Baños Services
MONEY

Many banks are located on Baños' main plaza, Parque Central. There is a Banco de Pichincha on the corner of Halflants and Ambato streets (daily 9 a.m.-5 p.m.). A Banco Bolivariano/BanRed ATM is on the Calle Maldonado side of the plaza. Banco de Pacifico has a branch on the corner of Halflants and Rocafuerte (Monday-Friday 8:30 a.m.-4 p.m.); it has an ATM on the Rocafuerte side.

KEEPING IN TOUCH

To stay connected, try Internet Solnet, centrally located on Calle Ambato, near the corner of Halflants ($0.80 per hour. daily 9 a.m.-10 p.m. Tel: 03-274-3212). It has 17 computers as well as several national and international calling booths. Send mail home from the town's post office, on the Calle Halflants side of Parque Central, next to Banco de Pichincha (Monday-Friday 8 a.m.-6 p.m., Saturday 9 a.m.-1 p.m. Closed Sundays. Tel: 03-274-0901).

TOURISM

Baños' tourism office is on the Calle Halflants side of Parque Central (Monday-Friday 8 a.m.-12:30 p.m. and 2-5:30 p.m., Saturday-Sunday 8 a.m.-4 p.m.); however, the staff is not particularly friendly or helpful. The police office is on Calle Ambato, near Calle Eloy Alfaro (Tel: 03-274-0101/0251).

MEDICAL

Baños' hospital is at Montalvo and Pastaza, and has 24-hour emergency care. Clinica Baños de Santa Agua (Ca. Montalvo and Eloy Alfaro, next to the SRI. Tel: 03-274-2447, Cel: 09-9904-0026) is also open 24 hours and accepts American Express credit cards.

There is a Farmacias Cruz Azul on Calle Ambato, between Eloy Alfaro and Halflants streets, in front of the Pasaje Artesanal (daily 7 a.m.-10:30 p.m. Tel: 03-254-0237, Cel: 09-8825-8230). A Sana Sana pharmacy can be found half a block from the bus terminal, on Calle Maldonado and Espejo.
Updated: Dec 03, 2012.

Volcanic Fears

Tourism in Baños hit a pretty serious bump when, in 1999, the Tungurahua Volcano burst to life and the city was evacuated. For almost two years, tourism was brought to an almost complete stand-still as residents and travelers alike held their breath and waited for the inevitable explosion. Luckily, disaster never struck, and life slowly trickled back to this small mountain town. More recently, in December of 2012 and July of 2013, Tungurahua began erupting again, so much that the inhabitants of Baños were urged to voluntarily evacuate by the government.

So the threat of volcanic activity still remains, and it's recommendable to check the level of activity before visiting Baños. A phone call to your hotel or tour operator will work, or www.volcanodiscovery.com/tungurahua_updates.html gives English updates to major volcanic events in Baños.

As much of Ecuador lives under the threat of volcanic eruption, you may be surprised at the relaxed attitude locals have toward their fiery neighbor.

Things To See and Do in Baños

With striking natural beauty and a range of companies catering to the adventuresome spirit, there's no shortage of things to do in Baños. You can rent a bike for the day and follow the mostly downhill road to Puyo through spectacular scenery and past several waterfalls, some of which splash onto your path. This can be a half-day or an all-day trip, depending on how fast you go and how far you take the path. To go all the way to Puyo is 60 kilometers (37 mi). Most travelers stop 17 kilometers (10.5 mi) down the road at the beautiful Pailón del Diablo waterfall.

Tour agencies are found along pretty much every single block in Baños offering every variety of adventure sports from swing jumping off bridges to rafting, canyoning and rock climbing. Spas are plentiful in Baños as well, so you can soothe your sore muscles after a long day of adventure sports with a massage or other rejuvenating treatment. Chiva tours to view the naturally illuminated Tungurahua Volcano depart every night and should only be taken on very clear nights so as to get the best views.
Updated: Jan 23, 2013.

El Refugio Spa ⌡

(PRICE: $2.50 and up) For a one-of-a-kind spa experience that won't break the bank, an afternoon at El Refugio is a must. The bohemian spa compound is nestled deep in the tranquil valley under the Tungurahua Volcano and overlooking the Río Pastaza, about two kilometers (1.24 mi) outside of Baños, just off the road to Puyo. Choose from a full menu of á la carte treatments, including mud baths, massages and ear candling. Treatments start with a visit to a lookout point facing a mountainside, where all are encouraged to release stress with a scream into the valley.

For a memorably invigorating experience, try the baños de cajón: you'll be seated in an enclosed sauna box with only your head poking out of the top while hot vapors deeply cleanse your pores. Every 15 minutes, you'll be doused with icy-cool water before returning to the warmth of the box. It's amazingly refreshing. Couple one of these cleansing sessions with a soothing hot-stone massage for a full-body experience. El Refugio accepts credit cards. Camino Real, Barrio San Vicente, Tel: 03-274-0482, Cel: 09-9785-0607, URL: www.spaecuador.com.
Updated: Nov 26, 2012.

Puenting/Swing Jumping

(PRICE: $10-20) While not quite as scary as a real bungee jump, puenting (swing jumping),which is similar to bungee jumping but with fewer bounces, is just scary enough to get your heart beating and your legs wobbly. An expert will strap you in and give you the choice of whether you want to jump off the bridge facing forwards or let yourself fall backwards. Falling backwards is not nearly as scary as going forward. You are harnessed

to a rope, so you will swing under the bridge instead of bouncing back up, which is not as jarring as bungee jumping. Puenting is typically done off of one of three bridges in the area, ranging from 25-100 meters (82-328 ft) high; falls are typically between 15 and 35 meters (49-114 ft). Prices depend on the height of the bridge, usually costing between $10-20 per jump. While no accidents have been reported, keep in mind you are jumping off a bridge and there is always an element of risk involved.
Updated: Nov 23, 2012.

Bike Ride to Puyo

(PRICE: $7-10) For the more athletic travelers, there is the option to rent bicycles and ride 60 kilometers (37.3 mi) from Baños to Puyo in a single day. While the ride is fairly mild, without too many large hills to climb, you can still catch a bus heading to Baños at any point on the ride and head back into town if you can't make it all the way.

In the first 20 kilometers (12.4 mi) or so, there are many different waterfalls of varying sizes that culminate in the powerful El Pailón del Diablo waterfall at about 17 kilometers (10.6 mi) into the ride. Your biking will take you along the river where you can stop to swing jump, also known as puenting, with locals. Further on, you can stop to ride several different cable cars across the valley to see other waterfalls or wander through the lush greenery and flowers.

A few things to know before you do the ride: you will be sharing the highway with speedy, if not suicidal, truck and bus drivers and at some points you will have to go through pitch black tunnels with the traffic. It can be very frightening. There is always the risk of your bike breaking down or being faulty in some way. It also may rain, leaving you in between towns with nowhere to take cover, so bring appropriate gear, just in case. The good news is you can always catch a bus and head back to Baños. The ride can take anywhere from five to eight hours, depending on how long you dilly-dally at each waterfall.
Updated: Jan 23, 2013.

Chiva Night Tour

(PRICE: $4) As you walk around Baños, you are bound to see signs announcing an imminent volcano eruption: The natural phenomenon is predicted nightly at 9 p.m. and 11 p.m. Don't be worried, though, as the signs are simply advertising the chivas (open-sided party buses), which take tourists on a ride to see Volcán Tungurahua. Most of these chivas head up to the Bellavista viewpoint, where on clear nights the volcano's lava can be seen. Unfortunately, most of the time you are unlikely to see Tungurahua erupting, or even be able to spot the volcano cone at all, due to cloud cover.

However, the views over Baños, in addition to the free canelazo (a hot beverage made with water, raw brown sugar, cinnamon and, if desired, aguardiente) and a spectacular fire show combine to make this a worthwhile and inexpensive nighttime activity (most agencies charge just $4). Booking a trip is extremely easy and most tour agencies will be able to reserve you a seat in advance. The chivas leave from the corner of 16 de Deciembre and Luis A Martínez; if you haven't got a ticket, try turning up a few minutes before 9 p.m. and you might be able to bargain the price down for a last-minute seat.
Updated: Nov 26, 2012.

Volcan Tungurahua

Volcan Tungurahua (5,023 m / 16,479 ft), situated in the Sangay Nacional Park, is one of Ecuador's most active volcanoes. Tungurahua, which means "throat of fire" in Quechua, is only 5 km (just over 3 miles) from the small tourist town of Baños, over which it looms ominously. After being quiet for over 90 years, Tungurahua burst dramatically back to life in 1999 with an eruption that resulted in the evacuation of over 25,000 people. Since that time the volcano has been continually active and regularly expels clouds of ash into the air, which can be seen for miles around. Although the last major eruption was on August 16, 2006, Tungurahua poses no immediate threat to the surrounding towns and villages. In fact, volcano-watching has become a popular tourist attraction in Baños. You can catch buses anddchivasat night (many leave around 9 p.m.) for the ride from town to see the volcano, although only plan a trip if the weather is clear.
Updated: Mar 12, 2013.

Hike to the Virgen del Agua Santa

The journey up to the Virgin del Agua Santa is similar to the Bellavista hike in that it's an uphill trek to an equally rewarding viewpoint, though this one involves hiking up hundreds of steps. Follow the blue signs to the end off Calle Juan Leon Mera and head up the first flight of 82 steps. There is a short dirt path before the second set of 54 steps, and then it's only another 539 more to the top! This hike can be combined with the Bellavis-

CENTRAL ANDES

ta hike to make a loop, which will take three to four hours depending on your pace. To do this, follow the route to the Bellavista cross, then backtrack down the path you came up until you see a sign to Café del Cielo. Follow this path steeply upwards until you reach the café (part of Luna Runtun Lodge), where can enjoy a coffee or snack and take a break. From here, the sign-posted track to the Virgin gently descends until you reach the concrete statue and lookout. To head back to town, just follow the steps down.
Updated: Nov 26, 2012.

Hike to Bellavista

The hike up to Bellavista starts at the south end of Calle Maldonado and is a steady climb up to a viewpoint, where there are two cafés with unpredictable opening hours. Although the hike is almost all uphill, there are regular wooden covered lookouts to break the climb, which make ideal rest spots. The view from the top is well worth the effort! This short hike can be also be combined with the hike to the Virgen del Agua Santa.
Updated: Nov 23, 2012.

Studying Spanish in Baños

Mayra Spanish School

Accredited by Ecuador's Ministry of Education, Mayra has been offering quality Spanish classes since 1998. The school offers courses of all levels and caters to individual student's needs. Classes are available morning, afternoon and evening. Those interested in volunteer work can join Mayra's Social Club; members teach English to local students in the area. The school also arranges various cultural and adventure activities for its students. For accommodations, Mayra offers homestays or student apartments, all within walking distance of the centrally located school. Montalvo and 16 de Diciembre, Tel: (593-3) 2742 850, E-mail: welcome@ mayraspanishschool.com, URL: http:// mayraspanishschool.com.
Updated: Nov 12, 2012.

Baños Tours

Baños has plenty of well-equipped tour agencies. Most tourists seek out agencies to book half-day or full-day adventure activities, including rafting, zip-lining, puenting (swing jumping), canyoning, rock climbing, kayaking or bird-watching. It is also possible to rent bikes, motorcycles or quads by the hour or day. For those looking for an extended adventure, many agencies run full-scale tours to the jungle, the Galápagos and other tourist destinations. At first, the amount of tour operators may seem overwhelming, but seek out recommendations at the tourism office or at your hostel to help direct you.
Updated: Nov 22, 2012.

Imagine Ecuador ❗

Specializing in extreme sports and adventure trips into the great outdoors surrounding Baños (but also throughout all of Ecuador - including the Galapagos). In addition, Imagine Ecuador is the only tour operator in the area to be certified by the Ministry of Tourism of Ecuador to sell tickets for Galapagos Cruises. They deal with packages that range anywhere from climbing, puenting (swing jumping, $25), rafting ($25) and canyoning ($25) all the way to trips around the country and more. They also provide all-day bike rentals for $7. With experienced guides and high-quality gear from Europe and the U.S., Imagine Ecuador has a reputation and image that's hard to beat in Baños. 16 de Diciembre Street, between Montalvo and Luis A. Martinez Streets, Tel: 03-274-3472 / 098-728-6625, URL: http://www.imagineecuador.com/.
Updated: Jun 11, 2013.

Rainforestur

RainForestur has been operating in Baños for over 15 years. The agency specializes in jungle, mountain climbing and adventure exhibitions. In addition to the standard one-day canyoning ($30) and rafting ($30) trips offered by most agencies, RainForestur also offers a full-day combined cycling and rafting trip. This extremely fun but strenuous tour allows you to experience the spectacular Baños scenery from two different perspectives and makes for a great day. You can also organize multi-day Galápagos and rainforest trips here ($40-60 per day). RainForestur also has an office in Quito. Monday-Saturday 8:30 a.m.-8:30 p.m., Sunday 10 a.m.-4 p.m. Ca. Ambato 800 and Maldonado, Tel: 03-274-0743, Cel: 09-8446-9884/8703-2952, URL: www.rainforestur.com.ec.
Updated: Nov 22, 2012.

Geotours

Although Geotours is not the cheapest agency in town, it has a good reputation for safety and only employs fully qualified, specially trained bilingual guides. Its full- and half-day tours include rafting on the Pastaza and Patate Rivers ($30 half day), puenting (swing jumping) from three different bridges of varying heights ($10-20), and canyoning ($30 half day, $45 full day). Geotours also offers a three-day beginners kayaking course

($70 per day; 9 a.m.-noon and 2-4 p.m.) for those who want to learn how to navigate the rivers near Baños. Its helpful staff can also arrange trips to the jungle, ranging from one to five days. Ca. Ambato and Halflants, Tel: 03-274-1344, E-mail: geotoursbanios(at)yahoo.es / info(at)geotours.com.ec, URL: www.geotoursbanios.com / www.geotours.com.ec. Updated: Nov 22, 2012.

Baños Lodging

Hotels in Baños are, in general, exceptionally affordable and abundant, except during Ecuadorian holidays when nationals flock to the area to enjoy the exceptional climate and numerous activities. During the holiday seasons, advanced reservations are a must, but the rest of the year, you will normally have your pick of where to stay in Baños. Hostels and hotels are available for every type of budget, but you get what you pay for, so don't hesitate to look around before deciding where to rest your head. There are several trendy hostels around for those who enjoy artistic surroundings or social atmospheres. Hotels cater to those with a bit more to spend and have excellent on-site amenities; restaurants, saunas, swimming pools and games rooms for the kids are commonplace. Updated: Jan 23, 2013.

BUDGET
Hostel Transilvania

($8 per person) At first, one wonders whether it's a good idea to opt for a hostel called Transilvania in the middle of Ecuador. But don't be mistaken by the name (which actually means "forest") because this hostel has a great reputation in Baños. In the morning, pull up a log seat and sit down at one of the five petrified wood tables where you will be served copious amounts of fruit with your choice of pancakes or granola. Owners, Itai and Janeth are very warm, as is the entire staff, many of whom speak not only English but also Hebrew. Rooms are bright and clean and have private bathrooms, but are a little cramped. However, leather "count" chairs line the halls and are perfect for out-of-room lounging. 16 de Diciembre and Oriente, Tel: 03-274-2281, Cel: 09-9428-1661, E-mail: hostal.transilvania@gmail.com, URL: www.hostal-transilvania.com. Updated: Nov 05, 2012.

Gala Hotel

($12 per person) Gala Hotel is located on a quiet street to the southeast of the center of Baños. The hotel has a sterile, modern feel, but what Gala lacks in character it makes up

for in comfort and cleanliness. The 20 rooms are spacious and all have TVs with cable. Ask for one of the two rooms with a balcony and view of the mountains and waterfall. The per person rate jumps a few dollars during holidays. Av. 16 de Diciembre and Juan Montalvo, Tel: 03-274-2870. Updated: Nov 21, 2012.

Princesa Maria

($7-10 per person) With big clean rooms and piping hot showers, Princesa Maria is your best budget option in Baños. It's a three-block uphill walk from the main strip, but has a small communal kitchen, a TV area with a DVD collection, and WiFi throughout. The owners are friendly and accessible, always more than willing to offer help in arranging tours, or just to chat. Princesa Maria has an 11 p.m. rule, where all guests must be quiet after 11 p.m., making it a good option for couples or solo travelers, but not for big groups of party-goers. It's also one of the few places in town that is wheelchair accessible on the ground floor. Corner of Rocafuerte and Mera, Tel: 03-274-1035, E-mail: holaprincesamaria1@hotmail.com. Updated: Nov 21, 2012.

La Petite Auberge

($12-20 per person) La Petite Auberge is a pleasant, peaceful hotel tucked in a garden with views of the mountains. You can relax in the garden, chat with other travelers by the fireplace or exchange books in English, French, Dutch, German and Hebrew (the deal is give two books, get one). Rooms come with or without a fireplace and private bathroom, and most have cable TV and terraces. All include a continental breakfast in Le Petit Restaurant with French bread, homemade marmalade, juice and coffee. Credit cards are accepted, though there is a $20 minimum and a 10 percent surcharge. Ca. 16 de Diciembre 240 and Montalvo, Tel: 03-274-0936, E-mail: lepetitbanos@yahoo.com, URL: www.lepetit.banios.com. Updated: Nov 05, 2012.

Hostal Chimenea

($8-11.50 per person) Set back a bit from the busier streets of Baños, the friendly, family-run hostel La Chimenea is conveniently located close to the hot springs. The rooms are basic, but very good value; they are all clean and functional, with comfy beds and private bathrooms. Breakfast is served in a bright, airy room on the roof terrace, and you can chose from an extensive menu of pancakes, giant fruit salads and omelets. There are three computers with free internet access for guests' use, as well as a small pool, Jacuzzi and steam bath (baño de cajon). Luis A. Martinez and Rafael Vieira, Tel: 03-274-2725/274-0830, E-mail: info@hostelchimenea.com, URL: www.hostalchimenea.com. Updated: Nov 05, 2012.

Hostal Alcazar

($8-15 per person) Located two blocks from the bus station in Baños, Hostal Alcazar has matrimonial, double, triple and family rooms, which are a bit dated but clean nonetheless. All have private bathrooms and cable TV. Rooms facing the street might be noisy for some guests, especially on weekends, so keep that in mind. The service is friendly and staff is willing to answer any questions you might have about the local attractions. The hotel offers good value for money, given its reasonable prices. Ca. Oscar Efrén Reyes and Oriente, Tel: 03-274-0436, E-mail: alcazarh@hotmail.com. Updated: Nov 21, 2012.

Magic Stone

($15-25 per person) This Danish-run guesthouse is small and cozy, with just two distinct rooms. The Blue Room has a double bed and blue accents, while The Red Room has one double bed and one single bed and red decorative touches. Both have cable TV, a private bathroom with hot water, and a private outdoor space with hammocks, making it a quiet, intimate choice for travelers. Breakfast costs extra, but is a filling mix of homemade bread, butter, jam and cheese with crepes, eggs or fruit salad, accompanied by a fresh fruit juice and coffee or tea. You can buy breakfast with homemade bread, butter, jam, cheese, juice and coffee or tea for just $5. Ca. Ambato, El Campamento Los Pinos,: The place is located in the far end of Calle Ambato (toward the waterfall)Calle Ambato, (the main-street) continues on the other side of the church and you just follow the street to the very end or ask for "El Campamento Los Pinos," Tel: 09-8443-3202/8441-5924, E-mail: magicstonebanos@yahoo.com, URL: www.magicstonebanos.com. Updated: Jan 30, 2013.

Hostal Residencial Lucy

($12.50 per person) A family-run hotel with some of the cheapest rates in Baños for private rooms, Hostal Residencial Lucy has dark, dank rooms with saggy mattresses and tiny bathrooms. On the plus side, it is well-located, right between the two plazas and half a block from the supermarket. Each room comes with cable TV. There is no checkout time; you can leave whenever you want. Prices raise during holidays. Rocafuerte 240 and 16 de Diciembre, Tel: 03-274-0466. Updated: Nov 21, 2012.

Hostel Plantas y Blanco's "World"

($5-12 per person) Hostel Plantas y Blanco "World" is three different hostels in one, all within a few blocks of one another. One part has a terrace, cafetería and a steam bath; the second has Internet/WiFi, a fireplace and a small garden; and the third has WiFi, a communal kitchen, a terrace with a small pool, a fireplace and a Turkish bath. Anyone staying at any of the three parts can use the facilities at all three hostels. In general, it has a relaxed backpacker atmosphere. Its cheap dorm beds are the most reasonably priced in town, but there are simple private rooms as well. Plantas y Blanco is very popular with foreigners; don't expect to meet many locals here. Luis A. Martínez and 12 de Noviembre (main hostel), Tel: 03-274-0044 (main hostel), 03-247-0648 (other reception), Cel: 09-8470-7433, E-mail: info@plantasyblanco.com / option3@hotmail.com, URL: www.plantasyblanco.com. Updated: Jan 30, 2013.

Ross Hotel

($12-14 per person) A four-story building on the main plaza, Ross Hotel was inspired by big-chain American hotels. Its 17 rooms all have private bathrooms and cable TV, and guests can borrow DVDs and a DVD player from reception to watch movies in their rooms. Ask for a room with a view of the plaza and the waterfall in the distance. Room service from the 24-hour restaurant downstairs can usually be arranged. Prices include breakfast.Ambato and 16 de Diciembre, Plaza de La Basílica, Tel: 03-274-1709/0852, Cel: 09-9804-4580, URL: ross-innhotel@hotmail.com. Updated: Nov 21, 2012.

MID-RANGE
Hotel Casa Blanca

($20 per person) If you happen to get into Baños late at night, you might find that many of the hostels will already be closed. Fortunately, Hotel Casa Blanca is only blocks from the bus station and has an open-door policy late into the night. Rooms are comfortable and roomy, with hot showers and a TV. The staff is extremely helpful, and there is always someone at the front desk to address any concerns, which might include noise: the walls

CENTRAL ANDES

are thin, so your neighbors might keep you up at night. Prices are all-inclusive and include access to Casa Blanca's pool, Jacuzzi and steam bath, as well as a daily breakfast. Corner of Maldonado and Oriente, Tel: 03-274-0092, E-mail: hcasablanca@latinmail.com. Updated: Nov 21, 2012.

La Petite Auberge

($12-20 per person) La Petite Auberge is a pleasant, peaceful hotel tucked in a garden with views of the mountains. You can relax in the garden, chat with other travelers by the fireplace or exchange books in English, French, Dutch, German and Hebrew (the deal is give two books, get one). Rooms come with or without a fireplace and private bathroom, and most have cable TV and terraces. All include a continental breakfast in Le Petit Restaurant with French bread, homemade marmalade, juice and coffee. Credit cards are accepted, though there is a $20 minimum and a 10 percent surcharge. Ca. 16 de Diciembre 240 and Montalvo, Tel: 03-274-0936, E-mail: lepetitbanos@yahoo.com, URL: www.lepetit.banios.com. Updated: Nov 05, 2012.

Hostal Donde Iván

($19 per person) The highlight of this place is its third floor restaurant with a spectacular panoramic view of the countryside. A terrace garden, located on the fourth and fifth floor, is also a great place to sit and relax with a good book or friends. The hostel has single, double and triple rooms, and a restaurant and cafeteria where you can eat your fill of traditional Ecuadorian fare. Laundry service and luggage store are available, and bicycle, horseback riding or rafting excursions can be arranged. A buffet-style breakfast is included in room price. Eloy Alfaro 10-22 and Espejo, Tel: 03-274-1285, Cel: 09-8464-5766, E-mail: dondeivanres@yahoo.com, URL: www.hostaldondeivan.com. Updated: Nov 21, 2012.

Volcano Hotel

(ROOMS: $55-168) The Volcano Hotel offers 12 clean, comfortable and well-priced rooms in single, double, triple and suite varieties. Rooms are simply decorated and many have big windows, allowing for lots of light and nice views of the surrounding nature. Some also have balconies. It is the sort of place you can get a feeling of luxury without a steep price tag—where you can enjoy extras like a nice pool, Jacuzzi, therapeutic massages, and an on-site restaurant and bar. A breakfast buffet, consisting of bread, marmalade, cheeses, meats, fruit, yogurt, granola, pancakes and eggs, is included in room prices. The restaurant also serves lunch and dinner. Ca. Rafael Vieira and Av. Montalvo, Tel: 03-274-2140, E-mail: volcano@sbabogados.com.ec, URL: www.volcano.com.ec. Updated: Nov 05, 2012.

Monte Selva Hotel

(ROOMS: $45.50-120) Located on five hectares (12.3 ac) of land, Monte Selva consists of 12 cottages surrounded by gardens, in addition to private rooms and suites, some with nice views and large bathtubs. All have private bathrooms and cable TV; rooms have WiFi but cottages don't, though common areas have both Internet and WiFi. It has several on-site restaurants, ranging from the poolside "Los Anturios," which serves food made with ingredients from its garden, to the all-you-can-eat weekend buffet at Asador "La Terraza." Other amenities at Monte Selva include heated outdoor pool and children's pool, thermal spa with yellow volcanic waters, Jacuzzi, sauna, massage services, sports field and nature trails. Thomas Halflants and Av. Montalvo, Tel: 03-274-0244, Cel: 09-9524-9081, Fax: 03-274-1411, URL: www.monteselvaecuador.com. Updated: Nov 05, 2012.

Hosteria Bascun

(ROOMS: $33-88) The Hostería Bascun offers natural beauty, warmth, comfort and tranquility for an unforgettable stay in Baños. It provides a large number of services, including free WiFi, airport pickup (for an extra charge), complimentary breakfast, an indoor and outdoor pool, meeting facilities, and a Jacuzzi. Bascun is also wheelchair accessible, child-friendly and allows pets. The friendly staff can arrange excursions around Baños and to other parts of Ecuador. 200 meters from El Salado Aguas Termales, Quito office: Atahualpa 1127 and Av. Amazonas, Edif. Buendía, 1st floor, Tel: 02-224-6521/03-274-0740, Fax: 03-274-0334, E-mail: bascunhosteria@gmail.com, URL: www.bascun.com.ec Updated: Feb 06, 2013.

Posada J

(ROOMS: $23-65) Previously called Posada El Marques, Posada J is a comfortable, friendly hotel at the end of a quiet street. Rooms are large and well-lit, with private bathrooms and cable TV, and a few rooms have balconies with views of the falls (ask for #12 if you can get it). Conveniently close to Piscina de La Virgen baths and next door

CENTRAL ANDES

to Posada del Arte restaurant, which has the best breakfast in town, Posada J also has a spa where you can pamper yourself with a massage. The hotel can also arrange salsa dancing classes and has a laundry service. Breakfast is included in room prices. Pasaje V. Ibarra and Av. Montalvo, Tel: 03-274-0053, Fax: 03-274-1710, E-mail: posada_marques@yahoo.com, URL: www.posada-j.com. Updated: Nov 05, 2012.

Hospedaje Higueron

(ROOMS: $25-35) Run by a friendly local climber and his wife, this B&B is immaculately clean and is removed from the hustle and bustle around the corner from it. The rooms are bigger than at the comparable Posada del Arte, only instead of art on the walls, there are climbing ropes!

A quiet alternative in Baños. Ca. Los Arrayanes and Oriente, heading east on Ambato from the church, you take the second left, an unnamed street that says "A Puyo" on it. walk down this street, which seems to have less and less houses on it, but have no fear, Higueron will be on the left, just before the coliseo. Tel: 03-274-1482. Updated: Feb 06, 2013.

La Posada del Arte ♪

(ROOMS: $32-112) For art aficionados and discriminating travelers, La Posada del Arte is certainly a Baños treasure. In addition to big, comfy beds, and plenty of hot water, the hostel has a cozy sala where you can relax, listen to music or read in front of an inviting fireplace. The hostel is also a showcase for Ecuadorian paintings, including work by artists like Whitman, Soriano, Rueda, Endara and Sanchez, and all of the artwork is for sale. The rooftop terrace boasts stunning views of the surrounding scenery, including a spectacular view of the nearby waterfalls.

When your tummy starts to rumble, head to the hostel's restaurant, which features traditional Ecuadorian dishes, and international plates like curries and pasta. Vegetarian options are also available. The American-style breakfast, fresh fruit juices and fruit salads are also highly recommended—some of the best breakfast in town. The owner is particularly knowledgeable about treks and trails through the area, and even has a notebook full of helpful maps he's made himself. Ca. Velasco Ibarra and Av. Montalvo, Tel: 03-274-0083, E-mail: artehostal@yahoo.com, URL: www.posadadelarte.com. Updated: Nov 21, 2012.

HIGH-END

Samari Spa Resort ♪

(ROOMS: $186-373) Samari Spa Resort is an upscale hotel and spa with cozy and characterful rooms. Thoughtful touches like carved dark wooden furniture and ceiling rafters, tiled floors, neutrally painted exposed brick walls, and fireplaces with sitting areas or rocking chairs give them a warm and romantic feel. The junior suite even has an en-suite Jacuzzi. Samari's spa has a heated indoor pool, sauna, Turkish bath and hydro-massage, and offers lots of different treatments, including massages, facials, aromatic detoxifying wraps, reflexology, and exfoliation with salt and honey or chamomile. The hotel also has a gourmet restaurant and an underground tavern located in a former monastery. Vía a Puyo Km. 1, Tel: 03-274-1855, Cel: 09-9930-8593, E-mail: welcome@samarispa.com, URL: www.samarispa.com. Updated: Nov 05, 2012.

Luna Runtun

(ROOMS: $184 and up) A gorgeous luxury hotel and spa set in the mountains above Baños, Luna Runtun offers breathtaking views of Tungurahua Volcano, Llanganates National Park and Baños below. Swiss-owned and managed, the service is consistently good and friendly. The hotel has a network of outdoor pools and Jacuzzis overlooking the spectacular view, and manages a nearby ecological reserve that is protecting the diverse habitat on the slopes of Tungurahua. Its spa offers body treatments like volcanic ash and salt exfoliation, honey exfoliation, massages, waxing, and manicures and pedicures. You can visit the spa even if you are not staying at the hotel. Luna Runtun also has an on-site restaurant (for guests only) and a poolside coffeeshop/bar called Café del Cielo (open to public, daily 1 p.m.-10 p.m.). Café del Cielo serves 34 types of coffee as well as tapas, crepes and sandwiches—all with a view of Tungurahua volcano, the Andes and the city of Baños. Caserío Runtun Km. 6, Luna Runtun is six kilometers (3.7 mi) off the main Baños-Puyo road. To get there from Baños, get a taxi, rent a car or make arrangements through a tour company, Tel: 03-274-0882/3/03-274-0655/0835, E-mail: sales@lunaruntun.com / carmen@lunaruntun.com, URL: www.lunaruntun.com. Updated: Feb 06, 2013.

Hotel El Belen

($7-10 per person) Hotel El Belen, about two blocks from the bus station on Calle Reyes, is a cozy and comfortable family-run hotel with cable TV in every room. All except two rooms have private bathrooms. Set around a colorful, plant-adorned courtyard, El Belen's rooms are a bit outdated and some could benefit from a fresh coat of paint, but many have mountain views. A small hot tub, steam bath, community kitchen and on-site garage are additional amenities. The hotel also has its own tour operator and can organize chiva tours. Oscar Efrén Reyes and Ambato, Tel: 03-274-1024, Cel: 09-9490-5281/9758-1665, E-mail: Info@hotelelbelen.com, URL: www.hotelelbelen.com. Updated: Nov 20, 2012.

Baños Restaurants

Baños is a popular tourist destination for both Ecuadorians and foreigners alike, so you shouldn't be surprised to find that the town has a great number of places to eat. Baños' main street is lined with restaurants that provide a wide range of options, including many fast food joints, bars and grills, ice cream parlors, and the central market where you can get a taste of cuy (guinea pig).

If you venture just one block away from the main street, you will find a great number of small Ecuadorian restaurants that offer typical almuerzos (set lunches) of soup, rice and chicken and a glass of juice for a few dollars. Baños also boasts a couple of high-quality restaurants, which have varied menus, international fare and vegetarian options. You will be able to find Mexican food, Swiss specialties, French cuisine, Spanish tapas, and pub chow all in this small town.

You may also notice many locals stretching taffy along Baños' main boulevards; this is called melcocha and is a regional specialty, be sure to try some before you leave! Updated: Jan 23, 2013.

La Tasca

(ENTREES: $6.50-7) This authentic Spanish eatery gets rave reviews for its tapas, paellas, cured sausages and cheeses, and wine. Bring along your family or friends and order a mix of tapas to taste, such as Galician-style octopus, Andalucia-style meatballs, shrimp in garlic sauce, grilled pork skewers marinated in ginger and cardamon, or chorizo cooked in red wine sauce. The mixed or seafood paellas are prepared for two people and have a 40-minute wait time to be made and served. Other mains include grilled llama steak and Basque fish stew. Ca. 12 de Noviembre and Av. Montalvo, Tel: 09-9988-8530. Updated: Jan 29, 2013.

Sativa Studio Café

(ENTREES: $3.75-4.50) Sativa Studio is located within a beautifully renovated abandoned garage and nearly the entire place is made with recycled materials; the floors and tabletops are mosaiced with salvaged tile from the town Cathedral and from a local high school art project. Sativa's small vegan menu includes a delicious black bean and potato veggie burger, vegan tamales and fried plantains with an organic salad. Its specialization is probiotic drinks such as kombucha, meads, herbal elixers and guarapos (like a natural sweet wine made with organic fruits), which are meant to energize the body and strengthen the immune system.

Sativa also has a variety of loose leaf herbal teas, Caribbean drinks made with hibiscus flowers, and the highly recommended rosemary lemonade. Chilled out and eclectic, Sativa features Afro-Caribbean art and music, an indoor garden and will eventually have a pottery studio out back. Monday-Saturday 11 a.m.-11 p.m. Closed Sundays. Ca. Luis A Martínez, across from Casa Hood, Tel: 09-9723-5598, URL: www.sativastudiocafe.com. Updated: Nov 22, 2012.

Stray Dog Brew Pub

(ENTREES: $4-7.50) Opened by the owners of the well-known Posada del Arte hotel and restaurant, Stray Dog Brewpub is a happy addition to the restaurant and bar scene in Baños. This microbrewery has four different (and excellent) beers, all brewed locally using Agua de la Vida spring water. Try one or a few, or opt for the sampler, where you can taste a little of each for $0.50 per small glass. Accompany your beer with an item off the pub food menu, which features delicious hot wings, pulled pork sandwiches, homemade lamb sausages, burgers and taco plates. You've been warned: the food service is extremely slow, but the food and beer is worthwhile. Tuesday-Sunday 3 p.m.-midnight. Closed Mondays. Corner of Ca. Maldonado and Rocafuerte, Tel: 03-274-0083, URL: www.straydogbrewpub.com. Updated: Nov 22, 2012.

Blah Blah Café

(SANDWICHES: $2-3.50) Blah Blah Café has graced Baños for more than 10 years and specializes in sandwiches. It is a nice spot for breakfast, a coffee or a quick but filling lunch. The sandwiches are on large baguettes and are stuffed with any combination of veggies, omelettes, cold cuts and cheese, having more than enough vegetar-

ian options. With magazines and books in English and Spanish, music and some board games like Chinese checkers, the café has a very relaxed and comfortable atmosphere. Corner of Halflants and Luis A. Martinez, Tel: 09-8402-3466.
Updated: Nov 22, 2012.

Mariane

(ENTREES: $6.75-11.50) Mariane is not a typical Baños restaurant. Hidden a block away from the main street is a small piece of Provence, where you can enjoy French-style cuisine and music in a cozy atmosphere. The food is of a high quality and includes favorites such as French onion soup and a range of steaks, which can be paired with South American wines. Some menu highlights include grilled steak with herbs de provence, Moroccan chicken with spicy harissa sauce, and cheese and meat fondue. Outdoor seating in the garden, which is lit up at night, is also possible. Although mostly open for dinner, Mariane's is sometimes open for lunch, from 1 p.m. on; call in advance to confirm. Monday-Saturday 6-10 p.m. Closed Sundays. Av. Montalvo, between Halflants and Eloy Alfaro, Tel: 03-274-1947, Cel: 09-9522-3555, E-mail: juliohotelmariane@hotmail.com.
Updated: Nov 21, 2012.

Café Hood

(ENTREES: $5.50-7) Not to be confused with Casa Hood, Café Hood is a small, brightly painted restaurant on the Calle Maldonado side of Parque Central. The café cooks up a range of international fare, including Greek and Hindu plates, Indonesian pork chops, and Pad Thai, along with pasta dishes, sandwiches and salads. Its breakfast menu includes options with pancakes, Belgian waffles or fruit salad. Overall, the food is decent and there is a good selection of vegetarian dishes, making it easy to please a crowd with mixed tastes and preferences. Monday-Tuesday and Thursday-Sunday 10 a.m.-10 p.m. Closed Wednesdays. Ca. Maldonado, between Ambato and Rocafuerte, Parque Central, Tel: 03-274-0537, Cel: 09-8469-5836, E-mail: cafehood@yahoo.com.mx.
Updated: Nov 22, 2012.

Coffee Bar Jota and Jota

(SNACKS: $1.20-5) Previously known as Rincón de Suiza, Coffee Bar Jota & Jota has since changed hands and names, but still has excellent coffee, homemade cakes, German specialties, and fruit juices and smoothies. Try the creative "Kaffee Tungurahua," which is coffee with milk foam and strawberry

sauce, made to resemble the lava-spitting volcano. At nighttime, it is also a chill place to enjoy some cocktails, wines, liquors and fine tobaccos. The establishment also has pool tables, table games and sofa corner, as well as an outdoor garden with tables. If you feel like reading, there are newspapers, magazines and a book exchange. Overall, Coffee Bar Jota & Jota has a pleasant and cozy atmosphere. Tuesday-Sunday 9 a.m.-midnight. Closed Mondays. Luis A. Martinez and Haflants, Tel: Cel: 09-9837-3240, E-mail: banios@coffeebarjotajota.com, URL: www.coffeebarjotajota.com.
Updated: Nov 22, 2012.

Casa Hood

(ENTREES: $4.50-6.50) Tucked away behind the market, the eccentric Casa Hood is part café/restaurant, part bookshop and part cinema. Its decorations, made up of family snapshots, leftover New Years masks and bizarre artwork, combine with the friendly and helpful staff to create a great atmosphere. The international food is truly delicious and very reasonably priced; try the blackened Cajun-style trout, falafel plate, spicy curry or Chinese black bean stir fry.

There are lots of options for vegetarians, including the daily set-price vegetarian menu consisting of a soup, main plate, dessert and juice. The book trade, free movie each afternoon at 4:30 p.m. (with $1.50 purchase), and end-of-the-evening happy hour (9:30-10:13 p.m.) make this place a do-not-miss spot. Closed Tuesdays. Ca. Luis A. Martinez, behind the Mega Santa Maria supermarket, Tel: 03-274-2668.
Updated: Nov 12, 2012.

Pancho Villa

(ENTREES: $4.50-8.50) Pancho Villa is the place to go for tasty Mexican food or some quality tequila. This cute upstairs restaurant with only a few tables is plastered with poetry, Mexican posters, framed pictures of Frida Kahlo and postcards from past patrons. The menu features favorites like burritos, chalupas, nachos, fajitas, and taco plates with beans, rice, meat and flour tortillas. Bring some friends along and order a few Coronas, margaritas, shots of tequila or a pitcher of sangria to complete the meal. If it is a nice day, you can sit at one of the two outdoor tables. Monday-Saturday 12:30-3:30 p.m. and 6-10 p.m. Closed Sundays.Ca. Luis A. Martínez and Eloy Alfaro, Tel: 03-274-2138, Cel: 09-9832-6403.
Updated: Nov 12, 2012.

Swiss Bistro

(ENTREES: $12 and up) Specializing in culinary creations from Switzerland, this restaurant features an extensive menu that is sure to please even the pickiest palates. While its meat and cheese fondues are a definite highlight, the beef stroganoff, chicken cordon bleu, fresh steamed trout and grilled hunks of meat do not disappoint. Complete your meal with one of Swiss Bistro's desserts; try the Swiss ice cream or banana flambé for a real treat.

The restaurant also features a variety of Argentine and Chilean wines, beers, juices and gourmet coffees. For the little ones, there is a set children's menu, which includes French fries and ice cream, sure to win over the little munchkin. Daily noon-11 p.m. Luis Martínez y Eloy Alfaro, Tel: 03-274-2262, E-mail: welcome@swiss-bistro.com, URL: www.swiss-bistro.com. Updated: Jun 13, 2013.

Café del Cielo

(SNACKS: $1-5) Perched on the side of Volcán Tungurahua, Café del Cielo (part of the Luna Runtun Spa complex) is one of the lights that shine out like a beacon above Baños. Through the giant glass windows, which make up two of the café walls, you can enjoy sweeping views of the town and the surrounding Andes.

The food menu is not extensive (though there are 34 varieties of coffee), but items are reasonably priced, making this a great place to enjoy a drink or a snack, as well as the main attraction: the view. Daily 1-10 p.m. Caserío Runtun Km. 6, Tel: 03-274-0882/3/655/835, URL: www.lunaruntun.com/english/cafe_bar_resta.html#cielo. Updated: Nov 05, 2012.

Banos Nightlife
Leprechaun Bar

This small but fun bar in the heart of Baños has no cover and a bumping dance floor blasting salsa, merengue, reggaeton, hip hop, rock and more. On crowded nights, the back patio opens up where there is an outdoor bar and big pit in the middle where a bonfire blazes.

Brave souls can order a "Bob Marley," a flaming shot of grenadine, mint liqueur and banana liqueur mixed with white rum. Monday-Saturday 8 a.m.-2 a.m. Closed Sundays. Ca. Alfaro and Oriente, Tel: 09-9901-1913, E-mail: petto_262@hotmail.com. Updated: Nov 22, 2012.

Around Baños
Things To See and Do Around Baños
Río Verde

Río Verde is about 17 kilometers (10.6 mi) south of Baños and is known for its waterfalls and lush vegetation. Most travelers see this area on a day trip from Baños by bike, tour bus, chiva, scooter or motorbike. The biggest waterfall in the area, El Pailón del Diablo, is the stopping point to the south for most tours from Baños and features a less than one-kilometer (0.6-mi) path leading through the forest to the waterfall as well as some restaurants and lodges set deep in the woods. Updated: Jun 13, 2013.

El Pailón del Diablo ⟩

A beautiful waterfall about one kilometer (0.6 mi) off the main road from Baños to Puyo, El Pailón del Diablo (the Devil's Cauldron) is well worth the visit. If you ride a bike from Baños (17 km/10.6 mi), you will pass several other waterfalls on your way. Park at the Restaurante Las Hortensias just after a small bridge and head downhill on a small footpath, which weaves through beautiful cloud forest until you reach a suspended bridge. You can view the waterfall from the bridge, or, for $0.50, pass through El Otro Lado restaurant and walk on their private path until you are almost close enough to touch the waterfall. There is great birdwatching here and you will see a variety of butterflies and orchids along the way.

If you biked down and don't relish the idea of biking all the way back to Baños (mostly uphill), the buses will help you stash your bikes or you can hitch a ride with someone passing through. Large flatbed trucks often park in front of Restaurante Hortensias, offering rides back to Baños (around $2 per person). The bus is much cheaper, but you will save the trek to the main road. 17 kilometers (10.6 mi) from Baños towards Puyo. Updated: Nov 23, 2012.

Lodging Around Banos
La Casa Verde

(ROOMS: $26-63) Owned by an accommodating Kiwi-Aussie couple, La Casa Verde is a peaceful, eco-friendly retreat along a river. About a 20-minute walk from the center of Baños (or a short taxi ride), La Casa Verde has beautiful views of the nearby river, valley and mountains, especially enjoyable from a hammock on its shared deck space. Comfortable rooms sleep one to five people, with the nicest and most expensive ones being those with private balconies. All have orthopedic mattresses and locally woven cotton sheets. Other amenities include a fully equipped communal kitchen, free drinking water, an extensive DVD and board games collection, and an on-site spa where you can get massages or other eco-friendly treatments. The included breakfast is delicious and filling. El Camino Real, Santa Ana. From the Baños bus terminal: Continue down the main road toward Puyo for approximately one kilometer (0.6 mi) until you get to Barrio San Vicente. Turn left off main road to enter Barrio San Vicente. Continue for 300 meters (984 ft) and you will reach a stone/dirt road (El Camino Real), before the paved road turns to the right. Go straight down El Camino Real and the hotel is 700 meters (2,297 ft) on the left-hand side (the river side). A taxi will cost $1.50 or it's a two kilometer (1.2 mi) downhill walk. Tel: 09-8659-4189, E-mail: staygreen@lacasaverde.com.ec, URL: www.lacasaverde.com.ec. Updated: Jan 23, 2013.

Hacienda Manteles

(ROOMS: $95-195) Located about a half-hour from Baños, Hacienda Manteles is an elegant, full-service hostería. First constructed in 1580, Hacienda Manteles is one of the oldest in Ecuador. The establishment is relatively small, with only 10 rooms, but each has a private bath and hot water. There is also an on-site restaurant specializing in traditional cuisine. The hacienda owns 200 hectares (494 ac) of primary cloud forest, and part of its profit goes to preservation. Due to the location, you can find several species of hummingbirds and orchids on the Manteles' grounds. The hacienda also offers activities such as horseback riding, birdwatching and "agriculture day," in which guests are encouraged to participate in the planting and care of local crops. Breakfast and a three-course dinner is included

in the price, along with a welcome cocktail and coffee. Hacienda: Km. 11 Vía Patate–Baños by La Ruta Turística Ecológica Patate; Quito office: Ca. General Eloy Alfaro 320 and García Moreno, Cumbayá, Tel: 02-603-9415, Cel: 09-9461-4275/9213-5309, E-mail: sales@haciendamanteles.com, URL: www.haciendamanteles.com. Updated: Nov 05, 2012.

Miramelindo ❗

($30-45 per person) Walking through the doors of Miramelindo is like walking into the colorful otherworldly scene of a Gonzalo Endara Crow painting. The hotel itself is a life-size work of art. It's truly a surprise to find such a fine hotel and restaurant in the tiny, remote town of Río Verde. Located right off the highway and next to the river, its a quick walk to the thundering Pailón del Diablo waterfall. Stay in one of the 13 cheery rooms or opt for the four- to six-person cabin. No matter which you choose, you will have access to Miramelindo's beautiful grounds, which include a garden with 2,000 orchid species, a pool and Jacuzzi, movie theater and gourmet restaurant. Additionally, its friendly-family service and excellent food (the included breakfast buffet is amazing) make this place highly recommended and an excellent-value option. **Río Verde**, Tel: 03-249-3004/3212, Cel: 09-9587-3307/8751-4617, E-mail: hosteriamiramelindo@gmail.com, URL: www.miramelindo.banios.com, Updated: Nov 05, 2012.

El Otro Lado

(ROOMS: $65) El Otro Lado is set within a private reserve of the same name, which is only accessible to hotel guests. The reserve has numerous nature trails that lead to waterfalls and cross rivers, and is home to many species of birds and butterflies. El Otro Lado has just three cabins, one of which is fully furnished with a kitchen and porch and can accommodate four people, and another which can accommodate two people. Both require a minimum stay of two nights. It also has a yoga and meditation cabin, adding to the relaxing atmosphere. Guests can cook in the communal kitchen as well, complete with basic ingredients. One kilometer (0.6 mi) off the main Baños-Puyo road: from Baños, take a bus ($0.40) or a taxi ($8) to the village of Río Verde, take the trail down to the famous waterfall "Pailon del Diablo," cross the suspension bridge and you will see El Otro Lado. E-mail: elotroladoreserva@gmail.com, URL: www.elotroladoreserva.com. Updated: Nov 23, 2012.

Hacienda Manteles

CENTRAL ANDES

Hacienda Leito

(ROOMS: $85-250) Whether you're an adventurer in search of a relaxing break or a couple looking for a romantic getaway, Hacienda Leito can cater to your needs. This spectacular hacienda is located just three hours south of Quito, and convenientlyclose to Ecuador's rainforest and the hulking Tungurhua Volcano. It offers a spectacular setting coupled with a warm, family atmosphere. Bright spacious rooms appointed with tasteful antique furniture boast soft, comfy beds that promise a restful sleep. (Did we mention that all rooms have a fireplace?) Kick back and relax in the charming social spaces, or request a tailor-made tour: the hacienda can arrange hiking, horseback riding, river rafting, paragliding, biking and cultural expeditions. From nature lovers and active travelers to families and photographers, this place has something for everyone, including a spa that offers a menu of 24 massages and therapies. Kilometer 10 on the way from Baños - Patate, Tel: 593-03-2859329/2859331, E-mail: info@haciendaleito.com, URL: www.haciendaleito.com.
Updated: Nov 05, 2012.

Restaurants Around Banos

El Pailón Restaurant

The owners of El Pailón have taken the initiative to create paths through the cloud forest leading to the waterfall Pailón del Diablo. For $1, you can take a walk through the orchid-lined forest until you are almost close enough to reach out your hand and touch the falls. The owners have also created a series of balconies over the base of the falls and there is even a path you can take to get behind the massive rush of waters (but you have to crawl). The restaurant itself doesn't have a view of the Pailón de Diablo waterfall, but has open-air seating looking out at the lush forest hills and a suspension bridge over the river. Río Verde 17 Km Via Banos, Tel: 03-288-4204.
Updated: Nov 23, 2012.

Restaurante Las Hortensias

Right off the main road from Baños to Puyo and near the entrance to the path down to Pailón del Diablo, Restaurante Las Hortensias offers typical Ecuadorian cuisine like trout, grilled chicken and churrasco (grilled or fried beef with a fried egg on top). This restaurant is a perfect place to park your bike or scooter and catch your breath before heading down to see the waterfall. Río Verde, Tel: 03-249-3016.

CHIMBORAZO

At 6,310 meters (20,702 ft), Chimborazo is the highest mountain in Ecuador and, thanks to the equatorial bulge, qualifies as the furthest point from the center of the Earth. Chimborazo is actually an extinct volcano that is believed to have last erupted some 10,000 years ago.

The volcano's massive glacier persists, but it has dwindled in recent years due to global climate change and ongoing eruptions of Tungurahua, which spews black ash onto the Chimborazo's eastern slopes. This causes it to conduct more of the sun's heat and thus melt at a greater than normal rate. Despite the snowcap's decline, Chimborazo's white crown is still among the most beautiful sights in Ecuador.
Updated: Apr 12, 2013.

Getting To and Away from Chimborazo

Chimborazo is located approximately 150 kilometers southwest of Quito. The best way to reach the mountain is via a dirt road that branches off southeast from the **Ambato-Guaranda** road.

Take the Pan American Highway south to Ambato and then head southwest towards Guaranda. About 56 kilometers from Ambato, you will arrive at a dirt road that leads to the Whymper refuge, named after Edward Whymper, the British climber who made the first ascent of Chimborazo in 1880. This juncture is sometimes referred to as "el cruce del Arenal" and is marked by a deserted block house. The road winds 12 kilometers across the windblown countryside to a parking area and lower refuge below the Whymper hut.

If you do not have a vehicle, you can take a bus to "el Cruce del Arenal" and walk to the lower refuge via the main dirt road. If you decide to take a cross-country route, walk southeast on the dirt road for about four kilometers until you come to a sharp bend where you must turn left and climb due east for approximately four more kilometers until you see the lower refuge and parking area. This takes approximately four hours.

You can also hire transportation from **Ambato** or **Riobamba**. Riobamba is more pleasant than Ambato and offers a better selection of accommodations and restaurants. The trip to the parking area directly from

Quito takes between three and four hours in a four-wheel drive vehicle. Hiking to the Whymper refuge is straightforward and takes about 45 minutes from the parking area. Updated: Apr 12, 2013.

Things To See and Do in Chimborazo

Chimborazo, is a magical full of life province, it has great touristic attractions, both cultural and natural, such as Chimborazo, and it´s meaning to the people, Tungurahua volcano and andean forests, tropical forests, waterfalls, clean rivers, and ever green valley. Updated: Apr 12, 2013.

Horseback Riding in Chimborazo

($55 x 1 day, $90 x 2 days) Head on out for a high altitude horse back adventure across the ruggedly beautiful Chimborazo highlands, known only to herds of wild Llamas and remote communities who live in the mountains far from civilization. Saddle up on a horse and witness the contrast between the rugged and rocky lunar landscapes of Chimborazo´s mountainous highlands and the lusciously green valleys of Bolivar province. At our journeys end we arrive at Salinas, a picturesque pueblo nestled within the verdant mountains. Its cobbled streets and quaintly colorful houses host an enterprising people whom export their iconic cultural heritage of hand woven clothing and exotic Ecuadorian chocolate all over the world. The intricately knitted sweaters, scarves, blankets, beanies and other clothing consist of only of the highest in quality Alpaca wool that sell for a fraction of the cost than its exported equivalent in Italy and France. Stay another day and explore the Salt Mines and Caves of archaeological significance close to this historically rich town. Offices are located on Avenida Daniel Leon Borja and Uruguay no. 21-60. Riobamba, Ecuador. Book via E mail, once in Riobamba you´ll be picked up from bus terminal, Lodging is usually included on the trip. Tel: 099-831-1282, URL: www.ecuadorecoadventure.com. Updated: Apr 12, 2013.

Summiting Chimborazo

Though Chimborazo is not Ecuador's most technically difficult climb, summiting it requires previous glacier experience,a complete array of climbing gear, stamina, and adequate acclimatization. Climbers should make ascents of other nearby peaks, such as Iliniza Norte and Cotopaxi, and consider spending a couple of nights at the Whymper refuge to properly acclimatize.

Chimborazo has five summits: Whymper Peak (6,310 meters), Veintimilla Summit (6,267 meters), North Summit (6,200 meters), Central Summit (6,000 meters) and Eastern Summit (5,500 meters). Most people that make the effort to climb Chimborazo try for its highest point, Whymper Peak. There are several routes to Whymper Peak, and they vary slightly year to year because of the ever changing glacier.

Climbers usually depart from Whymper refuge at midnight to make the eight to 10-hour slog to the summit. Generally, the route takes you to the left of Thielman Glacier to El Corredor, which begins just below some large rock outcroppings. Traverse right of these outcroppings and then climb left up a steep snowfield until you reach another large rock outcropping called El Castillo. From here ascend northwest toward the Veintimilla summit. The final leg of the climb changes frequently due to a shifting, large crevasse, so it is strongly advised to go with a local guide who knows the current route. The descent takes between two and four hours. Updated: Apr 12, 2013.

Chimborazo Lodging
Estrella del Chimborazo

($50 per person) The Historical "Tambo de Totorillas" (roadside inn) was once located in this place, along the old "Royal Road" between Guayaquil and Quito. The owners have rebuilt the inn, combining its traditional architecture with modern comfort and services. The name of the refuge, Estrella Del Chimborazo (Star of Chimborazo) is the name of a hummingbird that is endemic to the Chimborazo area. Decorated with photographs and illustrations of the natural and Andean history of Chimborazo, the shelter is at the center of the Base Camp and provides a place where guests can rest, eat and acclimatize comfortably and warmly.

There is capacity for 30 persons in the dining room. National and international cuisine is served on a daily basis. Professional mountain guides can be provided to help climb to the summits of the Chimborazo and Carihuayrazo, along with naturalist guides for excursions into the surrounding areas in the páramo. Km. 36 vía al Chimborazo / Comunidad Pulinguí-San Pablo / Valle de Totorillas, Tel: 02-236-4278 / 02-236-4258 / 02-296-4915, Fax: 5933 2969604, E-mail: marcocruz@andinanet. net, URL: www.expediciones-andinas.com. Updated: Apr 12, 2013.

RIOBAMBA

 2,754m 144,795  03

Broad streets and aging, but still-charming colonial buildings characterize this buzzing town, situated in the heart of the central Andes. The capital of Chimborazo Province, Riobamba is a commercial hub and cultural center for both nearby indigenous communities and the city's more European-styled constituents. Originally located 20 kilometers south — until an earthquake leveled it in 1797 — today's Riobamba features several attractive cathedrals, plazas and parks, including the noteworthy Parque Maldonado, Parque Sucre, Parque Guayaquil and Santa Bárbara Cathedral.

On clear days, the city boasts unparalleled views of five of the region's volcanic peaks: Chimborazo, Altar, Tungurahua, Carihuairazo and Sangay. (Find a hotel with a rooftop terrace and spend the morning savoring the stunning view). Saturday is market day, when indigenous people from across the region come to sell their wares.

While the market in Plaza de la Concepción (Orozco y Colón, south of the Convento de la Concepción) is geared towards tourists, the San Alfonso (Argentinos y 5 de Junio) and La Condamine (Carabobo y Colombia) markets are also worthwhile browsing-stops, especially if you're looking for fresh fruit or traditional textiles. Despite its agreeable, laidback-but-busy atmosphere, Riobamba is probably more known as a gateway to nearby sites than as a destination in and of itself. You can go off-the-rails with the famous Nariz del Diablo (Devil's Nose) train ride, venture into the wilds of nearby Chimborazo, or trail-blaze through the northern stretch of Parque Nacional Sangay. Updated: Apr 12, 2013.

Getting To and Away from Riobamba

Buses to Riobamba from **Quito** depart every half-our from the Quitumbe Terminal. The bus station in Riobamba is located about 2 km north of El Centro in Riobamba on the street León Borja. It is feasible to walk from the station to the city's center, but when it's late at night or you have a lot of luggage, you're probably better off just taking a taxi.

There are regular buses from the terminal in Riobamba to Quito (4.5 hours), **Guaya-**
quil (5 hours), **Cuenca** (7 hours), **Guaranda** (2.5 hours) and **Santo Domingo** (5.5 hours). As is usual with Ecuador, the fares will run about a dollar per hour.

Also, from Thursday to Sunday, a train departs at 8 a.m. from the train station (on the corner of Av. Daniel León Borja and Carabobo, Tel: 1-800-873637) to **Urbina** and **Colta**. The trips offer you the chance to either see the Ice Merchants or the Colta Lagoon and it's incredible surrounding landscapes. All train rides are round trip, and cost $11 for Urbina, and $15 for Colta. Updated: Apr 19, 2013.

Riobamba Tours

Ecuador Eco Adventure

Environmentalists, socially minded individuals and conscientious adventurers will want to check out the host of volunteer opportunities, sustainable tourist projects and guided adventures available with Ecuador Eco Adventure. Promoting ecotourism and cross-cultural understanding, this organization has options for participating in remote community work, reforestation projects, coastline regeneration, or wildlife rescue and sanctuary volunteer work. If you don't have time to volunteer, you can still enhance your trip to Ecuador with one of its off-the-beaten track archaeological adventures, horseback riding tours or professionally assisted trekking trips. Av. Daniel leon Borja 2160 and Uruguay, Riobamba, Tel: 03-296-8412, Cel: 09-9831-1282, URL: www.ecuadorecoadventure.com. Updated: Feb 07, 2013.

Things To See and Do in Riobamba

The capital of Chimborazo province, Riobamba and the surrounding areas are considered to be the heartland of Ecuador. It is an attractive if somewhat worn-out city, and on a clear day you can see five volcanoes: Altar, Tunguragua, Chimborazo, Carihuairazo and Sangay. Riobamba has much to offer the visitor. It has markets which sell native handicrafts, such as ponchos, baskets and blankets, and also finely carved tagua nuts. It has attractive plazas and parks, and is a good place from which to explore the Chimborazo region. There are also a few interesting museums in Riobamba.

La Balbanera Church

When the Spanish came to Ecuador, one of the first places they settled was Riobamba area (after conquering what was then part

CENTRAL ANDES

of the Inca empire). One of the first things they built was La Balbanera Church, a stone edifice that dates back to 1524.

Although the original building was destroyed in a massive 1797 earthquake and was rebuilt in the later reconstruction efforts, the church is still considered the oldest in Ecuador. La Balbanera, with its rough stone walls, simple adornments and crude bell tower, will not be the most dazzling stop on your trip. (If you're interested in intricate facades and are pressed for time, head to the near-by Catedral de Riobamba instead).

Still, if you're a history buff, or simply want to see one of the earliest signposts on the long road into Spanish-Ecuadorian history, La Balbanera Church is worth a quick visit. The church's arched entryway features low pillars, cherubs and rough religious imagery. Also worth noting are what appear to be nautical motifs, such as anchors. The church is located in Cajabamba, 18 km (11 miles) from the city of Riobamba near Lago Colta. Updated: Feb 08, 2013.

Horseback trip to Salinas

(PRICE: $75 per person) Near Riobamba, you can ride horses through the Chimborazo highlands, rounding the magnificent volcano, and crossing into the national reserve, where you can admire the wildlife of the páramo. To complete this Andean safari, plan to spend the night in the mountain town of Salinas. With any luck, you'll watch the brilliant sunset over the clouds of the tall sierra hills. In the morning, relax in the thermal waters of the volcano. Av. Daniel leon Borja 2160 and Uruguay, Riobamba, Tel: 03-296-8412, Cel: 09-9831-1282, URL: www.ecuadorecoadventure.com. Updated: Feb 07, 2013.

Parque Sucre

Parque Sucre was created in the Plaza de Santo Domingo to honor a hero of the Ecuadorian fight for independence, Antonio José de Sucre. The foundation stone for Parque Sucre was laid on Aug. 10, 1919, and the park was inaugurated on Nov. 11, 1924. In 1913, the inaugural year of Riobamba's municipal water system, the city celebrated with the installation of a large fountain in Plaza Santo Domingo. The fountain, which features the Roman god of the sea, Neptune, surrounded by cherubs, is a centerpiece of Parque Sucre. Visitors can locate the fountain just opposite Colegio Nacional Maldonado. Updated: Feb 08, 2013.

Catedral de Riobamba

Riobamba's original cathedral was destroyed in an earthquake that leveled the majority of the city in 1797. Elements of the baroque-style façade were rescued and reused in the reconstruction of the current edifice, which was finished in 1837. By 1967, the building had fallen into disrepair, and faculty from La Universidad Central de Quito agreed to help with reconstruction efforts. The building's limestone façade today is a striking mix of religious and pastoral scenes done in bas-relief. Inside, you'll find a mural of 1980 Nobel Peace Prize laureate Adolfo Pérez Esquivel. Also noteworthy is a mural on the nave of Christ with indigenous features, painted by artist Oswaldo Viteri. The Chapel of Santa Barbara is located to one side of the cathedral. Ca. 5 de Junio, between Ca. Orozco and Ca. Veloz. Updated: Feb 08, 2013.

La Virgen de la Merced

La Virgen de la Merced is a pretty white and red church on the corner of Eugenio Espejo and Guayaquil streets, across from the Riobamba food market. An inscription inside the vestibule reads "Señor, no nos dejes caer en la tentación" (Lord, lead us not into temptation) and the interior of the church features a large gold altar. Like many Riobamba attractions, however, La Virgen is usually closed. The church opens for services Tuesday through Friday (at 7 a.m.), Saturdays (7 p.m.) and Sundays (7, 9, 11 a.m. and 7 p.m.). Eugenio Espejo and Guayaquil. Updated: Feb 08, 2013.

Riobamba Lodging

The majority of tourists who visit Riobamba used to do so to ride through the famed Nariz del Diablo. For this reason, the majority of places to stay are concentrated around the train station. If you are on a budget, and will only be in town for a short while, there are a number of cheap options in Riobamba. Hostels may not have as many amenities as a fancy hotel, but for one night, they tend to do the trick. If you are planning on staying in town for a few days, have a larger budget, and are looking for a quiet holiday, it is worth staying at one of the hotels that are located outside of the city of Riobamba. Accommodations on the outskirts tend to be fancier, and the scenery is unforgettable.

Abraspungo

(ROOMS: $87-210) The Hacienda Abraspungo was built in traditional Spanish style and is set amid extensive, flowered grounds.

It offers 42 beautiful single, double and triple suites. Located 3.5 kilometers (2.2 mi) from Riobamba, it forms an ideal headquarters to explore the countryside. Horseback riding can be arranged and a small spa is under construction. The on-site restaurant-bar offers excellent food and has a pleasant atmosphere of casual elegance. The staff is friendly and helpful. Km. 3.5 1/2 Vía Riobamba - Guano, Tel: 03-236-4031/4274/5/6/7, Cel: 09-9768-3450, E-mail: info@haciendaabraspungo.com, URL: www.abraspungo.com.ec. Updated: Feb 07, 2013.

Hotel Rioroma

($10-20 per person) The rooms at Rioroma are first rate, with full carpeting, private baths, telephones and cable TV. It also provides private parking and a restaurant. Its 32 rooms come in simple, double and triple varieties. Cdla. Sultana de los Andes Mz. G 14-15 Panamerican Highway South Km. 1/2. Updated: Feb 07, 2013.

Hostería La Andaluza

(ROOMS: $66-98) This charming hotel is located about 10 minutes away from Riobamba and is the perfect place to stay if you want a quiet countryside experience in the area. Located near Chimborazo, you can enjoy the mountainous splendor from your hotel room here. The hostería offers suites and junior suites as well as regular rooms. All rooms feature a private bathroom, heating system and TV. On-site there is a gym, sauna, steam bath, bar and restaurant. Panamerican Highway North Km 16Vía Riobamba - Ambato, Chuquipogio Community, Tel: 03-294-9370/1/2/3/4/5, E-mail: welcome@hosteriaandaluza.com, URL: www.hosteriaandaluza.com. Updated: Feb 07, 2013.

Hotel Zeus Internacional

(ROOMS: $34-53) Hotel Zeus is one of the nicer hotels in Riobamba, and is of excellent value given its reasonable prices and long list of amenities. Polished wooden accents give the rooms a comfortable, earthly feel. All come equipped with LCD TVs with cable and DVD players, WiFi, duvets and electronic locks with key cards. The executive ones also have mountain views and high-end bathrooms with granite counter tops. There is also an on-site restaurant, bar and café, as well as a games room, a full gym and an events room. Av. Daniel León Borja 41-29 and Duchicela, Tel: 03-296-8036/7/8, E-mail: reservaciones@hotelzeus.com.ec, URL: www.hotelzeus.com.ec.

Hostal Montecarlo

(ROOMS: $25) Located only a few blocks from the train station, Montecarlo is a very convenient place to stay. Its rooms are comfortable; they are not the most elegant but are sufficient nonetheless. There is also a café on-site, where the included continental breakfast is served each morning. Av. 10 de Agosto 25-41, between García Moreno and España, Tel: 03-295-3204/296-1577, Fax: 03-296-0557, E-mail: montecarloriobamba@andinanet.net. Updated: Feb 07, 2013.

Hotel Tren Dorado

($17 per person) Clean bathrooms, spacious comfortable rooms, friendly service and an excellent location makes Hotel Tren Dorado a great place to lay your backpack for a few days while you explore Riobamba. Painted bright green and pink on the outside, Tren Dorado is hard to miss. Located on Carabobo, the hotel is just one block to the east of the Riobamba train station, and only blocks from the weekend markets, museums and the many restaurants that lie along Avenida Leon Borja. Tren Dorado serves up a delicious continental breakfast buffet of bread, fruit, granola, yogurt, coffee, juice and tea. Carabobo 22-35 and 10 de Agosto, Tel: 03-296-4890, E-mail: htrendorado@hotmail.com. Updated: Feb 07, 2013.

El Troje

(ROOMS: $65) Located in the pleasant countryside just 5 minutes from Riobamba, El Troje is a traveler's dream. Rustic meets modern in this lovely hostería, which boasts 48 stylish rooms (fully equipped with TV and phone) and spectacular views of Ecuador's highest peak, Chimborazo. Relax and unwind in the warm and cozy setting, where you can spend the day pampering yourself in the Turkish sauna or breaking a sweat on the basketball and volleyball courts. The more adventurous can organize a tour; mountain biking, hiking, trekking, and horseback riding expeditions are perfect for exploring the surrounding countryside.

After a hard day of trail blazing or lounging by the pool, head to El Troje's charming restaurant, La Arquería. Top-notch local and international cuisine paired with first-class service ensures a memorable dining experience. Lucky visitors may even catch one of El Troje's live Andean shows, complete with traditional folkloric music and dance. In addition to a great atmosphere, this place is family-friendly and equipped to handle weddings, banquets and conventions. Kilometer 4.5 via Riobamba-Chambo, Tel: 03-262-2200,1, 2and3, E-mail: reservas@eltroje.com / sales@eltroje.com, URL: www.eltroje.com. Updated: Feb 07, 2013.

Hotel San Pedro de Riobamba

(ROOMS: $71-162) Hotel San Pedro is an example of colonial republican Ecuadorian luxury. Built in the 20th century, this house belonged to a worker from the Ecuadorian railway company who provided lodging to early tourists. It was rebuilt a few years ago to preserve its original splendor and charm. The personalized attention makes for a unique and unforgettable stay. Av. Daniel León Borja 29-50, between Carabobo and Juan Montalvo, Tel: 03-294-0586/1359, E-mail: sanpedroderiobambahotel@hotmail.com, URL: www.hotelsanpedroderiobamba.com. Updated: Feb 07, 2013.

Riobamba Restaurants

There are not shortages of places to eat in Riobamba, however most of the restaurants are mom-and-pop-run holes in the walls. Their food usually is not bad, and is cheap, but sanitary conditions often seem questionable. If you are looking for a little nicer place to eat, a walk up the main street in town, Avenida 10 de Agosto, will lead you to most of your more upscale (and clean) options. Updated: Feb 08, 2013.

Café Orfeo

This café turns into more of a bar during the night. It is a great place to go if you want a more relaxing night out, instead of a drunken night at the discoteca. It tends to have live music often, especially on the weekends. It is located just one block off of 10 de Agosto, and is very close to the city center. Primera Constituyente and García Moreno. Updated: Feb 07, 2013.

Pizzería San Valentín

(PIZZAS: $10 and up) Pizzería San Valentín is a cozy pizza joint that has shadows of an old-school American pizza place, with tasty pizzas, chilled beers and a jukebox to boot. Besides the traditional slice, San Valentín also serves standard pizzeria-fare such as mozzarella sticks and special French bread calzones. San Valentín also serves Mexican food; while it's not the hot spicy food you may be craving, it's some of the better burritos and tacos you'll find in Ecuador. A favorite spot for locals to throw back a few beers and chill out, San Valentín also sees its fair share of gringos, as it is on Avenida Leon Borja, the main drag in town. Although a good, comfortable and casual restaurant for just about anyone, families going for dinner should get there early as the place fills up by about 9 p.m., and the music grows louder with each hour. Monday-Saturday 6 p.m.-midnight. Daniel León Borja 22-19 and Vargas Torres, 1 block from the train station, Tel: 03-296-3137, E-mail: sanvalentinclub6@hotmail.es. Updated: Feb 07, 2013.

Hollywood Coffee

Perhaps the most random coffee shop in Ecuador, Hollywood Coffee seems to be trying to be a Planet Hollywood meets Starbucks. Outside of the coffee shop, "hand prints" of famous people line the sidewalk. Inside it is decorated with various posters of quintessential celebrities such as Marilyn Monroe. The coffee is not great, but at least it is not NesCafé. Av. 10 de Octubre. Updated: Feb 07, 2013.

D'Baggio

(PIZZAS: $5-20) Anyone who has spent a reasonable amount of time in Ecuador probably knows that generally the pizza here is nothing to write home about. D'Baggios is the exception to this rule. This small restaurant's attempt to look like a quaint Italian eatery may not be spot on but is endearing. The pizzas are completely homemade in an area in the front of the restaurant. As you sit and wait for you meal, you can watch the chef flipping the dough in the air and whipping pizzas in and out of the wood oven. The delicious pizzas, all made with fresh ingredients. The restaurant also has a selection of pastas. Daily 1-10 p.m. Daniel León Borja and Miguel A León, Tel: 03-296-1832. Updated: Feb 07, 2013.

SALINAS (DE BOLÍVAR)

 3,560m   11,677 03

A windy bus ride on dirt roads through the Ecuadorian countryside brings you to the small town of Salinas. Not to be confused with the beach destination, its official name is Salinas de Bolívar or Salinas de Guaranda. If you are looking to see peaceful, relaxing country life in Ecuador, Salinas is the perfect place.

During Spanish colonial times, Salinas de Bolívar was a major producer of salt—thus its name. Since the 1970s, though, it has become famous for its cheese, chocolates, salamis and sweaters. Everything is made in fair-trade factories. One taste of the chocolates and cheeses, and you will be wondering if it would be acceptable to fill up an entire suitcase to bring home. That is, if you don't accidentally eat them all before you even leave Ecuador.

Salinas has few lodging and eating options. Nothing is five-star, but you can find clean and cozy accommodations and restaurants serving typical Ecuadorian cuisine, with daily almuerzo specials.

An entry of $2 is charged to enter Salinas de Bolívar village. It's another $5 charge to go and visit the village.
Updated: Oct 16, 2012.

When To Go to Salinas

The best time to visit the salt mines and do outdoor activities is during summer, July-October, when it is dryer and temperatures reach 12°C (54°F). If you come during the rest of the year, expect rains and cool temperatures (5-7°C / 41-45°F).

Like its neighbour, Guaranda, Salinas also celebrates pre-Lenten Carnaval in high fashion, with dance and music troupes, and gastronomic and artisan fairs. November is when this town celebrates its Festival Multicultural El Salinerito – a.k.a. Festival de Queso – with traditional dance, llama races, concerts and, of course, cheeses.
Updated: Oct 16, 2012.

Getting To and Away from Salinas

The most common way to arrive at Salinas de Bolívar is through **Guaranda**, 33 kilometers (20 miles) away. Transport to Salinas depart from Guaranda's Plaza Roja, and include buses (Monday-Friday 6 a.m.-4 p.m., weekends 6 a.m., 7 a.m.; 1 hr, $0.50) and shared taxis and pickups (leave when full, 45 min, $1.50). If you are coming from **Ambato**, you can go as far as Cuatro Esquinas, 10 kilometers (6 miles) before Guaranda, and wait for transport to pass.
Updated: Oct 16, 2012.

Salinas Services

Salinas de Bolívar has very few services. The Oficina de Turismo Comunitario provides information on lodging, restaurants, attractions and tour guides, and offers one to four-day tourist packages (Plaza Central de Salinas. Tel: 221-0042, Cel: 0994-040-

584, E-mail:turismosalinas@andinanet.net /fugjs@salinerito.com, URL:www.salinerito.com). Another useful website is:http://toursalinas.com.

The town has no bank, so be sure to stock up on cash before leaving Guaranda.
Updated: Oct 17, 2012.

Things To See and Do in Salinas

The biggest ticket in town is the fair-tradeco-operatives. However, other places await the curious traveller who happens to this remote village. In town are the Centro Intercultural Matiaví Salinas, where you can taste the locally produced goodies and learn about other aspects of the pueblo's culture, and an archaeological museum (Museo Arqueológico). To stretch your legs a bit, check out the nearby salt mines, archaeological sites and caves. Salinas de Bolívar is also a popular place for going horseback riding and doing sport fishing.
Updated: Oct 17, 2012.

Cooperatives

(PRICE: $5) Salinas de Bolívar is a living example of sustainable economic growth. It all began back in 1971, with the idea of Silesian priest Cándido Rada and Swiss volunteer José Duvach, and blossomed under the direction of Father Antonio Polo. Today over two dozen cooperatives open their doors to the public. The fair-trade factories produce foodstuffs – like cheeses, chocolates, marmalades, trout, salamis mushrooms, and turrón taffy – woollen clothing, buttons, soccer balls and other items. As well, the community has a hostel, Hotel el Refugio. If you can't make it to the factories, no worries; everything can be bought for the same price in a store called Tienda El Salinerito, right off of the main square.
Updated: Oct 17, 2012.

Salt Mines

On the outskirts of Salinas is the origin of this town's name: blocks of salt that glitter in the sun like giant granite boulders. A thin river winds across the páramo and licks the edges of the saline deposits. At dawn during the dry summer months (July-October), you can see the local women working these mines, much as their ancestors did many centuries ago. In the afternoons, they return to the village, leading donkeys bearing buckets of the precious salt. 1 kilometer (0.6 miles) from Salinas de Bolívar.
Updated: Oct 17, 2012.

Salinas Lodging

You can count the hotels in Salinas de Bolívar on one hand. Lodging options include community and family-run hostels that offer not only a cozy place to lay your head after a day of gorging on the yummy creations of the village's cooperatives, but also hikes and other tours to nearby attractions. If you are properly equipped, camping is also possible.

El Refugio

($7-14 per person) Located a short, two-block walk from the main plaza, this Ecuadorian-owned, eco-friendly hostel is probably your best option if you are planning to spend a night or two in Salinas. This hostel, run by the Fundación Grupo Juvenil Salinas (Salinas Youth Group Foundation), supports sustainable tourism by keeping its staff 100 percent local. Rooms include cable TV and private bath with hot showers. The hostel also offers saunas and therapeutic massages. The small, on-site restaurant serves breakfast, lunch and dinner. Be sure to call ahead if you are planning a visit, as the owners can be hard to find on-site. Vía Agua Mineral, Tel: 593-3-221-0044, Cel: 094040584, E-mail: turismosalinas@salinerito.com / turismosalinas@andinanet.net, URL: http://www.turismosalinas.com.
Updated: Oct 19, 2012.

Hostería Samilagua

($7-12 per person) Hostería Samilagua is another hotel option in Salinas de Bolívar. This small hostel provides comfortable, yet basic, shared and private rooms to travellers, and a common kitchen. The fireplace is the perfect place to curl up in front of on a chill evening. This inn also offers tourism packages, mountain biking expeditions, and outings to Chimborazo and to the subtropical lowlands. Tel: 221-0167, Cel: 0997-282-170 / 0983-125-356, E-mail: ecosamilagua@yahoo.es / hostalsamilagua@gmail.com, URL: www.facebook.com/hosteria.samilagua.
Updated: Oct 19, 2012.

Salinas Restaurants

Most of the restaurants in Salinas de Bolívar are located around the main plaza. Many use locally produced and grown ingredients. Local dishes to try are llapingachos (potato-cheese pancakes), empanadas, sancocho (a soup made with pork or mutton) and the famous Salinas cheeses. The cooperatives' salamis, cheeses and other offerings are perfect for preparing your own meals. Pick them up at the factories or at the Tienda El Salinerito, near the main square.

La Va-k Pizzaría

Just around the corner from Quesaría Salinas (the cheese factory) is La Va-k Pizzaría. This unassuming restaurant prepares mouth-watering pizzas in four sizes (small, medium, family and gigantic). Varieties include vegetarian, mushrooms, salami, ham, basil (albahaca) and two house specialties: especial and piklets. Va-K also whips up huge calzones. Only local ingredients are used. Near Quesaría Salinas.
Updated: Oct 17, 2012.

Scrop

Scrop, sitting right at the corner of the main square, is one of the nicer restaurants in town. It may be small, but it tends to be packed, particularly on the weekends. There is a TV in the corner with cable, which locals seem to enjoy sitting in front of for hours at a time. The food served is your classic Ecuadorian rice and meat, satisfying and well-priced. At night the place is transformed into a bar. The tables are pushed to the side so people can dance to the loud music. If you are spending the night, it is a great place to meet some locals and have a good time.
Updated: Oct 17, 2012.

GUARANDA

 2,668m 25,000  03

Guaranda is best known for its massive pre-Lenten Carnaval, celebrated with parades, parties and water throwing on the streets for about five days before Ash Wednesday. If you want to see the ultimate Ecuadorian Carnaval party, Guaranda is the place to go.

During the rest of the year, Guaranda is a pretty sleepy town that sees very few tourists. It is a good place to go if you want to see a more authentic view of what a typical life in Ecuador consists of. Be aware though, that you will be an outsider in town – Guaranda sees few foreigners throughout the year.

Guaranda is nicknamed "La Ciudad de las Siete Colinas," for the seven hills it is built upon. It was founded by the Spanish in 1571, with its first settlers being Jews fleeing from the Inquisition in Lima. The name may have come from the guarango tree, or the indigenous nation, the Guaranga, that lived in the area, or for a chief named Guaranga. Today, this largely Quichua town is the capital of Bolívar Province.

Guaranda is a good jumping off point for the village of Salinas. On the road to Ambato is the entry point for Reserva de Producción Faunística Chimborazo, home to Ecuador's highest volcano, which backdrops Guaranda. Updated: Oct 10, 2012.

When To Go to Guaranda

Guaranda has a humid temperate climate. It receives approximately 1,000 millimeters (39 in) of precipitation per year. The dry season is May-October. Daytime temperatures range 14-19°C (57-66°F), and at night 8-12°C (46-53°F), though it can get quite colder.

Carnaval is Guaranda's biggest fiesta. This moveable feast falls at the end of February or the beginning of March, and is the week before Ash Wednesday. The town's balconies are colorfully decorated, streamers and confetti flurry through the streets, and water douses everyone. Chicha and the local Pájaro Azul aguardiente (firewater) fuel on the festive air. Other annual observances of Guarandeños are:

- **April 23** – Founding of Bolívar Province.
- **July 29** -- Fiestas de San Pedro de Guanujo, the town's patron saint.
- **November 10** -- Independence of the city of Guaranda, from the Spaniards.

Updated: Oct 10, 2012.

Getting To and Away from Guaranda

Guaranda's Terminal Terrestre, located on Avenida Circunvalación, is a 20-minute walk from downtown. A taxi should cost about $1.

Several companies run half-hourly to **Quito** (3:30 a.m.-5:30 p.m., 5 hr, $5) and to **Guayaquil** (4 hr, $4.50). Buses also depart for **Riobamba** (2 hr, $2.50; passes by the entry to Reserva de Chimborazo), **Babahoyo** (2.5 hr, $3), **Quevedo** ($4.50), **Ambato** (2 hr, $2.50) and **Santo Domingo**.

Transport for Salinas departs from Plaza Roja: buses (Monday-Friday 6 a.m.-4 p.m., weekends 6 a.m., 7 a.m.; 1 hr, $0.50) and shared taxis and pickups (leave when full, 45 min, $1.50).
Updated: Oct 10, 2012.

Guaranda Services

TOURISM OFFICE

The city's tourism office, Centro de Información Turística, is a half-block Plaza Simón Bolívar (Ca. García Moreno, between Convención 1884 and 7 de Mayo. Tel: 298-5877,

URL:www.guaranda.gob.ec). The Policía Nacional is on Avenida Guayaquil (Tel: 298-0045).

MONEY

Banks in Guaranda are typically open Monday-Friday 9 a.m.-5 p.m., Saturday 9 a.m.-12:30 p.m. The following have ATMs:

- Banco de Guayaquil (Sucre and García Moreno)
- Banco del Pinchincha (Azuay, between 7 de Mayo and Convención 1884).

KEEPING IN TOUCH

The post office is about two blocks north of the main plaza (Pinchincha and Azuay). If e-mail is more your game, the town has several cybercafés. Likewise, cabinas (phone centers) are also common.

MEDICAL

The public health facility is Hospital Provincial Alfredo Noboa Montenegro (Selva Alegre s/n. Tel: 298-2840 / emergency: 298-0110, E-mail:hospitaldeguaranda@hanm.gob.ec). Farmacia San Andrés is open daily (9:30 a.m.-10:30 p.m. Ca. Sucre 401 and General Salazar. Tel: 298-3235).
Updated: Oct 10, 2012.

Things To See and Do in Guaranda

Guaranda has a few things of interest, if you happen to come outside of Carnaval-time. Parque Simón Bolívar, the main plaza, has a statue of the Libertador created by celebrated Ecuadorian artist, Oswaldo Guayasamín. The church on one side of the park is also interesting. The seven hills surrounding the town may be climbed for spectacular views of the countryside and Chimborazo. One of the hills, Cruz Loma, has El Indio Guaranga monument with a history-ethnography museum. The town also has a small anthropology museum (Escuela de Educación de la Cultura Andina, Calle 7 de Mayo and Almedo). Justa an hour away is Salinas.
Updated: Nov 22, 2012.

Guaranda Lodging

Guaranda accommodations are a bit sparse, understandably so since it is not a place that draws a huge amount of tourists. Several good, reasonably priced options around the town though – nothing fancy, but definitely acceptable. Guaranda's more expensive accommodations can be found above the city and many assist guests in arranging tours and excursions. For the least expensive options, check near Plaza Roja, especially on Calle García Moreno. Be aware that if you plan to visit Guaranda during Carnaval and do not book ahead, you could end up in a less than savory hotel. Updated: Oct 15, 2012.

Hostal de las Flores

(ROOMS: $17-35) Hostal de las Flores offers travelers a friendly comfortable stay in Guaranda. It is housed in a renovated old building, which includes a quaint, interior courtyard with tables and seating areas, where you may catch up on your journal. The 11 simple rooms are equipped for one to four guests, and include a television and telephone. Hostal de las Flores is located a few blocks south of Plaza Simón Bolívar, the town's main square, making it easy to get to restaurants in the area, yet far enough away that the area tends to be quiet. Pichincha 402 and Rocafuerte, Tel: 593-3-298-4396. Updated: Oct 11, 2012.

Hotel Bolívar

(ROOMS: $20-25) Hotel Bolívar, located two blocks from Parque Simón Bolívar, is a good choice for solo travelers, couples and families. It offers three floors of clean, quiet rooms around a nice courtyard. Each accommodation has private bathroom and cable TV. This hostel also has WiFi and a salon for meetings. Plus it has a restaurant-café, setting it apart from other hotels in the area. It is handy spot to relax with an afternoon coffee or catch a breakfast before a day of exploring the area. Sucre 704 and Rocafuerte, Tel: 298-0547, Fax: 298-5287, E-mail: hbguaranda@gmail.com, URL: http://hotelbolivar.wordpress.com. Updated: Oct 11, 2012.

Guaranda Restaurants

In general, Guaranda has the general small town Ecuador fare: lots of small restaurants serving meat and rice. They are usually a good value – just make sure you are comfortable with the cleanliness of the restaurant. If you are itching to try cuy, Guaranda has a handful of decent restaurants that sell it for a lower price than in bigger cities like Quito. Other typical Guarandeño dishes are tamales and chihuile, a cheese-filled tamale. Daily markets happen at Mercado 10 de Noviembre, on the south side of town, and Plaza 15 de Mayo, on the north side. Saturday is best.

Los 7 Santos

Los 7 Santos is probably the place with the most ambiance in Guaranda. It feels like the sort of coffee shop you might find in a hip neighborhood in New York, not in this small town. It offers coffee, snacks and light meals. Los 7 Santos is a great place to relax and plan out your day, with a good breakfast. The coffee is not the best ever, but that tends to be typical in Ecuador. Drop by in the evening, when live music might be playing. Open daily 9:30 a.m.-11 p.m., weekends until 2 a.m. Convención de 1884 and 10 de Agosto, Tel: 593-3-298-0612, E-mail: silarrea@interactive.net.ec, URL: http://facebook.com/lossiete.santos. Updated: Oct 15, 2012.

Pizzería Buon Giorno

(PIZZA: $5-15) If you are needing a break from the run-of-the-mill Ecuadorian fare and you aren't quite up to trying exotic cuy, then head over to Pizzería Buon Giorno for something international. Travelers say the service and atmosphere are good – and the pizzas not too bad, either. Choose between four sizes of pie or one of the pasta dishes. Buon Giorno is located across from the main plaza, Parque Simón Bolívar. Sucre, between 10 de Agosto and García Moreno, Tel: 298-3603. Updated: Oct 15, 2012.

Queseras de Bolívar

If you are unable to get over to Salinas during your stay in the area, definitely plan to visit this shop in Guaranda. It sells a wide selection of the cheeses, chocolates and other goods that are made in the Salinas area. The chocolates are smooth and milky and make a great gift for friends back home. That is, if they don't mysteriously disappear before you get home. They are hard to resist once you have a stash in your backpack. Open Monday-Saturday 8:30 a.m.-1 p.m., 2:30-6 p.m.; Sunday 8:30 a.m.-noon. Avenida General Enríquez, Tel: 298-2205. Updated: Oct 15, 2012.

La Nariz del Diablo

ALAUSÍ

 2,340m   9,563   03

Most tourists that end up in Alausí do so to take the famed Devil's Nose train ride. Besides the train ride, there is little to see in this sleepy countryside village. If you arrive on days when the train is not running, you will likely be the only visitor in town - a good opportunity to see typical small town life and chat to a few locals. There is a large statue of St. Peter here, which is worth hiking up to. Also, there is a hill near the statue which gives a wonderful view of the town.

There are a few restaurants in town, which all serve typical Ecuadorian food. There are also a couple of bars that are usually absolutely packed with local men enjoying a futbol game. The bus and train station are located right on the main strip, near all the restaurants, hotels, stores and banks in Alausí. Updated: Apr 15, 2013.

Getting To and Away from Alausi

Alausí's bus station is located on 5 de Junio, just three blocks down from the train station (where most visitors arrive) along the town's main street. Buses run throughout the day to and from smaller towns, and on set schedules to more popular destinations.

Bus to **Cuenca** (4.5 hours, $5): 6 a.m., 10 a.m., and immediately after the train arrives on tour days (Wednesdays, Fridays, and Sundays)

Bus from **Cuenca**: 5 a.m., 2:45 p.m. To **Quito** (5 hours, $5): 4:05 a.m., 8 a.m., 10 a.m., 1:30 p.m.

Bus from **Quito**: 7:25 a.m., 9:25 a.m., 2:15 p.m., 5:25 p.m.

To **Guayaquil** (4.5 hours, $5): 4 a.m., 9 a.m., 11 a.m., 1 p.m.

Bus from **Guayaquil**: 4 a.m., 6 a.m., 9 a.m., 1 p.m., 4 p.m.

Bus to and from **Riobamba**: (2 hours, $1.50): At least one bus runs every hour, between 5 a.m. and 7 p.m.

To get to the **Ingapirca** ruins in **Cañar**, get on any bus heading for **Cuenca**. You'll find the town just an hour and a half before Cuen-

ca. It is also possible to catch buses on the highway that runs above town; while these pass more frequently than those scheduled at the station, they are often full.

You can head to **Sibambe** via train (from the Alausí train station) and catch a magnificent view of La Nariz del Diablo (The Devil's Nose) along the way. The trip costs $25 (roundtrip) and takes 2.5 hours. Trains depart Tuesday to Sunday. 8:00 a.m., 11:00 p.m., and 3:00 p.m.
Updated: Apr 19, 2013.

Alausí Services
TOURISM OFFICES
Head on over to the train station of Alausí to find the local tourism office. Here you'll find general information on the area, as well as maps and details regarding the trails for bikes and hiking inside and around Alausí. Updated: Apr 18, 2013.

Things To See and Do in Alausi
La Nariz Del Diablo ❗
(TICKETS: $25-35) El Nariz del Diablo, or The Devil's Nose, is the highlight of a rail trip that meanders through the rich tapestry of cultivated fields and páramo in the southern half of Ecuador's 400-kilometer (29-mi) long Central Valley. The valley was aptly christened "The Avenue of the Volcanoes" in 1802 by the German explorer Alexander Von Humboldt. The people of Alausi have taken advantage of the growing fame of their stretch of rails by maintaining a series of autoferros (rail cars). Although the cars have train wheels and black-and-yellow striped cow catchers, the bodies are of decommissioned school buses.

Since travelers are no longer allowed to sit on top of the rail cars, competition for window seats is fierce. These rail cars are cheaper to take ($6.50) than the actual trains themselves, and are said to travel slightly faster. These only depart once a day however at 9 a.m. The train ride is different in that it is an actual train-car that includes a guide and a small cafe on-board, as well as entry into the station museum. Both trains and rail cars typically stop at several different points to allow travelers to disembark and take pictures.

The main attraction of the Devil's Nose ride is the series of switchbacks that engineers carved into the mountain as a way to allow trains to climb a gradient of 1-in-18 from 1,800 to 2,600 meters (5,905-8,530 ft), by going forwards then backwards up the tracks. As the rail cars and trains go forward and backward over the three or four zigzags, they will occasionally stop to allow another car to pass. A hundred years after it was constructed, the steep grade of the Devil's Nose stretch of track precludes its use as a freight or efficient passenger line, but is a way for present-day explorers to catch a glimpse of the rugged and breathtaking Ecuadorian countryside.

You can buy tickets on the train, but it is suggested to buy them a day earlier, a task for which you may need your passport

As of April 2013, here is the train schedule and info:

Trains leave every day except for Monday from the Alausi train station, and have an estimated travel time of 2.5 hours:

Departure from Alausí:
8 a.m, 11 a.m. and 3 p.m.

Return Departure from Sibambe:
10:30 a.m., 1:30 p.m., 5:30 p.m.

Arrive to Alausí:
10:35 a.m., 1:35 p.m., 5:35 p.m.

Due to safety concerns passengers are no longer allowed to ride on the roof of the trains. Estación de Alausí, Av. Eloy Alfaro and Sucre (corner), Tel: 02-293-0126 / 1-800-873637, URL: www.ecuadorbytrain. com/trainecuador.
Updated: Jul 16, 2013.

Alausí Lodging

Alausí's main street is full of hotels, though none of them are particularly appealing. Hotels here are not very expensive. There isn't very much to do in Alausí other than take a trip on the infamous Nariz del Diablo train and perhaps this is reflected in the overall standard and price range of accommodation in the town.

Hotel Europa

(ROOMS: $18-45) If you arrive by bus, the first thing that you will see in Alausí is the large pink building directly across from the station, which houses Hotel Europa. The hotel is as good a place as anywhere in town to lay your head. The rooms are arranged alongside an inner parking lot and vary in quality and size, but are clean and a good value in town. Ask to see your room before you pay. Av. 5 de Junio 175 and Orozco, Tel: 03-295-7327/293-0200, E-mail: info@hoteleuropa. com.ec, URL: www.hoteleuropa.com.ec. Updated: Feb 07, 2013.

Alausí Restaurants

Alausí does not have a great deal of quality restaurants. However, finding somewhere to eat is not a problem, as the main street is lined with inexpensive eateries. The cafés and restaurants nearest the station tend to be a little more tourist focused and therefore a bit more expensive.

Trigo Pan

If you are in the mood for a little snack, perhaps something to bring along with you on the train, Trigo Pan is the place to go. This panadería, or bakery, offers a variety of baked goods, including empanadas, rolls and cakes. It also takes orders for specialized baked goods, such as a birthday cake. Probably nothing the average backpacker is ever going to need, but you never know. 5 de Junio and Estaban Orozco, Tel: 03-293-1341.
Updated: Feb 07, 2013.

Llovy Burger

Conveniently located near the train station, Llovy Burger is the one place in town offering American food. If you can just not stand another dinner of rice and chicken, stop in for a hamburger or hot dog and fries. The food is not amazing, but is acceptable, about the grade of any American fast food restaurant out there. The prices are very reasonable, ranging from one to five dollars, depending on what and how much you want. 5 de Junio near the Train Stataion.
Updated: May 31, 2013.

Cafeteria La Higuera

Cafeteria La Higuera offers more or less typical Ecuadorian fare. However, its quality seems to be a bit better than most. The portions are large, and the food flavorful. It is in particular a good place to catch breakfast before a ride on the train. It has many breakfast special options, the most popular of which includes eggs, bread, juice, cheese and coff Updated: Feb 07, 2013.

Pekin Chifa Restaurant

While Alausí is not packed full of quality restaurants, the Pekin Chifa is a good choice and is one of the only places open on a Sunday night. The restaurant is on the main street in the same pink building that houses Hotel Europa. Pekin Chifa serves standard Chinese food in giant portions. Everything on the menu is cheap, but if you want even better value order a set meal. Av. 5 de Junio (next door to Hotel Europa). Updated: Mar 11, 2013.

CENTRAL ANDES

Southern Andes

Leaving the rugged, rumbling volcanoes of theNorthern Andes, and heading south along the Panamericana, one enters the softer and slightly more isolated scenery of the impressive Southern Andes. No longer bearing the scars of a violent volcanic past, this region is home to long, lonely stretches of untamed, sparsely inhabited, historically and culturally rich landscapes. Lower elevations give way to warmer, drier climates, which with the stunning countryside, make the Southern Andes supreme walking and trekking territory.

Vilcabamba is a good base for hikes and horseback treks, while the glimmering lakes and grand views of El Cajas National Park, or wild waterfalls and breathtaking scenery of Podocarpus Nacional Park offer some of Ecuador's finest backcountry adventures. Tucked neatly into the folds of this striking landscape are historical sites and cities steeped in centuries-old traditions, which make the region intellectually, as well as topographically astonishing.

The seat of southern culture, and the South's only large urban center,Cuenca is a remarkable city graced with spectacular colonial architecture and a wealth of local artesanía, including gold and silver jewelry, textiles, ceramics and of course the ill-named Panama hat. Just a short shot from Cuenca is Ingapirca, Ecuador's only major Inca ruins, where history buffs can contemplate the genius of Incan stonemasonry.

Slipping south of Cuenca, the traveler encounters more secluded, but no less surprising territory. Meander through the streets of Saraguro, where the locals maintain an age-old tradition of dressing in black, and take a stroll back in time. For a bit more action, head further south to Loja. A buzzing city known for its swift intellectual and cultural currents, Loja is also the piggy-back point for direct service to Peru. Draped in dramatic scenery and festooned in history and culture, the Southern Andes are amply armed to entertain intrepid trekkers and cultural explorers alike.
Updated: Mar 16, 2013.

CUENCA

 2,560m   330,000   07

If you measure a city on size or population alone, Cuenca ranks third in Ecuador. If you consider charm, beauty and the opinion of all Ecuadorians, however, Cuenca leaps into first place. The city is a colonial jewel, a neat, orderly city set in the picturesque rolling hills of southern Ecuador.

Like Quito, Cuenca has a centuries-old colonial center full of stunning architecture, venerable churches and well-kept parks. Unlike Quito, however, the colonial center is still the heart of the city: a place to be enjoyed by all cuencanos, day or night. As you wander around the center, notice the finely carved wooden doors—they're quite striking. The best hotels and restaurants are to be found here, as well as ice cream parlors, cafés, shops and more. Quiteños have abandoned the colonial heart of their city, at least at night; cuencanos still cherish theirs. They are immensely proud of the fact that their colonial downtown was named a UNESCO World Heritage Cultural site in 1999.

Cuenca is an ancient city, older than even the Spanish occupation. Long before this settlement became Cuenca, it was Guapondelig, a Cañari settlement. When the Incas came, they conquered the Cañari and changed its name to Tumipamba. The Spanish continued the tradition, building on the city of the vanquished Inca; they named it "Santa Ana de los Cuatro Ríos de Cuenca," or "Saint Anne of the Four Rivers of Cuenca." Four rivers do indeed flow through and around Cuenca, the most visible of these is the Río Tomebamba, which runs along the southern edge of the old city.

Cuenca has a lot of activities for travelers. Apart from the obvious architecture and colonial churches—they say that Cuenca has 52 churches, one for every Sunday of the year—Cuenca is used as the base for trips to the breathtaking El Cajas National Park as well as Ecuador's most significant Inca ruins,

Photo by: Alex Proimos
Cuenca

SOUTHERN ANDES

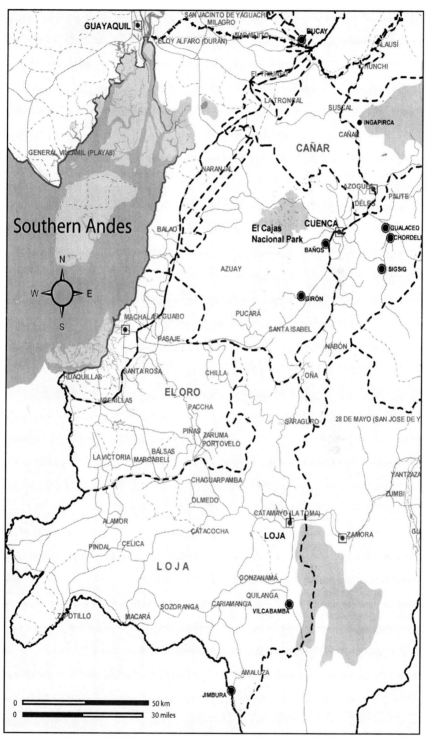

Southern Andes Highlights

Cuenca (*p. 260-281*): Ecuador's third largest city is also its most charming, with a centuries-old colonial center full of stunning architecture, venerable churches, interesting museums and well-kept parks. Cuenca has a mix of excellent hotels and restaurants, making it a great place to spend some time as you explore the surrounding artisan communities, archaeological sites and national parks.

El Cajas National Park (*p. 282-283*): Home to more than 250 glacier-fed lakes and inhabited by a diverse mix of wildlife and an interesting set of endemic plant species, El Cajas is a delight for hikers, bird-watchers and sport fishers. Over 15 hiking trails wind through the park's valleys, lagoons, highland vistas and rock formations, making for interesting landscapes with surprises at every corner.

Ingapirca: (*p. 281-282*) The most impressive set of Inca ruins in Ecuador, Ingapirca was once an important Inca military and religious center. Although they may not size up to the major Inca ruins in Peru, the ruins of Ingapirca are still interesting to visit and have a fascinating history. The Temple of the Sun is the focal point of the ruins, remaining the best-preserved structure in the complex.

Vilcabamba (*p. 296-302*): After just a few moments in the small bohemian village of Vilcabamba, you will probably realize why it is called the "Valley of Eternal Youth." As your stresses drift away into the gorgeous mountainous scenery and you put down your vegan truffle to start the day's yoga session, you may just forget about time altogether.

Saraguro (*p. 286-287*): Visit this small, rarely visited mountain town for a peek into Ecuador's best-preserved indigenous community. Saraguro is an exemplary model of what community tourism should be, and eager visitors can stay with a local family, tour weaving and traditional hat workshops, and learn about medicinal uses of sacred plants. Updated: Feb 15, 2013.

Ingapirca. Cuenca is also surrounded by many quaint villages, each of which is worth a visit: Gualaceo, Chordeleg, Sigsig, Bulcay, Girón and Jima.

The hotels in Cuenca are a great value for any budget. The best hotels are the converted colonial homes in the center of town. Cuenca's restaurants offer a great value and memorable dining experiences.

Cuencanos love food (particularly ice cream and other sweets) and there are many excellent restaurants in town. Regional fare is similar to the rest of Ecuador: a lot of pork, rice and potatoes, but it's very well done and there are always options, even vegetarian ones.

If Cuenca is lacking in anything, it's its nightlife: Cuenca is just not a party town. Still, there are places where you can go out and have a good time. Check out some of the other bars and cafés by the river.

Come for a visit and you'll see why Ecuadorians agree that Cuenca is one of the most beautiful cities in their country. Updated: Jan 15, 2013.

Safety

Most travelers and expats feel completely at ease in Cuenca and don't feel threatened by some of the annoyances and dangers that exist in other Ecuadorian cities. Especially compared to Quito and Guayaquil, Cuenca is a very laid-back and safe place, which adds to its overall appeal. However, that does not mean you should let down your guard completely, as it is a city after all. Just use common sense, go with your gut, and ask locals before venturing to areas off the typical tourist grid and you should be fine. It is always a good idea to leave documents and valuables in your hotel room instead of bringing them out with you and to keep an eye on your belongings at all times. At night, stay within well-lit areas and walk in groups. Updated: Feb 08, 2013.

Getting To and Away from Cuenca

From Quito, the fastest and most convenient way to get to Cuenca is to fly. Tame, Aerogal and Icaro offer regular 50-minute flights from Quito to Cuenca, at a cost of approximately $90-120, round-trip. Cuenca can also be reached via international flights with American and Continental Airlines, among others.

The ride from Quito to Cuenca by bus is 9-10 hours (usually overnight), and costs about $10. Panamericana Internacional (Tel: 02-255-7133/7134/9428) makes this trip. Cuenca's Terminal Terrestre (Av. España and Sebastián de Benalcazar) is several blocks away from the airport, making it easy to arrive in Cuenca and make travel arrangements for your next destination, hassle-free. The station has several ATMs, bathrooms, a few restaurants and even a hair salon. You need to pay $0.10 to leave the terminal after buying your ticket, so make sure you have the change on hand.

From the terminal, buses leave regularly for **Guayaquil**, **Loja**, **Quito**, **Machala**, and to **Máncora**, **Piura** and **Chiclayo** over in the country of **Peru**:

Buses to **Gualaceo** ($0.60) leave every 15 minutes between 6 a.m. and 10 p.m., and return every 15 minutes from 5 a.m.-8:30 p.m. Cooperativa Transporte Cañar (booth #4 in terminal) has two direct buses per day to **Ingapirca** (9 a.m. and 12:20 p.m.; 2 hr, $2.50). Flota Imbabura (booth #18) has buses to **Quito** (9 hr, $12) at 6:40 a.m., 5:30 p.m., 7:30 p.m., 8:30 p.m. (continues to **Tulcán**), 9 p.m., 9:15 p.m., 9:45 p.m., 10:40 p.m., 11 p.m. and 11:30 p.m.

Cooperativa de Transporte Loja (booth #19) has two buses per day to **Loja** (4.5 hr, $7.50), at noon and at 10 p.m. It also has one direct bus that heads up to **Lago Agrio** at 8 p.m.

Ejecutivo San Luis (booth #11) has buses to **Loja** (4.5 hr, $7.50) at 7:45 a.m., 11 a.m., 4 p.m., 7 p.m. and midnight. Viajeros Internacional (booth #10) also services the Loja trip, with more frequent departures (11 daily between 5 a.m. and 10:30 p.m.). Both companies' buses pass through **Saraguro** after three hours ($5).

Alianza-Atrain is the recommended bus company to **Guayaquil**. Buses go through either El Cajas (4 hr) or through **Cañar** (6 hr); both cost $8. Those through **El Cajas** leave every 20-40 minutes from 7 a.m.-7 p.m. and every hour from 7 p.m.-midnight and from 1 a.m.-7 a.m. The ones through Cañar leave every 15-30 minutes from 12:30 a.m.-9:40 p.m.

Super Semería (booth #3) also services buses to Guayaquil ($8), with eight leaving per day through **El Cajas** and nine per day through **Cañar**. Schedules change daily.

Pullman Sucre (booth #14) has the best international buses to **Peru**. It has three departures per day to **Piura**, Peru (7:15 a.m., 6 p.m., 9 p.m.; 10 hr, $15), which pass through **Máncora** after eight hours. Its buses to **Huaquillas** leave at 7 a.m., 9 a.m., noon, 3 p.m. and 9 p.m. ($7). It also has buses to **Machala** ($5.50) every 15-45 minutes from 5:15 a.m.-11 p.m.

Azuay Internacional (booth #5) has buses every 30 minutes to **Machala** ($5.50). It also has one bus to Zaruma at 4:45 p.m. (8 hr, $8) and one international bus to **Chiclayo**, Peru ($20) at 9:30 p.m., which passes through **Máncora** and **Piura**.

Turismo Oriental (booth #7) has 11 buses per day to **Macas** (7 hr, $8.50), with the first bus leaving at 6 a.m. and the last at 11 p.m. It also has six daily buses to **Quito**, with the last bus leaving at 11:15 p.m.

Cooperativa de Transportes Patria (booth #12) does a **Cuenca-Alausí-Riobamba-Quito** route eight times per day (4:15 a.m., 5:15 a.m., 9:40 a.m., 11:20 a.m., 2 p.m., 3:30 p.m., 5:30 p.m. and 7:15 p.m.). Buses pass through **Alausí** after four hours ($5) and through **Riobamba** after six hours ($6).

Cooperativa de Transporte "Express Sucre Internacional" (booth #13) has 13 buses per day to **Quito**, 11 per day to **Machala**, and five per day to **Santo Domingo** (7:15 a.m., 9:15 a.m., 12:30 p.m., 7:10 p.m., 9:50 p.m.; 10 hr, $12). Updated: Nov 08, 2012.

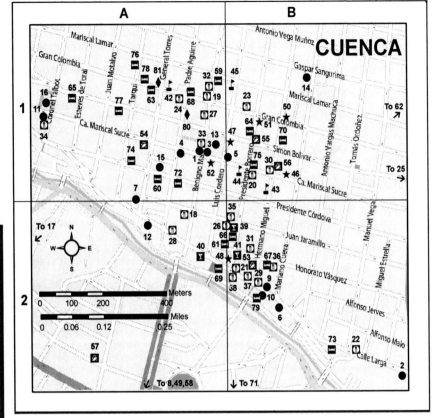

Getting Around Cuenca

Most of Cuenca's attractions are reachable by foot, especially if you are staying in the historical center. However, Cuenca also has a good, reliable local bus system which can take you around. Buses generally run from 6:30 a.m.-10 p.m. during the week, and buses pass each bus stop on their route every 15 minutes or so. Actual bus stops are labeled with blue signs that say "parada de bus." Each ride costs $0.25 and you must have exact change.

You can also purchase a refillable bus pass at any store with an "Urbania" sign; it costs $1.70, then you can charge it with as much money as you'd like.

The website www.cuencatransit.com has maps of all the bus routes, but you can also ask bus drivers if they pass where you are going when they stop at the bus stop. Several local buses go to the bus station, including bus #11, #18 (also goes to airport), #26 and #28; just look for an bus that says "T.

Terrestre." Taxis between the bus terminal and downtown (historical center) cost on average $2; trips around town in taxi should cost more than $3-5.
Updated: Nov 08, 2012.

Cuenca Services
MONEY

The city of Cuenca has many banks, so you will not have a problem accessing money while here. There are several banks concentrated along Avenida Mariscal Sucre, between Calle Hermano Miguel and Calle Mariano Cueva, which is only two blocks from Parque Calderón. You will find a Banco de Pacifico, Banco de Guayaquil (which also has 5 ATMs), Banco del Austro and Banco de Pichincha all on this strip. There are also Produbanco and Banco Internacional branches located nearby. Western Union has several locations in town as well, including one at Presidente Córdova 755 and Luis Cordero (Open Monday-Friday 8:45 a.m.-5:30 p.m., Saturday 9 a.m.-12:30 p.m. Closed Sundays).

Get the best rates and reserve your hotel or hostel at vivatravelguides.com/hotels/

Activities ●

1 Catedral de la Inmaculada A1
2 Central Bank Museum B2
3 Cuenca City Tour Bus A1
4 Flower Market A1
5 Iglesia El Sagrario B1
6 Iglesia Todos Los Santos B2
7 Mercado 10 de Agosto A1
8 Mirador Turi A2
9 Museum of Aboriginal Cultures B2
10 Museum of CIDAP B2
11 Museum of Modern Art A1
12 Panama Hat Museum A2
13 Parque Calderón A1
14 Plaza Rotary B1
15 Plaza San Francisco A1
16 Plaza San Sebastian A1
17 San Joaquín Neighborhood A2

Eating ⑪

18 Café Austria A2
19 Café Eucalyptus A1
20 Casa Do Brasil Café Cultural B1
21 Coffee Tree B2
22 ▤ Maiz Restaurante B2
23 ▤ Pavon Real B1
24 ▤ Pedregal Azteca A1
25 Good Affinity Restaurant
   and Tea House B1
26 Govinda's Vegetariano A2
27 Heladeria Holanda A1
28 Kookaburra Café A2
29 La Esquina B2
30 Maria's Alemania Café B1
31 Moliendo Café B2
32 Néctar A1
33 Raymipamba Café Restaurant A1
34 San Sebas Café A1
35 Tiestos B2
36 Villa Rosa B2
37 Wildhorse Café B2
38 Wunderbar Café B2

Nightlife ⓨ

39 Cacao y Canela Café Bar B2
40 Chiplote A2
41 La Compania B2

Schools ⌇

42 CEDEI A1
43 Escuela Amauta B1
44 Si Centro Spanish School B1
45 Símon Bolívar Spanish School B1

Services ★

46 Banco de Guayaquil B1
47 Farmacias Cruz Azul B1
48 Gr@n Net B2
49 Hospital Monte Sinai A2
50 Laundry B1
51 Post Office B1
52 Tourism Office A1

Shopping ⓩ

53 Carolina Bookstore B2
54 Centro Municipal Artesanal A1
55 ▤ Surtido Almacen de Musica B1
56 Libri Mundi B1
57 Tatoo Adventure Gear A2

Sleeping ▦

58 Casa Lloret Hostal A2
59 Casa Ordoñez A2
60 Cofradia del Monje A1
61 ▤ Cafecito A2
62 Hacienda Uzhupud B1
63 Hostal Chordeleg A1
64 Hostal La Orquídea B1
65 Hostal Posada del Angel A1
66 Hostal Santa Fe B2
67 Hostal Villa Del Rosario B2
68 Hotel Carvallo A1
69 Hotel Crespo A2
70 Hotel El Quijote B1
71 Hotel La Casona B2
72 Hotel Milan A1
73 Hotel Oro Verde B2
74 Hotel Santa Ana A1
75 Hotel Santa Lucía B1
76 Macondo Hostal A1
77 Mansión Alcázar A1 A1
78 San Andrés Hotel A1
79 Villa Nova Inn B2

Tours ♦

80 Cazhuma Tours Travel
   Agency A1
81 Expediciones Apullacta A1

SOUTHERN ANDES

KEEPING IN TOUCH

Staying in touch with family and friends while in Cuenca will not be a problem, as Internet cafés and international call booths abound. Some good ones include Gr@n Net (daily 9 a.m.-10 p.m. Borrero 4-48, between Ca. Larga and Honorato Vásquez), which has five modern computers equipped with Skype, and Cuenca Net (corner of Hermano Miguel and Ca. Larga. Tel: 07-283-7347).

The post office is located at the corner of Borrero and Gran Colombia (Monday-Friday 8 a.m.-6 p.m., Saturday 8 a.m.-noon). There is a DHL office a few blocks from the main plaza (Monday-Friday 9 a.m.-6 p.m., Saturday 9 a.m.-1 p.m. Gran Colombia 5-30 and Mariano Cueva. Tel: 07-283-6537), which is also a Western Union agent.

TOURISM

Cuenca's tourism office is located on the main plaza and has lots of helpful maps and brochures to guide you during your visit in and around the city. (Monday-Friday 8 a.m.-10 p.m., Saturday-Sunday 8:30 a.m.-1:30 p.m. Mariscal Sucre, between Luis Cordero and Benigno Malo. Tel: 07-282-1035, itur@cuenca.com.ec, URL: www.cuencaecuador.com.ec). There is also a satellite iTur office in the airport (Monday-Wednesday 7:30-11 a.m., 2-3:30 p.m. and 5-7 p.m., Thursday-Friday 7:30-11 a.m., 2-3:30 p.m., 4:30-7 p.m., Saturday 8 a.m.-noon. Tel: 07-286-2203, ext 162). The following countries have consulates in town:

Germany: Simón Bolívar 9-18 and Benigno Malo. Tel: 07-282-2783.

Brazil: Av. Gil Ramírez Dávalos 14-34 and Turuhuayco. Tel: 07-287-1870.

Chile: José Peralta y 12 de Abril, Edif. Acrópolis, 4th floor, office 403. Tel: 07-410-3630.

France: Tadeo Torres 1-92 and Av. Solano (Alianza Francesa). Tel: 07-284-8314.

Spain: corner of Gran Colombia and Luis Cordero, Edif. Torre de Negocios El Dorado, 4th floor. Tel: 07-283-2807.

Italy: Av. Huayna Capac 1-97 (Pasamanería Tosi). Tel: 07-283-2388.

Guatemala: Av. Carlos Tosi s/n and Miguel A. Narváez (Cuenca Bottling). Tel: 07-280-9093.

MEDICAL

Two of Cuenca's best medical facilities are Hospital Monte Sinai (Av. Miguel Cordero 6-111 and Av. Solano. 07-288-5595/281-4813, URL: www.hospitalmontesinai.org) and Hospital Santa Inés (Av. Daniel Córdova and Agustín Cueva. Tel: 07-281-7888/7889). There are many pharmacies scattered throughout the city, including large, nationwide chains. One branch of Farmacias Cruz Azul is located at Hermano Miguel 11-46 (daily 8 a.m.-10 p.m. Tel: 07-282-3993); another is located at the corner of Simón Bolívar and Luis Cordero, on the northeast corner of the main plaza (Tel: 07-288-2855).

LAUNDRY

Laundromats can be found throughout the city, and many of the city's hostels and hotels provide laundry service at an additional cost. There is a Lavandaría Nieves branch at Avenida Gran Colombia 5-84 and Hermano Miguel ($1.50 per pound. Monday-Friday 8 a.m.-6 p.m., Tel: 09-9085-8547) and a Durán e Hijos at the corner of Luis Cordero and Juan Jaramillo.

Updated: Oct 26, 2012.

Shopping in Cuenca

Are you a shopper? Great news! Cuenca is known for handicrafts. The most famous Cuenca handicraft is the Panama hat, which is, of course, made in Ecuador and not Panama. The hats are handwoven out of a special sort of straw—paja toquilla—which is native to the region.

Many families and individuals weave Panama hats as a full-time job or as a way to make extra money. A simple Panama hat can be woven in about two days and might fetch five to 10 dollars for the weaver, whereas a finely woven one can take weeks and can cost up to $500. Your best bet to see Panama hat makers at work is to go to the Homero Ortega factory or Barranco's factory in Cuenca, or the town of Sigsig.

Cuenca is also known for pottery and ceramics. Check out the Vega gallery near the Turi overlook, or browse the shops near the center of town.

If you're more a fan of textiles, arrange a tour to the town of Bulcay, where you can see the last of the ikat weavers. Silver is also worked in Chordeleg where you can't miss all the jewelry stores.

Updated: Jan 15, 2013.

Tatoo Adventure Gear

Tatoo Adventure Gear is a great place to pick up brand-name sportswear, trekking and camping equipment, biking accessories and more. Tatoo Cuenca carries a comprehensive selection of gear as well as travel guidebooks and maps. The knowledgeable staff is a great source of information on everything from adventure hotspots to the perfect hiking boot. Tatoo also has stores in Quito and in Cumbayá. Av. Remigio Tamariz 2-52 and Federico Proaño, Tel: 07-409-0438, Fax: 07-288-4809, E-mail: 07-288-4809, URL: http://cl.tatoo.ws/store?id=3.
Updated: Oct 11, 2012.

Libri Mundi

Established in 1971, Libri Mundi is a popular bookstore chain with a number of stores in Cuenca, and also in Quito and Guayaquil. They stock a wide variety of books but for the traveler, the most important thing is that they sell English-language books, including novels. Libri Mundi stocks some of the best-quality reads, in genres including art history, mystery, biographies and Ecuadorian literature. Not least, they sell guidebooks, and V!VA is proud to partner, so you can buy your V!VA guide here! Hermano Miguel 8-14 and Mariscal Sucre (Centro), Tel: 593-7-284-3782.
Updated: Oct 11, 2012.

Carolina Bookstore

Carolina Bookstore houses the self-proclaimed "largest selection of used books in Cuenca." Secondhand hardcovers and paperbacks in English and other languages—including Spanish, Italian, German and Dutch—are stacked on bookcases and tables throughout the store, with prices starting at just $2 (on a discount table in back!). Also, if you have some old books you'd like to leave behind, Carolina Bookstore gives $2 credit toward your next purchase for trade-ins, as long as they are in decent condition. Hermano Miguel 4-46 y Calle Larga, Tel: Cell: 097-794-057.
Updated: Oct 15, 2012.

El Surtido Almacen de Musica

El Surtido offers the largest selection of national and folkloric music for sale, if the any music you have heard in Ecuador has piqued your interest. The friendly, knowledgeable staff can help guide you in your selection. Also for sale are musical instruments and accessories, DVDs, music instruction booklets and sheet music. Borrero 8-68 and Bolivar, Tel: 593 7 2831 409/ 2841 949.

Centro Municipal Artesanal/ Casa de la Mujer

Casa de la Mujer is an artisanal market near the main plaza filled with stalls selling every type of craft typical to Ecuador, especially from the Azuay province. Products include knit sweaters from Otavalo, traditional Andean musical instruments, Panama hats, jewelry, ceramics and weavings. A more orderly and relaxed market than the nearby San Francisco market, you can browse the stalls at your own pace with no one pressuring you to buy anything. There are two stories of stalls and public bathrooms on the ground floor. General Torres 7-33 and Presidente Córdova, Located on General Torres and Mariscal Sucre, across the street from the Plaza San Francisco Market.
Updated: Oct 11, 2012.

Things To See and Do in Cuenca

Cuenca is one of Ecuador's most elegant and beautiful cities. The city is a UNESCO World Heritage Cultural site, a fact of which the locals are immeasurably proud. The easiest and most obvious thing to do in Cuenca is to simply stroll around the historic downtown, marveling at the architecture in and around the well-kept central park, Parque Calderón.

You can not walk far without running into a colonial church; Cuenca supposedly has 52, one for every Sunday of the year. The number of churches you visit will depend on your level of interest, but the La Inmaculada (the New Cathedral) and El Sagrario (the Old Cathedral), both on the central park, should not be missed.

There are also several museums of note, including the Pumapungo Museum complex (also known as the Central Bank Museum), which have very good exhibits for those interested in the complete history of the region and city.

No trip to Cuenca is complete without a trip to the Mirador Turi (Turi Overlook), where you can get an overview shot of the city. The lookout point is on a modest hill to the south of the city and on a clear day, the view is spectacular. There is a small church there and some coin-operated binoculars.

Outside of town, you can visit the spectacular El Cajas National Park, or visit the nearby artisan towns of Gualaceo, Chordeleg and Sigsig. Each of the towns has a unique market or artisan product, and all three can

be visited in one day. In Gualaceo, stop by the large produce and animal market; in Chordeleg, peruse the many stores selling fine silver products; and in Sigsig, visit one of the Panama Hat cooperatives.
Updated: Jan 15, 2013.

Plaza San Francisco

If you still want to shop, head over to Plaza San Francisco, a block away from the Flower Market to the west. You'll find a lot of low-quality stuff for locals, like shoes, but also some vendors from Otavalo selling the usual blankets, scarves and other artesanía. Some of the stores around the square sell clothes for religious icons, such as gold-embroidered capes.

On the western side of the plaza, you'll find the Centro Municipal Artesanal, or the Casa de la Mujer, a tidy collection of stands selling jewelry, Panama hats and other handicrafts. You will also find carts in the plaza selling fruit salad, coconuts and cevichochos, if you'd like to buy a quick snack while there. On Ca. Presidente Córdova, between Ca. Padre Aguirre and Ca. General Torres.
Updated: Oct 15, 2012.

San Joaquín Neighborhood

San Joaquín is a neighborhood in Cuenca that has emerged as the place to eat carne asada (grilled meat). Lining the dirt roads are family-owned restaurants where cuencano families come to devour savory lunches. This is one place in the city where you will be virtually the only foreigner. Many of the restaurants have playgrounds for children, can accommodate large groups, and have both indoor and outdoor seating.

San Joaquín is not ideal for vegetarians, though. Specializing in all types of grilled meat (pork, beef, chicken and guinea pig), most plates come with mote (hominy), potatoes, and humitas/tamales (steamed corn cakes). The most well-known restaurants are Las Palmeras, Las Cabañas de San Joaquin and El Tequila. Most plates cost no more than $4 and come with heaping amounts of food. The restaurants also serve beer..

You can get to San Joaquín by taxi, which takes about 15 minutes from the center; it shouldn't cost more than $3.50. Alternatively, you can take local bus #19 ($0.25) from the corner of Presidente Córdova and Juan Móntalvo or from the Feria Libre market. San Joaquín district.
Updated: Oct 22, 2012.

Museum of CIDAP (Inter-American Center of Popular Arts)

(ADMISSION: Free) El Centro Interamericano de Artesanías y Artes Populares, or Inter-American Center of Popular Arts, is a small but interesting museum dedicated to the popular crafts of the Americas. The upper floors where the administration is located display mainly textiles, while the lower floors are the museum proper. The spacious, brightly lit rooms display exhibits that change every month; sometimes ceramics, textiles or carvings, which are also for sale. Hermano Miguel 3-23 and Ca. Larga, La Escalinita, Tel: 593-7-282-9451, URL: www.cidap.org.ec.
Updated: Oct 15, 2012.

Central Bank Museum

(ADMISSION: Free) The Central Bank Museum is actually a complex of several smaller exhibits, each dedicated to a different aspect of Cuenca life or history. The museum is next to the Pumapungo archaeological site, an ancient Inca city. The ethnographic exhibit (on the 2nd floor) is based on the theory that a great deal can be learned about a culture through their everyday objects. There are informational displays about Ecuador's various cultures, including a series of shrunken heads from the Amazon.

The archaeological museum contains many pieces and relics unearthed nearby, mostly from the Inca and Cañari cultures, including an exhibit about the neighboring Pumapungo site, which you can visit. Also on the premises is an exhibit of religious art and a numismatic exhibit, which has extensive displays of coins and currency. The museum also has rotating displays, such as a series of photographs of famous locations in Ecuador. Ca. Larga and Av. Huayna Capac, Tel: 07-283-1255.
Updated: Oct 15, 2012.

Mercado 10 de Agosto

Once considered to be one of the more dangerous markets in town, in the last few years Mercado 10 de Agosto has had a tremendous facelift and is now a nice place to visit for an authentic local experience, or to buy cheap produce for cooking in hostels. Redesigned and cleaned up, it now proudly flaunts its new image; it also has the privilege of being the only market in Cuenca with an escalator.

For a taste of real Cuencan life, come here and meander down the aisles of women selling fresh fruit and vegetables or medicinal herbs. Sample one of the many juices or smoothies made here with fresh fruits, some exotic to foreigners. For a cheap and hearty lunch, head to the second floor. If you have any specific ailments, the far right hand section on the second floor is filled medicinal plants to make teas, and the women selling them will be happy to let you know what plant will best assuage your respective ailment. Calle Larga between Tarqui and General Torres.

Parque Calderón ❗

Cuenca's beautifully tended central park, Parque Calderón, is an attractive, expansive area of flowers and trees. The park is dominated by a monument to Abdón Calderón, a young cuencano who fought valiantly at the battle of Pichincha in 1822, a pivotal confrontation in Ecuador's struggle for independence.

According to local legend, a critically injured Calderón crawled to the summit of Pichincha Volcano, where he planted the Ecuadorian flag in defiance of the Spanish. This legend is probably embellished somewhat, but according to historical documents, he received four wounds in the battle yet continued to fight. Although he died in Quito five days later, to this day, Ecuadorian soldiers who show tremendous courage are awarded the Abdón Calderón medal.

The park is flanked on two sides by churches that are popular with tourists. To the east is the colonial El Sagrario Church and on the west is Cuenca's most famous building, the massive La Inmaculada Church, which is instantly recognizable by the blue domes that dominate Cuenca's skyline. Ca. Simón Bolívar and Mariscal Sucre and Ca. Benigno Malo and Luis Cordero.
Updated: Oct 11, 2012.

Barranco's Panama Hat Factory/ Museum

(ADMISSION: Free) El Museo del Sombrero de Paja Toquilla (Panama Hat Museum) is located in the Paredes Roldán family Panama hat factory, which has been producing the iconic hats for more than 60 years. The factory itself sells Panama hats in all shapes, colors and sizes, and can customize them to your personal preference in 30 minutes time.

Hats range from $20 to nearly $1,000, depending on quality and how fine the stitch is. The small museum, visited by a short tour led by one of the factory employees, displays the history and process of Panama hat-making, about the plant paja toquilla, how the hats are colored and molded, and why they are called Panama Hats. Afterwards, you can peruse the stacks of hats in the store and buy one, if desired. Calle Larga 10-41 between Padre Aguirre y General Torres (look for the giant hat outside)., Tel: 2831569, E-mail: panamahat@etapaonline.net.ec, URL: www. ecuatorianhat.com.
Updated: Oct 15, 2012.

Iglesia El Sagrario (Old Cathedral)

(ADMISSION: $2) The Iglesia El Sagrario, also known as the Old Cathedral, sits across the Parque Calderón from La Inmaculada, and is well worth a visit. If you wander inside, you'll see no pews or altars, but many interesting artifacts.

There is even a glass window in the floor through which you can see a small section of the catacombs below. The catacombs look sort of like a shallow well with several neatly arranged skulls. There is also a small museum inside. Luis Cordero and Mariscal Sucre, on Parque Calderón.
Updated: Oct 15, 2012.

Iglesia Todos Los Santos

Iglesia Todos Los Santos is the oldest church in Cuenca. The church has been in the process of renovations for the past few years and continues to be, but you can now visit it and see the statue of Santa Ana, patroness of the city, inside. Corner of Ca. Larga and Bajada de Todos Los Santos.
Updated: Oct 15, 2012.

Catedral de la Inmaculada (New Cathedral) ❗

(ADMISSION: $0.50) The massive brick facade and sky-blue domes of Catedral de la Inmaculada Concepción make the building one of the most recognizable (and photographed) in Cuenca. La Inmaculada, which is dubbed the "New Cathedral" to distinguish it from El Sagrario, dates to 1885.

The entrance of La Inmaculada is choked and filled to the brim with vendors selling candles and religious souvenirs. Inside, you'll find a large gold altar, the crowned Virgin Mary for which Inmaculada is known, and walls lined with religious statues (where you can light one of the candles you bought earlier).Benigno Malo and Mariscal Sucre, on Parque Calderón.
Updated: Oct 15, 2012.

Flower Market

Cuenca's Flower Market is located on Calle Mariscal Sucre, near Padre Aguirre, in front of the southern side of the Cathedral de la Inmaculada (New Cathedral), and wraps around on Padre Aguirre, between Plaza San Francisco and Calle Mariscal Sucre. This colorful market is filled with dozens of stands of women selling a variety of locally grown flowers. The entrance to La Carmen de la Asunción convent is there as well, where nuns sell religious items through a special window. The market is picturesque, but the sellers are a bit short with tourists who snap photos but don't buy anything, so keep that in mind.

Cuenca's Churches and Cathedrals

The streets of historic Cuenca are lined with many interesting colonial churches. While it may be difficult to pay a visit to all of the city's 52 sanctuaries, it's worthwhile to pick out a few to see while there. Two of the most famous, La Inmaculada (the New Cathedral) and El Sagrario (the Old Cathedral), are located opposite each other on either side of Parque Calderón. The other church popular with tourists is Todos Los Santos (All Saints).
Updated: Jan 17, 2013.

Plaza San Sebastián

Plaza de San Sebastián is a quiet retreat from the city streets and features both the Museo of Modern Art and, to the north, Iglesia San Sebastián (on Ca. Bolívar side). The church is best known for its large wooden doorway and for the Cross of San Sebastián, a colonial era tribute to Christianity that also marks the western limit of Cuenca's historical center. Coronel Talbot between Bolívar and Mariscal Sucre.
Updated: Oct 15, 2012.

Museum of Modern Art

(ADMISSION: Free) The Museo Municipal de Arte Moderno (the Museum of Modern Art), on the Plaza San Sebastián, has a permanent collection of contemporary paintings and sculptures. The artwork is displayed in separate rooms and within the gardens, spread around two delightful courtyards.

The buildings were previously a casa de la temperancia (house of temperance), a treatment center used for the rehabilitation of alcoholics. After years of neglect and general deterioration, the buildings were beautifully restored as a national monument. Photographs showing this are displayed within a separate exhibition. Well worth a visit. Ca. Mariscal Sucre 15-27 and Coronel Talbot, on Plaza San Sebastián.
Updated: Oct 15, 2012.

Museum of Aboriginal Cultures

(ADMISSION: $2) This cultural foundation displays over 5,000 archaeological pieces from the different indigenous cultures of Ecuador in a spacious, well-lit loft. You can see many classic items like painted jugs and pots with anthropomorphic handles, or more unusual ones like zoomorphic (animal-shaped) whistles and even a shrunken head. The museum is a little short on explanation signs, so you are best taking a tour, which can be done in English or in French. There also is an onsite restaurant, a library and a well-stocked souvenir shop. Ca. Larga 5-24, between Hermano Miguel and Mariano Cueva, Tel: 07-284-1540, E-mail: www.museoculturasaborigenes.tk.
Updated: Oct 15, 2012.

Cuenca City Tour Bus

(PRICE: $5) Especially if you are short on time, the Cuenca city panoramic bus tour is an excellent way to see the city. It leaves from Parque Calderón in front of the El Sagrario church (Old Cathedral) and passes by over 20 major city sights, including Catedral de la Inmaculada, Plaza de San Sebastián and the Museo de Arte Moderno, Iglesia de Todos Santos, the Banco Central Museum and Pumapungo, Iglesia Turi and Puente Roto, before swinging back around to let passengers off at the starting point. The entire tour takes about two hours and your ticket is valid for hop-on and hop-off at any of the stops for 24 hours. Tours leave Monday-Saturday at 10:30 a.m., 2:30 p.m. and 5:30 p.m., and on Sundays at 10:30 a.m. and 2:30 p.m. Leaves from Luis Cordero and Mariscal Sucre, Parque Calderón, in front of the El Sagrario (Old Cathedral) entrance, Tel: 07-288-3564, Cel: 09-9842-0807/9809-3718, E-mail: cotratudossa2003@hotmail.com, URL: www.cotratudossa.com/#!bturistico/c1omy.
Updated: Jan 17, 2013.

Plaza Rotary

Located about four blocks to the northeast of the central plaza in Cuenca, Plaza Rotary hosts an outdoor market of random, non-touristy handicrafts made by and for locals. Hand-tied rope, baskets made of old car tires, brass bells and more are for sale here. The spot is well worth a visit, but don't plan on buying much of anything: there just isn't much of interest for travelers. The

plaza stretches between the streets Hermano Miguel and Mariano Cueva east to west, and between the streets Gaspar Sangurima and Mariscal Lamar north to south.
Updated: Oct 11, 2012.

Mirador Turi

Turi, or "brother" in Kichwa, serves as a quick escape away from the center of the city. Most enjoyable at sunset, Turi sits atop a steep hill, providing gorgeous vistas of the city lights below and the mountains that surround it. You can usually count on a backdrop of pink and purple sky, cuddling couples and, at dusk traditional music blaring from the church loudspeakers. The actual lookout point is just in front of the church, the side of which is covered in interesting murals that depict daily indigenous life. On Sundays, Turi is filled with churchgoers and provides an interesting perspective of what town life is really about. Turi is located to the south of Cuenca. From the center of the city, a cab ride should not cost more than $3. By bus ($0.25), take any that say "Turi" from the intersection of Fray Vicente Solano and 12 de Abril. It is also included in the city bus tours ($5), which leave three times a day for Parque Calderón, in front of the Old Cathedral museum entrance.
Updated: Oct 15, 2012.

Studying Spanish in Cuenca

While not offering Quito's variety of options and competition, Cuenca has a good selection of Spanish schools. Studying here, as opposed to Quito, is appealing to many travelers due to Cuenca's smaller size and relative safety. You will also have more opportunities to interact with locals as you practice conjugations.

Many of the Spanish programs include cultural activities—such as salsa dancing, cooking classes, city tours and day trips to nearby attractions—and can set students up with homestays and/or volunteering opportunities to enhance language study. Cuenca is one of Ecuador's most expensive cities, but its quaint, colonial atmosphere will continue to attract Spanish students for years to come.
Updated: Jan 15, 2013.

CEDEI

CEDEI hosts international academic programs and teaches courses in Andean literature, business, environment and culture, as well as Spanish language classes. Around 20 universities from the U.S. have partnerships with CEDEI, allowing students to receive college credit for their coursework. It can also arrange volunteer programs and/or home stays to complement Spanish study. If only in town for a short amount of time, travelers can pay for Spanish classes per week, which typically consist of four hours of instruction per day ($10 per hour): two hours focused on grammar and two hours on conversation skills.

CEDEI is also Cuenca's largest English school, with three campuses in the city. Native English speakers with relevant teaching experience, references and a TEFL certification can contact Elisabeth Rodas (Tel: 07-409-2186, E-mail: erodas@cedei.org) for more information about securing a teaching job. Teachers typically work 12-20 hours per week. Gran Colombia 11-02 and General Torres, 3rd floor, Tel: 07-283-9003, URL: www.cedei.org.
Updated: Oct 15, 2012.

Si Centro Spanish School

Authorized by the Ecuadorian Ministry of Education, Si Centro is an efficiently run school that only employs university-trained Spanish teachers. The school is only two blocks from Parque Calderón. In addition to its professional teaching in quiet classrooms, the school also has a friendly atmosphere, with two cozy lounge areas and hosts cultural Fridays, where students can learn how to cook typical food and make local beverages. Si Centro offers lessons for all levels, from complete beginner to advanced Spanish for use in professional fields. Lessons are taught one-on-one or in small groups, usually in programs with 20 hours of classes a week, though 30-hour intensive courses are also available. Borrero 7-67, between Mariscal Sucre and Presidente Córdova, E-mail: sicentrocuenca@hotmail.com, URL: www.sicentrospanishschool.com.
Updated: Oct 15, 2012.

Símon Bolívar Spanish School

Just one and a half blocks away from Cuenca's central park, Símon Bolívar is ideally located right in the heart of the historic city. With four locations across Ecuador, Símon Bolívar is a well-respected chain of schools. The Cuenca location was founded in 2005 is now very well-established, employing only experienced, well-qualified Spanish teachers. The school recommends students take four hours of one-on-one lessons per day, however they do also offer group lessons (3-6 people). The school has free WiFi for students and also organizes extracurricular

SOUTHERN ANDES

activities such as dance classes, weekday excursions around Cuenca, and weekend trips to sites around the city, such as Ingapirca. Ca. Luis Cordero 10-25, between Gran Colombia and Mariscal Lamar, Tel: 07-284-4555, E-mail: info@bolivar2.com, URL: www.bolivar2.com.
Updated: Oct 15, 2012.

Escuela Amauta

This highly recommended Spanish school only provides private classes, except in the case that friends who are at the same level want to take them together. Classes are charged per hour ($9), but during high season, students are required to commit to two hours per day for a minimum of a week. Amauta organizes free activities for students in the afternoon, such as salsa dancing, city tours and cultural activities, and can also arrange volunteering and home stays.

The school is well-equipped, and students can use its computers with Internet for free and help themselves to coffee, tea and cookies in its cafeteria. All of Amauta's teachers are native speakers and bilingual. Located on Hermano Miguel 7-48, between Sucre and Presidente Córdova, Tel: 07-284-6206, URL: www.amauta.edu.ec/programs/04_school_cuenca.htm.
Updated: Oct 23, 2012.

Cuenca Tours

Cuenca has numerous tour agencies that can easily be found in the area around Parque Calderón. These agencies can arrange one- or multi-day trips around Ecuador as well as domestic and international flights. The most popular trips, which almost all the agencies offer, are city tours around Cuenca and one-day trips to the Inca ruins at Ingapirca and into El Cajas National Park.
Updated: Jan 15, 2013.

Cazhuma Tours Travel Agency

Cazhuma is a reputable Cuenca-based travel agency that offers trips around the southern Andes, all across Ecuador and even to Peru. This agency specializes in tours around the historical city of Cuenca and to all of the area's highlights, including one-day trips to Ingapirca, Cajas National Park, the valley of Yunguilla and waterfall of Girón, and the towns of Gualaceo and Chordeleg.

The agency can also arrange mountain biking, climbing, canyoning and horseback riding with reputable guides in the mountains surrounding Cuenca. Cazhuma

also organizes longer trips that range from three-day excursions and treks in the southern Andes to multi-day trips encompassing different regions of Ecuador. It also has an on-site Spanish school, which charges $6.50 per hour for private classes. Padre Aguirre 9-40 and Simón Bolívar-, Tel: 07-283-9959, E-mail: gabriela@cazhumatours.com, URL: www.cazhumatours.com.
Updated: Oct 15, 2012.

Expediciones Apullacta

Expediciones Apullacta is a very professional travel agency that specializes in domestic travel and shared tours. It runs one-day tours to Cajas National Park every day, to Ingapirca three times a week and to nearby artisans towns twice a week. Other options include camping in Cajas National Park, extreme sports around Cuenca, or visits to community tourism projects like the one in Saraguro. All of Apallacta's guides are bilingual. You can also book domestic flights here or tours to other parts of the country, including to the Galápagos Islands. Gran Colombia 11-02 and General Torres, 2nd floor, office 111, Tel: 07-283-7815/7681, Cel: 09-9960-4870/9975-0193/9977-1605, E-mail: info@apullacta.com, URL: www.apullacta.com.
Updated: Oct 15, 2012.

Cuenca Lodging

The picturesque city of Cuenca offers a wide variety of lodging options, from the luxury digs just outside of town to hostels that even the most tightfisted backpacker can afford. If you're going to Cuenca, you should consider staying at one of several converted old homes that are found in the center of town. Some of the most picturesque old mansions in Cuenca have been converted into hotels and guesthouses in recent years, and they provide charming places to stay that are close to the action of the city center. There are also some nice options along the Tomebamba River, which have rooms with river views.

If you're looking for a less intense, more relaxing trip, you might want to consider some of the lodging options outside of town, like in the town of Baños (not to be confused with the much larger town of Baños near Ambato) or in neighboring Ingapirca. The hotels located in these little towns offer good service and value, and are conveniently located near sites that are of plenty of interest, such as the Baños thermal pools and the ancient Inca ruins of Ingapirca.
Updated: Jan 15, 2013.

BUDGET

Hostal Santa Fe

($6-10 per person) A great option for those looking for a budget hostel in Cuenca, Hostal Santa Fe is set in between the town center and the Tombamba River. You can easily walk to all the main attractions in Cuenca from here, as well as to several Internet cafés and restaurants. Not all the rooms at Hostal Santa Fe have private baths, but there are two shared bathrooms downstairs. At first glance they seem unimpressive, but looks can be deceiving, as the showers are hot and powerful. For those traveling in groups or who want to save some money, Hostal Santa Fe also has one dorm with 12 beds. Borrero 5-57 between Juan Jaramillo and Honorato Vásquez, Tel: 07-282-2025, Cel: 09-9450-8837, E-mail: hostalsantafe2010@hotmail.com.

Hostal Villa Del Rosario

($10-12 per person) The family-run Villa del Rosario is located in an old colonial house that has been completely restored and remodeled. Private rooms equipped with armoires and mirrors are set around a nice courtyard and garden. There is also one room for six to eight people, which families or groups can reserve. Guests can use the hostel's kitchen, making it convenient for those who want to cook during their stay. Honorato Vásquez 5-25 and Mariano Cueva, Tel: 07-282-8585, Cel: 09-9225-3778, E-mail: hvillarosario@yahoo.com, URL: www.hvillarosario.com.
Updated: Oct 16, 2012.

Villa Nova Inn

(ROOMS: $35-100) Villa Nova Inn is located in front of Parque de la Madre and the Tomebamba River and offers 12 cozy rooms with private baths and showers with 24-hour hot water. The rooms with river views have nice terraces and cost more than those located in the interior. The complimentary breakfast is prepared with natural ingredients and is served either in your room, on the sunny terrace, or next door at its affiliate Sukara Restaurant overlooking the rushing Tomebamba River.

Villa Nova Inn also offers discounted lunches and dinners from Sukara, which specializes in Japanese food. The hostel's staff is bilingual and helpful. Paseo 3 de Noviembre 24-06 and Escalinatas, Tel: 07-283-6790, E-mail: info@villanovacuenca.com, URL: www.villanovacuenca.com.
Updated: Oct 16, 2012.

El Cafecito

($6-30 per person) El Cafecito is a decent option if you want a cheap dorm bed close to Cuenca's attractions and nightlife. However, it also has its own restaurant and bar in the colonial courtyard and the noise level often makes it hard to sleep. The private rooms are overpriced for what you get, but the hostel's social atmosphere still draw backpackers from around the world. The chilled-out café often becomes crowded and rowdy come happy hour time (daily 5-7 p.m.). El Cafecito also has locations in Quito and in Bogota, Colombia, but the one in Cuenca seems a bit more rundown than the other two. Honorato Vásquez and Luis Cordero, Tel: 07-283-2337, E-mail: cuenca@cafecito.net, URL: www.cafecito.net/Enghtml/cafecitoC.html.

Hostal La Orquídea

(ROOMS: $20-50) Hostal La Orquídea is a converted colonial home in downtown Cuenca with 25 rooms. The establishment's rates are lower than many of its competitors, so the place tends to fill up fast. If you plan to stay at La Orquidea, try to call ahead or arrive early. The hostel is quite pleasant and known for good service. Borrero 9-31 and Bolívar, Tel: 07-283-5844, E-mail: hostal-laorquidea@hotmail.com.
Updated: Oct 15, 2012.

Macondo Hostal

($21-33 per person) Macondo Hostal is a very nice mid-range option and serves sleepy backpackers well. Rooms are clean and comfortable, and are set around an outdoor garden. If you don't have your own laptop, you can borrow the hostel's for 30 minutes at a time, free of cost. Macondo also has a permanent art exhibit featuring artwork by local Ecuadorian artists, all of which are for sale, and sells artesanía and jewelry near reception. The hostel accepts credit cards, but charges an extra 5 percent to use them. Discounts are available to groups of eight or more. Prices include a buffet continental breakfast, and guests can use the hostel kitchen to prepare other meals. Tarqui 11-64 and Mariscal Lamar, Tel: 07-282-1700, E-mail: info@hostalmacondo.com, URL: www.hostalmacondo.com.
Updated: Oct 25, 2012.

Hotel Milan

(ROOMS: $20-48) Hotel Milan is a favorite place for foreign visitors to lay their heads in Cuenca, in no small part because the establishment is clean, centrally located and comes highly recommended by the local tourism bureau. Hotel Milan is so popular that the hotel fills up quickly, particularly during weekends, so you should call ahead to reserve a room before busloads of your fellow tourists arrive.

All 24 rooms have private bathrooms, cable TV, security boxes and telephones. The hotel also has a fourth-floor terrace for breakfast (a continental breakfast is included in the price), and a small restaurant at street level. The staff is also very friendly and helpful. Presidente Córdova 9-89 and Padre Aguierre, Tel: 07-283-1104/5351, E-mail: info@hotelmilan.com.ec, URL: www.hotelmilan.com.ec. Updated: Oct 15, 2012.

MID-RANGE
Casa Lloret Hostal

(ROOMS: $40-100) Staying at Casa Lloret feels more like staying at a friend's home than at a hotel. This small guesthouse close to the Yanuncay River has just seven private rooms and two family-style suites, some of which have balconies. Suites have fully-equipped kitchens and large flat-screen plasma TVs.

The whole place is decorated in soothing, autumn-like colors, and there is a lovely common sitting area with couches and a fireplace downstairs. Breakfast is included in room prices, and free coffee and tea is available all day. Carlos V 3-12 and Isabel La Católica, Tel: 07-288-6150, Cel: 09-9950-0777, Fax: 07-288-3010, E-mail: info@hostalcasalloret.com, URL: www.hostalcasalloret.com. Updated: Nov 08, 2012.

Casa Ordoñez

(ROOMS: $60-75) This charming, family-owned boutique hotel is actually an old mansion, beautifully restored to its original grandeur. Its comfortable rooms have large beds, goose down comforters and finely detailed decorations. With a characterful reading room, family room, living room and terrace, you will feel as if you staying at a friend's home instead of in a hotel.

The on-site restaurant, Los Abuelos, features gourmet Ecuadorian cuisine. Guests can use the free Internet and make international calls. Mariscal Lamar 8-59 and Benigno Malo, Tel: 07-282-3297, E-mail: casaordonez@gmail.com, URL: www.casaordonez.com. Updated: Oct 16, 2012.

Hostal Posada del Angel

(ROOMS: $44-99) One of the best mid-range options in Cuenca, the elegant Posada del Angel is a friendly, well-kept place that tries to maintain a family atmosphere. The hotel, which is housed in a restored colonial home, is laid-back and airy, and has 22 comfortable rooms with private bathrooms.

The place itself has a lot of character and is filled with small but cozy sitting areas to make you feel right at home. The staff is also very welcoming and helpful. Breakfast is included in room prices. Bolívar 14-11 and Estévez de Toral, Tel: 07-284-0695-282-1360, E-mail: reservas@hostalposadadelangel.com / posadadelangel@hotmail.com, URL: www.hostalposadadelangel.com. Updated: Oct 15, 2012.

Hotel Santa Ana

(ROOMS: $33-70) Hotel Santa Ana is very attractive and elegant, with 40 comfortable and modern rooms. Although it is no longer managed by Grupo Plaza Hotels and Tourism, it still retains most of its perks, including a pool and Jacuzzi, a space to host events, and a garage to guard your vehicle. It no longer has a restaurant, though. Room prices include an American breakfast. Presidente Córdova 11-49, between General Torres and TarquiCuenca, Ecuador, Tel: 07-282-3872/284-8138, E-mail: hotelsantaana77@yahoo.com. Updated: Oct 15, 2012.

Hotel El Quijote

(ROOMS: $35-76) Hotel El Quijote offers 33 rooms with a total capacity for 65 people. Rooms are small but sufficient and have private bathrooms and plasma TVs. There is a restaurant-bar on-site that cooks up Ecuadorian food and a conference space for 60 people that guests can rent out for an extra cost. Although not included in the room prices, guests can enjoy one of three different breakfast choices in the restaurant each morning. Parking is available, as is a laundry service. Hermano Miguel 9-58 and Gran Colombia, Tel: 07-284-3197/283-5031, E-mail: info@hotelquijote.com, URL: www.hotelquijote.com. Updated: Oct 16, 2012.

Cofradia del Monje

(ROOMS: $29-72) This elegant, small hostel is attached to Iglesia San Francisco, in front of Plaza de San Francisco. It has beautiful décor and friendly staff. Each room comes with private bath, hot water, comfy beds, cable TV and WiFi. Breakfast is included in the price and is served at its on-site restaurant and bar. The restaurant also serves cheap almuerzos ($2.50). Presidente Córdova 10-33 and Padre Aguirre, Tel: 07-283-1251, E-mail: reservas@hostalcofradiadelmonje.com, URL: www.hostalcofradiadelmonje.com. Updated: Oct 15, 2012.

Hostal Chordeleg

(ROOMS: $26-85) An excellent choice for those in the lower mid-range budget zone, Hostal Chordeleg is a converted colonial home in Cuenca's historical center. The courtyard, with its neat garden and wooden upper floors, is beautiful. Its rooms, which have clean bathrooms, are well-maintained and come with TV. Free on-site parking is available and there is WiFi throughout the hotel. Prices include breakfast. Gran Colombia 11-15 and General Torres, Tel: 07-282-2536/4611, E-mail: hostalfm@etapaonline.net.ec, URL: www.hostalchordeleg.com. Updated: Oct 15, 2012.

Mansión Alcázar

(ROOMS: $65-85) A little over a decade ago, the owners of this fine colonial mansion in central Cuenca renovated it into a modern, elegant hotel. The setting is quite pleasant and the rooms are large and comfortable, if a bit formal. There are a total of 15 rooms and nine suites, each of which is different and each of which has a different name. The hotel features an excellent restaurant and attractive courtyard where guests can relax. Definitely not for the backpacker set, if you're the sort of traveler who prefers to stay in "The Mirage Suite" rather than "room #4," this is the place for you. It also offers romantic packages for special occasions that include flowers, a box of chocolates and a bottle of champagne. Ca. Bolívar 12-55 and Tarqui, Tel: 07-282-3889, Fax: 07-282-3554, E-mail: info@mansionalcazar.com, URL: www.mansionalcazar.com. Updated: Oct 16, 2012.

San Andrés Hotel

(ROOMS: $49-89) Considering the quality of accommodation and prices, San Andrés is a good value. Spacious rooms feature oversized beds, elegant comforters and classic dark-wood furniture. Social areas are organized around classy cast-iron furniture and tastefully arranged décor, while the service is attentive. It also has a cafetería, where you can enjoy your breakfast each morning. Gran Colombia 11-66, between Tarqui and General Torres, Tel: 07-284-1497/285-0039, E-mail: info@hotelsanandres/net, URL: www.hotelsanandres.net. Updated: Oct 15, 2012.

HIGH-END

Hotel La Casona

(ROOMS $49-100) Between the Tomebamba and Yanuncay rivers, you'll find the beautifully restored house of Hotel La Casona. Its 28 rooms are equipped with private bathrooms, cable TV, WiFi, safety box and hairdryer. Some of the rooms are more spacious than others, so ask to see some rooms first if you would prefer one of the larger rooms. You can enjoy any meal of the day at La Casona's restaurant, which has both indoor and outdoor seating. Overall, you will find good service with personalized attention here, making it a nice place to stay if you don't mind being a bit further away from Cuenca's historic center. Miguel Cordero 2-124 and Alfonso Cordero (corner), Tel: 07-410-3501/3509/288-8869, Cel: 09-9882-1664, E-mail: info@lacasonahotel.com.ec, URL: www.lacasonahotel.com.ec. Updated: Oct 16, 2012.

Hotel Carvallo

(ROOMS: $134-244) Located in the beautiful historical center, this recently converted colonial home integrates classic charm with all the comforts of an elegant modern establishment. Warmth and refinement greet visitors at every corner, from the tastefully appointed furnishings to the stylish décor. The 30 rooms are spacious and airy, and feature large beds with fluffy comforters and plenty of throw pillows. And if the beds can't guarantee a good night's sleep, the hand-painted angels soaring above your head are sure to watch over you. Gran Colombia 9-5, between Padre Aguirre and Benigno Malo, Tel: 07-283-2063, E-mail: reservas@hotelcarvallo.com.ec, URL: hotelcarvallo.com.ec. Updated: Oct 16, 2012.

Hotel Crespo

(ROOMS: $77-118) One of the most popular hotels in Cuenca, Hotel Crespo is a converted family estate, dating back over 100 years, and is located close to the center of town. It is a gorgeous place, set right on the banks of the Tomebamba River. The hotel has 48 elegant, airy rooms, each of which has cable TV, phone and WiFi. Many of the rooms have been remodeled recently, but this has in no way decreased their charm. There is also a first-class restaurant featuring French and

SOUTHERN ANDES

Ecuadorian cuisine. Breakfast is included. The hotel will pick you up for free at the airport if you have reservations. Hotel Crespo is located at the southern edge of the old town on Calle Larga, overlooking the Tomebamba River, and some of the rooms have river views. Ca. Larga 793 and Luis Cordero, Tel: 07-284-2571, Cel: 09-8723-4333, E-mail: reservacioneshotelcrespo@yahoo.es. Updated: Oct 16, 2012.

Hotel Oro Verde

(ROOMS: $115-125) Hotel Oro Verde (the name translates as "Green Gold" in Spanish and refers to bananas) is Cuenca's most luxurious hotel. The establishment is a destination in itself, offering such amenities as a swimming pool, exercise room, fine dining, tennis and horseback riding. The Oro Verde has 77 rooms, so there is usually space available, even during busy seasons.

This hotel is one of several high-end Oro Verde branded hotels in Ecuador, and like the others, the complex features large, well-designed rooms, gorgeous gardens and elegant restaurants. The hotel is built on the banks of the Tombamba river, next to a small natural lake. Easily the fanciest hotel in Cuenca, Oro Verde is particularly popular with businessmen and deep-pocketed tourists. If you have the money, the Oro Verde is a good place to spend it. Av. Ordóñez Lazo s/n, Tel: 07-409-0000, Fax: 07-409-0001, E-mail: ovcuenca@ororverdehotels.com, URL: www.ororverdehotels.com/cuenca/index.htm. Updated: Sep 27, 2012.

Hotel Santa Lucía

(ROOMS: $98-156) Hotel Santa Lucía is a beautiful converted home in central Cuenca; the home once belonged to Don Manuel Vega Dávila, the first governor of Azuay province. The hotel is elegant, and the rooms are comfortable and modern, with luxurious amenities like plasma TVs with satellite cable, digital safes, mini-bar and free bottled water. Owned by the Veintimilla family, who also own other successful hotels and restaurants, Hotel Santa Lucía won an award for best building restoration in 2002. Its restaurant, which doubles as a café, is very good and serves Italian-Ecuadorean style food. A breakfast buffet in the restaurant and a welcome cocktail is included in the price. Antonio Borrero 8-44 and Mariscal Sucre, Tel: 07-282-8000, E-mail: info@santaluciahotel.com, URL: www.santaluciahotel.com/index2.php.

Hacienda Uzhupud

(ROOMS: $79-230) Located about 45 minutes outside of Cuenca, Hacienda Uzhupud is a good option for those who want to be near Cuenca but still have more of a countryside experience. The hacienda has hiking trails, horses for riding, tennis courts, a pool and sauna, in addition to soccer field, volleyball court and children's games. There is even a small orchid garden. It can also host meetings, conventions and other special events. On Sundays, it offers an impressive buffet lunch featuring local dishes such as hornado (roast pork).

On weekends and holidays, Uzhupud is popular with Ecuadorians who go to relax: you can pay day rates to use the pool and sauna area. Many tours to nearby Gualaceo and Chordeleg will stop for lunch at Uzhupud. The dishes are quite reasonably priced and the food is excellent. Try the yaguana juice: it's a fruit punch of sorts colored with the pinkish ataco plant. Km. 32 Via Paute; Cuenca office: Baltazara de Calderón 3-76 and Gran Colombia (3rd floor), Tel: 07-225-0339/0329, Cel: 09-783-0209; Cuenca office: 07-284-0615/285-0649, Cel: 09-362-0427, E-mail: reservaciones@uzhupud.com, URL: www.uzhupud.com. Updated: Jun 05, 2013.

Cuenca Restaurants

Cuenca is a great place to eat. The restaurants in the city center are diverse, and there are options that will appeal to every taste and budget. The best restaurants are often associated with hotels, but they're still quite reasonably priced. The city also has quite a few American-style and European-style cafés where you can find a taste of home. There are also several good vegetarian restaurants in Cuenca.

Regional food in Cuenca is similar to that of northern Ecuador: a lot of pork, corn, potatoes and rice. Cuenca is also a good place to sample cuy (guinea pig), and if you look around as you drive around town, you'll see women cooking them on sticks over open grills.

The San Joaquín neighborhood is known for having very good barbecued meat.

If you're feeling very adventurous, head to the local market for a meal. There, you'll see dozens of roasted pigs all lined up: for a couple of bucks, you'll get a steaming plate of pork with tasty yellow mashed potatoes known as llapingachos. Go ahead and try it if you've got a strong stomach, but be warned that recent arrivals in country, and those prone to digestive problems, will want to take a pass.

Café Austria

(ENTREES: $5.50-8.50) Café Austria is a charming café, perfect for a slice of Austrian cake and coffee in the afternoon, or for a delicious lunch or dinner. Run by the same owner as Wunderbar Café, the Austria locale is smaller and more reminiscent of a European café, filled with wooden tables and chairs. On Mondays through Saturdays, it has set lunches that change daily. At night, Café Austria fills up with patrons ranging from the young to middle-aged, both local and foreign; its happy hour runs from Monday to Friday from 7-8 p.m. On most weekends, it hosts live music performances or events such as poetry readings.
Updated: Oct 18, 2012.

Café Eucalyptus !

(ENTREES: $6-15) A staple for many foreigners living in Cuenca, as well as a local crowd, this restaurant offers comfort food you can't easily find elsewhere, including Pad Thai and Jamaican jerk chicken in addition to typical Ecuadorian food. It also has a long drink list. Located in a renovated colonial house and owned by an American woman, the restaurant fills two floors, with a full bar on the lower level and a dance floor in the covered patio. The back wall is filled with caricatures of all of the regulars that frequent the café. At night, the place fills up and there is often live salsa music, so be sure to bring your dancing shoes. This is also one of the only restaurant in town that is reliably open on Sunday nights. Gran Colombia 9-41 and Benigno Malo, Tel: 07-284-9157, URL: www.cafeeucalyptus.com.
Updated: Oct 17, 2012.

El Maiz Restaurante

(ENTREES: $5-8) One of the most tranquil restaurants in town, El Maiz is located in an old colonial building with a beautiful courtyard, and is a true place to soak up the peaceful atmosphere of Cuenca. With sunny rooms and outdoor seating, this restaurant specializes in typical Ecuadorian dishes and fresh juices, as well as more experimental but just as delicious fusion meals. Here you can order grilled cuy (guinea pig) with potatoes and hard-boiled egg along beef medallions in a naranjilla (local fruit) and red wine sauce. The restaurant is a close walk from the Museo del Banco Central, away from the bustle of the center of the city. Despite its upscale looks, the prices are surprisingly affordable. Ca. Larga and Ca. Bajada de Los Molinos 1-279, Tel: 284-0224, Cel: 09-9902-8098, Fax: 593 7 2840224, E-mail: elmaiz17@etapanet.net / elmaizrestaurante@hotmail.com, URL: http://www.facebook.com/pages/RESTAURANTE-EL-MAIZ/131285656883886.
Updated: Oct 16, 2012.

El Pavón Real

(ENTREES: $3.75-6) El Pavón Real is a simple restaurant serving a mix of typical Ecuadorian plates and international dishes. It has cheap set-price lunches with three different options for the main course during the week. Here you can also try motepillo, a cuencano specialty of fried hominy mixed with scrambled eggs, which you can order alone or accompanying grilled chicken or pork. Others options include vegetarian pizza, chicken sandwich, shrimp risotto and BBQ chicken wings. Gran Colombia 8-33, between Benigno Malo and Luis Cordero, Tel: 07-284-6678, Cel: 099-262-8060, E-mail: elpavonrestaurante@gmail.com, URL: http://pavonreal.blogspot.com.
Updated: Oct 22, 2012.

El Pedregal Azteca

(ENTREES: $5.50-15) Craving some deep-fried Mexican? Then check out the town's popular Mexican-owned restaurant, which serves up specialties like flautas, tacos, chile rellenos (stuffed chili peppers) and chicken in a mole sauce. The set lunch menus are a good deal: choose between a burrito, chili or eggs with chorizo, each accompanied by a salad and soda, or two enchiladas with beans and guacamole, served with a soda and ice cream dessert.

The place fills up on weekend nights, when the restaurant hosts live Mariachi bands. Top off your meal with a house margarita or tequila shot. Gran Colombia 10-29 and Padre Aguirre, Tel: 07-282-3652/283-3627, E-mail: pazteca@hotmail.com, URL: www.pedregalazteca.com.
Updated: Oct 18, 2012.

Heladeria Holanda

(ICE CREAM: $0.60-1) This is unanimously considered the best place to get ice cream in town. Although it has recently changed locations, you can still sample dozens of different flavors here, including many only found in Ecuador. Grab a fresh scoop, or

opt to sample the delicious yogurts, cakes and sandwiches. Besides its food, Heladeria Holanda offers a great place to people-watch as it's a popular rendezvous point for many cuencanos.
Updated: Oct 18, 2012.

Raymipamba Café Restaurant

(ENTREES: $4.50-8) Perhaps the most famous restaurant in Cuenca, it is hard not to stop in, if just for a coffee or dessert. With terraced seating and windows facing out onto Parque Calderón, this café is perfect for a break in a busy day. The menu offers anything from crepes and fresh juices to pastas, humitas, tamales, chaulafan (fried rice), and ceviche. Make sure to steal a peek at the walls adorned with old photos of Cuenca. Raymipamba is just as much a magnet for locals as it is for foreigners, but the prices are higher than in other establishments with similar food. Benigno Malo 8-59 and Mariscal Sucre, Parque Calderón, Tel: 07-283-4159/282-4619, E-mail: raymi859@hotmail.com.
Updated: Oct 17, 2012.

San Sebas Café

(ENTREES: $3.75-5.75) San Sebas Café has delicious Arabica 7 coffee, awesome American-style breakfasts that are served all day long, and gourmet sandwiches, wraps, soups and salads. Menu items include BLT on focaccia bread, California chicken sandwich with basil mayo, Greek salad, and five different burger/veggie burger options. Breakfast options range from oatmeal banana pancakes and breakfast scrambles to a French toast sandwich, where two eggs and two slices of bacon are sandwiched between slices of vanilla cinnamon French toast. San Sebas is decorated with local artwork, which is all for sale, and it hosts live music every Friday night from 7-9:30 p.m. The café is located on the corner of Parque San Sebastián by the Museum of Modern Art. Corner of Mariscal Sucre and San Sebastián, Parque San Sebastián, Tel: 07-284-3496, URL: www.sansebascuenca.com.
Updated: Jan 15, 2013.

Villa Rosa !

(ENTREES: $10-16) Villa Rosa is one of Cuenca's most elegant restaurants, and one of the best that is not affiliated with a hotel. Located in a converted colonial home not too far from the center of town, the restaurant is attractive and the service is excellent. Villa Rosa specializes in a mix of Ecuadorian and international cuisine, serving dishing like

beef in mushroom sauce, sea bass in caper sauce, octopus prepared to your liking, and a number of pasta dishes. All of the food is well-prepared and tasty. Accompany your meal with a bottle off the extensive wine list, and finish it all off with a dessert like flambeéd bananas. It also has a tourist menu, available both for lunch and dinner, where you can choose an appetizer, main course and dessert for a set price. Gran Colombia 12-22, Tel: 07-283-7944, URL: www.villarosarestaurante.com.
Updated: Oct 18, 2012.

Wildhorse Café

(ENTREES: $2-7) Owned by an American couple who served as Peace Corps volunteers in Ecuador from 2008-2010, this recently opened café is a small breakfast and lunch spot, as well as a community gathering space. Specializing in baked goods, Wildhorse is a place to enjoy a delicious slice of walnut bourbon pie or rhubard custard pie, and the only spot in town that serves real thick milkshakes and malts. Lunch options include sloppy joes, pita pockets stuffed with hummus, or veggie burgers made with beets, brown rice and beans. Every Tuesday morning (9 a.m.-noon), the café hosts a Buddhist study group, and on Sunday mornings (at 9 a.m.), it leads a Tibetan Buddhist meditation session. On Mondays, a knitting group meets, and on Saturday afternoons (at 1 p.m.), people gather to play Scrabble. Ca. Larga 6-16 and Hermano Miguel, Tel: 09-8030-0736/8640-7359, E-mail: www.facebook.com/WindhorseCafe.
Updated: Jan 29, 2013.

Kookaburra Café

(ENTREES: $2-5) Kookaburra is an excellent place to start your day. Order a bottomless cup of real, high-quality coffee or a pot of cinnamon and orange tea and sip it alongside an order of pancakes with bananas, fruit with yogurt, or a fried egg on toast with sauteed mushrooms. At lunchtime, Kookaburra offers a daily special, such as a hearty soup with artisan bread or chard pie with a small salad. It even has peanut butter and jelly or peanut butter and banana sandwiches on the menu. Sweets include cinnamon rolls, chocolate mocha cake with chocolate frosting, caramel nut bars and carrot cake. The café also rents a few nice rooms—some of which are suites with kitchenettes—upstairs for a minimum of three nights. Ca. Larga 9-40, between Padre Aguirre and Benigno Malo, URL: http://kookaburracafe.typepad.com.
Updated: Oct 23, 2012.

Néctar

(ENTREES: $2.70-4) Néctar specializes in vegetarian and raw food, with dishes ranging from pita pizzas and quinoa tabbouleh to gazpacho and zucchini linguine with pesto sauce. It also has a wide selection of fresh fruit juices, batidos (made with soy milk) and teas, such as the banana tahini batido; the pineapple, ginger, apple, beet and carrot juice; and the chocolate mate tea. Néctar is only open for lunch, except on Thursday, Friday and Saturday evenings, when it is also open for dinner from 6-9 p.m. and when it sometimes hosts events such as live jazz music. You can either choose the day's set lunch for a cheap price, which includes a soup, main plate, juice and a small dessert, or order off of the main menu. Located on Benigno Malo 10-42, between Gran Colombia and Mariscal Lamar, Tel: 07-284-4118, E-mail: nectarcuenca@vegemail.com. Updated: Oct 25, 2012.

Maria's Alemania Café

(SNACKS: $1.50-5) Unlike most bakeries found throughout Ecuador that have dry cakes and crumbly cookies, the baked goods at this German bakery are moist, dense and absolutely delicious. It sells the best bread in town, with shelves filled with white and whole wheat varieties, as well as chocolate- or vanilla-covered mini cake loaves. The chocolate- and fruit-filled pastries are scrumptious and go well with a coffee in the morning in the outdoor courtyard. For those who favor savory over sweet, Maria's Alemania Café also has empanadas, crepes with meat, lasagna and pizza. Hermano Miguel 8-09 and Sucre, Tel: 07-283-4684, Cel: 09-9296-3712. Updated: Oct 25, 2012.

Govinda's Vegetariano

(ENTREES: $1.50-4) A favorite vegetarian restaurant among Cuenca's non-meat eaters, Govinda's Vegetariano has an inventive menu incorporating Indian, Italian and Asian influences. The place itself is clean and eclectic, with only a few tables, and plays relaxing world music. Choose from plates like vegetarian paella, eggplant parmesan, vegetables in curry sauce, or tempeh in a mushroom sauce. During the week, you can opt for the affordable daily menu, consisting of soup, main plate and juice, which is healthy and satisfying. Juan Jaramillo 7-27 and Borrero, Zip: 07-282-2036, Cel: 09-9833-3518, E-mail: govindasvegetariano@hotmail.com. Updated: Oct 25, 2012.

La Esquina

(ENTREES: $11-18) This upscale Argentine restaurant with funky décor cooks up typical food from rural Argentina in traditional discos de arado (plow discs, similar to cast-iron skillets), as well as high-quality beef topped with chimichurri sauce. You can order plow disks full of mixed meat, mixed vegetables or cazuela española (seafood, fish, potatoes, white wine and homemade tomato sauce), in addition to many other options. All of the these dishes come with a side of rice and salad.

La Esquina is a great place to bring a date or your spouse, as most of the low disk plates are prepared for two people to share, but they can be made for one person for a slightly higher cost. La Esquina also has an extensive wine and cocktail list with over 18 different types, mostly Malbecs. Corner of Ca. Larga and Hermano Miguel, Tel: 07-284-5344, Cel: 09-9865-0914, E-mail: la_esquina_ec@hotmail.com, URL: www.laesquina.ec Updated: Feb 2, 2013

Moliendo Café

(AREPAS: $2.30-3.50) Moliendo Café is one of the city's most popular lunch spots, and with good reason. This simple Colombian restaurant with friendly Colombian owners has cheap but filling set lunches, and a menu with large arepas (Colombian corntortillas) topped with everything from meat and guacamole to a lentil hamburger with salad. If you are feeling hungry, order the bandeja paisa, a typical Colombian platter consisting of ground meat, sausages, beans, rice, avocado, plantains, fried eggs and an arepa. Don't forget to ring the bell on your way out to let the chefs and owners know you liked your meal! Honorato Vásquez 6-24 and Hermano Miguel, Tel: 07-282-8710, E-mail: moliendocafexj@hotmail.com. Updated: Jan 15, 2013.

Tiestos !

(ENTREES: $9.20-17.30) Tiestos is pure culinary genius. Besides exquisite family-style food prepared in huge ceramic hot plates, you will find that the chef is extremely personable, making rounds to each table as guests eat. To really spoil yourself, order the degustación (tasting)menu for two people, which includes five courses and two glasses of wine for each person, featuring gigantic prawns in a garlic butter sauce, tender beef in parmesan cream sauce and chicken in curry macadamia sauce.

All meals come with nearly a dozen sides, including Israeli couscous, hot pepper sauces with fruit, pearled onions and rice. Although you will be stuffed by the end, do not miss out on the exceptional desserts, like the brownie topped with chocolate-coffee mousse with passion fruit ice cream! Reservations are required, whether for lunch or dinner, because this place has quite the reputation in town. Juan Jaramillo 7-34 and Borrero, Tel: 07-283-5310, Cel: 09-8723-3063, E-mail: jcsj71@hotmail.com / tiestosjj7-34@hotmail.com.
Updated: Oct 25, 2012.

Coffee Tree

(ENTREES: $3-7.50) The popular yet commercialized Coffee Tree, which has several locations in Quito, has now opened its doors in Cuenca's Old Town. Some come for the varied—though overpriced—menu with eight different breakfasts, sandwiches, salads, crepes and pasta dishes. Others enjoy taking advantage of the bar's daily drink specials, which are 2x1 on one particular cocktail all day long. Coffee Tree's biggest perks are probably its central location, convenient hours and outdoor seating, which makes it a good place to meet a friend for a coffee or drink to catch up. Ca. Larga 7-92 and Borrero, Tel: 07-283-0350, E-mail: coffeetreecu@gmail.com.
Updated: Oct 26, 2012.

Casa Do Brasil Café Cultural

(SNACKS: $1-5) Casa do Brasil is a welcoming upstairs café and cultural space opened by Brazilian transplants. Besides being a place to enjoy a coffee, snack or drink, Casa do Brasil offers Portuguese classes as well as Brazilian cooking and dance classes, and hosts a language exchange every Friday night where locals and travelers can mingle and practice English, Spanish and Portuguese. Its walls double as a rotating art gallery, with international artwork for sale, and it often has live music and other fun events. Come to chat over some caipiriñhas, the national cocktail of Brazil made with cachaça (sugar cane rum), sugar and lime, or to learn Portuguese and more about Brazilian culture. Happy hour is every night from 4-8 p.m., and caipiriñhas are 2x1 on Fridays with a purchase of tapas or snacks. Ca. Antonio Borrero 7-90 and Mariscal Sucre, 2nd floor, Tel: 09-8421-0128, E-mail: casadobrasilcafecultural@gmail.com, URL: www.facebook.com/pages/Casa-Do-Brasil-Caf%C3%A9-Cultural/176907029028780.
Updated: Jan 17, 2013.

Good Affinity Restaurant and Tea House

(LUNCH: $2.50) This vegetarian restaurant is a peaceful retreat from the noisy streets. Owned by a Taiwanese couple, the restaurant is filled with calming music and has outdoor seating surrounded by bamboo and bonsai. The basic but tasty lunch comes with soup, juice and a plate of rice accompanied by some sort of vegetables and soy meat. It also serves soy milk and sells bags of soy meat. Good Affinity is only open for lunch from 11:30-3 p.m. Monday-Saturday. Gran Colombia 1-89 and Capulies (opposite Banco del Pacifico), Tel: 07-283-2469.
Updated: Oct 18, 2012.

Cuenca Nightlife

People don't come to Cuenca to party, though there are plentiful places to grab a beer or coffee and listen to live music most weekend nights. Almost any night of the week, you will be able to find happy hours or drink specials, and there are several places that host weekly gringo nights where foreigners can meet and mingle.

There are several salsa clubs and big dance discotecas for those who want to extend their evenings; asking the locals is a good way to find out about the best places to go.
Updated: Jan 15, 2013.

Wunderbar Café !

(ENTREES: $3.50-7.50) This funky German-owned café is a crowd-pleaser, both for its international food and for its fun drinking atmosphere. Wunderbar has a menu packed with plates like spaghetti alfredo and pasta in bolognese sauce, hamburgers, and baguettes stuffed with chicken, steak or eggplant. There is also a set lunch menu Monday-Thursday. If it is a nice day, you can choose to eat outside in the garden. At night, the bar comes alive, and there is sometimes live music on weekends. Wunderbar has drink specials Monday-Saturday from 11:30 a.m. to 6:30 p.m., when cocktails are $2. Accompany your drinks with a game of Jenga or foosball, or just relax in the funky setting. Hermano Miguel 3-43 and Ca. Larga (Escalinata), Tel: 07-283-1274, E-mail: cafewunderbarcuenca@yahoo.es, URL: http://wunderbarcafe.wordpress.com.
Updated: Oct 22, 2012.

Chiplote

(ENTREES: $3-8) Chiplote is knows for its subs and shots, and is a popular happy hour spot. Greasy pub grub, including beef chili,

quesadillas, bacon cheeseburgers, cheesesteak sandwiches and Italian subs, go great with Chiplote's cold beers and cocktails, which are 2x1 from 4-10 p.m. Monday-Saturday. Females get the additional privilege of 2x1 shots from 6-7:30 p.m. every day. Additionally, Chiplote has a special on Monday-Thursday, when a bowl of chili and a Corona go for $6.50. This is also a great place to watch a fútbol game. Ca. Larga 8-15 and Luis Cordero, Tel: 09-8417-7521.
Updated: Oct 26, 2012.

Cacao and Canela Café Bar

(DRINKS: $3.50-12) Cacao and Canela is a delightful café serving, as the name suggests, all things chocolate and cinnamon. The menu consists of a long list of every kind of hot chocolate imaginable. The cacao used to make the chocolate is grown in Ecuador. Also available is beer, mixed drinks, sandwiches and salads. During the daytime, the café serves as a quiet place to read a book or chat with a friend but at night it fills up and the volume rises. Seating is limited as the place is quite small, but you can take advantage of the loft space and the owners always find a way to squeeze you in. Happy hour is from 7 - 8 pm. Borrero 5-97 and Juan Jaramillo, Tel: 07-282-0945.
Updated: Oct 16, 2012.

La Compañía

(BEER: $2.25-4.50) Cuenca's only microbrewery is a relaxed place to drink a few artisanal beers, providing a nice alternative to all the other local establishments that only serve bottles of Pilsener and Club. Choose from four different types of beer on tap: stout, Irish red, extra golden, brow ale or Weizenbock. If you are not a beer drinker but want to accompany your beer-drinking friends, La Compañía also has cocktails. You can also chow down on bar food like nachos with guacamole, French fries and hamburgers. Borrero 4-58/4-62 and Honorato Vásquez, Tel: 09-9887-4099.
Updated: Oct 23, 2012.

Around Cuenca

There is as much to do outside of Cuenca as within it. Apart from the obvious architecture and colonial churches, Cuenca is close to the breathtaking El Cajas National Park and reserve, as well as Ecuador's most significant Inca ruins - Ingapirca. This city is also surrounded by quaint villages, each of which is worth a visit: Gualaceo is a small town with colonial roots and a pleasant river park. Chordeleg is known for the numerous silver shops lining the main street and park.

Sigsig is a bit far off, but a good place to see Panama hats being made in the traditional way. Bulcay is the last place to see the dying art of ikat weaving: there are less than 30 weavers who still practice it today. Girón boasts colonial architecture and the nearby waterfall of El Chorro. The nearby town of Jima is developing a fledgling tourism industry: it offers good hikes. Many tours will stop for lunch at the beautiful Hosteria Uzhupud.
Updated: Jan 15, 2013.

INGAPIRCA

Although those who have already seen the impressive ruin complexes in Peru (or Mexico and Guatemala, for that matter) may be disappointed by Ingapirca, it is still a site that's worth the trip, particularly if you are already in Cuenca or a ruins buff.

Things To See and Do In Ingapirca

Ingapirca Ruins

(ADMISSION: $6) Ingapirca is the most impressive and significant set of Inca ruins in Ecuador. That being said, the ruins at Ingapirca are not very impressive when compared to Macchu Picchu or other pre-Columbian ruin complexes in Peru. Ingapirca was once an important Inca military and religious center, but over the centuries the site was cannibalized by the Spanish who used the finely chiseled stones to build their own homes and churches. Before the arrival of the Incas, the site had been an important Cañari observatory. Today, the best-preserved structure is an oval-shaped platform known as the Temple of the Sun. Efforts are underway to restore the site.

Ingapirca is located in the middle of nowhere, about 90 kilometers (56 mi) away from Cuenca. Guided tours to the site can be arranged in Cuenca, or if you get there by yourself (wheel and deal with the taxis in Cuenca, and make sure they stick around to take you back), there are guides hoping for clients at the entrance to the ruins. Alternatively, there are two daily buses from Cuenca to Ingapirca with Cooperativa Cañar, leaving at 9 a.m. and 12:20 p.m. from the terminal and returning at 1:15 p.m. and 3:45 p.m. during the week. On weekends, the second departure to Ingapirca leaves at 1:15 p.m. instead of 12:20 p.m. The ride is two hours and costs $2.50 each way. It is also possible to take any Quito-bound bus and ask to be let off at El tambo, from where you can take another local bus or hire a truck to bring you to the ruins entrance. Plan on spending about two hours visiting the ruins.
Updated: Jan 15, 2013.

Ingapirca Lodging
Posada Ingapirca/Ingapirca Inn

(ROOMS: $55-92) The hotel is a surprisingly attractive converted 200-year-old hacienda: it features 23 rooms, elegant social areas and well-kept gardens. There is more to do than just see the ruins: the posada can arrange hikes along the Inca trail that passes through the area, and there is a billiard room on the premises. Staying here is an appealing option for someone who wants to see the ruins and who also would like to escape the cities for the quiet, elegant night away. Prices are quite reasonable for a converted hacienda.

Posada Ingapirca is managed by the Grupo Santa Ana, which also manages the Victoria Hotel and El Jardin Restaurant in Cuenca: information is available at the hotel. Right up the hill from the ruins / Ca. Larga 6-93 and Borrego (Cuenca office), Tel: 07-282-7401/283-1120/0064, Fax: 07-283-2340, E-mail: gstaana@etapanet.net, URL: www.grupo-santaana.net.
Updated: Jan 15, 2013.

EL CAJAS NATIONAL PARK !

El Cajas National Park and Reserve (Parque Nacional El Cajas) is a starkly beautiful wilderness of valleys, lakes, highland vistas and rock formations that consists of 29,000 hectares (70,000 ac) of páramo (grassy highland generally unfit for cultivation). Located close to Cuenca, El Cajas is a great place to head for a day of hiking or trout fishing.

The park is known for its glacial-fed lakes (there are more than 250) and for the diversity of its wildlife, which includes spectacled bears, pumas, gray-breasted mountain toucans and Andean condors. In the mid-1990s, wild llamas were also reintroduced to the El Cajas.

Head up into the volcanic terrain and you'll also be able to find hairy puya bromeliads, paper (polylepis) trees, and quinua trees, a tiny species that can survive higher than any other. The best time to go is during the August to September dry season.

On an excursion through the park, you might also stumble across the remains of a major Inca highway, which used to run through the area, or one of the many tambos (way stations) that the Incas built at strategic points around El Cajas.

On your visit to the park, stop first at the information center next to Laguna Toreadora. There, you'll be given a basic map of the park and major hiking routes. There are several trails of interest, most of which are medium in terms of difficulty level. If you're going on a multi-day hike, make sure to bring emergency supplies, supplemental maps of the region and enough clothing to keep you warm through the below-freezing temperatures that often occur at night.

Note that fog and rain are common in El Cajas National Park, so pack accordingly. There are several tour operators in Cuenca who offer guided day tours to El Cajas National Park and Reserve. Admission to the park itself is free.

To get to the park independently, head to the South Terminal and catch one of the Transporte Occidental buses (45 minutes). Buses leave for El Cajas daily at 5:30 a.m., 6:15 a.m., 7 a.m., 10:20 a.m., noon, 1:30 p.m., 2 p.m., 4 p.m. and 5:45 p.m. It costs $1.25 each way. You can also take any Guayaquil-bound bus via El Cajas from the main bus terminal,

El Cajas National Park

which leave approximately every hour, but you will be charged the entire fare to Guayaquil ($8). To get back to Cuenca, just flag down any Cuenca-bound bus on the highway in front of the park entrance. Updated: Jan 15, 2013.

BAÑOS (CUENCA)

Eight kilometers (5 mi) southeast of the city of Cuenca is the small town of Baños, not to be confused with the larger tourist town of the same name near Ambato. Baños-Cuenca is a pleasant, peaceful little village named for the hot thermal waters there. The water is channeled into four different commercial complexes, the best of which is the Balneario Durán (daily 7:30 a.m. - 8 p.m., closes earlier Wednesday and Sunday).

Once you're done at the thermal baths, you can explore the small town, the highlight of which is probably the church, from which there is a good view of the valley. If you wish to have a bite to eat or even stay overnight, your best bet is the Hostería Durán.

Getting To and Away from Baños

To get to Baños-Cuenca, take bus number 11 from Avenida Solano and Avenida 12 de Abril. Alternatively, take a taxi from downtown, which should cost around $5. Updated: Jan 15, 2013.

Baños Lodging

Often confused with the tourist mecca of the same name, Baños (Cuenca) is still a great place to visit. It too has thermal hot springs, as well as some great hiking around town. Unfortunately there isn't much in the way of lodging, and Baños hotels do not exist. However, the Hostería Duránis a quality place, and has competitive rates compared to Cuenca.

Hostería Durán

(ROOMS: $67-131) Hostería Durán is a surprisingly large hotel and visitor complex with four hot springs, Turkish baths, a gym, a football fields and tennis court, water slides, a games room and more. It is far and away the best place to stay in the tiny town of Baños and stacks up well against hotels in Cuenca, too. Reservations can be made online, or call in advance. The upscale, award-winning on-site restaurant serves a mix of national and international plates, accompanied by an extensive Chilean wine list. Its cafetería and snack bar offers quicker, lighter meal options such as sandwiches, salads, ceviche and fast food staples. Av. Ricardo Durán, Tel: 07-289-2485/2486, E-mail: reservaciones@hosteriaduran.com, URL: www.hosteriaduran.com. Updated: Jan 15, 2013.

BULCAY

About half an hour outside of Cuenca, the tiny town of Bulcay is home to the last remaining weavers of the ikat tradition. The women weavers use traditional hand looms (often handed down from generation to generation) to produce strikingly colored shawls and sweaters (as well as purses, shoulder bags, etc.). They commonly use cotton, wool and alpaca for their creations and crafts, which they then sell from their homes or to agents who later sell them in markets or shops over in Quito.

Sadly, the ikat (pronounced "ee-cot") tradition is dying out. There are only about 30 weavers still producing the textiles today. The Orellana family has a home on the highway in Bulcay, a cozy, simple place surrounded by well-tended flower gardens and poinsettia trees. Ligia Orellana, one of the few remaining weavers, learned the technique from her mother, and in her family weaving goes back four generations. She says that ikat weaving does not appeal to the young women of Bulcay: "The young people today want to do easy things," she said.

There are many reasons for the decline of ikat weaving. Ligia Orellana and her sister suffer from persistent back pain, the result of hours at the loom or embroidering. Bulcay doesn't get many visitors: "There's very little tourism here," Orellana admits. The ikat weavings are fine, colorful and well-made, yet because of the costs associated with bringing them to market and the level of competition with other Ecuadorian handicrafts, prices must be kept low.

Bulcay itself is a pleasant little town, but there is little to see or do besides visiting the homes of the weavers, a perk which is generally only possible if you're on a tour from Cuenca.

Bulcay is on the way to Gualaceo, and tours may stop there if you ask them. The modest Pachaíma hotel in town is the only one, but Bulcay is only a few minutes from the Hostería Uzhupud and Gualaceo. Updated: Jan 15, 2013.

CHORDELEG

Chordeleg is a small town about one hour from Cuenca, often combined with Gualaceo (6 km/3.7 away) for day trips. It is known for the many jewelry stores that line the streets and main square: there must be at least 20 of them. The jewelry—particularly the silver—is made locally and there is an impressive selection of pendants, bracelets, earrings and other items.

Other than shop, there isn't much to see and do in Chordeleg. Most of the tours take visitors to have lunch at the nearby Hosteria Uzhupud.

Buses leave Cuenca regularly for Gualaceo (from the corner of Españaand Benalcázar), where it is easy to catch a second bus to Chordeleg. There are also direct buses to Chordeleg from the main bus terminal ($0.75).
Updated: Jan 15, 2013.

JIMA

Jima is a small charming town an hour and a half southeast of Cuenca. Seated at the foot of a steep green mountain ridge, this is the place to go if you are tired of all the tourist traps. With the help of a Peace Corps volunteer and the Fundación Turistica Jima, the town has developed its own community-based tourism, so you know that the money you spend here will go directly back to the community members, not to a big company. From Jima, there are a number of trails and hikes with varying lengths and difficulty. Many of these go to the peaks of the mountains surrounding the town, where you will be rewarded with beautiful views. To cool off after a hike, try taking a dip in the cool and clean Rio Moya.

An hour from Jima is the primary cloud forest, Bosque de Tambillo, which has hundreds of different animal species and more then 200 types of orchids. There is also a three- to four-day hike that takes you from the Sierra to the Oriente. The hike begins 22 kilometers (13.6 mi) east of Jima in the Cordillera Moriré and drops 1,800 meters (5,900 ft) by the time you reach the Oriente. It is also possible to rent horses and camping gear in Jima.

Unfortunately, lodging options in Jima are meager, and hotels do not exist. There are two options for places to spend the night.

One is the Hostal Chacapamba (07-241-8035/046), a two-story house with a balcony. The other option is to spend the night in a building owned by the local high school (07-241-8398): rooms with shared bathroom cost $5. All of the proceeds go towards improving the schools in town. You can also make reservations for rooms at the information center (07-241-8270).
Updated: Jan 15, 2013.

SIGSIG

Sigsig is a small agricultural town 60 kilometers (37.2 mi) southwest of Cuenca that sits in a valley surrounded by steep mountains. It is best known for being the source of many of the Panama hats sold within and outside of Ecuador. A quick walk around town will give you a glimpse of the many stages of paja toquilla hat production.

Arriving from Cuenca, you will be let off in the first of two of the town's parks. This park is filled with soccer fields and basketball courts and is dominated by two enormous and eerie welded statues of angels on stilts. To get a glimpse of the scenery and to orient yourself, walk up the flight of stairs toward the basketball court on the hill, where you will be able to take advantage of the height and enjoy the vistas.

The town is very straightforward, and by walking around for about an hour or so, you can cover just about all of the streets. The streets are laid out in a grid formation, with the uphill side of town being north, and the downhill side, toward the market, being south. The houses are old colonial buildings with flowers dripping off balconies. There are not many formal activities to entertain you with in Sigsig, but walking around the town and peeking into doors where women are weaving hats can be quite interesting. Toward the east of town there is another park with a statue dedicated to Cacique Duma, the chief of the Cañari Confederation from Sigsig who defeated the Incan conquistadors from Cuzco.

If you get tired of walking around town, head toward the south of town where a five- to 10-minute walk will lead you to the "playa," or bank of the river. Along the way you can stop at the Asociación de Toquilleras Maria Auxiliadora and take a look at the Panama hat production. If you are interested in buying, this is probably the best place to look. The "playa" is a refreshing stop, surrounded by eucalyptus trees and steep green mountains, and a perfect place to picnic. Swimming and fishing are allowed, but some spots can get deep, so be careful.

Those interested in exploring the surrounding areas should visit the Zhavalula and Chobshi caves, once used by the Incas. These can be reached in about five to ten minutes by pick-up truck, which you can hire (about $3-4) either at the southeast corner of the park when you first arrive in town, or at the market. If you would like to walk there, follow the road to the "playa" then stay straight and follow signs to the caves.

For a good and cheap bite to eat in Sigsig, try Chunucari Bar Restaurant, located on Calle Davila between Sucre and Bolivar. Open for breakfast, lunch and dinner, this restaurant serves delicious meals in the courtyard of a rustic colonial house. Lunch includes a large bowl of soup, a rice plate with vegetables and fish or meat, juice and dessert for $1.50. There is also a small gift shop attached to the restaurant.

There are not many hotels in Sigsig, but if you do plan on spending the night you can stay at Residencial Lupita (07-266-257).

To get to Sigsig, take a "Cenepa" bus from the terminal in Cuenca. Buses run daily from 5 a.m. to 7 p.m. and cost $1.25 each way. Updated: Jan 15, 2013.

GUALACEO

An attractive little village on the river of the same name, Gualaceo is known as "The Garden of Azuay" (Azuay being the name of the province). Located about an hour away from Cuenca, this village is in the heart of a fertile agricultural region known for its fruit.

The best time for visitors is Sunday, market day. Gualaceo's market is small but picturesque, and shoppers can find handmade baskets and other articles. There is a pleasant little park along the river that is excellent for a stroll. If you go far enough, you'll come across the remains of a Spanish aqueduct from the colonial period.

Buses to Gualaceo leave from Cuenca's bus terminal every 15 minutes between 6 a.m. and 10 p.m., returning to town every 15 minutes between 5 a.m. and 8:30 p.m. ($0.60). "Santiago de Gualaceo" and "Santa Barbara" are the two companies that run this route.

Also, travel agencies in Cuenca offer tours that normally include the towns of Gualaceo, Chordeleg and (sometimes) Sigsig. Updated: Jan 15, 2013.

GIRÓN

Girón is a small sleepy town nestled into the mountains 45 km southeast of Cuenca. Just an hour drive to the town, the climate is significantly milder than its larger neighbor. Most of the old colonial houses that line the street have not been remodeled in years, but this antiquity is what gives the town much of its charm.

There is a quaint central plaza with a somewhat out-of-place modern church. If you have time, it is worth walking around town and on the outskirts, where the paved roads quickly turn to dirt and you are soon walking in farmland. Girón has a huge emigration rate to the US; don't be surprised if some of the townsfolk speak surprisingly good English.

One of the main draws to the vicinity of Girón is El Chorro, the waterfall that flows down the cliffs outside of town. The walk to the waterfall makes for a nice day hike, including beautiful views of the valley below and trails in dense forest. There are two options to reach the waterfalls: one is by walking up a 5 km dirt road, which takes about two hours (ask for directions in town); the other is a bit hardier, along an uphill trail through the woods. This second hike gets you to a higher waterfall, much more isolated, but well-worth the sweat.

From Cuenca, buses to Girón ($1) leave from the terminal at the Feria Libre market every hour. You can also take any bus that heads towards Machala or Santa Isabel and ask the driver to let you off at Girón. The ride takes 45 minutes to an hour. Updated: Jan 15, 2013.

South To Loja

Riddled with potholes and assaulted by the occasional landslide, the road from Cuenca to Loja boasts its fair share of obstacles. But dodge the ditches and sail past the landslides and you'll be stunned by the scenery unfolding before your eyes. On a clear day, as the road climbs in altitude, a remarkable panorama of mountain ranges and verdant valleys stretches out below. Only occasionally does a traditional pueblo pop up among the otherwise uninhabited landscape. These sleepy little towns, such as Saraguro, offer a rare glimpse of life in rural Ecuador, as untouched by tourism as the land is by people. Meandering past the quiet backcountry communities and cutting across the barren but beautiful landscape, the road continues its serpentine route south towards Peru, astounding the onlooker with more breathtaking views around each twist and turn. This is a drive not to be missed.

SARAGURO

Arriving in Saraguro is a one-of-a-kind experience; there is no place like it in the world. What makes this small town so unique are the inhabitants, the Saraguros. The Saraguros are distinctive in their dress, traditions and history, and are unlike any other indigenous group in Ecuador.

Originally from the Lake Titicaca region in Peru, the Saraguros were moved to their present location by the Incas as part of the Mitimae system. As a result, the Saraguros have maintained their age-old traditions and have become leaders in the indigenous movement, both in Ecuador and internationally, and remain the best-preserved indigenous group in all of Ecuador. In fact, Saraguro is the only indigenous group in the province of Loja to survive Spanish conquest.

Saraguro is famous for its beautiful weaving and jewelry, which can immediately be observed upon arrival. The typical dress of the women includes a long black pleated skirt, which covers a more colorful embroidered one, together with a black shawl held closed by an intricately designed metal tupu, or pin. Around their waists are brightly woven belts, and their colorful, beaded necklaces are often so large that they hang over their shoulders. The dress of the men is most notable for the calf-length black pants and ponchos. Both men and women traditionally wear heavy white wool hats with flat, wide brims—but many now wear short-brimmed black hats instead—and their hair in a long braid.

To really get a feel for Saraguro, it is worth hiring a guide take you not only through the city, but to the surrounding towns, which hold just as much culture. Saraguro also refers to the canton that encompasses all of the small communities around it, including Namarín, Las Lagunas and Ilincho. In these towns, you can visit a traditional weaving workshop, a workshop that makes traditional Saraguro hats, organic gardens that grow medicinal plants, or sacred waterfalls where traditional ritual cleansing is still performed.

It is not possible to visit these places independently (except for the baños de Inca/Inca baths $2.50), as you need permission from the communities first and transportation can be complicated. These tours should be booked at least a day in advance through Saraurku, the only tour operator in town (Monday-Friday 8:30 a.m.-12:30 p.m. and 2-6 p.m. Ca. 18 de Noviembre s/n and Av. Loja. Tel: 08-594-7476/07-220-0331, E-mail: saraurku@turismosaraguro.com, URL: www.turismosaraguro.com).

Saraurku works closely with Fundación Kawsay (URL: www.kawsay.org), which set up the community network 'Saraguro Rikuy,' a community tourism project to promote sustainable tourism and funnel money back into the communities themselves. The profits of this organization go directly to the different communities visited, so you know exactly where your money is going. And if you have a hankering to pick up some Kichwa, this is the place to do it, as most people in the area, especially in the surrounding towns, speak this native language.

One of the more interesting aspects of the community tourism project is the ability to arrange a home stay with one of six local families. Also organized through Saraurku, home stays cost $27, and include accommodation, three meals a day and family activities. Meals are made with ingredients from the family's garden and are mostly vegetarian. Grains, corn, potatoes, mote (hominy), cheese, quinoa and empanadas are common. Family activities may include tending to the family's garden and animals, helping cook meals, assisting with carpentry project or making typical jewelry.

Alternatively, if you would like more independence during your stay in Saraguro, you can stay instead at the community-run hostel, Hostal Achik Wasi (Tel: 07-220-0058), which has a capacity for 34 people (rooms: $17-75). The hostel has the most luxurious rooms in the area with Direct cable TV, private bathrooms with hot water, and pretty views of Saraguro and the surrounding countryside. There is no WiFi in the rooms, though. A continental breakfast is included in the room price.

SOUTHERN ANDES

If you would like to come on a weekend and take advantage of a home stay or local tours, be sure to do so in advance. On Sundays, Saraguro has a nice produce market that may be of interest. Another special time to come visit Saraguro is during its annual Inti Raymi celebration, or Festival of the Sun, each June 20-21, when locals bath in sacred baths, host cultural events and dancing ceremonies, barbecue cuy (guinea pig) and drink chicha (a drink made from fermented corn).

In the town of Saraguro, there are a few hostels, restaurants, ATMs, pharmacies, artisan shops and Internet cafés on or near the main plaza. Saraguro's iTur office (Monday-Friday 8 a.m.-1 p.m. and 2-5 p.m. Av. 10 de Marzo, near Av. Loja, on main plaza. Tel: 07-220-0100) also has a small exhibition about Saraguro culture, music and dress. A decent place to eat is Mama Cuchara (Monday-Friday 6:30 a.m.-8 p.m. Corner of Av. El Oro and Av. Loja. Tel: 09-9329-9342), which has cheap set lunches for $2-2.50.

The only bus office in Saraguro is for Viajeros Internacional (Av. Azuay and Av. El Oro). Buses to Loja (1.5 hr, $1.75) leave every hour-1.5 hour from 8 a.m.-9:45 p.m., and buses to Cuenca (3-4 hr, $5) leave every one to two hours from 6:30 a.m. to 10:45 p.m. The 4:45 p.m., 7:45 p.m. and 10:45 p.m. buses also continue on to Quito ($13). There are no direct buses from Cuenca to Saraguro; just take any Loja-bound bus and ask to be left off in town. Updated: Jan 15, 2013.

LOJA

 2,060m 185,000 📞 07

Founded in 1548 by Alonso de Mercadillo, Loja is somewhat of a political and cultural island, surrounded by mountains and stranded at the far southern end of Ecuador. Besides being the provincial capital, Loja warrants recognition as the first city in Ecuador to generate electricity (1897). Today, Loja is an intellectually and architecturally unique city, boasting two universities set among a peculiar mix of urban concrete and colonial structures.

Approximately 500 meters (1,640 ft) lower than most southern cities, Loja enjoys noticeably warmer weather—an appropriate complement to its congenial cultural climate and exuberant atmosphere.

Situated around the sprawling palm-tree studded central park are a number of interesting buildings, including the Cathedral, Casa de Justicia, which houses the Museo del Banco Central, and the modern Municipal Building, with its pleasant courtyard and vibrant murals, which play out various indigenous scenes.

Beyond the park, further south along Bolívar from the Iglesia Santo Domingo, is the Plaza de la Independencia, where the citizens of Loja gathered on November 18, 1820, to denounce the Spanish Crown and assert their independence. Perhaps the most attractive section of the city, the square is enlivened by the brightly painted facades of colonial-style buildings, and neatly framed by resplendent hills rising in the distance.

Between the historic center of the city and the northern areas, you'll find the Entrada a la Ciudad, a towering structure designed to look like a medieval castle gatehouse. The building houses an art museum and snack bar and is worth a quick visit.

Beyond the city center and its magnificent squares are the Parque de Recreación Jipiro, Parque La Argelia and Jardín Botánico Reynaldo Espinosa, all perfect for day-strolls. For stunning panoramic views of the city, head up to the statue of the Virgen de Fátima, sitting in the hills east of the city. Located just beyond Loja, Parque Nacional Podocarpus offers more sweeping views and stunning landscapes to explore.

Most visitors to Loja are delighted to discover that the city is still quite inexpensive. You can stay and eat for less money than you can in most of the rest of Ecuador. Restaurants in Loja tend towards the regional. Most of the food you'll find is heavy southern Ecuadorian fare, heavy on the soups, tamales and pork, but there are a few places that feature international cuisine.
Updated: January 12, 2013

Getting To and Away from Loja
BY AIR
The closest airport to Loja is **Camilo Ponce Enríquez Airport** in nearby **Catamayo**. Flying from **Quito** to Lojas is the fastest way to get to Loja, but it comes at a considerably more expensive price than ground transportation. Roundtrip tickets can vary in price, ranging anywhere from $90-120. TAME is the most frequented operator.

SOUTHERN ANDES

BY BUS

Getting to Loja by bus from **Quito** is a long, 12- to 15-hour trip, best taken overnight. Panamericana (Av. Colón and Reina Victoria. Tel: 02-255-7133/34) makes the trip from the Mariscal. Loja Internacional has a more comfortable (and more expensive) express overnight bus to Loja (Av. Orellana between Juan de Velazco and 9 de Octubre. Tel: 02-222-4306), leaving from the Mariscal and also from Quitumbe). Many more buses leave for Loja from Quitumbe. A bus ticket to Loja costs about $14-20, depending on the operator, quality of bus and how fast it makes the trip.

The bus station in Loja is called Terminal Terrestre "Reina de el Cisne," and has a 24-hour restaurant, bathrooms and other basic services. Buses leave for Quito, Cuenca, Vilcabamba, Zaruma, Zamora, Machala, Guayaquil and Peru, among other destinations.

Transportes Vilcabambaturis has buses to **Vilcabamba** ($1.30) every 15 minutes from 6 a.m.-7:45 p.m. and every 30 minutes from 7:45-9:15 p.m.

Cooperativa TAC has one departure per day to **Zaruma** (12:45 p.m.; 5 hr, $6) and Piñas (3 p.m.; 5 hr, $5). Cooperativa TAC's bus is the only direct bus to Zaruma from Loja; all of the others change in **Catamayo**.

Unión Yanzatza services buses to **Zumba** (10:45 a.m, 9:45 p.m.; 6 hr, $7.50), **Huaquillas** (6:40 p.m.; 6 hr, $6) and **Machala** (10:45 a.m., 9:35 p.m.; 5.5 hr, $6).

Nambija Interprovincal goes to **Zamora** (21 buses per day from 3:15 a.m.-11:15 p.m.; 1.5 hr, $2.40), **Zumba** (12:50 p.m., midnight; $7.50), **Huaquillas** (9:30 a.m., 12:40 p.m., 11:45 p.m.; $12-12.50), **Machala** (7:45 a.m., 11:45 a.m., 10:40 p.m.; $6-7.50) and **Guayaquil** (9:45 p.m. 10:45 p.m.; 8 hr, $9.45-10.45).

Loja Internacional has many daily departures to Quito (9 buses, last one at 10 p.m.; $14-20), **Guayaquil** (8 buses, last one at midnight; $10), **Machala** (11 buses, last one at 11 p.m.; $6), **Cuenca** (4 buses, last one at 2:30 p.m.; $7.50), **Piura** (3 buses, last one at 11 p.m.; 8 hr, $10) and **Macará** (7 buses, last one at 11 p.m.; 5 hr, $6). It also has two buses per day to **Lago Agrio** (8 a.m., 2:30 p.m.; $22) and **Huaquillas** (9:30 p.m., 11:15 p.m.; $6) and one per day to **Santo Domingo** (7 p.m.; $15).

Viajeros Internacional has the most frequent buses **Cuenca**, leaving every hour to hour and a half between 4 a.m. and 12:30 a.m. You can also catch one of its buses to **Quito** (3:30 p.m., 6:30 p.m., 9:30 p.m.; $15) or **Zamora** (7 a.m., 6:30 p.m., 9:15 p.m.).

Unión Cariamanga Internacional services buses to **Machala** (3:30 a.m.), **Huaquillas** (10:15 p.m.), **Zaruma** (1 p.m., 6:15 p.m.), **Zumba** (9 a.m., noon, 4 p.m., 11:30 p.m.) and **Zamora** (5:30 a.m., 7 a.m., 10 a.m., 2:30 p.m., 5 p.m.). It also has two buses per day to **Piura, Peru**; the one at midnight goes via **Catacocha**, while the one at 6 a.m. goes via **Cariamanga**. Both pass through **Macará**.

Cooperativa Transportes Santa does the **Loja-Cuenca-Ambato-Quito** route five times per day, at 3 p.m., 6 p.m., 6:45 p.m., 7:15 p.m. and 8:40 p.m.

Cooperativa Transporte Piñas goes to **Piñas** (5 hr, $5) at 6 a.m., 9:15 a.m. and 3 p.m. every day.
Updated: Feb 25, 2013.

Getting Around Loja

If you spend most of the time in the city's center, you will find walking to be the best mode of transportation. However, if you would like to venture to other neighborhoods or visit some of the city's parks, you will need to take a local bus or taxi. The local buses only go north-south along two of Loja's main avenues: Avenida Universitaria and Avenida Emilio Ortega. All bus rides cost $0.25, regardless of where you hop on and off. Most destinations within the city itself cost $1-1.50 via taxi. A taxi between the city center and the bus terminal costs $1. Alternatively, shared taxis leave from Ciudadela Yaguarcuna and cost only $0.25 per person; those along the "Ruta La Pradera" go to the bus terminal.
Updated: Jan 17, 2013.

Loja Services
MONEY

Banco de Pichincha has a branch on the corner of Valdivieso and 10 de Agosto, on Plaza de la Independencia (Monday-Friday 9 a.m.-4:30 p.m., Saturday 9 a.m.-1 p.m. Closed Sundays). It has three ATMs. There is also a **Banco de Guayaquil** with two ATMs on Eguiguren, between Valdivieso and Olmedo (Monday-Friday 8:30 a.m.-5 p.m., Saturday 9 a.m.-1 p.m. Closed Sundays). **Produbanco** is on the corner of

Get the best rates and reserve your hotel or hostel at vivatravelguides.com/hotels/

Valdivieso and Eguiguren, also on Plaza de la Independencia (Monday-Friday 9:30 a.m.-4 p.m.). **Western Union** is located on Sucre, between 10 de Agosto and Rocafuerte (Monday-Friday 9 a.m.-6 p.m., Saturday 9 a.m.-1 p.m. Closed Sundays. Tel: 07-256-0108).

KEEPING IN TOUCH

Loja's post office is on the corner of Sucre and Colón (Monday-Friday 8 a.m.-6 p.m., Saturday 8 a.m.-noon. Closed Sundays). There are many Internet cafés in Loja, including Cyber Speed JC, on the 18 de Noviembre side of Parque Bolívar ($0.80 per hour. Daily 9 a.m.-10 p.m.). It has 17 modern computers, some with Skype, and three calling booths.

MEDICAL

The city's best clinics are Hospital Clínica San Augustín (Av. Azuay, between 18 de Noviembre and Sucre. Tel: 07-258-8027-257-2164) and Clínica Abendaño (corner of Olmedo and Leopoldo Palacios. Tel: 07-255-0076). Both are open 24 hours from emergencies. Farmacias Cruz Azul has locations on two corners of Plaza de la Independencia, both on Avenida Mercadillo. There is another one on the corner of Colón and 18 de Noviembre, on Parque Bolívar (Monday-Friday 7:30 a.m.-11 p.m., Saturday 7:30 a.m.-9 p.m., Sunday 7:30 a.m.-1 p.m. Tel: 07-257-1174).

TOURISM

Loja's tourism office, iTur, is located on the main plaza (Monday-Friday 8 a.m.-1 p.m. and 3-6 p.m., Saturday 9 a.m.-1 p.m. Closed Sundays. Tel: 07-257-0407, ext 220).

LAUNDRY

It is hard to find a laundromat near Plaza de la Independencia. If you need to drop your laundry somewhere, try Lavandaría Lava Mass, at the corner of Juan de Salinas and Sucre ($0.89-0.95 per lb. Monday-Saturday 8 a.m.-8 p.m., Sunday 6:30-9 p.m.). It also has a delivery service ($2), if that is more convenient.

PHOTOS

There are two photo shops on Plaza de la Independencia, one of which is Digital Photo Express (Monday-Friday 8:30 a.m.-7 p.m., Saturday 8:30 a.m.-1 p.m. Closed Sundays. Bolívar, between Eguiguren and 10 de Agosto). It sells camera batteries and memory cards, as well as Canon cameras and camera cases, and has three quick stations to print photos instantly. You can also have passport photos taken here.
Updated: Oct 31, 2012.

Things To See and Do in Loja

Most visitors to the city of Loja are just passing through on their way to peaceful Vilcabamba, which is a pity: Loja is a charming city in its own right, with lots to see and do. If you're planning on passing through, you should consider spending a day or two checking out what Loja has to offer.

Jipiro Park is located to the north of the city and hugely popular with Lojano families, especially on weekends. The park is low-cost entertainment at its friendly best: check out an ultra-cheesy planetarium show for 25 cents, rent a paddle boat for a dollar or watch the locals play soccer. The park is full of small replicas of famous buildings: St. Basil's Cathedral has slides for kids, an Arabic mosque hosts the planetarium, and the bathrooms are in the Polynesian Tiki House.

There are several other parks surrounding the city, including Parque Universitario la Arquelia and the Reinaldo Espinoza Botanical Garden.

Loja's historic downtown, while not as nice as Cuenca's, is still worth a visit. There are several cathedrals and city squares and a number of interesting museums, including the Music Museum and the Central Bank Museum. You may also want to walk down Calle Lourdes, Loja's oldest street, which is filled with colorful building in their original architectural style; the street is lined with a few small cafés and artisan shops.
Updated: Jan 17, 2013.

Entrada a la Ciudad

(ADMISSION: Free) Also known as Puerta de la Ciudad (Portal de la Ciudad), the Entrada a la Ciudad de Loja is without a doubt Loja's most recognizable landmark. Built to look like a medieval gatehouse, complete with (fake) portcullis, the Entrada a la Ciudad straddles Sucre Street as it leaves downtown to the north. The Entrada crosses a very small river (it seems like overkill, in fact: you could probably jump over the "river") and there is a small park-like area on either side.

Inside the castle-like structure, you'll find a free art museum, a snack bar (3rd floor), and a wandering maze of stairways, balconies and towers. There is a small information desk. The gatehouse is well-kept, attractive and more than a little fun: you'll want to stop and see it, and you'll only need about 20 minutes. Across the street to the south are two dazzling murals dedicated to Simón

SOUTHERN ANDES

Bolívar and José Antonio de Sucre, heroes of Ecuadorian independence. Av. Universitaria, intersection of Ca. 18 de Noviembre and Ca. Sucre, Tel: 09-9527-9746/8607-0730. Updated: Oct 31, 2012.

Parque Jipiro

One of the best known parks in Loja, Jipiro is north of the city and spans 10 hectares (25 ac). There is a lake, sports fields, a "cyber train" with Internet service, a zoo and pools, as well as many replicas of the world's great buildings. It is a great place to take a stroll. On the weekends it fills up with Lojano families who come for the many activities and events. One of the buildings houses a planetarium, with shows playing continually (whenever the seats fill up) and lasting about 15 minutes. Masochists will enjoy an interesting ride where a guy straps you into a gyroscope-looking thing and give you a hearty spin. The paddle boats are also fun for a couple of bucks. Tel: 07-258-3357 (ext 251), To get there, head to the north of the city, a few blocks east of the bus terminal. Getting there by bus takes five minutes from city center aboard the bus marked "Jipiro" from corner of Juan José Peña and 10 de Agosto ($0.25). Alternatively, take a taxi there ($1).
Updated: Oct 31, 2012.

Museo de la Música

(ADMISSION: Free) This small museum set around a sunny courtyard is dedicated to the musicians and composers of Loja. The displays include many of their original instruments and sheet music. The museum also has occasional musical performances (stop by for schedule) and a nice café that serves fresh juices, coffee, and typical Lojano snacks, such as tamales. It also has some CDs for sale. Bernardo Valdivieso 09-42 and Rocafuerte, Tel: 07-256-1342.

Municipal Building

Stretching across the whole Avenida Eguiguren side of Plaza de la Independencia and wrapping around the corner down Calle Simón Bolívar, Loja's Municipal Building is a good reference point and offers a wealth of information. The creme building with green accents houses a public library (Monday-Friday 8 a.m.-1 p.m. and 3-8 p.m., Saturday 9 a.m.-1 p.m. Closed Sundays), which includes a braille library, as well as the city's tourism office. Next to the iTur office is a beautiful mural of traditional musical life in Loja, painted by Oswaldo Mora, that is worth visiting.

Museo de la Cultura Lojana

(ADMISSION: Free) Previously known as the Museo del Banco Central, this museum still contains an extensive collection of archaeological pieces, including 10,000-year-old weapons and tools from the region around Loja, and other objects pertaining to the most well-known cultures of Ecuador, such as Valdivia, Machalilla and Chorrera.

There is also an ethnographic section that focuses on the region of Loja and Saraguro, as well as a fine arts section with religious art and contemporary pieces. It also has a room to commemorate famous Lojanos. 10 de Agosto 13-30, between Bolívar and Bernardo Valdivieso.
Updated: Oct 31, 2012.

Parque Universitario La Arquelia

La Arquelia is a beautiful 90-hectare (222-ac) park on the edge of the city. There are seven kilometers (4.3 mi) of excellent hiking trails that go through forest, streams and the parámo. There is a small museum and information center, and, at the entrance to the trails, there is a map that shows the various hikes. Also part of the park, with an entrance across the street, is the impressive botanical garden, including many species of plants native to Ecuador, such as cinchona trees, various medicinal plants and an orchid garden. La Arquelia is on the road from Loja to Vilcabamba.

Take any bus heading toward Vilcabamba and get off at the gate (12 min, $0.60). Or take a local bus that says "La Argelia" (10 min, $0.25) that drops you off at the campus. From there, it is a 10-minute walk. A taxi ride there from downtown will cost $1.50.
Updated: Oct 31, 2012.

Mercado Centro Comercial Loja

This huge market stretching along 18 de Noviembre, between 10 de Agosto and Rocafuerte, sells everything you could ever need. The ground floor is split up into sections of stalls selling fresh produce, flowers, fish, red meat, chicken and blocks of cheese, making it a one-stop shop for groceries. There are also people selling baskets, sneakers, posters, sunglasses, watches, socks and other miscellaneous items. Upstairs has an heladería and dulcería, where you can buy local sweets or ice cream before perusing small shops stocked with clothes and kitchen appliances. Continue roaming and you will come across several hair salons and small restaurants serving cheap lunches and ceviche. There is also a pharmacy on the third floor. All along 18 de Noviembre, outdoor stores sell a mix of power tools, art supplies and jewelry. Main entrance: 18 de Noviembre, between 10 de Agosto and Rocafuerte. Updated: Nov 08, 2012.

Museo De Arte Religioso

(ADMISSION: $1) Housed in an old monastery that was founded in 1597 by a bishop from Quito named Luis López de Solís, the Museo de Arte Religioso displays a collection of Loja's most important religious artwork. It features paintings, sculptures, carvings, and gold and silver works from the colonial era, including characteristic pieces from the Escuela Quiteña, or Quito School.

There is a painting collection dedicated to the biblical Mary, a room of sculptures with different interpretations of Jesus, and an assortment of sacred ornaments from over 300 years, including church choir cloaks and garments worn by former Roman Catholic ministers and priests. The museum has two floors and takes about 30 minutes to visit. 10 de Agosto 12-78 and Valdivieso, Tel: 07-256-1109.
Updated: Jan 14, 2013

Loja Tours
Tucan Travel

Tucan Travel specializes in unique one- to two-day tours to places in or around Loja, so visitors can appreciate the natural beauty and cultural richness of the southern Andean region of Ecuador. With Tucan Travel, you can visit a nearby indigenous community to observe their way of life, participate in some of their traditional rituals, and try a typical meal.

You can tour a local ceramic or weaving workshop, a center for panela (sugar cane) and aguardiente (sugar cane alcohol) production, or a town that produces recycled paper products and beeswax candles. Adventure tours include going hiking to the waterfalls, fishing for tilapia, biking or horseback riding in Loja's environs. You can also check out the best of Loja's churches, parks and museums on a full-day city tour. Trips can be arranged to Saraguro, Podocarpus National Park and nearby religious pilgrimage sites as well . José María Peña, between Venezuela and Espíritu Santo Correa, Tel: 07-257-4025, Cel: 09-8075-4816, URL: www.ecuadortucantravel.com.
Updated: Jan 17, 2013.

Aratinga Aventuras

Aratinga Aventuras is the birding specialist in town and organizes bird-watching tours around Loja. You can book a bird-watching trip to the tropical forest of Podocarpus National Park in Zamora province, to the Tapichala Reserve, to the Utuana Reserve, to the Buenaventura Reserve, to Vilcabamba or to the Cajanuma cloud forest. The operator's quality guides will point out the area's diverse birds, with the opportunity to see the Masked Trogon, tanagers like the Lacrimouse Mountain Tanager, many different hummingbirds, and endangered species such as the Bearded Guan and the Grey-breasted Mountain Toucan. Lourdes 14-80, between Sucre and Bolívar, Tel: 07-258-2434.
Updated: Oct 30, 2012.

Loja Lodging

Loja has a variety of lodging options for visitors. If you're looking to sleep cheap, head to the Old Town. West of the central square, you'll find an array of budget Loja hostels in varying states of upkeep and cleanliness. The Old Town is a bit noisier than other areas of Loja, but if you're on a tight budget, you're pretty much stuck there. Loja is still an inexpensive town, and there are several good hotel deals in the mid-range category. Unless you are on the tightest of budgets, you may want to spend a little more for a more comfortable stay. For the cost of a lower mid-range hotel in Quito, you can stay at a nice mid-range or business-class hotel in Loja. Of course, there are elegant, higher-end options as well, the nicest of which are in converted colonial homes.

Casa Lojana

(ROOMS: $75-130) Casa Lojana is one of Loja's best high-budget options. The building that houses the hotel was once an elegant home, which has since been converted. There are gardens, balconies, a fine restaurant and luxurious, well-decorated rooms. The hotel is efficiently run by the University of Loja, who use the business as a learning tool for their students in hotel industry courses. The hotel is located outside of town on a hilly street. The rates are quite high for inexpensive Loja, however, a night at a place like Casa Lojana would be much more expensive in Quito or other parts of the world, making it a good place to splurge if you're on a mid-range budget. Casa Lojana is relatively small: it only has 12 rooms, so booking ahead is suggested. París 00-08 and Zoilo Rodríguez, Tel: 07-258 5984, E-mail: casalojanahotel@utpl.edu.ece.

SOUTHERN ANDES

Copalinga

(ROOMS: $23.50-55) Located three kilometers (1.86 mi) from Podocarpus National Park, Copalinga is a mecca for birders and nature lovers. The hotel is surrounded by a complex network of trails with bird viewing spots. Six cozy cabins house up to 12; four smaller doubles each have private bath, hot showers and a balcony. There are also more budget "rustic" cabins with bunks and a shared bath.

The owners will make you meals in an on-site restaurant and bar, but make reservations ahead of time if you plan to eat. Located halfway between Zamora and Copalinga, on the road to the Podocarpus National Park, from Zamora, you can take a taxi ("yellow cab" or "white pick-up truck") to Copalinga. Copalinga is located halfway (3 km/1.86 mi) on the road to the Podocarpus National Park. The place is locally also known as "El Oso." Most taxi drivers know the place., Tel: 09-347-7013, E-mail: info@copalinga.com, URL: www.copalinga.com / jacamar@impsat.net.ec.
Updated: Sep 27, 2012.

Zamorano Real Hotel

(ROOMS: $71-95) Zamorano Real is a really good value given its modern facilities and extra amenities. Its rooms are spacious and decorated in soothing earth tones with contemporary touches and big plasma TVs. Not only do they look spotless, but they have the scent of a freshly cleaned room as well. The nicest suites have big bathrooms with marble counter tops, new appliances, hairdryers and Jacuzzis. All have mini-bars with a complimentary bottle of water. Room prices include a buffet breakfast. The hotel also has two equipped conference rooms for business or social events, in addition to a gourmet restaurant. Miguel Ríofrío 14-62, between Mariscal Sucre and Bolívar, Tel: 07-257-0921/0722/0923, E-mail: reservas@zamoranorealhotel.com / info@zamoranorealhotel.com, URL: www.zamoranorealhotel.com.
Updated: Nov 08, 2012.

Hostal Aguilera Internacional

(ROOMS: $25-55) Located directly across the street from the impossible-to-miss Entrada de la Ciudad, the Hostal Aguilera Internacional is an airy, bright hotel with small but clean rooms. The hotel has an array of other amenities, including free parking, a social room (for wedding receptions, etc.), a yard with a basketball court where kids can play, a conference room and a restaurant. There is even a sauna, steam room and gym. Aguila Internacional is a significant step up from similarly priced downtown hotels, and the view from the rooms is much better than downtown: you'll see the surrounding hills instead of a brick wall. However, the downtown area is still within walking distance from the hotel. Sucre 01-08 and Av. Emiliano Ortega, Tel: 07-258-4660/257-2892/2461/2894, Fax: 07-257-2477, E-mail: hostal_aguilera@hotmail.com.
Updated: Oct 22, 2012.

Hostal Las Orquídeas

($10 per person) Probably the all-around best low-budget lodging option in downtown Loja, Las Orquídeas is a small but clean and friendly hostel just around the corner from the central park. The rooms are neat and tidy and the service is friendly. It's also about the most economical place to stay in Loja that still features private bathrooms. The interior is not nearly as gloomy as most of the other downtown hotels, and efforts have been made to liven it up with plants, wall art, etc. Bolívar 08-59, between 10 de Agosto and Rocafuerte, Tel: 07-258-7008, E-mail: hlorquideas@easynet.ec.
Updated: Oct 22, 2012.

Hotel Acapulco

($10-15 per person) Dank and dismal, the Hotel Acapulco is about as cheery as a morgue. Presumably the building once saw better days, but those days are a fading memory. The rooms are slightly brighter than the murky passageways and stairwells, but the bathrooms smell funky enough to make you wonder if cleanliness is really a priority. The service, while not exactly friendly, is at least efficient and polite. As hotels in the area go, there are worse values. The best that can be said about the Acapulco is that it is well-located, being only a couple of blocks from most of the attractions in downtown Loja. Sucre 07-61 and 10 de Agosto, Tel: 07-257-0651/9652/0199, E-mail: hacapulco@easynet.net.ec, URL: www,hotelacapulco.com.
Updated: Oct 22, 2012.

Hotel Libertador

(ROOMS: $50-70) The Hotel Libertador is the best of the hotels located in Loja's historic district. The interior is dimly lit and gloomy, and the whole place has a "seen-better-days" feel to it, but the rooms are nice, the service is very good, and there are a variety of extras that other hotels in the area do not have, such as a swimming pool, sauna, steam room and restaurant. The Libertador also offers free Internet for guests, cable TV and parking, which is a bonus in the chaotic Loja city center. A large hotel, the Libertador has almost 60 rooms and suites. The place is especially family-friendly, but solo, budget and business travelers can find better bargains elsewhere in Loja. Colón 14-30 and Bolívar, Tel: 07-256-0779/257-8278, E-mail: reservas@hotellibertador.com.ec, URL: www.hotellibertador.com.ec.

Hotel Londres

($6 per person) The Hotel Londres is located in an old, unassuming building that was obviously cut in half at some point in the past. Tall and narrow, the hostel has 12 rooms with a varying number of beds in each, all at rock-bottom prices. Bathrooms are spread through the building and are shared (none of the rooms has private bath). Happily, the bathrooms are spotless. There is a small community kitchen in back. The old wooden floors are sort of charming, though and there is even a little nook where guests can hang out. Sucre 07-57 and 10 de Agosto, Tel: 07-256-1936.

Podocarpus

(ROOMS: $30-80) Located near the central plaza, Hotel Podocarpus is comfy and modern, making it one of your better options while staying in Loja. It offers spacious rooms with hot water, private bathrooms and cable TV. Guests can dine at the on-site restaurant El Tucán, or socialize in "Romerillos," the central hotel lounge. Internet and international calls are also available. José A. Eguigeren 16-50 and 18 de Noviembre, Tel: 07-258-1428, E-mail: info@hotelpodocarpus.com.ec, URL: www.hotelpodocarpus.com.ec.

Quo Vadis

(ROOMS: $49-114) The Quo Vadis is modern, reasonably priced and well located within walking distance of Jipiro Park and the bus terminal. Its rooms are very nice, comfortable and clean, and the hotel is very tastefully decorated. As an added bonus, the Quo Vadis is one of very few places in Loja to get a decent expresso or cappuccino, which is an important consideration for java-heads. On Sundays, the restaurant at the Quo Vadis has a lunch buffet popular with locals and guests alike. Av. Isidro Ayora and Av. 8 de Diciembre, Tel: 07-258-1805/256-0964, E-mail: quovadishotel@gmail.com, URL: www.quovadishotel.com.ec.

Loja Restaurants

Loja does not have a whole lot of variety when it comes to restaurants. Most serve typical Lojano snacks, including tamales, humitas, quimbolitos and empanadas de verde. The good news is that restaurants offering cheap fixed-priced almuerzos (lunches) during the week are on nearly every corner, so you won't have to spend much to fill up at lunchtime.

Head to the sector "El Valle" to sample some local cuisine, including cuy asado (grilled guinea pig), cecina (pieces of pork dried in the sun then grilled), aguado de gallina (a traditional chicken and rice soup with potatoes and onions) and repe (a traditional creamy soup made with green plantains and cheese). One recommended place to eat there is Salón Lola (Salvador Bustamante Celí and Guayaquil. Tel: 07-257-5603). Taxis to "El Valle" cost $1 from downtown. Updated: Oct 31, 2012.

Casa Lojana Restaurant

(ENTREES: $7-15) Casa Lojana is a fancy hotel and restaurant located outside of Loja in a converted home. It is owned and operated by the University of Loja, which uses it as a teaching tool for its students involved in the hotel and restaurant industries. The restaurant is classy and well decorated and offers a complete menu. Some of the food is experimental: you can order, for example, grilled ribs in a pineapple-honey-eucalyptus sauce.

The prices were high for Loja, which means that they're ridiculously low for anywhere else. There is an impressive wine list as well. The restaurant is a great place for a treat for anyone but those on the tightest of budgets. París 00-08 y Zoilo Rodríguez, Zip: 593, Tel: 07-258 5984/5985, E-mail: casalojanahotel@utpl.edu.ec. Updated: Jan 07, 2013.

Topoli

(SNACKS: $1.25-6) Be sure to check out Topoli if you are looking for a quick fix to satisfy your sweet tooth or an appetizing way to cool down on a hot Loja morning. Serving a variety of cakes and ice cream sundaes, along with the best coffee and yogurt in town, this small cafeteria also offers basic sandwiches, personal pizzas, and waffles topped with fruit and whipped cream. It also has three different breakfast options. Service is friendly and the prices are reasonable. Bolívar 13-78 and Riofrío, Tel: 07-258-8315.

SOUTHERN ANDES

Restaurant Riscomar

(ENTREES: $4.50-11) One of the fanciest places in town, Restaurant Riscomar is perfect for a romantic or celebratory meal. The extensive menu goes way beyond the options at the majority of other establishments in town and has some fusion items, featuring dishes like grilled chicken and pineapple in a sweet and sour sauce, seafood risotto and ropa vieja (a Cuban dish made with shredded beef in a tomato sauce). Corvina, or sea bass, is the star of 10 different dishes, and can be prepared in a coconut sauce or with bacon in a mustard sauce. Besides the food, you will also find attentive service and a classy interior. Rocafuerte and 24 de Mayo, Tel: 07-5258-5154, Cel: 09-9150-6840, E-mail: info@riscomarloja.com, URL: www.riscomarloja.com.
Updated: Oct 23, 2012.

Las Chavales Café

(TAPAS: $1.30-3.50) This small Spanish place, hidden in a passageway close to Plaza de la Independencia, brings a new set of flavors and sounds to Loja. With just a few small tables, Las Chavales transports diners and drinkers to Spain with its Spanish music and menu filled with Spanish specialties and tapas, such as patatas bravas (fried potatoes with a spicy tomato sauce), croquetas de pollo (chicken croquettes) and tortilla española (Spanish omelette with potatoes). You can accompany your tapas or small sandwiches with wine or beer. Monday-Friday 9 a.m.-2 p.m. and 4-11 p.m., Saturday 9 a.m.-11 p.m. Closed Sundays. 10 de Agosto 14-10 and Simón Bolívar, Pasaje Bolívar Centro Comercial, Tel: 09-8081-8541.

El Tamal Lojano

(BREAKFASTS: $3-4) El Tamal Lojano probably has the best traditional regional food in town. Its menu is simple, with three different breakfasts, and specialty snacks like tamales, humitas, quimbolitos, bolónes, and empanadas de verde. The tamales and empanadas can be prepared with cheese, pork or chicken. Do as the locals do and accompany one of the above with a piping hot cup of black coffee or cappuccino, or wash it down with a fruit juice. This place gets very crowded around dinner time and you may have to wait for a table. Make sure to order and pay first at the counter, or you will be waiting to be served for, well, forever. Daily 8 a.m.-noon and 3-8 p.m. 18 de Noviembre 05-12 and Imbabura, in front of Parque Bolívar, Tel: 258-2977, Cel: 09-8772-1143/9196-4812

A Lo Mero Mero

(ENTREES: $3-6) A Lo Mero Mero is the place to go for Mexican food in Loja, whether you want flautas, fajitas, enchiladas or burritos. The taco or burrito with soda combos are a pretty good deal. At lunch time, A Lo Mero Mero also serves a good set-price almuerzo, which includes soup, a main plate, a juice or grain-based drink, and dessert. Those watching their waistline can order the "light" lunch, which comes with fresh salad, brown rice and no dessert. On Saturdays, the restaurant additionally has typical Ecuadorian food like encebollado (a fish and onion stew). Sucre 06-20 and Colón, Tel: 09-9451-4357
Updated: Oct 23, 2012.

Molino Café

(SNACKS: $0.90-2) This modern café serves six different types of breakfasts, including a "French breakfast" with a piece of cake, hard-boiled egg, juice and coffee; and a "Spanish breakfast" with a Spanish potato omelette, juice and coffee. It also prepares 15 different coffees from around the world, such as the café asiático (Asian coffee)—made with coffee, cognac, condensed milk, cinnamon and liquor—and the café irlandés (Irish coffee)—made with coffee, whiskey and whipped cream. However, you can opt for a simpler latte or expresso if you wish instead. Molino Café also has a plain frozen yogurt machine with a toppings bar and serves typical lojano snacks like tamales, humitas and empanadas de verde. Ca. Euguiguren 15-20 and Sucre, Tel: 07-254-0460.
Updated: Oct 23, 2012.

Forno Di Fango Pizzería

(PIZZA: $3-5.50) The best pizza place in town, Forno di Fango has four locations throughout the city, with the most central being on the corner of the streets 24 de Mayo and Azuay. All have an identical menu; pizzas come in five different sizes and can be topped with just veggies or pepperoni, or with more creative toppings such as the Mexican pizza, which has ham, bacon, onion, beans, jalapeño peppers and nachos. Otherwise, Forno di Fango has lasagna, spaghetti and cannelloni dishes, and sandwiches. You can also order pizza or pasta for delivery online or via telephone. Tuesday-Saturday noon-10:30 p.m., Sunday noon-10 p.m. Closed Mondays. Corner of 24 de Mayo and Azuay, Tel: 07-258-2905/257-6474, E-mail: info@fornodifango.com, URL: www.fornodifango.com.
Updated: Oct 24, 2012.

SOUTHERN ANDES

Around Loja
Podocorpus Notionol Pork   !

Podocarpus National Park is one of the jewels of Southern Ecuador and is named after the Podocarpus tree, the only native conifer in the Ecuadorian Andes. Spanning 1,462 square kilometers (564.5 sq mi) of Andean cloud forest, the park hosts five different microclimates and provides drinking water for Loja, Zamora and a number of smaller towns in the region. The park ranges from 900 to 3,600 meters (2,953-11,811 ft) and is home to toucans, spectacled bears, mountain tapers, pigmy deer and over 600 species of birds; 97 percent of the park's fauna is invertebrate.

There are two main access points to the park: from Loja and from Zamora. To access the high zone, travel 15 kilometers (9.3 mi) along the highway between Loja and Vilcabamba until you reach the Cajanuma Ranger Station.

From this point, head 8.5 kilometers (5.3 mi) along a smaller road until you reach the administration center. From here, there are four main self-guided trails: "Oso de Anteojos," 400 meters (1,312 ft) long, moderately steep and easily accessible; "El Bosque Nublado," 750 meters (2,460) long, medium difficulty; and "El Mirador," 1.5 kilometers (0.9 mi) long, medium difficulty. For a daylong hike, you can continue along "El Mirador" for 3.5 kilometers (2.2 mi), however some parts of this trail are very difficult. The "Lagunas del Compadre Trail" is 15.5 kilometers (9.6 mi) one way and is very steep. For this trail you must bring good camping gear and warm waterproof clothes, and for your safety, advise the park that you will be hiking this trail.

The access to the low zone is 6.8 kilometers (4.2 mi) from Zamora. The last 0.8 kilometers (0.5 mi), you must hike along an easy trail to the Bombuscaro refuge, where there are four different trails. Two lead to waterfalls: "La Chismosa," 200 meters (656 ft), and "La Poderosa," 450 meters (1,476 ft). The other two trails are "La Urraquita," 600 meters (1,969 ft), and "Los Higuerones," 3 kilometers (1.9 mi). All of these trails are of medium difficulty. Entrance to the park is free.

Tours to Podocarpus can be arranged in either Loja, Zamora or Vilcabamba. Otherwise, it is easiest to catch a taxi ($10 from Loja, $4 from Zamora, $15 from Vilcabamba) from any of those towns to either of the access points. It is a good idea to arrange for the same taxi driver to come back to get you at a set time to bring you back to town. If you want to save money or don't know how long you'd like to stay in the park, you can also walk the eight kilometers (5 mi) downhill from the refuge to the main highway, where you can flag down a bus to Vilcabamba. From Vilcabamba, it is also possible to rent bikes to bike to the park.
Updated: Jan 17, 2013

Puyango Petrified Forest

The largest field of exposed petrified wood in the world is found just south of the Ecuadorian city of Loja, not far from the Peruvian border: its name is El Bosque Petrificado de Puyango, or the Puyango Petrified Forest. Massive stone logs, 80 million years old cross the trails, fallen giants from a bygone age. Petrified forests are rare: wood usually decomposes once it dies, and Puyango is considered a very significant source of information by scientists, especially as most of the trees are in the Araucarias family, which are rarely fossilized. There are marine fossils in the park as well, a remnant of a time even before the trees, when the area was a shallow sea.

There is more to Puyango than petrified wood. In the local language, Puyango means "dry, dead river," and for good reason. The region is considered a dry tropical forest, a rare ecosystem since most forests in the tropics tend to get a good deal of rain. The area is a protected national park, and features a diverse ecosystem with interesting wildlife. There are more than 130 species of birds that call the park home during all or part of the year, and it is also known for being home to many pretty species of butterflies.

For some, the best part will be the fact that Puyango is well off the gringo trail: it's very remote, and the nearest city of any size i Loja, about four hours away. It's possible to day trip from Loja, but it will be a very long day. The nearest town with any sort of tourist facilities is Alamor.

Puyango Petrified Forest stretches over 2,569 hectares (~6,570 acres). The oldest fossils in the park are marine fossils estimated to be about 500 million years old; the area was once underwater. The tree fossils are considered to be about 65-80 million years old. The park is open from 8 a.m. to 4 p.m. every day with good local guides available.

From December to May is the rainy season, and the dry season is from June to November. It's preferable to visit during the dry season. It is suggested to bring water, hat, light clothes and sunscreen. There are decent trails through the park. You camp in the park; ask about it at the information center. To get there, you can either arrange a tour with a tour operator in Loja, Zaruma or Machala. Alternatively, you can independently take a local bus to the village of Puyango, then a taxi or pick-up truck to the entrance of the park. Updated: Jan 17, 2013.

VILCABAMBA

Highly publicized as "The Valley of Eternal Youth" for its sprightly 70- and 80-year-old inhabitants, Vilcabamba is a growing hot spot on the gringo trail. It is a must for anyone keen to meet up with fellow travelers or indulge in homemade hippy treats and pamper themselves with a massage or steam bath. For some time, it was thought that residents regularly lived beyond 100 years, however, it is now thought that this is unlikely. At one time a small, isolated village, Vilcabamba is now more of an expat-haven, rich in gringo-run businesses catering to backpackers, than a place equipped to administer a shot of local culture.

Boasting a warm, pleasant climate, set among spectacular scenery and an agreeable atmosphere, Vilcabamba is popular among Lojano weekenders, as well as foreign travelers. This is the place to head for excellent horseback riding, walking, hiking or just plain hanging out. Just outside of town, the scenic Mandango trail makes a great day-hike, while a number of private nature reserves and the famed Podocarpus National Park sit just beyond the village, offering even more opportunities to explore the local landscape. Come between June and September, when the climate is drier and warmer.

Getting To and Away from Vilcabamba

Located near the southern tip of Ecuador, the easiest way to get to Vilcabamba is to fly to Loja, the nearest major city, and take a bus from there. However, currently the airport is closed for renovations.

There are no direct buses to Vilcabamba. All travelers coming from Quito, Cuenca, Guayaquil or any other destination will have to take a bus to Loja and change there. Transportes Vilcabambaturis has buses to Vilcabamba from **Loja** (1 hr. 15 min, $1.30) every 15 minutes from 6 a.m.-7:45 p.m. and every 30 minutes from 7:45-9:15 p.m. The same company does the return trip every 15 minutes from 5:45 a.m.-7:45 p.m., then every 30 minutes until 12:15 a.m. Alternatively, you can take a taxi or white pick-up truck between Loja and Vilcabamba for about $15-20 one way. Updated: Nov 06, 2012.

ECUADOR-PERU BORDER CROSSING

Due south of Vilcabamba is a crossing into Peru, convenient for getting to Cachapoyas, Peru. This journey has been described as adventuresome and beautiful, through a landscape of cloud-bathed jungle mountains strewn with orchids. Expect delays due to landslides (especially December-April) and roadwork. You will need two days; hotels exist in every transfer point, though Jaén is best.

From Vilcabamba, starting at 6-6:30 a.m. there are several buses called Cooperativa "Sur Oriente" that pass in front of Hosteria Izhcayluma and head to Zumba (5-6 hrs, $6.50).

From Zumba to La Balsa there are several open-air buses called "rancheras" or "chivas" that will take you there (1.5 hrs, $1-2). Once in La Balsa, either catch a bus to the border or take take a taxi there for $20. The border is open on both sides from 6:00 a.m. to 6 p.m., and there are moneychangers available as well.

From the Peruvian border you can get to San Ignacio via a colectivo taxi (2 hrs, 15 soles/$5.50). Then from San Ignacio take a combi (microbus) to Jaén (3 hrs, 12 soles/$4.50). From Jaén head to a Bagua Grande in a one hour-taxi colectivo ride (8 soles, $3). From Bagua Grande you can get to Chachapoyas via colectivo taxi (3 hrs, 25 soles/$9); or alternatively, catch a combi

SOUTHERN ANDES

to Pedro Ruiz (1 hr, 22 soles/$8) and then ride another combi to Cachapoyas (2 hrs, 8 soles/$3).
Updated: Apr 12, 2013.

Vilcabamba Services

MONEY

There is a Banco de Guayaquil ATM next door to the tourism office, on Diego Vaca de Vega, near Bolívar. Another ATM is located on Luis Fernando de la Vega, between Bolívar and Sucre, next to the church.

KEEPING IN TOUCH

Internet cafés are scattered along all four sides of Vilcabamba's central park. Most charge $1 per hour. There is one on Diego Vaca de Vega, between Bolívar and Sucre (daily 7 a.m.-10:30 p.m. Tel: 07-264-0491), that has seven computers with webcams and headphones, and two calling booths. It also has a laundry service ($1 per kilogram) in the back, making it a convenient stop. On Sucre, near Diego Vaca de Vega, there is another Internet café called Nico's Net Cyber (daily 7 a.m.-10 p.m. Tel: 07-264-0378, Cel: 09-8804-2576). It has six computers equipped with Skype, as well as copying and fax services.

MEDICAL

The town's hospital is at the corner of Avenida Eterna Juventud and Calle Miguel Carpio (Tel: 07-264-0188). If it is an emergency after 4 p.m., call the hospital's number and enter extension 111 for medical attention. Better hospitals are located in Loja.

Several pharmacies can be found in Vilcabamba. Two that are located near the central park are: Farmacia Su Salud (Monday-Thursday 7 a.m.-10 p.m., Friday-Sunday 7 a.m.-11:30 p.m. On Bolívar, near Luis Fernando de la Vega, 1/2 block from central park. Tel: 07-264-0171 (day)/264-0336 (night)) and Farmacia San Andres (daily 7 a.m.-10 p.m. On Sucre, near Luis Fernando de la Vega. Tel: 07-264-0350). Both are open 24 hours one week a month, on a rotating schedule.

TOURISM

Vilcabamba's tourism office is located at the corner of Diego de Vega and Bolívar, on the central park (Monday-Friday 8 a.m.-1 p.m. and 3-6 p.m., Sunday 8 a.m.-1 p.m. Tel: 07-264-0090). The police station is near the corner of Bolívar and Agua de Hierro streets (Tel: 07-264-0089)
Updated: Oct 30, 2012.

Safety

Vilcabamba is a safe, happy-go-lucky place and most visitors will not encounter any troubles while here. However, it is recommended to take caution on the more remote hiking and biking trails, as robberies have been reported, especially on the popular Mandango trail. If alone, it is best to hire a guide or buddy up with someone at your hostel before venturing solo. Either way, leave valuables at your hostel, including cameras, important documents, jewelry and large sums of money. Updated: Jan 17, 2013.

Getting Around Vilcabamba

Vilcabamba is easy enough to get around on foot. Even the hotels a bit outside of the town itself are walkable, but you can just as easily hire a white pick-up truck to take you to and from town. Many also like to rent bikes to take advantage of the multitude of nature trails in the area or to go to Podocarpus National Park. Updated: Jan 17, 2013.

Things To See and Do In Vilcabamba

Vilcabamba's charm comes from its peaceful surroundings, which urge visitors to want to do nothing more than relax in a hammock and take in the beautiful mountain views. The town itself does not have much to do beyond strolling in and around its leafy central plaza with its fountain and small church, encircled by vegetarian restaurants, organic juice bars and hippie shops. However, active types and nature lovers will want to take advantage of the area's many hiking trails or rent a bike to explore the nearby Podocarpus National Park. Afterwards, you can soothe your sore muscles with a massage at one of the town's many spas. Vilcabamba has also gained quite the reputation as a spiritual center, so visitors can participate in various meditation sessions or traditional Andean ceremonies to renew their energies.

Horseback Riding

Horseback riding is popular in Vilcabamba, mostly due to the quality of local horses and the stunning natural beauty of the valley. There are rides for all levels and interests. Beginners will want to try a local two- or four-hour ride before committing to longer excursions. For more advanced riders, there are multi-hour to multi-day trips to Podocarpus National Park, outside of town. These trips are longer, go over some very rough terrain, and often involve some hiking. Talk to your guide about your level, confidence and what you would like to see and do.

SOUTHERN ANDES

If you go horseback riding in Vilcabamba, wear long sleeves, sunscreen and a hat, as sun can be strong. Your guide should bring water, but having a small bottle along isn't a bad idea. Carry as little as possible because when the horse starts to run, any cameras, backpacks, fanny packs, etc. will start to bounce up and down, which is very uncomfortable and irritating.

Most outfitters will provide rubber boots for you to use while riding, however, if you have very small or very large feet, you might want to bring your own.

There are several small agencies offering horseback rides in Vilcabamba; just have a look around the main square area and you'll see several to choose from. Two that have good reputations are Caballos Gavilán and La Tasca Tours.

A whole-day trip, including lunch, usually runs around $35: shorter trips are cheaper. Updated: Oct 30, 2012.

Centro De Meditación

Vilcabamba's Centro de Meditación is a bilingual Buddhist meditation center and retirement community offering free Anapansati breath meditation and Vipassana meditation sessions. It also leads Sweat Lodge ceremonies the second and fourth Saturday of each month (suggested donation: $5) and an all-day Vipassana meditation retreat (suggested donation: $25) on the second Saturday of each month.

The center has rooms that can be rented out per week ($100-140 per week) or month ($400-500 per month), or on a long-term basis. Prices include daily breakfast, WiFi, access to the communal kitchen and free meditation sessions. There is also a nice medicinal plant garden and organic fruit and vegetable garden out back. On Ca. Bolívar, a few blocks from central park, Tel: 09-8959-2880, E-mail: bernard@mindfulnessmeditationinecuador.org, URL: www. mindfulnessmeditationinecuador.org. Updated: Oct 31, 2012.

Traditional Andean Ceremonies

You will probably see many flyers around Vilcabamba posted by various people offering to clean your energies, renew your relationships with the Universe, encounter your ancestors and connect with your own consciousness. Call Santiago (Cel: 09-9389-5963), who has 18 years of experience, if you would like to make offerings to Mother Earth, or have a new house or workplace blessed.

You can hire him at Estación 14 jewelry store, next to Café Sambuca on the main square. Felicia (Cel: 09-9370-8341) is a female shaman that leads sacred medicine journeys with San Pedro cactus in Vilcabamba; you should have at least two full days in town to take advantage of the ceremony. Domos Vilcabamba (Cel: 09-8862-8163/8261-0707) also leads bi-weekly temazcal sweat lodge ceremonies ($10 donation, call for reservations) as well as individual and group drumming ceremonies. Updated: Jan 17, 2013.

Sacred Sueños Organic Farm

This organic farm is located on 90 hectares (222 ac) in the beautiful mountains that surround Vilcabamba. The farm is open to anyone interested in organics and willing to help out around the farm. A two-hour uphill hike from Vilcabamba, the farm is a joint effort to improve a degraded mountainside using permaculture and other sustainable practices.

There are many projects that need helping hands, including trail building, composting and mulching, animal care, building structures and furniture with local materials, planting trees, beekeeping, rainwater harvesting and gardening. Sacred Sueños requires a two-week minimum commitment ($10 initiation fee, $30 per week for food) from volunteers, and expects them to work six hours per day five days a week. Sacred Sueños also offers an interesting goat cheese apprenticeship, where you can learn about the production of organic, raw goat cheese. This one-month program costs $160 and runs 20 hours per week.

Those who give advance notice can be met in Vilcabamba and led to the farm; donkey service can be provided from the trailhead for your luggage. The hike up to the farm is of medium-difficulty, but the scenery is worth it, as is the peace and quite and amazing views on arrival. There is no electricity at the farm and most people sleep in tents, however there are also some beds available. It can sleep 8-14 people, and there is a communal kitchen, solar showers and composting toilet. Tel: 593-9-143-1689, E-mail: sacredsuenos@wildmail.com, URL: www. sacredsuenos.com. Updated: Oct 30, 2012.

SOUTHERN ANDES

Rasa Lila Yoga At Izhcayluma

Yogis will be delighted to know that Hostería Izhcayluma offers yoga sessions nearly every day of the week. Classes are taught in English and blend mantra chanting, breathing techniques, asana postures and chakra, and take place on Monday (8:30-10 a.m.), Wednesday (5-6:30 p.m.), Thursday (8:30-10 a.m.), Friday (10-11:30 a.m.) and Saturday (10-11:30 a.m.). Private ($10) and group ($5 per person) classes can also be arranged at alternative times. At Hostería Izchayluma, two kilometers (1.2 mi) outside of Vilcabamba, E-mail: rasalilayoga@gmail.com. Updated: Jan 17, 2013.

Hiking In Vilcabamba

Vilcabamba is a great place to hike as there are many marked trails in the area that range in length and difficulty, all offering views of the beautiful flora and fauna in the area.

The Chaupi Loop is the easiest trail of all and lasts about 3.5 hours, with views of the Vilcabamba River and Chaupi Valley. The Mandango Loop is probably the most popular route: a four-hour hike of medium-high difficulty to the Mandango mountain (2,040 m/6,692 ft), which affords spectacular views of the valley and its surroundings.

Due to a slew of robberies on this particular trail, it is recommended that you hire a guide. The Waterfall Hike is a six-hour trail of medium difficulty that follows along the Yambala River to a 15-meter (50-ft) high waterfall under which you can swim, if desired.

Other options include the Forgotten Road Trail, which is the hardest and undoubtedly the longest hike, lasting eight hours; the Izcayluma Loop, which is a five-hour hike of medium difficulty that passes through the village of Mollebamba, ascends a ridge from where you can enjoy overhead views of three valleys and sight the Mandango mountain, and descends into a riverbed; and the San José Trail, a three-hour hike of easy-medium difficulty that reveals beautiful views of Vilcabamba and Podocarpus National Park and passes through the nearby village of San José.

It is also possible to schedule a two-day camping hike through the cloud forest and Podocarpus National Park, with an overnight stay at the park's refuge. Hostería Izhcayluma has a binder with detailed instructions and maps for each hike. Updated: Jan 17, 2013.

Vilcabamba Tours

Caballos Gavilán

New Zealander-turned-longtime Ecuadorian resident Gavin Moore offers excellent day and overnight trips on his well-kept and reliable horses. He leads two- or three-day tours that combine hiking and horseback riding with overnight stays at his cabin in the nearby cloud forest, which include delicious gourmet meals. Shorter tours, for two ($25), four ($25) or six ($35) hours, can also be arranged. Galiván also offers introductory horseback riding lessons for those who want to learn how to groom, mount and ride horses. Ca. Sucre 10-30, between Diego Vaca de la Vega and Agua de Hierro, Tel: 07-264-0209. Updated: Oct 30, 2012.

La Tasca Tours

La Tasca is a small tour operator with over 20 years of experience, located just off of Vilcabamba's main square. It specializes in horseback riding tours to Podocarpus Park and offers a few different options, ranging from two hours to three days or more. The owner of the agency, René León, is also owner of a very large private reserve that borders Podocarpus. Due to this, La Tasca has access to parts of Podocarpus that other agencies do not. There is a waterfall, known as Los Helechos ("The Ferns") on the land, and on the longer day trip, you can go to see it. La Tasca takes excellent care of its horses, giving them proper rest for a few days between trips and keeping them healthy. Ca. Bolívar, between Diego Vaca de la Vega and Fernando de la Vega, Tel: 09-8556-1188/8127-3930. Updated: Oct 30, 2012.

Tienda De Bicicletas "el Chino"

Another way to see Vilcabamba's surrounding countryside or to visit Podocarpus National Park is by bicycle. Tienda de Bicicletas "El Chino" are the bike and motorcycle experts in town. You can either rent a bike or motorcycle by the hour ($2 bike, $10 motorcycle), or sign up for one of the four-hour tours to Podocarpus that they organize ($25 per person 4 people, $35 per person 2 people). When you rent a bike, ask for the map that shows the various routes you can follow; it plots out six different options, ranging from one to four hours. The most difficult is the "Mollepamba Descent," so only attempt this one if you are an experienced rider. "El Chino" also repairs bikes and motorcycles. Ca. Sucre, between Agua de Hierro and Diego Vaca de Vega, in front of Jardín Escondido, Tel: 09-8187-6346.

SOUTHERN ANDES

Vilcabamba Lodging

For a pueblo of this small size, Vilcabamba offers a range of places to stay, each varying in style and price. Some of the most scenic and interesting places lie just a short distance (a few kilometers) outside of the town itself.

The nicest ones come equipped with pools, on-site restaurants and spas—but are still very affordable given their amenities. Many also offer yoga classes or meditation sessions, which is not surprising given the town's spiritual aura. There are also several opportunities to pitch in and stay at nearby working farms.
Updated: Dec 18, 2012.

Hostería Izhcayluma   !

(ROOMS: $10-56) Hostería Izhcayluma is situated on a hill approximately two kilometers (1.2 mi) outside of Vilcabamba, and enjoys spectacular vistas of the village and surrounding countryside. Guests are housed in beautiful bungalows, set well-spaced within the grounds and decorated in a minimalist style. Balconies and hammocks overlooking the stunning landscape are a very welcome feature of the rooms and add an already tranquil atmosphere to your stay, especially at the end of the day.

Relaxation is also possible while lounging by the pool, walking along the nicely decorated pathways, playing pool or table tennis, or simply enjoying a cold beer at the bar. Izhcayluma also has an on-site spa, with reasonably-priced treatments including facials, massages and reiki, and offers daily yoga classes. The hotel also has a restaurant, which serves big portions of both Ecuadorian and German specialties. An awesome buffet-style breakfast is included in the room price. Tel: 07-302-5132, Cel: 09-9915-3419, E-mail: izhcayluma@yahoo.de, URL: www.izhcayluma.com.
Updated: Oct 30, 2012.

Hotel Le Rendez-Vous

($10-20 per person) Le Rendez-Vous was set up by a French couple who fell in love with and chose to settle in Vilcabamba after traveling extensively throughout South America. The grounds feature eight adobe cabins with private bathrooms and 24-hour hot water. Each has a pretty terrace where you can kick back and relax in your hammock, while enjoying views of the manicured garden below. Before you settle in and swing away, grab a book from the library, which has books in English, French, German and Spanish. There are also five rooms along the patio with either private or shared bathroom. Breakfast and taxes are included in the room price. Diego Vaca de la Vega 06-43, Tel: 09-9219-1180, E-mail: rendevousecuador@yahoo.com, URL: www.rendezvousecuador. Updated: Oct 30, 2012.

Jardín Escondido   !

(ROOMS: $12-35) In addition to the sizzling Mexican and international fare offered at its restaurant, Jardín Escondido has 13 pleasantly appointed rooms—singles, doubles and family rooms—with private baths. The hotel, as the name would suggest, features a beautiful hidden garden with an inviting pool for taking a dip or lounging about. The owners are friendly and accommodating, a nice match for the warm atmosphere and peaceful grounds. Ca. Sucre, between Diego Vaca de la Vega and Agua de Hierro, Tel: 07-264-0281, E-mail: jardinescondido@yahoo.com/, URL: www.jardinescondidovilcabamba.com.
Updated: Oct 30, 2012.

El Descanso Del Toro

(ROOMS: $65-175) This brand-new lodging option in Vilcabamba brings a bit of luxury to this bohemian town. El Descanso de Toro has 17 spacious rooms, each with a private in-room Jacuzzi. The hotel's multi-storey wooden structures surround its large heated pool—the undeniable focal point—complete with a small waterfall and a stone indoor cave leading to a more private pool area, which is all illuminated at night. Other facilities include steam bath, sports field, gym, small movie theater, games room and restaurant. The on-site spa offers treatments like massages, aromatherapy and therapy sessions incorporating chocolate or clay. Diego Vaca de Vega, passing Río Chamba (Vía principal a Yamburara), Tel: 07-264-0007/302-6398, Cel: 09-8088-2809/2722, E-mail: descansodeltoro@hotmail.com, URL: www.descansodeltoro.com.

Madre Tierra

(ROOMS: $25-120) A highlight of any stay in the Vilcabamba region for those who wish to shell out a little cash, Madre Tierra offers outstanding accommodation and first-class service. To relax and recharge for a couple of days, head to the health spa and indulge in a luxurious facial or massage, along with more exotic treatments. Set around a landscaped organic garden, each room features its own colorful style. Prices include breakfast and snacks, and veggie-maniacs will be glad to hear that Madre Tierra's restaurant (daily 8:30 a.m.-8:30 p.m.) features a different veggie option each day. Its on-site conference hall can hold over 100 people and hosts theater, dance and workshops. Tel: 07-264-0269/0087, Cel: 09-9446-4972, E-mail: info@madretierra.com.ec, URL: www.madretierra.com.ec. Updated: Oct 30, 2012.

Rumi Wilco Nature Reserve and Eco-Lodge

($7-15 per person) Rumi Wilco is only a 10-minute walk from the center of Vilcabamba, but you feel like you are miles away. This nature reserve (admission: $2) was created by an Argentinian couple, Alicia and Orlando Falco, in an effort to reverse the environmental degradation caused by slash-and-burn agriculture. The reserve encompasses a beautiful mountainside with 12 different trails for day hiking. There is also an eco-lodge on the reserve with well-kept rustic adobe cabins with kitchens.

A third of what you pay goes toward various management programs on the reserve, such as protection and reintroduction of native species, nature trails and scientific research. You are also welcome to volunteer on the reserve for a discounted stay. Orlando, a bilingual naturalist with decades of experience in Ecuador, can take you on a guided excursion. Homemade organic granola, marmalade and coffee grown in their own tree-shaded orchard are also for sale. Turn left on the dirt road at the end of Calle Agua Hierro, go on in the gully (sometimes with water, you may jump on rocks or walk on the new rocky wall built on the left side of the gully), then walk along the bank. E-mail: rumiwilco@yahoo.com, URL: www.rumiwilco.com. Updated: Oct 30, 2012.

Vilcabamba Restaurants

Vilcabamba is a tiny town, so the restaurant selection is equally small. However, the main park is surrounded by several cute cafés, juice bars and eateries where you can get a satisfying snack or meal. Many of the restaurants use fresh, organic ingredients from their own local farms, so there will be plenty of options for vegetarians, organic-only eaters and those with healthy lifestyles. Quite a few of the town's hostels also have on-site restaurants with good international food, including Mexican and German food as well as the all time classic - pizza. Updated: Jan 17, 2013.

Café Sambuca

(ENTREES: $5-7) Café Sambuca has its own organic farm in Vilcabamba. Although the restaurant does have a menu featuring organic salads, pizza and Mexican food, Café Sambuca's owner and chef, Raul, can also personalize dishes based on the day's fresh ingredients from the farm. So come on in, say what you are in the mood for, and leave the rest to him. All dishes are made to order, so be patient. The café also has an extensive juice menu, blending some with spinach or microgreens for a healthy twist. It is also possible to arrange volunteering at Café Sambuca's farm; contact Raul for more information. Closed Wednesdays. Ca. Bolívar and Luis Fernando de la Vega, Tel: 09-8592-7081, E-mail: raul@vilcabambasambuca.com / raulahora13@yahoo.com, URL: www.facebook.com/vilcabamba.sambuca. Updated: Oct 30, 2012.

Jardín Escondido

(ENTREES: $4.50-9.50) Jardín Escondido is a tranquil restaurant and part of the hotel of the same name. The locale, truly a "hidden garden," has tables spread throughout a lush courtyard. The Mexican food here is highly recommended, as the burritos, fajitas, tacos and enchiladas are well-seasoned, flavorful and even a bit spicy. However, if you aren't in the mood for Mexican, Jardín Escondido also has typical Ecuadorian food and international cuisine. There is live music some Saturday nights, and the owner also sells original, handmade masks. The only complaint is the slow service, but the food is worth the wait. Ca. Sucre, between Diego Vaca de la Vega and Agua de Hierro, Tel: 07-264-0281, E-mail: jardinescondido@yahoo.com, URL: www.jardinescondidovilcabamba.com. Updated: Oct 30, 2012.

La Terraza

(ENTREES: $4.25-9) La Terraza is a lovely small restaurant with outdoor seating facing the central plaza and with striking views of the mountains in the distance. The service is friendly and the menu covers most of the staple meals in Ecuador as well as international fare, including Asian, Mexican, Italian and Mediterranean dishes. This is a good place to good if you are not sure exactly what you are in the mood for or are in a group with varying tastes, as you can order plates of rice or noodles with veggies and tofu alongside spaghetti in pesto sauce, Greek salad, fajitas or grilled chicken. Diego Vaca de la Vega and Bolívar, on central plaza, Tel: 09-9132-2614.

SOUTHERN ANDES

Cafeteria Coffeeshop Layseca's

(SNACKS: $1.50-4.50) This cafetería is popular for its downright delicious *dulces* (sweets), variousbreads and three different types of homemade granola, all made with organic ingredients. Sweet tooths will be delighted to find slices of carrot cake, orange cake, banana cake and portions of tres leches here, in addition to homemade waffles and crepes filled with chocolate, dulce de leche (caramel) or marmalade. You can also enjoy pizzas, sandwiches, hamburgers and Mediterranean plates for a proper meal. Even if you are aren't hungry, swing on by to pick up a bag of granola, ground organic coffee from Vilcabamba or cookies to take on the road. Ca. Sucre and Diego Vaca de la Vega, Tel: 09-9395-6252, E-mail: laysecaleonor@hotmail.com.
Updated: Oct 30, 2012.

Natural Yogurt Vilcabamba

(ENTREES: $1-4.50) Natural Yogurt Vilcabamba is one of the best cafés around. Located right off the central park, the pleasant outdoor seating area is always filled, due to the restaurant's delicious yogurt-and-fruit breakfasts, tasty main meals and exquisite dessert crepes. There are lots of vegetarian options, such as quinoa soup, veggie burgers and potatoes with spinach in a cheese sauce, and the food is made with almost all organic ingredients—all for a great price. Order one of the many fresh fruit juices and batidos (made with milk)to wash it all down. Ca. Bolívar, near Diego Vaca de la Vega, near central park.
Updated: Oct 30, 2012.

Shanta's Café Bar

(ENTREES: $3-7) A laid-back rustic country café and bar, Shanta's is a nice break from the restaurants surrounding Vilcabamba's central park, and has some unique menu specialties, like sauteed frog's legs and "Snake's Juice" (made with sugar cane alcohol and fermented snake). Simpler palates can choose from plates of pasta or fish, or settle for a hamburger or personal pizza.

Shanta's is also a fun place to party come nighttime, with drink special available through the night. Hop on one of the horse saddle bar stools and let the mustached, cowboy hat-wearing bartender mix up a few drinks for you. Located about a five-minute walk from the center, over the bridge heading east on Ca. Diego Vaca de la Vega toward Yamburara.
Updated: Oct 30, 2012.

The Juice Factory Vilcabamba

(JUICES: $2.50-2) This juice and smoothie mecca blends up large glasses of healthy yet creative concoctions, including an organic goji berry, wild Andean blueberry, coconut water, organic cacao, matcha and almond milk smoothie. It also sells vegan treats like walnut chai spice balls, raw vegan peppermint truffles and organic kale chips. In the back, there is a small natural shop selling hard-to-find items like fresh kefir, garam masala, organic raw cacao butter and ghee. Each day, it also prepares a different vegetarian soup and salad, making for a nice light lunch. Ca. Sucre and Luis Fernando de la Vega, on central park.
Updated: Jan 29, 2013.

Timothy's Café Bar

(ENTREES: $3.50-8) Timothy's Café Bar is eclectically decorated with the owner's personal collection items, including U.S. sports jerseys, international flags, international beer bottles and bottle caps, hats and soda cans. A great place to catch a game, Timothy's has a big plasma TV with a cable sports package. The food served here is typical bar grub, such as hamburgers, onion rings, nachos, buffalo chicken wings and BBQ ribs, and plates are named after sports references and personalities. Many come for Timothy's pancake breakfasts or to fill up on its brunch special, which consists of fried steak, gravy, eggs, French fries and juice. The bar serves a mix of local and imported beers (Budweiser, Beck's, Stella Artois, Negra Modelo, etc.) and has a bunch of cocktails, including passion fruit margaritas and mojitos. It has a happy hour every day from 4-8 p.m., when two cocktails go for $5. Diego Vaca de la Vega and Eternidad Juventud 10-51, Tel: 09-9341-2069/9593-7099, E-mail: timothybar@aol.com, URL: www.facebook.com/pages/Timothys-Bar-and-Grill/109315745802824.
Updated: Oct 30, 2012.

!!!!!

Amazon Basin

The Amazon River Basin, or El Oriente to Ecuadorians, is the biggest region in Ecuador. Ecuador has 2% of the Amazon Rainforest and makes for a convenient jump from major cities. Tourist infrastructure is well developed, and most destinations are less than a day's journey from Quito.

A plethora of tour operators based out of Quito, Tena and Baños can help you find a tour that meets your needs, be it a comfy lodge with three-course meals and hot showers, or a mud-up-to-your-knees trekking and camping adventure.

More life hums, buzzes, chatters and bubbles in the Amazon Rainforest than anywhere else on the planet. One Amazonian tree can host more ant species than all of the British Isles put together, one hectare of forest boasts about as many frog species as all of North America and the great expanse of the jungle contains more than twenty percent of the earth's vascular plant species. Here you can find a monkey small enough to sit on your fingertip, an eight-pound toad, a spider that eats birds and the world's largest snake, the 30-foot anaconda.

The Amazon is home to thousands of indigenous inhabitants, who make up nearly 200 distinct nations, including the Siona, Secoya, Cofan, Shuar, Zaparo, Huaorani and Quichua. Having lived there for more than 10,000 years, they know its trees, its animals and its rhythms better than anyone.

Oil companies are a serious threat to the rainforest today. Even at lodges deep in the jungle, plumes of smoke coming from oil refineries smudge the otherwise untouched horizon day and night. You can learn more about indigenous forest peoples and the rainforest itself joining one of the many community-based eco-tourism programs offered in the Ecuadorian Amazon or by becoming a volunteer with one of the many nonprofits working in the region.

Safety

Along your trip through the Amazon Basin, you might come across several instances of make-shift zoo's and self-proclaimed 'nurseries' inviting you to come in and take a look as well as even get a chance to pet the 'local' wildlife. You must avoid these wildlife rehab places (particularly near the Yanacocha Reserve) at all costs. These are solely money making ventures and do not rehab or intend to release the animals at any time.
Updated: May 10, 2013.

When To Go

Down in the Amazon Basin, rainfall is quite frequent during most months, but August and December to March tend to be the driest times of the year. Note that sometimes a shortage in rainfall can make the rivers run dry and passage becomes tougher for some lodges.

Amazon Tours

There are two basic Ecuadorian tours to the Amazon Rainforest Basin: lodge-based tours and canoe-based tours. In both, you pay a base price at the beginning which includes guides, all meals, transportation from the nearest major town to the launching spot and usually special equipment like boots and rain ponchos. The guides expect tips at the end of your tour.

Lodge-based tours tend to be a bit pricier and more comfortable. They are best booked out of Quito, where most have their main offices or arrangements with tour agencies. You can expect a variety of quality and comfort: everything from shared bathrooms with cold water to steamy private baths and gourmet meals. The prices for these tours range right around $60-100 per night.

Canoe tours are great for those willing to rough it. You usually travel by day, stopping to spot flora and fauna along the way and enjoy picnic meals. At night you either camp out or stay in a local community where there will be a small hotel. Sometimes homestays are provided on these tours. Canoe tours can be booked in Quito, or for a discount, plan to book in the towns where your tour will begin. Choose from: Puyo, Tena, Coca or Lago Agrio for trips to the nearby reserves. These tours are significantly cheaper than a lodge-based tour.

Manatee Amazon Explorer

A massive river cruise boat offering four to ten-day trips with a variety of itineraries that take passengers through Yasuní National

AMAZON BASIN

Amazon Basin Highlights

Baeza (*p. 306-307*): Frequently skipped by those going further into the jungle, Baeza features spectacular landscapes of the Quijos River Valley, where there is world-class kayaking and rafting. Just two hours east of Quito, on the road to Tena, this small town is the perfect base for exploring the surrounding cloud forest, Reventador Volcano, Sumaco National Park, and San Rafael Falls, Ecuador's largest waterfall.

Isla Parque Amazónico (*p. 319*): Located on a small island between the Tena and Pano rivers in the city of Tena, this conservation project has gardens, small waterfalls, and a diverse mix of typical Amazonian plant life and wildlife, allowing visitors who are unable to go deeper into the jungle a chance to see and learn about the region's unique ecosystems.

Limoncocha National Reserve (*p. 311-312*): This reserve, located on the north shore of the Napo River, is one of the most biodiverse areas of the world, and is home to a small population of Quichua families. The reserve's focus point is the Laguna Limoncocha, which is famed for being an excellent bird-watching site. Past petroleum activities have negatively affected the reserve so ecotourism is common here.

Yasuní National Park (*p. 312*): Yasuní is Ecuador's largest mainland national park and a UNESCO-declared International Biosphere Reserve. The park protects 982,000 hectares (2.4 million ac) of pristine rainforest, which is home to an impressive diversity of vegetation and animals, and encompasses native Huaorani ancestral lands. Yasuní is bisected by five major rivers and contains some of Ecuador's nicest jungle lodges.

Cuyabeno National Reserve (*p. 309-310*): Accessed from Lago Agrio, Cuyabeno National Reserve has over 500 recorded bird species, 450 species of fish and 15 species of monkeys, not to mention an abundance of endemic plant species. The reserve contains six different ecosystems as well as a network of lagoons connected by several major rivers and their tributaries. Some of the most budget-friendly Amazon tours are those available to Cuyabeno.

Updated: Feb 18, 2013.

Park, the Terra Firmae Forest, Limoncocha Biological Reserve, up the Cuyabeno river, and into various jungle lakes and gorges. The trips are typically all-inclusive and are quite the adventure. Quito Office: Av. Gaspar de Villarroel 1100 y 6 de Diciembre Edif. Ritz Plaza Esquina, Tel: (593 2) 336-0887 / 336-0888 / 336-0889 ext 16 Cell Phone 593 8 7752868 USA: 786-469-7744, Fax: (593 2) 336-0774, E-mail: marketing@advantagecuador.com Skype : advantagetravel, URL: http://www.advantagecuador.com http://www.mantarayalodge.com http://www.manateeamazonexplorer.com.
Updated: May 11, 2012.

Ikiam Expedition

Ikiam Expedition is an authentic and exceptional travel experience. After traveling from Quito to Puyo to Shell, you depart for Shiona in a five-passenger Cessna. Upon arrival, you take a 30-minute canoe ride to reach the territory of the Shiwiar, an indigenous community deep in the Ecuadorian jungle. With Ikiam, you become a part of the Shiwiar community, learning and living among this community only accessible by air. The Shiwiar are only a bit westernized, live in a non-monetized society, and continue to practice the rituals and beliefs they have cultivated over thousands of years.

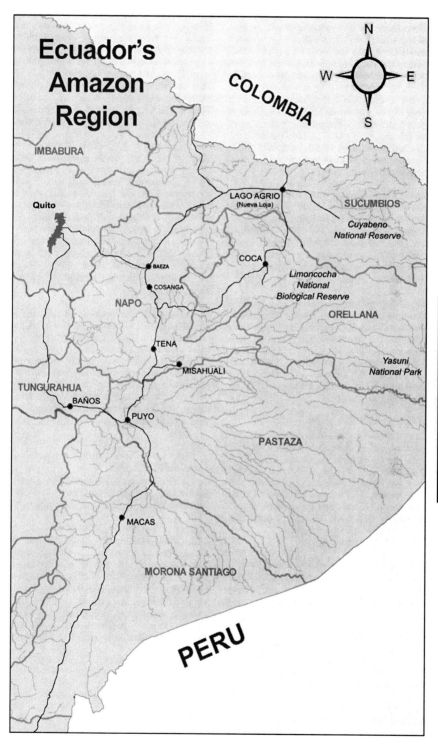

Ecuador's Amazon Region

Here, there are no expensive meals, no spacious suites: you sleep simply in a traditional house (mosquito net included!) and participate in the daily life of four Shiwiar families, helping to make handicrafts and prepare food. There is no set tour or agenda; you are free to explore the forest, view the amazing diversity of species or swim in the river at your leisure. Only five outsiders are allowed on the site each week. In Shiwiar territory, you are not viewed as a tourist or a client, but as a friend who has come to the jungle to help and to learn.

Ikiam Expeditions is committed to showing the outside world the beauty of the Shiwiar way of life, without compromising their existence. The company is devoted to ecotourism and is locally owned. The goal of the community and of the company is to defend this territory from oil exploitation and to preserve the Shiwiar culture.

Ikiam Expeditions is pricier than many of the ecotour companies you'll find in Ecuador, but the level of cultural immersion that you are sure to experience should be more than enough to make up for the extra cash. Tel: 09-9099-1941/9815-6132, E-mail: fundacionshiwiar@yahoo.es / ikiamp21@hotmail.com, URL: www.ikiam.info.
Updated: Feb 18, 2013.

Great Tours CIA LTDA

Great Tours CIA LTDA is a travel operator specializing in adventure trips, especially trekking in national parks and camping in Cuyabeno and Yasuní. This tour operator can also arrange Galápagos yachts and rafting, mountain biking and climbing in Ecuador. Quito Office: Juan Leon Mera N23-84 y Wilson, 2nd floor, Tel: 593-2-222-8405, URL: www.hotspots-tours.com.
Updated: Mar 13, 2013.

Amazon Rainforest Lodges

The Amazon rainforest basin, or El Oriente, is a popular tourist destination, and a number of jungle lodges are located here. Most of them are centered aroundTena,Puerto Francisco de Orellana (Coca), or Nueva Loja (Lago Agrio), which are transportation hubs in Ecuador's eastern lowlands. Although each is quite unique, activities and basic features don't vary too much, unless you splurge on a high-end option.

Location is the first consideration for a trip to the Amazon rainforest. Hotels and lodges near Tena, such as Cotococha, are more eas-

ily accessible than those near Coca or Lago Agrio, but have significantly less wildlife. Getting from Quito to Tena is a relatively easy six-hour bus ride, whereas the buses from Quito to Coca or Lago Agrio take at least 10 hours. There are also flights to all major launching points in the jungle to and from Quito. Flights to both Coca and Lago Agrio take about 25 minutes and cost $120 round trip.

Another consideration is comfort. If your idea of a vacation always includes a pool, a buffet table and hammocks, there are jungle lodges that will provide that. If you're more interested in animals and birds than comfort, you should check out the more remote lodges, such as lodges in the Cuyabeno Reserve. If you're willing to pay, there are lodges that offer both comfort and good animal-watching. Still others offer a closer look at local jungle communities, which can be fascinating as well.

Of course, it is also possible to stay in the region's major towns instead of one of the jungle lodges in their outskirts. Whether you want to spend a night or two in Lago Agrio, Coca or Tena before or after your jungle tour, or prefer to base yourself in Tena, Puyo or Misahuallí and take day trips from there, each town has enough of a tourist infrastructure to provide a selection of lodging options.
Updated: Feb 18, 2013.

BAEZA

Baeza is a small town about two hours to the East of Quito passed through by most people traveling by land to the Amazon region.

Located at the fork in the road that goes to Tena, Baeza features the Napo Province to the south, and Lago Agrio and the Sucumbios Province to the north. It is blessed with the spectacular landscapes of the Quijos River Valley (where there is world class kayaking and rafting). Baeza can be used as a base to explore the surrounding bird-rich cloud forests, Ecuador's highest waterfall- San Rafael Falls, Volcan Reventador and Sumaco National Park.
Updated: Mar 12, 2013.

Hiking Reventador

Reventador Volcano has been erupting intermittently since 2002 so the route has been changing and it may even be too dangerous to climb. However, it is a unique geo-

AMAZON BASIN

Did a unique trek? Got way off the beaten path? Tell other travelers at vivatravelguides.com

logical and ecological landscape to visit. Its recent eruptive history and location on the edge of the Oriente have created interesting landforms and habitats that are rapidly changing.

Note: This volcano is currently erupting and extremely dangerous to climb. The refuge is still present and most of the trail is intact, but there are new lava flows and periodic ash eruptions. It is likely, however, that this volcano will evolve into a dormant status again in the next few years.

Check its status with the SAE, the Smithsonian Global Volcanism Program (www.volcano.si.edu) or the Instituto Geofi sico de Escuela Politécnica Nacional (www.igepn.edu.ec). For more information about Reventador, see the Ecuador: Climbing and Hiking Guide. Updated: Apr 22, 2013.

COSANGA

Cosanga is a small town and area that attracts bird-watchers, biologists and nature lovers to its expansive cloud forests and high-altitude rain forests. Located 20 kilometers (13 mi) east of Baeza on the road from Baeza to Tena, where the high Andes plummet down into the Amazon at about 1,800 meters to 2,400 meters (5,905-7,874 ft) in altitude, the Cosanga area is one of the most biodiverse areas on the planet.

The area is an important biological corridor connecting the Antisana National Reserve with the expansive Cayambe-Coca Reserve and served as a pre-Columbian route between the highlands and the Oriente. The area is one of the best studied and understood areas of the high Amazon basin, thanks mostly to the Yanayacu Biological Reserve and its steady stream of visiting biologists over the years.

The climate is humid (that means it rains a lot, so bring a light rain coat) and has a near perfect year-round temperature. The Camino de los Caucheros (2 km/1.3 mi west of the town of Cosanga off the main highway), is a beautiful drive or bike ride where several (mostly private) trails are accessible. The area is also excellent for hiking, road and mountain biking and advanced white water kayaking. Sumaco Volcano (an arduous three-day climb) and the Cordillera Guacamayo are also accessible from this area. Updated: Feb 18, 2013.

Cosanga Lodging

Cosanga is home to some of Ecuador's most beautiful Andean cloud forests and is fairly close to Quito. However, it has very limited lodging options. The place most people head to is the Cabañas San Isidro, located on its own nature preserve and home to over 300 species of birds. However, you'll have to pay a premium price for it, but you'll get what you pay for. Cosanga hostels are rare and underpublicized, making it a very difficult place to stay for budget travelers.

Cabañas San Isidro

($48-68 per person) Come for the birds, then stay for the food. World-renowned as a major stop on the Ecuador bird-watching circuit, Cabañas San Isidro is an exemplary model of how private reserves, scientific research and tourism can be sustainably used to preserve forest environments. Located a few kilometers outside of Cosanga on the Las Caucheras road, over 300 species of birds have been identified in the reserve's extensive network of trails and vast mature humid temperate forest. Excellent birding can be had next to the cabins (especially from 6-9 a.m.), and the most accessible Cock of the Rock lek in Ecuador is but a 20-minute walk from the cabins.

Several nearby birding hotspots enable birders to access higher and lower altitudes as day trips from the cabins. Renowned birding guide Mitch Lysinger can assist in planning birding trips to the area's hot spots. San Isidro's rustic farmhouse now serves as the dining room and kitchen where the non-avian magic takes place.

Manager Carmen Bustamante also doubles as a chef who melds local ingredients into creative, eclectic international delicacies. Quito office: Av. Siena 318 and Ca. A, Edificio MDX, office 310, La Primavera-Cumbayá, Tel: 02-289-1880/1883, Cel: 09-9358-1250/9924-6899, E-mail: info@cabanasanisidro.com, URL: www.cabanasanisidro.com.

LAGO AGRIO
(NUEVA LOJA)

 297m   28,522   06

Lago Agrio (officially Nueva Loja) is seven hours east of Quito by bus or 30 minutes by plane. The town got its unofficial name from Sour Lake, Texas (the original headquarters of Texaco Corporation) which began using it as an outpost for oil exploration in the 1960s. After more than four decades, Lago is a far cry from the lethargic jungle community that Texaco commandeered. Now it's a grimy frontier city that has flattened all greenery for kilometers in every direction to accommodate the oil pipelines that crisscross the once virgin landscape.

Despite being an eyesore and harboring some sinister vibes, Lago Agrio serves as the best jumping off point for visiting the Cuyabeno Reserve, a spectacular 603,380-hectare protected area that boasts unparalleled wildlife viewing opportunities. Buses departing to the various lodges in and around the reserve depart from Hotel D'Mario.
Updated: May 03, 2013.

When To Go to Lago Agrio

Lago Agrio, like any jungle town, has a hot, humid climate. During the day, temperatures reach 28-30ºC (82-86ºF). Nights are a tad brisk: 19ºC (66ºF). Annual precipitation measures 4,014 millimeters (159 in), with considerable rains every month. March-July are the wettest months, and December-February are the dryer ones.

Lago Agrio has three principle festivals:

February 12 -- Día del Oriente Ecuatoriano

June 6 – Fiestas de la Virgen del Cisne

June 20 -- Cantonización de Lago Agrio
A common sight in Nuevo Loja's celebrations are the gaily decorated carros alegóricos, or car floats.
Updated: Oct 08, 2012.

Safety

Despite the magnificent facelift Lago Agrio has undergone in the past 10 years, the close proximity to the Colombian border still makes this place a hot-zone for illegal trafficking of all kinds. With shady business not being as apparent in the day as it is at night, it's still strongly advised to avoid wandering

away from the main strip (Ave. Quito) during the day, especially after dark. The border up north is also probably one of the least recommendable places to cross into Colombia.
Updated: May 03, 2013.

Getting To and Away from Lago Agrio

The quickest and most convenient way to get to Lago Agrio is by plane, which only takes around 30 minutes. The airport is a little way out of town, so you'll need to take a taxi to the center. TAME and AeroGal offer flights throughout the week, but because of the town's importance in the oil industry, flights can get pretty booked up, so reserve early to be sure.

If you prefer to take the bus to or from Quito, the route is very scenic as you drive along colossal green hills and empty river banks, passing Papallacta along the way. Expect to be on the bus for about eight hours ($8). Buses from Lago Agrio also go to Riobamba, Cuenca, Guayaquil, Tena and Puyo. The bus terminal is located to the northwest of the town center ($1-2, 5 mins in taxi), and has buses that can take you further into the Cuyabeno Reserve to towns such as Dureno and Tarapoa.
Updated: May 03, 2013.

Lago Agrio Lodging

Lago Agrio, also known as Nueva Loja, is one of the most important cities in northern Ecuador due to its role as a the home base for oil extraction in the Amazon. As a result, there has been severe environmental degradation surrounding the city which is home to a continuously growing population. Lago Agrio hotels tend to be on the modest side, but most offer the essential amenities; hot water, air conditioning and cleanliness.
Updated: Jul 12, 2013.

Hotel Arazá

(ROOMS: $36-70) A little away from the main hub of hotels and restaurants, Hotel Arazá is long established and a good choice with pleasant, clean rooms. The rooms have hot water and TV, while the hotel itself is well-appointed, boasting a swimming pool and a gym. Av. Quito and Narváez, Tel: 06-283-0223, E-mail: arazahot@hotmail.com.
Updated: Feb 14, 2013.

Hotel D'Mario

(ROOMS: $15-55) The well-established Hotel D'Mario has a great location in Lago Agrio. Room facilities vary depending on the

AMAZON BASIN

price. The cheapest rooms include a continental breakfast and one hour of Internet use, while the more expensive rooms have a better finish and unlimited Internet use. Some rooms have cable TV, telephones and air conditioning, in addition to a mini-bar and hydromassage services.

The hotel also has a restaurant, gym, swimming pool, sauna, game room and laundry service. It can also arrange airport transfers. If you book through its website, the hotel will offer you a welcome cocktail on arrival. Discount rates can be negotiated for groups as well if you're travelling together. Av. Quito 2-63 and Pasaje Gonzanamá, Tel: 06-283-0172/0456, E-mail: info@hoteldmario.com, URL: www.hoteldmario.com.
Updated: Feb 14, 2013.

Hotel El Cofán

(ROOMS: $24-55) Named after a local indigenous group of the Amazon, Hotel El Cofán is centrally located. The rooms are pleasant, with air conditioning, safe box, radio, mini-bar and satellite TV. The hotel also has a restaurant and bar. Other services in the hotel offers includes laundry, parking, money exchange services, room service and a game room. Ca.12 de Febrero 1915 and Av. Quito, Tel: 06-283-0526/2409, Cel: 09-9914-2913, E-mail: onlyneto@hotmail.es.
Updated: Feb 14, 2013.

Hotel Gran Colombia

($12-25 per person) The Hotel Gran Colombia is centrally positioned and offers reasonable rooms that are fairly good value for the money. Rooms come with fans or air conditioning and are clean. The hotel also has a pool table, bar and restaurant serving up the usual fare. Av. Quito and Gran Colombia, Tel: 06-283-1032.
Updated: Feb 14, 2013.

Lago Agrio Restaurants

Pizzería D'Mario

(ENTREES: $4-10) Adjoined to the Hotel D'Mario, the restaurant Pizzería D'Mario's main offering is exactly what the name suggests: pizza. In addition, the restaurant serves up other simple international options, including pasta and regional specialties. The restaurant is not bad; its menu items are fairly reliable staples and the breakfasts served here can be surprisingly scrumptious. Av. Quito 2-63 and Pasaje Gonzanamá, Tel: 06-283-0172/0456/2472/2308/3978, E-mail: info@hoteldmario.com, URL: www.hoteldmario.com/restaurant/index.htm.

CUYABENO NATIONAL RESERVE !

The Cuyabeno Reserve—or Reserva de Producción de Fauna Cuyabeno—is one of Ecuador's largest reserves and part of the Amazon Rainforest basin with over 6,000 sq. kilometers of rainforest. Because of the steep drop-off from the Andes mountains in the sierra region of Ecuador, the basin area is incredibly rich in flora and fauna. An excellent spot for bird lovers, the Cuyabeno reserve has over 500 recorded bird species, including the huatzin, which is known to be a direct descendent of prehistoric dinosaurs. Not only does the reserve have species that

survived the last ice age, but there is also an abundance of plant species only seen in the Amazon basin: tapirs, ocelots, 15 species of monkeys, as well as diverse aquatic wildlife like pink freshwater dolphins, turtles, five species of caiman, anaconda, manatee, giant otters, eels and around 450 species of fish.

There are several lodges to choose from when visiting the Cuyabeno Reserve ranging from rustic to hotel-like. All are reached by boat, usually a hand-carved motorized wooden canoe. A network of lakes and lagoons connect the two main black-water lake systems in the rainy season (April-October) and eventually lead down to the Napo River which leads to the Amazon River. In the dry season (November-March), many of the lodges close down for all but the hardiest tourist who are willing to walk along the dried up river bottom, or what is known as flooded forest, to reach the lodge.

Getting To and Away from Cuyabeno

Most tour operators will provide transportation from Lago Agrio and from the entrance to the Cuyabeno Reserve to the lodge. **Bring your passport.** If you take the bus, you will have to get out at a military checkpoint near the border with Colombia.

AMAZON BASIN

Cuyabeno Lodging

The Cuyabeno National Reserve covers more than 6,000 sq. kilometers of pristine Amazon rainforest. It attracts tourists of all tastes and budgets, and there are Cuyabeno hotels that are able to meet most needs (don't expect to find a Four Seasons). Some lodges offer diminutive amenities while providing great access to wildlife, while others cater to tourists that like dependable toilets and hate bugs. Some provide both, but at a premium price. You can also choose to live with an indigenous group, although these tours cost a lot of money.
Updated: Feb 18, 2013.

Cuyabeno Lodge

($250: 4 days/3 nights in dorm - $450: 5 days/4 nights in superior room) The Cuyabeno Lodge, run by Neotropic Tours, is a popular eco-lodge with minimal impact on the environment. Each cabaña has a thatched roof, with a roughly two-foot space between the wall and roof. Mosquitoes are not a serious problem as the rivers are blackwater rivers that do not inhabit mosquitoes. Most tours are four or five days but special arrangements can be made for groups. Three meals a day; free tea, coffee and water; and transportation from Lago Agrio to the lodge are all included.

A typical tour includes bird-watching at dawn, piranha-fishing, dolphin-watching, visit to a community, tours of the rivers by boat, afternoon swims and sunset viewing, and several walks through the rainforest by day and night. Cuyabeno Lodge's guides are all bilingual, certified guide nature specialists. Between November to March, the lagoon could dry up and transportation from the park entrance to the lodge may be difficult. Be sure to ask ahead of time before booking in these months. Quito Office: Pinto E4-360 and Av. Amazonas, Tel: 02-252-1212, Cel: 09-9980-3395, E-mail: info@neotropicturis.com, URL: www.neotropicturis.com.

Jamu Lodge

($177.50: 3 days/2 nights - $305: 5 days/4 nights) Jamu Lodge is by far the best "bang for your buck" if you're planning on exploring the Amazon jungle. This economical choice is nestled deep in the rainforest, unlike many of the other inexpensive lodges in the Cuyabeno area, which aren't even in the jungle. From the Cuyabeno bridge, where you pay entrance to the reserve, you will be transported into another world. Sailing for two hours down the Cuyabeno River in the

lodge's motorized canoe feels like a scene straight out of a movie. The experienced guide has "jungle eyes" that will spot out animals you would have never seen on your own, from butterflies to bird to monkeys.

The trip also includes a visit to the village shaman, who presents and explains his medicinal healing and traditional dances—an experience unlike any other. Also, you will visit a local village, go piranha fishing, swim in the beautiful Laguna Grande at sunset, search for caiman alligators, and explore the jungle at night. Beware of the tarantulas!

As for the lodge itself, it features nine separate cabañas with thatched roofs, bunk beds and cold showers. There are many hammocks to relax in between your excursions. The staff and guides at Jamu are friendly and helpful, whip up delicious and filling meals, and stay up with you in case there is anything needed. Calama E 6-19 and Reina Victoria, Tel: 02-222-0614, Cel: 09-9528-1035 / 099-971-7295, E-mail: ecuadorverdepais@hotmail.com / contacto@ecuadorverdepais.com.ec, URL: www.cabanasjamu.com.

Tapir Lodge

Tapir Lodge is located in Cuyabeno Reserve, and has a capacity for 32 guests in single, double or triple ooms, all with private bathrooms, hot water and electricity. Rooms are spread throughout the floors of two 15-meter (49-ft) towers rather than in typical huts or cabañas that most other lodges have. Tapir was built in 1999 with members of the Siona community, keeping ecological conservation in mind; the lodge's electricity come from solar panels. It has an on-site restaurant, and guests usually come as part of four-, five- or seven-day itineraries that include rainforest activities and all meals. Quito office: Av. Eloy Alfaro N29-235, between Italia and Alemania, Edificio Fortune Plaza, office 812 B, Tel: 02-380-1567, E-mail: info@nomadtrek.com, URL: www.tapirlodge.com.

COCA
(FRANCISCO DE ORELLANA)

 300m   40,730   06

Popularly known as Coca, this city's official name is Puerto Francisco de Orellana, being named after the Spanish conquistador, Francisco de Orellana, who managed to explore the Amazon River from the Ecuadorian jungle all the way to the Atlantic Ocean. One of Eastern Ecuador's largest cities and capital of Orellana Province, Coca perches right on the edge of where the Coca, Napo and Payamino Rivers converge.

In the 1980s, with the discovery of petroleum in the surrounding jungle, Coca grew from a sleepy little Amazon outpost into a sprawling oil boomtown. Tourists had no reason to visit Coca during the first two decades of this urban transformation, but in the late 1990s the municipality began a program to make itself more appealing to travelers, and with it the crowds began to flow in. Today, while it's still not the most attractive city, Coca has become an essential hub for the serious ecotourist, serving as the gateway to Ecuador's best ecological lodges along the Napo River.

Coca serves as the jumping-off point into the Yasuni National Park and UNESCO International Biosphere Reserve that encompasses nearly one million hectares of pristine primary rainforest and also serves as the entrance into Huaorani territory - one of the world's most isolated indigenous tribes and an amazing cultural experiences for travelers. Other protected areas and places accessed from Coca are Reserva Biológica Limóncocha, Bosque Protector Napo, Payamino, Bosque Protector Subcuenca Río Pacayacu, and - for those wanting a serious expedition - Iquitos, Peru.
Updated: May 02, 2013.

When To Go to Coca
Coca has a very humid tropical climate. Yearly precipitation ranges 2,800-4,500 millimeters (110-178 in), with March-July being the wettest months. The driest time of the year is December-February. Expect daytime temperatures of 29-31°C (84-88°F) and cool evenings of 19-21°C (66-68°F). Coca's biggest celebration is its Fiesta de Cantonización, April 30. During the last week of April, the city hosts a beauty pageant, artisan and agricultural fairs, and a variety of sporting, social and cultural events.
Updated: May 03, 2013.

Getting To and Away from Coca
Coca is fairly well serviced by road and air. The most convenient way to travel to Coca is flying to the Francisco Orellana airport from Quito's Mariscal Sucre Airport. Flights take around 30-40 minutes, and typically cost $40-60. The main airlines that service this route are TAME and AeroGal with flights departing daily (from both Quito and Coca airports) throughout the week.

For those preferring a cheaper, more scenic route, buses can be taken from the Quitumbe terminal in the South of Quito. Transportes Baños offers daily service to Coca, departing every hour beginning at 6 until noon; and then, following that, buses leave intermittently, roughly every 3-4 hours until 11 p.m. The journey lasts about 8 hours ($10) so be prepared to lose nearly a half a day.

Buses from Coca go to Tena, Lago Agrio, Puyo, Guayaquil, Machala, Santo Domingo and Loja. These buses depart from the Northern end of town at the terminal there. It is also possible to take a boat to Iquitos in Peru during certain times of the year – information regarding this can be obtained via Fausto's Canoe Tours, or simply inquire at the docks.
Updated: May 03, 2013.

Things To See and Do in Coca
Malecón
If you have time, you may want to head to the waterfront to see the Municipality's Malecón Project, which includes a Tourism center (iTur) that is run by locals. The Malecón and the Tourism center overlook the Napo River in front of the Port Authority, known in Spanish as the "Capitanía." Both initiatives hope to further develop tourism as an alternative to the oil industry, which the Municipality has wisely recognized will not be around forever.
Updated: May 03, 2013.

The Limoncocha National Reserve
The Limoncocha Reserve, located on the north shore of the Napo River between the Coca and Aguarico rivers, is on mostly level ground characterized by the presence of wetlands and swamps. The Limoncocha Reserve is one of the most bio-diverse areas in the world, but its flora and fauna are continually threatened by increasing oil activity. Scientific studies have identified over 450 bird species in the area, and unique trees such as the giant ceibo, cedars, laurel, the balsa and

AMAZON BASIN

the Pambil are common. The Reserve also contains the Laguna Limoncocha, which is famous for being an excellent birdwatching site.

Lowland Quichua families live nearby the lagoon and mostly farm for a living. Petroleum activities during the 1980s and 1990s have negatively impacted this region and its people. Therefore, the community is open to eco-tourism and other alternative uses of their fragile environment.

The best way to access the Reserve from Quito is by taking a plane to Coca or Lago Agrio. Buses also travel to these two destinations as well as directly to the town of Limoncocha. There is also water transportation from Coca to two small ports (Puerto de Palos and Puerto Pompeya). Updated: Mar 20, 2013.

Journey to the Border

For the adventurous, there is the possibility of traveling by commercial barge or private canoe down the Napo River to Nuevo Rocafuerte and across the border to Peru. The service is constantly changing, so anybody wishing to try this should check with the Capitanía Port Authority to find out current schedules and prices; tour operators also sometimes offer this as a tour option as well. It should be made clear that such an endeavor is not for the faint of heart; the trip, while surely exhilarating, is fraught with discomfort and perils. Updated: May 03, 2013.

Yasuni National Park !

Designated as a UNESCO Biosphere Reserve in 1989, this enormous bosque protegido (protected forest) encompasses an area of 9,820 square kilometers (6,100 mi), along with the Huaorani indigenous people's ancestral territory, and several uncontacted indigenous tribes (such as the Tagaeri and the Taromenane) – the latter areas are referred to as intangible zones due to them being off limits to oil extraction, logging and in some cases even tourism.

The park itself is one of the most biologically diverse places on Earth, with several hundred different species of trees, birds and wildlife capable of being found just within a square kilometer of the entire park. It also also holds a world record of having 150 amphibian species (for places with comparable landscapes) living amongst a plethora of other creatures.

The Yasuni National Park has, however, been under constant threat from international oil companies that intend to cut into its jungle with roads and machinery in order to extract the fossil fuels it rests over. In an incredibly ingenious environmental compromise, the government of Ecuador has pledged to leave the forests untouched and exempt from oil extraction with a project known as the Yasuni ITT initiative. In return for the lost revenue by doing so, the international community will pitch in to provide a compensation fund equivalent to at least 50% of the profits that it would have otherwise gained from drilling throughout the reserve. Unfortunately, on August 15, 2013, Correa announced that due to the lack of support for the initiative, the government of Ecuador is now obliged to enter and extract the oil they need to keep their heads above an unstable world economy. He has promised, however, to only touch 1% of the entire park in doing so.

The La Selva Jungle Lodge and Yasuni Kichwa Ecolodge are the only lodges located inside the National Park; the latter is run by the local Añangu community which seeks to preserve its tradition and the natural setting while providing a lodge for visiting tourists, specifically those tourists whom wish to experience the Añangu's culture and its ways.

Access to the National Park is best done via a tour operator either in Quito beforehand or Coca (see Amazon: p. 303 and Coca Tours). Updated: Aug 27, 2013.

Coca Tours

Aside from staying in luxurious lodges or eco-retreats, an alternative way to visit the Ecuadorian Amazon is to spend time in a Huaorani community. The Huaorani only came into contact with the outside world in the 1950s, however, they have largely maintained their traditional way of life, living a similar hunter-gatherer lifestyle as they have done for hundreds of years. A few operators offer this type of tour. Their main offices are in Quito, so you will need to book in advance. Updated: Jun 18, 2013.

Otobo Amazon Safari

Otobo is a Huaorani native and bilingual naturalist guide in Yasuní National Park, and he and his family run one-of-a-kind tours deep into the Ecuadorian Amazon. Itineraries typically last eight or five days, and start with a charter flight into the jungle from Shell or Puyo to the Huaorani village of Bameno (or an 11-hour motorized canoe

ride split up into two days with a night of camping). Led by a local Huaorani guide, visitors experience cultural immersion and adventure in small groups, participating in treks through the forest and canoe rides on the Río Cononaco, learning about medicinal plants, and spotting lots of wildlife. Guests stay in tents at the Otobo campsite and interact with locals on a daily basis, eating typical food, witnessing traditional dance and even trying out a real blowgun.   URL: www.rainforestcamping.com.
Updated: Feb 18, 2013.

Tropical Ecological Adventures

Tropical Ecological Adventures offer tours to experience life with a Huaorani tribe, staying in tents close to the community. The company has been offering this experience since 1994, and there are chances to learn about the Huaorani culture and their practical and spiritual relationship with the forest. Participants can also understand the medicinal properties of plants and learn about the traditional handicrafts that are practiced. The experience lasts for six days and starts and ends in Quito. The price of $900 per person includes meals, activities, guides and community entrance costs. This price is based on four travelers. Quito office: Pasaje Sanchez Melo Oe1-37 and Galo Plaza Lazo (also known as 10 de Agosto), Tel: 02-240-8741/281-4658, URL: www.tropiceco.com.
Updated: Feb 14, 2013.

Amazonpanki Tours

With tours encompassing the Limoncaocha Reserve, Shirpuno River and Yasuni National Park, Amazonpanki tours offers visitors the chance to embark on a journey (or two) that'll treat you to all the wonders near Coca - and beyond. Guides are local and savvy, with a keen eye on all the critters and fauna that are typically invisible to the untrained eye. With their tours, you'll also get a chance to participate in the traditions and customs of natives from the forest such as Shuaras, Kichwas and Waoranis. Package deals include food, aquatic transportation, water and guide; and can either last for one day or several. Tel: 099-104-1745 / 06-288-1805, E-mail: info@amazonpanki.com / pankitour@hotmail.com, URL: http://www.amazonpanki.com.
Updated: May 03, 2013.

Fausto's Canoe Tours

Fausto Andi is a local tour guide with a thirst for adventure and exploration in and around the local Napo River as well as beyond. His main specialty is coordinating extended-trips in canoe aimed at taking travelers all the way east across the border into Iquitos, Peru. The journey centers around examining the wildlife (among them: monkeys, birds and caimans) as well as camping along the riverbed at night, with the trip typically lasting anywhere from 8 to 10 days. The ride includes pretty much everything: from food and water all the way to boating equipment and camping gear - all aboard his private canoe. Discounts are available with larger groups. Tel: 099-437-8383.
Updated: May 07, 2013.

Coca Lodging

El Coca is the capital of the Francisco de Orellana province, and is home to about 40,000 people. The town is an important hub for visitors to the Amazon and its respective lodges due to its relatively large size and riverside location (making it a good embarcation point). El Coca hotels do not vary much in quality or price, but most places offer what you need; a firm bed, clean bathroom and cozy atmosphere. There aren't many luxury accommodations in towns, so travelers looking for a posh trip to the jungle should look at booking within lodges located inside the Amazon.
Updated: Jul 12, 2013.

URBAN LODGING
Hotel El Auca

($33-44 per person) Long established in Coca, with a convenient location on the main strip, Hotel El Auca is a reliable traveler's favorite. The staff is pleasant and can provide help to find local guides, or to store baggage. The hotel is well-presented and has a rustic charm. It also has a pretty garden courtyard surrounded with interesting looking plants, where you can kick back in the hammocks while watching the macaws. Rooms are clean and simple, and come with private bathroom and fans. The hotel has a decent restaurant too, serving regional cuisine. Ca. Napo and Garcia Moreno, Tel: 06-288-0600/0127, E-mail: ventas@hotelelauca.com, URL: www.hotelelauca.com.
Updated: Feb 14, 2013.

Hotel La Misión

(ROOMS: $31-75) A popular haunt, Hotel La Misión is situated on the riverside and is a pleasant enough place to lay your head for the night. This hotel is frequently used by tour groups who pass through on their way to or from the lodges. Rooms are well-presented, with hot water and private bathrooms. The hotel has a swimming pool, perfect for splashing down after a sweaty day on the bus. The food at the restaurant-bar is some of the best that Coca has to offer. Central Malecón and 12 de Febrero, Francisco de Orellana, Tel: 06-288-0544, Fax: 06-288-0547, E-mail: :info@hotelamision.com, URL: www.hotelamision.com. Updated: Feb 14, 2013.

Hotel Oasis

($11-20 per person) Located away from the hub of the town center, Hotel Oasis is often used by lodges such as Yuturi and Yarina to accommodate travelers who stay overnight at the beginning or end of their stay in the jungle. The hotel is a little worse for wear; there are 10 rooms in total and breakfast is not included in the price. However, it is a decent budget choice for those pinching pennies. Camilo de Torrano and Alejo de Vidania, Tel: 06-288-0206/0619. Updated: Feb 14, 2013.

Hotel San Fermin

($14-18 per person) Centrally located, the Hotel San Fermin is well-positioned for travelers staying in Coca. The hotel is tastefully designed from wood and concrete, using vegetation for a more natural finish. The San Fermin offers single, double and triple rooms, as well as cabins, with hot water and air conditioning. In case you arrive by car, the hotel also has a large parking lot. There is a living room for chilling out and meeting up with other travelers to talk about jungle adventures. Av. Quito and Bolívar (corner), in front Banco de Pichincha, Tel: 06-288-0802/1848, URL: www.amazonwildlife.ec. Updated: Feb 14, 2013.

JUNGLE LODGING

Yarina Lodge

($270: 3 days/2 nights - $450: 5 days/4 nights) Yarina Lodge is an eco-lodge set in the wilds of the Amazonian jungle near Yasuni National Park, in the zone reserved for indigenous Kichwas. The lodge was started in an attempt to alert both foreigners and Ecuadorians to the cause of environmentalism in the Amazon.

The park is now one of the most important environmental centers in the area, in conjunction with Yuturi Conservation Group and San Carlos Foundation. Yarina Lodge contains 27 huts for travelers (single, double, triple and quadruple accommodations), all complete with private bathrooms and

showers. The huts are constructed with materials native to the area. The lodge offers a plethora of activities; whether you're interested in fishing for piranhas or visiting a local shaman, you can certainly do it here. On the Napo river, only 60 minutes by covered motorized canoe from Puerto Francisco de Orellana (Coca). Quito Office: Av. Amazonas N24-240 and Av. Colón, Tel: 02-250-4037/3225, E-mail: info@yarinalodge.com, URL: www.yarinalodge.com. Updated: Feb 18, 2013.

Yachana Lodge

($759: 4 days/3 nights - $1,001: 5 days/4 nights) Yachana Lodge, the only officially certified eco-lodge in Ecuador's Amazon by the Ministry of Tourism, means "a place for learning" in the local indigenous language. It does a good job of making guests comfortable in its spacious and modern facilities, while teaching them about local communities and the challenges they face. Unlike many other rainforest lodges, all of Yachana's rooms are fully enclosed with screened-in windows. The bathrooms have 24-hour hot water and potable water from the tap. Activities include rainforest hikes, visits to indigenous communities, participation in traditional ceremonies, and a trip to a nearby cacao farm, where Yachana Gourmet harvests for its chocolate production. However, don't expect to see as many large animals as other Ecuadorian reserves; the area has been highly populated for some time and much of the large wildlife has been hunted or chased deep into the forest. Quito office: Reina Victoria N21-226 and Vicente Ramón Roca, Tel: 02-252-3777, Fax: 2-252-3327, E-mail: sales@yachana.com, URL: www.yachana.com. Updated: Feb 18, 2013.

Sani Lodge

(4 days/3 nights: $470 (camping)-$1,020 (single), 8 days/7 nights: $950 (camping)-$1,860 (single)) Sani is located on a secluded lagoon off of the Napo River on 37,000 hectares (92,500 ac). It is remote: visitors must first get to Coca and from there take a three-hour motor canoe ride to a point on the Napo. If the water is high, smaller canoes can take guests right to the lodge, otherwise, you may have to hike from the drop-off point on the Napo.

In spite of its remoteness, Sani is quite comfortable. Guests are lodged in triple or double cabins, with a summer camp sort of feel to them. The cabins are comfortable: they are screened against insects and each bed is equipped with a mosquito net. Each room also has candles, as it only tends to run the generator until about 10 p.m. The communal dining room offers hearty, solid fare; meals are done family-style.

Sani has a prime location for wildlife viewing. In many places along the Napo, mammals like monkeys have been hunted or driven away from entire areas. But the lagoon is protected, and home to many animals including endangered black caiman. At night, guides take tourists out in the canoes to try to see them. It is also possible to see 13 different species of monkeys, toucans, parrots, macaws and tanagers from the comfort of the lodge, which has an open wall to permit viewing. There is a 90-foot canopy observation tower built around the trunk of a mighty kapok tree nearby for bird-watching. Other activities include hikes, canoe rides and even piranha fishing!

Sani lodge is 100 percent owned by the Quechua community, who work in the lodge and serve as guides. Much of the money raised by Sani Lodge is returned to the local community in one way or another. Sani does package tours for 4 days/3 nights or 8 days/7 nights. It may be possible to arrange trips of other durations, though. Sani Lodge has a maximum occupancy of about 20 people: if you're interested in a visit, be sure to check ahead with plenty of time. On the Napo River, 2 to 3 hours from Coca on motorized canoe. Quito office: Jorge Washington E4-71 and Av. Amazonas, Edificio Rocafuerte, office 3 PB, Tel: 02- 222-8802/3800, E-mail: info@sanilodge.com, URL: www.sanilodge.com. Updated: Feb 18, 2013.

Napo Wildlife Center

($1,000 all-inclusive) The Napo Wildlife Center is located on the Napo River and is about two hours by motor canoe from Coca. As jungle lodges go, Napo Wildlife Center is one of the more deluxe. The center boasts 10 cabañas with large, pleasant rooms. Every cabaña has a porch, private bath, ceiling fan, and is well-screened to keep insects out. There is a communal area with a library, a bar, and a 50-foot viewing tower for those who wish to do some birding from the lodge itself.

The Napo Wildlife Center is far enough away from "civilization" that it is possible to see many birds and animals: 565 species of bird have been seen in its reserve, and a fortunate tourist can also hope to see monkeys and river otters. It is also near a parrot lick: on a sun-

ny day, hundreds of parrots will visit the lick to get certain nutrients they cannot get elsewhere, making for a memorable experience.

A modern, responsible eco-lodge, nearly 50 percent of the Napo Wildlife Center is owned by the nearby Quichua Añargu community, members of which work in the lodge as support staff and guides. The community produces handicrafts such as traditional pottery, which are sold in the lodge, with profits going directly to the artists. Activities included guided hikes, canoe rides, bird -atching tours, night hikes and visits to a local community. Guides are provided by the lodge. Usual stays are Monday-Friday (5-day/4-night) and Friday-Monday (4-day/3-night). These all-inclusive packages include all meals, transportation, park fees, guides, boots, etc. The flight from Quito to Coca, alcoholic beverages, and tips for guides and staff are not included. Quito Office: Yánez Pinzón N26-131 and La Niña, Edificio Las Carabelas, office 101, Tel: 02-600-5893/5819, E-mail: info@napowildlifecenter.com, URL: www.napowildlifecenter.com. Updated: Feb 18, 2013.

Sacha Lodge

($1,050: 6 days, 5 nights - $2,290: 9 days, 8 nights) Sacha Lodge, opened in 1992, is located on the Napo River, about two and a half hours from Coca by motor canoe. As far jungle lodges go, Sacha has a slightly more academic focus than most: it boasts a butterfly farm and an ornithology research base. There is also a 135-foot canopy observation tower, built around a mighty kapok tree. Complimenting the observation tower is a suspension bridge located deeper in the forest that stretches out over and above the canopy; with a remarkable span of 275 meters, (900 feet) long and 36 meters (120 feet) above the forest floor, you'll be awed by the views it provides.

Lodging is in 26 single- and double-occupancy cabins. The cabins are a perfect hybrid between luxurious and rustic, and are quite comfortable, each with private bath and screens to keep the bugs out. Sacha Lodge owns 2,000 hectares (5,000 acres) of private reserve, so be assured that there's plenty of excellent animal-viewing to be had. Not to mention, the savvy and friendly guides will fill you in on all the sights and secrets contained with the forest.

Staying at the lodge is typically structured around itineraries or set packages that span over the course of several days, and have you exploring the jungle and surrounding areas by foot or canoe. Among the activities included are: caiman-spotting in canoe (at night), swimming in the lake, night hikes, zip lining and more.

All meals are included with your stay and are incredibly delicious, with barbecues held twice a week right by the lake at night. Quito office: Ca. Julio Zaldumbide 397 and Valladolid, Tel: 02-256-6090/250-9504/9115 ext.23, Fax: 02-223-6521, E-mail: info@sachalodge.com, URL: www.sachalodge.com. Updated: May 03, 2013.

La Selva Jungle Lodge 』
($765: 4 Days/3 Nights in Traditional Huts -, $1,370: 5 Days/4 Nights in Superior Suites) La Selva Jungle Lodge is 97 kilometers (60 mi) down the Napo River (2.5 hours by canoe) from the town of Coca. Located within Yasuní National Park, the lodge has 18 thatched cabins and a striking dining room with bar/lounge area overlooking Garzacocha Lake. Each of the cabins has a private bathroom, mosquito nets and a hammock for relaxing.

La Selva was completely remodeled and reopened in July of 2012, and has become one of the premier luxury eco-lodges in the Ecuadorian Amazon. As one of the more deluxe jungle lodges in the area, each of the La Selva cabins has filtered water and hot water in the showers. The lodge also takes great pride in its food and the restaurant at La Selva is possibly the best restaurant in the country east of Quito.

La Selva offers many activities common to jungle lodges. There are various trails, guided hikes during the day and at night, canoe trips. Nearby is a salt lick where parrots and macaws congregate. There is also a butterfly farm and as a new feature, there is the Spa housed inside the butterfly farm. If guests wish, they can spend the night out deeper in the wilderness at a camping facility. Native guides are available to show guests the hundreds of species of birds in the park, and it is also common to see monkeys, caimans and a variety of insect life. Guides are available in English, French and German. Quito Office: Foch 265 and Leonidas Plaza, Sonelsa Building, 6th floor, Tel: 02-254-0427/5425/255-0995/Toll Free US/Canada: 1-866-687-3109, E-mail: info@laselvajunglelodge.com / sales@laselvajunglelodge.com, URL: www.laselvajunglelodge.com. Updated: Apr 09, 2013.

Coca Restaurants

La Finca
(ENTREES: $5-12) This cheery, intimate restaurant serves a mix of international food, with a specialty in different meats. Meals range from the typical chicken or beef plates to more exotic dishes featuring ostrich. Salmon and other fish mains are other options. At breakfast and lunch time, multicourse set menus are available for the work crowd. La Finca has a capacity for 25 people and can also host special events. There is happy hour on Mondays and Wednesdays from 6-7 p.m. Road to Agua Potable (parallel to Ca. Alejandro Labaka), Tel: 09-8929-4305, E-mail: lafinca@mail.com, URL: www.turisaven.com/lafinca.

La Casa Del Maito
(ENTREES: $5-7) Aside from having an open grill right outside the restaurant, used to cook up fresh fish brought out from the Amazon rivers, there isn't much that sets La Casa del Maito apart from many of the other places to eat in town. Nevertheless, this little restaurant is a decent place to come sit down and enjoy the Amazon's aquatic bounty, along with the amusing sight of all sorts of locals walking by along the street right outside. Espejo, between Quito and Napo, Tel: 06-288-2285/348. Updated: May 02, 2013.

Ocaso
(ENTREES: $5-7) With plenty of plates and appetizers to have you set and filled for the remainder of your day, Ocaso is a pretty simple restaurant. With the only real distinguishing feature from all the other places in town being the park outside, Ocaso won't bring you any major culinary epiphanies to boast about, but will nevertheless satisfy your hunger with a warm and flavorful meal. Plates mainly consists of meat and rice. Eloy Alfaro, between Amazonas and Quito, right in front of the park. Updated: May 02, 2013.

Frutilandia
(SMOOTHIES: $1.50-4) With a correspondingly colorful facade right outside, Frutilandia is a place full of sweets, fruits and shakes. The place boasts a wide array of all sorts of blends that you can have concocted with whatever fruit or ice-cream you desire. Batidos (smoothies) are their forte, so be sure to come in and have one, especially on any one of Coca's typically hot days. Corner of Quito and Espejo. Updated: May 02, 2013.

AMAZON BASIN

Did a unique trek? Got way off the beaten path? Tell other travelers at vivatravelguides.com

Food Alley

(PLATES: $3.50) More like a tunnel in the wall than just a mere individual hole, this alley serves as the cooking grounds for a number of individual barbecue stands and their tenants whom happily welcome the public.

Fresh fish (talapia) wrapped in banana leaf is grilled over hot coals, and then served promptly along with yuca and salad. It's definitely an experience that shouldn't be missed, despite how dingy and unkempt the entire strip might seem at first. Malecón, right beside the old one-lane bridge. Head west if you're facing the river.
Updated: May 02, 2013.

Como En Casa

(ENTREES: $3-6) Popular among the locals for having decent and satisfying desayunos and almuerzos (set breakfasts and lunches), Como En Casa is a pretty safe bet for getting your fill on at a pretty cheap price. Homestyle food and river food (brought out from the Amazon nearby) in the form of fish and poultry are typical here. Quito, between Espejo and Eloy Alfaro.
Updated: May 02, 2013.

TENA

Five hours southeast of Quito, Tena is the perfect launching point for a jungle trek or a rafting or kayaking trip down one of the countless rivers that pass within reach of town. Once an important colonial trading post in the Amazon, Tena is now the commercial center and capital of the Napo Province. The rainforest surrounding Tena supports a large population of lowland Kichwa indigenous people.

Significant numbers of Quijos and Chibcha Indians live further out in the green expanse that stretches as far as the eye can see. It is possible to visit many of these communities and to observe and sometimes participate in traditional dancing, the preparation of chicha (an alcoholic drink made by masticating maiz, rice or yucca and fermenting the juice), shamanic rituals and blowgun competitions.
Updated: Jan 22, 2013.

When To Go to Tena

Considering its location in the rainforest, Tena's climate is surprisingly comfortable; it is cooler and drier than most people expect. There is rainfall year round, and the heaviest rains come in June, July and August. Even in this very wet time, it does not necessarily rain every day or all day when it does rain. The rain is pleasant and warm, like the rain that those of us from the northern hemisphere only get in the sweltering heat of summer. Plus, it often makes for better rafting opportunities. In addition to other Ecuadorian holidays, Tena celebrates the Napo River Festival every January 5-11 and the foundation of Tena on November 15, among others.

Getting To and Away from Tena

BY BUS

Tena's bus terminal is located on Avenida 15 de Noviembre between Calle Montero and Avenida del Chofer. The terminal is unattractive but don't be too quick to judge the rest of the city based on its appearance, the northern part of town is much nicer and boasts and increasing number of interesting shops and decent restaurants.

Over the past several years, roads that lead to the Amazon have been greatly improved and travel times between destinations have been significantly cut. From Tena, you can catch buses to **Misahuallí**, **Baeza**, **Quito** (via Baeza), **Baños**, **Puyo**, **Riobamba**, **Ambato** and **Guayaquil**, as well as several smaller nearby jungle towns.

Cooperativa Transporte y Turismo Baños has buses to **Quito** daily at 2:30 a.m., 9 a.m., 10 a.m., 11:10 a.m., 1 p.m., 1:50 p.m., midnight.

Cooperativa de Transportes Amazonas has six buses to **Quito** each day in the mornings only, leaving at 1 a.m., 2 a.m., 3 a.m., 5:30 a.m., 9:30 a.m. and 11:45 a.m.

Cooperativa de Transportes Riobamba has six buses per day that stop in **Puyo**, **Baños** and **Riobamba**: 2 a.m., 3 a.m., 4 a.m., 9 a.m., 3 p.m. and 6 p.m.

Flota Pelileo goes to **Ambato** daily at 7 a.m., 8:30 a.m., 12:30 p.m. and 4 p.m., and to **Guayaquil** each night at 7:30 p.m.

Expreso Baños has seven buses per day to **Ambato**, with the first one leaving at 1 a.m. and the last at 7 p.m.; it also has five daily buses to **Quito** between 4:30 a.m. and 5 p.m.

BY PLANE

There is a small airport outside of Tena but there are no commercial flights, only short flights over the jungle.
Updated: Jan 23, 2013.

AMAZON BASIN

Getting Around Tena

Tena is small enough so that you should not have too much trouble getting around. It is divided in two by two rivers: the Río Tena and the Río Pano. Two bridges, one for pedestrians and one for automobiles, connect the two halves. There is also a nice riverside walkway on the western bank of the Río Tena.

Walking around town is easy and convenient, but you can also catch a taxi to bring you from point A to point B, if you prefer. Almost everywhere in town costs just $1 in a taxi. Taxis can also be hired to take you to lodges outside of Tena reachable by road or to some of the nearby attractions, and typically charge $5-10, depending on distance.

Tena Services

MONEY

There is a Banco del Austro (Monday-Friday 9 a.m.-5 p.m., Saturday 9 a.m.-1:30 p.m. Tel: 06-288-6446) on the corner of Avenida 15 de Noviembre and Díaz de Pineda, between the footbridge and car bridge. It has a 24-hour ATM. Another Banco del Austro is located at the PS gas station at the "Y" where Avenida 15 de Noviembre splits. A Banco de Pichincha (Monday-Friday 8:30 a.m.-4 p.m., Saturday 10 a.m.-1 p.m.) with three ATMs is half a block south of the gas station on Avenida 15 de Noviembre, near Calle Tena.

KEEPING IN TOUCH

Lots of small Internet cafés are scattered throughout Tena. Most charge $0.60 per hour. Café Tortuga conveniently has WiFi, if you have your own laptop. If not, Chipos-Net is right around the corner, at the foot of the footbridge. The post office is at the corner of the streets Olmedo and Moreno.

MEDICAL

Tena has many pharmacies where you can stock up on bug spray and sunscreen before your trip further into the jungle. There is a Farmacias Comunitarias (daily 8 a.m.-10 p.m.) conveniently located on Avenida 15 de Diciembre, across from the footbridge and next door to the tour operator River People.

A Su Farmacia is on the corner of Avenida Amazonas and Olmedo. For emergencies, head to Hospital José Maria Velasco Ibarra (Av. 15 de Noviembre and Eloy Alfaro. Tel: 06-288-6305).

TOURISM

Tena's tourism office (Monday-Friday 7 a.m.-5 p.m. Tel: 06-288-8046) is located on Avenida Rueda. The staff will gladly give you some information and tips about Tena and its surroundings. The police station is at Avenida Muyuna and Calle Gonzalez Suarez (Tel: 06-288-6101).

LAUNDRY

A recommended laundromat, Trapitos Lavandaría (Monday-Friday 7:30 a.m.-1 p.m and 2:30-7:30 p.m., Saturday-Sunday 8:30 a.m.-4 p.m. Cel: 09-9523-3919/5960-9655), can be found on Avenida 15 de Noviembre, half a block closer to the car bridge from Banco del Austro. Some of the hostels and hotels here also offer laundry service. Updated: Dec 20, 2012.

Tena Tours

There is a good chance that if you have ended up in Tena you are interested in venturing into the jungle, and there is no shortage of guides willing to take you. Whether you want a day trip to a nearby community or a multiday, full-immersion deeper into the jungle, Tena's tour operators can arrange it for you. Many have offices at the northern end of town on Avenida 15 de Noviembre.

Tena has lots of tour agencies, though, so it best to give yourself some time to visit a few to confirm credentials and find the perfect trip for you; be sure to inquire about certifications.

Don't be afraid to compare excursions or ask for reviews other travelers have left, and be sure to agree on what exactly is to be provided prior to the trip. The jungle is an incredible place and with a little research, you will take more than a few unbelievable memories home with you.
Updated: Jan 23, 2013.

The River People

River People Rafting provides exhilarating day and multi-day trips into the jungle for rafting, hiking, kayaking and fun. Experts on all the twists and turns of Ecuador's wildest rivers, River People guides are all certified and most are also bilingual. Day trips cost around $55-75 per person per day, and most can be extended with overnight stays in communities or with camping. It also offers a four-day kayaking school. Additional activities include wilderness hikes, horseback riding, bike riding and visits with indigenous people. 15 de Noviembre (across the street from the footbridge), Tel: 06-288-8384, E-mail: riverpeople@hotmail.com, URL: www.riverpeoplerafting.com.
Updated: Nov 28, 2012.

Amarongachi Tours

Amarongachi Tours have two ecological jungle lodges: the Cabañas Amarongachi and the Cabañas Shangrila (were in maintenance at time of writing). The former is specializes in adrenaline-pumping adventure, while the later is a place of nature-inspired relaxation. Between the two cabañas, Amarongachi is able to provide multi-day tours that combine the perfect amount of excitement and tranquility.

It charges $50 per per person a day for both, though rates are discounted for longer stays. Daytime activities include trekking with indigenous guides, canyoning up waterfalls, jungle handicrafts, survival skills, panning for gold, swimming in lagoons and river rafting. Av.15 de Noviembre 438 and 9 de Octubre, Tel: 06-288-7433, Cel: 09-9274-7496, E-mail: amorangachi@yahoo.com, URL: www.amarongachi.com. Updated: Nov 28, 2012.

Rios Ecuador

At the heart of Ríos Ecuador is a team of internationally certified guides that were born and grew up in and around Tena. Its guides are focused on skill and safety, and trips are guaranteed to be unforgettable. Rios Ecuador offers rafting trips on the Río Napo (Class III), the Río Misahuallí (Class IV), the Río Jondachi (Class IV) and the Río Anzu (Class II & III). The Río Napo is the most popular trip at $59 per person and promises big water and big thrills. The Río Misahuallí is one of the most challenging day trips offered in Tena and costs $69 per person. Rios Ecuador also offers kayak lessons and trips on all classes of rapids. Day trips for beginners, intermediate and expert kayakers cost $60-140 per person. You can also combine your rafting or kayaking adventure with a jungle stay at one of three nearby lodges. Monday-Friday 8:30 a.m.-1 p.m. and 2:30-6 p.m., Saturday 8:30 a.m.-12:30 p.m. Closed Sundays. Ca. Tarqui 230 and Días de Pineda, Tel: 06-288-6727/02-260-5828 (Quito), Cel: 09-9680-4045, URL: www.riosecuador.com. Updated: Nov 28, 2012.

Akangau Jungle Expeditions

Akangau Jungle Expeditions is a 100% indigenous-owned travel agency with no foreign investment. It is run by Misael Cerda, a Kichwa-licensed native guide who speaks Spanish and English and has 13 years of experience; he is passionate about preserving the jungle that he calls home. Akangau Jungle Expeditions offers authentic jungle tours steeped in the culture, heritage and traditions of his people. Its tours stand apart from other tour operators because they are a true cultural exchange and a real chance to experience Kichwa community life. Tour options include one-day and multi-day jungle tours, rafting and canoe trips, fishing expeditions, shaman ritual experiences, homestays in Kichwa communities, wildlife viewing, and visits to the primary rainforest, giant ancient ceibo trees, or to nearby waterfalls, lagoons or caves. 12 De Febrero and Augusto Rueda, Tel: 06-287-0464, Cel: 09-8617-5641, E-mail: akangautour@yahoo.com, URL: www.akangau.com. Updated: Jan 22, 2013.

Things To See and Do in Tena

Tena's claims to fame is its surrounding rainforest and rivers. The jungle, especially if you get outside town 15 or 20 kilometers (9.3-12.4 mi), is incredibly impressive. First-timers will be changed forever after they lay their eyes on a pristine stretch of Amazon. Tena has reached near legendary status with whitewater enthusiasts and boasts the best rafting and kayaking in Ecuador and, some say, the world. The jungle rivers on the Amazon side of the Andes are bigger and have more consistent flows than their west-Andean counterparts. They are also the cleanest and most scenic rivers in Ecuador.

Isla Parque Amazónico

(ADMISSION: $2) Isla Parque Amazónico, located on a small island right in the middle of Tena, was established in 1996 as part of a local an effort to conserve the natural splendor of the Amazon's plants and animals. Since the park was established, over 135 species of trees, plants and flowers have been identified on the island. The plant life is intermixed with gardens and waterfalls, and there is access to the river. Although some areas of the park seem a little neglected, it's a worthwhile visit, and the park is big enough to make you forget that you're in Tena. There are many different kinds of birds, butterflies, insects and other animals; some, such as the boa constrictors and turtles are caged, while others, including monkeys and tapirs, are free to roam. Currently, the footpath is being reconstructed and access to the island is by a 30-second boat ride across the river. The entrance is somewhat hidden by construction work, but it is there: walk west of the footbridge and look for a stone flight of steps leading down to the river. Between the Tena and Pano Rivers (just west of the footbridge). Updated: Jan 23, 2013.

AMAZON BASIN

Jumandy Cavernas

(ADMISSION: $5) Don't let the entrance to the Jumandy Caves deter you from going inside. Yes, you will have to enter through a water park. Yes, you will have to make your way through screaming kids to the café counter to ask for a guide. Yes, it will cost $5 for your guide and flashlight, and yes, you will wonder, "What the heck am I doing here?" As soon as you are 30 meters (100 ft) into the cave, you will forget what you left behind as you concentrate on working your way deep into the earth without slipping.

Your guide will lead you through the creek that has carved out the caves over the years, and at times, you will have to swim through it. You will climb over waterfalls, see sleeping bats and touch stalactites and stalagmites. If you get there early enough and a 45-minute trek through the caves isn't enough for you, there is a cave that takes four hours to get through. Make sure you are comfortable with your guide's knowledge and abilities if you embark on this four-hour adventure, though. Head lights and life vests should be provided, even for the shorter trek, so don't commit without being given either. 5 km/3.1 mi from Archidona, 7 km/4.3 mi from Tena, you can take a $6-8 cab ride from Tena, or hop on a bus in town to get out to the Jumandy Caves. Be sure to mention to the bus driver that you would like to be dropped off there. Updated: Jan 23, 2013.

AmaZOOnico

The animal rehabilitation center, amaZOOnico, is located in the middle of a protected jungle preserve and makes huge efforts to shelter a number of different animals, some in danger of extinction. The station was built in 1993, and has grown since as a hidden but popular place to come see wildlife up close.

The animals arrive at the shelter in a number of ways, the majority coming from individuals who have found them or from the police (who have confiscated the animals from illegal traffickers). Most of the animals arrive at amaZOOnico in bad condition: malnourished, wounded due to being tied up, and very often full of parasites. Following their recovery, the majority of them eventually end up being set free. The remaining half must remain at amaZOOnico – either living free in the area, or in enclosures to protect them from other animals and hunters.

Along with this, the Zoo is quite a spectacle, with plenty of animals existing within inches from you - many that you'd otherwise have to trek deep into the jungle to (hope to) see. The Zoo also provides internship and volunteer opportunities for those interested. Puerto Barantilla (45 km east of Tena), from Tena you take the 14:30 bus in direction Puerto Barantilla / SANTA ROSA DEL NAPO and tell the driver, that you want to get out at Puerto Barantilla, the bus stops only 30 meters from the river. Normally the Amazoonico canoe will already be waiting there if you've contacted them in advance. Tel: 09-980-0463, E-mail: amazoonico@gmail.com, URL: http://www.selvaviva.ec/amazoonico/index.php?l=en. Updated: Jun 04, 2013.

La Isla de Los Monos

(ADMISSION: $2) La Isla de los Monos has been declared a protected rescue area for monkeys and other wildlife. It is located at the convergence of the Napo and Misahuallí rivers and encompasses seven hectares (17.3 acres) of forest. Before you even enter, you may hear the competitive cry of the howler monkey from nearly a mile away. In the trees overhead, you can see many different species of monkeys as they chase each other in an endless game of tag.

A few of the friendlier monkeys won't hesitate to drop on down to meet you, tease you and run off with your things if you let them. Besides the playful antics of the monkeys, you can hold a boa constrictor and view brightly colored birds, jungle cats and countless other interesting species. There is also a hostería here with comfortable cabins, a tasty restaurant and a bar. There are pools to take a dip in when the sun gets too hot, and there are trails throughout the forest that allow you to get close to nature. Puerto Misahuallí, 20 minutes from Tena. Updated: Jun 04, 2013.

Tena Lodging

Tena has a booming tourism business, and there are several hostels and hotels in town to accommodate visitors. Many choose to stay outside of town at one of the jungle lodges in the rainforest nearby. The lodges near Tena have pros and cons. On the plus side, they are not very remote and are easy to reach by bus from Quito, which can save you time, money and hours on a bus. On the negative side, most of the cool wildlife like monkeys, great cats and birds have all been hunted out of the Tena area long ago and your chances of seeing anything really memorable are slim.

Did a unique trek? Got way off the beaten path? Tell other travelers at vivatravelguides.com

URBAN LODGING
Hotel Caribe

($8-12 per person) Hotel Caribe is located in the southern end of town, a few blocks from the bus terminal but a bit far from the footbridge and its surrounding restaurants and tour operators. Also, since it is near industrial areas on the main street, it is sometimes difficult to sleep due to noise. The hotel has 33 rooms in double, triple and matrimonial varieties. All have a private bathroom with hot water and cable TV. There is also air conditioning, which is not a luxury found in most accommodation options here. The rooms are pieced together with mismatched furniture and linens, but they do have all the basic comforts and are clean. Its on-site restaurant serves cheap breakfasts (not included in room price), lunches and dinners. Out back, there is a bar and covered area where folkloric dances are often held. Av. 15 de Noviembre, Barrio Eloy Alfaro, Tel: 06-288-6518, E-mail: hotel_caribe@yahoo.es.com. Updated: Nov 28, 2012.

A Welcome Break

($7-13 per person) A Welcome Break has a great location, just off Tena's main street. The hostel is cozy and simple, with all the basic amenities. Although the shared kitchen looks a little run down, it is clean. Rooms are also clean and have either private or shared bathrooms (all with hot water). There is also an outdoor patio with hammocks to relax in. This is known as a kayaker hostel, so it is a good place to meet and mingle with other kayakers. If you are interested in organizing a tour, the certified on-site travel agency Lefer Turismo can assist. WiFi is another perk. Corner of Ca. Augusto Rueda 331 and 12 de Febrero, Tel: 06-288-6301, E-mail: a_welcome_break@yahoo.com, URL: www.awelcomebreakecuador.com Updated: Nov 28, 2012.

Hostal Limoncocha

($7-10 per person) Even though Hostal Limoncocha is somewhat removed from the footbridge and "happening" end of town, it's hard to beat the views. Here you can watch the sunset from a hammock on the patio and fall asleep to all the jungle sounds. The rooms are spacious, clean and comfortable—a really good value given the cheap prices. Rooms with shared bathrooms are several dollars cheaper, and some of the ones with private bathrooms also have cable TV. There is a small communal kitchen on the third floor and one computer with Internet on the first floor that guests can use for 30 minutes. Breakfast is not included, but a few different options are served daily for a small added cost. The hostel also runs its own tour agency, which you can use to book jungle or rafting trips. Av. del Chofer (300 m/984 ft uphill from the bus station), Tel: 06-284-6303, Cel: 09-8705-3185, E-mail: limoncocha@andinanet.net, URL: http://limoncocha.tripod.com. Updated: Nov 28, 2012.

Hostal Los Yutzos

($24-49 per person) The Hostal Los Yutzos is a family-oriented hotel that is located on a quiet street in the middle of the most peaceful residential area of Tena. Many of the rooms overlook the Pano River and guests can hear the soothing sounds of the river just below their balconies. The hostal is pleasant and clean, with spacious and comfortable rooms that make for a wonderful stay. All rooms have private bathrooms, hot water, cable TV, telephone and WiFi. Ones with air conditioning are a bit more expensive. The staff is friendly and helpful. Breakfast is included in the price. Los Yutzos accepts Visa and Mastercard credit cards. Ca. Augusto Rueda 190 and 15 de Noviembre, Tel: 06-288-6717/6769, E-mail: yutzos@uchutican.com, URL: www.uchutican.com/yutzos. Updated: Nov 28, 2012.

Hostal Canela

($12 per person) There are 12 double, triple and quradruple rooms at the clean and comfy Hostal Canela. They are spacious and have everything a worn out traveler may need, including private bathrooms with hot water, cable TV, telephone access, WiFi and a garage. Corner of Av. Amazonas and Abdón Calderón, Tel: 06-288-6081, E-mail: canela-hostal@yahoo.com. Updated: Nov 28, 2012.

JUNGLE LODGING
La Casa del Suizo

($99 per person) La Casa del Suizo jungle lodge is one of the most luxurious lodges in Ecuador's Amazon. Located a short distance from Tena, La Casa has an outdoor swimming pool and 75 rooms with electricity, ceiling fans, private terraces and hot water. The hotel's restaurant serves sprawling buffets of international cuisine, and the bar has a full menu of tropical drinks. There is international phone service available for guests, but it is costly. The hotel began as just a lodging house in 1985 and slowly expanded over time to the luxury hotel it is

AMAZON BASIN

now. Itineraries are flexible and include typical lodge activities like hikes through the rainforest, canoe rides and visits to communities. The rainforest surrounding the lodge is primary forest. La Casa del Suizo is only 15 minutes from the town of Punta Ahuano and can be reached by bus or car from Quito. Quito Office: Julio Zaldumbide N25-42 and Valladolid, Tel: 02-250-9504, Fax: 02-223-6521, E-mail: info@lacasadelsuizo.com, URL: www.casadelsuizo.com. Updated: Feb 18, 2013.

Huasquila Amazon Lodge

($55-99 per person) This family-run eco-resort offers nine luxury cabins, built with local materials in Kichwa Style, within the Sumaco Biosphere Reserve. Each cabin has a private bathroom, hot water, amazingly comfortable beds, and wide interior spaces and porches from where you can enjoy the fascinating views of the Amazon. Huasquila is also perhaps the only Amazon eco-lodge in Ecuador to cater to visitors with disabilities, and can accommodate groups of up to 30.

Huasquila offers personalized tours and activities including caving, jungle walks to identify medicinal plants, and visits to petroglyphs, an animal rescue center, Kichwa communities, and much more. This lodge offers first-class attention in a family atmosphere, including bar service with exotic cocktails, as well as a show featuring traditional dances.

You will be served three- and four-course meals everyday for breakfast, lunch and dinner with delicious national and international dishes. This lodge is ideal for small groups with individual interests looking for a relaxing way to experience the beauty of the jungle. Km 3.5 via Huasquila, Cotundo, Take one of the several buses that head toward Tena from Quitumbe in Quito and ask to be let off in Cotundo (2 towns before Tena). From Cotundo, hire a camioneta (there are no taxis) for $3 to take you to Huasquila. Quito office: Av. Amazonas 743 and Veintimilla, Edificio Espinoza, office801, Tel: 02-237-6158, Cel: 09-8764-6894, E-mail: info@huasquila.com / reservations@huasquila.com, URL: www.huasquila.com. Updated: Feb 18, 2013.

Hostería Hakuna Matata

(ROOMS: $60-72) This private lodge, just 10 kilometers (6 mi) from Tena, rests along the shores of the crystalline Río Inchillaqui. Sensibly located between the Andes and the Amazon, the lodge is free from tropical diseases, providing guests a safe environment to freely explore the 150-hectare (371-ac) tropical playground. This eco-friendly retreat works hard to respect the natural beauty and culture that surrounds it, from conservation/reforestation efforts to projects supporting the local community. The 36-guest hostería offers three accommodations: Cabañas Hakuna Matata, Hakuna Lodge, or the luxury Hakuna Supreme. All rooms include hot water, private terrace and private bath, along with breakfast and a gourmet three-course dinner included in the price. WiFi is free when available.

For a dose of tranquility, lounge in a hammock or splash around in the unique palm-tree-shaped swimming pool, which offers breathtaking views of the Llanganati Mountains. The pristine river with a small private beach is ideal for relaxing baths or horseback riding. Nature enthusiasts can wander the area on one of the several marked nature trails, which are densely packed with a variety of flora and fauna.

For adrenaline-seekers, the lodge organizes customized rafting, kayaking and canyoning trips. Via Chaupi Shungo Km 3.9, ArchidonaPost address: Apartado Postal # 165 Correo Central Tena Napo - Ecuador, From Quito: Just past Archidona on the main road to Tena, follow the yellow signs on your right hand side just across the bridge, 4 km/2.5 mi from main road. From Quito, the trip is about 4 hours.From Baños/Tena: Main road to Archidona/Baeza, before Archidona follow the yellow signs just before the bridge on your left hand side, 4 km/2.5 mi from main road. From Baños, the trip is about 3 hours. Tel: 06-288-9617, Cel: 09-9337-7441, E-mail: info@hakunamat.com / ecuadorparadise@gmail.com, URL: www.hakunamat.com. Updated: Nov 28, 2012.

Cotococha Lodge ⟩

($235: 3 days/2 nights - $550 5 days/4 nights) One of the more easily accessible jungle lodges, Cotococha is located in the upper Amazon basin on the Napo River between Tena and Puyo. This is a good location, as it is therefore accessible from both Baños and Quito. It has 21 well-built, comfortable bungalows with differing capacities. Each one has a private bath, a balcony and a hammock. There is a cozy lounge area with a bar, gardens, a social area and an open-air restaurant. Cotococha owns four hectares (9.9 ac) of rainforest. Activities are flexible,

AMAZON BASIN

allowing guests to create their own itinerary and customize their experience. Some suggestions are nature walks, visits to local indigenous communities, canoe trips, night hikes, rafting, exploring nearby caves and visiting waterfalls. Guides are available. Cotococha Lodge's packages include food, guides, rubber boots, etc., but not transportation to and from Quito. Quito Office: Amazonas N24-03 and Wilson, 2nd floor, office 3, Tel: 02-223-4336, Cel_ 09-9904-4419, Fax: 02-252-7721, E-mail: reservas@cotococha.com, URL: www.cotococha.com. Updated: Feb 18, 2013.

El Establo De Tomas
($20-42 per person) If you want the experience of staying in the jungle outside of Tena but can't afford the higher prices of the all-inclusive lodges, El Establo de Tomas is an excellent alternative. Set in extensive grounds a 15 minute drive from the center of Tena, the hotel consists of several individual wooden cabins, pretty gardens frequented by toucans and talkative parrots, river access, a volleyball court, a small lagoon, and communal areas with a dining area, bar, pool table, cable TV and free WiFi. The cabins are simple but well-kept with mosquito nets, and each has a private bathroom with a shower heated by solar-power. A hearty breakfast (bread rolls, eggs, ham or cheese, yuca, fruit, juice, tea and coffee) is offered for an extra $4, and dinner can be arranged for $6-8.

Unfortunately however, there have been reports of animal trafficking at the hotel. Rio Lupi, Muyuna, Tena (4 km/2.5 mi northwest of Tena), The hotel is located four kilometers (2.5 mi) out of Tena. Take the road that runs past the airport and onto Muyuna. Once in the small town of Muyuna, take a left at the suspension bridge over the river (there's a sign for the hotel by the bridge). On the other side of the bridge go down a gravel road for around 100 meters. The hotel is on your right just before a pedestrian bridge. Tel: (062) 888-926/886-318/Cel: 099-000-914, E-mail: tomaslodge@andinanet.net, URL: www.tomas-lodge.com. Updated: Aug 16, 2012.

Arajuno Jungle Lodge
($180: 3 days, 2 nights - $365: 4 days, 3 nights) A family-owned jungle lodge located on a private forest reserve next to the Jatun Sacha Biological Field Station on the banks of the Arajuno River, Arajuno Jungle Lodge offers package stays for three or four days.

Packages range from economic to deluxe options. Spacious wooden cabins with big screened windows and tiled bathrooms look out over the river. The whole place is run with environmental conservation in mind, down to an intricate solar electric lighting system.

There are lots of neat things to do here also, from playing on the Ecua-volleyball court to a climbing the high canopy lookout tower and trying out the rope swing. On Arajuno River, about 45 minutes from Tena: From Tena, go south on the road to Puyo. After about 15 minutes, you will cross the bridge over the Río Napo. After crossing the river, on the south side of the bridge, take an immediate left turn. Follow this paved road until it becomes unpaved (approx 20 km/12.4 mi). At this point, keep going straight for anther 5 km/3.1 mi until you reach the only large bridge over the only large river. You have arrived at the Arajuno River. Cross the bridge and park your car at the small store on the right hand side just past the bridge. Tel: 06-301-8762, Cel: 09-8268-2287, E-mail: larstom@gmail.com, URL: www.arajuno.com. Updated: Nov 28, 2012.

Tena Restaurants
The majority of Tena's eateries are located near the footbridge over the river. Most commonly, you will find Ecuadorian fare, fried fish, pizza and rice—lots of rice. The restaurants cater to travelers who have worked up a hearty appetite on the river or in the jungle, and prices are cheap for the adventurists.

Don't expect to find upper-class restaurants in Tena, this is a thrill seeker's town with an appetite for adventure—not award-winning cuisine. That said, food is decent and you'll have no problem refueling for tomorrow's activities.
Updated: Dec 04, 2012.

The Marquis Restaurant
(ENTREES: $9-18) The Marquis Restaurant, owned by a Colombian chef with over 40 years of culinary experience, has a reputation as one of the nicest eateries in town. However, if you're picturing an upscale restaurant with speedy service and top-notch food, you may be a little disappointed. The menu has mainly grilled meats and seafood as well as dishes like beef in red wine sauce, chicken in apple sauce and grilled prawns over pasta.

Plates vary in quality but portions are generous and there is a good selection of wine. Marquis also cures its own meats and sells

AMAZON BASIN

them by the pound. It is highly recommended to make a reservation, as 80 percent of clientele call ahead. Daily noon-4 p.m. and 6-10 p.m. Closed Sundays if there are no reservations. Av. Amazonas 251 and Olmedo, Tel: 06-288-6513.
Updated: Nov 28, 2012.

Restaurante Safari

(ENTREES: $2.75-6.50) Restaurante Safari is located about 10 minutes south of the footbridge on Tena's main street. This little restaurant has a limited menu, featuring items like seco de pollo (typical dish of chicken in sauce) and chaulafan (fried rice), in addition to cheap fixed-price lunches and dinners.

It is a good place for a quick and filling, albeit not especially healthy, meal. The lunches and dinners usually include a large mound of white rice and a piece of fried meat. Monday-Saturday 7 a.m.-10 p.m., Sunday 7 a.m.-3 p.m. Corner of Av. 15 de Noviembre and Federico Monteros, Tel: 06-288-8257.
Updated: Nov 28, 2012.

Chuquitos

Popular with locals and tourists alike, Chuquitos overlooks Tena's main plaza. Be sure to grab a table on the balcony if you can to get a nice vantage point of the area as you enjoy your meal. The grotty stone steps that lead up to this second-floor restaurant belie the pleasant, airy surrounding. The friendly service and the tasty menu of seafood, meat and traditional Ecuadorian dishes are crowd pleasers, making the place tends fill up during mid-day. Be sure to come early and grab a seat while its avaialble if you can. Ca. Garcia Morena (on the main plaza, by the river).
Updated: Aug 13, 2012.

Café Tortuga

(ENTREES: $2.50-5) Right on the riverfront is Café Tortuga, a favorite foreigner hangout. This small café's charm comes from its attentive staff and simple, good food, including sweet and savory crepes, large sandwiches, soups, avocado stuffed with chicken or cheese, and beef chili.

Many come for its yummy and filling breakfasts (served from 7 a.m.), while others come to cool off with an iced coffee, fresh fruit juice or homemade iced tea. There's free WiFi and a book exchange available too. Monday-Saturday 7 a.m..-7 p.m., Sunday 7 a.m.-1 p.m. Malecón Francisco de Orellana, Tel: 09-9529-5419, E-mail: cafetortuga@yahoo.com.
Updated: Nov 28, 2012.

MISAHUALLÍ

Misahuallí is a little port village located on the Napo River, just 45 minutes east of Tena. Despite having lost the bulk of its commercial river trade in the 1980s due to the completion of a road connecting Coca and Tena, Misahuallí has stayed alive thanks to its reputation with ecotourism.
Updated: May 06, 2013.

Getting To and Away from Misahualli

Roughly 7 hours southeast of Quito, Misahualli, like nearby Tena is a popular destination for weekend jungle excursions. From **Quito**, Cooperativos Amazonas has direct buses to Misahualli leaving at 11:30 am and returning from Misahualli at 8:30 am everyday ($7).

Should you want more flexibility, your best bet is to take a bus to **Tena** via **Baeza** (5 to 6 hours, runs frequently) and make the connection to Misahualli from there. Try to book in advance – buses tend to fill up on the weekends. Tena is also a good base from which to make other long distance connections.
Updated: Mar 13, 2013.

Misahuallí Tours

There are many guides and travel agencies offering tours up to 12 days into the jungle, including everything (rubber boots, canoe, food, etc.) Be sure to always ask guides for their license and pay half (or less) of the total cost up front. Pay the balance upon completion. Make sure that everything is included on the trip before signing, or giving away any up front payment. The average cost per day is between US$30 to US$70 per person depending on number of tour participants.

TeoRumi Travel Agency

Teo Rumi is an indigenous guide specializing in medicinal plants and poisonous snakes. He is licensed through the Ministry of Tourism in Ecuador and offers exciting jungle adventures out of Misahuallí. He offers one-, two- and three-day tours into the surrounding jungle. Activities include motor canoeing to the Shiripuno Community, typical dances, artisan demos, lunch, jungle walks, forest and waterfall viewings, medicinal explanations, and swimming. The multi-day tours also include shaman rituals and visits to the cultural museum and animal rescue shelter. In front of the central park, Tel: 06-289-0203, Cel: 09-8701-6852, URL: www.teorumi.com.
Updated: Feb 18, 2013.

Selva Verde

Luis Zapata is a super-friendly guide with over nearly 20 years of experience guiding. He has five guides: three that speak English and two that speak Spanish and Quichua who lead adventures into the jungle. Trips are one-day to multi-day and include jungle tours, piranha fishing, bird-watching, canoeing, kayaking, butterfly education, gold panning, and ceramic and handicraft lessons. Prices range from $40-70 per day, depending on the activities and duration of the trip. He also offers day trips canoeing on the river, jungle walks, museum visits and shaman rituals. Av. José Antonio Santander, across from the central park, Tel: 06-289-0165, Cel: 09-9821-5710, URL: www.selvaverde-misahualli.com. Updated: Feb 18, 2013.

Ecoselva

Ecoselva is a reputable tour operator located in Misahuallí. Adventurists can choose from a variety of tours from single day to 10-day tours (some to the Peruvian border!). There is usually a minimum of five people required. Tours include: hikes, night walks, bird-watching, body rafting, swimming, motor canoeing, flora and fauna explanations, piranha fishing, museum visits, cultural activities with native Quichua tribes, overnight stays in jungle cabins, and essentials such as food, water and equipment. Ecoselva also participates in volunteer programs associated with working in schools, medical volunteers and the butterfly projects. Its guides are licensed and experienced. In front of the central park, Tel: 06-289-0019. Updated: Feb 18, 2013.

Things To See and Do in Misahuallí

Any number of local tour operators and guides sell inexpensive excursions into the rainforests of the Upper Napo River Region. This area of the Ecuadorian Amazon has more jungle lodges than anywhere else in the country.

There isn't a lot to do after ferreting out your jungle tour, but that's not necessarily a bad thing: take a moment to sip a cold drink while absorbing the sights and sounds of this old Amazon settlement. Updated: Nov 15, 2012.

Butterfly Farm

(ADMISSION: $2) If you find yourself with a little free time and have tired of watching the gang of monkeys run around Misahuallí, be sure to stop in and visit the Butterfly Farm for some interesting information on butterflies and the metamorphosis process. There are some beautiful species of butterflies to observe. Across from Misahuallí high school, Tel: 06-289-0019. Updated: Feb 18, 2013.

La Cascada Latas

(ADMISSION: $2) If you board a bus headed towards Tena from Misuahallí and ask the driver to drop you off at the Camino de las Cascadas (approximately 15 minutes outside of Misuahallí and 25¢ fare depending on the mood of the driver) you'll find yourself on your way to see a pretty waterfall, nice picnic areas and a little swimming hole. Its a 40-minute hike to the actual falls. Its very slick and muddy at spots so wear good shoes and you may also find yourself wading through the river. The trail can sometimes be hard to pinpoint and you don't want to find yourself alone and lost in the jungle, so bring a friend. El Camino de las Cascadas. Updated: Mar 13, 2013.

Misahuallí Lodging

Misahualli is a popular spot for tourists visiting the Amazon because it is fairly accessible from Quito. The town itself isn't much to see, but there are playful monkeys everywhere, which makes any place on earth significantly better. Accommodations are fairly modest, but you can find a clean room with air conditioning and hot water for about $15. There's not much to splurge on in Misahualli; hotels aren't nearly as luxurious as those found in larger cities. But if you're on a budget and have reasonable standards, you'll be fine.

In addition, there's the option of heading out to any one of the lodges nearby so you can plunge just a bit deeper into the Amazon and a little further away from civilization. Updated: Jan 12, 2013.

URBAN LODGING
Hostal el Paisano

($15-20 per person) Hostal El Paisano could almost be deemed luxurious for jungle standards. It is located just a block off the Parque Central (central park) and is clean and fresh. The hostel has a very open-air feel about it, with rooms opening onto an outdoor patio. Generally quiet, El Paisano sometimes gets noisy when the community's herd of playful monkeys scampers across the tin roof. It can accommodate 37 people in double and triple rooms, and each one is equipped with mosquito nets and a sparkling private bathroom with hot water. There is a restaurant on-site serving all meals for cheap prices. Guillermo Rivadeneira and Tandalia (front of the school), Tel: 06-289-0027, Fax: 06-289-0115, E-mail: reservations@hostalelpaisano.com, URL: www.hostalelpaisano.com. Updated: Feb 18, 2013.

Hostal Clarke

($15 per person) This cheery hostel is on the south side of the main road into Misahuallí. It is just one block from the community's main square. Rooms are bright with colorful (though peeling) walls and mismatched blankets. The hostel has 35 beds total: six doubles, three triples, four matrimonials and the rest are quads. Each room has a private bathroom, hot water, television and fans. There are areas for lounging outside of the rooms, and there is a restaurant that is open when large groups are on-site. In the evening, guests can partake in karaoke in the bar downstairs while drinking cocktails and imported liquors.

Hostal Clarke also has its own licensed travel agency that can set up jungle tours, visits with nearby Quichua tribes or shamans, rafting, tubing, motor canoe rides and more. Juana Arteaga and Antonio Santander, Tel: 06-289-0085/0002, E-mail: douglasclark-expediciones@yahoo.com / jungle_boyec@yahoo.com / chaman380@hotmail.com. Updated: Feb 18, 2013.

Hostal Shaw

($8-12 per person) Hostal Shaw is a one-stop shop for all of your jungle-getaway needs. Located in the center of the village on the north side of the park, travelers, diners and guests have front row seats to view the antics of the herd of monkeys that affectionately terrorize the community. Rooms are comfortable, with private bathrooms, mosquito nets, 24-hour hot water and all your basic needs. The windows are kept locked up tight when nobody is in the room to keep the monkeys from coming in and messing up the bed sheets and tearing down the mosquito nets.

Downstairs there is a delicious restaurant that serves up vegetarian and meat dishes in addition to typical Ecuadorian fare. Feel free to browse the local native jewelry for sale, pick a movie to watch or a book to read, or simply be entertained by the playful monkeys out front that will try anything to slip into the restaurant for a snack. The reputable EcoSelva Travel Agency is also located here and offers tons of activities including nocturnal navigation, night walks, jungle hikes, canoeing, swimming, bird-watching and body rafting, and can also organize trips into the jungle. Across from the central park, Tel: 06-289-0163, Cel: 09-9701-2911. Updated: Feb 18, 2013.

JUNGLE LODGING

Misahuallí Amazon Lodge

($70-104 per person) The Misahuallí Jungle Lodge was founded by a local pioneer of the Amazon on a beautiful plot of land in the jungle. The lodge can accommodate up to 100 guests in cabañas, doubles, triples and quadruples. The rooms are cozy and made of natural materials of the region. Each cabaña has a private bathroom, hot water, ventilation and 24-hour electricity. The restaurant on-site serves local specialties and international cuisine, all prepared with purified water. Any special requests pertaining to diet can be accommodated.

Packages are offered that blend the beauty of the surrounding jungle with adrenaline-pumping activities. Enjoy tranquil hikes, jungle facts, visits with indigenous peoples, shaman rituals, bird-watching or a trip to the rescue center. Follow these activities with rafting, mountain biking, swimming, caving or canoeing. Quito office: Enrique Iturralde Oe3-44 and Av. de La Prensa., Tel: 02-252-004 /224-9651, Cel: 09-9179-1952, E-mail: info@misahualliamazonlodge.com, URL: www.misahualliamazonlodge.com. Updated: Feb 18, 2013.

El Albergue Español

($105: 2 days, 1 night - $220: 5 days, 4 nights) This Spanish-run jungle bunker is situated on a hill overlooking the Río Napo. Views of the river make this location ideal for a village experience. The hostel sleeps 50 people in rooms with private baths, solar-heated hot water, fans, laundry, Internet, parking lot and safes. Stop off on the first floor at the restaurant for a good meal. Jose Antoño Santander and Juana Arteaga (a block west of the central park), Tel: 06-289-0127, E-mail: alb_esp@uio.satnet.net / reservas@alberguespanol.com, URL: www.alberguespanol.com. Updated: Feb 18, 2013.

France-Amazonia Guesthouse

($18-30 per person) France-Amazonia is a small, peaceful jungle lodge run by a lovely couple who will make you feel right at home. The hotel can host up to 36 people in 16 rooms, all with private bathrooms and hot water. There is also a swimming pool, a bar, private parking and private access to the Napo River. Tour packages are arranged with a native-certified, English-speaking guide and include kayaking, rafting, hiking, and visiting the nearby jungle and indigenous villages. The prices are very competitive and equipment, such as rubber boots and rain ponchos, is included. Tel: 06-289-0009, Cel: 09-8023-6364, E-mail: franceamazonia@gmail.com, URL: www.france-amazonia.com. Updated: Feb 18, 2013.

Banana Lodge

($8 per person) Banana Lodge is located on the bank of the Misahuallí River and bears its name for the banana plants growing in its territory. It is just a 10-minute walk from the central park of Puerto Misahualli. The lodge has three cozy rooms with private bathrooms, as well as a hut with hammocks, a BBQ and a fireplace. Guests can grill up their own meals during their stay. The area surrounding the lodge grows cacao, coffee, bananas, oranges, limes and other plants. You can swim in the river or sunbathe along its shores, or go deeper into the jungle; the staff can help arrange tours. Via al Pununo: 800 meters (2,625 ft) from Misahuallí's central park, toward Pununo. Tel: 06-289-0190, Cel: 09-9888-5169, E-mail: barantseva@gmail.com, URL: www.bananalodge.com. Updated: Feb 19, 2013.

Hamadryade Lodge

(ROOMS: $300-600) Hamadryade Lodge is a high-end ecolodge surrounded by beautiful vistas and nature, nestled in the heart of the Ecuadorian Amazon Rainforest. The lodge has five luxurious and spacious bungalows, which makes it ideal for those in search of adventure but not quite ready to compromise on quality and comfort in the pursuit. Each room, with majestic views of the jungle, can host two to three persons; with their biggest bungalow holding up to six people.

Staff here are very professional and courteous, and the main lodge offers a hub for relaxing or socializing by the restaurant and mini-library. The lodge also organizes all types of activities, from rafting and jungle hikes, all the way to visits to local Kichwa and Waorani communities. Tel: 098-590-9992 / 08-590-9992, E-mail: lodge@hamadryade-lodge.com, URL: http://www.hamadryade-lodge.com. Updated: May 06, 2013.

Suchipakari Jungle Lodge

($160: 3 days/2 nights - $340: 5 days/4 nights) Suchipakari Jungle Lodge is a little paradise in the Ecuadorian Amazon Basin. Whether you are looking for adventure or just a place to relax and discover the beauty of the jungle, Suchipakari can make it happen. The lodge is located 25 minutes from Puerto Misahualli, on the shores of the Pusuno River. The lodge has 10 typical cabañas and seven rooms, all with private bathrooms. There is also a dining room, a bar, a common area to relax with hammocks, and a private beach at the river. The kitchen offers several delicious and fairly priced menus, including local dishes. The hotel staff members come from nearby communities and are very friendly. You can either book lodging only or an all-inclusive tour. At the shores of the Napo and Pusuno rivers in the province of Napo. It is a 50-minute drive from the capital of this province, Tena.; Quito office: Venezuela N6-09 and Mejía, Centro Histórico, Tel: 02-295-9042, Cel: 09-9271-7038/8053-5854, E-mail: info@suchipakari.com, URL: www.suchipakari.com. Updated: Feb 19, 2013.

Misahuallí Restaurants

As travelers are drawn to Misahuallí for the adventure, not necessarily the gastronomy, there are just a few options for dining. Fringing the Parque Central are a handful of restaurants and the typical shops selling snacks and ice cream. Almost all of the hostels and lodging in Misahuallí have restaurants or bars on-site and serve standard Ecuadorian fare.

Restaurante Doña Gloria

(ENTREES: $2-5) Overlooking the central park, this warm little restaurant is family-owned and cooks typical Ecuadorian fare. The restaurant is clean and has a nice beachy feel to it. Breakfast is just a few dollars and includes bread with butter and marmalade, eggs, meat, coffee and juice. Lunch is a set menu of soup, the main course (meat with rice), juice and a dessert. Dinner comes with your choice of tilapia, chicken, apanados de carne (breaded chicken or beef) or churrascos (fried thin slice of meat topped with fried egg)(with rice and sides, of course). Ca. Juana Arteaga and Guillermo Rivadeneira (central park), Tel: 06-2890-100. Updated: Feb 19, 2013.

EkoKafe Bar and Restaurant

(ENTREES: $2-6) EkoKafe Bar and Restaurante is a delicious restaurant that serves up vegetarian and meat dishes in addition to typical Ecuadorian fare. Feel free to browse the local native jewelry for sale, pick a movie to watch or a book to read, or simply be entertained by the playful monkeys out front that will try anything to slip into the restaurant for a snack. On José Antonio Santander, across from the central park, Tel: 06-289-0163. Updated: Feb 19, 2013.

PUYO

Until recently, Puyo was nothing more than a stopover on the way into the depths of the Amazon Jungle. However, it has begun to earn a reputation as a tourist destination. It is in particularly popular with those who either don't want to, or can't, venture deeper into the rainforest. It offers visitors a taste of jungle life in Ecuador, while still slightly in the Andes Mountains.

The city is located relatively near popular tourist destination Baños, which has helped put its name on the map. Puyo's increased popularity has lead to a greater selection of good places to stay and eat in the area. There may not be as great of a selection as other tourist towns, but that is part of its appeal: it is more off the beaten track.

Safety

Paseo los Monos should be avoided, given that there have been several reported incidents of the monkeys biting visitors. Dont swim in the Puyo river either, as it is quite contaminated with fecal matter; Dique de Pambay at end of Quito street is probably your best best for swimming (safely and cleanly) if you need to satisfy your urge. Updated: May 10, 2013.

Getting To and Away from Puyo

Puyo is often a starting out point to the jungle, so there are regular buses to the area from Quito's Quitumbe station (5.5 hr, $6). Additionally, there are buses that leave from the city of Baños (1.5 hrs, $2) - making short day-trips to Puyo from **Baños** quite easy and cheap. If you want a more adventurous trip to Puyo from Baños there is a popular day-long bike ride from the city that is run by operators there (see **Baños**, p. 233).

From Puyo, buses go to **Tena** (2 hr, $2.50), **Macas** (3.5 hr, $5), **Quito** (5.5 hr, $6), **Ambato** (2.5 hr, $3), **Coca** (7 hr, $9), **Guayaquil** (7-8 hr, $9) and *Riobamba* (3.5 hr, $3.75). Updated: May 10, 2013.

Puyo Services

MONEY

Most banks and ATMs are concentrated to the center of town. Banco de Pichincha is on Calle 10 de Agosto, between Atahualpa and Francisco de Orellana (Monday-Friday 8:30 a.m.-4 p.m., Saturday 9 a.m.-noon. Tel: 03-288-6792/795/). There is a Banco del Austro on Calle Atahualpa, between 9 de Octubre and 27 de Febrero (Tel: 03-288-3931). A Banco de Guayaquil is on the corner of Avenida Ceslao Marin and Avenida 24 de Julio.

KEEPING IN TOUCH

Many Internet cafés can be found on Calle 9 de Octubre, between Orellana and Atahualpa. Kodak (Monday-Friday 9 a.m.-8 p.m., Saturday-Sunday 9 a.m.-3 p.m. Tel: 03-288-7037), on the corner of Francisco de Orellana and 9 de Octubre, doubles as a photo shop. It has eight computers with Internet and webcams ($0.75 per hour), and can process and print digital photos in 30 minutes ($0.20 per photo). The post office is at Calle 27 de Febrero and Atahualpa.

MEDICAL

Several Farmacias Comunitarias surround the Municipal Building the the center of town. There is also a Farmacias Cruz Azul on Calle 20 de Julio, between the 4 de Enero and Bolívar (daily 8 a.m.-11 p.m. Tel: 03-288-9710). Puyo does have hospitals, but better medical facilities are located in nearby Shell. If you must get emergency medical assistance in Puyo, Hospital Puyo (Tel: 03-288-3871) is located on Calle Eugenio Espejo and Ramiro Fernandez.

TOURISM

Puyo has three iTur offices: one in the Municipal Building (9 de Octubre and Francisco de Orellana, 2nd floor. Tel: 03-288-5122, ext 111), one on the Malecón Río Puyo in Barrio Obrero (2nd floor of the watchtower) and one in the bus terminal. All are really helpful and have extensive information on the area's attractions. All of the locations are open Wednesday-Friday 9 a.m.-6 p.m. and Saturday-Sunday 9 a.m.-1 p.m. They are closed on Mondays and Tuesdays. You can reach the police office at 03-288-5101.

LAUNDRY

Drop your dirty clothes off at ServiClean Lavandería, on Calle 20 de Julio, next to Farmacias Cruz Azul. It charges $0.40 per pound and can wash and dry it within two or three hours (daily 6 a.m.-9 p.m. Tel: 09-8423-3327). Updated: Nov 29, 2012.

Did a unique trek? Got way off the beaten path? Tell other travelers at vivatravelguides.com

Puyo Tours

Puyo's tour operators are focused on providing trips into the jungle, but adventure sports like canyoning or whitewater rafting can also easily be arranged. Some even book trips to other destinations in Ecuador, including to the coast and to Cotopaxi National Park. Many of the jungle tours from Puyo visit nearby Kichwa, Huaorani or Shuar communities, where visitors can participate in shaman rituals, try traditional food and help make typical artesanía. No matter what amount of time you want to spend in the area, Puyo's tour operators can help you get a taste of the jungle or organize a full-on, multi-day jungle experience.

Selva Vida Travel

Selva Vida specializes in activities and adventures near Puyo. It organizes one- to three-day excursions to the Hola Vida Reserve, 30 kilometers (18.6 mi) from Puyo, as well as five-day trips to the further-away Yasuní National Park via canoe or plane. Additionally, Selva Vida leads guided tours to several nearby caves, including the Jumandi Caves, and heart-pumping whitewater rafting on the Pastaza River. For those who want to try Ayahuasca, Selva Vida offers an overnight itinerary where you can participate in the sacred ritual led by a shaman. Ca. Ceslao Marin and Vilamil, La "Y" sector, next to Banco de Fomento, Tel: 03-288-9729/279-2005, Cel: 09-9135-3487, E-mail: selvavidatravel@hotmail.com, URL: www.selvavidatravel.com. Updated: Nov 27, 2012.

Papangu Tours

If you are interested in really immersing yourself into the communities and cultures of the Amazon, Papangu may have the tour for you. Specializing in community tourism, Papangu Tours organizes three- to six-day trips to Shuar and Kichwa communities, reachable only by small plane or several-hour canoe rides. Fifty percent of all tour costs go directly to the communities themselves to assist with improving infrastructure and education, nature conservation and other local projects. Tours cost around $70-90 per person per day, not including transportation. Ca. Sucre and 27 de Febrero, Tel: 03-288-7684, URL: www.papangutours.org. Updated: Nov 27, 2012.

Madre Selva

Registered with the Ecuadorian Ministry of Tourism and claiming to be an ecotourism operator, Madre Selva offers a whole range of tours for one to five days. Here you can book a day trip to a nearby Kichwa community or opt for a more in-depth six-day/five-night jungle experience to a Huaorani community reachable by small plane. Adventurous types can arrange canyoning, whitewater rafting or zip-lining. Unlike some of the other operators in town, Madre Selva also offers tours to other parts of Ecuador, including to Mindo, Quilotoa, Cotopaxi, Atacames and Cuyabeno Reserve. Daily 9 a.m.-7 p.m. Ca. Ceslao Marin 668 and 9 de Octubre, 2nd floor, in front of Tía Supermarket, Tel: 03-288-9572, Cel: 09-8766-1172, URL: http://madreselvaecuador.com. Updated: Nov 27, 2012.

Things To See and Do in Puyo

Puyo itself does not have a slew of tourist attractions, but it isn't a bad place to spend a day before venturing further into the jungle. While in town, you will probably want to spend most of your time near the Puyo River, rather than in the busier and dirtier town center. You can stroll along the Paseo Turístico Río Puyo, get an introduction to the jungle at Parque Etnobotánico Omaere or visit the impressive Jardín Botánico Las Orquídeas. Just outside of Puyo, on the way to either Tena or Macas, there are waterfalls, jungle viewpoints, caves and animal refuges that you can arrange to visit independently or with a guide. Updated: Jan 23, 2013.

Parque Etnobotánico Omaere !

(ADMISSION: $3) Located about five minutes walking from the northeast edge of Puyo, el Parque Etnobotánico Omaere gives those who do not have enough time to go deeper into the jungle the opportunity to experience an Amazonian forest. The park stretches over 15 hectares (38 acres) and contains an impressive collection of the most important plants to Amazonian indigenous peoples, together with an impressive variety of uncaged birds, butterflies and other animals. Guided walks typically last one to two hours.

Omaere is also culturally enriching, as the guide will explain in traditional houses about the ancestral life of the Shuar and the Waorani (2 tribes that were never conquered) and show some of their artifacts. The admission fee includes a guided tour, making it a great value. The walk may also be in English, especially if reserved. Volunteers are welcome for generally at least a month. Natural medicine is prepared and ecological sanitation is explained. Barrio Obrero: From the Malecón del Río Puyo, cross a metal and

AMAZON BASIN

cement footbridge, continue along the Paseo Turístico del Río Puyo (paved with bricks), past the Flor de Canela Hotel, for 200 meters (656 ft) and it´s just before a metal suspension footbridge. Tel: 03-288-3174/7656, E-mail: omaere@gmail.com, URL: omaere.wordpress.com. Updated: May 14, 2013.

Jardín Botánico Las Orquídeas

(ADMISSION: $5) During your time in Puyo, the Jardín Botánico La Orquideas is a must-add to your travel itinerary. Located in the suburb of Intipungo, which is about a 15-minute car ride from Puyo, this garden has an amazing selection of flora. What really makes this attraction is its owner, Omar Taeyu, who is always eager to share his love of plants with visitors. Daily 8 a.m.-6 p.m. south of Puyo, on road to Macas, Tel: 06-288-4855. Updated: Nov 08, 2012.

Handicrafts

This handicraft co-op is run by women of the Huaorani indigenous community. You'll find a nice array of all sorts of crafts and wares here. Atahualpa and La Marin, on first floor of Hotel Amazonico. Updated: May 10, 2013.

Finca Sarahi

Raised with the "green" and "optimistic" people of the planet in mind, Finca Sarahí is an example of agro- and sustainable tourism happening around Puyo. The main highlight of their property is their enormous and varied collection of fresh-water fish that they exhibit in their aquarium, including the biggest fish in the world (know as paiche, which can grow up to be 5 meters long!). The ironic catch of the whole place? You can go fishing in their exclusive pools filled with tilapia fish to reel in your days' lunch. They provide an onsite restaurant for cooking your catch or simply grabbing an alternative meal as well. For additional fun, there are swimming pools to bathe or relax in as you take in the lush, green scenery of the surrounding amazon jungle. Km. 2 via Shell-Te Zulay-Madre Tierra, Tel: 099-199-5700, URL: www.fincasarahi.com. Updated: May 13, 2013.

Ethno-archaeological Museum

Located within the Youth House of the Municipal Government of the Pastaza province, this little museum presents the history and culture of Puyo along with its inhabitants and the surrounding areas. Focusing mainly on the Tupi Guarani culture that came through the Amazon and later reached Pastaza, you'll still find a number of well preserved archaeological samples and artifacts belonging to the ancestral indigenous tribes from the Amazon region. 9 de Octubre and Atahualpa. Updated: May 13, 2013.

Rio Puyo Malecón

Stroll down this pleasant little strip of pedestrian walkway that runs along - and parallel to - the Puyo River to absorb scenes of the city along with an amazonian backdrop. Best done during the day, given that later at night it might get somewhat unsafe to walk down its path - especially if you're alone. Malecón. Updated: May 13, 2013.

Hola Vida Waterfall

This beautiful waterfall is hidden (but found) a little bit south of Puyo and provides a nice natural setting to come and rest your weary bones by. You can even go for a dip if you're willing to submerge yourself into the chilly waters, and then bathe under the falling cascade. On road to Macas km 16, take road to pomona by Altos de Pastaza.

Puyo Lodging

Puyo has quite a few accommodation options in the town itself, and several more on its outskirts in the jungle. It may be a bit hard to find a dorm bed here, but luckily you can get a private room with a shared or private bathroom and even a TV for just a few dollars more than a dorm bed in many other Ecuadorian towns.

If you shell out a bit more, you can secure a nicer place with a spa and/or pool. Lodges outside of town have the additional benefit of being embedded in beautiful natural surroundings, where you can enjoy more privacy and peacefulness. Updated: Jan 23, 2013.

URBAN LODGING

El Pigual

(ROOMS: $40-200) For what El Pigual offers its guests, it is a bit overpriced. There are other places in the area that offer similar, if not better, accommodations for a much better price. However, if there is nothing else available and you have money to spare, it is not a bad place to end up at all. All rooms, ranging from singles to seven-person family rooms, have private bathrooms with hot water, cable television, telephones and a mini-bar. Most also have their own terraces with hammocks. Those with air conditioning cost a few dollars more. There is also a restaurant, hot tub and pool on-site. End of Ca. Tungurahua s/n, Barrio Obrero, Tel: 3-288-7972/6137, E-mail: elpigual@hotmail.com, URL: www.elpigualecuador.com. Updated: Nov 27, 2012.

Hostal Las Palmas

($15-20 per person) Hostal Las Palmas is a simple and convenient lodging option in Puyo. All rooms have private bathroom, hot water and cable television, and some have big balconies. Cabin-style rooms are a bit more expensive but are roomier and have more furniture. The onsite cafeteria, where the included breakfast is served, also serves drinks and dinner. There is also a natural garden and a couple of social areas with hammocks, which are nice places to relax after a jungle hike. WiFi is available throughout, or you can pay to use the downstairs Internet café. Ca. 20 de Julio and 4 de Enero, Tel: 03-288-4832, Cel: 09-8520-5039. Updated: Nov 27, 2012.

El Jardín !

($35-38 per person) Probably the nicest place to stay in Puyo, El Jardín has achieved a tropical yet sophisticated ambiance. Located on the other side of the swinging footbridge from the Paseo Turístico along the river, El Jardín maintains a relaxing and secluded feel. As the name suggests, the entire place is set within a lush garden, with stone pathways and natural huts that serve as communal areas. One of the highlights of the hotel is the medicinal Japanese baths that are available to all guests. Rooms are large and have either hammocks or outdoor furniture on a balcony. Only one of the rooms is a matrimonial; all the others are doubles and triples with separate beds. The on-site restaurant serves creative and delicious fusion meals. Paseo Turístico del Río Puyo, Barrio Obrero (cross swinging footbridge), Tel: 03-288-7770, E-mail: info@eljardinrelax.com.ec, URL: http://eljardinrelax.com.ec. Updated: Nov 27, 2012.

Posada Real

($30 per person) Posada Real's rooms are cozy and elegantly decorated, with comfortable beds complete with plush linens and pillows. All rooms have cable TV. It is located near the main center of Puyo, making for a short walk to restaurants and shopping, but is far enough away to maintain a quiet, safe and relaxed feel. Other amenities include an on-site garage with security system and laundry service. Out front, there is a nice outdoor patio with tables and couches. Considering the quality, this place is a good-value option. Ca. 4 de Enero and 27 de Febrero, Tel: 03-288-5887, Cel: 09-9510-2430/8400-3340, E-mail: posada_real@hotmail.com, URL: www.posadareal.pastaza.net. Updated: Nov 27, 2012.

Hostería Turingia

(ROOMS: $28-150) Hostería Turingia, which was named after the German city its owners were born in, is a fine accommodation option in Puyo. This modern hotel can accommodate 88 people in 40 different rooms, some in quaint wood-paneled bungalows. Mini-suites and suites are also available for one or two people. All rooms have private bathrooms with hot water, cable TV, WiFi, fan and room service. Turingia also has a restaurant, bar, conference space, pool, Jacuzzi and sauna. Ca. Ceslao Marín 294 and Francisco de Orellana, Tel: 03-288-5180/6344, Fax: 03-288-5384, E-mail: turingia@andinatel.net, URL: www.hosteriaturingia.com. Updated: Nov 27, 2012.

JUNGLE LODGING
Altos del Pastaza Lodge and Reserve

($86 per person) This several-year-old eco-lodge is located on a private 65-hectare (160.6-ac) reserve and has been verified by the Rainforest Alliance for its sustainable practices. Altos del Pastaza offers packages that include accommodations, meals and some guided activities ranging from two days/one night to five days/four nights (longer itineraries can also be arranged). Some activities include walks to natural pools and waterfalls, observation of flora and fauna, and visits to local indigenous communities.

The lodge, built with natural materials and cleaned with eco-friendly products, has 24 rooms with private bathrooms, some with views of the Pastaza River. It also has a swimming pool, restaurant, bar, game and TV room, and several viewpoints. Puyo-Macas road, Km 16, 40 minutes from Puyo, Tel: 09-9168-7130 (English)/09-9767-4686/9876-5653 (Spanish),, E-mail: info@altosdelpastazalodge.com / altosdelpastaza.lodge@yahoo.com, URL: www.altosdelpastazalodge.com. Updated: Nov 27, 2012.

Huella Verde Rainforest Lodge

(ROOMS: $39-108) With capacity for nine people, Cabañas Huella Verde consists of two spacious wooden cabins (one with capacity for four, the other for five). The cabins are spaced nicely away from one another and border on the jungle (expect a wake-up call from monkeys or birds!), each with a large terrace and comfy hammocks. Huella Verde is a bit difficult to get to, as it is a one-kilometer hike outside of Canelos. However, what it lacks in convenience, it makes up for in peaceful seclusion and proximity to wilderness. Plus, the Swiss-Ecuadorian owners are extremely accommodating and will pick you up at the bus station in Canelos free of cost.

The Bobonaza River is just a small walk from the hotel and makes a great place to cool off and relax. There is also a restaurant that serves large, delicious portions of international and local food. Renacer Amazónico, Pitirischka, Canelos, Tel: 03-278-7035, E-mail: christof.tononi@huella-verde.org, URL: www.huella-verde.org.
Updated: Nov 27, 2012.

Kapawi Lodge

($839: 4 days/3 nights - $1509: 8 days/7 nights) Kapawi, one of the more socially responsible and well-known eco-lodges, was founded in 1993 to help the Achuar people, who live in the surrounding area. For years, the lodge was operated by the Achuar people with the aid of outside hotel experts, but on January 1, 2008, total ownership and responsibility for the lodge passed to the Achuar. The lodge is located in Achuar territory, on the Pastaza River near the Peruvian border.

The architecture of Kapawi is Achuar-based: the complex boasts several thatched-roof cabins that are quite solid and comfortable. The rooms are attractive and come with balconies, hammocks, private bath and mosquito netting. The lodge can accommodate up to 50 guests in double and triple cabins. There is also an attractive main lodge with a bar, library and dining room. Kapawi is a true eco-lodge, featuring recycling programs, solar energy and minimal-impact boat motors, to name a few practices.

There are many activities at Kapawi lodge, including bird-watching (540 different species have been seen in the area), hiking, canoe rides, camping and visits to the Achuar communities for you to partake in on any of the days you're there. Quito office: Av. de los Granados E14-958 and Charapa, Edificio Los Granados, office 2A, Tel: 02-600-9333, Fax: 02-600-9334, E-mail: info@kapawi.com, URL: www.kapawi.com.
Updated: Feb 18, 2013

Puyo Restaurants

Puyo does not have a great variety of restaurants. However, there are plenty of places to try reasonably priced local cuisine and traditional Amazonian food. Head to the Malecón Río Puyo if want to sample the city specialty: ceviche volquetero (ceviche made with pieces of tuna, chochos, toasted corn, fried plantain chips and onions). The Malecón has lots of cevicherías and "fuentes de soda" where you can grab a meal along the river. Otherwise, you can settle for one of the fast food or pizza joints, or splurge on one of the delicious fusion dishes at El Jardín.
Updated: Nov 29, 2012.

Kiwa Pishku Micuna

(ENTREES: $3-8) This is a nice little place for food that is customary of the Amazon region, where you'll be sampling exotic endemic fish and soups. It's s a great place to stop by for traditional goodies, especially *maitos de pescado* (fish cooked in banana leaf) and *chicha de yuca* (manioc liquor). The food here is very fresh and well prepared, and is your best bet for sampling some authentic and traditional *oriente* (amazonian) food. Orellana and Amazonas.
Updated: May 14, 2013.

El Jardín

(ENTREES: $7.80-14) El Jardín Restaurant, which is located in the hotel of the same name, is arguably the best place to eat in town. The chef has won awards and strives to create dishes that are both traditional and unique, such as pork chops in plum sauce, tilapia in ginger sauce and chicken in a light cinnamon sauce.

If you would like to sample dishes that are reminiscent of Amazonian cuisine, this is a great place to do so; the food is delicious and very safe to eat. Plus, it has several healthier options. Besides indoor tables, it also has a covered outdoor seating area surrounded by a small garden and stream nearby, making it a relaxing place to enjoy a meal. Open Monday-Saturday noon-4 p.m. and 6-10 p.m. Paseo Turístico del Río Puyo, Barrio Obrero (cross swinging footbridge), Tel: 03-288-7770, E-mail: info(at)eljardinrelax.com.eceljardin-relax.com.ec, URL: eljardinrelax.com.ec.
Updated: Nov 27, 2012.

Pizzería Buon Giorno

(SMALL PIZZA: $5.90-8) Pizzería Buon Giorno is a pizza restaurant chain that can be found throughout Ecuador. It is known for its decent pizzas at relatively good prices, and is a consistently safe option, especially if you are not in the mood for Ecuadorian or Amazonian food. Buon Giorno has many different pizza options and you can customize simpler pizzas by adding extra ingredients for a small extra price. Pizzas come in sizes small and medium only. Salads and lasagnas are alternative menu options. Ca. Francisco de Orellana and 27 de Febrero, Tel: 03-288-3841. Updated: Nov 27, 2012.

MACAS

Macas is located in the eastern part of Ecuador, six hours south of Puyo. This jungle town was founded at the end of the 16th century as a missionary outpost. Today, it serves as a center for exploring the natural and cultural riches of the area.

Macas is in the midst of Shuar territory. Once known as the "head-hunting" Jívaro, these indigenous people allow visits to traditional villages only with approved guides, in order to learn about their misunderstood culture. At the confluence of the Kapawari and Pastaza rivers is the Kapawari Ecological Reserve, working in cooperation with the local community. The Achuar-styled complex is set in an area rich in biodiversity, and is reached by plane and canoe.

Tour agencies may arrange short or long treks into the jungle or Sangay National Park, whitewater rafting on the Río Upano, or other adventures. A few kilometers north, on the Cupueno River, is La Cascada, which offers great swimming, a water slide and a picnic area.

Macas offers an alternative route into the cultural and natural richness of the Ecuadorian Oriente. Whether to visit a Shuar community, or merely to gaze upon Sangay glowing on the horizon, a visit to this town promises to be unforgettable.

When To Go to Macas

Macas' higher altitude makes it a bit cooler than other destinations in the Amazon basin. Daytime highs only reach 25-28°C (77-82°F), and at night it drops to 12-14°C (54-57°F). It receives 2,414 millimetres (95 in) of rain per year. Although it rains every month, the wettest ones are April-July. Expect less precipitation December-February.

Besides the holidays celebrated in other parts of Ecuador – Carnaval, Semana Santa,

Christmas and New Year's Eve – Macas has a few of its own festivities. This city fêtes its patron saint, the Virgen Purísima de Macas, on February 18 (when it is called "Fiesta Jurada") and August 5. On February 12 is Día del Oriente Ecuatoriano.

Macas' founding is observed May 23-29, with civic and military parades, as well as cultural and folkloric events.
Updated: Oct 08, 2012.

Getting To and Away from Macas

It is possible to fly to Macas, a trip that takes 45 minutes. Tame offer flights every day except Saturday at 09:30 in the morning, arriving at 10:15. The return journey leaves on the same days at 17:00 and is the same duration. Buses run to Quito a couple of times per day and the journey takes around ten hours. Buses also run to nearby towns such as Sucua, and some buses head to other parts of the Oriente such as Puyo and Tena.
The Terminal Terrestre is situated on Amazonas and 10 de Agosto.

Macas Limitada (tel. 270-0869) goes to **Cuenca** (7 hours, $8.50) at 11:15 p.m., 11:45 p.m., 12:20 a.m., to **Guayaquil** (10 hours, $10) at 8:40 p.m. and 11 p.m., to **Quito** at midnight, to **San Luis** (1 hour, $0.50) at 7 a.m., 10 a.m., 11 a.m., 1 p.m., 4 p.m., to **San Isidro** (30 minutes, $0.25), at 5.30 a.m., 7 a.m., 9 a.m., noon, 1:45 p.m., 4 p.m.

Turismo Oriental (tel. 270-0159) goes to **Cuenca** via **Guarumales** at 7 a.m., 8 a.m., 11:30 a.m., 12:40 p.m., 4 p.m., 8 p.m., 9 p.m., 10 p.m., 11 p.m., to **Cuenca** via **Limon** at 5 a.m. and 5:30 p.m.

Transportes **Baños** (tel. 270-3111) go to Quito (7 hours, $8) at 10:30 p.m. and 2 a.m.

Cooperativa Sucua (tel. 270-0396) goes to **Guaraquiza** (8 hours, $8), at 12:30 p.m. and 10:40 p.m., to **Morona** ($8) at 9:45 a.m., 5:45 p.m., to **Cuenca** ($8) at 3:30 a.m., 5:30 a.m., 2:30 p.m., 8:30 p.m. and 10:30 p.m.

Compañia Riobamba (tel. 270-1381) goes to **Riobamba** (5 hours, $5) at 7 a.m. and 4 p.m., and to **Guayaquil** (9 to 10 hours, $10) via **Riobamba** at 3 a.m., 10 a.m., 1 p.m. and 9 p.m.

Centinale del Oriente (tel. 270-2490) goes to **Puyo** ($5) at 6:30 a.m., 8:30 a.m., 9:30

a.m., 10:30 a.m., 11:30 a.m., 1:30 p.m., 4 p.m., 7 p.m. and to Quito ($8) via Puyo in coche cama (reclining seats) at 11 p.m., to **Tena** ($7.50) at 9:30 a.m. and 1:30 p.m.

Cooperativa San Francisco (tel. 270-0995) goes to **Puyo** ($5) at 7 a.m., 10 a.m. and 2 p.m., to **Guayaquil** ($12) via **Puyo** at 6 p.m., to **Quito** ($8) via **Puyo** at 3 a.m., 12:30 p.m., 8 p.m. and 9 p.m., to **Riobamba** at 5 a.m. and 1 p.m.

Orientur goes to **Yaupi** ($6.50) at noon, to **Limon** ($3.75) at 4.40 p.m., to **Mendez** ($2.50) at 1:45 p.m., to **Gualaquiza** ($8) at 6:40 p.m.

Valle del Lupano (tel. 270-1095) goes to **Mendez** ($2.50) at 11:15 a.m. and 3:30 p.m., to **Logroño** ($1.80) at 10:30 a.m. and 1:30 p.m., to **Yaupi** ($6.50) at 8:50 p.m. Updated: Mar 25, 2013.

Things To See and Do in Macas

Tienda Fundación Chankuap

This fair trade shop founded by a Salesian father distributes crafts and organic food products made by the Shuar and Achuar communities of the Morona province. All the cosmetics and herbal infusions are made from aromatic plants picked in the Amazon basin, and the jewelry incorporates seeds, feathers and natural fibers as well as tagua (vegetal ivory). Also on sale are brightly colored woven bags, wooden spears, jams, coffee, cheese, spices and much more, all at very reasonable prices. Bolívar, between Soasty and 24 de Mayo (behind Banco de Fomento), Tel: 07-270-1176.
Updated: Feb 19, 2013.

Museo Arqueológico Municipal

This small museum has a small collection of artifacts. They are not presented in the most attractive manner, but they are interesting. There is a collection of feather adornment and headdresses, blowpipes, baskets and a replica of a shrunken head. If you happen to be in Parque Recreacional on a weekday it is worth a stop in, after all it is free.
Updated: May 21, 2013.

Cathedral

This massive modern church gives its visitors a nice view of the city. The building also features twelve elaborate stained glass windows which depict the store of the Virgen Purísima de Macas. The cathedral, which was completed in 1992, was constructed to celebrate the 400 year anniversary of this Virgen. At the back of the church one can see the Pio Upano valley, and a number of swallows swooping by. Near Parque Central.
Updated: Mar 13, 2013.

Huerto Eden wildlife rescue center

(ADMISSION: $2) Just four kilometers (2.5 mi) outside Macas, in a lovely five-hectare (12.3-ac) park, retired veterinarian Dr. Vázquez and his family have created a wildlife sanctuary for all the wild animals that were once bought as pets and then discarded: turtles, parrots, a dozen different monkeys, a coati, a couple of boas, an ocelot, a young puma, a capybara (the world's largest rodent) and more. The animals, all species native to the Amazon basin, are tended to, then when rehabilitated, are set free again in the forest, though a few of the smaller monkeys and parrots are simply too adapted to domestic life and stick around the center where they roam free. When taking you on a tour of the place, the owners will call each animal by its name, and while explaining about the creature's mating and feeding habits, will regale you with tales about the animal's individual character. Doctor and Señora Vázquez are also very knowledgeable about the flora of the area, and will point out the cinnamon trees, cocoa pods and other plants in the park. Proaño, Km 4.5 de la Vías a San Isidro, 300 metros (984 ft) from Proaño's central park, Tel: 07-304-5227.
Updated: Feb 19, 2013.

Parque Nacional Sangay

Parque Nacional Sangay, which almost doubled in size in 1992 with the addition of 245,000 hectares to the south, includes vast tracts of high-altitude páramo and lush, lower-level cloud forest. Its original, northern section is listed as a World Heritage site. Within the park and (more specifically) around the area of the Sangay Volcano, there exists one of the last sizeable refuges for the mountain, or woolly mountain tapir.

This species is listed as endangered and until the last two decades, the area supported a healthy population. Hunting is the major cause of the population decline, despite the laws prohibiting it. Many areas of the park are beginning to open up to hikers, with the implementation of new guidelines and services by the parks department. For now though, Volcán Sangay, Tungurahua (in Baños) and El Altar, all in the western zone of the park, remain the primary attractions for park visitors. Although information can

AMAZON BASIN

be obtained about the park in Quito at the Ministerio de Ambiente offices or at Fundacíon Natura, the main office for the park is located in Aloa. There should also be guard stations in Aloa (Volcán Sangay, El Placer), Atillo (Guamote-Macas Trail), Candelaria (El Altar), Pondoa (Tungurahua), and Río Negro (cloud forest). For more information about Parque Nacional Sangay, see the Ecuador: Climbing and Hiking Guide.
Updated: Sep 2012.

Hiking El Altar

El Altar, the fifth highest mountain in Ecuador, undoubtedly involves some of the most technical climbing and has one of the longest approaches. El Altar is an extinct volcano which at one time was probably higher than Cotopaxi, but a huge ancient eruption almost totally destroyed the cone, leaving a steep-sided and jagged crater three kilometers in diameter. Despite repeated attempts by many climbers, the icy ramparts of El Altar withstood all assaults until July 7, 1963, when an Italian expedition led by Marino Tremonti conquered the last unclimbed 5,000-meter (16, 405 ft) mountain in Ecuador. For more information on this climbing El Altar, see the Ecuador: Climbing and Hiking Guide.
Updated: Sep 2012.

Macas Lodging

Macas is a fairly large city in southeastern Ecuador, and offers a great starting off point for an Amazon expedition. In Macas, accommodations don't vary to widely in terms of price or quality, and most find a happy medium between budget and luxury. However, you will find some places that offer amenities such as spas and pools, and other ones that are barely passable. However, there are plenty of options and if you're dissatisfied with one, you can always head down the street.
Updated: Jul 12, 2013.

Cabañas del Valle

($15-20 per person) The Cabañas del Valle, just on the outskirts of Macas, are ideal for groups, large families or events. The nine functional cabins, all with private bathrooms, hot water and TVs, can accommodate between three and six people. Choose carefully, though, since the mattresses range from spongy to hard; the rooms at the rear of the building have wooden floors and are more cheerful. There is a swimming pool and a large restaurant area, as well as slides and a ping-pong table. Judy and Marcelo, the friendly owners, also run a travel agency that organizes rafting and hiking trips, as well as visits to the nearby Shuar communities. Av. 29 de Mayo, Km 1.5 on the road to Cuenca, Tel: 07-232-2393/2396, E-mail: hosteriadelvalle@yahoo.com / cabanasdelvalle@gmail.com, URL: www.hosteriacabanasdelvalle.com.
Updated: Feb 19, 2013.

Casa Blanca

($15-20 per person) The Casa Blanca, is as the name suggests, a white building. It offers 13 rooms set across two floors. The hotel has a fairly decent restaurant, and breakfast is included in the price. Casa Blanca is centrally positioned and convenient for local eateries and Internet cafés. Soasti and Sucre, Tel: 07-270-0195, Fax: 07-270-1584, E-mail: jsamaniego_75@yahoo.com.
Updated: Feb 19, 2013.

Hotel Heliconia

($13-30 per person) Just one block from the bus terminal, Hotel Heliconia is a decent and convenient choice. The six-story building has a bright yellow exterior and a number of the rooms have balconies facing onto the street. The hotel has 23 rooms with hot water and private bathrooms. The friendly and helpful staff are able to speak English to some degree. The hotel also offers a number of useful amenities, including a restaurant serving regional cuisine, a garage, Internet and telephone service. Ca. Soasti and 10 de Agosto, Tel: 07-270-1956, Fax: 07-270-0441.
Updated: Feb 19, 2013.

Manzana Real

(ROOMS: $20-35) The Manzana Real is located away from the center of things, but is well equipped, including facilities such as a hydromassage, a sauna, a swimming pool and a gym. The place has 26 well-appointed, pleasantly furnished rooms, and the hotel offers Internet to guests. You've got it all here–have a swim before dinner, eat in the on-site restaurant and then dance off the calories in the hotel's discotheque. The hotel also offers parking to guests, which is just as well, given its location. Cap. de Villanueva and Sor María Troncati, Tel: 07-270-0191, Fax: 07-270-2728, E-mail: gerencia@hmreal.com, URL: www.hmreal.com.
Updated: Feb 19, 2013.

Macas Restaurants and Nightlife

If you're cruising the streets of Macas with an empty stomach, you will find that there are few real dining options, apart from street food. There are a couple of Chinese and Ital-

ian places, but your best bet is to follow the locals, in which case you will find yourself filling up at the carb-heavy Napolitana or at the Sports Café Bar and Grill, or chilling at the warm and friendly Maravilla, just next door on Soasti.
Updated: Mar 13, 2013.

Balcón del Río

Balcón del Río, located a 15-minute drive from town, features a large terrace and pool, a mini zip-line, a swing, a sauna and a bar. At night, the large area beneath the rotunda turns into a full night club, with disco ball and strobe lights, where the young and not-so-young of Macas strut their stuff to the sound of loud salsa, bachata and reggaeton. Road to Puyo, Km 5, sector de Las Flores, Tel: 07-270-2508, Cel: 09-9317-0649/9244-1723, E-mail: balcondelrio@gmail.com. Updated: Feb 14, 2013.

La Maravilla

(ENTREES: $2.50-8) The aptly named La Maravilla ("the marvel") is undoubtedly one of the best places to have a drink and snack in Macas. Set in a fairy tale-like wooden house, the friendly and inviting café/bar is decorated with indigenous artifacts and photos from the region. Sitting on the small veranda or in the warm glow of the lamps inside, you can order plates of cheese and other snacks para picar (to pick on). The meat dishes are served with yucca and are very reasonably priced; the restaurant also has hot and cold drinks, including guayusa, a traditional infusion that can come spiked with a shot of cane alcohol. There even is a room for playing cards. Ca. Soasti and Sucre, across from Hostal Casa Blanca, Tel: 07-270-0158, URL: www.facebook.com/MaravillaGuayusabar. Updated: Feb 14, 2013.

La Napolitana

La Napolitana is a vast restaurant and is a good choice if you're ravenous. The restaurant is patronized by families and by Macas teenagers, who wolf down pizzas the size of cartwheels and then wash them down with bottles of soda. On the menu are also mega-parilladas (huge BBQ meat platters) ($42), to share between five people, or filling dishes like pastas or rice with shrimp. The fish (tilapia, trout or sea bass) comes highly recommended. Service is rather slow, though. Av. Amazonas between 29 de Mayo and Tarqui, Tel: 07-270-0486, E-mail: lanapolitanamacas@gmail.com, URL: www.lanapolitanamacas.com. Updated: Feb 14, 2013.

Sports café, bar and grill / Tutto Freddo

(ENTREES: $3-8) Don't be put off by the neon signs and annoying TV screens, this restaurant/ice-cream-parlor is a great place to satisfy any sugar craving. If you can muster the patience for the excruciatingly slow and despairingly clumsy service, the diner at the back serves decent pollo a la plancha, (but avoid the lasagnas, obviously industrially-made and served in an aluminum dish which ruins the taste), and a selection of sweet pancakes and ice-cream sundaes so wide that the desserts menu unfolds like a roadmap. For a lighter (and faster) treat, head to the Tutto Freddo counter, which offers a dozen different flavors of helados, including "quita pena", a rum and raisin cream. Soasti and Bolivar.
Updated: Mar 13, 2013.

The Northern Coast and Lowlands

Few that visit Ecuador come solely to see the beach, however, those who find themselves with time to head to the coast will find that the region boasts some of the world's most diverse rain forests and cloud forests, uncrowded beaches, tiny fishing villages, the ruins of ancient civilizations, and a cultural richness much different than the other regions of Ecuador.

The Northern Coast, which is filled with lush green vegetation, is considerably closer to Quito than the cities of the Southern Coast. In addition to this, the drive to the beach goes past some fascinating cities. Mindo, for instance, is internationally renowned for its bird watching. Santo Domingo is a sprawling transportation hub which itself is nothing spectacular, but nearby indigenous sites prove to be very interesting.

Popular destinations on the actual coast include Atacames, which is known for its lively nightlife and Canoa, which has a really chill surfer scene, spectacular sunsets over the ocean and some phenomenal cuisine. If you want surf and sun without the crowds, Mompiche is an excellent choice, offering big waves, beautiful beaches and an ultra-relaxed atmosphere. The larger cities of the area, such as Esmeraldas and Manta are less popular with visitors, mainly due to their dirty industrial feel, but serve as highly important starting points for many travelers due to their airports and bus terminals.
Updated: Apr 05, 2013.

When To Go

Winter is typically from January to May, when rains are more common and – contrary to the season's name - the heat tends to go up (25-30 C) rather than down. Summertime lasts from June to December, which is when you'll find temperatures cooling off (20-25 C). September to November, and then starting again in April up until the end of June is low-season for accommodations along the coast.

Semana Santa (Holy Week, last week of March) provides tourists with a chance to experience Danza Afro (African-inspired dance), music and traditional food in Esmeraldas. Mid-August offers a similar spectacle, except that this time you'll find Esmeraldeños selecting and parading their beauty queen around town. Carnaval (mid-February) is peak season for the Coast, a

many Ecuadorians from the highlands flock to the beaches to soak themselves in sun and water - both inside the ocean and out on the streets with water balloons.
Updated: Apr 05, 2013.

MINDO

 2,400m  2,500   02

Mindo is set in breathtaking cloud forests (including 47,444 acres of the nationally protected reserve, Bosque Protector Mindo-Nambillo) teeming with birds. Over 350 species have been identified in the areas around Mindo alone. Tubing is a popular activity on the low-level rapids, as well as waterfalls, which are ideal for snapping photos, wading in the nearby pools and jumping into the icy waters just below the falls – a 10 m (33 ft) leap!

One of the most ecologically-aware towns in Ecuador, Mindo has recently seen a huge tourist boom. Weekends bring an increase in visitors- make sure you have reservations! Holidays and long weekends will often find the road entering Mindo with bumper-to-bumper traffic. As a result, the town exists almost entirely on tourism. Many private homes will paint a sign "Hostal" and hang it on their fence, offering rooms for really decent prices.

A strong local government and an even stronger common awareness of ecology and environmental protection have so far saved Mindo from exploiting this tourist niche too far. Much of the tourist activities here work to promote ecologically-aware activities.
Updated: Apr 12, 2013.

When To Go to Mindo

Mindo is small and very popular; therefore, it is essential to plan your trip right, or you may be stuck in stopped traffic before you even get in the entrance to town. The high tourist season is from July to October and holiday weekends, when Quiteños flee the city en masse in search of some fresh air. The climate in Mindo tends to be milder than the weather in Quito, with temperatures ranging from about 15°C – 24°C (60°F – 75°F) year-round. Rain storms are common, so bring proper gear. There is no true dry season, but the climate tends to be driest from May until the end of September.

NORTHERN COAST

Loved it? Loathed it? Write a review and help other travelers

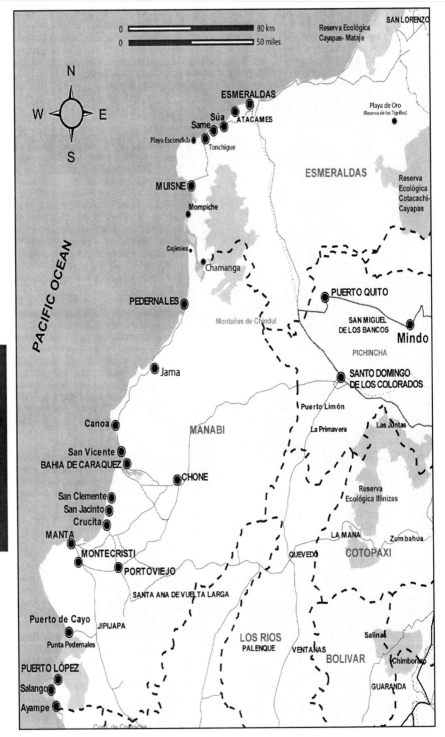

The Northern Coast and Lowlands Highlights

Mindo (*p. 337-348*): A paradise in the cloud forest, Mindo is a nature-lovers dream, and has some of the best bird-watching in all of South America. Stay at one of the lodges on the town's outskirts and indulge in outdoorsy activities like tubing or zip-lining, visit one of the orchid gardens or butterfly farms, or take a tour of a local organic chocolate producer.

Visit a Tsáchila Community (*p. 350*): One of the most offbeat yet interesting experiences near Santo Domingo, visiting a Tsáchila community gives insight into the lifestyle and shamanistic rituals of a distinct indigenous group of the region. Tsáchila men are most recognized for dying their hair red with native achiote seeds.

Canoa (*p. 383-389*): A favorite destination for foreigners and Ecuadorians alike, Canoa has the perfect balance of relaxed beach bum atmosphere and liveliness. Its long stretch of beach is lined with brightly colored tents that provide shade from the sometimes blistering sun, and beach-side cabañas serve cervezas alongside some of the most delicious food on the coast.

Mompiche (*p. 371-376*): This once-sleepy fishing village is now a haven for surfers and hippies from all over the world. Yet it continues to maintain its rustic charm, with just a few basic bungalows providing accommodation in town. The beach itself is encircled by palm trees and emerald green forests, and the neighboring untouched beach El Portete is reachable via a long dirt road and a brief canoe ride.

Playa Escondida (*p. 369*): A secluded beach along a beautiful bay, this hidden retreat is located within a 100-hectare (247-ac) ecological refuge meant to protect the surrounding area from threats to its fauna and flora. With capacity for just 30 people and the option of camping, Playa Escondida is an intimate escape from the more crowded and touristy beaches nearby.

Fiestas de Mindo (Mindo's yearly city celebration) begins the second weekend in May and goes until the end of the month. The festivities begin with the election of a city beauty queen (La Reina de Mindo) in the town convention center, just off the main drag near El Rincon del Río restaurant. Updated: Apr 11, 2013.

Getting To and Away from Mindo

If you have access to a private car, or don't mind paying up to $45 for one-way private transportation, the drive to Mindo is beautiful. There are lots of places to stop along the way, like the **Pululahua Volcano**, the Bellavista Lodge and nature reserve and a handful of lookout points.

However, if you're on a budget, taking a bus to Mindo is a convenient and inexpensive option. The only buses that go directly into the town of Mindo are called Cooperativo **Flor de Valle** (also known as Cayambe buses, but be sure the bus isn't headed to Cayambe, as this is in the complete wrong direction) and leave from **Ofelia** in northern Quito. Ofelia can be reached on the Metrobus (at a

NORTHERN COAST

Loved it? Loathed it? Write a review and help other travelers

cost of $0.25, Ofelia is the last stop) or in taxi at the cost of $4- 5 from central Quito.

The bus schedule is as follows:

QUITO – MINDO
Monday – Friday: 8a.m., 9a.m., 4p.m.
Saturday: 7:40a.m., 8:20a.m., 9:20a.m., 4p.m.
Sunday: 7:40a.m., 8:20a.m., 9:20a.m., 2p.m., 3p.m.

MINDO – QUITO
Monday – Friday: 6:30a.m., 1:45p.m., 3p.m.
Saturday: 6:30a.m., 2p.m., 3p.m., 5p.m.
Sunday: 6:30a.m., 2p.m., 3p.m., 4p.m., 5p.m.

These buses tend to fill up, so it is smart to get to the station at least 10 minutes early or you might not get a seat. The Mindo station, located on the main drag across from the grocery store, is open Monday to Friday from 6 to 6:30 am, from 9 am to 12 pm and from 1:30 to 6:30 pm. On Saturdays and Sundays, the office is open until 7 pm.

If you miss these buses, buses from the Terminal Terrestre **Carcelén** (main bus station in Northern Quito) leave about every 2 hours headed to the coast by way of Los Bancos. The main companies that run this line are: Cooperativa Kennedy, Cooperativa San Pedro, and Cooperativa Aloag.

The disadvantage of using this option is that you have to request your bus driver to let you off at the turn-off to Mindo. The road into Mindo is all downhill, but is a long hike, so if you aren't in the mood for a good hour of walking, hitchhike or try to hail a cab (good luck!).

Several hotels will pick you up for an extra cost if you let them know well in advance when you are arriving, so call ahead. Sometimes caminonetas (private trucks) park at the top of the road and pack everyone for the rest of the trip down into town. The ride costs $1, but hop in quickly if you want a seat in the cab rather than in the truck bed.
Updated: Jan 12, 2013

Things To See and Do in Mindo

Most of the activities in Mindo take advantage of its spectacular natural setting and rich variety of flora and fauna. If you are in search of a little adrenaline, there's plenty of outdoor activities to do that are sure to get you your fix. With a little bartering too,

sometimes, you can even get discounts on big groups.

Bird watchers, nature lovers, and people interested in learning a little more about flora and fauna in the area can hire a local biologist guide either through their hotel, an international or Quiteño travel agency. If you choose to find a guide locally, you probably won't be able to get a bilingual guide, but you will learn a lot about local politics and life. Among the rare bird species spotted in Mindo are the toucan-barbet, the cock-of-the-rock and the golden-headed quetzal.

El Quetzal de Mindo Chocolate Tour

(PRICE: $5) Just short walk up above the town, you'll find this coy little restaurant that specializes in all sorts of cacao-based treats and baked goodies to delight in. The tour is a basic overview of the cacao-making process (from pod all the way to the nibs and finally - the exquisite fudge, ranging from 60-100%).

The tour, while short, does portray an interesting glimpse into the modest cacao operation that they have running up in Mindo (apparently the only one), and it's still quite a treat to get to sample every step that goes into making the final piece of chocolate. Prepare yourself for the exquisite bonus at the end, which involves sampling all sorts of cacao-based syrups, percentages and a deliciously moist brownie. 9 de Octubre, Mindo. Walk to the lowest corner of the park and head up the dirt/cement road that goes upwards into the jungle above. Tel: 02-217-0034, E-mail: info@elquetzaldemindo.com, URL: www.elquetzaldemindo.com.
Updated: April 12, 2013

Horseback Riding
Horseback riding can also be done in Mindo, although quality of horses is often questionable, inquire at any one of the Hostels for more information.
Updated: Apr 12, 2013.

Cable Car (Tarabita)
(ADMISSION: $5) A ride on the *tarabita* (cable car) from one mountainside to another costs $5 per person if you just want a round-trip ride. It offers excellent photo opportunities and spectacular views of the cloud forest and river surrounding Mindo, as well as providing access to a private reserve on the other side, with paths that lead all the way down to the waterfall.
Updated: Apr 12, 2013.

NORTHERN COAST

Biking

(RENTALS: $8 per day) Bike rentals are available at several different spots around town. You can bike to the waterfalls on two different paths – one mostly uphill, and one a little longer but less difficult.
Updated: Apr 12, 2013.

Tubing

(ADMISSION: $5-7) Tubing is a popular sport and involves reclining on several inner tubes tied together with rope down the mellow rapids on Río Mindo. The price includes the drive up to the launch point, helmet, guide, life jacket and, of course, the tubes. Inquire at any of the Hostels around town for more information.
Updated: Apr 12, 2013.

Mariposario

(ADMISSION: $6) The Mariposario (Butterfly Farm) is 3 km (2 miles) outside of town on the road headed to the waterfall, along natural paths and a few hotels.
Updated: Apr 12, 2013.

Orchid Garden

(ADMISSION: $2) The Mindo Orchid Garden is a private collection of plants replanted from the nearby cloud forest. There are over 200 orchids on display, some large and easily-spottable, others so tiny you need a magnified glass to find them.

When entering the garden, you'll pay the small admission fee at a rickety shack for admittance to the garden and rental of a magnified glass. A guide—usually Hugolindo, the owner of the garden—will give you a private tour, explaining the names of each of the orchids and some of their key characteristics. His garden is truly a labor of love, and he beams proudly whenever travelers stop to snap pictures of the flowers. Tours are only conducted in Spanish, but if you only know a little bit you can just smile, nod, and take pictures. The Orchid Garden is located just behind the soccer field, easily walkable from the center of town.
Updated: Feb 08, 2013.

Canopy Tour ♪

(ADMISSION: $15) If you like the idea of flying above and across Mindo's cloud forest, like a modern-day Tarzan, a canopy tour is definitely for you. Canopy Adventures, a company with over 10 years' experience in Costa Rica, has installed a circuit of 11 different zip lines spanning the valleys and hills above Mindo. Securely harnessed to the cable, you literally zip along, at a height varying from three to 120 meters (9.8-394 ft), just above the treetops, from one platform to the next. For an extra rush, try doing the headfirst "Superman" or the upside-down "mariposa" while harnessed to a guide. The total length of the circuit is 3,500 meters (11,483 ft) and takes between 1.5 and 2 hours, depending on the crowds. The ride is open to kids from age 5 and up. Km 2.5 vía las Cascadas, Tel: 09-9453-0624/09-8542-8758, URL: www.mindocanopy.com.
Updated: Apr 16, 2013.

Mindo to Lloa Trek

This is a two-day trek for hikers and perhaps a four-day trek for birders and botanists. The eruptions of Guagua Pichincha between 1999 and 2002 have altered parts of this trail, and there is a risk of debris flow if Guagua becomes active; check for current conditions on the trail before hiking. The route takes you from the agricultural town of Lloa through cloud forest into western slope rainforest, skirting the southern edge of Bosque Protector Mindo-Nambillo. There has been some clearing in the river valleys for cattle, but a large amount of primary forest remains.

In the late 1980s a road was planned and partially constructed for this route, but it was abandoned when it became clear that the construction maintenance costs due to unstable slopes and frequent landslides were not worth the benefits that the road would provide. Undoubtedly the area would have been deforested if the road had been constructed and, hopefully, the road will never be completed. There is plenty of water, but remember to treat it. You quickly drop to warmer elevations, so one sweater is probably sufficient, but proper rain gear is essential. The trail is very muddy, so rubber boots are recommended. Check out the V!VA Ecuador: Climbing and Hiking Guide for more information on this route.
Updated: Apr 12, 2013.

Cascadas Hike ♪

One of the few good hiking opportunities around Mindo can be found at the waterfalls tour a few kilometers out of town. You reach the beginning of the path by zipping over the valley in the cable car (tarabita), an exhilarating ride which offers grand views of the cloud forest and of the river snaking below. When you reach the other mountainside, you can turn right on a path towards the Cascada Reina, the area's largest waterfall. As the guides will tell you, the hike takes one hour to get there and one hour to get back. Along the rather slippery path (wear appropriate foot gear), you can see many butterflies, giant caterpillars, bromelias, as well as birds flying through the thick forest.

The other hike, to left from the tarabita platform, is much shorter (under 30 minutes) and will take you to the Sanctuario de Cascadas and to the Cascada Nambillo. You can take a very refreshing dip in the ice-cold pools beneath all of the waterfalls, but watch your toes – it is not easy keeping your balance on the rocks while the current drags at you. Updated: Mar 19, 2012.

Frog Concert

(ADMISSION: $4.50) One of the activities you might hear about during your stay in Mindo is the area's "frog concert." This show takes place nightly at 6:30 p.m., just outside of town at a lodge called Mindo Lago. While the event has an enticing title, the concert unfortunately does not actually involve any frogs putting on a performance. Instead, you take an hour-long walking tour, lit by flashlight. The tour starts by visiting a frog pool, then proceeds around the lake into the woods, where the knowledgeable guide explains all about the flora and fauna of the cloud forest.

The guide can even show you an unbelievable fungus that makes rotting wood naturally glow in the dark, frog-eating spiders, armadillo holes, giant crickets, and a species of lightning bug that has glowing eyes. The tour concludes back at the lodge, overlooking the lake, with a complimentary glass of wine.

As an introduction to the cloud forest, the tour may be worth checking out; Mindo does not offer much else in the way of nightlife. The best time to go is shortly after or during rain, when all the frogs come out to sing. Mindo Lago Hostería, Tel: 02-217-0201/254-7139, Cel: 09-9709-3544, URL: www.mindolago.com.ec. Updated: Jan 28, 2013.

Mindo Tours

A strong local government and an even stronger common awareness of ecology and environmental protection have so far saved Mindo from exploiting this tourist niche too much. A lot of the tourist activities work to promote ecologically-aware activities, and typically involves a healthy dose of adventure (hiking, walking) and nature guides thrown into the mix.

Verdecocha Expeditions

Verdecocha, just an hour from Quito on the Nono-Mindo road, is a playground for bird-watchers and nature lovers. Verdecocha is located on a private reserve at the head of the "Paseo del Quinde" route. The Verdecocha Expeditions—organized by a foundation of the same name—arranges horseback riding, mountain biking and llama trekking tours with round-trip transportation from Quito. The reserve contains an incredibly rich biodiversity that you can view from trails that loop past waterfalls, thermal baths, prairies and riverbeds. Quito Office: Murgeón OE3-236 and Av. America, Tel: 02-255-1508/254-8939, Fax: 02-225-6348, E-mail: funubesierra@verdecocha.com, URL: www.verdecocha.com. Updated: Jan 29, 2013.

Mindo Bird Tours

Mindo Bird Tours is completely devoted to providing birders with the best possible experience. It leads tours in Mindo and throughout Ecuador, as well as all over South America. The guides are knowledgeable about wildlife and are bird-watching experts. The company is very flexible, able to provide guides and transportation for as little as one person on one day up to large groups for a month. The scheduled tours generally have less than 10 participants. Mindo Bird Tours also offers tours where participants can view rare butterflies in their natural habitats. Quito office: Av. Brasil N45-283 and Zamora, Tel: 09-9735-1297, E-mail: mindobirds@gmail.com, URL: www.mindobirds.com.ec. Updated: Jan 29, 2013.

Mindo Lodging

A popular destination for birdwatchers and outdoor lovers, tourists and locals alike are drawn to Mindo, Ecuador. Hotel and hostel accommodations are easy to come by here. This small town offer lodging for everyone from people just looking to get out of Quito for a weekend or hardcore birders and outdoor enthusiasts. Sited as one of the most ecologically friendly places in Ecuador, there are no shortages of eco-lodges and environmentally friendly lodgings.

Weekends are busy for Mindo hotels and hostel so it's a good idea to make reservations before you go. During holidays and long weekends several private homes open up to visitors. You can spot these places by looking for the sign that says "Hostal." Updated: Apr 11, 2013.

NORTHERN COAST

BUDGET

Dragonfly Inn

(ROOMS: $27-82) With beautiful woodwork and clean, ample rooms, the Dragonfly Inn is a perfect blend between rustic and modern with great views and sounds of the river and forest (if staying on the appropriate side of the hostel). Conveniently located right on the mainstreet of town, the inn gives you quick and easy access to touring the greater part of the village and surrounding areas. In addition, it has plenty of hummingbirds that pay a near-continuous visit to it (thanks to the numerous birdfeeders). Only drawback for some travellers might be the noise that comes in off the mainstreet and other rooms, due to thin walls. This problem is easily circumvented though by simply getting a room that faces the stream and forest, if there are any available. Added bonus is the impressive movie collection available to guests. Main street, Tel: 02-217-0426 / 099-238-2189, E-mail: DragonflyInn.Mindo@gmail.com, URL: www.dragonflyinn-mindo.com/index.html. Updated: Apr 16, 2013.

Cabañas Bambu

(ROOMS: $15-80) Cabanas Bambu is an incredibly clean and immaculate place to stay in the middle of Mindo's cloud forest, just a 5 minute taxi ride ($2) from town. This haven is a place ideal for travelers looking to soak in the tranquility, silence and the nature embellishing it. With access to Wi-fi in the middle of a cloudforest, along with a pool and jacuzzi, this is a remarkable little piece of lodging not to be passed up on, even if its just a little out of the way. 800 meters away from the village, Tel: 02-217-0216 / 099-969-1213, URL: http://www.hotelbambuecuador.com/pages/mindo.html. Updated: Apr 16, 2013.

Birdwatcher's House

(ROOMS: $15-20) The Birdwatcher's House was designed as a place to relax. It has a central location with easy access to Mindo's bus stop and all of the area's major birding sites, up slope and down slope. Comfortable, secure and clean single and double rooms have private bathrooms, Jacuzzi and hot showers. Meals are served according to birders' schedules; box meals and snacks available, and vegetarian or other diet restrictions can be catered to. Av. Los Colibris, El Progreso Neighborhood, Tel: 02-217-0204, Cel: 09-9947-6867, E-mail: birdwatcher-tower@hotmail.com, URL: www.birdwatchershouse.com. Updated: Apr 20, 2013.

La Casa de Cecilia ♪

($8-10 per person) Tucked away on a dirt path a few minutes south of the plaza, La Casa de Cecilia is a clean and cozy lodge. This place is a real steal for the budget traveler. Its main lodge and cabins are spread along a rocky riverside, and the river's rushing waters provide a soothing soundtrack to travelers lounging in one of the balcony's hammocks. The main lodge has several rooms to accommodate singles or groups. Across the street are two cabins that cater more to families and couples (ask for the matrimonial). Rooms either have shared or private bathrooms, all of which have hot water. Cecilia whips up breakfast for $2-3.50 each morning in the open-air restaurant. Laundry service, luggage storage and activity/excursion tips are all available. Two blocks past the plaza. Turn left at the fork in the road., Tel: 09-9334-5393. Updated: Jan 28, 2013.

Hostal Melyang

($8 per person) Hostal Melyang (also know as Tia Mely), is a clean, friendly, family-run bargain, with cheap rooms with private bath. The rustic building boasts an impressive tropical garden sprinkled with tables, chairs and hammocks. Beware: the walls are thin, and the hotel can get quite loud. If you're worried about noisy neighbors, this may not be the place for you.

They have beautiful murals painted on the walls, so it's worth it for people to go there to see the murals. It is clean, private bathrooms with hot showers in each room. Av. Quito 260 across from "Colegio Tecnico Ecuador de Mindo," just on your left as you enter Mindo by bus. From the bus station, backtrack several blocks, across the bridge and up the hill, and you find that the hostel will be on your right. Updated: Apr 11, 2013.

El Descanso ♪

($12-16 per person) Located off the main drag (to the right if you are entering from the main access road), El Descanso is a little more expensive than its many hotel neighbors, but has clean, fresh rooms with hardwood floors and lofts. An open-air café and lounge looks out onto a lovely garden, where staff has spotted up to 18 different species of hummingbird. The lounge also has games for guests. Staying in the open-air attic loft with a shared bathroom is the cheapest option. Prices include breakfast, but if you'd rather not eat there, you can get a discounted price

Loved it? Loathed it? Write a review and help other travelers

without breakfast. It's a good idea to bring slippers or flip flops because there are no shoes allowed on the hardwood floors. Tel: 02-217-0213, Cel: 09-9482-9587, E-mail: info@eldescanso.net.
Updated: Jan 28, 2013.

Cabañas Armonía

($15 per person) Cabañas Armonía is a friendly family hostel and orchid garden established more than 10 years ago, in the midst of pure tranquility. Its cabins are scattered around a garden and have various layouts, all with private bathrooms with hot water, a balcony and a hammock. There are also four rooms, all of which share one bathroom. Prices are the same per person, whether you stay in a cabin or room. All include breakfast, a tour of the orchids garden, and access to the bird-watching area. Two blocks from the main street, to the right of the church. Just behind the stadium., Tel: 02-217-0131, Cel: 09-9488-6444/9943-5098, E-mail: cabanasarmonia@hotmail.com, URL: www.birdingmindo.com.
Updated: Feb 04, 2013.

El Rocio

($8-10 per person) Just a five-minute walk from the center of Mindo, El Rocio is a welcoming, creaky wooden hostel set among hummingbird-filled trees. The bedrooms on the first floor and the seven-bed dorm on the second floor smell musty, but they are clean, as are the shared bathrooms. However charming an all-wood house may be, the walls are very thin and it gets awfully noisy when people walk around with hiking shoes or even just talk loudly, so this hostel is a better bet on a quiet weekday than on a busy weekend. Owner Claudia speaks excellent English and can set up canopy tours, as well as tubing and other activities for you. Claudia also features what she proudly calls "super breakfasts" for an additional $2.50. From Mindo's main street, follow the unpaved road opposite the church for five minutes. The hostel is about 300 meters/984 feet past the football field. Tel: 02-217-0141, Cel: 09-9822-7359, E-mail: elrociomindohostal@hotmail.com.
Updated: Jan 28, 2013.

Caskaffesu Hotel

($15 per person) Located behind the attached restaurant and visible from the outdoor patio are the colorful adobe buildings that make up the Caskaffesu Hotel. Its eight rooms, spread out over two stories, are set in a semi-circle around a small garden. Clean and secure, with private bathrooms, the rooms are among the nicer options in Mindo. While they are a bit dark inside, the use of adobe in the construction, rather than wood and thatch, means the rooms also manage to avoid much of the mustiness that pervades other establishments. Ca. Sixto Durán Ballén s/n and Av. Quito, Tel: 09-9386-7154, E-mail: caskaffesu@yahoo.com.
Updated: Feb 04, 2013.

Hospedaje Arasari

($20 per person) Arasari lodge offers tourists a beautiful and peaceful environment, surrounded by mountains, and away from the noise. The hotel offers cabins designed for your comfort. The rooms have private bathrooms with warm water. There are green areas, fields, and a restaurant where you will find delicious national food prepared with local products. Hospedaje Arasari is on the border of the Tideland Saguambi, and is close to all tourist activities. 600 m/1,969 ft from Mindo's central park, near Hacienda Yahuira, Tel: 02-207-1880, cel: 09-9634-3236, E-mail: hospedajearasari@hotmail.com.
Updated: Feb 08, 2013.

Hostería Kumbha Mela

(ROOMS: $18-35) Hostería Kumbha Mela is a sprawling compound of cabins and rooms located across the road from Río Mindo. The hostel is a good option for those who want more of a solitary retreat and can afford to pay a bit more for the privilege. The five cabins, which range in capacity from two to eight people, feature their own private porches with hammocks.

Kumbha Mela also has a lodge, with seven dorm rooms and space for 16 people, which faces a heated, outdoor swimming pool. Kumbha Mela is closer to the main attractions (tubing, canopy tours and hikes in the Santuario de Cascadas) than many of its competitors, but the hostel is also a kilometer walk from restaurants in Mindo.

The hostel has a secure parking area and an on-site bar and restaurant; the staff can arrange visits to the area attractions. A sauna, Turkish bath and hydro massage are in the planning stages. Since space at the Kumbha Mela is limited, particularly during weekends, the owners recommend you make reservations ahead of time. 1 km/0.6 mi outside of Mindo on the road to Río Mindo and Vía Nambillo: make a right after Parque Central de Mindo on the road to the waterfalls (via a la cascada). After 1 km/0.6 mi, the hostel will be on your left., Tel: 02-217-0210, Cel:

09-9522-4000, E-mail: cheza.herrera@hosteriakumbhamelamindo.com, URL: www.hosteriakumbhamelamindo.com.
Updated: Feb 04, 2013.

MID-RANGE

Mindo Gardens

(ROOMS: $59-110) Mindo Gardens is owned by a huge Ecuadorian corporation. You wouldn't know it by looking at this quiet, isolated hotel, though, which is 1 km past the Butterfly Farm (about a half-an-hour drive down an unpaved road from the main center of Mindo). The hotel complex is set in a 300 hectare (741 acres) private reserve of secondary cloud forest, rivers and waterfalls. From the parking lot, walk down the main path to the reception, restaurant and main lounge, which has games, a pool table and a TV. The paths continue to different cabins, each of which has 3 rooms. There is a total capacity for about 52 guests. The Mindo river runs along the edge of the cabins and provides a melodic soundtrack to your stay.

The rooms of various sizes are colorful, clean and comfortable; although punctuated with obnoxiously bright curtains and bed covers. The restaurant is spacious and ideal for large groups. The regular menu is quite limited – with a couple of pizzas and traditional Ecuadorian dishes – but for large groups, more food selection is offered. Quito Office: Av. Rep. de El Salvador N35-82 Edif. Twin Tower P.B., Tel: 099-722-3260 / 099-733-1092, E-mail: contact@mindogardens.com, URL: www.mindogardens.com.
Updated: Apr 11, 2013.

El Quetzal de Mindo

($26 per person) El Quetzal de Mindo is located only a few blocks from the Parque Central de Mindo, yet is still in a quiet area with a river view. From the hotel, you can see hummingbirds, toucans, parrots and quetzals. It consists of just a few upstairs rooms, which come in deluxe king and deluxe queen varieties. All have private bathrooms with hot water and unlimited purified water. The deluxe king has a large private balcony with a hammock and views of the Canchupi River and mountains. Downstairs is the on-site café/restaurant and where the chocolate production is done; El Quetzal is also an artisan chocolate producer with a cacao plantation out back. Ca. 9 de octubre, Tel: 02-217-0034, Cel: 09-8626-3805, E-mail: info@elquetzaldemindo.com, URL: www.elquetzaldemindo.com.
Updated: Feb 04, 2013.

Mindo Rio Hosteria

(ROOMS: $45-65) Mindo Río Hostería is an all-inclusive resort lodge in Mindo offering elegant and comfortable rooms with private baths. Couples and parents can enjoy the adults-only pool while the children go for a splash in the kiddie pool. As a means for relaxing, they have a sauna and hydromassage available. The pleasant and airy on-site restaurant offers both local specialties and international cuisine. In addition, the hosteria can host conferences and conventions as well. Quito office: Aparicio Rivadeneira E7-23 and El Morlán, Tel: 02-241-9029/241-6511, Cel: 09-9324-9622/8741-0989, E-mail: info@mindorio.com, URL: www.mindorio.com.
Updated: Jan 30, 2013.

El Gallo de la Peña Hotel

($15 per person) This larger hotel on the edge of the main plaza in Mindo and at the beginning of the road headed to the Butterfly Farm offers lots of extra services and a reasonable price. The hotel includes a large outdoor pool, a hot tub with views of the surrounding mountains, a restaurant and a lounge. Each of the rooms has a private bathroom with hot water. With space for 150 guests, this hotel is ideal for big groups or travelers wanting to meet others. Staff can also help you with arranging tours around Mindo or bike rentals. Parroquia de Mindo, Km. 78 vía Calacalí, Tel: 02-217-0129, Cel: 09-9349-4740, E-mail: pmarcelosoria@yahoo/com, URL: www.mindorainforest.com/gallo.php.
Updated: Jan 28, 2013.

Biohostal Mindo Cloud Forest

(ROOMS: $15-18) Just 200 meters (656 ft) from the central park of Mindo, Biohostal offers an atmosphere of peace and tranquility. It has 10 spacious rooms with private bathrooms with hot water, and there is an on-site restaurant, café and bar. The hostel is complete with social areas, gardens overflowing with local plants, an outdoor BBQ grill and some scenic views.

Other facilities include on-site parking, a laundry service and a cinema; it is possible to host conventions or seminars here. Tourist information is also available in multiple languages including: Spanish, English and German. Biohostal aims to be the main study center of biodiversity in all of Mindo. Av. 9 de Octubre and Los Colibries (200 m/656 ft) from central park, Tel: 02-223-2783, Cel: 09-9854-5891, E-mail: biohostamindol@hotmail.com, URL: www.mindobiohostal.com.
Updated: Feb 04, 2013.

NORTHERN COAST

Loved it? Loathed it? Write a review and help other travelers

HIGH-END
Mariposas de Mindo

(ROOMS: $189) This family-run hotel two kilometers (1.2 mi) from the town of Mindo is surrounded by butterfly gardens and is dedicated to sustainable tourism and education about the surrounding region. Pleasant rooms and cabañas with spectacular views of the forest house up to 26 guests. Its pretty restaurant serves up exotic regional dishes, which are included in package rates. Besides accommodation and three meals a day, the two-night packages also include two cocktails per person and activities including a visit to the Butterfly Farm, cable car to the waterfalls, zip-lining, a chocolate tour, tubing and horseback riding. Transportation to all activities is also included. Parroquia de Mindo, Km. 2 Vía Mindo Garden S/N, Sector Yaquira, Tel: 02-224-2712, Cel: 09-9751-1988, E-mail: info@mariposasdemindo.com, URL: www.mariposasdemindo.com. Updated: Jan 29, 2013.

Casa Divina Lodge

(ROOMS: $100-265) Casa Divina sits on 2.7 hectares (6.5 ac) of secondary cloud forest and boats three two-story luxurious finished wood cabins. Each room has a private porch with hammock, spacious living quarters and an elegant bathroom with full-size bathtub. Rooms can accommodate from one to four guests. In the main house, guests can relax with a good book in the reading nook, take meals in the family-style dining room, and enjoy great music and its house cocktail (the Divina Capirinia) at the bar. On the property, there are also two short self-guided hikes that offer great lookout points. You will be amazed by the bird-watching possibilities here, where you can sight tanagers, quetzals, toucans and hummingbirds right outside the lodge's windows. 1.2 Km toward Cascada Nambillo, Tel: 09-9050-9626/9172-5874/U.S. number: 650-843-9164, E-mail: info@mindocasadivina.com, URL: www.mindocasadivina.com. Updated: Feb 04, 2013

Hostería Séptimo Paraíso

(ROOMS: $91-140) This hotel is set in a private reserve toward the top of the access road to Mindo, closer to the main highway, and has acres of untouched cloud forest, private paths for bird-watching, a hummingbird garden, a lovely open-air café, and even a jungle gym for kids. Its 22 rooms have the feel of a country home and are good for those who like more comfort than most eco-lodges of the region offer. Everything is of excellent quality and all of its naturalist guides are bilingual. The owners preserve the surrounding cloud forest via a non-profit organization and are involved in local conservation issues. Hostería Séptimo Paraíso has lots of extras like a pool, a sauna, satellite television, private transportation, Internet facilities and more. 2 Km/1.24 mi from the "Y" of Mindo, Tel: 09-9368-4417/18/20/21, E-mail: info@septimoparaiso.com, URL: www.septimoparaiso.com. Updated: Jan 29, 2013.

El Monte Sustainable Lodge ♩

($96 per person) The most ecologically friendly hotel in this incredibly environmentally conscious town, El Monte is a comfortable, full-service lodge with spectacular views. It's set on a 44-hectare (109-ac) private nature reserve with a rich secondary cloud forest, excellent bird- and wildlife-watching and a river full of rapids for tubing and waterfalls for cliff-jumping.

El Monte earns it's eco-lodge status by maintaining a number of eco-friendly projects. The farm produces some of the vegetables and fruits served to guests, no red meat is served, and most meals are vegetarian. The electricity for El Monte comes from a small hydro plant, which interacts with the grid. Guides teach guests about the importance of preservation in the area, the facilities build awareness, and the private reserve protects a good portion of Mindo's cloud forests from development and destruction.

There are three two-story cabañas and three larger one-story cabañas which sleep five people each. Décor is minimalist, allowing nature to be the focus. The quality of the cabins is excellent, quite luxurious even. El Monte lodge limits its occupancy to one party, so you won't have to share with strangers. The cabins are spaced far enough apart along the river banks so that you can feel completely isolated and even bird-watch from the comfort of your own bed. The service is pretty friendly and attentive, responding to whatever inquiries or concerns you might have. El Monte is owned by an American/Ecuadorian couple, who often join guests for meals and make themselves available for conversation, assistance, guiding and transportation. Quito Office: Roca E4-49 and Amazonas (Pasaje Chantilly), Tel: 02-254-6348/217-0102, Cel: 09-9308-4675, E-mail: elmontelodge@gmail.com, URL: www.ecuadorcloudforest.com. Updated: Feb 04, 2013.

Mindo Restaurants

Most restaurants in Mindo are nothing special, offering Ecuadorian cuisine as opposed to international. Some of the typical dishes you will find in Mindo are: tilapia – a type of fish usually served with rice, salad, and patacones (plantain chips); ceviche de palmita: the typical cold soup made with heart of palm, lime, diced onion, tomato and cilantro; and trucha al ajillo: fresh trout in a garlic sauce, usually served with rice, salad and patacones. If you are craving international cuisine, probably the best you will get is pizza. Updated: Apr 11, 2013.

El Quetzal

(LUNCH: $5) El Quetzal prepares plates made with fresh products harvested from its own organic gardens out back. Delicious Ecuadorian dishes are served alongside international food, and vegetarian options are always available. Its American-style breakfasts are a great way to start the day, with options like pancakes, granola with yogurt and fruit, and eggs. Sandwiches and more substantial fish, chicken, beef and pasta dishes are served for lunch and dinner, and there is always a special of the day. El Quetzal is an artisan chocolate producer and makes many decadent chocolate products that you can try here, including its rich, fudgy brownies. It also roasts its own Ecuadorian coffee, which is excellent. Products like chocolate bars, ginger syrup, teas, coffee beans and more are for sale. It leads chocolate tours daily. Ca. 9 de Octubre, Tel: 02-217-0034, Cel: 09-8626-3805, E-mail: info@elquetzaldemindo.com, URL: www.elquetzaldemindo.com. Updated: Feb 04, 2013.

Hostería Séptimo Paraíso Restaurant

(ENTREES: $6-7) Even if you are not staying here, it's worth at least stopping by for lunch or dinner. Located off the main access road to Mindo in the middle of acres of protected cloud forest, the open-air cafe is lovely. Spend some time walking off your meal on any of the paths around the lodge, playing on the jungle gym, or observing hummingbirds and other rare bird species from the garden. Hostería Séptimo Paraíso has several dining experiences in one: an elegant bar-restaurant with national and international dishes, a relaxed bar area with a pool table and darts, and a casual restaurant that serves coffee and a la carte items. Just off Av. Quito (the main road into Mindo), Tel: 09-9368-4417/18/20/21, E-mail: info@septimoparaiso.com.

Fuera de Babylonia

(ENTREES: $6-8) Fuera de Babylonia is a hidden treasure of a restaurant. The eatery, which occupies the lower floor of a chalet, has slightly off-kilter post and beam walls decorated with driftwood art. The tables consist of large slabs of polished wood with tiny stools for seats. While the service is slow, and the side dishes are relatively uninspired, the mains will more than make up for wait. The trout options, steamed or fried, are particularly delicious (be careful with the tiny bones inside). The fish is caught daily and then kept in barrels at the back to keep it fresh. During dinner, the restaurant also serves cold raspicuña, a local drink made from cane liquor, sugarcane and lemon juice. Open from 8 a.m. to 9 p.m. Located on a side street, to the left of Parque Central de Mindo, Tel: 091-32-6572 / 099-475-7768. Updated: Apr 11, 2013.

El Nomada !

(PIZZAS: $7-10) Several restaurants along Mindo's main strip have neon pizza signs, but venture a little further up the road (on way to the waterfalls) and you'll find El Nomada, a cozy Italian joint whose back room is dominated by a brick pizza oven. Like many other area establishments, El Nomada is set inside a rustic wood and thatch building; the plank tables and stools are arranged in alcoves, which heightens the intimate feel of the eatery. Although the menu has a range of Italian dishes—from lasagna to cannelloni and ravioli—the fresh, thin-crust pizzas are the real attraction. Toppings range from ham and pepperoni to eggplant and red peppers. There are vegetarian options as well, but if you can't find what you want, Nomada is more than happy to make pizzas to order. Daily noon-10 p.m., sometimes earlier on Monday nights. Its bar is open until midnight Monday-Thursday and until 2 a.m. on Friday and Saturday nights. 30 meters/98 ft from the park on the road to the waterfalls., Tel: 02-217-0160, Cel: 09-9331-1939, E-mail: nomada_mindo@yahoo.com. Updated: Feb 04, 2013.

Caskaffesu

(ENTREES: $7-10) Caskaffesu's dining area is spacious and modern, with lots of natural light, dark wood and a fireplace. A small outdoor patio nearby has room for another eight people or so and has views of the colorful Caskaffesu hotel rooms. Main plates are centered around proteins like steak, chicken or whole fish, but several vegetarian options are available. Smaller meals like grilled cheese or soup are satisfying alternatives. It also has a bunch of coffee options made with local coffee, which go great with a sweet for a mid-afternoon snack. There is also an extensive wine and liquor menu. Lunch-sized portions are a bit small, considering the price but are tasty nonetheless. Ca. Sixto Durán Balién s/n and Av. Quito, Tel: 09-9386-7154, E-mail: caskaffesu@yahoo.com, URL: www. caskaffesu.com. Updated: Feb 05, 2013.

Mindo Gardens Restaurant

(ENTREES: $5-10) Even if you do not stay at Mindo Gardens, its restaurant gives you a good excuse to check out this beautiful private reserve full of paths, gardens, bird-watching opportunities and a good portion of the Río Mindo. That said, the food at the restaurant is not amazing. A very limited menu offers a couple of pizzas and some traditional Ecuadorian soups and dishes. Large groups have the advantage of an extended menu and plenty of space to enjoy it. Upstairs from the restaurant is a casual lounge with games, a pool table and a TV. Daily 8-10:30 a.m., 12:30-3:30 p.m., 7-9:30 p.m. Quito Office: Av. Rep. de El Salvador N35-82, Edificio Twin Tower P.B., Tel: 09-9722-3260, Fax: 593-2-225-3452, E-mail: contacto@mindogardens.com, URL: www. mindogardens.com. Updated: Feb 08, 2013.

Around Mindo
Lodging Around Mindo

Bellavista Cloud Forest Reserve and Lodge !

(ROOMS: $54-121) Bellavista is a private 700-hectare (1,730-ac) cloud forest reserve and lodge. A variety of clearly-marked trails take you through the forest to hidden canyons and spectacular viewpoints. The reserve offers naturalist guides and specialist bird guides, and the self-guided educational trail awaits the curiosity of young people of all ages. The truly original lodging facilities include the Geodesic Dome, Bamboo House, Gingerbread House, House in the Woods and Gloria's Honeymoon House. Budget facilities are available at the Research Station, and it also offers camping areas.

Gourmet food includes local trout and chicken, as well as vegetarian options. Transport-inclusive packages from Quito or elsewhere are available every day. Quito office: Jorge Washington E7-25 and Av. 6 de Diciembre, Tel: 02-290-3166/223-2313/211-6232

(lodge), Cel: 09-9949-0891, E-mail: info@ bellavistacloudforest.com, URL: www.bellavistacloudforest.com. Updated: Feb 04, 2013.

El Encanto

($43-69 per person) El Encanto is a luxurious resort set right on the equator, a special location that inspires experiments and tricks unique to this latitude to awe guests. The 17 rooms come with private bathrooms, and there is a pool and spa with a Turkish bath. It is a good place from which to go on hikes through the rainforest, where guides will point out orchids and hummingbirds. Resort: Km. 7 On the way to Valle Hermoso, San Miguel de los Bancos, North West of Pichincha / Quito office: Av. América 45-60 and Mañosca, conjunto Jardines de las Américas # 2, Tel: 02-277-0707 / 02-227-8764 / 02-224-2553 / 099-956-4254, E-mail: info@elencantoresort.com.ec, URL: www.elencantoresort.com.ec. Updated: Jan 25, 2013.

Urcu Puyujunda Eco-Lodge

(ROOMS: $45-155) The Urcu Puyujunda (cloudforest in Quechua) Eco-Lodge is a small ecological reserve privately owned and run by an Ecuadorian couple. Located within the Choco-Andes region, this lodge offers you the chance to observe the amazing ecosystem that the cloud forest represents. As well as bird-watching for over 350 species, you can also follow hiking trails, go horse riding and fishing, milk cows, visit a butterfly farm, and take part in tubing and rappelling. The lodge also organizes volunteering programs for visitors and works on conservation projects, such the reforestation of the local area. Accommodation is in wooden cabins, made with environmentally-friendly materials typical of the area. Single and double rooms both come with private bathroom and balcony. There is a restaurant on-site serving international and local dishes, as well as a bar, games room and reading room. Quito office: Marcella E8-45 and Shyris, Tel: 02-226-5736, Cel: 09-9833-4489 / 098-265-0335, E-mail: urcupuyujunda@ cloudforestecuador.com, URL: www.cloudforestecuador.com. Updated: Jan 29, 2013.

Hostería el Paraiso

(ROOMS: $60-70) Hostería el Paraiso is an attractive, fun country resort about 120 kilometers (75 mi) from Quito along the road that leads to the coast, not far from the town of Los Bancos. The sprawling hostería has lots of fun things to do, including fishing, tubing in the river, a river beach, horseback riding, games, sports and more. Price includes breakfast. Km 116 via Calacali - La Independencia; Quito office: Av. 10 de Agosto N21-214 and Roca, Edif Intriado, 10th floor, Tel: lodge: 02-239-2437/239-2879; Quito office: 02-255-8617/8/9; Cel: 09-9832-6046/9705-5575, E-mail: informes@hosteriaelparaiso.com. ec, URL: www.hosteriaelparaiso.com.ec. Updated: Feb 04, 2013.

Sapos y Ranas Hotel

(ROOMS: $80-177) Sapos y Ranas (Toads and Frogs) is a friendly lodge located in the heart of the El Chocó region. The Chocó is at a strategic biodiversity point, with nearly 160 species of birds. The lodge is surrounded by sub-tropical forests, orchid nurseries, rivers and trails. There are also over 2,000 signature figurines and sculptures of frogs and toads from all over the world that adorn the complex. The establishment's pretty gardens, thermal pools, hiking trails and a Turkish bath make for a relaxing ending to a day exploring the natural wonders of the area. It also has a canopy or a games room.

Package deals include all meals, some activities and full use of hotel facilities. On the road toward Las Mercedes, 15 km/9.3 mi from Los Bancos; Quito office: Av. Gaspar de Villarroel E4-50 and Av. Amazonas, 2nd floor, Tel: 02-224-5871/225-1446, Cel: 09-9206-0197, Fax: 02-245-4087, E-mail: info@saposyranas.com / reservas@saposyranas.com, URL: www.saposyranas.com. Updated: Feb 13, 2013.

Tandayapa Bird Lodge !

(ROOMS: $140-325) Tandayapa, the self-proclaimed "ultimate birding destination," was built in 1999 on a pasture on the edge of the cloud forest outside of Mindo. The lodge has since planted over 30,000 trees to fill in the areas of the cloud forest that had been destroyed. Tandayapa, which is stacked with birding gear and viewing equipment, features a viewing deck, extensive trails throughout the forest and full-time guides willing to set out in search of birds at all hours of the day.

There are several options for different day trips, each with a list of bird species found in those areas. Tandayapa has 12 rooms in the main building, all with hot water, private bathrooms and electricity. 6 km/3.7 mi off Calacalí-La Independencia road

Km 52; Quito office: Félix Oralabal N45-55 and Zamora, Estupiñan building, 3rd floor, Tel: 02-244-7520, Cel: 09-9923-1314, E-mail: tandayapa@tropicalbirding.com, URL: www.tandayapabirdlodge.com. Updated: Feb 04, 2013.

SANTO DOMINGO (DE LOS TSÁCHILAS)

 625m   300,000   02

Located in the lush central lowland area of northern Ecuador, Santo Domingo de los Colorados is a huge transportation hub that links Quito and the Sierra to the coastal regions of Ecuador. The city is 129 kilometers (80 mi) from Quito and the area is of great importance to the banana industry, hence the good road links.

The city itself is dusty, noisy and polluted, not unlike other coastal lowland towns. However, the surrounding forests offer fabulous opportunities for bird watching, and form part of the Choco biodiversity region, meaning there's lots of wildlife to see.

The population of the town itself is an interesting mix. The area has been a major draw point for Colombian immigrants that come south in search of better opportunities. Additionally, the area is famed for its Tsáchila indigenous people, well-known for their use of an achiote dye to color their hair red. The people no longer wear their traditional outfits, except for special occasions. Updated: Apr 05, 2013.

Getting To and Away from Santo Domingo

The bus terminal is about 1.5 kilometers north of the central part of town, if you head out of town along Avenida de los Tsáchilas. The bus station is actually just off Avenida Abraham Calazacón. For convenience, take a taxi to get to and away, especially if arriving or leaving at night. Due to its central location in Ecuador, getting to and away from Santo Domingo de los Colorados is easy—you can get buses to most other parts of the country from this bus terminal, but it is especially easy to get to coastal towns from here.

If you're headed north to **Esmeraldas** and the beach, the journey takes around three hours. To hit the coast further south of Es-

Loved it? Loathed it? Write a review and help other travelers

meraldas, you can get a bus to Pedernales, which takes three hours, or to **Bahía** de Caráquez (four hours) or to **Manta**, which takes around six hours. If you are going to **Guayaquil**, the bus travels via **Quevedo** and the journey takes four hours. As a general rule, expect to pay approximately one dollar per hour of journey.
Updated: Apr 11, 2013.

Things To See and Do in Santo Domingo

Visit a Tsáchila Community ♪

One really worthwhile trip if you're at a loose end in the area is to head out to a Tsáchila community. The group is known for the fact that the men dye their hair red with achiote. A typical visit would include a tour where you are shown their dress, their bamboo homes, weapons and learn more about their history and beliefs, particularly the shamanistic ritualism aspects. Contact a community to find out more, they're usually located around town.
Updated: Feb 18, 2013.

Santo Domingo Lodging

Santo Domingo de los Colorados hotels are plentiful, however, choose with care as quality varies considerably. A large number of hotels are centered around one of the main streets (29 de Mayo). However, in general these are not recommended as this street is busy, hence very loud. You may find it worthwhile to try to find somewhere off this main strip in order to get a decent night's sleep, but if you feel compelled to stay in this part of town, try to get a room facing away from the main street. If you´re looking for luxury hotels, Santo Domingo doesn't have many options except for the Milenio Hotel, which has a spa offering hydro-massages.
Updated: Apr 11, 2013.

Hotel del Pacifico

(ROOMS: $33-56) Hotel del Pacifico is conveniently located in Santo Domingo de los Colorados. Since the hotel is on Avenida 29 de Mayo, the space can be fairly noisy. Rooms are of a decent size and are comfortable, with private bathrooms and hot water, TV and a telephone. The hotel has a bar and restaurant, and all guests are given a welcome cocktail. Hotel del Pacifico also provides a laundry service and parking. Room prices include breakfast. Prices do not include tax and service charge, but breakfast is provided. Av. 29 de Mayo 510, between Ibarra and Latacunga, Tel: 02-275-2806/276-0373, E-mail: hotel.delpacifico@hotmail.com.

Hotel Sheraton

(ROOMS: $10-30) Not to be confused with the luxury chain in the U.S., Hotel Sheraton sits conveniently from the main bus terminal in Santo Domingo, but other than that, there's not much of a draw to the hotel. The five-story building houses a complex labyrinth of tiled hallways and staircases, and rather unglamorous rooms with hot water, basic toiletries and cable TV. Although nothing fancy, the hotel provides good quality lodging at a low price. Located on Av. Abraham Calazacón, just across from the bus terminal, Tel: 02-275-1988.
Updated: Feb 08, 2013.

Hotel Zaracay

(ROOMS: $58-125) Hotel Zaracay is a pleasant hotel and is a fairly reliable choice. The hotel has plenty of amenities, including a nice swimming pool, which comes in handy in the sweltering heat. There are also areas for playing football, basketball, tennis and volleyball. The hotel boasts a little aviary, a gym, a bar and good restaurant that serves regional and international cuisine. To get to Zaracay, head along the Quito road, and the hotel can be found approximately 1.5 kilometers (0.9 mi) from the center of town, in front of the new Recinto Ferial. Av. Quito 1639, Km 1.5, in front of the Recinto Ferial, Tel: 02-275-0316/1023, Fax: 02-275-4535, E-mail: hotelzaracay@hotmail.com, URL: www.hotelzaracay.com.
Updated: Feb 08, 2013.

Milenio Hotel

(ROOMS: $22-45) The well-presented Milenio Hotel is a bit of a splurge, but perhaps worth it. Spread over five floors, the rooms come with air conditioning, which is helpful in the humid coastal climate, plus private bathroom and cable TV. In case you didn't watch enough telenovelas (soap operas) in your room, there is also a common TV room. If you're done with the TV, head to the Turkish bath, sauna and hydromassage area, where you can kick back and soak after a long bus journey. The hotel also has a garage and a bar. The hotel restaurant called is called Chelo's and serves an array of meat and seafood options. Road to Quevedo and Juan Pío Montufar, Tel: 02-371-0516/17/18, E-mail: marco.v.rojas@hotmail.com.
Updated: Feb 08, 2013.

Tinalandia

(ROoms: $86-135) Built in the 1940s as a farm and later converted for tourism, Tinalandia was one of Ecuador's first eco-lodges.

Modestly sized, Tinalandia has 16 comfortable rooms and capacity for 30 guests. The lodge attracts birdwatchers from around the globe and is a personal favorite of Paul Greenfield, illustrator of "The Birds of Ecuador," which is considered the definitive book of its kind. More than 350 species of birds have been sighted at Tinalandia. Just hanging out at the dining hall, you're certain to see several species of hummingbird as well as (if you're lucky) some tanagers and toucans that come to feed at a special bird feeder designed by the owner.

Tinalandia is also the best place in Ecuador to experience the latest thing in eco-tourism: butterfly watching. There are hundreds of species of butterfly native to Tinalandia, and the owner has been cataloging them in a nifty binder with photos. Butterflies are sensitive, and their presence (or lack thereof) can tell a researcher much about a climate zone. Many nature lovers the world around are taking up butterfly-watching as an alternative to birdwatching, and in Ecuador, Tinalandia it is the best place to start by far.

The area around Tinalandia has more than just birds, however. The cloud forest is of interest to biologists and hikers. One of the world's few remaining moss forests is within hiking distance. The staff can arrange for whitewater rafting trips, and there is even a nine-hole golf course on the premises. Tinalandia can also arrange for guides for hiking or bird watching excursions, if you give the lodge advance notice. Km 85 Vía Aloag - Santo Domingo de los Colorados, Tel: 02-244-9028, Cel: 09-9946-7741, E-mail: info@tinalandia.com, URL: www.tinalandia.com. Updated: Feb 08, 2013.

Santo Domingo Restaurants

Chef Sheraton Restaurante

(ENTREES: $4-7) Chef Sheraton Restaurante offers an abnormally large amount of options for appearing to be a typical Santo Domingo food joint. It serves pastas, several meat dishes and a little bit of Chinese, but the quality is the issue. It's not the greatest meal you'll have, but if you're looking for something quick and convenient, right across from the bus terminal, this is a safe bet. The restaurant is located directly beneath the Hotel Sheraton (not to be confused with the luxury hotel chain), and is easily spotted along the main avenue. Av. Abraham Calazacón, just across from the bus terminal, Tel: 02-275-1988, Cel: 09-9319-6710. Updated: Feb 08, 2013.

El Rincón del Che

(ENTREES: $5-8) This is definitely the place to try parrillada, the assortment of meat cuts on individualized grills. Ask any local in Santo Domingo, a city famed for its meats, and they will probably point you in the direction of El Rincón. Perpetually crowded with families, often ordering up to five grills at a time, you might be hard pressed to find a table. Once you do, though, immediately order one for yourself. From traditional cuts of steak to cow udder, try it all (really!), as well as a jar of the restaurant's lemonade to go with your meal–there is absolutely no way you'll leave dissatisfied. Av. 6 de Noviembre and Bartolomé Ruiz, across from Colegio Pío XII, Tel: 02-276-0220/5519. Updated: Feb 08, 2013.

PUERTO QUITO

This little town squatting on the shores of the Río Caoni was, ironically, originally intended to be the capital's port (hence the name). Today, it sits smack dab in the middle of the main circuit to the coast vía Quito, Calacalí and La Independencia.

An area of extreme natural beauty, bisected by the Caoni and its tributaries, the lands surrounding Puerto Quito are divided by a number of reserves and dotted with good resorts. Due to its natural resources as well as its growing ecological and economic infrastructure, Puerto Quito is ideal for going wild in the wilds: from bird watching to river rafting, kayaking and swimming to walking this is the place to clear the mind and the lungs. Updated: Jun 15, 2013.

Getting To and Away from Puerto Quito

Puerto Quito is easily reachable from **Quito** via a four-hour bus ride. Trans Esmeraldas has four buses per day that leave for the city of **Esmeraldas**, passing Puerto Quito on the way (12:30 a.m., 3:30 p.m., 8:40 p.m. and 11:55 p.m.). Tickets cost $4 each way. Some of its buses to **Atacames** also stop in Puerto Quito; confirm at the ticket office.

Trans Esmeraldas buses leave from both **Quitumbe** bus station (02-382-4791) in the south of Quito and from a more central location in the **Mariscal** neighborhood: Santa Mariá and 9 de Octubre (Tel: 02-250-5099). To get to the lodges outside of Puerto Quito, you will need to take a taxi, if you do not have your own car. Updated: Feb 18, 2013.

Loved it? Loathed it? Write a review and help other travelers

Puerto Quito Lodging

Puerto Quito hotels mostly fall into the eco-lodge variety, due to the numerous tropical reserves and parks around the town. You'll find most places to be spread out amongst a few acres of tropical forest, with quaint bungalow-style accommodations. There aren't a lot of options in Puerto quito, hostels are rare and luxury hotels are even more so. Updated: Jul 12, 2013.

Arashá Spa

(ROOMS: $105-200) This internationally recognized resort and spa is located in the heart of Ecuador's tropical forest, a hot spot of biodiversity and natural beauty. The surroundings themselves would be enough to attract travelers, but the sheer luxury of Arashá Spa, with its self-indulgent spas and ecologically sensitive bungalows make it an engaging and undeniably extravagant experience. You won't be roughing it here. Besides lavish accommodation and cuisine to please even the most discerning palate, Arashá offers a number of activity packages, from Wellness Experiences to Eco-Education Expeditions and Family Experiences.

Activities range from primary and secondary forest treks and trips to nearby cascades, to exotic birdwatching and juice making. And of course, everyone can relax and unwind in the spring-fed natural pool. All-inclusive packages include taxes and transportation, three meals per day and drinks (yes, that includes alcohol!), one spa treatment/person and guided tours. Note: Some tours require 72 hours advanced notice reservations. Km. 121 Vía Quito - Calacalí - La Independencia, Pedro Vicente Maldonado; Quito Office: Av. De los Shyris 39-41 and Río Coca, Edificio Montecarlo X, 8th floor., Tel: 02-225-3937/67, Cel: 09-9198-2122, E-mail: info@arasharesort.com, URL: www.arasharesort.com Updated: Feb 08, 2013.

Cucuya Eco-Lodge

($5-15 per person) The Cucuya Eco-Lodge is the perfect spot to unwind in nature—to savor its sounds and flavors, to relax under starlit skies, to rest alongside a gently flowing river, and to become aware of nature's rhythms. Each cozy canopy room of the wooden lodge was designed to accentuate the breathtaking beauty of the exotic landscape and river flowing alongside it. The tropical climate of this region is characterized by a balmy temperature of 22°C (72°F) year round. As part of a dedication to sustainable tourism, Cucuya Eco-lodge employs only people from the local community and is committed to environmentally sound practices. A wide variety of guided tours and individual activities are also available. Road to Achiote, Km 2, Puerto Quito, Tel: 02-215-6233, Cel: 09-9978-0431, E-mail: preventas1@hotmail.es, URL: www.cucuyaecolodge.com. Updated: Feb 08, 2013.

Kaony Lodge

(ROOMS: $70-270) Spread out along the Rio Caoni, Kaony Lodge is a private ecological reserve of over 30 hectares of tropical forest. Cabins are rustic but cozy, and constructed entirely from local materials in order to blend in with the surroundings. As well as rest and relaxation, the lodge offers ample opportunity to get out and about in the area. Excursions include swimming, horseback riding and nature walks, which can be followed with a dip in the jacuzzi. Also attached to the grounds is a first-class restaurant, specializing in typical dishes like trout and tilapia, but which also serves international dishes. Quito office: Av. 12 de Octubre 2449 y Orellana (Edificio Jerecio), 1st floor,, Tel: 099-469-0302, URL: www.kaonylodge.com. Updated: Apr 11, 2013.

Esmeraldas (Province)

In the northwestern corner of Ecuador, African and indigenous cultures come together amidst jungle, river, and sea. The African heritage for many of Esmeraldas' residents comes from a shipwreck off the coast of a slave ship. According to legend, about two-dozen slaves made their way to land and to freedom. You will notice the influence of eastern African dress, music and customs in Esmeraldas.

European feet first touched this coastal piece of Ecuadorian soil here when the Spanish landed on the Pacific Coast in 1526. The conquistadors were astounded to find Indians bedecked in emeralds awaiting them on shore. Convinced that the region was abundant in the brilliant gems, they named it Esmeraldas.

While today's Esmeraldas harbors few emeralds, it does live up to its other name, the "Green Province." The northernmost of all the coastal provinces that frame Ecuador, Esmeraldas is also the greenest, riddled with estuaries, mangroves and densely flooded tropical forest. Its wild and remote inland areas, that are accessible only by canoe,

NORTHERN COAST

make Esmeraldas the ideal staging ground for a river safari. Gliding past frontier towns that suddenly appear out of the dense green tangle of jungle, you will be reminded of scenes from "The African Queen" and "Heart of Darkness."

If you would rather vegetate than bushwhack your way though thick vegetation, Esmeraldas also boasts some of the coast's most vibrant beaches with small towns scattered among them. There is a whole range in accommodation here, as it is one of the closest beach areas to Quito and Ibarra and city folk of all income levels love to spend weekends at the beach.

The Esmeraldas province offers an array of beach town options. If you want to party, check out Atacames. If it's peace and quiet that you're looking for, the sleepy towns of Same, Sua, Tonchigue or Muisine should be explored. Surfers should head to Mompiche. Those looking for a variety of things to do could stay in Chamanga and explore the surrounding area.

PLAYA DE ORO

RESERVA DE LOS TIGRILLOS

($50 per day, all-inclusive) The Afro-Ecuadorian community of Playa de Oro, the last settlement on the Rio Santiago, has the region's first ecotourism project. The project is designed to protect a 10,000-hectare (24,710-ac) reserve of pristine rainforest, which is the only Margay (jungle cat) reserve in the world, and is considered one of the most important areas in the world for endemism in birds.

Playa de Oro offers guests the option of either staying in wooden cabins in the heart of their community, or taking a half hour trip upriver to the Reserva de Tigrillos Lodge. The Reserva de Tigrillos Lodge—an abandoned military barracks converted into a lodge by the locals and set back 100 meters (328 ft) from the water—is totally surrounded by protected jungle, except for the river side, where there is a "food forest" made up of tropical fruit trees (banana, anona, papaya), sugar cane and pineapples.

The lodge is rustic (built of rough-hewn wood), but is as comfortable as anything you will find anywhere in the Ecuadorian rainforest. Rooms are simply furnished, with a bed, a table, a stool, shelves for clothes and a large lock-box for valuables. The rooms are screened and beds are mosquito-netted. The dining room and kitchen are downstairs, where the two wings of the lodge meet.

Upstairs, the big corner rooms are the library and the hammock lounge. The library has a small collection of books and some interesting information on the area. The village has constructed three wooden cabañas, set apart from each other and overlooking the river on the edge of the village. A path runs past the cabañas and down to the beach, and continues through the trees to the village football pitch (daily matches can get quite roudy!) The cabañas are luxurious by jungle standards, with spacious balconies. There are two doubles or triples and a large cabaña that can accommodate up to eight people.

Being close to the village, the cabañas have electricity from 6 p.m. until 10 p.m. every day. Food is served in a family house. While in Playa de Oro, you can learn about the life and culture of the Afro-Ecuadorians and experienced village guides will take you out on their many jungle trails for hikes that range from one to four hours.

The treks are a great opportunity to experience the rich flora and fauna that abounds in their untouched reserve (the area is particularly good for birdwatching), and will take you to some beautiful sites. In addition to the hikes, there are relatively short boat trips (1 hour or less) upriver to more remote parts of the reserve; for example, to an interesting rock formation called La Cathedral, or to explore rocky beach areas. The river is great for swimming and playing in mild rapids, and if the conditions are right, don't miss the opportunity to free float down river.

Reservations must be made two weeks in advance. The only way into Playa de Oro is by their boat, so they need advance notice to send the boat to pick you up. There is a $10 per person reserve entrance fee. The boat transport is $160 for round-trip transport from Selve Alegre to Playa de Oro. There are some additional fees if you need use of the boat during your stay. Fees must be paid in cash to the Playa de Oro treasurer before your departure.

To get to Selva Alegre you need to get to Esmeraldas first, which has regular connections from all over the country. From there you need to get a bus to Selva Alegre with Del Pacifico (at 10 a.m.) or La Costeñita (6:10

NORTHERN COAST

a.m. or 1:10 p.m.). Costs $4.50 and takes 4 hours. Community of Playa de Oro (Luis Vargas Torres), Rio Santiago, Tel: 09-9960-6918, E-mail: jramirobuitron@gmail.com, URL: www.touchthejungle.org.
Updated: Feb 08, 2013.

ESMERALDAS (CITY)

 15m   165,216   06

Despite its rather alluring name, there is nothing much to attract even the most daring adventurer to Esmeraldas. The city is a dirty, depressing industrial port. Part of the blame must reside with a series of mudslides in 1997-1998, which destroyed much of the town and area. Whatever the reason, the city of Esmeraldas is no one's idea of a tourist destination. Oppressive heat and humidity, paired with a reputation for being unsafe, mean the city is more suitable for brief stopovers than longer stays. Dusty streets packed with a mechanical menagerie of buses, cars and taxis crisscross through town, passing street vendors, mom-and-pop stores, fruit and vegetable stalls and a variety of look-alike local restaurants along the way.

The region, however, is culturally rich and home to one of Ecuador's earliest communities: La Tolita. The island by the same name, located to the north, is an important archaeological site - the artifacts of which you can view at the town museum. In addition, Afro-Ecuadorean culture is very much alive and well in Esmeraldas, and is best sampled through its marimba music and dance, or local cuisine, which relies heavily on coconut and plantain (in various forms).

The road from Quito to more appealing beach towns such as Same, Súa, and Atacames passes through Esmeraldas, so some travelers will inevitably wind up there. That's actually the best way to see Esmeraldas: through the window of a moving bus. Change buses if you must, but otherwise don't plan on spending too much time there.
Updated: Apr 04, 2013.

Getting To and Away from Esmeraldas

Servicio directo (executive service) buses run to and from **Quito** and **Guayaquil**, and are the best option as they don't stop to pick up passengers along the way, tend to be more comfortable, and are way faster. To/

From Quito: $6.00 regular / $8.00 servicio-directo (6-7 hours). Trans-Esmeraldas has buses that depart from Quito at their station over on Santa Maria 870 and 9 de Octubre in **La Mariscal**. Tel: 02-250-5099, www.transesmeraldas.com. Be sure to drop in or call to confirm departure times and seat-availability, especially on weekends.

A good paved road runs from Esmeraldas to **Borbon** and **San Lorenzo** to the north, continuing on to **Ibarra** in the northern Andes. Buses run frequently to the south as well. Esmeraldas has a bus terminal from which you can catch these buses. Buses to **Atacames**, leave every 20 minutes, $.60, 1 hr. Buses to **Muisne** leave every 30 minutes, $2, 2 hours.
Updated: Apr 05, 2013.

Safety

Olmedo, Colon, Sucre and Bolivar streets are safe during the day and in the early parts of the evening. Esmeraldas has more police on the streets now than it did previously, but it's best not to walk alone – especially if you're a solo female traveler – late at night. The Las Palmas Malecon is best avoided in the late evening, as the restaurants and bars there start closing up early sometimes and taxis can get rather scarce.
Updated: Apr 05, 2013.

Esmeraldas Services
MONEY

Banco de Pichincha: Corner of Bolivar and 9 de Octubre.

TOURISM

The "iTur" Office will provide you with general information on the area. There Offices are located on Bolivar and 9 de Octubre, 5-21. Tel: 06-272-7340, jestupinan@municipioesmeraldas.goc.ec, www.municipioesmeraldas.goc.ec.

MEDICAL

Farmacias Cruz Azul: Olmedo and 9 de Octubre. Farmacias Económicas: Olmedo and 10 de Agosto.
Updated: Apr 04, 2013.

Things To See and Do in Esmeraldas

If you find yourself stuck in the city for a night or two, catch a bus or taxi to Las Palmas, the Esmeraldas version of an upscale beach. You can also drop by the city museum to peruse its artifacts or check out the plazas for some really great people watching.
Updated: Apr 05, 2013.

Museo y Centro Cultural Esmeraldas

(ADMISSION: Free) Numerous examples of the ceramic heritage of Esmeraldas are housed here. Split up into different eras that define the region throughout history, you'll find a number of archeological objects here (some replicas, the majority are authentic – and in incredibly good shape). Piedrahita and Bolívar, Tel: 06-272-7076.
Updated: Apr 04, 2013.

Getting Around Esmeraldas

Buses run up and down Olmedo ($0.25), some heading towards the Malecon Las Palmas, others to the bus terminal. Make sure to verify what their destination is by looking at the signs displayed on their front window. Taxi cabs to the Malecon cost $1-2, and are $3 if you want to head to the bus terminal.
Updated: Apr 04, 2013.

Esmeraldas Lodging

Hotels in Esmeraldas are surprisingly clean and friendly considering the general appearance of the city itself. A good option, if you can afford to spend a few more clams, is to spend the night over by Las Palmas near the beach. All in all, this area offers some fairly nice accommodations, including a couple of luxurious ones too.
Updated: Apr 05, 2013.

Hotel Roma

($8-16 per person) Located on the ever-busy Olmedo street, Hotel Roma offers very simple but clean accommodations. Rooms are air-conditioned, with private bathrooms and 24-hour running water. If you're looking to block out noise from the street below, each room also has cable TV. Although not particularly pleasing on the eyes, this hotel feels reasonably safe and the staff are extremely friendly (if your Spanish is up to it, ask them for restaurant recommendations). The adjacent restaurant is open for breakfast and lunch, and if you need to make a phone call or recharge a cell phone card just head to the shop conveniently located beneath the hostel. Olmedo and Piedrahita, Tel: 06-271-1511.
Updated: Feb 08, 2013.

Hostal El Cisne

($15 per person) Set back from the main road, Hostal El Cisne is a quiet place to rest your head for the night. A large blue and yellow concrete building, the hotel lacks the character of smaller hostels but more than makes up for it in value and comfort. Clean, bright rooms come with a big bed, tiled floors, air conditioning, TV, and clean, private bathrooms with cold-water showers. They do lack windows though. A parking lot will serve those with cars, and the hotel is conveniently located near the main street. This is probably one of the best value hotels in Esmeraldas. Note: most rooms are concrete blocks, with tiny slits for windows at the top of the ceiling, but unless you're one for postcard views of sagging rooftops, there's not much to see in Esmeraldas anyway. 10 de Agosto 416, between Olmedo and Colón, Tel: 06-272-1588/3411/271-3627, URL: www.hotel-elcisne.com.
Updated: Feb 08, 2013.

Residencial Zulema

($12 per person) Despite a grand external appearance, this hostel doesn't seem to put its money where its mouth is. The multistoried building with beehive-stacked windows boasts dingy, dark rooms, some with a shared bathroom and a TV. For the price, you're better off staying in one of the other places in town, but the staff does seem friendly. If your choices are slim or you're in a rush to get settled, try Zulema. Av. Olmedo and Piedrahita, Tel: 06-272-3826.
Updated: Feb 08, 2013.

Hostal Estefania

($12-15 per person) Hostal Estefania is one of the friendlier and cleaner places to stay in town. Walls adjacent to the staircase bear various brightly colored paintings, and most rooms feature reprints of Ecuador's great master Guayasamín. Rooms are clean and simple, with private bathrooms, air conditioning and a remarkably safe feel, especially considering other buildings in Esmeraldas tend to look fairly decrepit. An unadorned reception area boasts a large TV. Owner Washington Guashpa Roano and his staff are friendly and sure to assist you in anything you need. Ca. Sucre and Juan Montalvo, Tel: 06-272-3893.
Updated: Feb 08, 2013.

Hostal Sultana de Los Andes

($10 per person) This budget hostel along the Olmeda drag can be reached via a set of stairs from the street. The walls around the reception area have been painted a cheerful purple color, which matches the friendly woman who will show you available rooms. As in most of the lodgings in Esmeraldas, the rooms are slightly run-down but for the most part clean and tidy. Beware that rooms overlooking the street can be noisy, so don't expect a vacationer's retreat. What you will get

NORTHERN COAST

is a bed with clean sheets, private bathroom with 24-hour hot water, and a relatively safe night's sleep. Av. Olmedo and 9 de Octubre, Tel: 06-272-6778.
Updated: Feb 08, 2013.

Hotel Perla Verde

($48 per person) Hotel Perla Verde is truly a pearl compared to the otherwise lackluster accommodations available in Esmeraldas. The hotel is centrally located, and offers hot water, WiFi, private bathrooms, firm beds and an American breakfast is included. The hotel is sports a modern, sleek feel in the midst of Esmeraldas' dusty, crowded streets. This is one of the most luxurious options in Esmeraldas city. Ca. Piedrahita, between Olmedo and Sucre, Tel: 06-272-3820/5924, Fax: 06-271-2841, E-mail: reservaciones_perlaverde@hotmail.com, URL: www.hotelperlaverde.com.
Updated: Feb 08, 2013.

Hotel Casino Palm Beach

(ROOMS: $45-55) The brand-new Hotel Casino Palm Beach is one of the most luxurious of Esmeraldas' lodging options. The hotel isn't exactly beach front, but it's about 100 meters away from the palm-lined Las Palmas beach. The staff is extremely friendly and courteous, and the manager is always glad to chat. The owner has French and Italian roots, and the decor and restaurant menu reflect this Mediterranean influence. Rooms are spacious, clean and bright, and offer a minibar, flat screen television, high-quality linens and mattresses and hot water in the private bathrooms. Most have a partial or full view of the beach, and there's a Jacuzzi on the first floor. The place is relatively new and has to work out some kinks, but it has a very pleasant feel about it and is a good option if you have the money. Breakfast is included in the price as well. Av. Kennedy, Just above the Malecón at Las Palmas, Tel: 06-246-1708 / 099-100-7770, E-mail: palmbeach_esme@hotmail.com, URL: www. palmbeachecuador.com.
Updated: Apr 04, 2013.

Hotel Colon Palace

(ROOMS: $50-110) This is one of the newest hotels in Esmeraldas. As a result, it's the most modern-looking and pristine of the bunch. Offering accommodations that seem oriented more for business-folk, Hotel Colon still welcomes tourists and backpackers alike with great service. Rooms are spacious with practically immaculate bathrooms and linens, satisfying just about anyone's cleanliness standards. You're pretty much guaranteed a fresh and clean night's sleep here, albeit with minimal decor. And with plasma TV's and direct-TV, A/C, Wi-fi and hot water, you'll find plenty of what business travelers favor. Not to mention, the hotel is complemented by what would has to be one of the ritziest bars and restaurants in town just downstairs, connected to the hotel itself. Colon and Rocafuerte, Tel: 06-271-4405/1409, E-mail: jeniferguilcapi@hotmail.com / hotelcolonpalace@hotmail.es.
Updated: Apr 04, 2013.

Esmeraldas Restaurants

Besides buses and cars, the city is packed with look-alike local eateries and hole-in-the-wall restaurants, each serving its own special plates and most offering street side seating around plastic tables and chairs.

There are a few nicer joints in town, especially if you're in the mood for steak, and if you're up for seafood there are a number of places in Las Palmas. Just be aware that due to Esmeralda's mammoth project to renovate the entire Malecón Las Palmas (Paseo las Palmas), some of the restaurants listed below may no longer be around by the time you visit them.
Updated: Apr 04, 2013.

Bar y Cevicheria Oh! Mar

(ENTREES: $4-7) An open-air restaurant facing the sea, this place offers one of the nicest views you'll get while in Esmeraldas. Dining is simple and only slightly classier than in town: the plastic tablecloths and glass-top tables are clean and inviting. Specials include the standard range of seafood dishes, but ceviche, langosta and the regional specialty encocado are among the best options. If you're in the mood for something a bit more hearty, try one of the arroz dishes. Prices are a tad more expensive than in town, but then none of the inland dives can offer palm tree-studded ocean views. Main strip Las Palmas, Tel: 06-246-0791.
Updated: Apr 04, 2013.

Parrilladas El Toro

(ENTREES: $8-20) In a town where the words ramshackle and overcrowded seem to accompany any observation, Parrilladas el Toro is a breath of fresh air. Walking through the glass front doors and into the spacious, marble-floored dining area is like entering a king's quarters. Precisely set tables with wooden-back chairs spread out across the room, astride a classy bar area

NORTHERN COAST

and walls decorated with Guayasamín reprints. This is the perfect spot for a romantic rendezvous, or to share a bottle of wine and a few drinks with friends. An open-air seating area located toward the back, the centerpiece of which is a lovely fountain, is a great place to breeze through a meal. The warm and welcoming staff is another bonus. Ca. 9 de Octubre 423, between Olmedo and Colón, Tel: 06-272-7925.
Updated: Apr 04, 2013.

D'fernando Restaurante
(ENTREES: $5-12) Along the Malecón of Las Palmas, you will find a row of seemingly identical seafood joints with plastic furniture and lazily-oscillating fans. D'Fernando is no different, but its menu options are a bit more varied. In the adorably-mangled Spanglish menu, you can find a variety of coastal favorites. "Seafaring rice," "prawns to the iron," etc. The service is decent and the food isn't anything to write home about, but it's a solid option if you're in the mood for some seaside seafood. Malecón of Las Palmas.
Updated: Aug 03, 2013.

Perla Verde Restaurant
(ENTREES: $6-20) Set beneath the Hotel Perla Verde, the restaurant is just as clean and modern as its bigger sibling. The menu has plenty of variety, including seafood and international dishes, and the prices are reasonable. The restaurant seems out of place with the rest of Esmeraldas, almost sterile in comparison to the dust and grit on the streets outside. Or you could look at it as a respite, which it definitely is: air conditioning, good service and cleanliness might be the first three things you notice about this place and wont pass up. Ca. Piedrahita, between Olmedo and Sucre, Tel: 06-272-3820 ext 112.
Updated: Feb 08, 2013.

Gustos Del Paladar
(ENTREES: $3.50-5) This little hole in the wall – as unappetizing as it looks from the outside – is in fact quite fulfilling once you sit down, order and eat any one of the plates they have listed on their mini-billboard menu outside and inside. A variety of ocean and land meats smothered in coastal sauces will get you your fix over a mound of rice. And, if for some reason that still doesn't manage to cut it, just know that there's a ton of food stands serving fries and burgers right outside at the city park. Olmedo, between Jose Mejia and Salinas, right in front of the plaza, Tel: 06-245-6451.
Updated: Apr 04, 2013.

Things To See and Do in Esmeraldas
If you find yourself stuck in the city for a night or two, catch a bus or taxi to Las Palmas: the Esmeraldas version of an upscale beach. Also, go check out the city's museum and plazas.
Updated: Apr 04, 2013.

Malecón Las Palmas
Las Palmas is the main street that borders the beach, hosting a few bars and seafood restaurants along its lane, as well as boasting excellent sea views and providing a good place to grab a cold beer and sample the local fare. Be warned, however, that this is not the best place to hang around alone at night. Note: Las Palmas was undergoing substantial construction and renovation at the time of this writing, as the new Paseo las Palmas is set to open its doors to an array of new restaurants, bars, stores, and recreational facilities at the end of 2013. To get to Las Palmas head to Olmedo and catch a bus with red, green and white lettering with "Las Palmas" as its destination. Alternatively, just cab it there for $1-2.
Updated: Apr 05, 2013.

Esmeraldas Plazas
There's two miniature central parks that reside within Esmeraldas. Parque Central 20 de Marzo is the city's main park, while Parque Luis Cervantes is more of a recreational park. On early evenings at the end of the week or during the weekend, head on over to the latter to watch the locals duke it out in a game of Ecua-Volley, or sample the fried food, and amuse yourself with the community dance workouts. Both parks are found on Bolivar and 10 de Agosto / Olmedo and Jose Mejia, respectively.

ATACAMES

 5m   15,526   06

Spread across an expansive stretch of fine gray sand, Atacames is a beachside playground for Ecuadorians. Foreigners are more the exception than the norm. Part hustler, part street-side vendor and welcoming hotel owner, Atacames is a town with many faces, which seem to change as the sun moves across the sky.

Families can be seen with toddlers lagging along at their sides and young couples walk wrapped in each others arms. Pods of young

NORTHERN COAST

Ecuadorians meander through the streets or stake claim to a squat of beach. Volleyball matches and soccer games sporadically appear along the beach where mothers, brothers, sisters, girlfriends and happily single males mingle or lounge across beach chairs.

At sunrise, the beach is practically empty, which seems to draw another crowd: older couples and families with small children. This is the time to stroll the beach strip and enjoy Atacames for its inherent natural beauty: seemingly endless coast set amidst rolling green hills that tumble into brown cliffs that plunge into the sea.

At night, of course, all such attributes disappear beneath a blanket of sky, the only lights being an occasional beach bonfire and the neon glow of Malecon's bouncing bars and hopping restaurants. To taste all of Atacames, you'd have to rise early, party hard and be prepared to spend a hefty dime or two. Besides over-priced cocktails, the town specializes in encocado dishes, coconut-based deserts and ice cream sundaes served in carved out pineapples.
Updated: Apr 08, 2013.

When To Go to Atacames

During Carnaval, Quito empties, and most Quiteños head to the beach. Atacames is the first to fill up: expect hotel rates to at least triple (if you're lucky enough to find one). In the daytime, the beach is so packed, you'll be hard pressed to find a place to lay out a bandanna, let alone a towel.

Atacames (and most of the other seaside resort areas) has two seasons: temporada alta (high season) and temporada baja (low season). As you might have guessed, hotel prices tend to rise by at least 10-15% during peak season, generally August to December and big holidays like Semana Santa and Carnival. If you're planning a trip during these times, it's best to reserve a room ahead of time, as the best places fill up quickly. Remember, too, that bargaining is always an option; whether you can successfully knock off a few bucks is another question.
Updated: Mar 20, 2013.

Getting To and Away from Atacames

Trans-Esmeraldas offers daily, direct service to Atacames from **Quito** and **Guayaquil**. To get to Atacames from Esmeraldas, grab a taxi ($3) to the Esmeralda Bus Terminal from which buses depart every 20-minutes

to Atacames ($1-1.50, 1 hour). The other (and faster) option is to walk down to Orellana and grab a bus ($0.25) that's either heading to "Terminal" and/or "Tolita la Y," making sure to tell the conductor that you're headed to Atacames.

The 10-minute bus ride will have him drop you off at the piggy-back point between Esmeraldas and Atacames, at which point you can grab a taxi there for just $1 (20 mins). Note: If travelling solo, you must wait for the taxi cab to fill up completely with other passengers before the ride to Atacames can begin, that is of course unless you want to pay the full $4 fee. The road to Atacames boasts a network of picturesque green hills, frequently interrupted by simple dirt roads or the orange flame-bearing pipes that mark the site of an oil refinery.
Updated: Apr 05, 2013.

Safety

Safety is always an issue, as crowds and money seem to go hand-in-hand with crime and petty theft. Always keep an eye on your bag, never carry anything you'd be sad to lose and stay with the crowds: areas to the far east and west of the Malecon are noticeably less crowded, but also seem to attract more assaults. Traveler be warned: Walking the beach alone at night is not recommended, so if you plan on bar hopping all night you'll probably want to stick to the Malecón.

While there are plenty of hotels running east and west of the main Malecon strip, it's best to stay close to the action if you're in a small group or plan on walking to and from your hotel later at night.

Inside the discos, don't accept drinks from unknown people, and beware of pickpockets on crowded dance floors. It is even unwise to drive on the roads near Atacames after dark to nearby towns like Same and Sua, as local thieves have learned that wealthy young Quiteños often travel those roads on their way back to the posh hotels and resorts in those towns after a night of partying in Atacames.
Updated: Apr 05, 2013.

Atacames Services

If you're strapped for cash, there are two ATM's on the Malecon. If you're in search of phone cards, inquire at one of the convenience stores or head to Hotel El Tiburon on the northern end of Malecon. You'll also find internet-cafes spread out along the Malecon itself if you need to get in touch via web ($1

NORTHERN COAST

for 1 hour), so just walk along the avenue or ask around to find one.

For general inquiries and pamphlets, the "iTur" Office will provide you with general information on the area. Located on Av de las Acacias, it's the tall green building on the corner of the bridge and road that goes to Súa. Emails:camara.atacames@gmail.com, info@atacames.travel, Tel: 06-273-1333, 06-276-0232.
Updated: Apr 05, 2013.

Things To See and Do in Atacames

With more bars and restaurants per square meter than palm tree or patch of available sand on the beach, Atacames serves as more of a platform to come drink, party, have fun and soak in the sun rather than partake in any culturally/geographically enlightening tours or activities. That's not to say there's anything wrong with having fun, though! Just know that you won't find much here in terms of sights to see or places to go, if that's what you're looking for.
Updated: Apr 05, 2013.

Tubing and Boat Tours
(PRICE: $2-3) On the beach in Atacames, you will find an abundance of motorboats anchored just past the shore-break. These boats will pull you around on giant inflatable tubes for a price of about a dollar or two per 15 minutes. Be careful, if the water is choppy it might be a bit uncomfortable. Don't hesitate to bargain.

In addition to this, ask about tours to the nearby islands or fishing, and they'll probably be able to arrange something. Prices vary depending on the size of the group, but expect to pay anywhere from $10-20 per person. Walk out on the beach, and look for turquoise or green motor boats sitting in the surf.
Updated: Apr 05, 2013.

La Vida Del Mar Museum and Aquarium
(PRICE: $1.50) Probably one of the rarer things available to any visitor of Atacames is an Aquarium. But this small and modest locale offers newcomers a chance to look at a variety of species that are native to the ocean right out front. Get a chance to look at their remarkable collection of seahorses and/or sea turtles, which they keep them in temporary captivity before letting them out into the ocean again. Structurally speaking, the museum is nothing spectacular, but it's

nice to walk into something that's completely different from all the bars and restaurants that seem to overwhelm Atacames at times. Northern end of the Malecon, in front of Hotel Tahiti. Tel: 02-276-0237 / 099-945-3931.
Updated: Apr 05, 2013.

Handicraft Market
It's typically during high-season and weekends that you'll find artists from all over the place coming and selling their goods here, ranging anywhere from coastal clothing to tiny, hand-carved souvenirs.
Updated: Apr 05, 2013.

Atacames Lodging
Accommodation options in Atacames run from cheap backpacker dives offering little more than a bed all the way to more luxurious resorts featuring courtyard pools, air-conditioned rooms and on site restaurants and bars. Those with a budget don't necessarily need to suffer through their stay, as a few new places have recently gone up that are reasonably priced and offer brand new, ultra-clean facilities. You're better off scouting out the area (and prices) before choosing to throw down your pack. Most places are located on the Malecón.

Hotel Club Del Sol
(ROOMS: $61-76) Club del Sol is one of the few places in Atacames that has the distinct feel of a large hotel chain: artwork-adorned walls, precisely made beds with matching nightstands, and that ever-so-friendly paper tab wrapped around the toilet to signal no one has used it since the last cleaning. Besides modern bathrooms and air conditioning, Hotel Club del Sol offers a host of other trademark resort amenities, such as a restaurant/bar, pool, game room and flat-screen TVs.

Although significantly more expensive than the simple rooms up for grabs on the Malecón, the price is right if you're looking for something private, beach-front and secure. Av. 21 de Noviembre s/n, Nueva Granada neigborhood; Quito office: Av. Universitaria Oe5-84 and Av. 18 de Septiembre, Tel: 06-276-0660/1/2/3, Cel: 09-9859-6136, Quito office: 02-252-9412/6865, E-mail: club-sol@interactive.net.ec / hclubdelsol@andinanet.net, URL: www.hotelclubdelsol.com
Updated: Feb 13, 2013.

Hotel Juan Sebastian
($60 per person) Hotel Juan Sebastian lies at the eastern end of the Malecón and features an unmistakable sign mimicking the

NORTHERN COAST

Walt Disney logo. The hotel tries to live up to this association with its five abnormally large pools interconnected by narrow channels in the center of the grounds. A number of room options are available, from cabin-like bunks to first-class suites. Rooms are a bit shabby for the price, but the location, pool and friendly staff make up for it. Plentiful parking is also available if you brought a car with you. The main pool area is a large, wide open space surrounded by palm-thatched huts where you can picnic or imbibe. Av. 21 de Noviembre, east end of Malecón, with the main entrance found on the street behind but parallel to the boardwalk; Quito: Ca. Wilson E8-22 and Av. 6 de Diciembre, Tel: 06-273-1606/7, Quito: 02-256-1990/3243/3192, E-mail: recepcionjs@hembassy.com, URL: www.hoteljuansebastian.com. Updated: Feb 13, 2013.

Hostería Cayapas

($10-15 per person) Tucked away from the main strip, Hosteria Cayapas is significantly quieter and more expensive than other options in town. The area outside looks a little worse for wear, and you might expect more of the rooms considering the price, but in general, Hostería Cayapas isn't a bad deal. Rooms come with private bathroom, air conditioning and cable TV, and facilities include a swimming pool and recreation area. Parking is also available. Cayapas is a good option for those wanting to avoid the noise without sacrificing having a beach right out front. The hosteria only offers cabañas that easily house five people, so don't expect to find a single room here. Av. 21 de Noviembre, on beach near Hotel Cielo Azul and Rincon del Mar, Tel: 06-273-1047, URL: www.hotelcayapas.com. Updated: Feb 13, 2013.

Hotel Orus

($20-60 per person) Hotel Orus is one of the few modern-looking, multistoried hotels in Atacames, and features a terrace-top pool overlooking the ocean. Rooms are simple but clean, with private bathrooms and hot water. Unfortunately, this otherwise modern hotel lacks air conditioning, so you might have to make frequent trips to the terrace for a dip. The hotel also owns Nagiba Bar, on the beach side of Malecón. The entrance is around the corner from the street-facing bakery and is a nice place for Nescafé coffee or fresh-baked treats. Central Malecón, on the left side of Hotel Tiburón, Tel: 06-273-1314, E-mail: cesar-manjarres@hotmail.com.

Hotel Carluz

($18-23 per person) Located across the street from Hotel Club del Sol, at the quieter western end of Atacames, Hotel Carluz seems to occupy its own peaceful space. The hotel is significantly smaller and better maintained than other options nearby and is the perfect place for those in search of a slightly cozier, more intimate place to stay. Rooms are clean and bright with cheerful, colored sheets, white tiles, spacious modern bathrooms, and amenities like air conditioning and a mini-fridge. There is a courtyard pool outside. The adjacent restaurant is similarly appealing in class and tastefulness, but might remain shut when there aren't many people. If you do get a chance to dine at Carluz, you'll be delighted by both the atmosphere and the menu, which offers a range of local and international cuisine, from ceviche and seafood to chicken, meat and past. Av. 21 de Noviembre and Intersección C, next to the stadium, Tel: 06-273-1456/1272, Fax: 06-273-1272, E-mail: info@hotelcarluz.com, URL: www.hotelcarluz.com. Updated: Feb 08, 2013.

Hotel Cielo Azul

(ROOMS: $30-71) In terms of price, location and facilities, Hotel Cielo Azul is probably one of the best mid-range choices in Atacames. The hotel is tucked away from the Malecón's noise and crowds, and the rooms overlook the beach and a central courtyard with a small pool. Follow a sandy walkway from the hotel and relax on the beach, or mosey back to the pool area where you can stake claim to a lawn chair and order a drink from the poolside bar. Rooms are clean and bright, with air conditioning, private baths and tiled floors, and the coral hues add to the tropical feel. As one might expect from a place like this, the hotel fills up during high season so be sure to reserve a room in advance. Av. 21 de Noviembre, on the beach, Tel: 06-273-1813, Cel: 09-9466-2783, E-mail: cieloazulatacames@yahoo.es, URL: www.hotelcieloazul.com. Updated: Feb 13, 2013.

Chill Inn

($8-16 per person) This small, Swiss-run hostel is clean and friendly, with nice rooms that sleep two to eight people each. All have comfortable beds, private bathrooms and fans. Several common areas to chill out in provide a pleasant ambiance for travelers, small groups, couples and families. In the small beach-style bar, guests can enjoy exotic drinks, fresh fruit juices and salads. Chill Inn is ideally situated on a quiet street only 50 meters (164 ft) from the beach, near all kinds of shops and just around the corner from the nightlife on the Malecón. The Swiss owner speaks several languages. Free parking is also available. Salida del Paco Foco, Diagonal al Bachita, located a few steps away from the famous and bustling Malecón. Where the artisanal market ends you take left for leaving the Malecón and after around 50 m/164 ft you will find the Hostal Bar Chill Inn on your left. Tel: 06-276-0477, E-mail: yoliboegli@gmx.net, URL: www.chillinnecuador.com. Updated: Feb 13, 2013.

Hotel El Marques

(ROOMS: $79-147) Hotel El Marques is one of Atacames' largest and most luxurious hotels. Just a few years old, the hotel exudes luxury, with its seven-story presence and large courtyard pool. Everything about the hotel is maintained well, and rooms offer hot water, cable TV, and firm beds with nice linens, and most have a view of the ocean. The hotel sits on prime real-estate, directly on the Malecón, but is separated by plexiglass walls from the street's hubbub. This is one of the nicest options in Atacames, but probably a bit noisier than other high-end places. Malecón and Los Crotos, Tel: 06-276-0182, E-mail: reservaciones@elmarqueshotel.com / info@hotelelmarques.com.ec, URL: www.hotelelmarques.com.ec. Updated: Feb 13, 2013.

Hotel Oceano

($15 per person) Hotel Oceano sits a few buildings off of the Malecón and offers pretty meager amenities. Some rooms do not have windows and none have hot water, but there is cable, an oscillating fan in each room, and a few arcade games. The front desk also doubles as a small convenience store. This shouldn't be high on your list of places to stay, as there are plenty of other options at a lower cost. Make sure to ask to see your room before agreeing to anything. Los Crotos and Malecón, on the second-to-last side street on the western end of the Malecón, Tel: 06-273-1244, Cel: 09-9192-9025, E-mail: deycaros@yahoo.es. Updated: Feb 13, 2013.

Hotel Mira Valle

($10 per person) Hotel Mira Valle sits right off of the western end of the Malecón and offers basic rooms for a fairly cheap price. However, there is no hot water and some rooms have no windows. The building itself lacks any sort of charm and long, dark hall-ways give it a drab feel. The location is good, however.and there is cable TV and a fan in each room. This is a decent option if you're on a budget and low-maintenance. Corner of Atacames and Las Acacias, a few pointers are that the hotel lies on the western end of the Malecón and is a fairly tall building. The entrance itself is unassuming, but there is a large sign that will help you find it. Tel: 06-273-1138, Cel: 09-9744-9509. Updated: Feb 13, 2013.

Arco Iris Hotel

(ROOMS: $50-150) The 11-story Arco Iris Hotel offers everything in the way of luxury accommodation in Atacames. The hotel sits on the quieter eastern end of the Malecón, and almost every suite has a view of the ocean. There are no small rooms here; each suite has a small kitchen, a firm bed, a balcony and hot water. The hotel has two pools, a game room and a large parking garage. Los Delfines and Malecón, Walk east along the Malecón until you see two tall towers. Hard to miss. Tel: 02-207-5381, Cel: 09-9294-1017/8392-9100, E-mail: fmorales@arcoirisatacames.com, URL: www.arcoirisatacames.com. Updated: Feb 13, 2013.

Malecón Inn

($15-20 per person) Looking like a miniature skyscraper, Malecón Inn has a commanding view of the Malecón strip and the beach. Walk through the glass door and up the stairs and you'll be pleasantly surprised by how clean, modern and safe the hotel feels, but it lacks any sort of charm. Offering simple but immaculately kept rooms with air conditioning, hot water and TV, this place is certainly one of the best deals in town.

Walls and floors look so new you'd think the hotel had just opened. A bright yellow hallway leads into violet-colored rooms with new beds and nightstands. Sheets and mattresses look like something out of a mall display and the bathrooms are sparkling. There's a parking garage nearby. Corner of Malecón and Ca. Sua, in front of beach., Tel: 06-273-1508. Updated: Feb 08, 2013.

Hotel San Jose

($7-10 per person) If you're looking for a place in town but set away from the Malecón's noise, this is an ideal option. You might have to inquire next door at the convenience shop, as the entrance is often unattended. This is a solid place to spend the night: rooms with clean sheets, private bathroom, fan and TV. Those with bad backs

NORTHERN COAST

should probably seek other accommodation, as the beds lack a little give. Rooms are windowless, so don't expect ocean views or much light coming into it either, but that doesn't really matter if you like to sleep in! Ca. Las Acacias, turn left at the far west end of Malecón, on the left among a row of other hostels. Tel: 06-273-1072.
Updated: Feb 08, 2013.

Rincon del Mar

($10-15 per person) This sprawling complex is located on the beach behind a gruesome-looking chain link fence. Its small, shabby-looking rooms with private bathrooms and multiple bunks open onto ocean views, while an adobe complex to the back offers more rooms by the pool. Compared to other hotels in the same location, Rincon del Mar is a deal and would be particularly good for small groups looking for a quiet escape from the noise of Atacames. The pool appears clean, as do the rooms, but other places in town are slightly brighter. If you're traveling alone, consider something closer to town; it's quite a walk down either a relatively deserted street or strip of beach to get here. There was no indication that owners could speak either French or German, as they've advertised. Still, the place appears to be popular with foreign travelers. Av. 21 de Noviembre and Acacias, on the beach., Tel: 06-276-0360, Cel: 09-9137-3187, E-mail: rincondelmar1@yahoo.es.

Hotel El Tiburón

($15 per person)Hotel El Tiburón, located behind a conspicuous purple and white façade, is a friendly and economical option for families and groups of friends. The hospitable staff and central location are a bonus, as are both the hammock-lined courtyard restaurant and indoor pool area. Rooms are nothing to brag about—dated wooden beds and dark bathrooms—but, for the price, El Tiburón not a bad place to end up for a day or two. Malecón, next to the Le Cocotier Restaurant, Tel: 06-273-1145/1622 /1653, Cel: 09-9168-4716, E-mail: antonia@hoteltiburonatacames.com, URL: www.hoteltiburonatacames.com.

Hotel Miramar

($12 per person) If you plan on hitting Atacames with a group of four or more, then Hotel Miramar (formerly Hotel Ximena Inn) is your best bet. Suites include clean, modern rooms with screened windows (a plus considering the mosquitoes) and large, tiled bathrooms. Caribbean and coral colors add a splash of flavor to the already appealing hotel, and, if you didn't get enough of the beach, you can always hang out on the private balconies that come with the rooms. If the owner is out of town, you'll probably be greeted by his sister, Noemi Pico, who's as accommodating as the rest of the place. Unfortunately, there is only one double room so the hotel is not the most economical option for less than three or four people. Call ahead for reservations during high season. Corner of Malecón and Tolitas, Tel: 06-273-1363, E-mail: hotelmiramar@hotmail.com, URL: www.hotelmiramar.com.
Updated: Feb 08, 2013.

Andy Hotel Internacional

($8-15 per person) The concrete building perched above the Malecón strip might be considered an eyesore, but in terms of value for money, travelers will find this place appealing. Rooms are simple, with bunks, TV, fan, and private bathrooms, and most offer a seaside view through screen-less windows (beware of mosquitoes). Bathrooms are nicely tiled and relatively clean, though hot water doesn't always appear. Although in need of a good back-breaking once-over clean, the rooms are cozy and tidy and the staff extremely friendly. The hotel is also centrally located, so this is one of the safer options. Also, if you're visiting during high season, it always helps to negotiate with the owner, who might knock off a few dollars. Malecón and Ostiones, Tel: 06-276-0221/0228, Cel: 09-9915-0633, URL: www.hotelandyatacames.com.
Updated: Feb 08, 2013.

Hotel Galleria

($8-20 per person) Like a number of places in Atacames, Hotel Galleria has seen better days. The small, dark rooms are in a conspicuously large, sagging wooden building and offer little more than a bathroom, simple bunks and maybe-works ceiling fan. Despite appearances, however, the hotel is not without its charms. Balconies feature slivers of seaside views and the restaurant downstairs has an extensive menu, specializing in pizza and pasta, as well as streetside and ocean views. While the rooms might not be to your taste, the restaurant is a perfect spot for sharing a few drinks with friends or just people-watching. Ask owner Milton Altamirano about the package deal—a real steal considering the Atacames location: room and breakfast, lunch and dinner for a good price. Malecón, near Hotel Tiburón, Tel: 06-273-1149.

Atacames Restaurants

As you might expect from a popular resort town, Atacames has its fair share of restaurants, each featuring its own menu (and prices). Whether you're bustin' for pizza and pasta, or hangin' out for surf and turf, restaurants in this town are bound to satisfy your craving. Like the hotels, most places are easy to find: just take a stroll down the Malecón. Prices from one place to another vary little, so you're more likely to choose a restaurant for its menu and atmosphere rather than by how many clams it will set you back.

One of the big things in Atacames is cocada, which is a treat consisting of sweetened coconut shards rolled into balls, cut into squares, or spread on toast. Streets are literally filled with vendors, each selling similar-looking packets, stacked on a table. Ecuadorians never fail to grab several when they're leaving town and heading back to the city. Updated: Apr 05, 2013.

Gabilo's Helados

(TREATS: $1-3) If you are looking for something a little more unique, or are wary of street stuffs, then pay a visit to Gabriel Ruiz Diaz at Gabelo's Helados. For the past 11 years, Gabriel and his wife have been producing these cocout delights en masse, carefully monitoring each batch for taste and quality.

The cocada de manjar sold here is more expensive but softer, richer and tastier than its street cousins. The shop also sells hot dogs, ice cream and gigantic ice cream sundaes. For $1.50, you can get a hot dog and a cola. Gabelo's is easy to find, just look out for a large picture of a jovial middle-aged man on the west end of the Malecón. Updated: Mar 20, 2013.

Restaurante Oh Mar!

(ENTREES: $6-16) Just off the Malecón, you'll find Restaurante Oh Mar!, a mid-range seafood joint with ample seating and an abundance of options, most of them containing seafood. The place seems to be really popular with the locals, which is always a good sign. Try the ceviche, which is the restaurant´s specialty. Av. 21 de Noviembre and Los Crotos, Tel: 06-273-1637. Updated: Feb 13, 2013.

Shamu Restaurante

(ENTREES: $9-20) The Shamu Restaurante occupies part of the massive Hotel El Marques' ground floor, but you there is easy access through the Malecón entrance. The restaurant has a wide variety of options, mostly oriented around seafood and meat. Shamu lacks any sort of local character, and the dining room is a rather sterile looking room with a view of the Marques' pool. There is also an ice cream shop, Heladería Dulcefrío, attached to the restaurant where you can get some pretty scrumptious ice cream treats. Overall, the restaurant is a safe bet, but you're not going to have any sort of culinary epiphany here. Western end of the Malecón., Tel: 06-273-1172/1560. Updated: Apr 05, 2013.

D'Lyly Restaurant

(ENTREES: $5-9)This little place isn't much different from other seafood diners along he malecon have to offer. Prices might seem a little unreasonable given the small portions of rice and meat your served with your meal, but it's quite striking when you realize it fills you up. It's open entrance allows for streets vendors selling coconut water and sweets to enter, so don't be ashamed to opt for their beverages rather than what's listed on the menu to the place. Malecón, Tel: 098-546-0218. Updated: Apr 05, 2013.

Cevicheria Plaza

(CEVICHE: $4-6) Grab a bowl of delicious ceviche at the food plaza here, and watch as it's prepared directly in front of you - and don't worry, all the seafood is precooked. Look for the roofed, open air place along the beach by the street, with waiters holding menus out. Updated: Apr 05, 2013.

Der Alte Fritz

(ENTREES: $5-10) Der Alte Fritz is loved by travelers and guidebooks alike and is a sure win if you're in the mood for something German, something Ecuadorian, or simply something a little classier than what the rest of Atacames can offer. The menu is extensive, and is written in three languages so almost everyone can understand. If you still can't read the selections, ask the stalwart-looking fellow with glasses and long hair: Captain Martin Einhaus speaks five languages and will most likely be able to answer you. The restaurant's seafood is likely fresher than the stuff they serve up along the beach, and changes with the season to ensure quality. The menu also features various pastas and special Austrian pancakes. This eatery even beats restaurants in the big city; people travel from as far as Guayaquil just to sit and nibble on the most authentic German food in the region. Above the restaurant are numerous simple but tasteful rooms for

about $15 a night; Der Alte Fritz is the place to come to stay and stay to eat. Malecón., Tel: 099-470-7538 / 06-273-1610, E-mail: meinhaus@deraltefritzecuador.com, URL: www.deraltefritzecuador.com.
Updated: Apr 05, 2013.

Pizzeria da Giulio

(ENTREES: $7-20) There are a couple of pizza restaurants in town, but Pizzeria Da Giulio is probably the most gourmet. Owner Giulio was born in Italy and spent 14 years working in Milan. Whether or not his background contributes to the restaurant's authenticity is something you'll have to decide for yourself. The Italian-Ecuadorian owners go to great lengths to ensure their ingredients are fresh and true to Italian form, something easier said than done in a country where rice, plantains and meat are the staples. Cheese is bought from a specialty store in Quito and the mushrooms are hand-chopped and marinated in a special mix of olive oil and garlic. Although pizza is the specialty, the restaurant also offers a variety of fish, chicken and meat dishes, all of which can be enjoyed with an ocean view. Central Malecón, next to Disco Scala, Tel: 06-273-1603. Updated: Feb 13, 2013.

El Tiburon

(ENTREES: $5-6) A popular locals' joint, this restaurant is small but tidy, with colorful decorations and friendly service. The house recommends Bandeja de Mariscos, which can be shared between three people. The rest of the menu is pretty typical Atacames fare, with various ceviches, and fish, meat and chicken dishes. Those who aren't up for fish or game can treat themselves to a simple spaghetti dish. If you're up early and feeling hungry they also serve breakfasts, but be aware that this party town doesn't get going much before 09:00. Malecón, Tel: 06-273-1145/1622/1653.
Updated: Apr 05, 2013.

Atacames Nightlife

Atacames serves up its fair share of drinks and bombastic sounds. Just take your pick of the bamboo and thatched-roof bars fronting the beach. Each varies only slightly in style, music played and how the drinks are served, and popularity seems to rotate night-to-night. Early in the evening families can be seen, while the night drives a rowdier and younger crowd. Prices seem to vary little from bar to bar, and the cocktail list is pretty extensive at each and every one. Some have DJ's, some just have a playlist.

At the far eastern strip of Malecón, Friends Bar seems to be a popular joint, offering pumping music and weekend Marimba. The guys at Jamaica Bar, a bit further west, know how to make a good cocktail. As with every other place, the juice is fresh-as, but here drinks ($2-4) are artfully prepared and topped off with sliced fruit and tied-napkins. The atmosphere here is chilled out, like the music. At night, on the other side of the street, Tsunami Bar seems to be the most popular Ecuadorian draw. If you're looking for deals, just walk the main strip and grab any of the fliers being handed out like candy.
Updated: Apr 05, 2013.

SÚA

Set in a pleasant cove behind the picturesque green hills, cradling Atacames and separating it from nearbySame, Súa is a slightly — albeit not much — quieter version of its bar-infested big brother to the north. Talk to travelers and you're bound to get mixed reviews about this place: either it's a chilled-out place to throw back a few beers, enjoy the beach and rest your head, or it's a lackluster, lonelier version of Atacames. Contrary to some guidebooks, Atacames locals say Súa is more dangerous, as there are fewer people and beach-prowlers tend to be more aggressive — but this could just be a ploy to lure back tourists attempting to avoid their notoriously crowded beach.

The town is a bit scruffy, with the same unruly Reggaeton blasting from generic bamboo beachside bars; and you'd think the street vendors had just pushed their cart over the hill. To give credit where credit's due, the beach is less crowded and surprisingly picturesque, considering the shabby shops and hotels fronting its shores: expanses of fine gray sand stretch towards the sea, curling into a quiet cove at the far end.

If you make it to this side of Atacames, head over to the massive cliffs dropping abruptly into the sea on the western side of the bay. Known as Peñón del Suicida (Suicide Rock), the rock is named after Princess Súa and conquistador Captain de León — Ecuador's own Romeo and Juliet — who leapt headlong into the sea after a forbidden love affair gone awry. At night, their ghosts are said to wander along the beach, but by dawn these legendary specters slip back into the sea and the day shift arrives: shrieking pelicans, blue-footed boobies and frigate birds stake out the cliffside, occasionally swooping down on unsuspecting fisherman and their haul.

Between June and September, you can catch a boat from here to spot humpback whales off the coast, near Punta Galera (about 40-60 minutes by boat). Simply look to the shores for fishermen - sometimes they'll even have inflatable barges/tubes - and ask them if they can take you out. There's also the nearby Isla de los Pajaros (Island of the Birds) that's worth checking out via boat. Updated: Apr 05, 2013.

Súa Services

Heads up: There are no banks or ATM's available in Súa, so be sure to stock up on cash in Atacames before you head South. There's an Internet Café with a red sign that reads "Claro! Cabinas Internet Banda Ancha" where you can reconnect for $1/1hr, located around the block fom Buganvillas Hotel. There's also a farmacy on the main road that leads into town on the corner of Malecón. Updated: Apr 05, 2013.

Getting To and Away from Súa

You can easily get to **Atacames** for an evening of revelry by catching a motorcycle rickshaw to Súa for about a dollar or two per person (bargaining isn't very effective, but there are so many rickshaws buzzing around you'll have no problem finding an honest driver). Have patience with the machines as they sputter up the large hills outside of town, it takes awhile for the atrophied engines to climb them.

During the day, there's green buses that head down from Atacames to Súa (and vice-versa) every 10-15 minutes, just flag one down as it comes into town off the main coastal route into Avenida de las Acacias. Travel time to Súa is about 5 minutes ($0.25). Alternatively, take a normal taxi to Súa for $3.

If you want to head North or South from Súa, Costeñita buses run every 15-20 minutes down the main coastal route. South to **Muisne**, North to **Esmeraldas**, $1. Estimated travel time to Muisne is about 1 hour, to Esmeraldas: 40 minutes. Also note that depending on the time of the day, you might not have seating for the length of the journey given a lot of people commute on weekdays. Updated: Apr 05, 2013.

Súa Lodging

Súa hotels are all about the same in terms of price and quality. All cost less than $15 a night, and none have hot water. However, the majority of them are beach-front and possess enough charm to make a stay worthwile. The town itself doesn't have much in the way of activities, but the beach is gorgeous, uncrowded and much more relaxing than in the larger towns along the coast. Updated: Aug 02, 2012.

Hotel Chagra Ramas

($8-12 per person) Like everything else in Súa, Hotel Chagra Ramas is a bit run-down and in need of some work. However, its ocean views can't be beat. Brightly-painted cabins line the hillside in tiers, while a large open restaurant sits at the bottom, but all sections overlook the sea. Bare essential rooms come with dated wooden beds, dark bathrooms reminiscent of high school locker rooms and television equipped with spotty cable. The restaurant is, like the rest of the place, oversized and under-nourished; a large seating area appears empty, except for a few patrons and the staff. Meals are cheap and range from stock standard rice, meat, and chicken plates to the only slightly more expensive encocado and ceviche dishes. Two types of breakfast are served. However, Chagra Ramos provides the most secluded atmosphere of Súa's options, and has a few hammocks lying around. You can also rent sea kayaks for $5 an hour. Note; on weekends the hotel sometimes throws parties that last until dawn, so unless you're the heaviest sleeper there is (or looking for an all-night beach party), consider staying somewhere else during the weekend. Main street, occupies entire right side of main street at beach, Tel: 02-473-3106, E-mail: hotelsierranomo_79@hotmail.com. Updated: Apr 05, 2013.

Hotel Los Jardines

($10-16 per person) Los Jardines is set back from the beach, on the street leading beach-front. The hotel is a decent budget option with bare but clean, rooms that surround an appealing pool and attractive garden. Don't be surprised if the entrance is unattended, just knock or say hello and someone is sure to come. Los Jardines is an option if you're in need of a place to stay and are looking for something slightly better than a bed with sheets. However, almost every other option in Súa is on the beach, and charges similar prices. Street signs and names are not really used in Súa, but the hotel is easily found on the main street heading towards the beach, very close to where the bus drops you off. Tel: 06-247-3037/3081 / 099-904-2796, URL: http://www.hotellosjardines-sua.com. Updated: Apr 05, 2013.

Sol De Súa

($8-15 per person) Sol de Súa sits towards the western end of the Malecón, right across from the beach. There are about ten cabañas spread out on about an acre of dusty land that backs up to a small river. The place has a nice charm to it, but the rooms are pretty threadbare; no television (warning: there isn't much to do in Súa, a TV is important!), no hot water and only a small fan. However, there is plenty of space outdoors to relax, and the place labels itself as an eco-lodge. It's a good option if you aren't high-maintenance. Western end of Malecón, Tel: 06-247-3090. Updated: Apr 05, 2013.

Hostal Buganvillas

($10 per person) Glowing with a faded joy that it might've still had thirty years ago, Hostal Buganvillas retains at least some of its charm through chipped paint and faded, bare-boned rooms. Despite its lackluster looks however, Buganvillas is pretty tidy and clean. Mattresses are pretty comfortable, and linens are cleaned periodically. Rickety fans and netted windows will keep you safe from the exteriors, just don't come expecting a lavish interior. Amenities include: a well-maintained pool and a super convenient store that's actually part of the hotel itself. Malecón, Tel: 06-247-3008 / 099-932-2217, URL: www.hostallasbuganvillas.com. Updated: Apr 05, 2013.

Súa Restaurants

Súa has just a couple of family-run restaurants along its Malecon, all of them specializing in seafood. Step outside any one of them after you're done eating and walk across the street to have a drink or two at any of the wooden bars that line the waterfront.

Kike's Restaurant

(ENTREES: $4-15) Set in a large airy room featuring glass-top tables with napkin-bearing cranes, this is one of the cleaner, nicer restaurants in town. The menu is pretty standard seaside fare, but slightly cheaper than the stuff served up in Atacames. Specialties include Mariscos and encocado dishes. While the street action outside might feel otherwise, Kike's restaurant gives off a pleasant family atmosphere. Central Malecón, Tel: 099-385-8406. Updated: Apr 05, 2013.

Restaurante Malibu

(ENTREES: $5-12) The majority of restaurants in the small beach towns of Ecuador's coast have the same vibe; open air, plastic chairs and quality seafood. Malibu is no different, and there isn't much that sets this place apart from anywhere else along the strip. The encocado dishes are decent, and breakfast is a bit cheaper than elsewhere. Central Malecón, Tel: 06-247-3230 / 098-013-4137. Updated: Apr 05, 2013.

SAME

 6m   4,301   06

Located on a secluded strip of beach away from the blaring bars and packed streets of Atacames, Same is little more than a quiet stretch of exclusive apartment buildings for vacationing Quiteños, with the odd hotel squeezed in among them. Although it can feel a bit deserted, it's a nice spot to spend the day.

Those prepared to blow a few bucks can head up to Club Casablanca, which spreads out across the adjacent hillside like a white fortress for the wealthy. This is not the place for backpackers and penny-pinchers, but certainly a great getaway for those with means. Back beachside, there are a couple of options for sleeping and eating, though availability seems to depend more on the owner and time of year than physical presence of a room to spare. Updated: Apr 09, 2013.

Getting To and Away From Same

To get to Same from Atacames, head to the main highway that cuts through Atacames north and south. Buses run frequently to Súa, Same ($0.50, 30 minutes) and Muisne. Just flag the bus down and it'll pull over. Alternatively, take a taxi to Same for $5. Updated: Apr 09, 2013.

Same Lodging

Same hotels cater to those with more money than the average backpacker. You'll find most options to be fairly pricey, given cheap dives are not as prevalent as in Súa or Atacames.

However, for a bit more than you'd pay for a bare bones joint in Atacames, you can find a great beach-side room on one of Ecuador's nicest beaches. Same is very quiet, and therefore its lodging options are fairly limited. Make sure to book in advance if you plan on heading out there during the holidays. Updated: Mar 21, 2013.

La Terraza

($15-25 per person) La Terraza's white adobe building is reminiscent of the more expensive places perched on the hillside, and the rooms inside are bright and breezy. Private bathrooms are immaculate and rooms open onto a terrace overlooking the sea. The next-door cabins, also part of La Terraza, are slightly more economical but far less attractive (they are, however, almost on the beach). The hotel offers mosquito nets and hot water, and some rooms have a small fridge. Those in search of food can wander a few steps further to La Terraza's restaurant, one of the nicer and more affordable places in town. The owners, Alexandra and Pepo, are friendly and helpful and suggest bargaining regardless of the season, though in high season solo travelers would probably have to pay for all the beds in a room. Western end of the Malecón, Tel: 06-247-0320, Cel: 09-9732-4405, E-mail: pepol@hotmail.es. Updated: Feb 13, 2013.

Hotel Cabanas Isla del Sol

(ROOMS: $34-183) Hotel Cabanas Isla del Sol is an oceanfront hotel concealed by palm trees. The hotel offers accommodations for one to seven people with rooms that include cable TV, fridge, hot-water, and fan or air conditioning. There are also two-room cabins with complete kitchens, which are perfect for families. Hotel amenities include a swimming pool for adults and one for children, a bar/cafeteria, a basketball court, private on-site parking, laundry service and WiFi service by the front desk. Tours to go whale-watching or to visit the Isla de los Pájaros are also available. Southern point of Same, seafront; from Same, ask your bus driver to drop you of at Cabanas Isla del Sol, (on the main road after the 2nd main access to the beach), Tel: 06-273-3470, Fax: 06-247-0563, E-mail: info@cabanasisladelsol.com, URL: www.cabanasisladelsol.com, : From Same, ask your bus driver to drop you of at Cabanas Isla del Sol, (on the main road after the 2nd main access to the beach). Updated: Feb 13, 2013.

Same Restaurants

Same attracts the wealthy Ecuadorians, and likewise its dining options have adapted to higher culinary expectations. You can find a couple of really nice restaurants here, most serving up local seafood and some international dishes. There are also a few cheap restaurants scattered around where you'll find the standard coastal dishes. Updated: Mar 20, 2013.

Sea Flower

(ENTREES: $10-25) Catering mostly to the money-wielding folks vacationing in the high-rise apartment complexes of Same, the Sea Flower offers an expensive menu known for its gastronomic, more than economic, appeal. Dishes are carefully prepared and served in style, and seafood is the focus of the menu. The restaurant has a unique sea-captain feel, with dark polished wood and a bewildering array of artifacts strewn about the room. Outside seating among carefully set tables is also available. Although this place is also reputed to be a hostel, the owner has recently decided to pursue only the restaurant business. One block away from the beach, Tel: 06-247-0369, E-mail: ateneobolivar@hotmail.com. Updated: Feb 13, 2013.

La Terraza Restaurant

(ENTREES: $6.50-8.50) This split level thatched-roof building fronting the beach offers great ocean views and an enticing menu, which includes Italian, Spanish, and Ecuadorian fare. There's a bar towards the back and walls bear a sporadically placed collection of 1950s style posters. Owner Alexandria claims all dishes are excellent, but recommends the paella or the encocado mixto. A jack of all trades, Alexandra also sells handmade artesanía and beach clothes (the shop is located in the restaurant).The restaurant is connected to La Terraza Hotel as well. On the beach, Tel: 06-247-0320 / 09-9732-4405. Updated: Mar 21, 2013.

Bernabe Cevicheria y Restaurante

(ENTREES: $6-15) This open, airy restaurant with simple wood floors, seaside views, and a basic menu is a good option, and one of the few in Same. Specialties include Cazuela Mixtos, but you'll also find traditional Ecuadorian seaside fare like rice and fish, and rice and shrimp dishes. If you're up for a splurge, they also serve langosta (lobster) in a variety of ways. Typical breakfast options are also served. Updated: Aug 03, 2012.

Noe Sushi Bar

(ENTREES: $9-20) Nestled on the eastern end of Same's beach and adjacent to the Casablanca villas lies Noe Sushi Bar. The place

NORTHERN COAST

caters to the wealthier crowd, as it does in Quito and Guayaquil where there are also locales. Right on the water, the restaurant serves up its fair share of fish, and as the name implies -an array of high-quality sushi. Drinks can be a bit expensive but delicious. The restaurant is not on the main strip, so once you get to the beach, turn right and walk until you see a sort of jetty with buildings rising up behind it on the cliff. East end of Same beach, Tel: 09-9358-3772/8074-0227, E-mail: eventos@noesushibar.com, URL: www.noesushibar.com. Updated: Mar 20, 2013.

TONCHIGÜE

 2m   1,508   📞 06

A world away from the busy beaches and bars further North, Tonchigüe is little more than a sleepy fishing village with a modest beach. About 2 kilometers south of town, the road heads west, following the coast towards Playa Escondida and Punta Galera, eventually running into Quingüe, Estero del Plátano, San Francisco and Bunche. Rarely trekked by tourists, this area is abundant in visually arresting and culturally interesting sites, from tiny villages and quiet coastal landscapes to remote forests and hidden waterfalls. More than anything, Tonchigue serves as key access point to get to Playa Escondida. Updated: Apr 09, 2013.

Getting To and Away from Tonchigüe

If you are coming by bus from **Esmeraldas**, **Atacames**, **Súa**, **Same** or **Tonchigüe**, there are 2 bus lines (Costeñita and River Tabiaso) that make trips - North to South - throughout the day. Just head on over to the main road and flag any one of them down. Buses depart from Esmeraldas: 7:00 a.m., 8:00 a.m., 12:00 p.m., 2:00 p.m., 4:00 p.m. These buses get to Atacames in 45 minutes, and then Tonchigue another 30 minutes later, and then they take about an hour and a half to reach the gates of Playa Escondida from there. Return buses pass the Playa Escondida gate: 6:30 a.m., 8:00 a.m., 12:00 p.m., 2:00 p.m., 4:00 p.m. Located at Km 14, Via Tonchigue-Punta Galera. Watch for the sign just three kilometers 1.8 mi) past Tonchigue to ensure that you don't miss the abrupt right hand turn toward Playa Escondida. Updated: Apr 09, 2013.

Tonchigüe Lodging

Playa Escondida

($10-30 per person) Playa Escondida is located in a beautiful bay, just 10 kilometers from Tonchigüe and 6 kilometers from Punta Galera. The words "Playa Escondida" mean hideaway beach and, indeed, it is way off the beaten track. The ecological refuge based here is large, covering nearly 100 hectares, and boasts a variety of flora and fauna. As an ecological retreat, Playa Escondida is not just for tourists: it is committed to protecting the surrounding plants and animals from local hunters, logging, cattle and shrimp farming, and commercial tourism. The retreat currently has capacity for 30 people. There is a camping area with plenty of shade and showers. There are no cooking facilities, but small campfires are allowed. For something a bit more private, ask to stay in Casa Wantara, a large house with its own kitchen and private bathroom ($25/person). Tel: 06-273-3122 / 099-973-3368, E-mail: judithbarett@hotmail.com, URL: http://www.playaescondida.com.ec. Updated: Apr 09, 2013.

MUISNE

 4m   👤 28,047   📞 06

Seen from the mainland across the opaque Río Muisne, the town of Muisne sits cheerfully but quietly on the other side. With it's array of brightly colored, fluorescent buildings lining the pier, one might think that their about to set foot into a town with cartoons, let alone people. But this is all just a mere facade, really.

Beyond the dock and behind the colored riverside with its painted structures and new playground, Muisne sheds it cheerfulness to reveal a rather lackluster town. Pallid and windowless buildings line the street, where chickens and children roam freely. A single road, Isidro Ayora, stretches away from the docks, past the aging shop fronts, and ends abruptly at the stunning palm-studded stretch of beach on the opposite end of town. It is here, on this strip of clean, quiet beach, that one begins to understand why travelers make the detour and cross-river trek to such a tired little town.

Anyone coming from Atacames is sure to appreciate the peace, and even surf and sand snobs will have something positive to say about the beach (though if you're into surfing, Mompiche is a better bet). With a stretched out seaside presenting clear views of beach inhabited only by resident palm trees, you're bound to breathe easy and let worries wash away like shells with the tide. Although the town and beachfront can feel a bit deserted at times, Muisne radiates a relaxed "enjoy-today-and-worry-tomorrow" island attitude that can charm even tight-fisted travelers into having just one more beer. Updated: Apr 05, 2013.

Getting To and Away from Muisne

A good paved road heading south from Muisne to Pedernales simplifies (to some extent) travel down the entire length of Ecuador's coast. **El Salto**, a dusty one-horse-type town, is the main hub for bus travel to and from Muisne and places to the south. From El Salto, the road heads 56 kilometers south, before hitting the turn-off for **Mompiche** and continuing on to Chamanga, a link-up town for buses to Pedernales. From El Salto, grab a bus heading to Muisne. You'll be dropped off at the docks, from which you can hop on a boat to Muisne, across the Río Muisne. Once you get to the other side, take an EcoTaxi to the beach on the other end of town ($1.00/5 minutes).

To get out of Muisne, the earliest boat leaves around 06:00. Once on the other side, walk up the cement steps and either catch a bus back to **Quito** (Trans-Esmeraldas, 8 hours/$9, Tel: 06-248-0661) or to **El Salto** ($0.50/30 minutes). In El Salto change buses to **Chamanga** ($1.70), the bus to Chamanga drops you off at entrance to the road into **Mompiche**, it's a 3 kilometer walk from here or you can wait to hitch a ride or pay a pick-up truck $1. From Chamanga you can catch a bus to **Pedernales** ($2.00). If you're hungry there are a number of food stalls and cheap eateries around Pedernales bus station, mind the hygiene and your bags. From Pedernales you can catch a bus to **Canoa** ($2.50). Updated: Apr 05, 2013.

Safety

Despite it's peaceful appearance, Muisne is gradually recovering from a devastating crime wave that swept its beaches five years ago, during a time when tourism was slowly gaining traction in the area. What many saw as a godsend to the town, tourism actually became one of the main causes behind the rise in crime, with wealthy tourists provoking some of the more impoverished people in town to assault and steal. Things have gradually gotten way better however, and the town itself is now caught in the faint afterglow of a past it so strongly wishes to erase. Its people are incredibly kind and conscientious of the newcomer, and will go out of their way to help you with anything you need; and the streets are much safer now at night with law enforcement in town now. Needless to say, avoid walking alone at night and make sure that your room is locked before going out.

The Northern and Southern tips of the island - despite being within walking distance along the shore (45 mins.) - is an area of the beach which we strongly recommended not walking down alone as assaults have been reported. It's advised that you stick to the main, populated areas and the ocean in front of them if you want to go swimming. Updated: Apr 05, 2013.

Things To See and Do in Muisne

People come to Muisne usually to lay back and soak in the incredibly mellow atmosphere, but there are plenty of things to go check out around the island. The manglares (mangroves) tend to be the biggest attraction. For boat tours contact Tomás (Tel: 098-990-1416) or simply head on over to the docks and hire a fisherman to show you around for $10 per person. Updated: Apr 08, 2013.

Isla De Las Mancha (Isla Bonita)

You'll find the beach here is home to calm and quiet waters most of the time, the shores of which are supposedly visited by more than 150 species of birds per year. In addition, the small island is home to a group of people that form a substantial part of Muisne's history as they're the once that cradle the myths and legends surrounding the region. Isla Bonita can be reached via boat or land (when the tide is low enough, but still not recommended). Updated: Apr 08, 2013.

Manglares (Mangroves)

The few mangroves that exist today around Muisne are but one-tenth of what they were in 1980's. After shrimp farming caught on, entire areas of mangroves were cut down to make way for the shrimp farms themselves. This has been one of the low-points in Muisne's history, given that the town formerly thrived off of low-impact fishing and gathering within the mangroves themselves. Fortunately, the people have made an effort to put

NORTHERN COAST

Loved it? Loathed it? Write a review and help other travelers

an end to this in recent years, securing what mangroves remain in the area. Be sure to get a boat tour of them before leaving.
Updated: Apr 08, 2013.

Muisne Lodging

Don't come here expecting lavish tropical bungalows with king-sized beds and travel-sized shampoos and soaps; what you will find is a comfortable accommodation well within range of any backpacker's budget. The salty sea breeze and ocean sounds are complimentary with any place fronting the beach.
Updated: Apr 05, 2013.

Hotel Galápagos

($10 per person) Certainly the biggest, most hotel-looking place in Muisne, Hotel Galápagos features large, clean rooms organized around a modest central garden. Owner José Miguel Ochoa is an older gentleman, in charge of maintaining the property himself, and he goes great strides to make guests feel comfortable. Originally from Loja, he is also keen to pass an afternoon chatting about local politics, so if you're one for getting the lowdown on places you visit, pull up a chair. Due to a recent decline in Muisne tourism, he has been forced to close the hotel's restaurant, but everything else about this place is open and ready for business. While Hotel Galápagos may not feature ocean views, the grounds are immaculate and the beds are comfortable. This is a good spot for families or large groups looking for something a bit more private than the hostels on the beach. Ca. Manabí, on the way to the beach, Tel: 06-248-0289/0523, E-mail: hotel-galapagos@hotmail.com.
Updated: Feb 13, 2013.

Hostal Calade

($8-12 per person) A beach garden area appointed with a few scattered hammocks greets visitors entering this quiet little place just off the beach. Rooms are clean enough, offering good beds with clean sheets but zero ventilation (besides the breeze that may or may not come in through the window). The place too, can seem rather rickety and run-down for the most part (some might even saying it's falling apart). Owners claim to run ecological tours, and sport fishing trips, but nothing much seemed to be going on at the time of writing so if you want to organize something, you might have to take the initiative and ask. While not the best option in town, it is a good budget option that's sits quietly on the fringe of town, with soothing beach views and sounds. Beachfront, West-

ern end of Malecon. Tel: 099-794-1355 / 02-248-0279, E-mail: hotelcalade@gmail.com/ polo330_2000@yahoo.com.
Updated: Apr 05, 2013.

Las Olas Hostal

($10-20 per person) You wouldn't think it by the looks of the noisy bar and restaurant downstairs, but Las Olas Hostal is actually a decent and clean place to stay at when the music isn't blasting downstairs. It's also your best bet for an ocean-view hostel in all of Muisne. Ideally, try getting a room upstairs (away from the noise) and with a terrace. Beachfront, Tel: 06-248-0161 / 099-898-9008.
Updated: Apr 05, 2013.

Cabañas Bellavista

($60 per person) Rustic is the key theme surrounding these cabins. If you've never felt like a peace corps volunteer before and you'd like a taste of it, this might be your shot. Lovely, attentive and incredibly kind William Chila and his family run Cabañas Bellavista, which is an initiative to help ecotourism grow and prosper within Muisne. Anywhere from tours of the palm-shaded forests nearby, to fishing out in the open ocean or getting a closer look at the mangroves on the outskirts of the island, William includes a full-on tour and number activities to keep you entertained throughout your stay. Not to mention, he is a master of cocada-making, which will give you a firsthand chance to see the process that goes into making these popular coastal treats.

In addition to all this, you'll be eating fresh cacao, bananas and coconut picked from his orchard (depending on the harvest) as snacks. The cabins aren't anything remarkable, but the experience definitely is. Just be sure to call ahead to confirm availability and let him get everything arranged before your arrival. The price includes tax, breakfast, lunch, dinner as well as all the tours and activities throughout the day. Northern end of town, simply ask any of the moto-taxi's to take you to William Chila's house ($1.50). Tel: 06-248-0076 / 098-284-8512, E-mail: teodoro_11@yahoo.es.
Updated: Apr 08, 2013.

Muisne Restaurants

Located just off the popular tourist circuit, Muisne maintains its local flavor and is a great spot to try traditional coastal fare like ceviche and encocado (dishes steeped in coconut sauce). There are a number of food stalls lining the main street, Isidro Ayora, but the beachside restaurants have a bit more atmosphere and definitely better views. Plates offered and prices vary little from place to place so your decision on where to dine will probably be based more on appearance and atmosphere than anything else. Note that most restaurants operate on beach time, meaning they tend to open and close according to the flow of patrons.

Las Palmeras.
(ENTREES: $4-7.) With a nice little palm-covered eating area outside, and a cement floored alterntive inside, this place provides hot and fresh seafood goodies. Dig your toes into the sand during the day as you lick your fingers from the shrimp with coconut sauce, or remain alert at night while you eat as the club next door blasts its beats out from its tiny interior on weekends. Either or, finish it off with a cold beer or two. Malecón, Tel: 06-248-0786 / 097-946-4996.
Updated: Apr 17, 2013.

La Riviera
(ENTREES: $3-15) An unassuming façade leads into a small kitchen area where they prepare stock-standard coastal fare (try the camaron apanado: breaded shrimp) for anyone hungry and looking for a meal. Although its name may conjure images of fancy candle-lit dinners and men in striped shirts rowing gondolas, the restaurant bears the family name and dining here is an informal affair, more like eating than dining out. Even if you're not in the mood for rice and fish it's a good place to just chill out with a beer and watch the beach comings and goings. The restaurant is the first on the left as you approach the beach from town, Tel: 099-344-0679 / 02-648-0149.
Updated: Apr 08, 2013.

Restaurante Santa Martha
(ENTREES: $3-8) This place seems to be the local favorite, recommended by motor-taxi drivers and extended-stay tourists. At a glance there is little to set it apart from the other restaurants, except that polished wood has replaced the ever-popular plastic tables and chairs. Inside, owner Martha greets patrons with a broad smile and warm air that makes even the newest islander feel welcome. The food is typical coastal cuisine (seafood served in soup, mixed with rice, or smothered in coconut sauce) but served with a distinct down-home flavor. Martha's ever-chatty husband Lois is a good source of information on the island and more than eager

to pass his knowledge on to anyone with an open ear. He can also organize impromptu horseback riding and boat excursions. If you're curious: Martha recommends the Bandeja Marinera, while Lois favors the Encocado Marinero, both look appetizing. On the Beach, Tel: 06-248-0307 / 06-986-7345.
Updated: Apr 08, 2013.

MOMPICHE

  2m   28,047   06

A well-guarded secret among surf enthusiasts, Mompiche is quite possibly the nicest spot to drop your bags, grab a beer, and bum around for a few days. Located in a sheltered bay, this once-sleepy fishing village has awakened to a burgeoning tourist industry, leading to a number of beach bungalows and even all-inclusive resorts popping up in recent years. And it's not hard to see why: a backdrop of emerald green hills encircles the stunning seven-kilometer stretch of dark sand beach. Surf gurus say this is the best break in Ecuador, but even those who would rather hang out than hang ten will find the surf and sand of Mompiche agreeable.

Considering its mythic status in the travel community, it should come of no surprise that Mompiche harbors a secret of its own: ask around town for boat rides to a nearby, even more remote (and from what we hear, more beautiful) island off the coast. We'd love to tell you more, but travel to such a spot seems to be a rite of passage granted only to those adventurous enough to ask.
Updated: Apr 08, 2013.

Getting To and Away from Mompiche
Buses run almost every 20 minutes along the highway in front of Mompiche, heading north to **Atacames** (1 hour, $1.50) and then on to **Esmeraldas** (3 hours, $4) starting at 6 a.m. Getting to Mompiche from other destinations in Ecuador involves changing buses in one of these two towns. From **Quito** buses run daily to Esmeraldas (6 hours, $8) and **Atacames** (6.5 hours, $7-8). If coming from **Muisne**, you'll have to transfer buses in **El Salto**.

NOTE: Over half of the south bound buses that head to **Chamanga** don't go into Mompiche town. These buses stop at the entrance into Mompiche on the main road, around 5km from the town. Unless you fancy a long walk or waiting for a ride into town (10 mins, $1), confirm that the bus you are taking actually runs all the way into Mompiche town.

The nearest airport to Mompiche is the Aeropuerto General Rivadeneira (ESM) in Esmeraldas. Tame (www.tame.com.ec) makes the 30 minute flight daily between Quito and Mompiche (around $60 each way).

To head further south down the coast via bus, get to the entrance of Mompiche and wait by the highway. Flag down any one of the buses that's headed to **Chamanga** (45 minutes, $0.50). In Chamanga, transfer buses to get to **Pedernales** (1 hour, $1.50). Updated: Apr 08, 2013.

When To Go
The waves roll in typically between early November and end of February, December usually being the prime-time for some really great waves. Outside of those months, Mompiche is rather flat and the waters are noticeably more tranquil and cooler, as is the temperature. Tourism tends to die down as well. Updated: Apr 08, 2013.

Safety
Mompiche is relatively safe at night, even sleepy. It's best to keep to the Malecón and mains street after dark however, and it's definitely not a good idea to wander over to the southern end of the beach alone at night. When surfing, just know that at the point the waves break over a rock-filled bottom, not a sandy one, so keep this in mind when riding at low-tide. Updated: Apr 08, 2013.

Things To See and Do in Mompiche
Mompiche is teeming with activities and things to do around its small, modest town. From riding through the jungles up above the town and seeing monkeys fool around, to exploring its coast and shores, Mompiche offers tons of adventure to the newcomer. You can even wind down with a fantastic massage afterwards.

Note: Mompiche's growth in popularity - for tourists as much as investors - has brought about as many blessings as misfortunes in recent years. Investors and contractors in the area are now dealing some incredibly dramatic and devastating blows to the environment, mainly due to construction and excavation in and around town. Given the case, it's sad to say that Mompiche might not

remain the same for long, so be sure to check it out before a greater part of its beaches are altered forever. Updated: Apr 09, 2013.

Surfing in Mompiche
Those who grew up in Mompiche have surfing ingrained in their blood from an early age. So, don't feel bad if you decide to try riding the waves and six-year-olds are flying past you looking like they were born on a board. The Mompiche Bay and Point break are the ideal places for novice surfers and pros, where you'll find them all clustered in different areas across the water during high season. There are three sections to catch the waves; only go to the outermost area by the point if you are confident in your surfing abilities and know the etiquette properly.

Punto de Encuentro or La Facha Hostel offer surf classes ($20 for two hours) and rents boards ($15 for a day, and $8 for half a day, or if you're in a real hurry - $4 per hour). Additionally, if you're looking for classes in English, contact Sol (E-mail: solfunkfoto@gmail.com, Tel: 097-961-1991), who offers them at $25 for 2 hours and has special long boards to learn on. Best to take surfing classes earlier on in the morning when the waves are more frequent and there are less people in the water to get in your way. Updated: Apr 16, 2013.

Portete Beach
Portete is a virtually untouched and uninhabited beach that sits hidden a ways behind the main shore. Palm groves border the beach as far as the eye can see, yielding to green hills on your right and stunning rock formations etched out by the sea. If you come to Portete, please respect and preserve its natural beauty. There are no trash cans, so please take all your trash away with you. Access is via a long dirt road and brief canoe ride. It's about an hour on foot, 10 or 15 minutes by car. If you're walking, bring a water bottle, plenty of sunscreen and maybe a few snacks. If you'd rather go the easy route, you can rent a 4x4, or, preferably, bum a ride from a pickup truck along the way.

To get to Portete, go all the way to the south end of the main beach, toward the cliff and rocks. You will see a dirt road heading into the tree line, this is the entrance. Head down the road for about an hour, passing a major turn-off on your left and continuing straight. Keep going past a few more hills and the Royal Decameron until you reach the end of the road. At the end of the road, hand $0.50 to a boatman who will ferry you across the river. You can try to swim it, but the current is very strong and becomes outright dangerous the closer it comes to the sea.

Above the river you'll notice the twisted, rusty remnants of a metal bridge that was abandoned midway through construction. The lack of direct access by car is probably what has kept Portete so pristine. After being dropped on the opposite shore, walk past a handful of little houses, through a cluster of palms at which point you'll come out onto an immense stretch of white sand and beach with crystal clear water. It's a good idea to bring water, sunscreen, snacks, and any other beach gear you might desire.
Updated: Apr 09, 2013.

Playa Negra

You can walk from one end of Playa Negra to the other in under five minutes. But you'll probably have the whole place to yourself: a smooth sheet of shimmering black sand to play on, unbroken save for a few hulking pieces of driftwood. This sand is not only remarkable for its color, rather, it is its texture that makes it so special. This is the softest sand you may ever set foot on. Pick up a handful. It's heavy and slick, almost like a silky black mud. There isn't much to this beach other than the sand, sea and trees, but to many visitors it will be a treasure worth basking in.

To find Playa Negra, go all the way to the south end of the main beach, toward the cliff and rocks. You will see a dirt road heading into the tree line, this is the entrance. Head down the road for about 30-40 minutes, passing a major turn-off on your left and continuing straight. Keep going past a few more hills, and you will find the path to Playa Negra on your right, indicated by two posts, and swinging gate (if you hit the Royal Decameron Resort you've gone too far). Trek down the hill from here and you'll discover this little piece of paradise. You can only access Playa Negra during low tide.
Updated: Apr 08, 2013.

Boat Tours

($10-20 per person) Boat tours are offered throughout the week, typically you'll find the boatmen advertising their tours along the Malecón during high season. If they're not, just head on over to the beach (southern end of Malecón) and inquire with any one of the fishermen (a trip to Isla Jupiter or Portete can cost about $10-20 per person). Adven-

ture tours can also be arranged at La Facha Hostel, with excursions ranging anywhere from heading up the mountainside, exploring the coast or kayaking to the mangroves.
Updated: Apr 09, 2013.

Horseback Tours with Doña Fabiola

(PRICE: $15-20) Charming and incredibly calm in her demeanor, Doña Fabiola is an animal lover and the owner of some 20+ horses that she keeps in Mompiche. She offers guided tours (3-4 hours) of the mountain on horseback, letting you gauge the incredible level of fauna that resides above Mompiche; you'll spot monkeys and tucans as you cross tiny rivers and small farms along your journey. She can also take you all the way to Portete and Playa Negra along a private path.

For those already experienced in horseback, just ask and show her your skills, and she'll let you run freely across the 4 km (2.5 miles) stretch of beach out front. It's highly advised to call ahead (at least 2 hours in advance) to notify Fabiola so that she can reserve your horses and get them ready. To get the there, head to the southern end of the beach just before the cliffs and rocks, over by the cabins and run-down shacks. Shout out for Doña Fabiola, or give her a call if you have a phone. Tel: 099-139-8467, E-mail: fabiolaminda@hotmail.com.
Updated: Apr 09, 2013.

Casa Yarumo

Want to relax extra hard while at the beach? Then head on over to casa Yarumo to get an incredibly relaxing rub. German owner Katharina gives some really great shiatsu massages at $15 and hour, or $8 for a half hour. Best to call ahead to set up an appointment. They also offer a small beach-side cabin for two people. Way Northern end of Mompiche's beach. Just know that you'll have to cross the river at low-tide to get there. It's about a 20-30 minute walk from town, just past Mompiches Land Hotel (look for the red-colored roofs). Tel: 098-867-2924 / 099-683-0687, URL: www.casayarumomompiche.com.
Updated: Apr 08, 2013.

Mompiche Lodging

Mompiche may be a tiny beach town with a couple of dirt roads, but it still has a decent range of accommodations, from surfing hangouts to bungalows and adobe-walled getaways all the way to an all-inclusive hotel. When you first arrive, spend a few minutes walking through town (a few minutes is all it takes) to find the place that's best suited to you.

NORTHERN COAST

Loved it? Loathed it? Write a review and help other travelers

De Mompiche Con Amor

($8-15 per person) De Mompiche Con Amor is a great building made from wood and bamboo, typical of the Mompiche style. It has a lower level with budget rooms, a second story with private rooms with a small living room/kitchen area, a third level great for hanging out and taking in the view (complete with hammocks), and a look-out deck above. Facing the ocean on the main-street, go North 10 meters up Calle La Fosforera (one street back from the Malecon). Tel: 06-244-8063. Updated: Apr 08, 2013.

Hotel San Marena

($10-15 per person) While most Mompiche accommodations are rustic, relying heavily on thatch and bamboo, San Marena is more in line with the clean, budget hotels found in the United States (Day's Inn or Red Roof spring to mind). The rooms are large and have fans, televisions and DVD players. Guests can also buy Internet cards for their computers at the reception desk. The hotel has space for 46 people in 14 rooms, all of which have private bathrooms and balconies, including one room for five or more people with an extra-large patio. The restaurant downstairs is one of the only places in Mompiche where you can order chicken and meat, in addition to seafood dishes. The only drawback is that San Marena is about a five-minute walk from the beach (the furthest in town) and has no ocean views. The hotel is also across from the town's busy little store. Loacted on the main road heading into town. Tel: 06-244-8032, Cel: 09-9421-3947, E-mail: mercedes.camacho5@yahoo.es. Updated: Feb 13, 2013.

Hosteria Gabeal

Hosteria Gabeal, separated from the rest of town by a large archway, offers a variety of accommodations right on the beach. Up a sandy, palm-lined drive, you'll find private bungalows, a building with multiple rooms and an al fresco dining area, all built in the bamboo and thatch style that's common in Mompiche. Since it's steps from the beach, the hostería has outdoor showers and taps where guests can wash off the salt and sand. The rooms have insect netting over the beds and clean, private bathrooms with indoor showers. A main building doubles as a reception area, bar and kitchen (seafood is available between 1 and 4 p.m.). You can rent one of the hotel's surfboards for $4 per hour (surf lessons are available in town) or arrange to ride a horse down the beach. During the summer months, Gabeal also offers whale-watching tours. The hotel also has a small, thatched bar with wooden saddle seats that it opens during high season. Facing the ocean on the main-street, go North 50 meters up Calle La Fosforera (one street back from the Malecon) Hosteria Gabeal is located at the end of the road through an archway. Tel: 06-244-8060, Cel: 09-9969-6543, E-mail: mompiche_gabeal@hotmail.com. Updated: Feb 13, 2013.

Iruña

(ROOMS: $45-85) Located three kilometers (1.9 mi) outside of the sleepy town of Mompiche (as you go north along the beach), Iruña (formerly Las Pigualas) is a peaceful place to relax for a couple of days. This little-known spot has cabins that are simple but sufficient and unusually come complete with a fridge. Each cabin has a hammock out front for kicking back after a tough day at the beach. Friendly owner Teresa cooks up a tasty breakfast, and lunch and dinner too if you like. You can arrange kayaking trips and whale-watching in season. Access is only possible via the beach, so if you're driving you need to find out when high tide is. If you're not driving, the owners will pick you up from town at your request. 3 km/1.9 mi north of Mompiche, accessed via the beach, Tel: 09-9947-2458/9497-5846, E-mail: teremompiche@yahoo.com. Updated: Feb 13, 2013.

La Facha Hostel

($10 per person) The hotel has a rustic yet pristine feel to it, given how well it's maintained and run by owner Tito himself, a laid-back surfer and cook. In addition to that, La Facha has a really mellow vibe surrounding it that compliments the beach or a long-day of surfing quite well. The mini-book/movie collection upstairs and below offers guests a nice selection of entertainment to amuse themselves with when the waves are flat or when evening rolls in. The greatest bonus is their excellent restaurant downstairs. On the Main Avenue, go right on Calle La Fosforera (one street before reaching the Malecón) about 15 meters (50 feet)., Tel: 06-244-8024 / 099-804-4604, E-mail: lafachamompiche@gmail.com, URL: www.lafachamompiche.com. Updated: Apr 09, 2013.

Cabañas La Cotona

($10-18 per person) Quietly tucked away from the street, Cabañas La Cotona offers backpackers a little more than just your standard hostel around town. Clean and tidy rooms will make you feel satisfied with your stay, but you'll also feel more at home by having access to the communal kitchen (should you want to prepare/store your own food rather than eat out).

Wifi is readily available, as well as 24-hour hot water. Fans and mosquito nets in the rooms are a godsend on some nights. They also offer a two-story Cabana ($45, fits three), which has got to have one of the best beachfront views in all of Mompiche. On the Main Avenue, go right on Calle La Fosforera (one street before reaching the Malecón) and walk about 15 meters (50 feet). Tel: 099-046-9231 / 099-739-6244, E-mail: mompiche@gmail.com.
Updated: Apr 09, 2013.

Bernabeth Mompiche Beach
(ROOMS: $80-100) If your ready to throw all your worries away and have everything catered to you, then spend a night (or more) at Bernabeth Hotel. This all-inclusive hotel is brand new in the town of Mompiche, and with it's giant neon sign visible from the beach, it definitely stands out from the rest of the rustic lodging available. Come here if you're expecting upper-scale services and rooms, with all you can drink and eat available throughout the day. North end of Malecon, right beside Hosteria Gabeal. On the fringe of town., Tel: 098-978-4916 / 06-244-8047, E-mail: info@hotelbernabeth.com.
Updated: Apr 09, 2013.

Mompiche Restaurants
Culinary delights here are quite diverse, which can be rather surprising given the size of the town. Typical seafood fare comes in fresh out of the waters, but vegetarian options are available as well. To top it off, the town has a fantastic little place to go grab dessert after you've gotten your main-course out of the way.

El Economico
(ENTREES: $4-7) This is a typical almuerzo (lunch) restaurant that specializes in breakfast. For two bucks, take the big plunge and get the breakfast (supposedly smaller, but note the dripping sarcasm) portion of fried or shrimp al ajillo (garlic) that comes with rice, menestras (typical coastal beans) and patacones (fried plantains).

You can also get a more traditional breakfast for the same price: eggs, two rolls, coffee and juice. No worries, the service is kind of random and a little slow, but you are at the

beach so look out at the waves, chill out, and your hearty meal will eventually show up. Corner of Malecón and the main street that leads into town., Tel: 099-432-3960.
Updated: Apr 08, 2013.

Batidos del Negrito
(SMOOTHIES: $2-4) In the middle of a hot day at the beach cool off with some blended, fruit goodness courtesy of Batidos del Negrito. Order a mix of your favorite fruits at the juice and batidos (blended juice and milk) stand on the road in to town. It is amazing to watch the juice man as he bounces to the high-volume Latin beat coming from the stereo, manages at least three blenders at once, takes orders and cuts watermelons, bananas and pineapples to garnish your drink.

If you are ready to let loose for the day, ask him to throw some alcohol in the mix or just bring your own bottle. This juice stand is on your right if you are standing on the road into town and looking out at the water. It is directly across from Atardacer del Mompiche. It is hard to miss, just listen for the loud music. Tel: 099-086-8617.
Updated: Apr 08, 2013.

El Punto De Encuentro
(ENTREES: $4-12) Check out this surf shack at the southern end of the street that runs parallel to the beach. Morongo, a local who grew up in Mompiche, runs his surf school and quasi restaurant out of his thatched-roof hut. If you are looking for quick, filling grub before or after a long day at the beach, then this is the place.

If you are facing the water and standing at the crossroads, take a left. Walk all the way down until the street turns into sand and look for the thatched hut on your right. Tel: 095-923-9054, E-mail: morongoenmompiche@gmail.com.
Updated: Apr 08, 2013.

La Langosta
(ENTREES: $5-15) La Langosta is a small but extremely popular restaurant right on the beach. If you want to be guaranteed a spot it's best to go around noon because the place gets packed every day from about 1 to 4 pm. The food is good and fresh, but the menu is limited, and options tend to run out as the day goes on. Note that lobster typically in season between mid-july to mid-January. Lunch plates, which include your main plus rice and patacones, are somewhat expensive for Mompiche. La Langosta is known for

NORTHERN COAST

its langostinos (prawns), but you may have trouble finding them in stock if you don't get there early enough. Situated close to the south end before you reach the rocks and thick foliage that close off the shore, on the sand in front of the ocean, past all the fishing boats. Updated: Apr 08, 2013.

La Chocolata

(PIES: $1.50-5) You might be blown away by how good the sweets and pastries sold at this little place are. Run by a motley crew of Argentinians, La Chocolota spans the length of scrumptious pastries and pies all the way to warm, invigorating beverages. The locale, slightly dingy but overwhelmingly charming, is a cozy blend of ambiance and character to remind you that these treats weren't produced at some bakery in Europe or North America far, far away, but right here in the heart of Mompiche. Small events and music nights are usually held towards the end of the week. On the Main Avenue facing the ocean, go left on Calle La Fosforera (one street before reaching the Malecón) about 10 meters (30 feet). It's the wooden house on your left. Tel: 06-244-8077. Updated: Apr 09, 2013.

La Facha Restaurant

(ENTREES: $3-12) With a fusion of Peruvian, Argentinian and Ecuadorian tastes, La Facha serves up a vegetarians galore with plates that revolve around anything from quinoa, to lentils, to ginger and more. Burgers and sandwiches are a must try. There's a bar here too that will serve up some rather exquisite drinks, should you feel the need to wind down or get your night started. On the Main Avenue facing the ocean, go right on Calle La Fosforera (one street before reaching the Malecón) about 15 meters (50 feet)., Tel: 06-244-8024 / 099-804-4604, E-mail: lafachamompiche@gmail.com, URL: www.lafachamompiche.com. Updated: Apr 09, 2013.

Doña Mary

(ENTREES: $2-8) Apparently there's "world famous" Bolon de Verde (fried plantain balls with cheese and pork) served here, whether or not this is true is up to your palette to decide. Needless to say, owners Mary and Tacito are genuinely nice and devoted to their craft, capable of cooking up a storm in their kitchen if need be. The seafood fare offered here is pretty typical from what the rest of town serves, but don't miss out on the bolones or empanadas just in case your palate really does agree with the international recogni-

tion they've gotten. If you overfill yourself, find some solace in knowing that they run a small little hostel out back which you can amble over to after you've eaten, with beds for $10 a person. On the Main Avenue, go left on Calle La Fosforera (one street before reaching the Malecón) about 20 meters (65 feet). The restaurant will be on your left, past an expanse of garden., Tel: 098-276-9343. Updated: Apr 09, 2013.

La Chillagua

(ENTREES: $3-10) This little family-run restaurant boasts your typical array of seafood plates, but it's the incredibly cheap almuerzos (set lunches) that make this place pack a culinary punch. From noon until 2 p.m. Doña Rosa will cook up a seafood concoction fit for the ravenous, at a price you can't beat on the coast, let alone find right by the water. Seaside view and the sound of waves can serve as a dessert if need be. Head down the main avenue that goes into town and turn right when you hit the Malecón, walk 10 meters (30 feet). Tel: 098-148-6131. Updated: Apr 09, 2013.

Choco

(ENTREES: $5-10) If you've ever wondered what a blend of Californian and Ecuadorian coastal cuisine might look like, then this might be your chance to find out. The restaurant is an incredible piece of work crafted in bamboo, built principally by restaurant owner Sol himself, who can often times be seen in the kitchen cooking up a storm. Plates here range from fish tacos to your traditional coastal seafood and rice plates. Note that this restaurant is only open during high-season (November to April, July and August). Calle La Fosforera, in front of La Facha, Tel: 097-961-1991, E-mail: solfunkfoto@gmail.com. Updated: Apr 16, 2013.

CHAMANGA

Situated south of Muisne and Mompiche, Chamanga is a lively place, featuring houses built on stilts over the estuary. While there is not much going on in this grungy little town, this is a key piggy-back point to more interesting beaches down south and other sites nearby, such as the majestic mangroves and walking trails. The Reserva Ecológica Mache Chindul, managed by the Jatun Sacha Foundation, stretches across the provincial boarder offering unique flora and fauna to explore. For volunteer opportunities and more information, check outwww.jatunsacha.org. Updated: Apr 09, 2013.

Manabí (Province)

South of Esmeraldas rests the coastal province of Manabí. The beach cities along the Manabí coast are very popular during holidays and summer months for their mellow surfing towns, big waves and, of course, excellent seafood.

The Parque Nacional Machalilla is in Manabí and features excellent wildlife, possibly Ecuador's most beautiful beach, Los Frailes, whale watching, kayaking and horseback riding tours, and some campgrounds. La Isla de la Plata, just off the coast of Puerto López and part of the Parque Machalilla, is nicknamed "The Poor-Man's Galapagos" for its variety in birds also found in Galápagos and great snorkeling and diving. Enjoy excellent whale watching from July to October when humpback whales finish their long trip from as far south as Antarctica. The first whales arrive off the coast of Ecuador in July, when they give birth and spend the summer in the warm currents off the coast of Manabí. The whale watching season ends in late September or October when the humpbacks head south as soon as their babies are big enough to make the long return trip.
Updated: Apr 08, 2013.

Getting To and Away from Manabí

Reina del Camino offers the most direct bus service available from to Manabí and Guayas. Choose between clase ejecutivo (first class, $10) and clase económico (standard, $8). First-class buses are usually overnight trips and have strict rules for safety (i.e. no stops along the way) and most items are stored underneath the bus. Passengers are also frisked before boarding. **Quito**, El Ejido Station: Manuel Larrea and 18 de Septiembre. Tel: 02-321-5824 / 02-321-6633, Terminal Terrestre Cumanda: Of. No. 111, **Manta** Tel: 05-262-2474. **Guayaquil** Tel: 04-213-0030 / 04-230-0757.
Updated: Apr 10, 2013.

Things To See and Do In Manabí

Parque Nacional Machalilla

Parque Nacional Machalilla (136,000 acres) is a nationally protected area which includes a stretch of beach and dry tropical forest as well as two islands, Isla de la Plata and Isla Salango north of Puerto López and south of Puerto Cayo in the Manabi province. Highlights are the unique wildlife like blue-footed boobies, sea lions, iguanas, which can also

be seen in Galápagos. Humpback whales procreate just offshore every year from July to October and can be seen from several inland points and up close on special tours or on your way to and from Isla de la Plata. We recommend skipping the whale-watching tours as you get the exact same experience on the Isla de la Plata tour plus you get to see the island!

Other tours in Parque Machalilla include horseback riding, kayaking, fishing, snorkeling and diving. If you are planning to visit Isla de la Plata and the mainland areas of Parque Nacional Machalilla, buy the combined entrance ticket for the island and the mainland for $20 ($5 for Ecuadorians). Otherwise, entrance to the island is $15 for foreigners and $3.50 for Ecuadorians and entrance to the mainland park areas are $12 and $2 for Ecuadorians. There are also multi-day passes. The park is best during the month of July when the weather is still sunny and the whales are arriving.

Three miles off the main highway in the park and 7.5 miles north of Puerto López, there is a small local community with ancestors dating back to the Manteña Culture who inhabited the land from 800 to 1532. The Agua Blanca Community and their small museum can be visited with a guide.

Tours introduce you to the ancient burial customs, typical dress and religious practices on a mile-walk through the forest where you can also bird-watch and catch views of the river valley and lagoon.

Isla de la Plata

One of the highlights of the Parque Nacional Machililla, Isla de la Plata has earned the nickname of the Poor Man's Galapagos because of the unique variety of birds, seals and iguanas that are found in both spots. From July to October you can see humpback whales.

The best spot to find a tour to the island is in Puerto López where several tour operators offer day trips including lunch and snorkeling, diving or fishing.

If you are planning to spend some time on the mainland areas of Parque Nacional Machililla, you should go ahead and buy the combined entrance ticket for the island and the mainland for $20 ($5 for Ecuadorians). Otherwise, entrance to the island is $15 for foreigners and $3.50 for Ecuadorians.
Updated: Mar 19, 2013.

Loved it? Loathed it? Write a review and help other travelers

Los Frailes

Relaxing and remote, Los Frailes is widely considered one of the most gorgeous beaches along the Pacific coastline, and it's easy to see why: its lovely landscape includes pristine waters and sweeping white sand, beautifully backdropped by lush, forested bluffs. From Puerto Lopez you can visit the beach through a guided tour or on your own. The Machalilla National Park entrance fee includes Los Frailes, and many people maximize their ticket by exploring Isla de la Plata and Los Frailes. If you decide to just visit the beach, you'll still have to shell out cash. Once you pass the entrance gate, it's a 3.2 km (2 mile) trek to the beach.
Updated: Mar 13, 2013.

Punta Gorda Reserve

About a five mile beach walk outside of Bahia de Caráquez is Punta Gorda Reserve where volunteers can work on the last bit of the Tropical Dry Forest while getting away from the gringo trail, busy bus lines, always on the go travel style. The Cabin Tortuguita "Small Turtle" is perched high on a cliff overlooking the Pacific Ocean to the west. We were there for a week. We were able to discover many old pottery laden fields from thousands of years ago, hike, maintain the trails, fish with the only subsistence fishing family for miles, try out some surfing on the board provided, and just relax on the hammocks with the cool breeze. Bahia de Caráquez is easily accessible and weekly there are giant ultimate Frisbee games which was also a novelty for the trip. Over all, Punta Gorda is a great place if you really just want to relax with the books you brought to Ecuador, and the crash of the waves below. Best of all the money goes to the preservation of these lands and the food is free! We paid 50 dollars a week per person. www.projectsforpeace.org/puntagorda.
Updated: Apr 08, 2013.

PEDERNALES

 8m   46,876   05

Not much distinguishes Pedernales from other coastal towns. While it features the same bamboo beachside bars as Atacames, it lacks the line of hotels and hostels that might give it more of a welcoming, resort feel. Instead, it remains more of a bustling commercial hub and crossroads for traffic north and south rather than a desirable destination in itself. That said, the town is not a bad option if you're looking to break up a trip

from Esmeraldas, Canoa, Bahía or Manta. The beach, while not spectacular, is certainly picturesque enough to pencil in some time for sand and sun.

Getting To and Away from Pedernales

The bus terminal is located on Juan Pereira, just two blocks northeast of the main square. Buses leave every 20 minutes for **Santo Domingo**, with connections to **Quito** (5-6 hours). Connections south include **Guayaquil** ($8, 9 hours) and **San Vicente** ($3, 2.5 hours). You can also grab a Coactur bus that head to closer towns like **Jama** (1.5 hours, $1.50) and **Canoa** (3 hours, $3), departing every other hour from 5am – 6pm.
Updated: Apr 09, 2013.

Pedernales Services

Heads up to all travelers passing through: This is your chance to refill your wallets with cash at the nearest ATM, because the next one isn't until Bahia (3+ hours south) or Atacames (4 hours). Head on over to Banco de Guayaquil and stock up on cash. Plaza Costa and Lopez Castillo.
Updated: Apr 09, 2013.

Safety

Be alert and attentive with your belonging when at the bus terminal, the constant flux of people and movement through this area can lead to distractions and petty theft. Pedernales itself is a rather run-down place, so just be wary of individuals who walk up to you. Be sure to stick to areas that are well lit. The Malecón and plaza are probably the safest areas in town.
Updated: Apr 09, 2013.

Getting Around

Motorcycle taxis are the quickest way to get around town and they shouldn't cost you more than $1-3 to get you from place to place.

Pedernales Lodging

Pedernales is growing quickly, and new hotels open all the time. They top out at about three stars: a couple have pools, which is a bonus. The cheapest ones are located a block or two off the beach, although there are a couple of dives at the south end of the malecón that might be classified as jails more than hostels.

On holidays and weekends, the cheesy bars try to out-do one another by blasting their speakers throughout the night, so if you intend to get any sleep at all, steer clear of hotels on or near the Malecón.

NORTHERN COAST

Royal Hotel

($25-35 per person) The Royal Hotel is a modern mid-range accommodation option located at the south end of the Malecón. It has air-conditioned rooms, Internet and a swimming pool. The rates are very reasonable, and the staff is friendly and helpful. Visit quick before they figure out that it can raise its rates! Garcia Moreno and Malecón, Tel: 05-268-1218/0532, Cel: 09-9711-5474, E-mail: royal.hotel@hotmail.com, URL: www.royal-hotel.com.ec.
Updated: Feb 13, 2013.

Hostal Agua Marina

(ROOMS: $50-175) Clean and friendly, Hostal Agua Marina is clearly one of the most comfortable options in town. It has a pool and the tidy rooms are air conditioned. Rates are reasonable for its facilities and level of service. There are two drawbacks: one is that it is not on the beach, but about a four-block walk away (this means it's quieter, however, as the beach bars blast music all night). Also, the rooms are a little cramped: the suite that can sleep seven features two bunk-beds; seven adults will find the quarters a little tight. If you can afford it and you don't care about being close to the beach, Hostal Agua Marina should be your first choice in Pedernales. Ca. Jaime Roldós Aguilera 413 and Velasco Ibarra, Tel: 05-268-0492, Cel: 09-9765-7309, Fax: 05-268-0491, E-mail: hostalaguamarina@hotmail.com, URL: www.hostalaguamarina.com.ec.

Orion Hotel

($10-15 per person) Planted on a hill overlooking the sea, Orion Hotel and its brightly painted blue and white façade are easily spotted from the road leading down from the bus station. One of the more modern-looking joints in town, the hotel features an on-site cafetería, flower-adorned terraces, hot water, private bathroom, and cable TV. It's also very close to the public swimming pool, which is nice. Av. Juan Pereira and Malecón, Tel: 05-268-0136, , Cel: 09-9879-4408.
Updated: Feb 13, 2013.

Hotel Yam Yam

($6-8 per person) A blocky building a couple blocks off the beach, Hotel Yam Yam doesn't have much going for it, which is why owner Yandre Arteaga has lowered the room rates and offers additional services. He is a friendly local with good knowledge of the area, and he does unofficial tours with hotel guests. He'll take you to see the nearby Isla de Cojimies or the Chindul waterfall, fishing or whatever else you want to do. Hotel Yam Yam will appeal to those who want to go to the beach but don't want to be out on the sand 24/7, or for those who want to stay close to the bus station. Your best bet: call or e-mail ahead, ask Yandre what's going on, and work out a deal on the room you want. You can also ask to stay at the nearby Cabañas Yam Yam, which has a restaurant that opens in high season, a swimming pool, a game room and other amenities. Note that prices tend to rise to $12-15 per person during high season. Av. Gonzáles Suárez and Juan Pereira, Tel: 05-268-0566/1359, Cel: 09-9705-2326, E-mail: yandre_arteaga@hotmail.com.
Updated: Feb 13, 2013.

Pedernales Restaurants

Ask most Ecuadorians, and they'll tell you that the food in the province of Manabi is the best in the country. Huge langostinos (giant shrimp), fresh sea bass, red snapper and swordfish, tasty lobsters in season...throw in a cold beer and what more could you want? Pedernales hosts several good restaurants, most of them on the malecon across from the ocean.

Prices are cheap: you can get a plate of fresh fish, rice and patacones (cooked green banana) for $4...and that's at one of the expensive places. If you're not afraid of street food, feel free to help yourself to a 'Pincho' (a skewer of meat or sausage). At any of the restaurants, be sure to check out the 'menu,' a low-cost option that usually includes soup, main course, dessert and a glass of fresh juice for as little as $2.

El Costeñito

El Costeñito is an airy, friendly, family-run restaurant located right in the middle of the malecon, the main drag in Pedernales. Like most restaurants in town, it specializes in fresh seafood, available in a variety of sauces. A la diabla is a shrimp sauce, a la diabla is a mildly spicy red sauce, al ajillo is a creamy garlic sauce and encocada is a coconut sauce, famous on the coast. You may simply prefer your seafood "a la plancha" which is grilled in a bit of oil. The seafood is so good and fresh that it doesn't need any sauces or spices. Malecon and Eloy Alfaro, Tel: 05-268-0513 / 099-369-4407.
Updated: Apr 09, 2013.

La Choza

(ENTREES: $3-10) Like most of the coastal towns, Pedernales features its own set of generic beachfront restaurants and bars.

Loved it? Loathed it? Write a review and help other travelers

In terms of gastronomy, La Choza fits right in; however, its well-appointed dining area, complete with a collection of wine bottles spread across the back wall, give it a bit more atmosphere than the other seafood dives in town. Calling itself a restaurant of 4 b's—bueno, bonito, barato and bastante—this place seeks to serve its customers a bit of everything good with a side of better than the rest. The menu includes 50 different plates, so even the picky palates should be able to find something here. Specialties include mariscos and ceviches, meat, chicken, fish, rice and pasta dishes. Malecon and Eloy Alfaro, Tel: 099-436-1582 / 098-060-6152. Updated: Apr 09, 2013.

JAMA

 14m   23,253   05

Sitting slightly inland, amid humid pasturelands, is the unassuming town of Jama. Though this market center offers little in the way of beaches and bars, it does present visitors with the opportunity to experience the rural countryside and its inhabitants. Jama is a great stopover spot for those looking to escape the crowds and wander into nature without straying too far from the sand and surf.

The town has an old cowboy-western feel to it, with weathered wooden houses, smiling faces peering from their upstairs windows, and locals riding into town on their horses sometimes. It also has a soccer stadium as well as a tiny museum.

Don't come looking for discos or such other kinds of distractions, Jama is where you stop chasing life. Linger around the plaza for people-watching on Sundays, when vendors crowd the square to peddle sundry objects. You can also catch a collective taxi for $2-3 to nearby Playa El Matal, though remember not to wait too late in the day to catch a return taxi back to town! Updated: Apr 09, 2013.

Getting To and Away from Jama

No direct buses exist between Jama and Quito or Guayaquil. Visitors will need to go to **Pedernales** first (6 hr from Quito, 7 hr from Guayaquil), then take a COACTUR or Costanorte bus south to Jama from the bus station there. The trip between Pedernales and Jama is approximately one hour via bus and costs $1-2.

If you have your own car, the best route to take from **Quito** is Quito-Santo Domingo-Pedernales-Jama, which should take around six hours. From Guayaquil, the best route is Portoviejo-Pedernales-Jama, which should take five or six hours. Updated: Feb 18, 2013.

Safety

With Jama's small-town vibe bringing everyone into a close-knit community (and consequently, everyone pretty much knowing everyone), it's actually remarkable how safe the town is during the day, and even after dark.

Stick close to the plaza and outlying areas, but don't wander out into the outskirts and unlit places. Do not stay at the beaches after dark either, specifically because the chances of getting a ride back to Jama drop exponentially, and the walk back is long, dark and unsafe. Updated: Apr 09, 2013.

Getting Around Jama

Getting around Jama is relatively easy via Motorcycle Taxi. These can also take you out to the nearby beach El Matal ($3), and quite possibly - if they're up for going that far - to the wonderful and extensive shoreline of La Division ($6). Updated: Apr 09, 2013.

Jama Services

Jama has no banks, and only has one small tour office located at the Casa Blanca (White House) on the corner of Av. Bernardo Espinar and Pacifico Centeno. For general inquiries on what to do around Jama, just stop by and ask. Tel: 099-784-6605, E-mail: erikaormaza1912@hotmail.com. Updated: Apr 09, 2013.

Jama Tours

There are no official tour operators in Jama, but the locals (specifically Xavier) are more than happy and delighted to show you around. Updated: Apr 10, 2013.

Outdoor tours with Xavier

Xavier Cevallos, a natural, kind and patient guide, gives an incredible tailored outdoor/nature service. Horseback riding to the beach, canoe trips down Rio Jama, checking out the waterfalls, whale watching - even specialized tours of his family's shrimp ponds are a few options if you want to decompress in the Jama area. Call or e-mail him in advance to set something up. Tel: 098-837-9369, E-mail: xavier-cevallos1@hotmail.com Updated: Apr 09, 2013.

Things to See and Do in Jama

You'll be delighted to find that despite Jama's inland and rather barren location, there's a few beaches nearby worth checking out. In addition, the town itself has a modest pair of museums you can peruse during the day. Not to mention, the dry forest awaits just north of town.

Bosque Seco Lalo Loor

Just 20 minutes south of Pedernales (by bus) and a short jaunt north of Jama is a network of trails winding through unique coastal dry forest, past a stunning variety of flora and fauna and spectacular views of the expansive Pacific Ocean. Bosque Seco Lalo Loor is a great place to get out and about in nature: a number of self-guided trails introduce visitors to dry forest ecology, as well as the area's endemic wildlife, which includes white-fronted capuchin monkeys, mantled howler monkeys, red-masked parakeets, Pacific royal-flycatchers, boa constrictors, jaguarundi and a mixed bag of frogs and lizards.

Bird fans and orchid aficionados will also find the area full of interesting sights and sounds. The 45-minute Mariposa Trail begins at the reserve's entrance, winding past tumbling waterfalls, while the Pacifico Trail starts from the Biological Station, eventually climbing a number of ridge lines and presenting visitors with some spectacular ocean views. Lodging is available in the Biological Station. The station can accommodate up to 24 people, providing basic lodging for visitors, researchers and volunteers, as well as serving as a research center for reforestation and conservation projects.

To arrange a visit, contact CFTC (Ceiba Foundation for Tropical Conservation). For a few more creature comforts, you can also arrange to stay at Punta Prieta Guesthouse, just a few kilometers south of the reserve, or Hacienda Camarones that's just a 20-minute walk south from the reserve.

While in the area, be sure to check out the wave-carved natural monument, El Arco del Amor (Tasaste Beach), located three kilometers (1.9 mi)south of the reserve, along the coast road toward the town of Tasaste. For maps of the reserve and its trails, visit www.ceiba.org/loormaps.htm. To arrange a visit or volunteering, contact CFTC: Eugenio de Santillán N34-248 and Maurián (Quito), Tel: 02-603-5904 (Quito), URL: www.ceiba.org. Updated: Feb 13, 2013.

El Matal Beach

This fishing village is right on the fringe of Jama, and would seem to have an average tourist to fishing boat ratio of 1:50. All in all, it offers a rather narrow coastline with some delightful views of the ocean and warm waters to bathe in. Just remember to head back before dark, given that transportation back into town is hard to find as the day comes to an end. To get there take a motorcycle taxi for $3, and you'll get to ride past green pastures and the countryside on the way. Updated: Apr 10, 2013.

Tasaste Beach

You'll find this beach wedged between the cliffs up north (20 mins) that form part of Jama's coastline. It's a local and favorite hangout for residents, who make the trip to come and sunbathe, relax, and have BBQ's (huts with grills, open to the public, are available). You might think that it's the turtle-shaped shack that's the main attraction, when really – just right around the corner of the beach to the north - you'll find a pretty fascinating rock formation that the locals call El Arco del Amor (The Love Arch). Its name comes from the fact that the ancestral, indigenous communities of the area used to hold their wedding ceremonies underneath it. Additionally, you can typically rent a boat for an hour ($10) from any of the fishermen and get a different vantage point of this bit of coastline, or go swimming out in open water for a while. Access to this beach is incredibly limited, with moto-taxi's incapable of getting there due to the distance and terrain. The only way to get there is to hire a truck to take you there (and arrange a pick up time as well). Ask around town, or any of the moto-taxi's if they can hook you up. Updated: Apr 10, 2013.

Town Hall and Museum

Located at the Casablanca (white house) of town is a tiny and modest museum housing the artifacts that have been discovered in and around Jama, dating back to pre-Inca cultures and communities that lived along the coast of Ecuador centuries ago. Av. Bernardo Espinar and Pacifico Centeno. Updated: Apr 10, 2013.

Artesanal Store

This small museum and store that's located right by the entrance into town houses several more (in addition to what the Town Hall has) artifacts that are native to the lands in and around Jama. In addition, it sells handicrafts and artisan goods. Right beside the

Loved it? Loathed it? Write a review and help other travelers

entrance into Jama off the main road, best to take a motorcycle taxi there, ask them to the take you the *Tienda Artesanal*.
Updated: Apr 10, 2013.

La Division Beach

La Division beach is Jama's longest and most extensive shoreline, with a beach that's incredibly clean and home to only a couple of the kind-hearted locals than run tiny restaurants and tienditas (stores) along its shore. Tranquil and almost always empty, this incredible expanse of beach feels almost like a well guarded secret that no one ever even whispers about, and is practically all yours should you come to visit. Have a motorcycle taxi take you there for $3-4, making sure to coordinate with them on how to get back as well.
Updated: Apr 10, 2013.

Jama Lodging

El Ciragan

(ROOMS: $20) Clean, tidy rooms with air conditioning and cozy beds are what make this place a haven for beaten and tired travelers. Hot showers (via an electric shower head) will be sure to wash away your stresses and dirtiness, and wi-fi is super convenient for reconnecting with friends and family. In addition to all this, the TV will be your sole source of entertainment after the town shuts down around 8 pm. The hotel is conveniently located right beside the town hall/museum and two blocks from the bustling plaza, where you'll find all the life at. Lovely hand painted décor garnishes each room, and you'll be sure to get a good night's rest here given how separated and quiet it is from the heart of town. Av. Bernardo Espinar 606 and Pacifico Centeno, Tel: 099-711-6800, E-mail: carmensaker@hotmail.com, URL: www.hosteriaciragan.com.
Updated: Apr 10, 2013.

Punta Prieta Guesthouse

(ROOMS: $20-80) Miles from the nearest village and filled with the sound of waves crashing into its cliffs, Punta Prieta calms the restless and soothes the burdened. This guest house offers creature comforts, fresh seafood, and all of those intangibles that go with its location: a salty breeze that rejuvenates the spirit, a deserted beach that begs for company, and an atmosphere that makes relaxation no chore. Punta Prieta is a tourist-free oasis in the middle of a stretch of coast between Pedernales and Canoa (outskirts of Jama) that attracts many Ecuadorians and foreigners alike in search of peace and solitude. The comfortable rooms come with with fans and simple but inviting decor, with use of the shared kitchen and refrigerator included in the price. Via del Pacifco, km 36 from Pedernales to Jama, Tel: 098-342-3811 / 098-640-1298, E-mail: puntaprieta@ hotmail.com, URL: www.puntaprieta.com.
Updated: Apr 09, 2013.

Hostal Río Jama

(ROOMS: $10-15) Located right beside the lively plaza, this small and family-run hostel is probably your cheapest bet in all of Jama which does not sacrifice cleanliness. Rooms come with a private bathroom, TV, and fan. In addition, there's lower-rate rooms with a shared bathroom as well. Mind you, if you're not a heavy sleeper, just know that the noise outside might mean you'll be waking up with the town rather to your own accord in the mornings. Jama Ave. and Marco Cevallos. In front of the town park., Tel: 05-241-0188 / 098-968-7264.
Updated: Apr 10, 2013.

Jama Restaurants

La Esquina Del Cheo

(ENTREES: $5-8) With an open-air terrace and a view of the ocean, you'll find that the vista here compliments the food they serve here quite nicely. Given El Matal is a fishing town, you're pretty much guaranteed the freshest seafood there is in all of Jama. Just know that Cheo's has no menu, and the man himself – kind owner and seafood connoisseur – will typically be the one taking your order after reciting a list of specials for the day. Don't be shy about asking for any options outside of what he states, it just might be that they have it, or at most – they can go fetch it. Located on the corner of the main street that leads into El Matal and the Malecón., Tel: 096-971-1441.
Updated: Apr 10, 2013.

Restaurant Exclusivo

(ENTREES: $3-7) Right by the main plaza is where you'll find this small but immensely popular "upscale" hole-in-the-wall serving up some pretty satisfying cuisine. Ranging from your traditional seafood fare to spaghetti, chicken and even Asian chaulafan (rice plates), the portions here (especially rice) are served larger than what's typically expected. Desayunos and almuerzos are available for about 2.50-3.50, just know that due its popularity this place tends to fill up at midday. Jama Ave. and Marco Cevallos Valencia, Tel: 05-241-0400 / 099-237-6197.
Updated: Apr 10, 2013.

CANOA

 6m   4,476   05

Mompiche may have the surfer's hearts and Atacames may have the bars, but Canoa is sure to romance almost anyone into a stupor with its long stretches of white sand, chilled surf, and easy-going town. Whether you like long walks on the beach or lengthy chats in bars and restaurants, Canoa's spell-binding atmosphere is bound to capture your attention for a day or two - or more; it's not uncommon for travelers to come for the night and stay for a month.

Quiet dirt roads crisscross through town, running into the main street and beach front, lined with restaurants and hostels that fill to the brim with foreign and Ecuadorian travelers alike on the weekends. During the week, however, Canoa maintains an unhurried pace which settles nicely with the hushed sound of waves breaking and the palm fronds shifting in the breeze.

Adventures and activities are close at hand too, given Canoa offers a range of services in getting you on a horse, or canoe, or mountain bike, or surfboard (post-yoga session).

Getting To and Away from Canoa

To get to Canoa, you can travel direct from **Quito**, or to either **Bahía de Caráquez** or **San Vicente**, which sit across a small bay from each other. Canoa is about 20 minutes down the beach from San Vicente.

From **Quito**, a Reina del Camino bus (Manuel Larrea & 18 de Septiembre, Tel: 02–321-6633) leaves for Canoa around 10:45 p.m. (6-7 hr, $10). Reina del Camino buses also leave at 11:30 p.m. for **San Vicente** (7-8

hr, $8). From San Vicente, either take a taxi ($5) or a local bus or open-air chiva ($0.30), which run every 30 minutes to Canoa. Note, that Reina del Camino is the only bus company the goes to Canoa, San Vicente and Bahía de Caráquez from Quito.

However, the main transport hub in this area is Bahía de Caráquez, located on the other side of a bay from San Vicente, which is now connected to the rest of the coast by a bridge; in fact, it is the longest bridge in Ecuador. From Bahía, buses operate regularly to **Quito** (8 hr, $8), **Guayaquil** (6 hr, $5), and locations all around the region. On all of these routes, the fancier ejecutivo buses also run, which will cost around $1-2 more than the regular service.

Buses to **San Vicente** and **Bahia** leave from the plaza Antonio Aveiga (central park) in Canoa every 20 minutes, and are the ones labeled 'Tosagua.' The trip costs $1 and lasts around 45 minutes.

There are rumors that Bahía's airport will be welcoming commercial flights in the near futurel; however, for now, to get to Canoa by air you have to fly to Manta's Eloy Afaro airport (MEC), and then catch a bus to Bahía (3 hr, $3). Tame (www.tame.com.ec), Aerogal (www.aerogal.com.ec) and Icaro (www.icaro.aero) fly daily to Manta from Quito for around $100 return.
Updated: Apr 11, 2013.

Canoa Services

There are no banks in Canoa, the closest ones being in San Vicente and Bahia.

LAUNDRY

Laundry Ashley: $1 x 1 kilo. Javier Santo and Ciriaco Valdez. 098-663-2046

KEEPING IN TOUCH

Cyber Surf Rider: $1 x 1 hour. Javier Santo and Ciriaco Valdez.

MEDICAL

Farmacy Farmacia Vida Sana: Javier Santo and 30 de Noviembre.
Updated: May 03, 2013.

Safety

As with any other beach along the coast, don't take valuables with you to the beach, or at most - don't ever leave them unattended (especially after sunset). Walking alone along the beach at night is not advised either.
Updated: Apr 11, 2013.

Photo by: Athena Lao

NORTHERN COAST

Loved it? Loathed it? Write a review and help other travelers

Things To See and Do in Canoa

The easygoing beach town of Canoa offers a little something for everyone: travelers looking for a laid-back vacation and thrill-seekers alike. Post up in one of the many hammocks that line the sand, go horseback riding down the coastline or into the dry jungle, hit the waves on a surfboard, take Spanish classes with the locals, sail above the city on a paraglider or hang glider, or just enjoy the sunset views from one of the many bars at happy hour.

Surfing

Surf board rentals throughout Canoa are pretty much set at: $15 all day, $10 for half a day. You can rent them at almost any of the hotels around town (even the internet cafe "Cyber Surf" rents out boards). A popular place to rent them out at is Surf Shak.
Updated: Apr 11, 2013.

Betty Surf and Yoga Camp

The Betty Surf & Yoga Camp presents eclectic classes for women (and men too!) focused on Yoga, Meditation and Surf. Patricia White is the on premise Yoga instructor, holding accreditation from the Yoga Alliance as a certified Core Power instructor. She teaches vinyasa flow with modifications to make the class accessible for beginners to practiced yoga people alike, available in a power class or as a moderated stretch. Her specialty is Yoga for Surfers, focusing on shoulder opening, hip opening and stretching of the lower back and lumbar.

After a long day of paddling out and riding, this is the perfect way to wind down or power up for your next surfing session. Surf and yoga camps/retreats are offered throughout the year (typically between June and August). Otherwise, sign up for a daily session. Courses vary in price, with an $1300, 9 day, all-inclusive package available. Alternatively, it's $20-30 for a 2-hour yoga and surf lesson. Offices are located right next to the Bambu Hostel at the corner of the Malecon, Tel: 098-974-4830, URL: http://www.bettyadventures.com. Updated: Apr 10, 2013.

Rio Muchacho Organic Farm

Situated in the Río Muchacho river valley, just a short distance from the chilled beaches of Canoa, Río Muchacho Organic Farm focuses on environmental and cultural awareness with an affinity towards community development and sustainable tourism.

Owners Nicola and Dario have not only created a self-sufficient organic farm based on the practices of permaculture, but have also cultivated a strong relationship with the local community.

Due in part to their hard work and constant toil, the area (in Bahia and Canoa) now has 13 eco-schools, which cater to nearly 900 children. Foreigners, as well as locals, can benefit in uncountable ways from a visit to the farm—whether to volunteer for a couple weeks, or to attend agricultural courses for a few months. It is a unique opportunity to offer up one's time and labor in return for valuable knowledge and insight into rural Ecuador, its land and its people.

From dawn to dusk, this place offers ample opportunity to learn and grow. The farm runs a number of programs and tours, but perhaps the best way to make the most of your experience is to volunteer for a few weeks. The farm is always on the lookout for Spanish-proficient volunteers to head up programs in the environmental schools. See Guacamayo Tours for more information.
Updated: Apr 11, 2013.

Horseback Riding

(PRICE: $25) Head on over to Hostal Coco Loco and ask for Elizabeth, who offers horseback tours of the ranches up and around Canoa, finishing up with a walk (or gallop) across the beach. The horses are hers, and she pridefully takes great care of them. Riders of all skill levels are welcome. Hostal Coco Loco, Malecón, Tel: 099-243-6508, E-mail: hostalcocoloco@yahoo.com.

Spanish Classes

(PRICE: $600-800) Private Spanish classes for travelers interested in learning while enjoying the beach are available. One on one tutoring or group classes are available by the hour, or choose a one to four week package deal for a discount. Located 2 km south of the town center of Canoa on the highway to San Vicente. Price is for a four-week program with room and meals included. Price depends on private or shared room and lessons. E-mail: canoaschool@hotmail.com, URL: www.ecuadorbeach.com/spanish_school.

Alternatively, for private lessons that are held locally in town, contact Andrea: Tel: 095-927-1025, E-mail: andreacoronado.27@gmail.com.
Updated: Apr 10, 2013.

Canoa Tours

Guacamayo Tours !

In association with the Río Muchacho Organic Farm, Guacamayo Tours is one of the main operator in Canoa and has a variety of exceptional eco-oriented treks and tours. Dedicated to responsible tourism and environmental work, the company is owned by Ecuadorian Dario Proaño and New Zealander Nicola Mears, who dedicate every waking hour to exploring new ways to facilitate socially and environmentally sustainable tourism in the area. The educational tours are the perfect opportunity to learn about fair trade, sustainable development, and even how tourists can leave a positive imprint on the places they visit. Their office also sells local crafts, recycled paper, organic honey and other fair trade products. Calle Javier Santos (Main Street, on the corner in front of the park), Tel: 05-258-8108 / 099-796-1466, URL: www.guacamayotours.com.
Updated: Apr 11, 2013.

Canoa Thrills

Canoa Thrills is an adventure tourism company based out of the popular Surf Shak restaurant. Eclectic and energetic, this young company offers a variety of adventures, ranging from half-day kayaking to a cave to week-long excursions. A must is a paragliding trip over Canoa at sunset, where you can get a birds-eye view of the town and beaches. Other offerings include a booze cruise to Cabo Pasado, a deserted beach close by, day trips to nearby reserves, and fishing excursions.

Beach bums (and babes) visiting Canoa should definitely stop by Canoa Thrills: it rents a slew of surf and sand equipment, including body boards, fins, surfboards, longboards, kayaks, mountain bikes and motorbikes by the hour or all day. You can also take lessons or courses in surfing, kayaking and tandem paragliding. Want to learn how to fly? Brave souls can stay for a few weeks and receive their paragliding certification USH-GA P-1 & P-2. Surf Shak on the Malecón, Tel: 098-101-1471, URL: www.canoathrills.com.
Updated: Apr 10, 2013.

Canoa Expeditions

From surfing to mountaing biking to kayaking and ecotourism, Canoa Expeditions is your outlet to partake in any one of these adventurous activities. Go whale or bird watching if you're interested in doing something more passive. Either way, you'll end up soaking in plenty of Canoa's surrounding area across the seas or through the forests. Instructors are available as well. Calle Filomeno Hernandez, right beside Pais Libre Hotel, Tel: 099-817-0832, URL: www.21671.com/canoaexpeditions.
Updated: Apr 11, 2013.

Canoa Lodging

Canoa is a backpacker haven, geared towards cheap to mid-range accommodation right on the beach. Recently, a number of new places have gone up in town, giving most of the older places a run for their money in terms of quality, service and style. Like all places on the coast, Canoa overflows with people on weekends, so you'd be smart to make reservations early. Don't expect to cruise into town on Saturday night or an Ecuadorian holiday and find a place to stay.
Updated: Jan 20, 2012.

Amalur !

($12 per person) This is one place in Canoa which you can't help but be changed by when you walk through its doors. Maybe its the Spanish accents that the hosts charm you with, or the incredible hospitality they provide you with, or maybe the fact that somehow - and in a subtle way - it doesn't even feel like Ecuador anymore, because it actually feels more like a little piece of Spain. Needless to say, the rooms here are incredibly tidy and well maintained, not to mention there's a cool terrace up top that gives you a nice view of the ocean across the small town of Canoa.

A little set back from the beach (but no more than a 5 minute walk from its shores), there's still plenty of room here to stretch, relax and soak it all in with unbeatable hospitality. San Andreas Street in front of the football field., Tel: 098-303-5039, E-mail: amalurcanoa@hotmail.com, URL: www.amalurcanoa.com.
Updated: May 03, 2013.

Coconut Bungalow

(ROOMS: $10-40) Located 1.5km south of Canoa on the road from San Vicente, Coconut Bungalow offers rooms with balconies and views of the ocean, and owns its own stretch of beach, reserved only for guests. Relax in the shade of the hotel´s beach tents, or eat to your heart´s content in their restaurant, which caters to both traditional and international tastes. Located on the beachfront, 1.5 km south of Canoa. Tel: 06-922-8715, E-mail: sailingandcoconuts@gmail.com, URL: http://www.coconuthotelcanoa.com.
Updated: Apr 10, 2013.

NORTHERN COAST

Hostería Canoa

(ROOMS: $67-143) Hostería Canoa, sprawled across its own section of private beach a few kilometers from town, offers a slightly more intimate setting than some of the smaller places in Canoa. Clean, modern and colorful rooms are set around a courtyard swimming pool and restaurant and bar area. The restaurant, in particular, is a spacious but stylish place for a meal. Cabins are perfect for larger groups or families, and come with the same well-appointed rooms and modern bathrooms. Although the hotel is pricier than the joints down the road, Hostería Canoa is still a good value considering the facilities and location. Main entrance. Road to San Vicente Km. 1, Tel: 05-258-8180/82, Cel: 09-9977-4747/9995-5401, E-mail: hosteriacanoa@gmail.com, URL: www.hosteriacanoa.com.
Updated: Feb 14, 2013.

Cabañas Mar y Paz

($10-20 per person) At Cabañas Mar y Paz, clusters of modest cabins surround a spacious yard equipped with a volleyball court and picnic tables. The facilities make the hotel the perfect setting for friendly reunions and family excursions. The ever-amiable owners, Catalina and Jaime, aim to please and (with prior notice) are happy to organize local tours or cater for special events, including slow food events accompanied by live music. The cabins are rustic but relatively comfortable, with simple bunks and wooden floors. A fun family atmosphere is complemented by plenty of open space and small gardens in which to sit and socialize. Cabins fill up quickly during high season and special holidays so it's wise to call ahead and book early. Ruta de Sol, 3 minutes from Canoa town, Tel: 05-258-8185/302-0539, Cel: 09-9895-4458/9358-4168, E-mail: carohe47@hotmail.com / jaimesolisch@yahoo.es, URL: www.cabanasmarypaz.info.
Updated: Feb 14, 2013.

Hotel Bambu !

(ROOMS: $10-120) Commanding a quiet, sandy corner of the main street, Hotel Bambu is a popular traveler hangout and good place to rest your head. Accommodation ranges from cheap to more expensive (by Canoa standards), from a dorm bed to a more elaborate room with private balcony and bathroom, and a big comfy bed. Camping spots and private cabins are another option. There is a restaurant and bar (daily 8 a.m.-9:30 p.m.; entrees: $5-10), which serves a tempting array of national and international dishes, including salad, crepes, sandwiches and ice cream. Travelers seem to congregate around the beach-like yard, where beach chairs, hammocks, and wooden tables make cozy spots to relax. Ever environmentally conscious, the bar does not sell beverages in plastic bottles due to ecological concerns and a free cocktail is the reward for turning in a bag full of trash collected from the beach. The owner also runs Casa Bambu in Quito and Cabañas Bambu in Mindo. Main street, far north end of beach, Tel: 05-258-8017, Cel: 09-9926-3365, URL: www.hotelbambuecuador.com.
Updated: Feb 14, 2013.

Coco Loco

($8-25 per person) A big Swiss-family Robin-esque bamboo house, Hostal Coco Loco is one of the most popular spots to spend the night in Canoa. A true traveler's meeting ground, Coco Loco provides all the comforts of home for an international crowd. It is easy to spend a morning, afternoon or evening idling around the kitchen counter, swapping travel stories and shooting the breeze.

Of course, this place isn't all talk: newly built and smartly styled rooms bear crisp clean sheets, new mattresses and high-tech fans, which combined with a fresh sea breeze are certain to relax the limbs and produce droopy eye-lids. Rooms are built around mock-beach area, complete with white sand and palm trees, and perfect for lounging about, or catching up on some pleasure reading. Accommodation ranges from shared bunks (themselves a steal with doors that open onto a sea-view porch hung with comfy hammocks) to large white-walled private rooms. And you're bound to sleep soundly with the knowledge that you'll wake to one of the best breakfasts in Canoa: eggs benedict, chorizo and eggs, or fruit and granola are just a few of the options. Beachfront, Tel: 099-243-6508.

Hotel Sol y Luna

($10 per person) Located at the far south end of the beach, Hotel Sol y Luna is an aging but good-value place. It is built hacienda-style around a courtyard swimming pool which boasts excellent seaside views. A modest garden adds a splash of color to the site, and rooms are big, clean and well-maintained, with modern bathrooms. The on-site restaurant serves a range of traditional and international dishes, and paragliding tours can be arranged. Far south end of the beach, Tel: 05-261-6363 / 099-850-9203.

La Vista

(ROOMS: $26-38) A grand hotel fronting the main beach, La Vista is a new place boasting big beds and polished wooden floors. The private balconies all have hammocks and a stunning sea view. Rooms are open and airy, and emit a chilled-out but classy feel that even the grungiest backpacker will appreciate. The staff is friendly and the bar downstairs serves a variety of hard and soft drinks, a good spot to pull up a stool and contemplate one's luck at finding a place so beautiful and well priced. Bar open daily 14:00 - 22:30. Main street, next to Coco Loco, Tel: 099-228-8995.
Updated: Apr 10, 2013.

Hostel Shelmar

($8-12 per person) Located one block from the beach, Hostal ShelMar offers basic but bright rooms and private bathrooms upstairs and a good, cheap restaurant downstairs. This isn't the best place in town, but still good value, clean and comfortable. Laundry service is available for both patrons and non-patrons. Active travelers looking to stretch their legs for a while can also rent bikes from here. Javier Santos 304 Av. Principal, Tel: 098-450-5391, E-mail: shelmar66@hotmail.com.
Updated: Apr 10, 2013.

La Posada de Daniel

($10-18 per person) A popular Canoa fixture, La Posada de Daniel offers comfortable cabins, which are perfect for large groups, and equipped with mosquito nets, private bathrooms and fans. The cabins also have balconies with views of the town and a bit of sea. Calm, quiet and cozy, this place also features an on-site restaurant, and the staff can organize both horseback riding excursions and local tours. The owner, once a slick surfer himself, gives lessons to anyone interested. As if the views weren't enough, this place also has satellite internet, a swimming pool and vegetarian restaurant. If you're up for a drink head to the hotel-owned Iguana Bar for "crazy" hour from 8 to 9 p.m. 150 meters back from the beach, by the town square., Tel: 05-258-8108 / 098-126-0537.
Updated: Apr 10, 2013.

Sundown Inn

($8-12 per person) The Sundown Inn is very popular for its Spanish lesson programs and isolated, private beach location. Located a 20-minute walk, or a quick five-minute bus ride to Canoa, The Sundown Inn is a great escape for couples or travelers looking for seclusion and tranquility, with only the sound of the waves crashing on the shore. The rooms are comfortable and modern, with hot water and hammocks on their beach-side balconies. Guests can also camp on the sand in front of the inn, make a bonfire with driftwood or play beach volleyball. While there is a restaurant on-site that provides complimentary breakfasts, it is not always open during the off-season. The Canoa Spanish Language School run from here offers one-on-one or group classes for $4-6 an hour, with discounts for students who plan to stay for awhile. Road to San Vicente, Km. 2, Tel: 09-8309-5218/9744-4484/8270-5006/9143-6343/8063-8078, E-mail: majuli@live.com, URL: www.ecuadorbeach.com.
Updated: Feb 14, 2013.

Cabañas Baloo

(ROOMS: $11-44) Located on the south end of the beach, down the street from the music of the bars and restaurants, Cabañas Baloo offers a quiet place to rest. You can either stay in one of its pleasant cabins with porches, private bathrooms and a fan, or book one of the private rooms in the main house, which are cheaper and have a shared bathroom. Baloo has an on-site restaurant where breakfast, lunch and cocktails are served; on Saturday nights, it also hosts steak night where you can choose your cut, grill it up and enjoy it with a baked potato and salad. The central gazebo is filled with hammocks—a wonderful place to unwind or curl up with a book. South end of beach, Tel: 09-8556-5952, E-mail: baloo_canoa@yahoo.com, URL: www.baloo-canoa.com.

Canoa's Wonderland

(ROOMS: $70-120) Run by a Dutch family, this few-year-old hotel offers some of the best high-end accommodation to be found in the small village of Canoa. The hotel occupies a prime location at the end of the main street, right on the beach, though it is a bit of an eyesore compared to the other rustic accommodation options that are built with natural materials blend in with the beach.

The rooms are clean and spacious, have TVs and DVD players, and are cooled by either fans or air conditioning, but the highlights of the hotel are undoubtedly the communal areas. There is a plush bar, a restaurant, a roof-top terrace with great views across the sea, and a heated swimming pool, which sits right on the beach.   Although this is one of Canoa's more expensive hotels, if you're

NORTHERN COAST

looking for an easy place to relax, Canoa's Wonderland might be the perfect place for you. Malecón and Ca. San Andrés, Tel: 05-258-8163, Cel: 09-9456-3854, E-mail: canoaswonderland@hotmail.com, URL: www.hotelcanoaswonderland.com.ec.
Updated: Feb 14, 2013.

Canoa Restaurants

From fresh fruit salad to Spanish entrees, this little town has got the culinary circuit pretty much covered. And, of course, you'll have no trouble finding typical coastal fare, including ceviches and platos encocados. Prices between places don't vary much.
Updated: Apr 10, 2013.

Amalur Spanish Restaurant !

(ENTREES: $5-8) Amalur is a must-stop for visitors and locals alike looking to get their fill of traditional Spanish cuisine. Set back from the beach, Amalur is a great location for a quiet date or intimate dinner party. Start with the organic salad and French bread with a tasty tomato & garlic spread, indulge in the Spanish meatballs and a glass of vino tinto (red wine), and finally, round out the night with some decadent chocolate truffles. Other good dinner options are the breaded eggplant, grilled pork, Galician-style octopus, and squid in its own ink. Open from noon-10 p.m. Amalur is located behind the football field in central Canoa. From the beach, walk down main street, and turn right towards the field., URL: www.amalurcanoa.com. Ca. San Andreas (right beside the football field), Tel: 098-303-5039/812-9486, E-mail: amalurcanoa@hotmail.com.

Surf Shak

(ENTREES: $5-10) If a big, juicy, American-style burger and steak fries is what you're craving, look no further than Surf Shak. Co-owned by three friendly Americans and a Dutchman, the restaurant offers some classics very few others have been able to successfully accomplish on this side of the equator. On a street lined with seafood restaurants facing the beach, this joint full of English-speaking staff can provide a nice break to someone looking for a bit of American fare.

In addition to its thick burgers, Surf Shak also offers a delicious assortment of pizzas served hot from the oven. A variety of board games keep visitors entertained as they wait for food and happy hour, which lasts from 6-8 p.m. every night, and 4-8 p.m. on Fridays. Trivia Night on Thursdays

at 8:30 mustn't be missed. And lo' and behold dear traveler, this place is the only one (within miles, quite possibly) that serves pretty good IPA Beer! In the morning before the surf breaks, grab your laptop and stop by the Surf Shak to check your email with their free WiFi. American-style breakfasts like pancakes, French toast, and eggs with hash browns can be enjoyed with a cup of delicious French-press coffee for a wonderful start to your day. Malecón, Tel: 09-8101-1471, E-mail: pete@canoathrills.com, URL: www.canoathrills.com/surf-shak.
Updated: Apr 10, 2013.

Saborearme

(ENTREES: $4-10) Occupying a prime location on the beach front, this cevicheria serves up a variety of seafood dishes, including a wide range of ceviches served with plantain chips. Reasonably priced, high-quality seafood is exactly what you should expect to find at the beach, and this open-air bamboo hut with a sandy floor is the ideal place to enjoy it. Try regional specialties like camarones encocados (shrimp in coconut sauce) or camarones al ajillo (shrimp in a garlic lime sauce), served with a mound of white rice and patacones (fried plantains). Malecón.
Updated: Feb 14, 2013.

Comedor Jixy

(ENTREES: $4-7) This unassuming place set back from the beach is one of the most popular spots to settle the stomach and sample local seafood. Serving good value set meals and cheap mains, Comedor Jixy also knows how to satisfy the budget. There's not much in the way of atmosphere here, but its hard to argue with the prices, or the sea breeze. Set back from the beach, on the corner of the main road and the Malecon.
Updated: Feb 16, 2013.

Freedom Bar & Restaurant

($3-10) A terrific spot to watch the sunset with beers in hand and incredibly cool decor around (hammock chairs hanging from the ceiling, plush bean bags to lay down on), Freedom B&R has a lounge-by-the-sea thing happening that you can't miss out on. The owner runs a terrific restaurant and bar, serving up some amazing home-style mashed potatoes with gravy! Take a taxi ride ($2) there from Canoa, and leave all your worries behind as you bask in what Freedom has to offer. They even have movie nights with free popcorn every now and then. Kilometer 12.5, on the road to San Vicente. Tel: 05-737-1351.
Updated: April 31, 2013

Coco Loco Restaurant

(ENTREES: $2-8) The charismatic food fare served here is bound to bring a smile to your face while eating, especially if you come during happy hour to see and/or meet some really extroverted travelers. Fish tacos during the evening are a house specialty, but know that this is the place that you should come to for some exquisite early morning breakfasts ranging from eggs benedict to French toast. Hostal Coco Loco, Beachfront, Tel: 099-243-6508.

Bambu Restaurant

(ENTREES: $3-15) For a more romantic breakfast, lunch or dinner by the seaside head on over to Bambu. Once seated, you can simply dig your toes into the sand and bask under the sun or stars to the sounds of waves, along with the flavors that it'll have you swirling across your palette. They serve some rather classy concoctions here ranging from shrimp with tequila all the way to the traditional seafood fare, but you'll be pleasantly surprised to find that their in-house specialty is crepes. Don't missing out on having one, even if only for a dessert! Northern corner of the Malecon, Tel: 05-258-8017, Cel: 09-9926-3365, URL: www.hotelbambuecuador.com. Updated: April 20, 2013

Totem

(SANDWICHES: $2-7) If you need a change from all the seafood plates and rice you've been eating along the coast, this place is sure to offer you your fix nudged in between a homemade baguette. It doesn't end there either - sample their array of sweets from cheesecake to maracuya mousse. This place is incredibly popular with locals as much as it is with the foreigners, so don't miss out on at least sampling what it has to offer. Beachfront.

Macondo Lodge (Restaurant)

(BREAKFAST: $3) For a deal-breaker breakfast and what has to be the best banana pancakes (done right!) in town, head over to Macondo Lodge's restaurant, run by friendly owner Felix who cooks up the meals himself. For a price that's hard to beat, you get pancakes, toast, fruit, juice and coffee. Alternatively, you can ask for the equally delicious hash-browns, bacon and eggs combo which is just as scrumptious. For the extra hungry, simply order both! Xavier Santos and Antonio Aveiga, right in front of the Central Park, Tel: 08-309-0111, E-mail: anibalmacondo@gmail.com. Updated: April 20, 2013

BAHÍA DE CARÁQUEZ

 12m   52,158 05

This clean and breezy town, sitting on a slender peninsula reaching into the Río Chone, boasts a quiet atmosphere accompanied by tall white-fronted apartment complexes and broad tree-lined avenues. Locals in San Vicente say the best thing about Bahía is the view from San Vicente. To a certain extent, the city does seem a lot more impressive from afar than up-close. Once a holiday haven for high-heeled Ecuadorians, Bahía was tormented by unrelenting El Niño rains in the late 1990s. Severe flooding, coupled with a double earthquake, destroyed buildings and roads, triggered landslides and pretty much washed out tourism in the area. The city has made a brilliant recovery, and along with the repaired roads and reconstructed buildings came the growth of a new urban trend: ecotourism.

Navigating the town is relatively easy: the Malecón wraps around the edge of the peninsula, eventually becoming Circunvalación as it approaches the shore. Some of the best and most popular eateries line the riverside, close to the ferry, in an area touted as Malecón 69. Lying within striking distance of tropical dry forests, mangrove islands and remote beaches, Bahía is a good place to get down with nature, or just spend a pleasant afternoon meandering along the Malecón.

Getting To and Away from Bahía de Caráquez

Bahía de Caráquez is well connected to destinations all across Ecuador, and all long-distance buses leave from the Bahia de Caráquez bus terminal at the sound end of the Malecón ($2 taxi ride to get there, 5 minutes). There are regular, daily bus services to **Guayaquil** (5 hours, $5), **Quito** (7 hours, $8), **Manta** (2 hours, $2), **Portoviejo** (1-1.5 hours, $1.20) as well as many other smaller destinations.

Reina del Camino offers the most direct bus service available from **Quito** to Bahia ($10, 7 hours). Quito Tel: 02-321-6633 / 02-321-5824 / 02-238-2487. Manuel Larrea and 18 de Septiembre.

To get to the popular beach destination of **Canoa**, buses ($1, 45 mins) leave regularly from the bus terminal in Bahia. This trip crosses the bridge to **San Vincente** - a

NORTHERN COAST

town which sits on the opposite side of the Río Chone from Bahía - and affords you with beautiful views of the beach and bluffs along the way.
Updated: Apr 19, 2013.

Bahía de Caráquez Services
MONEY
Banco De Guayaquil. Riofrio and Bolivar, Tel: 05-373-0100.
Updated: Apr 10, 2013.

KEEPING IN TOUCH
Cyber Bahia. Av. Bolivar and Arenas.
Updated: Apr 10, 2013.

Bahía de Caráquez Tours
Guacamayo Tours
In association with the Río Muchacho Organic Farm, Guacamayo Tours is the main operator in Bahia (as well as Canoa) and has a variety of exceptional eco-oriented treks and tours. Dedicated to responsible tourism and environmental work, the company is owned by Ecuadorian Dario Proaño and New Zealander Nicola Mears, who dedicate every waking hour to exploring new ways to facilitate socially and environmentally sustainable tourism in the area. The educational tours are the perfect opportunity to learn about fair trade, sustainable development, and even how tourists can leave a positive imprint on the places they visit.

They've also been garnering support for the Bahía Eco-City projects, designing programs for organic recycling (including eco-paper recycling in the city), developing community training eco-camps, and even establishing an environmental primary school so that even the youngest generation is educated on new techniques for sustainable farming, recycling, waste management and reforestation. The main office, fittingly located in the eco-city of Bahía, also sells local crafts, recycled paper, organic honey and other fair trade products. Bolívar 902 y Arenas, Tel: 05-269-1412 / 05-269-1107, URL: www.guacamayotours.com.
Updated: Apr 11, 2013.

Things To See and Do in Bahía de Caráquez
Although Bahía´s bay is nothing to brag about, the town is lively and friendly on weekends (though a bit deserted during the week) and there are a number of interesting sites (even a hidden beach) nearby. The Río Chone estuary consists of several islands and mangrove habitats; this unique area is a bird's and birder's paradise. During mating season, from August to January, visitors can observe the male frigate bird and his characteristic red-puffed chest, among other winged residents, nesting in the mangroves. For some excellent culture and history head to Museo del Banco Central.
Updated: Apr 11, 2013.

Isla Fragatas
Just a 15-minute boat ride from Bahía, Isla Fragatas is a bird paradise and mangrove haven. Check out this unique island ecosystem, and see La Tortuga Miguelito (the local 93-year old Galápagos turtle and mangrove mascot) and Saiananda Park. A portion of the tour fee is reserved for conservation. Island excursions need to be arranged through Guacamayo Tours.
Updated: Apr 11, 2013.

Isla Corazon
Located just a stone's throw from Bahía is Isla Corazon, home to endangered mangroves and numerous bird species. Learn about the local Mangrove Forest and estuary ecosystem, while interacting (and giving back to) the locals. The ever-friendly and outgoing guides Julio and Luciano can point out resident bird species, and explain the importance of this rare Río Chone estuary ecosystem. Tours include an introduction to the area, a boat and boardwalk tour of Isla Corazon and a traditional lunch (usually viche, a peanut-based seafood soup). Come for mating season (August to January) when you can spot the puffed red sacks of male frigate birds and appreciate the age-old search for a suitable (or willing) spouse. Island excursions need to be arranged through Guacamayo Tours.
Updated: Apr 11, 2013.

Sainanda Park
(ENTRANCE: $2) Owned by biologist Alfredo Harmsen, Saiananda is a private park situated along the waterfront, just 5 kilometers from Bahía. In addition to striking views of the sea, the park also features an intriguing menagerie of native and domestic animals and birds. Park residents include itinerant sloths, coatimundi, deer, ostriches, rabbits, macaws, peacocks and geese, all of which freely interact with their human guests. The Japanese bonsai garden, eclectic cactus collection, and variety of other plants are equally worth a visit. The entire area encompasses a spiritual center offering comfortable to out-and-out lavish accommodation and a first-class vegetarian restaurant. Spiritual cleansing and relaxation retreats can be or-

NORTHERN COAST

ganized too. Park excursions need to be arranged through Guacamayo Tours. Tel: For reservations contact Guacamayo Tours in Bahía. Tel: 05-398-331.
Updated: Apr 11, 2013.

Punta Bellaca

As you walk along Bahia's Malecón you'll probably wonder where the beach is exactly. Just 5 minutes from Bahia in car is Punta Bellaca, or Bahia's missing beach. It's here that you'll find an incredibly laid back and peaceful atmosphere alongside its beautiful sandy shores, away from the noise and crowds that make up the city; and perhaps even find yourself grateful that Bahia's hidden beach isn't right up against civilization. Located on the backside of Bahia. $2 in taxi. Just be sure to coordinate with the driver on getting back/having a pick-up time.
Updated: Apr 10, 2013.

Museo Del Banco Central

(ADMISSION: $1) This place houses an excellent collection of archaeological artifacts from a variety of pre-hispanic coastal societies, and is definitely worth checking out if you have more than half a day in town. Malecón, Alberto F Santos between Aguilera and Peña, Tel: 05-269-0817 / 05-269-2285.
Updated: Apr 10, 2013.

Bahía de Caráquez Lodging

The choice of hotels in Bahía is not nearly as extensive as in Canoa—and if you like to fall asleep to the sound of waves breaking, you're better off crashing in Canoa and day-tripping to Bahía—but depending on your budget there are a couple of higher-tier hotels that offer a little more luxury than the smaller places in Canoa.

Hotel Italia

(ROOMS: $30-50) Hotel Italia, set back from the beach, is a multi-storied hotel offering clean but dated rooms which, for the price, are a bit lackluster. The restaurant downstairs has a modest selection of national and international dishes, and in the morning you can grab a simple breakfast for $3. Av. Bolivar and Ca. Checa, Tel: 05-269-1137, E-mail: hotelitalia@gmail.com.
Updated: Feb 14, 2013.

La Herradura

(ROOMS: $55-70) Aged but atmospheric, La Herradura offers simple rooms set around an attractive Spanish-style building. The front porch and restaurant area face the sea, and there are vaulted ceilings with clean white walls, all of which create a bright and breezy spot to sit, sip a drink and share a meal with friends. The neatly set tables, with burgundy and white tablecloths and wine glasses, add a touch of elegance. Bar Michelangelo is a nice place to pull up a stool and start the night with a drink. The hallways are a bit dark compared to the more spacious front area, but tastefully trimmed with an eclectic collection of art and artifacts. During the week, La Herradura is quiet, almost deserted, but on weekends and in high season, the hotel's rooms are full and restaurant is buzzing. Av. Bolívar and Daniel Hidalgo, Tel: 05-269-0446, E-mail: hotelherradura@hotmail.com, URL: www.herradurahotel.com.
Updated: Feb 14, 2013.

Hostal Bahía Bed and Breakfast

($5-10 per person) A bit of love and affection, plus a little artistic flair, infuse the otherwise dark and drab space of Hostal Bahía with life. Climb the sagging wooden stairs from the street entrance and you'll find yourself in a spacious reception area surrounded by walls painted with creeping vines and delicate pink flowers. Clearly, the building has seen better days, but the owners have worked hard to keep the hostel clean, and little touches—like hand-painted walls, clean-swept floors and a hammock-filled porch area—make aging and run-down feel more like old-fashioned and unique. The building is 120 years old and the dour faces looking back at you from the walls are members of the owner's family. Very modest but clean rooms come with bunk beds and either shared or private bathrooms. If you're keen, Spanish classes are also available; ask for Jacob or Jairo. The attached restaurant is open for breakfast only. Ascasuvi 316 and Montufar, Tel: 05-269-0146, Cel: 09-9220-7412, E-mail: hc4js@ecua.net.ec.
Updated: Feb 14, 2013.

Hostal Coco Bongo !

($8-25 per person) A hotspot for expats that live in the area of Bahia and international travelers that pass through, Coco Bongo is a quaint and cozy little hostel located right near the Malecón. It's hosted by the lovely owners - a small family of which gives this place somewhat more of a bed and breakfast-vibe. The lounge and restaurant downstairs can be an incredibly fun outlet for swapping stories, participating in trivia nights on Fridays or simply hanging out and reading a book. The age of the place might deter from the overall image of cleanliness, but if you can muster a few wrinkles in aes-

Loved it? Loathed it? Write a review and help other travelers

thetics here and there, this place is a must. A delicious breakfast is served in the mornings for $3. Malecón, Alberto F. Santos 410 and Arenas, Tel: 098-544-0978 / 05-269-1084, E-mail: cocobongobahia@yahoo.com, URL: www.cocobongohostal.com.
Updated: Apr 10, 2013.

Hotel La Piedra
(ROOMS: $128) Hotel La Piedra, one of the most lavish places to stay in Bahía de Caráquez, features stunning views and classy modern facilities. A large complex sprawling across the seafront, this place puts on all the airs of a first-class hotel, with valet parking, marble-floored reception area, and spacious rooms appointed with double beds, new furniture and large modern bathrooms. The first-floor restaurant, El Faro, has glass doors that open to a seaside terrace, creating a pleasant, airy place in which to take in a meal and enjoy the local cuisine. Circunvalación Virgilio Ratti 803, in front of the sea; Quito office: Av. Naciones Unidas E6-99 and Shyris, Edificio Banco Bolivariano, 3rd floor, office 1, Tel: 05-269-0780/0154/1473, Cel: 09-9711-0584, Quito office: 02-224-5267/5268, E-mail: reservaciones@hotel-lapiedra.com.ec / repcion@hotellapiedra.com.ec, URL: www.hotellapiedra.com.ec.

Bahía de Caráquez Restaurants

Bahía boasts quite a few options for taking in a meal or two, though the most popular places stick to the same coastal cuisine characteristic of the region. Meat lovers will be glad to hear that there are a number of parrillada joints (just follow your nose). Quite a few places are clustered around the Malecón 69, conveniently located next to the ferry.

El Muelle Uno
(ENTREES: $4-35) Boasting superb views of the water and San Vicente, El Muello Uno also serves up generous plates of traditional coastal fare, like fish and shrimp. This is a lunch or dinner spot, especially if you've got a hankering for barbecue meat (parrilladas are their specialty). Vegetarian options are available, though nothing too extravagant. Malecón, by the ferry, Tel: 098-989-8927.
Updated: Apr 10, 2013.

La Terraza
(ENTREES: $2.50-20) Inexpensive grilled meat and rice dishes or local seafood plates are offered up at this older, but clean place by the docks. Little sets La Terraza apart from its neighbors—the menu is traditional

barbecued meat and Manabi coastal cuisine—but the prices are slightly lower than the other Malecón joints. The set lunch menu is also a fine option for a cheap midday meal. Malecón, next to El Buen Sabor, Tel: 093-973-6152.
Updated: Apr 10, 2013.

El Buen Sabor
(ENTREES: $2-10) A similar style restaurant as the others lining the Malecón, El Buen Sabor offers typical meat and seafood dishes, served in an open and airy atmosphere with water views. Service is fairly fast and friendly, and the food is delicious if you're up for traditional meat and seafood plates. Malecón, next to El Muelle Uno, by the ferry, Tel: 098-677-6838 / 099-934-7700.
Updated: Apr 10, 2013.

Brisas del Mar
(ENTREES: $3.50-6) Set in a kitty-corner close to the sea, Brisas del Mar is a cozy little place, perfect for sharing a bottle of wine and watching the sun set. Decor consists of plastic chairs tucked under wooden tables and spread across a tiny room colored with a few paintings and randomly placed wine bottles. Atmosphere is more cheap seafood than casual romantic, but the view is bound to romance the unromantic regardless. Av. Virgilio and Daniel Hidalgo, next to Hotel Herradura, Tel: 05-269-1511.
Updated: Feb 04, 2013.

SAN CLEMENTE

San Clemente is the quintessential sleepy fishing village with long, expansive beaches and friendly locals that is only recently being discovered by international travelers. Less than an hour north of Manta, San Clemente and neighboring San Jacinto are worth a stop if a few days of relaxing on the beach are in order.

San Clemente Lodging

Palmazul
(ROOMS: $117-170) Palmazul is simply paradise. Situated right on the beach of the tiny fishing village of San Clemente, this luxury hotel and spa is a place to relax and forget about the rest of the world. Walks on the beach and through the dry forest above the hotel accompany a wide array of spa treatments, swimming on the kid-safe beach, and lounging with a cocktail at the expansive infinity pool. The Cocomar Restaurant serves some of the finest food in the region and is an excellent value. They have traditional lo-

cal breakfasts (included with room price), exquisite seafood dishes and pool side barbeques.

All rooms have ocean views and the sound of the ocean makes for an exceptionally restful stay. Tastefully redecorated in 2011 by a Norwegian-Ecuadorian couple, the new hotel offers one of the highest levels of service in all of Ecuador and is the only hotel in Ecuador where you can drink the tap water due to a desalination water purification system.Behind the hotel is a condo development called Vista Azul owned mostly by foreigners whom always seem to have an interesting tale or two to tell about how they got there and their experience living there. Ask if there are any units left, as you may not want to leave. Av Quito S/N y secundaria, 500 meters from Calle Principal via Punta Bikini, Tel: (593) (2) 254-9721, E-mail: info@palmazulecuador. com, URL: http://www.manabihotel.com. Updated: Sep 12, 2012.

CRUCITA

 18m   3,683   05

About 30 minutes from Manta, Crucita boasts a pleasant ribbon of dark sand beach, and a Malecón with plenty of seafood restaurants. Quiet and relaxed during the week, the town atmosphere shifts to slightly noisier and ecstatic on weekends. Massive cliffs and good wind conditions are conducive to airborne activities.

As such, Crucita has become a popular place to launch paragliding and kite surfing classes and tours. A lovely place with wonderful sunsets, and a few adrenaline-pumping daytime activities, Crucita grows bigger and better every year.
Updated: Apr 11, 2013.

Getting To and Away from Crucita

From Bahia, head to the bus terminal and take a Turistico bus (they leave every hour or two) to **Rocafuerte** ($2, 1.5 hours). From Rocafuerte, transfer over to a **Crucita** bus (30 minutes, $0.50).

If coming from Manta, head to the bus terminal there and catch a Crucita bus north (45 minutes, $0.75). Alternatively, a taxi from Bahia to Crucita costs you $35, taken from Manta it's $45.
Updated: Apr 11, 2013.

Things To See and Do In Crucita
Paragliding
(PRICE: $35) Feel like getting a radically different perspective of the coast line? Or tackling your fear of heights? Either take a brief, 15-minute tandem paragliding tour or sign up for class and get your certification within 5 days! Either-or, you get equipment, helmet, radio and a seasoned (and certified) instructor to keep your fears at bay. $35 for a 15-minute tour, $380 for a 4-5 day course. Hostal Voladores, Calle Principal and Nueva Loja, Far soutern end of the Malecón, right behind the high rise apartment building., Tel: 05-234-0200 / 09-399-4781, E-mail: hvoladores@hotmail.com, URL: www.parapentecrucita.com.
Updated: Apr 11, 2013.

Crucita Lodging
Hostal Voladores
($8-15 per person) Both tall and small at the same time, Hostal Voladores offers two very different kinds of accommodations in the same place. You can either choose the incredibly rustic rooms that are a bamboo extravaganza below (with no fan, but given the winds in Crucita, that's usually not necessary), or go for something literally more concrete and opt for one of the rooms that are housed above within cement walls - and have fans included as a result. A nice little pool separates the two different styles of accommodation, along with a restaurant/communal kitchen that's available right beside it. Wifi, towels and soap are a nice little bonus. Calle Principal and Nueva Loja, Far southern end of the Malecón, right behind the high rise apartment building., Tel: 05-234-0200 / 09-399-4781, E-mail: hvoladores@hotmail.com, URL: www.parapentecrucita.com.
Updated: Apr 11, 2013.

Crucita Restaurants
Alas Delta
(ENTREES: $5-12) Offering a vista with your meal, this place sits up against the Malecón and offers two floors-worth of majestic ocean views. Meals range across the usual coastal, flavorful fare at a reasonable price. For an extra view of the town, head upstairs and gaze at the horizon or the Malecon as it bends northward and flows with all sorts of people and commotion. This restaurant is not to be confused with the other 'Alas Delta' that try to imitate it with numbers after the same name. Malecón, Southern End, Tel: 099-216-0118.
Updated: Apr 11, 2013.

NORTHERN COAST

MANTA

 6m    217,553   05

Compared to the hippy haven of Montañita, or peaceful unpopulated beach coasts and coves further north, Manta is only better than average — that is, unless, your idea of a good beach is an overabundance of restaurants and bars backed by skyscraper-like hotels and holiday homes.

Manta is divided almost in half by the Río Manta, with the up-market Playa Murciélago to the west and considerably less swanky Playa Tarqui to the east. Running along the coast, and connecting both beaches is the Malecón, Manta's main drag. In general, hotels to the west are more expensive (and the neighborhoods quieter and safer), but that's not to say you can't find good value, budget-friendly places. The beaches here are OK, but you'll have to share your seaside view with the cranes and hundreds of port boats moored offshore; Manta is an extremely important port in Ecuador and is the second largest port after Guayaquil.

Overlook the eyesore that is maritime Manta, however, and you'll see a vibrant, pulsing city packed with trendy restaurants, bars and upscale hotels. While it's not the most spectacular place to stay, Manta is not without its own unique charms. Spend a day chilling on the beach, then take a stroll along Playa Murciélago, the place to grab a cool beer or tropical drink, and take in a meal and a sunset at one of the popular seaside-seafood restaurants. History buffs can spend a few hours poking around the Museo del Banco Central, while market lovers can meander to the city center, where there are a couple of fruit and vegetable markets. During the day, Tarqui is an interesting place to wander, but you'd be wise to catch a taxi back to your hotel as this is not a safe area at night.

Getting To and Away from Manta

Several bus companies (Reina del Camino and Panamericana Internacional) operate from Quito to Manta; the trip lasts 8 to 9 hours and costs $8-10. Tame (www.tame.com.ec), LAN (www.lan.com) and Areo-Gal (http://www.aerogal.com.ec) also fly daily to Manta from Quito for around $100, roundtrip. From Manta most buses head towards the commercial and travel crossroads of **Portoviejo** and **Jipijapa**, but an infinitely more appealing option is to find a bus

bound for the scenic stretch of road heading south towards **San Lorenzo** and **Puerto Cayo**. This paved route features unparalleled views of Ecuador's coast: uninhabited stretches of soft sand bound by turquoise waters and imposing cliffs.
Updated: Apr 11, 2013.

Manta Services

MONEY
ATM's located along Calle Flavio Reyes, between the Ca. 17 and 19.

TOURISM
Av 3 y Calle 11 towards Malecón Escencia (Paseó Jose María Egas).

Things To See and Do In Manta

Museo Del Banco Central
(ADMISSION: $1) Visit the newly renovated Archeological Museum in town, home to an excellent collection of archaeological pieces, remnants of seven different civilizations that inhabited the coast from 3500 BC to 1530 AD. You'll find all the information you need regarding their legends as well as getting to view some of the authentic artifacts that characterized these pre-hispanic groups. The museum also houses a gallery presenting the national and international works of 12 different artists. Malecón between Calle 9 and Avenida 2, Tel: 05-262-2956, URL: www.museos-ecuador.com.
Updated: Apr 11, 2013.

Manta Schools
Spanish And Surfing
The Superpacifico school offers a variety of courses, including medical Spanish or Spanish and Surfing. A two-week program with 20 hours of instruction and homestay will set you back approximately $800. 24 Ave. and 15 St. Barre Building 3rd. Floor, Tel: 05-261-0838 / 099-918-4735, E-mail: info@ecuadorsspanishschools.com / surpacifico@easynet.net.ec, URL: http://www.surpacifico.k12.ec.
Updated: Apr 11, 2013.

Surf and Kitesurf, Ecuador
(CLASSES: $15-40 per hour) The kitesurfing on a beautiful beach near Manta called Santa Marianita (Playa Bonita) is world-class, and the surrounding areas also have great surf. Manta Kitesurf is a great school based right on the wide, almost deserted beach. It offers surf and kitesurf courses for any level, equipment rental and surf tours, and sells equipment too. There is one hostel/restaurant here, which is of a high standard, and

right next to the kite school. A great spot! From the city of Manta, its 20 minutes or so south to the tiny town of Santa Marianita. The hostel and surf/kite school are before you get to the town, along the beach away from the road. There are micro buses from the manta market, or a taxi is $6. A beginners kitesurf course of 4 days (8-10 hr) is $280 all-inclusive, 1-hour class is $40. Equipment rental $30/hour. Surf: Board rental $10/day. A 4 day course (10 hours) is $70. A 2 hour class is $15.Tel: 09-9806-6703, URL: www.ecuadorkitesurf.com. Updated: Feb 14, 2013.

Shopping in Manta City

There are two main markets within Manta City that in paticular cater to your every culinary need. La Baviera Market is an upscale market, this is a good place to get lunch meat, fresh bread and produce, which you can take for a picnic on the beach. You'll also find a range of imported meats and cheese, and treats like sauerkraut and pickled onions and olives. It is located on 16th Street and 6th Ave.

Early risers should head to the massive Mercado Municipal in the center of town, where you can watch Manta inhabitants prepare for the day. Grab some fresh bread from the Colombian bakery, which will also provide Nescafé coffee if you ask. The market opens at 05:00 and by 05:15 it has dropped its sluggish, sleepy pace and swung into full gear; grab a seat and observe people scurrying from stand to stand with factory-like precision, arms full of fresh produce, bread, or bags of rice.

Energy like this doesn't last long, though, and by noon this place has pretty much exhausted itself and returned to the quiet, relatively empty sector of town that it was before dawn. This is an excellent spot for cheap eats, especially if you're feeling adventurous and go for a set meal ($1.00). For even cheaper produce head to Tarqui Market at the east end of town, open every Monday and Thursday, Calle 12 and Av. 16. Updated: Feb 14, 2013.

Manta Lodging

Host to a wide range of hotels and hostels, Manta is bound to suit any traveler's needs, from backpacker dives to 5 star luxury retreats. If you can swing it, find a place in the Oro Verde section of town (named after the lavish hotel of the same name). Situated on a hill in a quiet residential section of Manta, close to Playa Murcielago and Malecón Escénico, the places in this area tend to be safer and more stylish than those located over the Río Manta. And in some cases, staying here is only slightly more expensive than spending the night in Tarqui. If you're really pinching pennies, however, it might be best to start looking in Tarqui. While not considered to be as safe as its western counterpart, this area is full of character and is ready to greet guests with some pretty good budget hotels as well as nearby local restaurants. Updated: Apr 11, 2013.

BUDGET

Hostal Del Mar

($8-10 per person) A dated entrance leads into a dark hallway and upstairs to a modest reception area. Rooms, like the hotel, are aging but offer clean sheets and bathrooms. This is a good no-frills option for those on a budget. Restaurant del Mar (daily 7 a.m.-10 p.m.), located beneath the hotel, serves good cheap breakfasts and set meals, but don't expect shiny silverware and spotless glasses. Av. 105 and Ca. 104 (corner), Tel: 05-261-3155. Updated: Feb 14, 2013.

Hotel ArenaMar

(ROOMS: $12-30) Hotel ArenaMar is a solid option for those on a budget and looking to stay at the east end of Manta. The hotel has a professional, modern-looking reception area that leads upstairs to large rooms with cable TV, telephones, surprisingly large modern bathrooms and the capacity to sleep as many as 12 people. The rooms are tidy and clean, despite over-washed 1980's style comforters and aged facilities. Calle 101 and Av. 106 and 107, near bridge to Westside, Tel: 05-261-2856 / 02-262-3163. Updated: Apr 11, 2013.

Hotel Las Rocas

(ROOMS: $15-42) This large hotel facing the sea is, like most of the hotels in Tarqui, in need of a face-lift but still manages to offer clean and comfortable accommodation. Rooms are large and those streetside boast good views of the port. Faded, but clean sheets conceal older beds, which match the Victorian-style dresser drawers. Bathrooms are large and spotless, always a good sign. Air conditioned rooms are slightly nicer, with newer furniture and art on the walls. Las Caraconas, the attached restaurant lacks style but is clean, cool, and offers nicely set tables and good cheap food. Entrees: $2-5. Calle 101 and Av. 105, Tel: 05-262-0607, E-mail: hotellasrocas@hotmail.es.

NORTHERN COAST

Loved it? Loathed it? Write a review and help other travelers

MID-RANGE

Hostal Manakin

(ROOMS: $49-80) This lovely building set in a peaceful residential neighborhood has been renovated and revamped and now houses one of the nicest hostels on this side of town. Modest rooms are tastefully appointed with new beds, bedspreads and furniture, and brand new gizmos like remote-control air conditioners and TVs. Bathrooms are small, but are modern, clean and equipped with shining sinks and plenty of hot water. In the morning, head to the stylish dining area or down to the breezy courtyard where you can start your day with a plate of bread and jam, fruit (fresh from the local market) and coffee. Comfy but classy accommodation at reasonable prices and in a stellar location would be enough to make any traveler stay a while, so the extremely friendly staff is just another bonus that, like breakfast, is included in the price of the room. Av. 12 and Ca. 20, across from TV Cable, Tel: 05-261-2437/262-0413, Cel: 09-8436-2435, E-mail: hostalmanaquin@hotmail.com, URL: www.hostelmanakin.com.
Updated: Feb 14, 2013.

Panorama Inn y Su Cascada Suite

(ROOMS: $23) Panorama Inn, one of the more modern places to stay in Tarqui, offers rooms overlooking a courtyard pool that has been decked out in an island theme. Ask for the suites across the street, which are even nicer, though a bit steeper in price, and have new comforters, small but tidy bathrooms, and doors that open onto the pool deck. Both sections are a popular draw for Ecuadorian families and young couples. An attached cafetería is dated but clean and airy, serving typical Ecuadorian fare (daily 7 a.m.-10 p.m.; entrees: around $3). Av. 103 and Ca. 105, Tarqui, Tel: 05-261-1552, URL: www.hotelpanoramainn.com.
Updated: Feb 14, 2013.

Hotel Las Gaviotas

(ROOMS: $30-90) A peeling blue façade leads into a surprisingly professional-looking reception area, where a friendly staff is ready and waiting to help. Rooms are well-appointed, clean and spacious, making Hotel Las Gaviotas one of the better value options in the area. The attached restaurant, La Barca, maintains a sea-captain theme, with an assortment of sea mariner paraphernalia decorating the walls, and dark polished tables and chairs. While not the best budget option, it does offer a pool area and nicer views of the beach than other places nearby.

Tarqui Malecón. Ca. 109, seafront, Tel: 05-262-7240, E-mail: reservas@hotelgaviotasmanta.com / hotelgaviotasmanta@gmail.com, URL: www.hotelgaviotasmanta.com.
Updated: Feb 14, 2013.

Hotel Miami

(ROOMS: $29-40) Located at the far end of Tarqui's Malecón, Hotel Miami is a popular spot for young Ecuadorians looking for a cheap place close to the beach. An aging, yellow colored reception area leads upstairs to drab but clean rooms with private bathrooms and cable TV. The pool area could use a little love and attention, but still seems to be a popular retreat from the sun and surf out front. While not always pleasant on the eyes, Hotel Miami doesn't hurt the wallet either. The attached restaurant is convenient and has a solid menu of traditional set meals. Malecón Tarqui and Ca. 108, Tel: 05-261-1743, E-mail: cdlacruz_17@hotmail.com.
Updated: Feb 14, 2013.

HIGH-END

Hotel Balandra

(ROOMS: $77-150) Balandria is a self-sufficient paradise tucked away in a quiet residential neighborhood only 50 meters (164 ft) from Murciélago Beach, and the hotel offers stylish and comfortable lodging that is perfect for families or large groups. The mock-cabin studios, topped with green roofs and wooden balconies, overlook plenty of greenery and a peaceful garden and pool area. The cabins are nicely constructed and mildly reminiscent of a luxury jungle lodge. You won't find monkeys here, though, just a friendly staff and smartly decorated two-level suites. The hotel's on-site restaurant (daily 6:30 a.m.-11 p.m.; entrees: $10) also cooks up a delightful range of dishes, served on peach-colored table cloths with sparkling wine glasses and precisely set cutlery. From the veranda, you can take in stunning sea views while you dine. The menu is extensive—crepes and beef stroganoff even make an appearance—and is well-priced for the surroundings. Av. 7 and Ca. 20, Cordova neighborhood, Tel: 05-262-0545/8144 ext 121, E-mail: balandra@hotelbalandra.com, URL: www.hotelbalandra.com.
Updated: Feb 14, 2013.

Hotel Costa del Sol

(ROOMS: $67-172) Perched on a high cliff overlooking the sea, the hotel's romantic setting is somewhat marred by the its circus-style construction. Rooms, however, are tasteful and the staff stylish. A modern reception area with marble floors and modern art decorating the walls ushers visitors toward large, modern rooms with all the amenities one might expect from a chain-like hotel: mini-fridge, phone, cable TV, air conditioning, and a spacious bathroom with tiled floors and a sliding glass shower door. Relax and unwind in the swimming pool and sauna area, grab a Turkish bath, or make your way directly to the beach. When you get hungry, head to the hotel's bar and restaurant where you can sample traditional Manabí fare, or enjoy more familiar ethnic cuisine. Av. Malecón 1 and Ca. 25, Tel: 05-262-0019/0025/4852, E-mail: info@hotelcostadelsol.com, URL: www.hotelcostadelsol.com.ec. Updated: Feb 14, 2013.

Vistalmar Cabañas Boutique

(ROOMS: $70-130) The view itself would be worth a chest of gold, but this Manta wonder also offers a unique setting so tranquil even the air seems more relaxed up here, leaving visitors with the feeling that time might be found just around the corner, relaxing in the bamboo bungalow. Vistalmar, which is graced with various art and artifacts from around the world, is somewhat of a museum by the sea, as well as peaceful retreat. An architectural anomaly squeezed between holiday high rises, the delicate cabañas share the same ocean view as their lofty neighbors, but offer tasteful rooms built with local materials and decorated with both internationally flavorful art and a Southeast Asian flair. The art and architecture, combined with the well-groomed garden and an infinity pool overlooking the sea, create a luxurious but intimate setting in which to unwind. Considering the view and atmosphere, Cabañas Boutique is worth the splurge. Ca. M-1 and Av. 24, El Murciélago neighborhood, Tel: 05-262-1671/1617, E-mail: reservaciones@hosteriavistaalmar.com, URL: www.hosteriavistaalmar.com. Updated: Feb 14, 2013.

Manta Restaurants

Playa Murciélago is the place for seafood and rows of restaurants line the beachfront, each serving similar fare at only slightly varied prices. Over the bridge in Tarqui, you'll find another set of seafood restaurants, without the well-clad customers and fancy fanfare of its neighbors to the west.

Beach Comber

(ENTREES: $5-20) The smell of grilling meat is overwhelming even before Beach Comb-er's flashy neon sign or thumping music have a chance to hit your other senses. Good luck finding a place to sit here around dinner time; the eatery is one of the most popular joints in the area, and rightfully so. Spectacular food (parrilladas are the house specialty) is served in a lively atmosphere that will lift the spirits of even the most jaded traveler. Calle 20 and Av. Flavio Reyes, Tel: 05-262-5463, E-mail: beachcomber_79@yahoo.es. Updated: Apr 11, 2013.

OH Mar

(ENTREES: $5-19) A seafood chain with a sister restaurant in Salinas, OH Mar is a good choice for standard Ecuadorian meat and seafood dishes. Not the best place if you're looking for character and ambiance, but the space is clean and airy, and in terms of food you can't go wrong. Portions are hearty and prices digestible, at least by Manta standards. Group discounts available. Malecón Escénico Playa El Murciélago Local 9, Tel: 05-261-0360, URL: dorys.02@hotmail.com. Updated: Feb 14, 2013.

El Cormoran

(ENTREES: $8-42) Laid out like an amusement park, this sprawling restaurant complex is popular with Ecuadorian families and large groups. If the large sign at the entrance doesn't give you a clue, parrilladas (BBQ meat plates)are the house specialty, among other traditional coastal dishes. You're bound to find something tasty on the menu, that is if you're in the mood for anything surf and turf and served with rice. Picky eaters can make do with the simple pasta dishes, but don't expect Tuscany. The daring (or anyone searching for a seafood fix) can try the corvina en salsa de mariscos (sea bass in seafood sauce), while meat eaters can chow down on a parrillada. Av. 24 and Ca. M-2, Tel: 05-262-9816. Updated: Feb 14, 2013.

Mamma Rosa Bar and Restaurant

(ENTREES: $5-25) Somewhat of a local fixture, Mamma Rosa keeps the people coming with its over 246 different dishes, top-notch service, and an atmosphere that even Italy would find hard to create. Owner Jiorjio carried his culinary secrets with him when he came over from Genova and now Ecuador gets the pleasure of sampling his time-tested and lovingly prepared dishes, including real garlic bread. Mains cover just about every gastronomical possibility, from vegetarian lasagna to grilled meats like marinated venison and rabbit.

NORTHERN COAST

Loved it? Loathed it? Write a review and help other travelers

The atmosphere is almost as delicious as the meals; delicate gravel walkways lead to a terrace-like seating area decorated with flowering plants and miniature street lamps, giving the feeling that you have gone for a romantic stroll rather than restaurant meal. Wine is served chilled in silver stands and waiters scurry about in black and white uniforms accented by neatly arranged bow ties. As one might expect, desserts here are not to be outdone by the mains.

A true culinary gem, Mama Rosa's has all the necessary ingredients for a truly pleasurable dining experience. If you're still dubious about just how good this place is, then consider this: Jiorjio exports his ravioli and bread to markets in Spain and Italy. Special dishes can be ordered a day ahead. Av. Flavio Reyes and Perimetral, Umiña neighborhood. Across from Umiña Park., Tel: 05-262-6076, Cel: 09-9964-6067/9233-3500, E-mail: chlaura22@hotmail.com. Updated: Feb 14, 2013.

Mediterraneo

(ENTREES: $4-15) This lovely restaurant distinguishes itself from other Manta eateries, not just by location, but in style and service. While it may not boast beach views, Mediterraneo has bragging rights to the best Spanish and Ecuadorian influenced plates in town, which is no surprise considering owner Martin is from Barcelona, Spain.

Meat from Texas is ordered from a specialty shop in town and then matured on-site to ensure each meat dish explodes with flavor; try the cordon bleu, chatubriou or filet mignon. The non-meat dishes are just as flavorful, but then again doesn't everything taste a little better when its served by candlelight? For a romantic night out share a bottle of wine and the tapas, a sure way to melt any heart. Open, airy and affordable, this is one of classiest, most colorful places to eat in town. Ca. Flavio Reyes, between Ca. 29 and Ca. 30, Tel: 05-262-8512. Updated: Feb 14, 2013.

Las Velas

(ENTREES: $6-12) While differing little in appearance from other places on the Malecón strip, Las Velas is apparently the place to be seen if you're somebody in Manta. At night, well-dressed Ecuadorians chattering beneath the outdoor umbrellas and the sound of clinking glasses is a common occurrence. This is also a good place to come for no-frills continental or americano breakfasts. Playa Murciélago, Local 8, Tel: 05-262-9396 / 099-862-8494, E-mail: lasvelascia@hotmail.com. Updated: Apr 11, 2013.

Ocean Delight

(ENTREES: $4-11) A slight change from the dominant plastic seating, this place offers neatly arranged wooden tables and chairs, and walls graced with panama hats. From the outside it looks a slight step up from other places nearby, however, the menu consists of typical Ecuadorian coastal cuisine and prices vary little from those on nearby menus. This is a solid option if you're in the mood for seafood and sea views. Playa Murciélago, Local 15, Tel: 098-021-7990 / 099-231-7601, E-mail: oceandelight15@hotmail.com. Updated: Apr 11, 2013.

Jireh Bar and Restaurant

(ENTREES: $5-15) Decked out in simple but stylish décor, Jireh Bar is one of the more popular places to eat on restaurant row. Open-air seating allows for a cool sea breeze and beach views, and meals are heaping, served still steaming from the kitchen. Jireh is as good a spot as any to try viche, a typical Manabí soup with fish, peanuts and plantain dumplings, or to dig into other traditional Ecuadorian dishes. Anyone indecisive, or hoping to try a little of everything, can opt for the combo plates, which mix and match culinary creations. Eating here isn't a black-tie affair, but the service is fast and friendly and the food is delicious. Malecón Escénico Local 11, Tel: 05-262-3061, E-mail: jirehale@hotmail.com / apec87@hotmail.com. Updated: Feb 14, 2013.

Restaurante Arena Caliente

(ENTREES: $8-20) Located on the terrace of Hotel Costa del Sol, this classy bar offers some of the best views of Manta. From up here life looks good, and with a smooth drink and sumptuous plate of food things only seem to get better. The view is always here so whether you're an early bird looking for breakfast or a night owl just starting out, head here to fuel up and check out the beach bums below. Considering the location, prices are almost as good as the view. Hotel Costa del Sol, Avenida Malecón 1 y calle 25., Tel: 02-262-0025/4852, E-mail: hostelcostadelsol@hotmail.com, URL: hotelcostadelsol.com.ec. Updated: Apr 11, 2013.

))))!

NORTHERN COAST

The Southern Coast

The Southern Coast of Ecuador stretches south of Manta in Manabi all the way through the new Santa Elena province to Guayas and El Oro.

The highlight is Ecuador's only protected coastal zone, Machalilla National Park. Further south are the busier beach resorts of La Ruta del Sol (The Route of the Sun). Most famous is the surfer's sweet spot, Montañita, with some of Ecuador's best waves on the coast and a lively, Bohemian atmosphere.

About three hours inland by bus is Ecuador's largest city, Guayaquil. Although still not a very popular tourist destination for foreigners, the city has undergone an award-winning redevelopment in recent years. With a stunning waterfront, new museums and glitzy malls, there is more than enough

SOUTHERN COAST

The Southern Coast Higlights

Parque Nacional Machalilla (*p. 402-403*): Ecuador's only coastal national park is most easily visited from Puerto López. Spend a day sunbathing at the stunning and secluded Los Frailes beach, boat over to Isla de La Plata and interact with some Galápagos wildlife, or visit the indigenous community of Agua Blanca. From June to September, book a whale-watching tour to see gigantic humpback whales up close and personal.

Learning to Surf in Montañita (*p. 418-419*): There is no doubt that Montañita is one of the best places to learn how to surf in the country, with makeshift surf schools and surf equipment shops at every corner. Settle down for a few weeks and take some lessons before renting a board and attempting to ride in the waves of La Punta solo.

Ayangue (*p. 428-420*): Few know about this beautiful beach surrounding a bay-like part of the Pacific, where waters are warm and calm and locals are friendly. Prime scuba diving is possible at the nearby Islota del Pelado and cheap lobsters are a local specialty, making this offbeat destination worth a visit.

Seafood in Salango (*p. 409-410*): There is one major reason to come to Salango: seafood. This tiny fishing town serves up bold plates of *mariscos*, with the unique *precebes* (goose barnacles) taking center stage. Pull up a chair, order a few plates and savor every bite.

Biking the Ruta del Sol: Rent a bike or bring your own and pedal your way down the Ruta del Sol, which is dotted with chilled-out beaches within close reach of one another. Whether you cycle this part of the coast in a day or a few months, you will be rewarded at each stop with ample sunshine, seafood and surfing opportunities.

to keep tourists busy for a couple of days en route to the beach or the Galapagos. South of Guayaquil the highway soon reaches the most convenient crossing to the Peruvian border at Huaquillas.
Updated: Apr 08, 2013.

La Ruta del Sol

La Ruta del Sol is a strip of some of the most beautiful and popular beaches in Ecuador, with some of Ecuador's best surfing. The area is best from December to June, when the weather is hottest. However, this also coincides with the often torrential rainy season between January and April. After July the temperatures drop and it can be surprisingly cool at times. Prices are often cheaper and hotels are emptier, which can be peaceful or depressing, depending on your taste. You could spend months chilling in backpacker hang-outs like Montañita or beach-hopping

along countless undiscovered beaches. However, a shorter trip is more common by taking advantage of the rapidly developing tourist infrastructure. The public transportation is fairly extensive and inexpensive, and there are also several tour agencies that offer package deals to highlighted spots along the coast, though these tend to be overpriced.
Updated: Mar 31, 2013.

PUERTO LÓPEZ

 4m   18,000   05

Puerto López is one of the more established towns along the Ruta del Sol and the main hub for travelers visiting Isla de la Plata and Parque Nacional Machalilla. The towhasa growing selection of hotels, some good restaurants, and reliable agencies to book whale-watching tours, trips to the island and

hikes in the national park. However, while many travelers enjoy staying here for a day or two, you may find it surpisingly ragged in places. The pot-holed dirt roads and garbage on the beach are not the best advertisement for the tourist center of Ecuador's only coastal national park.
Updated: Sep 04, 2012.

When To Go to Puerto López

Puerto López sees tourists all year long, but tourism swells during whale-watching season, which runs June to mid-September. Accommodation prices are also higher during this time. It is also important to note that tours to Isla de la Plata are different during the wet and dry seasons. During the wet season, the island is green and the majority of the birds are seen flying overhead or on the cliffs; during the dry season, the plants dry up and land birds can be seen walking around the island itself.

The town of Puerto López also celebrates several holidays each year. June 23-25 is the Festival de las Ballenas Jorobadas (Festival of the Humpback Whale) and August 31 is the Aniversario de Cantonización (the Town's Anniversary). Also, every year from June 27 to 30, fisherman in the province of Manabí do processions in honor of their patron saints San Pedro and San Pablo.
Updated: Sep 05, 2012.

Getting To and Away from Puerto López

Although Puerto López is situated in a relatively remote location, the town is reasonably well connected to other parts of Ecuador. The nearest airport, in **Manta**, is two hours to the north, though many people chose to fly to **Guayaquil** and make their way up the coast from there.

From Puerto López, it is very easy to travel by bus to destinations up and down the coast. Cooperativa Manglaralto buses run every 15-30 minutes, starting at 4:35 a.m., both north to **Manta** (2 hr, $3) and south to **Santa Elena** (2.5 hr, $3), passing through **Montañita** after 1.25 hours. Buses leave from Avenida Machililla, near the corner of General Córdova, diagonal from the church.

Buses run hourly to **Guayaquil** (4 hr, $5), with the last bus leaving at 5:05 p.m. There are also five buses per day to **Quito** from Puerto López (11 hr, $13). All buses to **Quito** also stop in **Portoviejo**. Reina del Camino has a direct overnight bus service between Quito and Puerto López, which leaves from Quito at 7:30 p.m. and from Puerto López at 8 p.m. The buses in Quito leave from Reina del Camino's office at 18 de Septiembre between Manuel Larrea and Pérez Guerrero. For those who would prefer to travel during the day, Carlos Aray has a 6:10 a.m. bus to Quito and Reino del Camino has an 8 a.m. bus to Quito.

Prices and times change regularly, though; if you have to catch a bus, inquire at the individual bus companies to find out the exact times at which buses will be passing through the town.
Updated: Sep 06, 2012.

Puerto López Services
MONEY
Banco de Pichincha is the only bank in town and has two 24-hour ATMs. It is located on Malecón Julio Izurieta, near the corner of Mariscal Sucre and is open Monday-Friday 9 a.m.-4:30 p.m.

TOURISM
Puerto López's **tourism office** (Tel: 05-230-0102, Cel: 08-662-2171/09-452-4976) has lots of information about the activities around town, and has maps of Puerto López and the whole Ruta del Sol. It is located on Avenida Machililla, diagonal from Cruz Azul pharmacy. Parque Nacional Machalilla also has its **headquarters** (Tel: 05-230-0170. Daily 8 a.m.-5 p.m.)in Puerto López, at Calle Eloy Alfaro and García Moreno, in front of the market. It also has a small museum about the park. The **police office** (Tel: 06-948-0221) is next door to the tourism office.

KEEPING IN TOUCH
Puerto López has several Internet cafés around town, including **Cyber Surfer** ($0.80 per hour. Daily 8 a.m.-11 p.m. Mariscal Sucre, between Machalilla and Rocafuerte) and **Whale Cyber** ($1 per hour. Daily 8:30 a.m.-9:30 p.m. General Córdova and Malecón Julio Izurieta. Tel: 09-058-0158). **La Heladería**, attached to the Farmacias Cruz Azul on Avenida Machalilla has several *cabinas* from where you can make national or international calls. The not-so-reliable **post office** is on the Malecón, between General Córdova and Mariscal Sucre.

MEDICAL
Puerto López's **Centro de Salud** (Tel: 09-158-1597) is located at the town's entrance and is open 24 hours. There are three pharmacies on Avenida Machalilla, between Alejo

SOUTHERN COAST

Lascano and Atahualpa, across from Centro Comercial Julio Izurieta Figueroa. **Farmacias Cruz Azul** is open daily 7:30 a.m.-10 p.m. and **Farmacia Lisbeth** is open daily 6:30 a.m.-10 p.m.

LAUNDRY

Lavandaría Burbujas, on Malecón Julio Izurieta next to Banco de Pichincha, does laundry and drying in three hours. It charges $4 per load, no matter the weight. A few of the hotels in town also offer laundry services.
Updated: Sep 05, 2012.

Getting Around Puerto López

Most people will find that walking around Puerto López is the easiest way to get around. Of course, if you would like to get from point A to point B faster, or get safely home at night, you can hire any one of the many *mototaxis* (motorcycle rickshaw) in town. They all charge $0.50 to go anywhere within Puerto López itself. A few agencies in town rent bikes and kayaks, which you can use to get to nearby beaches or other sites in Parque Nacional Machililla.
Updated: Sep 05, 2012.

Puerto Lopez Tours

Several registered tour operators line Malecón Julio Izurieta, offering similar trips to places within Parque Nacional Machilila. You must take a tour to Isla de la Plata, but it is easy to visit Agua Blanca or Los Frailes independently. Isla de la Plata tours include round-trip boat transport, snorkeling equipment, guided hikes on the island along with a light lunch.

These companies also offer whale-watching tours in season, though Isla de la Plata tours include whale-watching and tend to be more worthwhile. Additionally, most can organize kayak rental, scuba diving, paragliding, sport fishing, and biking trips to surrounding beaches, as well as jungle excursions.
Updated: Sep 05, 2012.

Exploramar Diving

Explormar Diving are the diving experts in town and operate two excellent boats for island tours and scuba diving. Its highly qualified PADI scuba instructors lead open-water diver courses for PADI certification, supervise beginner-level dives, provide divemaster training and teach rescue diver classes. It provides excellent, well-priced services, and the staff is very friendly and speaks several languages. The head office is in Quito, but the operator organizes diving in Parque

Nacional Machalilla and in the Galápagos. Alemania N32-71 and Mariana de Jesús, Quito/Operations: Malecón Julio Izurieta, Puerto López, Tel: 02-256-3905/4342 (Quito)/05-230-0123 (Puerto López), Cel: 09-950-0910, URL: www.exploradiving.com.
Updated: Sep 05, 2012.

Naturis

This tour operator specializes in community tourism and cultural experiences. Activities include fishing, kayaking, horseback riding as well as the standard whale-watching and island tours. It also offers tours to San Sebastián, and a three-day, two-night package of Parque Nacional Machalilla, including accommodation, food, transport and guides for $159 per person. General Córdova and Juan Montalvo, Tel: 05-230-0218, Cel: 08-495-1841/09-460-0108/09-470-4641, E-mail: puertolopez@gmail.com, URL: www.naturis.com.ec.
Updated: Sep 05, 2012.

Machalilla Tours

Machalilla Tours seems to have its name plastered all over town. That said, its whale-watching tours and tours to Isla de la Plata are pretty identical to the others offered by competing tour operators along the Malecón. However, it can also arrange half-day horseback riding trips to nearby beaches and forests, *parapenting* (paragliding), biking tours to Agua Blanca or Los Frailes, and surf and scuba diving classes as well. Visitors can also rent mountain bikes or kayaks from the agency per hour or for the whole day. All tours include transportation from Puerto López, a guide and light lunch. Malecón Julio Izurieta and Eloy Alfaro, Tel: 05-230-0234/672-2686, Cel: 09-492-5960, URL: www.machilillatours.org.
Updated: Sep 05, 2012.

Things To See and Do In Puerto López

Although the town itself does not have many activities beyond relaxing on the beach or visiting the morning fish market, Puerto López is the ideal spot to spend a few nights while visiting the surrounding area. It is the most convenient town from which to visit Parque Nacional Machalilla, where you can sunbathe on one of Ecuador's most beautiful beaches, visit an archaeological community or go wildlife-watching. Thousands of tourists also come here every year just to take whale-watching tours that are made off of Puerto López's shores.
Updated: Sep 04, 2012.

Los Frailes ♩

Relaxing and remote, Los Frailes is widely considered one of the most spectacular beaches along the Pacific coastline, and it's easy to see why. Its pristine waters and perfect crescent-shaped beach are flanked by terracotta cliffs against a backdrop of lush, forested hills. There are also two other adjacent beaches, which are considered part of Los Frailes: La Tortuguita and La Playa Negra. The latter refers to the darker-sand beach 3.2 kilometers (2 mi) away, which offers good snorkeling; it is accessible by an easy walk from Los Frailes beach. Don't miss the Las Fragatas Mirador lookout point, accessible by a 25-minute walk along the same path to La Playa Negra, where there are gorgeous overhead views.

As of January 2012, Machalilla National Park, which includes Los Frailes, no longer has an entrance fee. Since it is part of a national park, there is a cap of 1,500 people who can visit Los Frailes per day. You are also not allowed to smoke or drink alcoholic beverages on the beach. It is open daily 8 a.m.-4 p.m.

From Puerto López, you can easily visit the beach on your own. Take any Jipijapa-bound bus from Avenida Machalilla in Puerto López ($0.50, 20 min) and ask to be let off at the Los Frailes entrance. From there, you will either need to walk about 45 minutes on a dirt road to reach the beach, or can hire a *mototaxi* at the entrance to take you there ($1 per person).

At Los Frailes, there are bathrooms and changing areas with showers. Sometimes vendors sell water and ice cream by the beach entrance, but come prepared with enough water and food for the day. The sun can be really strong here, so be sure to bring high-spf sunscreen and apply often.
Updated: Aug 25, 2012.

Parque Nacional Machalilla

Parque Nacional Machalilla (55,037 hc/136,000 ac) is a nationally protected park in Manabí province that includes a stretch of beach and dry tropical forest as well as two islands, Isla de la Plata and Isla Salango north and south of Puerto López respectively. The park also encompasses Agua Blanca, a small community with a worthwhile archeological museum. Aside from the island tours, other activities include horseback riding, kayaking, fishing, snorkeling and diving. The park is best during the month of July, when the weather is still sunny and the whales are arriving. As of January 2012, Parque Nacional Machalilla has free entry.
Updated: Sep 04, 2012.

San Sebastián

Further inland from Agua Blanca, the dry forest rises 800 meters (2,625 ft) up to the cloud forest of San Sebastián. Highlights include orchids, bamboo, howler monkeys, anteaters and some 350 species of birds. You can explore it on a hike with a guide hired either in Agua Blanca or on a day-trip from Puerto López. You can also camp overnight or stay with local villagers.
Updated: Sep 04, 2012.

Agua Blanca

(ENTRANCE: $5) The best place to explore Machalilla's dry forest is at Agua Blanca. Five kilometers (3 mi) off the main highway in the park, 12 kilometers (7.5 mi) north of Puerto López, there is a small local community with ancestors dating back to the Manteña Culture who inhabited the land from 800 to 1532.

The entrance fee includes a local guide who will show you around the community and the small archaeological museum. Tours introduce you to the ancient burial customs, typical dress and religious practices on a 1.5 kilometer (1 mi) walk through the forest,where you can also bird-watch, take in spectacular views of the surrounding hills and go for a relaxing but pungent dip in an ancient sulfur pool, considered sacred by the local indigenous people. It is also possible to stay in the community for $8-10 per person per night.

To get to the community, take any Jipijapa-bound bus north from Puerto López and ask to be left off at Agua Blanca. Then you will need to walk the unpleasant five-kilometer (3.1-mi) trail up a dirt track, or you can hire a mototaxi for $5 one-way. There are not many mototaxis at Agua Blanca, so you can pay the mototaxi $5 per hour to wait for you there and bring you back to Puerto López. Another option is to hire a bike at one of the agencies on the Malecón and bike to Agua Blanca and back.
Updated: Sep 04, 2012.

Isla de la Plata

(TOURS: $30-40) This small island, 37 kilometers (23 mi) northwest of Puerto López, has earned the tag "The Poor Man's Galápagos." Comparisons are rather unfair but

SOUTHERN COAST

Isla de la Plata is well worth a day-trip to see the abundant bird-life. We also recommend skipping the whale-watching tours as you get a similar experience on the Isla de la Plata tour, plus you get to see the island. The island is home to blue-footed boobies, masked boobies and *fragatas*, and these are the species most frequently seen. There are also red-footed boobies and waved albatrosses, sometimes seen April to October. The island has a small colony of sea lions but you will be very lucky to see them.

You need to book a tour to see Isla de la Plata. Operators along the Malecón all offer similar tours, which include boat transport to the island, a guided walk on one of the bird-watching trails, a simple lunch of fruit and sandwiches, and snorkeling.
Updated: Sep 04, 2012.

Whale-Watching

(PRICE: $20-25) Whale-watching can be arranged from any number of tour operators with offices along the Malecón. The season is June to September, when the humpback whales arrive in the warm coastal waters looking for a mate or to protect their young. Boats generally set off mid-morning, around 10 or 10:30 a.m., and return around 2 p.m., but some operators offer afternoon tours that leave at 2 p.m. and return at 5 p.m. You may see individual whales, pairs, or small groups of up to eight, and the massive whales can sometimes be observed jumping out of the water or flapping their tails. Most whale-watching also include a short snorkeling session and small snack. These tours can also be arranged from other coastal towns, including Mompiche, Puerto Cayo, Manta, Montañita, Ayampe and Salinas.
Updated: Aug 25, 2012.

Puerto López Schools
Clara Luna Spanish School

Clara Luna is not only about Spanish language education, it also seeks to teach students about ancient Ecuadorian cultures, Ecuadorian coastal food and environmental issues in the area. Its bilingual teachers are also naturalist guides in Parque Nacional Machalilla and have at least three years of experience teaching. The school offers several unique programs, some that combine Spanish lessons with surfing classes, scuba diving, visits to nearby attractions, stays at organic farms and volunteer work. Spanish classes are 20 hours per week, and many include daily breakfast in the school's restaurant, free WiFi, and organic coffee and tea.

Clara Luna also hosts a language exchange on Wednesdays at 5:30 p.m. and yoga classes. South of the Puerto López beach, Tel: 09-062-5479, E-mail: info@claraluna.com.ec, URL: www.claraluna.com.ec.
Updated: Sep 06, 2012.

Puerto López Lodging

Since Puerto López sees lots of tourism due to the beautiful natural surroundings, there is a pretty big selection of accommodation options given its small size. Lodging ranges from budget places offering dormitories for backpackers to nicer cabañas on the beach, some of which have pools and good on-site restaurants. Prices tend to be per person, and always rise during high season. Most of the places are now equipped with WiFi too, although few choose to include breakfast in the room price.

BUDGET
Sol Inn

($8-15 per person) Sol Inn has a mellow beach bum atmosphere with a friendly, energetic owner. You can relax in the outdoor lounge area with couches and a pool table, find out information about or book tours, exchange books in several languages (for a $1 charge per book), or cook in the communal kitchen. The rooms are clean and creatively painted. It is also possible to camp in the yard or crash in one of its hammocks for $4 per person. There is WiFi throughout the hostel and even a computer to use if you didn't bring your own. It is also the only place in town that sells rolling papers. Juan Montalvo and Eloy Alfaro, Tel: 593-05-230-0248, E-mail: hostal_solinn@hotmail.com., URL: www.hostalsolinn.com.
Updated: Sep 04, 2012.

Hostal Fragata

($10-15 per person) This cozy hostel has a great sense of family. The owner's two sisters have restaurants less than half a block away that will bring you food if requested and her daughter has a tour operator that will offers whale-watching tours. The owner is also happy to share a spacious kitchen near the reception area for those who want to prepare their own meals and will even let you come back to use the bathroom and showers after you have checked out. The rooms are a bit of a squeeze, though, and only a few have air conditioning (and are more expensive). There is capacity for about 70 guests. Eloy Alfaro and Malecón Julio Izurieta, Tel: 04-230-0156, Cel: 08-896-9832/09-360-3338, E-mail: yaquymenendez@hotmail.com.

SOUTHERN COAST

Hostería Itapoâ !

($12-15 per person) Named after the owner's favorite beach in her home country of Brazil, Hostería Itapoâ is about one block from Puerto López's beach and has a comfortable, tranquil atmosphere. When you first enter, it feels a little like you are trespassing into someone's backyard. Press on and you will see several cabañas on the left and rooms in a small building on the right of the main garden and eating area. The cabañas are nicer than the other rooms and have private porches with hammocks. Room prices include breakfast, which is served at tables in the raised café with ocean views. Maria's husband, Raúl, who is a biologist, also runs a reforestation volunteer project near Puerto Quito for just a small weekly fee. Part of the project includes generating income for jungle and rural communities by making and selling chocolate. Blocks of 100 percent pure cacao are for sale at the hostel. Malecón Julio Izurieta Norte, Tel: 09-314-5894/478-4992, E-mail: itapoa_25@hotmail.com, URL: www.itapoareserve.com.
Updated: Sep 04, 2012.

Hostal Yemayá

($8-15 per person) This new hostel is centrally located on a pedestrian street, only half a block from the beach. It has one dorm with seven beds and two bathrooms, as well as 10 private rooms with tiled floors, exposed brick walls and clean private bathrooms, some of which have a TV with cable and air conditioning. Those that don't have air conditioning have fans. There is an internal garden, terrace with ocean views, a common area with a TV and games for guest use, and WiFi throughout. Downstairs there is a surf school that offers classes. General Córdova and Cristo del Consuelo, across from the fire station., Tel: 05-230-0122, Cel: 08-864-6118, E-mail: www.hostalyemaya.com, URL: yemayahostal@hotmail.com.
Updated: Sep 04, 2012.

Hostal Tuzco

($10-15 per person) Hostal Tuzco is one of the longest-standing hotels in town and is run by a very sweet and accommodating local woman. The price per person doesn't rise during high season, which is a definite perk in Puerto López. Rooms are clean but a bit outdated and uninteresting, and there is a common roof area with hammocks and patio furniture with views of Puerto López and the beach in the distance. Unfortunately it is a fair distance (300 m/984 ft) up a hill from the beach and main strip of Puerto López.

This place is especially great for groups, as there is an attached pharmacy and a recreational area across the street with a pool table, football field, pool with water slide and games to borrow in the lounge area. General Córdova and Juan Leon Mera, Tel: 05-230-0120, E-mail: jasalazar1@hotmail.com, URL: www.hostaltuzco.com.
Updated: Sep 04, 2012.

MID-RANGE

Hostería Mandála

(ROOMS: $36-153) Located on a quiet stretch of beach north of the town's center, Hostería Mandala offers a convenient escape without having to venture far. Guests can relax in private, individual cabañas surrounded by the grounds' extensive, dense tropical garden that is filled with exotic flowers, trees and plants. Inspired by local culture, history and nature, the German and Italian owners have gone on to decorate each cabin with unique artistic designs made of wood, bamboo and bits of stone.

Each is also equipped with fans, hot water, hammocks, private baths and porches. The hotel's restaurant serves a variety of Ecuadorian and Italian dishes, and even makes its own fresh bread and ice cream from scratch. Guests can form their own band in the community lounge, which has a variety of instruments from Esmeraldas, duel one another with the 60+ free games available, or relax with a good book in the extensive library. Hostería Mandala is also handicap accessible. Malecón Julio Izurieta Norte, Tel: 593-05-230-0181, E-mail: info@hosteriamandala.info, URL: www.hosteriamandala.info.
Updated: Sep 04, 2012.

Hotel Pacífico

($15-30 per person) A clean and spacious hotel, Hotel Pacífico is a good option and one of the few places that accepts all credit cards. The rooms with air conditioning are double the cost of rooms with a fan but have great ocean views and a common balcony with hammocks and patio furniture. These more expensive rooms also have WiFi and phones to order room service from the adjacent restaurant. The rooms toward the back of the hotel have fans and are definitely more moist and musty than the rooms facing the beach. The view-less rooms do have the advantage of easy access to the lovely outdoor pool. All rooms also have cable TV. Malecón Julio Izurieta and Gónzalez Suárez, Tel: 593-09-399-5977.
Updated: Sep 04, 2012.

Hostería La Terraza

(ROOMS: $15-73) The remarkable impressions of a trip are often received outside the well-known tourist sites. Just above Puerto López, you will find the Hostería La Terraza, which is known as a sanctuary for its peacefulness and its hospitality. The wind on the hill makes for a pleasant climate with a refreshing breeze. From the hostel, which is surrounded by green, you have a picturesque view of the small fishing village. You can reach Puerto López by path.

Lying in a hammock in front of the rooms of one of the three guesthouses, or on the terrace of the main house, you will have an unforgettable view of the sun going down over the pacific. An ideal place for bird-watching is the garden of "La Terraza" where you can find a variety of birds from small parrots to ospreys. Cdla. Luis Gencón-Calle San Francisco s/n, getting there from the center by Mototaxis or by foot takes 5-10 mins. Tel: 05-230-0235, Cel: 08-855-4887, E-mail: info@laterraza.de, URL: www.laterraza.de. Updated: Aug 22, 2012.

Oceanic

($20-25 per person) Situated at the far north end of the beach, this is one of the best options in Puerto López to get away from it all, surrounded by small hills and a quieter, cleaner stretch of beach. Accommodation in cabins, made in part with natural materials, will allow you to enjoy all of the comfort that you desire. The hostel has a restaurant with a full view of the ocean, and the chef prides himself on producing great national and international cuisine. There is also a massage room and a very pleasant swimming pool with miniature waterfall. Breakfast is included. Malécon Julio Izurieta Norte, Tel: 593-08-259-8631, E-mail: hosteriaoceanic@gmail.com, URL: www.hosteriaoceanic.com. Updated: Sep 04, 2012.

Hotel Piedra del Mar

(ROOMS: $36-100) This newer hotel adds a pinch of boutique chic into dusty Puerto López, mixing classic colonial architecture with rustic touches such as the pebble-dashed walls, which give the hotel its name. The hotel has a peaceful courtyard with small pool and Jacuzzi, overlooked by a small bar-terrace.

The hotel is linked to the tour operator Ecuador Amazing. Rooms are well-presented and have cable TV and private bathrooms with hot water. Guests have access to free WiFi and can even make free calls to the U.S. and Canada from here. General Córdova and Cristo del Consuelo, across from the fire station, Tel: 05-230-0250/0227, Cel: 09-984-8585, E-mail: reservas@piedradelmarhotel.com, URL: www.piedradelmarhotel.com. Updated: Sep 04, 2012.

Hostería Nantu

(ROOMS: $22.50-84) At the north end of the beach, Hostería Nantu is a very appealing mid-range option. Rooms, ranging from singles to family-style suites for six people, are spacious and have tiled floors, and are well-equipped with cable TV, hot water and firm beds. Some have fans and others have air conditioning. The Hosteria is pretty clean and makes an effort to keep it that way.

There is a small swimming pool in the courtyard available as well and a restaurant serving breakfasts in the morning and seafood throughout the day. Malécon Julio Izurieta Norte, 150 meters (492 ft) from the fishing terminal, Tel: 05-230-0040, Cel: 09-781-4636/529-4524, E-mail: reservas@hosterianantu.com, URL: www.hosterianantu.com. Updated: Sep 04, 2012.

HIGH-END
Mantaraya Hotel

(ROOMS: $90-300) This absolutely beautiful lodge is located about 1.5 kilometers south of Puerto López on the main highway. Mantaraya's 15 single, double, triple and quadruple rooms are spacious and cheery, and all have large windows that open up onto spacious private balconies, allowing for lots of natural light to come in. Its stunning architecture has a Mediterranean feel to it, but the biggest highlight is perhaps the refreshing outdoor pool, complete with a small waterfall and surrounded by a tropical garden that you can be relaxed by..

The on-site restaurant is one of the best in the area, and guests can enjoy meals or cocktails on their balconies or poolside, in addition to eating in the indoor dining room. All-inclusive rates include land transportation to and from Manta, naturalist English/Spanish-speaking guide, visits according to the itinerary, accommodations and meals (set menu), and trip to Isla de la Plata on board Mantaraya II. Quito office: Gaspar de Villarroel 1100 and Av. 6 de Diciembre, Edificio Ritz Plaza, Tel: 02-336-0887/0888/0889 (Quito office), E-mail: info@advantecuador.com, URL: www.mantarayalodge.com. Updated: Feb 18, 2013.

Puerto López Restaurants

Since Puerto López is a fishing village, seafood is the name of the game in this coastal town. In the early morning, the area on the beach near the fishing boats transforms into a seafood market where fishermen slice and sell their fresh catch. All along the beach, cabañas serve up *ceviche* and *cervezas*, as well as fresh fruit juices and *batidos*, for bargain prices.

Along the other side of the Malecón, restaurants with both indoor and outdoor seating grill, fry and sauteé fish, shrimp, calamari and octopus. Rice and fried plantains accompany nearly every main dish. Near the center of town, where buses come and go, there is also a market where several stands offer cheap seafood soups and *ceviche*. A few Italian restaurants are on the Malecón for those who want a change of taste, and some foreign-owned places are scattered about, offering international fare.

Note, that while *spondylus*, a spiny oyster, used to be on many menus in this area, it is now all but illegal to serve unfortunately, as it is an endangered species.
Updated: Sep 05, 2012.

Hotel Pacífico Restaurante

(ENTREES: $6-10) Hotel Pacífico restaurant is just next door to the entrance of the hotel of the same name. The restaurant features an open-air porch overlooking the beach and is one of very few places to eat in Puerto López that accepts credit cards. The food is a little pricier, but is very well prepared. Daily 7:30 a.m.-8 p.m. Malecón Julio Izurieta and Gónzalo Suárez, Tel: 09-399-5977, E-mail: hotelpacificoecuador@gmail.com, URL: www.hotelpacificoecuador.com.
Updated: Sep 04, 2012.

Espuma del Mar

(ENTREES: $4.50-10) Located right on the Malecón overlooking the beach, Espuma del Mar could not be in a better location. There is a porch and plenty of seating as well as tacky, ocean-themed decor. It has a few different standard breakfast options and offers a cheap fixed-price lunch and dinner.

If you are staying at the Hostal Fragata, you can order food from this restaurant to be delivered to your door. The owners are sisters. Daily 8 a.m.-9 p.m. Malecón Julio Izurieta and Eloy Alfaro, Tel: 05-230-0187, Cel: 08-638-3271.
Updated: Sep 04, 2012.

Carmita Restaurant and Bar

(ENTREES: $5-20) Restaurant Carmita is one of the best restaurants in town. The large menu includes ceviches as well as shrimp, fish, calamari and octopus prepared several different ways. Try one of the dishes smothered in *salsa de maní*, a delicious peanut sauce with white wine and a bit of a kick. Some chicken and beef dishes are also available for those who need a break from seafood. Although the prices are a bit higher than that of the surrounding restaurants, the cozy ambiance and large portions of delicious food make it worth the extra cents. This is one of the few restaurants that accepts all major credit cards as well. Daily 10 a.m.-11 p.m. Malecón Julio Izurieta and General Córdova, Tel: 09-372-9294, URL: www.restaurantcarmita.com.
Updated: Sep 05, 2012.

Patacón Pisa'o

(ENTREES: $3-9) For a refreshing change from seafood, head to the friendly little Patacón Pisa'o, a half a block from the Malecón. Run by a family of Colombians from Cali who have lived in Puerto López for years, it serves up large platefuls of the Colombian version of *patacones*, or crispy plantain pancakes, topped with a variety of meats in *hoga'o* (onion and tomato) sauce.

Other options include arepas, kebabs, crepes, soups and salads. It also has eight different breakfast options and serves real Colombian coffee. Plus, there's WiFi! Monday-Saturday 9:30 a.m.-9:30 p.m., shorter hours during rest of the year. General Córdova and Juan Montalvo, Tel: 09-127-4206/377-1915, E-mail: pataconpisaoec@hotmail.com, URL: www.pataconpisao.blogspot.com.
Updated: Sep 04, 2012.

Bellitalia

(ENTREES: $7-12) Bellaitalia occupies an upstairs space on the Malecón and cooks up some tasty Italian dishes in an airy, candlelit atmosphere. Here you can choose from several different types of pasta, such as spaghetti, fusilli or homemade tagliatelle, and match it with one of your favorite sauces like pesto, bolognese or tomato sauce. If you are looking for pizza, though, head elsewhere; no pizza is served here.

The mains are very filling, so no need to start off the meal with one of the soups and salads, though accompanying it with a glass of wine while looking out the balcony onto the beach is a relaxing way to end the day. Daily

6-10 p.m. June-September. Closed Sundays rest of the year. Malecón Julio Izurieta and Alejo Lascano, upstairs from Palo Santo Tours, Tel: 09-242-0448.
Updated: Sep 05, 2012.

Restaurante "russo"

(ENTREES: $2-8) New to Puerto López's restaurant scene, Restaurante "Russo" specializes in Russian cuisine and cooks up comforting specialties like *pelmeni* (dumplings with ground meat), *deruni de papa* (potato pancakes) and *brizol frita* (similar to a Spanish tortilla with meat inside). The owner also makes homemade Russian bread. Although the place is small—with only three tables covered in red tablecloths—portions tend to be big and are always made to order. Spaghetti dishes, crepes, fried prawns and pork chops are alternative menu options. Daily 8 a.m.-8 p.m. Located on Juan Montalvo and General Córdova.
Updated: Sep 05, 2012.

Whale Café

(ENTREES: $6-10) This popular America-owned café no longer serves breakfast but has lots of vegetarian options, including a variety of salads and wraps, some with Asian influences. Try the Thai chicken wrap, avocado and shrimp salad, or hummus with garlic toast for a taste of home. The owners go to Manta once a week to buy the freshest produce, so beyond large portions, you can also expect tasteful food.

The wife also makes some delicious baked goods, including brownies, chocolate cake and apple pie, and these alone make it worth the walk to the southern part of the Malecón. In addition to indoor tables, Whale Café also has a comfy sitting area with couches and a book exchange. During high season, it is open Monday-Wednesday 1-9 p.m. and Thursday-Sunday 5-9 p.m. Malecón Julio Izurieta Sur, Barrio San Pedro, Tel: 09-660-6836, E-mail: dianehillis@yahoo.com.
Updated: Sep 05, 2012.

Clandestino

(SNACKS: $1-4) Created as a place to connect with others and engage in conversation, this small café and bar is a nice place to unwind. It is probably the only place in town where you can enjoy organic coffee, hot chocolate, and a variety of local teas—including chocolate mint tea and pomegranate green tea—while listening to reggae, rock or trance music. Friendly local owner Javiar, who is also a guide in Parque Nacional Machalilla, has a book exchange, where you can trade one book for a coffee and an hour of salsa lessons with him—not a bad deal. At night, Clandestino also serves beers, mojitos and other alcoholic drinks. At any time of the day, you can accompany your warm or cold beverage with *tostadas* (hot toasted sandwiches), fruit salad with yogurt and granola, or desserts like *tres leches* or apple crumble. Daily 10 a.m. until people leave. Cristo del Consuelo and General Córdova, Tel: 09-566-6398, E-mail: clandestinobarpuertolopez@hotmail.com.
Updated: Sep 05, 2012.

Etnias

(SNACKS: $2-4) This earthly little French-owned café with a pebbled floor and bamboo furniture has great breakfasts. Beyond the typical continental-style breakfasts served around town, Etnias also has crepes and waffles topped with nutella, peanut butter or fruit, as well as fruit with yogurt. Those who favor savory can order crepes with ham and cheese, hamburgers, quiche or salads. It also has organic coffee from Loja, hot chocolate made with organic chocolate and fresh fruit juices.

Attached is a store by the same name that sells *artesanía* and organic food products-from Puerto López and all of Ecuador, including *tagua* jewelry, ceramics from Cuenca, natural cosmetics, wool products from Salasaca and chocolate bars. The café is open Tuesday-Sunday 8:30 a.m.-7 p.m. and the store is open Tuesday-Sunday 9 a.m.-noon and 4-7 p.m. General Córdova and Juan Montalvo, Tel: 09-797-1230/057-7662, E-mail: etnias1@hotmail.com.
Updated: Sep 05, 2012.

Restaurante Spondylus

(ENTREES: $3.50-7.50) This endearing laid-back place is a great-value option with colorful murals and an informal atmosphere. The menu contains a range of seafood and ceviches as well as a variety of spaghetti, meat and burgers, if you're tired of the fish. Prawns or lobster are delicious choices if you have a bit more money to spend, mind you the latter is only available during specific parts of the year (otherwise, lobster is known to be in "veda," or banned so as to promote the breeding of their species). Desserts include brownies, banana splits and a lovely apple pie. Malecón Julio Izurieta and General Córdova, Tel: 08-562-7536, E-mail: richardspondylus01@hotmail.com.
Updated: Sep 04, 2012.

SOUTHERN COAST

SALANGO

A small fishing village just six kilometers (3.7 mi) south of Puerto López, Salango's main features are its excellent seafood and an archaeological museum, Museo Salango. The town has a nice beach but the view is spoiled by the eyesore of a large factory.
Updated: Sep 06, 2012.

Getting To and Away from Salango

There are no direct buses to Salango from Quito or Guayaquil; you will need to go to **Puerto López** first. From Puerto López, **Cooperativa Manglaralto** buses leave every 15-30 minutes from Avenida Machalilla, near the corner of General Córdova, diagonal from the church. Take any south-bound Cooperativa Manglaralto bus and ask to be let off at Salango's town entrance, just five minutes away. Alternatively, you can take a taxi or bike there.

From Salango, you can easily head elsewhere up or down the coast by flagging down a north- or south-bound Cooperativa Manglaralto bus from the town entrance.
Updated: Feb 18, 2013.

Things To See and Do In Salango

Museo Salango

(ADMISSION: $2.50) What better place to have an archaeological museum than in a town that boasts 5,000 years of history and culture. This small museum has artifacts from the area's pre-colonial cultures, including the Valdivia, the Machalilla, the Chorrera-Engoroy, the Bahía, the Guangala and the Manteña.

The exhibit includes 245 pieces of pre-Columbian pottery as well as a collection of spondylus shells, sculptures and jewelry. Additionally, it has information about each culture's lifestyles and the methods of agricultural production. Daily 8 a.m.-5:30 p.m. Head toward the water and Malecón, and you will see the museum halfway down the road on the right side, Tel: 05-258-9304, URL: www.salango.com.ec.

Salango Lodging

Salango is a small fishing village, and its lodging options are equally few in number. There aren't many places to stay, and you won't find any hotels, just hostels and locally run cabins. Interestingly, Salango runs a community tourism project that operates 12 cabins, which have a total capacity for 45 people ($15 per person; Tel: 05-258-9304, Cel: 09-8557-8096, E-mail: info@salango.com.ec / comsalango@yahoo.es). The cabins are made from typical materials such as brick, reeds and wood, and have private bathrooms with hot water. Depending on what type of experience you are seeking, you may be better off spending the night in nearby Puerto López and coming here just for the day to sample the seafood and maybe visit the small archaeological museum.

Hostería Islamar

($21-45 per person) Hostería Islamar's five luxury cabañas are located on top of a hill facing Isla Salango. Each can sleep up to eight guests and has a private balcony overlooking the water. Beyond the cabañas, Islamar has a recreational area with a volleyball court, a children's playground, and a restaurant serving local seafood dishes as well as international food. This place is especially appropriate for families or groups, but can also easily accommodate couples. Altos de Punta Piedra Verde Km 669 Ruta del Pacífico. You need a car to arrive here. Head to the watchtower of Salango, called "Mirador de Salango," and go up the hill for five minutes. E-15, Tel: 04-228-7001, Cel: 09-385-7580, Fax: 04-220-2346, E-mail: info@hosteria-isalmar.com.ec, URL: www.hosteria-islamar.com.ec.
Updated: Aug 20, 2012.

Salango Restaurants

For such a small village, Salango sure has a reputation for its seafood. In the past, people from all over the Ecuadorian coast stopped here to fill up on fresh fish and to try the local specialty, *spondylus*. However, this spiny oyster is now banned from menus due to its endangerment status and *precebes* have taken center stage. This alternative offers an interesting, barnacle-like crustacean to your palatte, and is considered a delicacy in Salango. It's also one of the few places along the Ruta del Spondylus where you can try it.
Updated: Sep 06, 2012.

El Pelícano

(ENTREES: $5.50-20) In direct competition with the popular Delfín Mágico Restaurante, El Pelícano offers the same fare of fresh-off-the-boat seafood at more reasonable prices and with speedier service. Try the fish in *salsa de maní* (peanut sauce)—you'll be dreaming about it for days. Hard-to-find scallops are also on the menu, as well as Salango's specialty, *precebes*. El Pelícano has a very simple atmosphere with thick wooden picnic tables and boat decor. The highlight is the fresh, deliciously prepared seafood. Daily 8 a.m.-8 p.m. Ca. Principal and La Plaza, Tel: 09-185-1812, URL: www.pelicanos-tours. com/restaurant-el-pelicano.php. Updated: Sep 06, 2012.

Delfín Mágico
(ENTREES: $8-22) People come from all corners of Ecuador for a taste of Delfín Mágico's famous seafood plates. Fresh prawns, lobster, shrimp, scallops and octopus are meticulously prepared several different ways. The specialty, though, is *percebes*, or goose barnacles, which come with an exquisite lime sauce. These rare sea creatures are harvested by hand at low tide. This place gets rave reviews so you are bound to love whatever you order. Daily 10 a.m.-8 p.m. Ca. Principal, in front of the central park., Tel: 04-278-0291, Cel: 09-9114-7555, E-mail: antoniovrt@hotmail.com / info@delfin-magico.com, URL: www.facebook.com/profile.php?id=100001334157094. Updated: Jan 21, 2013.

PUERTO RICO
Blink and you might miss Puerto Rico, it´s such a small village. Set about ten kilometers (6.2 mi) south of Puerto López, along the Ruta del Sol between Salango and Las Tunas, Puerto Rico is best-known for one of its biggest hotels – Cantaelmar - but also has a great stretch of beach that you might very well may have all to yourself, given how tiny this little town is and how often it's overlooked by other tourists. Updated: Apr 18, 2013.

Things To See and Do In Puerto Rico
Museo Marino
The museum is located in the Jambeli Islands. To get to this island you catch a boat from the Puerto Bolivar part of El Oro. The island offers restaurants, cabins and places to stay and enjoy the beach and night life. The exhibit is made of over 500 pieces on display, divided into mollusks, crustaceous, echinoderms, corals, algae, fishes, whale bones and sea fossils. Almost 90 percent of the collection was found along the Ecuadorian coastline nearby. Located 300 meters (984 feet) south (left) of the main entrance of the beach, Tel: 593-9-383-6307, E-mail: geomertierramar741@hotmail.com. Updated: Apr 05, 2013.

Puerto Rico Lodging
Along Ecuador's Ruta del Sol lies Puerto Rico, a secluded beach town in its early stages of tourism development. There are a couple of nice places to stay here, but you won't find any hotels. Puerto Rico has a nice beachy vibe with long, beautiful stretches of quiet beach.

Hostería Cantaelmar
(ROOMS: $30-64) Cantaelmar Hostería Holistica is one of the few true ecologically friendly lodges along the Ruta del Sol. Water is recycled for watering plants and compost is also used for fertilization purposes. The organic garden provides most of the fresh food in the restaurant. Cantaelmar also makes an effort to preserve the native culture. With capacity for about 100 guests, Cantaelmar has Robinson Crusoe-esque architecture and a clever treehouse play-area for children.

Cabanas are divided into tall, wooden structures with rooms for one to four guests each. There is also camping space at $15 per person. The open-air restaurant lets you appreciate the natural setting while dining on organic specialties from Cantaelmar's own garden and seafood from local fishermen. Internet is available for emergency use (you'll have to ask for it). Note that this hotel is pretty popular during holidays and booking in advance is highly recommended. Km. 12, Puerto Lopez to Salinas / Quito office: Inglaterra N3-57 and Av. República, Tel: 05-234-7028 / 02-224-5432 / 099-495-8962, E-mail: info@hosteriacantaelmar.com, URL: www.hosteriacantaelmar.com. Updated: Apr 18, 2013.

Puerto Rico Restaurants
UVVA
Just across the lobby at Hostería del Mar you'll find the island-renowned Uvva Restaurant. With its tropical ambiance and its breathtaking views of the Atlantic, this International Creative Cuisine Restaurant serves everything from healthy sandwich wraps to succulent filet mignon. Open from 8 a.m. to 10 p.m., Uvva Restaurant is the perfect venue for a romantic dinner, casual lunch with friends or those low-key business meetings away from the office. Seating at Uvva is available inside, outside on the sun deck or down the steps on the beach. Calle Tapia Ocean Park, San Juan-Puerto Rico, Zip: 00911, Tel: (787) 727-3302, E-mail: hosteria@caribe. net, URL: http://www.hosteriadelmarpr. com/Restaurant/Restaurant.html. Updated: Apr 05, 2013.

LAS TUNAS

Las Tunas is a small beach town between Puerto Rico and Ayampe along the Ruta del Sol, about a 10-minute bus ride south of Puerto López. A very quiet town with a fair stretch of beach and a small Malecón, Las Tunas is still in the very developmental stages as far as tourism goes. If you come for a swim, wear water shoes as the beach can be fairly rocky.
Updated: Sep 17, 2012.

Las Tunas Lodging

Many of the Las Tunas hostels are tucked away on secluded plots along the beach, and have great views of the ocean. Prices are decent, in that you get good value for your dollars, but there aren't many truly budget places to stay around here.

Hostería Tsafiki

(ROOMS: $50-130) Hostería Tsafiki does a good job of being fairly luxurious without sacrificing personality, maybe because of its inspired name, which means "the tongue of the real man" in a native Ecuadorian coastal language. Cabañas have terraces, fresh flowers, and hypoallergenic mattresses, pillows and blankets. The main lounge has great ocean views, a pool table, an English and Spanish book exchange, and a restaurant with outdoor seating. Prices include breakfast. Ca. Principal s/n - Cdla. 12 de Octubre, Tel: 05-234-7057.
Updated: Sep 18, 2012.

Hosteria La Barquita

($12.50-40 per person) The main draw of this well-known hosteria is the boat-shaped main building from which it gets its name (little boat). Here you can exchange books in four languages, shoot pool in the upper decks or sip cocktails in the bar followed by sumptuous food from the restaurant. The Swiss owners are very friendly, hands-on and full of advice for guests. There is a relaxing, new swimming pool, plus a tree-house and adventure playground, frequented by the owners´ children. The boat theme is carried out in the architecture of the cabanas, with porthole mirrors, rounded doors and natural stone locks, although some of the rooms could do with a bit of freshening up.

You can also get reasonably priced tours and rental equipment from La Barquita. Horse rental is $5 an hour, whale watching tours are $25 per person and tours to Isla de la Plata are $40 per person plus the park en-trance fee of $15. Even if you don´t stay here, you should stop off to eat in this unique setting. With open-air seating and views overlooking the ocean, it's the next best thing to eating on the open water. The seafood is excellent and specialities include brochettes (nicknamed "harpoons"), great ceviches and cazuela manabita (a steaming peanut and plantain flavored fish stew). Transfers from Manta and Guayaquil are also provided by the hotel as well. Km 88 of Ruta del Sol, Zip: EC131950, Tel: 05-234-7051/7063, E-mail: reserva@hosterialabarquita.com, URL: www.hosterialabarquita.com.
Updated: Nov 15, 2012.

Equus Erro

(ROOMS: $75-120) Equus Erro Hostería's main draw is the view of the ocean, which can be seen from almost all the rooms. With seven rooms and two suites equipped with saunas, this little coastal inn is homey and relaxed. The hostería also has four- to six-person cabins for rent. There are several entertainment areas with ping pong, darts and a pool table, as well as a seafood restaurant. It has an on-site animal rescue center that protects macaws, parrots and monkeys from animal trafficking, and is involved in a number of other social and environmental projects. Inquire about its many volunteer opportunities. Prices include breakfast as well. Ca. Libertad Ciudadela and Cdla. 12 de Octubre, Tel: 05-234-7081, Cel: 09-456-6629, E-mail: info@equuserro.com, URL: www.equuserro.com.
Updated: Sep 18, 2012.

Hostería La Perla

(ROOMS: $25-94) This family-owned B&B on the beach takes sustainable tourism seriously and has earned a certificate from the Rainforest Alliance for its environmental practices. It is the ultimate place to relax, with private beach access and a spa that offers massages and morning yoga classes. Some months, La Perla has two-day/two-night all-inclusive packages that include accommodation, detoxifying meals, meditation and yoga. Both the private and family-style rooms have porches, fans and private bathrooms with hot water. There is an artsy outdoor sitting area that shelters a large wood-burning oven, and a funky, rustic restaurant for guests inside La Perla's main colorful structure. Ca. Principal s/n, Cdla. 12 de Octubre, Tel: 05-234-7001, Cel: 09-994-6372, E-mail: monfabara@hotmail.com, URL: www.hosterialaperla.net.
Updated: Sep 17, 2012.

SOUTHERN COAST

Cabañas Viejamar

(ROOMS: $24-70) Viejamar's cabins, which are built with natural materials, sleep one to four people and are set in a nice, large garden, giving it a very relaxed—even jungly—feel. The garden grows a mix of herbs, including mint and basil, which all have labels and make the place smell quite fragrant. The cabins themselves are a bit dark and musty, with limited windows, but are cozy nonetheless. It also has a small outdoor pool, a private beach entrance, a BBQ, a TV with satellite cable, and an outdoor social area with couches, books to read and board games. A simple breakfast is included in the price, and the hostel's restaurant serves seafood the rest of the day. Viejamar can also arrange surfing lessons, surfboard rentals and horseback riding. Ca. Principal s/n, Cdla. 12 de Octubre, Tel: 05-234-7032 / 08-781-7310, E-mail: viejamar@hotmail.com, URL: www.viejamar.com.
Updated: Sep 17, 2012.

Azuluna Eco-Lodge !

(ROOMS: $56-120) Azuluna Eco-Lodge is a set of cheery ecological cabins perched on a hill overlooking the ocean. The lodge employes local workers, sells organic Ecuadorian coffee and locally made handicrafts, and is involved in a number of community projects. In fact, 10 percent of all room costs is funneled back into Las Tunas to facilitate these projects. All of the cabins are well-built with natural materials and have views of the ocean, and some are handicap accessible. They come in the standard, superior, suite and deluxe suite varieties, depending on your taste and budget. Each is uniquely decorated. Its restaurant serves fixed-priced breakfasts, lunches and dinners. Ca. Principal - Cdla. 12 de Octubre, up the hill, Tel: 05-234-7035/7093, Cel: 09-951-0542/08-371-5281, E-mail: info@azuluna-ecuador.com, URL: www.azuluna-ecuador.com.
Updated: Sep 18, 2012.

Cabañas Mirada al Mar

($12.50-15 per person) This two-storey, locally owned bamboo hotel is ideally located directly on Las Tunas' Malecón. Its eight rooms are clean but basic with private bathrooms and fans, and are ideal for those on a budget. It has a communal kitchen and a terrace with hammocks and ocean views. Some of the rooms also have views of the ocean, but those that do cost a bit more per person. Malecón, Barrio San Vicente, Tel: 05-234-7011, Cel: 09-484-1948.
Updated: Sep 17, 2012.

Las Tunas Restaurants

Tsafiki's Wahoo Restaurant

(ENTREES: $3-15) Located in the main building of Hostería Tsafiki and overlooking the water, Wahoo Restaurant is a great spot to relax and enjoy fresh seafood and other local favorites. It has continental breakfasts as well as fixed-priced lunches and dinners that rotate daily. Items off the menu cost a bit more. Choose a beverage from the fairly extensive drink menu to accompany your meal. Daily 9 a.m.-10 p.m. Ca. Principal s/n - Cdla. 12 de Octubre, Tel: 05-234-7057.
Updated: Sep 18, 2012.

Gacebo Equus Erro

(ENTREES: $6-12) Gacebo Equus Erro specializes in exquisitely prepared, gourmet seafood. The vast wine list presents endless possibilities for pairing flavors. The kitchen says its desserts are "like paradise"; you be the judge. While it may be fine dining, Restaurant Gacebo caters to all tastes. A special kids' menu is available to please the little ones as well. Daily 8 a.m.-9 p.m. Ca. Libertad Ciudadela and Cdla. 12 de Octubre, Tel: 05-234-7081, Cel: 09-456-6629, Fax: 593-4-278-0571, E-mail: info(at)equuserro.com, URL: www.equuserro.com.
Updated: Sep 18, 2012.

AYAMPE

Ayampe is a tiny sleepy fishing village that just recently awakened to the wave of tourism flowing through the area. The town is surrounded by rain forest, excellent views and top-notch surfing. It's the perfect place to get away from the crowds of Montañita futher south, and simply relax in nature or meet the friendly local fishermen. The beach is clean and always free of crowds, but bring water shoes or grit your teeth, as the bottom here is fairly rocky and spiky. The currents however are exceptionally strong and great care must be taken while swimming or even wading in the ocean.
Updated: Jan 14, 2013.

Getting To and Away from Ayampe

Ayampe is a 30-minute bus ride from **Puerto Lopez** (or **Montañita** in the other direction). **Manglaralto** buses, which follow the coast south to Montañita and further, leave every half hour or so from the main street of Puerto Lopez and will leave you at the entrance of Ayampe's entry road.
Updated: Apr 18, 2013.

SOUTHERN COAST

Things To See and Do In Ayampe

Besides lying on the beach, there are a few different nature trails and bike routes you can explore while in the area; you can rent bikes in town. One goes along the river, another through the forest, and yet another to nearby Las Tunas. Ayampe also has a good reputation among surfers, and there is at least one surf school where you can take lessons. The surf school also gives yoga classes and Spanish classes, so you can have more excuses to stay.
Updated: Jan 14, 2013.

Otra Ola

Otra Ola is a laid-back school for travelers interested in learning Spanish, practicing yoga, or surfing while visiting Ecuador's southern coast and an organic restaurant and café. Both Spanish and surfing classes (at any level) are available by the hour or at a discounted rate for multi-session packages. Spanish lessons can be arranged in private or group settings, and the general curriculum can be personalized to your interests and wants. You can also choose to rent short or long surfboards here by the day or for longer periods of time.

To clear your mind, try one of Otra Ola's group or private yoga classes, which incorporate poses and sequences that focus on areas that are involved in surfing and traveling. The school also provides free English classes to the local community and encourages visitors to get involved as well—a great opportunity to meet local people, practice Spanish and give back to this little piece of paradise. Tel: 09-8884-3278, E-mail: info@otraola.com, URL: www.otraola.com.
Updated: Dec 19, 2012.

Ayampe Lodging

Ayampe still has the qualities of a quiet fishing village but word is getting out about its charm and excellent surfing. Its tourism industry is slowly taking off and several new hotels have opened up as a result. There are many comfortable lodging options, whether you prefer a private room, cabin or tent. Most are situated right on the beach or just a few minutes walk away, and many have gardens or green spaces for a secluded feel. The nicest ones come equipped with TVs, air conditioning, private porches, and/or spa facilities. Overall, the majority of hostels in town have a laid-back atmosphere suitable for backpackers and surfers.
Updated: Jan 14, 2013.

Cabañas La Tortuga

($16-50 per person) With capacity for 78 people in cabins and suites, plus camping space in three military-size tents, Las Cabañas Tortuga is a clean, spacious and child-friendly spot. Beyond a place to sleep, La Tortuga has a game room, a children's area, a pool table, a ping-pong table, and a TV with a satellite cable and a selection of DVDs. Right out front is a private beach entrance, or you can opt to sun-bathe by its own pool. Private transportation is available from Guayaquil, Manta and some of the other nearby cities. There are kayaks for rent as well, and horseback riding or trips to Isla de la Plata are arranged. Tel: 05-258-9363/9378, Cel: 09-433-0052/383-4825, E-mail: info@latortuga.com.ec, URL: www.latortuga.com.ec.
Updated: Sep 19, 2012.

Cabañas La Iguana

($12.50-15 per person) Cabañas La Iguana has a relaxed atmosphere with a common kitchen area and lounge with hammocks. The owner is a musician with a passion for book collecting. As a result, you will find a collection of CDs, books and musical instruments in the reception area, which are for exchange or for sale. La Iguana has a large garden that grows a variety of fruits, herbs and vegetables and guests can take in-season produce like oranges, coconut, papaya and passion fruit to eat or make juice or teas with. There is a BBQ area and a camping area ($5 per person) as well. Beach access is through Cabañas La Tortuga, just across the way. Tel: 05-258-9365, E-mail: laiguana2@gmail.com, URL: www.hotelayampe.com.
Updated: Sep 19, 2012.

Finca Punta Ayampe

($16-23 per person) Finca Punta Ayampe is secluded in the middle of the forest just south of Ayampe and has beautiful views of the ocean. The lodge itself maintains the natural, rustic feeling of the surroundings, which have lots of lovely flowers and plants. It has a total capacity for 38 people in private double- or quadruple-occupancy rooms and in five cabins set apart from the main building. These are more expensive but worth the privacy and views. The main lounge features various sitting areas, board games and satellite TV, with an eclectic mix of decorations, including bongos, hand-painted canvases, and large dreamcatchers. Tel: 02-222-3206/252-5849, Cel: 09-189-0982/077-6163, E-mail: info@fincapuntaayampe.com, URL: www.fincapuntaayampe.com.
Updated: Sep 19, 2012.

SOUTHERN COAST

Bungalows La Buena Vida

($25-30 per person) Built with surfers in mind, this small resort handcrafted with local materials consists of six modern, ecological bungalows. The rooms are comfortable and spacious, with orthopedic memory foam mattresses and glass sliding doors. Some also have air conditioning and TVs. Private bathrooms come equipped with towels, shampoo, toothpaste and bottles of water. La Buena Vida's restaurant serves awesome, American-style breakfasts all day long, and breakfast is included in the room price. It also has a mini-spa that offers massages, manicures and pedicures, and a personal trainer that can lead fitness classes. Owned by an American couple, the husband, Keith, is the lead surf instructor and runs hourly classes. La Buena Vida also offers all-inclusive surf packages. Tel: 09-486-3985, E-mail: info@surflabuenavida.com, URL: www.surflabuenavida.com.
Updated: Sep 19, 2012.

El Campito Lodge

(ROOMS: $70-120) El Campito is a complex of cabins lauded as an ecological art lodge, and is surrounded by primary and secondary rainforest (as opposed to the area's predominant dry forest). It is just a few minutes away from the beach of Ayampe, retaining a private and secluded feel. The high-end bungalows with exposed brick interiors and earthly tones all have private porches with hammocks. The nicer ones have king-sized beds and flat-screen TVs with Direct TV, and the VIP suite even has a private outdoor Jacuzzi. However, there is also a pool and a Jacuzzi that any of the guests can use. El Campito's common area—with intricate wood-carved statues, wicker furniture and pool tables—combines nature and art really beautifully. Tel: 09-449-5228, E-mail: contacto@elcampitoartlodge.com, URL: www.elcampitoartlodge.com.
Updated: Sep 19, 2012.

Los Orishas

($10-15 per person) Owned by a group of welcoming Italian and Ecuadorian friends, Los Orishas is a quiet and comfortable place to rest your head in Ayampe. Located across from a lagoon and just steps from the beach, the Los Orishas' rooms are spacious and clean, with private bathrooms and queen-sized beds.

For the price, you may be surprised to find thoughtful details like filtered water in the rooms as well as towels and a bar of soap—happy surprises for tired travelers. Los Orishas also doubles as a pizzeria at night, serving brick-oven pizzas, pasta and seafood dishes after 7 p.m. ($6-15) in a chill outdoor seating area. It also has wine, beer, cocktails and sangria to sip on as you eat. In high season, breakfast is included in room prices. There is WiFi inter offered throughout the place as well. Camping is also possible. Ca. La Laguna, Malecón de Ayampe, Cel: 09-9966-9129/8677-9792/8001-7662, E-mail: info@losorishashostal.com, URL: www.losorishashostal.com.
Updated: Jan 14, 2013.

Ayampe Restaurants

Slowly more restaurants are opening up in Ayampe. Most of the hostels in town have their own restaurants, making it convenient to go from bed to beach to brunch. However, a few other places have popped up, providing a nice change of atmosphere. Several foreign-owned restaurants are now part of Ayampe's food scene, so you will be able to find awesome American-style breakfasts, brick-oven pizza, organic vegetarian plates and Mexican-style food, in addition to the standard seafood plates.
Updated: Jan 14, 2013.

Picantería El Paso

(ENTREES: $5-12) This bright and breezy beach shack-style restaurant owned by a local family might not look much, but the seafood here is as fresh as it gets, the portions are generous and the food is mighty tasty. Moreover, with not many eating options available in Ayampe, El Paso makes a great change from eating at your hotel. Fill yourself up on prawns, squid, fish, burritos, chicken or pasta; all of the dishes are made to order. It also makes great juices and milkshakes, or has beers and cocktails to accompany your meal instead if you'd prefer to get a buzz. Daily 8 a.m.-10 p.m. Located along the main road in Ayampe running from the highway to the beach, diagonal the football field, Tel: 08-916-7035.
Updated: Sep 19, 2012.

Pizzarte Trattoria

(PIZZAS: $8-15) This quiet eatery with just five outdoor tables cooks up 10 different kinds of artisanal pizzas in its large wood-burning oven, including *tres quesos* (three cheese), vegetarian, Hawaiian (jam, pineapple and cheese) and pesto. The Peruvian owner also makes fresh, homemade ciabatta bread, and each day, there is a "pasta of the day" option that changes. Wash it all down with a glass or pitcher of delicious sangria. On Thursdays, PizzArte runs Bingo night, and during high season, it sometimes hosts live bands. The place itself is also a rotating art exhibit showcasing the work of local artists, and has much of the artwork for sale. Wednesday-Monday 6:30 p.m. on. Tel: 08-642-2705, E-mail: patybazo@aol.com.

Surf Restaurant Ayampe

(ENTREES: $3-7) Owned by Finca Punta Ayampe, this colorful restaurant right on the beach has a bunch of vegetarian options. Big glass windows look out onto the ocean, which can be seen from nearly every table, or you can sit outside on the balcony and eat your meal to the sound of waves. Inside, there are also three elevated platforms where you can sit on cushions instead of chairs. Quirky details like fabric Moroccan lanterns, classic rock posters of Jimi Hendrix and the Grateful Dead, and psychedelic artwork give it a funky vibe. Surf Restaurant Ayampe serves typical international fare like quesadillas, hamburgers, pizza and gigantic burritos, and has breakfasts and desserts; the food is decent, but nothing spectacular. Monday and Wednesday-Sunday 8:30 a.m.-10 p.m. Malecón, Tel: 09-189-0982/08-626-8967, E-mail: urf.restaurant.ayampe@gmail.com, URL: www.fincapuntaayampe.com / www.facebook.com/pages/Surf-Restaurant-Ayampe/341763029181427. Updated: Sep 19, 2012.

MONTAÑITA

 8m   1,653   04

The lively beach town of Montañita is a mecca for surfers, hippies and party-goers, and has grown quite the reputation among foreigners. About 3.5 hours north of Guayaquil and a little over an hour south of Puerto López along the Ruta del Sol, Montañita is one of the few Ecuadorian beach towns with a great selection of international restaurants and hostels for all budgets and indeed at times you may forget you're in Ecuador, such is the international vibe of the town.

When To Go

Prices tend to be higher from December to the beginning of April, when the weather is the warmest and best, and the Ecuadorian beach season flourishes with Guayaquileños fleeing from the city en masse. Later in the year, prices and temperatures drop and it´s generally overcast. During Carnival (in February) Montañita hosts water sports events that include bodyboarding, scuba diving and windsurfing - all of which attract tourists and locals in huge numbers.

Montañita has gained it's place among popular destinations along the international surfing circuit thanks in large part to its strong, consistent waves. Exceptional tubes, typically from January to March, make this place a thrill for experienced and new surfers alike, breaking at up 2 meters (6.5 feet) sometimes. Normally however, the waves are no more than half a meter to a meter (3 feet) high throughout the year. Updated: Apr 18, 2013.

Getting To and Away from Montañita

BY BUS

Montañita does not have a bus station. Only **Cooperativa Libertad Peninsular**,which services regular buses between Montañita and **Guayaquil** (3 hr, $5.50), has an office on Avenida Vicente Rocafuerte, diagonal from Escuela José Maria Laquencia, from where its buses leave:

Montañita to Guayaquil: 4:45 a.m., 5:45 a.m., 10 a.m., 1 p.m., 3 p.m., 5 p.m.

Guayaquil to Montañita: 5 a.m., 6 a.m., 7 a.m., 1 p.m., 3 p.m., 8:30 p.m.

Before you buy your ticket, confirm that the bus you want to go on is direct, as not all are and those that are not make many stops along the way, taking at least 30 minutes longer to arrive.

Otherwise, you can catch any north- or south-bound green Manglaralto bus or blue-and-white CITUP bus that passes the Carretera Principal, or Ruta de Spondylus, every 15-30 minutes. These buses go up and down the coast between Manta and Santa Elena. The bus stop in Montañita is on the Ruta de Spondylus, near the corner of Avenida Vicente Rocafuerte.

There are no direct buses between Quito and Montañita. There are a few options: take an overnight bus to **Puerto López** with Reina del Camino (11 hr, $13), then another bus down the coast (1.25 hr, $2.50); travel to **Manta** by bus (8 hr, $9-10) and then south down the coast (3.5 hr, $5); go to **La Libertad** with TransEsmeraldas (9 hr, $10), then catch one of the frequent buses up the coast

SOUTHERN COAST

(1.25 hr, $2.50); or take a bus to **Guayaquil** (8 hr, $9) and go up from there (3 hr, $5.50).

BY AIR

The fastest way to get to Montañita from **Quito** is by plane. Most people fly to **Guayaquil** (45 min-1 hr, around $100-150 round-trip), then take the three-hour bus from there. However, it is also possible to fly to **Manta** (45 min, $110 round-trip) and travel down to Montañita on a local bus or by private transport.

BY TAXI

Since many of the destinations on the coast are located within close reach of each other, it is also feasible (and more convenient if traveling with lots of luggage) to take taxis between them. Taxis from Montañita to the nearby towns of Olón and Manglaralto cost $1.50, while those to Dos Mangas cost $5. It is also possible to take taxis to further-away destinations, such as Puerto López ($25), Los Frailes ($30, plus $10 per hour to wait), Salinas ($35) and Guayaquil (around $80). Updated: Sep 13, 2012.

Getting Around Montañita

Montañita is a walkable town and everything you should need will be within close reach. If you are staying at La Punta, it is recommended that you take a taxi to town or back after dark; the ride costs $1.50. Although buses frequently pass along the Carretera Principal, or Ruta de Spondylus, to destinations north and south along the coast, you can also hire a taxi to take you.

The company **Taxi Convencional Montañisol** (Tel: 04-206-0144, Cel: 09-8378-2643/8279-5312, E-mail: montañisol@gmail.com) has a stand at the corner of Avenida Segundo Rosales and Vicente Rocafuerte. It costs around $1.50 to Olón or Manglaralto, $5 to Dos Mangas, $25 to Puerto López, $30 to Los Frailes (and $10 per hour to wait, if you want the same taxi to bring you back), $35 to Salinas and $80 to Guayaquil.

Montañita Services

MONEY

Montañita only has one bank, **Banco Bolivariano** (Guido Chiriboga, near corner of Ca. Segunda, next to Hotel Montañita), with pretty inconvenient hours (Monday-Saturday 10 a.m.-1:30 p.m. and 2-3 p.m.). It usually has long lines, so plan accordingly. Next door, there is an ATM. Another ATM (Banco de Guayaquil) is located on Calle Segunda, between Guido Chiriboga and 10

de Agosto. Across the street is a **Western Union** booth (daily 9 a.m.-5 p.m.), where you can send or receive money. On Vicente Rocafuerte, near the corner of 15 de Mayo, you can find a **MoneyGram** booth (Monday and Thursday-Sunday 10 a.m.-10 p.m., Tuesday-Wednesday 10 am.-8 p.m.).

TOURISM

There is no official tourism office in Montañita, but the tour operator **MontañiTours**, at the corner of Avenida Guido Chiriboga and Rocafuerte (Tel: 04-206-0043), has friendly-English-speaking staff with lots of information about the town and its surroundings. The **police station** (Tel: 09-586-0991) is on 10 de Agosto, a block from Farmacias Cruz Azul and right in front of the football field.

KEEPING IN TOUCH

It shouldn't be too much of a problem staying connected while in Montañita; most restaurants and hotels here are equipped with WiFi. One of the nicest Internet cafés in town is **Shemesh.net**, which has eight modern computers with Skype and webcams ($1.50 per hour. Monday-Friday 9 a.m.-10:30 p.m, Saturday-Sunday 8 a.m.-10:30 p.m. Ca. 10 de Agosto and Ca. Segunda, diagonal Hola Ola). You can also store your bags in a locker here for $0.50 for an hour or $3 for the day. **"Mis Cabinas"** also has several computers with Skype and phone booths from where you can make national or international calls (daily 8 a.m.-midnight. Av. Primera A and Guido Chiriboga). Calls to the U.S. here costs $0.32 per minute and the Internet costs $1 per hour. Montañita does not have a post office.

MEDICAL

Montañita does not have a hospital; the closest one is in Manglaralto, three kilometers (1.9 mi) away. **Hospital Manglaralto** (Tel: 04-290-1192) is open 24 hours and is a free clinic. There are plenty of pharmacies around town, including **Farmacias Cruz Azul** (Daily 8 a.m.-1 a.m.; open 24 hours one week per month on rotating system) at Avenida 10 de Agosto and Rocafuerte.

LAUNDRY

The most reliable and recommended laundry place in town is **"Lavandaría Juanita,"** next to the taxi station on Calle Segundo Rosales (Tel: 09-741-3763). She charges $0.50 per pound, and if you drop your laundry off in the morning, she can have it washed and dried by the afternoon.

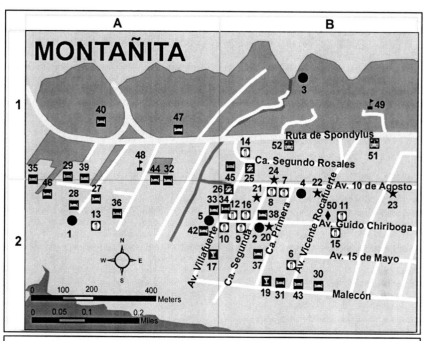

MONTAÑITA

● Activities

1 Escuela del Surf A2
2 Local Pro Surf School B2
3 Montañita Canopy B1
4 Montañita Spa B1
5 Surf and Fitness Gym A2

🍴 Eating

6 Bar-Restaurante El Punto B2
7 Hola Ola B2
8 Kapadonkia B2
9 Karukera B2
10 La Casa Blanca B2
11 Mamapacha B2
12 Papillón Crepería B2
13 RestoBar Guacamayo
   Grill and Wok A2
14 Soluna Café   B1
15 Tiburón B2
16 Tiki Limbo B2

🍸 Nightlife

17 Caña Grill A2
18 Hola Ola (See 7)
19 Nativa Bambu B2

★ Services

20 Banco Bolivariano B2
21 Banco de Guayaquil ATM B2
22 Farmacias Cruz Azul B2
23 Police Station B2
24 Shemesh.net B1

🖼 Shopping

25 Soluna Artisana B1
26 Tagua 950 B2

🛏 Sleeping

27 Cabaña Comuna Montañita A2
28 Cabañas Arena Guadua A2
29 Casa del Sol A1
30 Charo's Hostal B2
31 El Centro del Mundo B2
32 Hostal Esperanto A1
33 Hostal Pakaloro A2
34 Hostal Papaya B2
35 Hotel Baja Montañita A1
36 Hotel Kundalini A2
37 Hotel Montañita B2
38 Hotel Tsunami B2
39 La Balsa Surf Camp A1
40 La Barranca A1
41 La Casa Blanca (See 10)
42 Majagua Adventure
   Boutique Hostel A2
43 Mochica Sumpa B2
44 Paradise South A1
45 Rivera Suites Hotel B1
46 Rosa Mistica A2
47 Swisspoint Montañita A1

↗ Spanish Schools

48 Mar Azul Spanish School A1
49 Montañita Spanish School B1

♦ Tours

50 MontañiTours B2

🚍 Transportation

51 Bus Stop B1
52 Cooperativa Libertad
   Peninsular B1

SOUTHERN COAST

PHOTOGRAPHY

Foto Estudios Gutierrez (daily 8 a.m.-10:30 p.m. 15 de Mayo and Av. Javier Ledesma. Tel: 09-413-9357) sells memory cards, film and batteries for cameras, and can quickly print photos from USB drives and memory cards. It also does passport and visa photos if you need either ($6 for 4 photos).

SPORTS

Custom-Made Surfboards and Repair

Interested in specially handmade balsa surfboards? If *si*, visit local, renowned shaper, Victor Garcia. Victor's been making *tablas de surf* (surfboards) for over 35 years. Locals and tourists come from all over for a board or repair work. Victor is a simple, humble, kind soul who pays passionate detail to his boards; he falls in love with each one. He has also started a new apprenticeship program where you can pay to learn how to make your own board; contact him directly for more details. Victor's *taller* (workshop) is located between Montanita and Manglaralto in a three-story treehouse with a green tin roof. Victor has no set schedule, calling ahead is preferable, but not necessary. Between Manglaralto and Montanita, off Kamala Rd.;North of the bridge from Manglaralto: turn left on Kamala Road, take 1stright, Tel: 09-9484-2426/6969-0092, E-mail: vicgarmanglar(at)hotmail.com, URL: www.facebook.com/vicgarshaper.
Updated: Jan 18, 2013.

Things To See and Do in Montañita

Most people come to Montañita for sun and surf. However, you can pass your time many other ways here, whether it be receiving a spa treatment, pumping some iron, studying Spanish or participating in adventure sports. **Casa del Sol**, near La Punta, is Montañita's only yoga studio and has dance, yoga, martial arts and nia classes. The "**Local Pro Surf Shop**" also hosts salsa classes every Monday through Friday 8-9 p.m. ($15). If you'd like to get out of town, you can visit some of the nearby beaches, like Olón or Manglaralto, or hire a local guide in the community of Dos Mangas.
Updated: Dec 19, 2012.

Montañita Spa

(SESSION: $8-40) Montañita Spa is the place to pamper yourself after a long day of surfing or a crazy night of partying—or just because you want to. On Mondays and Tuesdays, it has a manicure and pedicure deal for $10. All week long, you can combine a 20-minute massage with a mind-clearing session in its sauna for $15. Otherwise, you can get your hair cut in the upscale salon, get your eyebrows or bikini line waxed, or enjoy a relaxing massage or reflexology treatment. 10 de Agosto and Ca. Primera A, near Farmacias Cruz Azul, Tel: 08-951-3779.
Updated: Sep 13, 2012.

Surf and Fitness Gym

(SESSION: $4 per day) If you want to maintain your beach body while in Montañita, you can go to this centrally located gym. Surf & Fitness has lots of weight machines, free weights and stationary bikes, but no treadmills or ellipticals. It also has personal trainers who can assist with specialized workout plans, and offers some classes, including spinning, aerobics, power abs and crossfit. You can pay per day or get a monthly pass, depending on how long you will be in town. Ca. Villafuerte and Av. Guido Chiriboga, next to Majagua Adventure Boutique Hostel and across from Hostal Papaya.
Updated: Sep 14, 2012.

Surfing

Montañita has quite the reputation among surfers of all levels of experience. Not only is it one of the best places in Ecuador to learn surfing, but La Punta (The Point)—which is at the northern end of Montañita's beach—is known for having the longest right surf break in Ecuador and has waves that reach up to three meters (9.8 ft) high in good conditions. Every year, Montañita also hosts a national surfing championship.

Especially on the beach between the town center and La Punta, it seems as if there is a surf school every few meters. Most offer two-hour lessons for $20-25 and surfboard rentals for $4-6 per hour. The lessons usually include a technical land component and a supervised in-water session.

Two recommended schools are:
"**Escuela de Surf**"—on the beach north of Montañita's town center. Tel: 09-232-7110. It has six instructors, some of who speak English and one who was selected to surf in Montañita's surfing championship.

"**Local Pro Surf Shop**"—daily 8 a.m.-7:30 p.m. Av. Guido Chiriboga, between Ca. Segunda and Av. Primera A. Tel: 08-860-2545. Certified by the International Surfing Association, this surfing school—which opened in 1996—has national and international surfing

champions as instructors. It also doubles as a surf shop and sells surfboards, wetsuits and other equipment.
Updated: Sep 14, 2012.

Montañita Canopy

(PRICE: $10-20) It seems like zip-lines have been strung between the treetops of almost every popular tourist destination in Ecuador, and Montañita is no exception. Cables stretching 2,840 meters (9,318 ft) provide the ultimate adrenaline rush for visitors wanting to mix beach time with extreme sports. No matter if you choose to whiz across four, six or nine cables, everything will seem much more fun and adventurous from 80 meters (262 ft) in the air. You can book with Montañita Canopy directly or with any of the number of tour operators in town. Daily 9 a.m.-6 p.m. Located one kilometer (0.6 mi) from Montañita's center, in Barrio El Tigrillo, Tel: 08-003-0950.
Updated: Sep 14, 2012.

Montañitours

MontañiTours has a knowledgeable, English-speaking staff that can help you participate in local activities and plan your onward trip, whether it be elsewhere in Ecuador or internationally. It specializes in local extreme sports, and rents out scooters, dirt bikes and quads in addition to organizing paragliding, sport fishing, horseback riding, zip-lining and surfing trips. MontañiTours also reserves spots on whale-watching tours in Parque Nacional Machalilla, sells packages to the Galapágos, and works with tour agencies in Quito to book adventures in the Andes. You can also buy long-distance bus tickets to Peru or Colombia here as well as airline tickets. Monday-Friday 8:30 a.m.-10 p.m., Saturday 8:30 a.m.-4 pm. Closed Sundays. Corner of Av. Guido Chiriboga and Vicente Rocafuerte, Tel: 04-206-0043, Cel:09-133-1171, URL: www.montanitours.com.
Updated: Sep 13, 2012.

Shopping in Montañita

Montañita is filled with shopping opportunities, whether you want to buy a custom surfboard, some beachwear, a hand-woven bracelet by hippies, or any other souvenir. In the town center, especially near the main intersections, tables are typically overflowing with crafts along with vendors selling identical items, including pipes, hammocks, ashtrays, and jewelry made of shells. Prepare to be bombarded on the beach by wishful people and traveling artists selling pretty much anything under the sun.

If you'e looking for a one-of-a-kind piece, though, stop by **Soluna Artisana** (Monday and Thursday-Sunday 11 a.m.-midnight. Ca. Segundo Rosales and Simpilio Santo), diagonally across from Soluna Café. This small shop is chock-full of eclectic items, including jewelry, dresses, paintings, sculptures and furniture, some of which are from India or China and others that are made by local artists or visitors who have come through town. **"Tagua 950"** (daily 11 a.m.-8 p.m. Av. Villafuerte and 10 de Agosto. Cel: 09-9366-6484, URL: www.tagua950.com) has a beautiful collection of designer *tagua* (a palm tree seed native to the area) products, including necklaces, rings, earrings and key chains. The friendly Espinel couple, who owns the company, runs a tagua workshop in nearby Manglaralto, where they work with 10 families from the rural communities surrounding the town of Montañita.
Updated: Dec 19, 2012.

Studying Spanish in Montañita

There are only two official Spanish schools in Montañita: Montañita Spanish School and Mar Azul Spanish School. Some local tour operators may try selling Spanish classes, but these are essentially just booked through one of the two schools at a higher price. It is best to arrange any Spanish study through the individual schools themselves. During high season, book the classes with anticipation, because they tend to fill up.

Mar Azul Spanish School

Mar Azul Spanish School is a smaller, alternative option to studying Spanish with Montañita Spanish School. In addition to weekly programs, Mar Azul offers hourly group ($6 per hour) and private lessons ($8 per hour), which makes it easy to fit in a few hours of Spanish study without having to revolve your time in Montañita around it. Classes are either one-on-one or in mini-groups, which are capped at three people, and can be catered to any level of Spanish background. However, if you'd prefer to combine studying Spanish with yoga or surfing, that is also a possibility. Mar Azul can also arrange homestays with local families. Five minutes walking distance from the town center or bus station along the main road, walking north. The school is located down the second dirt passageway after crossing the bridge, Tel: 04-206-0001, Cel: 08-186-8213, E-mail: marazulspanishschool@gmail.com, URL: www.ecuador-spanishschool.com.
Updated: Sep 11, 2012.

SOUTHERN COAST

Montañita Spanish School !

If you want to get more out of your visit than lazing around and partying, Montañita Spanish School has friendly, innovative teachers and staff. You can learn Spanish for two hours in the morning and two hours in the afternoon, and enjoy the rest of what the town has to offer in between and later on. The school also combines learning Spanish with surfing classes, diving courses, salsa dancing lessons, volunteer opportunities and even yoga. It also offers accommodation with beautiful cabañas, a swimming pool and Jacuzzi, or can organize homestays with two meals per day. Take Avenida Vicente Rocafuerte to the main highway, cross the Ruta del Spondylus, and walk up the hill, Tel: 09-758-5207/04-206-0116, E-mail: info@montanitaspanishschool.com, URL: www.montanitaspanishschool.com. Updated: Sep 11, 2012.

Montañita Lodging

Lodging options in Montañita tend to be characterful and inexpensive because of the level of competition. A backpacker's paradise, the small town features one cheap hostel after another. If you don't like the look of one place, just keep on walking down the street. Especially during low season, prices can be flexible, so if you are traveling in a good-sized group or staying awhile, try to cut a deal. However, if you intend to sleep, consider staying outside of the town center. La Punta, which is north of the center, is a quieter spot with several nice mid-range options, and El Tigrillo, across the main highway, has some places where you can camp. Regardless of where you stay, expect for prices to rise during high season and on holidays (feriados) especially. Updated: Dec 19, 2012.

Hostal Pakaloro

($10-12 per person) Hostal Pakaloro is a multi-story structure with 28 private rooms, each with a spacious, meticulously designed wooden balcony and hammock. The hostel also has a nice grassy patio area to relax and meet other guests. Guests can use the communal kitchen and there is a laundry service available. Rooms are clean and all have private baths with hot water. It is very centrally located within town, and is only a short block away from the beach. Ca. Tercera and Guido Chiriboga, across from Hostal Papaya, Tel: 04-206-0092, Cel: 09-741-5413, E-mail: pakaloro2006@hotmail.com, URL: www.pakaloro.com. Updated: Aug 28, 2012.

La Barranca

($20-35 per person) La Barranca's rooms are spacious, clean and tranquil, each with a TV, air conditioning and private bathrooms. On the first floor you will find the restaurant, bar with satellite TV, and Jacuzzi. You can enjoy the beautiful view of the ocean and sunset from the hotel's terrace, which has hammocks. La Barranca is located a few feet away from La Punta, where you will find the best waves for surfing. If you are looking for a place to disconnect from the world, La Barranca is certainly an excellent option. Room prices include breakfast as well. La Barranca is located on the Ruta Del Sol between the center of Montañita and Olón's Santaury, across from the Points. It is five-minute drive away from the center of Montañita town, Tel: 04-206-0139, Cel: 08-850-6354, E-mail: info@labarrancamontanita.com, URL: www.labarrancamontanita.com. Updated: Aug 26, 2012.

Rosa Mistica Hostal

(ROOMS: $20-40) Rosa Mistica is one of several laid-back places in La Punta, right on the beach. It has two different room settings: four spacious and colorful cabañas close to the beach and several other nice but a bit more dated rooms set around a large garden with native plants. Almost all of the rooms have their own hammocks; the rooms closer to the beach have air conditioning, while the rest have fans. A definite perk is its restaurant called La Llamarada that sits right on the beach, just meters from the ocean, and has a retro feel to it. A simple breakfast, which is included in the room price, is served there every morning. Otherwise, it serves pizza, beer, fresh juices or batidos throughout the day. Ciudadela Bajo Montañita, La Punta, Tel: 09-798-8383/798-8383, E-mail: rosamisticahostal@yahoo.com, URL: www. hostalrosamistica.com. Updated: Aug 27, 2012.

Charo's Hostal

($15-20 per person) Charo's Hostal has modern rooms and is right on the boardwalk. The hotel is close enough to the center of town (one and a half blocks), yet at enough of a distance to offer a restful night's sleep. Rooms have either street or ocean views, but all of them come with private bathrooms, hot water and air conditioning. The rooms are very clean and the staff is friendly. The owners speak English and are very helpful. The property is quite large with manicured gardens, hammocks, a pool, hot tub, outdoor bar, and various plants and trees. At Charo's, you'll also find an excellent restaurant and bar with reasonable prices, great food and fast service. 15 de Mayo and Vicente Rocafuerte; there is also an entrance on the Malecón, Tel: 09-938-6474/04-206-0044, E-mail: charo117@msn.com, URL: www.charoshostal.com. Updated: Aug 28, 2012.

Hostal Papaya

($10 per person) The best rooms at Hostal Papaya are upstairs. There are a few downstairs rooms, one with a shared bath that knocks a few dollars off the price, but the upstairs rooms—especially on the third floor—are more colorful, spacious, and some have creatively hidden upper loft sleeping areas. Each room has its own balcony with a hammock and bathrooms with hot water. The hotel has a popular restaurant downstairs called Papillón Crepería. The staff speaks English, French and Spanish. Guido Chiriboga and Villafuerte, Tel: 09-607-0086, E-mail: hostalpapaya@gmail.com. Updated: Aug 27, 2012.

Swisspoint Montañita

(ROOMS: $40-50) Swisspoint Montañita is a charming thatched guesthouse a couple of blocks east of central Montañita. Rooms are bright and airy with colorful blankets, and all have air conditioning, satellite TV, and modern tiled bathrooms with hot water. There is a pleasant open porch area in the back as well as a small swimming pool, which is ideal for relaxing away from the noise that's typical of the town's center. Upstairs, there is a restaurant that serves filling multi-course Swiss breakfasts daily 9-11 a.m. ($6). Ruta del Spondylus, a few meters from the bridge, Tel: 09-132-8299, E-mail: swisspoint@live.de, URL: www.swisspointmontanita.com. Updated: Sep 12, 2012.

Majagua Adventure Boutique Hostel

($10-30 per person) Posing itself as an adventure boutique hotel, this brand new lodging option is part of a chain of boutique hotels throughout Ecuador. Opened in September of 2012, Majagua has 20 private rooms spread out over five brightly painted floors separated by sturdy bamboo staircases, including a huge fourth-floor suite with panoramic views of the ocean ($120). All rooms have plasma TVs with satellite cable, WiFi, soundproof windows and air conditioning, and are unlocked with magnetic card keys, giving it a very upscale feel. It also has one dorm with 20 beds, four bathrooms

and a small communal area with a TV. The whole place is very clean, and a restaurant and bar is expected to open up downstairs soon. Ca. Tercera and Guido Chiriboga, Tel: 04-206-0038/0046/02-228-0830, E-mail: info@hotelmontanitaecuador.com, URL: www.cialcotel.com. Updated: Sep 11, 2012.

Hostal Esperanto

($10-17 per person) This pentagonal wooden beach house-turned-hostel is a popular place for independent travelers. Rebuilt with recycled wood from the old house, Hostal Esperanto opened in March of 2011 and now offers six rooms with balconies and good mattresses. Downstairs, there is a fully equipped communal kitchen and a TV area with satellite cable and a collection of DVDs. The rooftop terrace has hammocks and an awesome view of the ocean and La Punta. If you aren't traveling with your own computer, the hostel has a laptop with Skype that guests can use for free. Although sociable, this is a quieter, more relaxed place than the party hostels in town. Two blocks from the bridge, toward the beach. Next to Paradise South, Tel: 09-970-4569, URL: www.esperantohostal.com. Updated: Sep 11, 2012.

La Balsa Surf Camp

($18-80 per person) A true surfer's haven, La Balsa Surf Camp has 12 private, spacious and well-lit rooms in sturdy cabañas that sleep two to eight people, just steps from the best waves in Montañita. They have big beds with comfortable mattresses and come equipped with fans and mosquito nets. The cabins are scattered throughout a garden with high leafy plants and come with huge balconies that have outdoor furniture and hammocks for relaxing outside.

La Balsa Surf Camp also logically runs a surf school ($25 for two-hour lesson) and offers board rentals ($5 for one hour, $8 for two hours). It also makes and sells custom balsa surf boards to those that are willing to spend a pretty penny on one. La Balsa's restaurant serves some typical coastal dishes, along with hamburgers, sandwiches and burritos to boot. Breakfast is included in the room price as an added bonus, and guests can choose from five different filling options to start their day. Located at La Punta, a 10-minute walk from the town center, Tel: 04-206-0075, Cel: 09-8971-4685/9757-2450, E-mail: balsasurfcamp@gmail.com, URL: www.balsasurfcamp.com Updated: Dec 19, 2012.

Don't want to leave? Never going back? Review it at vivatravelguides.com

Riviera Suites Hotel

(ROOMS: $108-161) One of the newest high-end hotels to open in Montañita, Riviera Suites Hotel is a modern and luxurious option that is especially good for families and groups. Centrally located in the middle of town and only a few blocks from the beach, Riviera Suites offers guests a slew of added extras, including access to the town's Surf & Fitness Gym and the steam sauna at Montañita Spa, air-conditioned rooms, filtered water, and a Jacuzzi with a view of the ocean. The hotel has 15 suites total—10 junior suites and five master suites—each with a living-dining room, kitchenette, spacious private bathroom, a LCD TV with cable, and a private balcony with views of the ocean and river. Malecón del Río, Tel: 04-206-0060, Cel: 09-9111-7777, E-mail: reservaciones@rivierasuiteshotel.com, URL: www.riviera-suiteshotel.com.
Updated: Dec 19, 2012.

Hostal Kundalini

($20-50 per person) If you would rather awake to the sound of waves than a nasty hangover, Hostal Kundalini may be the place for you. This relaxing, quiet place is located right on the beach, just a few-minute walk from the town center toward La Punta. In fact, Hostal Kundalini was one of the first beachfront houses built in Montañita and was previously a family vacation home. Its 18 rooms, which incorporate natural local materials like bamboo and decorative stones, are a bit rustic but generally clean, and each has its own private deck with hammocks and outdoor furniture. There is also a spacious, well-groomed lawn with trees, making it a nice oasis in this crazy town. On beach, a few-minute walk north of town center, Tel: 09-5950-5007, URL: www.hostalkundalini.com.ec.
Updated: Dec 19, 2012.

Hotel Montañita

($20-25 per person) Breaking from Montañita's classic hippy style, Hotel Montañita is a large, concrete block of rooms with a pool in the central courtyard. During high season, the Jacuzzi heats up on a deck overlooking the ocean. With space for around 170 guests and more than 10 years of history, the size and age seem to have faded away whatever personality Hotel Montañita could have had.

Rooms are fairly cramped, with thin mattresses and concrete bed bases, and are in desperate need of a good airing out. Discounts are available for groups of eight or more people. Guido Chiriboga and Av. Segunda, Tel: 04-206-0062, Cel: 09-913-7414, E-mail: hotelmontanita@hotmail.com, URL: www.hotelmontanita.org.
Updated: Aug 27, 2012.

La Casa Blanca

($10-20 per person) La Casa Blanca is at the northern end of Guido Chiriboga, about two blocks east of the beach. With capacity for about 50 people, this hotel has a relaxed, if somewhat old and musty atmosphere. The rooms are pretty standard bunkbed style, some with lofts, and one has ocean views. All have private bathrooms with hot water. There is also WiFi in the downstairs restaurant that guests can use. Guido Chiriboga and Villafuerte, Tel: 09-918-2501, E-mail: lacasblan@hotmail.com, URL: www.montanita-lacasablanca.com.
Updated: Aug 27, 2012.

Casa del Sol

($15-25 per person) Run by a Canadian yoga instructor, Casa del Sol is a relaxing and sociable hotel in front of La Punta, and the only yoga studio in Montañita. During high season, it hosts 15 yoga, dance, martial arts and nia classes each week in its bamboo studio, which cost $7 a session. It has a communal atmosphere, with rotating "family dinners" ($6-10) each week where the owner cooks healthy homemade meals, which are shared at wooden tables in an outdoor garden. Most nights, guests all gather around the downstairs bar and engage in conversation. Prices include real, rave-worthy breakfasts. This is a great place for solo travelers, or for those looking to disconnect and practice yoga on the beach. At La Punta, a 10-minute walk from the town center. There is an entrance on the beach, and another on the street., E-mail: info.casadelsolmontanita@gmail.com, URL: www.casadelsolsurfcamp.com.
Updated: Sep 10, 2012.

Paradise South

($8-25 per person) Paradise South is, ironically, just north of Montañita's town center. The hotel features cool, cave-like rooms with stone walls and iron frame beds, as well as a spacious lawn right close to the beach with a grill, pool and ping pong tables shaded by open-air huts. A small playground for kids and a simple weightlifting area are also on the grounds. Ask for a room in the cabañas closest to the ocean; they are the nicest. There is also one large cabin with a wood-and-stone interior for families, which has a private kitchen and bathroom. If you stay for

several days, you can negotiate a lower price. Two blocks from Montañita's bridge, toward the beach., Tel: 09-787-8925, E-mail: psmontanita@gmail.com.
Updated: Aug 27, 2012.

Cabañas Arena Guadua

($25 per person) With colorful and slightly sandy cabaña rooms right on the beach, Cabañas Arena Guadua (Bamboo Sand Cabins) is a relaxed, quiet spot. Smack between La Punta, where the best waves for surfing are found, and the hub for all-night parties in central Montañita, Arena Guadua is perfect for travelers who want a taste of both worlds. There are three cabañas that each sleep five people, which is especially convenient for families and groups. The beach bar serves pizza and burgers and has tables on a patch of private beach. Arena Guadua also has lounge chairs on the beach that guests can use. Prices include a continental breakfast. La Punta, Tel: 09-134-8791/08-273-6211, E-mail: arenaguadua@hotmail.com, URL: www.arena-guadua.com.
Updated: Sep 10, 2012.

Hotel Tsunami

($6-10 per person) Located on one of the biggest party streets in Montañita, Hotel Tsunami is reasonably priced with a fun atmosphere. Although you won't get an ocean view, there are rooms for large groups (including for eight or 10 people) with a private bath, colorful decorations and bamboo furniture. Downstairs, there is a pizzeria and bar with cocktails and hookah, which is open daily from 1 p.m. Guido Chiriboga and Avenida Segunda, Tel: 09-471-3853.
Updated: Aug 27, 2012.

El Centro del Mundo

($5-12.50 per person) El Centro del Mundo may just be the cheapest spot to sleep in Ecuador with ocean views. It is a three-story wooden building with dorm space for 27 people in the attic and plenty of porch space with hammocks to relax too. During high tourist season you won't want to lounge on your pile of mattresses (no real beds in the dorm space) for long; the rooms higher up get quite steamy even without solid walls. There is a communal kitchen as well for those who would like to cook food bought in town. It is located next door to one of the most popular nightclubs in town, so don't expect to sleep much here when it's late at night, either. Malecón and Vicente Rocafuerte, Tel: 08-619-3459.
Updated: Aug 27, 2012.

Hotel Baja Montañita

(ROOMS: $91-219) If you want to lord it in Montañita, then stay here at this high-class hotel north of the center of town on a quiet stretch of beach. Choose from rustic cabins, regular rooms or lavish suites. All come with air conditioning, cable TV and private bath. Enjoy the large swimming pool, gourmet restaurant and a range of spa treatments and you'll likely forget you're even in Montañita. Prices include buffet breakfast. Tel: 593-4-256-8840, URL: www.bajamontanita.com.ec.

Cabaña Comuna Montañita

($10-25 per person) If you are more interested in hearing the waves than the music of downtown, head north along the beach to this set of six thatched cabins. Situated right on the beach with a small bar but an otherwise tranquil atmosphere, they are great value for money and since they're only a few years old, you avoid the musty smell present in so much of the town's beaten-down accommodation. All have hot water, fans, hammocks, and tables and chairs. Each cabin sleeps four to six people. Carretera Principal via Olon, also entrance on beach north of the town center, near La Punta, Tel: 08-805-9111/08-058-8471.
Updated: Aug 27, 2012.

Montañita Restaurants

Montañita has so many restaurant options, it is not likely you will get bored of the food selection, even if you stay in town for a few weeks. Travelers from all over the world come to this party paradise, many who decide to stay and open up restaurants here, so you can find lots of international fare. Of course, being on the coast, the highlight is seafood, and you can sample delicious *ceviches* from stands on the beach or lining Avenida Vicente Rocafuerte between the Malecón and Avenida Guido Chiriboga. Vegetarians won't starve here, either. Most menus have at least a few vegetarian options, and there are even a few small vegetarian-only places scattered around town.

Karukera

(ENTREES: $6-15) Karukera has a similar menu to the other restaurants in the town center, serving *ceviches*, sandwiches, salads, and seafood and meat mains. Try the seafood platter in pineapple sauce for a taste of the tropics. It also has some French specialties like crepes and Chicken Cordon Bleu that complement the Ecuadorian coastal dishes featuring shrimp, octopus, calamari, fish and lobster. Karukera is also a bar that serves beers, cocktails and flaming shots, and sometimes hosts live music. Av. Guido Chiriboga and Costanera (corner), Tel: 09-427-0828/0737/212-7659, E-mail: karukerabar@hotmail.com. Updated: Sep 12, 2012.

Tiki Limbo

(ENTREES: $6-15) Serving up a little bit of everything delicious, Tiki Limbo is the place to go if you're not sure what you want, but know it better be good and plentiful. The restaurant prepares large-sized portions of oriental, Mediterranean, Italian and Mexican dishes, as well as six different types of burgers and several over-sized salads. If you are feeling a big indulgent, order waffles smothered with nutella or ice cream, or one of the big-enough-to-share desserts. Grab a seat in the island-themed indoor dining area or sit outside on the sidewalk to watch all the street action. Tiki Limbo also has a book exchange and WiFi. Av. Guido Chiriboga, between Ca. Segunda and Villafuerte, Tel: 09-954-0607, E-mail: info@tikilimbo.com, URL: www.tikilimbo.com. Updated: Sep 12, 2012.

Hola Ola Café

ENTREES: $6-16) This social hub is a popular restaurant by day and a bumping *discoteca* by night, making it easy to spend a good amount of time here while in Montañita. Its international menu has American-style breakfasts with pancakes and waffles that are available all day long, as well as salads, sandwiches, hamburgers, pizza and pasta. The promotion of a cheeseburger, wrap, salad or *milanesa de pollo* (chicken cutlet) with a soda and dessert is a good deal compared to the higher prices on the general menu. It has happy hour Monday-Friday 2-8 p.m., but if you'd prefer caffeine to alcohol, the cappuccinos are also really good. Also, when much of the rest of town is deserted on Sunday evenings, Hola Ola is open to feed you a filling meal. Ca. 10 de Agosto and Ca. Primera A, Tel: 09-494-9208/04-206-0118, E-mail: tomermadmoni@gmail.com, URL: www.holaolacafe.com. Updated: Sep 18, 2012.

La Casa Blanca Bar and Grill

($5.50-11.50) This centrally located restaurant on the ground floor of the hostel of the same name has two Peruvian chefs who whip up dishes native to Peru, like *tacu tacu de mariscos* (rice and beans with a seafood sauce), *tiraditos* (thin slices of raw fish in a spicy lime sauce) and *papas a la huancaína* (potatoes with a cheese sauce made with yellow chili peppers), in addition to filet mignon, grilled fish and risottos.

It has several large plasma TVs that play soccer games and a bar with an extensive cocktail list that has a happy hour from 3-7 p.m. every day. The restaurant also has some board games you can play while drinking or chowing down on a hamburger or *churrasco* (thin slice of meat topped with fried egg, usually accompanied by rice and French fries). Guido Chiriboga and Villafuerte, Tel: 04-277-7931, Cel: 09-318-3202, E-mail: lacasblan@hotmail.com. Updated: Sep 11, 2012.

Bar-Restaurante El Punto

(ENTREES: $5-7.50) A mellow beach bar and popular breakfast spot, Bar-Restaurante El Punto is right off the main drag in Montañita. El Punto brings the beach inside with its natural wood tables, coral centerpieces and a pebbled floor. In the mornings, travelers flock for the gigantic creole breakfasts and crepes with nutella. At night, the bar fills up with both locals and visitors as American music from the 70s and 80s plays on in the background. Daily 8 a.m. until people leave. Vicente Rocafuerte between 15 de Mayo and the Malecón, Tel: 09-953-1212, E-mail: barestaurantelpunto@gmail.com / exhibidoresbrillones@hotmail.com. Updated: Sep 11, 2012.

Mamapacha

(ENTREES: $4-6) Mamapacha is a small vegetarian restaurant with a rotating daily lunch menu consisting of soup, vegetables in a sauce over rice, and a glass of flavored ice tea. If you don't like the day's menu, or would like to dine here for dinner instead, Mamapacha always has veggie lasagna, soy burgers, burritos and salads. It also has five different breakfasts, including pancakes with lemon sugar or homemade bread with eucalyptus flower honey and butter.

Homemade desserts include carrot cake, brownies, orange cake and oatmeal cookies, and all are delicious. Accompany a slice with a cup of hot ginger-tea with lemon and honey or one of the many other teas available. The restaurant also has a two-for-one book exchange for those interested. Daily 8 a.m.-11 p.m. Guide Chiriboga, near Vicente Rocafuerte, two doors down from the pharmacy, Tel: 09-159-8856. Updated: Sep 11, 2012.

SOUTHERN COAST

Kapadokia

(ENTREES: $5-25) Kapadokia's stone archways and blue and white tones will make you feel as if you are dining on the Mediterranean Sea instead of near the Pacific Ocean. This upscale Mediterranean grill in the middle of Montañita serves authentic hummus, falafel plates, Turkish salads and shish kebab sandwiches beside plates of grilled lobster, chicken kebabs with rice, and tagliatelle with seafood. Splurge with an order of "surf and turf," ($19) and top it all off with a pitcher of sangria ($12) for the perfect meal. Daily noon-midnight. Corner of Ca. Segunda and 10 de Agosto.

Restobar Guacamayo Grill & Wok

(ENTREES: $2.50-5.50) At this artsy Argentinian-owned restaurant, you can customize stir fries or chow down on a grilled meat kebab right on the beach. Choose vegetables like broccoli, celery and carrots; mix them with spices like ginger, thyme and rosemary; and add in chicken, shrimp or bacon for a filling meal. Guacamayo also doubles as a cultural bar and hosts movies, theater, music festivals and artwork. It has outdoor seating on the beach at both tables and beds, which are covered by tents painted by unique artists who live in Montañita or those who have passed through town. At night, the bar serves beers and cocktails as well. Daily 11 a.m.-8 p.m., later when there are events. On the beach, north of Montañita's town center, toward La Punta., Tel: 08-299-5083.
Updated: Sep 12, 2012.

Papillón Crepería

(ENTREES: $3-12.50) Papillón Crepería has a mix of Ecuadorian, Argentinian and French food. As obvious from its name, it has many different crepe options, including a Mexican crepe stuffed with ground beef, rice and beans, and a tropical crepe filled with peaches, vanilla ice cream and sweetened condensed milk. Every day, between 4 and 7 p.m., if you buy one crepe, the second one is half off. On Wednesdays, all meals come with a free salad bar. Papillón has a drink special on Thursdays, where cocktails are three for $5.99 or $7.99, depending on the type. It also has eight different breakfast options. The whole place is painted in funky designs, and there is a colorful surfer mannequin jutting out of one of the walls that's supposed to be eye candy. Guido Chiriboga and Villafuerte, underneath Hostal Papaya, Tel: 09-352-1551/05-925-5763, URL: www.facebook.com/papillon.montanita.
Updated: Sep 12, 2012.

Tiburón

(ENTREES: $4-12) This small wooden restaurant does not look like much from the outside, but the menu is surprisingly eclectic and the owner is surprisingly friendly. Besides ceviches and other local specialties, it has lots of different types of homemade empanadas, including ones stuffed with cheese and seafood; ham, cheese and pineapple; and banana and chocolate. Some dishes have Thai influences, such as the green curry soup or the shrimp in a pineapple curry sauce. Risottos are also on the menu. Daily 10 a.m.-midnight. Guido Chiriboga and Vicente Rocafuerte, Tel: 09-359-2206.

Soluna Café ❗

(ENTREES: $4.50-8) This lovely little café on the eastern edge of town specializes in organic food and uses produce from its own organic farm in Dos Mangas. Here you can fill up on healthy, wholesome meals while listening to world music and sipping on ginger lemonade; it has plenty of vegetarian options. On Sundays, Soluna has a special brunch, with omelettes, eggs benedict or BLT sandwiches accompanied by fruit salad, fruit juice, home fries, and bloody marys, mimosas and bellinis. Every day after 4 p.m., Soluna's upstairs transforms into a cozy lounge with drinks and eclectic music. The owners are also involved in ecotourism and local charities, and can organize cheap tours to Dos Mangas. Monday and Thursday-Saturday 8 a.m.-2 a.m., Sunday 8 a.m.-9 p.m. Closed Tuesday and Wednesday. Av. Segundo Rosales, Tel: 09-214-9918.
Updated: Jan 29, 2013.

Montañita Nightlife

When it comes to nightlife, Montañita has it down pat. Most nights, excluding Sundays, you won't have a problem finding somewhere to drink a few cocktails or even go dancing. Avenida Villafuerte is better known as Calle de Los Cockteleros, or Street of the Cocktail Makers, and is lined from the Malecón to Avenida Guido Chiriboga with stands that sell large tropical cocktails for less than $5.

Several nightclubs are in the town center that have weekly parties and concerts, if you are looking for sweaty crowds and loud music, this will be your hotspot.

Otherweise, some of the other restaurants and cafés around town turn into more relaxed bars and lounges, providing quieter alternatives for those that seek it.
Updated: Dec 19, 2012.

SOUTHERN COAST

Hola Ola Discoteca

(COVER: $5-10) This open-air nightclub with a small pool and elevated stage really heats up on weekends, when it hosts all-night parties with live music and DJs. Thursdays are Ladies Night, when females can drink for free from 9:30 p.m.-midnight. On Fridays, Hola Ola has a Latin Party with an open bar and salsa, merengue and reggaeton music. Every Saturday night is the Wild On party with an open bar, dancers and jugglers. If you prefer singing to dancing, it also has karaoke nights on Tuesday and Wednesday. Ca. 10 de Agosto and Calle Primera A, Tel: 09-494-9208/04-206-0118, E-mail: tomermadmoni(at)gmail.com, URL: www.holaolacafe.com / www.holaolacafe.blogspot.com.
Updated: Sep 18, 2012.

Nativa Bambu Discoteca

Run by a Spanish entertainment company, Nativa Bambu is a multi-story, European-style *discoteca* right on the beach. With a capacity for 1,000 people, this thumping nightclub also has an upstairs lounge with outdoor seating. Tuesday night is Montañita Night, when there is live rock music upstairs and ladies can drink free sangria all night, and Wednesday night is Caribbean Night, with drink specials and live DJs. No matter what happens earlier on, the club switches personalities after 1 a.m. and blasts electronic music until the wee morning hours. Nativa Bambu hosts different events each week, so check the calendar on its website to see what's up. Malecón and Ca. Primera A, Tel: 04-206-0095, URL: www.nativabambu.com/nativa.htm.
Updated: Sep 18, 2012.

OLÓN

Olon is a nice getaway beach where you can enjoy the calm Pacific waters with out the overcrowded, party-scene that is common in Montañita. The town itself is located about six miles from Santa Elena and 195 km from the town of Guayaqui, and just a 5-minute taxi ride from Montañita.

The sand here has a dark color along with a swell that's pretty decent. This might be a perfect place to come and practice water sports like surfing and windsurfing, while simultaneously deviating from the crowds and mainstream that tends to flow into all of Montañita up north.
Updated: Apr 18, 2013.

Olón Lodging

Samai Ocean Lodge Spa

(ROOMS: $45-115) Located on the San Jose Hill, with views of the sea stretching out 100 meters (330 ft) below, the Samai Ocean Lodge Spa combines holistic healing programs with comfortable accommodation, and is the place to go for a spiritual and emotional breath of fresh air. Natural accommodations with feng shui-oriented architecture complement the ocean views, while the restaurant offers delicious vegetarian food—so good, in fact, that even carnivores may be tempted to convert.

In conjunction with Sacred Journeys Inc., owners Ed and Tania Tuttle facilitate Shamanic adventures to the Andes and Amazon, where guests are introduced to indigenous healing techniques using traditional medicinal plants. Km 700 E15 Ruta del Spondylus, San Jose - Montañita, Tel: 07-281-4832, Cel: 09-462-1316, E-mail: sales@samailodge.com / samaispa@yahoo.com, URL: www.samailodge.com / www.sacred-journey.com.
Updated: Sep 17, 2012.

Hostería NJ

($12-20 per person) This is a pretty wholesome place that offers its guests activities/tours around Olon. It's well maintained and also has rooms available for rent across the month, downstairs is a lounge area for guests to gather and hang out before hitting the beach or checking out the town itself. A restaurant is also available inside the hostel. Olon, Ruta del Sol., Tel: 04-239-0643 / 08-424-9495, E-mail: j27261@yahoo.com, URL: www.hosterianj.com.
Updated: Apr 18, 2013.

Jardines de Olon

(ROOMS: $25-150) Fourteen miles of pristine sand beach, less than a hundred feet away from the private house. It is in exquisite condition with three bedroom and three bathrooms, which fits up to eight people, a grand balcony and lush gardens, all fully maintained and guarded. There is a vaulted, hardwood interior with breezeways throughout. Local attractions include whale watching (June through October), surfing, hiking, a nearby jungle canopy zip Line, tropical bird watching, fishing, shopping and international cuisine. The nearest airport is in Guayaquil (about two hours away), language and concierge services are offered. Tel: USA 760 325 5989, E-mail: globalcitizen@dc.rr.com, URL: http://ecuafriendly.com.
Updated: Sep 15, 2012.

Finca-Hostería El Retiro

(ROOMS: $61-244) The Hostería El Retiro is a great place to spend a weekend with kids. The comfy rooms and cabins open right onto the swimming pool. Once the tykes are tired of splashing around, there is still plenty to do with a bird-watching path, a zip line, a climbing wall, horse-drawn carts, and even a visit to a farm and beekeeping area. In the meantime, parents can relax with a massage ($25 for 1 hr), also given on-site. The hostería's restaurant serves breakfast, lunch and dinner, and has provides an outdoor area with ocean views. Km 1.5 vía San Vicente de Loja, Tel: 09-450-1520/910-4109, E-mail: reservations@elretiro.com.ec, URL: www.elretiro.com.ec.
Updated: Sep 18, 2012.

Hostería Susi's

(ROOMS: $25-30) Located right in the central square of Olon, in front of the town church, Hosteria Susi is a family run hostel that's charming and clean. What's convenient is how close this place is to the main artery that cuts across town, which sends you on your way to Montañita in bus or taxi in just 5 minutes. Note that this detracts from the level of quietness in general. Rooms have air conditioning, which is a godsend given how hot the place can get, even at night. Calle Othmar Stahalin 217, in front of Olon's church, Tel: 04-278-8034/0177 / 098-676-2861, E-mail: navgio@hotmail.com, URL: www.hosteriasusiboon.com.
Updated: Apr 18, 2013.

MANGLARALTO

Manglaralto is a coastal town three kilometers (2 mi) south of Montañita. It is a pleasant escape from the touristy crowd with a sleepy square and a relaxing bathing spot at the mouth of the river.

Note that the currents are particularly rough here so swimming in the sea itself is not advisable. Restaurant options are very limited so you're best either eating in your hotel or heading into Montañita. Manglaralto is also very convenient for trips to Dos Mangas and Cordillera Chongon. Updated: Jan 21, 2013.

Manglaralto Lodging

Staying in Manglaralto is a great alternative to spending the night in nearby Montañita, especially if you are more interested in relaxation than partying. By booking one of Manglaralto's few lodging options, you will get a higher-quality place for a cheaper price than equivalent hotels or hostels in Montañita. However, the selection is not nearly as varied, and you will need to go to Montañita for better services, restaurants and nightlife. Updated: Jan 21, 2013.

Manglaralto Sunset Hostel

($20-30 per person) This is a better-known accommodation option with little to set it apart from Hostal Manglaralto, except that it's right off the seafront, but unfortunately comes with a particularly uninspiring view. Rooms have large in-suite bathrooms with hot water and independent entrances with a multicolored hammock; some also have air conditioning. The hostel has WiFi throughout and an on-site café and bar. It accepts MasterCard and Visa as well. El Oro s/n and Constitución, Tel: 04-244-0797, Cel: 09-9440-9687/9750-5104, E-mail: manglaralto_beach@yahoo.com, URL: www.facebook.com/manglaralto.hostel.
Updated: Jan 21, 2013.

Kamala Hostería

($15-25 per person) This hippy hideaway is by far the most interesting accommodation option available in Manglaralto. The set of individual cabins, which can hold between two and six people, are set around a small swimming pool just yards from the beach north of town. It takes some time to get to but that's precisely the point - the farther you are, the more relaxing it gets. There's also a bar, restaurant, pool table, board games, volleyball and a dive school available to keep you entertained; you can also book horse-riding and massages on-site. Located just past the Manglaralto River, 3 km/1.9 mi away from the heart of Montanita, Tel: 09-9942-3754, E-mail: kamalahosteria@hotmail.com, URL: www.kamala-hosteria.minihostels.com.
Updated: Jan 21, 2013.

Hostal Manglaralto

($10-15 per person) Manglaralto has a scarcity of accommodation options but this hostel has sea views, which other options lack, and is good-value, particularly compared with Montañita. It has 23 suites that can sleep one to five people each. Rooms are comfortable with hot water, and some have ocean views. There is a small restaurant downstairs with friendly service that serves breakfast, lunch and dinner. Avenida Principal de ingreso de Manglaralto, Tel: 04-290-1369, URL: http://hotelmanglaralto.com.
Updated: Jan 21, 2013.

SOUTHERN COAST

VALDIVIA AND SAN JOSÉ

If you're traveling between Machalilla and Montañita, you could do worse than stop for a couple of hours at these two towns, which blend into one another.

The northern town, **Valdivia**, is rather unattractive but has a couple of attractions to keep you busy. Its museum, **Museo Valdivia** (Tuesday-Saturday 8 a.m.-6 p.m.; admission: $1 adults, $0.50 students), has a small but well-organized collection of pottery, figures and artifacts from the five ancient cultures of coastal Ecuador: Valdivia, Machalilla, Chorrera, Guangala and Manteña. There is also a small excavation site that contains a skeleton and remnants of altars. The aquarium next to the beach has penguins, blue-footed boobies, baby sharks, a sea lion, aquatic birds and a fish tank. However, you may feel that these animals would be better off in the Galápagos rather than staying cooped up in small enclosures.

San José, one kilometer (0.6 mi) to the south, has a beautiful stretch of beach with plenty of seafood restaurants and is a good place to stop for lunch and a dip in the sea. Updated: Jan 21, 2013.

Valdivia and San J. Lodging

Hostería Cuna Luna

(ROOMS: $60-85) This welcoming hostería is as relaxing as the name sounds: "cradle moon." Conceived as a relaxing retreat but also a community tourism project employing local people, it's well worth staying here to escape the tourism crowds in more popular resorts. The cozy but breezy thatched cabins all have sea views, balconies, hammocks and private bath, plus there are no TVs or air conditioning to maintain a calm, natural environment. The restaurant serves a variety of Middle Eastern and seafood specialties such as prawns in coconut and passion fruit sauces. The owners are a Ecuadorian-Lebanese couple. Breakfast is included. Tel: 04-278-0735, Cel: 09-961-0927, E-mail: info@cunaluna.com, URL: www.cunaluna.com. Updated: Sep 17, 2012.

PALMAR

South from Manglaralto and Ayangue, La Ruta del Sol continues to hug to coast as it sails toward Salinas. Both Palmar and its neighbor Monteverde have pleasant beaches and popular cafés. Stopping at either town is a good way to break up travels further south, especially if you are keen on sticking your feet in the sand and catching some rays for a while. Updated: Jan 21, 2013.

Angauel Hostería Playa Rosada

($18.50 per person) Hostería Playa Rosada is located on a remote stretch of Costa del Sol beach, about three kilometers north of Palmar, which in turn is located approximately midway between Salinas and Montañita (it is closer to Montañita). The hostería is a retreat of sorts, offering tranquility and a beautiful setting for artists and musicians. It offers meditation and tai chi as well as massages, snorkeling, archery and adventure travel. The comfortable six-person cabins have hot water and hammocks, and are surrounded by Palo Santo plants. There are also private twin ensuites for those traveling in couples or pairs. About three kilometers (1.2 mi) north of Palmar. To get there, proceed about three kilometers (1.2 mi) north of Palmar, turn toward the sea when in Pueblo Nuevo at the Santa Paola church. If you have a jeep or other off-road vehicle, you'll be better off, because the road is in bad shape. Proceed to the coast. If coming by bus, get off any of the north- or south-bound coastal buses at the Cruz de Palmar and take a taxi to the hostel ($3) Tel: 09-482-1171, E-mail: playarosadaecuador@gmail.com, URL: www.playarosadaecuador.com. Updated: Sep 17, 2012.

AYANGUE

A sheltered bay is a rarity on La Ruta del Sol with most of the beaches exposed to strong currents, but the petite fishing village of Ayangue is a notable exception. Here the sea is very calm and so warm it's like taking a bath, making it a family favorite. Ayangue is a well-kept secret from tourists because it's a couple of kilometers from the main highway. If you aren't keen on walking the distance with your backpack, you will have to wait for a taxi or friendly local to take you, but it's worth the effort. Updated: Sep 07, 2012.

Getting To and Away from Ayangue

From **Salinas** there are northbound buses that will take you to **Ballenita**, **Valdivia**, **Ayangue** and **Palmar**. From Montañita there's also buses that head south towards Salinas and can drop you off along the way. Updated: Apr 18, 2013.

SOUTHERN

Things To See and Do In Ayangue

Besides relaxing on the beach, Ayangue is a great place to go scuba diving. The nearby Islota del Pelado is known for its colorful coral and for a statue of Christ that is submerged underwater there. You can walk to Playa Rosada (Pink Beach), a beach located 3.5 kilometers (2.2 mi) away, which is named so because the sand is peppered with *spondylus* shells, making it look pinkish.

You can also hire a taxi for $2 to take you to a lookout point called Mirador de San Pedro, which has pretty views. Ayangue is also a good place to try *parapenting* (paragliding), which is best experienced between 2 and 4 p.m., when the winds are especially good. Updated: Jan 29, 2013.

Scuba Diving

One of the most popular activities in Ayangue is scuba diving, and people from all over Ecuador and the world come to this calm coastal village to plunge underwater and explore the colorful coral and sea creatures nearby. Ayangue Ray Aguila Dive Center, right on the beach, offers scuba diving courses of all levels as well as diving tours. The PADI certification course lasts three days and includes four different dives ($350). You can also arrange one two-hour diving session ($120) to visit the underwater statue of Christ or see the coral and manta rays around Islote El Pelado, 15 minutes off the coast by boat. The dive center also leads snorkeling tours for a minimum of four people ($20 per person), as well as surfing lessons, canopy tours and parasailing. On the beach, Tel: 04-291-6162, Cel: 09-9023-9104/9346-2834, E-mail: ayanguerayaguila@hotmail.com, URL: www.ayanguerayaguila.com. Updated: Jan 14, 2013.

Ayangue Lodging

Since Ayangue doesn't see as much tourism as other towns on the southern coast, accommodation options are a bit limited here. However, it appears as if this will change soon, as several places have recently opened up and a few more are under construction and will be ready to host guests within the next year. Camping is not permitted on the actual beach, but is possible at two of the hostels, which allows budget travelers to sleep restfully for just a few dollars a night.

Most of the lodging possibilities are located within a few meters from the beach or have ocean views. While they rarely fill up during low season, it is wise to make advanced reservations during high season and holidays, when families from around Ecuador come to unwind, swim and go scuba diving.

Hotel Sol y Mar

($10-15 per person) Hotel Sol y Mar's rooms are dated and characterless, but all have TVs and private bathrooms with hot water. While it is not nearly the nicest lodging option to stay in town, it wouldn't be a bad place to crash for a night, especially if in a group or on a tight budget. Several of the rooms can sleep up to six people. You can pay a bit more for air conditioning and a balcony. Downstairs, there is also a communal sitting area with a TV, though it isn't particularly inviting. Av. Raúl Falconí and Ca. Principal, one block inland from the beach, Tel: 04-291-4014, Cel: 09-325-7956. Updated: Aug 29, 2012.

Hostal Pangora

($15 per person) This wooden beachside hostel is good value for the money. Its matrimonial and family-style rooms are clean, airy and comfortable, and there is a pleasant terrace with large hammocks from where you can see Ayangue's bay or watch the sun set. The common area upstairs is rustic but stylish, with wooden walls and woven furniture with black, orange and creme tones. Spacious hammocks are out front as well for lounding out in, giving the whole place a very laid-back vibe. On the Malecón, Tel: 09-845-9036, E-mail: hosteriapangora@hotmail.com / helen_cariv64@hotmail.com. Updated: Sep 07, 2012.

Cumbres de Ayangue

(ROOMS: $75-180) If you have money to spend and want something a little special, then head up to the top of the hills south of Ayangue. This hotel has one of the most spectacular locations on the Ecuadorian coast, perched on the cliffs with jaw-dropping—often hair-raising—views. The setting of the swimming pool is particularly impressive, with sheer drops on either side. However, the rooms are nothing special for the price, but all do have ocean views; you are really paying for the location. If you're short on cash, you can just take a taxi up for lunch at the hotel's very good restaurant, take in the views and then stay elsewhere. Located just outside of the town of Ayangue, via Santa Elena–Manglaralto, Tel: 04-291-6041/6100, E-mail: info@cumbresdeayangue.com, URL: www.cumbresdeayangue.com. Updated: Aug 28, 2012.

SOUTHERN COAST

La Rica Ruca Eco-lodge

($10 per person) La Rica Ruca Eco-Lodge is the most organic place in Ayangue, offering rustic bungalows made with natural materials as well as a camping area. Guests can use the communal kitchen and BBQ, go bird-watching or take walks to a nearby forest where Palo Santo grows. The caretakers of La Rica Ruca also lead ancestral ceremonies using heated volcanic rocks, herbs and aromas to self-purify and spiritually reconnect with earth, water, air and fire. It also has a small organic vegetable garden and sells a few different types of pizza on-site or for delivery. Calle 1 de Mayo, up the hill from the beach, Tel: 04-291-1-6117, E-mail: diarte_ecuador@yahoo.ed, URL: www.facebook.com/pages/La-Rica-Ruca-Eco-Lodge/200627677103.
Updated: Sep 07, 2012.

Muyuyo Lodge

(ROOMS: $25-95) Muyuyo Lodge is a compound of three bamboo Polynesian-style bungalows situated on a cliff in front of Ayangue's bay. The lodge has a beautiful ocean view and has direct access to Ayangue's main beach where you can practice a variety of activities like diving, paragliding, whale and bird-watching, among others. Once in Ayangue, turn to the right on Avenida Raúl Falconí (parallel to the beach) and advance three blocks, Muyuyo Lodge is on the left side, Zip: 593, Tel: 09-158-8610, E-mail: info@muyuyolodge.com, URL: www.muyuyolodge.com.
Updated: Sep 07, 2012.

Oasis Ayangue

($15-25 per person) Owned by friendly retired couple from Canada, this recently opened B&B consists of just four private rooms in the upstairs of their house. Two of the rooms share a bathroom, while the other two have their own; all of the bathrooms are clean and spacious. Oasis has a small swimming pool, a shared balcony with hammocks, and a bar downstairs with a pool table.

The owners can also cook up international snacks like nachos, pizza and hamburgers, being just about the only place in town that offers an alternative to seafood. Located just a block from the beach, this is a great place for budget travelers, families and groups looking to stay in the area for a night or more. Breakfast is included in the price. Tel: 09-176-5613, E-mail: oasis1ec@hotmail.com, URL: www.oasisayangue.com.
Updated: Sep 07, 2012.

Hostel Playa Rosada

($10-15 per person) Hostería Angauel Playa Rosada is located on a remote stretch of Costa del Sol beach, about three kilometers (2 mi) north of Palmar. The hostería is a retreat of sorts, offering tranquility and a beautiful setting for artists and musicians. They offer meditation and tai chi, as well as massages, snorkeling, archery and adventure travel. To get there, proceed about three kilometers (2 mi) north of Palmar and turn toward the sea when in Pueblo Nuevo at the Santa Paola church. If you have a jeep or other off-road vehicle, you'll be better off because the road is in bad shape. 24 km from Montañita, Cerro de Playa Rosada. From Cruce de Palmar take a taxi to hostería Playa Rosada. The taxi ride costs about $3 or you can choose to take a bus to Santa Elena and then from there take a taxi to Hosteria Playa Rosada. Tel: Cel: 593-9-482-1171, E-mail: playarosadaecuador@gmail.com, URL: www.playarosadaecuador.com.

Ayangue Restaurants

Dozens of *comedores* (small outdoor restaurants) line the beach, most with nearly identical menus centered around seafood. Ayangue is especially known for its cheap *langosta* (lobster), and you can enjoy a entire lobster on the beach for as little as $8, compared to the typical $20 price tag in many other restaurants along La Ruta de Spondylus. One recommended place is called 'Comedor Panchita,' whose warm local owner Panchita prepares some excellent *ceviches*, *arroz marinero* (seafood rice) and fried fish, in addition to grilled lobster and lobster in garlic lime sauce. Note, most of the restaurants close around 6 p.m., and after this time, food options are very limited, so plan accordingly.
Updated: Sep 17, 2012.

Photo by: wogo

SOUTHERN COAST

SALINAS

 3m   28,731   04

A hotspot for the Guayaquil elite, Salinas is an overpriced and often overcrowded beach town that most adventurous travelers tend to avoid. If you come here, bring plenty of money, as cheap accommodation is thin on the ground and restaurants are more expensive than other resorts. Note that Salinas is very seasonally-based; it's heaving with young couples and families between Christmas and Easter, particularly weekends, but often dead after June. However, that's not to say that the largest of Santa Elena's resorts has nothing to offer.

The long stretches of white sand beach in Salinas and its sister town Chipipe to the south are the main attraction, but get there early in the morning or visit out of season because the beaches get extremely busy and the charm of the place can be lost. If you don't mind spending an extra couple dollars for a good meal, then the upscale restaurants that line the Malecón are well worth sampling. Most have outside seating and are a good vantage point to watch the fashion-conscious Guayaquil rich set strolling beachside. Beyond the attractive Malecón, however, most of the town differs little from the characteristic dusty streets and aged concrete buildings found elsewhere along the coast and it's surprisingly ugly in places.

As the sun sinks behind the high rises, Salinas nightlife gets going and the town's discos and bars are another reason to stick around for a night or so. From July to September, another traveler makes its way to the shores off of Salinas: the Humpback Whale. Whale-watching tours can be arranged at offices in Salinas. If you miss whale season, you can also organize fishing and boat tours, water sports activities or city tours.
Updated: Sep 17, 2012.

Getting To and Away from Salinas

BY BUS

Transportes Occidentales (Ca. 18 de Septiembre OE2-14 and Versalles, Quito. Tel: 02-250-2734) has a direct bus to **Salinas** from **Quito** each night at 9:50 p.m., returning to Quito from Salinas at 8 p.m. **TransEsmeraldas** also has buses between Quito and Salinas, leaving Quito daily at 9:30 a.m., 8:50 p.m., 9:20 p.m. and 10:10 p.m.,
and from Salinas at 8 a.m., 7:45 p.m., 8:30 p.m. and 9:30 p.m. Alternatively, you can take a direct bus to La Libertad or Guayaquil and catch local transportation to Salinas.

Buses to **Guayaquil** (2.5 hr, $3.50) from **Salinas** leave every 15 minutes from 3 a.m. to 8 p.m. with one of three bus companies: Liberpesa, Cooperative Intercantonal Costa AzuL (CICA) or Cooperativa Libertad Peninsular (CLP). All leave from the small bus station on Avenida 5, between Calle 17 and Calle 18. To get to other destinations in the region, the best bet is to head to La Libertad, 30 minutes away from Salinas.

This is the transport hub for the whole of the Santa Elena Peninsular, and from here, regular buses head up the coast to **Manta**, passing through **Montañita** and **Puerto López** on the way. To get to **La Libertad** (30 min, $0.25), take a local La Transisca, Horizon Peninsular or Trunsa bus. Alternatively, you can take a taxi to La Libertad ($2) or Santa Elena ($3-4).

BY AIR

TAME has started offering flights from **Quito** to the General Ulpiano Paez Airport near Salinas since the end of January of this year. Alternatively, you can fly into **Guayaquil** and take a coastal bus from there. Flights to Guayaquil with TAME leave from Quito several times a day and end up costing around $85, round-trip.
Updated: April 14, 2013.

Salinas Services

Most of the services in Salinas are concentrated on the Malecón and the three streets located behind it, especially Avenida Gral. Ernesto Gallo (Av. 1).

MONEY

Several banks have branches on the Malecón. **Banco de Pichincha** is between streets 29 and 30, half a block from the Capitanía de Puerto (Monday-Friday 8:30 a.m.-4:30 p.m., Saturday 9 a.m.-1 p.m.). A **Banco de Austro ATM** can be found next to Yogurt Persa. A block away is **Banco de Guayaquil**, just past Calle 23 (Monday-Friday 8:30 a.m.-4:30 p.m., Saturday 9 a.m.-1 pm.).

KEEPING IN TOUCH

"**Claro Cabinas,**"on the Malecón next to Oh Mar and in front of the area where the boats are docked, has seven computers for Internet use. Internet costs $1 per hour (daily 8 a.m.-10 p.m.). It also has seven calling booths, from where you can make national or international calls. You can also download and print photos directly from your digital camera here.

MEDICAL

If there is a medical emergency, call 911, or 112 for an ambulance. The city's public hospital is located in Ciudadel Frank Vargas Pazos, next to the Salinas Country Club. It is open 24 hours and has free consultations; it is only OK for general consultations for those who speak Spanish, as it does not have a lot of specialists and the doctors there do not speak English.

A much better option is **Clínica Fae**, the military hospital, located in the Chipipe neighborhood (Av. Séptima s/n and Ca. Atahualpa. Tel: 04-277-3764). There is a pharmacy on the Malecón, near the corner with Calle 22 (daily 9 a.m.-10:30 p.m.). Another pharmacy, **Farmacía Sabano**, is located just one block from the bus station, at Avenida 18 s/n and Avenida Gral. Enrique Gallo (Monday-Thursday and Sunday 9 a.m.-10:30 p.m., Friday and Saturday 9 a.m.-midnight; longer hours during high season. Tel: 04-277-3602).

TOURISM

Salinas' iTur office is only open during high season, which runs December to April. The one in nearby La Libertad is open year-round. The city's **police office** is on Avenida Espinoza Larrea, in Barrio San Lorenzo (Tel: 04-277-5813).

LAUNDRY

You can bring your dirty laundry to **Lavandaria "Piky,"** on Avenida Gral. Enrique Gallo and Calle 24 (daily 9 a.m.-5:30 p.m. Cel: 09-9918-4582), which charges $0.40 per kilogram.
Updated: Dec 19, 2012.

Things To See and Do in Salinas

Salinas' biggest draw is its beaches, and that is where you will find its visitors most of the time. You can rent a beach chair at Playa de San Lorenzo for $3 for the whole day and relax under the sun while sipping coconut water from fresh coconuts, or spend time in the water, whether swimming or on a boat.

You can stop by the 'Centro Artesanal Permanente,' where vendors sell artesanía like hammocks and jewelry made of tagua or shells along Calle Armando C. Barreto S.,

half a block from Banco de Pichincha. Other activities in Salinas include visiting the small Museo de Ballenas (Whale Museum), complete with skeletons of humpback whales, and watching the rough waves crash at La Chocolatera - South America's most western point, geographically speaking.
Updated: Sep 25, 2012.

La Chocolatera

La Chocolatera is the most western point in South America. It is called La Chocolatera (Chocolate Pot) because strong currents converge and swirl into the shore here, bringing sand to the surface and giving the water a brown, chocolate-like color. On a sunny day, it is possible to see multiple rainbows in the powerful crashing waves. Within La Chocolatera, there is also a colony of sea lions and a black-sand beach suitable for surfing and water sports but not recommended for swimming. During whale-watching season (June-September), it is highly possible to see humpback whales off the coast just from La Chocolatera on the coast.

Interestingly, La Chocolatera is located within the Salinas Naval Base, so be sure to bring an ID or copy of your passport to leave with the guard when you enter. If you don't have your own car, you can hire a taxi to bring you to La Chocolatera, wait for you for an hour and then bring you back to town ($10).

Keep in mind that the sea lion colony is a substantial walk from the point with the lighthouse, so if you would like to see them, you may be better off hiring a local guide to take you there. The area is located inside the Salinas Naval Base.
Updated: Jan 14, 2013.

Water Sports

All along Salinas' waterfront, you can arrange to partake in different water sports, including banana boating (8-10 min, $2 per person), high-adrenaline rafts attached to speed boats (called 'La Bestia,' 8-10 min. $3 per person) and jet skiing (30 min, $20).

You can go on a leisurely 30- to 40-minute boat ride ($20 per person) from the waterfront to the bay, passing Playa de Chipipe, with an opportunity to see pelicans and go swimming. The boats hold 20-30 passengers. Most of the people organizing these activities are located on the beach in front of Banco de Guayaquil until the Yacht Club, and are there daily from 9 a.m.
Updated: Jan 14, 2013.

Salinas Tours

Tours in Salinas, like everything else, come at a premium, but if you have money to spend you can set enjoy some high quality tours, especially boat trips.
Updated: Apr 15, 2013.

Pesca Tours

Whether you're a landlubber or sea aficionado, you're bound to find something to suit your fancy with this company. It was established in 1958 by Knud Holst Dunn, an avid fishing fan determined to turn his favorite hobby into a successful business. Although sports fishing is its specialty (as the name may imply), other popular excursions include city tours, boating trips and whale-watching (June to September only). All-inclusive tours include airport transfers, hotel pick-up/drop-off. If you're keen to keep anything you catch, simply go ahead and ask *el capitán* in the office and he can arrange to have it sent to a taxidermist. Malecón 717, next to Café Bar Jetset, Tel: 04-277-2391, E-mail: fishing@pescatours.com.ec, URL: www.pescatours.com.ec.
Updated: Sep 24, 2012.

CarolTour S.A.

This tour company, conveniently located on the Malecón, organizes a range of tours and activities, and is a good place to stop by for information on things to see and do in the area. Depending on your time and budget, you can choose from simple city tours to trips up the Ruta del Sol and specialized excursions like whale-watching (July to September), sports fishing and water skiing. Those keen to see more of Salinas can take the city tour; this three-hour tour includes visits to Los Marinos, Punto St. Elena, La Chocolatera, Artesenías Genesis and Museo Farallón Dillon. CarolTours can also make hotel arrangements, organize special events and customize tours. Daily 9 a.m.-1 p.m. and 3-7 p.m. Malecón, Condominio El Alcazar, ground floor, Tel: 04-277-0475, Cel: 08-517-2987/09-214-1875/753-8202.
Updated: Sep 24, 2012.

Salinas Lodging

Anyone accustomed to cheap dorm beds and plentiful budget accommodation options will be in for a bit of a shock upon arriving in Salinas. Lodging is more expensive here and if often booked up in high season; it is best to plan ahead. Hostels in Salinas have rates that would be considered mid-range in most other places. If you are willing to splash out, then there are plenty of high-quality high-rise hotels, many of which cater to business travelers as much as those staying for some sand and sun. Mid-range options are also available, but at higher rates than those in the same category at most other beach towns along the coast.
Updated: Jan 21, 2013.

Big Ralph's Hostel and Restaurant

($15-25 per person) Big Ralph's is owned by a friendly Ecuadorian-English couple and provides clean, air-conditioned rooms with a TV and WiFi. All of the rooms, which surround a tiled outdoor patio, have private bathrooms with hot water and showers with excellent water pressure. It is located in a quieter area of the city, about a 10-minute walk from the Malecón and beach, where most of the action is. Ralph is a British-trained chef and brings a taste of England to the Ecuadorian coast at his excellent on-site restaurant, which specializes in traditional fish n' chips with homemade tartar sauce.

Other menu options include shrimp or chicken in Thai curry sauce, lamb chops, braised beef with garlic mashed potatoes, and sea bass topped with parmesan cheese (entrees: $7.50-10). The restaurant's opening hours are Wednesday-Saturday 5-10 p.m. and Sunday noon-4 p.m., but they vary depending on the season. Av. San Lorenzo and Av. Carlos Espinoza Larrea (Diagonal from the San Lorenzo church), Sector San Lorenzo, Tel: 04-293-0910, Cel: 09-9618-8111, E-mail: bigralphhostal@gmail.com, URL: www.bigralphhostal.com.
Updated: Jan 14, 2013.

Hostal Aqui !

($18.50-25 per person) Hostal Aqui is much more than just a place to stay. It is also an excellent restaurant serving American food, including juicy hamburgers, pulled pork sandwiches, chili and meatball subs; a sports bar; and a well-known gringo hangout. The hostel's eight rooms all have private bathrooms, air conditioning, cable TV, digital safes and wardrobes, and can sleep up to five people. It prides itself on being a pet-friendly facility, and has a large English-language book and DVD exchange. The friendly American owners also organize fundraisers for children's life-altering surgeries. Even if you don't stay here, you can stop by for BBQ ribs on Sunday night, for steak night on Thursdays, or for real American breakfasts any day of the week. Ca. 10 and Malecón, Tel: 04-293-1353, URL: www.hostalaqui.com.
Updated: Sep 24, 2012.

SOUTHERN COAST

Francisco II

(ROOMS: $37-79) Francisco II offers visitors the opportunity to enjoy their vacation in a friendly environment designed for relaxation. Guests will find a secure facility with a family-friendly atmosphere and comfortable common areas suitable for socializing.

Rooms are pretty basic but all have air conditioning and a small TV with cable, and since it is located on the Malecón, most have beautiful views of the ocean. Francisco II also has a hydro massage pool and a garage where guests can park for free. Malecón, between Ca. 17 and 18, Tel: 04-277-4133/3751, E-mail: hotelfco_ii@hotmail.com, URL: www.hotelesfrancisco.com.
Updated: Sep 20, 2012.

Barcelo Colón Miramar

($65-95 per person) Barcelo Colón is the snazziest, most expensive place in Salinas, where the who's who of Ecuador spend the night. If you can afford to spend the extra dollars, this place is a sure-win in class, comfort and style. The nicer suites have a living room, mini-bar, coffee machine, bathtub and ocean views. Barcelo Colón also has a cocktail bar and lounge, sushi bar, restaurant with Spanish and Mediterranean cuisine, casino, gym, spa, pool and crafts shop, so you may never even need to leave the hotel.

It also offers all-inclusive packages with three meals a day, cocktails and activities. Prices depend on day of the week and time of year. Malecón, between Ca. 38 and 40, Tel: 04-277-1575/1610, E-mail: colonmiramar@barcelo.com, URL: www.barcelocolonmiramar.com.
Updated: Sep 24, 2012.

Hotel Marnier

($10-18 per person) Located just four blocks from the beach, Hotel Marnier makes guests feel right at home, whether traveling for business or pleasure. It has WiFi in all of the rooms, as well as air conditioning, cable TV, hot water in private bathrooms, an on-site restaurant and a garage for private parking. Rooms come in the single, double, matrimonial and family-style varieties.

The hotel can arrange private transport to and from the airport and also between Guayaquil and Salinas. Group discounts are available. Avenida Principal de Salinas, Ciudadela Italiana 5 Mz Solar 5, Zip: 593, Tel: 04-277-9588, Cel: 09-9374-4790, E-mail: rjara@hotel-marnier.com, URL: www.hotelmarnier.com.
Updated: Jan 21, 2013.

Hotel Chipipe

($25-45 per person) Set back from the busy Malecón in a quiet but well-kept part of Salinas, the orange blocks of Hotel Chipipe don't look like much from the outside, but the modern facilities and attentive service make this one of the better places to stay. Besides having pleasant rooms with air conditioning and modern private bathrooms, the hotel also offers a nice pool area and first-class restaurant. Children between 4-10 years old pay half price. American-style breakfasts are included in room prices. Ca. 12 between Av. 4 and 5, Tel: 04-277-0550/51/53, Fax: 04-277-0556, E-mail: info@hotelchipipe.com, URL: www.hotelchipipe.com.
Updated: Sep 24, 2012.

El Carruaje Hotel

(ROOMS: $43-147) One of the nicer places to spend the night in Salinas, El Carruaje Hotel has clean, classy rooms with air conditioning. Those with ocean views cost extra. Centrally located on the Malecón, it is within close reach of Salinas restaurants and nightlife, and, of course, the beach. The restaurant downstairs serves excellent national and international dishes. Prices are a bit steeper than other places, but it's not a bad place to drop a buck. Malecón 517, Tel: 04-277-4282, E-mail: hotel.elcarruaje@live.com, URL: www.hotelcarruaje.com.ec.
Updated: Sep 20, 2012.

Suites Salinas

(ROOMS: $45-110) Black leather couches, glossy floors and a modern reception area greet travelers as they enter Suites Salinas. Rooms are clean and modern with new furniture, and bathrooms come equipped with miniature soaps and bottles of shampoo. If you're only staying the night and have some cash to spare, this is a good option. Breakfast is included, and the attached restaurant, Cafetería Gaudua, is good place for coffee and a bite to eat. Corner of Av. Enriquez Gallo and Ca. 27, Tel: 04-277-4267/1682, E-mail: salinashoteles@gmail.com.
Updated: Sep 24, 2012.

Travel Suites

(ROOMS: $20-40) A palm tree-shaded modern building located away from the main drag maintains Travel Suites, a set of apart-hotels that are especially ideal for longer Salinas stays. Rooms are bright, modern and spacious, with a small kitchen area fronted by a tiled counter and equipped with a mini-fridge and modest cooking facilities. An outdoor courtyard with a few scattered

SOUTHERN COAST

hammocks provides a peaceful alternative to sand and sun. Facilities and prices are good value compared to other places lining the Malecón, and the atmosphere is notably more relaxed, making this a good option for groups. Av. 5, between Ca. 13 and Ca. 14, diagonal the Cruz Roja, Chipipe, Tel: 04-244-8677, E-mail: info@salinastravelsuites.com, URL: www.salinastravelsuites.com.
Updated: Sep 20, 2012.

Cocos Hostal

(ROOMS: $24.50-122) The bright and cheerful Cocos Hostal is the best-value option on the Malecón. Modern art adorns the colorful walls, and the rooms are of very good standard for the price. All 48 rooms have private bathrooms, a TV and air conditioning, but those with ocean views and additional details are more expensive. There's a game room and a beautiful terrace available to all guests. The downstairs restaurant and bar has a varied menu, ranging from pizza, pasta and toasted sandwiches to BBQ meat and, of course, seafood. Book in advance because this is a very popular spot. Malecón and Fidón Tomalá, Tel: 04-277-0361/0367, Cel: 09-948-9336, URL: www.cocos-hostal.com.
Updated: Sep 20, 2012.

Hotel Yulee

($8-15 per person) The cheaper rooms in this hotel are among the most economical in town. Housed in an old colonial-style building sitting behind the high-rises, Hotel Yulee is a charming architectural throwback. Bright yellow paint enlivens a sagging wooden façade, which leads into a modest but well-appointed dining area on the first floor. Upstairs, there are three levels of rooms. The cheapest are smaller with fans and shared bath; you pay a higher rate for spacious rooms with private bath and air conditioning. It does not have Internet facilities or WiFi. Av. Eloy Alfaro and Mercedes Molina, Chipipe, Tel: 04-277-2028/4325.
Updated: Sep 20, 2012.

Hostal Las Olas

(ROOMS: $15-25) A modern entrance leads into a simple reception area adorned with antique chairs and a few plants. Rooms are standard hostel-style but clean and equipped with private bathrooms, TV and air conditioning. If you're in Salinas and pinching for pennies, this is one of your most comfortable, best-value options. Ca. Las Palmeras 252 and Av. 5, in front of Cevichelandia, Tel: 04-277-2526.
Updated: Sep 20, 2012.

Hotel Oro del Mar I, II, and III

($12-15 per person) The first Oro Del Mar must have done fairly well, because Salinas now has two others of the same name. Spread out across Salinas, these hotels are a good budget option, offering simple, clean rooms with well-maintained private bathrooms and TVs. Air conditioning is also available in some rooms. Reception is friendly and helpful, and compared to some other budget options, the hotels feel relatively safe. Prices are the same for all three hotels. Hotel I: Ca. 23 and Gral. Enriquez Gallo, Hotel II: Ca. 18 and 2da Av., Hotel III: Av. 12 and Ca. 38, Tel: Tel: Hotel I: 04-277-1334, Hotel II: 04-277-1389, Hotel III: 04-278-6057.
Updated: Sep 17, 2012.

Hostería Ecológica El Faro

($45-50 per person) For a completely opposite experience to the glitzy Miami-wannabe vibe of the rest of Salinas, head to the northern end of Malecón and stay at this colorful eco-lodge. High-rise modernity is swapped for leafy jungle vibes and people-watching swapped for wildlife-watching. The gardens are filled with pines, palms and exotic flowers as well as birds, squirrels, tortoises, parrots and monkeys. The spacious rooms are decorated with local artwork and pine furniture, and the restaurant serves high-quality seafood. It's not cheap staying here but it will certainly be memorable. Breakfast included. Cdla La Milina, block G, Tel: 04-277-7334/293-0680, Cel: 09-787-4580, E-mail: hosteriaecologicaelfaro@gmail.com, URL: www.hosteriaelfaroecolodge.com.
Updated: Aug 21, 2012.

Salinas Restaurants

Salinas' restaurants are mostly concentrated along the Malecón or on the streets right behind it, though they can be found all throughout town—it is a city after all. Since the clientele in Salinas is known for being wealthier, most restaurant prices reflect such, and you may need to veer away from the touristy area to find a good deal. That said, there are plenty of places to eat, most of which specialize in seafood, and many of which have ocean views. Additionally, since Salinas is growing popularity among the foreign expat set, you can now find several gringo-owned restaurants where you can enjoy a taste of home. These places are great if you want to meet other travelers or expats, or just need a break from seafood. You will also find that most of the city's nicest hotels have their own on-site restaurants.
Updated: Jan 21, 2013.

SOUTHERN COAST

Yogurt Persa

(SNACKS: $1.50-4.50) For something to temper the Salinas sun, head to this hole-in-the-wall place specializing in frozen treats. An Ecuadorian chain, Yogurt Persa specializes in frozen yogurts and various types of *pan de yuca* (a cheesy bread made with yucca flour). You can also indulge in cheap (and greasy) fast-food fare like pizzas, hamburgers and hotdogs. It is only open in the afternoons, from 2 p.m. on. Malecón.
Updated: Sep 25, 2012.

Hotel Chipipe Restaurant

(ENTREES: $5-17) Located in the classy Hotel Chipipe, this restaurant bears the same style as its commercial neighbor. Tables are carefully set with maroon and white tablecloths, fanned napkins and wine glasses. Prices are excellent, considering the atmosphere and facilities, and the menu is extensive. Mains include sauteéd beef, *milanesas* (breaded chicken or beef cutlets), beef cordon bleu, curry chicken and spaghetti. It also accepts credit cards. Ca. 12, right between Av. 4 and 5, Tel: 04-277-0550/51/53, E-mail: info(at)hotelchipipe.com, URL: www.hotelchipipe.com.
Updated: Sep 25, 2012.

Jetset Bar and Discotec

An unassuming Malecón resident during the day, this place fills up when the sun goes down and remains bumping until the early morning hours. While probably not the most family-friendly place in town, it's a popular haunt for hip young Ecuadorians looking to drink and dance the night away. Malecón, next to La Bella Italia.
Updated: Sep 24, 2012.

Luv N Oven

(ENTREES: $4.50-10) While you could easily pass this place on the Malecón without giving it a second look, you'd be missing out on some of the best food in Salinas if you did. The friendly, English-speaking owner from Esmeraldas cooks up large portions of coastal favorites, like *ceviches, cazuela* (seafood stew), black clams in coconut sauce and oysters au gratin. While their forte is seafood, in the mornings you can also enjoy creole breakfasts with *bolónes* (fried balls of mashed plantains with cheese) and black coffee. Although a bit out of place on the menu, Luv N Oven also has risottos and spaghetti alfredo, for pickier eaters. Daily 8 a.m.-10 p.m. Malecón and Rumiñahui, Tel: 04-277-0513, Cel: 09-957-8101.
Updated: Sep 24, 2012.

Brasa Club

(ENTREES: $5-20) Going for a tropical theme, this restaurant, which is the Bar-Restaurant of Coco's Hostal, consists of thatch-roof buildings seemingly pulled right off the beach. The menu features 15 different types of broiled meat and paellas, so anyone in the mood for meat should definitely consider dining here.

You'll also find typical coastal cuisine on the menu as well as various soups, sandwiches and pasta dishes. At nighttime, Brasa Club is also a popular drinking spot where you can down a few cocktails or beers right on the Malecón. Daily noon-1 a.m., sometimes later. Malecón and Fidón Tomalá, Tel: 04-277-0361/0367, Cel: 09-948-9336, URL: www.cocos-hostal.com.
Updated: Sep 25, 2012.

Cafetería del Sol

(ENTREES: $4-15) This classy cafetería is the perfect place to sit and spend some time people-watching and enjoying the view of the beach. Start your day off with a cup of real coffee here, whipped up using an authentic cappuccino machine. Come later in the day if you'd prefer to sample one of its traditional meat, chicken, seafood and rice dishes, or want to calm a craving for international food like burritos, pizza or hamburgers. If you still have room for more, select one of the home-baked treats sitting devilishly behind the glass counter.

Prices are standard to expensive, but the atmosphere is certainly more laid-back at this end of the Malecón and there's room to breathe. Try the house special: *paella mixta* (paella with mixed seafood), if you have a partner to share with. Cafetería del Sol accepts credit cards. Daily 7 a.m.-midnight. Malecón, Playa de San Lorenzo, next to Banco de Pichincha, Tel: 04-277-2159/2307.
Updated: Sep 24, 2012.

La Ostra Nostra

(ENTREES: $3.50-12) Except for its Italian-looking sign out front, this place is pure Ecuadorian. La Ostra Nostra serves up a variety of traditional coastal fare, from fish and seafood to soup and meat dishes. The restaurant is a popular gastronomical hangout with a flair for anything fried or served with fish and a side of rice. Almost always packed, the restaurant has a busy fast-food buzz to it and is a good bet if you're up to trying some local cuisine, but don't want to swallow the Malecón prices. Try the house special, *Os-*

tras al Limon (oysters with lime). Av. El Eloy Alfaro and Los Almendros (Ca. 12), Tel: 593-4-277-4028, Cel: 593-9-413-7736, E-mail: ostranostra@hotmail.com.

La Bella Italia

(ENTREES: $4-12) La Bella Italia's façade, made to look like a little slice of Italy, leads into a spacious seating area and well-appointed wooden tables. A large brick oven occupies the front, near a street side window, so patrons and potential customers alike can watch how the mouth-watering dishes are created. Specialty dishes include antipasto, Calamare Allarabiata and Cannelloni Bella Italia—and of course, pizza. The chef also suggests *pescado en salsa de mariscos* (fish in seafood sauce). Its second-floor seating has excellent sea and street views, and is a good place to sip some wine and savor the gastronomical scene. Soccer fans should head here on game nights, when the restaurant fills with patrons proudly sporting their team's colors and all eyes are on the big screen TV in front. At night, it also has karaoke. Malecón and Ca. 17, Tel: 04-277-1316. Updated: Sep 24, 2012.

Oh Mar Comida Manabita

(ENTREES: $6.50-17) This simple restaurant serving traditional food from the province of Manabí has an extensive menu offering various ceviches and soups, including *viche* (a peanut-based fish soup)and *cazuela* (a seafood stew). Additionally, it has grilled or fried fish, seafood rice, crab-stuffed sea bass, shrimp in garlic lime sauce or coconut sauce, seafood paella and lobster. Meat options range from *churrasco* (thin slice of grilled beef topped with fried egg) to plates of grilled beef or pork chops. The best part is that it is located on the Malecón and has outdoor seating, so you can enjoy your meal to the sound of the waves. Malecón, in front of the palm trees (Building Sai Tómas), Tel: 04-277-2896, Cel: 09-748-9374.

Restaurant Carloncho

(ENTREES: $3-8) Simple but savory Manabí fare is on offer at this popular haunt just off the Malecón. Relatively unassuming during the day, the restaurant kicks into high gear at night when the rows of outside grills overflow with meat, corn and various fried treats, and the white plastic tables and chairs fill up with hungry Ecuadorian families. During peak times, the smell of grilling meat and sound of light-hearted chatter linger in the pleasant outdoor courtyard. You won't find black-and-white clad waiters or spar-

kling wine glasses that accompany some of the classier joints in Salinas, but the food is hearty and the atmosphere is like its meat: sizzling. Opens at 6 p.m. daily. Ca. 27, between the Malecón and Gral. Enriquez Gallo.

Cafetería Roberto

(ENTREES: $2-7) Almost always packed with hungry patrons, Cafetería Roberto is one of many outdoor street stalls in Cevichelandía, an outdoor market serving cheaper plates of seafood and, of course, *ceviche*. This seems to be a popular choice, especially for locals during lunchtime, so follow the crowds and try a ceviche or seafood soup here. If nothing else, it will be a more authentic experience than eating at any one of the swanky Salinas restaurants on the Malecón, but the food is also quite tasty. Monday-Friday 8:30 a.m.-5 p.m., Saturday-Sunday 8:30 a.m.-7:30 p.m. In Cevichelandía, Ca. de Las Palmeras. Updated: Sep 24, 2012.

GUAYAQUIL

 4m   2,530,000   📞 04

Guayaquil used to be a place to avoid with little to offer tourists, but Ecuador's largest city and commercial hub now has more than enough to keep you busy for a couple of days. The 3km-long riverside Malecón is a triumph of local organization, mixing cultural and recreational attractions; the bars and art galleries of the regenerated Las Peñas district are ideal for a stroll in the evening and there are plenty of museums as well as extravagant malls to cool off. If you're travelling along the coast or en route to the Galapagos it's convenient to stop over here, but keep things in perspective: as much as Guayaquil has improved in recent years, the oppressive heat could certainly affect your enjoyment and the city remains dangerous in places, particularly at night. Luckily, though, the main tourist areas are very safe and well-patrolled.

Getting To and Away from Guayaquil

Along with Quito, Guayaquil is one of Ecuador's two major transport hubs, both nationally and internationally. From here it is possible to get to almost anywhere in the country. Even if you don't plan on visiting the country's largest city, you may find yourself passing through the bus station or airport.The new airport and renovated bus station are both conveniently located in the north of the city, just a few blocks from each other, making connections between air and land transport extremely easy. Much to the locals' pride, these two new facilities give Guayaquil a definite edge over Quito.

BY AIR
José Joaquín de Olmedo International Airport

Guayaquil's Simón Bolívar Airport closed in 2006 when it was replaced by the brand new José Joaquín de Olmedo International Airport (GYE), named after Guayaquil's first mayor. This terminal is the "Best Airport in Latin America and the Caribbean," according to Business Week Magazine, an accolade it's won several times. The clean, well-organized, and airport is located five kilometers (3 mi, $4 taxi ride), north of the city center, right next to the old airport building. A modern stone and glass building houses both the Domestic and International Terminals, from where it is possible to fly to destinations all across Ecuador (including the Galápagos), in addition to international destinations in Europe and North and South America.

BY BUS
Terminal Terrestre Guayaquil

Along with a new airport, Guayaquil has also just acquired a brand new bus terminal, just north of the airport (Av. Benjamín Rosales and Av. de las Américas, Tel: 04-213-0166 & 7 Ext. 1 / www.terminalterrestreguayaquil.com). The new bus station is clean, relatively hassle-free and contains a pleasant shopping mall, the Outlet Shopping Center. From the Terminal Terrestre, buses run to destinations all across the country, as well as some international destinations, such as **Lima**, Peru. Purchase your ticket at the offices located downstairs before heading upstairs to find your bus. Regular buses make the eighthour journey to **Quito**, the five-hour trip to **Cuenca** and the 3.5-hour journey up the coast to **Montañita**.
Updated: Feb 21, 2013.

Getting Around Guayaquil

Because of the heat, you won't want to walk around Guayaquil for very long. There are three options for getting around: public bus, Metrovia or taxi. The public buses ($0.25) are variable in quality and the system is chaotic and confusing, so if it's anything more than a simple, short journey then you're better off avoiding them. The new Metrovia system was modeled around Quito's own system and is a good way of getting from the bus terminal to downtown.

Avoid rush hour though, when it is jampacked. Taxis are never in short supply in Guayaquil but few use their meters and will usually try to overcharge foreigners. Most taxi rides around the city should be $2-4. Always negotiate in advance, never take unmarked cabs (very dangerous) and take extra care at night.

Many hotels and restaurants will have cards of private taxi companies, which tend to be safer and more reliable. Note that the standard of driving is notoriously bad in Guayaquil so take extra care when crossing the road and check the taxi has a seatbelt before getting in. Also know that most of the time the taxi's here won't make use of their taxi meters, so it's best to ask about the price before you start moving.

Car Rentals in Guayaquil

To rent a car in Guayaquil, all you need is a valid drivers license from your home country. Some companies require you be at least 25, others ask for a security deposit, sometimes as much as $2000 in the form of a hold on your credit card.
Updated: Jul 15, 2013.

Guayaquil Services
TOURISM

The local tourist office at Pedro Icaza 203 (Mon–Fri 9am–5pm; 04/259 9100, www.visitaguayaquil.com) has friendly staff and up-to-date maps and brochures. The tourist office produces a general tourism guidebook and a specialist gastronomy guide, so ask if they have any in stock.
Updated: Apr 15, 2013.

LITERATURE
Libri Mundi

Established in 1971, Libri Mundi is a popular bookstore chain with a number of stores in and around Quito, and also in Cuenca and Guayaquil. They stock a wide variety of books but for the traveler, the most important thing is that they sell English-language books, including novels. Libri Mundi stocks some of the best quality reads, from art history to mystery and biographies to Ecuadorian literature. Not least, they sell guidebooks, and V!VA is proud to partner, so you can buy your V!VA guide here! Centro Comercial San Marino: 2nd floor, local 10, Francisco de Orellana y Av. Plaza Dañin, Tel: 04-208-3202 / 3207 / Centro Comercial Riocentro: Entre Ríos Local 48A, Tel: 04-283-2723/44, Email: entrerios@librimundi.com.
Updated: Feb 25, 2013.

Guayaquil Tours

Guayaquil cannot rival Quito in terms of quantity of travel agencies but if you're stopping here, there are plenty of reputable companies to arrange tours to the Galapagos, jungle and elsewhere in Ecuador. The following list is a selection rather than a comprehensive list.

Amazonas

Cdla. Entre Ríos, Av. Río Guayas and Calle Primera, Mz. X1 S, 04-283-1251. www.viajesamazonas.com.

Canodros

Urb. Santa Leonor, Mz 5, Solar 10, Vía al Terminal Terrestre, 04-228-5711. www.canodros.com .

Cetitur

9 de Octubre 109 and Malecón, Piso 1, 04-232-5299. www.cetitur.com.

Dream Kapture

Alborada, Doceava Etapa, Juan Sixto Bernal, Manzana 02, Villa 2104-224-2909. www.dreamkapture.com.

Ecoventura

Miraflores, Av Central 300A, 04-283-9390, www.ecoventura.com.

Galasam

Gran Pasaje building, bottom floor, 9 de Octubre 424 and Cordova, 04-230-4488, www.galasam.com.ec.

Guayaquil Vision

This company specializes in quick and inexpensive open-top bus tours, which are a great way to see several parts of the city. The tour company offers three regular routes, with different levels of amenities and services: the Scenic City Tour, Grand Guayaquil Tour and Noche de Fiesta Tour. Av. de las Américas # 406, Centro   de Convenciones de Guayaquil, Centro Empresarial Of. 11, Tel: 04-228-0732 / 04-230-0744 ext 114 / 098-906-4033, E-mail: info@guayaquilvision.com, URL: www.guayaquilvision.com. Updated: Feb 21, 2013.

Things To See and Do In Guayaquil

Malecón 2000 !

The multi-million dollar Malecón 2000 project was begun by former Mayor León Febrés Cordero in the late 1990s and is an astonishing achievement. This 3km public space is by far the biggest attraction in the city for tourists. The cool breezes off the river and the watchful eye of security guards make the Malecón the most relaxing place to spend time in Guayaquil. The obvious starting point is La Plaza Cívica at the end of 9 de Octubre. The highlight is La Rotonda, a statue depicting a famous meeting of South America's two most prominent liberators, José de San Martín and Simón Bolívar. This semi-circular monument is a spectacular night to behold at night.

South of La Rotonda are towers dedicated to the four elements, the Guayaquil Yacht Club and the Moorish Clock Tower, constructed in 1931. Just down from the clock tower is the Henry Morgan, a replica of a seventeenth-century pirate ship. A one-hour trip on the river costs $5 (afternoons and evenings only, late-night trips at weekends). South of this is the shopping area. It's bland and mainly sells modern items rather than artisan wares but it's a good place to escape the heat. On the other side is an outdoor food court with countless cheap restaurants serving fast food and traditional Ecuadorian specialities, notably seafood. Further south is the quietest part of Malecón at Plaza Olmedo, named after the city's first mayor and beyond that a small artisans' market.

North of La Rotonda is a large children's play area leading to a beautifully laid out set of botanical gardens with more than three hundred species of plants and trees. This is one of the highlights of Malecón so it's worth getting lost in the greenery and stopping for a drink at Aroma Café. Above the gardens are 32 transparent panels with the names of more than 48,000 citizens who contributed to the Malecón project. North of the botanical gardens is the new Museo Guayaquil en La Historia (open 10am–6.30pm daily; $2.50), which packs a history of the city from pre-historic times to the present into 14 dioramas. Above the museum is one of South America' only IMAX cinemas with a 180-degree screen. It's a unique but somewhat disorientating experience.

At the far north end of Malecón, just below Las Peñas, is the impressive Museo Antropológico y de Arte Contemporáneo (MAAC) (04-230-9383 Tues–Sun 9am–5pm. Free entrance), which has an exhibition on ancient history and a huge collection of pre-Columbian ceramics as well as modern art. If you're not visiting the mountains but want to stock up on handicrafts and indigenous clothes, head a couple of blocks in from the

SOUTHERN COAST

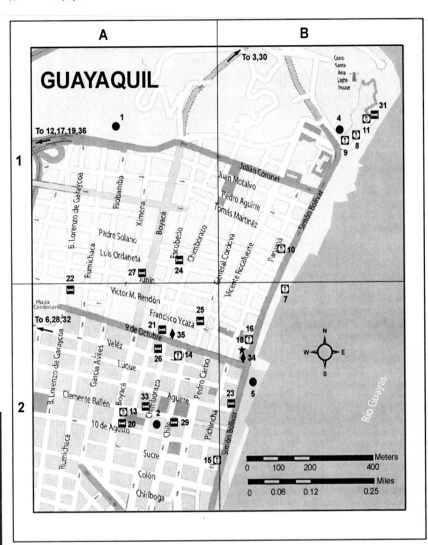

north end of Malecón along Calle Loja to the huge, enclosed Mercado Artesanal. Prices are higher than in the Sierra so haggle away if you're up for buying things. Further information about Malecón can be obtained from the Fundación Malecón's office in Sargento Vargas 116 and Av. Olmedo, Tel: 593-4-252-4530 / 4211, URL: www.malecon2000.com. Updated: Feb 21, 2013.

Malecón del Salado

As if the huge Malecón 2000 project weren't enough, it now has a junior version at the opposite end of 9 de Octubre. The Malecón del Salado is named after the tributary of the river Guayas that it straddles. Citizens used to bathe here in the 19th century but it's far too dirty nowadays. However, the pleasant walkway, which undulates up and down bridges, makes for a pleasant stroll and if you work up an appetite there is a cluster of good seafood restaurants at the end. Updated: Feb 21, 2013.

Las Peñas and Cerro Santa Ana

The north end of Malecón blends conveniently into the colorful artistic district of Las Peñas. This area has been completely regenerated in recent years and is almost as impressive an achievement as Malecón itself. It's a relaxing place to hang out during the day but best enjoyed in the evening

Activities ●

1 General Cemetery and Flower Market A1
2 Guayaquil City Center A2
3 Guayaquil Historical Park B1
4 Las Peñas and Cerro Santa Ana B1
5 Malecon 2000
6 Malecón del Salado A2

Eating

7 Aroma Café B2
8 Arturs Café B1
9 Diva Nicotina B1
10 Frutabar B1
11 La Paleta B1
12 La Parilla del Nato A1
13 La Pepa De Oro A2
14 Las 3 Canastas A2
15 Menestras del Negro A2
16 Sweet and Coffee B2

Services ★

17 Libri Mundi A1
18 Tourism B2

Sleeping 🛏

19 Dreamkapture Inn A1
20 Gran Hotel Guayaquil A2
21 Hampton Inn Guayaquil A2
22 Hostal Linda A2
23 Hostal Manso B2
24 Hotel Andaluz A1
25 Hotel La Fontana A2
26 Hotel Las Peñas A2
27 Hotel Mar de Plata A1
28 Hotel Oro verde A2
29 Hotel Rizzo A2
30 Hotel Suites Guayaquil B1
31 Mansion del Rio Boutique Hotel B1
32 Tangara Guest House A2
33 Unipark Hotel A2

Tours ◆

34 Cetitur B2
35 Galasam A2
36 Guayaquil Vision A1

SOUTHERN COAST

when the steep climb up 444 steps is more comfortable and can be broken up by visits into the many welcoming cafes, bars and restaurants. At the top is an open-air museum Museo El Fortín del Santa Ana which has original cannons and replicas of Spanish galleons. There is also a small chapel and replica lighthouse at the top of the hill, but the main attraction is the fabulous view over the city and Guayas estuary.

An alternative to climbing the hill is to walk around to the right from the foot of the steps along the cobbled street of Numa Pompillo Llona, named after the Guayaco who wrote Ecuador's national anthem. There are several art galleries and one of the city's most interesting bars – La Paleta. Further on, the old district blends into the modern Puerto Santa Ana, which is already impressive but as yet incomplete. In addition to the shops and cafes lining the riverside, there will soon be an extensive marina overlooked by luxury apartments.

Guayaquil City Center

Beyond Malecón and Las Peñas, the center of Guayaquil is a bit hit and miss with the heat and heavy traffic often marring your sightseeing experience. The center is also sadly lacking in historic architecture, the legacy of several devastating fires, notably in 1896. However, there are a couple of attractions that you shouldn't miss. Top of the list is the small Parque Seminario, most commonly known as the Parque de las Iguanas. If you're on your way to the Galapagos, this will be an amusing hors d'oeuvre and if you're not, it's certainly a memorable experience to get up close and personal with these lethargic creatures.

The iguanas lounge around on the grass and in the trees, remarkably unconcerned by the crowds of people. There's also a small pool filled with turtles. The park is dominated by the monument to liberator Simón Bolívar on horseback at its center and the huge white Neo-Gothic Cathedral, rebuilt in 1948, towering over the west side of the square. Between the park and Malecon there is a pleasant square, Plaza de la Administración, surrounded by the elegant buildings of the local municipal government. North along Pedro Carbo will take you to another attractive square, Plaza San Francisco, dominated by the church of the same name and a statue of Pedro Carbo on top of a large fountain.

Don't want to leave? Never going back? Review it at vivatravelguides.com

One block to the south-west of Parque de las Iguanas is the Museo Municipal (Sucre and Chile, free). This is the oldest museum in Ecuador, it's still the city's best and as it's free, what do you have to lose? The Pre-Hispanic room hosts a collection of fossils, including the tooth of a mastodon, dating back ten thousand years. There are also sculptures from Ecuador's oldest civilization, the Valdivia, and a huge Manteña funeral urn. Upstairs is a room of portraits of Ecuadorian presidents and a small exhibition of modern art. There are five shrunken heads on display in a closed room upstairs, which can only be viewed on a guided tour. Free English-speaking tours are available on request. Updated: Feb 21, 2013.

General Cemetery and Flower Market

Guayaquil's General Cemetery is among the most elaborate in the Americas. The grounds include neo-classical architecture and sculpture from noted Spanish and Italian artists of the 20th century. Each turn through the labyrinth of mausoleums brings more surprises, such as marble angels weeping or standing over the decorated graves. You can also see Guayaquil's Masonic influence in the nooks and crannies of the cemetery. The lavish decoration and expensive materials of the tombs on one side of the General Cemetery are a sharp contrast to the wooden crosses on the western side of the hill, where the almost vertical graves seem to have been piled one on top of the other. The west side is where those unable to afford a niche in a cement mausoleum buried their relatives during the night. At the main entrance is the grandiose tomb of Victor Emilio Estrada, a banker and former President of the Republic. Legend says that he made a pact with the devil, exchanging his soul for wealth and power. As a result, his spirit is not at peace and wanders the nearby streets at night. Taxi drivers tell ghost stories in which one of them picks up a man who is walking alone and the passenger then asks to be dropped off at the cemetery entrance, near his tomb.

The flower market is in front of this main entrance, where Calle Machala meets Julián Coronel. The main entrance is next to the "salones de velorio," the place where the families of the deceased mourn for 24 hours before crossing the footbridge to the cemetery. Note that robberies have been reported so do not travel to the cemetery alone and avoid it completely after dark. Located on Julián Coronel and Machala.

Guayaquil Historical Park

Guayaquil historical park is a great place to go if you want to learn more about the city's history and the culture of the coastal region. The park is separated into three main sections: the wildlife zone, the urban architecture zone and the traditions zone. The wildlife zone consists of elevated paths through natural mangroves. You pass enclosures of animals such as tapir, caiman, deer, sloths, toucans and monkeys. The urban architecture zone has reconstructions of houses and a church from the 19th and early 20th century. The traditions zone gives a glimpse of what life is like in rural parts of the coast, where people continue to live in bamboo homes. This area also includes the "Granja urbana solidaria" program, which promotes communities and families working together to grow healthy produce and curative plants.

The highlight is the boisterous programme of theatrical performances at weekends. Even those who do not understand Spanish will enjoy the spectacle of these lively shows, which reenact traditions and legends from 100 years ago. Characters range from cacao plantation owners to a French-educated Ecuadorian heiress to a hoofed devil disguised as a gentleman. When you're done with the show, the kiosk at the 'peasant's house' offers a variety of tasty traditional snacks. The park is 20 minutes from the city center across the bridge. There are occasional buses from the Terminal but it's easier to simply take a taxi there ($5). Km 1 1/2 Vía a Samborondón, Av. Esmeraldas (junto a Cdla. Entre Ríos), Tel: 04-283-5356/2958, URL: www.parquehistorico.gob.ec. Updated: Feb 21, 2013.

Cerro Blanco

Cerro Blanco is a protected forest that's easily accessible by bus and is a great day trip from Guayaquil. Visitors can take advantage of a self-guided tour along the two trails, or request a trained guide for a more educational experience. Administered by the Fundación Pro-Bosque, Cerro Blanco protects a section of dry forest that is a biodiversity hotspot. There are more than 500 vascular species of plants and one of the highlights is seeing the ceibo or kapol trees up-close: their green, human-like trunks seem to come right out of a Dr. Seuss book.

The park is located on the edge of a city that has three million inhabitants and harbors populations of jaguar, ocelot, agouti, peccary and other mammals. Birdwatchers will be excited by the opportunity to see mora, with more than 200 species, of which 20 are endemic. The forest is home to a dozen endangered bird species, including the Guayaquil subspecies of the great green macaw (locally called the "papagayo de Guayaquil").

For those looking to stay a while, there is a camping and picnic area with flush toilets, showers and cooking grills. Alternatively, you can enjoy the comfort of a two-bedroom sustainably built cabin. If you're interested in volunteering at the forest, contact the very helpful director of the foundation, Eric Horstman. To get here from Guayaquil, catch a Salinas bus from the terminal and ask to be dropped off at this location. It takes about 20 minutes. Km 16 off the Guayaquil-Salinas highway, Tel: 593-4-287-4947, E-mail: bosqueprotector@yahoo.com.
Updated: Apr 16, 2013.

Puerto Hondo Mangroves
Just one kilometer (.62 mi) west of the entrance to the Cerro Blanco forest reserve is Puerto Hondo, a dry, beaten down town that sits on the edge of a slender saltwater estuary. Although the village itself is of little interest, the nearby mangrove swamps around the estuary are worth a visit. You can make the trip there via motorized canoes as part of a tour organized by a local guide association and the Pro Bosque Foundation.

To get there, catch a bus heading toward the Cerro Blanco forest reserve and ask to be dropped off at the Puerto Hondo turnoff. From there, head south; it is about a five-minute walk from the highway.
Updated: Apr 16, 2013.

Playas
The closest beach to Guayaquil is Playas (officially called General Villamil), about 1.5 hours by bus. This is the opposite of Salinas, attracting the lower and middle class Guayacos rather than the rich and that is part of its appeal. Like all south coast resorts, it's heavily seasonal – jam-packed on national holidays and weekends between Christmas and Easter, and very quiet the rest of the year.

Unlike Salinas, the beach is very long but not sheltered so currents can be strong so take care. It's best as a day trip and you can enjoy cheap, fresh seafood from the scores of restaurants lining the beach. There are plenty of well-priced hotels along the Malecon if you choose to stay here.
Updated: Apr 20, 2013.

Puerto El Morro
A few miles east of Playas lies this small port with abundant marine life. It's an enjoyable day trip from Guayaquil and can easily be combined with a dip in Playas to cool off afterwards. The main attractions are the mangroves, birdlife and the dolphins swimming in the estuary. The shorter route (1.5 hours, $5) takes in the mangroves, dolphins and some fishing, while the longer route (3 hours, $8) includes a longer boat trip and a walk on the Isla de los Pájaros. Both can be arranged with a community tourism project Ecoclub Los Delfines de Puerto el Morro. Take a bus from Guayaquil's main terminal to Playas and then change for Puerto El Morro (1.5 hours). Tel: 593-4-252-9496, E-mail: puertoelmorro@yahoo.com, URL: www.puertoelmorro.blogspot.com.
Updated: Apr 20, 2013.

Guayaquil Lodging
Guayaquilis still not a very popular destination with budget travelers, probably because decent cheap or mid-range accommodation is less abundant than in Quito or Cuenca.

There are plenty of high-class hotels to blow your budget. With a handful of in-house restaurants and even a beauty parlor, one Guayaquil hotel where you can really pamper yourself is Hotel Oro Verde. Rooms at this chain hotel start around $130 per night.

In the mid-range, Guayaquil accommodations tend to cost between $40-60. Places to stay in this range are called 'guest houses' or 'hostals' instead of hotels, even though they are much more classy establishments than the backpacker hostels most travelers are accustomed to. Hostal Linda has marble floors and elegant furnishings, while the more homey Tangara Guest House has peaceful gardens and a shared kitchen.

Your options are fewer if you're shorter of cash when in Guayaquil. Hostels such as Hostal Manso are more like a boutique hotel than a place where backpackers flock. Hostal Manso has a bar and decently designed rooms, as far as Ecuadorian standards go. Prices start around $25 per night. Note that it's best to avoid the cheapest hotels or Guayaquil hostels in the center of town because many are seedy, unfriendly 'motels,' frequented by locals for secret amorous encounters. The following budget options do not fit into this category.
Updated: Jun 30, 2013.

BUDGET
Dreamkapture Inn

($11-40 per person) Guayaquil is sadly lacking in good-quality budget accommodation but Dreamkapture, located in a northern suburb Alborada, is a notable exception It's a few miles from the city center but secure, well-maintained and good value for the price. Choose from dorms, rooms with shared bath up to more comfortable rooms with air conditioning and private bath. There is a small waterfall and pool, hammocks to relax in and a small travel agency. and tourism information desk. The manager is American and very helpful. Alborada Doceava Etapa, Calle Juan Sixto Bernal, Manzana 02, Villa 21, Tel: 04-224-2909, E-mail: info@dreamkapture.com, URL: www.dreamkapture.com. Updated: Feb 20, 2013.

Hostal Manso

(ROOMS: $12-90) Boutique hotels are very hard to find in Guayaquil and you could easily miss Hostal Manso. It's small front door is snuggled into a large block opposite Malecón. Venture up the stairs and you'll find a welcoming slice of Arabia. The maroon décor of the lounge, the seating on cushions and the hammocks in the bar all make for an eclectic mix of originality. The rooms are individually colored and designed (in descending order of price) amber, white, orange, blue, green and pink. The best rooms have private bath and air conditioning, and the cheapest do not. Don't come here expecting to get luxury though; you are paying for the atmosphere and original designs rather than for extra comfort. There are regular theatrical and musical performances hosted in the lounge area and the rooms are closed every three months while the hotel is being converted into an Arabian-style bazaar. Malecon 1406 and Aguirre, upper floor., Tel: 04-252-6644, E-mail: reservas@manso.ec, URL: www.manso.ec. Updated: Feb 20, 2013.

Ecovita

(CAMPING: $22 per day) Ecovita is an organic farm camping site located in Pallatanga, two hours from Guayaquil, promoting projects geared toward community efforts and raising awareness about conservation. The name "ecovita" itself means "ecological life," fitting for a place dedicated to agrotourism and environmental education. Comfortable tents are equipped with mattresses and bug nets, and there are several simple double rooms with baths. Lots of areas for relaxing and play are available, stocked with hammocks, a natural pool, volley ball court, soccer field, pool and ping pong tables, mountain bikes, and even go-kart racing. Pallatanga-Panamericana Sur, Km 139 Guayaquil - Riobamba road, Tel: 04-288-8196 - 099-908-5226 / 099-730-0558, E-mail: info@vivecovita.com, URL: www.vivecovita.com. Updated: Feb 20, 2013.

Hotel Andaluz

(ROOMS: $25-34) Located just a few blocks from Malecón and 9 de Octubre, the elegantly designed Hotel Andaluz is perhaps the best mid-range deal for travelers who want to be in the middle of everything in downtown Guayaquil. The hotel provides all of the basic amenities: private bath with hot water, air conditioning, and a living room area with leather sofas and TV. One of the hotel's highlights is its garden-like roof terrace. Decoration is simple with a splash of Ecuadorian art. Rooms off the street may be best for those sensitive to noise, since the hotel is located in a rather busy area. Baquerizo Moreno 840 and Junín, Tel: 04-230-5796, Fax: 04-231-1057, E-mail: hotel_andaluz@yahoo.com, URL: www.hotelandaluz-ec.com. Updated: Feb 20, 2013.

Hotel Mar de Plata

(ROOMS: $25) This is one of the best budget options in the centre of town. Most of the options cheaper than this are dirty, seedy and generally unbearable. The rooms are simple but clean with a private bathroom and cable TV, and the hotel is very conveniently located for sightseeing. Junín 718 and Boyacá, Tel: 04-230-7610. Updated: Feb 21, 2013.

Hostal Linda

(ROOMS: $25-40) The rooms at this mid-range hotel are a cut above the competition with elegant furnishing, plush décor and marble floors. It's one of the newest hotels in the center and coninvently located overlooking Parque Centenario. Lorenzo de Garaicoa 809 and Victor Manuel Rendón, Tel: 04-256-2495. Updated: Feb 20, 2013.

MID-RANGE
Hotel Rizzo

(ROOMS: $40-73) It's not as endearing inside as Andaluz but Hotel Rizzo's position is perfect, right on Parque de las Iguanas. The rooms are well-appointed, some have small balconies and others overlook the park. Downstairs there's a good if slightly pricey café Jambelí which serves set menus for

SOUTHERN COAST

breakfast, lunch and dinner. Clemente Ballén 319 and Chile, Corner, Tel: 04-601-7500, E-mail: reservas@rizzohotel.com, URL: www.rizzohotel.homestead.com.
Updated: Feb 21, 2013.

Hotel Las Peñas

(ROOMS: $60-90) Hotel Las Peñas, located above the bakery "Panadería California" and just one block from Av. 9 de Octubre, is a nice mid-range option if you want a comfortable place to stay. Rooms have a hotel-chain feel to them without the hefty price. They come with private bath, air conditioning, mini-bar, cable TV, telephone and room service. Laundry and private shuttle service are also available. Light sleepers might want to request an inside room to avoid Guayaquil's street noise. Breakfast is included. Escobedo 1215 between Av. 9 de Octubre and Vélez, Tel: 04-232-3355, E-mail: ventas@hlpgye. ec, URL: www.hlpgye.ec.
Updated: Feb 20, 2013.

Hotel Suites Guayaquil

(ROOMS: $49-56) Hotel Suites Guayaquil is located in the center, near Malecon del Salado. They are comfortable suites ideal for people looking for more privacy and independence than a hotel can offer. Prices include tax and Internet is free. Airport pick up is also included, just call Mario to set an arrival time. There is a sister hotel located next to the airport. 305, 3rd. Av and 8th St. Cdla. Ferroviaria (railway, near Guayaquil Malecón of El Salado, Tel: 04-239-1120 / 04-239-8305 / 04-220-8089 / 098-624-4077 / 099-961-6161 / 099-768-9186 / 099-791-1246, E-mail: info@suitesguayaquil.com, URL: www.SuitesGuayaquil.com.
Updated: Feb 20, 2013.

Tangara Guest House

(ROOMS: $40-60) Located in a residential area on the outskirts of downtown, the Tangara Guest House offers a homely hostel atmosphere not easily found in Guayaquil. The communal kitchen and gardens make for a pleasant extended visit. The guesthouse owners also run a tour agency as well, so they're quite savvy on things to do in the area. Breakfast included. Ciudadela Bolivariana, block "F" house 1. Manuela Sáenz & O'Leary streets., Tel: 04-228-2828and9 / 04-228-4445 / 098-129-5186, E-mail: tangara@gye.satnet.net / reservastangara@cablemodem.com.ec / aperroneg@gmail.com, URL: www.tangara-ecuador.com.
Updated: Feb 20, 2013.

Hotel La Fontana

(ROOMS: $45-56) Situated in Guayaquil's downtown banking district (a.k.a. "a well-guarded area") just three blocks from Malecón 2000 and one block from 9 de Octubre, Hotel La Fontana is the best located hotel in its price range and its boutique style is a breath of fresh air from the mundane chain hotels. Rooms have air conditioning, private bath with hot water, cable TV and a telephone. On the corner of Francisco de P. Icaza and General Córdova, Tel: 04-230-7230, E-mail: gerencia@lafontana-ecuador.com, URL: www.lafontana-ecuador.com.
Updated: Feb 20, 2013.

HIGH-END
Hampton Inn Guayaquil-Downtown

(ROOMS: $110) Boasting 95 rooms and a 24-hour business center, the Hampton Inn Guayaquil-Downtown offers all the necessities for business or pleasure. Dining options inside the hotel include Japanese cuisine at the Bonsai Sushi Bar, a la carte lunch and dinner at the Kafe Boulevard Restaurant and a gourmet deli and French bakery at the Deli Boulevard. This family-friendly hotel offers babysitting services, cribs and family package deals. Included in the price of the room are a breakfast buffet, airport shuttle, use of the spa and fitness center, lap pool, Jacuzzi, sauna, valet parking and free WiFi anywhere on the property. Av. 9 de Octobre 432 and Baquerizo Moreno, Tel: 04-256-6700, Fax: 04-256-6427, URL: www.guayaquil.hamptoninn.com
Updated: Feb 20, 2013.

Hotel Oro Verde

(ROOMS: $130) Centrally located and only 10 minutes from the airport, the Oro Verde is a plush choice for those with money to burn. This chain hotel boasts spotless well-furnished rooms, complete with cable TV, Internet, radio, telephone, safe and mini-bar. A couple of days at this hotel would give you just enough time to try out the numerous eateries in the building: El Patio, the Gourmet Deli, La Fondue, Bar El Capitan and the Gourmet Restaurant. The culinary choices are varied enough to satisfy almost anyone's palate and the buffet breakfast is a delicious way to start the day. Aside from eating, you can get pampered in the beauty parlor or head to Oro Fit, the place to work off that heavy breakfast or lunch. Other services include 24-hour room service, laundry, dry cleaning, currency exchange, airport transfer, valet parking and limousine service. A

SOUTHERN COAST

sister hotel is located in Manta. 9 de Octobre and Garcia Moreno, Tel: 04-232-7999, Fax: 04-232-9350, E-mail: reservas_gye@oroverdehotels.com / ventas_gye@oroverdehotels.com / ov_gye@oroverdehotels.com, URL: www.oroverdeguayaquil.com. Updated: Feb 20, 2013.

Mansion Del Rio Boutique Hotel

(ROOMS: $109-125) We are located in the Barrio Las Peñas, important center of tourism development and one of the most representative traditional neighborhoods of the city of Guayaquil, Mansion del Rio Boutique Hotel provides pleasant space. All of our rooms are decorated with an antique European style, enabling our customers to have the experience of live in the 20th century with the comforts of the present time, making our rooms and suites unique in the city with a splendid view of the river Guayas. Enjoy a friendly atmosphere full of art and delicious Ecuadorian and international food with excellent wines in our restaurant. 120, Numa Pompilio Llona St., Las Peñas neighborhood, next to Puerto Santa Ana, in front of Guayas River., Tel: 04-256-6044 / 04-256-5827 / 04-256-5983 / 04-230-3576, E-mail: reservas@mansiondelrio-ec.com, URL: www.mansiondelrio-ec.com. Updated: Feb 20, 2013.

Grand Hotel Guayaquil

(ROOMS: $98-110) The ageing concrete of Grand Hotel Guayaquil looks very uninviting from the outside but inside it lives up to its name, featuring a spacious reception area and excellent service. Centrally located, it's convenient for the city sights and a great place to indulge for a day or two. Activities include splashing in the pool, relaxing in the sauna, massage or working out in the rooftop gym. Rooms are tastefully decorated and have cable TV, telephones, internet connection, hair dryers, radio alarms and in-room coffee machines (always a nice perk). For a bite to eat, head to La Pepa de Oro, the 24-hour coffee shop; alternatives are the 1822 Restaurant, the Turtle Bar and the Barbecue Restaurant. Boyaca between Clemente Ballen and 10 de Agosto, Tel: 04-232-9690, Fax: 04-232-7251, E-mail: reservas@grandhotelguayaquil.com / info@grandhotelguayaquil.com, URL: www.grandhotelguayaquil.com. Updated: Feb 22, 2013.

Unipark Hotel

(ROOMS: $89-200) Convenient for a leisurely stroll to the Malecón, this upscale hotel is owned by the Oro Verde chain. Smack in the middle of the central commercial district, the hotel is spread across two towers accommodating 139 rooms, including wheelchair accessible room options. The hotel has several restaurants including the UniCafé, UniBar, the Uni Deli and the Sushi Bar, the latter of which has an all-you-can-eat promotion on Wednesdays. Rooms are comfortable, well-serviced and include telephone, voice mail, cable TV, mini-bar, Internet, hair dryer and safe. Airport transfers are available as well. There is also a small shopping center next door with a Banco de Guayaquil ATM. This is a good option for families as the hotel also offers a babysitting service upon request and connecting rooms are also available. Clemente ballen 406 between Chile and Chimborazo, Tel: 04-232-7100, Fax: 04-232-8352, E-mail: unipark@oroverdehotels.com, URL: www.uniparkhotel.com. Updated: Feb 26, 2013.

Sol de Oriente

(ROOMS: $93-111) This is a simple, yet sleek hotel whose various oriental inspirations make it stand out against other characterless hotels in the area. Its 56 rooms come equipped with air conditioning, cable TV, WiFi, and a mini-fridge. Hotel Sol del Oriente has four event rooms that can accommodate anywhere between 40 and 180 guests. The hotel has various dining options, including the Great Wall, which serves international fare, and the Oriental Corner, the in-house breakfast buffet. For a tranquil end to the day, visit the hotel's spa. Those wanting to test out their vocal chords can head to the on-site karaoke bar. There's also an Internet café, international phone booths, printers and other technical support available. The hotel can also set up airport transfers. On the corner of Aguirre and Escobedo., Tel: 04-232-5500 / 04-232-8150, E-mail: info@hotelsoloriente.com, URL: www.hotelsoloriente.com. Updated: Feb 20, 2013.

Hotel City Plaza

($85-135) The newest addition to Guayaquil's top-range accommodation is this modern, sleek business-like hotel. It's a touch more economical than the city's more grandoise options but the rooms are still immaculately presented just like any of the other options around town and the service is equally attentive. Located on Boyaca 922 and V. Manuel Rendon, Tel: 04-230-9209, E-mail: reservas@hotelcityplaza.com.ec, URL: www.hotelcityplaza.com.ec. Updated: Feb 20, 2013.

SOUTHERN COAST

Guayaquil Restaurants and Nightlife

Finding somewhere to eat in Guayaquil is not as relaxed an experience as in Ecuador's more tourist-friendly cities. Many of the restaurants in the center are either bog-standard or else overpriced, attached to high-class hotels. However, look hard enough and you will find some very appealing options.

Away from the center, head up to Las Peñas for the most relaxed evening experience or, alternatively, to the northern district of Urdesa, which has plenty of good restaurants along the main street Victor Emilio Estrada. After dinner, Las Peñas has plenty of bars to have a civilized drink. If you want something more raucous, head to la Zona Rosa along Rocafuerte between Roca Rodriguez and Juan Montalvo, but don't stray from the main street and always take a taxi back to your hotel.
Updated: Apr 16, 2013.

La Pepa de Oro

(ENTREES: $3-9) With service 24/7, The Grand Hotel's La Pepa de Oro is the perfect place to safely grab a bite in Guayaquil if you arrive into town late. Choices range from typical coastal dishes like sea bass ceviche to American options such as a club sandwich. Only a few blocks from the Malecón, it also makes a refreshing stop while taking a walking tour of the downtown area on a sunny Guayaquil afternoon. On Thursday, Friday and Saturday nights, meals are accompanied by traditional "pasillo"music. The menu is in English and includes a brief history of the Ecuadorian Cacao Boom that inspired the restaurant's décor. Boyaca between Clemente Ballen and 10 de Agosto, Tel: 04-232-9690, URL: www.grandhotelguayaquil.com.
Updated: Feb 21, 2013.

La Parrilla del Ñato

La Parrilla del Ñato is an enticing restaurant for meat lovers who want to indulge in a barbecue. Most people come for the parrillada (grilled meats), but be careful when ordering from the untranslated menu and make sure that if you ask for "morcilla" or "chinchulín" that you are ready to eat blood sausage or intestines.

Eating with a vegetarian? The ravioli in a rich, four-cheese sauce is a great option and the pizza is also popular. If there is any room left after dinner, try one of the desserts such as a coconut flan (queso de coco) or an after-dinner drink from the bar. This local chain

of restaurants is extremely popular at weekends and there's a large restaurant on Victor Emilio Estrada in Urdesa a couple of miles north of the center. Luque 104 and Pichincha (corner), Tel: 04-232-1649.
Updated: Feb 25, 2013.

Sweet and Coffee

Many Guayacos like to pretend they live in Miami, so it's no surprise that this chain has been a huge success in recent years. Large slices of walnut cake, chocolate Oreo cheesecake and lime meringue pie can be accompanied by a frothy vanilla latte or an iced coffee drink. You pay more than other coffee places, but the quality cannot be questioned. Sweet and Coffee also packages and sells its own brand of whole bean or ground coffee. If you want to eat something more authentically Ecuadorian, try an humita (steamed mashed corn with cheese). Malecón 2000, Galería C. Updated: Apr 20, 2013.

Menestras del Negro

(ENTREES: $3 and up) Menestras del Negro may seem like a strange, even offensive name ("The Black Guy's Beans" just does not translate well into English), but in Ecuador "El Negro" is often considered an endearing nickname. What the restaurant's name tries to inspire is that they know what they are doing when it comes to making beans. "Arroz con menestra" (Red beans or lentils and rice) is one of the most common dishes on the Ecuadorian coast. It can be eaten with just a few "patacones" (fried plantain wedges) or more frequently it is also accompanied by thin, well-cooked slices of beef, chicken, or pork. This is a fast-food restaurant, so prices are fairly low, though ordering the same thing at a hole-in-the-wall restaurant around the corner might be almost half the price. On the corner of Malecón and Sucre streets.
Updated: Feb 21, 2013.

Frutabar

(ENTREES: $5-10) Frutabar feels like a piece of Montañita has been transplanted to the big city. Instead of waves crashing, you might catch a view of the Guayas River slowly drifting by, but surfboards converted into tables definitely recall the beach. This café serves light fare like turkey sandwiches and humitas but the highlight is the selection of large batidos (milkshakes). Flavors range from strawberry and peach to coconut and mango or you can create your own. For an extra kick, try the borojó—a dark-brown, endemic fruit paste locally known as an aphrodisiac. Estrada 608 between Las Monjas and

SOUTHERN COAST

Ficus. Tel. 04-288-0255- CENTRO Malecón 514 between Tomás Martinez and Imbabura. Tel. 04-230-0743- SUR C.C. Centro Sur. Chile between el Oro and Azuay. Tel. 04-244-402, URL: www.frutabar.com. Updated: Feb 25, 2013.

Aroma Café

(ENTREES: $5-10) To break up a hot day of sightseeing, it's hard to beat the location of this open-air restaurant, nestled in the cool, shaded atmosphere of the botanical gardens of Malecón. The café serves a wide range of Ecuadorian meat and seafood specialities, all cooked to perfection and well-presented. If you're not that hungry, it's great for snacks, desserts and of course a wide selection of coffee. Jardines de Malecón 2000, Tel: 04-239-1328, E-mail: aromacafe01@yahoo.com, URL: www.actiweb.es/aromacafegquil. Updated: Feb 25, 2013.

Artur's Café

(ENTREES: $10) Wander up to the right along Numa Pompillo in Las Peñas to find this dramatically located café/restaurant perched over the river. The open windows make for a fresh, breezy experience and the menu offers all the Ecuadorian staples but it's also good for a quiet drink. Evenings only. Numa Pompillo Llona 127, Las Peñas, Tel: 04-231-2230 / 256-1017, E-mail: arturscafe@hotmail.com / info@arturscafe.com, URL: www.arturscafe.com. Updated: Feb 25, 2013.

Diva Nicotina

(ADMISSION: $5-7) At the bottom of the steps of Las Peñas, this bar is either quiet or heaving, depending on the live music offering, which is its main attraction. The management are quite selective about who plays here and acts mainly play original songs, so for a entrance charge of $5-7 you can catch some great live music - from Cuban Habanera to jazz. The bar is stocked with every liquor imaginable and they specialize in cigars if you want to puff away while you listen. Moran de Buitron (Malecon), Las Peñas.

Chapus

This rustic, wooden bar is one of the oldest in the northern district of Urdesa. You can have a quiet drink upstairs early in the evening or shake it up on the dancefloor downstairs later on. It gets very busy at weekends and you're guaranteed a fun, raucous evening. There is usually a cover charge for men at weekends. Victor Emilio Estrada (Las Monjas), Urdesa. Updated: Feb 25, 2013.

Hotel Oro Verde

Guayaquil's top hotel also hosts many of its best restaurants. Choose from French haute cuisine at Le Gourmet, Ecuadorian specialities at El Patio, Swiss dishes including the obligatory cheese fondue at Le Fondue, and cakes and pastries at Le Gourmet Deli. None of it is cheap, but that's precisely the point – you splash out on something special. Le Gourmet is probably the pick of the bunch. 9 de Octubre and Garcia Moreno, Tel: 04-232-7999, URL: www.oroverdeguayaquil.com. Updated: Feb 25, 2013.

Las 3 Canastas

(ENTREES: $2.50-4) This Guayaquil institution has a few branches dotted about the city. It's a colorful, informal café specializing in pastries, fruit salads, ice creams and of course traditional Ecuadorian specialities. You get big portions and it's half the price of many of its rivals in the center. There's a smaller café on the corner of Pedro Carbo and Clemente Ballen between Parque de las Iguanas and Malecon. Panama and Junin. Updated: Apr 16, 2013.

La Española

If your standard hotel breakfast hasn't quite hit the spot then head to this spotless Spanish bakery. It's a cool escape from the city's heat with reasonable prices and friendly service. It has a wide selection of delicious cakes, pastries and sandwiches so it's also a good option for a light lunch or treat. Located on Junin and Boyaca. Updated: Apr 16, 2013.

La Paleta

You wouldn't happen upon this place by accident, hidden mid-way up Numa Pompillo in Las Peñas, but you should certainly make a beeline for it because it's quite possibly one of the most interesting bars in all of Guayaquil. It epitomizes the Bohemian, artistic atmosphere of Las Peñas with an eclectic, colorful décor, low ceilings, nooks and crannies, and a wide-ranging menu of cocktails and tapas.

Guayaquil's creative and eccentric crowd tends to head here even weeknights, and if you're not in Guayaquil for long, this is one place you shouldn't miss at all. Note: Although that it's not open-air like other bars in Las Peñas, it still gets quite smoky later on as the evening rolls in with plenty of drinks and dance. Open 8 p.m.-3 a.m. Numa Pompillo Llona 174, Tel: 04-231-2329. Updated: Feb 25, 2013.

El Oro

El Oro stretches from Guayaquil to the Peruvian border and most people don't stop en route. Admittedly, this area has no must-see attractions but the main city Machala is worth a look, if only to say you've visited the "banana capital of the world". Machala is also a convenient starting point for exploring the mangrove circled town of Puerto Bolívar, the markets of Santa Rosa, the gold-mining community of Zaruma and the peninsula beaches of Jambelí. On the Río Zarumilla, on the border with Peru, sits Huaquillas, the busiest crossing point between the two countries. Huaquillas offers little more than a checkpoint and a shopping destination for Peruvians looking for bargains.
Updated: Apr 20, 2013.

UPLANDS OF EL ORO

Head inland from Machala and you will discover a peaceful corner of the country, relatively free of tourists. Scenic roads meander through the countryside, winding past quiet colonial cities and the characteristic gold mines that give the region its name. A network of trails crisscrosses the landscape, running to hidden waterfalls and through expansive tracts of forests. As a transition zone between the rugged mountains of the Andes and the smooth sandy beaches of the coast, this region presents travelers with a unique climate conducive to walking and trekking.
Updated: Apr 20, 2013.

MACHALA

Machala, the capital of El Oro Province, is an important city for Ecuador's banana production. In fact, because of the area's mass banana production and exportation, it is sometimes referred to as the "banana capital of the world." There is even a World Banana Festival in late September that includes the Banana Queen of Machala contest. Head to the cities outskirts and you'll find seemingly never-ending banana plantations growing out in every direction.

Although Machala is an important hub for business in Ecuador - and thus home of a decent amount of conventions and meetings - it is not often frequented by foreigners. Most travelers pass through here on their way to the border or up to Guayaquil, but there are definitely worse places to stop over if you decide to linger and it's certainly a more preferable place compared to Huaquillas.
Updated: Apr 20, 2013.

Getting To and Away from Machala

Although Machala doesn't have a major bus station, all the bus companies have their own small stations located in the center of town. In general each company goes to a certain area of the country. To get to **Guayaquil**, there are several options: Cifa (Tel: 593-7-293-3735, URL: www.cifainternacional.com), Ecuatoriano Pullman (T. Córdovez, Tel: 593-7-293-0197) or Rutas Orenses (R. Gómez, Tel: 593-7-293-7661). Panamericana (T. Córdovez and Santa Rosa, Tel: 593-7-293-0141,) has six comfortable buses daily to Quito ($10, 12hr). For **Cuenca** ($5, 5hr) try Trans Azuay, (T. Córdovez and Santa Rosa, Tel: 593-7-293-0539), which has eight daily buses. Updated: Apr 20, 2013.

Things To See and Do Around Machala

ISLA DE JAMBELI

On Isla de Jambeli, one of Ecuador's southermost beaches, you'll find adequate accommodations, most of which have a laid back, rustic feel. To get to this island you need to get a boat ride from the Puerto Bolivar part of El Oro province in Ecuador. All of the Isla de Jambeli hotels are beachfront, but you only have a few to choose from. You can also stay in Puerto Bolivar, where there are more options available.
Updated: Jul 12, 2013.

Hostal Solar del Puerto

This is great hostel to use as a take-off point for Jambeli Island. Great service, helpful staff, clean, comfortable rooms, hot water, nice sitting areas on each floor and upstairs there is an open patio with a view of the ocean! Breakfast is included and tasty. They have a secure parking lot, so you can leave your car when you go over to the island. Av. Gonzalo Cordova y Henriquez, Tel: 593-7-292-8793/8796, E-mail: solarpto@ecua.net.ec, URL: www.hostalsolardelpuerto.com.ec. Updated: Jun 10, 2013.

Museo Marino

The exhibit is made of over 500 pieces on display, divided into mollusks, crustaceans, echinoderms, corals, algae, fishes, whale bones and sea fossils. The majority of the collection was found in the Ecuadorian coastline and a 10% from other countries. Geomer Garcia Poma, Owner and Director. 300 meters south (left) of the main entrance of the beach. Tel: 593-9-383-6307, E-mail: geomertierramar741@hotmail.com. Updated: Mar 20, 2013.

SOUTHERN COAST

Machala Lodging

Machala's largest draw is its thriving banana trade, whereas the beach and town itself are not much to see. There are a few luxury Machala hotels to accommodate the businessmen, as well as a number of lower price options for the travelers and tourists. However, there aren't too many places to stay in Machala, so make sure to book in advance. Updated: Jul 12, 2013.

Hotel Ines

($10-20 per person) If you are looking for a place that is budget-friendly, Hotel Ines is a good bet. It may not be the fanciest or the newest place, but it is perfectly acceptable. Most rooms have air conditioning and cable TV. Juan Montalvo 1509 and Pasaje, Tel: 593-4-7293-2301.
Updated: Apr 20, 2013.

Hotel Oro Verde

(ROOMS: $129-350) Hotel Oro Verde may be by far the nicest hotel in Machala, but it is the sort of place where you are paying for luxury, rooms start at $129 bucks a night. However, if your budget allows this sort of prices, and you want to have a relaxing couple of days, this is the perfect place to stay. The hotel's décor is meant to be reminiscent of New Mexico, with adobe and bright colors. On site there is a coffee shop, two restaurants, a laundry room, a deli, a gym and Turkish baths and a whirlpool. Circunvalación Norte y Calle Vehicular, Tel: 593-7-2933140, Fax: 593-7-2933150, E-mail: ov_mch@oroverdehotels.com.
Updated: Jun 04, 2013.

Oro Hotel

(ROOMS: $27-40) For a bit more comfort, this is a better bet with spacious rooms, friendly service and a pleasant café. Breakfast is included. Sucre and Juan Montalvo, Tel: 593-7-293-7569, URL: www.orohotel.com. Updated: Apr 20, 2013.

Border Crossings To and From Peru

Tumbes, Peru / Huaquillas, Ecuador

The most popular border crossing between Ecuador and Peru is a bridge over the **Río Zarumilla**. Note that before crossing the border you need to get the exit stamp from the Ecuadorian immigration office (open 24hr, Tel: 593-7-299-6755), inconveniently located 3km north. If you're coming from Machala, ask the driver to stop here, or take a taxi ($1.50). Then take a bus or taxi to the bridge, which must be crossed on foot, then get your passport checked by Peruvian officials on the other side. Note that the entry stamp is usually obtained at the main Peruvian immigration office at **Zarumilla** a couple of kilometres away ($1 by mototaxi). There are regular direct buses to **Tumbes, Piura, Trujillo** or **Lima**. A taxi to Tumbes costs $5-7. Ensure you get an exit stamp from the country you are leaving and an entry stamp for the country you are arriving in, otherwise you could have big legal problems.

Besides the to-be-expected contraband running, dangers await at the border for the unsuspecting. For many decades, travelers of all nationalities have reported that they were given counterfeit notes by border money changers, robbed on the route between border posts, charged extra fees by corrupt border officials (all official transactions are free) and taxi drivers (who may demand a $20 "road tax" at gunpoint) and, unfortunately, even assaulted and raped. Many international travelers are now choosing to use the other border crossing near La Tina. However, for those whose next destination is on the coast, Huaquillas remains the most logical point to cross into Peru.

We don't recommend crossing in the evening, but if events conspire to leave you in Huaquillas at dusk, there are some safe accommodation options. Grand **Hotel Hernancor** (Tel: 593-7-299-5467) and **Hotel Vanessa** (Tel: 593-7-299-6263, next to each other on 1 de Mayo 323 and Hualtaco, offer decent mid-range rooms with private bathroom, cable TV and air conditioning for $24 (doubles).

Finally, there is direct international service direct between **Piura, Peru** via **Tumbes** crossing via **Huaquillas** to **Machala** or **Guayaquil**. This bus stops at both border posts then on to the final destination. The most reliable service is provided by **Cifa** (Tel: 593-7-293-3735, URL: www.cifainternacional.com). From Guayaquil all the way to Piura takes 9 hours and costs $10-12. Buses between Huaquillas and Machala run several times hourly so if there's no bus direct to Guayaquil, take the first bus to Machala and change there.
Updated: Apr 20, 2013.

)))))

SOUTHERN COAST

Galápagos Islands

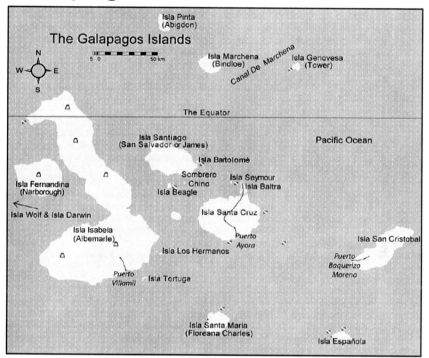

The Galapagos Islands

Leaving behind the smog, traffic and fast food of Quito, an airplane flies two hours west and eons backward in time. The Galápagos Islands are a land that time forgot, a rugged and unforgiving paradise where the air, land and sea are home to species found nowhere else on earth. It is a zoo without cages: each island is its own harsh laboratory of evolution, adaptation and competition. The marine iguanas understand this—stoic black dragons that seem to have crawled out of the volcanic rock itself, they share the lordship of these islands with the birds, tortoises and sea lions. They were here first, and they will permit you to visit, but they know that you couldn't stay even if you wanted to. You're not tough enough to share their rocky bit of paradise.

Fun and sun? Surf and sand? Forget it. If that's what you're looking for, go to Cozumel. A visit to Galápagos is an expedition, a chance to walk in the footprints of Charles Darwin. It's not about the beach entirely; it's about the birds, fish and animals, and simply put, there is no better place to see them up close and personally than here.

In a sense, there are no species that are purely native to the islands. The islands were never connected to any continent—every resident reptile, mammal, bird and fish arrived after the islands were born of thunderous volcanic upheavals in the deep crevasses of the Pacific Ocean. Once these animals found themselves on these rock-strewn, desolate islands, survival dictated the long process of adaptation. Ages later, the island species no longer even resemble their cousins on the continent.

There are dozens of species on Galápagos, animals that can be found nowhere else on earth. Not counting Lonesome George, there are 10 surviving species of giant Galápagos Tortoise: four more have gone extinct. The Galápagos Penguin is the only penguin to live north of the equator. The Flightless Cormorant has lost its wings to evolution—there are few predators to flee. The iguanas are marvels of adaptation—the land iguanas eat spiny cacti with ease, while the marine iguanas can survive a 15 degree drop in body temperature while they eat underwater algae. Even the

GALÁPAGOS

nondescript little finches have their share of the fame: Darwin used the 13 different endemic species of finch as an example to prove his theories (one variety can suck blood!). Even many marine species are endemic: the Galápagos Shark is a gray reef shark only found in the islands.

Young Sea Lions, Española

For all the rugged vistas and parched, rocky trails, Galápagos is actually a very fragile ecosystem. The first settlers released goats and pigs into the wild. This did provide food in the short term, but now they're considered an ecological disaster: they destroy the vegetation and ruin the habitat of other native animals; the tortoises and iguanas in particular have been badly affected. Introduced plants such as the sour apple and blackberry have taken over acres of park area, forcing out native plants in the process. Domestic dogs and cats that escape and breed in the wild are considered a serious problem as well. Efforts to control these animals and plants have met with mixed success: for example, goats have been successfully eradicated from some of the islands.

There is hope—concerted efforts of park staff, international organizations and tourism operators have helped greatly in recent years to protect the islands and the animals that live there. And don't be dismayed by the history of the islands! As long as you closely follow the instructions that your specially trained naturalist guide gives you, you won't cause any damage.

There is a reason why the Galápagos Islands are one of the top three visitor destinations in South America on any list you check: they're magnificent. Enjoy the white sand beaches, lounge on a luxurious cruise ship, but bring extra rolls of film or digital memory cards for the real stars of the islands—the flora and fauna of one of the the last original places in the world!

Planning Your Galápagos Trip

A visit to the Galápagos is the trip of a lifetime, and it needs to be planned accordingly! There are a limited number of visitors who are allowed to go to the islands every year and the cruise ships tend to fill up at certain times of the year. You'll want to start planning long before your actual trip. Here are some of the questions you need to ask yourself while still in the early planning stages.

WHEN TO GO?

Galápagos is always nice, but there are other factors such as animal life cycles and high/low tourism seasons to consider. See the following section for details (p. 454).

HOW MUCH CAN I AFFORD TO SPEND?

Unless you have a minimum of about $1500 for a five-day trip, not counting airfare from wherever you are to Ecuador, you will not be able to afford a cruise and will have to see the islands while staying in Puerto Ayora or one of the other towns.

That's not necessarily a bad thing; many people choose to see them this way. Just bear in mind that Galápagos is expensive. Even if you're already in Quito, it will cost you some $600 for the flight and park entrance taxes...just to set foot in Galápagos!

If you can afford a little more, services improve greatly the more you spend, and you're more likely to have a memorable time.

WHAT DO I WANT TO DO WHILE I'M THERE?

Do you want to spend a day SCUBA diving? Then you'll need to stay in one of the towns for a while. Do you want to shop for souvenirs? You'll want to go to Puerto Ayora or Puerto Baquerizo Moreno. Want to try some local food? Puerto Ayora is your best bet. Need a few days on the beach? Head for Isabela Island.

This goes for the animals, too. Do you want to see a Galápagos Penguin? They are only at certain visitor sites. Same goes for the albatrosses, cormorants, tortoises and land iguanas. If you desperately want to see one of these species, look closely at our Wildlife and Visitor Sites sections (p. 480 and 521) while planning your trip, and only go on a cruise that visits those sites.

To get the most out of your time at the islands and explore as much as possible, taking a cruise (p. 464) over the course of a week is the best thing to do.

Did a unique trek? Tell other travelers at vivatravelguides.com

WHO DO I BOOK WITH?

There are countless tour agencies and travel agents that offer trips to Galápagos. Your friendly hometown travel agency can help, but if you want someone with a little more experience in the islands, I personally recommend the following:

Haugan Cruises: Haugan Cruises operates the catamarans Ocean Spray and Cormorant, two of the nicer ships in Galapagos. They can also set you up on other cruises and get last-minute deals if that's what you're looking for. Reliable, responsible and professional, Haugan cruises is a big step up from the places in Mariscal. URL: www.haugancruises.com.

Opuntia Eco Journeys: Contrary to all the hype and fuss over cruises, Opuntia aims to organize a well-rounded experience that's based around taking in the wildlife, nature and adventure that's to be found in land-based tours of the islands. The moments you do spend in the water will only involve either going from island to island quickly or checking out the wildlife below with snorkeling, rather than spending it on a cruise. As added karma, Opuntia is also recognized by the Rainforest Alliance as a sustainable tour operator. Their guides are top-notch and the tours are meant to give you a thorough experience of the Galapagos islands and its highlights, rather than just a passing visit which cruise-based tours are prone to giving. Manuel Sotomayor E17-105 and Flores Jijón Tel: 1-800-217-9414, URL: www.opuntiagalapagostours.com.

Andean Discovery: Experts in putting together your Andean "dream trip," Andean Discovery sets out to take care of all the logistics involved in arranging an itinerary for you and filling your time in Ecuador (or even Peru). Their interest and devotion in taking you off the beaten path is what makes them quite exceptional, showing you places many others rarely get to see. Their itineraries can also convert just about any set of variables (budget, interests, schedule, group size, etc.) into an unforgettable and solid experience. The guides are well-trained English speakers and will be there to offer you a safe and memorable experience as well. Tel: 1-800-893-0916, E-mail: info@andeandiscovery.com, URL: www.andeandiscovery.com.

Metropolitan Touring: Metropolitan is an Ecuadorian agency which has been working in Galápagos for decades. They have international offices and agents and can combine your Galápagos tour with visits to mainland Ecuador, Peru (Machu Picchu!), Argentina or other South American points of interest. Metropolitan is best for those with a little more money to spend who want to hire one of the top local agencies to make sure there is always someone to meet them at the airport, make sure their tour van is ready to go, etc. URL: http://www.metropolitan-touring.com.

Columbus Travel: Based in Quito, Columbus specializes in Galápagos and trips to mainland Ecuador. They are experienced and professional and have a long track record of satisfied clients. Columbus is best if you know you want to go to Ecuador and Galápagos but don't know exactly what you want to do: their staff will patiently talk you through any questions you may have and find the right cruise/tour/itinerary for you. They know all of the ships, and therefore any budget level is welcome to book with them. URL: http://www.galapagosisland.net.

Come to Galápagos: Based in Puerto Baquerizo Moreno (San Cristóbal Island), Come to Galápagos is run by an American/Ecuadorian couple who are residents of the islands and therefore have local knowledge other agencies lack. They specialize in land-based tours (as opposed to cruises) and pride themselves on individual attention. They also sponsored the first ever Galápagos marathon! Best for those who want a land-based tour or who prioritize helping local communities, a foundation of Come to Galápagos. URL: http://www.cometogalapagos.com.

Galápagos Travel Center: GTC is a reliable operator with an office near the corner of Foch and Reina Victoria in Mariscal. They specialize in personalized service and good prices. They do all things Galápagos: land tours, diving, cruises - you name it. Combination tours with mainland attractions are also possible. URL: www.galapagosislands.com.

Galápagos Travel Line is run by Rodrigo Miño (formerly of Columbus Travel) who has a great many years of experience in the industry and contacts with boats and operators. Miño and his team are friendly, helpful and accommodating in finding you a trip to suit your needs and budget. URL: http://www.galapagostraveline.com.

Updated: July 31, 2013

GALÁPAGOS

Galápagos Island Highlights

Wildlife (p. 480) Visitors to the Galápagos do not come for the great beaches, delicious food, or lavish accommodations - althought these are a plus - they come to see the world's most amazing cage-less zoo. Travelers in the Galápagos can observe (without binoculars) the unique and often unusual characteristics and behavior of species not found anywhere else in the world.

Diving (p. 462) The Galápagos is consistently ranked among the best overall dive sites in the world. Because of the combination of cool and warm water ocean currents and a high level of ecosystem protection, the variety and abundance of Galápagosfish and marine mammal species is astounding.

Puerto Ayora (p. 493) The majority of land tours, scuba diving tours and adventure tours originate and/or are based in Puerto Ayora. Travelers with more time than money can often save up to 50 percent by booking a last-minute cruise in this quaint port town. Puerto Ayora has a wealth of hotels, restaurants, bars, stores, tour agencies, dive shops, internet cafés and phone cabinas.

Cruise Tours (p. 464) The most popular way to see the islands is a boat tour through the archipelago. These boats become the visitor's home for the duration of the tour, and all activities originate from these ships.

Visitors Sites (p. 521) Travelers in the Galápagos will be amazed by the number and vriation of visitor sites throughout the archipelago. There are over 50 accessible visitor sites in the Galápagos National Park Territory. Each offers its own unique history, landscape, vegetative characteristics and faunal features. When taken in tandem, visitors can begin to understand the complex evolutionary process that has shaped island biogeography. Read on to see each visitor site listed along with a map including island wildlife, paths, fauna and dive sites.

GALÁPAGOS

When To Go to the Galápagos

There is no bad time to visit the Galápagos Islands. There is always something interesting to see and the weather is usually great. Still, there are a few variables you may want to consider.

WEATHER

The Equator passes through the islands, so it's never frigid, but there are significant seasonal variations. From June to November, currents bring cool water and air to the islands. The islands are cooler, there is more rain or mist (garúa), and water temperatures are cool enough that you may want a wetsuit while snorkeling. From December to May, the islands get hotter (sometimes it's quite brutal) and there is more rain. The highlands of San Cristobal and Santa Cruz can get cool any time of year.

WILDLIFE

There are cycles and patterns to the wildlife as well, and you should bear this in mind if seeing a particular type of animal or behavior is important to you. For example, the tortoises migrate into and out of the highlands; if you want to see them in their natural habitat, it's best to go between January and June. If you want to see a Waved Albatross, don't go from January to April, because they won't be there. If you want to see a specific animal, your tour company should be able to tell you or see our wildlife section.

Did a unique trek? Tell other travelers at vivatravelguides.com

Galápagos History

For years, tourism was limited to a few stray boats that visited, and there were really no controls. It wasn't until the 1950s that tourism began to be a serious industry in the islands, and not until the 1970s that it started to show signs of the boom that it is now. Although tourism was embraced by some of the islanders, most notably the descendants of the salty German settlers of the early 20th century, most viewed it with a mixture of suspicion and resentment. As tourism increased, Ecuadorian and foreign experts came to the islands and began telling the islanders what to do: "Don't eat the tortoises! Don't kill the sharks! Don't plant non-native plants!" For a rugged people that had been totally ignored by mainland Ecuador for decades, this new do-what-we-say attitude was offensive.

Conflicts between the two major industries—fishing and tourism—continued to grow. In the islands, the two are often at odds with one another; the aggressive fishing of sharks (for their fins) and sea cucumbers has crippled the island ecosystem, which in turn means less wildlife for tourists to see. Fishermen have been known to blockade certain islands in order to have their demands for more liberal quotas met by the government.

Historically, the biggest complaint of the islanders with tourism is that much of the money that comes into the islands does not stay there. Many visitors book their cruises and flights abroad, come to the islands, pay their park fee, and go right to their ship. Locals rarely see much money from these sorts of tourists. Only those who work on the ships or sell the occasional souvenir in town see any profit.

In the late 1990s, several initiatives were passed to allow the islanders to take more control over the tourism industry. One of the first laws to be passed was one specifying that guides must be Galapagueños, and could no longer come from abroad or the Ecuadorian mainland. Even those non-native guides who were grandfathered in under the new law are being muscled out by aggressive unions. This law had the desired effect, as many locals became guides and started to earn very good money working for the tour companies.

Unfortunately, the overall quality of guides suffered, because the foreign and mainland guides in general are better educated and speak more languages than the locals. Also, once the law was passed, the pool of available guides decreased dramatically and ships were forced to grossly overpay unqualified guides in order to meet park regulations. In some cases, guides that were repeatedly accused of sexually harassing visitors continued to easily find work, simply because there was no one else to take their places.

More initiatives have passed to benefit the islanders. In the future, all ships must have all-Galápagos staff and even be at least 51% locally owned in order to operate.

A new $100 tax on all arriving tourists will be divided among the three towns in the islands: it should add up to millions of dollars. Within a few years, the entire tourism industry should be controlled locally.

There is a new attitude among the islanders. They feel that for too long they were ignored or bossed around by the mainland, and now they are ready to seize control of the lucrative tourism industry for themselves. Ask any islander about it and they will rant and rave about the injustices of the past, when rich tourists came to the islands but all their money stayed in Quito and Guayaquil. Some of them are quite militant and hostile about the whole issue.

GALÁPAGOS

TOURISM

If it's your plan to go to the islands and either island hop or try to find a good last minute deal, you'll want to do so during low tourist season. Try May-early June or late September-October. Early December is also a good time to go. If you go during high season, hotels and last minute deals will be much harder to find.

Galápagos Budgeting and Costs

Once you've paid for your Galápagos tour and flights, you don't need any more money, right? Wrong! There are still some costs you'll need to consider.

OFFICIAL FEES AND TAXES

All adult foreigners must pay a $100 entry fee to Galápagos. The majority of this income (over 95%) goes to the maintenance and conservation of the Galápagos National Park. The Instituto Nacional Galápagos is now charging visitors an additional $10 fee for the issue of "Transit Control Cards." The new cards will keep better track of tourist numbers on the islands and monitor both arrival and departure dates. You get your card in the airport in Quito or Guayaquil.

Leaving the pier on Isabela Island (on a ferry to Puerto Ayora) will cost you $10.

EXPENSES ON CRUISE SHIPS

If you're on a cruise ship, most of your expenses will be paid for. Most likely you'll only be paying for drinks such as alcohol or soda. There may in some cases be a small fee to rent gear such as fins or wetsuits. Most of the larger ships have gift shops with T-shirts, playing cards, etc. There has been some talk of charging cruise-going visitors an additional $100, but this fee has not yet been implemented. Recently, a "fuel surcharge" has been added to cruise costs, but it's generally just factored in when you pay.

TIPPING YOUR GALÁPAGOS

GUIDE AND CREWS

Tipping guides and ship crews is customary in Galápagos. This is always a delicate subject, since tips are generally meant to be a reflection of services rendered and not an obligation.

Some people recommend giving the crew between $20 and $50 per passenger per week, and giving the guide as much as half of that amount. Others suggest tipping as much as $10 per passenger per day, which can add up. Each boat has its own system for accepting tips—two envelopes, a communal tip box, the honor system—but the crew, not the tourist, is responsible for dividing the tip money among the individual members.

If any of the crew members were exceptional, feel free to give them an individual display of gratitude, monetary or verbal.

Guides, staff and crew can make or break your Galapagos cruise experience!

SHOPPING IN GALÁPAGOS TOWNS

When you are in Puerto Ayora or Puerto Baquerizo Moreno the potential for spending money is high. A tourist's necessity items—camera supplies and sunscreen, to mention a few—are two to three times more expensive in Galápagos than in the United States, or even on the mainland, so stock up before you come.

Souvenir shops abound in both major towns. Visitors can select from Galápagos T-shirts, coffee mugs, hats, playing cards, posters and much more. Prices for these tend to run relatively high; figure on $12-20 for a T-shirt, three postcards for a dollar, etc. Selection is pretty good, so getting little gifts for friends back home is easy. Savvy Galápagos souvenir shoppers may want to check out the little stuffed boobies, sea lions and other animals; some of these are actually made in Galápagos out of recycled material and make great gifts.

Major credit cards are accepted in many of the nicer hotels, restaurants, gift shops and tour centers, but they often charge for use of this particular service.

There is one bank in Puerto Ayora, the Banco del Pacífico, which gives cash advances on MasterCards, changes traveler's checks (with a minimal surcharge), and has a MasterCard and Cirrus-compatible ATM. The bank is open from Monday to Friday (8 a.m.-3:30 p.m.) and Saturday (9:30 a.m.-12:30 p.m.). There are also some stores on Avenida Charles Darwin that will change your traveler's checks for you. Make sure before you come that you will have the ability to withdraw money; otherwise, bring more cash than you think you will need—small bills are preferred. You are more likely to spend all of your cash than have it stolen!

There are also ATMs in Puerto Baquerizo Moreno (San Cristóbal Island), but note that **there is no ATM on Isabela**. There isn't much to buy there, as there are no souvenir stores, but you'll want to bring enough cash with you to cover your hotel, food, tours, etc. For decades, Galápagos was a backwater province, a place no decent Ecuadorian wanted to go. A few hundred hardy pioneers, half-cracked German settlers and irredeemable criminals in penal colonies scratched a meager living out of the volcanic rocks. They were subsistence farmers and fishermen, and thought nothing of eating the tortoises, birds and other animals that the islands are now famous for. The Ecuadorian government was far away and frankly couldn't have cared less about them.

STAYING IN GALÁPAGOS

If you're staying in the cities instead of on a cruise ship, your budget can vary greatly. Hotels run from as little as $10 per night on up into the thousands of dollars. Restaurants are similar: it's possible to eat dinner for anywhere from $4 to $30. In general, it's tough to economize in Galápagos. As a bare minimum, plan on spending $50 per day in Galápagos, including the most basic hotels and food and a day trip to a snorkeling spot, beach or nature trail with guide. Some of the best visitor sites are free: if you're saving, look for those!

DAY TRIPS

Packaged tours may offer any combination of trips to local visitor sites. You can book individually (with one or a few companies) or you can book a weekly tour package comprised of a series of day trips, which can include land sites, snorkeling/dive sites, surf sites, or all three.

Daily tours to island sites range in price from $30 to $115 per person per day when booked individually, depending on the services provided by the tour company and the sites visited. Daily tours to dive sites have less variable prices; most dive centers charge a standard $100 to $150 per person per day, according to the site. The price of combination tour packages range from $800

to $1,200 per week, including guided trips, hotel and meals. You can arrange these types of trips from your home country or from the mainland, following the same guidelines outlined for navigable tours.

For some companies that offer land-based or snorkeling tours, visit our Galápagos Tours page for an overview and list of operators.

A typical island day trip begins at dawn, with a walk to the dock or a bus trip to the canal, where you meet the boat that will take you to your destination. You spend a short time sailing to the predetermined visitor site. Once there you will spend the majority of the day touring the island with a naturalist guide, eating lunch, and (if available at the island site) swimming and snorkeling from the beach. You return to town via the same route in the early afternoon.

There are plenty of day trip operators in Puerto Ayora (fewer in Puerto Baquerizo Moreno) who will accept reservations until the day preceding the excursion. Day boats can vary in quality and comfort, but since most island sites are close and you spend a relatively longer period of time on-site, it is probably more important to shop for day trips by destination. Most day trip destinations from Puerto Ayora include visitor sites on the central islands of Santa Cruz, Santa Fé, North Seymour, South Plazas and Bartolomé. Different boats visit different islands on different days, so plan accordingly.

DIVE DAY TRIPS

Galápagos is a world famous dive destination and many visitors will want to spend a day or more diving. This is easily done with one of the many dive shops in both major towns. Visit our Galápagos Diving section for more information.

LAND-BASED VS. CRUISE TOURS

There are certain benefits associated with land-based tours, the most important of which is the comfort of stationary hotel accommodations versus mobile staterooms. You are not limited to on-board facilities and services, gaining access to a wider variety of port town restaurants, nightlife and shops. Finally, your community and associated social outlets extend to town visitors and residents, not just the other passengers on your boat. Being on land also allows you to pick and choose where you want to go instead of being tied to an itinerary mandated by the national park.

GALÁPAGOS

There are downsides to land-based tours relative to navigable tours. A considerable time is spent sailing back and forth to visitor sites; you are limited to visiting the close, central islands; only one (versus two) site is visited per day; and there is no chance of visiting sites either very early or late in the day.

Galápagos Packing List

Most things travelers need are available in Galápagos, but at a much higher price than on the mainland. You should plan on bringing what you'll need.

CLOTHES

There is no dress code on most boats or in island towns, so pack casual yet comfortable clothing. Bring lightweight, breathable items for day hikes and a sweater or jacket for cool evenings on the boat. Terrain on some islands is rough and rocky, so pack comfortable sneakers or hiking boots with good traction. Tevas, Chacos or any other types of sandal with a security strap are great for beach sites and less rugged trails. On the boat, you will keep your shoes in a communal bin and either walk barefoot or in flip-flops. A good hat, preferably with a wide brim, is a must.

LUGGAGE

If you are on a cruise tour, it is a good idea to pack as lightly and compactly as possible, since there is only a finite amount of space in your cabin and on board. Backpacks are the most portable through all of the required land-water transfers, but suitcases and duffel bags are fine.

Your boat will send representatives from the crew to meet you at the airport, collect your bags, deliver them to the boat, and ultimately place them in your cabin. So if you have bulky or awkward pieces of luggage, the burden of transporting them will fall upon the helpful and gracious members of the crew.

Because you will have day excursions on the islands, it is essential that you bring a day pack or fanny pack so that you can have water, sun protection, photographic equipment, rain gear and any other items you may need with you at all times.

SWIMMING/SNORKELING GEAR

You will have a number of opportunities to swim, snorkel or scuba dive in Galápagos, oftentimes more than once a day. As such, you should bring a swimsuit, a towel (most ships provide beach towels but the cheap ones might not), and beach attire (a sarong or beach wrap is perfect for women).

Because you can get cold and sunburned very easily in Galápagos waters, it is also a good idea to bring a lightweight neoprene wetsuit or dive skin, if you have one, or some other quick-dry outfit that you don't mind wearing in the ocean. Wetsuits are available for rental on most of the reputable cruise ships— check once you've booked. If not, you can rent one in Puerto Ayora or Puerto Baquerizo Moreno.

Many boats have their own snorkeling equipment, which is complimentary or available for rent, but the quality and maintenance may be sub-par and the sizes available may be limited. If you are on a boat with scuba diving capability, you will probably have more luck, but you should still bring your own if you have it.

SCUBA DIVING EQUIPMENT

If you plan on scuba diving and have your own equipment, bring it. You will need at least a 6mm wetsuit, boots, gloves and possibly a hood, in addition to a regulator, BCD, computer, fins and mask. All of the dive shops will include equipment in the price of their packages, but the quality and size availability vary from place to place. Some dive shops replace their equipment every year, keep a variety of sizes and styles and maintain their gear in stellar condition. Others have older, worn-out equipment—a sticky regulator, a leaky BCD, ill-fitting apparel, etc.—that is still usable but less desirable for many recreational divers. The conditions in Galápagos can be challenging for many divers, so if you are at all nervous about your abilities, ease some of your worries by bringing your own gear.

MEDICAL

If you use any prescription medications, be sure to bring plenty, as they can be tough to find in the islands. You'll also want seasickness tablets if you tend to suffer from it, as well as aspirin, anti-diarrheal medicine such as Lomotil, and other basics. You'll definitely want sun protection: sunscreen, hats, sunglasses, after-sun lotion, etc.

PHOTOGRAPHY

Galápagos is an excellent place—even for novices—to take magazine-quality photographs and to make exciting home videos. Because much of the wildlife in Galápagos is close to the trails, you can get very good

GALÁPAGOS

results with even the most basic cameras. Although you probably don't need anything larger than a standard lens, you can get some stunning close-up results if you bring a zoom lens.

Make sure you have plenty of memory space; you'll be taking a lot of photos. Bring a memory stick as well, to help with sharing photos with fellow guests and new-found friends. If you know you will be making a stop in Puerto Ayora during your cruise, you can plan to download photos from your memory card onto a CD at any of the internet cafés in town. Some cruise ships offer this service as well. Back up your favorite photos: more than one camera has accidentally found its way to the bottom of Galapagos waters!

You should also bring an underwater casing for your camera (if you have one) or an underwater camera. Although capturing the underwater landscape and bigger creatures is best with a video camera or a camera with a strobe, the smaller digital cameras with flash are great for macro shots of fish, seascapes or coral. If you own binoculars, this is the time to bring them.

In Summary ... A basic packing list of the essentials in Galápagos:

- Sunhat
- sunglasses
- sandals (for the boat)
- sneakers (for dry landings and rocky shores) Teva-style sandals (for wet landings)
- swimsuit
- umbrella (for sun protection during island hikes or the occasional downpour)
- high factor, waterproof sunscreen
- binoculars
- flashlight or head lamp
- water bottle
- plastic Ziploc bags to keep things from getting wet
- snorkel and mask if you aren't renting
- beach towel and bath towel
- wind resistant jacket
- light sweater or sweatshirt (nights can get rather cool and you don't want to miss stargazing on deck)
- twice as much film or memory cards as you think you will need
- extra batteries
- underwater camera
- motion sickness pills
- Water can be very cold so you may want to bring a dive skin or wetsuit

WHAT NOT TO BRING:
Although there are mosquitoes in Galápagos, none of them are carriers of malaria or dengue fever, so you don't have to worry about bringing medicine. Parts of mainland Ecuador are risky for malaria and other ailments, so if your trip will take you to other parts of Ecuador, you may want medicine.

Galápagos Health and Safety

Touring Galápagos can be a mentally and physically exhausting vacation. The long flights, extended periods of time on a moving boat and drastic changes between land and sea temperatures can all take their toll on the body. Here are some tips for keeping healthy.

COMMON MEDICAL PROBLEMS
The two most common ailments for Galápagos visitors are overexposure to the sun and seasickness. Sunscreen and motion sickness medicines are available in Puerto Ayora or Puerto Baquerizo Moreno, but it's better to bring your own.

MEDICAL FACILITIES IN GALÁPAGOS
Medical facilities and pharmacies on Puerto Ayora are decent. The town's hospital offers basic medical services, but it is not very modern or well-stocked. There is a 24-hour clinic on San Cristóbal and a small clinic on Isabela as well. You can usually find an English-speaking doctor at the hospitals.

The hyperbaric chamber/clinic in Puerto Ayora offers 24-hour care for diving emergencies and serious burns. Dr. Gabriel Idrovo and Dr. Ramiro López specialize in hyperbaric medicine, but they also provide general medical consultations during their regular office hours (9:30 a.m.-1:30 p.m. and 3:30-7:30 p.m.). Since it is a private facility that counts on only a small percentage of its funding from local scuba-diving operators, they may ask tourists that use the clinic to give a small contribution in addition to the $20-30 consultation fee.

SAFETY IN GALÁPAGOS
Mainland Ecuador has its share of problems with crime and poverty. Fortunately, Galápagos is a different matter. You really only need to be watchful of unattended things—do not leave valuables behind at public beaches or snorkeling sites, or purses or cameras unattended on restaurant tables. Belongings left

behind in hotel rooms will usually be pretty safe, but lock them up if there is a strongbox in your room. Cruises are generally safe in terms of things stolen from rooms, but if you're on a budget cruise, keep an eye on your stuff.

Galápagos Transportation

Transportation on Galápagos is mainly based on boats and planes. In the two main towns, there are some cars and taxis.

Transportation to the islands from mainland Ecuador is only by plane, given no boats offer transportation. All flights to the islands leave from Quito or Guayaquil.

Once you are on the islands, most visitor sites are reached by boat. We have divided this section into: "transportation to and from Puerto Ayora," "transportation around Puerto Ayora" and "transportation around the Galápagos Islands."

TRANSPORTATION TO AND FROM THE GALÁPAGOS ISLANDS

Flights to the main Galápagos airports in San Cristóbal and Baltra depart from Quito and generally stop en route in Guayaquil. The Quito-Guayaquil flight lasts about 40 minutes, and the Guayaquil-Galápagos flight takes just under two hours. The archipelago is one hour behind mainland Ecuador.

Three airlines, LAN, TAME and Aerogal, service the Galápagos Islands. Children and infants do receive a discount. According to TAME, the low tourist season is from May 1 to June 14 and from September 15 to October 31. Times vary and change in different seasons, but the prices are fixed, so there's no need to comparison shop.

If you book a cruise, the travel agency generally arranges your flight for you. Even though there is usually some availability on flights to the Galápagos, it is a good idea to make independent flight reservations at least a few days in advance.

Travel agencies will block seats for their all-inclusive tours, but then release them on the day of the flight if there are cancellations or unsold tour spaces. So if you are desperate to get to (or return from) the Enchanted Islands, you should be able to find spaces last-minute, especially during low-season.

Since flight prices are fixed, you can usually change the date of your ticket after purchasing it without penalty.

This policy can come in handy if you—like many other tourists—get caught up in the small-town charm of Puerto Ayora and decide to extend your stay; just stop by the TAME office anytime before your flight to make alternative arrangements.

Furthermore, if you decide after sunbathing for a week that you want to spend more time in coastal climes, you can easily change your final destination to Guayaquil. This requires simply checking your luggage to Guayaquil; no ticket change is needed.

It is not feasible to take a boat from mainland Ecuador to the Galápagos: it is a three-day trip over rough waters and there are currently no ships or agencies selling this service.

TRANSPORTATION TO AND FROM PUERTO AYORA OR PUERTO BAQUERIZO MORENO

After you deplane in Baltra, you will either meet the naturalist guide leading your pre-arranged tour or you will head off individually towards Puerto Ayora. If you have an organized cruise tour, you will go with your guide and boat-mates on a five-minute TAME or Aerogal bus ride to the *muelle*, or dock, where you will take a ferry to the other side. Once there, transportation will take you to the pier over in Puerto Ayora where your boat is anchored. The drive there takes 20 mins.

If you are on your own and heading to Puerto Ayora, you can ride the same TAME or Aerogal bus to the canal (for free) and take the same ferry to Santa Cruz ($1 one-way). Once you get across the channel to Santa Cruz, you can either catch a taxi (about $20 per truck, so try to share) or public bus ($3) to take you the final leg to Puerto Ayora. The trip takes approximately 45 minutes by bus, and 20-30 if going in taxi.

Ideally, the ferries and buses are scheduled to coincide with flights landing and taking off, so you should not have to wait long to catch transportation in that direction. The taxi or bus will drop you off in any of the most frequented central spots—like the main pier or boardwalk—or the hotel you specify to the driver.

If your point of arrival is Puerto Baquerizo Moreno (San Cristóbal) it's not nearly as complicated. The airport is right on the edge of town. There are plenty of taxis there to take you to your hotel and the ride should cost less than $2.

Did a unique trek? Tell other travelers at vivatravelguides.com

TRANSPORTATION BETWEEN ISLANDS

Inter-island transportation is relatively straightforward. You can travel between Santa Cruz and the other main islands of San Cristóbal and Isabela either by plane, ferry or private boat. Itineraries and prices can change. The small airline, EMETEBE, flies a small plane between the main islands every day, if there are passengers. Tickets can be purchased at any of the airports or at the EMETEBE office near the port supermarket in Puerto Ayora (hours: 7:15-10:45 a.m., 2-6 p.m.; telephone: 05-252-6177). The flight costs about $160 one-way and lasts about 30 minutes.

Most people simply use the ferry. Every day, a handful of private ferries will leave Puerto Ayora for Isabela or San Cristóbal and vice versa. Some are better than others, so book your ferry ahead of time with a tour agency in town. You'll see signs on the travel agencies that say "Ferry Isabela San Cristóbal" or something similar. Stay away from the cheesy little hole-in-the-wall agencies near the dock and **never** buy a ferry ticket from a "tour operator" in the street. It's possible to buy a return ticket when you book your ferry, but it's not necessary.

The "system" of ferries is a little hectic. There are several small boats that go between the islands, and some are better than others. Some are quicker, and some have less fumes or have more comfortable seats. There is a co-operative of these ferries loosely overseen by the Galápagos park service. Here are the steps you must take:

- Decide when you want to travel. You can buy your ferry tickets a couple of days in advance.

- Purchase your ticket. They cost $30, or sometimes a little less. There are several places to buy them; many little tour agencies will have signs out front that say "Tickets San Cristóbal & Isabela" or something similar.

- Do not buy them on the street, or from the cheesy little tour agencies close to the pier. Many hotels will help you: if your hotel has this service, use it.

- You do not need to purchase your return ticket when you buy your departure ticket. You can, but it's just as easy to get it in Puerto Villamil or Puerto Baquerizo Moreno, and in fact may save you some hassle.

- To get back to Santa Cruz from Isabela, book a return ticket at the ferry co-op office on the main square. In San Cristóbal, any tour agency can sell you a return ticket.

- The tour operators know which are the better boats, and a good vendor will help you get on one of the more comfortable ones.

- You'll need to arrive at the old tourist pier (next to the Proinsular supermarket) by 1:30 p.m. on the day of your departure, because the park service must inspect your bags before you board. Stand in the "line" and wait your turn: when the park official determines that you are not smuggling illegal plants from one island to the other he or she will put a little tag on your bag.

- Find your ferry. The vendor might have told you which one to look for, or it might say on your ticket. Sometimes, the vendors will accompany you to the pier and help you find the right one.

- Get comfortable for the two-hour ride!

TIPS FOR THE FERRY RIDE:

The water can get quite rough on the two-hour ferry ride, especially during the colder months of June-October. If you are prone to motion sickness, don't eat anything after 10:00 a.m. or so and take a motion sickness pill about 45 minutes before the ferry leaves. Motion sickness pills are called "mareol" in Ecuador and are available at any pharmacy. On the bright side, you'll know quickly how bad the waves will be: within 15 minutes of leaving port you'll be in open water and you'll know how rough it will be for the rest of the trip.

Also, if you get motion sick, sit near the back of the boat, as it moves less. Sometimes, the water is not your worst enemy. Many of the ferries are small and covered and quickly fill up with fumes from the engines. If you feel yourself getting lightheaded, sit where you can get some air.

Ferry times: Puerto Ayora-San Cristóbal: Daily, 2 p.m.

San Cristóbal-Puerto Ayora: Daily, 6:30 a.m.
Puerto Ayora-Isabela: Daily, 2 p.m.
Isabela-Puerto Ayora: Daily, 6 a.m.

All ferries leave from the municipal docks and cost $30 one-way.

GALÁPAGOS

If you are in a hurry or cannot acquire a space on the ferry, you can contract a private boat in any of the port towns. Private transportation will be more expensive. Prices are negotiable, but you should expect to pay between $80 and $100 one-way to either San Cristóbal or Isabela. However, it will be faster and most certainly guided, since local boat-owners love to share their knowledge with tourists. The capitanía, or port captain, should also be able to tell you which boats are going to these islands and their expected departure times, or just ask around.

Galapágos Lodging

There has been a hotel boom in Galapagos in recent years, and for better or for worse, new places have been popping up like mushrooms on a fallen log. Some of these places are quite nice, whereas others...well, you get the idea.

Okay, picture this in your mind's eye. A square room, about fifteen feet (five meters) across. Wall off one corner, roughly 30% of the total space of the room. Inside this area, put a new, tiled bathroom with toilet, sink and shower. In the main room, put in three single beds, wherever they will fit. There is a small, dusty TV bolted to a platform, plugged in and connected to a cable. There is one small refrigerator. A hole has been cut in the wall near the door, and there is a battered air conditioner there. One lone print hangs in a frame: it's of something nautical, but you forget what it is –a ship, maybe – as soon as you look away.

Got it? Congratulations! You've just imagined about 80% of the available rooms in Galapagos. Some won't have cable, some will have a double bed instead of two or three singles, and some will have a small piece of ugly furniture like a dresser or night table, but they're all essentially the same. This room will cost you approximately $25/night in any of the three towns in Galapagos.

The reason is this: most of the hotels in Galapagos are owned by old-time Island families who have built them on their family land in town. Many hotels are literally in someone's backyard. It's a good business for them, because mainland and foreign competitors are no longer allowed to build or operate hotels in the islands. These families are not very creative and don't care much about return business, so there's little reason for them to make the rooms memorable. They also stuff as many beds as they can into the rooms, so they can make more money, but don't worry: you'll still only pay for a double if you have two people in a room with three beds. Naturally, some families take their business as hoteliers more seriously than others, and some of these rooms are not too bad and not unreasonably priced.

Your options tend to be on either price side of the $20-30 range. If you stay at one of the $10/night places, the rooms will have plenty of character, such as stained sheets, doors falling off the hinges and creepy-crawly guests. If you have a little more money to spend, you can get a very nice, breezy room that is tastefully decorated and comfortable for as little as $60 per night. If you really want to go crazy, there are a couple of hotels in the over $200/night range which have every modern convenience and are extremely well-done and classy.

Feel free to bargain with the hotels: their prices are most definitely not set in stone. If you're with a group or if you're staying more than one night it's often possible to wheel and deal a little. Suggest prices that are about 20% discounted and see if they go for it, or simply ask "descuento?" Often that's enough to do the trick. Low tourism season is also a good time to get a deal. High season tends to be between mid-June to mid-Setpember and then mid-September to the end of October), it pays to books ahead of time, as the islands swell with tourists and it may be harder to find a room of your choice. While most Galápagos Islands visitors prefer to spend their tiem cruising around by boat, booking a hotel on any one of the islands is a great way to relax and experience the simple joys of island life.

Air conditioning is much more important in the warm season (December-April). The rest of the year, it's quite cool, and a fan should suffice.

Many hotels (particularly on San Cristobal) advertize "agua caliente" or hot water, but they're referring to the sub-lethal "ducha electrica" or "electric showers" which consist of a heating unit where the shower head should be (picture a cross between a shower head and a toaster, and plug it in). They're not dangerous and do provide tepidly warm water, but they're far from "hot water" as most visitors would define it.

Galapágos Island Diving

The Galápagos are consistently ranked among the best overall dive sites in the world. Because of the combination of cool and warm water ocean currents and a high level of ecosystem protection, the variety and abundance of Galápagos fish and marine mammal species is astounding. Observant divers can expect to see both small reef fish like the endemic gobies and blennies common throughout the islands, and the big draws, like hammerhead, white-tipped and black-tipped reef sharks, Galápagos sharks, green sea turtles, manta and eagle rays, and if you are lucky, a whale shark.

The most frequented dive sites are Gordon Rocks, Daphne Minor, North Seymour (punta and canal), Floreana (Devil's Crown, Champion, and Enderby), Cousin's Rock, and Academy Bay, each of which offers a uniquely spectacular experience. There are also some interesting sites on San Cristobal island, such as Kicker Rock and Isla Lobos. Dive shops in Puerto Baquerizo Moreno can take you there.

Although any open-water certified diver is permitted to dive, strong surge, a dramatic thermocline, and varying water conditions make Galapagos best for experienced divers. All of the dive shops will require for safety purposes (and to check your weight) that you complete a check-dive in a shallow, sandy area near your dive site, but it is your responsibility to recognize your own capabilities and dive (or sit on the boat) accordingly.

It used to be that you could dive and explore island visitor sites on the same cruise, but that is no longer an option. Your best bet is to organize a few daily dive tours from Puerto Ayora either before or after your tour.

If you're a die-hard diver and uninterested in land tours, you'll want to find a live-aboard dive cruise, preferably one that goes to the remote islands of Darwin and Wolf.

GALAPÁGOS TOURS

There are basically three kinds of tours in the Galapagos: 1) yacht cruises, or "navigable tours," around the archipelago, land-based, or 2) "combination tours," to sites near the islands' main towns, and 3) adventure tours, which can run the gamut and are usually sponsored by private entities, hotels, or individuals as alternatives to the other tours.

We have also included a section on avoiding problems and frustrations, (p. 469) which outlines some useful tips that may just save your vacation and thousands of dollars!

Navigable Galapagos tours are organized so that all visitor activities take place from an autonomous tourist vessel: tourists visit the island sites, eat their meals, and sleep on their boat. This is the most popular option, because it allows tourists to visit a wide-range of islands in the archipelago and because it is the most promoted by tour agencies.

Combination tours are organized in conjunction with hotels in Puerto Ayora on Santa Cruz and to a lesser extent, Puerto Baquerizo Moreno (San Cristóbal). Combination tours based in Puerto Ayora venture to various visitor sites on the island of Santa Cruz, on other central islands, and in the water, returning to the same hotel each night.

Many day tours are thematic, like surfing tours and scuba-diving tours, but most can be arranged according to the visitors' interests, combining local sites, nearby island sites, and dive sites.

Galapagos Adventure tours are still in their beginning stages and include activities like kayaking, hiking, horseback riding, mountain biking, scuba diving, snorkeling, and wildlife viewing, to name a few. These are generally promoted by individuals among the local population and are more flexible than their more expensive counterparts - organized tours arranged internationally.

Land-Based Galápagos Tours

ombination tours, or land-based tours, are similar to navigable tours in that they combine visits to land and marine sites in the archipelago. The major difference is that combination tours include lodging on land and are limited to sites within a finite radius of the hub town, either Puerto Ayora or Puerto Baquerizo Moreno. These tours are based in certain hotels, which have partnerships with various tour agencies, dive centers, and transportation services. As cruise prices (and taxes on them) have gone up, more and more Galapagos visitors are choosing land-based trips.

Packaged tours may offer any combination of trips to local visitor sites. You can book individually (with one or a few companies) or you can book a weekly tour package comprised of a series of day trips, which can include land sites, snorkeling/dive sites, surf sites, or all three.

Daily tours to island sites range in price from $30 to $115 per person per day when booked individually, depending on the services provided by the tour company and the site visited. Daily tours to dive sites have less variable prices: most dive centers charge a standard $100 to $120 per person per day, according to the site. The price of combination tour packages range from $800 to $1000 per week, including guided trips, hotel, and meals. You can arrange these types of trips from your home country or from the mainland, following the same guidelines outlined for navigable tours.

For some companies that offer land-based tours, visit our Galapagos tours page for an overview and list of operators.

LAND DAY TRIPS

A typical island day trip begins at dawn, with a walk to the dock or a bus trip to the canal, where you meet the boat that will take you to your destination. You spend a short time sailing to the pre-determined visitor site. Once there you will spend the majority of the day touring the island with a naturalist guide, eating lunch, and (if available at the island site) swimming and snorkeling from the beach. You return to Puerto Ayora via the same route in the early afternoon.

There are plenty of day-trip operators in Puerto Ayora (fewer in Puerto Baquerizo Moreno) who will accept reservations until the day preceding the excursion. Day boats can vary in quality and comfort, but since most island sites are close and you spend a relatively longer time on-site, it is probably more important to shop for day trips by destination. Most day trip destinations from Puerto Ayora include visitor sites on the central islands of Santa Cruz, Santa Fé, North Seymour, South Plazas, and Bartolomé. Different boats visit different islands on different days, so plan accordingly.

DIVE DAY TRIPS

Galapagos is a world-famous dive destination and many visitors will want to spend a day or more diving. This is easily done with one of the many dive shops in both major towns. Visit our Galapagos diving page for more information.

LAND-BASED VS. CRUISE TOURS

There are certain benefits associated with land-based tours, the most important of which is the comfort of stationary hotel accommodations versus mobile staterooms. You are not limited to on-board facilities and services, gaining access to a wider variety of port town restaurants, nightlife and shops. Finally, your community and associated social outlets extend to town visitors and residents, not just the other passengers on your boat. You can also pick and choose where you want to go instead of being tied to an itinerary mandated by the national park.

There are downsides to land-based tours relative to navigable tours. A considerable time is spent sailing back and forth to visitor sites; you are limited to visiting the close, central islands; only one (versus two) site is visited per day; and there is no chance of visiting sites either very early or late in the day.

dventure tours basically encompass all tours not covered by the other two categories. These tours are usually self-styled and formulated in conjunction with a local individual, small company, or hotel and often include activities like kayaking, hiking, wildlife viewing, mountain biking, horseback riding, scuba diving and/or camping.

GALÁPAGOS ADVENTURE TOURS

Although the infrastructure for this type of tour is still in its initial stages, you will probably witness a boom in the coming years: entrepreneurs and tourism sector employees looking to venture into unexplored niches in the informal economy and generate income that stays in the islands (as opposed to foreign tour companies) have been developing creative tour opportunities. Since most residents of the major towns know their islands inside-and-out, the extreme to this type of unofficial touring is to contract a local guide or taxi driver to take you on your own, individual tour. This is often a surprisingly informative, unique, and cost-effective option for Spanish speakers.

CRUISE TOURS

The most popular way to see the islands is by boat, which become the visitors' homes for the duration of their tour, and all activities (eating, sleeping, relaxing, partying, etc.) take place onboard. Due to the increasing popularity of the Galápagos, some 75 vessels are now available for cruises, ranging from small but charming sailboats, to elegant, custom-designed motor yachts and luxurious, mid-sized cruise ships.

ITINERARIES

Because park rules limit the number of ships visiting each island, each cruise carries a fixed trip length and itinerary. Voyages vary in length from four to fifteen days, although currently most cruises are excursions lasting four to eight days, counting the days you arrive and depart at the airport.

Did a unique trek? Tell other travelers at vivatravelguides.com

Ship tours combine land and marine visits on the islands. Tourists usually visit two different land sites and one or two snorkeling sites on each full day of the tour. Usually, guests staying a full week get to spend some time in the highlands of Santa Cruz or the visitor center on San Cristóbal while the guides pick up new passengers and drop off those who are departing.

You can get a taste of the Galápagos in four days, but since each island has its own unique characteristics, you will see a broader variety of plants and animals with each additional day's visit. Besides, since the first and last days of the tour include a morning flight, a four-day tour yields only two full days and two half-days in the islands. Because of travel time required on each end of the trip, a longer trip is recommended.

In 2011, many ships switched to a 15-day cycle, divided into three crusies of six, six and five days. Basically, this change was made to reduce wear and tear on major visitor sites. That's great for the boobies, but not for the tourists, who can no longer see all the major islands in one week.

Generally, the three tours are divided into Western Islands (Isabela and Fernandina), Eastern and Southern Islands (Española, San Cristobal and Floreana) and Central and Northern Islands (Santa Cruz, Genovesa and Santiago). Each of these tours has its highlights, but unfortunately if you want to see all of Galápagos you'll need to spend two weeks on board!

Checking the ship's itinerary should definitely be an important part of your booking process. Itineraries change frequently and are partially controlled by the park service, so make sure you're looking at information that is up-to-date.

See this book's section on visitor sites to help you make up your mind. For instance, those interested in birds will want to prioritize ships that visit Española to see the Waved Albatross and Genovesa to see Red-Footed Boobys. Those who want to snorkel with sea lions will want cruises that stop at the Devil's Crown (Floreana) or Isla Lobos (San Cristóbal).

Between the visitor sites and the itineraries, you should be able to quickly pick a good cruise and price for all of what you want to see and do.

GUIDES

Each boat is required to have one or more naturalist guides—each guide is responsible for up to 16 passengers—who is in charge of providing daily island briefings, natural history information on flora and fauna of the islands, and suggestions for island conservation.

There are over 200 certified naturalist guides in the Galápagos (not all work concurrently), who are qualified with a level I, II, or III according to their educational background.

Generally speaking, level I guides have their high school diploma; level II guides have a bachelor's degree and some foreign language training; and level III guides have an advanced degree or specific training in the biological sciences and fluency in a foreign language.

Lamentably, these are fairly arbitrary designations that do not take into account years of experience in Galápagos, naturalist behavior, or group facilitation style.

Guides can make or break a tour, so it is prudent to ask for additional recommendations and/or qualifications that clarify the ranking of the guide assigned to your cruise. Unfortunately, since most guides are hired on a tour-to-tour basis (some have semi-permanent placements on boats), visitors have very little control over guide selection.

CREW

Galápagos cruisers are crewed almost exclusively by Ecuadorians, most of them from the Galápagos. There will be captains mates, cooks, panga drivers and in some cases engineers and even doctors. Most of the time, the crews are very friendly and professional,but there are a few bad eggs.

Some visitors have reported sexual harassment and petty theft. In many cases, it all comes down to getting what you paid for. The higher the cruise class you choose, the less likely it is that you'll have a bad experience.

Most crew members only speak Spanish, but they're usually able to communicate with just about anyone despite the language barrier. This often becomes an interesting game of charades with some crew members. In general though, ships have one crew member for every two or three passengers.

Remember to tip them if they provide you with good service!

GALÁPAGOS

Choosing a Galapágos Cruise

The things to consider when selecting a cruise are your expectations for price, boat quality, trip length and itineraries. In the Galápagos, the adage "you get what you pay for" is most definitely true.

Because new tourist boats occasionally arrive in the Galápagos, antiquated boats stop running tours, and Galápagos boats are periodically renovated or rebuilt, the class system is dynamic. Tourist boats can move up, down, or straddle the line between two categories in the class hierarchy according to specifications set in a particular period of time.

SHIP CATEGORIES

The tourist vessels in the Galápagos Islands are regularly inspected and categorized according to a set of fixed standards, including facilities, amenities, construction, maintenance and safety. V!VA Travel Guides divides Galápagos ships into six categories: cruise ships, luxury ships, first class, mid-range, budget and diving ships. This is to help you decide which category of ship best suits you.

LARGE CRUISE SHIPS

There are a handful of large cruise ships in Galápagos, each carrying between 48 and 100 passengers. These ships are known for great stability and service, comfortable accommodations and superior food (lunch buffet? Woo-hoo!). Because they are larger than the others, they have ample public areas like bars and sun decks.

The cruise ships are fairly expensive, matching prices with first-class and luxury-class ships, but their facilities are comparable. They all have air conditioning, ocean-view cabins, gift shops and other luxurious facilities.

Cruise ships are best for those travelers who tend to get seasick, as there is considerably less motion as they cruise around the islands. They often have doctors on board, so they are a good choice for elderly or unwell travelers. They are also best for meeting people: obviously, if there are 90 passengers on your ship, you're bound to make some new friends!

Typical cruise ship rates run about $500-$900 per person per day, depending on season, what sort of room you want, etc. An eight-day cruise can cost $4000-$7000/person. Prices vary greatly among the big cruisers: La Pinta and the Eclipse are significantly more expensive than some of the others.

LUXURY YACHTS

Luxury yachts are the most expensive, since they have the most lavish accommodations, the most professional crews, the highest quality food, and the most in-demand naturalist guides. Yachts receiving this designation have air conditioning, hot water, ocean-view cabins with private facilities, and spacious social areas (dining room, living room, sun decks).

Eight-day luxury cruise tours generally cost between $4,000 and $7,000, or around $600 to $900 per day. Four- and five-day tours aboard the luxury yachts are not as common, but they do exist.

The newest ships in Galápagos usually fall into this category. Many of the best luxury yachts are catamarans, which makes them more spacious and almost as stable as the cruise ships.

The luxury class is best for those travelers for whom money is not an object. If you want the best there is and are willing to pay, these are the ships for you. A great, memorable experience is practically guaranteed.

FIRST-CLASS

First class cruise yachts have spacious, comfortable and handsome accommodations, very experienced crews, gourmet food and some of the most knowledgeable naturalist guides. Yachts in this category also have air conditioning, hot water, ocean-view cabins with private facilities, and spacious social areas. Although first-class yachts have unique, distinctive features that contribute to an extra-pleasurable experience, they lack the extravagant perks that would catapult them into the luxury class. These boats can range in size, but most are well-designed, stable and fast.

Prices for eight-day tours aboard these yachts range from $2,900 to $4,300, or about $350 to $550 per day. Four- and five-day tours are more common on first-class cruise boats, and they range in price from around $1,600 to $2,200 for four days or $2,000 to $2,800 for five days (all prices per person). Again, these are cruise prices only and do not include airfare, national park fees or beverages.

First-class ships are best for those who want to splurge a little bit on a good experience but who don't want to break the bank. The crew and staff will be very professional and the guides very good.

GALÁPAGOS

MID-RANGE

Boats in the mid-range category tend to be slightly smaller, less private and less fancy. Yachts receiving a mid-range designation have air conditioning and hot water (although it may not be fully functional), double cabins with private facilities that may be below deck or with access to the outside, and moderately spacious social areas. These boats have good quality food and a professional crew. Occasionally ships in the mid-range category will save money by hiring guides with less experience or questionable language skills. A good example of a mid-range ship might be a past-its-prime yacht with a professional crew that tries hard to keep it shipshape and make the passengers happy.

Prices range from $2,300 to $3,500 for an eight-day tour, or $300 to $450 daily. Four-day tours cost about $1,300 to $1,800. Five-day tours cost about $1,800 to $2,200 or so. Last-minute cruises on these yachts are common.

Mid-range ships are best for those with just enough money to climb out of the murky waters of the budget category. If you can spare an extra couple hundred bucks to take a mid-range cruise instead of a budget-level one, it will be money well spent.

BUDGET

Budget-class ships are the least expensive, and as such, offer the lowest level of service. Conditions can be cramped, uncomfortable and primitive. These yachts often do not have air conditioning or hot water (or any water at all); double, triple, or quad cabins with private or shared facilities; and small social areas. The food, crew, naturalist guide and itinerary are all decent but pale in comparison to the higher category yachts.

These yachts offer budget travelers and last-minute shoppers (these boats often have availability) an opportunity to experience the wonder of Galápagos by ship, but unless you have a thriving spirit of adventure and zero claustrophobia, it is worth spending a few hundred extra dollars to travel comfortably. Economy class boat tours cost between $1,800 and $2,500 for eight days, or $225 to $300 per day. Four-day tours cost around $900 to $1,300, and five-day tours are about $1,150 to $1,500. Shorter itineraries are almost always offered in this class (and may just coincide with the maximum length of time you can tolerate the sub-par conditions!).

Horror stories on budget-class ships are not uncommon. Visitors who arrive to find that their ship has been overbooked and they have been placed on another one (with no say in the matter and no refund if the second ship is worse than the original), defective air conditioning that causes passengers to sleep on the deck, or snorkeling equipment that is unacceptable are some of the usual complaints. Breakdowns, bedbugs and cabins that reek of diesel are the norm on the less scrupulous budget ships.

If you do have a problem aboard a budget-class cruise, it is nearly guaranteed that the management will completely ignore any complaints or demands that you make. The crew and captain of the ship will usually be fair, but the guide may not speak English or other languages besides Spanish. The bottom-of-the-barrel guides find work on budget ships: you may even find guides who have been blackballed from superior ships for things such as sexual harassment of guests, gross incompetence or drunkenness. Petty theft is common, so lock up your valuables as best you can.

The worst-case scenarios described above may not apply: hundreds of visitors annually have good experiences aboard these ships. In recent years, complaints about the budget ships seem to be decreasing, possibly because some of the worst offenders have gone out of business (or sank, to tell the truth). Budget-class ships are best for backpackers and those who wish to see the Galápagos for the lowest possible price.

DIVING SHIPS

Serious divers will want to consider a live-aboard cruise. There are a select few ships in the Galápagos which offer live-aboard diving trips. They're usually quite comfortable and have top-notch gear and guides. Most of the dive ships correspond in price and service to first-class land tour yachts. All of them will have gear for rent and skilled divemasters with years of experience. Prices vary, but are comparable to first-class cruises.

The diving in Galápagos is unforgettable, and these live-aboards offer the chance to head out to the remote islands of Darwin and Wolf, where seeing Whale Sharks, Hammerheads, Manta Rays and other spectacular marine life is commonplace.

Note that these dive ships are not allowed to visit traditional landing sites, so guests will not get to see tortoises, land iguanas, etc.

GALÁPAGOS

Where To Book Your Galápagos Cruise
FROM ABROAD

Most visitors arrange their tours before arriving to the islands. Since the Galápagos are becoming ever more popular and high-season tours sometimes fill up over a year in advance, arranging your tour early is often the only guarantee that you will get what you want. You can do this through a travel agency in your home country, but understand that while the process may be more efficient, you will pay more (commission cost, package fees, national taxes, etc.) and have fewer options (only those boats partnered with your home agency—usually the top-end boats).

You can also contact the boats directly, via the internet: pick a ship you're interested in by searching our Viva Travel Guides database or the list in this book, and go to the official website for the tour company that owns or operates the ship.

Many of the first class and luxury boats focus promotion on pre-arranged tours with foreign groups, making them unavailable to independent (or budget) travelers.

ON THE MAINLAND

You can arrange tours (from luxury to economic) in Guayaquil or Quito, either through the boats' city offices or through any number of travel agencies. During the low season, you may find a well-priced tour with openings leaving in only a few days, but expect to have to wait a month or more for availability during the high season.

If you have a few extra travel days in one of the big cities, go to a number of different agencies to inquire about tour availability and prices. You may happen upon a cancellation or a tour looking to fill spaces on departures leaving right away may offer you a last-minute bargain (especially in the low season). If you're really lucky, you may find a travel agent who works directly with boat owners and offers you the at-cost (no commission) tour price.

ON THE ISLANDS

During the low season, some visitors opt to organize their Galápagos tour from Puerto Ayora or Puerto Baquerizo Moreno. Tour agencies based in the islands will often offer last-minute deals on cruises, which can save you up to 50%.If you have substantial travel time and a limited budget, you may save some money by flying to the islands, staying in an inexpensive hotel and trolling the tour agencies in town.

The best-case scenario: you fly to Puerto Ayora and immediately find a first-class ship leaving the next day with an opening, and you pay a fraction of what you would have had you booked ahead. Worst-case scenario: you spend the week looking for a ship with an opening and find nothing, so you do day trips and some SCUBA diving. Still not too bad. Finding boats in the high season is exponentially more difficult.

Special Galapágos Cruises

Tour boat companies—in conjunction with private agencies—sometimes offer special tours for families, scuba-divers, photographers, students, and scientists. Most of the time, these tours are coordinated by private organizations, which charter a boat to meet their special needs, and thus are not available to individual tourists. This mostly applies to photographic, student, or research expeditions.

If you have a special interest in Galápagos that cannot be stimulated within the realm of the general tour your best option is to organize a charter (six months to a year in advance) with others that have the same interest.

Family tours are not uncommon in the Galápagos. A few boats—especially the bigger cruise ships—will have special family promotions in order to attract (and concentrate) younger visitors. Although the Galápagos vacation is more meaningful for visitors who can understand the evolutionary dynamics of island biogeography, students of all ages, young and old, can learn important lessons from their Galápagos tour.

If you want to bring young children, it is worth your while to look for a family tour: other families will be present with playmates for your children, and your guides will have some experience with younger visitors.

Extreme diving aficionados also have the option of booking a live-aboard scuba tour to the outlying islands of Darwin and Wolf. These trips organize two to three daily immersions in some of the archipelago's most amazing (and remote) dive sites along the route. Live-aboard scuba-diving tours in the Galápagos do not incorporate on-land excursions, instead focusing 100% on cultivating

GALÁPAGOS

the marine experience. You will, however, get interesting views of rarer island sites while you are navigating.

Avoiding Problems and Frustrations

Since there is always the possibility that things go wrong on any vacation and the potential for rough sailing in the Galápagos exists, it is impossible to make a comprehensive section on how to avoid any negative situation. However, we've tried to cover the basics and address the most common problems that travelers face in the Galápagos Islands.

In order to better guarantee you will get what you pay for, especially if you are booking from abroad, make sure the agency you are using gives you a detailed contract outlining payment schedules and refund policies and that it, or its Ecuadorian counterpart, is registered with the government with a specific RUC-number.

It is also a good idea to do your homework: search for information published in written or electronic form and ask for references. Many tourists with combination tours have complained that the hotel, dive center, or day-tour company associated with their package offers a sub-standard service relative to what is provided by others in Puerto Ayora. By organizing your trip outside of the tour context, you can avoid feeling locked in to any aspect of your vacation that may prove to be dissatisfactory.

However, you should recognize that seeking out the perfect set of options will require more time - even though the services and accommodations are generally concentrated on one street in Puerto Ayora. It may also take a bit more money although you will have the benefit of not paying for things you don't want.

People have also criticized economy-class cruise tours for bottom-of-the-barrel services and accommodations, so if you are not willing to chance it, pay the few hundred extra dollars for a nicer, more comfortable, medium-class boat. This is a small price to pay for an upgrade, especially when you consider the total price of the trip.

Even people traveling on more expensive boats have reported problems—anything from sinking ships to sexual harassment. The most common complaints are last-minute boat changes - which the fine-print of the contract allows; overbooking and/or last-minute cancellations; changes in the itinerary; a poor crew; mechanical trouble; and general dissatisfaction with the quality of the experience relative to the price of the trip.

If you experience problems once you are on your trip, register your complaints with the port captain at the capitania or at the Cámara de Turismo (Chamber of Tourism; infocptg@capturgal.org.ec) in Puerto Ayora. They will take your reports seriously and make sure the problems are not repeated on subsequent tours.

GALÁPAGOS ISLAND CRUISE BOATS

The following is a fairly comprehensive list of the ships that currently offer cruise tours in the Galápagos Islands. They are organized according to class: cruise, luxury, first class, mid-range, budget and diving. Ships may change their categorization as they improve (or diminish) the quality of services provided.

Please visit the V!VA Travel Guides website-after your tour and be sure to rate your boat and add comments so our reviews can stay as accurate and up-to-date as possible!

Galápagos Cruise Ships
• Eclipse
• Silver Galapagos
• Galápagos Legend
• Isabela II
• National Geographic Islander
• National Geographic Endeavor
• La Pinta
• Santa Cruz
• Xpedition

Eclipse
If it's space you're looking for, the Eclipse is your ship. This luxury ship claims to be the most uncrowded vessel of its size in the Galápagos. The Eclipse has a capacity for 48 passengers, housed in four suites, eight staterooms, 13 doubles and two singles. All rooms are indeed very large and have a private bathroom with hot shower and are fully air-conditioned. Dining Eclipse-style is alfresco, with the dining area located around the 20-foot (six-meter) pool.

Other amenities include a library/video room, an on-board shop and an observation deck. Tours of the islands are broken down into groups of no more than 12, divided between the naturalists on-board. The Eclipse offers a variety of tours from four to eight days. The Eclipse offers special family cruises in March, April, July, August and December where there are games and special activities for kids. URL: www.eclipse.com.ec. Updated: May 14, 2013.

Galapagos Silver

Formerly named the Galápagos Explorer II, Galapagos Silver is a 100-passenger cruise ship with 50 ultra-elegant suites, each with television, DVD, mini-bar, and satellite communication, in addition to the standard private facilities, hot water and air conditioning. It is one of the fastest, most modern and most luxurious tourist vessels in the Galápagos, blending comfort, adventure and environmental preservation. Social areas—including sun decks, a bar and lounge, and a library—offer the amenities of a world class cruise liner. The Explorer II was purchased in 2012 by the prestigious international cruise company Silversea Expeditions, which immediately refurbished, refitted and renamed it. They also set about poaching the best guides from other cruise ships, showing that they're serious about providing a good experience for their guests. URL: http://www.silversea.com/expeditions/silver-galapagos/ Updated: May 3, 2013

Galápagos Legend

The 90-passenger expedition ship, Galápagos Legend, is a well-regarded cruise ship known for good service, good food and well-maintained facilities. There is a kids' room, which should come in handy for families. Deluxe amenities—including numerous sun terraces, a small swimming pool, an outdoor bar area, mini-cinema, music lounge, and a well-stocked library—may make you want to stay onboard and forget about blue-footed boobies and hammerhead sharks. URL: www.kleintours.com/en/Galápagos-legend.html. Updated: May 10, 2013.

Isabela II

The 40-guest Isabela II, with 20 spacious cabins with private bathrooms, hot water and air conditioning, offers an elegant yet relaxed atmosphere for experiencing the full adventure of the Galápagos. It has three public decks, stocked with a bar-salon, dining room, sun deck and jacuzzi. It also has a complete reference library, with a large selection of books on Ecuador and the Galápagos, nature and conservation videos, and nightly multimedia presentations and lectures. Tours are divided into northern, southern and central islands. URL: www.metropolitan-touring.com. Updated: Nov 2, 2012.

National Geographic Islander

The Islander is a small cruise ship with capacity for 48 guests. It has a very good reputation in the islands for service, facilities and quality guides. All rooms and common areas are air conditioned, elegant and tastefully decorated. The mahogany and brass fixtures give the Islander a real classic shippy vibe. It has internet, an on-board doctor and videographer. The food is excellent: it's international with just enough Ecuadorian dishes to give you a taste of local life. Snorkeling gear is available and well-maintained. It is run by the internationally known Lindblad Expeditions in partnership with National Geographic. URL: www.expeditions.com. Updated: April 17, 2013

National Geographic Endeavor

The Endeavor, a classy veteran of cruises all over the world, has settled nicely into the blue waters of Galapagos. Run by the reputable Lindblad Expeditions in conjunction with National Geographic, good service and facities are guaranteed. A spacious, massive cruiser, the Endeavor has room for 96 guests. The extras are nice: quality snorkeling gear, a full time photographer/videographer, kayaks and a glass-bottom boat. Guides are top-notch. Often sold as part of larger combination tours to Machu Picchu and other South American highlights. URL: http://www.expeditions.com/our-fleet/endeavour. Updated: May 8, 2013.

The Pinta

The Pinta is a roomy, recently renovated cruiser with space for 48 guests in comfortable, luxurious double cabins. Owned by Metropolitan Touring, which has decades of experience in Galápagos, the Pinta features outstanding service, dedicated crew and knowledgeable guides. Its large size makes it stable, so it's good for those who are prone to seasickness. The facilities are top-notch and include a TV room, bar/salon, briefing room, restaurant, deck and individual air conditioning for rooms. The Pinta also prides itself on being a good cruise for families and kids, in part because some of their

GALÁPAGOS

cabins inter-connect, a rarity on Galápagos ships. Check the itineraries carefully to make sure the ship visits the places you want to see. URL: www.yachtlapinta.com. Updated: May 2, 2013

The Santa Cruz

The Santa Cruz, a 90-passenger cruise ship, is one of the only large vessels exclusively designed for exploring the Galápagos. The 47 cabins are well-maintained and relatively spacious, each equipped with private facilities, hot water and air conditioning. Comfort is a priority on the Santa Cruz, which has three decks filled with lounge chairs, a solarium, Jacuzzi, reading room, and well-stocked bar and lounge.

The Santa Cruz has gained worldwide recognition for its excellent standards, including superb service, expert crew, the most knowledgeable multilingual naturalist guides and menus that feature the very best Ecuadorian and international cuisine. Quality snorkeling equipment is provided free of charge. URL: www.metropolitan-touring.com. Updated: May 4, 2013

Celebrity Xpedition

A large cruiser with capacity for 92 guests, the Xpedition is roomy, classy and elegant. It's what you'd expect from a cruise ship: spacious with nice social areas and comfortable rooms. The crew and guides are first-rate. It has a hot tub, sauna and other amenities that simply won't fit on smaller vessels. Cabins are strategically placed to minimize rocking and seasickness. It offers room service, something you see on very few ships in the Galápagos. A good fit for those who want a larger ship with a touch of luxury. One bonus: access to the pangas from the ship is better than on most of the other large ships, so elderly or less-mobile passengers may prefer the Xpedition. Their website is useful but a little confusing. URL: http://galapagosxpedition.co.uk/ Updated: May 8, 2013

Luxury Class Galápagos Cruises

- Anahi
- Athala II
- Cormorant
- Evolution
- Grace
- Ocean Spray

Anahi

The Anahi is a classy catamaran with luxurious cabins and ample public areas. It has a Jacuzzi, bar area, sundeck, lounge, restaurant, etc. Staff to guest ratio is high, assuring a comfortable trip. The Anahi is one of the more affordable catamarans in its class, but does not skimp on comfort or service. It's operated by Andando Tours, a reputable company owned by the Angermeyer family, pioneers in Galapagos. URL: http://www.visitgalapagos.travel/index.php/anahi-galapagos-cruise. Updated: May 10, 2013

The Athala II

The Athala II is a spiffy new catamaran that has been drawing rave reviews from visitors. As a recently built catamaran, it is very spacious for a 16-passenger vessel and quite stable. The Athala is somehow roomy without losing the intimacy of a smaller boat: it's a great choice for someone who wants just the right amount of space vis-à-vis the other passengers and crew. It features eight tastefully furnished double cabins, each with private bath, air conditioning, hot water and closet. The ship itself has a bar area, Jacuzzi, library, TV/DVD, and sunny observation deck in addition to the dining area. The food is outstanding and the staff and guides are very competent and professional. The Athala II tends to book up early, so make your plans in advance. URL: http://www.sanctuaryretreats.com/galapagos-cruises-athala-ii Updated: May 12, 2013

Cormorant

The Cormorant, sometimes referred to for reasons unknown as the Cormorant Evolution, is a classy catamaran which has been serving Galapagos since being built in 2011. Its prices are good for a ship in its class, so it tends to fill up. It has six spacious cabins and two luxurious suites, each with a private balcony. It's very well designed, with ample space in public and private areas. It's operated by the reputable Haugan Cruises, based in Quito. Not to be confused with the ill-fated Cormorant II, which sank in 2009. URL: http://www.haugancruises.com/cormorant-galapagos-cruise/index.html. Updated: May 9, 2013

M/V Evolution

The M/V Evolution, with a capacity for 32 passengers, has 15 total twin and double cabins and two suites, each beautifully furnished with private facilities, hot water, air conditioning and more. The Evolution caters to passengers seeking rest, relaxation and lavish accommodations, as well as families or charters.

A few important extras—most notably an open-air dining area, small heated pool, multimedia room, and infirmary—set this cruise experience apart in terms of comfort. It also has ample deck space for sunbathing and a boutique for shopping. The design of the boat is reminiscent of the 1920s, but charming details and deluxe amenities provide modern-day comforts. URL: http://www.galapagosexpeditions. com/cruises/evolution-galapagos-ship.php Updated: May 13, 2013

Grace

If you like a bit of history with your ship, the Grace is for you. Originally built in 1928, the Grace has sailed for many owners under many names: she is currently named for onetime owner Princess Grace of Monaco. She even served some time in World War Two and saw plenty of action, sinking an enemy submarine before being refitted as a hospital ship!

Today, Grace is a stately yacht, known for service, good food and all of the amenities you'd expect, such as good snorkeling gear, kayaks, top-notch guides, etc. The large staterooms are quite posh if you can afford them. URL: http://www.galapagosexpeditions. com/cruises/grace-galapagos-ship.php. Updated: May 10. 2013

Ocean Spray

The Ocean Spray is one of the newest luxury catamarans in Galápagos, and as such offers top-of-the-line service and comfort. Ocean Spray makes the most of being a large catamaran: the spacious cabins each have a balcony, large windows and air conditioning. The common areas are also roomy and tastefully done.

Details are always looked after: the snorkeling equipment is in good shape, there is a welcome cocktail, guests have access to airport VIP lounges, etc. The guides and crew are first-rate. Four to fifteen day itineraries include stops at visitor favorites like Punta Espinoza and Punta Suárez and memorable snorkeling spots like Vicente Roca Point. All of the major Galápagos species, including finches, giant tortoises, Flightless Cormorants and Galápagos Penguins can be seen at least once during the longer itinerary. URL: http://www.haugancruises.com/ocean-spray-galapagos-cruise/index.html Updated: May 15, 2013.

First Class Galápagos Cruises

- The Beagle
- Beluga
- Cachalote
- Coral I and Coral II
- Eric
- Flamingo I
- Galápagos Voyager
- Galaxy
- Letty
- Mary Anne
- Millenium
- Queen of Galápagos
- Sea Man II
- Tip Top II
- Tip Top III
- Tip Top IV

The Beagle

The Beagle is a 105-foot, two-masted, steel-hulled schooner/motorized sailboat with enough space to comfortably accommodate 13 passengers in its seven double cabins, each with private bathroom, hot water and air conditioning. Snorkeling equipment is available. It's good for families or other groups and is available for charters. The crew prides itself on personal service and great food. Although it is motorized, it has a distinct sailboat vibe to it, even if it rarely sets sail. URL: http://www.thebeagle.com.ec/Beagle.htm. Updated: May 10. 2013

Beluga

The Beluga is a deluxe, 110-foot, steel-hulled motor yacht, which accommodates 16 passengers in eight double staterooms, each with private bathroom, hot water and air conditioning. It is very spacious, with lots of deck space, a sun deck, a dining room, a bar and a galley. It has twin dining rooms, each for eight passengers. It also has TV with DVD player and all the other modern amenities you'd expect. As a bonus, it's relatively fast, which will allow visitors more time visiting the islands and less time chugging from one island to another. The crew is well-trained and professional and takes very good care of their guests onboard and ashore. It's run by Enchanted Expeditions (they also operate the Cachalote), a member of Smart Voyager, the Latin American Travel Association and other certifying organizations for responsible travel. URL: http://www.enchantedexpeditions.com/english/galapagos/beluga.html. Updated: May 4, 2013

Cachalote

The ketch-rigged motor sailor Cachalote has capacity for 16 passengers in eight

handsome double bunk cabins decorated in dark teakwood. Each cabin has two porthole windows, private bath, hot water and air conditioning. Other amenities include a large dining room, salon, bar and three ample wooden decks. The Cachalote was rebuilt and refurbished in 2002 to provide more space and to add modern touches to its Victorian style. Cabins are still a bit tight, but that's the norm for ships in this class. The attractive design of the Cachalote, its professional crew and excellent cuisine produces an ambience that enhances the character of the Enchanted Islands. Snorkeling equipment is available. URL: http://www.enchantedexpeditions.com/english/galapagos/cachalote.html.
Updated: May 9. 2013

Coral I and II

The Coral I and Coral II are both owned by Klein Tours: the Coral I is a larger (36 Passengers) version of the Coral II (20 passengers). Both ships are well-run and hire excellent crew and guides. The Coral I is a spacious motor yacht with standard (bunk-style), superior (twin double), and deluxe cabins, all of which have outside access, carpeted floors, handsome wooden furnishings, private bathroom, hot water and air conditioning.

The Coral II is also a three-deck ship which, like her twin yacht, provides privacy, personal attention and comfortable accommodations. Decorated in the same dark teakwood and sparkling bronze, the Coral II adds a touch of refinement to an open and spacious design, complete with ample social areas, large picture windows and an expansive observation deck. Both Coral ships pride themselves on their excellent food and service. URL: www.kleintours.com/en.
Updated: Sept 18, 2013.

Eric

The Eric, in conjunction with her nearly-identical sisters, Letty and Flamingo I, was custom-designed for cruising the Galápagos archipelago. These three ships are reliable and consistent: they've been chugging around the Galapagos since 1991, leaving a trail of satisfied guests. Each of the three can accommodate 20 passengers in 10 double cabins on three decks—seven with two twin lower beds and three with one double bed—each equipped with private bathroom, hot water, air conditioning, intercom system and hair dryer. An ample dining space, a sun deck stocked with lounge chairs, and a conference area with television, DVD, stereo system, video collection and library add comfort, relaxation and modernity. Crew members provide dedicated and professional service, and naturalist guides—one per ten passengers—offer extensive and personalized information. Snorkeling equipment, sea kayaks, and beach towels are provided at no extra cost. URL: www.ecoventura.com.
Updated: May 2, 2013

Flamingo I
See the *Eric*.

Galápagos Voyager

One huge perk of the Galápagos Voyager: all staterooms are on the upper and middle decks, which means no lower-deck rooms which are often noisy and/or smell like fuel. All rooms also have ocean view and modern conveniences like individual music controls, in addition to private bathrooms (roomy showers!) and air conditioning. The social areas are also well-designed: there are two sun decks, a restaurant and lounge with TV/DVD. Their web site is rather quirky and not terribly informative. URL: http://www.galapagos-voyager.com/
Updated: April 29, 2013

Galaxy

The Galaxy is an attractive, single-hulled yacht well-suited for 16 passengers. It's classy, elegant and reasonably-priced for a ship in its class. The rooms are cozy but not cramped, and feature air conditioning and private baths. Social areas are ample and comfortable. The English-language part of the website is confusing and poorly-written, but clients generally have only positive things to say about the ship and her crew. The southeastern island itinerary is particularly good. URL: http://www.galapogosisland.net/cruises/galaxy-first-class/.
Updated: May 7, 2013

Letty
See the *Eric*.

Mary Anne

The Mary Anne, a three-masted barquentine, is probably Galapagos' most easily recognizeable ship. If you want the experience of cruising the Galapagos on a genuine sailing ship, the Mary Anne is for you. It does have a motor, and usually chugs from one island to the next. It only rarely actually sets sail. Nevertheless, it does have a sort of "pirate shippy" vibe to it. Sailing vessels are

GALÁPAGOS

notoriously cramped, so they compensate by having mostly individual cabins. It's run by the reputable Andando Tours, owned by the Angermeyer family, which has been doing tours in Galapagos as long as anyone. URL: http://www.visitgalapagos.travel/index.php/mary-anne-galapagos-cruise. Updated: May 8, 2013

Millenium

A classy and comfortable motor catamaran (making it one of the more stable cruises to ride on) with capacity for 16 passengers, the Millenium has six spacious double cabins with a private balcony view. Rooms are private with bathtub, hot water and air conditioning, and two suites also have a Jacuzzi included. Millenium also has ample social areas with views of the sea: a plush salon, communal dining room, well-stocked bar and four solaria. Crew and staff work hard for guests, but guides have gotten mixed reviews. URL: http://www.millenniumyacht.com/ Updated: May 7, 2013

Queen of Galápagos

Queen of Galápagos is a modern, stately catamaran featuring lots of space in cabins and common areas. The rooms all have private bathroom, air conditioning and other modern amenities, including TV with DVD player. It's designed for 16 passengers in double occupancy. The Queen of Galápagos is one of the speedier ships in Galápagos: this is a good thing, as you'll spend more time snapping photos of iguanas and less time cruising from one island to another. As a catamaran, it's much more stable than the older yachts in the islands, good news for those who turn a little green while out at sea. Popular with families. URL: http://queenofgalapagos.com. Updated: May 13, 2013

Sea Man II

The Sea Man II (you'll also see it listed as Seaman and Seaman Journey) is a roomy catamaran featuring nine large, beautiful and comfortable double cabins with outside views, private bathroom, cold/hot water, locker and closet, comfortable dining room, two bars and a lounge, library, full air conditioning with control in each cabin, TV, DVD, stereo, first aid, ice maker, water purifier, observation deck, and spacious sun deck with chairs for sleeping and relaxing. URL: http://www.galapagosisland.net/cruises/seaman-ii-luxury-cruise/index.html. Updated: May 7, 2013

Tip Top II

The Tip Top II is a modern, steel-hulled motor yacht with a capacity for 16 passengers in eight double cabins—four below and four above deck—and one single cabin. Each double cabin has two twin beds, private facilities, hot water and air conditioning. It also has ample social spaces: a carpeted interior salon with fully-equipped bar, television, DVD player and full sound system, a plush dining room area, an extensive covered deck (perfect for relaxing or dancing the night away), open top-deck for star-gazing, and diving platform.

Common areas are well-decorated and clean; food is well-prepared and varied; and navigational equipment is well-maintained and modern. SCUBA-diving facilities are available for two or more passengers. The Tip Top ships are operated by the locally famous Wittmer family: they give a lot back to the Galápagos community, so if that's important to you, give them a look. URL: www.rwittmer.com. Updated: Nov 1, 2012.

Tip Top III

The Tip Top III is the slightly more spacious equivalent of her sister ship, the Tip Top II. It also has capacity for 16 passengers, but in ten double cabins with two lower twin beds, private facilities, hot water and air conditioning. The Tip Top III is more modern, having been built in Guayaquil in 2001. Unusual for a small ship, different cabins have different prices: be sure to check when booking. URL: www.rwittmer.com. Updated: Nov 1, 2012.

Tip Top IV

The flagship of the Tip Top fleet, the Tip Top IV is one of the newer vessels in Galápagos, having been built in Guayaquil in 2006. It is an attractive, sleek vessel with airy common areas and spacious cabins. Naturally, the cabins and social areas are air conditioned and the ship features all other modern conveniences.

Tip Top has decades of experience in Galápagos, and it moved all of its best captains, crew and guides to this ship when it first launched, so you can be assured of great service and professionalism while onboard the ship! Snorkeling gear costs extra, so pack it if you have it. URL: www.rwittmer.com. Updated: May 10, 2013

GALÁPAGOS

Mid-Range Galápagos Cruises

- Aida María
- Angelito I
- Daphne
- Eden
- Estrella del Mar
- Fragata
- Galaven
- Monserrat
- San José
- Xavier III

Aida María

The 16-passenger Aida María was designed to combine style, comfort and efficiency. Eight double bunk cabins—each with outside access—are minimalist yet classy, and equipped with private bath, hot shower and air conditioning. Ample dining and social areas (most notably an expansive external sun deck) provide plenty of space for passengers to make themselves at home. Although it has some of the problems common for ships in its class (some have complained of rooms smelling of diesel), the Aida María has a pretty good reputation. This has much to do with a hardworking crew who keep the Aida María shipshape. The price puts it right on the line between budget and mid-range. It's a good value and a smart upgrade from the cheapest ships. Contact them through their website for last-minute deals. URL: http://www.aidamariatravel.com/galapagos-cruises/aida-maria.html. Updated: May 10, 2013

Angelito I

The Angelito I is a comfortable, 16-passenger motor yacht with eight double bunk cabins, each with private bath, hot water, air conditioning and outside access. Four of the cabins are below decks.Frill-less yet efficient, the Angelito I has a professional crew, attentive service and excellent food. Social areas are roomy, but communal, so it provides the perfect atmosphere for groups or for making new acquaintances.

Snorkeling equipment is provided free of charge. The Angelito is a very respectable, reliable and professional ship for its class. Angelito guides and chefs have gotten mixed reviews, but the crew is usually very good. Popular with German travelers, the website is also in German. URL: http://www.angelitogalapagos.com/ Updated: May 7, 2013

Daphne

The Daphne is a 16-passenger motor yacht with seven smallish but fully-equipped double-occupancy cabins and one fancy suite. Other amenities include a restaurant/bar, a small library, television and DVD, and solarium. Social areas and sun deck are surprisingly spacious given the Daphne's small size. Naturalists and crew are professional and experienced. It is one of very few Galápagos cruisers actually built in the islands. The Daphne is certified by SmartVoyager, which recognizes contributions to the local community. May rock in rough seas. Squarely in the mid-range of ships, the Daphne is comfortable and unmemorable, which can be a very good thing, if you think about it. The web site is confusing, but should get you the information you need to know. URL: www.daphnecruises.com. Updated: May 7, 2013.

Eden

The 16-passenger Eden is equipped with eight tight but comfortable double cabins, each with private bath, hot water and air conditioning. Her elegant interior and refined details—complemented by a library, television, DVD and full bar—provide a touch of class to enhance the cruise itinerary. An ample sun deck and accessible upper deck provide added comfort to an already luxurious trip. The Eden is relatively classy and well-appointed for a ship in its class. The dining area is particularly well-done. Snorkeling gear and wetsuits are available. URL: http://www.aidamariatravel.com/galapagos-cruises/eden-yacht.html Updated: May 7, 2013

Estrella del Mar

The Estrella del Mar is a well-designed motor yacht with capacity for 16 passengers. Double cabins have private bathroom, hot water, air conditioning and views of the sea. Wood-paneled staterooms have twin beds instead of bunks, which means a little more elbow room. The Estrella del Mar also has a comfortable lounge and dining areas with plush booth seating. Ample sun decks are well-stocked with cushioned lounge chairs. Some of the indoor social areas are also air conditioned, a nice touch for when it gets hot. There is, of course, a TV with DVD player in one of the lounges. The Estrella del Mar has been in Galápagos for some 20 years, so it's getting a little

GALAPAGOS

weary, but the crew keeps it in good shape and most customer comments seem to be positive. URL: http://www.galasam.com/cruises-estrellademarI.php.
Updated: May 7, 2013

Fragata

The Fragata, a 16-passenger motor yacht with eight fully-equipped double cabins, is outfitted to provide comfortable cruising, fine dining and attentive service. Rebuilt in 2003, the Fragata combines modern style with spaciousness and comfort. It contracts experienced naturalist guides and maintains a professional crew, including talented chefs who take pride in the food. The Fragata sits on the line between mid-range and first-class: it's a good value, as the air contitioning usually works and the common areas are nice. Cabins have twin or bunk beds. URL: http://www.fragatayachtgalapagos.com.
Updated: May 7, 2013

Galaven

Galaven is a 20-passenger motor yacht featuring eleven cabins, each with private bath. The main deck cabins are a little tight, and two of them are right next to the engine room (=noisy), so avoid them if you can. Check their website for special deals and last-minute trips. Reviews of guides, service, food, etc. are almost always positive. One bonus: as a 20-passenger ship, it must have two guides, which means more quality time with your naturalist. It's pricing puts it squarely into the mid-range class. URL: http://www.gala-vengalapagos.com/index.html.
Updated: May 8, 2013

Monserrat

The Monserrat is a 91-foot (28-m) motor yacht with capacity for 16 passengers in eight double cabins. The spacious cabins are equipped with double beds and upper berths or twin lower berths, private facilities, hot water and air conditioning. Social spaces include a comfortable lounge area with television and DVD, as well as a bar, communal dining room and sun deck. The upper deck cabins are greatly superior to the lower deck ones, so get into those if you can (it'll cost you an extra $300 but may well be worth it). The crew is attentive and professional. All in all, a solid choice in the mid-range category. URL: www. Galápagosislands.com/mid-range-cruises/monserrat/monserrat-yacht.html.
Updated: May 7, 2013

The Monserrat

San José

The San José is a large, stable, and comfortable motor yacht accommodating 16 passengers. The San José was built in Ecuador in 2003, so it's fairly modern and in good shape. The eight spacious double cabins on main and upper decks are equipped with two lower twin berths, outside access and windows on both sides of the stateroom, private facilities, hot water and climate control. Cabins are very large for a ship in its class. They're also located near the dining room (as opposed to near the engine) which makes them less noisy.

Social areas are ample and comfortable. The indoor lounge has television, DVD, video collection and stereo system. The dining area has three communal tables and the covered observation deck is well-stocked with plush lounge chairs. Snorkeling equipment is available. A good bargain and a savvy choice for a ship in its class. URL: http://www.galapagosisland.net/cruises/san-jose-first-class/index.htmlUpdated: May 7, 2013

Xavier III/GAP IV

The Xavier III is a small ship, but it somehow seems to have a spacious deck and the cabins aren't too bad. How do they do it? Magic, maybe. It's built for 16 in eight double-occupancy cabins, each with private bath and either a porthole or window, so they all get at least a little natural light. The crew is solid (they even have formed a band and occasionally play for/with the guests) and the food is particularly good for a ship in its class. The Xavier occasionally has good last-minute deals, so ask about it if you're shopping for a good bargain and can go aboard on short notice. URL: http://www.galapagosisland.net/cruises/xavier-yacht/index.html
Updated: May 7, 2013

GALÁPAGOS

Budget Galápagos Cruises

- Amigo I
- Darwin
- Encantada
- Floreana
- Golondrina I
- Guantanamera
- Merak
- New Flamingo
- Pelikano/GAP Adventure I
- Princess of Galápagos

Amigo I

The Amigo I is a battered, 16-passenger motor yacht with eight double cabins, each equipped with private bath and hot water. A small external sun deck provides a good place to catch some sun while cruising. The Amigo provides an adequate visitor experience for a reasonable price, offering seniors, students and groups special discounts. The Amigo has a kind of roly-poly Noah's Ark look to it and is not great for those who get seasick in rough weather.

Food is good, but portion size may leave something to be desired. Quality of guides/crew is patchy. Bugs have been reported by passengers, but most agree that the crew works hard to keep the ship clean. Air conditioning is inconsistent. All in all, the Amigo seems to get fewer complaints than the others in its class, which is probably a good thing, right? URL: http://www.galapagosisland.net/cruises/amigo-budget-class/index. Updated: June 7, 2013.

Darwin

The Darwin sits at the top of the list of budget-class ships with slightly better facilities (and corresponding slightly higher prices) than some of the others in its class. The 16-passenger motor yacht has eight spacious double cabins, each with private bath, hot water and air conditioning. It also has plenty of comfortable social areas: a plush dining room, living room area, bar and sun deck. Snorkeling equipment is also provided.

The guides on board have gotten mixed reviews. The Darwin has the distinction of being one of the few ships actually built in Galápagos. A good place to look for last-minute deals if you want to save some money and avoid the bottom-of-the-barrel ships is this vessel. URL: http://www.darwinyacht.com/ Updated: May 7, 2013

Encantada

The Encantada is a candy-apple red, 12-passenger, motorized sailing boat (it never sails, by the way, preferring to chug between islands with its motor). It has six double bunk cabins with private bath, a small conference room with television and DVD player, a sun deck, and an internal and an exterior dining room. Like other boats of its class, it is cramped and noisy, and the facilities on board are not always in working order (i.e. intermittent hot water). Some passengers have complained of roaches, bedbugs and cabins that reek of diesel. Decent food and cheerful crew make up for some of the discomfort. Guides get mixed reviews (at best). Not advisable for those prone to seasickness. Generally popular with backpackers and those who wish to find the cheapest cruise they can, regardless of comfort. URL: http://www.encantadasailboat.com/. Updated: May 5, 2013

Floreana

The Floreana is a motor yacht that accommodates 16 passengers in eight double cabins containing private facilities and hot water. Amenities include comfortable bar and lounge areas equipped with television and DVD, sun deck, and indoor and outdoor dining areas. Quality snorkeling gear is available. It was formerly known as the San Juan. The Floreana, with dark wood paneling and tasteful social areas, is more attractive than most other ships in its class. It has a good reputation for helpful crews and good facilities. Guides have been described as "adequate," which is actually a ringing endorsement in this class of ship. It's a family operation: your captain may well be the owner. The Floreana is at the top-end of the price range for the budget class of ships, but it's probably money well invested to get you out of the dregs. URL: http://www.galapagosisland.net/cruises/floreana-tourist-yacht/index.html Updated: May 8, 2013

Golondrina I

The Golondrina I is another option for visitors who do not require privacy or posh rooms. With capacity for 10 passengers in double bunk cabins with shared bathrooms, the Golondrina I provides only basic comforts and facilities. Still, it has a good reputation, based on the crew trying hard to make up for what the ship lacks in comforts. For a small yacht, it does have a sizable sun deck and a comfortable dining room. The cook specializes in Ecuadorian dishes and seafood. URL: http://www.galapagosisland.net/cruises/golondrina-tourist-yacht/index.html. Updated: May 7, 2013

Guantanamera

The Guantanamera has capacity for 16 passengers, distributed among two below-deck matrimonial suites—with double lower and twin upper berths, two below-deck double cabins, and four upper-deck double cabins. Each mid-sized, simple cabin is equipped with private bathroom, hot water, and oftentimes frigid air conditioning, which passengers must adapt to since they cannot control it from their staterooms. External deck space is fairly ample, with a few front-facing lounge chairs providing excellent sunbathing and dolphin-watching opportunities, and a covered conference area with tables and chairs.

Unfortunately, this is the limit of the social space: the indoor lounge consists of two cushioned benches directly in front of the television/video and minimalist library facilities, while the dining/bar area includes three cramped—but plush—booths and a hallway doubling as a buffet area. Not for those with weak stomachs, the Guantanamera is somewhat top-heavy and tends to wobble in high seas. Crew members are friendly and competent. Guides get mixed reviews. URL:http://www.galapagosisland.net/cruises/guantanamera-tourist-yacht/index.html Updated: May 7, 2013

Merak

The Merak is a small motor sailboat with limited lounging space and privacy. It has four double cabins, accommodating eight passengers, and two shared bathrooms. Social areas include a communal dining area and outdoor solarium. The Merak caters to small groups looking for the intimacy of their own sailboat at a reasonable price. Like others in its category, it is cramped, and air conditioning and hot water do not always work. There have been complaints about bugs, surly crews and clueless guides. The motor is loud and usually runs even on those extremely rare occasions when the Merak uses its sails. Although the Merak has snorkeling gear, it's not reliable, so bring your own. Brace yourself, keep your expectations low

and if the trip turns into hell on Earth, remind yourself of the money you saved by booking here. URL: http://www.galapago-scruise.com.ec/merak-yacht. Updated: May 9, 2013.

New Flamingo

Look out! There are two cruise ships named Flamingo working in Galápagos, and there is quite a difference between them. The Flamingo owned by Ecoventura is a first-class luxury yacht, and not to be confused with the "New Flamingo," which is most definitely not. The 10-passenger New Flamingo offers your typical economy-class amenities: five tiny double bunk cabins, which are all below deck, a small bar and dining room, a sun deck that also serves as the upper deck (or roof) of the boat and almost no public space. Privacy is at a minimum. By the way, there's nothing "new" about it except the name: it's actually sort of old, saggy and worn-out.

Passengers have reported power outages, no hot water, noisy generators, bugs and not-infrequent problems with the ship itself. (One passenger reports that a screw came loose on the rudder and the ship went in circles until the captain himself dove down to fix it!) By most reports, the crew tries hard to make up for these deficiencies. It's also priced accordingly, and is definitely among the least expensive ships to cruise the Galápagos. Caveat emptor. URL: http://www.galapagosisland.net/cruises/flamingo-economic-cruise/index.html. Updated: May 8, 2013

Pelikano

The 16-passenger Pelikano (a.k.a. GAP Adventure I) is one of the more comfortable of the lower-priced yachts, with eight double cabins, each with private bathroom and showers. Cabins are frill-less and small—although all of them have easy access to the eating area—and social space is limited to the dining room and upper deck areas, causing conditions to feel a bit cramped.

If you are friendly, adventurous and on a strict budget, the Pelikano is one of your better options. Snorkeling equipment is provided. Reviews of service and guides are generally good. Price is at the high end of the budget range. URL: http://www.galapagosisland.net/cruises/pelikano-yacht/index.html. Updated: May 10, 2013

GALÁPAGOS

Princess of Galápagos

The Princess of Galápagos (also known as the San Juan II) is fairly small for a 16-passenger ship, yet somehow they have managed to squeeze in eight double cabins with private bath, hot water and air conditioning. Try to get one of the upstairs rooms, as some passengers have complained that the lower ones smell of fuel. The Princess of Galápagos has two decks, a sun deck and a roof deck, and the dining area is open-air towards the stern. Princess of Galápagos is sort of in the middle of the budget category: it's not the bottom-of-the-barrel, but it will most likely leave you underwhelmed. URL: www.princessofgalapagos.com. Updated: Nov 2, 2012.

Galápagos Live-Aboard Dive Cruises

- Aggressor I and II
- Buddy Darwin and Buddy Wolf
- Deep Blue
- Humboldt Explorer
- Sky Dancer/Galápagos Sky

Aggressor I and II

Custom-built for Galápagos diving, the Aggressor I and II have been operating in the islands since the early 1990s, so there is a lot of experience on board in the form of captain, crew and divemasters. They're part of a world-wide diving fleet. Both ships prioritize diver safety and have taken steps to minimize their impact on the local ecosystem. Their week-long itinerary takes them to most of the best sites in Galápagos, including remote Darwin and Wolf. They have all the gear a diver will need available for rent. The ships are nearly identical. Both have room for 16 passengers, well-appointed, wood-paneled social areas, well-designed diving deck and partially-covered sun deck which also serves as the bar. There are two different kinds of stateroom available: one is larger and therefore more expensive, but even the cheaper ones are fairly roomy. All staterooms have air conditioning and private bathroom. A reliable, professional dive operation. URL: www.aggressor.com. Updated: May 3, 2013

Wolf Buddy/Darwin Buddy

The Wolf Buddy and the Darwin Buddy are twin dive cruisers relatively new to the islands. They offer elegant cabins with air conditioning and DVD player, a roomy dive deck and cassy social areas. Prices are higher than some of the other dive cruisers

(and go up during the May-December "Whale Shark Season"), but these cruisers are first-class and designed for those who want to dive and cruise in comfort. They rent all the gear any diver could need. URL: http://www.buddydive-galapagos.com. Updated: May 12, 2013

Deep Blue

The Deep Blue is a well-designed diving cruiser with airy dive deck, eight double cabins, nice social areas and library with TV/DVD player. The food is quite good (and plentiful). Service is professional and the divemasters know what they're doing. The Deep Blue hits all the usual Galápagos diving sites, including Darwin and Wolf. It's currently one of the least expensive diving live-aboards in the Galápagos, but the service hasn't seemed to suffer, and the itinerary is just the same as the other ships (plus, the Whale Sharks won't know how much you paid!). They can rent gear. The crew is good but may get a little pushy when it comes to the tip box. URL: www.deepbluegalapagosdiving.com. Updated: Oct 20, 2012.

Humboldt Explorer

A shiny, new dive cruiser, the Humboldt Explorer is a luxurious, 16 passenger yacht designed and built for diving in the Galápagos. All eight double cabins are roomy, with air conditioning, private bath, TV and ocean view. The social areas are well-done and the lounge is also air conditioned. There is a Jacuzzi and even a BBQ grill! The Humboldt Explorer goes to Darwin, Wolf and all of the other major dive sites. It has a satellite phone for making calls worldwide while on the trip (in case you want to gloat to your diver friends back home). Divemasters are professional and have all of their licenses up to date. It's a popular dive ship, and tends to book up, so look for space ahead of time if you're interested. URL: http://humboldtexplorer.com. Updated: Nov 16, 2012.

Sky Dancer/Galápagos Sky

The Galápagos Sky is a well-outfitted diving ship that hits all of the major Galápagos dive sites, including a trip to far-flung Darwin and Wolf Islands. The Sky features eight double cabins for a maximum of 16 passengers (each with private bath and all the amenities), an ample stern deck for ease of water entry and exit for divers, and spacious social areas including a bar, lounge and restaurant. The food is excellent. But of course, divers don't care about food: They want hammerheads! The crew and divemasters

GALÁPAGOS

onboard have been doing these dive trips for a very long time and they are excellent at what they do. Expect to be pampered after every dive with towels, bathrobes and juice handy. The captain and divemasters speak good English, but the crew does not. It's operated by the same people who run the first-class cruisers Eric, Letty and Flamingo, so service is a priority and customer satisfaction is important. All in all, a professionally-operated ship which will most likely leave divers very happy and satisfied. URL: www.ecoventura.com. Updated: Nov 20, 2012.

GALÁPAGOS WILDLIFE GUIDE

As spectacular as the waters, islands and beaches of Galápagos are, there is no doubt about what visitors have come to see: the animals. Because the archipelago was undiscovered until very recently (geologically speaking), the endemic species of Galápagos never learned to fear humans, as animals and birds did in every other corner of the globe. In other words, the animals on the islands see the lumbering hairless monkeys that smell like sunscreen, but do not identify them as something predatory or dangerous.

For this reason, you can get very close to them before they spook and run away. Some animals are more skittish than others: migratory birds, including many of the shore birds, will not let you get too close, because they've encountered mankind in other parts of the world. Other animals, like marine iguanas, barely seem to notice you at all.

Many careless travelers have accidentally stepped on them—they blend right in with the black lava rocks. The sea lions will let you get fairly close, as will most of the sea and land birds, but watch out. Get too close, and a sea lion or booby will give you a good nip!

Galápagos is home to several species of reptiles, including the giant tortoise, marine iguana and land iguana. However, there are very few native mammals in the archipelago, the most noteworthy of which is the Galápagos Sea Lion.

The birds of the Galápagos are easily divided into categories. Land birds are generally seen inland where they feed and nest. Some endemic Galápagos land birds include the Galápagos Hawk and different species of Darwin's Finches. Shore birds may nest farther inland, but they are most commonly seen along the shoreline and in tidal pools and mangroves where they feed. Sea birds nest on land but feed exclusively on fish, squid and other marine life.

The marine life in Galápagos is impressive, which makes the snorkeling and diving in the islands world-class. There are many different fish, sharks and rays that are easy to spot and identify. Unfortunately, not all of the wildlife in Galápagos belongs there. Introduced species remain a major ecological problem, although scientists and park rangers are dedicated to removing them. Please note that there are many other species not included here—the islands are home to thousands of different kinds of animals, birds and fish, and there is only room in this guidebook to include the most common and interesting ones. Local Spanish names are given in parentheses where appropriate.

Sea Birds

Bird life is everywhere in Galápagos, and the marine species are particularly fun to watch and identify. Because of the cold-water currents that cruise through the archipelago, there is an unusual abundance of marine life, which in turn supports large colonies of different avian species.

The Galápagos bird species are specially adapted to working together. Take the three species of booby, for example. The Blue-footed Booby fishes close to shore—thrilling visitors by putting on a fantastic show of plummeting after fish. The Nazca Booby fishes at an intermediate range from shore and most visitors will never get to see them in action. The Red-footed Booby fishes far out to sea, often flying many miles simply to find a good fishing spot. In this way, the three booby species do not compete with one another for food resources.

Some species of sea birds are endemic to the Galápagos Islands. The three most noteworthy are the Flightless Cormorant, the Waved Albatross and the Galápagos Penguin.

Did a unique trek? Tell other travelers at vivatravelguides.com

There are many other sea birds in the islands. Shearwaters and petrels can be seen skimming the waves, if you look for them. There are plovers and terns, and other species of gull that are not endemic to the islands. A knowledgeable guide should be able to point out most of these species to you as you spot them.

Blue-footed Booby

The Blue-footed Booby (piquero patas azules) is most easily identified, as its name suggests, by its bright blue feet. It has brown upper plumage and white lower plumage, with wings that are a slightly darker brown than the rest of the body. Juveniles are completely brown and receive their coloration after about one year.

Males are slightly smaller than females and perform an elaborate, rather entertaining mating dance to attract a partner. He begins by lifting up his enormous clown feet, one-by-one, and then stops in a distinctive pose, beak raised skyward, announcing his studliness with a loud whistle, sticking out his tail and opening his wings. This is accompanied by a love-offering of sticks and twigs. Females join in the mating dance, following the same movements, but respond with a guttural honk. Besides their distinguishing sounds, the females also have larger eye pupils.

Breeding can take place at any time of the year when the food supply is abundant, and also varies from island to island. Up to three eggs are laid in a "guano ring," or circle of booby dung. When food is scarce, the oldest sibling will push younger sibling(s) out of the guano ring in an act of "cainism." This form of natural selection is effective, because chicks outside of the ring are refused care and ultimately perish. It is nature at its most cruel, but the stronger chick survives.

The young take two to six years to mature, at which time they will return to their island birthplace to mate. Meanwhile, they travel among the islands feeding on fish, which are caught in a graceful plunge dive. Watching the boobies fish—either from the air or underwater—is a major highlight in Galápagos.

Blue-footed Boobys are common throughout the archipelago and can be seen on several islands.

Red-footed Booby

The Red-footed Booby (piquero de patas rojas) can be easily identified by its distinctive red feet, blue-gray bill, pinkish facial skin and brown outer plumage. A certain percentage of them are mostly white instead of brown, but they're the same species. It is the smallest of the three booby species in Galápagos and nests in treetops and ledges, instead of on the ground.

Courtship among Red-footed Boobies is similar to the blue-footed variety, but it is performed in the trees. Unlike the Blue-footed Booby, the Red-footed Booby lays a single egg on a platform of twigs and guano. The egg is then incubated by both parents for 45 days. The chick is dependent on its parents for food for about a year. The Red-footed Booby feeds exclusively on fish, which are caught far away from land.

Red-footed Boobys are common throughout the islands, but best seen on Genovesa.

Nazca Booby

The Nazca Booby (Piquero Nazca) is alabaster white with a black tail and black ends to the primary feathers on the wing. Some black skin at the base of the bill serves as a distinctive Zorro-mask. The Nazca Booby is the largest of the three booby species in Galápagos.

Galápagos Nazca Boobies were once thought to be the same as Masked Boobies, but are now considered different enough to be their own species. Nazca and Masked Boobies look almost identical, and many in the islands (including some guides) may still refer to them as Masked Boobies.

As with other boobies, the Nazca Booby feeds entirely on fish and follows the same courtship ritual, although it's a bit less elaborate. Males and females look alike, so the best way to distinguish them is by their sounds: the males whistle and the females quack.

Nazca Boobies are commonly seen at Punta Suarez (Española), Punta Pitt (San Cristóbal), Daphne Major and Genovesa.

Frigatebird

There are two species of Frigatebird in the Galápagos, Great Frigatebirds and Magnificent Frigatebirds. They're hard to tell apart: both are large black birds with a long beak, hooked on the end.

Male Frigatebirds of both species are most recognizable by their dazzling red skin flaps, which they can inflate to volleyball-sized balloons to attract females. Immature Frigatebirds are known to have a white head and neck and a pale beak.

GALÁPAGOS

Males construct nests out of twigs in low trees or shrubs and wait in the nests with their pouches inflated until a female arrives to mate. Frigatebirds spend much of their time offshore, but return to land to mate, nest, and rear their young.

Since Frigatebirds do not secrete enough oils to waterproof their feathers, they cannot swim, even though they are sea birds. As such, they steal fish from other birds (especially the Blue-footed Boobies, who are excellent fishermen) or force them to regurgitate the food. Oftentimes, Frigatebirds will raise their young near Blue-footed Booby colonies so that they have a food source nearby and readily available. Because of this behavior, Frigatebirds are considered kleptoparasites or pirates.

In Galápagos, both varieties are most commonly seen on Genovesa and North Seymour.

Flightless Cormorant

The Flightless Cormorant (cormorán) is unmistakably recognized by its stubby vestigial appendages that were once wings. Although they cannot fly, they are excellent swimmers and feed on small fish, eels and octopuses. Adults have black upper feathers and brown under feathers, but they—like the juveniles—look completely black when wet. They also have short black legs; large, black webbed feet; brilliant turquoise eyes and a hooked, black bill. Although the cormorant is a common bird around the world, flightless ones are only found on Galápagos.

Like many other sea birds, Flightless Cormorants have an elaborate courtship display: pairs begin with an aquatic dance, followed by an unusual "snake necking" embrace, where necks are intertwined in a snake-like spiral. The mating ritual continues with some swimming back and forth, a continuation of the dance on land and a final presentation of a seaweed nest to the female by the male.

Most females lay their eggs between May and October. The eggs are then incubated for about a month before hatching, and the chick is reared for about nine months by both parents. If, however, food supplies run low, the female may leave the male to care for the chick while she looks for another, more apt, mate.

Flightless Cormorants can be seen in Punta Espinosa (Fernandina) and the western visitor sites of Isabela.

Galápagos Penguin

The endemic Galápagos Penguin (pinguino) is the only species of penguin found north of the equatorial line (a good trivia question!). At only 35 cm tall, the Galápagos Penguin is also one of the world's smallest penguins. Adults have black outer feathers, white under feathers, an irregular black band across the breast and a distinctive white stripe passing from the eye to the throat.

There are only about 1,000 monogamous pairs of Galápagos Penguins, which can breed at any time of year when resources are plentiful and water temperatures are cool. They lay one or two eggs in shady holes or caves nestled along the shoreline. Pairs take turns incubating the egg, for a period of about 40 days. Chicks can fend for themselves after two months, but often stay in swimming groups with the adults.

Galápagos Penguins can best be seen at Punta Espinosa (Fernandina), at various west coast Isabela visitor sites and Bartolomé.

Brown Pelican

The Brown Pelican (pelícano) is an unmistakable bird with a large, heavy body and an enormous, deep bill. Mating adult pelicans have a striking white head and maroon neck; when they do not have their breeding plumage, their necks are gray.

Brown Pelicans breed individually or in small colonies, making their nests in mangroves on virtually all of the islands in the archipelago. The female lays three large eggs, usually during the colder months of May to July, which are then incubated by both parents for about one month (if they are not eaten by the Galápagos Hawk). They feed mainly on large fish, which they catch by plunging straight into the ocean (a graceless but effective dive), filling their pouches with sea water and filtering the food out by draining the pouch.

Brown Pelicans are common throughout the islands. A good place to see them is at the fishermen's pier in Puerto Ayora as they try to mooch a free meal.

Red-billed Tropicbird

The Red-billed Tropicbird (ave tropical) is a spectacular, solitary bird with white feathers, black barring on the back and a bright red bill. Its most distinguishing characteristic, however, is its long white tail, which can reach up to a half-meter in length.

During the breeding season, which varies in the archipelago, the Red-billed Tropicbird performs a courtship flight characterized by a shrill, "knee-knee-knee" call. The female lays a single egg in a fissure of a cliff, which is then incubated by both parents for about six weeks.

Red-billed Tropicbirds are best seen off the cliffs of South Plaza, Española, Daphne Major and Genovesa.

Swallow-tailed Gull

The endemic Swallow-tailed Gull (gaviota de cola bifurcada) is the only nocturnal gull in the world. Adults have a distinctive black head with a red ring around the eyes; a black bill with a gray tip; a white, forked tail; and red, webbed feet. They often have white spots on their back, which resemble guano and help them to camouflage with their rocky cliff habitat. Immature gulls are white with dark brown spots on their backs and a black band on their tails.

Swallow-tailed Gulls nest in small colonies on islands concentrated in the eastern archipelago, breeding throughout the year. Their courtship ritual involves mutual preening, head-tossing and regurgitation of food by the male. The young have a recognizably harsh call, consisting of an initial scream that displays their red gape and tongue, an unnerving rattle, and a final clicking noise, which some experts think may also be used for echo-location during night feeding.

The most common places to encounter Swallow-tailed Gulls are Genovesa and South Plaza.

Shore Birds

One of the best places in all of Galápagos to see birds is right along the shoreline. Many of the most interesting species in Galápagos are wading shore birds who feast on small fish, crabs, snails, small marine iguanas and other creatures that live in the mangroves and tidal pools of the islands.

Since most of the visitor sites in Galápagos involve a transfer from the cruise boat to the island, usually by means of a zodiac or panga, visitors to the islands have a good chance of seeing one or more shore birds.

American Oystercatcher

The American Oystercatcher (ostrero americano) is a distinctive shore bird found up and down the eastern coast of North America,

the Gulf of Mexico and the western coast of South America. They are a common sight in Galápagos, where they can be seen on the coast poking around tidal pools and along rocky shores. Some ornithologists consider the Galápagos American Oystercatcher to be an endemic subspecies, known as Haematopus palliatus galapagensis.

The American Oystercatcher is easily identified by its red-rimmed eyes, black head, white body, grayish-black wings and white legs. Its most distinctive feature, however, is certainly its long, thick, bright orange beak, which looks, from afar, like a large plastic drinking straw.

As you might imagine, the preferred food of the American Oystercatcher is shellfish. Using its sturdy beak, an American Oystercatcher can pry apart an oyster, clam or mussel. It then snips the muscle that holds the shells together and eats the oyster at its leisure. Their long beak allows them to poke into small nooks in tidal pools that are too deep for other predators. American Oystercatchers are shy and will dart or fly away if closely approached.

American Oystercatchers can be seen on any island where there are tidal pools along the shore.

Greater Flamingo

The Greater Flamingo (flamenco) receives its characteristic pink color from the pigments consumed in its diet of crustaceans and shrimp larvae. Legs are gray or flesh-colored; feet are webbed for swimming; primary feathers are black; and bills are pink with a black tip. Young flamingos are pale white until about three months, when they begin to feed on their own and become a richer pink color.

This species of flamingo is thought to have arrived from the Bahamas during a one-time intense tropical storm. Since they did not have the flying capacity to return, they made their homes in the brackish lagoons of the archipelago.

Around July and August, the male flamingoes perform their courting ritual: they join in fixed lines, moving and swaying together in a sensual, flamenco-like dance. Monogamous pairs will lay their eggs in cone-shaped mud nests nearly 25 cm high, which have a 28-day incubation period before hatching in September and October. Chicks are born with

GALÁPAGOS

a straight bill, but it starts to curve after about three weeks. They live about 20-30 years.

There are currently about 500-600 flamingoes on the various islands. They are most commonly found at Punta Cormorant (Floreana), Puerto Villamil (Isabela) and Las Bachas Beach (Santa Cruz).

Yellow-crowned Night Heron

The distinctive Yellow-crowned Night Heron (garza nocturna) can be easily identified by its yellow crown and a white stripe under its eye. They are gangly birds, with heads that seem a little too large for their bodies. During the day, they can often be seen poking around rocky shorelines. They are more active at night and sometimes even come into the towns to feed near streetlights.

Yellow-crowned Night Herons can be found all over North America and in northern South America. Those in Galápagos are considered by some scientists to be a sub-species.

The Yellow-crowned Night Heron mostly feeds on crabs, which it snatches off the rocks and downs in one big gulp. They're also known to eat shellfish, snails, fish and small reptiles. They nest in branches and mangroves that hang over water. They can be seen on just about every island, but they're most common on Genovesa.

Lava Heron

Scientists are currently debating whether or not the Lava and Striated Herons are, in fact, separate species. While we all wait for them to make up their minds, your guides will probably refer to them as two different types of heron, and we'll list them separately here for now.

The Lava Heron (garza de lava) is very similar in appearance to the Striated Heron: they're the same size and shape, and have roughly the same coloration. You can tell them apart easily, however—the Striated Heron has a black crown and dappled wings, whereas the Lava Heron is a uniform gray color. Some experts believe that the heron has adapted to blend in easily with the lava rocks of Galápagos. During mating season, male Lava Herons develop brightly colored feet and their beaks turns a glossy black. The Lava Heron is also called the Galápagos Heron because it is endemic to the islands.

The Lava Heron perches on rocks or branches in mangroves, tidal pools and along any shore where small crabs and fish can be found. It waits, still as a stone, before suddenly lunging forward to snatch up its prey. They are very efficient hunters and fishers—some Lava Herons have been observed catching up to three small crabs per minute.

Lava Herons are less shy than their cousins, the Striated and Great Blue Herons; if you move slowly, you can get quite close to them before they spook and fly off.

Lava Herons can be seen on any of the islands.

Striated Heron

The Striated Heron (garza estriada) is a fairly common sight in Galápagos tidal pools, mangroves, ponds and rocky shores. Similar in size to a Lava Heron, the Striated Heron is also rocky gray in color.

Striated Herons are common around the world, from Japan to South America, Africa and Russia. They usually perch on a branch or rock near the water's edge, head back, waiting for small fish or crustaceans to swim by. They then lunge forward, trapping their prey in their sharp beaks and quickly gobbling it up. The Striated Heron is a clever bird, occasionally dropping a leaf into the water and snapping up fish that come to look at it.

Striated Herons can be seen on most islands.

Great Blue Heron

Yes, the Great Blue Herons that you may have seen in the USA and Canada are the same as the ones in Galápagos. The Great Blue Heron (garza morena) is a large, majestic bird that is relatively common in the United States and Canada, as well as Mexico and the West Indies. They can be found in South America as well. Great Blue Herons living in Canada and the northern United States migrate south to spend the winter. They can be seen year-round in Galápagos.

The Great Blue Heron is a shore bird, and can often be seen wading in tidal pools looking for small fish. They have also been known to eat reptiles, turtles and even rodents. Great Blue Herons nest in colonies, occasionally with or near other heron species.

They tend to fish alone, however, stalking their prey both during the day and at night as well. Males can be identified by the small patch of feathers sticking out from the back of their heads.

Snowy Egret

The Snowy Egret (garceta blanca) is a long-legged white bird a little larger than a Lava or Striated Heron. It's native, but not endemic, to the islands. Their plumage is entirely white, with a dark beak and legs and a yellowish face. They're fairly common in North and South America, if you know where to look for them. They look an awful lot like the Cattle Egrets very common in the Galápagos highlands. The two species can be differentiated by the color of their beaks—Snowy Egrets have grayish bills while those of the Cattle Egrets are yellow. That, and Snowy Egrets consider hanging out with cows "uncool."

They're not easily seen in the islands, although you might get lucky in the highlands of those islands that have highlands. One good place to see them is the brackish pool in the town of Puerto Baquerizo Moreno (San Cristóbal) where the little creek empties out into the ocean.

Land Birds

There are relatively few land birds in Galápagos, and most of them are endemic. In general, their coloring runs in grays, browns and blacks, with the dazzling Vermilion Flycatcher being the most obvious exception. Like most Galápagos birds, they can be surprisingly tame and even friendly to humans. Darwin's Finches—the famous little birds that helped to inspire their namesake's evolutionary theories—are known to land on your dinner table (or in your hand, if there are crumbs in it). Mockingbirds like to land nearby and hop over for a closer look, perhaps even perching on your feet to ask for a drink of water.

Other Galápagos land bird species are less outgoing: the Galápagos Hawk prefers to soar and to majestically sit on the treetops rather than associate with lowly humans, the Short-eared Owl is usually busy looking for a meal, and the Galápagos Dove will dart away if approached. On the far end of the spectrum, the Galápagos Rail is shy and only very rarely seen.

Even though they're considered land birds, some of these Galápagos species are only one step or so removed from the sea. The hawk eats marine iguanas, the Yellow Warbler sometimes eats bugs at the waterline, the Short-eared Owl eats small sea birds, etc. This is one more reminder of how interconnected the island ecosystems can be despite their categorization.

Yellow Warbler

The Yellow Warbler (canario maria) is frequently spotted in Galápagos flitting across the trail or snapping up bugs near the water's edge. The Yellow Warbler is the only small, dazzling, yellow-colored bird with black stripes on its wings in the islands—you can't mistake it for anything else. Male Yellow Warblers have distinctive reddish stripes on their breasts and a reddish "cap" on top of their heads. Females are a little drabber and have duller stripes, or may lack them altogether. Their song sounds a little like "sweet, sweet, sweet."

Yellow Warblers are not endemic to Galápagos. They're found all over the western hemisphere, from Alaska to Peru. In other parts of the world, the tiny warblers prefer the edges of boggy wetlands and fields with trees. In Galápagos, you'd expect to see them feeding on the ground or in a low tree. Nevertheless, they have found that there are more insects along the shoreline than in the dry interior of the islands. They also occasionally feed on seeds or fruit. They're found throughout the islands: look for them at the Puerto Egas visitor site.

Darwin's Finches

The 14 species of Darwin's Finches (pinzón) that are found in the Galápagos are perhaps the most famous and sought-after land birds on the islands. This is probably due to the ecological significance of differences in the species' beak morphology and its link to feeding behavior.

All of the finches are sparrow-sized with mottled gray, brown, black or greenish feathers and short, rounded wings. Because all 13 species have similar superficial characteristics, it is difficult, and at times nearly impossible (even for naturalist guides), to distinguish them. The only clues they provide are the shape of their beak, the type of food they eat and the type of habitat they occupy.

Although they all originated from a single ancestor, individual species have formed as niche specialists: some eat seeds, some eat leaves, some eat cacti and some eat insects. One species found on Wolf drinks the blood of Nazca or Red-footed Boobies, a habit that has led to its being dubbed a "vampire finch."

Three other finch species—the small, medium and sharp-billed ground finches—have

GALÁPAGOS

the distinction of eating the ticks and mites off of reptiles.

There are even two species—the woodpecker and mangrove finches—that use twigs or spines as primitive tools to extract hidden insect larvae or grubs from holes in tree branches.

The mating season of finches generally begins after the first major rainfall of the rainy season (around February). The male courts the female by building an elaborate dome-shaped nest made of twigs, grass, bark, feathers and other materials, which he locates in his firmly established and highly protected territory. The male will continually attend to the female at the nest, while she lays and incubates her eggs (two to five, on average), and during the first weeks of the fledglings' lives.

Finches are found on all major islands, with each species distributed throughout the archipelago (and within the islands) according to its desired habitat. They are also common in towns, where they'll sit around at outdoor restaurants hoping for a handout. Darwin would approve of them adapting to this new food source!

Galápagos Mockingbird

There are four similar-looking species of endemic mockingbirds in very different home ranges throughout the Galápagos archipelago: The Charles Mockingbird (Nesomimus trifasciatus, cucuve de Floreana) is found near Floreana on the islands of Champion and Gardner. The Hood Mockingbird (Nesomimus macdonaldi, cucuve de Española) is found on Española. The Chatham Mockingbird (Nesomimus melanotis, cucuve de San Cristóbal) is found on San Cristóbal. The Galápagos Mockingbird (Nesomimus parvulus, cucuve de Galápagos), lives on most of the remaining major islands.

All four species of mockingbird are thrush-sized, long-tailed, gray and brown streaked land birds. The mockingbirds, especially the Hood variety, will greet you inquisitively with a loud, piercing call, loosely translated as "give me any liquid beverage—even your spit will do." Resist the temptation to quench their thirst: years of successfully begging tourists have caused an increasing reliance on them for water.

The mockingbirds have an extremely interesting social structure. During the breeding season, they form cooperative groups comprised of a breeding female, her mate and the offspring of her previous broods, all of whom participate in the raising of the next brood and maintenance of the territory.

During the rest of the year, large communal territories are formed with as few as nine and as many as 40 individuals, each contributing to territory defense.

It is a hoot (no pun intended) to watch these birds defending their territories; individuals will face off across the imaginary frontier in linear fronts, each enemy pair squawking, flicking their tails, and rushing at each other.

Mockingbirds are omnivorous, but they occasionally exhibit aggressive, predatory behavior. They will eat just about anything: seeds, insects, baby turtles, young finches and sea lion placenta.

Galápagos Hawk

The Galápagos Hawk (gavilán de Galápagos) is an impressive, large, dark brown bird of prey. Adults have a dark banded tail, yellow hooked bill and strong yellow talons. The female has the same general features but has a larger, more imposing stature. Juveniles are a lighter brown and heavily mottled.

Nests—large, disorganized conglomerations of twigs—are usually constructed in trees or on a rocky outcrop. Following an unusual mating system termed "cooperative polyandry," each female will mate with up to four males, who take turns incubating the two or three eggs in the nest and raising the young. Young birds are expelled from the territory after about four months and begin to breed two years later.

A fearsome predator and scavenger with no natural enemies, the Galápagos Hawk delights in a smorgasbord of foods, especially baby iguanas, lizards, small birds, dead goats or sea lions and sea lion placenta. It can often be seen flying or perching impatiently near an iguana nesting area during April and May, when baby iguanas begin to emerge from their eggs. The hawks are best viewed at Punta Suarez and Gardner Bay (Española), South Plaza, Santa Fé, and Punta Espinosa (Fernandina).

Short-eared Owl

The Short-eared Owl (lechuza de orejas cortas) is the most commonly seen owl in Galápagos. It is dark brown in color with light mottled markings, a dark facial disc, yellow eyes, and a dark bill. You are most likely to see the diurnal hunter in the early morning or evening, when it is out looking for its next meal of small birds, rats or mice.

It makes its nests on open ground, where it lays three to four eggs. This species is found on every major island except Wolf. The best place to see them is on Genovesa.

Galápagos Barn Owl

The Galápagos Islands are home to a thriving population of barn owls (lechuza de campanario). They're easy to spot with their distinctive owl faces and mottled brown and white coloring. Galápagos Barn Owls are not considered an introduced species and are actually a subspecies of the Common Barn Owl.

Although probably as common as the Galápagos Short-eared Owl, they're much harder to spot because of their nocturnal habits.

Like their mainland cousins, they like to nest in airy structures, including buildings and lava tubes. They feed mostly on rodents and smaller birds. Seeing one is rare, as most visitor sites are closed at night. Your only real chance is to spot one on the outskirts of one of the towns at night or in a lava tunnel during the day.

Galápagos Dove

The endemic Galápagos Dove is one of the more spectacular land birds, with a chestnut-brown back, reddish-brown head and belly, bright red legs, and a conspicuous pale blue ring around the eyes. They nest year-round, but peak breeding season usually starts in February. Courtship behavior includes exaggerated flying patterns, a bowing ceremony, and the males' deep, soft cooing call. The female will lay two eggs in nests built under rocks or nests vacated by mockingbirds.

The curved shape of the Galápagos Dove's bill is indicative of its chosen food: seeds picked from the ground, mainly dropped by the opuntia cactus. They will also eat caterpillars and insect larvae. The Galápagos Dove can be seen in the drier areas of most islands; a slightly larger subspecies is found on Darwin and Wolf. Puerto Egas (Santiago) and Prince Philip's Steps (Genovesa) are good places to look for them.

Galápagos Rail

Seldom seen by visitors, the elusive Galápagos Rail (pachay) is a medium-sized bird which prefers wooded and grassy highlands. It is black with a grayish breast and white spots on its back. Visitors who get close enough will notice its red eyes.

The Galápagos Rail is nearly flightless, preferring to dart quickly through grasslands and forests, digging in fallen leaves for invertebrates such as worms, amphibians and insects. It is considered a threatened species, as introduced animals such as cats, dogs, goats and pigs devastate its habitat and eat the birds and their eggs. Increased efforts to eradicate these introduced species seem to be having a positive effect on Galápagos Rail populations. They can be seen in the highlands, usually in the morning.

Inland Water Birds of Galápagos

Although the different islands that make up Galápagos are generally very dry and arid, there are a few ponds and streams, mostly in the highlands of the larger islands. These ponds and streams are home to a handful of species of water birds like ducks and grebes that visitors won't ever see out to sea or on the beach. The most famous is probably the endemic Galápagos Pintail Duck, which can be seen in the highlands of Santa Cruz, Isabela or San Cristóbal.

Common Moorhen

Also called the Common Waterhen and Common Gallinule, the Common Moorhen (gallareta común) is a familiar sight in many areas of the world. A member of the Rail family, it is a medium-sized bird somewhere between a pigeon and a chicken in size. It has black feathers with a few white ones in the tail and wings. It is most easily distinguished by its bright red "face" around the eyes and over the bill. It also has skinny, bright yellow legs.

The Common Moorhen eats small insects and plants, and can often be seen puttering around ponds and lagoons. El Junco Lake on San Cristóbal Island is a good place to spot one.

Pied-billed Grebe

The Pied-billed Grebe (zambullidor de pico grueso) is a water bird resembling a small grayish-brown duck. The easiest way to recognize them is the black stripe on their bills (which are pointier than that of a duck). It looks like someone put a black rubber band on its bill to keep it closed.

The Pied-billed Grebe can often be seen puttering around freshwater highland ponds or

GALÁPAGOS

brackish inland lagoons. They're pretty quiet and shy, preferring to quickly swim away if approached. They eat frogs, bugs and small fish. They can also eat their own feathers to aid in digestion.

Galápagos Pintail Duck

The Galápagos Pintail Duck (patillo de Bahamas) is a medium-sized duck with brown and white feathers. It is easily identified by its white cheeks and colorful red and blue bill. It is a subspecies of the Bahama or White-Cheeked Pintail and is endemic to the Islands.

Ducks are rare in Galápagos, but there are enough highland ponds and coastal lagoons for the Pintail to thrive. Like other endemic species, it has adapted well to Galápagos life, feeding and breeding opportunistically as conditions on the islands permit. Look for them in any inland lake or lagoon—the brackish pools on Isabela Island are a good place to find them.

Whimbrel

Brown, medium-sized birds commonly sighted along the seashore, Whimbrels (zarapito) are most easily identified by their long, narrow, curved beaks. They're common in Galápagos and in much of the world. Whimbrels migrate, preferring to nest in colder northern climes.

Whimbrels eat small fish, insects and crustaceans. They are commonly seen in or near tidal pools, poking around for a good meal.

Galápagos Reptiles

Reptiles dominate the animal scene in Galápagos, due to their ability to cross long distances (i.e., from the mainland to the archipelago) without food or water. Giant tortoises and large land iguanas play the ecological role of the larger mammals on the mainland. There are 23 species of Galápagos reptiles, 21 of which are endemic to the archipelago. In 2009, the Galápagos Pink Iguana was identified as a separate species, which split off from other iguana species about 5-6 million years ago.

Galápagos Giant Tortoise

The Galápagos Giant Tortoise (tortuga gigante) is the namesake of the archipelago. The word "galápagos" refers to an old Spanish saddle very similar in shape to the shell of one of the two major types of tortoises: saddleback and dome-shaped. The saddleback tortoises have long necks, are smaller in stature, and live in low areas with little vegetation. Dome-shaped tortoises live in the highlands of the larger islands. Males have longer tails and are bigger than the females. Within these two categories fall 14 subspecies (three of which are extinct) of Galápagos Giant Tortoise, each having evolved differently due to habitat isolation.

The Galápagos Giant Tortoise is most well-known for its immense size. It can grow to over 1.5 meters (4.92 ft) in length and up to 250 kilograms (551.2 lb) in weight. Growth ring approximations on their shells indicate a life span of at least 150 years. The rate of growth is controlled by the availability of food, their food of choice extending to over 50 species of plants, including poison apple, guava, cactus pads and more.

Female tortoises reach sexual maturity at between 25 and 30 years of age, at which time they will mate and then migrate to the lowlands, locate a suitable earthy area, dig a shallow pit and deposit between two and 16 ping-pong ball-sized eggs. They will cover the eggs with mud and urine and leave the eggs incubating for 120 to 140 days. The distance traveled by female tortoises to lay their eggs is the greatest distance any tortoise will travel in its lifetime; males only move 4-5 kilometers (2.5-3.1 mi) per year and can often stay for days in their mud holes without moving.

The most famous Galápagos Giant Tortoise was Lonesome George, the last of the Pinta Island subspecies and an important symbol of the plight of the tortoises due to human activity until his death in 2012. Because tortoise populations have been drastically reduced from predation by introduced species, the Charles Darwin Research Station has spearheaded a very successful captive breeding and reintroduction program.

The easiest places to see Galápagos Giant Tortoises are at the Charles Darwin Research Station or at the breeding centers on Isabela or San Cristóbal and in the wild in the Santa Cruz highlands.

Galápagos Lava Lizard

There are seven endemic species of Lava Lizard (lagartija de lava) in Galápagos. They are easily recognizable by their small size (up to 30 cm in length) and interesting coloring. Males and females of all species are wildly different. Males are up to three times heavier than females, have more patterned skin, and have a clearly visible black or yellow throat. Females, on the other hand, are smaller and have a bright red or orange throat.

GALÁPAGOS

All Lava Lizards also perform a characteristic "push-up" behavior to show territorial aggression or courtship tendencies. Interestingly enough, this display is a vivid example of character divergence among species. This is because each of the islands' populations (even ones harboring the same species) have a slightly different display pattern.

Lava Lizards feed primarily on small insects, but they are omnivores and can occasionally eat plant material or even blood if a nearby bird or iguana is bleeding. Activity is closely dependent on daily temperature fluctuations, so you will probably see most lava lizards during the cool morning and mid-afternoon hours.

Lava Lizards can be seen darting around underfoot on every major island.

Green Sea Turtle

The only marine turtle to breed in Galápagos is the Green Sea Turtle (tortuga marina verde), which has a hard, dark green to black shell and can weigh up to 150 kilograms (330.7 lb). Unlike the giant tortoise, the female is larger than the male.

Peak mating season is from November to January, when both males and females will choose various partners with which to mate. You can often see a mating couple bobbing offshore or swimming near the surface of the water.

The female then goes ashore to prepare her nest, a large "body pit" with a smaller flask-shaped pit inside where the eggs are laid. She may come ashore as many as eight times at two week intervals, each time depositing 70 to 80 eggs. The small hatchlings emerge after a three-month incubation period, only to be confronted immediately with the reality of their delectability—only about one percent will survive predation by crabs, birds, sharks, or introduced cats, dogs or rats.

Snorkelers will see Green Sea Turtles all over the archipelago. You can also look for them while taking panga rides in calm, shallow waters.

Galápagos Land Iguana

There are two endemic species of land iguana (iguana terrestre) in the Galápagos archipelago, not counting the Pink Iguanas of Isabela: the more common Land Iguana and the island-specific Santa Fé Land Iguana.

Both species look very similar, with pale to dark yellow coloring, but the Santa Fé Land Iguana is paler, has a more pronounced crest, and is covered with a distinctive pattern resembling military camouflage.

There are also rare examples of land and marine iguanas hybridizing, the result of which is a land-loving iguana with dark skin, light-colored bands, a small spinal crest and webbed feet.

During the period of reproduction (the end of the year), males take on a brilliant red color to attract the females and become extremely territorial. After a somewhat violent copulation, the females will then lay six to eight eggs in underground nests, usually between January and March. The eggs are incubated for about 45 to 50 days, after which time young iguanas face the formidable challenge of surviving natural and introduced predators (especially the Galápagos Hawk). It is estimated that 70 percent of young land iguanas survive. The average life span is 45 years.

Land iguanas have a fairly limited home range of about 100 meters (328.1 ft), which means that they feed in a small area, mostly on pads and fruit from the opuntia cactus, and thus can be affected by localized climatic changes. The best places to see them are at Cerro Dragon (Santa Cruz) and on North Seymour. Sometimes they are seen wandering around near the Baltra airport.

Galápagos Pink Iguana

First discovered in 1986, the Pink Iguana was thought for a long time to be a subspecies of the Galápagos Land Iguana. In early 2009, however, researchers at a university in Rome released a study declaring the Pink Iguana to be a different species.

There is only a very small population of Pink Iguanas in Galápagos, and they are all found on the slopes of Wolf Volcano, on the northern end of Isabela Island. They are considered critically endangered due to their small population, and efforts are under way to protect them. Currently, there are no visitor sites on Wolf Volcano, so visitors to Galápagos will not get to see them.

Galápagos Marine Iguana

Ask any biologist what they think is the most remarkable of the Galápagos reptiles and chances are he or she will tell you that it's the Marine Iguana (iguana marina). After all, it's the only sea-faring lizard in the world!

Adult Marine Iguanas are mostly black or dark gray, but some have a colorful red and green lichen-like covering on their backs, the result of their algal diet. They also have an elongated tail to help them swim, a flat head, a pronounced crest running the length of their backs, and large, webbed feet.

Marine Iguanas live on land, but they feed on red and green algae in the cool ocean waters. Smaller iguanas keep to the intertidal zone, but others venture to depths of up to 10 meters (32.8 ft) and stay submerged for up to 10 minutes looking for food. After a swim, they return to land to bask in the sun or huddle with others for warmth (they are cold-blooded) and perform an unforgettable sneeze-like snort in order to release an excess of salt from their nostrils.

Marine iguanas have the same general reproductive cycle as land iguanas, laying their eggs in the beginning of the year. Their mating behavior, however, is a bit different. Marine iguanas are polyganous, meaning female iguanas accept a number of male partners, often as many as 15. Females lay three eggs in their underground nests instead of one, which take up to three months to incubate.

Young Marine Iguanas face the same predatory threats when they hatch, but they have the added challenge of thwarting marine predators. If they survive through the formative period, they are expected to live for 40 years.

Mammals List

There are not many mammal species that are native or endemic to Galápagos, as getting there from the mainland is very hard. Reptiles, for example, are much more likely to live on some floating vegetation for the days or weeks necessary to make it to the islands than a mammal. Still, the islands are home to a handful of endemic and native mammal species, as well as some undesirable introduced species.

The endemic mammal most often encountered by visitors is without question the Galápagos Sea Lion. These friendly critters are found on every island and often seem to enjoy interacting with tourists, particularly when snorkeling. Their cousins, the Galápagos Fur Sea Lions, are much more reclusive and only can be seen at a handful of visitor sites. They can be tough to tell from the regular sea lions, but naturalist guides can spot the differences easily.

There were once several subspecies of the Galápagos Rice Rat, but pressure from the far more aggressive introduced Black and Norway rats have driven most of them to extinction and there are now only three subspecies left. Every effort is being taken to preserve them, but it's a difficult battle against the introduced rats, cats and dogs. Active only at night, Rice Rats are very rarely seen by visitors.

The Galápagos Bat, or Galápagos Red Bat, is the only endemic bat in the islands. There are Hoary Bats as well, but they're common elsewhere in the world. Both species nest in vegetation and mangroves and are active at night. The best place to see one is in one of the towns around dusk.

Galápagos is also home to several species of whales and dolphins. These are rarely seen from shore but occasionally from a ship. The strait of water between Isabela and Fernandina is a good place to see them. The most commonly seen ones are Bryde's Whales and Bottlenose Dolphins. Galápagos cruise ships will usually make an effort to see the whales if there are some in the vicinity.

There are, of course, several other mammal species in Galápagos, none of them helpful for the ecosystem. Early whalers and settlers brought domesticated animals to Galápagos, including pigs, dogs, cats, goats and donkeys. Unintentionally, they brought rats and mice as well. These introduced animals have become a true nuisance, destroying whole ecosystems and pushing Galápagos species to extinction. Aggressive extermination measures have greatly reduced the impact of these species, but the problem is not yet over.

Galápagos Sea Lion

The endemic Galápagos Sea Lion (lobo marino) is found all throughout the islands and is absolutely fearless of humans. You will definitely have the chance to watch some of the 50,000 inquisitive juvenile sea lions, playful adult sea lions, protective mother sea lions and competitive male sea lions found in the archipelago. Male sea lions can be aggressive and are potentially dangerous so be alert while in their presence.

Males, or bulls, can be distinguished from the females, or cows, by their thick necks, bumped foreheads, and immense size (full-grown males can weigh up to 250 kg). They jealously guard and protect their territory, a finite area covering land and water space, a harem of approximately 20 cows and any number of pups. When bulls lose land battles to other, more aggressive dominant males, they conglomerate in specific island sites, or bachelor pads, to heal and rest until the next challenge.

The mating season varies from island to island, but it generally occurs from June to November. Females give birth to four or five pups over their lifetimes, one every two years. Copulation usually takes place in the water four weeks after a birth, but due to "delayed implantation," the egg is not implanted into the womb for another two months. Gestation takes another nine months, thus finalizing the annual birth cycle.

Nine out of 10 sea lion pups are females. The males and females stay together in "kindergartens," swimming and playing in the shallow water. After five months, the pups can start fishing for themselves, although they still depend on their mothers. After three years, cows have reached sexual maturity and begin to reproduce. After five years, the slow-blooming males reach their adulthood. Most sea lions live for 15 years or so.

Sea lions feed mostly on sardines (the cause of their bad breath) and other small fish, for which they may travel 10 to 15 kilometers (6.2-9.3 mi) out from the coast over the span of days to hunt. It is in deep water that sea lions encounter and must defend themselves from their only natural predators, sharks.

Marine Life

The Galápagos Islands are an amazing place for exploring underwater habitats. Due to the collision of warm and cool ocean currents, there is an astounding diversity and abundance of Galápagos fish species. That does not mean, however, that mastering marine creature identification is impossible.

The following pages are an introductory guide to the most common shore animals, cartilaginous fish (sharks and rays) and bony fish that can be seen when snorkeling. Marine life is more diverse than land life, and there are hundreds more fish, mollusks, crustaceans, echinoderms and other watery critters than are listed here.

Sally Lightfoot Crabs

Sally Lightfoot Crabs (zayapa) are named for their ability to flitter across rock faces like the semi-mythological dancer. Adults have a dramatic red-orange color, with a blue underside. Since red is the first color to disappear underwater, this coloration serves to camouflage the crabs. Juveniles, which are heavily predated, also rely on camouflage—they are black so that they can disappear against the lava background that serves as their habitat.

They are found on rocky shores throughout the islands, but common sightings are in Las Bachas (Santa Cruz), Puerto Egas (Santiago) and Sombrero Chino.

SHARKS IN THE GALÁPAGOS ISLANDS

The White-tipped Reef Shark (tiburón aleta blanca) is a common sight in snorkel spots throughout the archipelago. It is easy to identify by its pointed nose, silvery-gray color, and the white tips on its tail and first dorsal fin. Most White-tipped Reef Sharks are about the same size as an adult human, 1.5 to two meters (6.56 ft) in length. They tend to rest around rocky inlays or in caves, often swimming very close to snorkelers. Don't worry about these sharks reenacting a scene from *Jaws*—they feed at night on small fish and are very docile.

They are commonly seen by snorkelers at North Seymour, Gardner Bay and Turtle Island (Española), and Devil's Crown (Floreana). The place most famous for them is Tintoreras Islet near Puerto Villamil (Isabela), where visitors can see hundreds at a time if they're lucky. You can sometimes see them from the beach at Punta Cormorant (Floreana) and Bartolomé.

The Black-tipped Reef Shark (tiburón aleta negra) is less common than the White-Tipped Reef Shark, but it can still be seen by snorkelers. It is easily recognizable by its pointed nose, silvery-gray color, and the black (instead of white) tips on its fins. It is the same size as the White-Tipped Reef Shark, but it is more blatantly unassuming, usually swimming away at the sight of humans.

These are sometimes seen at Devil's Crown (Floreana). Juveniles are common in Black Turtle Cove (Santa Cruz).

The endemic Galápagos Shark (tiburón de Galápagos) is a stout, silvery-gray to brown shark. Despite its smaller size (up to two meters/6.56 ft), it is, arguably, the most threatening of the Galápagos sharks both in appearance and behavior. It is an active carnivore, and known to eat other sharks. It is rarely seen in the typical snorkel spots, but you might get lucky at Devil's Crown (Floreana) and at Leon Dormido (San Cristóbal).

GALÁPAGOS

The Hammerhead Shark (tiburón martillo) is instantly recognizable by its flattened head, peripheral eyes and nostrils and large (growing up to 4 m long) physique. Galápagos is famous for its abundance of Hammerheads—divers often see them in large schools of up to 30 or 40 individuals or even more.

You are less likely to see them while you are snorkeling, but your best chance is at Genovesa. If you are extremely lucky, you may see juveniles in Black Turtle Cove (Santa Cruz) or Post Office Bay (Floreana).

The Whale Shark (tiburón ballena) is a massive (but harmless) shark found mostly around the western islands of Darwin and Wolf. Since divers tend to be the only ones to visit these outlying islands, they are the most likely to see one of these gentle monsters. It has a huge mouth (often lined with cleaner fish) that swallows vast quantities of plankton.

RAYS IN THE GALÁPAGOS ISLANDS

The Manta Ray (mantaraya), with its large lobes, long mouth, thin tail and massive three-meter wingspan, is an amazingly beautiful, graceful and unassuming creature. Watching it swim or jump out of the water to remove annoying parasites or remora is a truly unforgettable experience. They feed on plankton near the surface of the water, making visual sightings from the ship or dinghy a fairly common occurrence.

They are often seen in open water between the central islands, most often from the cliff at South Plaza or from the beach at Rábida.

Golden Rays (raya dorada) are usually between a half-meter to a meter across the wings. They are aptly named for their golden-colored tops, but they can also be recognized by their blunt heads and long, whip-like tail. They are often seen in the major snorkel sites swimming alone, but they also swim in large schools in quiet lagoons. The best place to see schools of Golden Rays is at Black Turtle Cove (Santa Cruz).

Spotted Eagle Rays (raya águila) are also commonly sighted schooling in small lagoons like Black Turtle Cove (Santa Cruz). They have pointed heads, long tails with a spiny point, and a wingspan ranging from one to two meters (3.28-6.56 ft), but their most distinguishing feature is the array of white spots that covers their black tops. They are occasionally seen by snorkelers at Turtle Island (Española) or off Floreana.

Stingrays (raya sartén) are common residents of shallow beach areas and deeper sandy bottoms throughout Galápagos. They are gray with a flat body and long, narrow tail, which has the nasty stinger at its base. The size and shape of stingrays can vary, from the smaller, angular "diamond stingray" to the larger (up to two meter wingspan), circular "marbled" stingray.

You can spot stingrays lurking on the sea floor of some shallower snorkel sites or hiding out in the surf at Punta Cormorant, Post Office Bay (Floreana) and/or Concha de Perla near the dock of Puerto Villamil.

Introduced Species

Ask any Galápagos guide or park ranger, and they'll tell you that the most serious problem currently facing the islands is the threat posed by introduced species. The animals that live in Galápagos have been there by themselves for centuries, allowing them to adapt to very specific island conditions. Some scientists estimate that if it were not for humans, one new species would arrive to Galápagos "naturally" once every hundred years.

But the presence of humans changed all that. Since the islands were first discovered in the 16th century, dozens of new species have been brought to the islands. Some of them were brought accidentally, like the Tree Frog (Scinax quinquefasciatus) or the Ship Rat (Rattus rattus), but many, such as goats and pigs, were brought intentionally. In centuries past, sailing ships such as pirates and whalers would often release goats, pigs and other animals on islands so that they could be hunted for food on return visits. Also, early settlers brought cats, dogs, donkeys and other domestic animals with them, which would often escape into the wild.

The damage wrought by these animals is tremendous. Introducing new animals into a closed ecosystem often greatly disrupts it. Take for example the endemic Galápagos Flightless Cormorant. It arrived ages ago to the islands and began evolving. Most cormorants around the world can fly and make their nests in trees or on cliffs. The Galápagos variety does not fly and makes only a rudimentary nest of twigs on the ground.

These adaptations were possible because the Galápagos Cormorants have only one natural predator: the Galápagos Hawk, which can occasionally snatch a juvenile cormorant if the parent is inattentive. But when cats, dogs and rats were suddenly introduced, the cormorant, nesting on the ground and incapable of flying away, suddenly became vulnerable. Although the cormorant populations on the islands are not in any immediate danger, there is no doubt that their numbers are reduced from where they were before man arrived.

Almost every introduced species has caused great damage in the islands. Goats, one of the worst offenders, can pick an area clean of vegetation, leaving slower tortoises and iguanas to starve. Aggressive, introduced rats have muscled out the timid Galápagos Rice Rat. Cats eat bird eggs, small iguanas, snakes, lava lizards, turtle eggs and birds. Even introduced birds such as the Smooth-billed Ani carry diseases which infect local species.

Many invertebrates have arrived in Galápagos as well, including fire ants, wasps and the Cottony Cushioned Scale (Icerya purchasi). The scale insect was doing so much damage to the mangroves that the ladybug was intentionally introduced simply to combat it.

PLANTS
Many visitors assume that the introduced animal species are the most harmful to the islands, but this is not the case. Introduced plants have been taking over the islands at an alarming rate, elbowing out native plants in the process. Most of the plants were brought for a reason, such as edible blackberries or the Red Quinine tree, which produces an anti-malarial medicine. These plants are extremely difficult to control or eradicate. It is easier to remove goats or even rats from an island than an invasive plant species.

HOW TO HELP
The various institutions that are in charge of the ecology of Galápagos, such as the national park and the Charles Darwin Foundation, are working aggressively to remove these invasive species and undo the damage they have caused. There have been some success stories. Feral donkeys, for example, have been eliminated entirely from the islands. Project Isabela, a ten-year, multimillion-dollar initiative, removed an estimated 130,000 goats from Santiago and northern Isabela. Next up: cats, rats and certain plant species, including the Red Quinine.

As important as eradication, of course, is controlling the arrival of new species to the islands. Airplane cargo holds are fumigated, fresh food is not allowed, and carry-on baggage can be inspected.

The Galápagos Islands are probably about the only place in the post-9/11 world where airport personnel are more concerned with people carrying pears and apples on board than bombs! So do your part: be sure to follow the posted restrictions when you visit Galápagos, so that it can be preserved just as it is.

Town in the Galapagos
PUERTO AYORA
The main town in Galápagos is Puerto Ayora, located on Santa Cruz island. It's a friendly, medium-sized town of some 20,000 inhabitants. The majority of land tours, scuba-diving tours and adventure tours originate and/or are based here.

Visitors intending to arrange cruise tours locally will stay here waiting for availability on boats to open up. Virtually every cruise tour makes a day stop here—usually near the half-way point of an eight-day trip or at the extremes of the four or five-day trip—so that visitors can visit the Charles Darwin Research Station and highlands and stock up on medicine, film, batteries and snacks if supplies were beginning to run low. Since Puerto Ayora caters to tourist activities, visitors can find almost any item unintentionally left behind. There is a wide assortment of hotels, restaurants, bars, stores, tour agencies, dive shops, and internet cafes. There is also a post office, airline offices, a basic public hospital and a hyperbaric chamber.

Puerto Ayora Services
PUERTO AYORA SHOPPING
For the most part, if you're shopping in Puerto Ayora, you're looking either for supplies, such as sunscreen, or souvenirs. Things like medicine, food and sunscreen are available, but expensive, so stock up on those things beforehand. There are plenty of souvenir shops in Puerto Ayora, each of them selling coffee mugs, T-shirts, postcards and other touristy stuff, most of which seem to have some sort of Booby joke printed on them. Feel free to stock up on things for friends and family back home. It's a big boost to the local economy.

Lately, there has been an increase in high-end shops specializing in jewelry, art and quality handicrafts from Ecuador and elsewhere. You can't miss the shops, which line Charles Darwin Avenue from the pier to the research station.

GALAPAGOS

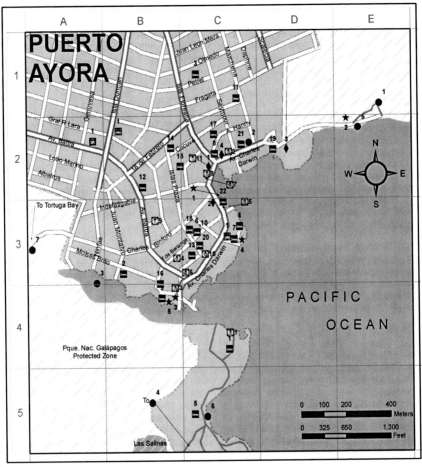

INTERNET IN PUERTO AYORA

There are literally dozens of internet cafés in Puerto Ayora scattered about, and they're spread out so you're bound to find one handy just about anytime. They're typically open throughout the day from 9 a.m. until later in the evening.

Rates for internet use are about $2 per hour, including use of Skype if you have it. Internet cafés are also a good place to make cheap phone calls home.

One good internet café is Galápagos On-line, on Charles Darwin Avenue across from the naval base. It's very popular with all the gringos that come through town.

Galápagos is not known for crime, but if you're surfing the net, best to keep an eye on your stuff while your at your computer.

Things To See and Do

There are lots of things to see and do in Puerto Ayora. There are a handful of semi-regulated visitor sites in and around the town and it's possible to visit them without a naturalist guide.

There are some good beaches in town and nearby. The most convenient is the Station beach, not far from the Charles Darwin Research Station, but the ones at Garrapatero and Tortuga Bay are much nicer. In the highlands, there are giant tortoises to view as well as lava tubes to explore. Hikers may want to visit Cerro Crocker, the highest point on Santa Cruz. Los Gemelos is a pair of sinkholes which are popular with birdwatchers.

If these sites aren't enough, it's possible to arrange day tours to nearby islands like Santa Fe or Floreana.

Did a unique trek? Tell other travelers at vivatravelguides.com

● **Activities**
1 Charles Darwin Research Station E1
2 Chi Spa C2
3 Laguna Las Ninfas A4
4 Las Grietas B5
5 Playa de la Estación E2
6 Playa de los Alemanes C3
7 The Miguel Cifuentes Arias Community Center A3

▥ **Eating**
1 Angermeyer Point C4
2 Café del Mar C2
3 El Descanso del Guía B4
4 Galápagos Deli B3
5 Garrapata C3
6 Henán Café C3
7 Il Giardino C2
8 Isla Grill C2
9 Kioskos B3
10 The Rock C3
11 Tintorera C2

★ **Services**
1 Bank C2
2 Galápagos National Park Office E2
3 Information Center (Itur) B4
4 Police C3
5 Post Office B4

▨ **Shopping**
1 Market A2

▬ **Sleeping**
1 Angermeyer Waterfront Inn C4
2 Casa del Lago B3
3 Casa Natura C1
4 Estrella del Mar C3
5 Finch Bay C5
6 Gardner C3
7 Grand Hotel Lobo de Mar C3
8 Hosteling 10-28 C2
9 Hotel Castro B4
10 Hotel España C3
11 Hotel Fernandina C1
12 Hotel Santa Cruz B2
13 Lirio del Mar C3
14 Maidith B2
15 Mainao B2
16 Ninfa B4
17 Pension Gloria C2
18 Red Booby C3
19 Red Mangrove D2
20 Salinas C3
21 Silberstein C2
22 Sol y Mar C3

♦ **Tour**
1 Galapagos Sub-Aqua C2
2 Moonrise Travel Agency C3
3 Scuba Iguana D2
4 Shark Friends C2

▦ **Transportation**
1 Airline B2, C3

The Charles Darwin Research Station

In 1959, the same year the National Park was established, the Charles Darwin Foundation—an international non-governmental organization—was formed. Its basic objectives were to promote scientific studies and environmental education in partnership with the Galápagos National Park, through the management of an on-site investigative facility, the Charles Darwin Research Station (CDRS). Since its foundation, the Charles Darwin Foundation and its Research Station have gathered baseline scientific data for a variety of conservation initiatives.

An important nexus of these conservation efforts has been the mitigation of the harmful effects of introduced species and the regeneration of native populations, a process that visitors to the CDRS can watch with their own eyes. Until his death in 2012, the station was home to Lonesome George, the last of the Pinta Island Giant Tortoise subspecies.

At the station you will also see the solution to the turtle population problem: a tortoise captive breeding center that has been successful in restoring healthy populations to the wild.

Other attractions at the CDRS include close-up views of several of the 11 subspecies of tortoise, land iguanas, and Darwin's Finches, paths through coastal and arid-zone vegetation, including salt bush, mangroves, prickly pear, and other cacti, an elaborate presentation and video of the station's conservation efforts in the Van Straelen Exhibition Center.

Check out the customary souvenir kiosk, whose profits go to support the station (since it is 100% privately funded, receiving zero support from the Ecuadorian government).

You can't miss the Research Station: it's right outside of town.
Updated: May 6, 2013

GALÁPAGOS

Playa de la Estación/Station Beach

Station Beach is a small, rocky beach located off of the road that leads to the Charles Darwin Research Station. It's the closest beach to town and the easiest one to reach, so sometimes it fills up. The small patch of white sand is bordered on either side by some jagged lava rocks, where you might see some shore birds like pelicans or gulls, and marine iguanas are common. It isn't the best beach, but it is close to town. It's free and there are no restrictions.

It's possible to snorkel here, and you may see some bright reef fish near the rocks on either side. Just don't bring any valuables to the beach, and if you do, keep a close eye on them.

Playa de los Alemanes

Playa de los Alemanes (German Beach) is an easy visit from Puerto Ayora and one of the better easily-accessible beaches. Simply take a water taxi (should cost about $1) to the pier on Angermeyer Point (just tell the water taxi guy that you want to go to Playa de los Alemanes). From there, it's an easy walk of five minutes; you'll pass some saline pools on the way, so keep your eyes open for some wading and swimming birds.

The beach itself is a crescent of white sand framed by a boardwalk behind and mangroves on either side. It's sheltered, so the water is great for swimming and snorkeling (although you shouldn't expect to see anything spectacular, like sharks). German Beach is great for kids.

There are no public changing or restroom facilities here. Nearby is the ultra-fancy Finch Bay Hotel—they'll probably let you sit in the shade at the bar and order a cool drink if you like, but the pool is only for guests.

As always, keep an eye on your valuables. German Beach is free and you do not need to be accompanied by a naturalist guide to visit. If you keep walking past the Finch Bay Hotel, you'll find the path to Las Grietas.

Las Grietas

A postcard-perfect swimming hole located in a lava crevasse on Angermeyer Point, Las Grietas is a great place to cool off on a hot Galápagos afternoon. The crystal clear blue water is as smooth as glass, and it's a great place for beginner snorkelers. It's very popular with daytrippers from Puerto Ayora but there isn't a lot of room to put your stuff. In fact, petty theft is common there when there are a lot of people, so you should only bring what you really need.

The trail to Las Grietas goes through a rocky, dry forest of tall cacti; you'll want good walking shoes and a bottle of water. Walking there will take you about 15-20 minutes from the Finch Bay Hotel. You'll pass a couple of salt lagoons, but don't expect to see a lot of wildlife on this trail.

Las Grietas is free, and you do not need to be accompanied by a naturalist guide. Hours: 6 a.m.-6 p.m.

Tortuga Bay

Tortuga Bay is a pristine, gorgeous white sand beach located within walking distance from Puerto Ayora. It's part of the park system, but it's free and you don't need a naturalist guide to go there. It's popular with locals and often you'll see families there on weekends.

The trail to get there leaves town not far from the Ninfas Lagoon. Just head further outside of town until you see signs for the Miguel Cifuentes Arias Community Center—the trail is right behind it. There are restrooms at the community center, but none at the beach, so plan ahead.

You'll have to pass through a sort of checkpoint where you'll sign in and out; this will also be your last chance to buy water, snacks, etc., as there is nothing at the bay. There are no trash cans there either, so plan on bringing back any empty bottles, chip bags, etc.

The trail emerges at Playa Brava, a wide and lovely beach that stretches for over a kilometer. You can surf there—several places in Puerto Ayora will rent you any gear you need. The mounds behind the beach are off-limits. That is where sea turtles nest. On a clear day, Carmaaño Islet (the Lobería) at the mouth of Academy Bay, Santa Fe Island and Floreana can be seen on the horizon.

The west end of Playa Brava, pools form at low tide. These are popular snorkeling spots for local school kids. The beach seemingly ends at a rocky point. A trail goes around this spit of land, full of marine iguanas—some of the largest you'll see so close to civilization. (Stay on the path, because this is also their nesting grounds). Offshore, you'll see sea turtles hanging out. The path loops around to the other side of the peninsula to Playa Mansa. Along this stretch, Blue-footed Boobies dance.

GALÁPAGOS

Playa Mansa is a perfect piece of paradise. The turquoise waters are perfectly tranquil. At times, even sea lions, Eagle Rays and mating sea turtles come to enjoy this warm cove. Between dips, rest on the makeshift benches beneath the trees. Occasionally there is a guy there who rents out kayaks, but there are no other vendors of any sort.

At the far end of Playa Mansa, past the mangroves, are some salt flats and marshes where a variety of waterfowl and shore birds, including flamingos, are seen.

Some petty theft has been reported at Tortuga Bay. Be sure to take care of your valuables. The path to the beach is paved, but long, and it can get quite hot. There are a few ups and downs. Bring bottled water for sure. Trail length: 2,500 meters (8,202 ft).

Puerto Ayora Tour Agencies and Dive Shops

There are many tour agencies in Puerto Ayora, ranging from competent, experienced professionals to sleazy con men on the street who would gladly sell their own mothers to a passing battleship if there was $5 in it for them.

To avoid the latter, stick to places that have a real office and NEVER deal with anyone who approaches you in the street. If you can, check the website of a place you're thinking of doing business with. If it looks serious and professional the place is probably okay. Stay away from the cheeseball hole-in-the-wall places near the old pier (close to the Proinsular supermarket). Many of the hotels have travel desks to help their guests. If yours does, take advantage of it. These are a great way to set up little tours, buy tickets for the ferry, etc.

For an in-depth look at dive sites see our Visitor Sites section on Puerto Ayora (p. 527).

Shark Friends

A relatively new dive shop, Shark Friends goes to all of the usual Puerto Ayora dive spots: Daphne, Seymour, Gordon Rocks, etc. They offer a variety of dive courses from discovery SCUBA for beginners to Dive Master. A two-dive day will cost you around $140, three dives $180, including gear, guide and lunch. Some of their packages are a good deal. See their website for details. They also do some basic local tours, such as biking, going to see the tortoises in the highlands, fishing, etc. Booking ahead is a good idea

if you can, but walk-ins are welcome. Tel: 593-05-252-6854/08-504-4995/683-7342, E-mail: sharksfriendsgalapagos@hotmail.com, URL: www.sharksfriends.com.

Academy Bay Diving

Academy Bay Diving is a locally owned and run business. They offer single and multi day dive packages, PADI courses—Open Water to Dive Master, island tours, last minute cruises and a wealth of local information. The crew is fun and professional, and the equipment is of good quality and regularly serviced. Av. Charles Darwin. Tel: 593-05-252-4164, URL: www.academybaydiving.com. Updated: Aug 09, 2012.

Moonrise Travel

A reputable local travel agency in central Puerto Ayora (It's more or less across the street from the Banco del Pacífico near the fishermen's pier), Moonrise is a good place to organize day trips such as highland tours, snorkeling, etc. You can also get tickets here for the ferries to San Cristóbal and Isabela. If you contact them before you go, they will help arrange tours, hotels, etc. Their website is a little problematic, but the form for contacting them should work. Charles Darwin 160 and Charles Binford. Tel: 593-5-526402,/526403/526348/526589, URL: www.galapagosmoonrise.com. Updated: Aug 09, 2012.

Puerto Ayora Lodging

As the main point of entry for Galápagos, Puerto Ayora has the best selection of hotels. You'll find everything from the battered Pensión Gloria ($10 per night) to the $1,000 per night Prince of Wales Suite at the Royal Palm Hotel with plenty of options in between. As in all of Galápagos, there has been a hotel boom recently, with most of the new construction taking place a couple of blocks off of the main drag, Charles Darwin Avenue. Some of the new hotels are quite nice and reasonably priced.

In Puerto Ayora, you'll find a couple of flat-out budget places, a glut of forgettable rooms in the $25 per night range, a few more for $40-60 or so, another glut of rooms in the $70-110 range, and a handful of excellent places for over $110 or so. Unless you're spending a wad of cash, you'll usually have to decide on some sort of trade-off. You may have to choose between being close to the main drag or having air conditioning, having a nice pool or having a nice view, etc. Look at the room options carefully!

GALÁPAGOS

Hotel rooms in Puerto Ayora tend to book up in the high season (June-September, December-January) but the town itself rarely gets so packed that nothing is available. You should book ahead to make sure you get your first choice of hotels and aren't settling for something sub-standard.

BUDGET

Pensión Gloria

(ROOMS: $5-10 per person) Pensión Gloria is the best option for the backpacker who has overstayed his welcome and overspent his budget. It is the least expensive—and least frilly—place to stay in the Galápagos, at $10 per person per day (you may get them as low as $5 per person if you stay for five or more days). There are a few (dark) rooms opening out to (an even darker) courtyard, each with fans and their own flair (the walls have painted Galápagos scenes). Bathrooms are shared, and kitchen facilities can be made available upon request. Av. Charles Darwin near Seymour. Updated: Aug 02, 2012.

Hotel Santa Cruz

(ROOMS: $7 per person) The Hotel Santa Cruz is popular with backpackers and low-budget Ecuadorians. It is a bit far from the boardwalk (in Puerto Ayora standards) and accommodations are basic. There are eight rooms—two singles, four doubles, one triple and one quadruple—with private bathrooms, tepid-water showers and portable fans. Some rooms have a TV, but no cable—local channels only. Av. Baltra and Indefatigable, near the market.Tel: 593-05-252-6573. Updated: May 12, 2013.

Hotel España !

(ROOMS: $15/person) Hotel España, the best budget option in Puerto Ayora, is clean, friendly and has been recently been renovated. The hotel is in a good location, plus the rooms are neat and tidy, and the mattresses have all been recently replaced. There is a new, attractive downstairs common area and even some hammocks for hanging out.

Most of the rooms have air conditioning (it costs a little more if you want to use it) and the showers are heated by gas heaters, not the lethal little "electric showers" most other hotels in the same price range have. The owner, Genoveva, is a friendly local lady who likes helping travelers find the right tours for them, and her daughter Esther is a SCUBA guide who can also answer any questions about the islands or about what you should see and do there. They help their guests with tours, ferry tickets, etc. The hotel tends to fill up, so you should either make reservations or call ahead before going to Puerto Ayora. Hotel España is priced comparably with the Hotel Gardner next door (although the hotels are not affiliated). The two hotels are probably the best value for budget lodging in town, so if one is full, your first stop should be the other. Tomas de Berlanga and Islas Plazas. Tel: 593-05-252-6108, E-mail: hotelesgalapagos@yahoo.es. Updated: Feb 22, 2013.

Hotel Gardner

(ROOMS: $25 per person) The Hotel Gardner is one of Puerto Ayora's better budget options. The rooms are spacious and neat. Some of the downstairs rooms are windowless, and can get quite dark. Ask for one of the sunnier upstairs rooms if they are available. Each room has a private bathroom, floor fans and TV, although only with local channels. There is a large room on the top floor with five beds in it: a good option if you're traveling in a larger group or with a family.

There is an attached travel agency next door operated by the owners: it's a good place to book simple daytrips like tours of Academy Bay. The Hotel Gardner is located next door to the Hotel España, which is similarly priced and also a very good value: the two hotels are not in any way affiliated. Islas Plazas between Bolivar Naveda and 12 de Febrero. Tel: 593-5-252-6979/8-800-3285, E-mail: hotelgardner@yahoo.com. Updated: Apr 07, 2013.

Hosteling 10-28

(ROOMS: $30 per person) Wedged in between a dive shop and a trinket store, Hosteling 10-28 is cramped but friendly, and efforts to improve the place seem to be ongoing, which is always a good sign. The tiny pool does not inspire much lounging about, but should suffice for a quick dip to cool off. There are only five rooms here, each suitable for 2-4 people. Rooms have cable TV, air conditioning, hot water and a small fridge. Tel: 593-2-255-0090/222-2156, URL: www.1028hostalgalapagos.com.

Hotel Lirio del Mar

(ROOMS: $15-45) A decent option for budget travelers, the Hotel Lirio del Mar is a three-story hotel with conspicuous orange walls and a second-floor terrace overlooking Academy Bay. Although its exterior is not

GALÁPAGOS

lacking for character, the rooms are fairly basic and ordinary. Twenty-four single, double, triple and quadruple rooms have private hot baths and fans. There is also a small, dark lounge area near reception that has sofas and a TV. Islas Plaza between Tomas de Berlanga and Av. Charles Darwin. Tel: 593-5-252-6212. Updated: Nov 22, 2012.

MID-RANGE

Hotel Salinas

(ROOMS: $25-78) Hotel Salinas is one of the more spacious and professional low-mid-range hotels in Puerto Ayora. It has 22 plain yet comfortable rooms with private baths, which are distributed on three floors. As you climb the courtyard staircase, you encounter more frills and perks. First floor singles and doubles have tepid water and fans. Second floor doubles, triples and quadruples have hot water and fans. Third floor suites have hot water, air conditioning and cable. This results in a bewildering array of prices. It almost seems as if each room has a different cost! It's best to go, see what they have available, and negotiate a price.

The hotel also offers 24-hour coffee, laundry, and tour information services. The small central garden also provides a refreshing area for sipping cold drinks or chatting with new friends. Price includes taxes and breakfast is included. All meals in the small attached restaurant cost $4.48 except platos á la carte which cost $7.84 (not including tax). Islas Plaza between Av. Charles Darwin and Tomas de Berlanga. Tel: 593-5-252-6107, E-mail: reservashotelsalinas@hotmail.com. Updated: Jan 12, 2013.

Hotel Castro

(ROOMS: $50-70) Hotel Castro is a pleasant surprise. It's a clean and friendly place in a good location and reasonably priced. The interior is a bit gloomy, and the 19 rooms are small and boxy, but overall the place is pretty good for the price, especially if it's hot out, as all rooms have air conditioning. If a/c is a must, this place might be your best bet in town if you're on a budget. Av. Los Colonos, near the old pier. Updated: Jan 12, 2013.

Hotel Estrella del Mar

(ROOMS: $47-83) The Hotel Estrella del Mar is the only mid-range hotel that can offer ocean views. Four of the hotel's 12 rooms face Academy Bay and receive fresh breezes off the water through their screened-in windows. All other rooms are ccomfortable, clean, and spacious, and have private hot showers and fan. A few select rooms have air conditioning and TV at the same prices, so request these rooms if you come between February and April and need solace from the unbearable heat. It is a friendly place near the water with a comfortable eating area (breakfast is available for a small price), self-service coffee bar, and lounge. 12 de Febrero, just off Academy Bay. Tel: 593-5-252-6427, E-mail: estrellademar@islasantacruz.com. Updated: May 12, 2013.

Casa del Lago

(ROOMS: $87-170) The Casa del Lago is part of an effort to offer tourists alternatives that emphasize social and cultural responsibility. Suites are rented on a daily, weekly or even monthly basis. Recycled glass fragments in window frames play with incoming light, hand-painted tiles add flair to showers and staircases and wild fabrics give the walls, ceilings and beds a spicy character.

The suites are all furnished with hot water, a private bathroom, cable and wireless internet. All suites have a private terrace with gardens. Breakfast is not included. Other meals in the caféteria range in price from $6-10. The residence is adjacent to the Casa del Lago Café Cultural and looks out on the Laguna Las Ninfas.

This is a comfortable and affordable option for travelers looking to venture outside the norm. The owner can also arrange custom-designed tours for student groups and other parties interested in educational tourism. Tours visit local hot-spots, farms and residences and generate proceeds that directly benefit Santa Cruz residents. Calle Moises Brito and Juan Montalvo, near the Ninfas Lake. Tel: 593-5-252-4116/9-971-4647, E-mail: info@galapagoscultural.com, casadellago@galapagoscultural.com,URL:www.galapagoscultural.com. Updated: Apr 28, 2013.

Hotel Silberstein

(ROOMS: $113-165) The Hotel Silberstein is a modern, intimate and beautifully-landscaped hotel. It has 22 clean, romantic rooms, each containing a private hot bath, ceiling fan and air conditioning, and a view toward the lush courtyard/swimming pool area. There are 11 matrimonial double rooms, eight double rooms with twin beds, and three triples. Comfort, style and attention to detail (not to mention price) are at a maximum at the Hotel Silberstein. A sandy space near the pool can serve as a playplace

GALÁPAGOS

for youngsters. The garden surrounding the open-air bar provides a diverse, eye-catching landscape (as well as interesting data for plant and bird surveys conducted by the Charles Darwin Research Station). The hotel partners with the Galextur to offer four to eight-day tours with overnight accommodations in Puerto Ayora. It can also arrange cruise tours and any sort of day trips. Av. Charles Darwin and Seymour. Tel: 593-5-252-6277, E-mail: blectour@iuo.satnet.net. Updated: Aug 02, 2012.

Maidith Galápagos Apartments and Suites ⟩

(ROOMS: $75-122) Don't let the name fool you, Maidith is a hotel, not a set of apartments or suites for long-term rental (although it seems they used to be). What's more, it's a very nice hotel and one of the best deals in Puerto Ayora.

Maidith is about as different from other Galápagos hotels as it is possible to be. That's a good thing. It's never blocky, boring, dull or forgettable. Instead, the hotel is a colorful maze of rooms and stairways, all different, all brightly but tastefully decorated with bits of tile and stone. It looks a bit like a candy house that someone made at Christmas come to life. Kids will love exploring the place. The rooms are all suites and each one is different and suitable for a different number of guests. The largest suite sleeps five.

There is a Jacuzzi and each of the rooms has all the expected comforts such as air conditioning, hot water, etc. There is a small kitchen available to some of the suites. Make sure you reserve the right room if you want it. Management is friendly and helpful. It's on a sleepy street a couple blocks off of the main drag; this is a boon for those who like it quiet. The website is Spanish-only but fairly easy to navigate if you want to see photos, make reservations, etc. Features: hot water, fridge, microwave, Jacuzzi, kitchen, TV cable, internet and restaurant. Tel: 593-8-456-8171/5-252-6311, E-mail: magreda@maidithgalapagos.com, URL: maidithgalapagos.com.

Hotel Ninfa

(ROOMS: $65) Remember that one spring break back in college, when you and a bunch of buddies went to Fort Lauderdale? And you had booked the cheapest hotel in town, because you figured, hey, I'll be too busy partying to care what the place looks like? And it had a pool, so how bad could it be?

And you got there, and found a squarish, whitewashed place with flaking paint, tired-looking palm trees and cracked tiles that looked like it had weathered one hurricane too many? Well, that hotel has been shipped brick-by-worn-out-brick down to the Galápagos, where it has been rebuilt and renamed the Ninfa. Right down to the sagging hammocks and broken pool table, it's all there.

I'm not saying this is a bad place. I'm just saying you shouldn't buy the "high-class luxury hotel" line that you'll get from their official websites and literature. The Ninfa owns a small cruise ship and package tours are available. Calle Los Colonos S/N. Tel: 593-5-252-6127. Updated: Dec 11, 2012.

Hostal Mainao

(ROOMS: $119-197) The Hostal Mainao (don't be fooled by the name; it's no hostal but a hotel) is a pleasant, clean, multi-story hotel located a couple of blocks off the main street in Puerto Ayora. The staff is friendly, the location is convenient, and the included breakfast is quite good. The rooms are clean, airy and comfortable, and the maids do a good job keeping them clean. There are 19 rooms, for a maximum capacity of about 45 people. The rates reflect different seasons: prices will go down May-June and Sepember-October. Check the hotel website for the latest information. The higher prices are for nicer suites. All of the rooms have air conditioning and fans to keep you cool. Prices are a bit steep for a hotel with no ocean view or cable TV. Still, the Mainao is quite nice and you're bound to find it charming. If you're looking for something upper mid-range in terms of price it's worth checking out. About two blocks off of the main drag in Puerto Ayora, turn near the fishermen's dock. Ca. Matazarnos and Indefatigable, Pelican Bay Neighborhood. Tel: 593-9-415-1847/8-921-8349, Fax: 593-252-7029/252-4128, URL: www.hotelmainao.com. Updated: Jan 15, 2013.

Hotel Red Booby

(ROOMS: $100-110) The dolled-up Red Booby occupies a very specific place on the food chain of Puerto Ayora Hotels. It's nice and expensive enough to keep out the riff-raff, but doesn't really hit the four-star status that it obviously desires. The bedspreads and curtains are very nice, but that can't change the fact that the rooms are boxy, bare and a little grim. Still, the pool is cool, as it occupies the whole top floor and has a great view. It's perfect if you want to spend a little more on a nicer hotel, but can't go

GALÁPAGOS

all-out and stay at a place like the Finch Bay. It will appeal to this 'tweener crowd only, however: most visitors will either decide to pony up a few more bucks for a nicer place or sacrifice the nice pool and pretty bedspreads for the sake of cutting their hotel bill in half and staying somewhere like the Hotel Castro.

P.S. In case you're confused, no, there is no such thing as a Red Booby—Red-footed Booby, yes; Red Booby, no. This apparent lack of creativity seems odd until you consider the Red Booby's motto: "Enjoy the comfort and elegance of Red Booby." I sure hope they didn't pay some ad guy very much for that one. Av. Plazas and Charles Binford Islas. Tel: 593-5-252-6485, E-mail: info@hotelredbooby.com.ec, URL: www.hotel-redbooby.com.ec. Updated: Mar 20, 2013.

Grand Hotel Lobo del Mar

(ROOMS: $82-158) The Grand Hotel Lobo del Mar may be "grand" in terms of size due to its recent four-story addition, but it is nowhere near grand in terms of service, despite the variety of activities it coordinates. The hotel has a day-boat and a cruise-boat and it also has partnerships with a variety of day-tour operators. This means that if you booked the cruise outside of Galápagos, you may wind up having to stay in the already paid for Lobo del Mar, and it is a toss-up whether you will be placed in the swanky, newer, more expensive section of the hotel or the lifeless, older, more economical section.

Academy Bay, Puerto Ayora

If you are lucky, you will have one of the newer rooms, complete with lush comforts, TV and air conditioning. Less fortunate tourists will get a room in the older, darker section, which comes with a fan and private hot bath. Communicating objections to reception staff over the location (and subsequent worth) of your room will result in the standard apology, graceless smile, and no change. 12 de febrero just off Av. Charles Darwin toward the bay. Tel: 593-5-252-6188, URL: www.lobodemar.com.ec. Updated: Apr 15, 2013.

Casa Natura

(ROOMS: $100-145) One of the better options in the upper-middle price range in Puerto Ayora, Casa Natura is a clean, attractive, well-run place a few blocks off of the main street. The rooms are spacious, airy and clean, there's a pool and a small restaurant, and the beds are comfortable. Like most of the nicer hotels, there is someone to help you book tours, buy tickets to the ferry, etc.

It's owned and operated by Via Natura, a growing Quito-based tour company with agencies in Peru and Chile. They also own the Monserrat yacht, a Galápagos cruiser. Booking combination packages with everything from Machu Picchu to Galápagos is possible. Via Natura is an eco-friendly organization and a member of the rainforest alliance and other eco-organizations. Petrel and Floreana. Tel: 593-2-246-9846/847, URL: www.vianatura.com, www.casanaturahotel.com.

Hotel Fernandina !

(ROOMS: $122-158) The Hotel Fernandina is a family-run place on the edge of town, but still not too far from where the action is. It's a great choice for the upper mid-range traveler who likes some luxuries. They have a swimming pool, jacuzzi, on-site restaurant and WiFi in the common areas. They have a travel desk and are happy to assist you in booking day trips and local tours. Try to get one of the upstairs rooms as they have a nicer view. Price includes taxes and buffet breakfast. Here's a bonus: the pool is available ($3) even if you're not staying there! Av. 12 Noviembre and Piqueros. Tel: 593-5-2526/499, URL: www.hotelfernandina.com.ec/eng.

HIGH-END

Hotel Sol y Mar

(ROOMS: $175-195) The Hotel Sol y Mar has 17 rooms, each with a private balcony and stunning sea view. The rooms are spacious, immaculate, and secure, and come with air conditioning and a bar. A small deck with picnic tables serves as a great resting or meeting area, with views of nearby Academy Bay. The on-site restaurant overlooks the bay. A family owned and operated establishment, Hotel Sol y Mar guarantees personalized, caring, and detail-oriented service. A mini buffet breakfast is included in the price. Av. Charles Darwin between Tomas de Berlanga and Charles Dinford (next to the Banco del Pacifico). Tel: 593-5-252-6281, Fax: 593-5-252-7015, E-mail: info@hotelsolymar.com.ec, URL: www.hotelsolymar.com.ec. Updated: Jan 20, 2013.

Red Mangrove Adventure Inn

(ROOMS: $192-550) The Red Mangrove Adventure Inn is one of Puerto Ayora's better hotels. Each room is clean, comfortable, and equipped with a private hot bath and ceiling fan. There is also a small pool, a meeting area with plush tables and chairs, a common room with television, and plenty of hammocks for lounging.

The Red Mangrove Adventure Inn is pricey, but it backs it up with good service and facilities. The inn coordinates a variety of tours, including camping, sea kayaking, fishing, mountain biking and horseback riding. As such, it offers excellent, custom-tailored alternatives to prearranged tours. The Red Mangrove has affiliated hotels on Isabela and Floreana and offers island-hopping packages. Av. Charles Darwin near the cemetery. Tel: 593-5-252-7011, Fax: 593-5-252-6564, E-mail: recepcion@redmangrove.com, URL: www.redmangrove.com. Updated: Aug 02, 2012.

Finch Bay Eco-Hotel ♪

One of the newer deluxe hotels in the islands, Finch Bay is owned and operated by the prestigious Metropolitan Touring, an Ecuadorian tour company that also owns three luxury Galápagos yachts. The Finch Bay hotel is a first class facility tucked away on Playa de los Alemanes, or "German Beach." The hotel is rather expensive, but it's the only hotel in Puerto Ayora on a beach, the pool is very refreshing, and the rooms are classy. Naturally, everything you could ask for is available. They do tours of the island, kayaking, snorkeling, birdwatching, etc; there is a fancy restaurant and bar on the premises; they'll send someone to get you at the airport; you name it. It goes without saying that the six suites and 21 regular rooms have air conditioning, hot showers, mints on the pillows, etc. Many people who stay at the Finch Bay have booked cruises on the Santa Cruz, Isabela or Pinta, Metropolitan's three Galápagos cruise ships, so sometimes the place fills up. Better make reservations well ahead of time. How to get there: It's on Playa de Los Alemanes on Angermeyer Point. You'll have to take a water taxi from the pier (just tell them Finch Bay). Costs: Finch Bay runs more on packages and specials than per night. Check their website for the latest deals, but assume approximately $300/night/person, but that includes tours, guides, etc. Features: Jacuzzi, outdoor pool, restaurant, bar, gift shop, ice machine , laundry, phone, fax, safe box, and hair dryer. E-mail: info@metropolitan-touring.com, URL: www.metropolitan-touring.com. Updated: Aug 02, 2012.

Angermeyer Waterfront Inn

(ROOMS: $175-350) Marine iguanas and plunging blue-footed boobies are a natural part of the landscape at this tranquil seaside inn. It is known for great service and facilities. For being one of the original Galápagos hotels, it's very modern. You can even check out photos and other information about them on Facebook. It has arguably the best location of any Puerto Ayora Hotel, right on a peninsula on Academy Bay. It is connected by land to Puerto Ayora, but due to the restrictions of the National Park it is not possible to walk there. Instead it can easily be reached by a 2 minute water-taxi ride right to their doorstep. Tel: 593-9-472-4955, E-mail: angermeyerwaterfrontinn@gmail.com, URL: www.angermeyer-waterfront-inn.com. Updated: Jun 01, 2013.

Puerto Ayora Restaurants

Along Avenida Charles Darwin in Puerto Ayora there are a variety of open-air cafés, restaurants and bars (or sites serving as all three). Seafood and Italian cuisine seem to dominate the food scene, but you can also find sandwiches, salads, amazing coffee and juices, and home-made ice cream. Even if you don't want to dine, stop in any street-side establishments, order a refreshing beverage, and watch the mesmerizing mix of people walk by. For less expensive eats, head away from Av. Charles Darwin and find a local eatery, where you can ask for the fixed menu (usually a lot of fish or chicken and rice). This will fill you up for under $5. There are also some food stands at the municipal market.

Note that most restaurants will add 10% service onto your bill. Look for it there, because if they have already added it, there is no need to leave a tip unless service was outstanding. Not all restaurants do this, so look at your bill closely. Also, not all restaurants will accept credit cards. If you're paying with plastic, it's always a good idea to ask before ordering.

ASIAN

Red Sushi

(ENTREES: $6-17) Red Sushi, in the Red Mangrove Adventure Inn, is a bar/restaurant specializing in Japanese delights. The sashimi and maki rolls are perfectly delectable, and popping them in your mouth in the colorful, waterfront establishment makes the dining experience truly enjoyable. There is also a selection of Japanese soups and main dishes, as well as a full menu of exotic drinks served at the bar. The menu also has steaks, pastas and other dishes for those not interested in raw fish. Av. Charles Darwin, near the cemetery. Updated: Jan 12, 2013.

ECUADORIAN/SEAFOOD

Kioskos

(ENTREES: $3-8) Eat at the kioskos, a series of outdoor food stands, and you will get the tastiest, most reasonably priced, and fastest fresh food in town. Most locals eat here, so don't be surprised if you have to fight for a seat during the dinner hour. Almost all of the stalls have the same menu: beef, chicken, fish, and/or shrimp prepared according to your tastes or encocado style, covered in a delicious coconut sauce. Most dishes come with rice, beans, and salad and cost around $5. Some stalls will also serve lobster, an especially tasty treat, for a pretty price. Ca. de los Kioskos, an extension of Charles Binford between Islas Plaza and Av. Baltra. Updated: Jan 12, 2013.

Restaurante El Descanso del Guia

(ENTREES: $5-8) The eclectic Restaurante El Descanso del Guia is a local staple. It is popular for breakfast. Try the bolon de verde, a giant ball of cooked plantain, it's about as 'typical' as it gets. Also good are the fruit salads and the secos de carne and pollo (chicken and beef soups) available for dine-in or to-go. A sign at the restaurant says "Rincon del Asado," so there may be some confusion about the name of the place. Av. Charles Darwin, next to the bus station. Updated: Jan 12, 2013.

Angermeyer Point

(ENTREES: $10-33) One of Puerto Ayora's finest restaurants was founded by the Angermeyers, one of the earliest colonist families. Set in the one-time cabin of Karl Angermeyer, it is decorated with photos and memorabilia of those early days of island life.

Argemeyer Point

On the deck facing the bay, you can enjoy an evening meal of fish or Galapagos beef, as succulent as that of Argentina. Meat portions are generous. The sides are delicious but disappointingly small. This is an unforgettable dining experience that is well worth the expense. Open evenings. Updated: June 01, 2013.

Il Giardino

(ENTREES: $5-13) One of the newest and best restaurants in Puerto Ayora, Il Giardino is a favorite of locals and visitors alike. The airy dining area is divided into several areas connected by a labyrinth of stairways and wooden walkways. Look around for a place you like (if the restaurant is empty enough for you to be choosy).

The menu features fresh seafood, pasta and more, with enticing daily specials. There is also a fine selection of ice cream and desserts. The owners also have another restaurant in the highlands, but they only open it for groups. Inquire if interested. Closed Mondays. Reservations may be needed on a busy night. On Charles Darwin and Charles Binford, across from Banco Pacífico and near the fishermen's pier.

Isla Grill

The Isla Grill is one more place on the restaurant-heavy stretch of Charles Darwin Av. near the Banco del Pacífico and the fishermen's pier. As its name suggests, it specializes in grilled meat and seafood. The grill itself is right inside the restaurant near the entrance, presumably so that the smells of fresh meat and seafood sizzling will lure in customers off the street!

In addition to grilled steaks and fish, they have burgers, pizzas and salads. The view is relatively lousy (you'll have a wonderful vantage point for observing the bank and traffic on Av. Charles Darwin), so if a romantic view is on your list, head over to Il Giardino instead. Av. Charles Darwin, across from the Banco del Pacífico.

The Rock

A hip, airy dining area, full menu and cool bar are the attractions at the Rock, named for the US airmen's nickname for Baltra in the 1940s. The food is pretty good, and the service isn't too bad (by Galápagos standards). It's a good place to kick off a fun evening with a drink or two. They sell T-shirts with their logo on them for those who really want to remember their trip here.

GALÁPAGOS

For some reason, locals seem to avoid The Rock. One nice bonus: their menu is online at their website www.therockgalapagos. com. Corner of Charles Darwin and Islas Plaza. Tel: 593-5-252-4176, E-mail: info@ therockgalapagos.com.

CAFÉS / BARS
Hernán Café
(ENTREES: $5-10) Hernán Café/Bar/Restaurante has a decent menu and a great location on a bustling corner not far from the new pier. The airy dining room and good food make it a favorite for locals and visitors alike. The menu has everything from sandwiches to pasta and is varied enough to be a good choice when your group can't agree on what to eat. Everyone will find something.

They sell ice cream at one end of the restaurant and locals often hang out there. It's one of the only places in all of Galápagos where you can get a decent cappuccino, not a small consideration for serious java-heads. Service can be lethargic enough that you may suspect that someone has put a waiter's uniform on a giant tortoise, so skip it if you're in a hurry or the sort to get irritated by wait staff watching soccer when you want to order. Av. Baltra and Charles Darwin.

DELI
Galápagos Deli !
Tucked away around the corner from the hospital is one of Puerto Ayora's best finds, Galápagos Deli. There they sell hot sandwiches and homemade ice cream, which is by far the best in the islands. Their menu is limited, but it's a great place to go for a snack or dessert. On Tomas de Berlanga near the corner of Baltra.

INTERNATIONAL / VEGETERIAN
Casa del Lago Café Cultural
(ENTREES: $4-9) The Casa del Lago Café Cultural serves organic coffee grown on the islands and fantastic coffee drinks, perfectly complemented by homemade ice cream. It also serves tasty and inexpensive breakfasts and vegetarian dishes, including healthy soups, salads, middle-eastern food and bagels.

Internet, musical instruments and board games are available for short-term use, and there are paintings and wooden crafts created by local elderly residents. Picture windows face the Las Ninfas Lagoon. Moises Brito and Juan Montalvo, near Las Ninfas. Tel: 593-9-971-4647, E-mail: info@galapagoscultural.com, casadellago@galapagoscultural. com, URL: www.galapagoscultural.com. Updated: Feb 20, 2013.

Garrapata !
(ENTREES: $10-15) Garrapata is often considered (by tourists and locals alike) to be the best restaurant in town. It serves fresh seafood and creative meat dishes, as well as different pastas. The restaurant also features a friendly waitstaff, ample bar, and candle-lit outdoor seating. If the food alone does not sell you, a stroll past the romantic atmosphere and full tables will convince you to stop in and eat before hitting the bar down the way. Try the lobster. Av. Charles Darwin between 12 de Febrero and Tomas de Berlanga. Tel: 593-5-252-6264. Updated: Mar 20, 2013.

Café del Mar
(ENTREES: $8-10) The aroma of grilled meats and the sizzle of the fire greet you as you walk into this brightly lit, cavernous space with bamboo walls and large, wood slab tables. On one wall, a TV screen usually shows Galápagos videos. Café del Mar is a parillada, or grill, restaurant. Vegetarians may want to go elsewhere.

There are some sandwiches and burgers for less than $5, and a heaping plate of meat will run you about $8-10. Try the grilled octopus. Prices are pretty competitive with the rest of the restaurants in Puerto Ayora. Café del Mar has a full bar. The wines are a bit overpriced. Open evenings after 6:30 p.m. Av. Charles Darwin, across from the WWF (World Wildlife Fund) offices. Updated: Nov 19, 2012.

GALÁPAGOS

Tintorera

(ENTREES: $5-12) Tintorera is a popular restaurant with a fresh, eco-friendly spin. Produce is organic and locally grown; cheeses are made locally; jams are produced by the Orgnization of Artisan Women in Isabela; and reusable glass soda bottles, not plastic throw-aways, are used. Ice cream, cakes and bread products, including bagels, are homemade and mouthwatering. Breakfast is the best meal here, not only because of the fresh baked goods, but also because you get a bottomless cup of tea or organic Galápagos coffee. Lunches, however, are not far behind: sandwiches on homemade bread, bagel sandwiches, veggie burgers, salads, soups and middle-eastern food provide delicious vegetarian options. Be sure to check out the executive lunch menu on the chalkboard if you're coming at lunchtime— it's a good deal. Av. Charles Darwin and Isla Floreana. Updated: Jan 12, 2013.

PUERTO BAQUERIZO MORENO

The capital and administrative center of the Galápagos, Puerto Baquerizo Moreno, has the second largest population in the archipelago after Puerto Ayora. Although the tourist infrastructure is less advanced here than in Puerto Ayora, visitors to Puerto Baquerizo Moreno are not without options. Hotels, stores, restaurants and travel agencies line the main street, and internet cafés, telephone centers and banks are common. There is also a small post office, police station and hospital. The Galápagos campus of the San Francisco University is also in Puerto Baquerizo Moreno, so university staff and students reside here.

Day trips to various onland, offshore and marine sites are available and can be arranged through travel agencies and dive centers located in town. Private vehicles (taxis) provide fairly inexpensive and reliable transportation and are often a good alternative to arranged tours when visiting highland sites. There are also infrequent public buses that run from Puerto Baquerizo Moreno to the village of El Progreso (8 km/5 mi to the east).

Some boats begin their tours here, and periodic closings of the Baltra airport for cleaning or maintenance can cause tourist activity to shift to San Cristóbal. As a result, visitor services and facilities are constantly improving in Puerto Baquerizo Moreno to provide alternatives for tourists and to meet tourist demand.

Services

Puerto Baquerizo Moreno is basically a smaller version of Puerto Ayora. There are shops, internet cafés, hotels and restaurants spread around along the main drag and nearby, none of which really stand out much.

SHOPPING

If you're in the market for T-shirts, playing cards, shotglasses and other tourist stuff, Puerto Baquerizo Moreno is the right place. They have all the same things as Puerto Ayora and it's a little cheaper. No fancy high-end stores yet, though.

INTERNET

Internet service is bad in town; apparently one lazy provider has quite a monopoly on the connection. There are internet cafés all over, but if one of them is down, they probably all are, a situation that is far too common. In general, the closer you are to the tourist pier, the more reliable the internet cafés are.

OTHER SERVICES

The post office is at the end of Charles Darwin Avenue near the sea lion beach. There are numerous places where you can drop off a bag of dirty laundry and they'll wash it for a couple bucks. The best place to make international phone calls is at the internet cafés: USA is $0.50 per minute, Europe slightly higher. There are a couple of ATM's near the tourist pier.

Things to See and Do

San Cristóbal (Chatham) is the fifth-largest (558 km2/346.7 mi2) and easternmost of the islands. Rapid development of tourist and educational facilities, as well as the existence of an airport, has caused island visitation to grow in recent years, with a corresponding boom in tourism services. You should definitely check out the visitor's center and the trails behind it, which lead to a great beach (Cabo de Hornos) and a superior snorkeling lagoon (Cerro Tijeretas). In the town, Playa Mann (across from the university) is as nice a beach as you can find in a town anywhere. La Lobería (see map, A3) is home to a very large pack of sea lions and some good surf.

Puerto Baquerizo Moreno is known for surfing, and there are several surf sites scattered

GALÁPAGOS

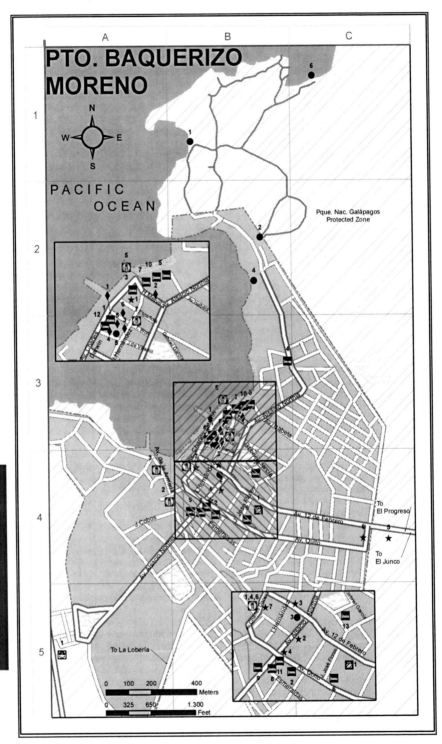

● **Activities**
1 Cabo de Horno B1
2 Centro de Interpretación B2
3 Cyber Dolphin B4*
4 Playa Man B2
5 Refugio del Pirata B3*
6 Tijeretas C1

🍴 **Eating**
1 Calipso B4*
2 Cormorant A4
3 La Playa A4
4 Miramar B4*
5 Muana Café B3*
6 Puerto Lobo B4*
7 Rosita B3*

★ **Services**
1 Bank B3*
2 Church B4*
3 Cruz Roja B4*
4 Hospital B4*
5 INGALA C4
6 Police C4
7 Post Office B4*

🛍 **Shopping**
1 Market B4*

▥ **Sleeping**
1 Albatros B3*
2 Algarrobos B4*
3 Bellavista B3*
4 Casa de Nelly B3
5 Casa Opuntia B3*
6 Hotel Cactus B4*
7 Hotel Casablanca B3*
8 Hotel Paraíso Insular B4*
9 Mar Azul B4*
10 Miconia B3*
11 Residencial Doña Pilo B4*
12 San Francisco B3*
13 Wilmar B4*

♦ **Tour**
1 Chalo Tours B3*
2 Dive and Surf Club B3*
3 Franklin Dive Center B3*
4 Galapagos Fishing Adventures B3*
5 Sharksky Tours B3*
6 Wreck Bay Dive Center B3*

▦ **Transportation**
1 Airport A5

* See inset maps

around the island, all of them accessible from town. There are good dive sites (Isla Lobos, Kicker Rock, Punta Pitt) nearby as well. For more information on these, see p. 530.

It's also possible to go to the highlands and hike to see only freshwater lake (El Junco) in all of the Galapagos. Some of the sites are only for cruise ships: these include Punta Pitt and Cerro Brujo. The rest can be visited from Puerto Baquerizo Moreno.

The Galápagos National Park Interpretation Center

The "Interpretation Center" on San Cristóbal is a small complex of buildings located at the far end of town, not far from Playa Mann and the university. It's a museum of sorts, with displays on the natural and human history of Galápagos—the human history part is by far the more interesting, although both are well done. It has fascinating displays on everything from the famous "Galápagos Affair" to the hardy Norwegians who settled Galápagos in the 1920s. The center is a must for anyone who wants to know more about the history of the islands.There is also a conference room and small open-air theater, both of which seem to be rarely used. Behind the interpretation center is the trail that leads to the Cabo de Horno/Punta Carola beach and Tijeretas Hill and snorkeling lagoon.

The trail itself is paved and well-marked—it's impossible to get lost.
Updated: Aug 15, 2012.

El Refugio del Pirata

El Refugio del Pirata ("Pirate's Refuge") is a liquor store and pool hall. There are two battered tables and it costs $2 per hour to play. They sell cold beer for carry-out as well. Eyepatches and parrots optional. Av. Jose de Villamil, a half-block from Avenida Charles Darwin.

Galapaguera Natural (Natural Giant Tortoise Breeding Center)

On the northern end of San Cristóbal Island is a natural protected zone for the San Cristóbal Giant Tortoises. A trail runs from the beach into the interior for about five kilometers (3 mi); visitors turn around and take the same path back out.

The trail is tough and most cruise ships do not include it on their itineraries (if your itinerary says "Galapaguera" it's probably referring to the one at Cerro Colorado, which is much easier to visit). The only way to do this trail is to contract a guide in Puerto Baquerizo Moreno, and the only way to reach the trail is by boat.

La Lobería

La Lobería is a beach and small island located not too far along the coast from Puerto Baquerizo Moreno. It's not technically part

GALÁPAGOS

of the Galápagos National Park, although the park rangers do help monitor it because of its ecological importance. It's a nice beach and home to a very large pack of sea lions. It is not necessary to have a guide; there is a trail to get there from near the airport which takes about a half hour on foot. Some cruise ships stop there. It's also possible to camp here overnight but you need previous permission from the National Park. La Lobería beach is known as a good place to surf: check with the surf shops in Puerto Baquerizo Moreno if you're interested. Updated: Jan 18, 2013.

Laguna El Junco/El Junco Lake

One of the few bodies of fresh water in Galápagos, El Junco Lake is located in the green highlands of San Cristóbal. Don't go there expecting to water ski or fish for salmon—in the USA they'd call it a "pond" instead of a lake. Still, it's the largest body of fresh water in the islands, and it's a great place to see birds that you won't see anywhere else. Many cruise ships go there, and it's possible to visit on your own from San Cristóbal, without a guide, by taking a taxi ($10 round trip from town, including waiting an hour for you to walk), or tours can be booked in Puerto Baquerizo Moreno.

The lake is a dormant volcanic caldera at 650 meters (2000 feet) above sea level and the only year-round lake in all of the islands. On a clear day, the 360 degree views are unparalleled. Visible on a hill in front of the lake are three wind turbines that produce around half of the electricity for the island in an innovative project financed by the E8, a consortium of some of the largest electricity companies in the world, and the United Nations.

Frigate birds frequent the lake to clean the salt from their wings and Pintailed ducks are frequently spotted feeding in the lake. Miconia, an endemic plant that traps mist from the air, covers most of the mountain but has been threatened by introduced blackberry. The National Park and the Jatun Sacha Foundation are reforesting with miconia, and volunteers can participate as well. Updated: Jan 18, 2013.

Playa Mann

The best of the beaches right in Puerto Baquerizo Moreno, Playa Mann is only a short walk from downtown. It's right across the street from the university. It's a gorgeous white-sand beach, and you can swim and snorkel to your heart's content. It's free and there is no need of a guide. Updated: Jan 18, 2013.

Puerto Chino

Puerto Chino is a remote beach on the southern edge of San Cristóbal Island, located not too far from the Cerro Colorado Tortoise Breeding Center. The trail from the road goes about 1,500 meters (4,921 ft) to the beach. The beach is great for relaxing and surfing but itself is smallish and surrounded by mangroves. Watch out for the poisonous Manzanillo trees. Most cruise ships don't visit Puerto Chino, and the only visitors are likely those who have booked a day surfing with a Puerto Baquerizo Moreno surf tour company. Updated: Jan 18, 2013.

Puerto Grande

Puerto Grande is a public beach on the coast of San Cristóbal Island not too far from Kicker Rock. It's accessible by boat from Puerto Baquerizo Moreno. It's popular with day-tripping families from town who have their own boat; cruise ships don't usually go there and it's unlikely to be included on any tour. It's a nice beach, and the swimming and snorkeling there are pretty good.

According to some locals, there is pirate treasure buried at Puerto Grande, although no one has ever found any. Most likely, the "treasure" is one of the best beaches in Galápagos!

Punta Carola

Located on the trails behind the visitor's center, Punta Carola is about a 45 minute walk from Puerto Baquerizo Moreno. Bring good walking shoes as the trail is rough. It's a small, sandy beach, home to sea lions and shore birds.

It's possible to snorkel there, but it can get a little rough; it's far better to walk 15 minutes over to the lagoon at Tijeretas. There's more space here, however, so if you're looking for a place to put down a towel and relax for a while, this is a better bet. Updated: Jan 18, 2013.

Puerto Baquerizo Moreno Tour Agencies and Dive Shops

Chalo Tours

Chalo Tours, conveniently located on the main drag across from the malecón, does a little bit of everything: SCUBA diving, snorkeling, day trips, surfing and more. They do dive courses and surfing classes as well. They rent all the necessary gear as well as other fun things like ocean kayaks and underwater cameras. Rates for excursions are reasonable for San Cristóbal—about the norm. Walk-ins welcome. Try the day trip to the highlands, with a downhill bike ride from El Junco Lake to the tortoise breeding center. Tel: 593-5-252-0953/430, Quito: 593-2-273-2416, E-mail: chalotours@hotmail.com. Updated: Jan 18, 2013.

Franklin Dive Center

Franklin Dive Center goes to all the usual dive sites near Puerto Baquerizo Moreno: Kicker Rock, Isla Lobos, etc. Rates are typical for San Cristóbal. They can rent all necessary gear and equipment. One feature of this dive shop is that they'll let you use their underwater camera at no extra charge; just bring your own chip and a CD and they'll burn you a copy of your photos! They also do snorkeling trips. Teodoro Wolf and Ignacio Hernandez. Tel: 593-5-252-1543, E-mail: franklindivecenter@hotmail.com. Updated: Jan 18, 2013.

Wreck Bay Dive Center

Wreck Bay offers a lot of services for a dive shop: they can help you get to and from San Cristóbal and set up just about any day trip you're interested in, including tours of the highlands. They can arrange island-hopping trips, too.

They do all the usual nearby dive sites, but for a large enough group they can go to sites which are further away, like Gardner Reef or Española. Walk-ins are welcome, or you can contact them before your trip and set something up. Charles Darwin and Teodoro Wolf. Tel: 593-5-252-1663/8-728-4164, E-mail: wreckbay_divingcenter@yahoo.com, URL: www.wreckbay.com. Updated: Jan 18, 2013.

Galápagos Fishing Adventures

Galápagos Fishing Adventures specializes, of course, in fishing. The owner has a couple of fishing boats, and different tours will have different costs. The fishing here is expensive ($1,300 for a day-long Marlin Fishing trip for up to three people) but they are by far the most experienced and professional fishing outfit in Galápagos. More economical tours are available as well.

They are also a dive shop and tour operator and can do day tours of the highlands and beaches on San Cristóbal as well as dives and snorkeling. Av. Jose de Villamil y Malecón. Tel: 593-5-252-1537/9-404-0714, E-mail: Gustavo@galafishing.com.ec, URL: www.galafishing.com.ec. Updated: Jan 7, 2013

Dive & Surf Club

Dive & Surf Club is pretty self-explanatory—it's a friendly dive shop that also has surfing stuff. San Cristóbal is well-known as a surfing destination, and Dive & Surf Club is your best bet of the places in town if you're going to hit the waves. They do courses (diving and surfing) and their dive shop visits all the usual San Cristóbal sites. They do snorkeling and day trips too. They also do some camping excursions out on the island. You might want to look them up if any of the above appeals to you. Ca. H. Melville and I. Hernandez. E-mail: Wendyadira81@yahoo.es, URL: www.divesurfclub.com. Updated: Jan 7, 2013

Come to Galápagos !

A full service travel agency based out of San Cristóbal, Come to Galápagos is run by an American/Ecuadorian couple. They do everything from arranging your flights to finding hotels, booking tours and hiring your guides. They don't really do walk-in business: you should plan on contacting them long before your trip and setting something up. The fact that they are based in the islands is an enormous bonus, as they'll deal directly with your hotel or guide and any problems are resolved very quickly.

They recently sponsored the first ever Galápagos Marathon, which was a big hit. They hope to make it an annual event. This travel agency is particularly involved with the community, so if you want a place that is making a positive difference, this is it. Tel: 593-5-252-1251/9-115-2102, E-mail: rickandbere@cometogalapagos.com, URL: http://cometogalapagos.com, http://galapagosfamilyvacations.com. Updated: Jan 7, 2013

Puerto Baquerizo Lodging

Of all the three towns, Puerto Baquerizo Moreno is the one with the highest percentage of bland, square rooms for about $25 per night. There are a couple of cheaper options, however, as well as some nicer places for those with a little more to spend.

Many of the hotels in San Cristóbal are clustered along the waterfront, including, oddly enough, almost all of the high end AND extreme budget options. Get away from the water and all of the hotels start looking the same. It seems like feast or famine for the Puerto Baquerizo Moreno. The hotels are usually mostly empty, as visitors tend to go to the centrally located

Puerto Ayora or the more hip Isabela. They can fill up fast, however, if there is a conference of some sort going on– remember, Puerto Baquerizo Moreno is the capital of Galápagos.

It also may fill up during the annual Galápagos marathon. In other words, book early, even though you may find when you get there that the town is nearly devoid of tourists.
Updated: Sept 13, 2012.

BUDGET

Hotel Albatros

(ROOMS: $10 per person) The Albatros, along with its next-door-neighbor the Hotel San Francisco, represents the least expensive lodging option in Puerto Baquerizo Moreno. The rooms are all located on the third floor or higher, making this a bad choice for those who can't climb a couple flights of stairs. The rooms are basic, although most have TV (there are five or six local channels only) and a fan. If you want hot water, a couple rooms have it, but it will cost you more. The location is quite good, on the main drag across from the Malecón. It's really about what you'd expect for the price. Tax is included, but not breakfast. Av. Charles Darwin y 9 Octubre, across from the Malecón. Tel: 593-5-252-0264, E-mail: Marita0422@hotmail.com.

Hotel San Francisco

(ROOMS: $8-12/person) At the bottom end of the hotel spectrum is the Hotel San Francisco, a basic, no-frills place that happens to be the cheapest place in town. It's well-located, right on the main drag across from the malecón. Rooms are blocky and unattractive, but most of them have a TV with five or six local channels (no cable) and a fan (no air conditioning). There is no hot water. If your goal is to spend the least amount of money possible, this is your place (or the similar Albatros next door). If you can budget an extra $10 per night, you might consider an upgrade, if only for the sake of a hot shower. They do not have E-mail or a website, so if you wish to make reservations, you'll need to call. Av. Charles Darwin across from the Malecón. Tel: 593-5-252-0304. Updated: Sept 27, 2012.

Residencial Doña Pilo

(ROOMS: $15/person) A half-step up from the cheapest places in town, Residencial Doña Pilo is a small, family run place only a couple blocks off of the main drag. It's upstairs from the cheery Kicker Rock Cafetería. There are only four rooms, each of which has three or four beds each, so getting a single might prove

problematic unless the place is mostly empty. The rooms have fans but no air conditioning, hot water (electric shower) and cable TV. There is a kitchen available. It's a pleasant enough little place, and probably worth the extra couple bucks that set it above the least expensive hotels in town. Av. Quito y Northia. Tel: 593-5-252-0409. Updated: Sept 27, 2012.

Residencial Wilmar

(ROOMS: $20/person) It doesn't look like much from outside, but the Residencial Wilmar isn't your worst choice in town. The place is clean, the owners are friendly, and it's $5 cheaper than comparable places, probably because it's a couple of blocks from the main drag. The rooms are the typical San Cristóbal cells with a walled-off bathroom, a TV (no cable), small fridge and an air conditioning unit. Look at all the available rooms (there are only 6 in total). Some rooms have a bad view of the neighbor's ugly house, while other rooms have an even worse view of a cement brick wall. The best part is the covered rooftop terrace with a great view of the town and Shipwreck Bay. The friendly owners will help you arrange local tours and day trips if you ask. Features: small common area, air conditioning, TV, private baths, and access to a kitchen. Cost includes taxes but not breakfast. However, breakfast can be arranged if you're there with a large group. No credit cards accepted. Ca. Gabriel Garcia Moreno and Vicente Rocafuerte. Tel: 593-5-252-0135, Cel: 593-8-555-4518, E-mail: rafaelr@easynet.net.ec.

Hostal Los Algarrobos !

(ROOMS: $25 per person) One of the top choices in the great glut of hotels that cost around $25 per person per night, Hostal los Algarrobos is located a couple of blocks off of Avenida Charles Darwin but worth the walk. The rooms are your standard San Cristóbal style—squarish, cell-like and forgettable— but the Algarrobos has two things the others do not, reliable free internet on three downstairs computers and a spiffy game room on an upper floor. There is a little restaurant as well and the top floor features a good view of the town and bay.

Hostal los Algarrobos is best for small groups who can take advantage of the triples or quads (one of the quads has a balcony) and want a nice place to hang out. The service at Algarrobos is professional enough that tour agencies in Quito will send groups there: their confidence speaks volumes about the place. Cost does not include taxes. Includes TV, cable, air conditioning, hot water with electric shower and a game room. Supposedly includes breakfast (I'm skeptical if there are not many guests there). Tel: 593-5-252-1010/252-0034, Cel: 593-8-582-9467, E-mail: hostallosalgarrobos@gmail.com, paulavera1969@hotmail.com. Updated: Sept 27, 2012.

Hotel Mar Azul

(ROOMS: $20-70) An undistinguished little place a couple blocks off of the main drag, the Mar Azul used to include the two buildings that are now the Grand Hotel Paraiso Insular, but for whatever reason the management split them up. The Mar Azul got the short end of the stick, settling for one low structure full of the same blocky rooms as everywhere else in town. The selling points are air conditioning, electric showers and a relatively noise-free neighborhood. They'll serve breakfast if the hotel is full. Bugs in rooms are sometimes an issue.

It's best for people looking for a cheap sleep and who don't plan on spending much time in their rooms or hotels. It's far away enough from the airport that you'll want to take a taxi ($1-2). You can walk there in ten minutes from the tourist pier, but if you have heavy luggage you'll also want a taxi. Avenida Alsacio Northia and Esmeraldas. Tel: 593-5-252-0107/252-0139, E-mail: marazul@seamangalapagos.com, URL: www.hosteltrail.com/hotelmarazul. Updated: Sept 27, 2012.

MID-RANGE

Grand Hotel Paraiso Insular

(ROOMS: $20-95) Don't let the fancy name intimidate you. The Grand Hotel Paraiso Insular is but an above-average hotel with two locations almost across the street from one another on Avenida Alsacio Northia. Try to get into the newer building if you can (it's the one a little farther from town). The rooms in the newer structure have gas-heated hot water as opposed to the "electric showers" at the older building. The rooms are your typical blocky San Cristóbal fare, mostly with cable TV and small refrigerators. Some have air conditioning, and some have a fan. Rooms with a/c cost about $20 more per night. Some of the rooms have a distant view of the ocean, but it's nothing to get too excited about. The hotel has many rooms, making it popular with groups and organized tours.

The Grand Hotel Paraiso Insular used to be affiliated with the "Mar Azul" hotel across the street, but no longer. The administration of the hotel is more or less professional. The girl in reception can help you book tours and trips if you can get her off the phone with her boyfriend. Unlike many of the other hotels in the low-medium price range, the Paraiso Insular can accept credit cards. Av. Alsacio Northia and Esmeraldas. Tel: 593-5-252-0091/252-0761/252-1573, E-mail: grandhotelparaisoinsular@hotmail.com, URL: www.grandhotelparaisoinsular.com. Updated: Sept 27, 2012.

Hostal Los Cactus

(ROOMS: $30-55) Los Cactus is a friendly little place located a few blocks off of the main drag in Puerto Baquerizo Moreno. The clean, comfortable rooms are a bit larger than the average in town, and there is one family room that sleeps four and has a little mini-kitchen. Owners are cheerful, speak some English, and seem to try a little harder than most places in town.

They can help you book tours, including fishing with a local guide, and they also have a restaurant in the San Cristóbal highlands which can be opened for larger groups. It's a good choice for couples or a family on a budget. The only drawback is the distance from the center of town, but it's only about four blocks. Rooms include Wifi, air conditioning, hot water, fridge, and TV (no cable). A 12% tax will be added to the bill. Service is not included. Breakfast is not included, but it can be for an additional $3. No credit cards accepted. Juan Jose Flores y Quito. Tel: 593-9-731-8278/5-252-0078, E-mail: Hostal_cactus@hotmail.com, URL: www.opuntiatravel.com.ec.

Hotel Casablanca

(ROOMS: $40-100) Casablanca is a pleasant, small (7 bedrooms) bed and breakfast conveniently located on the main street, across from the bay. The rooms are attractive, airy and eclectic. Each one is different and memorable. If you can afford it, the Cúpula suite is the way to go, as it features a terrace and ocean view. On the main street, not far from the pier. E-mail: jacquivaz@yahoo.com. Updated: Feb 18, 2013.

Bellavista !

(Rooms: $45-65) Bellavista is a family run hotel with a prime location in Puerto Baquerizo Moreno, right next to the tourist pier on the main street. Bellavista's waterfront location provides great sunset opportunities at

GALÁPAGOS

the memorable Wreck Bay. The hotel's nine rooms can accommodate up to 18 guests. Each room comes equipped with WiFi, cable TV, air conditioning, mini-bar, and 24-hour hot water. Charles Darwin Ave. and Hernan Melville. Tel: 593-5-252-1147/ 0352, E-mail: robertandradetorres@yahoo.com and agat74@yahoo.com.
Updated: Oct 19, 2012.

Hotel Miconia !

(ROOMS: $65-187) Hotel Miconia is one of the better visitor options in Puerto Baquerizo Moreno. The rooms are neat and airy, the staff friendly, and you'll find a Jacuzzi, small exercise room and bar available here. On mainland Ecuador the prices would be scandalous for what you get, but they're pretty fair by Galápagos standards and what's available.

The location is great, right smack in the center of what limited action Puerto Baquerizo Moreno has to offer. They'll even set up tours of the island if you wish. Av. Charles Darwin, more or less across from the pier . Tel: 593-5-252-0608, E-mail: hotelmiconia@yahoo.com, URL: www.miconia.com.
Updated: Feb 09, 2013.

Casa de Nelly

(ROOMS: $20-30/person)This friendly hotel has a B&B sort of feel to it. The rooms are your standard San Cristóbal cell-like affair, but an effort to keep them airy and attractive has been made, and there is a large marine mural on the wall downstairs adding a splash of color to the place. There are a variety of rooms available, all with air conditioning, TV and gas-heated water. The owner, Nelly, used to rent out suites and apartments on a monthly basis, but they're moving away from that.

There are still little mini kitchens spread around, so if you want to use one, just ask for a room with one attached or nearby. Even though she's officially out of the apartment-renting business, this would be a good place to try if your stay is a little longer. Casa de Nelly is close to the university, and visiting professors often stay there.

The best part is the rooftop deck with hammocks. This hotel is located close to the trails behind the interpretation center. If you plan to visit the beaches and snorkeling sites there frequently, you should check this place out. Av. Alsacio Northia (sector Playa del Oro). Tel: 593-5-252-0112/982, E-mail: saltosnelly@hotmail.com.
Updated: Sept 27, 2012.

HIGH-END

Casa Opuntia Hotel

(ROOMS: $89-163) San Cristóbal's newest luxury hotel occupies a privileged spot on the refurbished boardwalk within walking distance of the Playa del Oro beach. The beachfront rooms offer a spectacular view, and the pool, bar area and airy, air-conditioned rooms offer a welcome respite from the harsh Galápagos climate. The attached gourmet restaurant is worth a visit even if you're not staying there.

The Casa Opuntia will mainly appeal to travelers who want to spend a couple of extra days in Galápagos after a multi day luxury cruise, or for those who don't want a cruise but prefer to island hop in style. For the latter travelers, the Opuntia hotels group offers lodging at the Angermeyer Waterfront Inn in Puerto Ayora and the Iguana Crossing Hotel in Puerto Villamil. There are photos of the hotel on their website and on Facebook as well for those who want a peek before booking. There are only 10 rooms, so book in advance. Pasaje Cordova N23-26 and Wilson (Quito). On the waterfront (San Cristóbal). Tel: USA/Canada: 1-800-217-9414, Ecuador: 593-2-222-3720/252-0647 Fax: 593-2-254-4073, Email: info@opuntiagalapagoshotels.com, URL: www.opuntiagalapagoshotels.com.
Updated: Jan 22, 2013.

Casa Baronesa

(ROOMS: $1,00 for 2 people / $1,400 for 6 people) Casa Baronesa is a gorgeous, two-story and three-bedroom house which overlooks its own little piece of the beach right on the waterfront of Puerto Villamil. The creature comforts and service that are catered to your individual (or group) needs here are remarkable. Ranging anywhere from tours and activities around the island all the way to having a personal chef come over to cook you a delightful meal, Casa Baronesa truly serves as a platform for being pampered. The place also comes with packaged deals that include romantic meals for the honeymooners; or just come in a group and you can all share and cherish this wonderful little house to yourselves. On the waterfront, Tel: 1-800-217-9414 / 02-604-6800, Email: cs@ecuadoradventure.ec, URL: www.opuntia-galapagostours.com.
Updated: Aug 1, 2013 .

Grand Hotel Chatham

(rooms: $60-$216) The Grand Hotel Chatham is about as close to a luxury hotel as you'll find in Puerto Baquerizo Moreno. It has a pool, the rooms are pleasant enough and the prices can be a bit steep during high season. It's recently (2011) had a complete overhaul and renovation but it's already beginning to show a bit of wear. Room costs vary greatly, depending on the season and how fancy a room you want: the lowest will run you about $50/person in a double, which is pretty fair, actually.

Services here are good and include wi-fi, on-site bar and restaurant, TV room, air conditioning and a small library. As with any halfway decent hotel here, they can help you plan day trips and small excursions. Service can be a bit sluggish, even by island standards. Book early, as this place fills up with tour groups. Avenida Armada Nacional and Alsacio Northia. Phone: (593) 5-2520 923. URL: http://www.grandhotelchatham.com. ec. Email: info@grandhotelchatham.com.

Restaurants Puerto Baquerizo

CAFÉS/BARS

Puerto Lobo

(ENTREES: $4-7) Living up to its name ("Sea Lion Port"), you'll probably have to step over or around several sea lions to enter this small, airy restaurant. Puerto Lobo serves mostly crepes, snacks and desserts—if you're looking for a steak, keep looking. The food, service and coffee are good, but a bit unreliable. It's open whenever someone is in there, and it's often closed at strange times.

If you're in the mood for a light lunch you might give it a shot, especially because it has a nice view over Shipwreck Bay. The evening shift likes to watch the Jesus channel on the lone TV there, so either bring your bible or avoid the place as you see fit. Crepes $4-7, breakfast $4.25, and desserts $2-5. Av. Charles Darwin at the end of the Malecón, downstairs from Miramar and around the corner from Calypso. Just follow the sea lions. Updated: Sept 27, 2012.

Muana Café

(ENTREES: $3-5) Located right on a major intersection across from the pier and downstairs from the Casa Blanca Hotel, Muana Café gets a lot of business. The food and coffee are good, and so is the ice cream. They don't have an actual printed menu; look on the chalkboard behind the counter to see what's available. It features mostly snacks, sandwiches and desserts. Across from the tourist pier and under the Casa Blanca Hotel. Updated: Sept 27, 2012.

Café del Mar

(ENTREES: $3-7) Café del Mar is easy to find: it's got the best location in Puerto Baquerizo Moreno, right on the seaward side of the main drag. It's a stand-alone, square-ish building, brightly painted – you can't miss it. It's a café and light restaurant: it has ceviches, burgers, sandwiches, pasta dishes, etc. Prices are reasonable, given the location. It also serves drinks and has live music at night, so it's as good a place as any to go out in sleepy San Cristóbal. No reservations needed. Charles Darwin, Malecón 593. Phone: (05) 252-0658. Updated: June 10, 2013

SEAFOOD

La Playa

One of the best restaurants in Galápagos, La Playa is a casual, laid-back place with an ocean view. Nothing about the restaurant's plain exterior will cause you to suspect how good the food is. Specializing in seafood, La Playa is a local favorite and often fills up on weekends. There is a full menu, with non-seafood options for those who wish. The service is a bit surly, and the prices are quite steep by Puerto Baquerizo Moreno standards, but you'll forget all about that when the food comes. If you're very hungry, try a plate of chicharrón de pescado—little fried bits of fish served with a dipping sauce—as an appetizer. Av. Armada Nacional. Tel: 593-5-252-0044,

Ceviches del Colorado

(ENTREES $9-15) A cheery little outdoor cevicheria with plenty of shade, Ceviches del Colorado has a limited menu of mostly seafood. It's good seafood, however, and you won't regret taking a break here on a hot day. Portion sizes are large. Open daily 9-4. Avenida Armada Nacional and Ignacio Hernández. Updated: June 10, 2013.

INTERNATIONAL

Restaurante Miramar

(ENTREES: $8-19) Miramar has a winning menu of tempting international food, and obviously is taking a shot at being a very fancy restaurant in a town that currently does not have one. The food (and prices) are spot-on: the entrees are tasty and priced where you'd expect, at about the $8-19 range. The service and facilities don't quite make the cut, however. You think of a fancy restaurant, what do you think? Candles, wine, fancy tablecloths, hostess, free water, elegant waiter, little basket of bread...right? Here you'll get no bread, no tablecloth, no candles, no water, no hostess and a waiter in sneakers (wine was available, though, so maybe they're starting to get it). The point is that depending on your definition of what makes an upscale restaurant, you may or may not be hugely disappointed by Miramar. The food is good and has some nontraditional options, such as Tequila shrimp, but the restaurant itself misses the cut by a mile. If you're all about the food, give it a shot. If style points matter, take a pass. I heard elsewhere in town that Miramar makes an effort to use locally grown produce and meat in an effort to help the island economy. If this is so, they don't advertise it at the restaurant itself. Av. Charles Darwin at the end of the Malecón, on the second floor above Puerto Lobo and around the corner from Calypso.

Calypso

(ENTREES: $5-17) Calypso is a happy little place that always seems packed with locals and visitors, which means the food must be really good, because its location is not great (a sort of half-basement next to a busy street) and prices are a bit high for Puerto Baquerizo Moreno. They have a good selection of burgers, pizzas, pastas and other main dishes. Come early or you might not get a seat. Patrons tend to linger, either because of the chilled-out atmosphere or because of the speed of Galápagos service. You can't miss Calypso: it's in the port authority building between Avenida Charles Darwin and the ocean at the end of the malecón. It's on the same block as Miramar and Puerto Lobo.

TRADITIONAL ECUADORIAN

Rosita

(ENTREES: $4-10) Restaurant Rosita is a friendly place, open and breezy, located a few blocks from the beach. It has a definite beachplace vibe to it, from the photos of fish on the walls to the ship's wheel hung near the bathrooms. The menu is varied enough to be interesting. The seafood and traditional Ecuadorian dishes are recommended here. They also have set menus at reasonable prices. It's as good a place as any in Puerto Baquerizo Moreno to unwind after a day of diving, exploring or snorkeling, even if it's just to have a cold beer served in a frosty glass! Corner of Hernandez and Villamil.

Cormoran

(ENTREES: $2-9) One of the classier budget eating options, Cormorán is located near the little creek that runs through town to empty into the ocean. It's an airy, family run place with a good variety of ceviches, sandwiches, seafood and even some vegetarian options.

There is a massive TV there and the place fills up with locals when an important soccer game is on. Open for lunch and dinner. Cross the bridge at the end of the malecon and it's right there. Down the street a bit from La Playa restaurant.

PUERTO VILLAMIL

The charming town of Puerto Villamil on Isabela Island is probably the best kept secret in Galápagos. It's very small and underdeveloped—none of the streets in town are paved—but there's a lot to see and do, and it's well worth spending a couple of days here if you're doing the whole island-hopping thing.

First stop, the beach. Puerto Villamil is located right on one of the best beaches in all of Galápagos, a spectacular two-mile stretch of silky bone-colored sand and palm trees. Since there are fewer than 3,000 full-time residents in Puerto Villamil, the large beach never gets packed, even on the hottest days.

Locals seem divided about the tourism boom. Some have embraced it, while others can still be a little surly to outsiders. Service in hotels and restaurants is by far the worst in the islands, as hotel operators and waiters seem at best clueless and at worst apathetic. There are a few notable exceptions. See the hotel and restaurant descriptions for suggestions.

Puerto Villamil Services

Services in town are pretty basic. There's a post office, some laundry places, a couple of internet cafés, one dive shop, a small hospital and an assortment of hotels, tour agencies and restaurants of varying quality; all of them conviniently located around the cetner of the town itself.

Although there is a co-op sort of bank, it is worth remembering that **there is no ATM in Puerto Villamil**, and if you run out of cash here, it's next to impossible to get more. According to locals, the bank did put an ATM in once in response to their complaints, but it was a fake one—simply a front with a screen that said "Out of order, please come back later!" Eventually they even took that away.

Things To See and Do

Puerto Villamil is a paradise for those who like outdoor activities. It's possible to snorkel in several nearby places, including La Calera, Tintoreras and Concha de Perla. Just hiking around town will lead you past a couple of salt lagoons often filled with swimming and

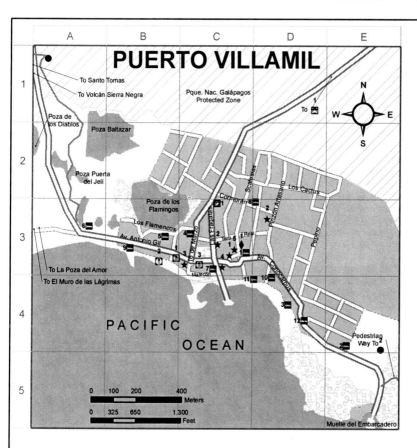

PUERTO VILLAMIL

● **Activities**

1 Centro de Crianza A1
2 Concha Perla E4

🏠 **Eating**

1 Aloha Betsy B3
2 Bar de Beto B3
3 Cesar's C3

★ **Services**

1 Bank C3
2 Church C3, D3
3 Medical Center C3
4 Police C3
5 Post Office C3

◼ **Shopping**

1 Market C3

■ **Sleeping**

1 Brisas del Mar C3
2 Hospedaje Plaucio E4
3 Hostal La Casa de Marita D4
4 Hostal Villamil C3
5 Hotel La Laguna B3
6 Iguana Crossing A3
7 Pensión Albemarle C3
8 Pensión San Vicente D3
9 Pink Iguana B3
10 Red Mangrove Isabela Lodge D4
11 Sol Isabela D4
12 The Wooden House D4

♦ **Tour**

1 Isabela Dive Center C3

▣ **Transportation**

1 Airport D1

GALAPÁGOS

wading birds. Popular hikes include the Sierra Negra Volcano, the trail to the visitor center and a coastal walk to the Wall of Tears, built by convicts during the time that Isabela was home to a penal colony.

Concha de Perla

Concha de Perla is a gorgeous lagoon located not far from the new municipal dock of Puerto Villamil. There is a trail through a dense mangrove to get there, but they've made a sort of boardwalk so it's an easy five-minute walk from the main dirt road.

The lagoon is perfect for swimming and snorkeling, as it's protected from the ocean surf and currents. Lucky swimmers will get to see plenty of fish and probably a couple sea lions or rays.

Note that the pier at the end of the trail is very small: there isn't much room to hang out or leave your stuff, so if you go there at a popular time—say, on a sunny weekend afternoon—the little pier will be full of locals lounging around and taking up all the space. You'll be able to squeeze past them into the water, but don't plan on laying out a towel or anything. Also, there have been some reports of petty theft, so don't bring anything valuable with you. It's perfectly acceptable to go there in your swimsuit with your towel and snorkeling gear only. You won't need your wallet.

El Muro de las Lagrimas (Wall of Tears)

The Wall of Tears serves as a bleak reminder of Galápagos' darker history. Located on Isabela Island, the wall was constructed by convicts from a penal colony that inhabited the island between 1946 and 1959. Building the wall was a form of punishment, as moving huge blocks of lava in the searing heat was torturously difficult. Many of the convicts, denied proper nourishment and medical care, were worked to death building the wall.

The Wall of Tears is not a protected visitor site—anyone can go. Just follow the trail outside of town or ask any local how to find it. It's about seven kilometers (4.3 mi) outside of town, and you can reach it (1 hour) by bike, which are easy to rent in town. Going on foot takes considerably longer. Bring plenty of water and sunscreen. Along the way you'll also find at fantastic look-out point perched atop of a hill, just hop off your bike and head on up the steps up to check it out.

The Wall of Tears is generally included in any tour of Puerto Villamil, but cruise ships stopping in town rarely go there, so don't expect to be taken there if you're on a boat.

El Estero (Humedales/Wetlands)

The Humedales, or "wetlands," are a can't-miss for those staying a couple days in Puerto Villamil. The humedales consist of a good trail through mangroves, pools, beaches and rocky shores. It's well worth a visit, as many different types of birds nest there.

The trail also ends up at Isabela's old cemetery, which is interesting because some of the earliest colonists are buried there. You'll also find the Wall of Tears not to far from here.

Along the trail you'll find Orchilla Hill, which is an easy climb. From the top there is a nice view of town and Isabela's volcanoes. Also look for "La Playita," a small, secluded beach. The park has released some Giant Tortoises into the wild near here, so keep an eye open for them too! There is a picnic area popular with locals, but don't plop down just anywhere, out of respect for the nesting birds.

The trail is long if you're travelling by foot (1-2 hours) but that time can be cut in half if you're going on bike. Either way, be sure to bring plenty of water. El Estero is also on the way to the Wall of Tears.

Centro de Crianza "Arnaldo Tupiza"

The Centro de Crianza (or "Rearing Center") is a sort of nursery for Giant Tortoises located within walking distance from Puerto Villamil. There are several pens housing grown tortoises, mainly from the different volcanoes on Isabela Island, as well as dozens of young tortoises in protected cages. Look for the ones from Cerro Paloma—the adults there were the only six left of their species in 1994, although now there are some little ones at the center.

An easy paved path leads through the penned-in area and ends up at an information center (and gift shop, naturally).

Unlike the Charles Darwin Research Station, the pens here are not open and you can't go in with the tortoises to have your photo taken. The walk is shadier though.

Although you can take a taxi to the Centro de Crianza, it's much more fun to walk. The trail leads outside of Puerto Villamil near the Iguana Crossing Hotel and winds through mangroves, swamps and

Did a unique trek? Tell other travelers at vivatravelguides.com

salty lagoons where you can see ducks, flamingoes, herons and other wading and swimming birds. The trail takes about 40 minutes to walk, but it's in good shape and pretty easy. You do not need a guide to walk on the trail or visit the Centro de Crianza.

You can book a half-day tour in Puerto Villamil which will include the trail, the Center and the Wall of Tears for about $20, but this is all as long as there are enough people who want to do it.

It isn't a bad idea, as a guide will help spot wildlife and tell you about the plants and animals that you're sure to see on the trail as well as the history of the wall. The center is a popular stop with cruise ships that visit Puerto Villamil.

Puerto Villamil Tour Agencies and Dive Shops

Isabela Dive Center

There's only one dive shop in Puerto Villamil, and that's the Isabela Dive Center, where divemaster/owner Pablo Constante will be happy to show you the best nearby dive sites. There are basically three places he goes to regularly: Roca Viuda, Cuatro Hermanos and Isla Tortuga (see descriptions of these under Diving Visitor Sites, p. 534). Isabela Dive Center can do basic certification courses. They can also do snorkeling and other guided day trips.

Dive prices vary depending on the number of divers and the destination. You're better off in a small group. One example is Isla Tortuga. It'll cost you $120 per person with three or more, but $140 per person for two (and presumably much more expensive for only one diver if they'll go at all). They have all the gear you'll need, including masks, fins, weight, air tanks, etc. Escalesia and Antonio Gil. Tel: 593-9-466-6568/5-252-9418, E-Mail: info@isabeladivecenter.com.ec, URL: www.isabeladivecenter.com.ec.

Puerto Villamil Lodging

There are certain laws in Galápagos which make it very difficult for outsiders—that is, anyone not from the Islands—to own or operate any sort of business there. Nowhere are the effects of this law in greater evidence than on Isabela Island, which began to boom long after the law had taken effect. The law has prohibited outsiders from coming in and setting up fancy hotels and restaurants, and instead has left such activities up to the people of Puerto Villamil, with mixed results. It seems everyone within a couple of blocks of the beach has built a hotel in their back yard. The rooms are mostly the same. Twenty dollars will get you a square room with one to three beds and a walled-off bathroom in the corner. At least they're all new, so they're all still in pretty good shape.

Most of the hotel owners still don't "get it," and by "it" I mean the whole concept of hotel service. They don't answer their phones. You'll show up and no one is at the hotel. They'll say they'll pick you up at the pier and they don't. If there's a soccer game, they'll blow off all their guests to go play. I'm sure this carefree attitude is great for their blood pressure, but it's bad for yours. At least if you're expecting a complete lack of professionalism, you won't be shocked by it. Don't say I didn't tell you!

There are exceptions, of course. A couple of the hotels are indeed managed by responsible tourism professionals—these will usually be noted in the hotel description. There are no "neighborhoods" as such in tiny Puerto Villamil and all of the hotels are within a few blocks of one another.

BUDGET

Hospedaje Plaucio

(ROOMS: $10/person) Plaucio is an eccentric local artist who has built a couple of concrete rooms near his home, which is located on the main street leading from town to the new municipal dock. What the four simple rooms lack in amenities, they make up for in character, thanks to the friendly, one-of-a-kind Plaucio, who is happy to sit and chat about anything. He has decorated the rooms and grounds with paintings and knick-knacks, and the hospedaje is friendlier than it looks from the road.

There is a flat space out back where he'll let you pitch a tent (negotiate a price) if you have one with you. There's a small kitchen and a sink and clothesline for doing your own laundry. It's rustic and "different" and most people will either love it or hate it. The rooms have a fan and electric shower, but no air conditioning. Look for the sign on the road between the new dock and the town, or ask anyone—everyone knows Plaucio.
Updated: Sep 24, 2012.

Hostal Villamil

(ROOMS: $15 per person) Hostal Villamil is a tiny hotel almost lost on a side street, but it's

GALÁPAGOS

worth checking out if you're on a budget. It's located next to the larger George's Corner Inn. The seven rooms face out onto a tiny courtyard. Like most places in town, it's family run. It's clean, neat and bright and the location isn't too bad. Some of the rooms have air conditioning. Rooms are all doubles and triples. 16 Marzo y los Flamencos. Tel: 593-5-252-9180/186/9-121-0686, E-mail: hostalvillamil@hotmail.es. Updated: Sep 24, 2012.

Brisas del Mar

(ROOMS: $15-20/person) Brisas del Mar is a typical Isabela Hotel, insomuch as it's a concrete bunker in someone's backyard. That being said, it's not too bad. An effort has been made to make the rooms as attractive as possible, the management lady who lives there is friendly and the prices are reasonable for what you get. There are two parts to the hotel, an older part in front and a newer sort of tower in back. The newer rooms are nicer, have air conditioning and cost an extra $10.

The older rooms are smaller and a little grim, and the façade of the hotel could use some work (I thought the hotel was not in service until I went around back). Some of the rooms can sleep up to five people. Try to bargain for a discount if you find yourself with a group. There is a large patio with hammocks, but you'll probably prefer to hang out at one of the bars on the beach, given it's proximity to them. It's only a block or so from both the beach and the main park. Conocarpus and Escalecia, Barrio Central. Tel: 593-5-252-9376, Cel: 593-8-697-4657/9-172-4391, E-mail: Yo.r.yex@hotmail.com. Updated: Sep 24, 2012.

Pink Iguana !

(ROOMS: $15 per person) An endearing little hostal run by a cast of characters right out of a sitcom, Pink Iguana is not to be confused with the Iguana Crossing Hotel down the street. The two are as absolutely unalike as it is possible for two hotels to get. Pink Iguana is a laid-back place popular with backpackers, surfers and dudes. It's right on the beach and there are plenty of hammocks and benches strewn around for folks to make themselves at home. There are some board games and puzzles inside for those so inclined. Prices are as low as you can get, and the place fills up fast. It is by far the least expensive place on the beach. The area to one side serves as the bar as well, and the happy hour is worth a visit even if you're not staying there. The hostel gets its name

from the hundreds of marine iguanas that live on the premises, climbing up its fluorescent pink walls to get some sun. Ask the owner to tell you the story of "Gringo Juan" if you can. The hostal is also known to locals as the "Pink House" (la Casa/Caleta Rosada). Tel: 593-5-252-9336, E-mail: info@caletaiguana.com. Updated: April 2, 2013.

George's Corner Inn/Rincón de George

(ROOMS: $20 per person) Yet another half-assed family affair with blocky rooms, George's Corner Inn is located across from the municipal buildings and central park. On my visit, the owner passed on answering my questions to run off and play soccer. I think that's all you need to know about the level of professionalism you can expect. There is no reception area for the place, either. However, there is a "boutique" on the ground floor instead. The rooms aren't too bad and the bathrooms are relatively nice, and if you run out of other options you might consider it. Just don't go by if there is a soccer game going on somewhere. Services include air conditioning, fridge and TV. 16 Marzo, across from the municipal buildings and the park. Tel: 593-5-252-9214. Updated: Sep 24, 2012.

San Vicente !

(ROOMS: $20-25/person) For a tourist class hotel on Isla Isabela, San Vicente does a pretty good job. Picnic tables and hammocks line the courtyard and a raised, open-air dining room serves both breakfast and dinner to guests. Single and double rooms come with air conditioning and private bathrooms. Singles go for $25 a night with breakfast included; doubles and triples are $20 per person. San Vicente also organizes daily horseback riding tours to the Sierra Negra Volcano as well as tours of the bay. Service here is very professional, a welcome break from the rest of Puerto Villamil. Cormorant and Escalecias. Tel: 593-5-252-9439, E-mail: ventas@hotelsanvicentegalapagos.com. URL: www.hotelsanvicentegalapagos.com, www.isabelagalapagos.com.ec.

MID-RANGE

Hotel La Laguna

(ROOMS: $60-168) One of the newer and spiffier places in town is La Laguna, which offers a view of one of the salt lagoons instead of the ocean. The rooms are clean and neat, and offer just about everything a traveler could want, such as hot water, private bathrooms, air conditioning, cable TV, etc. It's operated by the same people who run the efficient Hotel San Vicente, so you can be sure of professional service. The best part is the airy terrace restaurant. La Laguna can help you arrange island tours and trips on Isabela and also help you get there and back from Puerto Ayora. All in all, a good choice in the mid-budget range. Services include WiFi, air conditioning, cable TV, tour desk, restaurant, bar, hot water, private baths, Jacuzzi and airport pick-up. Tel: 593-2-290-8725/5-252-9140/9-274-7880, E-mail: hotelsanvicentegalapagos@hotmail.com, URL: www.accommodationgalapagosisabela.com, www.sanvicentegalapagos.com. Updated: Sep 24, 2012.

La Casa de Marita ⌐

(ROOMS: $45-180) Back in the day, the Casa de Marita was just about the only place you could stay in tiny Puerto Villamil. Marita and her family had a head start on other lodging options in town, and they have made good use of it. What was once a little guesthouse has evolved into a classy, well-run beachfront hotel. If you were there years ago, you may not recognize it. It's gone upscale, with nice rooms, a fancy restaurant and prices to match. It's well-located on the beach and the rooms are clean, airy and nice. The suites all face the ocean. It's best for middle or high-end travelers who want to spend a few days on Isabela and who want to save some money by avoiding the much more expensive Iguana Crossing and Red Mangrove Hotels. The staff there will help you book trips while on Isabela. Even if you're not staying there, the hotel restaurant is very good, with locally produced food. The hotel includes a restaurant, bar, laundry and room service, private bathrooms, hot water, air conditioning, minibars, hair dryers, telephones and WiFi. Tel: 593-5-252-9201/301, E-Mail: info@casamaritagalapagos.com, URL: www.casamaritagalapagos.com. Updated: Sep 24, 2012.

Hotel Albemarle

(ROOMS: $122-305) Location is everything, and Hotel Albemarle has the best location of any hotel on Isabela Island. It's right between the beach and the main park, where all the action is (or whatever action tiny Puerto Villamil has to offer, anyway). It has an impressive façade, and the interior is stately, if a little small and oddly structured. Check out the ocean view from the roof deck. Prices for the rooms vary depending on whether they face the ocean or not. The ground floor restaurant has good food and service. There is a small swimming pool near the restaurant. Like most upscale hotels on Isabela, Albemarle can help set up tours and transportation. The Hotel Albemarle (and the restaurant) is one of the only places in town that will take credit cards, an important thing to remember if you forgot to bring cash with you. Services include hot water, air conditioning, private baths, restaurant, cable TV, phones in the rooms, safes, WiFi, travel info desk, pool and Jacuzzi. Tel: 593-5-252-9489, E-mail: info@hotelalbemarle.com, URL: www.hotelalbemarle.com. Updated: Sep 24, 2012.

Hotel Sol Isabela

(ROOMS: $70) A friendly, airy, whitewashed beach hotel with a good location, Sol Isabela is a good choice in the middle price range, especially as it's flanked by the much more expensive Red Mangrove and Casa de Marita. It's located a half-block from the old pier, so it has good access to town. Of the 11 rooms, eight somehow face the ocean and three do not. Make sure you know which you are getting. There are some hammocks hung around for excellent lounging opportunities. Sol Isabela does not have a restaurant, but it's right next to places that do. The website is a little wonky. Services include air conditioning, hot water, kitchen, fridge and bottled water. URL: www.hotelsolisabela.ec, Tel: 593-5-252-9183, E-mail: info@hotelsolisabela.ec. Updated: Sept 24, 2012.

The Wooden House
La Casa de Palo ⌐

(ROOMS: $70) The Wooden House is a small but nice-looking hotel on the outskirts of Puerto Villamil on the way to the new municipal dock. As of recently it is under new, more professional management who have made a lot of positive changes to the place. As you might guess from the name, it's made of volcanic stone and attractively painted and stained wood. It has a sort of rustic yet comfortable feel and there is a nice second floor lounge for hanging out.

There is a small but inviting pool. Try to get a room on the second floor, as they're brighter. It's on the main drag outside of town on the way to the municipal dock. Tel: Quito 593-2-250-3740, Isabela 593-5-252-9235/9-949-2624, E-mail: info@woodenhouse.com, info@scubagalapagos.com, URL: http://woodenhousehotel.com/index.html. Updated: Sept 24. 2012

GALÁPAGOS

HIGH-END

Red Mangrove Isabela Lodge

(ROOMS: $200) The original Red Mangrove Hotel is in Puerto Ayora, but in recent years they have opened "branches" on Isabela and Floreana and now offer island-hopping tours. The Red Mangrove Hotels are all professional and offer high-quality facilities and service...at a corresponding price, of course. The Isabela branch is no different. The rooms are spacious with two queen size beds in each one. The rooms supposedly all face the beach, although some may actually open out onto mangroves. The Red Mangrove can help you book tours. In fact, if you're staying here you're probably booked through Red Mangrove and staying with them throughout your Galápagos trip. The Red Mangrove also features one of the better restaurants on Isabela. Prices are not listed here. Depending on the package you get and how many Red Mangrove hotels you're staying at on the various islands, the cost will vary. It is possible to book this hotel directly without staying at other Red Mangrove Hotels or taking tours with them. Check prices, but it's around the $200 per night range. Walk-ins may be treated rudely. Av. Conocarpus on the beach. Tel: 593-5-252-9030, URL: www.redmangrove.com/lodging/isabela.html. Updated: Sept 24, 2012.

Iguana Crossing Hotel

(ROOMS: $200-400) Located at the southern edge of town where the National Park starts, the Iguana Crossing hotel has enviable beach access in addition to good views of the ocean and Sierra Negra Volcano. Modern, clean and cool, the rooms at Iguana Crossing benefit from central air conditioning, which is a big bonus in Puerto Villamil, which can get quite toasty. The Iguana Crossing Hotel is expensive by Ecuadorian standards, and will appeal to luxury travelers who want to spend a couple of days in Galápagos after a cruise, or to those who wish to go island hopping in style. The hotel can arrange for guides to take visitors on day trips to official sightseeing spots on Isabela Island or other western Galápagos Islands. For island hoppers, Iguana Crossing is affiliated with the upscale Casa Opuntia Hotel on San Cristóbal and the Angermeyer Waterfront Inn in Puerto Ayora. Package deals to visit all three are available through their website or via phone. Av. Antonio Gil, on the road to the tortoise breeding center. Tel: 593-5-252-9484, Fax: 593-5-252-9485, E-mail: info@iguanacrossing.com. ec, URL: www.iguanacrossing.com.ec. Updated: Sept 24, 2012.

Puerto Villamil Restaurants

Puerto Villamil has a handful of look-alike restaurants, all serving seafood and simple plates. If you want something fancy, you'll have to head to one of the upscale hotels like the Iguana Crossing or Red Mangrove and eat there.

But why would you? You're in a remote fishing village, after all. Head down to one of the ramshackle places on the waterfront around the time the locals like to dine (they eat around 8 or 9 p.m.), have a seat and order up a plate of the fish of the day.

There isn't really such a thing as "regional food" on Isabela, so there's nothing you must try, just order what looks good. Meals are surprisingly expensive (around $10-12 for an entree off the menu at one of the beach places), but if you go with the lunch or dinner of the day (just ask what they have) it will usually be much cheaper.

Cesar's

(ENTREES: $6-12) Cesar's is one of four or five look-alike restaurants on the main drag across from the park. It's popular with locals and gringos alike for the good, simple seafood dishes. They have a decent menu to choose from, including chicken, fish, shrimp, etc. Ask for whatever fish they caught that day if you're going for the seafood. Updated: Aug 15, 2012.

Aloha Betsy

(ENTREES: $6-22) Located just off the main park, Aloha Betsy features typical beach-side fare—plenty of seafood with rice and plantains. It's family run and has a laid-back atmosphere very typical of Puerto Villamil. The $4 set lunches are a good deal. They also have a good selection of juices. Located on Antonio Gil across from the Park Office. Updated: Aug 15, 2012.

Bar de Beto

Beto's beach bar is a far cry from the overly commercial Puerto Ayora. Here, the beach is the bar. Wooden tables set in the sand are warmed nightly by a log-fed bonfire. Cocktails are pricey, but no more so than in any other part of the Galápagos.

Four dollars will buy you a caipirinha, cuba libre or gin and tonic. The décor and ambience is great, but with one caveat, the music is similar to a Starbucks' playlist. Norah Jones, Jack Johnson and Joan Osbourne played back to back. On La Playa Grande next to El Cormorán Cabins. Tel: 593-5-252-9015. Updated: Aug 15, 2012.

GALÁPAGOS VISITOR SITES

Visitors to Galápagos will be amazed by the number and variety of visitor sites throughout the archipelago. There are over 50 visitor sites in Galápagos National Park territory, each offering its own unique history, landscape, vegetation and fauna. By seeing these sites, visitors can begin to understand the complex evolutionary processes that have shaped island biogeography. Most cruise tours generally visit two island sites and one or two additional snorkel sites per day.

We have divided island and marine visitor sites into four regional categories: northern island sites, central island sites, southern island sites, and western island sites.

Northern Visitor Sites

Visiting the northern islands can be a special experience for tourists, because it involves a rite of passage across the equatorial line. Unfortunately, Marchena and Pinta are off-limits to tourists, but Genovesa is most certainly a Galápagos highlight. It is one of only two islands where you can see groups of Red-footed Boobies, and the surrounding bay is a great snorkeling site.

Although Santiago, Bartolomé (and nearby dive-site Cousin's Rock), Sombrero Chino and Rabida are closer to the central island of Santa Cruz than the three northern outliers, we consider them "northern islands," because they are located outside the central island conglomeration. These islands are geologically interesting and offer some of the best photographic opportunities in the Galápagos Islands.

GENOVESA

Also known as Tower, Genovesa is north of the equator in the northeastern extreme of the archipelago. Because it's so remote, it's impossible to go there on a day-trip from Santa Cruz or San Cristóbal; you'll have to take a cruise. If you are interested in sea birds and exciting snorkeling opportunities, you may want to prioritize this island on your itinerary when selecting cruises.

Because it is isolated from the other islands, Genovesa became home to colonies of birds, but relatively few land animals. For example, no Giant Tortoise species ever developed on Genovesa.

Due to Genovesa's relative isolation and lack of fresh water, it has remained uncontaminated by invasive species, and naturalist guides will likely ask guests to take extra care not to track anything into the delicate Genovesa ecosystem.

Genovesa is fairly flat and round, with a large, almost landlocked cove on the south side called Darwin Bay. During the dingy ride from your boat to one of the visitor sites, Prince Philip's Steps, you will have a good view of Red-billed Tropicbirds, Great Frigatebirds, Swallow-tailed Gulls, Nazca Boobies and Red-footed Boobies flying, fishing and potentially nesting in cracks in the seaward side of the cliff.
Updated: Aug 2012.

Darwin Bay

Darwin never visited Genovesa (Tower) Island in the northern part of the Galápagos archipelago, but he would have loved the bay named after him. The landing site is a spacious sandy beach with trails wending through mangroves and lava rock formations.

The birds are a marvel to see. Frigates with their dazzling chest sacs, Blue-footed and Red-footed Boobies, Swallow-tailed Gulls and more populate the sheltered bay. Genovesa is nicknamed "Bird Island" for good reason!

The easy trail winds in and out of nesting colonies of different bird species, allowing close-up photos of seldom-seen Galápagos species such as the Red-footed Booby or the Lava Gull. At one end of the trail, look for deep tidal pools, which occasionally trap a sea turtle or ray.

El Barranco/Prince Phillips' Steps

El Barranco (a.k.a. Prince Philip's Steps) is a memorable site located on the flat area above the cliffs in Darwin Bay. After a challenging scramble up a rocky crevasse, the rest of the trail is very easy.

The first part of the trail goes through some scrubby trees and brush where you're likely to see some boobies (of all three varieties if you're lucky), Frigatebirds and Galápagos Doves. The trail then continues to a long stretch of rocky dune, on the ocean side of

GALÁPAGOS

which it's possible to see the Short-eared Owl. Although the Short-eared Owl is fairly common in Galápagos, it's only seen at a handful of visitor sites, so make the most of the opportunity! They're hard to spot, so be patient and stay close to the guide. If you have binoculars or a major zoom lens for your camera, this is the place for it. Updated: Aug 2012.

Snorkeling

Because of the steep underwater terrain of Genovesa, snorkeling conditions can vary. If you like to dive and can hold your breath for extended periods of time, you may see interesting bottom-dwellers, tropical fish found only in the northern archipelago, or even a hammerhead shark.

MARCHENA

Also known as Bindloe, Marchena is a large, (130 km²/80.78 mi²) active shield volcano located due west of Genovesa. Although it is the seventh-largest island, it has a fairly desolate terrain and absolutely no visitor sites. There are some good scuba sites nearby, so you may get to see the island up close if you are on a dive tour. Updated: June 12, 2013.

PINTA

Also known as Abington, Pinta is an elongated shield located northwest of Marchena that used to serve as Lonesome George's abode. Visitation to the island is limited to researchers, who must get a permit before landing there. Updated: June 12, 2013.

SANTIAGO

Also known as San Salvador or James, Santiago is the fourth largest island at 585 square kilometers (363.5 mi). This island is especially interesting for people interested in geology, volcanology or succession. Visitor sites include Buccaneer Cove, Puerto Egas and Sullivan Bay. Updated: May 30, 2013

Buccaneer Cove

Buccaneer Cove, as the name suggests, is a small, sheltered bay once popular with whalers and pirates, who could re-stock fresh water and tortoises there while they repaired their ships. As a visitor site, it's a large cliff where you can see many birds, including blue-footed boobys and Brown Noddies. In general, ships don't land at Buccaneer cove:

the visit consists of a panga ride and some snorkeling, which is quite good when the water is clear.

Puerto Egas

Puerto Egas is a favorite visitor site, as it's a good place to see animals and birds and the hike itself is very easy. It's named for a man named Egas who had a salt mine there in the early 1960s; parts of the mine are still there, although they're not on the trail. Ask your guide to tell you the story of the crazy mine guard who remained there for some years after the mine folded.

Visitors disembark on a sandy beach and then head for the circular trail. Part of the trail heads into the interior of the island, and the scrubby brush is a good place to look for Darwin's Finches and other birds, including the pesky introduced Smooth-billed Ani. Near the landing site, look for sea lion pups.

The trail loops around once it hits the coast. The coastal walk features many tidal pools, which are a good place to look for marine life and shore birds like herons. You may even see a Yellow Warbler or two skipping along the seashore, nipping up bugs.

Another highlight along the seaside trail is "Darwin's Toilet," which is a small, rocky pool fed by invisible underground channels: as the waves crash, the "toilet" fills and drains.

Near Darwin's Toilet, look for the rare Galápagos Fur Sea Lion. Your guide will point them out: they look just like regular sea lions, but their coat is a bit thicker and their snout more blunt.

Ship crews are always happy to visit this site because there is a soccer field there and they can go play: join in if you're fit enough. Updated: Oct 28, 2012.

Sullivan Bay

The eastern side of Santiago Island was volcanically active relatively recently (about 100 years ago) and Sullivan Bay is a great place to see lava, sometimes edged with black volcanic glass (obsidian). There is a small colony of Galápagos Penguins at the landing site as well, but visitors with their hopes bent on seeing a lot of wildlife will be disappointed. On the sun-baked lava, insects and lava lizards may hop around, but there's little else to add to it.

GALÁPAGOS

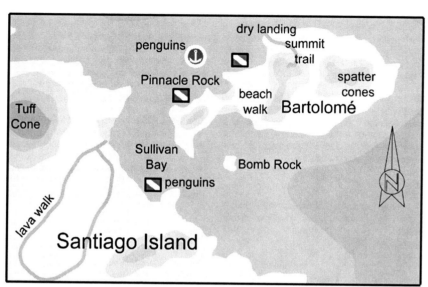

Sullivan Bay

Still, the geology of the area is very interesting. You can see the path of lava flow as well as the various igneous rock structures formed from varying rates of flow, temperature of formation, and pressure. Here you can see examples of three lava types—pahoehoe (braided), aa (jagged and painful), and schrict (ropy). You can also find hornitos, little ovens, formed when bubbles escape from hot lava to form mini-volcanoes. Your guide may even point out holes where trees were vaporized by the hot lava!

The regeneration of the island is ongoing. Pioneer plants such as Brachycereus cactus and Mollugo carpetweed can be seen as well as colonizer animals like insects, lizards and snakes. The bay is also a good snorkeling site—fortunate visitors will get to take a dip after taking the lava hike.
Updated: Oct 28, 2012.

BARTOLOMÉ

Bartolomé, a small islet (1.2 km²/0.75 mi²) just off Sullivan Bay on Santiago, is probably the most recognizable point in Galápagos—literally. On one side of Bartolomé is the famous Pinnacle Rock, a rocky formation pointing skyward. Legend has it that Pinnacle Rock was bombed into shape in the 1940s by American servicemen testing their ordinance. There's a hike to the top of a hill where you'll have a great view of Pinnacle Rock and there is a small beach with excellent snorkeling.

La Escalera/The Stairs
"La Escalera" is a long, winding wooden staircase which leads up to the peak of the island, where visitors are rewarded with a magnificent view. Along the way, visitors hike through an arid, rocky landscape of reddish volcanic rocks that has caused many people to speculate if the surface of Mars looks similar. Naturalist guides will point out the hardy pioneer plants that are slowly making the arid island livable for other species.

Other than the geology, there isn't much to see. Once away from the landing spot, there is little in the way of wildlife—look for Lava Lizards and brightly colored grasshoppers. The magnificent view at the top of Bartolomé is worth the climb, however. Don't forget your camera! There are usually Marine Iguanas, Sally Lightfoot Crabs and sea lions near the landing site.

The Beach
Bartolomé Island is home to a beautiful white sand beach with a gentle surf. The beach is at the base of the famous Pinnacle Rock, the unmistakable rock formation allegedly blasted into shape by American forces during World War II.

Bartolomé is very narrow at this point, and there is a short, easy trail which leads to a scenic beach on the other side. The beach is nice, but you shouldn't miss the opportunity to snorkel while here.

Beginners can putter around in the sheltered cove of the beach, but if you head out and

GALÁPAGOS

around Pinnacle Rock, you'll be rewarded with some truly awesome underwater life. Look for penguins, octopuses (they're tough to see but they're there), sea lions, sharks, rays and much more.

Even the underwater rubble from the bombing is now grown over with algae and seaweed and makes for memorable seascapes. If you're on one of the larger ships, they may have a glass-bottom boat for those who do not wish to snorkel.

RÁBIDA

Also known as Jervis, Rábida is a small island (5 km²/3.1 mi²) south of Santiago whose colorful splendor makes it a photographer's dream. Visitors will be struck by the sharp contrasts between the turquoise waters, maroon sandy beach, beige rock substrate, white trees and lush green highlands. There is only one visitor site on Rábida.

There is a wet landing onto the long, red beach where sea lions lounge, pelicans nest and the occasional manta ray jumps in the distance. A short walk away from the beach takes you to a brackish lagoon, where you can sometimes see flamingoes, despite the fact that sea lion fecal contamination has killed off most of the lagoon's crustaceans, the flamingoes' food source.

A 0.75 kilometer (0.46 mi) circular trail begins at the lagoon, winding through cacti (look for one shaped like Mickey Mouse). The walk offers amazing views of the sea as well as the island's 367 meter (1,204 ft) volcanic peak.

You can also snorkel from the beach or take a dingy ride along the cove to look for green sea turtles, marine iguanas, and fur sea lions. The deep-water snorkeling off of Rabida's walls is fantastic.

SOMBRERO CHINO

Sombrero Chino, or Chinese Hat, is a small islet which gets its name from its appearance—a yellowish, nearly perfect cone like hat worn in parts of Asia. Located off the southeastern tip of Santiago, Chinese Hat is a fairly recent volcanic cone with a few small but intact lava tunnels. The 400-meter trail starts on a small, white-sand beach, where you can often see American Oystercatchers and sea lions. The trail continues along the cove, passing marine iguanas, Sally Lightfoot Crabs, and Lava Lizards. The trail is a good place to observe different lava formations—ask your guide for details.

If you visit during the cold season (May/June-November/December), the island may have some small tide pools lined with green algae, which attract more marine iguanas. From the beach you can swim in tranquil blue waters along the cove, playing with sea lions and spotting tropical fish.

Sombrero Chino is considered a fragile visitor site, and only certain cruise ships (those which don't carry many passengers) are allowed to visit; if you want to include Sombrero Chino in your itinerary, be sure to sign up with one of the cruise ships that goes there or ask a tour agency in town.

Central Island Visitor Sites

The central islands of Santa Cruz and Baltra serve as the hub of tourist traffic, since the main town of Puerto Ayora and the airport are located here. The majority of organized tours and independent travelers begin and end their adventures here.

The surrounding islands of Daphne Major and Minor, North Seymour, South Plaza (and the nearby dive site of Gordon Rocks), and Santa Fe are thus the most visited by tourists due to their close proximity to Puerto Ayora. But they also offer some of the best opportunities for seeing sea birds and large marine creatures, such as hammerhead sharks and sting rays.

SANTA CRUZ

Tourist-friendly Santa Cruz (Indefatigable) Island is not only the home of Puerto Ayora, it's also the most centrally located island, meaning more visitor sites, dives and tours are available. Because the main airport is on nearby Baltra, most visitors to the Galápagos Islands will wind up in Puerto Ayora at some point, and the town has the best hotels, restaurants and nightlife in the islands. It's also home to the Charles Darwin Research Station, former home of Lonesome George and a must-see for any visitor to Galápagos.

Santa Cruz is more than just Puerto Ayora, however. There are 22 land and marine visitor sites on and around the island. The lush green highlands are home to tortoises and birds, the beaches are among the best in the islands, and even Puerto Ayora's Academy Bay is worth checking out.

There are several dive sites near Puerto Ayora, and plenty of dive shops in town to take you there. The best known site is probably Gordon Rocks, where different sharks, including hammerheads, are often seen.

Santa Cruz is a great place to see Giant Tortoises. There are some at the Charles Darwin Research Station, but it's better to go to the highlands to see them in their natural habitat, munching on vegetation, wallowing in mud and lumbering around. El Chato reserve is a good place to start: in addition to the tortoises, there is a freshwater lagoon that attracts ducks and other birds, and some lava tunnels that can be explored. Also in the highlands, Los Gemelos ("the twins") refers to two sinkhole craters formed by collapsing underground lava tunnels. They're a great place to see birds (keep an eye open for the brilliant red Vermillion Flycatcher) and native plants.

Some of the visitor sites on Santa Cruz are only for cruise ships, while others are open to the public. Of all the sites listed here, Las Bachas and Cerro Dragón are only for cruise ships and off-limits to day trippers from Puerto Ayora; the rest of the sites are either public or visited from Puerto Ayora as part of a tour. For more local sites that are within walking distance of Puerto Ayora, see the section on Things To See and Do in P. Ayora (p. 494).

Playa Ratonera

From Playa de la Estación, a path leads south to Playa Ratonera. This white-sand beach is a perfect place to watch the sun set over Academy Bay. Despite the rocky outcrops, this is a favorite place for Puerto Ayora's surfers. Often sea lions swim by to wave to anyone hanging out. When the sea goes out, tidal pools form in the lava-rock basins in which sea slugs, eels, octopus and a myriad of fishes may be studied. Shore birds are also frequent visitors. At the north end are mangrove stands. Beach morning glory, saltbush and sea purslane embroider the sand.

Laguna Las Ninfas

Laguna las Ninfas is a crystal blue lagoon located only a block away from a busy street in Puerto Ayora. For many years, it was run-down, full of garbage and a favorite place for surly Puerto Ayora teenagers to hang out and grumble about how much their lives sucked.

I'm happy to say that has all changed. The garbage is out of the lagoon and there is a lovely boardwalk most of the way around it with interesting signs describing the local plant and animal life. Even the teenagers are gone,

perhaps because the lagoon is no longer a depressing place. You can swim in the lagoon now, although some locals say that runoff from farms upriver makes doing so questionable.

Las Ninfas is a brackish lagoon: in other words, it's where sea water meets a creek bearing freshwater. As such, it is home to some fish, animal and plant species you may not see elsewhere. Seeing Las Ninfas won't take more than an hour and I highly recommend it if you're spending a couple days in Puerto Ayora. It's off the main drag near the Casa del Lago Hotel. Any local will give you directions to find it. Updated: May 6, 2013.

The Miguel Cifuentes Arias Community Center

Located a short walk from the main road and at the head of the trail that goes to Tortuga Bay, the Miguel Cifuentes Arias Community Center is a small complex of buildings housing some classrooms (would-be islanders must take a short class there before receiving their residency) and a tiny museum dealing with the marine reserve. There are some informational displays as well as a couple of aquariums with lobsters and eels in them.

It's named for Miguel Cifuentes Arias, former head of the Charles Darwin Research Station, director of the Galápagos National Park and Mayor of Puerto Ayora. It's worth a quick stop on your way to or from Tortuga Bay. Seeing the marine reserve room shouldn't take you more than 15 minutes. Also, there are bathrooms here, the closest ones available to the beach at Tortuga Bay.

Playa de los Perros

The "Beach of the Dogs" is a quick, 10-minute boat ride from Puerto Ayora. It's a pleasant enough white sand beach, with a nearby pool where you can see White-tipped Reef Sharks if you're lucky. Playa de los Perros is often included with tours of Academy Bay.

Lava Tunnels

Lava Tunnels are natural volcanic rock formations left behind when a stream of lava flows out of a volcano. The outer magma cools while the inner magma continues to flow, resulting in an underground stone tube of sorts. There are lava tunnels all over Galápagos, in all shapes and sizes.

There are several lava tunnels in the highlands near Puerto Ayora. They're often located near the farms where the Giant Tortoises hang out,

GALÁPAGOS

so tours to see the tortoises will usually stop at a lava tunnel as well. The ones usually visited by tourists either have lights installed or are short enough that visibility is not a problem. The lava tunnels are interesting, but not so much so that you'd really want to go out of your way to see one unless you're a geology buff. Best to catch one on a tortoise or highland tour. The tunnels are popular with barn owls, so keep your eyes open near the entrance. Updated: Aug 10, 2012.

Cerro Crocker

Cerro Crocker (Crocker Hill) is the highest point on Santa Cruz Island, which isn't saying much (860 m/2,821.5 ft). It's fairly easy to hike, and you'll be rewarded at the top with a good view of Puerto Ayora. The terrain is leafy and green (and muddy when it rains, so bring good shoes). Part of the trail goes through agricultural areas, and part is the Galápagos National Park.

A guide is legally not needed, but you'll definitely want one so that you don't get lost. Also, the trail winds its way through several vegetation zones, including some rare endemic plants and introduced species. Without a guide to tell you what they are, you might just assume that they are just some plants and walk right past them!

The Cerro Crocker hike is your best chance to see the elusive Galápagos Rail, a bluish purple-black bird that hangs out mostly on the ground. Updated: May 6, 2013

El Chato Reserve

Located in the green, hilly highlands of Santa Cruz Island, the El Chato Reserve is one of the best places in the islands to see the Giant Tortoises in their natural habitat. The reserve is free and open to the public, but a guide is highly recommended, as in recent years some visitors have gotten lost, and one died before he could be found.

The tortoises are easy to spot, lumbering around eating grass and leaves and wallowing in the small pools that are common in the reserve. You may also spot some highland birds, like Cattle Egrets, mockingbirds, finches or flycatchers.

There is a trail through the reserve, leaving from the little town of Santa Rosa. From the "caseta" or little house where it begins, figure on about a three or three and a half hour hike round trip. It's possible to hire horses and guides in Santa Rosa. There are also several

lava tunnels in the reserve, a couple of which are open to the public. There is also a small lagoon covered in red algae.

In addition to the El Chato reserve, there are a couple of private farms in the highlands where visitors can see the tortoises. That's another reason to go with a guide, as they'll tend to know where the tortoises are at any given moment. Updated: Aug 20, 2012.

Los Gemelos

Located in the Santa Cruz highlands, Los Gemelos ("The Twins") refers to two large sinkholes which were formed by collapsing underground lava tunnels. As paths to and around the sinkholes have improved, they have become more popular with visitors, who are kindly asked to stay far from the edges of the sinkholes and not to throw anything (i.e. rocks) into the craters themselves.

The big attraction here is the Scalesia forest. Scalesia is a sort of tree endemic to Galápagos. Many endemic and native species call Los Gemelos home.

Los Gemelos is the best place in Galápagos to see the dazzling, elusive Vermillion Flycatcher. Darwin's Finches are also commonly sighted there. Los Gemelos is often combined with trips to other highland locations to see Giant Tortoises. Updated: Aug 20, 2012.

Las Bachas Beach

Las Bachas is a beautiful white-sand beach on the northern coast of Santa Cruz Island. There isn't much to do there except lounge on the sand, go for a stroll or do some easy snorkeling in the gentle surf. Rough, right?

There are a couple of salt lagoons behind the sandy berm—lucky visitors will spot a flamingo or two. You can also look for a rusted pontoon, a relic of the Second World War. In fact, "bachas" is a poor pronunciation of "barges," two of which were wrecked offshore at that time.

Sea Turtles lay their eggs at the edge of the vegetation—be sure to obey the signs to stay away.

It's possible to snorkel in the gentle surf; you're unlikely to see much, given the sandy bottom and cloudiness of the water, but if you stay near the rocks you should see some fish, or a shark or turtle if you're lucky. Updated: Nov 10, 2012.

GALÁPAGOS

Did a unique trek? Tell other travelers at vivatravelguides.com

Cerro Dragón/Dragon Hill

The aptly named Cerro Dragón ("Dragon Hill") is a memorable visitor site and one of the best places in the islands to see land iguanas. The site is on the other side of the island from Puerto Ayora and consists of a trail in a sort of lasso shape: a trail leads inland to the hill, up and around the hill, and then back out the same trail to the beach.

Along the trail, it is possible to see land iguanas and several species of birds. It's lucky that there are land iguanas on Santa Cruz at all. As the most inhabited island, it is also the one most plagued by introduced species such as goats, cats and dogs, all of which wreak havoc on land iguana populations. Goats eat up all the available vegetation, cats eat baby iguanas and eggs, and a pack of dogs can gobble a fully grown iguana.

These introduced pests were devastating the Santa Cruz iguana population, to the point that researchers and Park Service officials relocated some of the iguanas to a nearby islet (with no dogs, cats or goats) so that if the Santa Cruz population were wiped out, they would be able to repopulate it.

Fortunately, intensive efforts to remove the offending introduced species have been successful, and the resident "dragons" are no longer seriously threatened. Efforts to control introduced plants and animals on this part of Santa Cruz are ongoing, and Cerro Dragón is one of few places on the islands where tourists and scientists may cross paths.

The path is one of the longer ones in Galápagos. From the top of the small hill is a nice view, and the trail itself goes through Palo Santo trees and cacti forests. There is a saltwater lagoon where lucky visitors may see Pintail Ducks or Flamingos.

Garrapatero Beach

Located outside of Puerto Ayora, Garrapatero Beach is a favorite among locals and visitors alike. It's a gorgeous white sand beach perfect for swimming, lounging or even a bit of snorkeling. There are mangroves around it and even the little trail to the beach is interesting.

Getting there is a bit of a trick; you'll have to take a taxi and the ride is about 40 minutes or so. The taxi will not wait for you, but will come back for you if you tell him when. There are usually no taxis waiting there. Once you reach the parking lot, there is a 15 minute walk to the beach along an easy trail.

You can also get here by bike—it's about a two hour ride from Puerto Ayora. There are no souvenir stands, restaurants, drink vendors or anything else at the beach— that's the whole charm of it, but be sure to bring everything you need. There are no trash cans either, so bring a bag for your garbage and be sure to take it out with you.

Beware of the manzanillo trees: they're poisonous. They're labeled, so just don't eat the little apples or sleep under the tree.

Although it's part of the park system, it's public access, so anyone can go there from Puerto Ayora with no need of any naturalist guides. There is sometimes a park ranger patrolling the area to make sure all regulations are complied with. Keep an eye on any valuables as petty theft is not unheard of.

Dive Sites Near Puerto Ayora

Puerto Ayora is by far the best of the three towns for divers. There are several dive shops to choose from, all of which go to the same sites. Perhaps because of its central location, the variety of sites is very good: you could stay a week in Puerto Ayora and not dive the same site twice

North Seymour

There are five different immersion sites on North Seymour, a small island not far from Puerto Ayora, making it good for all levels of diving skill. Currents can be strong. Highlights include a garden eel colony and a chance of sharks including Galapagos Sharks and Hammerheads.

Distance by boat from Puerto Ayora: 1 ½ hours.

Floreana Island

There are nine sites off of Floreana, which is good because if the water is rough at one site, the divemasters will usually just go to another one. There are sea lions at some of the sites and it's possible to watch them frolic underwater. It's also one of the only places in the Islands with significant coral formations.

Distance from Puerto Ayora: 1 hour, 45 mins.

Bartolomé Island/Cousins Rock

Bartolomé Island is usually combined with nearby Cousins Rock when organizing dives. Both dives are wall dives, best for intermediate to advanced divers. Highlights include the chance to see frogfish, sea horses and sharks.

Distance from Puerto Ayora: Two hours.

GALÁPAGOS

Academy Bay

Often overlooked, Academy Bay—the wide bay that serves as home for Puerto Ayora—is a superlative dive site in itself. There are five sites scattered around the bay, none of which is more than 20 minutes away from town by boat. It's good for beginners, and when people are staying for a few days, dive shops like to warm up here before heading to more difficult and remote sites. Good for rays, sea lions and perhaps a Galapagos Shark.

Distance from Puerto Ayora: n/a.

Santa Fe Island

The waters off of perennial favorite Santa Fe are calm and clear but still full of marine life, making it a must-do for divers of all levels. There are four different sites here, and your divemaster will pick the one most likely to have lots of marine life. Look for rays, eels, turtles and sharks.

Distance from Puerto Ayora: One hour.

Gordon Rocks

Another must-do, Gordon Rocks is a submerged tuff cone that consistently draws rave reviews from diving magazines and websites. Two of the four dive sites there are good for beginners, but the other two can be very challenging. It's a wall dive, and the wall goes very deep. Schools of Hammerhead Sharks are frequently seen, but other large marine life like rays and other shark species are common. Gordon Rocks is sometimes done in conjunction with North Seymour or Mosquera.

Distance from Puerto Ayora: One hour.

Mosquera

A good site for beginners, Mosquera Islet is home to a huge Garden Eel colony. The dive follows the reef which connects Mosquera to Baltra Island. There are other types of eel there, too, as well as sea turtles, a variety of rays including Manta Rays and a chance to see sharks. The currents can get strong sometimes.

Distance from Puerto Ayora: 1.5 hours.

Daphne

There are three dive sites spread out in this smallest of islands including Daphne Major, Daphne Minor and El Bajo. One of the sites is perfect for mixed groups, as beginners will find it possible to do and experts will find lots of marine life to see. Dive shops often take "Discovery Divers" (uncertified divers doing one or two dives only under the close supervision of a divemaster) to Daphne. The other sites can get a little rough, so beginning level divers should consult with the divemaster to make sure they're going to the right one!

Distance from Puerto Ayora: One hour.

NORTH SEYMOUR ISLAND

North Seymour is a small, flat island located near Baltra and Santa Cruz; it's possible to visit from Puerto Ayora as a day trip. It's a popular visitor site, as it is home to several species of birds as well as land and marine iguanas and sea lions.

The trail is about two and a half kilometers (1.6 mi) long and is rocky and treacherous in places. Following the trail along the beach, you should see Blue-Footed Boobies and pelicans fishing, Swallow-Tail Gulls and frigatebirds flying, and marine iguanas resting on the rocky shore. If you take a rest on the rocks and patiently look out at the sea, you will probably see a sea lion or two surfing the waves.

Regardless of the time of year you visit, you are likely to observe some kind of courtship, mating, nesting or chick nesting on North Seymour. And since both boobies and frigatebirds often make their nests close to the trail, you may get a very good close-up shot. It's also not uncommon to catch frigates and boobies doing their courtship rituals. Further along the trail, you will see flocks of male frigate birds nesting—attracting females with their inflated red sack—and the occasional land iguana.

The land iguanas are found inland, where they feast on low-hanging cacti. Your guide will help you spot the bright yellow lizards among the plants and rocks off the trail. The iguanas here have an interesting history—they were brought here from Baltra in the 1930s and they thrived. Later, the Baltra population of land iguanas went extinct, but was repopulated by bringing some iguanas back from North Seymour!

The waters off of North Seymour Island provide some of the best diving and snorkeling opportunities in the islands. From the surface, you are bound to see White-tipped Reef Sharks, Triggerfish, Surgeonfish, and other colorful fish. If you are diving in the Canal, you are likely see a host of Galápagos garden eels, moray eels, and the occasional diamond, golden, or manta ray.

GALÁPAGOS

Did a unique trek? Tell other travelers at vivatravelguides.com

BALTRA

Most visitors to the Galápagos archipelago arrive by plane to Baltra, also known as South Seymour. Baltra once served as a US military base. There are no visitor sites or accommodations on Baltra and the only facilities available relate to air traffic and transportation. From the airport you can catch a bus to the canal, where you catch the ferry to Santa Cruz, and to the port, where visitors with pre-arranged tours meet their boat.

SANTA FE

Located about 20 kilometers (12.4 mi) southeast of Santa Cruz, the small island of Santa Fe (Barrington) is a popular destination for day trips and cruises. The trail consists of two loops separated by a walk of a couple hundred meters. The first loop, a 300-meter (984 ft) circuit, takes you to one of the tallest stands of opuntia cacti in the archipelago, some reaching heights of over 10 meters (32.8 ft). Look for the elusive Santa Fe subspecies of land iguana. You also might see a park project of fire ant control. The other loop goes through a Palo Santo Forest, where you can also look for land iguanas.

Santa Fe is home to one of the two remaining species of endemic Galápagos Rice Rats, although it's very unlikely that you'll see one. There was once a species of Giant Tortoise on the island, but it has unfortunately gone extinct.

Santa Fe is a popular day trip from Puerto Ayora because of the excellent snorkeling in the cove. Note that only cruise ships are allowed to land on the island itself; if you're a day tripper, you'll come, snorkel and return without seeing the iguanas. It's also a popular SCUBA diving site.

MOSQUERA

Only about 600 meters long by 160 meters wide (1,968.5 ft by 525 ft) at its widest point, Mosquera is a small, rocky islet located between Baltra and North Seymour. It was once an underwater reef when a geologic force known as an uplift pushed it up above the water, forming an island. Because of this, Mosquera is very flat, not at all conical like other small islands in Galápagos.

There is a good beach on Mosquera, as well as a trail leading past a huge sea lion colony and a nesting area for Lava Gulls. It's possible to snorkel off of the beach, and there's a good chance swimmers will be joined by one of the numerous sea lions who make the island their home. Mosquera is a popular dive site with operators from Puerto Ayora.

SOUTH PLAZA

South Plaza is a small island off the east coast of Santa Cruz. The small size of the island combined with interesting geology, flora and fauna make it a definitive highlight for cruise travelers or for day trippers from Puerto Ayora.

There is a dry landing onto a shore covered with white rocks, polished to a brilliant sheen by the oily sea lions as they travel up and down the shore. A one-kilometer (0.62 mi) trail circuit leads you through an opuntia cactus forest frequented by land iguanas, Yellow Warblers and finches.

There is also a land/marine iguana hybrid that has been hanging out at the beginning of the trail since 2003, but it is only rarely seen. South Plaza is one of the best places to see land iguanas in Galapagos. The trail continues along a 25-meter (82 ft) high cliff, which provides excellent vistas of neighboring Santa Cruz as well as sights of numerous sea birds. You may also see a conspicuous line of mullets swimming offshore and, if you are lucky, a shark or two lurking in the rocks below or a manta ray jumping in the distance.

Further east along the trail, you will encounter a sea lion bachelor colony, where males defeated in the battle for territory kick back for a bit before returning to challenge once again. The final part of the trail passes through a sea lion nursery, where you may see newborn pups (if arriving in October-December) or playful juveniles (February-April).

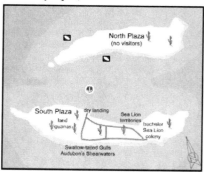

GALÁPAGOS

DAPHNE MAJOR AND MINOR

If you have the opportunity to visit Daphne Major, the island home where Rosemary and Peter Grant conducted their study on Darwin's Finches that inspired the novel, *The Beak of the Finch*, consider yourself among select company: the island is only accessible to one scientific group per month in order to mitigate erosion. It is clear from the beginning of the visit—a landing which requires stepping from the moving dinghy onto a vertical cliff face and scrambling up the rocks to the head of the steep, rocky trail—that a trip to Daphne is a special experience.

The short trail leads up the side of the volcanic island to a 120-meter (393.7 ft) high summit, passing Nazca Boobies, Swallow-tailed Gulls, and finches along the way. At the top of the cone are two small craters, where hundreds of Blue-Footed Boobies and Frigatebirds settle to find their mates (a veritable bird motel!).

Daphne Minor is fairly eroded and not accessible to tourists, although the surrounding waters are a very popular dive site. The underwater geology of Daphne proves very interesting to those inclined to dive, with recesses and steep cliffs, and a high possibility of seeing sharks as well —White-Tipped, Galápagos, and occasionally even Hammerheads—along with sea turtles and rays here and there.

Southern Island Visitor Sites

The three southern islands of San Cristóbal, Española, and Floreana provide some of the most exciting, unique and unforgettable visitor sites in Galápagos. San Cristóbal and its main port town, Puerto Baquerizo Moreno, have the best surfing spots in the archipelago. There is good diving and snorkeling nearby, as well as some good beaches. Española is famous as the only place in the world where the Waved Albatross nests. You can see their awkward waddling take-off during the months of the year when they are there.

Finally, the island of Floreana boasts one of the best snorkel spots in the islands, Devil's Crown, as well as some of the most interesting human history.
Updated: Aug 12, 2012

SAN CRISTÓBAL

San Cristóbal (Chatham) is the fifth-largest (558 km²/346.7 mi²) and easternmost of the islands. Rapid development of tourist and educational facilities, as well as the existence of an airport, has caused island visitation to grow in recent years, with a corresponding boom in tourism services.

San Cristóbal boasts the largest large freshwater lagoon in the archipelago, as well as beautiful beaches, amazing snorkeling and scuba-diving opportunities, and some of the best surfing spots in Galápagos.

The island also provides an interesting socio-environmental element missing from other islands—visitors interested in the human component of the Galápagos Islands can see colonial architecture, visit organic coffee plantations and other agricultural centers, and even check out local politics in the provincial capital, Puerto Baquerizo Moreno.

Some of the sites are only for cruise ships: these include Punta Pitt and Cerro Brujo. The rest can be visited from Puerto Baquerizo Moreno.

San Cristóbal Dive Sites

San Cristóbal is known mostly for surfing, but there are a few dive shops in town and they go to some pretty cool sites.

Kicker Rock/León Dormido

The distinctive, boot-shaped Kicker Rock is a favorite Puerto Baquerizo dive site. It's for beginner-intermediate level divers. There are actually two rocks there, and the dive takes you down between them to the bottom, about 80 feet (25 meters). Along the way, you'll see numerous fish and possibly Hammerhead Sharks. It's possible to snorkel on the surface here, so snorkelers and divers can take the same trip.

Isla Lobos

A fun dive for beginners, Isla Lobos is located just up the coast from Puerto Baquerizo Moreno. There is a long, narrow island separated from the coast by a short distance. Between the island and the coast is a little lagoon of sorts, full of sea lions and marine iguanas. It's only about 30 feet (10 meters) deep, and there is little current. Most dive shops combine Lobos with Punta Pitt or Kicker Rock. Also great for snorkeling.

Distance from Puerto Baquerizo Moreno: 20 minutes

GALÁPAGOS

Five Fingers

Located just outside of Shipwreck bay, Five Fingers is a great place for colorful reef fish. It's a wall dive off of a very small island and there are some coral formations, but the walls go too deep to go to the bottom of them except in a couple of places. Be careful with the sharpness of them.

Distance from Puerto Baquerizo Moreno: 20 Minutes

Caragua

The Caragua is a 100-year-old wreck located just outside Shipwreck Bay. It has formed an artificial reef and is home to many fish, seahorses, coral, sea lions and more.

There is a moderate current, but the wreck isn't too deep, only being in about 15 meters (50 feet). It's just about the only wreck worth diving in the Galápagos.

Distance from Puerto Baquerizo Moreno: 15 minutes

ESPAÑOLA

The southeasternmost of the Galápagos Islands, Española is also the oldest in geological terms. Like the others, it was created as the earth's crust moved over a geological "hot spot," spawning volcanoes which eventually created solid land. Española (known to the British as "Hood") moved away from the hot spot long ago and is no longer volcanically active.

Española's main claim to fame is that it is the only nesting site of the Waved Albatross, a large, stately bird endemic to Galápagos. It's also where you'll find a subspecies of the Marine Iguana: the Española "Christmas Iguana" so named because the larger ones turn a distinctive red and green color during mating season.

There are two visitor sites on Española: Punta Suárez (Suárez Point) and Gardner Bay. Punta Suárez is one of the most memorable sites in all of Galápagos—it's the only place to see the brightly colored iguanas and the Waved Albatross. Gardner Bay is a gorgeous white sand beach known for friendly sea lions and good swimming and snorkeling. Updated: Jan 18, 2013.

Gardner Bay/Tortuga Rock

Gardner Bay is one of the best beaches in Galápagos—a stunning stretch of white sand

rocked by gentle waves, which dozing sea lions will grudgingly share with you. There's not much to see in the way of wildlife and no trail to follow: just a great beach to spend a couple of lazy hours. Observe the signs, which will keep you out of a sea turtle nesting area. If you go to the far end of the beach (where the black rocks are) you have a good chance of spotting a Marine Iguana or two.

It's possible to snorkel in the fairly calm waters of the bay, but don't expect to see much. Sea lions may get close enough for a good look, and rays are common in the area. Stingrays lurk on the sandy bottom; look for them starting just a few feet from shore. Manta and Spotted Eagle Rays occasionally pass through. You'll see some fish as well or a sea turtle or White-tipped Reef Shark if you're lucky; look for fish near rocks.

Just offshore, however, is Turtle Rock, the remains of a volcanic crater that, when viewed from the right angle, looks like a turtle surfacing. The snorkeling around Turtle Rock is excellent. On the calm (no current) side of Turtle Rock, look carefully in the sand for camouflaged Stone Scorpionfish lurking on the sandy bottom. Although there is a current, Turtle Rock is a good place for intermediate snorkelers because one side of it is always sheltered from wind and waves. A good swimmer can make it from shore to Turtle Rock and vice-versa.

Punta Suárez

One of the best visitor sites in the islands, Punta Suárez is the only place where visitors can see the famous Waved Albatross. It's also a great place to see Boobies, Tropicbirds and other birds. Look for the red-and-green "Christmas Iguanas." There are a couple of sandy beach areas and a monument which is also a popular perch for the Galápagos Hawk. The trail is a loop; your guide may lead you to the left along the beach and into the interior, or to the right along the rocky coast. Either way, you'll get to see the whole trail.

Heading counter-clockwise along the coastal trail, you pass colonies of Blue-footed Boobies and Nazca Boobies nesting on the cliffs, most likely spot a finch or two, and probably see a few sea birds—the Red-billed Tropicbird or Swallow-tailed Gull—flying right offshore.

You'll also immediately learn to avoid all the Lava Lizards darting under your feet as well as the Mockingbirds that continuously beg for water.

GALÁPAGOS

Next, walk down to the beach where waves crash up on the rocks in a breathtaking display and where hordes of marine iguanas monitor the eggs they have laid between the months of January and March. If you arrive when the eggs begin to hatch, chances are you will see a Galápagos Hawk hovering around this area, waiting to prey upon the new hatchlings.

Just beyond lies a flat section of the trail, an "airport" where, from late March until late December, Waved Albatrosses can take flight, land, await the return of their mates from the mainland, or proceed with their elaborate courting rituals.

Further along the trail is a blowhole, a slit in the rocky coastline through which waves force water to spout about 20 meters (66 ft) in the air. Here you can sit on the cliff and watch the spectacle, relax and reapply sunscreen (you have probably already been walking for an hour!), and watch sea birds flying overhead.

The rocky trail back to the beach cuts inland through the dry vegetation of the island, where more albatrosses may be hiding. This part of the trail is the hardest, as the rocks can be treacherous and it gets very hot during certain times of the year.

FLOREANA

Floreana (Charles) is one of the more historic islands in Galápagos, although there is little left there today to remind visitors of the past. Charles Darwin visited the island in 1835; at the time there was a penal colony there, with between 200 and 300 prisoners.

Floreana had many Giant Tortoises at the time, and they were taken as food by the prisoners and by passing ships, eventually becoming extinct. Perhaps because of the abundant tortoises, Floreana was popular with pirates and whalers who could take on food and water easily there. One remnant of this time is Post Office Bay, where whalers would leave letters for home (and pick up any if they were headed back). There is still a place to leave postcards and letters, and other visitors will deliver them for you!

Floreana was also the site of the infamous 1934 "Galápagos Affair" that left five people dead or missing in a few short months. The Wittmer family, which was involved in the affair, still lives on Floreana. Floreana is

also known as Santa María or Charles. The island was named for Juan José Flores, the first President of Ecuador. He never visited Galápagos.

Because of the long human history on Floreana, it is also one of the worst off in terms of introduced species. The island has always suffered from more than its share of introduced vermin, including mice, wasps, fire ants and more. The island also has a problem with introduced plants, such as the blackberry. In many places on Floreana, it is possible to see efforts to remove them, as Floreana has been targeted by the Charles Darwin Research Station for urgent removal of these dangerous species.

There are several places to visit on Floreana. The first is the tiny town of Puerto Velasco Ibarra, the smallest settlement in Galápagos, with fewer than 200 inhabitants. There is now a small hotel there, so it's possible to spend the night. Post Office Bay includes a look at the famous post office site and some lava tunnels. The Baroness Lookout is a great site with a nice view. Punta Cormorant is a nice ocean walk and a good place to see flamingos. The Devil's Crown is one of the best snorkeling sites in the islands. Offshore, Champion Islet is a superlative snorkeling spot.

PUERTO VELASCO IBARRA

The tiny town of Puerto Velasco Ibarra has no more than 200 inhabitants, but does have a small hotel, restaurant and store operated by the Wittmer family, descendants of hardy German settlers who arrived in the 1930s, just in time to take part in the sordid "Galápagos Affair."

Most visits to the town take visitors up the hill to a lush area once owned by the Wittmer family; there is a small spring there, and you'll probably spot some birds.

Cerro Alieri/Alieri Hill
Cerro Alieri is outside of Puerto Velasco Ibarra, the tiny town of Floreana Island. To get there, it's a 15-minute ride in a truck followed by a two-hour hike (round-trip). The hike up to the top of Alieri hill is primarily notable for vegetation: most of the plant species are either native or endemic and the hike will be of great interest to botanists.

One of the plants is the endemic Scalesia tree, which was once abundant on Floreana.

Now there are only a few trees scattered around; their decline is due to pressure from goats and early settlers, who cut down the trees to make their homes. For Galápagos, Cerro Alieri gets a lot of rainfall. The trail may be muddy, so pack accordingly.

La Lobería/Sea Lions Area

About one kilometer (0.62 mi) away from Puerto Velasco Ibarra is a small beach which is home to a colony of sea lions, as well as some marine iguanas. It's possible to walk there from the town for some recreational snorkeling. If you're lucky, the sea lions will come out to join you! Extremely fortunate snorkelers may spot a ray or a shark. It's also a popular spot for sea kayaking. You don't need a guide. Updated: Feb 01, 2013.

Asilo de la Paz/Asylum of Peace

The Asilo de la Paz hike on Floreana Island is primarily of historical interest for guests. It goes past a cave allegedly once used by maroonee Patrick Watkins and also visits a freshwater spring which served as a source of water for early settlers.

The hike, which can be done from the small town of Puerto Velasco Ibarra (or you can contract for a ride to take you most of the way), goes through the heart of Floreana's agricultural region. Early settlers planted trees including tamarind, plums and particularly citrus trees (according to legend, it was Watkins himself who introduced citrus trees to the Island).

The cave allegedly used by Watkins was later home to the famous Dr. Ritter and his girlfriend Dore Strauch. After Ritter died, the Wittmer family lived there for a time. Near Asilo de la Paz, there is a place where the Park Service has built a corral of sorts for Giant Tortoises. As the Floreana Island subspecies of Giant Tortoise is extinct, the corral houses specimens from other islands.

Look out for the introduced Polistes Versicolor Wasp—it's aggressive and common all over Floreana. You don't want to mess with them!

Punta Cormorant

"Cormorant Point" is poorly-named, as there are no cormorants to be seen here. The other wildlife more than makes up for it, however. After a wet landing on a beach, visitors hike along a small trail over to the other side of the island. Along the way, there is a brackish lagoon where flamingoes feed and nest—there are a couple of good outlook points.

Watch the vegetation—you may see some wasp traps set out by the Park Service, as Punta Cormorant is a targeted area for getting rid of these introduced pests. The park advises visitors not to wear bright colors or use fragrant lotions or sunscreens, as these will attract the wasps, which sting.

On the other side of the island is a wide beach with a gentle surf, great for a leisurely barefoot stroll. Keep an eye on the water and you may see rays, turtles or sharks. Obey the signs to stay out of the area where sea turtles lay their eggs. Between the two beaches and the shallow lagoon, Punta Cormorant is one of the best places in the islands to see wading birds such as Whimbrels, Herons, Stilts, Pintail Ducks, etc. The beach where the zodiacs land is special; it gets its distinctive greenish color from olivine minerals only found in certain parts of Galápagos.

Post Office Bay

Post Office Bay is a popular stop with visitors, who get to soak in a little bit of the human history of the islands, which can be refreshing after days of natural history and animals. Centuries ago, whaling ships would spend years at sea hunting and rendering whales for their valuable fat. Needless to say, the sailors would miss home, and they would send letters to loved ones. The best way to do this was to drop the letters at places frequented by other whalers in the hopes that some other ship heading for your home port would take the letters with them. Apparently the system worked, because Post Office Bay was used by sailors for almost a century.

The traditional simple wooden barrel is more elaborate and decorated now, but still serves the same function. Just write a postcard or letter with an address and drop it in. No stamps needed! In theory, the next person who lives close to you will take it home and hand-deliver it. It's a great way to make new friends!

Visitors are encouraged to sift through the pile of outgoing mail and take a letter or two home. Remember, traditionally letters and post cards are hand-delivered, so only take something close to home. Taking a letter and then putting a stamp on it and mailing it is against the rules!

Post Office Bay also includes the ruins of a canning factory and a soccer field (your

GALÁPAGOS

ship's crew will probably come and play, and visitors are usually encouraged to join in, but watch out—they're good!). There's also a lava tube: a cave-like tunnel formed ages ago. There's a pool in the tube, good for a nice swim in the dark.

Champion Islet

A small island off the coast of Floreana, Champion is one of the top snorkeling spots in the islands (the island itself is off-limits to visitors). Occasionally, dolphins are sighted as the boats approach the shore.

The snorkeling is truly phenomenal. Lucky visitors will get to see White-tipped Reef Sharks, Galápagos Penguins, sea turtles, eels, and more in addition to the usual selection of dazzling reef fish.

Champion Island is special because it is one of two places where the nearly-extinct Charles (Floreana) Mockingbird is still found. The other is Gardner Island, also off the coast of Floreana. When Charles Darwin visited the islands in 1835 Floreana Mockingbirds were common, but hunting and introduced species on Floreana caused them to become extinct on the main island, and the only survivors are now on Champion and Gardner. Conservationists want to re-introduce them to Floreana, but conditions there are not yet right for the birds, which would not survive for the same reasons they died off there in the first place.

Walking on Champion is not allowed, but most operators will take visitors on panga rides around it, and lucky visitors may get to spot a Charles Mockingbird or other bird species such as Swallow-tailed Gulls, Nazca Boobies or Brown Noddies.

Champion Islet is also a popular SCUBA diving site, easily reached by Puerto Ayora Dive shops.

Western Island Visitor Sites

The western islands of Isabela and Fernandina are the least frequented by tourists due to their distance from the main islands. However, if you are lucky enough to visit them, you will have the rare opportunity to witness volcanology in action, to see the unusual Flightless Cormorant, and maybe even to cross paths with pods of whales and dolphins!

The islands of Darwin and Wolf are even more remote, so scuba-diving tours here offer an extra-special occasion to experience some of the most abundant and diverse marine life in the world.

You also have the best possibility of encountering the big attractions, like whales, Hammerhead Sharks and Whale Sharks.

ISABELA

Isabela (Albemarle) is by far the largest island, and there are several great visitor sites there. Most cruise ships will go up along the western coast of the island to see some of the sites there and also visit Fernandina Island. There are essentially two sorts of visitor sites on Isabela: the ones that you can only get to if you're on a cruise, and ones that are do-able from the town of Puerto Villamil. Most of the cruise ship ones are on the western side of the island.

Cruise-only sites include Tagus Cove, Urbina Bay, Punta Vicente Roca and Punta Moreno. Sites very close to the town include Concha de Perla Lagoon, Tintoreras, the Centro de Crianza, Humedales and the Wall of Tears. The sites of Sierra Negra Volcano, Sucre's Cave and the Sulfur Mines are further away from town, but tours from Puerto Villamil can be arranged. Occasionally cruise ships will visit Puerto Villamil and see some of the nearby sites, but if you're staying in town, you're not allowed to visit cruise-only sites like Tagus Cove or Urbina Bay.

Tagus Cove

A visitor favorite, Tagus Cove combines a panga ride around the cove with a hike along a stony trail to see lava formations and salty Lake Darwin. The cove is a good anchorage historically used by pirates and whalers who would carve or paint the names of their ships into a small cave near the beginning of the trail. Seeing this centuries-old graffiti is a highlight of the hike (nowadays the Park Service would kick any graffiti-carvers out of the islands!).

The hike is a fairly easy one, less than two kilometers (1.2 mi), and it leads past lava formations up the side of a volcano. Several small land birds can be seen, such as finches. The trail winds through arid-zone vegetation before climbing for a great view. Volcanic formations can be seen, including spatter cones and tuff cones.

GALÁPAGOS

The panga ride is a lot of fun: lucky visitors will get to see Galápagos Penguins, Flightless Cormorants and other marine birds.

Punta Moreno

Located on the western shore of Isabela Island, Punta Moreno is a popular site where a lot of wildlife can be seen. The trip usually begins (or ends) with a panga ride along the rocky shore: keep your eyes peeled for Galápagos Penguins sunning themselves on the rocks. If you look in the water, there is a chance that you'll see sea turtles, rays or other marine creatures.

Once on shore, the trail winds its way through lava formations, mangroves and crystal-clear tidal pools. It's in these little pools where the action is—check them all out to see what was trapped there the last time the tide was high. There will certainly be all sorts of colorful fish, crustaceans and echinoderms, but there may be something spectacular such as a turtle, ray or shark.

Punta Vicente Roca

Punta Vicente Roca (Vicente Rock Point) is a popular marine visitor site: there is no trail on land here. Typically, cruise ships will send passengers on a panga ride along the rocky shore, where they can often see Galápagos Fur Sea Lions, Galápagos Sea Lions and Galápagos Penguins. Lucky visitors might see a Flightless Cormorant too.

The highlight of the panga ride is a visit to a large, yawning cave; look for some birds nesting on the cave walls. After the panga ride, visitors can snorkel in the area. It's a good place to see some sea turtles and sea lions, and maybe sharks or the famous Pacific Sunfish in the cave area or out a little deeper.

Urbina Bay

One of the more fascinating Galápagos visitor sites, Urbina Bay (sometimes spelled Urvina Bay) was caused by a geological phenomenon in 1954. An area that was previously underwater suddenly was thrust up into the air 5 meters (16 ft.), creating land where there had previously been none. Local fishermen discovered it because of the odor of rotting marine life that had been too slow to escape! The hike therefore winds through coral formations and recent pioneer plants, giving geologists and botanists an illuminating look at how new lands are colonized by plants and animals in Galápagos.

Located at the base of the Alcedo Volcano, the trail is over 3,000 meters (9,843 ft) long and can be taxing for weaker hikers, especially on hot days. It's one of the few places to see grasshoppers. Look for land iguanas feeding on manzanilla apples: deadly poison for humans, but a tasty snack for an iguana! It's possible to snorkel at Urbina Bay and many ships allow their passengers to do so; it's not the best snorkeling in the Galápagos as the water is often cloudy, but a lucky snorkeler might see a green sea turtle or a stingray.

Las Tintoreras

Las Tintoreras is a memorable visitor site for those who get to go there. It's a small trail along a rocky island in the harbor off of Puerto Villamil. The trail goes past several channels and tidal pools, which for some reason are home to White-tipped Reef Sharks, sometimes as many as dozens of them. "Tintoreras" is, in fact, the local name for the White-tipped Reef Shark. The sharks usually hang out in a shallow, narrow channel, allowing visitors to get quite close and take good photos.

The trail itself is rocky but not too long or difficult. In addition to the sharks, it's common to see other marine life such as rays in the tidal pools, and sea lions and marine iguanas are abundant.

Once you're done, you can snorkel around the rocks nearby (you cannot snorkel in the little channel, and even though the sharks are harmless you probably wouldn't want to, especially if you've ever seen *Jaws*).

There is also another crevasse nearby where you can go if you're with a guide. Chances are good that you'll see more sharks while snorkeling around the rocks or in the other crevasse.

Some cruise ships will visit Las Tintoreras, but not all of them are permitted to snorkel there. Check and see if swimming alongside dozens of sharks appeals to you. If you're staying in Puerto Villamil, it should be pretty easy to find a guided group headed there; it usually costs about $25 or so, and is well worth it. Updated: Sep 22, 2012.

Centro de Crianza "Arnaldo Tupiza"

The Centro de Crianza (or "Rearing Center") is a sort of nursery for Giant Tortoises located within walking distance from Puerto Villamil. There are several pens housing grown tortoises, mainly from the different volcanoes on Isabela Island, as well as dozens of young tortoises in protected cages. Look for the ones from Cerro Paloma—the adults there were the only six left of their species in 1994, although now there are some little ones at the center.

An easy paved path leads through the penned-in area and ends up at an information center (and gift shop, naturally).

Unlike the Charles Darwin Research Station, the pens here are not open and you can't go in with the tortoises to have your photo taken. The walk is shadier though.

Although you can take a taxi to the Centro de Crianza, it's much more fun to walk. The trail leads outside of Puerto Villamil near the Iguana Crossing Hotel and winds through mangroves, swamps and salty lagoons where you can see ducks, flamingoes, herons and other wading and swimming birds. The trail takes about 40 minutes to walk, but it's in good shape and pretty easy. You do not need a guide to walk on the trail or visit the Centro de Crianza.

You can book a half-day tour in Puerto Villamil which will include the trail, the Center and the Wall of Tears for about $20, but this is all as long as there are enough people who want to do it.

It isn't a bad idea, as a guide will help spot wildlife and tell you about the plants and animals that you're sure to see on the trail as well as the history of the wall. The center is a popular stop with cruise ships that visit Puerto Villamil.

Sierra Negra Volcano

Sierra Negra Volcano is the closest one to Puerto Villamil and it makes for a popular hike. It's a day-long affair and you'll definitely want to have a guide because it's possible to lose the trail, especially if it gets rainy or foggy, which it often does.Usually trips will take a van or truck to a dropping-off place found near the base of the mountain and then go from there.

Sierra Negra is the oldest of Isabela's volcanoes, and was active as recently as 2005. The hike passes through several different vegetation and geological zones. Generally, guided tours will reach the summit of Sierra Negra and also visit the nearby Volcán Chico. The trip takes half a day.

It's possible to rent horses for the same trip; they usually cost about $10 more. Typically, you'll pay roughly $35 for a tour of Sierra Negra on foot and $45 if you want a horse. Sierra Negra last erupted in 2005, so if you rent a horse, make sure to ask for the fastest one they have.

Sucre's Cave

Located in the farmlands outside of Puerto Villamil on Isabela Island, Sucre's Cave is actually a visitor site protected by the National Park. More than just a cave, the hike, about a half kilometer (0.31 mi) in length, is mostly designed to show the ongoing restoration efforts of the humid rain forests in Isabela's agricultural zone.

Along this path, scientists and rangers have been working hard to eradicate introduced species and reintroduce native and endemic ones. Visitors will get to see the plant nursery used to repopulate the area as well as a small home for rangers and volunteers. There is, of course, a cave as well; it's a relatively small lava tunnel but fun and interesting to explore. It's possible to volunteer to work at this site; see rangers or Park Service for details. **Tips:** Bring a flashlight to explore the cave.

Isabela Dive Sites

The SCUBA diving in Isabela is much more limited than in Puerto Ayora or Puerto Baquerizo Moreno. There is only one dive shop in Puerto Villamil—Isabela Dive Center—so you're pretty much stuck with it, at least for now. It basically only go to three dive sites: Tortuga Island, Cuatro Hermanos and Roca Viuda, although if you're staying there for a few days and want to dive more, it's possible the dive center could find some more places to go. Isabela has excellent snorkeling, so it's a good place to go if some members of your group dive and some prefer to snorkel.

Tortuga Island

A moderate to strong current, but the underwater landscape is spectacular and the chance of seeing impressive marine life is good. Look for Hammerheads, Galápagos Sharks and large rays in addition to dazzling fish like Moorish Idols and Parrotfish.

Distance from Puerto Villamil: 30 minutes.

Cuatro Hermanos

Cuatro Hermanos is a spectacular site, where you're likely to see seahorses, including the Giant Pacific Seahorse. There is an underwater cavern here, too, and there's a good chance of seeing sharks and rays there. Enormous Manta Rays are also often seen as well as lobsters, octopus and, of course, plenty of colorful fish.

Distance from Puerto Villamil: 45 minutes.

GALÁPAGOS

Roca Viuda

The charmingly-named "Widow Rock" is one of the most challenging dives in Galápagos and only for advanced divers: it's on a wall and the currents are quite strong, occasionally carrying divers away from the site! Sometimes it's worse than others. Those who do it are rewarded with a truly astounding collection of reef fish: thousands of them literally everywhere. Not so many sharks and large rays, but the pretty fish make up for it.

Distance from Puerto Villamil: 25 minutes.

FERNANDINA

Fernandina (Narborough), the westernmost (and youngest, geologically speaking) of the main islands is situated directly above a geologic hot spot and as such, has the highest volcanic activity of any of the islands. Many eruptions have been recorded since 1813, with the most recent one having occurred in early 2009.

There is one visitor site, Punta Espinosa, where Flightless Cormorants, pelicans, penguins, sea lions, and an abundance of marine iguanas reside.

The marine ecosystem around Fernandina, where the cold Cromwell current has its greatest impact on water temperature and nutrient upwelling, hosts organisms not found in other sectors of the archipelago.

In fact, Bryde's Whales, Pilot Whales, and Bottlenose Dolphins feed here, so keep your eyes open when you are cruising! This area is resource-rich and has been declared a Whale Sanctuary.
Updated: Jan 4, 2013.

Punta Espinosa

Fernandina's only visitor site, Punta Espinosa is a great place to see some Galápagos wildlife that you don't often see. Most noteworthy is the endemic Flightless Cormorant, which is only found in the western islands. After a dry-ish landing on a rocky shore, visitors will have the opportunity to peek into some tidal pools, which often are home to interesting marine life. You may even spot a ray or sea turtle in the lagoon.

After the landing, you'll head to the main trail, passing a large colony of marine iguanas as you do. Stop for some photos, and then head along the trail past a sea lion nursery to see the cormorants. If you're lucky,

you'll be able to get a good look at them as they swim and flap their vestigial wings to dry them off. The other end of the trail leads to some interesting lava formations, an abandoned ship's engine and some more lagoons. Along the rocky shore near Punta Espinosa, visitors will occasionally see the rare Galápagos Penguin. If you're lucky, your cruise ship will send pangas or zodiacs along the shore, where your keen-eyed naturalist guide will help you spot the penguins—they're difficult to see against the black lava background.

DARWIN AND WOLF

Darwin (Culpepper) and Wolf (Wenman) are two tiny, outlying islands in the northwest archipelago that harbor an incredibly diverse and abundant marine life. As such, the islands are only visited on live-aboard scuba diving tours.

Certain species of tropical Indo-Pacific fish and coral can only be found here, but the main attraction for divers is the high possibility of seeing big stuff, and lots of it, like whales, Hammerhead Sharks, and Whale Sharks.
Updated: Jun 04, 2013.

!!!!!

GALÁPAGOS

Index

INDEX

Loved it? Loathed it? Write a review and help other travelers.

INDEX

INDEX

Loved it? Loathed it? Write a review and help other travelers.

INDEX

INDEX

Loved it? Loathed it? Write a review and help other travelers.

INDEX

Loved it? Loathed it? Write a review and help other travelers.

Like VIVA on facebook.com/VTGEcuador for news and updates

Why reserve your hotel or hostel with V!VA ?

- Hand-picked recommendations on the best places to stay by V!VA's on-the-ground writers.

- Get a free e-book download for every reservation made.

- Get a 35% discount on book purchases when you reserve.

- Your reservation helps V!VA improve this guide.

www.vivatravelguides.com/hotels

INDEX

PACKING LISTS
(* indicates something that might not be available in Ecuador)

GENERAL PACKING LIST
There are a number of items that every traveler should consider bringing to Ecuador:

- ☐ **Medicines and prescriptions** (Very important. Bringing all relevant medical info and medicines may well save you a lot of grief in Ecuador)
- ☐ **Photocopies of passport** and other relevant ID documents
- ☐ Paperback novels or E-book (sometimes you'll be sitting on buses, in aiports, or wherever else for a long time. Bring some books with you so you're not bored. It is possible to find and/or exchange books in several places in Ecuador, but don't count on much selection)
- ☐ A good camera (see photography section)
- ☐ Water bottle (bottled water is readily available in Ecuador, but you may want your own bottle)
- ☐ Sunglasses
- ☐ Motion sickness medicine
- ☐ Lip balm
- ☐ *Tampons (difficult to find outside the major cities)
- ☐ Sun hat
- ☐ Condoms and other contraceptives
- ☐ *Foot powder
- ☐ Antacid tablets, such as Rolaids
- ☐ Mild painkillers such as aspirin or ibuprofen
- ☐ *GPS device (especially for hikers)
- ☐ Watch with alarm clock
- ☐ Diarrhea medicine (i.e. Imodium)
- ☐ Warm clothes (Quito and the highlands are cooler than you think)

BACKPACKER PACKING LIST:
- ☐ All of the above, plus:
- ☐ Rain poncho
- ☐ Plastic bags
- ☐ *Swiss army knife / leatherman
- ☐ Toilet paper
- ☐ *Antibacterial hand gel
- ☐ Small padlock

RAINFOREST PACKING LIST
- ☐ Rubber boots (most jungle lodges have them, call ahead)
- ☐ *Bug spray (with Deet)
- ☐ Flashlight
- ☐ Waterproof bags
- ☐ Rain poncho
- ☐ First aid kit
- ☐ *Compass
- ☐ Whistle
- ☐ Long-sleeved shirt and pants
- ☐ Malaria / yellow fever medicine
- ☐ Original passport
- ☐ Mosquito net (if your destination does not have one; call ahead)
- ☐ Biodegradable soap

INDEX

Like VIVA on facebook.com/VTGEcuador for news and updates

GALÁPAGOS PACKING LIST

- ☐ Extra film/camera supplies
- ☐ Waterproof disposable camera for snorkeling
- ☐ Sunscreen
- ☐ Good, wide brimmed hat
- ☐ Long pants, lightweight
- ☐ Long-sleeved shirt, lightweight

ADDITIONAL ITEMS

- ☐ _____
- ☐ _____
- ☐ _____
- ☐ _____
- ☐ _____
- ☐ _____
- ☐ _____
- ☐ _____

ANTI-PACKING LIST: THINGS NOT TO BRING TO ECUADOR

- x Expensive jewelry. Just leave it home.
- x Nice watch or sunglasses. Bring a cheap one you can afford to lose.
- x Go through your wallet: what won't you need? Leave your drivers' license (unless you're planning on driving), business cards, video-club membership cards, 7-11 coffee club card, social security card and anything else you won't need. The only thing in your wallet you'll want is a student ID, and if you lose it you'll be grateful you left the rest at home.
- x Illegal drugs. You didn't need us to tell you that, did you?
- x Stickers and little toys for kids. Some tourists like to hand them out, which means the children pester every foreigner they see.
- x Really nice clothes or shoes, unless you're planning on going to a special event or dining out a lot.

INDEX

Loved it? Loathed it? Write a review and help other travelers.

USEFUL SPANISH PHRASES

CONVERSATIONAL

Hello	Hola
Good morning	Buenos días
Good afternoon	Buenas tardes
Good evening	Buenas noches
Yes	Sí
No	No
Please	Por favor
Thank you	Gracias
It was nothing	De nada
Excuse me	Permiso
See you later	Hasta luego
Bye	Chao
Cool	Chévere
How are you (formal)	¿Cómo está?
" " (informal)	¿Qué tal?
I don't understand	No entiendo
Do you speak English?	¿Habla inglés?
I don't speak Spanish.	No hablo español.
I'm from England	Soy de Inglaterra
" " the USA	Soy de los Estados Unidos

FOOD AND DRINK

Breakfast	Desayuno
Lunch	Almuerzo
Dinner	Cena
Check please	La cuenta, por favor
Main Course	Plato Fuerte
Menu	La Carta
Spoon	Cuchara
Fork	Tenedor
Knife	Cuchillo
Bread	Pan
Fruit	Fruta
Vegetables	Verduras
Potatoes	Papas
Meat	Carne
Chicken	Pollo
Beer	Cerveza
Wine	Vino
Juice	Jugo
Coffee	Café
Tea	Té

HEALTH/EMERGENCY

Call a....	¡Llame a...!
Ambulance	una ambulancia
A doctor	un médico
The police	la policía

It's an emergency	Es una emergencia
I'm sick	Estoy enfermo/a
I need a doctor	Necesito un médico
Where's the hospital?	¿Dónde está el hospital?

I'm allergic to...	Soy alérgico/a a...
Antibiotics	los antibióticos
Nuts	nuez
Penicillin	la penicilina

GETTING AROUND

Where is...?	¿Dónde está...?
The bus station?	la estación de bus?
The train station?	la estación de tren?
A bank?	Un banco?
The bathroom?	El baño?
An ATM?	un cajero automático

Where does the bus leave from?	¿De dónde sale el bus?
Left, right, straight	Izquierda, derecha, recto
One city block	Un cuadro
Ticket	Boleto

ACCOMMODATION

Where is a hotel?	¿Donde hay un hotel?
I want a room	Quiero una habitación
Single/Double/Marriage	Simple/Doble/Matrimonial
How much does it cost per night?	¿Cuanto cuesta por noche?
Does that include breakfast?	¿Incluye el desayuno?
Does that include taxes?	¿Incluye los impuestos?
Is there 24-hour hot water?	¿Hay agua caliente veinicuatro horas al día?

Like VIVA on facebook.com/VTGEcuador for news and updates

V!VA TRAVEL GUIDES BRINGS YOU A TEAR-OUT LIST OF USEFUL CONTACTS IN ECUADOR

Feel free to photocopy this sheet for your use, to give to your dog, or to wallpaper your room.

EMERGENCY NUMBERS

All emergencies (Quito only)	911	Police	101 (24 hrs)
Fire	102	Red Cross	131

HOSPITALS / DOCTORS / PHARMACIES

Hospital Vozandes
Villalengua 267 at 10 de Agosto
Tel: 593-2-226-2142 ext. 3052 / 3050
Has American and Ecuadorian physicians
24 hr emergency room
www.hospitalvozandes.org

Hospital Metropolitano
Mariana de Jesus y Nicolás Arteta
Tel: 02-399-8000
24 hr emergency room

Doctor: Dr John Rosenberg, Med Center Travel Clinic, Foch 476 and Almagro speaks English and German
Tel: 593-2-252-1104 ex. 310 / 9-973-9734

24 hr Pharmacy: Fybeca – 24hr branches at Av. Amazonas and Tomás de Berlanga (Tel: 593-2-245-9082 / 244-5175), Av. 6 de Diciembre and Irlanda, at Estación Sur in the south (Tel: 593-2-265-1154 / 6182) and C.C. Plaza del Valle (Tel: 593-2-286-1030).

ENGLISH SPEAKING LAWYERS IN QUITO (CRIMINAL)

Estudio Juridico Andrade Lara
Asunción 1031 and Canadá
Tel: 02-222-4933   Fax: 593-2-255-0782
Tel: 09-779-1954
E-mail: jorgeandradelara@hotmail.com

TRAVELER GUIDANCE: V!VA Travel Guides: www.vivatravelguides.com

South American Explorers (SAE)
Jorge Washington E-64 and Leonidas Plaza
Tel/Fax: 02-222-5228
E-mail: quitoclub@saexplorers.org
www.saexplorers.org

Ministry of Tourism
El Telégrafo E7-58 and de Los Shyris Ave.
Tel: 02-399-9333
E-mail: info@turismo.gov.ec
www.turismo.gov.ec

POST OFFICE (CORREOS DEL ECUADOR)
Japón N36-153 y Av. Naciones Unidas
Tel: 02-299-6835
Old Town – Guayaquil 935 y Espejo
Tel: 02-228-7134
Colon and Reina Victoria in Torres de Almagro
Tel: 02-250-8980

INTERNET CAFES
Papaya Net: Calama and Juan León Mera
Stop 'n' Surf: Av. Mañosca and Veracruz
Kantuñ@ Net: Venezuela and Chile

TRANSPORT
Taxis: City-taxi, Tel: 02-284-6208; Taxi Amigo, Tel: 02-222-2222; Taxi Galaxia, 02-340-0200; Taxi Batan, 02-328-1000.

Bus Terminal: Main bus terminal is Terminal Quitumbe, Av. Cóndor Ñan & Av. Mariscal Sucre

Complete the sections below for your convenience:

My tour operator:

My hotel address:

INDEX

Loved it? Loathed it? Write a review and help other travelers.

AIRLINES:

Aerogal (Ecuadorian)
Av. República del Salvador N34-107 and Suiza.
Brescia Bldg., Lobby
Tel: 02-294-3100
www.aerogal.com.ec
customerservice@aerogal.com.ec

American Airlines (US)
Av.de los Shyris N35-174 and Suecia
Renazzo Plaza Bldg., Lobby
Tel: 02-299-5000
Mon-Fri, 9 a.m.-6 p.m.
*Also located in Mall El Jardin in N. Quito

Avianca/TACA (Colombian)
Av. Rep. de El Salvador N36-139 and Naciones Unidas
Tel: 1-800-00-8222
Mon-Fri, 8:30 a.m.-5:30 p.m.

United/Continental Airlines (US)
12 de Octubre and Cordero
Tel: 02-2-255-7290
World Trade Center
Mon.-Fri. 9 a.m.-6 p.m.

Iberia (Spanish)
Eloy Alfaro 939 and Amazonas
Finandes Bldg., 5th Floor
Tel: 02-222-9454
Fax: 593-2-256-6199

KLM (Dutch)
12 de Octubre and Abraham Lincoln
Building Torre 1492, Office 1103
Tel: 02-396-6728
Mon.-Fri., 8:30 a.m.- 12:30 p.m., 2 p.m.- 5 p.m.

Lan (Chilean)
Av. La Coruña 1527, corner of Av. Fco. de Orellana
Tel: 1-800-10-10-75
Mon. – Fri., 9 a.m.-4 p.m.
*Also located on the ground floor of C.C. Quicentro

TAME (Ecuadorian)
Amazonas N 24-260 and Colón, 2nd Floor
Tel: 02-396-6300
www.tame.com.ec

EMBASSIES IN QUITO:

Canada
Av. Amazonas 4153 and Unión Nacional de Periodistas
Eurocenter Building, 3rd Floor
Tel: 02-245-5499
E-mail: quito@international.gc.ec

France
Leonidas Plaza 127 and Patria
Tel: 02-294-3800
E-mail: consulat@embafrancia.com.ec

Germany
Avenida Naciones Unidas E10-44 and Rep. de El Salvador
Citiplaza, floors 12-14
Tel: 02-297-0820

Ireland
Calle Yanacocha N72-64 and Juan Procel
(Sector el Condado)
Tel: 02-357-0156
E-mail: dominiquekennedy@gmail.com

Italy
Calle La Isla 111 and Humberto Albornoz
Tel: 02-232-11322
E-mail: archivio.quito@esteri.it

Japan
Avenida Amazonas N39 - 123 and Calle Arizaga
Edf.Amazonas Plaza, 11th floor
Tel: 02-227-8700

Russia
Reina Victoria 462 and Roca
Tel: 02-252-6361
E-mail: embrusia_ecuador@mail.ru

Switzerland
AJuan Pablo Sanz and Avenida Amazonas N35-17
Edificio Xerox, 2nd floor
Tel: 02-243-4949

Spain
Francisco Salazar E12-73 between
Isabel La Católica and Toledo
Tel: 02-322-6296
E-mail: emb.quito@maec.es

United Kingdom
Naciones Unidas Avenue and República de El Salvador
Citiplaza Building, 12th and 14th floors
Tel: 02-297-0800/801

United States of America
Avigiras E12-170 and Eloy Alfaro Ave. (next to SOLCA)
Tel: 02-398-5000
E-mail: contacto.usembuio@state.gov

INDEX

Like VIVA on facebook.com/VTGEcuador for news and updates

CPSIA information can be obtained at www.ICGtesting.com
Printed in the USA
BVOW04s1348261213

340114BV00010B/431/P